Great Ideas
Conversations between Past and Present

THOMAS KLEIN, BRUCE EDWARDS, THOMAS WYMER
Bowling Green State University

Harcourt Brace Jovanovich College Publishers
Fort Worth   Philadelphia   San Diego
New York   Orlando   Austin   San Antonio
Toronto   Montreal   London   Sydney   Tokyo

Publisher	Ted Buchholz
Acquisitions Editor	Michael Rosenberg
Project Editor	Catherine Townsend
Production Manager	Kathleen Ferguson
Art & Design Supervisor	Vicki McAlindon Horton
Text Designer	Art Ritter
Cover Designer	Michael Niblett
Composition	University Graphics

Library of Congress Cataloging-in-Publication Data
Klein, Thomas D.
    Great ideas : conversations between past and present / Thomas Klein, Thomas Wymer, Bruce Edwards.
        p.   cm.
    Includes index.
    ISBN 0-03-030514-4
    1. College readers.   2. English language—Rhetoric.   I. Wymer, Thomas L.   II. Edwards, Bruce
L.   III. Title.
    PE1417.K555   1991
    808'.0427—dc20   90-20835
                                                                                                 CIP

ISBN: 0-03-030514-4

Address Editorial Correspondence To: 301 Commerce Street, Suite 3700, Fort Worth, TX 76102

Address Orders To: 6277 Sea Harbor Drive, Orlando, FL 32887
1-800-782-4479, or 1-800-433-0001 (in Florida)

Printed in the United States of America

    3 4   090   9 8 7 6 5 4 3

Harcourt Brace Jovanovich, Inc.
The Dryden Press
Saunders College Publishing

PREFACE

To the Student

In this book, we invite you to venture into the past to see the present anew. By examining the "old" ideas that have shaped our cultural traditions and ultimately who we are, we seek not to withdraw from the present but to obtain a better understanding of it, to renew it, and to give a resonance and clarity to its possibilities.

We would not be surprised if you have found the study of the past unpleasant. Today, it has become a perilous undertaking to write or speak about the past; in fact, any study of ideas characterized with words like "classic," "great," "perennial," "enduring," or even "old" is immediately suspect of bias, superficiality, pedantry, naïveté, or overenthusiasm. We have some sympathy for such feelings; the study of the past, its history of cultural and intellectual traditions, is far too often dry, dull, and tedious. Another problem in studying the past is that certain groups, viewpoints, and values may be unknowingly privileged at the expense of excluding others. Even so, we believe in a deep obligation to take the risk and to open the pages of history.

We must not avoid the study of history, for the past exerts a strong hold on us, primarily in the form of the ideas we inherit. Change—mending the world—is possible only when we understand that hold and its inheritance. Study of the past can operate paradoxically. It can result in intolerance and rigidity if the study inspires a return to and reapplication of old values, regardless of their context or soundness. On the other hand, study of the past can result in an openness and flexibility if the object of such study is the historical context of old ideas. By learning how various ideas came into existence, how they were applied, and how they affected daily life, we can perhaps open our lives to fresh perspectives, to at least the lessons of the past, and the hope of improvement. Such study can also liberate us from our ignorance and the tyranny of the present, from fads and narrow-mindedness, and from the stereotypes and judgments inherent in every culture. A very thin line divides these two results, and the purpose of this text is to explore both sides of that line. We all carry with us the past; in our customs, rituals, attitudes, and values, we embody, for instance, the central values of religion, humanism, science, and democracy. We ought to become aware of what affects us so profoundly.

In a society in which young people can often name more brands of beer than titles of books, when many spend more hours before television than in school, when many of the worst fears Aldous Huxley expressed in *Brave New World* seem to have come true, all of us risk losing our common past, which would be an irreparable loss because the past is the best mirror we have in looking at ourselves. But education has failed to hold this mirror up to past realities. When we, the editors of this text, look at our colleagues and students, we sometimes see too much that is cynical, pessimistic, self-indulgent, narcissistic, and downright discouraged. We see few who hold out hope for a better future and little energy to tackle the great problems of society. We see too little careful reflection among our colleagues and students. We fear that the legacies and truths of the past may be lost.

This text, then, is our testimony to hope. As an introduction to intellectual forces that have shaped Western culture, it invites you to enter into the battle of ideas. That is what we have tried to present here: an opportunity for you to enter the great conversations of history. We believe that by listening to men and women of influence, and by being able to respond in thoughtful ways, you, too, will begin to share in that influence.

To the Instructor

The reading of ancient texts, for instance, from Plato's *Republic*, written in the fourth century B.C., to Virginia Woolf's *A Room of One's Own*, written in the twentieth century, is not always met with enthusiasm or interest by our students. They are perhaps overly influenced by our twentieth-century media to value reading and books less than videos, movies, or CDs. Our students ask, what can someone who lived centuries, even decades, ago possibly tell us about life in the modern, technological, tumultuous 1990s? What, indeed, did anyone "back then" know about our particular challenges, problems, hopes, and dreams?

One answer to this compelling question begins first by asking another: what is it about being human that is unique to time and place? That is, why should we assume automatically that someone who lived centuries ago did not share our aspirations, dreams, and problems? While admitting that our ancestors perhaps had to deal with their peculiar circumstances somewhat differently than we do, is there any reason to suspect that they prized peace, family, success, or vocation any less than we do? The problem with assuming the past has nothing to say to us is summed up well by C. S. Lewis: "There is no magic about the past. People were no cleverer then than they are now; they made as many mistakes as we. But not the same mistakes. They will not flatter us in the errors we are already committing; and their own errors, being now open and palpable, will not endanger us."[1] In other words, the past can serve as a barometer—a means of measuring the progress or lack thereof that the human community has made over time and through many different cultures. As we come to understand and celebrate what it means to be human, the past is for us an invaluable reference point, marking where we have been and how far we have to go in constructing a society that shares a common reverence for truth, for life, for each person's individuality, and for the accompanying blessings of peace and harmony.

In constructing *Great Ideas*, our aim has been to combat what Owen Barfield has called the twentieth century's "chronological snobbery," that is, the view that because our times are "our" times, it follows that they are, therefore, the best,

---

[1]Lewis, C. S. "On the Reading of Old Books," *God in the Dock*. Grand Rapids, Mich.: Eerdmans, 1970, p. 202.

the most enlightened, informed, important, and so on. Such notions are often based on the assumption—some would say *myth*—of "progress," that things naturally "get better" with the passage of time. But, as C. S. Lewis would argue, reading the "old books," some of the very ones chosen for this text, forces us to note ideas, people, cultures, and times that do not share in such "snobberies" and as such can assist in a better assessment and understanding of our own times. The alternative is to live only in the "now," guided only by the current wisdom or the received popular knowledge; this is, in fact, what our students, and perhaps many of us, are only too ready to do. Thus, it might be useful to suggest two modest principles we advocate for teaching students how to view historical texts—principles, at least, that will increase our confidence in the validity or relevance of our inquiry.

The first is the simple belief that a "recovery" of the past that allows historical texts to speak to us out of their own times is possible. With linguistic and historical research, we can provide the necessary contexts and backgrounds that allow us to see the past at least as clearly as we see any phenomenon in our times. Even granting that every observer will bring prejudices or tendencies into the readings, a startlingly fresh wind can blow through the centuries when we read a selection without too much of our twentieth-century bias or snobbery getting in the way.

The second is the notion that multiple perspectives may be applied to a text, yielding different, but not necessarily mutually exclusive, interpretations. For instance, a devout believer may hold that the historical fact of ancient Israel's departure from Egypt was entirely the result of God's miraculous intervention. A less literal believer or even nonbeliever may understand Israel's flight as a result of "natural" circumstances that have other explanations. Both readings can be respected and regarded as "true" within the framework of each reader's experience, faith, and historical understanding. Because all of us operate from finite fields of vision that supply both unique perspective and characteristic blind spots, we can expect to find lively debate, which will include informed as well as uninformed, even dogmatic, opinions among readers. Even so, as we deal with our students' reading experiences and their responses, it will be important for us to assure them that their efforts can generate real insight and to warn them that their inexperience may sometimes create faulty or partial views that will need to mature over time with further reading and reflection.

What we seek for our students in this group excursion into the past is not a consensus of response; rather, our goal is to elicit from our students an honest, individual struggle with these great ideas and to encourage them to find meaning in the past or the present, wherever it may be found.

Acknowledgments

In the development and completion of *Great Ideas*, each of us owes debts to colleagues, friends, and family for which formal acknowledgment here only begins to express our appreciation. But it is an ancient principle, worthy of practice in our times, of "giving honor to whom honor is due." Thus, each of us in turn would like to express our gratitude to those individuals who have helped shape and bring into being this book.

Tom Klein I dedicate this book to my wife, Dianne, whose many great ideas and insights I ashamedly stole for this book, and to my son, David, who had to put up with my pedantry and my constant distraction.

It should be apparent that a project with the scope and ambition of this text requires the collaboration of countless individuals whose goodwill, foresight and patience foster genuine innovation. This text has its genesis in the year-long discussions that took place in 1985 and 1986 on the campus of Bowling Green State University. About fifteen faculty and administrators whom I can only now call visionary gathered for the weekly lunches in order to develop a course that would respond to many of the ills of university education. The Great Ideas Program, whose centerpiece is the Great Ideas course represented in this text, was the result of our deliberations.

From the earliest stages of the program, when the bold idea of selecting a limited number of intellectual revolutions that contribute to the shaping of our culture was still being born, Kendall Baker, Jim Bissland, Alan Emery, Jim Litwin, and Ryan Tweney (who has recently assumed responsibility as Program coordinator) were indispensable; it was their faith in the project and their willingness to risk failure that has made the Great Ideas Program successful, and, eventually, has led to its being required in a number of large majors on our campus.

After the course successfully passed the planning stages, many faculty generously gave time as consultants in summer training sessions for peers, and they deserve our deepest thanks: Roger Anderson, Bill Baxter, Ellen Berry, Fr. James Bacik, Lawrence Daly, Karen Gould, Richard Hebein, Steven Ludd, Michael Maggiotto, Fred Miller, Vivian Patraka, Fred Rickey, and Ryan Tweney. In addition, Roger Anderson, Tom Attig, Bill Baxter, and Ellen Berry provided invaluable advice on individual chapters of the book. Finally, our faculty and graduate students bravely tested the course and tirelessly contributed to the incessant yet vital curriculum debates: Beth Casey, Neil Browne, Sheila Harrington, Craig Hergert (whose *Instructor's Manual* to accompany this text is a masterpiece of wisdom and pedagogical insight), Robert Jackson, Stuart Keeley, Jack Nachbar, Michael Peslikis, William Reichert, Jerry Streichler, Peter Schreffler, Marjory Kinney, David Skaggs, Susan Willis, and Ralph Wolfe. Thanks to Sue Ellen Campbell for a pivotal idea that helped us over the edge of confusion when we needed it.

Also, we appreciate the critical and careful responses from our reviewers: Nancy Barry, University of Iowa; Beth Basham, University of Louisville; Elizabeth Fifer, Lehigh University; Jane Follis, University of Southern Indiana; Lynn Grow, Broward Community College; Judith Lee, The American University; Mark Reynolds, Jefferson-Davis Junior College; Maria Valeri-Gold, Georgia State University; Julia Walther, Grambling State College, and Jayne A. Widmayer, Boise State University.

Finally, thanks to our friends and editors at Holt, Rinehart and Winston, Inc., who consistently kept our feet to the fire: Cathy Townsend, Chris Caperton, Mary Pat Donlon, Fritz Schanz, and Michael Rosenberg.

Tom Wymer   To my wife, Penny, whose able reading kept me aware of my audience; to my consultants, Alan Emery and Richard Hebein for Humanism, William Baxter for the Scientific Revolution, and David Roller for Marxism, whose critical eyes and expert suggestions helped with accuracy and focus; and to Carol Stevens, who reminded me that issues of racism and sexism had to be continually confronted and not merely relegated to their respective sections.

Bruce Edwards   My contribution to this book is dedicated to my mother, Betty Lou Edwards (1930–1988), whose life taught me that great ideas must be lived, as well as believed, to have meaning. It is important for me to acknowledge that my editorial contributions to *Great Ideas* were completed in part with the financial support of the Lynde and Harry Bradley Foundation of Milwaukee, Wisconsin, as I served as a Bradley Resident Scholar at the Heritage Foundation in Washington, D.C., 1989–1990. Special thanks to Charles L. Heatherly, vice-president for Academic Relations at the Heritage Foundation, and to my fellow Bradley Scholars for their encouragement and their insights into the processes that link history and ideas. In addition, I would like to thank my wife, Joan, and four children, Matt, Mary, Justin, and Michael, for the part they have played in this book project and four previous ones: keeping me sane and teaching me what longsuffering means. Third, I am also greatly indebted to Tom and Alice Cook, Bowling Green, Ohio, God's spies, whose gracious counsel and earnest skepticism continually challenge my thinking and provoke me toward a sounder analysis of the great ideas broached in this book. Special appreciation is extended to two consultants who worked with me on the Judeo-Christian and Freud chapters, respectively Rev. James Jordan of Biblical Horizons, Inc., and Carol O'Shea, Director of the Writing Lab at Bowling Green State University. Finally, I wish to thank my indefatigable colleagues, Tom Klein and Tom Wymer, for inviting me into the project and for their informed appreciation of the impact of ideas over time on culture and society.

Tom Klein
Tom Wymer
Bruce Edwards

CONTENTS

CHAPTER SIX
THE DEMOCRATIC REVOLUTION 343

The Formative Ideas 407

CHAPTER SEVEN
MARXISM AND ECONOMICS 409

CHAPTER EIGHT
FREUD AND STUDY OF THE MIND 509

CHAPTER NINE
EXISTENTIALISM 564

CHAPTER TEN
ETHNICITY AND CIVIL RIGHTS 614

CHAPTER ELEVEN
FEMINISM 679

Introducing the Great Ideas

Chapter One

CONFRONTING THE GREAT IDEAS

WHAT ARE THE GREAT IDEAS AND WHY STUDY THEM?

Before answering the question of why we created a set of readings on great ideas and why one should study them, we must ask what great ideas are. In other words, what makes the ideas we have chosen for this text (the four "fundamental" ideas—the Judeo–Christian Tradition, Humanism, the Scientific Revolution, and the Democratic Revolution, and the five "formative" ideas—Marxism and Economics, Freud and the Study of Mind, Existentialism, Ethnicity and Civil Rights, and Feminism) great in the Western world? Why did we not choose another set of ideas, events, or phenomena, like agriculture, Protestantism, Puritanism, impressionism, behaviorism, capitalism, the computer, or even the Hoola Hoop and the Pet Rock?

Each of these phenomena has had considerable impact on millions of persons, but some are not so much ideas as applications (the computer), some are short lived (the Hoola Hoop and the Pet Rock), and some are highly derivative. For instance, Protestantism is simply an extension of ideas that will be examined under Judeo–Christian Tradition; Puritanism may be seen as an emphasis within Protestantism; behaviorism is an outgrowth of and response to ideas that will be examined under both the Scientific Revolution, and Freud and the Study of Mind.

If we can assume that a great idea is not merely an application, is not a short-lived phenomenon, and is not essentially a derivation, and if we can assume that it is something that has had a great impact on many people, we still need to

3

examine how that impact occurs. How do influential ideas develop? Why do some ideas gain power, whereas others recede into the forgotten corridors of history? Why do so many people today consider as "great" and, therefore, worthy of study the nine ideas we have chosen? Why would other people choose a very different list? Did these ideas rise to the surface because they were and are inherently better than others? Or do ideas, like politicians, come and go according to the often capricious events of history?

To answer these questions, we must, first, acknowledge that we cannot see or evaluate the past (and, thus, the ideas that developed in the context of the past) outside of how we see ourselves in our own contexts, cultures, and values. What is great to one person may be despicable and potentially dangerous to another. For example, Christianity is seen by many as a great idea at the center of which is a forgiving and ennobling love. Others see it as an idea system that contributed to the excommunication of Galileo and to the teaching of anti-Semitism, which eventually, after hundreds of years, planted the roots for the Holocaust. Science, for many, is deemed almost worthy of worship and is considered a direct route to a higher standard of living and the good life; others see it as a force leading to polluted air, land, and water; massive highway death; and to a greater means of destruction on an ever larger scale.

Second, we need to acknowledge that great ideas grow out of dialogue and, very often, very bitter conflict. Power and dominance have much to do with how ideas fare in history, as we can see from the bloody struggles of the American, French, and Russian Revolutions. Ideas are fought over, and often the stronger force, by virtue of its victory, vanquishes an opposing idea. Indeed, history is generally written by the victors; history appears very different when the "losers"—whether they be peasants, serfs, gypsies, or disenfranchised women—tell their stories.

Many would follow this line of reasoning, then, in suggesting that what is "great" is almost entirely in the eye of the beholder and that value may be "constructed" by those who have the power to do so. Those who follow an opposing line of reasoning would say that great ideas have absolute and universal qualities and that the inevitable progress of such ideas in history, not political power and group dominance, will determine what is indeed great.

Despite all these difficulties inherent in defining a great idea, we have, with some necessary arbitrariness, selected nine ideas and have divided them into two groups. What is the basis for this selection and grouping? What features, for instance, have we used in selecting the most basic or *fundamental* ideas? All ideas, of course, are derivative to some degree. Science, for example, has many roots in Greek humanism and so does democracy. However, because both ideas have so profoundly changed how humanity views the world and society and because those changes did not become fully defined or begin to affect human culture worldwide until many centuries after the era of Greek humanism, we consider them *fundamental* contributions to the world of ideas.

What we consider to be *formative* ideas represent profound innovations in thought that have significantly transformed our world and continue to do so. We have distinguished between fundamental and formative ideas only to indicate that the four fundamental ideas historically preceded the five formative ones. Another term we might have used for "formative" is "derivative." Freud's work, for example, is an extension of the Scientific Revolution (and therefore is derivative), but his research contained significant and far-reaching new views of the inner workings of the mind that changed scientific opinion in his time and continues to do so (and therefore is formative). Similarly, feminism can be seen as a mere extension of democracy, but our sense of sexuality is so basic to our language and behavior, to our image of ourselves, and to our personal, social, and political relations that this idea must also be recognized as formative.

Thus, we can identify the distinguishing characteristic of great ideas: they have exerted a primary effect on the way people think and behave. The four ideas we have classified as fundamental have done so since an early period of recorded history and continue to do so. The five ideas we have classified as formative are more recent developments, to some extent outgrowths of the fundamental four, but representing similarly profound and far-reaching innovations.

This nine-part arrangement, of course, cannot pretend to be definitive, but it provides a basic framework and sufficient variety to initiate the process of seeking out and critically examining those guideposts by which our lives and culture have been shaped. The mathematician and philosopher Jacob Bronowski suggests in a selection in Chapter 2 that animals are "creatures" of the landscape, whereas humans are "shapers" of the landscape. With each stage of human development over the past several thousand years, we have invented and formulated ideas that have become revolutionary in guiding and shaping our lives. Great ideas, whether in the hands of great and powerful leaders or percolating through the masses of population, are so potent that they have been used to rule or plunder, to build or devastate.

Marxism, for example, as a radical idea attempting to explain the conflict of economic classes, originated a little more than one hundred years ago and has affected governance systems among two-thirds of the world's population. Science, the source of so many "miracle" cures as well as lethal weapons, surely exerts an equally strong influence on billions of people. We regularly make decisions about the environment or the regulation of human conduct that depend directly on science. Yet, we as citizens may collectively know little about either the origins or development of science or Marxism, let alone their effects.

Thus, we must warn students that the great ideas are not easily mastered and, in fact, tolerate very few true experts. Great ideas operate on so many levels and require so many different types of understanding that we are not likely ever to believe we have finally mastered the concepts and questions involved. That their meaning cannot be exhausted should not be a discouragement; on the contrary, tackling the great questions should be a source of challenge and wonder. Although there have been few experts on each of these very demanding ideas, there have been many inquiries into them. All of us have had direct experiences with faith, reason, science, and the other ideas. Although we may not know the particular history of each idea, we do have our attitudes and biases, and on that foundation, we can build greater clarity and understanding. It is intriguing that the so-called great minds have grappled with the questions raised by great ideas without achieving a final and successful understanding, and you are fully capable of and invited into this same effort.

A final, important point concerns the origins of great ideas. Great ideas do not erupt spontaneously—they spring from questions that humans have asked for millennia: What does it mean to be human? Where have we come from? What will we become? How shall we organize our community? Who will govern and how? What is right, and what is wrong? What is evil, and why is it so widespread? What does it mean to be male or female? Is there a God or gods? If so, what kind or kinds? What difference would the existence or nonexistence of God make? And, last, how will we know the answers to these questions? Do we decide on the basis of faith, reason, a more empirical method of inquiry, or some combination thereof? These are great questions because they arise again and again for every culture of every time and because their answers guide and shape our lives.

Thus, we raise our opening question again: what are great ideas and what makes them great? The nine we have chosen have emerged powerfully through the conflicts of the past four thousand years. They are vehicles we use to confront the great questions that have always and will always be with us. They contain answers, not always the "right" answers, to the issues that we confront, but, perhaps more importantly, these great ideas represent attempts at discovering truth. The great appeal and perceived value of these ideas is manifested by the fact that cultures and subcultures return to them time and again, and great thinkers throughout the ages have given them powerful forms relevant to their particular cultures. Even so, these ideas do not necessarily offer us the last word, and it is important, therefore, not to treat them as self-evidently true and not to accept them blindly without testing their validity over time. Therefore, we invite you to look critically at all of these ideas from a variety of viewpoints, including the context in which they were written and a present day perspective.

Why create a set of readings on great ideas? The answer takes us to the very essence of what it means to be human. Reading and writing about great ideas helps us become better thinkers and better learners, and supports us in our quest to lead full and meaningful lives. The person who lacks the cultural literacy built on these great ideas is cut off from the past and, therefore, lives in only a small fraction of the present. Much like a person with no memory, who lives only in the present and is a creature solely of his five senses, the culturally illiterate person cannot fully participate in the mainstream of his culture. Imagine a person walking through a museum of fine arts and gazing at paintings by great artists of the past yet knowing nothing about history, mythology, or literature. That person's experience would be empty and barren. The same is true of a person walking through the twentieth century without a critical and heightened knowledge of our common past.

STRATEGIES FOR READING AND WRITING ABOUT THE GREAT IDEAS

The reading that follows in this chapter of the text will serve two purposes: one, it will introduce you to strategies for reading and understanding the great ideas; two, it will introduce you, first, to what one contemporary writer has said about our need to become conversant with the great ideas and, second, to the debate being waged at many colleges and universities over the merit of "great books" courses.

But before introducing you to this debate formally, we want to walk you through a model of an effective reading process to identify successful reading strategies. These strategies include

1. Breaking the Ice: Undertaking an Initial Reading
2. Zeroing In: Doing a Close Reading
3. Getting Things Clear: Searching for a Logical Pattern
4. Celebrating: Committing One's Ideas to Writing and Speaking

Having a plan or set of reading strategies is important, and strong and experienced readers rely on them, whereas weak and developing readers do not. Weak readers often take shortcuts, easy ways to what they consider success; they often quickly read through selections only once, focusing on particulars and details and failing to see the larger issues and structure of the reading. Stronger readers use a more systematic and involved approach, often writing and taking notes in the process. They know that single readings are inadequate in developing a fuller understanding, and they take the time to absorb the text over several readings. We strongly recommend the latter alternative.

This section, then, will walk you through a sample text to illustrate that time and effort must be invested to develop a careful reading of a text, and that a text can be read in different ways and is approached much more systematically by trained readers than by untrained ones. Also, by reading the texts in this section, you will be introduced to some of the fundamental issues addressed in the chapters that follow.

Breaking the Ice: The Initial Reading

Before we travel to a new place or meet a new person, we intuitively try to find out something about that place or person. We do this because some prior knowledge makes it easier for us to engage and enter the novel situation. With the benefit of a broad context, we can more easily fit the particulars into some pattern or developing whole.

Likewise, before reading a text, we would find it helpful to know something about the author, his or her background, audience, other writings, and apparent intentions in writing the piece at hand. Therefore, we have provided general historical and philosophical overviews of each idea and brief biographical sketches of each author to help you become more informed about the context you are entering. These should be read carefully.

Keep these goals in mind while you perform the initial reading:

1. Identify your purpose. Are you reading the text with a particular task (writing or discussion, perhaps) in mind? Are you to connect the text to some other reading or lecture? If so, would a review of those other materials be helpful?

2. Size up your source. What do you know about the author? about the occasion for the writing? about the historical period and current thinking at the time of the writing? and about the intended audience and purpose of the writing?

3. Perform a fast first reading. Keep in mind that you are exploring and skimming only to obtain a general and cursory sense of the territory carved out by the writing.

4. Identify what you know after a first reading. In a short and informal writing, collect your first impressions, your prior knowledge of and experiences with the ideas, and a list of what you do not know about the reading. Asking questions and boldly identifying what has confused you (for most, admissions of ignorance today seem to be very bold!) will often be a step toward mastering the text.

Now, try an initial reading of an essay by Harold Morowitz, "Prison of Socrates." Do not spend too much time on this exploratory stage.

▼

Prison of Socrates
HAROLD J. MOROWITZ

1   It is not my usual custom to write an essay while sitting on a rock on the Acropolis; nevertheless the reasons are compelling. The architectural splendor of the Parthenon and surrounding ruins by themselves might inspire poetry rather than this hesitant prose, but I have just come from the supposed site of one of enlightenment's earliest martyrdoms, the prison of Socrates. I had experienced some difficulty in finding the exact place. There are no signs, no monuments; only ΣΩΚΡΑΤΕΣ scratched in the stone, graffiti-like, informed me that I had arrived at my destination. The path to the prison started at the foot of the Acropolis and passed near a small church that echoed with ageless liturgical chanting. Drawn to the chapel door, I was distracted from my mission for a few minutes of listening. Nearby stood a small restaurant where a kindly waiter, with whom I did not share a common language, responded to my inquiry after Socrates by escorting me to the porch and pointing out a walkway leading up a hill.

The prison cell was the simple two-room cave described by Plato. Iron grill-   *2*
work closed off the entrance, and I peered inside, feeling a strange admixture
of past and present. The dimly remembered words of Plato somehow emblazoned themselves on the here and now, creating a surrealistic timelessness:
"Were you yourself, Phaedo, in the prison with Socrates on the day when he
drank the poison?" "Yes, Echecrates, I was."

It is strange that the location of such an important happening should go   *3*
unmarked. In the half hour that I was there, not a single tourist appeared to
experience this shrine. Could it be that the descendants of the citizens of Athens who voted the death of Socrates do not wish to advertise the matter? That
is a charming notion, but it is probably more ideal than real. Perhaps there is
too much uncertainty about the authenticity of the location. I don't know, and I
am fully prepared to leave the mystery unsolved, being content with the good
fortune of visiting the place in tranquility, uninterrupted by the constant comings and goings that characterize such a popular attraction as the Parthenon.
One of the chief reasons for including Athens on our itinerary had been to see
the prison where the great philosopher had met his noble end. The motivation
was a long-time attraction to Socrates' doctrine that the beginning of wisdom is
the realization of how little we know. It is a necessary antidote to the tendency
to regard ourselves as wise and to consider present knowledge as the final
word.

Still somewhat dazed by having walked on the stones that had known the   *4*
sandals of the famous philosophers of antiquity, I climb the Acropolis and look
out over the modern city of Athens. In my mind's eye I try to sense the scene
as it must have been in the days of Pericles, but something obtrudes on that
fantasy. Hovering over the city is a dark cloud of pollutants so obscenely dirty
that it blots out all visions in a reeking miasma of filth. I have seen that cloud
floating over many great cities. Yet viewed from the Parthenon, it takes on a
new significance, for in looking back at the past, we are tempted to look toward
the future. The events of the morning are forcing me to move from the Golden
Age of Greece, to modern Athens, to some dim beyond.

It is simply not true that the past is good and the present is bad, as some   *5*
romanticists would maintain. The trial and death of Socrates is in itself evidence enough that classical Greece was something less than a utopia. Yet there
is an interesting contrast between one lone man sipping poison for ideological
reasons and an entire city of several million slowly inhaling a lethal mixture as
the price of a life-style committed to certain technological and material wants
that have become needs. Even here the comparison is informative. What is
done for modern Athens by pollution-causing machinery was done for their
ancestors by slaves. The simple notion of good and bad begins to slip away,
and we focus instead on the issue of what a modern society wants. How have
we arrived at these goals? What price are we willing to pay?

We can, in this context, begin to understand what made Socrates so different *6*
and classical Greece so unique. He dared constantly to raise the questions:
What is justice? What is the good life? What are the responsibilities of the

state? By obstinately placing these difficulties before his fellow citizens, he kept them from falling into the rut of merely accepting a way of life for its own sake. He forced each Athenian to look inward, even if just a little, and ask why he was doing the things he was doing. Modern Athens lacks a living conscience, a public nuisance who will force the citizens to pause and question the most fundamental assumptions of their lives.

7   Classical Athens was what it was because most of the citizens knew Socrates personally. Present-day nations are so large that individuals know only their small circle of acquaintances, and the state is an abstraction that can be comprehended but not touched emotionally. Most of the great social writings of antiquity deal with relations of individuals at a one-on-one level of interaction. The Ten Commandments deal with parent and child, man and wife, neighbor and neighbor. These interactions, while immensely important, have been overshadowed by social patterns that relate the individual to his world in a statistical and impersonal way. We are now faced with problems where each person's contribution is minute, but the aggregate is potentially disastrous. The black cloud over Athens is such an issue. Concerning these moral dilemmas, the most cherished writings of antiquity stand mute, since the problems have only arisen with the industrial revolution and the enormous population growth of the last 200 years.

8   If wisdom does not provide us with answers, it does suggest that we should not cease from asking the questions. In the performance of this task our societies are lacking. We turn our attention to such pragmatic features as manufacture and transportation, but we do not inquire what we should be making or where we should be going. A highly diverse culture will no doubt offer many answers to such challenges, and arriving at conclusions will be exceedingly difficult. It is naive to suggest that a few simple Socratic queries and replies will suddenly turn us on to the right road. I do maintain, however, that if we do not constantly labor over the major points of social ethics, we will surely miss the mark, for the guidance of the past does not fully encompass the present.

9   The world is in need of annoying, troublesome, Socratic-like thinkers who will keep us from intellectual and spiritual slumbers brought on by lethargy, hyperstimulation, self-satisfaction, or simple discouragement over the magnitude and complexity of the challenges that have been set before us. Such philosophers are needed in education, journalism, television, movies, and every other public forum. They will trouble us and cause us sleepless nights, and I suppose that from time to time we shall imprison them or worse. But in the end they are national treasures, and if their graves or the sites of their martyrdom are unmarked, their ideas are the catalysts that enliven life and keep us from stagnation.

10   It is a very emotional experience sitting here on the Acropolis, and I wish not to let the event pass without finding deeper meaning in life. "Tell me, Reader, what do we mean by a good society?"

An initial reading might yield these kinds of impressions: Morowitz is a twentieth-century scientist addressing an educated, but not a technical, audience. He is describing his travels in Athens to the prison of one of the great philosophers of the Western world, Socrates. This is a very personal and reflective essay, a meditation on the dramatic changes that have occurred in the past two thousand five hundred years. Although Morowitz is a molecular biophysicist by profession, he is interested in philosophy and history. After having visited Socrates' prison cell and while sitting above Athens and ingesting its smog, he uses the occasion to reflect on the changes in our notions of the good society. He is concerned about the cloud of pollution over Athens and considers it a metaphor for a host of modern ills, including the pursuit of material want, alienation of the individual in large societies, and disillusionment. He wishes each of us to ask disturbing questions that awaken our intellectual and spiritual senses to action. Perhaps we can ask one of the great questions: what is a good society? And by asking, we can help our society to achieve what is good. In this essay, there seems to be less emphasis on imparting information (for Morowitz says little about the writings of Socrates or even about the technical nature of pollution) than on raising urgent moral and social issues.

Zeroing In: Doing a Close Reading

As a relationship with another person develops, we break through the often illusory and deceptive first impressions. We observe one another more closely, weighing words and gestures carefully. We ask questions of one another and examine behaviors and events from numerous points of view. Reading is no different. It, too, is a relationship that must be developed over time; a second reading gives us the chance to see more and to delve more carefully into the text and, thus, avoid the pitfalls of first impressions.

When performing a close reading, then, keep these goals in mind:

1. Perform a careful second reading of the text. That is, do not merely skim the text as in the initial reading. The emphasis now is on active mental participation and precise analysis of the text as illustrated in steps 2–4.

2. Underline or highlight important terms and ideas; always read with pencil, pen, or highlighter in hand. If you use highlighters, try a color-coded system, marking the important generalizations in red and the supporting details in blue.

3. Annotate the reading in the margins. Try this system: in the left margin, summarize each paragraph in one or two sentences or phrases; in the right margin, record questions about what puzzles or provokes your thought. Although writing on every paragraph sounds unnecessarily tedious, it will help beginning readers and writers. As ominous as it sounds, skipping this step may endanger your success in academic life, unless you have already mastered the art of reading.

4. After completing steps 1–3, look over what you have underlined or highlighted and written. Now, generate a condensed list of what you know and what you still need to know about the text. If this reading is to become part of a larger research project, go to the library (for a biography, encyclopedia entry, or book

review), a classmate, or your instructor to pin down what you do not know. From your condensed list, try to summarize and clarify the reading by stating the author's purpose in two or three sentences.

When a paragraph has more than one main point, which often is the case, the annotation in the left margin should reflect this complexity. It is not important to gain a sense of the essay's overall purpose or organization at this stage. That will come later when you begin to put the parts together. At this stage, try only to perceive the parts accurately, that is, the sentences and the paragraphs.

You have already skimmed through Morowitz's essay on Socrates. Now, closely reread each paragraph. Summarize its main points in the left margin, and put questions in the right margin. Then, read our sample annotations and compare them to yours.

▼

Prison of Socrates
HAROLD J. MOROWITZ

WHAT I KNOW

Par. 1
Morowitz is in Athens to visit Socrates' prison. S was a great philr put to death for asking too many questions of the young.

It is not my usual custom to write an essay while sitting on a rock on the Acropolis; nevertheless the reasons are compelling. The architectural splendor of the Parthenon and surrounding ruins by themselves might inspire poetry rather than this hesitant prose, but I have just come from the supposed site of one of enlightenment's earliest martyrdoms, the prison of Socrates. I had experienced some difficulty in finding the exact place. There are no signs, no monuments; only ΣΩΚΡΑΤΕΣ scratched in the stone, graffiti-like, informed me that I had arrived at my destination. The path to the prison started at the foot of the Acropolis and passed near a small church that echoed with ageless liturgical chanting. Drawn to the chapel door, I was distracted from my mission for a few minutes of listening. Nearby stood a small restaurant where a kindly waiter, with whom I

WHAT I DO NOT KNOW

Par. 1
Why would Morowitz want to find Socrates?

did not share a common language, responded to my inquiry after Socrates by escorting me to the porch and pointing out a walkway leading up a hill.

Par. 2
M describes S's prison cell.

The prison cell was the simple two-room cave described by Plato. Iron grillwork closed off the entrance, and I peered inside, feeling a strange admixture of past and present. The dimly remembered words of Plato somehow emblazoned themselves on the here and now, creating a surrealistic timelessness: "Were you yourself, Phaedo, in the prison with Socrates on the day when he drank the poison?" "Yes, Echecrates, I was."

Par. 3
M wonders whether the cell is unmarked because the Greeks do not want the publicity of S's martyrdom or because of a lack of historical record. M interested in S because he knows beginning of wisdom is realization of our ignorance.

It is strange that the location of such an important happening should go unmarked. In the half hour that I was there, not a single tourist appeared to experience this shrine. Could it be that the descendants of the citizens of Athens who voted the death of Socrates do not wish to advertise the matter? That is a charming notion, but it is probably more ideal than real. Perhaps there is too much uncertainty about the authenticity of the location. I don't know, and I am fully prepared to leave the mystery unsolved, being content with the good fortune of visiting the place in tranquility, uninterrupted by the constant comings and goings that characterize such a popular attraction as the Parthenon. One of the chief reasons for including Athens on our itinerary had been to see the prison where the great philosopher had met his noble end. The motivation was a long-time attraction to Socrates' doctrine that the beginning of wisdom is the realization of how little we know. It is a necessary antidote to the tendency to regard ourselves as wise and to consider present knowledge as the final word.

Par. 3
How would realization of our ignorance help?

Par. 4
The pollution of Athens forces M to think of to-day's Athens in contrast to its "Golden Age."

Still somewhat dazed by having walked on the stones that had known the sandals of the famous philosophers of antiquity, I climb the Acropolis and look out over the modern city of Athens. In my mind's eye I try to sense the scene as it must have been in the days of Pericles, but something obtrudes on that fantasy. Hovering over the city is a dark cloud of pollutants so obscenely dirty that it blots out all visions in a reeking miasma of filth. I have seen that cloud floating over many great cities. Yet viewed from the Parthenon, it takes on a new significance, for in looking back at the past, we are tempted to look toward the future. The events of the morning are forcing me to move from the Golden Age of Greece, to modern Athens, to some dim beyond.

Par. 4
Was Athens' Golden Age in the fifth century B.C.?

Par. 5
Athens' past is not really all good. Slavery and S's death demonstrate that. Simple notions of ancient good and present bad will not hold up. Important question is what do we want and what is the cost?

It is simply not true that the past is good and the present is bad, as some romanticists would maintain. The trial and death of Socrates is in itself evidence enough that classical Greece was something less than a utopia. Yet there is an interesting contrast between one lone man sipping poison for ideological reasons and an entire city of several million slowly inhaling a lethal mixture as the price of a life-style committed to certain technological and material wants that have become needs. Even here the comparison is informative. What is done for modern Athens by pollution-causing machinery was done for their ancestors by slaves. The simple notion of good and bad begins to slip away, and we focus instead on the issue of what a modern society wants. How have we arrived at these goals? What price are we willing to pay?

Par. 5
Where is M going with these ideas on good and bad?

Par. 6
Socrates forced Athenians to look inward and ask about the good and just life. Moderns do little of that.

We can, in this context, begin to understand what made Socrates so different and classical Greece so unique. He dared constantly to raise the questions: What is justice? What is the good life? What are the responsibilities of the state? By obstinately placing these difficulties before his fellow citizens, he kept them from falling into the rut of merely accepting a way of life for its own sake. He forced each Athenian to look inward, even if just a little, and ask why he was doing the things he was doing. Modern Athens lacks a living conscience, a public nuisance who will force the citizens to pause and question the most fundamental assumptions of their lives.

Par. 6
Is it true that moderns (us) do little self-reflection?

Par. 7
The ancients had personal relations with the great sages and leaders; our mass society prevents that. Pollution is one example of the disaster that may result from impersonality.

Classical Athens was what it was because most of the citizens knew Socrates personally. Present-day nations are so large that individuals know only their small circle of acquaintances, and the state is an abstraction that can be comprehended but not touched emotionally. Most of the great social writings of antiquity deal with relations of individuals at a one-on-one level of interaction. The Ten Commandments deal with parent and child, man and wife, neighbor and neighbor. These interactions, while immensely important, have been overshadowed by social patterns that relate the individual to his world in a statistical and impersonal way. We are now faced with problems where each person's contribution is minute, but the aggregate is potentially disastrous. The black cloud over Athens is such an issue. Concerning these moral dilemmas, the most cherished writings of antiquity stand mute, since the problems have only arisen with the industrial revolution and the enormous

Par. 7
How is pollution the result of a lack of personal relations?

population growth of the last 200 years.

Par. 8
We may never get an-
swers, but we must ask
the questions on social
ethics. The past guides
us but is never sufficient.

If wisdom does not provide us with answers, it does suggest that we should not cease from asking the questions. In the performance of this task our societies are lacking. We turn our attention to such pragmatic features as manufacture and transportation, but we do not inquire what we should be making or where we should be going. A highly diverse culture will no doubt offer many answers to such challenges, and arriving at conclusions will be exceedingly difficult. It is naive to suggest that a few simple Socratic queries and replies will suddenly turn us on to the right road. I do maintain, however, that if we do not constantly labor over the major points of social ethics, we will surely miss the mark, for the guidance of the past does not fully encompass the present.

Par. 8
What does he mean by
social ethics? Could it
relate to anything (prob-
lems) created by a group
of people? How do we
supplement the wisdom
of the past?

Par. 9
The world needs gad-
flies to keep us mentally
and spiritually alive.

The world is in need of annoying, troublesome, Socratic-like thinkers who will keep us from intellectual and spiritual slumbers brought on by lethargy, hyperstimulation, self-satisfaction, or simple discouragement over the magnitude and complexity of the challenges that have been set before us. Such philosophers are needed in education, journalism, television, movies, and every other public forum. They will trouble us and cause us sleepless nights, and I suppose that from time to time we shall imprison them or worse. But in the end they are national treasures, and if their graves or the sites of their martyrdom are unmarked, their ideas are the catalysts that enliven life and keep us from stagnation.

Par. 9
Are gadflies critics of
modern society? Who
are our gadflies?

Par. 10
M concludes by asking
us what we mean by the
good society.

It is a very emotional experience sitting here on the Acropolis, and I wish not to let the event pass without finding

deeper meaning in life. "Tell me,
Reader, what do we mean by a good
society?"

After the close reading, this is what we know of the essay and what still puzzles us: it appears that Morowitz's purpose here is to ask us to puzzle over the nature of the good society, especially to warn us that easy generalizations of good and bad are dangerous. He contrasts life in ancient Athens to life now, pointing out several advantages and disadvantages in each and warning against romanticizing either. He uses the death of Socrates to suggest that the Golden Age of Greece was not so golden. Also, even though its skies were not polluted, this was so because it used slave labor rather than machines to get work done. Apparently, Morowitz wants us to question, as would gadflies, the balance of social goods and evils present today. Is this age any more or less golden than Socrates'?

Getting Things Clear: Searching for a Logical Pattern

Most of us make critical decisions about relationships very cautiously because we are skeptical of our first impulses and inclinations. That is why, for instance, we choose roommates or spouses so carefully. We often try to distance ourselves emotionally from the relationship, perhaps with a neutral observer to review our thoughts and feelings rationally. The third stage in reading is much like that process of reviewing a relationship. We look for a logical pattern that indicates the direction of an argument or exposition and that assists us in understanding the ultimate purpose of the text we are reading (much as we would weigh the patterns and direction of a relationship and come to a final understanding of it). In uncovering this "inner logic" to the text, we are better able to decide whether we agree, disagree, or need more information about the author's conclusions.

When searching for a logical pattern in a reading, keep these goals in mind as you read:

1. Although searching for a logical pattern is often performed as part of the second (the close) reading, it may be helpful to perform this as a third, separate reading. Its central characteristic is synthesis, that is, reconnecting the parts and verifying earlier impressions.

2. In this form of reading, search for one central issue and formulate it as a question. Then, identify the author's conclusion and his main points that support this conclusion.

3. Determine the central intention of the essay, which normally will be either to inform (to clarify a point of view) or to persuade (to change the beliefs of the audience), or a combination of the two. Ascertaining the author's intention (and the success in achieving it) is the key to evaluating the text for effectiveness.

4. Finally, convert your marginal notes and condensation from the close read-

ing into an outline or summary form. This form should be of use for the particular writing or discussion activities your instructor defines.

What follows is the thinking process you might use in searching for a structure.

In searching for a structure and verifying response to a text, note the most obvious ideas. In the process (and this is where a third or even fourth reading really pays off), amazing subtleties sometimes reveal themselves.

"Structure" can be an intimidating word, but here this concept comes to our aid. In most rhetorical structures, the two most important parts are the beginning and the ending, the places where the central concern of the work and its chief substance are usually expressed. After having gained some sense of what the work is about by noting these two sections, you can carefully analyze each step along the path the author has led you, and once you have finally arrived at the intended destination, you can analyze what you were supposed to have learned. Then, you can consider the author's strategy and how effective it is.

In the first two paragraphs, you might notice that Morowitz sets the scene by taking us with him on his search for Socrates' prison, "finding the exact place." You now know that this essay is about both the relevance of Socrates to the present and the difficulty of defining that relevance. With this in mind, this quest takes on additional overtones that reinforce this view and confirming details begin to emerge. For example, the ruins of the Acropolis suggest the expanse of time separating us from Socrates; the liturgical chant from a nearby church, most likely Greek Orthodox, which distracts us for a while, suggests some of the major cultural changes, especially religious ones, that might obscure both the relevance and our understanding of this pre-Christian thinker; the waiter who speaks no English suggests the language barrier between us and Socrates. Are we surprised to discover that to find the place we must climb a hill?

More of the dimensions of this struggle for understanding are suggested at the beginning of paragraph 2. We find the prison cave, and yet we do not, for an iron grillwork prevents our entry. The remembered words of Plato are "somehow emblazoned . . . , creating a surrealistic timelessness" that challenge our reason and imagination with the question of whether it is possible for us to be there, like Phaedo, "in the prison with Socrates on the day when he drank the poison."

In the last two paragraphs, Morowitz' point is to challenge us to be there *now*, not *then*, to carry the spirit of Socrates into the modern world. Clearly, his purpose is more to persuade than to inform. We are told that the world needs "annoying, troublesome, Socratic-like thinkers," and we are urged to ask ourselves a central Socratic question, that is, what we ourselves mean by a good society, and to struggle with finding an answer.

Now, after obtaining an understanding of the author's purpose, you can see in the essay's middle how Morowitz leads us to his conclusion. First, in paragraph 2, Morowitz explores how to "be with" Socrates (and invites us to do so likewise) by recalling Phaedo's lines about being with Socrates on the day of his death. The issue of being with Socrates will be accomplished by reenacting some of Socrates' thought processes, which means first, in paragraph 3, to ask a question, why more tourists were not looking for Socrates' prison cell. More important than the actual question at this point, however, is Morowitz' inability to answer and his recollection of a major Socratic idea: recognizing ignorance is the beginning of wisdom.

From that position of the beginning of wisdom, we are able to see more clearly, that is, to see more questions. In paragraph 4, we climb with Morowitz/Socrates to the top of the Acropolis and discover the smog, but now, rather than serving as another barrier between us and the past like those we saw in paragraphs 1 and 2, the smog generates new questions, turning our attention from the past to the present and to the future.

Paragraph 5 warns us of a false road we might follow, that is, to think of the difference between the past and the present as a simple contrast between good and bad. Here, the threads of the argument Morowitz is pursuing begin to come together. The recognition of our ignorance is not wisdom, only its beginning. We are closer to real wisdom when we begin to recognize *what* questions *need* to be asked and how to frame them. And Morowitz asks some of these questions at the end of this paragraph: what [does] a modern society want[?] How have we arrived at these goals? What price are we willing to pay?"

In paragraphs 6, 7, and 8, you can see both the value of Socrates in his time and in ours, that is, the value of asking the difficult questions and of serving as a living conscience and the difference between his questions and ours. You can also see the need to determine how to frame the difficult questions that need to be asked. The conclusion that has already been noted follows in the final paragraphs to reinforce and reiterate these points and to turn the questioning over to the readers.

Celebrating: Committing One's Ideas to Writing and Public Discussion

Close, active reading alone will not necessarily result in a knowledgeable and authoritative ability to demonstrate what you have discovered. Close reading, however, accompanied by writing will often result in such an ability. These activities are mutually beneficial, are interdependent, and will provide the best opportunity for understanding and evaluating a text. Writing and public or classroom discussion allow you to articulate and celebrate your discoveries and measure them against the evaluations others have given the same material. In this textbook, you will encounter two kinds of writing tasks designed to enrich your thinking about your reading. First, at the end of each reading selection, there are three sets of questions; each set is designed to provoke a brief and particular kind of reflection upon the respective text. (Typical questions and responses are illustrated below.) Second, at the end of each chapter, there are questions that require longer responses, and these will assist you in synthesizing the various ideas and contexts of each reading and in drawing conclusions about the present-day cogency, impact, and relevance of these readings.

The short writing tasks attempt to focus even further what you have already discovered in close reading, to prompt your expression, and to uncover additional insights by requiring your thoughts on paper. These tasks, thus, allow you to explore, expand, and explain to yourself (and to your classmates) the meanings and implications suggested by the texts you read. These tasks also permit you to complete your cycle of reading and reflecting with something concrete—something in writing that will give your classroom discussion more substance and clarity.

Most writers clarify, evaluate, or respond to a text according to three modes: *informative, persuasive,* and *personal writing.* We have designed short writing tasks for each of these modes. *Informative writing* is used to probe a text, to clarify its meaning and intention, and to determine its main thesis and the implications of that thesis for the audience (original and present day). Informative writing is used inevitably to focus on the text itself, explaining as objectively as possible what it says and why. *Persuasive writing* is used to argue in favor of or against a particular point of view that is promoted by a text. Persuasive writing takes a stand; that is, it marshals evidence from the text and the writer's own context to support a specific thesis, anticipates possible objections, and offers counter arguments to alternative views. Third, *personal writing* responds directly to a text, and it allows the writer to examine his or her own feelings and associations, to ground them in a text, and to evaluate the selection on the basis of personal convictions and beliefs. Personal writing, while informed and sensitive to context and audience, is a much more expressive attempt to react, apply, and evaluate the ideas of a particular text.

In the following examples, questions and short responses are provided for informative, persuasive, and personal modes of writing. Each type of writing elicits a different purpose, approach, and style.

Informative Writing

What does Morowitz mean when he says that Athenian society, despite its reputation for democracy and equality, was really no more intrinsically ethical and better off than our own society?

In comparing ancient Athens with modern American culture, Morowitz is suggesting that one should not be too intimated by the history books and their glowing treatment of "the birthplace of democracy" and its vaunted golden age of philosophy. The city of Athens was filled with corruption and social ills: slavery, inequality for women and youth, and, most notably, an aristocracy that feared the power of a gadfly like Socrates. This fear of philosophical inquiry—in this case, the probing of a culture's soul—lies at the heart of Morowitz's own critique of Athenian democracy and, thus, our own. America, like Athens, has its blind spots, not the least of which is its preoccupation with mass media and the information it packages for our consumption. Morowitz, thus, ponders the true lack of self-reflection and critical thinking that the present form of our democracy fosters. No democracy—simply because its government bears that label—is necessarily responsive to and respectful of the needs and aspirations of its citizens. Athens had its slaves; we have had—and perhaps still do have—ours. Perhaps it is the case then, as he argues, that our security as a people lies not so much in finding answers as in asking the tough questions. For the "gadfly" keeps us mentally and spiritually alive, forces us to see what we would rather not see. The epitome of such a gadfly, as Morowitz ably points out, is the venerable Socrates; it is ironic, in retrospect, to note that he is still serving that function (in an inspirational sense), 2000 years after his death. Ancient Athens could silence his voice but not his spirit.

Persuasive Writing

Argue that "gadflies," those social critics who probe and critique and thereby provide both a conscience and a means for retooling society where it falters, are essential to any society that strives for fair treatment of all its citizens. Who are some prominent gadflies in our times?

Clearly, all cultures need gadflies, that is, people in all walks of life who are willing to "blow the whistle" on error, immorality, and general unethical decision making. In our mass-media culture, it is easy to be swayed by the flood of public opinion that is bleated out on television and other media. For instance, during the most recent presidential campaign, each political party had what were called "spin doctors" to make sure that "we the people" understood what interpretation we were to place on the debates, stump speeches, and controversies. The spin doctor is, in effect, the opposite of a gadfly, for the gadfly owes no allegiances and is willing to remain skeptical and distant from the status quo. Thus, we need gadflies willing to stand against prevailing opinion and to articulate alternative views—just as Socrates did. Quite often in American culture, the "adversary press" plays this role—witness the demise of Gary Hart's campaign and of certain "televangelists." However, sometimes the press itself is in need of a whistle blower who points out a biased or incomplete treatment of an issue or story. Thus, the fact remains that in any would-be democracy, involved citizens must have a little gadfly in them, that presence of mind and quality of spirit that compels them to question, debate, and probe both the source and the validity of the received wisdom.

Personal Writing

When you think of what constitutes the "good society," what comes to mind? Is theorizing about the "good society" beneficial? What personal experiences contribute to your view of a healthy and just society?

I believe that too much brooding or soul searching over what "society is or does" can be counterproductive, that is, a waste of time. I am not sure myself whether "society" in the "national" sense really exists anyway. (I sometimes wonder if it isn't something the sociology department made up to attract more majors!) But I do agree that there can be better and worse goals and plans for groups of individuals, neighborhoods, and so on. It seems to me that theories about "the good society" have their impact more at the local level—not as "policy" but as the basic spirit or theme of the individuals living in a particular time and place. In the multiethnic neighborhood in which I grew up in Cleveland, we seemed to share an unconscious set of principles and dreams that transcended racial, religious, and class boundaries. When I was 12 years old, I remember that Mr. O'Malley's grocery store was robbed, and everyone on my street was outraged— old and young, black and white, factory workers and business executives. "The good society" in East Cleveland meant, among other things, that you did not hurt your neighbor and did not risk the welfare of the community for the benefit of one selfish individual. Things could have been tense and suspicion could have swarmed over the streets, but our common belief in each other and our sense of heritage in the neighborhood compelled us to rally around the O'Malleys and to show our support for their business and their lives. That's the good society in action, not as theory.

As you read through these sample paragraphs, you can discern the differences in approach and effect. In the *informative* example, the writer expresses an understanding of the text itself; he refers and defers to it for evidence and then articulates a reasoned summary of the author's point of view. The aim is to "explain" the meaning of the text rather than merely "react" to it in a personal sense. In the *persuasive* example, the writer argues a thesis; that is, he makes a particular point and attempts to support that point not only from the text itself but also from his own personal experience and general knowledge. The aim is to "persuade"—to change, to cause to adopt, or to reinforce the views of a reader on the topic. In the *personal* example, the writer is much more expressive and idiosyncratic; his is a "response," as opposed to an explanation or an argument, based on how the reading affected him. The personal text expresses sincere, individual feelings and reflections and is generally less bound by the rhetorical conventions of expository or persuasive writing.

Remember, of course, that these short writing tasks can be thought of not only as ends in themselves—important tools for uncovering your opinions—but also as the foundation and building blocks for discussion and classroom inquiry and for the long writing tasks at the end of each chapter. In these long writing assignments, your instructor will be exhorting you to synthesize ("bring together") in a fuller, more comprehensive way the informative, persuasive, or personal responses you have made to each chapter's great idea. The short and the long writing tasks will sharpen your reading skills and will strengthen your confidence and your ability to use the information you come in contact with during your college career and thereafter.

Chapter 2

MEMORY AND CIVILIZATION

Our relationship to the past is something most of us think little about. However, a few moments of reflection will remind us of how important the past is. The essays, articles, and reports in this chapter are all concerned with the past, or, in other words, with memory. Today, we face a threat to the civilized world, the loss of memory. Demonstrating one of the forms this threat takes, a recent report found that it was possible to be graduated from 38% of our nation's universities without a course in history, 45% without a course in British or American literature, 78% without a course in Western civilization, 62% without a course in philosophy, and 77% without a foreign language. (*Undergraduate General Education and Humanities Requirements*, Higher Education Surveys #7 [Rockville, MD: Westat, Inc., 1989])

One of the greatest threats to democratic life is precisely this loss of our past. The leadership in China has, at least at the time of this writing, suppressed the events of June 3 and 4, 1989 in Tiananmen Square, and therefore destroyed the memory of the brutal government attack on the people. George Orwell, Ray Bradbury, and Aldous Huxley, in their respective novels *1984, Fahrenheit 451,* and *Brave New World,* all warn us of how close modern, advanced industrial cultures have come to totalitarianism that either cuts off the past or controls it entirely to satisfy the ends of tyrannical leaders. You may recall that books were either burned or banned in *Fahrenheit 451* and *Brave New World;* in *1984,* there was a "past," but it was wholly fabricated to serve the oppressive political purposes of the leaders. These novels demonstrate that the freedom to know the past is critically important in choosing who and what we want to be. In this chapter, exploring this issue of our relationship to the past should achieve two distinct purposes: it will help us to see our present lives more clearly, and it will open the doors to the great ideas themselves.

An analogy is useful here to explain why a critical knowledge of the past is necessary to any culture, especially if that culture is to survive with its best traditions of justice, truth, and equality intact. Try to imagine what a person would be without a past. Some persons who survive catastrophic automobile accidents lose parts or all of their memories; perhaps this is the mind's way of protecting them from the awful memory of the accident. Such a person may still be capable of rudimentary functioning, but she may be incapable of normal relationships and behaviors. We consciously and unconsciously draw on meanings and values developed in our past as we live from day to day. We make plans for travel, careers, or encounters with friends, based on the attitudes developed over years. Our past personally operates as a kind of context from which we draw to make judgments about what is good or evil, healthy or neurotic, and selfish or devoted to the greater good of the community. Without our past, in other words, we are morally, emotionally, and intellectually lost.

Countries operate similarly. The United States may have avoided a fuller entry into the civil conflicts in Central America because the memory of the war in Vietnam is still vivid. On the other hand, the Sanctuary Movement, in which persecuted Central Americans were secretly transported to and hidden in this country by concerned citizens, may, once exposed, have had some success in encouraging the United States to become more involved to the degree that we guiltily recall the boatloads of Jews we turned away in World War II, at the cost of most of their lives in the Holocaust.

The readings in this chapter fall into three sections. In the first section, four readings very broadly address our relationship to the past and the consequences of shutting it out. Assuming that an unobstructed view of the past is a healthy and necessary component of life in a democratic society, we provide readings that examine how successful our society has been in this regard. In the first selection, novelist and essayist Tom Wolfe describes several recent events involving groups or individuals who lacked knowledge of the past. The next three readings come from educators. Vermont high school teacher Garret Keizer, University of Chicago professor Allan Bloom, and education researchers Chester E. Finn and Diane Ravitch claim that we have not done enough to promote what has come to be called "cultural literacy," that is, knowledge about culture that is necessary if individuals are to function effectively in society.

The second section contains three readings concerned with the challenge of recovering the past, specifically why a broad historical framework is necessary for knowing ourselves. Mathematician and philosopher Jacob Bronowski believes that humans are unique in nature in that we are not just products of our surroundings, but we are also shapers of those surroundings. As shapers, we carry a great burden of responsibility. English professor E. D. Hirsch argues that young people today are culturally deficient, and he goes one step further in identifying those pieces of cultural information deemed necessary to "thrive in the modern world." George Steiner, in reviewing Hirsch's book *Cultural Literacy*, takes Hirsch to task on several important points, including the basis for defining cultural literacy and for selecting those pieces worthy of study. Steiner wonders whether Hirsch is pushing for an "adjustment," via information collection, to the modern world of "Himmler and Pol Pot."

The chapter concludes with three readings that address the decisions involved in developing a university curriculum and the ethical issues involved, specifically those dealing with cultural bias. First, Kenyan novelist and teacher Ngugi Wa Thiong'o argues against imposing one society's literature on another and calls this an act of imperialism and racism. The remaining article and editorials from Richard Bernstein, *Wall Street Journal* editorial writers, and letter from Charles Junkerman, a Stanford University dean, all deal with a debate that occurred recently at Stanford University over its course in Western civilization. The Stanford debate illustrates the passions and values involved in arguing for one version or another of cultural literacy.

▼

The Great Relearning Heralds 21st Century
TOM WOLFE

In 1968, in San Francisco, I came across a curious footnote to the *1*
psychedelic movement. At the Haight-Ashbury Free Clinic there were doctors who were treating diseases no living doctor had ever encountered before, diseases that had disappeared so long ago they had never even picked up Latin names, diseases such as the mange, the grunge, the itch, the twitch, the thrush, the scroff, the rot.

Why had they now returned? It had to do with the fact that thousands of *2*
young men and women had migrated to San Francisco to live communally in what I think history will record as one of the most extraordinary religious experiments of all time.

The hippies, as they became known, sought nothing less than to sweep aside *3*
all codes and restraints of the past and start out from zero. At one point Ken Kesey organized a pilgrimage to Stonehenge with the idea of returning to Anglo-Saxon civilization's point zero, which he figured was Stonehenge, and heading out all over again to do it better. Among the codes and restraints that people in the communes swept aside—quite purposely—were those that said you shouldn't use other people's toothbrushes or sleep on other people's mat-

tresses without changing the sheets or, as was more likely, without using any sheets at all or that you and five other people shouldn't drink from the same bottle of Shasta or take *tokes* from the same cigarette. And now, in 1968, they were relearning the laws of hygiene . . . by getting the mange, the grunge, the itch, the twitch, the thrush, the scroff, the rot.

4   This process, namely the relearning—following a Promethean and unprecedented start from zero—seems to me to be the *leitmotif* of our current interlude, here in the dying years of the 20th century.

5   "Start from zero" was the slogan of the Bauhaus School. The story of how the Bauhaus, a tiny artists' movement in Germany in the 1920s, swept aside the architectural styles of the past and created the glassbox face of the modern American city is a familiar one, and I won't retell it. But I should mention the soaring spiritual exuberance with which the movement began, the passionate conviction of the Bauhaus's leader, Walter Gropius, that by starting from zero in architecture and design man could free himself from the dead hand of the past. By the late 1970s, however, architects themselves were beginning to complain of the dead hand of the Bauhaus: The flat roofs, which leaked from rain and collapsed from snow, the tiny bare beige office cubicles, which made workers feel like component parts, the glass walls, which let in too much heat, too much cold, too much glare, and no air at all.

6   The relearning is now under way in earnest. The architects are busy rummaging about in what New York painter Richard Merkin calls the Big Closet. Inside the Big Closet, in promiscuous heaps, are the abandoned styles of the past. The current favorite rediscoveries: Classical, Secession, and Moderne (Art Deco). Relearning on the wing, the architects are off on a binge of eclecticism comparable to the Victorian period a century ago.

7   In politics, the 20th century's great start from zero was one-party socialism, also known as communism or Marxism-Leninism. Given that system's bad reputation in the West today (even among the French intelligentsia), it is instructive to read John Reed's "Ten Days That Shook the World"—before turning to Alexander Solzhenitsyn's "Gulag Archipelago."

8   The old strike hall poster of a Promethean worker in a blue shirt breaking his chains across his mighty chest was the vision of ultimate human freedom the movement believed in at the outset. For intellectuals in the West, the painful dawn began with the publication of the "Gulag Archipelago" in 1973. Solzhenitsyn insisted that the villain behind the Soviet concentration camp network was not Stalin or Lenin (who invented the term concentration camp) or even Marxism. It was instead the Soviets' peculiarly 20th-century notion that they could sweep aside not only the old social order but also its religious ethic, which had been millennia in the making ("common decency," Orwell called it) and reinvent morality . . . here . . . now . . . "at the point of a gun," in the famous phrase of the Maoists. Today the relearning has reached the point where even ruling circles in the Soviet Union and China have begun to wonder how best to convert communism into something other than, in Susan Sontag's phrase, Successful Fascism.

9   The great American Contribution to the 20th century's start from zero was

in the area of manners and mores, especially in what was rather primly called "the sexual revolution." In every hamlet, even in the erstwhile Bible Belt, may be found the village brothel, no longer hidden in a house of blue lights or red lights behind a green door but openly advertised by the side of the road with a thousand-watt back-lit plastic sign: *Totally All-Nude Girl Sauna Massage and Marathon Encounter Sessions Inside.*

Until several years ago pornographic movie theaters were as ubiquitous as *10* the Seven-Eleven; these theaters included outdoor drive-ins with screens six, seven, eight stories high, the better to beam all the moistened folds and glistening nodes and stiffened giblets to a panting American countryside. But since then, in the last two years or so, the pornographic theaters have begun to be replaced by the pornographic videocassette, which could be brought into any home.

Up on the shelf in the den, next to the set of "The Encyclopaedia Britan- *11* nica" and the great books, one now finds the cassettes: "Shanks Akimbo," "That Thing with the Cup." My favorite moment in Jessica Hahn's triumphal tour of Medialand this fall came when a 10-year-old girl, a student at a private school, wearing a buttercup blouse, a cardigan sweater, and her school uniform skirt, approached her outside a television studio with a stack of "Playboy" magazines featuring the famous Hahn nude form and asked her to autograph them. With the school's blessing, she intended to take the signed copies back to the campus and hold a public auction. The proceeds would go to the poor.

But in the sexual revolution, too, the painful dawn has already arrived, and *12* the relearning is imminent. All may be summed up in a single term, requiring no amplification: AIDS.

The Great Relearning—if anything so prosaic as remedial education can be *13* called great—should be thought of not as the end of the 20th century but the prelude to the 21st. There is no law of history that says a new century must start 10 or 20 years beforehand, but two times in a row it has worked out that way. The 19th began with the American and French revolutions of the late 18th. The 20th century began with the formulation of Marxism, Freudianism, and Modernism in the late 19th. And now the 21st begins with the Great Relearning.

The 21st century, I predict, will confound the 20th century notion of the *14* Future as something exciting, unexpected or radiant; as Progress, to use an old word. It is already clear that the large cities, thanks to the Relearning, will not even look new.

Quite the opposite; the cities of 2007 will look more like the cities of 1927 *15* than the cities of 1987. The 21st century will have a retrograde look and a retrograde mental atmosphere. People of the next century, snug in their Neo-Georgian apartment complexes, will gaze back with a ghastly awe upon our time. They will regard the 20th as the century in which wars became so enormous they were known as World Wars, the century in which technology leapt forward so rapidly man developed the capacity to destroy the planet itself—but also the capacity to escape to the stars on space ships if it blew.

16   But above all they will look back upon the 20th as the century in which their forebears had the amazing confidence, the Promethean hubris, to defy the gods and try to push man's power and freedom to limitless, god-like extremes.

17   They will look back in awe—without the slightest temptation to emulate the daring of those who swept aside all rules and tried to start from zero. Instead, they sink ever deeper into their Neo-Louis bergeres, content to live in what will be known as the Somnolent Century of the 20th Century's Hangover.

WRITING AND DISCUSSION QUESTIONS

Informative

1. What does Wolfe mean by "the relearning—following a Promethean and unprecedented start from zero" (paragraph 4)? How do the examples from architecture, politics, manners, and mores support this conclusion?
2. What predictions does Wolfe make about the twenty-first century? How does he arrive at these predictions?

Persuasive

1. Argue that Wolfe is or is not right in describing the "great relearning." Cite your own examples to assess the quality of his thinking. Has he overstated his case?
2. Argue for or against questioning the past or of starting over. What advantages are there in not being bound to the past?

Personal

1. Can you identify with the "amazing confidence, the Promethean hubris" of the twentieth century in your own immediate life and culture?

▼

A Promised Land
GARRET KEIZER

Mister, I ain't a boy, no, I'm a man,
And I believe in a promised land.
                    —BRUCE SPRINGSTEEN,
                    "The Promised Land"

1   When the great cathedral of Notre Dame de Chartres burned in 1194, enthusiasm for its restoration swept through France. Among those who organized for the work were troops of children and teenagers who descended

on Chartres like harbingers of the apocalypse. Unfortunately, it is more accurate to speak of them as precursors of the Children's Crusade, which left for the Holy Land in 1212, and arrived instead at the slave markets of Baghdad and Cairo, thanks to two unspeakable merchants named Hugh the Iron and William the Pig.

We hear such stories and their modern parallels, and we shudder at the 2
enormous energy and credulity of youth. We sigh our thanks for living in a better place and time, and we send the kids off to the video arcade.

But the energy remains. That its use has often been tragic does not make its 3
waste any less tragic. That we do waste it, that we have allowed it to be perverted into a subculture of obnoxious mannerisms and indiscriminate consumerism does not make it any less marvelous to consider.

These young people need a challenge—that is one of our great clichés—but 4
our conception of challenge has become so bland that we might as well be saying they need their vitamins or their sleep. We frequently approach the education of our youth with the implied assumption that they do not want to learn, or that they will learn only in terms of the latest movies, records, and posters, which were designed, of course, not by rebellious fifteen- and sixteen-year-olds, but by comfortable twenty- to forty-year-olds desirous of being more comfortable. We assume that the only poetry our students will read is on an album jacket, the only research they will do concerns marijuana or the major leagues, and the only novel they will study is about a prostitute with pimples. We accept their initial groans at the introduction of anything different as sincere and insurmountable, not realizing that they are only reacting as they have been taught to react by a few moronic TV sitcoms which they themselves but half enjoy.

I accept the groans as points of etiquette, and proceed. My freshman 5
English classes read *Antigone, The Odyssey, Macbeth,* Hardy's *Return of the Native*—none of these abridged or paraphrased. I begin our study of these works by stating that I can think of several reasons why we shouldn't study them and that other persons have supplied me with several more, that I reject the reasons out of hand and that we are going to study the classics come what may. I will not pretend that the books are not difficult, and I will not pretend that they are without passages which most modern readers will find tedious— but I will also not pretend that tripe is profound or that people lack sensibility simply because they are fifteen and live "in the sticks." So we begin to read. And the response from the majority of students is one of mature commitment, unfeigned enjoyment, and surprising insight.

Of course one does not tackle *Macbeth* in remedial English. But the princi- 6
ple behind tackling it elsewhere remains in full force here. For several years I taught a class called Reading and Writing, which had been designed for students with difficulty in both. Halfway through one semester I announced to my "lovable thugs" that we were abandoning the worksheets and undertaking the writing of a book. The size of the class—three boys—had been something of an accident, and I realized almost too late that such an accident with all its possibilities was not likely to happen ever again. For their part, the boys sank ever

lower in their seats, presumably in a quandary over whether to kill themselves or me. I went on to tell them that when the book was written we would probably have it printed and sell it to the school population and to local libraries. They were relieved: something in the teacher had obviously "snapped" and he would be committed before any of this actually happened. But we did write a book, a hot-rod picaresque called *Born to Run*, or, as I nicknamed it, "Smokey and the Bandit Meet Strunk and White"—though nothing in the Good Ol' Boy genre has moments as touching and near to sublime as *Born to Run*. We sold out in two lunch periods and got reviewed in the local paper; the authors received an award at the June assembly. Years later I still get questions about "them guys that wrote the book." Them guys have been placed among the stars.

7   But when they were still on earth, one of them said to me, "I told my mom what we're up to, and she said, 'You can't even spell—how the hell are you gonna write a book!'" This was just my point. If a kid can't spell, have him write a book. If a kid can't clear the low hurdles, give him a shot at the high.

8   That he will frequently clear the high is not so mysterious as it seems. Kids are no different from other human beings in that they want to matter. Recently the son of some dinner guests, bored by our conversation, asked if I had any work around for him to do. I told him he could throw some firewood from a smaller pile into a larger one. I could tell he did not believe that was something I really needed done, and he came back in five minutes claiming to be tired. I wound up doing the job myself that Saturday. Had I asked him to block and split ten cords of tree-length logs with a chain saw and maul, he doubtless would have worked into the dark. But he refused to be "kept busy," and I respect him for that. He wanted to engage in something purposeful. He was willing to work, but only if I was willing to take a risk.

9   I have sometimes said that the best way to handle the kids who pose the biggest discipline problems in a school is to put them in charge of discipline. I am only half fooling. I think a major problem in our schools is not that kids are too brash and nervy but that we are not brash and nervy enough.

10   Nowhere is this more apparent than in our insipid campaigns for "school spirit" and "student leadership." We vainly hope to make a treadmill look like a sacred quest; we ask kids to be excited in a void of ideas, because only in talking about nothing can we be sure not to arouse any controversy. We don't even talk to them about patriotism anymore. We ask kids to take a stand in all the places where we have been taking a nap. Then, when we have few takers, we complain about the apathy of youth.

11   The so-called "rebelliousness" of youth—which often appears as little more than the hard edge of apathy—may also come from our failure to issue a significant challenge to our young. In public education, as in popular entertainment, we have sold our kids a curious bill of goods on the subject of rebellion. First we tell them that rebellion is basically good, creative, liberating. The bright lights of science, art, and politics were all rebels. Second, we tell them that rebellion is the natural attitude of youth. It's healthy, inevitable, and to some extent tolerable for the young to rebel. Assuming we're right on the first two

points, we ought to add a third: that rebellion is only as good, creative, and liberating as its opposition is strong, coherent, and not totally disarmed by points one and two. To quote the poet Hugh MacDiarmid, somewhat out of context: "You cannot strike a match on a crumbling wall." Take classicism away from the Romantics who rebelled against it and what does one have left? A few surly extras on the set of *Rebel Without a Cause.* Take away every claim of authority from our pronouncements, and thus any clear point of departure for a young thinker, and what does one have left by way of youthful rebellion? A few mannerisms less original than James Dean's.

An interesting observation in this regard is my students' understanding of 12 the word "radical." The term arose in discussion one day, and it was not long before I realized that my students and I were talking about two different things. Finally I asked them what a "radical" is. As nearly as I can quote their definition, a radical is an outrageously fun-loving person. At first I was amazed at their innocence. But in retrospect I am even more amazed at how accurately they had described their own predicament—and for that matter, how accurately they had intuited the nature of so much American middle-class "radicalism." In the absence of any real challenge, given or received, when opponents assume postures more than they take stands, we're pretty much left with "fun," aren't we? If reaching or redefining a promised land is not the "radical's" business, then all that remains is to raise a little hell.

Our failure to challenge kids to purposeful leadership, or even to provoke 13 them to creative rebellion, is matched by a still more significant failure to acquaint them with great ideas. It is not simply our school assemblies and slogans that are so bland and pointless, but the tenor of our curriculum. Kids are shockingly unaware of the religious and political ideas that have shaped their history and are even now revolutionizing their world. In a century torn by ideological struggles we seem to think that the best favor we can do for our young is to have them ignorant of all ideology. I wonder if any of them assume what their elders seem to have asumed, that the safest way to assure pluralism is to bury it in nihilism.

A bright student came to me several years ago with a question on her mind. 14 She'd been watching a television series on the Holocaust. "What's a Jew?" she asked. "They don't believe in God, right?" As gently as I could, I explained that her phrase "believe in God" was essentially a Jewish invention, or discovery if she preferred. She acknowledged the debt with an "oh!" but then wanted to know why the Nazis were so anti-Semitic. Like many other students, she thought that the Nazis had invented anti-Semitism. And like many other students, she probably could have located Israel on a map, named its prime minister, and recited the dates of its wars and founding. She would have been able to do the same for Iran and the Soviet Union. She just could not tell me in any detail what many a Jew, Muslim, or Marxist has lived and died for.

Admittedly, we often shy away from acquainting students with ideas because 15 we fear indoctrinating those ideas, or distorting them with a teacher's bias. That is a good fear to have. I know of a school in the Northeast Kingdom where a young girl, who may one day be an important scientist, was persecuted in a science class for her beliefs on the origins of humankind. Her ideas were quite conventional: she accepted Darwin wholeheartedly. Her teacher, if I must call him that, disagreed—and argued his case for "creationism" by repeatedly making monkey noises at the girl, an argument her less-evolved classmated found easy to copy. Apparently his understanding of ethics was as profound as his definition of *science*. Those who may seem overly zealous to prevent this kind of travesty are not such extremists after all. But the same vigilance we exercise to keep science classes from turning into Sunday school classes needs to be exercised to prevent legitimate fears from turning into superstitions. It is possible for students and teachers to explore "alien" ideologies (provided they are not utterly alien to the discipline being taught) without alienating one another.

16   Once a girl in my class decided to do a research paper on the John Birch Society. Her father was a Bircher, as she herself was soon to become, so this her first major research paper was a rite of passage as well. Perhaps because I was enthusiastic over her choice of a topic, she assumed I was also sympathetic to her political point of view. Almost conspiratorially she confided to me her worries about a history teacher who would also be reading her paper and giving it a grade. "Mr. M———is a pretty liberal guy, and I'm worried how he'll mark it," she said.

17   I assured her that Mr. M———would insist, as I would, on an objective presentation of factual material and on sources other than publications of the Society, but that our insistence did not in any way imply a prejudice against her or her work. "As far as politics go," I told her, "mine are probably a good deal to the *left* of Mr. M———'s, and look how excited I am about your paper." I had meant to put her at ease, but my mistake was immediately evident from the blood leaving her face. From where she stood, Mr. M——— looked as pink as a piece of rare prime rib, and I was to the *left* of that? Removing my glasses so as to blur even the slightest resemblance I might have to Trotsky, I smiled with great benevolence. "It's going to be a wonderful paper," I said. It's going to be the end of my life, she thought.

18   Well, it was a wonderful paper, and working on it with her was the beginning of one of the warmest relationships I ever enjoyed with a student. I tried not only to help her see different points of view, but also to give depth to her own. I introduced her to the novels of Ayn Rand. I found quotations from Lenin that she could use as ammunition. Rummaging at a barn sale I found a paperback entitled *The God That Failed,* an anthology of American writers and intellectuals who had become disillusioned with the Left. I paid the ten cents and bought it for her. That was the best bargain I ever got on a book, because for several years thereafter she presented me with a new book every Christmas.

19   What I saw in this girl—what I see again and again in young people that enables them to rebuild cathedrals and defy monkey-mimicking science teachers—was the ability to believe in something more than survival, gratification, and success. It was her having some conviction, aside from any content of the conviction itself, that I strove to reinforce. I think it was Toynbee who said that

the values of Sparta and Valhalla are preferable to no values at all. And a misfired challenge to the young may be preferable to allowing their need for challenge and commitment to go unmet.

A couple of years ago, my colleague Bob Ketchum and I attempted to take   *20*
our experience with student tutors and his experience in the Peace Corps one step further by using young people to teach adults in the community. If teenagers in Nicaragua could reduce illiteracy by tens of percentage points, why couldn't teenagers perform similar wonders in northeastern Vermont? And with the performance of even a dubious wonder, what questions might they be led to ask about democracy, education, and the meaning of a life? So we and a handful of students founded S.A.L.T.—Students and Adults Learning Together. Our members included my John Bircher and a very determined young man who would later join the Marines for some of the same reasons that he volunteered to be a Vermont *Brigadista*—because he believed he had a purpose beyond keeping fast food in his belly and gas in his car.

As a matter of prudence and courtesy—I hope not of timidity—we decided   *21*
to begin by offering our services as auxiliaries to an adult-ed program already in place: we were welcomed, given mixed signals, stalled, then told before we had even begun that our services were not needed. William the Pig strikes again. The idea needs to rest awhile before being revived, and then we shall need to revive it more assertively—but that is not my point. My point is that a handful of Vermont teenagers were ready to give up lunch periods, after-shool time, and weekends to tutor their neighbors, mind their tutored neighbors' kids, and take numerous risks, not least of all the risk of accomplishing nothing, and to make this commitment without the incentives of money, awards, privileges, or grades. Where we saw possiblities, they saw promise.

Working with students like these and like the boys who wrote *Born to Run,* I   *22*
have come to the conclusion that the recent invention called adolescence appeals to them about as much as it appeals to me—not much at all. Puberty is beautiful; adolescence can be as cheap and trashy as the interests that prey upon it. As an idea, it is far more apealing to ten-year-olds who want to talk "dirty" and to certain thirty-five-year-olds who want to live the way the ten-year-olds talk. The hearts of most sixteen-year-olds are made of finer stuff. They do not want to be adolescents. They want to be young women and men. They believe in a promised land. And if we are not inclined to believe in something like the same thing, our every effort to help them amounts to a betrayal.

WRITING AND DISCUSSION QUESTIONS

Informative

1. What evidence does Keizer cite to conclude that our youth are in trouble? How serious and widespread do you think these problems are?
2. What does Keizer blame for the tragic waste of youth?

Persuasive

1. Keizer believes that a large part of the remedy for our wasted youth lies in studying the classics and great ideas. Argue for or against them as a remedy.
2. Keizer claims that schools and communities prefer students to be ignorant of all ideology (paragraph 13). Argue for or against this claim.

Personal

1. How does your own experience in school confirm or contradict Keizer's ascerbic criticisms of American education?
2. Keizer ends his chapter on an idealistic, optimistic note. Do you think such optimism is justified?

▼

Books
ALLAN BLOOM

1   I have begun to wonder whether the experience of the greatest texts from early childhood is not a prerequisite for a concern throughout life for them and for lesser but important literature. The soul's longing, its intolerable irritation under the constraints of the conditional and limited, may very well require encouragement at the outset. At all events, whatever the cause, our students have lost the practice of and the taste for reading. They have not learned how to read, nor do they have the expectation of delight or improvement from reading. They are "authentic," as against the immediately preceding university generations, in having few cultural pretensions and in refusing hypocritical ritual bows to high culture.

2   When I first noticed the decline in reading during the late sixties, I began asking my large introductory classes, and any other group of younger students to which I spoke, what books really count for them. Most are silent, puzzled by the question. The notion of books as companions is foreign to them. Justice Black with his tattered copy of the Constitution in his pocket at all times is not an example that would mean much to them. There is no printed word to which they look for counsel, inspiration or joy. Sometimes one student will say "the Bible." (He learned it at home, and his Biblical studies are not usually continued at the university.) There is always a girl who mentions Ayn Rand's *The Fountainhead*, a book, although hardly literature, which, with its sub-Nietzschean assertiveness, excites somewhat eccentric youngsters to a new way of life. A few students mention recent books that struck them and supported their own self-interpretation, like *The Catcher in the Rye*. (Theirs is usually the most genuine response and also shows a felt need for help in self-interpretation. But it is an uneducated response. Teachers should take advantage of the need expressed in it to show such students that better writers can help them more.)

After such sessions I am pursued by a student or two who wants to make it clear that he or she is really influenced by books, not just by one or two but by many. Then he recites a list of classics he may have grazed in high school.

Imagine such a young person walking through the Louvre or the Uffizi, and   *3* you can immediately grasp the condition of his soul. In his innocence of the stories of Biblical and Greek or Roman antiquity, Raphael, Leonardo, Michelangelo, Rembrandt and all the others can say nothing to him. All he sees are colors and forms—modern art. In short, like almost everything else in his spiritual life, the paintings and statues are abstract. No matter what much of modern wisdom asserts, these artists counted on immediate recognition of their subjects and, what is more, on their having a powerful meaning for their viewers. The works were the fulfillment of those meanings, giving them a sensuous reality and hence completing them. Without those meanings, and without their being something essential to the viewer as a moral, political and religious being, the works lose their essence. It is not merely the tradition that is lost when the voice of civilization elaborated over millennia has been stilled in this way. It is being itself that vanishes beyond the dissolving horizon. One of the most flattering things that ever happened to me as a teacher occurred when I received a postcard from a very good student on his first visit to Italy, who wrote, "You are not a professor of political philosophy but a travel agent." Nothing could have better expressed my intention as an educator. He thought I had prepared him to see. Then he could begin thinking for himself with something to think about. The real sensation of the Florence in which Machiavelli is believable is worth all the formulas of metaphysics ten times over. Education in our times must try to find whatever there is in students that might yearn for completion, and to reconstruct the learning that would enable them autonomously to seek that completion.

In a less grandiose vein, students today have nothing like the Dickens who   *4* gave so many of us the unforgettable Pecksniffs, Micawbers, Pips, with which we sharpened our vision, allowing us some subtlety in our distinction of human types. It is a complex set of experiences that enables one to say so simply, "He is a Scrooge." Without literature, no such observations are possible and the fine art of comparison is lost. The psychological obtuseness of our students is appalling, because they have only pop psychology to tell them what people are like, and the range of their motives. As the awareness that we owed almost exclusively to literary genius falters, people become more alike, for want of knowing they can be otherwise. What poor substitutes for real diversity are the wild rainbows of dyed hair and other external differences that tell the observer nothing about what is inside.

Lack of education simply results in students' seeking for enlightenment   *5* wherever it is readily available, without being able to distinguish between the sublime and trash, insight and propaganda. For the most part students turn to the movies, ready prey to interested moralisms such as the depictions of Gandhi or Thomas More—largely designed to further passing political movements and to appeal to simplistic needs for greatness—or to insinuating flattery of their secret aspirations and vices, giving them a sense of significance. *Kramer vs. Kramer* may be up-to-date about divorces and sex roles, but anyone who does not have *Anna Karenina* or *The Red and the Black* as part of his viewing equipment cannot sense what might be lacking, or the difference between an honest presentation and an exercise in consciousness-raising, trashy sentimentality and elevated sentiment. As films have emancipated themselves from the literary tyranny under which they suffered and which gave them a bad conscience, the ones with serious pretensions have become intolerably ignorant and manipulative. The distance from the contemporary and its high seriousness that students most need in order not to indulge their petty desires and to discover what is most serious about themselves cannot be found in the cinema, which now only knows the present. Thus, the failure to read good books both enfeebles the vision and strengthens our most fatal tendency—the belief that the here and now is all there is.

6   The only way to counteract this tendency is to intervene most vigorously in the education of those few who come to the university with a strong urge for *un je ne sais quoi*, who fear that they may fail to discover it, and that the cultivation of their minds is required for the success of their quest. We are long past the age when a whole tradition could be stored up in all students, to be fruitfully used later by some. Only those who are willing to take risks and are ready to believe the implausible are now fit for a bookish adventure. The desire must come from within. People do what they want, and now the most needful things appear so implausible to them that it is hopeless to attempt universal reform. Teachers of writing in state universities, among the noblest and most despised laborers in the academy, have told me that they cannot teach writing to students who do not read, and that it is practically impossible to get them to read, let alone like it. This is where high schools have failed most, filled with teachers who are products of the sixties and reflecting the pallor of university-level humanities. The old teachers who loved Shakespeare or Austen or Donne, and whose only reward for teaching was the perpetuation of their taste, have all but disappeared.

7   The latest enemy of the vitality of classic texts is feminism. The struggles against elitism and racism in the sixties and seventies had little direct effect on students' relations to books. The democratization of the university helped dismantle its structure and caused it to lose its focus. But the activists had no special quarrel with the classic texts, and they were even a bit infected by their Frankfurt School masters' habit of parading their intimacy with high culture. Radicals had at an earlier stage of egalitariansim already dealt with the monarchic, aristocratic and antidemocratic character of most literary classics by no longer paying attention to their manifest political content. Literary criticism concentrated on the private, the intimate, the feelings, thoughts and relations of individuals, while reducing to the status of a literary convention of the past the fact that the heroes of many classic works were soldiers and statesmen engaged in ruling and faced with political problems. Shakespeare, as he has been read for most of this century, does not constitute a threat to egalitarian right think-

ing. And as for racism, it just did not play a role in the classic literature, at least in the forms in which we are concerned about it today, and no great work of literature is ordinarily considered racist.

But *all* literature up to today is sexist. The Muses never sang to the poets   *8* about liberated women. It's the same old *chanson* from the Bible and Homer through Joyce and Proust. And this is particularly grave for literature, since the love interest was most of what remained in the classics after politics was purged in the academy, and was also what drew students to reading them. These books appealed to eros while educating it. So activism has been directed against the content of books. The latest translation of Biblical text—sponsored by the National Council of the Churches of Christ—suppresses gender references to God, so that future generations will not have to grapple with the fact that God was once a sexist. But this technique has only limited applicability. Another tactic is to expunge the most offensive authors—for example, Rousseau—from the education of the young or to include feminist responses in college courses, pointing out the distorting prejudices, and using the books only as evidence of the misunderstanding of woman's nature and the history of injustice to it. Moreover, the great female characters can be used as examples of the various ways women have coped with their enslavement to the sexual role. But never, never, must a student be attracted to those old ways and take them as models for him or herself. However, all this effort is wasted. Students cannot imagine that the old literature could teach them anything about the relations they want to have or will be permitted to have. So they are indifferent.

Having heard over a period of years the same kinds of responses to my   *9* question about favorite books, I began to ask students who their heroes are. Again, there is usually silence, and most frequently nothing follows. Why should anyone have heroes? One should be oneself and not form oneself in an alien mold. Here positive ideology supports them: their lack of hero-worship is a sign of maturity. They posit their own values. They have turned into a channel first established in the *Republic* by Socrates, who liberated himself from Achilles, and picked up in earnest by Rousseau in *Emile*. Following on Rousseau, Tolstoy depicts Prince Andrei in *War and Peace,* who was educated in Plutarch and is alienated from himself by his admiration for Napoleon. But we tend to forget that Andrei is a very noble man indeed and that his heroic longings give him a spendor of soul that dwarfs the petty, vain, self-regarding concerns of the bourgeoisie that surrounds him. Only a combination of natural sentiment and unity with the spirit of Russia and its history can, for Tolstoy, produce human beings superior to Andrei, and even they are only ambiguously superior. But in America we have only the bourgeoisie, and the love of the heroic is one of the few counterpoises available to us. In us the contempt for the heroic is only an extension of the perversion of the democratic principle that denies greatness and wants everyone to feel comfortable in his skin without having to suffer unpleasant comparisons. Students have not the slightest notion of what an achievement it is to free oneself from public guidance and find resources for guidance within oneself. From what souce within themselves would they draw the goals they think they set for themselves? Liberation from the heroic only means that they have no resource whatsoever against conformity to the current "role models." They are constantly thinking of themselves in terms of fixed standards that they did not make. Instead of being overwhelmed by Cyrus, Theseus, Moses or Romulus, they unconsciously act out the roles of the doctors, lawyers, businessmen or TV personalities around them. One can only pity young people without admirations they can respect or avow, who are artificially restrained from the enthusiasm for great virtue.

10   In encouraging this deformity, democratic relativism joins a branch of conservatism that is impressed by the dangerous political consequences of idealism. These conservatives want young people to know that this tawdry old world cannot respond to their demands for perfection. In the choice between the somewhat arbitrarily distinguished realism and idealism, a sensible person would want to be both, or neither. But, momentarily accepting a distinction I reject, idealism as it is commonly conceived should have primacy in an education, for man is a being who must take his orientation by his possible perfection. To attempt to suppress this most natural of all inclinations because of possible abuses is, almost literally, to throw out the baby with the bath. Utopianism is, as Plato taught us at the outset, the fire with which we must play because it is the only way we can find out what we are. We need to criticize false understandings of Utopia, but the easy way out provided by realism is deadly. As it now stands, students have powerful images of what a perfect body is and pursue it incessantly. But deprived of literary guidance, they no longer have any image of a perfect soul, and hence do not long to have one. They do not even imagine that there is such a thing.

11   Following on what I learned from this second question, I began asking a third: Who do you think is evil? To this one there is an immediate reponse: Hitler. (Stalin is hardly mentioned.) After him, who else? Up until a couple of years ago, a few students said Nixon, but he has been forgotten and at the same time is being rehabilitated. And there it stops. They have no idea of evil; they doubt its existence. Hitler is just another abstraction, an item to fill up an empty category. Although they live in a world in which the most terrible deeds are being performed and they see brutal crime in the streets, they turn aside. Perhaps they believe that evil deeds are performed by persons who, if they got the proper therapy, would not do them again—that there are evil deeds, not evil people. There is no *Inferno* in this comedy. Thus, the most common student view lacks an awareness of the depths as well as the heights, and hence lacks gravity.

WRITING AND DISCUSSION QUESTIONS

Informative

1. What does Bloom mean when he says "There is no printed word to which they [today's students] look for counsel, inspiration or joy" (paragraph 2)? How does

Bloom use the analogy of the Louvre to describe the condition of a young person's soul?
2. What uses of the past does Bloom suggest in this chapter of his book *The Closing of the American Mind?* What dangers does he suggest in seeing the present in the absence of the past?
3. What is Bloom's criticism of feminism, and how does he see feminism [as the struggle against sexism] as more dangerous than the struggles against racism and elitism?

Persuasive

1. Argue for or against Bloom's conclusion that the present situation with the young is bad.
2. Bloom contends that the young have a contempt for the heroic, that they prefer egalitarianism, and that they have no defense against conformist thinking (paragraphs 9–10). Argue for or against these contentions.

Personal

1. If you think Bloom is esentially right in his indictment of the young, search your own experience to identify events and persons who have contributed positively or negatively to your book education. Identify two or three salient influences and comment on them.
2. Has the American mind closed and has it happened as the result of a retreat from books? Is this an oversimplification? What is in the American scene to make you think the culture is open or closed minded?

▼

No Trivial Pursuit
CHESTER E. FINN, JR., AND
DIANE RAVITCH

Good teachers have long sensed that background knowledge is vital *1*
if readers and listeners are to comprehend what they read and hear. Newspaper reporters, editorial cartoonists, and speech makers agree. But the only currently available gauge of background knowledge—what E. D. Hirsch terms "cultural literacy"[1]—is the National Assessment of Educational Progress (NAEP) appraisal of American students' knowledge of history and literature. Administered in 1986, this assessment marks the first systematic attempt to determine the extent to which students across the country possess basic information about American history and about some of the best-known writers and

---

[1]E. D. Hirsch, Jr., *Cultural Literacy: What Every American Needs to Know* (New York: Houghton Mifflin, 1987).

works of literature. Our book, *What Do Our 17-Year-Olds Know?*,[2] describes the creation of this assessment and analyzes the results.

2   The NAEP administered the history and literature assessment to a sample of 7,812 students in grade 11 who were representative of the national population according to sex, race, region, type of community, and attendance at public or nonpublic school. The test used a multiple-choice format in which most questions offered four potential answers: one clearly right, the others unambiguously wrong. Thus a random guesser would achieve a score of 25%. Here are some samples of the kinds of questions asked:

1. When was the Civil War?
   _____ Before 1750   _____ 1850–1900
   _____ 1750–1800   _____ 1900–1950
   _____ 1800–1850   _____ After 1950

2. The idea that each branch of the federal government should keep the other branches from becoming too strong is called (what)?
   _____ strict constructionism   _____ federalism
   _____ the system of checks and   _____ implied powers
         balances

3. What European nation was primarily responsible for exploring and settling the East Coast of the United States?
   _____ England   _____ France
   _____ Portugal   _____ Italy

4. *Julius Caesar* by Shakespeare is a play about Caesar's
   _____ discovery of and escape from a plot to kill him
   _____ ultimate triumph in the Gallic wars
   _____ death and the fate of his assassins
   _____ love affair with Cleopatra

5. In which novel did a 16-year-old boy who was expelled from school go to New York City for a weekend to find himself?
   _____ *A Catcher in the Rye*   _____ *The Sun Also Rises*
   _____ *A Tree Grows in Brooklyn*   _____ *A Separate Peace*

6. What is the novel *1984* about?
   _____ The destruction of the human race by nuclear war
   _____ A dictatorship in which every citizen was watched in order to stamp out all individuality
   _____ The invasion and ultimate takeover of the earth by creatures from outer space
   _____ A man who went back into time and changed history[3]

---

[2]Diane Ravitch and Chester E. Finn, Jr., *What Do Our 17-Year-Olds Know? A Report on the First National Assessment of History and Literature* (New York: Harper & Row, 1987).

[3]The percentages of correct responses to these questions were: 1. 32.2%; 2. 59.9%; 3. 60.6%; 4. 48.0%; 5. 22.5%; 6. 35.5%.

WHAT THE PRESS SAID

News accounts of the NAEP findings predictably dwelt on some by-now-famil-   3
iar "horrible examples" of shaky student knowledge:

- Nearly one-third of the high school juniors in the U.S. cannot identify the purpose of the Declaration of Independence or say in which 50-year period it was signed.

- Almost half of them are unaware of who led the Soviet Union during World War II, the meaning of the term *laisez-faire*, or the aim of the Monroe Doctrine.

- The majority do not recognize basic information about the U.S. Constitution, Sen. Joseph McCarthy, Reconstruction, *The Federalist* papers, Thomas Paine's *Common Sense*, The *Dred Scott* decision, the Emancipation Proclamation, or the Scopes trial.

- More than two out of three do not know the purpose of Jim Crow laws, the years of Lincoln's presidency, or the half century in which the Civil War was fought.

    These items were not particularly challenging or complex; most asked for   4
rudimentary information that high school students ought to be familiar with,
especially considering the fact that most 11th-graders—78% of those sitting
for this assessment—were enrolled in an American history course. Yet the
average score was just 54.5% correct.

    The literature results were even dimmer: the average score was only 51.8%   5
correct. The learning area committee that compiled the questions for the literature assessment was aware that all English classes across the country do not
read the same works or writers and that, unlike history, there is no real consensus on what literature American students *ought* to read. For that reason, the
literature assessment was in some sense a test of the curriculum rather than of
the students because the results reflected which authors, plots, novels, short
stories, and quotations the students had encountered.

    However, the findings suggest that many students have had little or no   6
acquaintance with major literary works, authors, characters, and themes. For
example:

- Nearly one-half of the high school juniors don't know who Oedipus was, what "Achilles' heel" means, or who said, "Ask not what your country can do for you."

- More than half of them are unaware of what *Julius Caesar, Macbeth, The Old Man and the Sea, Walden,* or *The Grapes of Wrath* are about.

- Nearly two-thirds have apparently never heard of Job or Walter Mitty, are unfamiliar with the plots of *1984* and *Lord of the Flies,* and do not recognize Sodom and Gomorrah.

- Fewer than one in five can match Joseph Conrad, Ralph Ellison, Fyodor Dostoyevsky, James Joyce, or Alexis de Tocqueville with their best-known works.

WHAT WAS NOT REPORTED

7   The dismal averages and painful examples captured most of the headlines. They always do. But what has been generally ignored is perhaps the most important part of our findings: the variability and mutability of student performance.

8   As expected, the children of college-educated parents generally scored highest. Also as expected, Asians and Whites generally outscored blacks and Hispanics. But there were exceptions. Ten percent of the black students scored in the top quartile of all students in history. It would have been far better, of course, had a full quarter of the black students turned up there. But that a significant number did is ample evidence (in case anyone needs reminding) that race does not foreordain educational success or failure and that averages can be deceiving.

9   Nor does family background invariably determine outcomes. Forty-four percent of all students in the top quartile of the assessment have parents who did *not* graduate from college. A sizable fraction of high-scoring students come from families in which *neither* parent had *any* formal education beyond high school. (On the flip side, however, 25% of students in the bottom quartile are children of college graduates.) These findings remind us that students are not locked into academic failure—or success—by the circumstances of their birth. Unpromising conditions can be overcome, and the average scores of a population group do not determine any individual's performance.

10   Certain student behaviors and habits are clearly associated with their test scores. The more regularly students attend school and the less they watch television, the higher their scores, regardless of race, parental education, or anything else.[4] No surprise here. What's important, though, is that watching television and attending school are things that parents, teachers, policy makers, and students themselves can do something about.

11   And there are others. The more eras of American history that students have

---

[4]The relationship between television and school success is actually rather complex. For some groups, such as Hispanics and students in rural areas, two or three hours of television viewing per day are associated with higher scores, perhaps because television exposes these youngsters to a culture and vocabulary that they might not otherwise encounter. Children in poor communities who watch *no* television tend to have lower scores than their peers from the same neighborhoods who watch television, whereas children in affluent suburbs who watch *no* television tend to have higher scores than their peers who watch television. Even in well-to-do communities, two to three hours of television a day are not associated with low scores; students who do relatively well on the assessment watch this much. Beyond three hours a day, however, television watching is associated with lower scores for everyone.

encountered in their coursework, the higher their history scores. The more time spent on literature in their English classes, the higher their literature scores. Again, no surprise. Students tend to learn what they have been taught, and they tend to learn it in rough proportion to the amount of time they spend studying it.

That is why we were not startled by the link between homework and knowl-   12 edge. Nearly 25% of the students in the bottom quartile on the history test claimed that they do not have—or never do—any homework. None. Just 12% of students in the top quartile made this claim. Whereas 26% of students in the bottom quartile on the history test said that they hit the books outside of school for two or more hours a day, 40% of those in the top quartile claimed to do this much homework.

The assessment reveals that 11th-graders don't read much for enjoyment.   13 Fewer than half read for their own purposes even once a week. Yet there is a clear relationship between leisure reading and knowledge of literature. One out of three students in the top quartile reads for pleasure on a daily basis; only one out of eight in the bottom quartile does so.

A commonsense equation is at work here: the more youngsters read, the   14 more regularly they attend school, and the more serious content they study while they are there, the more they tend to know about history and literature. Our results show that, to a significant extent, it is what students *do*, not just who they are, that determines how much they end up knowing. And what they do depends greatly on what the significant adults in their lives oblige them to do.

It would be wonderful if all parents read to their children, talked with them,   15 and took them to museums, concerts, and plays. Alas, we cannot count on all homes to instill the lore of history and the love of literature in their children. But we ought to be able to rely on *all* our schools to do the one thing that no other institution in this society was designed to do: transmit the knowledge that can open doors to upward mobility for the poor, the disadvantaged, minorities, and anyone else.

WHAT WE RECOMMEND

From the students' descriptions of their courses, we concluded that they had   16 not spent enough time studying history. Apparently, the way history is taught today does not afford sufficient opportunity to examine important events and issues in depth or to see history as an important and exciting subject.

Simply put, we need more history and literature at all grade levels: more   17 teaching, more studying, and more learning. Beginning in the primary grades, children should hear and begin to read legends and myths, heroic tales, fables, and folklore. The distinction between fact and fiction should become clear as youngsters in the upper-elementary grades begin to read significant literature and to encounter the elements of American history, world history, and ancient civilizations. In every grade, historical studies should be correlated with geography, literature, and social sciences.

18   Narratives, journals, and biographies ought to be used in each history course to enliven events and to illuminate concepts. It is the stories of individuals (heroes and villains alike) that bring history to life. It seems only common sense—though it is surely not common practice—to organize course content *chronologically*, stressing how one thing leads to the next, how changes occur over time, and how causes and effects are related.

19   Of course, it is impossible to give a clear picture of what happened *when* without also considering *where* it occurred. Geography should be an integral part of every history course.

20   At present there is not enough time in the curriculum for the study of world history. Nearly half of the high school juniors surveyed said that they had studied one year of world history. That is not enough; a minimum of two years is needed. Students need to understand the evolution of the democratic political tradition in the West and the history of the major civilizations in Asia, Africa, and Latin America.

21   As for literature, more should be taught throughout the school years. All students should get healthy servings of the best classic writers and works, along with outstanding contemporary ones.

22   This is a large challenge, but it is not an unrealistic one. California recently adopted a new framework for history and social science that will do much to strengthen the teaching and learning of history, geography, and civics by requiring three years of world history, three years of American history, and—in the primary grades—historical activities (such as constructing a family history or a history of the local community). California has also published a curriculum guide for literature that is filled with recommendations of excellent works and suggestions for teaching them at various grade levels. If this sprawling and diverse state can reach reasonable consensus on the content of these often fractious subjects, then it can happen in other places, too. Changes of this magnitude in the curriculum will have a domino effect and are likely to lead to changes in the preparation of teachers and in the content of textbooks.

23   But such change occurs slowly, and policy makers dare not sit around waiting for it to happen. Improving the teaching and learning of history and literature requires strong medicine. Here is part of our prescription:

- States and school systems should reorganize their curricula in social studies and language arts around a core of history and literature.

- Teachers and administrators must spell out coordinated objectives for these two subjects at every grade level, kindergarten through 12th grade.

- The schedule of the school day and year, as well as homework policies, need to be adjusted so that there will be enough time to *study* both history and literature in depth.

- Tracking should be abolished, and good literature should be taught to all students, not just to those bound for college.

- History ought to be taught chronologically and in context, so that students see particular events and individuals as part of larger social and political developments.

- Only individuals holding degrees in history and English should be hired to teach those subjects.

- Teachers of history and literature should be encouraged to collaborate and to use original materials, such as journals, autobiographies, narratives, stories, and historical documents.

- Expert assistance in the teaching of history and literature ought to be obtained from libraries, museums, historical societies, universities, and other organizations.

WHAT THE CRITICS SAID

Most of the commentators who have remarked on our report thus far have deemed the test results to be indisputable evidence of the need to improve the teaching and learning of history and literature in the schools. From some quarters, however, the book has elicited strong negative reactions—some so outlandish that we have occasionally felt as if we'd passed through the looking glass into a world in which things are not what they seem, a world in which the important is treated as trivial. It is a world that most parents and legislators would find bizarre indeed. [24]

By way of orientation, let us escort readers past seven signposts that we have come across most often in that strange world during the months since the book appeared. [25]

1. *The format is flawed, so the findings are worthless.* Some critics have dismissed the assessment results because, they contend, multiple-choice tests don't really measure what students know. Others have contended that nothing really worth knowing can be systematically measured and that, if something can be tested, it isn't important. This viewpoint suggests that no one should bother even trying to appraise the condition of American education, because any outcome that can be quantified will be trivial.

We're none too pleased with the limitations of the multiple-choice format. Our book makes this plain. We hope that future assessments will find other ways to appraise students' deeper understandings. But we believe that this assessment demonstrated serious gaps in students' background knowledge. No matter how students have been taught, no matter what methods have been used, there are some facts that all students should possess by the time they are juniors in high school.

Future assessments should certainly evaluate subtler and more complex understandings, but this is not easy to accomplish on a mass scale. It tends to be costly and to invite disputes over causation among people who have no trouble agreeing on the facts. But devising better assessment instruments and methods is not an impossibility and is well worth doing. In the meantime, data from the current assessment establish a baseline for future attempts to gauge whether students have learned anything at all about significant people, places, events, and ideas.

2. *So's your old man.* Some critics dismiss the findings because grownups don't know much about history or literature either. "Is it possible," asks Stephen Graubard of *Daedalus* and Brown University, "that American 'children' are not all that different from American adults, that we are finding fault with one when we ought to be looking at all?"[5] Other critics have charged us with "kid bashing." But our book stresses the fact that the youngsters are *least* culpable. We place the blame for their ignorance squarely on the shoulders of the grownups who determine what is taught and how well it is learned.

We hold no illusions that the person-on-the-street is a history expert or a literature whiz. We have no comparable data about what 17-year-olds knew 50 years ago. But this is beside the point. Far too many young people (and adults) today know too little about the past to understand the complex issues of the present and to participate as knowledgeable citizens of our democracy. The best way to improve the situation is not by throwing up our hands in despair but by beginning with those still in school.

Moreover, we find it surprising that some people reject the notion that future generations should be expected to *surpass* the knowledge of their predecessors. Had we followed such counsel in the past, we would have no electric lights, no automobiles, and no polio vaccine. Scientists seeking applications for superconductors or cures for AIDS might as well go back to plowing behind oxen.

3. *What matters is not what you know, but whether you can think.* Critics who level this charge see knowledge and information as of scant importance. To them, only reasoning, problem solving, and other "higher-order thinking skills" matter. Such people tend to see learning as a process of acquiring intellectual skills independent of content.

As we explain in our book, to separate skills from content or facts from concepts is to create false dichotomies. Children and adults need both skills and knowledge, facts and concepts. As Lauren Resnick writes in a thoughtful new report, reading is a skill that relies on "a combination of what is written, what . . . [the reader] already knows, and various general processes." The reader, Resnick explains, "*adds* information needed to make the message coherent and sensible," for written texts leave out some things that are essential to the mean-

---

[5]Stephen R. Graubard, "Alarmist Critics Who Cry Beowulf," *New York Times*, 1 October 1987, p. A-27.

ing "on the assumption that readers will fill them in. If this assumption is not met, comprehension fails."[6]

A variant of this signpost asserts that the modern "knowledge explosion" renders specific facts so rapidly obsolete that actually learning any of them is pointless. Whatever you need to know can be looked up, we are advised, and modern technology makes this process faster than ever before. But we can't expect people to watch television or read the newspaper with an encyclopedia or a computer at their sides to look up every reference.

4. *People don't really need to know that stuff to do their jobs.* According to this argument, because knowledge of history and literature is not directly applicable in the workplace, it isn't important. Vocational or technical skills, say these critics, are all that matter.

But the aim of formal education is to prepare students for much more than gainful employment. Schools help ready students to become competent citizens, informed voters, and responsible participants in community affairs. The study of history and literature contributes to these goals. Besides, knowledge of history and literature is immensely useful. Acquiring such knowledge sharpens students' intellectual skills and improves their ability to think rationally about causes and effects and about character and motivation. This kind of disciplined thinking may be the *most* useful part of every student's education, far more valuable in the long run than training for a job.

5. *What do you mean, "shared heritage"?* Some commentators believe that it is impossible to weave together the many strands of American history and literature into a coherent pattern that all children, regardless of ancestry, ought reasonably to be expected to learn. But American history *is* multicultural and pluralistic. It is the story of many races, religions, and ethnic groups striving to become one society under one government. It is a story filled with conflict and compromise, achievement and disappointment in the continuing effort to redefine what it means to be an American.

Of course, literature taught in American schools must reflect the diversity of the American people. Among other things, good literature helps youngsters become sensitive to the experiences of people who are different. Classic writers (e.g., Hawthorne, Whitman, Dickens, Twain, Shakespeare) should be part of the core reading for all students, but so should such superb writers as Frederick Douglass, Richard Wright, Ralph Ellison, Zora Neale Hurston, Adrienne Rich, Kate Chopin, and numerous others, both contemporary and classic.

6. *Not all students need a liberal education.* Those who take this view reject the idea of teaching all children knowledge that was once largely the intellectual property of the well-born and the well-to-do, the only ones able to afford to pursue a liberal education in the "good old days." Learning such "elitist"

---

[6]Lauren Resnick, *Education and Learning to Think* (Washington, D.C.: National Academy Press, 1987), pp. 8–9.

knowledge is said to be an unworthy pursuit for members of an egalitarian society.

If we acted in accordance with this line of reasoning, we would only *preserve* bastions of intellectual privilege and discourage upward mobility in society. Throughout history, elites have striven to insure that their progeny acquired enough of the knowledge, cultural lore, and intellectual traits associated with success in their societies. Although social status, wealth, business acumen, public office—or whatever other gauge of success one chooses—may not follow automatically from being "culturally literate," one's prospects of success are certainly enhanced by it. The well-to-do generally do their best to make sure that their children acquire such knowledge and attend schools that respect it. The challenge to educators is to see that these opportunities are available to *all* youngsters.

7. *Trash the whole rotten society.* The familiar radical or neo-Marxist critique of everything has turned up as a response to our book, too. It is most conspicuous in an essay by former "Weatherman" William Ayers.[7] If the society is basically corrupt, founded on unsound principles, and devoted to illegitimate goals, Ayers wonders, why oblige children to learn anything about it other than how horrid it is?

Along the same line of reasoning, we find Etta Mooser, an educational researcher, writing that "the world as experienced by this generation seems a far more treacherous place than the Ozzie and Harriet world of my generation." She suggests that, instead of assessing students' knowledge of history and literature, we would be better advised to test teachers about "the culture in which their students live," asking them to identify Bob Dylan or the Fat Boys or to answer such questions as "What is the most common punishment for first-time train-painting offenders?"[8]

Not many people would agree with Mooser, and we doubt that her plea for cultural trivia will win many converts. But in our wanderings in the world on the other side of the education looking glass we have often encountered a milder version of this kind of thinking. It goes something like this: the schools cannot reasonably be held responsible for serious cognitive outcomes, because we must first attend to such matters as income distribution, health care, prejudice, and so on. But this willingness to let the education system off the hook, while we wait for other social goals to be achieved, troubles us. It is a prescription for doing nothing. There are changes that we can and should make to improve the education system now.

26   These seven signposts appear along the lanes and boulevards of the world beyond the looking glass. They were there before we wrote our report, of

---

[7]William Ayers, "What Do Our 17-Year-Olds Know? A Critique," *Education Week*, 25 November 1987, pp. 24, 18.
    [8]Etta Mooser, "What They Do Know," *The Nation*, 9 January 1988, p. 4.

course, and would have been there even if we hadn't written it. But our book—
and some of the other recent studies, reports, and reform efforts that deal with
the woebegone state of history and literature—have drawn an uncommonly
strong reaction from individuals and groups that have heeded the messages on
those signposts.

This is true not just of individuals but also of influential education organiza-   27
tions. At its most recent annual meeting, the National Council of Teachers of
English adopted a resolution opposing curricula that reduce literature to "the
accumulation of particular facts, such as titles, names, phrases, and dates."
Perhaps we were the unnamed target of this resolution; perhaps it was E. D.
Hirsch; perhaps both. It doesn't really matter. What matters is that the resolution suggests a deliberate misreading of our message. it is the kind of distortion
that enables people to avoid dealing with what we are really saying: factual
knowledge is a *necessary but insufficient* element of literary and historical
learning.

Much the same reaction was evident at the most recent meeting of the   28
National Council for the Social Studies, where Jan Tucker, the NCSS president,
warned against the idea of cultural literacy, scorning it as the "nationalization
of knowledge." The kind of history-centered social studies curriculum that we
favor met with manifest hostility at that meeting. Merge the teaching of knowledge and process, facts and concepts? Devote class time to understanding the
past (and its relationship to the present) rather than musing about contemporary problems? Members of the NCSS bristled at such advice and objected
when examples of such curricula were brought up. Singled out for particular
obloquy was California's new statewide framework for history and social science, which amounts to a K-12 curriculum that is fully compatible with our
recommendations and likely to do a great deal to rectify the deficits that the
NAEP documented.

History and literature contain the keys to understanding ourselves and oth-   29
ers. Studying these subjects helps young people realize how the world they
know evolved and how people like them coped with challenges, sometimes successfully, sometimes not. These subjects introduce students to models of
achievement and courage, but they also provide cautionary tales of human evil,
error, and cruelty.

If we raise our children and their children without the illumination that his-   30
tory and literature shed on the culture they are heir to—perhaps with no culture at all save that conveyed by television, popular songs, athletic contests,
and *People* magazine—they will have little sense of how their society came to
be the way it is. They will be unable to place present events into larger contexts; they will be unacquainted with the ideas of the great thinkers and writers
who, over the centuries, have reflected on the fundamental questions and eternal dilemmas of humankind; and they will be unable to communicate with others because they will lack a foundation of shared knowledge and common
points of reference.

The study of history and literature is no trivial pursuit.   31

WRITING AND DISCUSSION QUESTIONS

Informative

1. What kinds of knowledge are Finn and Ravitch concerned with? In what sense, if any, is it important for all Americans to know about McCarthy, Jim Crow, or the Scopes trial? What serious deficiencies of knowledge are revealed by the cited press accounts? What kinds of knowledge would have to be called trivial?
2. What are the most important criticisms aimed at Finn and Ravitch's book? Which criticisms hold up despite the authors' explanations?

Persuasive

1. Argue that the kind of knowledge tested on the NAEP is or is not trivial and that we should or should not be deeply concerned about the poor results.
2. Choose one of the seven criticisms against the authors' book and expand on the authors' response, either supporting or refuting their position.
3. What dangers do you see in the Finn and Ravitch study? Argue that school could cause more harm than good in response to a perceived cultural literacy crisis.

Personal

1. Assess your own education in history, science, and English. What barriers to cultural literacy can you identify from your own experiences?

▼

Lower than the Angels
JACOB BRONOWSKI

1   Man is a singular creature. He has a set of gifts which make him unique among the animals: so that, unlike them, he is not a figure in the landscape—he is a shaper of the landscape. In body and in mind he is the explorer of nature, the ubiquitous animal, who did not find but has made his home in every continent.

2   It is reported that when the Spaniards arrived overland at the Pacific Ocean in 1769 the California Indians used to say that at full moon the fish came and danced on these beaches. And it is true that there is a local variety of fish, the grunion, that comes up out of the water and lays its eggs above the normal high-tide mark. The females bury themselves tail first in the sand and the males gyrate round them and fertilise the eggs as they are being laid. The full moon is important, because it gives the time needed for the eggs to incubate undisturbed in the sand, nine or ten days, between these very high tides and the next ones that will wash the hatched fish out to sea again.

Every landscape in the world is full of these exact and beautiful adaptations,   *3*
by which an animal fits into its environment like one cog-wheel into another.
The sleeping hedgehog waits for the spring to burst its metabolism into life.
The humming-bird beats the air and dips its needle-fine beak into hanging
blossoms. Butterflies mimic leaves and even noxious creatures to deceive their
predators. The mole plods through the ground as if he had been designed as a
mechanical shuttle.

So millions of years of evolution have shaped the grunion to fit and sit   *4*
exactly with the tides. But nature—that is, biological evolution—has not fitted
man to any specific environment. On the contrary, by comparison with the
grunion he has a rather crude survival kit; and yet—this is the paradox of the
human condition—one that fits him to all environments. Among the multitude
of animals which scamper, fly, burrow and swim around us, man is the only
one who is not locked into his environment. His imagination, his reason, his
emotional subtlety and toughness, make it possible for him not to accept the
environment but to change it. And that series of inventions, by which man from
age to age has remade his environment, is a different kind of evolution—not
biological, but cultural evolution. I call that brilliant sequence of cultural peaks
The Ascent of Man.

I use the word *ascent* with a precise meaning. Man is distinguished from   *5*
other animals by his imaginative gifts. He makes plans, inventions, new discoveries, by putting different talents together; and his discoveries become more
subtle and penetrating, as he learns to combine his talents in more complex
and intimate ways. So the great discoveries of different ages and different cultures, in technique, in science, in the arts, express in their progression a richer
and more intricate conjunction of human faculties, an ascending trellis of his
gifts.

Of course, it is tempting—very tempting to a scientist—to hope that the   *6*
most original achievements of the mind are also the most recent. And we do
indeed have cause to be proud of some modern work. Think of the unravelling
of the code of heredity in the DNA spiral; or the work going forward on the
special faculties of the human brain. Think of the philosophic insight that saw
into the Theory of Relativity or the minute behaviour of matter on the atomic
scale.

Yet to admire only our own successes, as if they had no past (and were sure   *7*
of the future), would make a caricature of knowledge. For human achievement,
and science in particular, is not a museum of finished constructions. It is a
progress, in which the first experiments of the alchemists also have a formative
place, and the sophisticated arithmetic that the Mayan astronomers of Central
America invented for themselves independently of the Old World. The stone-
work of Machu Picchu in the Andes and the geometry of the Alhambra in
Moorish Spain seem to us, five centuries later, exquisite works of decorative
art. But if we stop our appreciation there, we miss the originality of the two cultures that made them. Within their time, they are constructions as arresting and
important for their peoples as the architecture of DNA for us.

8   In every age there is a turning-point, a new way of seeing and asserting the coherence of the world. It is frozen in the statues of Easter Island that put a stop to time—and in the medieval clocks in Europe that once also seemed to say the last word about the heavens for ever. Each culture tries to fix its visionary moment, when it was transformed by a new conception either of nature or of man. But in retrospect, what commands our attention as much are the continuities—the thoughts that run or recur from one civilisation to another. There is nothing in modern chemistry more unexpected than putting together alloys with new properties; that was discovered after the time of the birth of Christ in South America, and long before that in Asia. Splitting and fusing the atom both derive, conceptually, from a discovery made in prehistory: that stone and all matter has a structure along which it can be split and put together in new arrangements. And man made biological inventions almost as early: agriculture—the domestication of wild wheat, for example—and the improbable idea of taming and then riding the horse.

9   In following the turning-points and the continuities of culture, I shall follow a general but not a strict chronological order, because what interests me is the history of man's mind as an unfolding of his different talents. I shall be relating his ideas, and particularly his scientific ideas, to their origins in the gifts with which nature has endowed man, and which make him unique. What I present, what has fascinated me for many years, is the way in which man's ideas express what is essentially human in his nature.

10   So these programmes or essays are a journey through intellectual history, a personal journey to the high points of man's achievement. Man ascends by discovering the fullness of his own gifts (his talents or faculties) and what he creates on the way are monuments to the stages in his understanding of nature and of self—what the poet W.B. Yeats called 'monuments of unageing intellect'.

WRITING AND DISCUSSION QUESTIONS

Informative

1. Explain what Bronowski means when he says "he [humankind] is not a figure in the landscape—he is a shaper of the landscape." What difference does he see between humans and animals like the grunion? What does Bronowski mean by "cultural evolution"?

2. In what sense does Bronowski speak of animal adaptation? Develop a definition of adaptation based on the examples Browowski gives or on your own examples.

3. Identify a recent discovery like evolution, the unconscious, the car, or the television. Explain how it rests on prior knowledge.

Persuasive

1. Bronowski calls the "brilliant sequence of cultural peaks" "The Ascent of Man," which is also the title of his book and his film series. Argue for the value in preserv-

ing a knowledge of human "achievements of mind." Argue that the cost of losing such knowledge cannot be afforded.

2. Idenfity one or two specific human achievements or great ideas originating before the twentieth century. Argue that these are just as important as a particular modern achievement or discovery, such as DNA, nuclear power, or flight.

3. In this reading, which is in the introductory section to *The Ascent of Man,* Bronowski emphasizes the idea of ascent. Argue the validity of claiming that human history has in fact been progressive. What examples from the twentieth century can you cite that suggest we have reverted to barbarian and inhuman ways despite our advanced technologies?

Personal

1. Choose a contemporary scientific or technological advancement—the car, the pill, television, and so forth, and examine its place in your own life. In what sense can you say it is a positive development? In what sense is it harmful?

2. View one of the films from Bronowski's series *The Ascent of Man,* especially "The Starry Messenger" [focusing on Galileo] or "Knowledge or Certainty" [focusing on Hiroshima, the Holocaust, and the dangers of a belief in absolute certainty]. Discuss ways in which Bronowski's thoughts relate to a contemporary issue like science versus religion or the threat of contemporary hate groups like the Nazi skin heads.

▼

Cultural Literacy
E. D. HIRSCH, JR.

PREFACE

Rousseau points out the facility with which children lend themselves to our false methods: . . . "The apparent ease with which children learn is their ruin."

—JOHN DEWEY

There is no matter what children should learn first, any more than what leg you should put into your breeches first. Sir, you may stand disputing which is best to put in first, but in the meantime your backside is bare. Sir, while you stand considering which of two things you should teach your child first, another boy has learn't 'em both.

—SAMUEL JOHNSON

To be culturally literate is to possess the basic information needed to thrive   *1* in the modern world. The breadth of that information is great, extending over the major domains of human activity from sports to science. It is by no means confined to "culture" narrowly understood as an acquaintance with the arts. Nor is it confined to one social class. Quite the contrary. Cultural literacy constitutes the only sure avenue of opportunity for disadvantaged children, the only reliable way of combating the social determinism that now condemns them to remain in the same social and educational condition as their parents. That children from poor and illiterate homes tend to remain poor and illiterate is an unacceptable failure of our schools, one which has occurred not because our teachers are inept but chiefly because they are compelled to teach a fragmented curriculum based on faulty educational theories. Some say that our schools by themselves are powerless to change the cycle of poverty and illiteracy. I do not agree. They *can* break the cycle, but only if they themselves break fundamentally with some of the theories and practices that education professors and school administrators have followed over the past fifty years.

2   Although the chief beneficiaries of the educational reforms advocated in this book will be disadvantaged children, these same reforms will also enhance the literacy of children from middle-class homes. The educational goal advocated is that of mature literacy for *all* our citizens.

3   The connection between mature literacy and cultural literacy may already be familiar to those who have closely followed recent discussions of education. Shortly after the publication of my essay "Cultural Literacy," Dr. William Bennett, then chairman of the National Endowment for the Humanities and subsequently secretary of education in President Ronald Reagan's second administration, championed its ideas. This endorsement from an influential person of conservative views gave my ideas some currency, but such an endorsement was not likely to recommend the concept to liberal thinkers, and in fact the idea of cultural literacy has been attacked by some liberals on the assumption that I must be advocating a list of great books that every child in the land should be forced to read.

4   But those who examine the Appendix to this book will be able to judge for themselves how thoroughly mistaken such an assumption is. Very few specific titles appear on the list, and they usually appear as words, not works, because they represent writings that culturally literate people have read about but haven't read. *Das Kapital* is a good example. Cultural literacy is represented not by a *prescriptive* list of books but rather by a *descriptive* list of the information actually possessed by literate Americans. My aim in this book is to contribute to making that information the possession of all Americans.

5   The importance of such widely shared information can best be understood if I explain briefly how the idea of cultural literacy relates to currently prevailing theories of education. The theories that have dominated American education for the past fifty years stem ultimately from Jean Jacques Rousseau, who believed that we should encourage the natural development of young children and not impose adult ideas upon them before they can truly understand them. Rousseau's conception of education as a process of natural development was an abstract generalization meant to apply to all children in any time or place: to French children of the eighteenth century or to Japanese or American children of the twentieth century. He thought that a child's intellectual and social skills

would develop naturally without regard to the specific content of education. His content-neutral conception of educational development has long been triumphant in American schools of education and has long dominated the "developmental," content-neutral curricula of our elementary schools.

In the first decades of this century, Rousseau's ideas powerfully influenced   6 the educational conceptions of John Dewey, the writer who has most deeply affected modern American educational theory and practice. Dewey's clearest and, in his time, most widely read book on education, *Schools of To-morrow*, acknowledges Rousseau as the chief source of his educational principles. The first chapter of Dewey's book carries the telling title "Education as Natural Development" and is sprinkled with quotations from Rousseau. In it Dewey strongly seconds Rousseau's opposition to the mere accumulation of information.

> Development emphasizes the need of intimate and extensive personal acquaintance with a small number of typical situations with a view to mastering the way of dealing with the problems of experience, not the piling up of information.[1]

Believing that a few direct experiences would suffice to develop the skills   7 that children require, Dewey assumed that early education need not be tied to specific content. He mistook a half-truth for the whole. He placed too much faith in children's ability to learn general skills from a few typical experiences and too hastily rejected "the piling up of information." Only by piling up specific, communally shared information can children learn to participate in complex cooperative activities with other members of their community.

This old truth, recently rediscovered, requires a countervailing theory of   8 education that once again stresses the importance of specific information in early and late schooling. The corrective theory might be described as an anthropological theory of education, because it is based on the anthropological observation that all human communities are founded upon specific shared information. Americans are different from Germans, who in turn are different from Japanese, because each group possesses specifically different cultural knowledge. In an anthropological perspective, the basic goal of education in a human community is acculturation, the transmission to children of the specific information shared by the adults of the group or polis.

Plato, that other great educational theorist, believed that the specific contents transmitted to children are by far the most important elements of education. In *The Republic* he makes Socrates ask rhetorically, "Shall we carelessly allow children to hear any casual tales which may be devised by casual persons, and to receive into their minds ideas for the most part the very opposite of those which we shall wish them to have when they are grown up?" Plato offered good reasons for being concerned with the specific contents of school-   9

---

[1]John Dewey and Evelyn Dewey, *Schools of To-morrow* (New York: Dutton, 1915 [14th printing, 1924]), 13.

ing, one of them ethical: "For great is the issue at stake, greater than appears—whether a person is to be good or bad."[2]

10   Time has shown that there is much truth in the durable educational theories of both Rousseau and Plato. But even the greatest thinkers, being human, see mainly in one direction at a time, and no thinkers, however profound, can foresee the future implications of their ideas when they are translated into social policy. The great test of social ideas is the crucible of history, which, after a time, usually discloses a one-sidedness in the best of human generalizations. History, not superior wisdom, shows us that neither the content-neutral curriculum of Rousseau and Dewey nor the narrowly specified curriculum of Plato is adequate to the needs of a modern nation.

11   Plato rightly believed that it is natural for children to learn an adult culture, but too confidently assumed that philosophy could devise the one best culture. (Nonetheless, we should concede to Plato that within our culture we have an obligation to choose and promote our best traditions.) On the other side, Rousseau and Dewey wrongly believed that adult culture is "unnatural" to young children. Rousseau, Dewey, and their present-day disciples have not shown an adequate appreciation of the need for transmission of specific cultural information.

12   In contrast to the theories of Plato and Rousseau, an anthropological theory of education accepts the naturalness as well as the relativity of human cultures. It deems it neither wrong nor unnatural to teach young children adult information before they fully understand it. The anthropological view stresses the universal fact that a human group must have effective communications to function effectively, that effective communications require shared culture, and that shared culture requires transmission of specific information to children. Literacy, an essential aim of education in the modern world, is no autonomous, empty skill but depends upon literate culture. Like any other aspect of acculturation, literacy requires the early and continued transmission of specific information in the form of symbols."[3] Only by accumulating shared symbols, and the shared information that the symbols represent, can we learn to communicate effectively with one another in our national community.

THE NATURE AND USE OF CULTURAL LITERACY

13 The documented decline in shared knowledge carries implications that go far beyond the shortcomings of executives and extend to larger questions of educational policy and social justice in our country. Mina Shaughnessy was a great English teacher who devoted her professional life to helping disadvantaged students become literate. At the 1980 conference dedicated to her memory, one of the speakers who followed me to the podium was the Harvard historian and

---

[2]Plato, *The Republic*, II, Stephanus 377, X, Stephanus 608.
[3]Dewey, *Schools of To-morrow*, 13.

sociologist Orlando Patterson. To my delight he departed from his prepared talk to mention mine. He seconded my argument that shared information is a necessary background to true literacy. Then he extended and deepened the ideas I had presented. Here is what Professor Patterson said, as recorded in the *Proceedings* of the conference.

> Industrialized civilization [imposes] a growing cultural and structural complexity which requires persons to have a broad grasp of what Professor Hirsch has called cultural literacy: a deep understanding of mainstream culture, which no longer has much to do with Anglo-Saxon Protestants, but with the imperatives of industrial civilization. It is the need for cultural literacy, a profound conception of the whole civilization, which is often neglected in talk about literacy.

Patterson continued by drawing a connection between background information and the ability to hold positions of responsibility and power. He was particularly concerned with the importance for blacks and other minorities of possessing this information, which is essential for improving their social and economic status.

> The people who run society at the macro-level must be literate in this culture. For this reason, it is dangerous to overemphasize the problems of basic literacy or the relevancy of literacy to specific tasks, and more constructive to emphasize that blacks will be condemned in perpetuity to oversimplified, low-level tasks and will never gain their rightful place in controlling the levers of power unless they also acquire literacy in this wider cultural sense.

Although Patterson focused his remarks on the importance of cultural literacy for minorities, his observations hold for every culturally illiterate person in our nation. Indeed, as he observed, cultural literacy is not the property of any group or class.

> To assume that this wider culture is static is an error; in fact it is not. It's not a WASP culture; it doesn't belong to any group. It is essentially and constantly changing, and it is open. What is needed is recognition that the accurate metaphor or model for this wider literacy is not domination, but dialectic; each group participates and contributes, transforms and is transformed, as much as any other group. . . . The English language no longer belongs to any single group or nation. The same goes for any other area of the wider culture.[4]

As Professor Patterson suggested, being taught to decode elementary reading materials and specific, job-related texts cannot constitute true literacy. Such basic training does not make a person literate with respect to newspapers or other writings addressed to a general public. Moreover, a directly practical drawback of such narrow training is that it does not prepare anyone for technological change. Narrow vocational training in one state of a technology will not enable a person to read manuals that explain new developments in the same

14

---

[4]Orlando Patterson, "Language, Ethnicity, and Change" in S. G. D'Eloia, ed., *Toward a Literate Democracy: Proceedings of the First Shaughnessy Memorial Conference, April 3, 1980,* special number of *The Journal of Basic Writing* III (1980): 72–73.

technology. In modern life we need general knowledge that enables us to deal with new ideas, events, and challenges. In today's world, general cultural literacy is more useful than what Professor Patterson terms "literacy to a specific task," because general literate information is the basis for many changing tasks.

15   Cultural literacy is even more important in the social sphere. The aim of universal literacy has never been a socially neutral mission in our country. Our traditional social goals were unforgettably renewed for us by Martin Luther King, Jr., in his "I Have a Dream" speech. King envisioned a country where the children of former slaves sit down at the table of equality with the children of former slave owners, where men and women deal with each other as equals and judge each other on their characters and achievements rather than their origins. Like Thomas Jefferson, he had a dream of a society founded not on race or class but on personal merit.

16   In the present day, that dream depends on mature literacy. No modern society can hope to become a just society without a high level of universal literacy. Putting aside for the moment the practical arguments about the economic uses of literacy, we can contemplate the even more basic principle that underlies our national system of education in the first place—that people in a democracy can be entrusted to decide all important matters for themselves because they can deliberate and communicate with one another. Universal literacy is inseparable from democracy and is the canvas for Martin Luther King's picture as well as for Thomas Jefferson's.

17   Both of these leaders understood that just having the right to vote is meaningless if a citizen is disenfranchised by illiteracy or semiliteracy. Illiterate and semiliterate Americans are condemned not only to poverty, but also to the powerlessness of incomprehension. Knowing that they do not understand the issues, and feeling prey to manipulative oversimplifications, they do not trust the system of which they are supposed to be the masters. They do not feel themselves to be active participants in our republic, and they often do not turn out to vote. The civic importance of cultural literacy lies in the fact that true enfranchisement depends upon knowledge, knowledge upon literacy, and literacy upon cultural literacy.

18   To be truly literate, citizens must be able to grasp the meaning of any piece of writing addressed to the general reader. All citizens should be able, for instance, to read newspapers of substance, about which Jefferson made the following famous remark:

> Were it left to me to decide whether we should have a government without newspapers, or newspapers without a government, I should not hesitate a moment to prefer the latter. But I should mean that every man should receive those papers and be capable of reading them.[5]

Jefferson's last comment is often omitted when the passage is quoted, but it's the crucial one.

---

[5]Letter to Colonel Edward Carrington, January 16, 1787, taken from *The Life and Selected Writings of Thomas Jefferson,* ed. A. Koch and W. Peden (New York: Random House, 1944), 411–12.

Books and newspapers assume a "common reader," that is, a person who   19
knows the things known by other literate persons in the culture. Obviously,
such assumptions are never identical from writer to writer, but they show a
remarkable consistency. Those who write for a mass public are always making
judgments about what their readers can be assumed to know, and the judgments are closely similar. Any reader who doesn't possess the knowledge
assumed in a piece he or she reads will in fact be illiterate with respect to that
particular piece of writing.

Here, for instance, is a rather typical excerpt from the *Washington Post* of   20
December 29, 1983.

> A federal appeals panel today upheld an order barring foreclosure on a Missouri farm, saying
> that U.S. Agriculture Secretary John R. Block has reneged on his responsibilities to some debt
> ridden farmers. The appeals panel directed the USDA to create a system of processing loan
> deferments and of publicizing them as it said Congress had intended. The panel said that it is
> the responsiblity of the agriculture secretary to carry out this intent "not as a private banker,
> but as a public broker."

Imagine that item being read by people who are well trained in phonics,   21
word recognition, and other decoding skills but are culturally illiterate. They
might know words like *foreclosure,* but they would not understand what the
piece means. Who gave the order that the federal panel upheld? What is a federal appeals panel? Where is Missouri, and what about Missouri is relevant to
the issue? Why are many farmers debt ridden? What is the USDA? What is a
public broker? Even if culturally illiterate readers bothered to look up individual words, they would have little idea of the reality being referred to. The
explicit words are just surface pointers to textual meaning in reading and writing. The comprehending reader must bring to the text appropriate background
information that includes knowledge not only about the topic but also the
shared attitudes and conventions that color a piece of writing.

Our children can learn this information only by being taught it. Shared liter-   22
ate information is deliberately sustained by national systems of education in
many countries because they recognize the importance of giving their children a
common basis for communication. Some decades ago a charming book called
1066 and All That appeared in Britain.[6] It dealt with facts of British history
that all educated Britons had been taught as children but remembered only
dimly as adults. The book caricatured those recollections, purposely getting the
"facts" just wrong enough to make them ridiculous on their face. Readers
instantly recognized that the book was mistaken in its theory about what Ethel-
red-the-Unready was unready for, but, on the other hand, they couldn't say
precisely what he *was* unready for. The book was hilarious to literate Britons as
a satire of their own vague and confused memories. But even if their school-
child knowledge had become vague with the passage of time, it was still functional, because the information essential to literacy is rarely detailed or precise.

[6]W. C. Sellar and R. J. Yeatman, *1066 and All That: A Memorable History of England, Comprising All the
Parts You Can Remember, Including 103 Good Things, 5 Bad Kings, and 2 Genuine Dates* (London: Methuen,
1947).

23   This haziness is a key characteristic of literacy and cultural literacy. To understand the *Washington Post* extract literate readers have to know only vaguely, in the backs of their minds, that the American legal system permits a court decision to be reversed by a higher court. They would need to know only that a judge is empowered to tell the executive branch what it can or cannot do to farmers and other citizens. (The secretary of agriculture was barred from foreclosing a Missouri farm.) Readers would need to know only vaguely what and where Missouri is, and how the department and the secretary of agriculture fit into the scheme of things. None of this knowledge would have to be precise. Readers wouldn't have to know whether an appeals panel is the final judicial level before the U.S. Supreme Court. Any practiced writer who feels it is important for a reader to know such details always provides them.

An Abridged List for Cultural Literacy

1066
1492
1776
1861–1865
1914–1918
1939–1945

abbreviation (written
   English)
abolitionism
abominable snowman
abortion
Abraham and Isaac
Absence makes the heart
   grow fonder.
absenteeism
absolute monarchy
absolute zero
abstract expressionism
academic freedom
a capella
accelerator, particle
accounting
AC/DC (alternating
   current/direct current)
Achilles
Achilles' heel
acid
acid rain
acquittal
acronym

acrophobia
Acropolis
Actions speak louder than
   words.
active voice
act of God
actuary
acupuncture
A.D. (anno domini)
Adam and Eve
Adams, John
Adams, John Quincy
adaptation
Addams, Jane
ad hoc
ad hominem
adieu
Adirondack Mountains
adjective
Adonis
adrenal gland
adrenaline (fight or flight)
Adriatic Sea
adultery
adverb
AEC (Atomic Energy
   Commission)
Aegean Sea
Aeneas
Aeneid, The (title)
aerobic

Aeschylus
Aesop's Fables (title)
aesthetics
affirmative action
affluent society
Afghanistan
aficionado
AFL-CIO
Africa
Agamemnon
aggression
Agnew, Spiro
agnosticism
agreement (grammar)
agribusiness
air pollution
air quality index
Akron, Ohio
Alabama
à la carte
Aladdin and the Wonderful
   Lamp (title)
Alamo, the
Alaska
Alaska pipeline
Albania
Albany, New York
albatross around one's
   neck
Alberta
Albuquerque, New Mexico

alchemy
Alcott, Louisa May
Aleutian Islands
Alexander the Great
Alexandria, Egypt
alfresco
algae
Alger, Horatio
Algeria
Algiers
Ali, Muhammad
alias
Alice in Wonderland (title)
Alien and Sedition Acts
alienation
alkaline
Allah
Allegheny Mountains
allegory

allegro
Alliance for Progress
Allies (World War II)
alliteration
alloy
All roads lead to Rome.
All's fair in love and war.
All's well that ends well.
All that glitters is not gold.
All the world's a stage
   (text)
allusion
alma mater
alpha and omega
Alps
alter ego
alternator
alto
altruism

Amazonian
Amazon River
ambiguity
American Legion
American Stock Exchange
America the Beautiful
   (song)
amicus curiae
Am I my brother's keeper?
amino acids
amnesia
amnesty
amniotic sac
amoeba
amortization
amp (ampere)
ampersand (written
   English)

WRITING AND DISCUSSION QUESTIONS

Informative

1. Hirsch claims that speaking, reading, and participating in democratic life intelligently and effectively requires mastery of much background information. (See the sample list of terms.) Explain in what ways such knowledge is helpful. You might examine personal life, family life, civic life, and the world of work.
2. Hirsch claims that cultural literacy, "the basic information needed to thrive in the modern world," will chiefly benefit disadvantaged youth. What assumptions about the disadvantaged is he making here and how does he think cultural literacy will benefit that group?

Persuasive

1. Many persons have criticized Hirsch for presenting cultural literacy in the form of a list of terms (63 pages in length, part of that list appears above). Argue for or against such a list and whether such a list benefits or harms education.
2. Hirsch defends himself against critics who argue that he is imposing a white, male, and middle class standard on students. The critics further point out that we live in a pluralistic and diverse society in which all groups should be represented. Argue the validity of this criticism.

Personal

1. Examine the required general and major courses for your major program. What kinds of knowledge would or are you learning in this curriculum? How much of it is

related to a particular profession? How would Hirsch judge the curriculum, given his goal of a broad cultural literacy for all?

▼

Little-Read Schoolhouse
GEORGE STEINER

1   The indictment is by now widely known, but it remains appalling. Some fifty per cent of American teen-agers can identify neither Churchill nor Stalin. Two-thirds of American seventeen-year-olds do not know that the Civil War took place between 1850 and 1900. Geography is to almost three-quarters of high-school juniors and seniors a black hole: they can neither identify the less salient states on a map of the U.S.A. nor make even an informed guess as to whether Ireland is east or west of England. One qualified witness could not find a single high-school or college student in Los Angeles able to tell him the years in which either World War was fought. Only two could locate Chicago "even in the vaguest terms." A junior at U.C.L.A. opined that Toronto must be in Italy; a pre-law student confidently situated the nation's capital in the state of Washington. How, one student asked, can Latin be called a dead language when there is a country called Latin America?

2   But these are only pinpricks. The best evidence is that at least one-third of the adult citizens of the United States are illiterate; that is, they are unable to read at all or can decipher only rudimentary bits of written information. The instructions on most medicine bottles, let alone tax forms, driver's licenses, and insurance policies, are wholly beyond their grasp. Of the remaining two-thirds of our citizens, it is thought that at least one-half, while technically literate, scarcely read at all, or read only print of the simplest and most ephemeral kind. Even people at the top of the educational and social pyramid fall, on average, well below the standard of cultural recognition taken to be essential in Japan and Western Europe. The schooling in mathematics and language in the Soviet Union is sharply ahead of that in all but the most selective and privileged of American schools. Learning by heart—note the depth and power implied in that eroded idiom—is crucial to Russian, Japanese, and European education. It has all but vanished from American mores. Instead, there is throughout primary and secondary schooling a planned amnesia.

3   The consequences are manifold. It is to the lowest common denominator that the mass media and the marketplace make their pitch. A deafening emptiness pours out of the television screens, radios, and jukeboxes that spangle the land. The press, except for a rather restricted mandarin sector, knows that the world must be blazoned to skimming readers in words of one syllable. Dependent clauses introduce into life a hostile mystery. Vital information—vital in the

sense that it must inform sane political debate and decision—remains blocked in the conduits of the specialists. In a context of illiteracy and semiliteracy, the Ciceronian-Jeffersonian program for a republic founded on the articulate discussion of demanding and evolving issues, for a free polis based on remembrance of the historical past and on the dissemination of new knowledge, breaks down. The problem is not only that the United States is being outstripped in both the volume and the quality of economic production by rival societies, or that it can no longer recruit into its military and administrative cadres men and women of even minimal intellectual calibre; it is that the axiom of mature perception and debate on which the great, proud experiment that is the United States is conceived may crumble into a morass of demagogy and apathy.

The alarm bells have been ringing since Sputnik. It is to the imperative task   4 of remedy that E. D. Hirsch addresses himself. His "Cultural Literacy" (Houghton Mifflin; $16.95) is a brief, crystal-clear, and condignly urgent tract. Even within its brevity, it is repetitive. But this is a legitimate device of impatient virtue. The hour is late.

Professor Hirsch sets forth his postulate as follows: 5

> We Americans have long accepted literacy as a paramount aim of schooling, but only recently have some of us who have done research in the field begun to realize that literacy is far more than a skill and that it requires large amounts of specific information. That new insight is central to this book.

One is left mildly numbed by this solemn, almost Mosaic promulgation of a "new insight." Did it truly require recent research (one hears the deep, supportive breath of the relevant foundations and of national powwows) to discover that human beings cannot read intelligently—cannot make sense of a message—unless they have mastered a more or less extensive corpus of previous background knowledge? Is it a novel discovery that semantics—the structure and performative means of meaning—is almost invariably "contextual," that it depends on a measure of familiarity with the codes and objects of reference, with the preceding "textuality," from which it derives its own sense? The very notion of uninformed reading is one of those idiotic spooks conjured by hayseed populism and by psychologists in American departments of education. Never mind. Whether his insight is original or not, Hirsch is emphatically right.

Who are the villains of the piece? Again, Professor Hirsch's answer is unam-   6 biguous: Jean-Jacques Rousseau and John Dewey. It is they who preached a "content-neutral" schooling for children. It is they who held up the mirage of the development of a child's capacities by means of vaguely defined and roseate stages of personal exploration, of, as Dewey puts it, "personal acquaintance with a small number of typical situations with a view to mastering the way of dealing with the problems of experience, not the piling up of information." That we find here a drastic misreading of Rousseau—whose education toward solitude in "Émile" is one of the most complex and tragic analyses of human defeat ever argued—is immaterial. Hirsch is surely right in asserting, over and over, that the evacuation of concrete knowledge—names, dates, texts, the vocabulary and grammar of one's own language and others—from American education in the name of pastoral license and utopian play has been sheer catastrophe. It is, moreover, exponential: when almost nothing is known, nothing further can be learned.

7   Hence the pressing need for a return to more traditional ideals and practices. Hirsch argues, "It isn't facts that deaden the minds of young children, who are storing facts in their minds every day with astonishing voracity. It is incoherence—our failure to ensure that a pattern of shared, vividly taught, and socially enabling knowledge will emerge from our instruction." The establishment of this pattern of minimal shared reference—of "common readership," to borrow Virginia Woolf's designation—constitutes the heart of Hirsch's manifesto. What ought every American child to be taught so that as an American adult he can exercise his talents, his political rights, his spiritual and emotional maturity within a coherent community of values and of recognitions? It is this delineation of an essential "cultural literacy" that is proving to be the most widely noticed and most controversial element in Professor Hirsch's case.

8   Actually, the proposals he makes are not easy to encapsulate. There is in them more than a dash of the Great Books program developed by Mortimer Adler and Robert Hutchins in those palmy days at Chicago. There are (though these precedents are passed over entirely in silence) echoes of the visionary plea in Paul Goodman's classic "Growing Up Absurd" and of the pioneering work on illiteracy in America by Jonathan Kozol. Hirsch's trump card comes from an impressive background of psychological and sociological research, and from a certain specificity. It is his dream (that Martin Luther King phrase sounds and resounds through the book) that the greatest possible number of American men and women be educated to the linguistic-contextual level required to read intelligently the news stories and editorial page of a serious, adult newspaper—say, the *Times*. The ingenuity and the advantage of so focussed a target are clear. If we take this particular standard of performance as canonic, we can fairly readily establish the vocabulary needed, the syntax that has to be internalized, and much of the "primary content"—historical, geographical, political, literary, and scientific—to which an American reader must have unforced access if he is to understand both his own national life and, to a certain degree, that of the planet at large. He must, even to make sense of the sports pages, be able to identify "Waterloo" if a home team is said to have suffered one; he must be able to make out what is meant by a "Pyrrhic victory" if the hockey game has resulted in excessive injuries. To characterize either of these events as a "Donnybrook" would, on the other hand, represent an instance of editorial preciosity beyond what might be reasonably expected of the normal reader.

9   This example derives from a list supplied by Hirsch and two of his colleagues at the University of Virginia, Joseph Kett, a historian, and James Trefil, a physicist, of basic words, terms, names, and proverbial tags that all literate Americans must be capable of grasping and locating accurately if literacy is to

be regained. The list is intrinsically fascinating. A wicked soul could construe
from it a psychobiography of E. D. Hirsch and his two associates. On a more
serious level, it represents a peculiarly graphic image of the American liberal
imagination—of the national mythologies of common sense—at a certain point
in our history. Having only this listing to hand, future historians, sociologists, or
political theorists could go a long way toward formulating with some accuracy
the ways in which the United States in the later nineteen-eighties looked upon
the past, upon its own institutions, and upon the outside world. Here was a
society that had to remember Orestes but not Electra; Dickens but not Thack-
eray; the massacre at My Lai but not that of St. Bartholomew's Day; George
McGovern but not Adlai Stevenson. Lee Iacocca makes the roll, but not Louis
Sullivan, the originator of the skyscraper; John Philip Sousa, yes, but not
Charles Ives, the most inventive figure in American music; Emily Dickinson is
of the pantheon, Ezra Pound not; the oratory of Webster is assured inclusion,
but not that of Demosthenes. The ideological reflexes discernible in this catalogue are sometimes transparent: Verdi is home and dry, but Richard Wagner,
the greatest aesthetic influence on modernity, goes unnamed. Auschwitz must
(praise God) be part of basic literacy, but not the Gulag. Wittgenstein is, haunt-
ingly enough, part of the cultural alphabet for Americans, but not Heidegger,
the begetter of modern existentialism and of all deconstructive movements, and
a presence who more and more towers over twentieth-century thought. Irregular verbs must be identified, but not irrational numbers; Spiro Agnew is
assigned a place in the echo chambers of the literate; syphilis endures, but her-
pes is not yet listed.

One could play this game ad absurdum (a tag omitted, while "ad hominem"   *10*
is present). Nor is it a trivial game, for it is precisely via this basic lexicon and
primer of cognizance that Professor Hirsch lets one divine what he has in mind.
It is only here that one can make out the material and psychological contours
of that "middle ground of cultural knowledge" which must be mastered and
universally shared if the republic is to accomplish its promised destiny. There
is a deliberate politics—almost a metaphysics—in the principles of selection
which array Betty Friedan next to Milton Friedman or put "Pilgrim's Progress"
immediately above the Pill. What emerges is the profile of a well-schooled man
or woman with not only a sound knowledge of American history and of the
numerous popular and populist elements alive within that history but also a
quite remarkable alertness to science: mesons, quarks, pulsars, nucleic acids
are postulated as indispensable signals. Nothing less will insure "that new generations will continue to be enfranchised in our medium of national communication as securely as they are enfranchised at the polls."

The attacks on Professor Hirsch's entire conception of a central cultural lit-   *11*
eracy—of an indispensable core of shared learning—have, predictably, come
from the spokesmen for ethnic and sex-polarized diversity. Those who regard
Mohican history as being at least as important as the sort of history that compels a child to know something about Julius and Augustus Caesar do not acquiesce in Hirsch's assumption of Judeo-Christian or European and Anglo-Saxon
centrality. Radical feminism lays claim to its own syllabus of long-neglected

facts and allusions. (In turn, how betrayingly characteristic it is of an academic in arcadian Virginia to include in his primary baggage of awareness Joe Louis but not Rocky Marciano!) Any canonic content is, in short, a piece of more or less naked power politics. Given the stridency and the personal tenor of the current ethnic, feminist, and minority-group polemics in the United Stated, Professor Hirsch is both elusive and defensive in his plea. The core must, he agrees, be flexible. It must be open to the currents of diversity in the singular mixture of races, inheritance, and historical provenance that make up the American mosaic. Classical markers will fade away as new configurations arise from American political and social experience. Booker T. Washington and Paul Robeson *must* appear on today's vade mecum (unlisted), even if Toussaint-Louverture does not. Nevertheless, insists Hirsch, there are prime numbers, as it were, that cut across all claims of splintered singularity. A play by Neil Simon is, if fundamental civility and civilization are at stake, never a substitute for one by Shakespeare.

12   Other polemics are bound to come from the more pessimistic and conservative right. Is it really evident that certain levels of linguistic manipulation and abstract thought are accessible to all human beings, or even to the overwhelming majority? What level of coaching, of continued education, of directed reading is necessary if some two hundred million Americans are to be able to cope even on a modest plane—to have a nodding acquaintance—with the Fourth Gospel, with the art of Vermeer, with the concept of a quantum leap or that of genetic recombination (all of which figure in the cardinal catalogue)? Is E. D. Hirsch's whole program not going to water down to the level of a bland digest those very virtues and fascinations of culture, of textuality, which have always been the possession and the joy of the few? It would not, I imagine, be difficult for Professor Hirsch to counter that the sheer informational demands of modern American life call for a heightened ambition in regard to human capacities, and that there is no definite evidence—certainly not on biological grounds— that such capacity is denied to any given group, class, or ethnic component of our society. Such a reply *may* be erroneous, but hope and decency must underwrite it.

13   My own uneasiness is twofold. "To be culturally literate," proclaims Hirsch, "is to possess the basic information needed to thrive in the modern world." The postulate is unashamedly Benthamite. I am not certain that thriving in the modern world—in the palpably economic and socially integrated sense intended by Hirsch—is an unquestionable ideal. And I am fairly certain that it is essential for a genuine inward culture to be acutely critical of the information and the values offered it by the body politic. The "modern world" is, in fundamental respects, a fairly hellish place. We inhabit the century of Himmler and Pol Pot. The nuclear arsenal has long since spiralled into homicidal lunacy. We are laying waste what is left of the natural resources and the vestiges of the Edenic on our planet. In many of its fundamental motions of spirit and of policy, the era of the superpower and the terrorist is one not of progress, as Hirsch seems to imply unexaminedly, but of reversion to barbarism. "Animal

kingdom" is immediately preceded by "angst" in the Hirsch lexicon. To "thrive" in these conditions and to do so via "information" are perfectly arguable predications, but they need to be argued.

The second point is more of a luxury. Here is an important tract on behalf *14* of eloquence—that of Cicero, of Jefferson, of Lincoln, of Martin Luther King. There is not in it an eloquent, a memorable sentence. Here is a plea for literacy in a dynamic, even joyful, sense, a plea for eyes that will light not only at the name of Shakespeare but at that of Rabelais. There is not a phrase, not a passage in this book that sings, that makes the language come alive with its matchless magic. When Bacon composed his "Advancement of Learning," when John Stuart Mill and Matthew Arnold discussed education and culture, they demonstrated by their very means of discussion just what was at stake. Perhaps it is now too late for that in the American circumstance. Perhaps it is, indeed, one of the merits of Professor Hirsch's discourse that it is as gray, as joyless, and as utilitarian as the realities and needs it addresses.

WRITING AND DISCUSSION QUESTIONS

Informative

1. Steiner criticizes some of Hirsch's basic premises but seems to agree with his central thesis and its implications. How does Steiner see this thesis, and how does he define cultural literacy?
2. Steiner cites certain historical, literary and cultural terms that Hirsch excludes from his list. What concerns Steiner about these exclusions? Which of these seem to be serious omissions?
3. Why is Steiner uneasy with Hirsch's views, saying that "thriving in the modern world" [by mastering a cultural literacy] is not clearly the ideal?

Persuasive

1. Argue that Hirsch's list is more than a "trivial game."
2. Argue the advantage or disadvantage of teaching from Hirsch's immense list of terms and the complex concepts behind those terms (numbering almost 5000). Also, argue whether or not such a list would, because of sheer numbers, become a "bland digest."
3. Steiner's review of Hirsch's book is essentially positive, except for two areas of concern. Reread Steiner's last two paragraphs and argue whether these concerns outweigh the positive aspects of Hirsch's work.

Personal

1. Make up your own list of 10 terms that suggest basic information and concepts needed to succeed in your college or hometown community. What social, political, literary, or scientific knowledge would you need? Explain why you chose these terms.

▼

The Canon in Africa: Imperialism and Racism
NGUGI WA THIONG'O

If the great works of literature convey the cultural beliefs of the society that calls those works great, then imposing the literature of one society upon another is a form of cultural oppression. According to this line of reasoning, each culture or group of people should have its own canon as part of its own culture, a canon that will represent local feeling and values.

In recent decades such thinking emerged most clearly in the newly independent countries of Africa, Asia, and the Caribbean. Until the middle of this century these areas were still largely colonies of European countries. The children who went to school were taught the literature of their European masters. Schoolchildren in Nigeria, India, and the Bahamas all read the great works of British literature. In Senegal, Algeria, and Vietnam French literature was the ideal.

Ngugi Wa Thiong'o (b. 1938) is a novelist and professor of literature at the University of Nairobi, Kenya. Here he describes the literary situation in Kenya in the 1970s, a decade after independence from Britain in 1963. He writes about the persistence of romantic British nature poetry and racism in the literary landscape of a tropical black African nation. He argues for the importance of a country developing its own sense of literature and not being the victims of foreigners' beliefs. The canon taught in school is crucial to cultural identity.

Ngugi originally presented this argument in 1973 to a conference of teachers of literature in Nairobi. He spoke not just of literary analysis and theory, but of what the audience must do. Although much writing on literature is academic and nonpolitical, critics and writers at times use their understanding of literature to analyze cultural issues and urge public action. Because literature conveys important understandings about the way we live, feel, and think, literary specialists are often accepted as authorities on social, cultural, and spiritual issues. Ngugi shares this belief about the social importance of literature, event though he rejects the literature of Europe.

Ignorant of their country, some people can only relate tales of ancient Greece and other foreign lands.

—MAO TSE-TUNG

If we want to turn Africa into a new Europe, then let us leave the destiny of our countries to Europeans. They will know how to do it better than the most gifted among us.

—FRANTZ FANON

1   The subject of our three days gathering and discussion is the place and the teaching of African literature in our schools. I hope that the very title will provoke us to anger and protest: how come that it has taken ten whole years after constitutional independence, Uhuru wa Bendera, for us native sons and daughters to meet and to debate for the first time on the subject—the

place of our literature in our education system? And why do we find it necessary to qualify this literature with the word 'African', for what else should it be?

A Russian child grows under the influence of his native imaginative litera-   *2*
ture: a Chinese, a Frenchman, a German or an Englishman first imbibes his national literature before attempting to take in other worlds. That the central taproot of his cultural nourishment should lie deep in his native soil is taken for granted. This A B C of education is followed in most societies because it is demanded by the practice and the experience of living and growing.

Not so in Africa, the West Indies and the colonized world as a whole,   *3*
despite the crucial role of the twin fields of literature and culture in making a child aware of, and rediscover his environment.

Let me give you three examples: *4*

The other day I found my own son trying to memorize a poem by William   *5*
Wordsworth. I contained my disappointment and held the book for him while, with a face tortured with the effort, he recited:

> I wander'd lonely as a cloud
> That floats on high o'er vales and hills,
> When all at once I saw a crowd,
> A host, of golden daffodils
> Beside the lake, beneath the trees,
> Fluttering and dancing in the breeze.

I asked him: What are daffodils? He looked at the illustration book: Oh, they are just little fishes in a lake!

Three years ago on a sunny hot afternoon, Okot p'Bitek and I went to a   *6*
school where one of our former students was teaching. The children hated poetry, she told us: Couldn't we convince them that though poetry was difficult it was a distillation of human wisdom and thought? A gigantic request since we had only one hour between us, but we would do our best. For a start we asked them what poems they had already learnt. Thereupon they told us about a poem of fourteen lines called a sonnet written by one William Shakespeare comparing old age to Winter!

I know of a leading school in Kenya where, on top of Sheridan's *School for*   *7*
Scandal, Paul Gallico's *The Snow Goose* and other literary vintages in the same vien, (not a single African writer, though they had possibly heard of Chinua Achebe's *Things Fall Apart* and no doubt of Charles Manqua's *Son of Woman*—the latter through the girls' own initiative) they have a text whose title I cannot recall which tells the story of Queen Victoria and how she used to cough and sneeze and eat pudding, and pull her dog's ears and of course anglicize (or is it civilize?) her German husband.

These would be fit cases for jokes and laughter were they not the general   *8*
practice in our schools. Indeed until a few years ago, the departments of literature (then called English departments) in Nairobi, Dar-es-Salaam and Makerere Universities would only teach British authors from Chaucer through Oliver

Goldsmith to Graham Greene. That is how most of us were brought up under the old colonial system administered from the University of London: but is there any reason why our children in this day and age should be brought up on the same impoverished diet administered in the so-called English departments, often headed by some retired biology teachers or retired army majors or men of God, whose main qualifications for the posts are a white skin, long residence in the country, and of course an acquaintance with *The London Book of English Verse*, or *A Penguin Book of English Verse?*

9   Why was this pattern so in our time? Why does it still persist? Has it all been an accident of content, time, place and persons?

10   Let us not mince words. The truth is that the content of our syllabi, the approach to and presentation of the literature, the persons and the machinery for determining the choice of texts and their interpretation, were all an integral part of imperialism in its classical colonial phase, and they are today an integral part of the same imperialism but now in its neo-colonial phase. Cultural imperialism, which during colonialism often affected the population and the country unevenly depending on the colonial policies of the marauding powers and the degree of resistance in each country and in different parts of the country, becomes the major agency of control during neo-colonialism. . . .

11   In [novels by people like Rudyard Kipling and Rider Haggard, the] European emerges as the hero, the superman, Batman, Tarzan, who can wipe a thousand thick-lipped, big-nosed, curly-haired blacks. The blacks, especially in Rider Haggard, are always of two kinds: the evil ones who are so described that a picture of a devil forms in a reader's mind,[1] and whose one characteristic is an insane hatred of white benefactors out of sheer spite and motiveless envy; or the good ones who are always described in terms of grinning teeth and who always run errands for the white man, tremble in fear when the white man frowns in anger, or show an 'Uncle Tom' face of humility and gratitude for any favour bestowed on them by the European master.[2]

12   You get a variation of Haggard's two types in the novels of the racist apologist for European settlerism in Kenya—Elspeth Huxley—especially in her two novels, *The Red Strangers* and *A Thing to Love*. Only now her bad evil Africans are those educated in western schools and instead of thanking the Lord for small mercies, actually demand political rights and urge the simple-souled African to violence and sabotage.

13   Karen Blixen is another writer in the racist tradition. An aristocrat from Denmark she came to Kenya at the beginning of this century and acquired a

---

[1] Note the description of Gagool in *King Solomon's Mines* haunted Graham Greene all his life, at least so he says in his collected Essays. And Micere Githae Mugo has written: 'I can never forget *King Solomon's Mines* nor the weird portrait of Gagool which for a long time epitomized in my childish mind the figure of an African woman in old age. It is only recently that I have got over my dread and fear of old black women.' See her article, *Written Literature and Black Image*, in Gachukia and Akivaga's *Teaching of African Literature in Schools*.

[2] See the description of this in *King Solomon's Mines*.

farm in the now fashionable district of Nairobi still bearing her name. She enjoyed wild animals and naked rugged nature. Later in her book, *Out of Africa,* she was to write:

> When you have caught the rhythm of Africa,
> You find that it is the same in all her music.
> What I learnt from the game of the country was useful
> to me in my dealings with Africans.[3]

She protests her love for natives and animals in the same breath:

> As for me, from my first week in Africa, I had felt a great affection for the natives. It was a strong feeling that embraced all ages and both sexes. The discovery of the dark races was to me a magnificent enlargement of all my world. If a person with an inborn sympathy for animals had come into contact with animals late in life: or if a person with an instinctive taste for woods and forest had entered a forest for the first time at the age of twenty; or if someone with an ear for music had happened to hear music for the first time when he was already grown up; their cases might have been similar to mine.[4]

In all her descriptions of African characters she resorts to animal imagery. The African was really part of the woods and animals, part of Hegel's unconscious nature. She gives medicine to Kamante and after he is cured he becomes her very good cook.

> Kamante could have no idea as to how a dish of ours ought to taste, and he was, in spite of his conversion, and his connexion with civilization, at heart an arrant Kikuyu, rooted in the traditions of his tribe and his faith in them, as in the only way of living worthy of a human being. He did at times taste the food that he cooked, but then with a distrustful face, like a witch who takes a sip out of her cauldron. *He stuck to the maizecobs of his fathers.* Here even his intelligence sometimes failed him, and he came and offered me a Kikuyu delicacy a roasted sweet potato or a lump of sheep's fat—*as even a civilized dog, that has lived for a long time with people, will place a bone on the floor before you, as a present.*[5] (italics mine)

When she goes back to Denmark, her African characters keep on visiting her *14* in her dreams—but in the form of animals

> It was then that my old companions began to put in an appearance in my dreams at night, and by such behaviour managed to deeply upset and trouble me. For till then no living people had ever found their way into those dreams. They came in disguise, it is true, and as in a mirror darkly, so that I would at times meet Kamante in the shape of a dwarf-elephant or a bat, Farah as a watchful leopard snarling lowly round the house, and Sirunga as a small jackal, yapping— such as the natives tell you that jackals will do in times of disaster with one forepaw behind his

[3]Karen Blixen: *Out of Africa,* Penguin edition, p. 24.
[4]Ibid., p. 25.
[5]Ibid., p. 44.

ear. But the disguise did not deceive me, I recognised each of them every time and in the mornings I knew that we had been together, for a short meeting on a forest path or for a journey. So I could no longer feel sure that they did still actually exist, or indeed that they had ever actually existed, outside of my dreams.[6]

15   Her cosmos is hierarchically ordered with God at the top followed by the white aristocracy, ordinary whites, domestic animals, wild animals who are all in 'direct contact' with God. Africans don't figure anywhere in this cosmic picture except as parts of wood and stones, different only because occasionally they exhibit impulses towards animals.

16   Karen Blixen was once proposed by Hemingway for the Nobel prize in Literature.

17   I quoted from Blixen liberally because she was no ordinary drunken soldier or an uncouth frustrated missionary spinster come to Africa to fulfil herself in lording it over schoolgirls and terrorizing timid African teachers but a refined lady of some discrimination and learning. She belongs to the same tradition of great racists like Hume, Trollope, Hegel, Trevor-Roper and all other arch-priests of privilege, racism and class snobbery.

18   The last group of writers I want to mention are those who set out to sympathetically treat the African world either to appeal to the European liberal conscience or simply to interpret Africa for the Africans. But even among these, the African image is still in negative terms. For Joseph Conrad, the African characters in *Heart of Darkness* are part of that primitive savagery that lay below the skin of every civilized being. He was telling his fellow Europeans: You go to Africa to civilize, to enlighten a heathen people; scratch that thin veneer of civilization and you will find the savagery of Africa in you too. For Joyce Cary, the positive creative African in *Mister Johnson* is a clowning idiot whose desire and final fulfilment is having to be shot dead by an Englishman whom we are led to believe loves him well. We all love our horses and dogs and cats and we often shoot them to put them out of pain. So much for *Mister Johnson* and Master Joyce Cary. For William Blake, the little black boy, cries thus:

> My mother bore me in the southern wild,
> And I am black, but O, my soul is white
> White as an angel is the English child,
> But I am black as if bereaved of light.[7]

He longs for the day he will die and be freed from the burden of his skin colour, then he and the white boy will 'lean in joy upon our Father's knee':

> And then I'll stand and stroke his silver hair,
> And be like him, and he will then love me.[8]

[6]Isak Dinesen: *Shadows on the Grass* (John Murray, London, 1960), p. 45.
[7]William Blake: 'The Little Black Boy' (*The Complete Poems*, Longman, p. 58).
[8]Ibid., p. 58.

This is the white liberal's dream of a day when black and white can love one   *19*
another without going through the agony of violent reckoning. Liberalism has
always been the sugary ideology of imperialism: it fosters the illusion in the
exploited of the possibilities of peaceful settlement and painless escape from
imperialist violence which anyway is not called violence but law and order. Liberalism blurs all antagonistic class contradictions, all the contradictions between
imperialist domination and the struggle for national liberation, seeing in the
revolutionary violence of the former, the degradation of humanity:

> Liberalism rejects ideological struggle and stands for unprincipled peace, thus giving rise to a
> decadent, philistine, attitude and bringing about political degeneration in certain units and indi-
> viduals (among the oppressed) . . . and objectively has the effect of helping the enemy [i.e.
> imperialism].[9]

And nowhere is liberalism so clearly manifested as in imaginative literature.

A written literature also develops alongside people's oral fighting literature   *20*
again as part of the cultural struggle and cultural assertion. In the case of
Africa, the very act of writing was itself a testimony of the creative capacity of
the African and the first tottering but still important steps by the 'educated'
elite towards self-definition and the acceptance of the environment from which
they had been alienated by western, Eurocentric imperialist education. But the
literature produced, because of its critical realism, also reflected the reality of
the African struggle against colonial domination.

Chinua Achebe is a case in point. His novels taken as a whole beautifully   *21*
delineate the origins, growth and development of a neo-colonial native ruling
class. This class has roots in the early Christian converts, the early *asomi* who
learnt to read and write; the court messengers; the policemen; the road over-
seers, in *Things Fall Apart* and *Arrow of God*. This class later becomes the
backbone of the business and civil service 'been to's' in *No Longer at Ease*. In
A Man of the People, the class inherits power and begins to fulfil its historical
mission of a messenger class, in the process looting the people. Where the
individual messenger was bribed by individual families in *Things Fall Apart;*
where the same individual messenger played one clan against another to confuse them about his messenger role and cloud it with nepotism and hence eat
the bribe in peace in *Things Fall Apart* and *Arrow of God,* the same class now
extorts bribes from the whole country in *A Man of the People* and plays one
ethnic community against others on a national scale, again to mystify its true
role and character as a messenger class. In *Girls at War*, the class involves the
whole country in bloodshed in its intraclass warfare for a share of the cake, the
left-overs, given to it by the master.

Such a literature, again at its critical best and most committed, defines a   *22*
people not in terms of always being acted on but in terms of actors. Okonkwo
and Ezeulu as representatives of the people and people's spirit of resistance

[9]Mao Tse-Tung: 'Combat Liberalism'.

make their own history. Okonkwo commits suicide rather than submit and live in a world where he is denied the right to make his own history through his control and development of the productive forces. His act of killing an imperialist messenger is as symbolic as it is prophetic. It is the new messenger class, the new errand boys of international monopoly capitalism that make total liberation difficult, for on the surface they do look like one of Okonkwo's own

23   people.

I believe that we as teachers of literature can help in this collective struggle to seize back our creative initiative in history. For this it is essential that we grasp the true function and role of literature in our society. We can help principally in three ways:

1. In all our schools, teacher training colleges and community centres we must insist on the primacy and centrality of African literature and the literature of African people in the West Indies and America. Central to this is the oral literature of our people, including their contemporary compositions.

2. Where we import literature from outside, it should be relevant to our situation. It should be the literature that treats of historical situations, historical struggles, similar to our own. It should be the kind of literature that rejects oppressive social-economic systems, that rejects all those forces that dwarf the creative development of man. In this case anti-imperialist literatures from Asia and Latin America and literature from socialist countries are very important. But anti-imperialist, anti-bourgeois literature and the pro-people literature of struggle from writers in imperialist countries can add a considerable contribution to our own struggles for a better world.

3. While not rejecting the critical demands of the more formal elements and needs of any art, we must subject literature whether oral, African or from other lands to a most rigorous criticism from the point of view of the struggling masses. We must detect what is positive, revolutionary, humanistic in a work of art, support it, strengthen it; and reject what is negative and anti-humanistic in the same or other works.

24   All this is not easy for it calls upon us to re-examine ourselves, our values, our own world outlook, our own assumptions and prejudices. Above all, it demands of us to re-examine our own stand and attitude to the struggle that still goes on in our continent: the struggle of our people against economic, political, and cultural imperialism of western European and Japanese capitalism, whose most ugly deformation is seen in South Africa, Rhodesia, Angola and Mozambique. It demands of us to adopt a scientific materialistic world outlook on nature, human society and human thought, and assume the standpoint of the most progressive and revolutionary classes (i.e. workers and peasants) in our society, for they are at the forefront in the struggle against imperialism and foreign domination, indeed against the suffocating alliance between the imperialist bourgeoisie and the local pro-foreigner *comprador* class.

In his last days in Conakry, Kwame Nkrumah wrote that the spectre of   25
Black Power was haunting the world. Black Power here does not mean a glori-
fication of an ossified past. Rather it means the true creative power of African
people through a people's control of their forces of production and equitable
distribution of the products of their sweat to enhance the quality of all their
lives. Seen in this light, Black Power is impossible outside a socialist context
and a total liberation of the African genius at all the levels we have been talking about. Literature, and our attitudes to literature, can help or else hinder in
the creation of a united socialist Black Power in Africa based on the just continuing struggle of peasants and workers for a total control of their productive
forces.

We writers and critics of African literature should form an essential intellec-   26
tual part of the anti-imperialist cultural army of African peoples for total economic and political liberation from imperialism and foreign domination.

WRITING AND DISCUSSION QUESTIONS

Informative

1. What argument does Thiong'o make against what he calls the "old colonial system" that prescribes a British canon of literature for the schools? What does he
   mean by calling it an imperialism in its "neo-colonial phase" [paragraph 11]?
2. Why does Thiong'o cite the writings of Karen Blixen? In what sense does he consider her a "great racist" (paragraph 20)? How are the writings of Chinua
   Achebe different in the mind of Thiong'o?
3. Thiong'o believes that liberalism offers the illusion of "peaceful settlement and
   painless escape from imperialist violence" [paragraph 23]. What is at the base of
   Thiong'o's antagonism toward liberalism?

Persuasive

1. Argue that the standard literature in American schools fairly or unfairly portrays
   ethnic and Native Americans. Does the literature taught in our schools underrepre-
   sent foreign cultures? If so, what are the consequences of such an ethnocentrism?
2. Argue that Thiong'o's three recommendations in paragraph 28 are essential to
   developing cultural identity and awareness in his country. What are their implications for your own course of study?

Personal

1. In paragraph 27, Thiong'o suggests that the best literature will define a people in
   terms of being actors rather than being acted on. Discuss a piece of literature that
   presents a particular group of people as actors or nonactors.

▼

In Dispute on Bias, Stanford Is Likely to Alter Western Culture Program

RICHARD BERNSTEIN

1 At Stanford University, they still talk of the day nearly a year ago when some 500 students, on a march with the Rev. Jesse Jackson, came up with a slogan for the next generation.

2   The students were celebrating a new course at Stanford, one that would stress the contributions of minorities and women to Western culture, and, they chanted: "Hey hey, ho ho, Western culture's got to go."

3   Student and faculty members these days assert that the slogan expressed no hostility to the likes of Plato and Saint Augustine, Rousseau and John Stuart Mill, all of whom are on Stanford's current list of required reading for freshmen. But in claiming a kind of equal time for minority contributions to American civilization, the chant did reflect a demand that is expected to be accepted by the faculty in the weeks ahead.

4   Responding to charges that the core reading list reflects what some have referred to as a "European-Western and male bias" and what others call "sexist and racist stereotypes," the Stanford faculty seems likely to approve a measure that would eliminate the Western culture course that is required of all freshmen. The course, which has been offered since 1980, is based on a list of 15 acknowledged masterpieces of philosophy and literature.

5   In its place would be a new yearlong requirement called "culture, ideas, and values" that would include the study of at least one non-Western culture and "works by women, minorities and persons of color."

RETURN TO CORE CURRICULUMS

6 The turmoil over the curriculum, with its overtones of 1960's protest, promises to reawaken a longstanding debate in American education. Some argue that by ignoring classics of Western culture, universities risk leaving students ignorant of the works of genius that lie at the heart of their own civilization. Others have said that Western culture is too restrictive a concept to be adequate in an ever more diverse world, and that students should be grounded, not just in the West, but also in a global culture.

7   In the past decade, as universities have returned to the idea of core curriculums, many of them, from Brooklyn College to Harvard, from Berkeley to

Columbia, have tried to thread their way between the two alternatives, offering students a selection of courses in both Western and non-Western cultures.

Stanford seems to be unusual these days in the sharpness of the anti-West- 8 ern attitudes among some students, who are asserting not only that the study of the West is incomplete, but also that it represents nothing less than the dominance of a particular white male view of history.

"I don't see black students at Harvard getting excited about this sort of 9 thing," said Nathan Huggins, chairman of the Afro-American studies department at Harvard. "It seems to me that the students at Standford are expressing the sense of ethnic diversity that is more conspicuous in California, which is close to one-third non-white, than elsewhere in the country."

'POLICY BY INTIMIDATION'

The anti-Western rhetoric at Stanford comes just as conservative voices—such 10 as those of Prof. Allan Bloom in his best-selling "The Closing of the American Mind" and William J. Bennett, the Secretary of Education—have contended that the failure of students to know the great works of the West's past has left them impoverished.

"This kind of debate has gone on before, and since it's going on at Stan- 11 ford, it may have a ripple effect," Mr. Bennett said in a telephone interview.

"They are moving confidently and swiftly into the late 1960's, and why any- 12 body would want to do that intentionally I don't know," he said. "It looks to me as though policy by intimidation is at work. Unfortunately, a lot of academic leadership is readily intimidated by the noisiest of its students and faculty."

Stanford's proposed new curriculum was forged at the end of a two-year dis- 13 cussion, involving numerous public meetings, written exchanges in various campus publications and a special student-faculty task force. The debate was spurred by the major black student organization, which was joined in its demand for change by feminists and groups representing other minority students.

The new course will begin in 1989 and, while its exact content remains 14 undetermined, will presumably spur a search for relatively unknown or underrated works by women and Africans to be included in the core list of acknowledged classics. But, whatever the course's final form, many students and faculty members believe, or at least hope that the decision to include the works of women and minority group members in no way is a repudiation of the idea that all students should be familiar with great works of Western civilization.

The set of suggestions expected to be adopted by the faculty were formu- 15 lated by the student-faculty task force. Members of the panel say they represent a middle ground, retaining many of the elements of the old Western culture course while paying more attention to the contributions to American civilization made by groups other than white males.

"Plato will not be banned from our republic of letters," said Barry M. Katz, 16 a historian and member of the task force. "Freshmen will not emerge from their first year steeped in the lore of Eskimos and Pygmies but ignorant of English composition."

17   "Put simply and bluntly," he added, "the existing course requirement asserts that we have a common culture and it asserts that it can be defined by a bit of reading in the great works. This has been an affront to a large number of students and faculty, to women and members of minority groups."

18   Nonetheless, it is clear that the recommendations have produced plenty of unease, even what William M. Chace, an English professor and vice provost for academic planning, called a mood of "disappointment and polite alienation" on the part of many in the faculty. Dr. Chace and others have indicated that the faculty, which is due to discuss the issue at a meeting this month, will vote for the changes, but more out of a sense of necessary compromise than intellectual enthusiasm.

19   Opponents of the changes have raised several objections. They say the old requirement, installed as part of Stanford's back-to-basics movement in the late 1970's, was among the most popular and successful in the university's 100-year history. They believe student pressure should play no role in devising curriculum. And, they think that to label history's most influential works as examples of a white male culture and little else is to make a travesty of Western culture itself.

'EDUCATION IS NOT A DEMOCRACY'

20   "It's a version of academic populism and populism is always dangerous for a university," Dr. Chace said. "Education is not a democracy. Students don't come here thinking that they know as much as their professors. There is a system of deference, and if the system breaks down, we're in real trouble.

21   "We owe it to our students to tell them, 'Here's the kind of thing you will find of long-term value. These are the things that thousands of people have lived their lives by.' To relegate them to the status of white male writing may be factually true, but it's of low significance."

22   Some maintain that dropping the old Western culture course marks the triumph of a kind of tyranny of the minority. They say proponents of the change were quick to label opposition as "racist."

23   "The overriding motivation for the change is political expediency," said Isaac D. Barchas, a classics student. "I think that the consequences will be the impoverishment of the undergraduate experience."

24   "What is a liberal education?" he asked. "It's an education that liberates people. And if there's a liberating idea in the Western tradition, it is that it doesn't matter if you're black or white or Jewish or Chinese, that there are truths that transcend the accident of birth. That's why the great books are important."

25   Many faculty members, including supporters and opponents of the new plan,

contend the demands of minority students, who constitute about one-third of freshmen classes, stemmed from a desire simply to be represented in a curriculum that excluded their own heritage's great figures.

The resentment and estrangement of some was expressed by Amanda 26 Kemp, former president of the Black Student Union who wrote in the student newspaper, The Stanford Daily, that the implicit message of the current curriculum is "nigger go home."

William King, the current president of the Black Student Union, said: "The 27 Western culture requirement has had a very significant impact because it's a course that every student at the university has to take. It's the one requirement that really says to us, we're different."

He added: "We want a sense that America, where we are now, is not just 28 the progress that came from England and France, that it wasn't only Thomas Jefferson and the Founding Fathers. Other groups contributed significantly."

In the debate other themes arose. Carolyn C. Lougee, a faculty member and 29 member of the task force, wrote that "the Western civ course is not a timeless, eternal distillate of human wisdom," which happens to be precisely what the core reading list's advocates believe it to be. Instead, she contended that it arose from a need of the United States, flooded by new immigrants after World War I, to forge "a myth of a West that transcended every ethnicity and embraced them all."

Faculty members here, aware of their university's importance and prestige, 30 have bristled at criticism of the change from elsewhere. The novelist Saul Bellow, for example, remarked in a recent issue of The New York Times Magazine that he did not know "the Tolstoy of the Zulus, the Proust of the Papuans." His remark provoked the ire of some professors, who charged him with insensitivity to the feelings of non-whites.

"I don't know much about the Zulus," John R. Perry, a philosophy profes- 31 sor and task force member, said, "but if his never having heard of a great author among them suggests that it's pointless to look for great ideas or things to teach from the whole African continent, then I find it sad."

WRITING AND DISCUSSION QUESTIONS

Informative

1. Critics have argued that the Stanford curriculum should be altered because our culture cannot be accurately defined by works or great books written primarliy by white, European males. What important reasons exist for guarding this heritage? What are some of the virtues of studying the works of Plato, Aristotle, Sophocles, Galileo, Jefferson, and so forth. What threat does "academic populism" (paragraph 20) pose?

2. What is the case for expanding the standard readings in a Western culture course to include readings from outside the European tradition?

Persuasive

1. Argue that a philosophy and literature curriculum composed solely of works by white males will or will not lead to sexual and racial cultural bias. What exactly is wrong, if anything, with a course that does not proportionately represent the writings of other groups?
2. Argue that the strong feelings many peoples have today against Western male or Eurocentric cultures are or are not warranted.

Personal

1. Investigate your university's freshman or sophomore requirements in literature, history, and philosophy. What does your university catalog say about liberal education and cultural literacy? Do the required courses measure up to the rhetoric of the catalog? How has your own campus participated in this national debate over cultural literacy?
2. Judge your own prior education: has it represented diverse racial, ethnic, and sexual groups? Has your education succeeded in providing you with cultural literacy?

▼

Editorial: The Stanford Mind
WALL STREET JOURNAL

1   Experience even in the Communist world has stilled the dreams of the 1960s, but at least one place continues to revere them—the ivory foxhole known as the American academy. A good example is Stanford University, which earlier this year caved into political pressure and cashiered its popular "Western Culture" course requirement for freshmen.

2   Stanford's educators promised to replace it with something better, and now we're learning what they had in mind. The course's eight traditional "tracks"—great works, history, philosophy and so on—will be redesigned to conform with "legislation" Stanford enacted for a new Culture, Ideas and Values (CIV) course. One of this year's "tracks," Europe and the Americas—an experimental prototype that could become permanent next year—certainly gives new meaning to the notion of "Great Books." As the Chronicle of Higher Education recently described it, "During this transition year, the term 'Western' is slowly being phased out."

3   Of the 15 great works previously required, only six remain. The rest have been replaced by lesser known authors. Dante's "Inferno" is out, for example,

but "I . . . Rigoberta Menchu" is in. This epic tracks Ms. Menchu's progress from poverty to Guatemalan revolutionary and "the effects on her of feminist and socialist ideologies."

Aquinas and Thomas More are out, but "Their Eyes Were Watching God"   4 by feminist Zora Neale Hurston is in. Ms. Hurston's book offers a critique of the male domination of American society. Locke and Mill go down the memory hole, replaced by such as the U.N. Declaration of Human Rights and Rastafarian poetry.

Virgil, Cicero and Tacitus give way to Frantz Fanon. Mr. Fanon's "The   5 Wretched of the Earth" celebrates violent revolution and is praised on its own book jacket "as a veritable handbook of revolutionary practice and social reorganization." Plato's "Republic" is said to illustrate "anti-assimilationist movements," whatever those are. Martin Luther and Galileo are out, but such timeless notables as Juan Rulfo ("The Burning Plain") and Sandra Cisneros ("The House on Mango Street") are in. And so on.

As for the six classics that survive, both the 20-page CIV course summary   6 (excerpted nearby) and the fall-quarter syllabus suggest they aren't taught like they used to be. Under this autumn's syllabus subject-heading titled Conventions of Selfhood, one discovers that Augustine's "Confessions" aren't a rumination on religious faith, but are read to accompany a lecture on "the body and the 'deep' interior self." Two days later the class discusses "multicultural selves in Navaho country." As the students move forward to the section on Making Other Cultural Selves, they will discuss "labor, gender, and self in the Philippine uplands," with readings that day from Genesis and Revelations. The 18-year-old freshmen end their first term at Stanford with seven classes on Forging Revolutionary Selves.

Much of this amounts to an intellectual fashion known as "deconstruc-   7 tion"—reading texts not as inherently worthy but to serve some professor's private agenda. We await the lecture that interprets Marx (still required) through the work of Groucho and Harpo.

Now, we're the first to defend the right of any private university to offer this   8 stuff with a straight face for $18,000 a year. And Stanford isn't apologizing. Charlie Junkerman, assistant dean for undergraduate studies, confirms to us that he told Mike Iwan and Norm Book of the Stanford Review, "We . . . think it is a challenging and probing comparative project. We couldn't have had any better people to construct a pilot CIV for us."

But perhaps Mr. Junkerman will forgive those who now snicker at Stanford's   9 earlier high-sounding defense of its course change as encouraging "diversity." The new course is a vindication of those who saw it as a capitulation to political intimidation. CIV's new curricula are "really quite wild," says French professor Robert Cohn, a voice in Stanford's intellectual wilderness. "The choices reflect a blatantly left-wing political agenda."

The new course rides the main hobby-horses of today's political left—race,   10 gender and class. The West is perceived not though the evolution of such ideas as faith and justice, but through the prism of sexism, racism and the faults of its ruling classes. The new course was also supposed to draw upon non-Western cultures, but "Europe and the Americas" still includes mainly Western authors. The difference is that rather than illuminate the West, the replacement authors mainly attack it.

11   In "The Closing of the American Mind," Allan Bloom describes the political conformity that now prevails throughout the American academy in the name of a fraudulent "diversity." As the West is "phased out" in Palo Alto, it's clear enough what's happening to Stanford's mind.

▼

Editorial: Stanford Slights the Great Books for Not-So-Greats
WALL STREET JOURNAL

1   *Stanford University decided earlier this year to replace its traditional freshman requirement, "Western Culture," with one titled "Culture, Ideas, Values." Preliminary to implementation of the new curriculum, some 50 students this year are taking a course that has been proposed for one of the eight "tracks" to replace the Western Culture curriculum. The following excerpts are taken from Stanford's outline for that course, entitled "Europe and the Americas."*

2   This course has been designed to meet the requirements for the new Area One requirement in Culture, Ideas, Values, which will take effect by 1989–90. The following remarks are intended therefore to make explicit the ways in which this course fulfills the spirit and the letter of the new legislation.

3   One of the main goals of this course [is to examine] culture in the context of complex relations between master and slave, colonizer and colonized, marginal and dominant, women and men. Indigenous views of Spanish and Christian values will be studied along with critical voices within European and Christian tradition. The negritude movement will be studied as a complex critique of Europe that uses languages and forms adapted from Europe. Contemporary writings by a range of North Americans show a wide variety of life experience, assumptions, and histories that coexist within this nation.

4   First quarter: The Spanish debate over indigenous rights raises issues around race as well as religion; readings on European enlightenment include Wollstonecraft on question of gender, and Flora Tristan on question of class. Race, gender and class are all thematized in Chungara de Barrios' autobiography and Anzaldua's poetic essays.

Second quarter: Race is a central focus of materials on the Haitian revolu- 5
tion, and materials from the twentieth century negritude movement which
developed in the post-emancipation context of modern "scientific" racism.
Gender is a central issue in Jamaica Kincaid's novel "Annie John," a mother-
daughter story. Roumain's "Masters of the Dew" plays out a class drama
around the conflict between traditionalist peasant culture and modern proletarian consciousness.

Third quarter: Marx and Weber are essential sources on class; Franz Fanon 6
on race; gender, ethnicity and class are central themes in Rulfo, Menchu,
Chavez and Anzaldua.

The syllabus includes instances of nearly every form mentioned in this sec- 7
tion. A partial list includes:

Poets: Jose Maria Arguedas, Pablo Neruda, Ernesto Cardenal, Audre Lorde, Aime Cesaire.

Drama: Shakespeare, Euripides.

Fiction: Garcia Marquez, Naipaul, Melville, Hurston, Findley, Rulfo, Ferre.

Philosophy and social theory: Aristotle, Rousseau, Weber, Freud, Marx, Fanon, Reta-mar, Benedict.

History: James, Guaman Poma.

Scientists: A number of social scientists, such as Benedict and Fanon, are included. Other material can be added if desired, such as readings on 18th century natural history, or late 19th century race science.

Diaries, memoirs, etc.: Columbus, Cabeza de Vaca, Equiano, Lady Nugent, Dyk, Augus-tine, Menchu, Barrios de Chungara.

Popular culture: Films on popular religion and healing in Peru ("Eduardo the Healer") and the U.S. ("The Holy Ghost People"); folk tale traditions of the trickster.

Painting, sculpture, music: Popular musical traditions in the Caribbean (Reggae lyrics, Rastafarian poetry), U.S. (corrido); Peru (Andean music); Peruvian folk painting *(retablos)*; 16th century iconographic depictions of the Americas.

Buildings, structures, machines: While not explicitly included, these will come up in discussion of plantations and plantation society.

This will be a five unit course. We propose to follow the "Great Works" for- 8
mat, with two lectures a week.

This syllabus was prepared with the support of the Stanford Humanities 9
Center.

[Descriptions of course readings:] 10

Shakespeare: "The Tempest"; Cesaire: "A Tempest"; "Song of Roland"; 11
Euripides: "Medea." Works of imaginative literature that establish paradigms
of the relationship between "European" and "other" will be analyzed, e.g.,
Euripides' "Medea," whose main character is both "barbarian" and female;
the medieval "Song of Roland," which polarizes Christian and pagan (Muslim)

sterotypes; Shakespeare's "Tempest," whose figure of Caliban draws on contemporary reports of natives in the recently discovered "New World"; Cesaire's "Une Tempete," an adaptation of the Shakespeare play that uses the Caliban-Prospero encounter as a model, in part, for colonizer/colonized relations.

12   Melville: "Bartleby, the Scrivener"; Marx: "The Communist Manifesto." Herman Melville's tale of the interplay between callous, uncomprehending bureaucratic-administrative rationality (to use a Weberian idiom) and the resistance of absolute refusal points both toward Weber and Marx. It underscores both the ambiguities of "rational" authority and the force of uncompromising resistance within a modern capitalist context.

13   Genesis and Revelations; Nora Zeale Hurston: "Their Eyes Were Watching God"; Film: "The Holy Ghost People." The Old Testament selections are discussed in their own right, and as a means of speaking about the distinctive Afro-American religious consciousness exemplified in Zora Neale Hurston's novel of the 1930s. This particular form of religiosity suggests comparisons and contrasts with Weberian themes. "The Holy Ghost People" portrays a southern white "snake handling cult" and suggests parallels and contrasts with Hurston's work.

▼

Letters to the Editor: Stanford's Philosophy Is an Open Book
WALL STREET JOURNAL

1   I found your Dec. 22 editorial "The Stanford Mind" fairly predictable in its application of arguments from Allan Bloom to the recent reform of our Western Culture Program. What was less predictable, and far more disturbing, was the apparent confidence you felt in publicly snickering at writers whose work I can be fairly certain you do not even know. It seems to me that your editorial is another instance of the closed American mind, and a further argument for the necessity of courses like "Europe and the Americas" in our colleges and universities.

2   Your attack on the "Cultures, Ideas and Values" (CIV) program is misinformed on several counts. For example, when you say that "Dante's 'Inferno' is out, but 'I . . . Rigoberta Menchu' is in," you imply that there was some sort of one-for-one swap, and that, further, Dante is not being taught in the CIV program at Stanford. You must remember that the "Europe and the Americas" course is a pilot for one of at least eight tracks in the CIV program. Other tracks will have emphases different from it, and many of them will teach Dante.

You must also recognize that "Europe and the Americas" has an ample representation of canonical "Greats" including Homer, Aeschylus, Euripides, Plato, Aristotle, Augustine, Shakespeare, Voltaire, Rousseau, Marx, Melville and Freud.

But I will not quibble, because your point is, in fact, a categorical one: that $\quad$ 3 all college students should receive a foundation course in the Great Books of the "Western" tradition. By citing Allan Bloom at the close of your piece, the reader is invited to supply arguments from "The Closing of the American Mind" that might be marshaled in defense of your position. Primary among these is Prof. Bloom's contention that there are a certain number of books that are considered (the agentless passive voice is necessary here for obvious reasons) to contain a measure of wisdom unavailable in lesser books, and that these "Great" Books should form the core of a liberal education.

Prof. Bloom's error, I believe, is to misconstrue the nature of the tradition $\quad$ 4 he champions. The truly vital tradition of liberal education has never been to read the same Great Books as one's predecessors, but to continue to ask the greatest questions one can pose. Questions are the beginnings of curricula and satisfactory answers are their destinations. It would be foolish to assume that we ought to ask the same questions as were posed 50 years ago when Robert Hutchins designed the University of Chicago's Great Books Program. But even if we do ask some of the same questions, it does not necessarily follow that we will all turn to the same books in search of our answers.

For example 50 years ago John Locke seemed indispensable in answering a $\quad$ 5 question like "What is social justice?" In 1989, with a more interdependent world order, a more heterogeneous domestic population, and mass media and communications systems that complicate our definitions of "society" and "individual," it may be that someone like Frantz Fanon, a black Algerian psychoanalyst, will get us closer to the answer we need.

In your editorial, you seem confident in your ability to distinguish between $\quad$ 6 writers who are "Great" and those who are "Not-So-Great." Into this second category, you sneeringly relegate "such timeless notables" as Rigoberta Menchu, Zora Neale Hurston, Sandra Cisneros and Juan Rulfo. On what basis, I wonder, do you dismiss them? Have you read any of them? Can you even place them in their countries of origin? I doubt it. I suspect strongly that it is solely on the basis of their names that you rank them as you do. This apparent inability to consider such writers seriously reveals an insidious prejudice: that people we have never heard of, people with "funny" names, cannot possibly have much of anything worthwhile to say to us. This kind of confident close-mindedness is just another piece of evidence that Stanford's curriculum reform is not only necessary but overdue.

Finally, you seem to feel no discomfort in totally disregarding the professors $\quad$ 7 who developed and are now teaching this course. You quote me as saying, "We couldn't have had any better people to construct a pilot CIV for us" without identifying the people involved. Perhaps you don't know who they are. In fact, all three of them have international reputations in their fields, and the combination of disciplines they represent gives them the scholarly scope needed to rethink how culture is taught in our universities: Gregson Davis, Classics and Comparative Literature; Mary Pratt, Spanish and Comparative Literature; and Renato Rosaldo, Anthropology. Any of the universities with which we compare ourselves would envy a team like this. Most of those universities are watching this course with a lot more understanding—and consequent approval—than you were able to muster in your editorial. Maybe this is because they assume that books are to be read and valued for what they have to say, not for the name-recognition of their authors.

CHARLES JUNKERMAN
Assistant Dean of
Undergraduate Studies
Stanford University

Stanford, Calif.

WRITING AND DISCUSSION QUESTIONS

Informative

1. The editorial writer objects to the change in the Stanford University's required curriculum from its "Western Culture" to its "Culture, Ideas and Values" sections. Analyze the stated and implied reasons for such a position. Note for example, the use of sarcasm and humor as well as explicit analysis of the politics of the situation.
2. Explain what the writer means in paragraph 10 (The Standford mind): "The new course rides the main hobby-horses of today's political left—race, gender and class. The West is perceived not through the evolution of such ideas as faith and justice, but through the prism of sexism, racism, and the faults of its ruling classes."
3. What objections to the editorial are presented by Stanford's Dean Junkerman in his rebuttal letter to the editor? What is his central objection?

Persuasive

1. Argue for or against the central thesis of the editorial that the changes at Stanford were made on political grounds and that the new curriculum would unfairly attack the West rather than equipping students with an understandings of its foundations.
2. Argue that a curriculum can or cannot be diverse and disinterested [objective and unbiased] at the same time.
3. Argue that Thiong'o would consider the Western Culture course a manifestation of imperialism and racism.
4. Junkerman claims that "questions are the beginnings of curricula." Argue the validity of such a position for teaching methodology and the selection of curricula.

Personal

1. In your opinion, what makes a writer great? In answering, examine the implied definitions of greatness in both editorials and Junkerman's response.

The Fundamental Ideas

Chapter Three

THE JUDEO–CHRISTIAN TRADITION

In this chapter, the trek into the past begins with some of the foundational and primary Biblical texts. Later in this chapter, works within the larger Biblical tradition are presented that expand and explore the meaning of these ancient texts for our times. In reading the ancient Biblical texts, we hope you will attempt to understand the relevance and meaning they held for those people who originally received them. Reading any ancient text, including the Bible, can be a tightrope walk between two extremes. The first extreme is the tendency to dismiss an ancient text out of hand because it *is* old and, therefore, seemingly out of date and irrelevant. The second extreme is the tendency to read into an ancient text our preconceptions about the age in which it was written and our twentieth-century bias, thus precluding it from speaking out of its own age directly to ours. Unfortunately, this tightrope walk is unavoidable and all the more perilous with regard to informed interpretations of sacred texts like the Bible.

UNDERSTANDING SACRED TEXTS

Sacred texts are writings that are revered by a community as documents that speak unique, universal truths about our lives as human beings and usually, though not always, are believed to be communications from a divine being. It is important to note that the *sacredness* of a given text is, therefore, only partly a function of what it contains; the reverence paid to any putatively sacred text is intimately related to the way it is *used* and *received* in a particular community.

89

Those inside a particular faith view the text from a different vantage point than do those outside the faith; what may be to one reader a merely interesting literary, political, or historical text may be to another reader an essential, transcendently significant text that places certain demands on him or her. The moral, political, and social impact of a text always, then, depends in large measure on the "acceptance" of its authority as a divinely inspired or uniquely insightful document. Nevertheless, even though a particular text may no longer be held "sacred" by a majority of people within a culture, it can continue to influence profoundly their views of the world and of how society should function. Some of the more important characteristics of *sacred* texts are as follows:

Sacred texts usually profess to be a product of *revelation* (divine inspiration) or *personal illumination* (contemplative discovery). For instance, the Bible authors often claim divine authorship of their words, while the insights of Gautama Buddha are usually traced to his disciplined meditation.

Sacred texts offer a *prescriptive pattern of life* (a set of moral codes, a "path," a list of duties, and so on) that provides a believer with guidelines for life in society. The Law of Moses and its elaborations in the Sermon on the Mount, the Parables of Jesus, and the numerous letters from the Apostle Paul clearly represent exhortations and moral governance that demand certain kinds of behavior and exclude others.

Sacred texts tend to be *anachronistic* (deliberately out of step with "the times") by offering a worldview that calls into question the predominant or existing one in a particular culture. The Pentateuch, the first five books of the Old Testament that are traditionally ascribed to Moses, are defiantly monotheistic and, thus, pitted against the polytheism of the pagan world; likewise, the Gospels of the New Testament uncompromisingly present Jesus as Messiah, Lord, King, and Judge.

Sacred texts often are *offensive to other sensibilities within the culture in which their authority is evoked*. This occurs usually because the text demands that its adherents return to a standard of conduct that is in direct conflict with the prevailing norms of their culture. This is true not only during the time when the sacred text is written, but also later. For instance, in the present, the Bible is increasingly criticized by feminist readers for its apparently "patriarchal orientation" in which certain social roles and positions of authority are viewed exclusively as male domains.

Sacred texts *are sometimes obscure, always demand careful interpretation, and frequently inspire considerable debate not only between nonbelievers and skeptics, but also among believers*. The reasons for these qualities are various, but they can involve such matters as the imperfection of language itself as an instrument for conveying a truth that is inherently mysterious; the difficulty of working with the ancient languages in which the texts are found, sometimes presenting scholars with puzzles of lexicon and syntax that make passages ambiguous; and the original process of collecting, copying, and preserving such texts. The Bible certainly faces each of these potential problems.

Sacred texts *usually generate a large body of secondary literature dedicated to their interpretation, both in terms of what the texts meant to their original readers and what they mean to present-day readers.* The Talmud, for instance, is a collection of ancient rabbinical writings that interprets the Torah, or Law of Moses, and the Mishnah, which itself is a collection of rabbinical expansions and applications of the Torah, and these provide the basis for religious authority in traditional Judaism. For some believers, these secondary texts sometimes take on an importance approaching the sacred text itself and become one of the means by which believers define, debate, and defend orthodoxy, or what legitimately constitutes the standards and practice of the faith itself.

THE BIBLE AS SACRED TEXT

The Bible, in its present form, certainly reflects the previously mentioned qualities of sacred texts. Much of the Bible explicitly rests its authority on its claim to ultimate, divine authorship—that God used human intermediaries to proclaim his will in both voice and text. Intermixed with history, poetry, prophecy, and biography are accounts of miraculous, supernatural events ascribed to God and accompanied by calls to obedience. Even a cursory reading of this formidable text reveals a remarkable unity of theme, given the various authors and ages that are represented within it. Perhaps the one clear message that the Bible conveys is that reality is multilayered and comprises more than the material world; that is, there is a supernatural dimension to existence that transcends the earthly plane, where a spiritual battle is taking place whose outcome determines the fate of the earth and its creatures. Readers of the Bible are consistently enjoined to trust in God and his representatives to avoid the destiny of the nonbeliever.

As we consider the heritage of Judaism and Christianity that is reflected in the texts chosen for this section, our terminology must be sensitive to believers within both traditions who rightfully regard their different faiths as unique and vibrant. We will use the term "Judeo–Christian tradition" as a shorthand for the foundational ideas and influence on subsequent Western culture that these two faiths are responsible for, with primary focus on the ideas that they share; for instance, *monotheism*—the belief that there is one, and only one, true deity—and the ethical core that is represented in the Torah, or Law of Moses. Nevertheless, our use of the term "Judeo–Christian tradition" should not be interpreted as an attempt to conflate or deny the distinctive elements of either faith or to imply there exists some consensus of principles derived from the two traditions. Indeed, Jewish and Christian scholars have questioned the usefulness of such a hybrid term. Although Christianity has clear roots in Judaism, and, indeed, was once thought of as an extension or revision of Judaism, it has its own unique features. Likewise, Judaism continues to be a significant and resilient faith in the twentieth century with its own dynamics and influence apart from whatever theology it may share with Christianity.

Structurally, the Bible (literally, "the Book") usually comes to us as two sets of "books" under one cover, and it remains one of the most obvious and important sources of the Judeo–Christian tradition. Both faiths respect the Hebrew Scriptures (the 39 books that make up what Christians traditionally refer to as the "Old Testament") as a revelation from God and, therefore, authoritative. (Jews generally prefer the term "Hebrew Scriptures" because *Old* Testament clearly suggests something outdated or obsolete.) Through the first century A.D., the early Christian church, in fact, knew only the Hebrew Scriptures, and these served as its "Bible"; the second set of books, usually referred to by later Christians as the "New Testament," consists of 27 documents that were eventually collected by the church as reliable testimony to the life and teaching of Jesus Christ, the central focus of Christian doctrine. (There are also the twelve disputed books of the Apocrypha, which are sometimes included in the canon of the Hebrew Scriptures by Catholic but usually not by Protestant or Jewish theologians and scholars.) The use of the word "testament" to label these two sets of books is derived from the idea of a covenant or agreement between God and a group of people in which each has stated responsibilities. The Hebrew Scriptures report the unique covenant made between God and the people of Israel through Moses, whereas the New Testament reports a subsequent covenant that Christians believe God made with the whole world through Jesus Christ.

The Hebrew Scriptures are traditionally classified according to three divisions: The Law (Torah), which includes the writings attributed to Moses; The Prophets, which contains history and prophecy, that is, the foretelling of events and exhortation to the people of Israel; and The Writings, which contains the wisdom literature of ancient Israel, including the Psalms, the Book of Job, and the Proverbs of Solomon. The narratives of the Hebrew Scriptures essentially comprise the story of God's mighty acts in history and his holy character as seen through the eyes of Jewish faith. These events include the creation of the world and the call of Abraham, who was God's special envoy to the world (Genesis); God's special covenant with a chosen people, the descendants of Israel, led by Moses (Exodus); God's passion for justice and righteousness in the earth (most of the Prophets); and God's desire for love and mercy in the nation of Israel and the world at large (the Proverbs and Psalms).

The New Testament includes four "gospels" that are essentially quasi-biographical narratives about the life and teaching of Jesus Christ, one historical work (Acts of the Apostles), and 22 letters written by early Christian leaders to their converts in various locations in Europe and Asia. These are read by Christians as a fulfillment of and companion volume to the Hebrew Scriptures. The general focus of these Scriptures is the life, death, and resurrection of Jesus Christ, whom Christians regard as uniquely the Son of God and the fulfillment of Hebrew prophecies about a coming Messiah. At the same time, New Testament

Scriptures paint a portrait of the early church and its battle for survival in an often hostile environment.

GREAT IDEAS AND THE JUDEO–CHRISTIAN TRADITION

In its impact on the development of Western culture and its institutions and social structures, the Bible, and the Judeo–Christian tradition that it underlies, surely qualifies as a great idea or, in fact, as many great ideas. Even a short list of its influences on the way we have thought and continue to think about ourselves, our environment, the just society, and the relationships between men and women and between individuals and their societies would fill many pages. The Bible has been read and enjoyed as a work of literature and cultural significance by countless readers in and out of Western culture.

However, it needs to be said that the Bible is, in some ways, not really a "Western" book in the sense that, say, Plato's *Republic* is. The Judeo–Christian worldview is decidedly less abstract and, therefore, less preoccupied with theoretical issues than is the Greek worldview. The Bible is intensely concerned with practical questions about how men and women should live in a community and in response to God. The core of the Biblical conception of God and the human community is that God has revealed what it means to be truly "human"; the believer is, in one sense, in search not of the "truth," but of the *determination* to believe and act on the "truth" as revelation from God.

Greek humanism, as will be seen in the next chapter, is profoundly more philosophical and interrogative in a way the Judeo–Christian tradition cannot be and still remain true to itself. If a typical question to the Greek mind is "What is *truth and beauty?*" a typical question to the Judeo–Christian mind would be "What is *righteous and just?*"

Nevertheless, the Bible has been appropriated by the West as a foundational document in shaping its society—its laws and government, its view of the family, its roles for men and women, and the treatment of the environment. Furthermore, regarded by writers, philosphers, artists, and musicians from many ages and nations as crucial to understanding European and American culture, the Judeo–Christian influence is evident in libraries, galleries, and popular media throughout the world. The question of whether the Judeo–Christian tradition can be legitimately considered a great idea must be more focused though; for instance, which great ideas are traceable to this heritage? In answering this, perhaps it is best to consider the kinds of questions the Bible and its readers raise and the quality of the answers they provide.

1. *Origins:* Whence came humankind, the world, and the universe? Who are we as male and female, parent and child, and brother and sister? Who is God? What does knowledge about God and humankind consist of?

2. *Promises:* What are the foundations of community and culture, of law and ethics? Why should we behave in one way as opposed to another? What are our obligations to our society, neighbors, and families?

3. *Destinies:* What should be the relationships between men and women and between nations? What lies beyond this life? What can we know about eternity and temporality?

4. *Authority:* Who or what is to be regarded as the source of norms or regulations for a society? In what sense is the Biblical text itself "true" or "valid" as history, science, and ethics? How should its pronouncements be read?

Surely, these are among the most profound questions that we can ask about ourselves and, in fact, are the kinds of questions that every human culture has raised in one way or another.

APPROACHING THE BIBLICAL TEXT

The Bible may, of course, be read in various ways: as a devotional text that enriches the spirituality of the reader; as a historical text that depicts the history of a people, a movement, or a set of ideas; and certainly as literature that narrates the lives of certain heroes and heroines, offers wisdom and poetry, or explains our origins and destinies in an uncertain world. Whatever your personal motives in reading, you may find the following approaches useful as a guide to interpreting the text. (1) Determine the historical context, purpose, and use of the excerpted text for its original readers. (2) Determine the kind of text the excerpted portion is: was it intended as history, prophecy, poetry, parable, myth, or scientific explanation? (3) Situate the text within the setting of contemporary issues, values, and needs you are confronting. How may the text speak out of its own time to provide guidance and answers to present concerns? How does the text attempt to "answer" the questions our culture is raising?

As you study these excerpts from the Bible and those later texts that build on its themes and messages, you will perhaps discover what it is within the Judeo–Christian tradition that continues to challenge and inform our Western ways of constructing and governing our society. In reading the short excerpts from the Bible provided in this text book, you may find it helpful, even essential, to obtain a complete Bible in order to have access to the larger context that will help in analyzing the events and people encountered in these selections.

THE HEBREW SCRIPTURES
Genesis 1–4, 6–9, 11–12 and Exodus 1–3, 19–20

Most of the Hebrew Scriptures were originally composed in the Hebrew language (a few passages were composed in Aramaic) and come to us in English through the work of translators. The importance of these works is indicated in the carefulness of their transmission and the continuing effort to provide accurate and sensitive translations of their meaning into countless world languages. The events depicted in the Pentateuch (the first five books of the Bible, traditionally attributed to Moses) are variously dated by Biblical scholars and archaeologists. Beginning with the person of Abraham, the earliest Biblical character whose identity can be subjected to historical corroboration, we can set the events of Genesis 12 (the call and journey of Abraham to the land God promised) at about 1900 B.C. The fully developed Law emerges with Moses sometime between 1450 and 1300 B.C., and the events in the life of David (see next section) presented in the Psalms occur approximately 930 B.C.

Genesis presents a world created by God in unspoiled beauty and grandeur; its human creatures are placed by God in the Garden of Eden to serve him in peace and harmony, only to have their world shattered through the introduction of temptation and sin. Expelled from the Garden, humankind multiplies and travels over the earth but is not abandoned by God, who calls men and women out of their native lands to do his will and forge a nation with an ethic that is new compared with cultures around it. Abraham and his family are among the first to be singled out in the Biblical story, and God promises him that his many descendants will occupy a land and become a blessing to the whole world. This is the people of Israel.

Exodus then tells the story of Israel's formation as a nation under slavery and the raising up of a leader (Moses) who leads them out of their slavery in Egypt and out to meet their God at the foot of Mount Sinai. Soon after committing themselves to the covenant, however, they break this word. Interceding for his people, Moses renews the covenant with Yahweh, the name by which God has revealed himself to Moses in Exodus 3:14, "I Am who I Am." Exodus portrays this deity as one who is everlasting and personal, a being outside of time who nevertheless cares for and identifies with the plight of peoples trapped in despair.

As heirs of God's covenant with Abraham, the "chosen" people are marked by a jealous God, and their rigid monotheism, a belief in a personal-infinite God who is both separate from his creation but immanent in it, distinguishes them from their idolatrous, polytheistic neighbors. The so-called pagan world in which the Israelites find themselves often seems to them a nightmare of cruelty, slavery, savage treatment of women and children, and general barbarism. Bound together with the Law recorded by Moses, Israel is called to be faithful to the covenant of their fathers and to be holy as God is holy.

The first five books of the Hebrew Scriptures—Genesis through Deuteronomy—are traditionally ascribed to Moses. However, there has been an ongoing debate in Biblical scholarship about the historical authenticity of the books, given their supernaturalism and emphasis on divine intervention in the affairs of humankind. Much post-Enlightenment Biblical scholarship of the late eighteenth and nineteenth centuries questions and reinterprets many of the miraculous accounts found in the Bible from a nonmiraculous, "natural law" perspective, attempting to make the Biblical narrative more "scientific" and less susceptible to unwarranted or ill-conceived religious use. Likewise, the debate regarding Mosaic authorship has often centered on the unity and coherence of Genesis as a literary document. For instance, the use of different names to refer to God in the narrative in the original language and the apparent repetitions of material in the creation account (Genesis 1–2) and the flood narrative (Genesis 9) is seen as evidence that the book is the product of several authors over a long period of time instead of the work of a single author like Moses; thus, the claim of Mosaic authorship has been disputed. A number of conservative responses to these important issues have been offered over the past 50 years that attempt to defend and articulate the traditionally received Mosaic authorship of the five books.

For some believers, the central issue is as much a theological one as a historical one. Many conservative Jewish and Christian groups rest the authority of the Bible as a whole on the inerrancy of each section of the Scriptures. Throughout the Hebrew Scriptures and the New Testament, the claim is made that Moses wrote the Pentateuch. Thus, the skepticism of "liberal" scholars is a problem for "conservative" believers. They are asked implicitly to choose between the sometimes abstruse scholarship of specialists in the field and their basic faith in the literal truth of the Bible. This challenge to faith by the scholarship based on disciplines operating outside of the text is emblematic of the confrontation between different ages, kinds of authority, and views of the world that are encountered throughout the great ideas of history.

The central themes and events in Genesis are the Creation of the universe (Gen. 1), the Creation of man and woman (Gen. 1–2), the Fall (Gen. 3), the first murder (Gen. 4), the Flood (Gen. 6–9), the Tower of Babel (Gen. 11), and the call of Abraham (Gen. 12). The central persons in Genesis are Adam and Eve, Cain and Abel (Gen. 1–4), Noah (Gen. 6–9), and Abraham (Gen. 12). The central themes and events in Exodus are the early life and call of Moses (Ex. 1–3), God's self-revelation (Ex. 3, 19–20), Israel's flight from Egypt (Ex. 12–15), and the Covenant, that is, the fulfilled promises to the patriarchs (Ex. 19), and the Law (Torah), that is, the creation of a kingdom of priests (Ex. 20). Important persons in Exodus are Moses, Pharaoh, Aaron, and Miriam.

▼

from *Genesis*

I. THE ORIGIN OF THE WORLD AND OF MANKIND

1. The Creation and the Fall

The First Account of the Creation[a]

1
2 1 In the beginning God created the heavens and the earth. ·Now the earth was a formless void, there was darkness over the deep, and God's spirit hovered over the water.

3
4 God said, 'Let there be light', and there was light. ·God saw that light was
5 good, and God divided light from darkness. ·God called light 'day', and darkness he called 'night'. Evening came and morning came: the first day.

6 God said, 'Let there be a vault[b] in the waters to divide the waters in two'.
7 And so it was. ·God made the vault, and it divided the waters above the
8 vault from the waters under the vault. ·God called the vault 'heaven'. Evening came and morning came: the second day.

9 God said, 'Let the waters under heaven come together into a single mass,
10 and let dry land appear'. And so it was. ·God called the dry land 'earth' and the mass of waters 'seas', and God saw that it was good.

11 God said, 'Let the earth produce vegetation: seed-bearing plants, and
12 fruit trees bearing fruit with their seed inside, on the earth'. And so it was. ·The earth produced vegetation: plants bearing seed in their several kinds,

---

[1]a. Ascribed to the 'priestly' source. . . . b. For the ancient Semites, the 'arch' or 'vault' of the sky was a solid dome holding the upper waters in check.

and trees bearing fruit with their seed inside in their several kinds. God saw
13 that it was good. ·Evening came and morning came: the third day.
14   God said, 'Let there be lights in the vault of heaven to divide day from
15 night, and let them indicate festivals, days and years. ·Let them be lights in
16 the vault of heaven to shine on the earth.' And so it was. ·God made the two
great lights:^c the greater light to govern the day, the smaller light to govern
17 the night, and the stars. ·God set them in the vault of heaven to shine on the
18 earth, ·to govern the day and the night and to divide light from darkness.
19 God saw that it was good. ·Evening came and morning came: the fourth day.
20   God said, 'Let the waters teem with living creatures, and let birds fly
21 above the earth within the vault of heaven'. And so it was. ·God created
great seaserpents and every kind of living creature with which the waters
22 teem, and every kind of winged creature. God saw that it was good. ·God
blessed them, saying, 'Be fruitful, multiply, and fill the waters of the seas;
23 and let the birds multiply upon the earth'. ·Evening came and morning
came: the fifth day.
24   God said, 'Let the earth produce every kind of living creature: cattle, rep-
25 tiles,^d and every kind of wild beast'. And so it was. ·God made every kind of
wild beast, every kind of cattle, and every kind of land reptile. God saw that
it was good.
26   God said, 'Let us^e make man^f in our own image, in the likeness of ourselves, and let them be masters of the fish of the sea, the birds of heaven,
the cattle, all the wild beasts and all the reptiles that crawl upon the earth'.

27   God created man in the image of himself,
               in the image of God he created him,
               male and female he created them.

28   God blessed them, saying to them, 'Be fruitful, multiply, fill the earth and
conquer it. Be masters of the fish of the sea, the birds of heaven and all liv-
29 ing animals on the earth.' ·God said, 'See, I give you all the seed-bearing
plants that are upon the whole earth, and all the trees with seed-bearing
30 fruit; this shall be your food. ·To all wild beasts, all birds of heaven and all
31 living reptiles on the earth I give all the foliage of plants for food.' And so it
was. ·God saw all he had made, and indeed it was very good. Evening came
and morning came: the sixth day.
1
2 **2** Thus heaven and earth were completed with all their array. ·On the sev-
    enth day God completed the work he had been doing. He rested on the
3 seventh day after all the work he had been doing. ·God blessed the seventh

c. Their names are omitted deliberately: the sun and the moon were worshipped by neighbouring poeples,
and here they are treated as no more than lamps to light the earth and regulate the calendar. d. 'Things which
crawl', a general term for small mammals, reptiles, amphibians and insects. e. Perhaps the plural of majesty:
the common name for God was *Elohim*, a plural form. But possibly the plural form implies a discussion between
God and his heavenly court. f. Man, *adam*, is a collective noun ('mankind'), hence the plural in 'Let them be
masters of . . .'.

day and made it holy, because on that day he had rested after all his work of creating.

4   Such were the origins of heaven and earth when they were created.

The Second Account of the Creation.[a] *Paradise*

5   At the time when Yahweh God made earth and heaven ·there was as yet no wild bush on the earth nor had any wild plant yet sprung up, for Yahweh God had not sent rain on the earth, nor was there any man to till the soil.
6   ·However, a flood was rising from the earth and watering all the surface of
7   the soil. ·Yahweh God fashioned man of dust from the soil. Then he breathed into his nostrils a breath of life, and thus man became a living being.

8   Yahweh God planted a garden in Eden which is in the east, and there he
9   put the man he had fashioned. ·Yahweh God caused to spring up from the soil every kind of tree, enticing to look at and good to eat, with the tree of life and the tree of the knowledge of good and evil in the middle of the gar-
10   den. · A river flowed from Eden to water the garden, and from there it
     divided to make four streams.[b] The first is named the Pishon, and this encir-
11
12   cles the whole land of Havilah where there is gold. ·The gold of this land is
13   pure; bdellium[c] and onyx stone are found there. ·The second river is named
14   the Gihon, and this encircles the whole land of Cush. ·The third river is
15   named the Tigris, and this flows to the east of Ashur. The fourth river is the
16   Euphrates. ·Yahweh God took the man and settled him in the garden of
17   Eden to cultivate and take care of it. ·Then Yahweh God gave the man this admonition, 'You may eat indeed of all the trees in the garden. Nevertheless of the tree of the knowledge of good and evil you are not to eat, for on the day you eat of it you shall most surely die.'

18   Yahweh God said, 'It is not good that the man should be alone. I will
19   make him a helpmate.' ·So from the soil Yahweh God fashioned all the wild beasts and all the birds of heaven. These he brought to the man to see what he would call them; each one was to bear the name the man would give it.
20   ·The man gave names to all the cattle, all the birds of heaven and all the
21   wild beasts. But no helpmate suitable for man was found for him. ·So Yah-weh God made the man fall into a deep sleep. And while he slept, he took one of his ribs and enclosed it in flesh. ·Yahweh God built the rib he had
22   taken from the man into a woman, and brought her to the man. ·The man
23   exclaimed:

> 'This at last is bone from my bones,
> and flesh from my flesh!
> This is to be called woman,[d]
> for this was taken from man.'

---

[2]a. From the 'Yahwistic' source. . . . b. Verses 10–14 are intended to fix the locality of Eden. However, the rivers Pishon and Gihon are unknown, and the two 'lands' named are probably not the regions designated elsewhere by the same names. c. An aromatic resin. d. In Hebrew a play on the words *ishshah* (woman) and *ish* (man).

24   This is why a man leaves his father and mother and joins himself to his wife, and they become one body.

25   Now both of them were naked, the man and his wife, but they felt no shame in front of each other.

The Fall

1 **3** The serpent was the most subtle of all the wild beasts that Yahweh God had made. It asked the woman, 'Did God really say you were not to eat
2 from any of the trees in the garden?' ·The woman answered the serpent,
3 'We may eat the fruit of the trees in the garden. ·But of the fruit of the tree in the middle of the garden God said, "You must not eat it, nor touch it,
4 under pain of death".' Then the serpent said to the woman, 'No! You will
5 not die! ·God knows in fact that on the day you eat it your eyes will be
6 opened and you will be like gods, knowing good and evil.' ·The woman saw that the tree was good to eat and pleasing to the eye, and that it was desirable for the knowledge that it could give. So she took some of its fruit and ate it. She gave some also to her husband who was with her, and he ate it.
7 ·Then the eyes of both of them were opened and they realised that they were naked. So they sewed fig-leaves together to make themselves loin-cloths.
8   The man and his wife heard the sound of Yahweh God walking in the garden in the cool of the day, and they hid from Yahweh God among the
9 trees of the garden. ·But Yahweh God called to the man. 'Where are you?'
10 he asked. 'I heard the sound of you in the garden;' he replied 'I was afraid
11 because I was naked, so I hid.' ·'Who told you that you were naked?' he
12 asked 'Have you been eating of the tree I forbade you to eat?' ·The man
13 replied, 'It was the woman you put with me; she gave me the fruit, and I ate
14 it'. ·Then Yahweh God asked the woman, 'What is this you have done?' The woman replied, 'The serpent tempted me and I ate'.

Then Yahweh God said to the serpent, 'Because you have done this,

'Be accursed beyond all cattle,
all wild beasts.
You shall crawl on your belly and eat dust
every day of your life.
15   I will make you enemies of each other:
you and the woman,
your offspring and her offspring.
It will crush your head
and you will strike its heel.'

16   To the woman he said:

'I will multiply your pains in childbearing,
you shall give birth to your children in pain.
Your yearning shall be for your husband,
yet he will lord it over you.'

17   To the man he said, 'Because you listened to the voice of your wife and
ate from the tree of which I had forbidden you to eat,

'Accursed be the soil because of you.
With suffering shall you get your food from it
every day of your life.

18   It shall yield you brambles and thistles,
and you shall eat wild plants.

19   With sweat on your brow
shall you eat your bread,
until you return to the soil,
as you were taken from it.
For dust you are
and to dust you shall return.'

20   The man named his wife 'Eve' because she was the mother of all those
21   who live.[a] ·Yahweh God made clothes out of skins for the man and his wife,
22   and they put them on. ·Then Yahweh God said, 'See, the man has become
like one of us, with his knowledge of good and evil. He must not be allowed
to stretch his hand out next and pick from the tree of life also, and eat some
23   and live for ever.' ·So Yahweh God expelled him from the garden of Eden,
24   to till the soil from which he had been taken. ·He banished the man, and in
front of the garden of Eden he posted the cherubs, and the flame of a flashing sword, to guard the way to the tree of life.

Cain and Abel

1   4 The man had intercourse with his wife Eve, and she conceived and gave
2   birth to Cain. 'I have acquired a man with the help of Yahweh'[a] she
said. ·She gave birth to a second child, Abel, the brother of Cain. Now Abel
3   became a shepherd and kept flocks, while Cain tilled the soil. ·Time passed
4   and Cain brought some of the produce of the soil as an offering for Yahweh,
·while Abel for his part brought the first-born of his flock and some of their
5   fat as well. Yahweh looked with favour on Abel and his offering. ·But he did
not look with favour on Cain and his offering, and Cain was very angry and
6   downcast. ·Yahweh asked Cain, 'Why are you angry and downcast? ·If you
7   are well disposed, ought you not to lift up your head? But if you are ill disposed, is not sin at the door like a crouching beast hungering for you, which
8   you must master?' ·Cain said to his brother Abel, 'Let us go out'; and while
they were in the open country, Cain set on his brother Abel and killed him.
9   Yahweh asked Cain, 'Where is your brother Abel?' 'I do not know' he

[3]a. The name Eve is explained as derived from the Hebrew verb, 'to live'.
[4]a. Folk-derivation of the name Cain from *qanah*, acquire.

10 replied. 'Am I my brother's guardian?' ·'What have you done?' Yahweh
asked. 'Listen to the sound of your brother's blood, crying out to me from
11 the ground. ·Now be accursed and driven from the ground that has opened
12 its mouth to receive your brother's blood at your hands. ·When you till the
ground it shall no longer yield you any of its produce. You shall be a fugi-
13 tive and a wanderer over the earth.' ·Then Cain said to Yahweh, 'My punish-
14 ment is greater than I can bear. ·See! Today you drive me from this ground.
I must hide from you, and be a fugitive and a wanderer over the earth. Why,
15 whoever comes across me will kill me!' ·'Very well, then,' Yahweh replied 'if
anyone kills Cain, sevenfold vengeance shall be taken for him.' So Yahweh
put a mark on Cain, to prevent whoever might come across him from striking him down. Cain left the presence of Yahweh and settled in the land of
16 Nod, east of Eden.

The Descendants of Cain

17   Cain had intercourse with his wife, and she conceived and gave birth to
Enoch. He became builder of a town, and he gave the town the name of his
18 son Enoch. ·Enoch had a son, Irad, and Irad became the father of Mehujael;
Mehujael became the father of Methushael, and Methushael became the
19 father of Lamech. ·Lamech married two women: the name of the first was
20 Adah and the name of the second was Zillah. ·Adah gave birth to Jabal: he
21 was the ancestor of the tent-dwellers and owners of livestock. ·His brother's
name was Jubal: he was the ancestor of all who play the lyre and the flute.
22 ·As for Zillah, she gave birth to Tubal-cain: he was the ancestor of all metal-
workers, in bronze or iron. Tubal-cain's sister was Naamah.
23   Lamech said to his wives:

'Adah and Zillah, hear my voice,
Lamech's wives, listen to what I say:
I killed a man for wounding me,
a boy for striking me.
24   Sevenfold vengeance is taken for Cain,
but seventy-sevenfold for Lamech.'

Seth and His Descendants

25   Adam had intercourse with his wife, and she gave birth to a son whom
she named Seth, 'because God has granted[b] me other offspring' she said 'in
26 place of Abel, since Cain has killed him'. ·A son was also born to Seth, and
he named him Enosh. This man was the first to invoke the name of
Yahweh.[c] . . .

---

[4]b. Folk-derivation of the name Seth *(Sheth)* from *shath,* he has granted. c. Other traditions put the revelation of the divine name later, in the times of Moses, Ex 3:14.

Sons of God and Daughters of Men

1 **6** When men had begun to be plentiful on the earth, and daughters had
2   been born to them, ·the sons of God, looking at the daughters of men,
3 saw they were pleasing, so they married as many as they chose. ·Yahweh
   said, 'My spirit must not for ever be disgraced in man, for he is but flesh;
4 his life shall last no more than a hundred and twenty years'. ·The Nephilim
   were on the earth at that time (and even afterwards) when the sons of God
   resorted to the daughters of man, and had children by them. These are the
   heroes of days gone by, the famous men.

2. The Flood

The Corruption of Mankind

5   Yahweh saw that the wickedness of man was great on the earth, and that
   the thoughts in his heart fashioned nothing but wickedness all day long.
6
7 ·Yahweh regretted having made man on the earth, and his heart grieved. ·'I
   will rid the earth's face of man, my own creation,' Yahweh said 'and of animals also, reptiles too, and the birds of heaven; for I regret having made
8 them.' ·But Noah had found favour with Yahweh.
9   This is the story of Noah:
10   Noah was a good man, a man of integrity among his contemporaries, and
11 he walked with God. ·Noah became the father of three sons, Shem, Ham
   and Japheth. ·The earth grew corrupt in God's sight, and filled with vio-
12 lence. ·God contemplated the earth: it was corrupt, for corrupt were the
   ways of all flesh on the earth.

Preparations for the Flood

13   God said to Noah, 'The end has come for all things of flesh; I have
   decided this, because the earth is full of violence of man's making, and I
14 will efface them from the earth. ·Make yourself an ark out of resinous wood.
15 Make it with reeds and line it with pitch inside and out. ·This is how to make
   it: the length of the ark is to be three hundred cubits, its breadth fifty cubits,
16 and its height thirty cubits. ·Make a roof for the ark . . . put the door of the
   ark high up in the side, and make a first, second and third deck.
17   'For my part I mean to bring a flood, and send the waters over the earth,
   to destroy all flesh on it, every living creature under heaven; everything on
18 earth shall perish. ·But I will establish my Covenant with you, and you must
   go on board the ark, yourself, your sons, your wife, and your sons' wives
19 along with you. ·From all living creatures, from all flesh, you must take two
   of each kind aboard the ark, to save their lives with yours; they must be a
20 male and a female. ·Of every kind of bird, of every kind of animal and of
   every kind of reptile on the ground, two must go with you so that their lives
21 may be saved. For your part provide yourself with eatables of all kinds, and

22 lay in a store of them, to serve as food for yourself and them.' ·Noah did this; he did all that God had ordered him.

1 **7** Yahweh said to Noah, 'Go aboard the ark, you and all your household, for you alone among this generation do I see as a good man in my
2 judgement. Of all the clean animals you must take seven of each kind, both
3 male and female; of the unclean animals you must take two, a male and its female ·(and of the birds of heaven also, seven of each kind, both male and
4 female), to propagate their kind over the whole earth. ·For in seven days' time I mean to make it rain on the earth for forty days and nights, and I will
5 rid the earth of every living thing that I made.' ·Noah did all that Yahweh ordered.
6 Noah was six hundred years old when the flood of waters appeared on the earth.
7 Noah with his sons, his wife, and his sons' wives boarded the ark to
8 escape the waters of the flood. ·(Of the clean animals and the animals that
9 are not clean, of the birds and all that crawls on the ground, ·two of each kind boarded the ark with Noah, a male and a female, according to the
10 order God gave Noah.) Seven days later the waters of the flood appeared on the earth.
11 In the six hundredth year of Noah's life, in the second month, and on the seventeenth day of that month, that very day all the springs of the great
12 deep broke through, and the sluices of heaven opened. ·It rained on the earth for forty days and forty nights.
13 That very day Noah and his sons Shem, Ham and Japheth boarded the
14 ark, with Noah's wife and the three wives of his sons, ·and with them wild beasts of every kind, cattle of every kind, reptiles of every kind that crawls
15 on the earth, birds of every kind, all that flies, everything with wings. ·One pair of all that is flesh and has the breath of life boarded the ark with Noah;
16 ·and so there went in a male and a female of every creature that is flesh, just as God had ordered him.

And Yahweh closed the door behind Noah.

The Flood

17 The flood lasted forty days on the earth. The waters swelled, lifting the
18 ark until it was raised above the earth. ·The waters rose and swelled greatly
19 on the earth. After a hundred and fifty days the waters fell, ·and in the seventh month, the earth so that all the highest mountains under the whole of
20 heaven were submerged. ·The waters rose fifteen cubits higher, submerging
21 the mountains. And so all things of flesh perished that moved on the earth, birds, cattle, wild beasts, everything that swarms on the earth, and every
22 man. ·Everything with the breath of life in its nostrils died, everything on dry
23 land. ·Yahweh destroyed every living thing on the face of the earth, man and animals, reptiles, and the birds of heaven. He rid the earth of them, so that

24 only Noah was left, and those with him in the ark. ·The waters rose on the earth for a hundred and fifty days.

The Flood Subsides

1 **8** But God had Noah in mind, and all the wild beasts and all the cattle that were with him in the ark. God sent a wind across the earth and the
2 waters subsided. ·The springs of the deep and the sluices of heaven were
3 stopped. Rain ceased to fall from heaven; ·the waters gradually ebbed from
4 the earth. After a hundred and fifty days the waters fell, ·and in the seventh month, on the seventeenth day of that month, the ark came to rest on the
5 mountains of Ararat. ·The waters gradually fell until the tenth month when, on the first day of the tenth month, the mountain peaks appeared.
6 At the end of forty days Noah opened the porthole he had made in the
7 ark and he sent out the raven. This went off, and flew back and forth until
8 waters dried up from the earth. ·Then he sent out the dove, to see whether
9 the waters were receding from the surface of the earth. ·The dove, finding nowhere to perch, returned to him in the ark, for there was water over the whole surface of the earth; putting out his hand he took hold of it and
10 brought it back into the ark with him. ·After waiting seven more days, again
11 he sent out the dove from the ark. ·In the evening, the dove came back to
12 him and there it was with a new olive-branch in its beak. So Noah realised that the waters were receding from the earth. ·After waiting seven more days he sent out the dove, and now it returned to him no more.
13 It was in the six hundred and first year of Noah's life, in the first month and on the first of the month, that the water dried up from the earth. Noah lifted back the hatch of the ark and looked out. The surface of the ground was dry!
14 In the second month and on the twenty-seventh day of the month the earth was dry.

They Disembark

15 Then God said to Noah, ·'Come out of the ark, you yourself, your wife,
16 your sons, and your sons' wives with you. ·As for all the animals with you,
17 all things of flesh, whether birds or animals or reptiles that crawl on the earth, bring them out with you. Let them swarm on the earth; let them be
18 fruitful and multiply on the earth.' ·So Noah went out with his sons, his wife,
19 and his sons' wives. ·And all the wild beasts, all the cattle, all the birds and all the reptiles that crawl on the earth went out from the ark, one kind after another.
20 Noah built an altar for Yahweh, and choosing from all the clean animals
21 and all the clean birds he offered burnt offerings on the altar. ·Yahweh smelt the appeasing fragrance and said to himself, 'Never again will I curse the earth because of man, because his heart contrives evil from his infancy.

Never again will I strike down every living thing as I have done.

22
'As long as earth lasts,
sowing and reaping,
cold and heat,
summer and winter,
day and night
shall cease no more.'

The New World Order

1 God blessed Noah and his sons, saying to them, 'Be fruitful, multiply
2 and fill the earth. ·Be the terror and the dread of all the wild beasts and
all the birds of heaven, of everything that crawls on the ground and all the
3 fish of the sea; they are handed over to you. ·Every living and crawling thing
shall provide food for you, no less than the foliage of plants. I give you
4 everything, ·with this exception: you must not eat flesh with life, that is to
5 say blood, in it. ·I will demand an account of your life-blood. I will demand
an account from every beast and from man. I will demand an account of
every man's life from his fellow men.

6
'He who sheds man's blood,
shall have his blood shed by man,
for in the image of God
man was made.

7 'As for you, be fruitful, multiply, teem over the earth and be lord of it.'
8 God spoke to Noah and his sons, ·'See, I establish my Covenant with you,
9
10 and with your descendants after you; ·also with every living creature to be
found with you, birds, cattle and every wild beast with you: everything that
11 came out of the ark, everything that lives on the earth. ·I establish my Covenant with you: no thing of flesh shall be swept away again by the waters of
the flood. There shall be no flood to destroy the earth again.'
12 God said, 'Here is the sign of the Covenant I make between myself and
13 you and every living creature with you for all generations: ·I set my bow in
14 the clouds and it shall be a sign of the Covenant between me and the earth.
15 ·When I gather the clouds over the earth and the bow appears in the clouds,
16 ·I will recall the Covenant between myself and you and every living creature
of every kind. And so the waters shall never again become a flood to destroy
all things of flesh. ·When the bow is in the clouds I shall see it and call to
mind the lasting Covenant between God and every living creature of every
kind that is found on the earth.'
17 God said to Noah, 'This is the sign of the Covenant I have established
between myself and every living thing that is found on the earth'.

3. From the Flood to Abraham

Noah and His Sons

18   The sons of Noah who went out from the ark were Shem, Ham and
19 Japheth; Ham is the ancestor of the Canaanites. ·These three were Noah's
sons, and from these the whole earth was peopled.
20
21   Noah, a tiller of the soil, was the first to plant the vine. ·He drank some
of the wine, and while he was drunk he uncovered himself inside his tent.
22 Ham, Canaan's ancestor, saw his father's nakedness, and told his two broth-
23 ers outside. ·Shem and Japheth took a cloak and they both put it over their
shoulders, and walking backwards, covered their father's nakedness; they
kept their faces turned away, and did not see their father's nakedness.
24 ·When Noah awoke from his stupor he learned what his youngest son had
25 done to him. And he said:

> 'Accursed be Canaan.
> He shall be his brothers'
> meanest slave.'

26   He added:

> 'Blessed be Yahweh, God of Shem,
> let Canaan be his slave!
27   May God extend Japheth,
> may he live in the tents of Shem,
> and may Canaan be his slave!'

28
29   After the flood Noah lived three hundred and fifty years. ·In all, Noah's
life lasted nine hundred and fifty years; then he died. . .

The Tower of Babel[a]

1   **11** Throughout the earth men spoke the same language, with the same
2   vocabulary. ·Now as they moved eastwards they found a plain in the
3 land of Shinar[b] where they settled. ·They said to one another, 'Come, let us
make bricks and bake them in the fire'.—For stone they used bricks, and
4 for mortar they used bitumen.—·'Come,' they said 'let us build ourselves a
town and a tower with its top reaching heaven. Let us make a name for ourselves, so that we may not be scattered about the whole earth.'
5   Now Yahweh came down to see the town and the tower that the sons of
6 man had built. ·'So they are all a single people with a single language!' said
Yahweh. 'This is but the start of their undertakings! There will be nothing
7 too hard for them to do. ·Come, let us go down and confuse their language

---

[11]a. A different explanation, from another source, of the diversity of peoples and language. b. Babylonia.

8 on the spot so that they can no longer understand one another.' ·Yahweh
scattered them thence over the whole face of the earth, and they stopped

9 building the town. ·It was named Babel therefore, because there Yahweh
confused[c] the language of the whole earth. It was from there that Yahweh
scattered them over the whole face of the earth.

The Patriarchs after the Flood

10   These are Shem's descendants:
    When Shem was a hundred years old he became the father of Arpach-

11 shad, two years after the flood. ·After the birth of Arpachshad, Shem lived
five hundred years and became the father of sons and daughers.

12   When Arpachshad was thirty-five years old he became the father of She-

13 lah. After the birth of Shelah, Arpachshad lived four hundred and three
years and was the father of sons and daughters.

14
15   When Shelah was thirty years old he became the father of Eber. ·After
the birth of Eber, Shelah lived four hundred and three years and became the
father of sons and daughters.

16   When Eber was thirty-four years old he became the father of Peleg.

17 ·After the birth of Peleg, Eber lived four hundred and thirty years and
became the father of sons and daughters.

18
19   When Peleg was thirty years old he became the father of Reu. ·After the
birth of Reu, Peleg lived two hundred and nine years and became the father
of sons and daughters.

20
21   When Reu was thirty-two years old he became the father of Serug. ·After
the birth of Serug, Reu lived two hundred and seven years and became the
father of sons and daughters.

22
23   When Serug was thirty years old he became the father of Nahor. ·After
the birth of Nahor, Serug lived two hundred years and became the father of
sons and daughters.

24   When Nahor was twenty-nine years old he became the father of Terah.

25 After the birth of Terah, Nahor lived a hundred and nineteen years and
became the father of sons and daughters.

26   When Terah was seventy years old he became the father of Abram,
Nahor and Haran.

The Descendants of Terah

27   These are Terah's descendants:
    Terah became the father of Abram, Nahor and Haran. Haran became the

28 father of Lot. ·Haran died in the presence of his father Terah in his native

29 land, Ur of the Chaldaeans. ·Abram and Nahor both married; Abram's wife
was called Sarai, Nahor's wife was called Milcah, the daughter of Haran,

30 father of Milcah and Iscah. ·Sarai was barren, having no child.

c. *Babel* is derived here from a verb meaning 'to confuse', but in fact the name means 'gate of the god'.

31   Terah took his son Abram, his grandson Lot the son of Haran, and his daughter-in-law the wife of Abram, and made them leave Ur of the Chaldaeans to go to the land of Canaan. But on arrival in Haran they settled there.[d]

32   Terah's life lasted two hundred and five years; then he died at Haran.

II. THE STORY OF ABRAHAM

The Call of Abraham

1   **12** Yahweh said to Abram, 'Leave your country, your family and your
2   father's house, for the land I will show you. ·I will make you a great nation; I will bless you and make your name so famous that it will be used as a blessing.

3
          'I will bless those who bless you:
          I will curse those who slight you.
          All the tribes of the earth
          shall bless themselves by you.'

4   So Abram went as Yahweh told him, and Lot went with him. Abram was
5   seventy-five years old when he left Haran. ·Abram took his wife Sarai, his nephew Lot, all the possessions they had amassed and the people they had acquired in Haran. They set off for the land of Canaan, and arrived there.
6   Abram passed through the land as far as Shechem's holy place, the Oasis
7   of Moreh. At that time the Canaanites were in the land. ·Yahweh appeared to Abram and said, 'It is to your descendants that I will give this land'. So
8   Abram built there an altar for Yahweh who had appeared to him. ·From there he moved on to the mountainous district east of Bethel, where he pitched his tent, with Bethel to the west and Ai to the east. There he built an
9   altar to Yahweh and invoked the name of Yahweh. ·Then Abram made his way stage by stage to the Negeb.

Abraham in Egypt

10   When famine came to the land Abram went down into Egypt, to stay
11   there for the time, since the land was hard pressed by the famine. ·On the threshold of Egypt he said to his wife Sarai, 'Listen! I know you are a beau-
12   tiful woman. When the Egyptians see you they will say, "That is his wife",
13   and they will kill me but spare you. ·Tell them you are my sister, so that they may treat me well because of you and spare my life out of regard for
14   you.' ·When Abram arrived in Egypt the Egyptians did indeed see that the
15   woman was very beautiful. When Pharaoh's officials saw her they sang her

d. Ur is in Lower Mesopotamia; Haran lies to the N.W. Mesopotamia.

16 praises to Pharaoh and the woman was taken into Pharaoh's palace. ·He
treated Abram well because of her, and he received flocks, oxen, donkeys,
17 men and women slaves, she-donkeys and camels. ·But Yahweh inflicted
severe plagues on Pharaoh and his household because of Abram's wife
18 Sarai. ·So Pharaoh summoned Abram and said, 'What is this you have done
19 to me? Why did you not tell me she was your wife? ·Why did you say, "She
is my sister", so that I took her for my wife? Now, here is your wife. Take
20 her and go!' ·Pharaoh committed him to men who escorted him back to the
frontier with his wife and all he possessed.

WRITING AND DISCUSSION QUESTIONS

Informative

1. Describe the relationships evident between God and humankind, and then
   between man and woman in this creation account. In what ways are man and
   woman related to nature? Is there any clue in the text as to what it means to be
   "made in God's image"?
2. Explain what happens to the human couple and their descendants after the Fall
   depicted in Genesis 3. What happens to them outside the Garden (Genesis 4)?
   How does the text picture the fate of humankind in rebellion against God (Genesis
   6–9)?
3. The specific promises offered by God to Abram (which means "father" in
   Hebrew and by which he was known before being referred to as "Abraham,"
   that is, the father of many nations) include land and a glorious progeny who
   would be a blessing to all peoples (Genesis 12). Explain how the story of Abraham may be seen as an antidote to the confusion and disintegration pictured at
   the Tower of Babel in Genesis 11.

Persuasive

1. There are a number of other creation stories extant from the ancient world, including several whose accounts bear some similarity to Genesis, but most of which are
   even less specific and detailed. Argue that Genesis 1–2 is a "mythological" or a
   "scientific" account of the origin of the universe. Consider its possible purpose for
   the original readers, and its impact on the values of contemporary believers who
   accept it literally, and the values of contemporary nonbelievers.
2. Archaeological expeditions have been launched many times in the past two centuries to recover possible evidence of the Genesis Flood and some remnant of the
   Ark. What would be the historical significance if indisputable evidence were
   found? Argue the question of whether such data, if verified, would alter the way a
   majority of readers view the Bible.
3. Argue the importance of a society having a common history or belief about its
   origins and destiny. In what way has Genesis served that role in the United States?

Personal

1. There are stories throughout history of bargains with Satan. Consider how the serpent tempts Eve. Why would she or anyone want to "be like God"? If you were presented with the seemingly diabolical proposition of becoming "like God," how would you respond?

2. From your point of view, is Genesis a credible account of the way the universe began? If not, what accounts for your twentieth-century skepticism? If so, how do you reconcile certain scientific theories that appear to explain the existence of the cosmos and to contradict the Biblical account?

3. Do you believe in such a thing as "sin"? Define the term and describe in your own words what constitutes the standard by which any particular action can be recognized and labeled as "sin"? How do you account for the origin of the idea of sin and its use in Western history?

▼

from *Exodus*

I. THE LIBERATION FROM EGYPT

A. Israel in Egypt

The Prosperity of the Hebrews in Egypt

1 These are the names of the sons of Israel who went with Jacob to Egypt, each with his family: ·Reuben, Simeon, Levi and Judah, ·Issachar, Zebulun and Benjamin, ·Dan and Naphtali, Gad and Asher. ·In all, the descendants of Jacob numbered seventy persons. Joseph was in Egypt already. ·Then Joseph died, and his brothers, and all that generation. ·But the sons of Israel were fruitful and grew in numbers greatly; they increased and grew so immensely powerful that they filled the land.

The Hebrews Oppressed

8 Then there came to power in Egypt a new king who knew nothing of
9 Joseph. 'Look,' he said to his subjects 'these people, the sons of Israel, have
10 become so numerous and strong that they are a threat to us. ·We must be prudent and take steps against their increasing any further, or if war should break out, they might add to the number of our enemies. They might take
11 arms against us and so escape out of the country.' ·Accordingly they put slave-drivers over the Israelites to wear them down under heavy loads. In
12 this way they built the store-cities of Pithom and Rameses[a] for Pharaoh. ·But

___

[1]a. The residence of Rameses II in the Delta; either Tanis or Qantir.

the more they were crushed, the more they increased and spread, and men
13 came to dread the sons of Israel. ·The Egyptians forced the sons of Israel
14 into slavery, ·and made their lives unbearable with hard labour, work with
clay and with brick, all kinds of work in the fields; they forced on them
every king of labour.
15 The king of Egypt then spoke to the Hebrew midwives, one of whom was
16 named Shiphrah, and the other Puah. ·'When you midwives attend Hebrew
women,' he said 'watch the two stones*b* carefully. If it is a boy, kill him; if a
17 girl, let her live.' ·But the midwives were God-fearing: they disobeyed the
18 command of the king of Egypt and let the boys live. ·So the king of Egypt
summoned the midwives. 'Why' he asked them 'have you done this and
19 spared the boys?' ·'The Hebrew women are not like Egyptian women,' they
answered Pharaoh 'they are hardy, and they give birth before the midwife
20 reaches them.' ·God was kind to the midwives. The people went on increas-
21 ing and grew very powerful; ·since the midwives reverenced God he granted
them descendants.
22 Pharaoh then gave his subjects this command: 'Throw all the boys born
to the Hebrews into the river, but let all the girls live'.

B. Early Life and Call of Moses

The Birth of Moses

1 There was a man of the tribe of Levi who had taken a woman of Levi as
2 **2** his wife. ·She conceived and gave birth to a son and, seeing what a fine
3 child he was, she kept him hidden for three months. ·When she could hide
him no longer, she got a papyrus basket for him; coating it with bitumen and
pitch, she put the child inside and laid it among the reeds at the river's
4 edge. ·His sister stood some distance away to see what would happen to
him.
5 Now Pharaoh's daughter went down to bathe in the river, and the girls
attending her were walking along by the riverside. Among the reeds she
6 noticed the basket, and she sent her maid to fetch it. ·She opened it and
looked, and saw a baby boy, crying; and she was sorry for him. 'This is a
7 child of one of the Hebrews' she said. ·Then the child's sister said to Pharaoh's daughter, 'Shall I go and find you a nurse among the Hebrew women
8 to suckle the child for you?' ·'Yes, go' Pharaoh's daughter said to her; and
9 the girl went off to find the baby's own mother. ·To her the daughter of
Pharaoh said, 'Take this child away and suckle it for me. I will see you are
10 paid.' So the woman took the child and suckled it. ·When the child grew up,
she brought him to Pharaoh's daughter who treated him like a son; she
named him Moses because, she said, 'I drew him out of the water'.*a*

b. The exact meaning is uncertain.
²a. Folk-derivation of the name Moses from *mashah*, to draw out.

Moses Escapes to Midian

11   Moses, a man by now, set out at this time to visit his countrymen, and he saw what a hard life they were having; and he saw an Egyptian strike a
12 Hebrew, one of his countrymen. ·Looking round he could see no one in
13 sight, so he killed the Egyptian and hid him in the sand. ·On the following day he came back, and there were two Hebrews, fighting. He said to the
14 man who was in the wrong, 'What do you mean by hitting your fellow coun-
15 tryman?' ·'And who appointed you' the man retorted ·'to be prince over us, and judge? Do you intend to kill me as you killed the Egyptian?' Moses was frightened. 'Clearly that business has come to light' he thought. ·When Pharaoh heard of the matter he would have killed Moses, but Moses fled from Pharaoh and made for the land of Midian.[b] And he sat down beside a well.
16   Now the priest of Midian had seven daughters. They came to draw water
17 and fill the troughs to water their father's sheep. ·Shepherds came and drove them away, but Moses came to their defence and watered their sheep for
18 them. ·When they returned to their father Reuel, he said to them, 'You are back early today!' 'An Egyptian protected us from the shepherds;' they said
19 'yes, and he drew water for us and watered the flock.' ·'And where is he?'
20 he asked his daughters. 'Why did you leave the man there? Ask him to eat
21 with us.' ·So Moses settled with this man, who gave him his daughter Zip-
22 porah in marriage. ·She gave birth to a son, and he named him Gershom because, he said, 'I am a stranger in a foreign land'.

The Call of Moses

God Remembers Israel

23   During this long period the king of Egypt died. The sons of Israel, groaning in their slavery, cried out for help and from the depths of their slavery
24 their cry came up to God. ·God heard their groaning and he called to mind
25 his covenant with Abraham, Isaac and Jacob. ·God looked down upon the sons of Israel, and he knew . . .

The Burning Bush

1 **3** Moses was looking after the flock of Jethro, his father-in-law, priest of Midian. He led his flock to the far side of the wilderness and came to
2 Horeb,[a] the mountain of God. ·There the angel of Yahweh appeared to him in the shape of a flame of fire, coming from the middle of a bush. Moses
3 looked; there was the bush blazing but it was not being burnt up. ·'I must go and look at this strange sight,' Moses said 'and see why the bush is not
4 burnt.' ·Now Yahweh saw him go forward to look, and God called to him

---

b. Midian lies S. of Edom and E. of the Gulf of Aqaba.
[3]a. Sinai; the alternative name used in the 'Elohistic' tradition.

from the middle of the bush. 'Moses, Moses!' he said. 'Here I am' he
5 answered. ·'Come no nearer' he said. 'Take off your shoes, for the place on
6 which you stand is holy ground. I am the God of your father,' he said 'the
God of Abraham, the God of Isaac and the God of Jacob.' At this Moses
covered his face, afraid to look at God.

The Mission of Moses

7 And Yahweh said, 'I have seen the miserable state of my people in Egypt.
I have heard their appeal to be free of their slave-drivers. Yes, I am well
8 aware of their sufferings. ·I mean to deliver them out of the hands of the
Egyptians and bring them up out of that land to a land rich and broad, a
land where milk and honey flow, the home of the Canaanites, the Hittites,
9 the Amorites, the Perizzites, the Hivites and the Jebusites. ·And now the cry
of the sons of Israel has come to me, and I have witnessed the way in which
10 the Egyptians oppress them, so come, I send you to Pharaoh to bring the
sons of Israel, my people, out of Egypt.'
11 Moses said to God, 'Who am I to go to Pharaoh and bring the sons of
12 Israel out of Egypt?' ·'I shall be with you,' was the answer 'and this is the
sign by which you shall know that it is I who have sent you . . . After you
have led the people out of Egypt, you are to offer worship to God on this
mountain.'

The Divine Name Revealed

13 Then Moses said to God, 'I am to go, then, to the sons of Israel and say
to them, "The God of your fathers has sent me to you". But if they ask me
14 what his name is, what am I to tell them?' ·And God said to Moses, 'I Am
who I Am. This' he added 'is what you must say to the sons of Israel: "I Am
15 has sent me to you".' ·And God also said to Moses, 'You are to say to the
sons of Israel: "Yahweh,*b* the God of your fathers, the God of Abraham, the
God of Isaac, and the God of Jacob, has sent me to you". This is my name
for all time; by this name I shall be invoked for all generations to come.

Moses Instructed for His Mission

16 'Go and gather the elders of Israel together and tell them, "Yahweh, the
God of your fathers, has appeared to me,—the God of Abraham, of Isaac,
and of Jacob; and he has said to me: I have visited you and seen all that the
Egyptians are doing to you. ·And so I have resolved to bring you up out of
17 Egypt where you are oppressed, into the land of the Canaanites, the Hittites,
the Amorites, the Perizzites, the Hivites and the Jebusites, to a land where
18 milk and honey flow." ·They will listen to your words, and with the elders of
Israel you are to go to the king of Egypt and say to him, "Yahweh, the God

b. The formula, 'I Am who I Am' becomes, in the third person, Yahweh, 'He is'.

of the Hebrews, has come to meet us. Give us leave, then, to make a three
19 days' journey into the wilderness to offer sacrifice to Yahweh our God." ·For
myself, knowing that the king of Egypt will not let you go unless he is forced
20 by a mighty hand, ·I shall show my power and strike Egypt with all the wonders I am going to work there. After this he will let you go.

The Egyptians to Be Plundered

21   I will give this people such prestige in the eyes of the Egyptians that when
22 you go, you will not go empty-handed. ·Every woman will ask her neighbour
and the woman who is staying in her house for silver ornaments and gold.
With these you will adorn your sons and daughters; you will plunder the
Egyptians.' . . .

III. THE COVENANT AT SINAI

A. The Covenant and the Decalogue

The Israelites Come to Sinai

1   **19** Three months after they came out of the land of Egypt . . . on that
2   day the sons of Israel came to the wilderness of Sinai.[a] ·From Rephi-
dim they set out again; and when they reached the wilderness of Sinai, there
in the wilderness they pitched their camp; there facing the mountain Israel
pitched camp.

Yahweh Promises a Covenant

3   Moses then went up to God, and Yahweh called to him from the mountain, saying, 'Say this to the House of Jacob, declare this to the sons of
4 Israel, ·"You yourselves have seen what I did with the Egyptians, how I car-
5 ried you on eagle's wings and brought you to myself. ·From this you know
that now, if you obey my voice and hold fast to my covenant, you of all the
6 nations shall be my very own for all the earth is mine. ·I will count you a
kingdom of priests, a consecrated nation." Those are the words you are to
7 speak to the sons of Israel.' ·So Moses went and summoned the elders of
8 the people, putting before them all that Yahweh had bidden him. ·Then all
the people answered as one, 'All that Yahweh has said, we will do.' And
Moses took the people's reply back to Yahweh.

Preparing for the Covenant

9   Yahweh said to Moses, 'I am coming to you in a dense cloud so that the
people may hear when I speak to you and may trust you always'. And Moses
took the people's reply back to Yahweh.

---

[19]a. According to tradition, Mount Sinai was at Jebel Musa, in the southern region of the Sinai peninsula.

10 Yahweh said to Moses, 'Go to the people and tell them to prepare them-
11 selves today and tomorrow. Let them wash their clothing and ·hold themselves in readiness for the third day, because on the third day Yahweh will
12 descend on the mountain of Sinai in the sight of all the people. ·You will
mark out the limits of the mountain and say, "Take care not to go up the
mountain or to touch the foot of it. Whoever touches the mountain will be
13 put to death. No one must lay a hand on him: he must be stoned or shot
down by arrow, whether man or beast; he must not remain alive." When the
ram's horn sounds a long blast, they are to go up the mountain.'
14 So Moses came down from the mountain to the people and bade them
15 prepare themselves; and they washed their clothing. ·Then he said to the
people, 'Be ready for the third day; do not go near any woman'.

The Theophany on Sinai

16 Now at daybreak on the third day there were peals of thunder on the
mountain and lightning flashes, a dense cloud, and a loud trumpet blast, and
17 inside the camp all the people trembled. ·Then Moses led the people out of
18 the camp to meet God; and they stood at the bottom of the mountain. ·The
mountain of Sinai was entirely wrapped in smoke, because Yahweh had
descended on it in the form of fire. Like smoke from a furnace the smoke
19 went up, and the whole mountain shook violently. ·Louder and louder grew
the sound of the trumpet. Moses spoke, and God answered him with peals of
20 thunder. Yahweh came down on the mountain of Sinai, on the mountain top,
and Yahweh called Moses to the top of the mountain; and Moses went up.
21 ·Yahweh said to Moses, 'Go down and warn the people not to pass beyond
their bounds to come and look on Yahweh, or many of them will lose their
22 lives. ·The priests, the men who do approach Yahweh,[b] even these must
23 purify themselves, or Yahweh will break out against them.' ·Moses answered
Yahweh, 'The people cannot come up the mountain of Sinai because you
warned us yourself when you said, "Mark out the limits of the mountain and
24 declare it sacred"'. ·'Go down,' said Yahweh to him 'and come up again
bringing Aaron with you. But do not allow the priests or the people to pass
beyond their bounds to come up to Yahweh, or he will break out against
25 them.' ·So Moses went down to the people and spoke to them . . .

The Decalogue[a]

1
2 **20** Then God spoke all these words. He said, ·'I am Yahweh your God
who brought you out of the land of Egypt, out of the house of
slavery.
3 'You shall have no gods except me.

---

b. But see ch. 29, which treats the investiture of priests as a later occurrence.

[20]a. This is the priestly version of the Ten Commandments; another version, the Deuteronomic, is found in
Dt 5, and it is the second which has been adopted by the Church.

4   'You shall not make yourself a carved image or any likeness of anything
5   in heaven or on earth beneath or in the waters under the earth; ·you shall
     not bow down to them or serve them. For I, Yahweh your God, am a jealous
     God and I punish the father's fault in the sons, the grandsons, and the great-
6   grandsons of those who hate me; ·but I show kindness to thousands of those
     who love me and keep my commandments.

7   'You shall not utter the name of Yahweh your God to misuse it,[b] for Yah-
     weh will not leave unpunished the man who utters his name to misuse it.

8
9   'Remember the sabbath day and keep it holy. ·For six days you shall
10   labour and do all your work, ·but the seventh day is a sabbath for Yahweh
     your God. You shall do no work that day, neither you nor your son nor your
     daughter nor your servants, men or women, nor your animals nor the
11   stranger who lives with you. ·For in six days Yahweh made the heavens and
     the earth and the sea and all that these hold, but on the seventh day he
     rested; that is why Yahweh has blessed the sabbath day and made it sacred.

12   'Honour your father and your mother so that you may have a long life in
     the land that Yahweh your God has given to you.

13   'You shall not kill.

14   'You shall not commit adultery.

15   'You shall not steal.

16   'You shall not bear false witness against your neighbour.

17   'You shall not covet your neighbour's house. You shall not covet your
     neighbour's wife, or his servant, man or woman, or his ox, or his donkey, or
     anything that is his.'

18   [c]All the people shook with fear at the peals of thunder and the lightning
     flashes, the sound of the trumpet, and the smoking mountain; and they kept
19   their distance. ·'Speak to us yourself' they said to Moses 'and we will listen;
20   but do not let God speak to us, or we shall die.' ·Moses answered the peo-
     ple, 'Do not be afraid; God has come to test you, so that your fear of him,
21   being always in your mind, may keep you from sinning'. ·So the people kept
     their distance while Moses approached the dark cloud where God was.

B. The Book of the Covenant

Law Concerning the Altar

22   Yahweh said to Moses, 'Tell the sons of Israel this, "You have seen for
23   yourselves that I have spoken to you from heaven. ·You shall not make gods
     of silver or gods of gold to stand beside me; you shall not make things like
     this for yourselves.

24   "You are to make me an altar of earth, and sacrifice on this the holo-
     causts and communion sacrifices from your flocks or herds. In every place

---

b. Either in a false oath or irreverently. c. This section probably should be read after 19:19; the Decalogue
itself is not linked to the narrative framework.

25 in which I have my name remembered I shall come to you and bless you. •If
   you make me an altar of stone, do not build it of dressed stones; for if you
26 use a tool on it, you profane it. •You shall not go up to my altar by steps for
   fear you expose your nakedness."

WRITING AND DISCUSSION QUESTIONS

Informative

1. Examine carefully the circumstances of Moses' birth and upbringing (Exodus 1–2).
   How does this auspicious beginning foreshadow his greater, climactic confrontation with God in Exodus 20?
2. Consider each of the Ten Commandments. How can they be grouped? How
   does each serve in the building of a nation or community? How does each contribute to the goal of stability and mutual concern? What is the particular contribution of the more "religious" commandments (Exodus 20:3–8)?
3. In what way is the founding of Israel a fulfillment of the land, nation, and "spiritual" covenant God made to Abraham in Genesis 12?

Persuasive

1. Many Biblical scholars argue that the pivotal event in Exodus really occurs when
   God reveals his "name" to Moses (Exodus 3). Argue that this event is significant
   in preparing Moses for his task and lends him authority when he later confronts his
   people.
2. The Ten Commandments (Exodus 20:1–17) provide the foundation for what many
   regard as "traditional American values." Provide evidence that these "laws" are
   the basis for family life and community and national ethics.

Personal

1. Moses is a prototypical "hero" to most cultures—daring, courageous, clever,
   and wise. Consider this tribute to the historical Moses' impact on Hebrew culture
   and the world's ethical system by theologian John Wenham: "No sense can be
   made of the history of the world unless Moses is recognized, not only as a historical figure, but as one of the greatest figures of all time. It can be safely said that
   the appearance in the world of the ethical monotheism of Judaism represents the
   most far-reaching influence in the whole history of mankind" ("Moses and the Pentateuch," *New Bible Commentary,* page 43). Do you agree with this assessment?
   Compare Moses to some of your own personal heroes.
2. The God depicted in the Hebrew Scriptures is sometimes caricatured as a God of
   wrath and vengeance. Does your reading of the excerpts in this section confirm or
   deny this view? In what way? Is there evidence to fuel a debate about whether
   there is a conflict between a vengeful and forgiving God in the passages you
   have read?

Psalms 8, 23, 51, 53

The Psalms of King David of Israel (ca. 930 B.C.) celebrate the dealings of God with the people of Israel and offer repentance, praise, and honor to the God they worship. David is a well-known Biblical figure whose exploits as a lowly shepherd boy rising up to defend his people against the Philistines and the taunts of the giant Goliath, and who is eventually anointed King of Israel, have made his name legendary in Western culture. A skilled soldier and leader, David is also traditionally thought of as a remarkably talented musician whose songs and psalms could alone provide the literary and historical foundation of the people of Israel. These selections from the Psalms provide a glimpse of the Israelite's view of humankind's place in God's universe (Psalm 8); their reverence for God as shepherd of their lives—a poignant image drawn from David's youth (Psalm 23); the lament for individual sin and the reception of forgiveness from God, another incident drawn from David's biography (Psalm 51); and the single-minded monotheism and devotion of the Israelites to the God who called them out of Egyptian captivity (Psalm 53). The Psalms also provide a window on poetic expression and music in ancient times, both of which are the center of Hebrew artistic culture and measurements of its vitality and variety.

▼

from *Psalms*

PSALM 8

The Munificence of the Creator

[a]For the choirmaster   On the . . . of Gath[a]   Psalm   Of David

1   Yahweh, our Lord,
       how great your name throughout the earth!

       Above the heavens is your majesty chanted
2   by the mouths of children, babes in arms.
       You set your stronghold firm against your foes
       to subdue enemies and rebels.

3   I look up at your heavens, made by your fingers,
       at the moon and stars you set in place—
4   ah, what is man that you should spare a thought for him,
       the son of man that you should care for him?

5   Yet you have made him little less than a god,
       you have crowned him with glory and splendour,
6   made him lord over the work of your hands,
       set all things under his feet,

---

[a]a. A musical instrument, or the name of a tune.

7   sheep and oxen, all these,
    yes, wild animals too,
8   birds in the air, fish in the sea
    travelling the paths of the ocean.

9   Yahweh, our Lord,
    how great your name throughout the earth!

PSALM 23

The Good Shepherd

Psalm   Of David

1   Yahweh is my shepherd,
        I lack nothing.

2   In meadows of green grass he lets me lie.
    To the waters of repose he leads me;
3   there he revives my soul.

    He guides me by paths of virtue
        for the sake of his name

4   Though I pass through a gloomy valley,
        I fear no harm;
    beside me your rod and your staff
        are there, to hearten me.

5   You prepare a table before me
        under the eyes of my enemies,
    you anoint my head with oil,
        my cup brims over.

6   Ah, how goodness and kindness pursue me,
        every day of my life,
    my home, the house of Yahweh,
        as long as I live!

PSALM 51

Miserere

For the choirmaster   Psalm   of David   When the prophet Nathan came to him because he had been with Bathsheba

1   Have mercy on me, O God, in your goodness,
        in your great tenderness wipe away my faults;

2 wash me clean of my guilt,
   purify me from my sin.

3 For I am well aware of my faults,
   I have my sin constantly in mind,
4 having sinned against none other than you,
   having done what you regard as wrong.

   You are just when you pass sentence on me,
   blameless when you give judgement.
5 You know I was born guilty,
   a sinner from the moment of conception.

6 Yet, since you love sincerity of heart,
   teach me the secrets of wisdom.
7 Purify me with hyssop*a* until I am clean;
   wash me until I am whiter than snow.

8 Instil some joy and gladness into me,
   let the bones you have crushed rejoice again.
9 Hide your face from my sins,
   wipe out all my guilt.

10 God, create a clean heart in me,
    put into me a new and constant spirit,
11 do not banish me from your presence,
    do not deprive me of your holy spirit.
12 Be my saviour again, renew my joy,
    keep my spirit steady and willing;
13 and I shall teach transgressors the way to you,
    and to you the sinners will return.

14 Save me from death, God my saviour,
    and my tongue will acclaim your righteousness;
15 Lord, open my lips,
    and my mouth will speak out your praise.

16 Sacrifice gives you no pleasure,
    were I to offer holocaust, you would not have it.
17 My sacrifice is this broken spirit,
    you will not scorn this crushed and broken heart.

18 Show your favour graciously to Zion,
    rebuild the walls of Jerusalem.*b*
19 Then there will be proper sacrifice to please you
    —holocaust and whole oblation—
    and young bulls to be offered on your altar.

---

[51]a. Plant used in ceremonial purification by sprinkling. b. In spite of the inscription at the beginning of this psalm, this stanza at least speaks of a time after the return from Exile.

PSALM 53

The Godless Man[a]

For the choirmaster   In sickness   Poem   Of David

1   The fool says in his heart,
      'There is no God!'
     They are false, corrupt, vile,
        there is not one good man left.

2   God is looking down from heaven
        at the sons of men,
     to see if a single one is wise,
        if a single one is seeking God.

3   All have turned aside,
        all alike are tainted
     There is not one good man left,
        not a single one.

4   Are they so ignorant, these evil men
        who swallow my people
     as though they were eating bread,
        and never invoke God?

5   They will be struck with fear,
        fear without reason,
     since God scatters the bones of the apostate,
        they are disgraced, for God rejects them.

6   Who will bring Israel salvation from Zion?
     When God brings his people home,
     what joy for Jacob, what happiness for Israel!

WRITING AND DISCUSSION QUESTIONS

Informative

1. Consider carefully the questions raised in Psalm 8. In answering the questions, consider how the psalmist's poetry reveals his conception of men and women and their relationship to God? How is the relationship similar to that depicted in Genesis 1–2? How is it different?

2. Psalm 23, the famous "shepherd" psalm, portrays God as a tender comforter of individual believers. Identify the imagery in the psalm that reinforces this theme, and discuss why the shepherd metaphor would have been a particularly endearing expression for God's dealings with the ancient Israelites.

---

[a] 53a. An edition of Ps 14 by an 'Elohistic' editor.

3. The anguish of Psalm 51 emerges from the biography of King David who, according to the Second Book of Samuel 11–12, arranged the death of one of his trusted soldiers so he could marry the soldier's wife, the beautiful Bathsheba. What references to this event are implied in the psalm? How does the psalmist refer to David's sin? What is proposed as a resolution to David's self-confessed crime?

Persuasive

1. Offer a picture of God derived only from the evidence offered by the psalmist, then argue that this God would be more loving or wrathful than the deity portrayed in other parts of the Hebrew Scriptures.
2. Argue that the religious message of Psalm 23 can be comforting and reassuring even if one is not an adherent of the faith from which it emerges. Is it possible to find solace in the faith of others who do not share yours in every specific detail?
3. In some ways, the psalmist of Psalm 53 appears quite intolerant of those who would disagree with him on the question of whether there is a God. Argue whether such a personal faith can become dogmatic and bigoted and breed enmity and strife. Is there a role for public faith and conviction? How should one's faith encourage participation in a society that does not share that faith?

Personal

1. Psalm 53 begins with the startling declaration, "The fool says in his heart, 'There is no God!'" In what sense may it be "foolish" to profess atheism? In what sense may it be "foolish" to confess belief in God?
2. Write a psalm of your own, modeled on the sample psalms here, that expresses your own sense of wonderment (Psalm 8), comfort (Psalm 23), anxiety (Psalm 51), or judgment (Psalm 53) or which parodies the theme, form, or style of one of these psalms.
3. How does the poetic form of the psalms make the reading of them more or less difficult than other Biblical passages? Does their presence in the Bible surprise you?

THE NEW TESTAMENT

Matthew 5–7, 26–28 and Luke 15

The Book of Matthew is regarded by many scholars as the most "Jewish" gospel, charting Jesus' lineage back to David and Abraham, emphasizing his association with the kingdom of God, and stressing Jesus' uniqueness as son and Messiah. In contrast, Luke's Gospel is often referred to as a work written for a Greco–Roman audience because of its sometimes more philosophical, contemplative nature. The explicit thesis of Matthew's Gospel is that Jesus is the logical conclusion and fulfillment of the Hebrew covenant and that he is the long expected Messiah. The Sermon on the Mount seems deliberately designed as a contrast to the then contemporary interpretation of the Torah, which Jesus regarded as a misconstruing of the Mosaic teaching. He responds with a call to return to a more balanced, traditional interpretation but with some special emphasis that he himself provides. Though the Sermon on the

Mount, presented in Matthew 5–7, is the ethical center of Jesus' teaching, it is only part of the larger purpose in his message, stressing a coming kingdom and his unique part in its establishment.

It should be pointed out that in Matthew 5–7 Jesus is entering into the kind of debate alluded to earlier in our introductory essay, namely, an attempt to define (or redefine) what constitutes orthodoxy. In effect, although Jesus' teaching style was basically modeled on the rabbinical tradition with which he was familiar, he nevertheless "taught them with authority" (Matthew 7:29). This "authority" focused not so much on his ability to debate rival teachers as on his personal integrity and powerful presence. In some ways, Jesus was the original populist, a public speaker appealing to his hearers with stories and simple, homely images—all poignant contrasts to the sometimes legalistic style more common to the Judaism of his time—a feature especially found in the parables in the Gospel of Luke.

In other ways, Jesus was simply an original, a charismatic and dynamic individual unafraid to challenge the status quo with outspoken pronouncements about his own authority ("You have learnt how it was said . . . But I say this to you . . . [Matthew 5:21]). This is but one manifestation of how Christianity would depart from the ethical monotheism of Judaism. Jesus overtly claimed to be God and appropriated to himself names and symbols previously attributed only to Yahweh, the God of Abraham, Isaac, and Jacob and the God of Moses and David. In short, whatever readers may make of him, Jesus clearly claimed a power and an authority that labeled him a blasphemer among the Scribes and Pharisees, the influential religious authorities of the first-century Jewish community. The betrayal, trial, and crucifixion narratives, as well as the crucial resurrection story, of Matthew 26–28 attest to the violently different opinions on his character and mission—opinions that are prevalent even today. Thus, these excerpts from Matthew and Luke focus on the completion of Jesus' ministry. In summary form, this mission involved the following: a period of startling teaching about God and Jesus' unique relationship to him; a confrontation with the religious and civil authorities that led to his crucifixion, a death to be seen as an atoning sacrifice for the sins of mankind; and, finally, his resurrection, a dramatic confirmation of his identity as the Son of God and the final evidence of his kingship.

The central themes and events in Matthew and Luke are ethics of the kingdom (Matt. 5–7), Jesus' betrayal and death (Matt. 26), the Resurrection (Matt. 28), the Ascension and commission (Matt. 28), and the parables about the kingdom (Luke 15, 18). Central persons in Matthew and Luke are Jesus, Peter, Judas, Mary Magdalene, Mary (Mother of Jesus), John, and Pilate.

▼

from *Matthew*

The Sermon on the Mount[a]

The Beatitudes

1
2   **5** Seeing the crowds, he went up the hill. There he sat down and was joined by his disciples. ·Then he began to speak. This is what he taught them:

[a]. In this discourse, which occupies three ch. of this gospel, Mt has included sayings which probably originated on other occasions (cf. their parallels in Lk).

3   'How happy are the poor in spirit;
         theirs in the kingdom of heaven.
4   Happy *the gentle:*[b]
         they shall have the earth for their heritage.
5   Happy those who mourn:
         they shall be comforted.
6   Happy those who hunger and thirst for what is right:
         they shall be satisfied.
7   Happy the merciful:
         they shall have mercy shown them.
8   Happy the pure in heart:
         they shall see God.
9   Happy the peacemakers:
         they shall be called sons of God.
10   Happy those who are persecuted in the cause of right:
         theirs is the kingdom of heaven.

11 'Happy are you when people abuse you and persecute you and speak all
12 kinds of calumny against you on my account. ·Rejoice and be glad, for your
reward will be great in heaven; this is how they persecuted the prophets
before you.

Salt of the Earth and Light of the World

13   'You are the salt of the earth. But if salt becomes tasteless, what can
make it salty again? It is good for nothing, and can only be thrown out to be
trampled underfoot by men.
14   'You are the light of the world. A city built on a hill-top cannot be hid-
15 den. No one lights a lamp to put it under a tub; they put it on the lamp-
16 stand where it shines for everyone in the house. ·In the same way your light
must shine in the sight of men, so that, seeing your good works, they may
give the praise to your Father in heaven.

The Fulfilment of the Law

17   'Do not imagine that I have come to abolish the Law or the Prophets. I
18 have come not to abolish but to complete them. ·I tell you solemnly, till
heaven and earth disappear, not one dot, not one little stroke, shall disap-
19 pear from the Law until its purpose is achieved. ·Therefore, the man who
infringes even one of the least of these commandments and teaches others to
do the same will be considered the least in the kingdom of heaven; but the
man who keeps them and teaches them will be considered great in the kingdom of heaven.

b. Or 'the lowly'; the word comes from the Greek version of Ps 37.

The New Standard Higher than the Old

20   'For I tell you, if your virtue goes no deeper than that of the scribes and Pharisees, you will never get into the kingdom of heaven.

21   'You have learnt how it was said to our ancestors: *You must not kill*[c] and
22 if anyone does kill he must answer for it before the court. ·But I say this to you: anyone who is angry with his brother will answer for it before the court; if a man calls his brother "Fool"[d] he will answer for it before the Sanhedrin;[e] and if a man calls him "Renegade"[f] he will answer for it in hell fire.
23 ·So then, if you are bringing your offering to the altar and there remember
24 that your brother has something against you, ·leave your offering there before the altar, go and be reconciled with your brother first, and then come
25 back and present your offering. ·Come to terms with your opponent in good time while you are still on the way to the court with him, or he may hand you over to the judge and the judge to the officer, and you will be thrown
26 into prison. ·I tell you solemnly, you will not get out till you have paid the last penny.

27   'You have learnt how it was said: *You must not commit adultery.*[g] ·But I
28 say this to you: if a man looks at a woman lustfully, he has already commit-
29 ted adultery with her in his heart. ·If your right eye should cause you to sin, tear it out and throw it away; for it will do you less harm to lose one part of
30 you than to have your whole body thrown into hell. ·And if your right hand should cause you to sin, cut it off and throw it away; for it will do you less harm to lose one part of you than to have your whole body go to hell.

31   'It has also been said: *Anyone who divorces his wife must give her a writ*
32 *of dismissal.*[h] ·But I say this to you: everyone who divorces his wife, except for the case of fornication, makes her an adulteress; and anyone who marries a divorced woman commits adultery.

33   'Again, you have learnt how it was said to our ancestors: *You must not*
34 *break your oath, but must fulfil your oaths to the Lord.*[i] ·But I say this to
35 you: do not swear at all, either by *heaven*, since that is God's throne; ·or by *the earth*, since that is *his footstool;* or by Jerusalem, since that is *the city of*
36 *the great king.* ·Do not swear by your own head either, since you cannot
37 turn a single hair white or black. All you need say is "Yes" if you mean yes, "No" if you mean no; anything more than this comes from the evil one.

38
39   'You have learnt how it was said: *Eye for eye and tooth for tooth.*[j] ·But I say this to you: offer the wicked man no resistance. On the contrary, if any-
40 one hits you on the right cheek, offer him the other as well; ·if a man takes
41 you to law and would have your tunic, let him have your cloak as well. ·And
42 if anyone orders you to go one mile, go two miles with him. ·Give to anyone who asks, and if anyone want to borrow, do not turn away.

43   'You have learnt how it was said: *You must love your neighbour* and hate

---

c. Ex 20:13 d. Translating an Aramaic term of contempt. e. The High Court at Jerusalem. f. Apostasy was the most repulsive of all sins. g. Ex 20:14 h. Dt 24:1 i. Ex 20:7 j. Ex 21:24

44 your enemy.*k* ·But I say this to you: love your enemies and pray for those
45 who persecute you; ·in this way you will be sons of your Father in heaven,
for he causes his sun to rise on bad men as well as good, and his rain to fall
46 on honest and dishonest men alike. ·For if you love those who love you,
what right have you to claim any credit? Even the tax collectors*l* do as much,
47 do they not? ·And if you save your greetings for your brothers, are you
48 doing anything exceptional? Even the pagans do as much, do they not? ·You
must therefore be perfect just as your heavenly Father is perfect.

Almsgiving in Secret

1 **6** 'Be careful not to parade your good deeds before men to attract their
notice; by doing this you will lose all reward from your Father in
2 heaven. ·So when you give alms, do not have it trumpeted before you; this is
what the hypocrites do in the synagogues and in the streets to win men's
3 admiration. I tell you solemnly, they have had their reward. ·But when you
4 give alms, your left hand must not know what your right is doing; ·your
almsgiving must be secret, and your Father who sees all that is done in
secret will reward you.

Prayer in Secret

5 'And when you pray, do not imitate the hypocrites: they love to say their
prayers standing up in the synagogues and at the street corners for people to
6 see them. I tell you solemnly, they have had their reward. ·But when you
pray, *go to your private room and, when you have shut your door, pray*ᵃ to
your Father who is in that secret place, and your Father who sees all that is
done in secret will reward you.

How to Pray. The Lord's Prayer

7 'In your prayers do not babble as the pagans do, for they think that by
8 using many words they will make themselves heard. ·Do not be like them;
9 your Father knows what you need before you ask him. ·So you should pray
like this:

> 'Our Father in heaven,
> may your name be held holy,
10 > your kingdom come,
> your will be done,
> on earth as in heaven.
11 > Give us today our daily bread.

---

k. The quotation is from Lv 19:18; the second part of this commandment, not in the written Law, is an Aramaic way of saying 'You do not have to love your enemy'. l. They were employed by the occupying power and this earned them popular contempt.
⁶a. Not a direct quotation but an allusion to the practice common in the O.T., see 2 K 4:33.

12　　　　And forgive us our debts,
　　　　　　as we have forgiven those who are in debt to us.
13　　　　And do not put us to the test,
　　　　　　but save us from the evil one.

14 Yes, if you forgive others their failings, your heavenly Father will forgive you
15 yours; ·but if you do not forgive others, your Father will not forgive your
failings either.

Fasting in Secret

16　'When you fast do not put on a gloomy look as the hypocrites do: they
pull long faces to let men know they are fasting. I tell you solemnly, they
17 have had their reward. ·But when you fast, put oil on your head and wash
your face, so that no one will know you are fasting except your Father who
18 sees all that is done in secret; and your Father who sees all that is done in
secret will reward you.

True Treasures

19　'Do not store up treasures for yourselves on earth, where moths and
20 woodworms destroy them and thieves can break in and steal. ·But store up
treasures for yourselves in heaven, where neither moth nor woodworms
21 destroy them and thieves cannot break in and steal. ·For where your treasures is, there will your heart be also.

The Eye, the Lamp of the Body

22　'The lamp of the body is the eye. It follows that if your eye is sound, your
23 whole body will be filled with light. ·But if your eye is diseased, your whole
body will be all darkness. If then, the light inside you is darkness, what
darkness that will be!

God and Money

24　'No one can be the slave of two masters: he will either hate the first and
love the second, or treat the first with respect and the second with scorn.
You cannot be the slave both of God and of money.

Trust in Providence

25　'That is why I am telling you not to worry about your life and what you
are to eat, nor about your body and how you are to clothe it. Surely life
26 means more than food, and the body more than clothing! ·Look at the birds
in the sky. They do not sow or reap or gather into barns; yet your heavenly
27 Father feeds them. Are you not worth much more than they are? ·Can any of
28 you, for all his worrying, add one single cubit to his span of life? ·And why
worry about clothing? Think of the flowers growing in the fields; they never
29 have to work or spin; ·yet I assure you that not even Solomon in all his rega-

30 lia was robed like one of these. ·Now if that is how God clothes the grass in
the field which is there today and thrown into the furnace tomorrow, will he
31 not much more look after you, you men of little faith? So do not worry; do
not say, "What are we to eat? What are we to drink? How are we to be
32 clothed?" ·It is the pagans who set their hearts on all these things. Your
33 heavenly Father knows you need them all. ·Set your hearts on his kingdom
first, and on his righteousness, and all these other things will be given you
34 as well. So do not worry about tomorrow; tomorrow will take care of itself.
Each day has enough trouble of its own.

Do not Judge

$\begin{smallmatrix} 1 \\ 2 \end{smallmatrix}$ **7** 'Do not judge, and you will not be judged;.·because the judgements you
give are the judgements you will get, and the amount you measure out
3 is the amount you will be given. ·Why do you observe the splinter in your
4 brother's eye and never notice the plank in your own? ·How dare you say to
your brother, "Let me take the splinter out of your eye", when all the time
5 there is a plank in your own? ·Hypocrite! Take the plank out of your own
eye first, and then you will see clearly enough to take the splinter out of
your brother's eye.

Do not Profane Sacred Things

6 'Do not give dogs what is holy;[a] and do not throw your pearls in front of
pigs, or they may trample them and then turn on you and tear you to pieces.

Effective Prayer

7 'Ask, and it will be given to you; search, and you will find; knock, and
8 the door will be opened to you. ·For the one who asks always receives; the
one who searches always finds; the one who knocks will always have the
9 door opened to him. ·Is there a man among you who would hand his son a
stone when he asked for bread? ·Or would hand him a snake when he asked
10 for a fish? ·If you, then, who are evil, know how to give your children what
is good, how much more will your Father in heaven give good things to
those who ask him!

The Golden Rule

11 'So always treat others as you would like them to treat you; that is the
meaning of the Law and the Prophets.

The Two Ways

12 'Enter by the narrow gate, since the road that leads to perdition is wide
and spacious, and many take it; ·but it is a narrow gate and a hard road that
leads to life, and only a few find it.

---

[7]a. The meat of animals which have been offered in sacrifice in the Temple; the application is to the parading
of holy beliefs and practices in front of those who cannot understand them.

False Prophets

13 'Beware of false prophets[b] who come to you disguised as sheep but underneath are ravenous wolves. ·You will be able to tell them by their fruits. Can people pick grapes from thorns, or figs from thistles? ·In the
14 same way, a sound tree produces good fruit but a rotten tree bad fruit. ·A
15 sound tree cannot bear bad fruit, nor a rotten tree bear good fruit. ·Any tree
16 that does not produce good fruit is cut down and thrown on the fire. ·I repeat, you will be able to tell them by their fruits.

The True Disciple

17 'It is not those who say to me, "Lord, Lord", who will enter the kingdom
18 of heaven, but the person who does the will of my Father in heaven. ·When the day[c] comes many will say to me, "Lord, Lord, did we not prophesy in your name, cast out demons in your name, work many miracles in your
19 name?" ·Then I shall tell them to their faces: I have never known you; *away from me, you evil men!*'
20 'Therefore, everyone who listens to these words of mine and acts on them
21 will be like a sensible man who built his house on rock. ·Rain came down, floods rose, gales blew and hurled themselves against that house, and it did
22 not fall: it was founded on rock. ·But everyone who listens to these words of
23 mine and does not act on them will be like a stupid man who built his house
24 on sand. ·Rain came down, floods rose, gales blew and struck that house,
25 and it fell; and what a fall it had!'

The Amazement of the Crowds

26 Jesus had now finished what he wanted to say, and his teaching made a
27 deep impression on the people ·because he taught them with authority, and not like their own scribes.[d] . . .

VII. PASSION AND RESURRECTION

The Conspiracy Against Jesus

1
2 **26** Jesus had now finished all he wanted to say, and he told his disciples, 'It will be Passover, as you know, in two days' time, and the Son of Man will be handed over to be crucified'.
3 Then the chief priests and the elders of the people assembled in the pal-
4 ace of the high priest, whose name was Caiaphas, ·and made plans to arrest
5 Jesus by some trick and have him put to death. ·They said, however, 'It must not be during the festivities; there must be no disturbance among the people'.

---

b. Lying teachers of religion. c. The day of Judgement. d. Doctors of the law, who buttressed their teaching by quotation from the scriptures and traditions.

The Anointing at Bethany

⁶
⁷ Jesus was at Bethany in the house of Simon the leper, when •a woman
came to him with an alabaster jar of the most expensive ointment, and
8 poured it on his head as he was at table. •When they saw this, the disciples
9 were indignant; 'Why this waste?' they said •'This could have been sold at a
10 high price and the money given to the poor.' •Jesus noticed this. 'Why are
you upsetting the woman?' he said to them. 'What she has done for me is
11 one of the good works*a* indeed! You have the poor with you always, but you
12 will not always have me. •When she poured this ointment on my body, she
13 did it to prepare me for burial. •I tell you solemnly, wherever in all the
world this Good News is proclaimed, what she has done will be told also, in
remembrance of her.'

Judas Betrays Jesus

14 Then one of the Twelve, the man called Judas Iscariot, went to the chief
15 priests and said, 'What are you prepared to give me if I hand him over to
16 you?' They paid him thirty silver pieces,*b* and from that moment he looked
for an opportunity to betray him.

Preparations for the Passover Supper

17 Now on the first day of Unleavened Bread*c* the disciples came to Jesus to
say, 'Where do you want us to make the preparations for you to eat the
18 passover?' •Go to so-and-so in the city' he replied 'and say to him, "The
Master says: My time is near. It is at your house that I am keeping Passover
19 with my disciples."' •The disciples did what Jesus told them and prepared
the Passover.

The Treachery of Judas Foretold

20
21 When evening came he was at table with the twelve disciples. •And while
they were eating he said, 'I tell you solemnly, one of you is about to betray
22 me'. •They were greatly distressed and started asking him in turn, 'Not I,
23 Lord, surely?' •He answered, 'Someone who has dipped his hand into the
24 dish with me, will betray me. •The Son of Man is going to his fate, as the
scriptures say he will, but alas for that man by whom the Son of Man is
25 betrayed! Better for that man if he had never been born!' •Judas, who was to
betray him, asked in his turn, 'Not I, Rabbi, surely?' 'They are your own
words' answered Jesus.

---

[26]a. As 'good works', charitable deeds were reckoned superior to almsgiving. b. 30 shekels, the price fixed
for a slave's life, Ex 21:32. c. Unleavened bread was normally to be eaten during the seven days which followed
the Passover supper; here the writer appears to mean the first day of the whole Passover celebration.

The Institution of the Eucharist

26   Now as they were eating,[d] Jesus took some bread, and when he had said
the blessing he broke it and gave it to the disciples. 'Take it and eat;' he
27   said 'this is my body.' ·Then he took a cup, and when he had returned
28   thanks he gave it to them. 'Drink all of you from this,' he said ·'for this is
my blood, the blood of the covenant, which is to be poured out for many for
29   the forgiveness of sins. ·From now on, I tell you, I shall not drink wine until
the day I drink the new wine with you in the kingdom of my Father.'

Peter's Denial Foretold

30   After psalms had been sung[e] they left for the Mount of Olives. ·Then
31   Jesus said to them, 'You will all lose faith in me this night,[f] for the scripture
says: *I shall strike the shepherd and the sheep of the flock will be scattered,[g]*
32   ·but after my resurrection I shall go before you to Galilee'. ·At this, Peter
33   said, 'Though all lose faith in you, I will never lose faith'. ·Jesus answered
34   him, 'I tell you solemnly, this very night, before the cock crows, you will
35   have disowned me three times'. ·Peter said to him, 'Even if I have to die
with you, I will never disown you'. And all the disciples said the same.

Gethsemane

36   Then Jesus came with them to a small estate called Gethsemane; and he
37   said to his disciples, 'Stay here while I go over there to pray'. ·He took
Peter and the two sons of Zebedee with him. And sadness came over him,
38   and great distress. Then he said to them, 'My soul is sorrowful to the point
39   of death. Wait here and keep awake with me.' ·And going on a little further
he fell on his face and prayed. 'My Father,' he said 'if it is possible, let this
40   cup pass me by. Nevertheless, let it be as you, not I, would have it.' ·He
came back to the disciples and found them sleeping, and he said to Peter,
41   'So you had not the strength to keep awake with me one hour? ·You should
be awake, and praying not to be put to the test. The spirit is willing, but the
42   flesh is weak.' ·Again, a second time, he went away and prayed: 'My
Father,' he said 'if this cup cannot pass by without my drinking it, your will
43   be done!' ·And he came back again and found them sleeping, their eyes
44   were so heavy. ·Leaving them there, he went away again and prayed for the
45   third time, repeating the same words. ·Then he came back to the disciples
and said to them, 'You can sleep on now and take your rest. Now the hour
has come when the Son of Man is to be betrayed into the hands of sinners.
46   ·Get up! Let us go! My betrayer is already close at hand.'

---

d. The Passover supper itself, for which exact rules for the blessing of bread and wine were laid down. The
'eating' of v. 21 is the first course, which came before the Passover itself. e. The psalms of praise which end
the Passover supper. f. 'be brought down': the regular expression for the losing of faith through a difficulty or
blow to it. g. Zc 13:7.

The Arrest

47 He was still speaking when Judas, one of the Twelve, appeared, and with
him a large number of men armed with swords and clubs, sent by the chief
48 priests and elders of the people. ·Now the traitor had arranged a sign with
49 them. 'The one I kiss,' he had said 'he is the man. Take him in charge.' ·So
he went straight up to Jesus and said, 'Greetings, Rabbi', and kissed him.
50 ·Jesus said to him, 'My friend, do what you are here for'. Then they came
51 forward, seized Jesus and took him in charge. ·At that, one of the followers
52 of Jesus grasped his sword and drew it; he struck out at the high priest's
53 servant, and cut off his ear. ·Jesus then said, 'Put your sword back, for all
54 who draw the sword will die by the sword. ·Or do you think that I cannot
appeal to my Father who would promptly send more than twelve legions of
55 angels to my defence? ·But then, how would the scriptures be fulfilled that
say this is the way it must be?' ·It was at this time that Jesus said to the
crowds, 'Am I a brigand, that you had to set out to capture me with swords
and clubs? I sat teaching in the Temple day after day and you never laid
56 hands on me.' ·Now all this happened to fulful the prophecies in scripture.
Then all the disciples deserted him and ran away.

Jesus Before the Sanhedrin

57 The men who had arrested Jesus led him off to Caiaphas the high priest,
58 where the scribes and the elders were assembled. ·Peter followed him at a
distance, and when he reached the high priest's palace, he went in and sat
down with the attendants to see what the end would be.
59 The chief priests and the whole Sanhedrin were looking for evidence
against Jesus, however false, on which they might pass the death-sentence.
60 ·But they could not find any, though several lying witnesses came foward.
61 Eventually two stepped forward ·and made a statement, 'This man said, "I
have power to destroy the Temple of God and in three days build it up"'.
62 ·The high priest then stood up and said to him, 'Have you no answer to that?
63 What is this evidence these men are bringing against you?' ·But Jesus was
silent. And the high priest said to him, 'I put you on oath by the living God
64 to tell us if you are the Christ, the Son of God'. ·'The words are your own'
answered Jesus. 'Moreover, I tell you that from this time onward you will
see the *Son of Man seated at the right hand of the Power* and *coming on the*
65 *clouds of heaven.*' ·At this, the high priest tore his clothes and said, 'He has
blasphemed. What need of witnesses have we now? There! You have just
66 heard the blasphemy. ·What is your opinion?' They answered, 'He deserves
to die'.
67 Then they spat in his face and hit him with their fists; others said as they
68 struck him, ·'Play the prophet, Christ! Who hit you then?'

Peter's Denials

69 Meanwhile Peter was sitting outside in the courtyard, and a servant-girl
70 came up to him and said, 'You too were with Jesus the Galilean'. ·But he

denied it in front of them all. 'I do not know what you are talking about' he
71 said. •When he went out to the gateway another servant-girl saw him and
72 said to the people there, 'This man was with Jesus the Nazarene'. •And
73 again, with an oath, he denied it, 'I do not know the man'. •A little later the
bystanders came up and said to Peter, 'You are one of them for sure! Why,
74 your accent gives you away.' •Then he started calling down curses on himself and swearing, 'I do not know the man'. At that moment the cock crew,
75 •and Peter remembered what Jesus had said, 'Before the cock crows you will
have disowned me three times'. And he went outside and wept bitterly.

Jesus is Taken Before Pilate

1
2 **27** When morning came, all the chief priests and the elders of the people met in council to bring about the death of Jesus. •They had him
bound, and led him away to hand him over to Pilate,[a] the governor.

The Death of Judas

3 When he found that Jesus had been condemned, Judas his betrayer was
filled with remorse and took the thirty silver pieces back to the chief priests
and elders. 'I have sinned;' he said 'I have betrayed innocent blood.' 'What
4
5 is that to us?' they replied 'That is your concern.' •And flinging down the
silver pieces in the sanctuary he made off, and went and hanged himself.
6 •The chief priests picked up the silver pieces and said, 'It is against the Law
7 to put his into the treasury; it is blood-money'. •So they discussed the matter
and bought the potter's field with it as a graveyard for foreigners, •and this
8 is why the field is called the Field of Blood today. •The words of the prophet
9 Jeremiah[b] were then fulfilled: *And they took the thirty silver pieces, the sum*
10 *at which the precious One was priced by children of Israel,* •*and they gave*
them for the potter's field, just as the Lord directed me.

Jesus Before Pilate

11 Jesus, then, was brought before the governor, and the governor put to
him this question, 'Are you the king of the Jews?' Jesus replied, 'It is you
12 who say it'. •But when he was accused by the chief priests and the elders he
13 refused to answer at all. •Pilate then said to him, 'Do you not hear how
14 many charges they have brought against you?' •But to the governor's complete amazement, he offered no reply to any of the charges.
15 At festival time it was the governor's practice to release a prisoner for the
16 people, anyone they chose. •Now there was at that time a notorious prisoner
17 whose name was Barabbas. •So when the crowd gathered, Pilate said to
them, 'Which do you want me to release for you: Barabbas, or Jesus who is
18 called Christ?' •For Pilate knew it was out of jealousy that they had handed
him over.

---

[27]a. The Jews had to approach the Roman governor for confirmation and execution of any sentence of
death. b. Actually a free quotation from Zc 11:12–13.

19   Now as he was seated in the chair of judgement, his wife sent him a message, 'Have nothing to do with that man; I have been upset all day by a
dream I had about him'.

20   The chief priests and the elders, however, had persuaded the crowd to
21 demand the release of Barabbas and the execution of Jesus. ·So when the
governor spoke and asked them, 'Which of the two do you want me to
22 release for you?' they said, 'Barabbas'. ·'But in that case,' Pilate said to
them 'what am I to do with Jesus who is called Christ?' They all said, 'Let
23 him be crucified!' ·'Why?' he asked 'What harm has he done?' But they
24 shouted all the louder, 'Let him be crucified!' Then Pilate saw that he was
making no impression, that in fact a riot was imminent. So he took some
water, washed his hands in front of the crowd and said, 'I am innocent of
25 this man's blood. It is your conern.' ·And the people, to a man, shouted
26 back, 'His blood be on us and on our children!' ·Then he released Barabbas
for them. He ordered Jesus to be first scourged[c] and then handed over to be
crucified.

Jesus is Crowned with Thorns

27   The governor's soldiers took Jesus with them into the Praetorium and col-
28 lected the whole cohort round him. ·Then they stripped him and made him
29 wear a scarlet cloak, ·and having twisted some thorns into a crown they put
this on his head and placed a reed in his right hand. To make fun of him
30 they knelt to him saying, 'Hail, king of the Jews!' ·And they spat on him and
31 took the reed and struck him on the head with it. ·And when they had finished making fun of him, they took off the cloak and dressed him in his own
clothes and led him away to crucify him.

The Crucifixion

32   On their way out, they came across a man from Cyrene, Simon by name,
33 and enlisted him to carry his cross. ·When they had reached a place called
34 Golgotha,[d] that is, the place of the skull, ·they gave him wine to drink mixed
35 with gall, which he tasted but refused to drink. ·When they had finished cru-
36 cifying him they shared out his clothing by casting lots, ·and then sat down
and stayed there keeping guard over him.

37   Above his head was placed the charge against him; it read: 'This is Jesus,
38 the King of the Jews'. ·At the same time two robbers were crucified with
him, one on the right and one on the left.

The Crucified Christ is Mocked

39
40   The passers-by jeered at him; they shook their heads ·and said, 'So you
would destroy the Temple and rebuild it in three days! Then save yourself! If
41 you are God's son, come down from the cross!' ·The chief priests with the

---

c. The normal prelude to crucifixion. d. The Aramaic form of the name of which Calvary is the more familiar
Latin equivalent.

42 scribes and elders mocked him in the same way. ·'He saved others;' they
said 'he cannot save himself. He is the king of Israel; let him come down
43 from the cross now, and we will believe in him. ·He puts his trust in God;
now let God rescue him if he wants him. For he did say, "I am the son of
44 God".' ·Even the robbers who were crucified with him taunted him in the
same way.

The Death of Jesus

45 From the sixth hour there was darkness over all the land until the ninth
46 hour.*ᵉ* And about the ninth hour, Jesus cried out in a loud voice, 'Eli, Eli,
lama sabachthani?' that is, *'My God, my God, why have you deserted me?'ᶠ*
47 ·When some of those who stood there heard this, they said, 'The man is call-
48 ing on Elijah', and one of them quickly ran to get a sponge which he dipped
49 in vinegar *ᵍ* and, putting it on a reed, gave it him to drink. ·'Wait!' said the
50 rest of them 'and see if Elijah will come to save him.' ·But Jesus, again crying out in a loud voice, yielded up his spirit.
51 At that, the veil of the Temple*ʰ* was torn in two from top to bottom; the
52 earth quaked; the rocks were split; ·the tombs opened and the bodies of
53 many holy men rose from the dead, ·and these, after his ressurection, came
out of the tombs, entered the Holy City and appeared to a number of peo-
54 ple. ·Meanwhile the centurion, together with the others guarding Jesus, had
seen the earthquake and all that was taking place, and they were terrified
and said, 'In truth this was a son of God.'
55 And many women were there, watching from a distance, the same women
56 who had followed Jesus from Galilee and looked after him. ·Among them
were Mary of Magdala, Mary the mother of James and Joseph, and the
mother of Zebedee's sons.

The Burial

57 When it was evening, there came a rich man of Arimathaea, called
58 Joseph, who had himself become a disciple of Jesus. ·This man went to
Pilate and asked for the body of Jesus. Pilate thereupon ordered it to be
59
60 handed over. ·So Joseph took the body, wrapped it in a clean shroud ·and
put it in his own new tomb which he had hewn out of the rock. He then
61 rolled a large stone across the entrance of the tomb and went away. ·Now
Mary of Magdala and the other Mary were there, sitting opposite the
sepulchre.

The Guard at the Tomb

62 Next day, that is, when Preparation Day*ⁱ* was over, the chief priests and
63 the Pharisees went in a body to Pilate ·and said to him, 'Your Excellency,

---

e. From mid-day to 3 p.m. f. Ps 22:1 g. The rough wine drunk by Roman soldiers. h. There were two curtains in the Temple; most probably this was the inner curtain which guarded the Most Holy Place. i. The day before the sabbath.

we recall that this impostor said, while he was still alive, "After three days I
64 shall rise again". ·Therefore give the order to have the sepulchre kept
secure until the third day, for fear his disciples come and steal him away
and tell the people, "He has risen from the dead". This last piece of fraud
65 would be worse than what went before.' ·'You may have your guard' said
66 Pilate to them. 'Go and make all as secure as you know how.' ·So they went
and made the sepulchre secure, putting seals on the stone and mounting a
guard.

The Empty Tomb. The Angel's Message

1 **28** After the sabbath, and towards dawn on the first day of the week,
Mary of Magdala and the other Mary went to visit the sepulchre.
2 ·And all at once there was a violent earthquake, for the angel of the Lord,
3 descending from heaven, came and rolled away the stone and sat on it. ·His
4 face was like lightning, his robe white as snow. ·The guards were so shaken,
5 so frightened of him, that they were like dead men. ·But the angel spoke;
and he said to the women, 'There is no need for you to be afraid. I know
6 you are looking for Jesus, who was crucified. ·He is not here, for he has
7 risen, as he said he would. Come and see the place where he lay, ·then go
quickly and tell his disciples, "He has risen from the dead and now he is
going before you to Galilee; it is there you will see him". Now I have told
8 you.' ·Filled with awe and great joy the women came quickly away from the
tomb and ran to tell the disciples.

Appearance to the Women

9 And there, coming to meet them, was Jesus. 'Greetings' he said. And the
10 women came up to him and, falling down before him, clasped his feet. ·Then
Jesus said to them, 'Do not be afraid; go and tell my brothers that they must
leave for Galilee; they will see me there'.

Precautions Taken by the Leaders of the People

11 While they were on their way, some of the guard went off into the city to
12 tell the chief priests all that had happened. ·These held a meeting with the
elders and, after some discussion, handed a considerable sum of money to
13 the soldiers with these instructions, 'This is what you must say, "His disci-
14 ples came during the night and stole him away while we were asleep". ·And
should the governor come to hear of this, we undertake to put things right
15 with him ourselves and to see that you do not get into trouble.' ·The soldiers
took the money and carried out their instructions, and to this day that is the
story among the Jews.

Appearance in Galilee. The Mission to the World

16 Meanwhile the eleven disciples set out for Galilee, to the mountain where
17 Jesus had arranged to meet them. ·When they saw him they fell down before

18 him, though some hesitated. ·Jesus came up and spoke to them. He said,
19 'All authority in heaven and on earth has been given to me. ·Go, therefore, make disciples of all the nations; baptise them in the name of the Father and
20 of the Son and of the Holy Spirit,[a] ·and teach them to observe all the commands I gave you. And know that I am with you always; yes, to the end of time.'

▼

from *Luke*

The Three Parables of God's Mercy

1 **15** The tax collectors and the sinners, meanwhile, were all seeking his
2 company to hear what he had to say, ·and the Pharisees and the scribes complained. 'This man' they said 'welcomes sinners and eats with
3 them.' ·So he spoke this parable to them:

The Lost Sheep

4 'What man among you with a hundred sheep, losing one, would not leave the ninety-nine in the wilderness and go after the missing one till he found
5 it? And when he found it, would he not joyfully take it on his shoulders ·and
6 then, when he got home, call together his friends and neighbours? "Rejoice
7 with me," he would say "I have found my sheep that was lost." ·In the same way, I tell you, there will be more rejoicing in heaven over one repentant sinner than over ninety-nine virtuous men who have no need of repentance.

The Lost Drachma

8 'Or again, what woman with ten drachmas would not, if she lost one, light a lamp and sweep out the house and search thoroughly till she found it?
9 ·And then, when she had found it, call together her friends and neighbours?
10 "Rejoice with me," she would say "I have found the drachma I lost." ·In the same way, I tell you, there is rejoicing among the angels of God over one repentant sinner.'

The Lost Son (the 'Prodigal') and the Dutiful Son

11 He also said, 'A man had two sons. ·The younger said to his father,
12 "Father, let me have the share of the estate that would come to me". So the
13 father divided the property between them. ·A few days later, the younger son got together everything he had and left for a distant country where he squandered his money on a life of debauchery.

---

[28]a. This formula is perhaps a reflection of the liturgical usage of the writer's own time.

14 'When he had spent it all, that country experienced a severe famine, and
15 now he began to feel the pinch, ·so he hired himself out to one of the local
16 inhabitants who put him on his farm to feed the pigs. ·And he would willingly have filled his belly with the husks the pigs were eating but no one
17 offered him anything. Then he came to his senses and said, "How many of my father's paid servants have more food than they want, and here am I
18 dying of hunger! ·I will leave this place and go to my father and say: Father,
19 I have sinned against heaven and against you; ·I no longer deserve to be
20 called your son; treat me as one of your paid servants." ·So he left the place and went back to his father.
21 'While he was still a long way off, his father saw him and was moved with pity. He ran to the boy, clasped him in his arms and kissed him tenderly. ·Then his son said, "Father, I have sinned against heaven and against you. I
22 no longer deserve to be called your son." ·But the father said to his servants, "Quick! Bring out the best robe and put it on him; put a ring on his
23 finger and sandals on his feet. ·Bring the calf we have been fattening, and
24 kill it; we are going to have a feast, a celebration, ·because this son of mine was dead and has come back to life; he was lost and is found." And they began to celebrate.
25 'Now the elder son was out in the fields, and on his way back, as he drew
26 near the house, he could hear music and dancing. ·Calling one of the ser-
27 vants he asked what it was all about. ·"Your brother has come" replied the servant "and your father has killed the calf we had fattened because he has
28 got him back safe and sound." ·He was angry then and refused to go in, and
29 his father came out to plead with him; ·but he answered his father, "Look, all these years I have slaved for you and never once disobeyed your orders, yet you never offered me so much as a kid for me to celebrate with my
30 friends. ·But, for this son of yours, when he comes back after swallowing up your property—he and his women—you kill the calf we had been fattening."
31 'The father said, "My son, you are with me always and all I have is
32 yours. But it was only right we should celebrate and rejoice, because your brother here was dead and has come to life; he was lost and is found." '

WRITING AND DISCUSSION QUESTIONS

Informative

1. What evidence is there in the Sermon on the Mount that Jesus was attempting to introduce a completely new ethic? What does he mean when he says that he has come not to "abolish" the Law [of Moses] or the Prophets, but to "complete" them (Matthew 5:17)?
2. Many of the sayings recounted in Matthew 5–7 have made their way into popular speech as code words and catch phrases, for example, "Do not judge, and

you will not be judged'' (Matthew 7:1). List those you recognize, and explain how their meaning may have changed since they were first recorded here.

3. How do the parables in Luke 15 (for example, The Prodigal Son) attempt to soften or ''humanize'' the God that Jesus was trying to portray to his hearers? What traits of God does Jesus emphasize? What is unique about the way Jesus teaches in these settings?

Persuasive

1. The Sermon on the Mount ends with a comment that the people were ''amazed'' at Jesus' teaching because he taught with ''authority.'' Argue that this text does or does not command the same response today.

2. The betrayal, crucifixion, and resurrection narratives of Matthew 26–28 are among the most evocative and influential texts in Western culture; artists and writers in the centuries since have attempted to depict these events and dramatize their significance. Argue that Jesus' sacrificial heroism is the source of the power and endurance of his story and its effects on art, literature, music, and drama. Or argue that the impact is based on the significance of his teaching. Speculate on the source of Jesus' continuing and influential presence in tradition and faith.

3. Had Jesus come to the twentieth-century, what would he find most troubling and in need of attention? Imagine a sermon he might address to a crowd of people in your hometown or on your college campus. Argue that the theme and focus of his sermon would or would not be those of the Sermon on the Mount. How might it compare with the ''word of God'' you have heard preached on television or on the radio?

Personal

1. Which of Jesus' sayings in the Sermon on the Mount is most out of step with your experience in contemporary American society, that is, which seems impossible for you to follow in our culture? Which ones are attractive to you?

2. It is said by some Christians that Christianity is not a set of ''views'' (an elaborate religious system of laws and rules) but ''news'' (the declaration of Christ's unique status as God's son who came to redeem humankind from its hatred and alienation from God). How useful is this notion in understanding the life of Christ? Is there any indication in Matthew 5–7, 26–28, and Luke 15 that the Gospel writers viewed Jesus' ministry in this way?

3. The term ''fundamentalist'' is sometimes used to describe a person who seems dogmatically and rigidly committed to a ''conservative'' religious point of view. Is ''fundamentalism'' a derogatory term? If so, does the term have any positive connotations? Can fundamentalists exist outside of religious faith? For instance, can there be fundamentalist democrats, feminists, or scientists? How might political, social, or scientific fundamentalism differ from religious fundamentalism? Is there a fundamentalist Marxist? republican?

FREDERICK BUECHNER, "JESUS" FROM *PECULIAR TREASURES*

Frederick Buechner (1926–) is a prolific writer of novels and theological volumes. Born and raised in New York City, Buechner began a successful writer's career in 1950 with the publication of *A Long Day's Dying*, which critics hailed as a remarkable first novel for a 24-year old. After completing two more works, Buechner underwent a dramatic conversion to Christianity and sought a seminary degree. Ordained as a Presbyterian minister, Buechner turned his attention to theological writing and to the crafting of novels whose plots and characterizations explored the meaning of the Christian faith in the twentieth century.

The primary audience for Buechner's work comprises two groups of readers—those for whom his personal Christian experience is both instructive and illuminating of their own faith and those who, with little regard for his religious conviction, admire his effortless prose and skillful depiction of the tensions and anxieties of modern life. Buechner has often said that his books are too religious for secular readers and too secular for religious readers. The truth is that throughout the winding path of his career, Buechner has had a consistently enthusiastic, though sometimes modest, readership among both groups. As an autobiographer, theologian, or novelist, Buechner refuses to explain away the tensions of faith or paint a simplistic portrait of the spiritual dimensions of life. In the following selection from Buechner's book *Peculiar Treasures*, Buechner is at his best, playfully, often uproariously updating and reconstructing the lives of prominent Bible characters in vignettes both to illustrate their timeless relevance to our own predicaments and to reveal their essential character, thus making the characters come alive out of the Bible and speak to our own times.

▼

Jesus
FREDERICK BUECHNER

1   Maybe any one day of a life, even the most humdrum, has in it something of the mystery of that life as a whole.

2   People had been flocking up to Jesus the way they always seemed to when word got around that he was in the neighborhood. A Roman officer came up to ask if he would do something for a paralyzed servant back home, and Jesus said he'd go have a look at him. When the officer said he hated to take that much of his time and asked if he couldn't just do something from right there where they were standing, Jesus was so impressed by the way the man trusted him that he told him he'd see to it that what he trusted would happen indeed, and when the officer got home, he found his servant up and around again. Later on, when Jesus dropped in at Peter's house, he found Peter's mother-in-law in bed with a fever, and all he did that time was touch the old lady's hand, but that turned out to be all it took.

3   A scribe showed up and in a burst of enthusiasm said he was all set to follow him any place he went, to which Jesus answered, "Foxes have holes, and

birds have nests, but if you stick with me, you'll find yourself out in the cold" *(Matthew 8:20)*. One of the disciples asked for a few days off to attend his father's funeral, and Jesus said, "Look, you've got to follow me. When life's at stake, burying the dead is for dead-heads" *(Matthew 8:22)*. When he saw a big crowd approaching, he figured he didn't have enough steam left to do much for them that day, so he went and climbed into a boat for a few hours' peace only to find that the disciples were hot on his heels and wanted to go along too. So he took them. Then he lay down in the stern of the boat with a pillow under his head, Mark says *(Mark 4:34)*, and went to sleep.

Matthew leaves out the details about the stern and the pillow presumably   4
because he thought they weren't important, which of course they're not, and yet the account would be greatly impoverished without them. There's so little about him in the Gospels you can actually *see*.

He didn't doze off in the bow where the spray would get him and the white-   5
caps slapped harder. He climbed back into the stern instead. There was a pillow under his head. Maybe somebody put it there for him. Maybe they didn't think to put it there till after he'd gone to sleep, and then somebody lifted his head a little off the hard deck and slipped it under.

He must have gone out like a light because Mark says the storm didn't wake   6
him, not even when the waves got so high they started washing in over the sides. They let him sleep on until finally they were so scared they couldn't stand it any longer and woke him up. They addressed him respectfully enough as Teacher, but what they said was reproachful, petulant almost. "Don't you see that we're all *drowning?*" *(Mark 4:38)*.

It was the wind rather than the disciples that Jesus seems to have spoken to   7
first, as soon as he'd gotten his eyes open. "He rebuked it," Mark says *(Mark 4:38)*. CUT THAT OUT!—you can almost picture him staring it down with the hair lashing his face as he holds on to the gunnels to keep from being blown overboard. He was gentler with the sea. "Take it easy," he said. "Quiet down." When it came the disciples' turn, he said, "Why did you panic?" and then "What kind of faith do you call that?" but they were so impressed to find that the wind had stopped blowing and the sea had flattened out again that they didn't get around to answering him *(Mark 4:39–41)*.

On the far shore there was a cemetery where a crazy man lived covered with   8
scars from where he was always smashing at himself with stones and from the chains they tried to tie him down with when he got even more violent than usual. As soon as the boat landed, he came gibbering out from behind the graves and went tearing down to the beach, but as soon as he saw Jesus, he stopped in his tracks and quieted down. They talked together a little, and then Jesus healed him.

The Roman officer, the sick old lady, the overenthusiastic scribe, the terri-   9
fied disciples, the lunatic—something of who he was and what he was like and what it was like to be with him filters through each meeting as it comes along, but for some reason it's the moment in the boat that says most. The way he lay down, bone tired, and fell asleep with the sound of the lapping waves in his

ears. The way, when they woke him, he opened his eyes to the howling storm and to all the other howling things that he must have known were in the cards for him and that his nap had been a few moments of vacation from. The helplessness of the disciples and the way he spoke to them. The things he said to the wind and to the sea.

10   Lamb of God, Rose of Sharon, Prince of Peace—none of the things people have found to call him has ever managed to say it quite right. You can see why when he told people to follow him, they often did, even if they backed out later when they started to catch on to what lay ahead. If you're religiously inclined, you can see why they went even so far as to call him Messiah, the Lord's Anointed, the Son of God, and call him these things still, some of them. And even if you're not religiously inclined, you can see why it is you might give your immortal soul, if you thought you had one to give, to have been the one to raise that head a little from the heard deck and slip a pillow under it.

(Matthew 8:5–34, compare Mark 4:35–41)

WRITING AND DISCUSSION QUESTIONS

Informative

1. Look carefully at the kinds of details Buechner chooses from the Biblical accounts in the life of Jesus. How does he manage to take the familiar and the assumed and make them seem unusual and contemporary? Analyze Buechner's method of characterization.

Persuasive

1. Argue that the Bible can or cannot be updated or made contemporary. Should it be left alone as a "sacred" text to speak to the present on whatever terms it can? Or, is it the business of Bible readers in our times to make such "translations"? How far can one go before the essential context and message of the original text is distorted?

2. Argue that Buechner is writing from a Christian point of view. Show where this Christian perspective is manifested in Buechner's choice of emphasis and interpretation of character.

Personal

1. Choose a Bible character and extend his or her story beyond the events and situations depicted in the Biblical account. What personality traits or tendencies can you identify and then use for your follow-up narrative? Write a vignette like Buechner's to amuse and enlighten your reader.

2. It has been said that the Bible does not attempt to prove that God exists, but assumes that he does, and its writers proceed along the assumption. In what way does that assumption—that God exists—affect your response to the Bible's sto-

ries and characters? How does your personal belief or lack of belief affect your willingness to read and interpret the Bible?

3. Buechner says in his vignette about Jesus, "something of who he was and what he was like and what it was like to be with him filters through each meeting as it comes along" (paragraph 9). What is it about Jesus that continues to intrigue people even 2000 years later? What attitudes, teachings, or incidents recorded in the Bible do you find significant about him?

▼

C. S. LEWIS, "MEDITATION IN A TOOLSHED" FROM *GOD IN THE DOCK*

C. S. Lewis (1899–1963) was a British scholar and writer who produced many and various works during his lifetime. A poet, literary critic, historian, and a writer of fiction, Lewis is probably best known as the author of the widely read *Chronicles of Narnia*, a seven-book series of the adventures of four schoolchildren in war-time Britain in the marvelous land of Narnia, and of the science fiction trilogy *Out of the Silent Planet*, *Perelandra*, and *That Hideous Strength*. Although much of Lewis's scholarly reputation rests on his meticulous scholarship in medieval and renaissance literature, he also became known as an ardent apologist of Christianity. His *Mere Christianity*, *The Problem of Pain*, and *Surprised by Joy* continue to stay in print and have influenced many present-day Christian believers.

In "Meditation in a Toolshed," Lewis broaches the question of why certain modes of thought and analysis dominate our approach to phenomena. He asks why, in particular, "looking at" (a more objective, "scientific" mode) seems to take precedence over "looking along" (a more subjective, "personal" mode) when we talk about love or religious faith. His aim is to level the ground of discussion a bit, to ask out loud if one mode of perception is intrinsically "truer" or "more reliable" than the other, and then to wrestle with the "either–or" question: must we always assume that "looking at" will yield the final truth? Or can we sometimes trust our intuitive sense of "looking along" to guide us?

▼

Meditation in a Toolshed
C. S. LEWIS

I was standing today in the dark toolshed. The sun was shining out-   *1* side and through the crack at the top of the door there came a sunbeam. From where I stood that beam of light, with the specks of dust floating in it, was the most striking thing in the place. Everything else was almost pitch-black. I was seeing the beam, not seeing things by it.

Then I moved, so that the beam fell on my eyes. Instantly the whole previ-   *2* ous picture vanished. I saw no toolshed, and (above all) no beam. Instead I saw, framed in the irregular cranny at the top of the door, green leaves moving on the branches of a tree outside and beyond that, 90 odd million miles away, the sun. Looking along the beam, and looking at the beam are very different experiences.

3   But this is only a very simple example of the difference between looking at and looking along. A young man meets a girl. The whole world looks different when he sees her. Her voice reminds him of something he has been trying to remember all his life, and ten minutes casual chat with her is more precious than all the favours that all other women in the world could grant. He is, as they say, 'in love'. Now comes a scientist and describes this young man's experience from the outside. For him it is all an affair of the young man's genes and a recognised biological stimulus. That is the difference between looking *along* the sexual impulse and looking *at* it.

4   When you have got into the habit of making this distinction you will find examples of it all day long. The mathematician sits thinking, and to him it seems that he is contemplating timeless and spaceless truths about quantity. But the cerebral physiologist, if he could look inside the mathematician's head, would find nothing timeless and spaceless there—only tiny movements in the grey matter. The savage dances in ecstasy at midnight before Nyonga and feels with every muscle that his dance is helping to bring the new green crops and the spring rain and the babies. The anthropologist, observing that savage, records that he is performing a fertility ritual of the type so-and-so. The girl cries over her broken doll and feels that she has lost a real friend; the psychologist says that her nascent maternal instinct has been temporarily lavished on a bit of shaped and coloured wax.

5   As soon as you have grasped this simple distinction, it raises a question. You get one experience of a thing when you look along it and another when you look at it. Which is the 'true' or 'valid' experience? Which tells you most about the thing? And you can hardly ask that question without noticing that for the last fifty years or so everyone has been taking the answer for granted. It has been assumed without discussion that if you want the true account of religion you must go, not to religious people, but to anthropologists; that if you want the true account of sexual love you must go, not to lovers, but to psychologists; that if you want to understand some 'ideology' (such as medieval chivalry or the nineteenth-century idea of a 'gentleman'), you must listen not to those who lived inside it, but to sociologists.

6   The people who look *at* things have had it all their own way; the people who look *along* things have simply been brow-beaten. It has even come to be taken for granted that the external account of a thing somehow refutes or 'debunks' the account given from inside. 'All these moral ideals which look so transcendental and beautiful from inside', says the wiseacre, 'are really only a mass of biological instincts and inherited taboos.' And no one plays the game the other way round by replying, 'If you will only step inside, the things that look to you

like instincts and taboos will suddenly reveal their real and transcendental nature.'

That, in fact, is the whole basis of the specifically 'modern' type of thought. 7 And is it not, you will ask, a very sensible basis? For, after all, we are often deceived by things from the inside. For example, the girl who looks so wonderful while we're in love, may really be a very plain, stupid, and disagreeable person. The savage's dance to Nyonga does not really cause the crops to grow. Having been so often deceived by looking along, are we not well advised to trust only to looking at?—in fact to discount all these inside experiences?

Well, no. There are two fatal objections to discounting them *all*. And the 8 first is this. You discount them in order to think more accurately. But you can't think at all—and therefore, of course, can't think accurately—if you have nothing to think *about*. A physiologist, for example, can study pain and find out that it 'is' (whatever *is* means) such and such neural events. But the word *pain* would have no meaning for him unless he had 'been inside' by actually suffering. If he had never looked *along* pain he simply wouldn't know what he was looking *at*. The very subject for his inquiries from outside exists for him only because he has, at least once, been inside.

This case is not likely to occur, because every man has felt pain. But it is 9 perfectly easy to go on all your life giving explanations of religion, love, morality, honour, and the like, without having been inside any of them. And if you do that, you are simply playing with counters. You go on explaining a thing without knowing what it is. That is why a great deal of contemporary thought is, strictly speaking, thought about nothing—all the apparatus of thought busily working in a vacuum.

The other objection is this: let us go back to the toolshed. I might have discounted what I saw when looking along the beam (i.e., the leaves moving and the sun) on the ground that it was 'really only a strip of dusty light in a dark shed'. That is, I might have set up as 'true' my 'side vision' of the beam. But then that side vision is itself an instance of the activity we call seeing. And this new instance could also be looked at from outside. I could allow a scientist to tell me that what seemed to be a beam of light in a shed was 'really only an agitation of my own optic nerves'. And that would be just as good (or as bad) a bit of debunking as the previous one. The picture of the beam in the toolshed would now have to be discounted just as the previous picture of the trees and the sun had been discounted. And then, where are you?

In other words, you can step outside one experience only by stepping inside 11 another. Therefore, if all inside experiences are misleading, we are always misled. The cerebral physiologist may say, if he chooses, that the mathematician's thought is 'only' tiny physical movements of the grey matter. But then what about the cerebral physiologist's own thought at that very moment? A second physiologist, looking at it, could pronounce it also to be only tiny physical movements in the first physiologist's skull. Where is the rot to end?

The answer is that we must never allow the rot to begin. We must, on pain 12 of idiocy, deny from the very outset the idea that looking *at* is, by its own nature, intrinsically truer or better than looking *along.* One must look both *along* and *at* everything. In particular cases we shall find reason for regarding the one or the other vision as inferior. Thus the inside vision of rational thinking must be truer than the outside vision which sees only movements of the grey matter; for if the outside vision were the correct one all thought (including this thought itself) would be valueless, and this is self-contradictory. You cannot have a proof that no proofs matter. On the other hand, the inside vision of the savage's dance to Nyonga may be found deceptive because we find reason to believe that crops and babies are not really affected by it. In fact, we must take each case on its merits. But we must start with no prejudice for or against either kind of looking. We do not know in advance whether the lover or the psychologist is giving the more correct account of love, or whether both accounts are equally correct in different ways, or whether both are equally wrong. We just have to find out. But the period of brow-beating has got to end.

WRITING AND DISCUSSION QUESTIONS

Informative

1. Examine Lewis' opening analogy about the toolshed. Explain what he means by "looking *at*" and "looking *along.*" How are they "very different experiences"?
2. Lewis says "people who look *at* things have had it all their own way; the people who look *along* things have simply been brow-beaten" (paragraph 6). Who makes up these two groups of people? According to Lewis, the "*at* people" have had what their way? In his view, what are the consequences of "looking *at*" things?
3. Although Lewis' essay is not explicitly a defense of religious faith per se, he clearly lobbies on behalf of the legitimacy of the "eyes of faith" ("looking *along*") as a useful and insightful mode of perception. Where does he make this argument? Is he essentially setting up a science versus faith dichotomy, or is he setting up something more elaborate?

Persuasive

1. Rhetorician Kenneth Burke has said that "a way of seeing is also a way of not seeing." Apply this maxim to Lewis's argument, and argue that one way of interpreting and experiencing the world could prevent one from learning truth from another or alternative view.
2. Argue that both "looking *at*" and "looking *along*" are necessary modes of thought and interpretation, using examples of phenomena that require a balanced approach to understanding them.
3. Lewis suggests that sometimes "looking at" becomes reductive or forces us to remove the very basis of rational thought: "You cannot have a proof that no proofs matter" (last paragraph). Argue in favor of or against this suggestion. Has

this tendency to becoming reductive occurred in your experience or education? Is it possible to avoid it?

Personal

1. Think of something that you tend to look *at* instead of *along* or vice versa. Use Lewis' distinction to change the way you would normally examine and respond to it. Record your experience, and account for the changes in perception and response created by the different way of looking at it.
2. Do you think it is true that people today tend to implicitly trust the scientific point of view on all matters? Do you regard scientists as infallible and science's pronouncements as the ''final word'' on a matter? When would you deliberately dissent from a ''scientific finding''?
3. Ultimately, Lewis' essay calls on us to examine carefully what we consider ''knowledge.'' We are, of course, not always, or even very much of the time, self-conscious about the truths and beliefs we hold as knowledge. Our presuppositions and assumptions rule us until something arises to challenge them. Sometimes this results in a ''conversion'' experience by which we suddenly see the world differently than before. Have you ever undergone such a conversion—religious or otherwise? If so, what triggered it, what were the most important influences? Can you identify a particular assumption you once held that you have since changed or rejected? Provide an account of this change and explain the process of replacing it.

▼

HUGH NISSENSON, "THE LAW" FROM *A PILE OF STONES*

Hugh Nissenson (1933–) is a Jewish–American writer who made his debut in 1965 with a collection of superbly crafted short stories, *A Pile of Stones*, that poignantly addresses such eternal issues as the meaning of existence, the brutality of life, humankind's ambiguous relationship with an apparently absent God, and the problem of living as a Jew in a world hostile to Judaism's heritage and beliefs. Unlike some other contemporary Jewish writers, Nissenson has declared that there is no redemptive power for the Jew who wishes to find a place in the modern world by returning to tradition or ancestral heritage. By this stance, Nissenson is a vivid contrast to another prominent Jewish writer, Isaac Bashevis Singer, whose stories call all people of faith to a recognition and theological appreciation of God's actions in history. Nissenson shares this much with Singer, however: a fascination with religious mythology, including Christian, Greek, Hindu, and Jewish—and he uses it effectively in the structure and imagery of his stories.

  A Pile of Stones is in many ways an autobiographical volume that explores the theme of free will or freedom of choice in the lives of Jewish men and women, and their children, who endured the horrible experience and memory of the Holocaust that took more than six million Jewish lives during World War II. This wrestling with destiny and the efficacy of one's choices in dealing squarely and forthrightly with the past is one of the major themes in "The Law," the first story in *A Pile of Stones*. Danny, a young Jewish boy facing adulthood, elects to embrace the heritage of his people even in the midst of his cousin Joe's skepticism and the haunted memories of his father's harrowing experiences in a Nazi concentration camp. Nissenson's concrete, sensitive portrayal of the generational differences between Danny and his father, Willi, and the intellectual distancing that separates Joe and Willi in their response to a common history make this story one of his best.

▼

The Law
HUGH NISSENSON

1   On and off, that whole summer, I wondered what my uncle Willi was going to do about his son. The boy, Danny, was going to be thirteen on the twelfth of July, and as early as February, I remembered, Willi was talking about having his Bar Mitzvah at their Temple in Queens; the whole works—a service in the morning and a party for the family and their friends in the afternoon at their home.

"Nothing ostentatious, you understand," he told me. "Drinks and hors d'oeuvres. You know: franks, little pigs in a blanket, or lox on pieces of toast."

I said that I thought that the party was a nice idea but, though it was really none of my business, maybe that was enough.

"I mean why the whole service? You don't want to make him go through all of that speechmaking."

2   "Ah, but he insists," said Willi.

"Does he?"

"So help me. He says he wouldn't think of having one without the other, and his doctor says it's all right. The doctor says if he really wants to speak, then by all means. Treat him normal."

"What doctor?"

"Rhinehart. Didn't I tell you? Rhinehart's been treating him since the Fall."

3   "Who's Rhinehart?"

"I thought you knew. Didn't Helene tell you? Speech therapy. One of the big speech men in New York. He's connected with the Medical Center. Just since September, and he's done wonders."

"I didn't know. I'm glad to hear it."

"Will you come to the service?" he asked.

"When will it be?"

4   "The weekend after the Fourth. That Saturday, in the morning. The Fourth is on a Monday. That Saturday, the ninth," he said.

"Sure."

"Ten o'clock in the morning. Don't you forget now. Mark it down." he said.

I never thought he'd go through with it. For as long as I could remember, 5
his son had a terrible stammer. Just to say "hello" was an effort. He had a
habit of closing his eyes as though he'd been told to visualize the word beforehand. It was agonizing to watch: the shut eyes, the deep breath, the pulse beating in his neck, the chin jerking spasmodically, and the spit gathering in the
corners of his mouth.

"H-h-h-hello, Joe," he'd greet me. "How-how-how are ya?"

Relaxed, silent, he seemed another kid, somehow altogether different-look- 6
ing, resembling his mother, with a placid oval face, and large dark eyes, beautiful eyes, with long curly lashes, and delicate hands with bitten nails that were
always in his mouth. To avoid speaking as much as possible, he had developed
the facility of listening attentively, fixing those eyes on you, with a faint smile
on his lips, nodding or shaking his head as the occasion demanded, so that he
gave the impression of following whatever you said with a kind of ravenous
intensity that made you self-conscious of being able to speak normally yourself.
An intelligent defense. That he was really brilliant, there wasn't any doubt.

"An 'A' average in school," Willi told me, throwing his arm about the boy's 7
shoulders, "He loves history," he added, as a kind of concession to me. A
pause, as though I was supposed to test the boy's knowledge. Helene, his
mother, glanced at me with alarm. I remained silent, smiling with a nod, and it
seemed to me that the boy himself gave me a look of gratitude that went unno-
ticed by his father. At the time, I was teaching American history to the tenth
grade in a private school on the Upper East Side. It was easy to imagine Danny's suffering in class, called upon by his teacher to recite, straining to express
himself, while the other kids laughed behind their hands, or mimicked him,
spraying the air with spit.

Anyhow, that was in February, as I've said. Came the summer and I didn't 8
see much of them at first. I spent most of my time in the Forty-second Street
Library doing research for my Ph.D. thesis on the Alien and Sedition Act. A
couple of times in May Willi called me on the phone to invite me out to dinner,
but I was too busy. He was really the only family I had left, but with one thing
and another, we were never really close. My mother's younger brother, a man
in his middle forties, short and powerfully built, running now to fat, with red
cheeks and a fringe of dark hair about the crown of his head that resembled a
monk's tonsure, he always reminded me of the picture of the jolly monk on the
labels of imported German beer. He had been born in Germany, as a matter of
fact. My mother had written and tried to persuade him to leave the country in
1935, but he intended to study law at Heidelberg, so the Nazis caught him and
deported him to Bergen Belsen where he managed to survive the war, coming
to this country in 1947, just before my mother's death. He had written a book
about his experiences—*Mein Erlebnis*—that was never actually published, but
everyone who knew him felt they had read it anyhow, from the way he constantly spoke of what had happened to him. When he spoke about the concentration camps, he sounded as if he was quoting from heart from a manuscript.
He generally loved to talk, and if it was a blow to his pride that his son had so

much trouble in getting a word out straight, he never let on, as far as I could see.

9   "Stammering? What's a stammer?" I once heard him tell the boy. "It's a sign of greatness. . . . Yes, I mean it. Demosthenes stammered, and Moses. *Moshe Ribenue.* Mose our Teacher himself."

"M-M-Moses?"

"The luckiest thing that ever happened, believe you me."

"H-h-how l-lucky?"

"How many Commandments are there?"

10   His son held up his ten fingers.

"Ten! There you are!" said his father. "Believe me, if he didn't have a stammer he would have given us a hundred. . . . Luck, eh? Luck or not?"

11   The boy laughed. His father had a way with words, there was no doubt of it, making a good living as a paper-box salesman for a company at New Hyde Park on the Island. I imagine he cleared over twenty thousand a year. He lived nicely enough, in one of those red-brick, two-story, semi-detached houses on Eighty-first Avenue in Queens, with a little rose garden in the back and a pine-paneled bar and rumpus room in the cellar where he intended to have the party after the Bar Mitzvah. I finally went out for dinner the second week in May. We had a drink downstairs.

12   "You can't help it," he said. "I figure about thirty, thirty-five people. What can I do? Helene's family, friends from the office, the kid's friends from school, the rabbi and his wife. Thirty-five, maybe more. . . . Helene says with that many we'll have to serve lunch. I thought maybe a cold buffet. We'll eat down here. I'm having it air-conditioned."

"It's a nice idea."

"It'll be a nice party, you wait and see. How about another Scotch?"

"Just a drop."

"Chivas Regal. Twenty years old. Like velvet water."

13   "Just a splash of water," I told him. "Where's Danny?"

"What's the time?"

"Just six."

"Be home any minute. He's at Hebrew school."

"How's he doing?"

14   "Wonderful. That rabbi does wonders. The boy can already read. Of course, it's all modern. To help him he has a recording of the Haftorah he has to say, put out by some company in New Jersey."

"Sounds like a wonderful idea."

"He's reciting from Numbers."

"I don't know too much about it."

"It's some of the Laws, and how they should organize themselves in the march through the desert."

15   "And Danny likes it?" I asked.

"You should hear him. The rabbi, the doctor, Rhinehart—I told you: everybody helps. Ask him yourself."

He came home about six-thirty, with his notebook under his arm. He had   *16*
grown a little since I saw him last, become a little leaner, with bigger hands
and feet, bony wrists. There was a slight down on his cheeks and upper lip, but
so far as I could tell his speech was about the same. He went through the convulsions just to say hello—the suspended breath and shut eyes, the blue veins
swelling on the sides of his neck. When we sat down at the dinner table, he
remained standing by his place, with a loaf of bread covered by a linen napkin
set before him, and a black silk skull-cap on the back of his bead.

"*B-b-b-b-aruch atar a-adonoi,*" he mumbled—the Hebrew blessing of the
bread—and when he finished, he looked pale and wiped the spit from his lips
with the back of his hand.

"How was that?" Willi asked me.

"Nice."

"Practice. Practice makes perfect."

His son lowered his quivering eyelids. Helene served the roast chicken and   *17*
wild rice, with little brown potatoes.

"You never learned the language?" Willi spoke to me again.

"I was never Bar Mitzvahed; no."

"Neither was I."

"Really?"

"In Germany, when I was growing up, it was—unfashionable to be given a   *18*
Jewish education." He tore at a chicken wing with his teeth. "Once in a while
in the camp I would run into somebody who could speak Hebrew. It's really an
ugly language. It's just that . . . I don't know. It was nice to hear it spoken. It
was *verboten,* of course, but still . . . how can I explain? It was something out of
our past, the really distant past. It somehow seemed to me to be the only part
of our consciousness that was left—uncontaminated. Not like Yiddish. . . . I
always hated Yiddish. I used to pride myself on my command of German, the
way I wrote particularly, a really educated style, but I learned to hate it. Sometimes for weeks I couldn't bring myself to say a word. The language of the
S.S. . . . ."

"T-t-t-tell about H-H-Heinz," interrupted his son.   *19*

"Eat your chicken," his mother said. The tone of her voice made me look at
her with surprise: black hair with a faint reddish tinge, and long curling eye-
lashes that shadowed her prominent cheekbones. Lucky enough to have been
spared the later horrors, she too was a refugee, coming from Germany in
1936. I suddenly sensed that she disapproved and was even a little frightened
of Willi's imposition of the whole thing on the boy's consciousness. In front of
me, though, "eat your chicken" was all that she said. We finished the rest of
the meal in silence—lemon meringue pie and coffee—and Willi, the boy, and
myself went into the living room and sat down on the sofa.

"Cigar?" Willi asked.

"No thanks."

He belched and lit up, and began to pick his front teeth with the folded cel-   *20*
lophane. "How about a little brandy?"

"That'd be nice."

21   "Napoleon: the best," he said, pouring some into two snifters that the boy had brought in from the kitchen. "Wonderful. . . . Too good. I'm getting too fat, I know. Soft," he said, patting his paunch. "The doctor tells me I ought to lose at least twenty pounds. An irony, eh? Did you know that when I got out of Belsen I weighed ninety pounds? Ninety, mind you, and now, like all the other Americans, I'm to die of overweight."

22   His eyes gleamed as though he derived some sort of satisfaction out of the thought.

"A living skeleton," he went on. "You must have seen photos after the liberation of a place like that. I don't have to tell you. . . ."

23   But he did, as I knew he would; he went on and on, while his son listened, his legs tucked under him, biting on one fingernail after the other.

"You can't know—thank God—not you, or Danny here, or Helene. . . . No one who was not there can even guess what it was like to be so hungry, to be literally starving to death on two slices of bread a day, and a pint of watery soup with a snip of turnip in it, if you're lucky. Twice a week a spoonful of rancid butter, and an ounce of sausage or cheese. . . . And the worst of it knowing that it's endless, knowing that no matter how hungry you are today there's absolutely no possibility of getting anything more to eat tomorrow but that the anguish will simply grow and grow and grow. . . . Words. . . ." He shrugged. "You aren't really listening and I can't blame you. What good are words to describe such things?"

24   He sucked on his cigar and screwed up his eyes to watch the smoke, as thick and white as milk, gather in the cone of light above the lamp on the coffee table. "There were two obsessions that everyone had. Ask anyone who was in such a place. Have you ever read any books about them? . . . Food first: dreaming about food, sitting down to a meal like we just had, and eating till you burst, and second: just staying alive so that you would be able to describe what was happening to you. Everyone wanted to write a book. Seriously. Just to tell the world, as though to convince ourselves as well that such things were really happening, that we were actually living through them. I wrote *Mein Erlebnis* in six weeks. . . ."

25   He waved the smoke away, and again his narrowed eyes had that peculiar gleam. The boy sat perfectly motionless, with his lips slightly parted in expectation of his father to continue, and for the first time I began to understand the nature of Willi's compulsion to talk so much about what he had endured. Triumph. There was a flash of triumph in his eyes as he regarded his son. It was as if I were listening to a mountain climber—what's his name, the one who climbed Everest—or the first man who will land on the moon and live to tell about it. He talked and talked, partly, I am sure, because it was essentially a personal victory that he was describing—and gloating over, in spite of himself. It was a display of prowess before his son; the supreme success, perhaps even the high point of his life, that he among all those millions managed to live through it all.

From the kitchen came the swish of water and the hum of the automatic   *26*
dishwasher. Helene came into the living room with a bowl of fruit.

"An apple, Joe?"

"No thanks."

Willi peeled a banana, and to be polite perhaps, or maybe because of his
wife's feelings about talking as he did in front of the boy, he began to ask me
about my work.

"The Alien and Sedition Act, eh?" he said. "Yes. . . . Yes, interesting and
significant. . . . When was it again?"

"S-s-seventeen n-ninety-eight," said Danny.   *27*

Willi questioned me with a raised eyebrow. "That's right," I told him.

He grinned. "I told you he loves his history."

"He's right a hundred percent."

"Who was it?" Willi went on. "President Adams, wasn't it? Against the Bill
of Rights—the first suspension of habeas corpus."

"And M-M-Marshall," began the boy.

His father laughed with his mouth full of banana. "You can see for yourself   *28*
he knows much more about it than me." The boy smiled, flushed to his temples with pride. "Still, I remember: No freedom of speech, hundreds of editors
thrown into jail for criticizing the government, the prisons packed with dissenters." From his voice, he sounded as though he momentarily somehow enjoyed
it.

"About twenty-five, all told," I said.   *29*

"You don't say. Just twenty-five?"

"That's it."

He grinned again. "How about that! America, you see?" he said to his wife.
"Imagine. A whole stink over that."

"There was more to it than that," I told him.

"Of course, but still—a crisis! Genuine indignation over the fate of just   *30*
twenty-five men. . . ."

"Yes, partly," I told him, suddenly weary, bleary-eyed from the dinner and
the drinks.

"And the Jews?" he asked me.

"I don't understand."

"There was no particular repression of the Jews, as such?"

"I never thought about it, to tell you the truth."

He laughed. "Seriously," I went on. "The law was directed against foreign-   *31*
ers, mostly—the British and the French. French spies, for example. There was
a lot of spying going on, and the law forced a lot of foreigners to leave the
country."

"But nothing was specifically directed against the Jews."   *32*

"No. Why should there have been?"

Another laugh. "What's so funny?" I asked him.

"Don't you know the joke?"

"Which one?"

33   "You must have heard it. . . . The S.S. man in Berlin who grabs a Jew by the collar and kicks him in the shins. 'Tell me, Jew, who's responsible for all of Germany's troubles?' The Jew trembles. His teeth absolutely chatter; his knees knock together. 'The Jews, of course,' he answers. 'Good,' says the S.S. man. 'The Jews and the bareback riders in the circus,' the little Jew goes on. 'Why the bareback riders in the circus?' the S.S. man asks. 'Aha,' comes the answer. 'Exactly! So *nu?* Why the Jews?'"

34   The boy laughed, slapping his thigh, guffawing until the tears came into his eyes, as if he were delighted to find a release in a sound that he could express without impediment.

35   "Yes, yes," Willi continued, taking a last bite of the banana and throwing the peel into an ashtray. "He laughs, and it's true, the absurdity, and yet there's something more. There's a reason. . . . Why the Jews? There's the psychology of a Heinz to contend with, and not an isolated pathological case either, but common. More common than you'd care to know."

36   The boy shifted his position, leaning toward his father with one hand on the arm of the sofa, and both feet on the floor.

"Have a piece of fruit," Helene told me.

"No thanks. Who's Heinz?" I asked.

37   "*Her Hauptsturmfuehrer Berger,*" said Will. "You know the type. Tall and blond, beautiful, really, the very image of manly perfection that you can see for yourself, today, just by going to the movies. . . . A movie star, so help me; six foot two at least, with straight blond hair, white flashing teeth, a positively captivating smile—dimples at the corners of his mouth—beautiful blue eyes. . . . The uniform? Perfection. Designed for him; tailor-made for that slim, hard body, broad shoulders. . . ." He spread his stubby hands in the air, reminding me more than ever of that monk making an invocation. "Black, all black and belted with what do you call them? Riding pants. Jodhpurs, and gleaming black boots. . . ."

38   "But I still don't understand," I said. "Who is he?"

"*Was,*" corrected Willi. "He was a guard in the camp. After the war the British caught him and he was tried and hanged. . . . *Was.* . . . Unfortunate. I mean it, too. Seriously. No one had the good sense to study him instead: how he used to stand, for example—very significant—with the thumb of one hand, his left hand, I remember, stuck in his belt, and the other grasping a braided riding whip that he would tap against those boots. The boots, the belt, the buckle, the buttons, all flashing in the sun—enough to blind you, believe me. White teeth, that dimpled smile. . . . He was convicted of murder. One day he killed a child, a little girl of seven. . . . In the camp, some of the barracks had three tiers of wooden beds along the wall, bare planks to sleep on, *boxen* in the jargon. We slept together packed like sardines. Often someone would die in the night, but it was impossible to move. We would sleep with the dead, but no matter. . . . Where was I?"

"The child," I said.

39   "Ah, yes. One of the *boxen* in the women's barracks was coming apart; one

leg was coming off. Three tiers, mind you; hundreds of pounds of timber. . . .
For some reason the child was on the floor, directly beneath it, on her hands
and knees. Perhaps he—Heinz—had ordered it so. I don't know. I don't think
so. She must just have been looking for something. A crust of bread, a crumb,
perhaps, and in walks the *Hauptsturmfuehrer* smiling all the while as though to
charm the ladies, immediately sizing up the situation; perfect. The child
beneath the rickety bed, the girl's mother, Frau Schwarz, in one corner, binding up her swollen legs with a few rags.

"'*Gnädige Frau* . . .' he greets her—the mother, who stands up nervously
twisting a rag about her wrist.

"'Hilda!' she screams. . . . Not even a Jewish name, mind you; a good Ger-   40
man name. . . . 'Hilda!' The child begins to rise, but it's too late. With a flick of
his boot, a movement of that polished toe, our Heinz has already acted, kicking
out the loose timber, bringing down the whole thing on the child's back. . . . A
broken back.

"'Mamma!' she cries. 'I can't move! My legs!' For a day and a half like that   41
until she goes into convulsions and dies in her mother's arms. The woman
comes to me and reproaches herself because she hasn't got the courage to
commit suicide.

"'After all,' she says, 'I have the means. . . .' She's referring to the rags that   42
she has woven into a noose. 'Just the courage is lacking. Mr. Levy, what's the
matter with me?' She goes mad, and before she dies she wanders about the
camp asking everyone to strangle her. . . . She even comes to Heinz. It was just
outside the latrines. I witnessed this myself. Apparently he doesn't even
remember who she is. He shoos her away, those beautiful blue eyes clouded
for just an instant in complete bewilderment.

"'*Verrüct*,' he tells me. 'Insane.' With a shrug. I'm busy on my hands and   43
knees scrubbing the concrete floor with a brush and a pail of lye and water, not
daring to look up, blinded by those boots.

"'Here, here, Levy. No; to the left. Put some elbow grease into it.'

"A fanatic for order and cleanliness, you understand. He used to speak with   44
me a great deal. I couldn't imagine why. Perhaps because we were both about
the same age. He would constantly ask me questions about the Jews—technical
questions, so to speak, about our beliefs, about the Torah, for example, all the
Laws. He seemed sincerely interested and, as far as I could tell, he was genuinely disappointed when he realized that I knew next to nothing and had been
educated like himself as a good, middle-class German—*Gymnasium*, and two
semesters at Heidelberg. One day he was absolutely flabbergasted to find out
that for the life of me I couldn't even recite the Ten Commandments. I couldn't
get more than five, and not in order, either. 'Tsk! Tsk! Levy.' He shook that
beautiful head and began reciting them all.

"'I am the Lord thy God who brought thee forth out of the land of Egypt,   45
out of the house of bondage. . . . Thou shalt have no other gods before me.'
Etc., etc. All of them, the whole business. . . . Imagine the scene. It was a Sunday, I remember, rest day, the one day off from mankilling labor the whole

week. I had gone outside the barracks to get a little sun. Imagine it, I tell you. A vast desert, our own Sinai surrounding us, rolling sand dunes, green wooden shacks set in rows. In the distance, the silver birch trees of the women's camp like a mirage. The wire mesh gate of the main entrance to my right that always reminded me of the entrance to a zoo. Here and there, scattered on the ground, all heaped together, the mounds of bodies, the living dead and the dead—stiff, open eyes, gaping mouths, all heaped together, indistinguishable. It was early spring, and warm, with a weak sun, gray clouds, cumuli, with a flat base and rounded outlines, piled up like mountains in the western sky. . . . I remember that distinctly—cumuli. . . . It was a matter of life and death, learning to tell one type of cloud from another—the promise of a little rain. There was never enough water. Just two concrete basins to supply the entire camp. We were slowly dying of thirst in addition to everything else. I remember thinking that if the rain does come I shall try and remain outside the barracks as long as I can after roll call, with my mouth open. Crazy thoughts. What was it? Chickens, young *Truthahnen*—turkeys drown that way in the rain, too stupid to close their mouths. . . . Insane, disconnected thoughts while, according to regulation, I stood rigidly at attention, with my chin in, and chest out, my thumbs along the crease in my striped prison pants, as Heinz drones on and on.

46   " 'Honor thy father and thy mother. . . . Thou shalt not murder. . . .' On and on to the end, and then, with what I can only describe as a shy expression on his face, the explanation:

47   " 'We live in Saxony,' he tells me. 'Absolutely charming, Levy. Do you know East Prussia? Ah, the orchard and the flower beds—roses, red and white roses, growing in front of the church. My father's church. A pastor, Levy, and his father before him and before that. Three generations of pastors. When I was young, I thought I would go into the Church myself. I have the religious temperament.'

    " 'Yes, sir. *Jawohl, Herr Hauptsturmfuehrer.*'

    " 'Does that astonish you?'

    " 'Not at all, *Mein Herr.*'

48   " 'It does, of course. . . . Sundays. . . . Ah, a day like today. The church bells echoing in the valley and the peasants in their black suits and creaking shoes shuffling between those rose beds to listen to Papa thunder at them from the pulpit, slamming down his fist. "Love, my friends! It is written that we are to love our neighbors as ourselves." The fist again. "Love!" he shouts, and I would begin to tremble, literally begin to shake. . . . Why, Levy? I often asked myself. You ought to know. Jews are great psychologists. Freud. . . .'

    " 'I don't know, *Herr Hauptsturmfuehrer.*'

49   " 'A pity. . . . He would preach love and all I could see from that front pew was that great fist—the blond hair on the backs of the fingers, the knuckles clenched, white. . . . That huge fist protruding from the black cuff like the hand of God from a thunder cloud. . . .' That was his image, I swear it. So help me, a literary mind. *'Die grosse Faust ist aus der schwarzen Manschette heraus ge-*

streckt wie Gottes-hand aus einer Sturmwolke. Yet, to be honest,' Heinz went on, 'he never struck me. Not once in my whole life, and I was never what you could call a good child, Levy. Secret vices, a rebellious spirit that had to be broken. . . . And obedience, was doubly difficult for the likes of me, but, as I've said, whenever I misbehaved, he never once laid a hand on me. . . . Love. . . . He spoke about love and was silent. Talk about psychology! That silence for days on end; all he had to do was say nothing and I would lie in my bed at night, trembling. Can you explain that, Levy? I would lie awake praying that he would beat me instead, smash me with that fist, flay my back with his belt rather than that love, that silent displeasure. He had thin, pale lips, with a network of wrinkles at the corner of his mouth. . . . No dimples. I get my dimples from my mother. . . . To please him, I would learn whole passages of the Bible by heart; your Bible, Levy.'

"He tapped his whip against the top of his boots.   50

"'Tell me, Levy. . . .'

"'Yes, sir?'

"I know the Jews; a gentle people. Tell me honestly. Did your father ever beat you?'

"'No, sir.'

"'Not once?'   51

"'Never, sir.'

"'A gentle people, as I've said, but lax in your education, wouldn't you say?'

"'Yes, sir,'

"'Well, then we must remedy that. . . .'"

For the first time, the flow of words faltered. Willi paused to relight his   52
cigar, and then, as though it had left a bad taste in his mouth, snubbed it out in the ashtray and picked a fleck of tobacco from the tip of his tongue. "Like some dog," he finally went on. "As if he were training some animal. . . . That whip across the back, the bridge of the nose, the eyes. . . . All afternoon I stood at attention while those clouds gathered and it began to rain, until I could repeat it all word for word. 'I am the Lord thy God who brought thee forth out of the land of Egypt.' He hit me in the adam's apple. I could hardly speak. The rain came down my face. . . ."

Another silence. The automatic dishwasher had long since stopped. Helene   53
bit into an apple and looked at her watch. Before she had a chance to speak, the boy shook his head.

"Never mind," she told him. "It's late. Past ten. Time for bed."

"Ten?" I repeated, standing up. "I've got to go myself."

"Say good night to Joe," said Helene to her son.

"You w-w-w-wanna hear my r-r-record?" He asked me. "It'll only t-t-take a minute."

"O.K.; for a minute."   54

His room was at the head of the stairs. I followed him up and he shut the door.

"Y-you never heard about H-H-Heinz before?"

"Never."

"I have; o-often. It used to give me b-bad dreams."

55   On top of his desk was a phonograph record. He put it on the portable phonograph that stood in one corner of the room. For a time, sitting on the bed
while the boy put on his pajamas, I listened to the deep voice chanting in the
unintelligible tongue.

"D-don't you understand?"

"Not much," I said.

"How—how come you were never B-B-Bar Mitzvahed?"

"I wasn't as lucky as you. My father was dead, and my mother didn't care
one way or the other."

56   "M-Mama doesn't care either," he said, tying his bathrobe around his waist.
He rejected the record and stood by the window that faced the rose garden,
biting his thumbnail.

"D-d-do you believe in G-G-God?"

"I don't know."

"I do—do."

"You're lucky there too."

"D-don't you ever pray?"

"No."

"I d-d-do; often."

57   I imagined that, rather like his laughter, that too must have been a wonderful relief; praying in silence, grateful and convinced that he was able to communicate something without a stammer.

"D-d-do you know what I p-pray for?" he asked me.

"What?"

"A-actually it's a s-s-secret."

"You can tell me if you like."

58   "S-sometimes, y-you know, when I think of all th-those people at the Temple—at the B-B-Bar Mitzvah, I mean—I get into a sweat."

"It'll be all right."

"There'll be h-hundreds of people there, M-Mama's whole family, G-G-
Goldman's parents and all his family, and all their f-f-friends."

"Who's Goldman?"

59   "He's a f-f-fink. Sammy Goldman. We're being B-B-Bar Mitzvahed together.
He's rich. His father owns a chain of delicatessens. He's t-told everybody about
me. He didn't want to g-go with me. He has p-pimples from p-p-playing with
himself."

"It's late," I told him, "I really ought to go."

"It's another m-m-month or so. More. Time enough. Anything can h-h-hap-
pen in time, don't you think?"

"It depends."

"If you b-b-believe enough?"

"Maybe so."

"The st-st-stammer, you know, is all psychological. Doctor Rhinehart says   *60*
so. It c-came all of a sudden. W-when I started school."

"I didn't know."

"Oh yes. And if it c-c-came that way, it can g-g-go too; suddenly, I mean.
That's l-l-logical, don't you think?"

"Anything is possible," I told him.

He smiled abruptly, and opened his mouth again, giving me the impression   *61*
that he wanted to say something more. But for some reason, maybe because he
was tired, he got stuck; his chin jerked spasmodically as he tried to force the
word from his mouth, and then he shrugged and gave up, holding out a moist
palm to say good night and good-by.

"Good luck," I told him.

About a week later his father gave me a ring. He had a customer in the gar-   *62*
ment district, on Seventh Avenue and Thirty-seventh Street, and he thought
that if as usual I was working at the Forty-second Street Library, we could
meet for a bite of lunch. I said fine. It was a hot day. His cheeks were purplish
from the heat and he breathed heavily. We had a sandwich and a soda at
Schrafft's and then he walked me back to the library where we sat for a while
on the granite steps under the trees around the flagpole at the north entrance
on the avenue. The place was jammed with shopgirls and clerks taking in a few
minutes of the sun before they had to go back to work. We sat and watched the
flow of crowds going into the stores; the cars and the buses and the cabs, the
cop at the intersection, wearing dark glasses and a short-sleeved summer uniform, waving the traffic on.

"How's the work?" Willi asked me.   *63*

"Coming along. How's the family?"

"Fine. They send their best."

"Send my love."

"I will." He smoked a cigar and coughed. The air was thick with fumes.
"You know, Danny doesn't say much, but he can't fool me."

"About what?"   *64*

"He's worried about the Bar Mitzvah. Speaking in front of all those people.
I told him to take it slow and everything would be all right. What do you
think?"

"You know best."

"Helene thinks I'm doing the wrong thing."

"It's hard for me to say."

"You heard me that night. . . . Sometimes I go on and on. She says I   *65*
shouldn't fill his head with that sort of thing, but I say that he has a right to
know."

"You may be right."

"He doesn't understand everything, of course. . . . That story about Heinz,
for example. . . . But he will in time. . . . It was a revelation to me. You know,
sometimes, in the camp, before I met Heinz, I used to wonder why it was all
happening. Why the Jews, I mean. . . .

66   "Oh, there are other factors, of course. . . . But don't you see? The Commandments. All the Laws. . . ." He flicked away his cigar ash. "The Law, more than anything. . . . He taught me that, that day in the rain. They were murdering, humiliating us because whether it was true or not we had come to—how shall I say it?—embody, I suppose . . . In some strange way, we had come to embody that very Law that bound them too—through Christianity, I mean— and in destroying us . . . Heinz, for example, hating his father, the pastor, who preached love—love thy neighbor, from Leviticus, you know. . . . Of course, there's the fist: love and hate all mixed together. I really don't understand that part myself, but I do know that what all of them hated, somehow, was the yoke that we had given them so long ago. The Law that makes all the difference, that makes a man different from a beast, the civilized . . ." He coughed, "Can't you see what I mean?"

67   "I'm not sure. I think so."

"It's hard for me to keep it all straight myself. . . . I just feel that the least we can do is pass it on, the way we always have, from father to son. The Bar Mitzvah. . . . Of course, now with Danny, he doesn't really complain, but he suffers, I know. I'm not sure just what to do."

"What can I tell you?"

"Nothing, I know. I just wanted you to understand. . . . You know the irony is that he hates me."

"Don't be absurd."

68   "It's true—at least partly. Oh, he loves me too, but Rhinehart says that stammering is very often—it's very complicated—a kind of expression of hostility, resentment, to those whom you're supposed to love. . . . It all started you know when he began school. He was very bright. I've always demanded too damn much of him."

"It'll be O.K."

"Oh, I know it, eventually. It's only that in the meantime . . . I told him yesterday that if he wanted to call the whole service off, I'd be glad to do it in a minute."

"What'd he say?"

"Nothing doing. What he's been saying all along. Definitely not. . . . As a matter of fact, he smiled."

"Did he?" I said. "What are you going to do?"

69   "Go ahead, I guess. But I made it as clear as I could that any time he wants to drop the speech and just have the party at home, it was more than O.K. by me."

"Well," I told him. "I've got to get back to the books."

"I know. I didn't mean to keep you."

"Thanks for lunch."

"My pleasure. . . . Joe, you're the only blood relative I've got left. People talk. I just wanted you to understand."

I nodded, and left him standing there, smoking and coughing, in the dazzling pattern of light and shadow cast by the sunlight streaming through the dusty leaves of the trees.

The weeks went by. Once or twice he called again to have me out to dinner, 70
and I asked him whether or not the service was still on. "Sure," he'd answer.
"He's studying away." I was too busy getting my notes into shape to go out
and see them. My work was going fairly well. I decided to attack the whole
problem from the point of view of Chief Justice Marshall—the origin of judicial
review—but with all of it, I got a good chunk of the reading done by the beginning of July, so that over the Fourth I was able to get away and spend the
weekend visiting a classmate of mine at Columbia and his wife who had taken a
cottage for the summer at Cape Cod. I got back Tuesday night. The service
was scheduled for the following Saturday, so I called Willi to make absolutely
sure once and for all that Danny was going to speak in the Temple.

"You bet," he told me. "You know, I think I've got a budding rabbi on my 71
hands."

"How do you mean?"

"Religious? My God, you ought to see him. He gets up at six in the morning
to pray."

The service was to be held at Temple Shalom on Seventy-eighth Avenue. I 72
hadn't bought a present yet and I was stumped. For the life of me I couldn't
think of anything original. In the end, I went to the bank and bought him a
series-E savings bond for $25.00. Somehow it didn't seem enough, so in addi-
tion I bought him fourteen silver dollars—one extra for good luck—and had
them packed in a velvet box with a clasp. I thought the kid might get a kick out
of it.

Saturday at last: hot and muggy, a promise of rain, with a peculiar diffused 73
light shining from behind the low gray clouds. It was too hot to sleep much the
night before. I was up at six-thirty and out of the house by a quarter to eight.
At first I thought that maybe I'd go out to the house and we'd all go to the
Temple together. I don't know why; I decided against it. I loafed around
instead, wasting time, and by the time I took the subway and arrived in Queens
it was a quarter to ten. The crowds were already arriving at the Temple, Goldman's relatives, most of them people I didn't know, all dressed up in dark
summer suits and light dresses, flowered prints and silks. It was so muggy that
the powder flaked on the women's cheeks. I finally recognized Helene's brother
and sister-in-law in the crush—a chiropodist who lived in Brooklyn. We chatted for a minute before they went inside.

"Willi here?" I asked.

"Not yet. I didn't see any of them," he said. "Maybe we ought to call up 74
and find out if they're really coming. Between you and me, I never thought the
kid would go through with it."

I waited alone just outside the big oaken doors. The air was stifling, and the 75
sun had shifted and faded from behind the clouds darkening the streets. It
began to rain. I went into the vestibule, and about three minutes of ten the
family arrived.

"A rabbi, I told you," said Willi, folding his dripping umbrella. "He didn't 76
want to take a cab on *Shabbos*. We had to walk here in the rain."

Helene took off her wilted straw hat. "Ruined," she said. The boy said noth- 77 ing. With a white-silk prayer shawl over his arm, he was dressed in a dark-blue suit that emphasized the pallor of his face. All the color had gone from his cheeks; his lips were drawn and white.

"Congratulations," I told him.

He nodded. "We're late," said his father. "We ought to get seated." He took his wife by the elbow and they went inside. The boy hung back and pulled at my sleeve.

"D-d-d-do you think they'll l-laugh?" he asked.

"Of course not."

He shook his head and shrugged.

"I p-p-p-prayed and p-p-prayed."

78   We all sat in the front pew, to the left of the Ark. There were baskets of red roses set on the marble steps. The bronze doors of the Ark were open and the rabbi, young and handsome, wearing horn-rimmed glasses and prematurely gray at the temples, conducted the morning service. He was sweating and, while the cantor sang, he surreptitiously plucked a handkerchief from the sleeve of his robe and dabbed at his upper lip. The service went on, mostly in Hebrew, chanting and responsive reading, the drone of voices and the tinkle of silver bells as Willi and Mr. Goldman were called upon to elevate the Torah over the heads of the congregation and lay it open on the mahogany podium set on the edge of the steps. The rain beat against the stained glass windows. Danny sat to my right, picking at the cuticle of his thumb. When it came time for the recitation of the Haftorah, the Goldman kid went first. He would do well and he knew it—chanting the Hebrew in a high singsong voice that was just beginning to crack; rather good-looking, and tall for his age, with reddish blond hair, full lips, and pimpled cheeks. His father, seated on the stage to the rabbi's left and next to Willi, beamed at the audience. Then it was Danny's turn. The crowd shifted perceptively in their seats, and as he stood up two women in the row behind us nervously began to fan themselves with their prayer books. Evidently he was right: the Goldman boy had told everyone about his stammer. You could sense it. You could hear everyone in the place take a deep breath as he mounted the three steps with the fringed end of his prayer shawl dragging along the floor. He stood behind the opened Torah, and with a bitten forefinger found his place. The rustle of silks; the audience had shifted again, with a faint murmur. The wooden pews creaked and the noise must have startled him, because he suddenly glanced up. For a moment he was up to his old tricks, trying to stare them down, but it was no use. No one said anything. All at once he was just listening to the sound of their labored breathing. They pitied him and he knew it, and they hated him, in spite of themselves, for the embarrassment that he was causing them, and he was aware of that too. The rabbi wiped the sweat from his upper lip. With his left hand rubbing the side of his nose, Willi sat looking at his feet. Then, for a moment more, wide-eyed, and with trembling lips, the boy continued to stare down at the crowd until he caught my eye. He blinked and shrugged his shoulders again, and hunched forward, as though before he began to stammer the blessing he had made up his mind to

assume the burden of what the reiteration of the Law of his Fathers had demanded from the first.

WRITING AND DISCUSSION QUESTIONS

Informative

1. Characterize the narrator's work, beliefs, and reactions to Danny and Willi. Why did Nissenson choose Joe to narrate the story?
2. The story seems to focus on Danny's stuttering and his refusal to let the ridicule he knows he will encounter at his Bar Mitzvah, the coming of age ceremony for 13-year-old Jewish boys, force him to back down. What do you think is meant by the last line of the story, which says Danny has chosen "to assume the burden of what the reiteration of the Law of his Fathers had demanded from the first"?
3. In a very broad sense, the story is about the problem of maintaining faith after the Holocaust, the destruction by the Nazis of six million of Europe's Jews during World War II. What part do Heinz and Willi's experiences in Bergen-Belson play in the story? How do such stories of atrocity affect Danny? What does Willi learn from Heinz?
4. What role does Heinz play in the story? How does his psychology suggest a cause of the Holocaust?

Persuasive

1. Hugh Nissenson himself professes to be a militant atheist who does not believe in God. Argue that this personal belief affects the way Nissenson constructs his characters' response to Judaism in "The Law". Is there one character in particular who represents the author's point of view?
2. Why does Willi find it unusual that Joe wishes to write his Ph.D. dissertation on the "Alien and Sedition Act," which involved the fate of "only twenty-five" British and French, but no Jews? In your answer, explain the point of the "joke" Willi relates about the S.S. man who harrasses a Jewish man and asks, "who's responsible for all of Germany's troubles?"

Personal

1. Danny appears to be more devout and more committed to his faith than his immediate family is; his father says with some pride mixed with humor, "I've got a budding rabbi on my hands." How do you feel around devoutly religious people? Do they make you uncomfortable or uneasy? Can you imagine yourself befriending Danny?
2. In handling the fact of the Holocaust, Joe has submerged himself in research about other people who were maligned and imprisoned. This could be an escape from

his heritage and his history, or it could be another way to help explain the tragedy of the Holocaust to himself and live with it. How would you react to the Holocaust if it were as close to you as it is to Danny and Joe?

▼

DOROTHY L. SAYERS, "THE GREATEST DRAMA EVER STAGED"

Dorothy L. Sayers (1893–1957) is best known as the creator of the popular detective characters Lord Peter Wimsey and Harriet Vane, who solve crimes in such Sayers mystery novels as *Strong Poison* and *The Unpleasantness at the Bellona Club.* In a varied career, Sayers was one of the first women to obtain a degree from the venerable Oxford University, England's oldest institution of higher learning. She later worked as a teacher at several women's schools and had a successful career as a translator; particularly successful was her "modern" translation of the works of the medieval Italian poet, Dante. What many of her readers do not know about her is that she was also a formidable theologian and wrote religious drama and poignant editorials about the recovery of orthodox Christian faith in Britain. One of her particular talents was her ability, derived from her translation skills, to explain the ideas and personalities of other historical periods and places in a way that seems alive and relevant to the present.

Some of her most important work involved what can be called the "translating" of Christian concepts and ideals for her contemporaries—whom she believed, if left to impose their own twentieth-century precepts on these ideals, would miss their point or would neglect them altogether. Sayers argues in the essay presented here, "The Greatest Drama Ever Staged," that many believe that the Christian faith needs to be "updated" and that it has been hindered by "dogma," which is intended to stand firm through the centuries without change. The key to its vitality is reaffirming that "dogma," which she posits is exciting and ever relevant. In this essay, Sayers achieves a clear and concise presentation of what the basic tenets of orthodox Christian faith involve in the twentieth century.

▼

The Greatest Drama Ever Staged
DOROTHY L. SAYERS

1   Official Christianity, of late years, has been having what is known as "a bad press." We are constantly assured that the churches are empty because preachers insist too much upon doctrine—"dull dogma," as people call it. The fact is the precise opposite. It is the neglect of dogma that makes for dullness. The Christian faith is the most exciting drama that ever staggered the imagination of man—and the dogma *is* the drama.

That drama is summarized quite clearly in the creeds of the Church, and if   *2*
we think it dull it is because we either have never really read those amazing
documents, or have recited them so often and so mechanically as to have lost
all sense of their meaning. The plot pivots upon a single character, and the
whole action is the answer to a single central problem: *What think ye of Christ?*
Before we adopt any of the unofficial solutions (some of which are indeed
excessively dull)—before we dismiss Christ as a myth, an idealist, a demagogue, a liar, or a lunatic—it will do no harm to find out what the creeds really
say about Him. What does the Church think of Christ?

The Church's answer is categorical and uncompromising, and it is this: That   *3*
Jesus Bar-Joseph, the carpenter of Nazareth, was in fact and in truth, and in
the most exact and literal sense of the words, the God "by whom all things
were made." His body and brain were those of a common man; His personality
was the personality of God, so far as that personality could be expressed in
human terms. He was not a kind of demon pretending to be human; He was in
every respect a genuine living man. He was not merely a man so good as to be
"like God"—He *was* God.

Now, this is not just a pious commonplace; it is no commonplace at all. For   *4*
what it means is this, among other things: that for whatever reason God chose
to make man as he is—limited and suffering and subject to sorrows and
death—He had the honesty and the courage to take His own medicine. Whatever game He is playing with His creation, He has kept His own rules and
played fair. He can exact nothing from man that He has not exacted from Himself. He has Himself gone through the whole of human experience, from the
trivial irritations of family life and the cramping restrictions of hard work and
lack of money to the worst horrors of pain and humiliation, defeat, despair, and
death. When He was a man, He played the man. He was born in poverty and
died in disgrace and thought it well worthwhile.

Christianity is, of course, not the only religion that has found the best expla-   *5*
nation of human life in the idea of an incarnate and suffering god. The Egyptian Osiris died and rose again; Aeschylus in his play, *The Eumenides*, reconciled man to God by the theory of a suffering Zeus. But in most theologies, the
god is supposed to have suffered and died in some remote and mythical period
of prehistory. The Christian story, on the other hand, starts off briskly in St.
Matthew's account with a place and a date: "When Jesus was born in Bethle-
hem of Judea in the days of Herod the King." St. Luke, still more practically
and prosaically, pins the thing down by a reference to a piece of government
finance. God, he says, was made man in the year when Caesar Augustus was
taking a census in connexion with a scheme of taxation. Similarly, we might
date an event by saying that it took place in the year that Great Britain went off
the gold standard. About thirty-three years later (we are informed) God was
executed, for being a political nuisance, "under Pontius Pilate"—much as we
might say, "when Mr. Joynson-Hicks was Home Secretary." It is as definite
and concrete as all that.

Possibly we might prefer not to take this tale too seriously—there are dis-   *6*
quieting points about it. Here we had a man of Divine character walking and

talking among us—and what did we find to do with Him? The common people, indeed, "heard Him gladly"; but our leading authorities in Church and State considered that He talked too much and uttered too many disconcerting truths. So we bribed one of His friends to hand Him over quietly to the police, and we tried Him on a rather vague charge of creating a disturbance, and had Him publicly flogged and hanged on the common gallows, "thanking God we were rid of a knave." All this was not very creditable to us, even if He was (as many people thought and think) only a harmless crazy preacher. But if the Church is right about Him, it was more discreditable still; for the man we hanged was God Almighty.

7   So that is the outline of the official story—the tale of the time when God was the underdog and got beaten, when He submitted to the conditions He had laid down and became a man like the men He had made, and the men He had made broke Him and killed Him. This is the dogma we find so dull—this terrifying drama of which God is the victim and hero.

8   If this is dull, then what, in Heaven's name, is worthy to be called exciting? The people who hanged Christ never, to do them justice, accused Him of being a bore—on the contrary; they thought Him too dynamic to be safe. It has been left for later generations to muffle up that shattering personality and surround Him with an atmosphere of tedium. We have very efficiently pared the claws of the Lion of Judah, certified Him "meek and mild," and recommended Him as a fitting household pet for pale curates and pious ladies. To those who knew Him, however, He in no way suggested a milk-and-water person; *they* objected to Him as a dangerous firebrand. True, He was tender to the unfortunate, patient with honest inquirers, and humble before Heaven; but He insulted respectable clergymen by calling them hypocrites; He referred to King Herod as "that fox"; He went to parties in disreputable company and was looked upon as a "gluttonous man and a wine-bibber, a friend of publicans and sinners"; He assaulted indignant tradesmen and threw them and their belongings out of the Temple; He drove a coach-and-horses through a number of sacrosanct and hoary regulations; He cured diseases by any means that came handy, with a shocking casualness in the matter of other people's pigs and property; He showed no proper deference for wealth or social position; when confronted with neat dialectical traps, He displayed a paradoxical humour that affronted serious-minded people, and He retorted by asking disagreeably searching questions that could not be answered by rule of thumb. He was emphatically not a dull man in His human lifetime, and if He was God, there can be nothing dull about God either. But He had "a daily beauty in His life that made us ugly," and officialdom felt that the established order of things would be more secure without Him. So they did away with God in the name of peace and quietness.

9   *"And the third day He rose again."* What are we to make of that? One thing is certain: if He was God and nothing else, His immortality means nothing to us; if He was man and no more, His death is no more important than yours or mine. But if He really was both God and man, then when the man Jesus died, God died too; and when the God Jesus rose from the dead, man rose too, because they were one and the same person. The Church binds us to no theory

about the exact composition of Christ's Resurrection Body. A body of some kind there had to be, since man cannot perceive the Infinite otherwise than in terms of space and time. It may have been made from the same elements as the body that disappeared so strangely from the guarded tomb, but it was not that old, limited mortal body, though it was recognizably like it. In any case, those who saw the risen Christ remained persuaded that life was worth living and death a triviality—an attitude curiously unlike that of the modern defeatist, who is firmly persuaded that life is a disaster and death (rather inconsistently) a major catastrophe.

Now, nobody is compelled to believe a single word of this remarkable story. *10* God (says the Church) has created us perfectly free to disbelieve in Him as much as we choose. If we do disbelieve, then He and we must take the consequences in a world ruled by cause and effect. The Church says further, that man did, in fact, disbelieve, and that God did, in fact, take the consequences. All the same, if we are going to disbelieve a thing, it seems on the whole to be desirable that we should first find out what, exactly, we are disbelieving. Very well, then: "The right Faith is, that we believe that Jesus Christ is God *and* Man. Perfect God and perfect Man, of a reasonable soul and human flesh subsisting. Who although He be God and Man, yet is He not two, but one Christ." There is the essential doctrine, of which the whole elaborate structure of Christian faith and morals is only the logical consequence.

Now, we may call that doctrine exhilarating or we may call it devastating; we *11* may call it revelation or we may call it rubbish; but if we call it dull, then words have no meaning at all. That God should play the tyrant over man is a dismal story of unrelieved oppression; that man should play the tyrant over man is the usual dreary record of human futility; but that man should play the tyrant over God and find Him a better man than himself is an astonishing drama indeed. Any journalist, hearing of it for the first time, would recognize it as news; those who did hear it for the first time actually called it news, and good news at that; though we are apt to forget that the word Gospel ever meant anything so sensational.

Perhaps the drama is played out now, and Jesus is safely dead and buried. *12* Perhaps. It is ironical and entertaining to consider that once at least in the world's history those words might have been spoken with complete conviction, and that was upon the eve of the Resurrection.

WRITING AND DISCUSSION QUESTIONS

Informative

1. Sayers begins her essay on a negative note: "Official Christianity . . . has been having what is known as a 'bad press.'" What does she mean by "Official" Christianity? In what way does her aggressive beginning prepare the reader for her argument that "The Christian faith is the most exciting drama that ever staggered the imagination of man"?

2. In Sayers' answer to what she considers the essential question of Christianity, "What think ye of Christ?" she lists such possibilities as myth, idealist, demagogue, liar, or lunatic, and then explains the historic creeds of Christianity (paragraph 2). Summarize her explanation.
3. Sayers emphasizes in her essay that whatever else the "dogma" or teaching about Christ is, it is a very good story or drama and that it may be revelation or rubbish but it is not dull. What incidents and personality traits of Christ does she cite to establish her point?

Persuasive

1. Toward the end of her essay, Sayers suggests that no one is compelled to believe a "single word of this remarkable story" (paragraph 10). To what extent has she persuaded you that this is, indeed, a "remarkable" story? Argue that her "translation" of the essential Biblical narratives does or does not make this dogma good drama.
2. Sayers seems to contend that Christianity is less a body of doctrines than a story about a particular person. Argue for or against her contention. Consider what associations and definitions come to mind when thinking of Christianity as a faith. Is the appeal of Christianity its ethics and belief system or Jesus? Is there a difference?

Personal

1. Imagine that you are a first-century journalist asked to cover the itinerant ministry of the man called Jesus Christ. Write an account of a typical day of traveling with Jesus and his disciples as you might for a twentieth-century national newspaper.
2. Consider yourself an anthropologist who is attempting to explain the religious behavior of Christians to an audience completely unfamiliar with the Christian tradition. Interview friends or relatives who consider themselves Christians, visit a church service, or watch a broadcast of a Christian evangelist. Write a factual account of this experience and then offer an objective, "clinical" report of this experience to your readers.

FLANNERY O'CONNOR, "GOOD COUNTRY PEOPLE" FROM THE *COMPLETE STORIES OF FLANNERY O'CONNOR*

Flannery O'Connor (1925–1964) was a renowned writer of short stories, one whose art was best suited to the medium of the short story simply because there her sharp, shocking, and grotesque characterizations could have full impact on the reader. Arguing that she wrote "by the light of Christian orthodoxy," O'Connor knew that the task of presenting the truths of Christianity as she saw them was difficult in a modern, secularized world. As a result, she chose unusual settings and characters to exemplify some of the tenets of her faith that most needed to be redeemed and brought to the attention of a reading public lulled to sleep by civil religion.

Born in Savannah, Georgia, O'Connor wrote about the people in the region she knew best—the American South. Though a devout Catholic, O'Connor tended, nevertheless, to write about the impact of "Bible-belt" or fundamentalist Christianity on the American landscape. But neither Christians nor non-Christians fare well in O'Connor's penetrating critique of the hypocrisy, empty faith, and false promises in much contemporary Christianity and in its secular replacements of art, science, or popular entertainment. She never tired of poking holes in the self-important and self-styled intellectuals who populated her stories, and in "Good Country People," the reader encounters one of O'Connor's most vividly drawn pseudoscholars in Hulga Hopewell. By placing Hulga's secularized, philosophically intense worldview beside the seemingly naive and simplistic worldview of Manley Pointer, O'Connor intends to highlight how the presence and absence of faith affect one's life.

▼

Good Country People
FLANNERY O'CONNOR

Besides the neutral expression that she wore when she was alone, *1* Mrs. Freeman had two others, forward and reverse, that she used for all her human dealings. Her forward expression was steady and driving like the advance of a heavy truck. Her eyes never swerved to left or right but turned as the story turned as if they followed a yellow line down the center of it. She seldom used the other expression because it was not often necessary for her to retract a statement, but when she did, her face came to a complete stop, there was an almost imperceptible movement of her black eyes, during which they seemed to be receding, and then the observer would see that Mrs. Freeman, though she might stand there as real as several grain sacks thrown on top of each other, was no longer there in spirit. As for getting anything across to her when this was the case, Mrs. Hopewell had given it up. She might talk her head off. Mrs. Freeman could never be brought to admit herself wrong on any point. She would stand there and if she could be brought to say anything, it was something like. "Well, I wouldn't of said it was and I wouldn't of said it wasn't," or letting her gaze range over the top kitchen shelf where there was an assortment of dusty bottles, she might remark, "I see you ain't ate many of them figs you put up last summer."

They carried on their most important business in the kitchen at breakfast. *2* Every morning Mrs. Hopewell got up at seven o'clock and lit her gas heater and Joy's. Joy was her daughter, a large blonde girl who had an artificial leg. Mrs. Hopewell thought of her as a child though she was thirty-two years old and highly educated. Joy would get up while her mother was eating and lumber into the bathroom and slam the door, and before long, Mrs. Freeman would arrive at the back door. Joy would hear her mother call, "Come on in," and then they would talk for a while in low voices that were indistinguishable in the bathroom. By the time Joy came in, they had usually finished the weather report and were on one or the other of Mrs. Freeman's daughters, Glynese or Carramae, Joy called them Glycerin and Caramel. Glynese, a redhead, was eighteen and had many admirers; Carramae, a blonde, was only fifteen but already married and pregnant. She could not keep anything on her stomach. Every morning Mrs. Freeman told Mrs. Hopewell how many times she had vomited since the last report.

3 Mrs. Hopewell liked to tell people that Glynese and Carramae were two of the finest girls she knew and that Mrs. Freeman was a *lady* and that she was never ashamed to take her anywhere or introduce her to anybody they might meet. Then she would tell how she had happened to hire the Freemans in the first place and how they were a godsend to her and how she had had them four years. The reason for her keeping them so long was that they were not trash. They were good country people. She had telephoned the man whose name they had given as a reference and he had told her that Mr. Freeman was a good farmer but that his wife was the nosiest woman ever to walk the earth. "She's got to be into everything," the man said. "If she don't get there before the dust settles, you can bet she's dead, that's all. She'll want to know all your business. I can stand him real good," he had said, "but me nor my wife neither could have stood that woman one more minute on this place." That had put Mrs. Hopewell off for a few days.

4 She had hired them in the end because there were no other applicants but she had made up her mind beforehand exactly how she would handle the woman. Since she was the type who had to be into everything, then, Mrs. Hopewell had decided, she would not only let her be into everything, she would *see to it* that she was into everything—she would give her the responsibility of everything, she would put her in charge. Mrs. Hopewell had no bad qualities of her own but she was able to use other people's in such a constructive way that she never felt the lack. She had hired the Freemans and she had kept them four years.

5 Nothing is perfect. This was one of Mrs. Hopewell's favorite sayings. Another was: that is life! And still another, the most important, was: well, other people have their opinions too. She would make these statements, usually at the table, in a tone of gentle insistence as if no one held them but her, and the large hulking Joy, whose constant outrage had obliterated every expression from her face, would stare just a little to the side of her, her eyes icy blue, with the look of someone who has achieved blindness by an act of will and means to keep it.

6 When Mrs. Hopewell said to Mrs. Freeman that life was like that, Mrs. Freeman would say, "I always said so myself." Nothing had been arrived at by anyone that had not first been arrived at by her. She was quicker than Mr. Freeman. When Mrs. Hopewell said to her after they had been on the place a while, "You know, you're the wheel behind the wheel," and winked, Mrs. Freeman had said, "I know it. I've always been quick. It's some that are quicker than others."

"Everybody is different," Mrs. Hopewell said.

"Yes, most people is," Mrs. Freeman said.

"It takes all kinds to make the world."

"I always said it did myself."

The girl was used to this kind of dialogue for breakfast and more of it for 7 dinner; sometimes they had it for supper too. When they had no guest they ate in the kitchen because that was easier. Mrs. Freeman always managed to arrive at some point duirng the meal and to watch them finish it. She would stand in the doorway if it were summer but in the winter she would stand with one elbow on top of the refrigerator and look down on them, or she would stand by the gas heater, lifting the back of her skirt slightly. Occasionally she would stand against the wall and roll her head from side to side. At no time was she in any hurry to leave. All this was very trying on Mrs. Hopewell but she was a woman of great patience. She realized that nothing is perfect and that in the Freemans she had good country people and that if, in this day and age, you get good country people, you had better hang onto them.

She had had plenty of experience with trash. Before the Freemans she had 8 averaged one tenant family a year. The wives of these farmers were not the kind you would want to be around you for very long. Mrs. Hopewell, who had divorced her husband long ago, needed someone to walk over the fields with her; and when Joy had to be impressed for these services, her remarks were usually so ugly and her face so glum that Mrs. Hopewell would say, "If you can't come pleasantly, I don't want you at all," to which the girl, standing square and rigid-shouldered with her neck thrust slightly forward, would reply, "If you want me, here I am—LIKE I AM."

Mrs. Hopewell excused this attitude because of the leg (which had been shot 9 off in a hunting accident when Joy was ten). It was hard for Mrs. Hopewell to realize that her child was thirty-two now and that for more than twenty years she had had only one leg. She thought of her still as a child because it tore her heart to think instead of the poor stout girl in her thirties who had never danced a step or had any *normal* good times. Her name was really Joy but as soon as she was twenty-one and away from home, she had had it legally changed. Mrs. Hopewell was certain that she had thought and thought until she had hit upon the ugliest name in any language. Then she had gone and had the beautiful name, Joy, changed without telling her mother until after she had done it. Her legal name was Hulga.

When Mrs. Hopewell thought the name, Hulga, she thought of the broad 10 blank hull of a battleship. She would not use it. She continued to call her Joy to which the girl responded but in a purely mechanical way.

Hulga had learned to tolerate Mrs. Freeman who saved her from taking 11 walks with her mother. Even Glynese and Carramae were useful when they occupied attention that might otherwise have been directed at her. At first she had thought she could not stand Mrs. Freeman for she had found that it was not possible to be rude to her. Mrs. Freeman would take on strange resentments and for days together she would be sullen but the source of her displeasure was always obscure; a direct attack, a positive leer, blatant ugliness to her face—these never touched her. And without warning one day, she began calling her Hulga.

12   She did not call her that in front of Mrs. Hopewell who would have been incensed but when she and the girl happened to be out of the house together, she would say something and add the name Hulga to the end of it, and the big spectacled Joy-Hulga would scowl and redden as if her privacy had been intruded upon. She considered the name her personal affair. She had arrived at it first purely on the basis of its ugly sound and then the full genius of its fitness had struck her. She had a vision of the name working like the ugly sweating Vulcan who stayed in the furnace and to whom, presumably, the goddess had to come when called. She saw it as the name of her highest creative act. One of her major triumphs was that her mother had not been able to turn her dust into Joy, but the greater one was that she had been able to turn it herself into Hulga. However, Mrs. Freeman's relish for using the name only irritated her. It was as if Mrs. Freeman's beady steel-pointed eyes had penetrated far enough behind her face to reach some secret fact. Something about her seemed to fascinate Mrs. Freeman and then one day Hulga realized that it was the artificial leg. Mrs. Freeman had a special fondness for the details of secret infections, hidden deformities, assaults upon children. Of diseases, she preferred the lingering or incurable. Hulga had heard Mrs. Hopewell give her the details of the hunting accident, how the leg had been literally blasted off, how she had never lost consciousness. Mrs. Freeman could listen to it any time as if it had happened an hour ago.

13   When Hulga stumped into the kitchen in the morning (she could walk without making the awful noise but she made it—Mrs. Hopewell was certain—because it was ugly-sounding), she glanced at them and did not speak. Mrs. Hopewell would be in her red kimono with her hair tied around her head in rags. She would be sitting at the table, finishing her breakfast and Mrs. Freeman would be hanging by her elbow outward from the refrigerator, looking down at the table. Hulga always put her eggs on the stove to boil and then stood over them with her arms folded, and Mrs. Hopewell would look at her— a kind of indirect gaze divided between her and Mrs. Freeman—and would think that if she would only keep herself up a little, she wouldn't be so bad looking. There was nothing wrong with her face that a pleasant expression wouldn't help. Mrs. Hopewell said that people who looked on the bright side of things would be beautiful even if they were not.

14   Whenever she looked at Joy this way, she could not help but feel that it would have been better if the child had not taken the Ph.D. It had certainly not brought her out any and now that she had it, there was no more excuse for her to go to school again. Mrs. Hopewell thought it was nice for girls to go to school to have a good time but Joy had "gone through." Anyhow, she would not have been strong enough to go again. The doctors had told Mrs. Hopewell that with the best of care, Joy might see forty-five. She had a weak heart. Joy had made it plain that if it had not been for this condition, she would be far

from these red hills and good country people. She would be in a university lecturing to people who knew what she was talking about. And Mrs. Hopewell
could very well picture her there, looking like a scarecrow and lecturing to
more of the same. Here she went about all day in a six-year-old skirt and a
yellow sweat shirt with a faded cowboy on a horse embossed on it. She thought
this was funny; Mrs. Hopewell thought it was idiotic and showed simply that
she was still a child. She was brilliant but she didn't have a grain of sense. It
seemed to Mrs. Hopewell that every year she grew less like other people and
more like herself—bloated, rude, and squint-eyed. And she said such strange
things! To her own mother she had said—without warning, without excuse,
standing up in the middle of a meal with her face purple and her mouth half
full—"Woman! do you ever look inside? Do you ever look inside and see what
you are *not*? God!" she had cried sinking down again and staring at her plate,
"Malebranche was right: we are not our own light. We are not our own light!"
Mrs. Hopewell had no idea to this day what brought that on. She had only
made the remark, hoping Joy would take it in, that a smile never hurt anyone.

The girl had taken the Ph.D. in philosophy and this left Mrs. Hopewell at a   *15*
complete loss. You could say, "My daughter is a nurse," or "My daughter is a
schoolteacher," or even, "My daughter is a chemical engineer." You could not
say, "My daughter is a philosopher." That was something that had ended with
the Greeks and Romans. All day Joy sat on her neck in a deep chair, reading.
Sometimes she went for walks but she didn't like dogs or cats or birds or flowers or nature or nice young men. She looked at nice young men as if she could
smell their stupidity.

One day Mrs. Hopewell had picked up one of the books the girl had just put   *16*
down and opening it at random, she read, "Science, on the other hand, has to
assert its soberness and seriousness afresh and declare that it is concerned
solely with what-is. Nothing—how can it be for science anything but a horror
and a phantasm? If science is right, then one thing stands firm: science wishes
to know nothing of nothing. Such is after all the strictly scientific approach to
Nothing. We know it by wishing to know nothing of Nothing." These words had
been underlined with a blue pencil and they worked on Mrs. Hopewell like
some evil incantation in gibberish. She shut the book quickly and went out of
the room as if she were having a chill.

This morning when the girl came in, Mrs. Freeman was on Carramae. "She   *17*
thrown up four times after supper," she said, "and was up twict in the night
after three o'clock. Yesterday she didn't do nothing but ramble in the bureau
drawer. All she did. Stand up there and see what she could run up on."

"She's got to eat," Mrs. Hopewell muttered, sipping her coffee, while she   *18*
watched Joy's back at the stove. She was wondering what the child had said to
the Bible salesman. She could not imagine what kind of a conversation she
could possibly have had with him.

He was a tall gaunt hatless youth who had called yesterday to sell them a   *19*
Bible. He had appeared at the door, carrying a large black suitcase that
weighted him so heavily on one side that he had to brace himself against the

door facing. He seemed on the point of collapse but he said in a cheerful voice. "Good morning, Mrs. Cedars!" and set the suitcase down on the mat. He was not a badlooking young man though he had on a bright blue suit and yellow socks that were not pulled up far enough. He had prominent face bones and a streak of sticky-looking brown hair falling across his forehead.

"I'm Mrs. Hopewell," she said.

20 "Oh!" he said, pretending to look puzzled but with his eyes sparkling, "I saw it said 'The Cedars' on the mailbox so I thought you was Mrs. Cedars!" and he burst out in a pleasant laugh. He picked up the satchel and under cover of a pant, he fell forward into her hall. It was rather as if the suitcase had moved first, jerking him after it. "Mrs. Hopewell!" he said and grabbed her hand. "I hope you are well!" and he laughed again and then all at once his face sobered completely. He paused and gave her a straight earnest look and said, "Lady, I've come to speak of serious things."

21 "Well, come in," she muttered, none too pleased because her dinner was almost ready. He came into the parlor and sat down on the edge of a straight chair and put the suitcase between his feet and glanced around the room as if he were sizing her up by it. Her silver gleamed on the two sideboards; she decided he had never been in a room as elegant as this.

22 "Mrs. Hopewell," he began, using her name in a way that sounded almost intimate, "I know you believe in Christian service."

"Well yes," she murmured.

"I know," he said and paused, looking very wise with his head cocked on one side, "that you're a good woman. Friends have told me."

Mrs. Hopewell never liked to be taken for a fool. "What are you selling?" she asked.

"Bibles," the young man said and his eye raced around the room before he added, "I see you have no family Bible in your parlor, I see that is the one lack you got!"

23 Mrs. Hopewell could not say, "My daughter is an atheist and won't let me keep the Bible in the parlor." She said, stiffening slightly, "I keep my Bible by my bedside." This was not the truth. It was in the attic somewhere.

"Lady," he said, "the word of God ought to be in the parlor."

"Well, I think that's a matter of taste," she began. "I think . . ."

"Lady," he said, "for a Christian, the word of God ought to be in every room in the house besides in his heart. I know you're a Christian because I can see it in every line of your face."

She stood up and said, "Well, young man, I don't want to buy a Bible and I smell my dinner burning."

24 He didn't get up. He began to twist his hands and looking down at them, he said softly, "Well lady, I'll tell you the truth—not many people want to buy one nowadays and besides, I know I'm real simple. I don't know how to say a thing but to say it. I'm just a country boy." He glanced up into her unfriendly face. "People like you don't like to fool with country people like me!"

25 "Why!" she cried, "good country people are the salt of the earth! Besides,

we all have different ways of doing, it takes all kinds to make the world go
'round. That's life!"

"You said a mouthful," he said.

"Why, I think there aren't enough good country people in the world!" she
said, stirred. "I think that's what's wrong with it!"

His face had brightened. "I didn't inraduce myself," he said. "I'm Manley
Pointer from out in the country around Willohobie, not even from a place, just
from near a place."

"You wait a minute," she said. "I have to see about my dinner." She went
out to the kitchen and found Joy standing near the door where she had been
listening.

"Get rid of the salt of the earth," she said, "and let's eat."

Mrs. Hopewell gave her a pained look and turned the heat down under the   *26*
vegetables. "*I* can't be rude to anybody," she murmured and went back into
the parlor.

He had opened the suitcase and was sitting with a Bible on each knee.

"You might as well put those up," she told him. "I don't want one."

"I appreciate your honesty," he said. "You don't see any more real honest
people unless you go way out in the country."

"I know," she said, "real genuine folks!" Through the crack in the door she
heard a groan.

"I guess a lot of boys come telling you they're working their way through   *27*
college," he said, "but I'm not going to tell you that. Somehow," he said, "I
don't want to go to college. I want to devote my life to Christian service. See,"
he said, lowering his voice, "I got this heart condition. I may not live long.
When you know it's something wrong with you and you may not live long, well
then, lady . . ." He paused, with his mouth open, and stared at her.

He and Joy had the same condition! She knew that her eyes were filling with   *28*
tears but she collected herself quickly and murmured, "Won't you stay for dinner? We'd love to have you!" and was sorry the instant she heard herself say it.

"Yes mam," he said in an abashed voice, "I would sher love to do that!"

Joy had given him one look on being introduced to him and then throughout   *29*
the meal had not glanced at him again. He had addressed several remarks to
her, which she had pretended not to hear. Mrs. Hopewell could not understand
deliberate rudeness, although she lived with it, and she felt she had always to
overflow with hospitality to make up for Joy's lack of courtesy. She urged him
to talk about himself and he did. He said he was the seventh child of twelve
and that his father had been crushed under a tree when he himself was eight
year old. He had been crushed very badly, in fact, almost cut in two and was
practically not recognizable. His mother had got along the best she could by
hard working and she had always seen that her children went to Sunday School
and that they read the Bible every evening. He was now nineteen year old and
he had been selling Bibles for four months. In that time he had sold seventy-
seven Bibles and had the promise of two more sales. He wanted to become a
missionary because he thought that was the way you could do most for people.

"He who losest his life shall find it," he said simply and he was so sincere, so genuine and earnest that Mrs. Hopewell would not for the world have smiled. He prevented his peas from sliding onto the table by blocking them with a piece of bread which he later cleaned his plate with. She could see Joy observing sidewise how he handled his knife and fork and she saw too that every few minutes, the boy would dart a keen appraising glance at the girl as if he were trying to attract her attention.

30   After dinner Joy cleared the dishes off the table and disappeared and Mrs. Hopewell was left to talk with him. He told her again about his childhood and his father's accident and about various things that had happened to him. Every five minutes or so she would stifle a yawn. He sat for two hours until finally she told him she must go because she had an appointment in town. He packed his Bibles and thanked her and prepared to leave, but in the doorway he stopped and wrung her hand and said that not on any of his trips had he met a lady as nice as her and he asked if he could come again. She had said she would always be happy to see him.

31   Joy had been standing in the road, apparently looking at something in the distance, when he came down the steps toward her, bent to the side with his heavy valise. He stopped where she was standing and confronted her directly. Mrs. Hopewell could not hear what he said but she trembled to think what Joy would say to him. She could see that after a minute Joy said something and that then the boy began to speak again, making an excited gesture with his free hand. After a minute Joy said something else at which the boy began to speak once more. Then to her amazement, Mrs. Hopewell saw the two of them walk off together, toward the gate. Joy had walked all the way to the gate with him and Mrs. Hopewell could not imagine what they had said to each other, and she had not yet dared to ask.

32   Mrs. Freeman was insisting upon her attention. She had moved from the refrigerator to the heater so that Mrs. Hopewell had to turn and face her in order to seem to be listening. "Glynese gone out with Harvey Hill again last night," she said. "She had this sty."

"Hill," Mrs. Hopewell said absently, "is that the one who works in the garage?"

33   "Nome, he's the one that goes to chiropracter school," Mrs. Freeman said. "She had this sty. Been had it two days. So she says when he brought her in the other night he says, 'Lemme get rid of that sty for you,' and she says, 'How?' and he says, 'You just lay your self down acrost the seat of that car and I'll show you.' So she done it and he popped her neck. Kept on a-popping it several times until she made him quit. This morning," Mrs. Freeman said, "she ain't got no sty. She ain't got no traces of a sty."

34   "I never heard of that before," Mrs. Hopewell said.

"He ast her to marry him before the Ordianry," Mrs. Freeman went on, "and she told him she wasn't going to be married in no *office*."

"Well, Glynese is a fine girl," Mrs. Hopewell said, "Glynese and Carramae are both fine girls."

"Carramae said when her and Lyman was married Lyman said it sure felt   35
sacred to him. She said he said he wouldn't take five hundred dollars for being
married by a preacher."

"How much would he take?" the girl asked from the stove.

"He said he wouldn't take five hundred dollars," Mrs. Freeman repeated.

"Well we all have work to do," Mrs. Hopewell said.

"Lyman said it just felt more sacred to him," Mrs. Freeman said. "The doc-   36
tor wants Carramae to eat prunes. Says instead of medicine. Says them cramps
is coming from pressure. You know where I think it is?"

"She'll be better in a few weeks," Mrs. Hopewell said.

"In the tube," Mrs. Freeman said. "Else she wouldn't be as sick as she is."

Hulga had cracked her two eggs into a saucer and was bringing them to the   37
table along with a cup of coffee that she had filled too full. She sat down carefully and began to eat, meaning to keep Mrs. Freeman there by questions if for
any reason she showed an inclination to leave. She could perceive her mother's
eye on her. The first round-about question would be about the Bible salesman
and she did not wish to bring it on. "How did he pop her neck?" she asked.

Mrs. Freeman went into a description of how he had popped her neck. She   38
said he owned a '55 Mercury but that Glynese said she would rather marry a
man with only a '36 Plymouth who would be married by a preacher. The girl
asked what if he had a '32 Plymouth and Mrs. Freeman said what Glynese had
said was a '36 Plymouth.

Mrs. Hopewell said there were not many girls with Glynese's common sense.   39
She said what she admired in those girls was their common sense. She said that
reminded her that they had had a nice visitor yesterday, a young man selling
Bibles. "Lord," she said, "he bored me to death but he was so sincere and
genuine I couldn't be rude to him. He was just good country people, you
know," she said, "—just the salt of the earth."

"I seen him walk up," Mrs. Freeman said, "and then later—I seen him   40
walk off," and Hulga could feel the slight shift in her voice, the slight insinua-
tion, that he had not walked off alone, had he? Her face remained expression-
less but the color rose into her neck and she seemed to swallow it down with
the next spoonful of egg. Mrs. Freeman was looking at her as if they had a
secret together.

"Well, it takes all kinds of people to make the world go 'round," Mrs.
Hopewell said. "It's very good we aren't all alike."

"Some people are more alike than others," Mrs. Freeman said.

Hulga got up and stumped, with about twice the noise that was necessary,   41
into her room and locked the door. She was to meet the Bible salesman at ten
o'clock at the gate. She had thought about it half the night. She had started
thinking of it as a great joke and then she had begun to see profound implications in it. She had lain in bed imagining dialogues for them that were insane
on the surface but that reached below to depths that no Bible salesman would
be aware of. Their conversation yesterday had been of this kind.

He had stopped in front of her and had simply stood there. His face was   42 bony and sweaty and bright, with a little pointed nose in the center of it, and his look was different from what it had been at the dinner table. He was gazing at her with open curiosity, with fascination, like a child watching a new fantastic animal at the zoo, and he was breathing as if he had run a great distance to reach her. His gaze seemed somehow familiar but she could not think where she had been regarded with it before. For almost a minute he didn't say anything. Then on what seemed an insuck of breath, he whispered, "You ever ate a chicken that was two days old?"

43   The girl looked at him stonily. He might have just put this question up for consideration at the meeting of a philosophical association. "Yes," she presently replied as if she had considered it from all angles.

44   "It must have been mighty small!" he said triumphantly and shook all over with little nervous giggles, getting very red in the face, and subsiding finally into his gaze of complete admiration, while the girl's expression remained exactly the same.

"How old are you?" he asked softly.

She waited some time before she answered. Then in a flat voice she said, "Seventeen."

45   His smiles came in succession like waves breaking on the surface of a little lake. "I see you got a wooden leg," he said. "I think you're brave. I think you're real sweet."

The girl stood blank and solid and silent.

"Walk to the gate with me," he said. "You're a brave sweet little thing and I liked you the minute I seen you walk in the door."

46   Hulga began to move forward.

"What's your name?" he asked, smiling down on the top of her head.

"Hulga," she said.

"Hulga," he murmured, "Hulga. Hulga. I never heard of anybody name Hulga before. You're shy, aren't you, Hulga?" he asked.

She nodded, watching his large red hand on the handle of the giant valise.

"I like girls that wear glasses," he said. "I think a lot. I'm not like these people that a serious thought don't ever enter their heads. It's because I may die."

"I may die too," she said suddenly and looked up at him. His eyes were very small and brown, glittering feverishly.

47   "Listen," he said, "don't you think some people was meant to meet on account of what all they got in common and all? Like they both think serious thoughts and all?" He shifted the valise to his other hand so that the hand nearest her was free. He caught hold of her elbow and shook it a little. "I don't work on Saturday," he said. "I like to walk in the woods and see what Mother Nature is wearing. O'er the hills and far away. Pic-nics and things. Couldn't we go on a pic-nic tomorrow? Say yes, Hulga," he said and gave her a dying look as if he felt his insides about to drop out of him. He had even seemed to sway slightly toward her.

48   During the night she had imagined that she seduced him. She imagined that

the two of them walked on the place until they came to the storage barn beyond the two back fields and there, she imagined, that things came to such a pass that she very easily seduced him and that then, of course, she had to reckon with his remorse. True genius can get an idea across even to an inferior mind. She imagined that she took his remorse in hand and changed it into a deeper understanding of life. She took all his shame away and turned it into something useful.

She set off for the gate at exactly ten o'clock, escaping without drawing Mrs. 49 Hopewell's attention. She didn't take anything to eat, forgetting that food is usually taken on a picnic. She wore a pair of slacks and a dirty white shirt, and as an afterthought, she had put some Vapex on the collar of it since she did not own any perfume. When she reached the gate no one was there.

She looked up and down the empty highway and had the furious feeling that 50 she had been tricked, that he had only meant to make her walk to the gate after the idea of him. Then suddenly he stood up, very tall, from behind a bush on the opposite embankment. Smiling, he lifted his hat which was new and wide-brimmed. He had not worn it yesterday and she wondered if he had bought it for the occasion. It was toast-colored with a red and white band around it and was slightly too large for him. He stepped from behind the bush still carrying the black valise. He had on the same suit and the same yellow socks sucked down in his shoes from walking. He crossed the highway and said, "I knew you'd come!"

The girl wondered acidly how he had known this. She pointed to the valise and asked, "Why did you bring your Bibles?"

He took her elbow, smiling down on her as if he could not stop. "You can 51 never tell when you'll need the word of God, Hulga," he said. She had a moment in which she doubted that this was actually happening and then they began to climb the embankment. They went down into the pasture toward the woods. The boy walked lightly by her side, bouncing on his toes. The valise did not seem to be heavy today; he even swung it. They crossed half the pasture without saying anything and then, putting his hand easily on the small of her back, he asked softly, "Where does you wooden leg join on?"

She turned an ugly red and glared at him and for an instant the boy looked 52 abashed. "I didn't mean you no harm," he said. "I only meant you're so brave and all. I guess God takes care of you."

"No," she said, looking forward and walking fast, "I don't even believe in God."

At this he stopped and whistled. "No!" he exclaimed as if he were too astonished to say anything else.

She walked on and in a second he was bouncing at her side, fanning with 53 his hat. "That's very unusual for a girl," he remarked, watching her out of the corner of his eye. When they reached the edge of the wood, he put his hand on her back again and drew her against him without a word and kissed her heavily.

The kiss, which had more pressure than feeling behind it, produced that 54 extra surge of adrenalin in the girl that enables one to carry a packed trunk out of a burning house, but in her, the power went at once to the brain. Even before he released her, her mind, clear and detached and ironic anyway, was regarding him from a great distance, with amusement but with pity. She had never been kissed before and she was pleased to discover that it was an unexceptional experience and all a matter of the mind's control. Some people might enjoy drain water if they were told it was vodka. When the boy, looking expectant but uncertain, pushed her gently away, she turned and walked on, saying nothing as if such business, for her, were common enough.

55   He came along panting at her side, trying to help her when he saw a root that she might trip over. He caught and held back the long swaying blades of thorn vine until she had passed beyond them. She led the way and he came breathing heavily behind her. Then they came out on a sunlit hillside, sloping softly into another one a little smaller. Beyond, they could see the rusted top of the old barn where the extra hay was stored.

The hill was sprinkled with small pink weeds. "Then you ain't saved?" he asked suddenly, stopping.

The girl smiled. It was the first time she had smiled at him at all. "In my economy," she said, "I'm saved and you are damned but I told you I didn't believe in God."

56   Nothing seemed to destroy the boy's look of admiration. He gazed at her now as if the fantastic animal at the zoo had put its paw through the bars and given him a loving poke. She thought he looked as if he wanted to kiss her again and she walked on before he had the chance.

"Ain't there somewheres we can sit down sometime?" he murmured, his voice softening toward the end of the sentence.

"In that barn," she said.

57   They made for it rapidly as if it might slide away like a train. It was a large two-story barn, cool and dark inside. The boy pointed up the ladder that led into the loft and said, "It's too bad we can't go up there."

"Why can't we?" she asked.

"Yer leg," he said reverently.

58   The girl gave him a contemptuous look and putting both hands on the ladder, she climbed it while he stood below, apparently awestruck. She pulled herself expertly through the opening and then looked down at him and said, "Well, come on if you're coming," and he began to climb the ladder, awkwardly bringing the suitcase with him.

"We won't need the Bible," she observed.

59   "You never can tell," he said, panting. After he had got into the loft, he was a few seconds catching his breath. She had sat down in a pile of straw. A wide sheath of sunlight, filled with dust particles, slanted over her. She lay back against a bale, her face turned away, looking out the front opening of the barn where hay was thrown from a wagon into the loft. The two pink-speckled hillsides lay back against a dark ridge of woods. The sky was cloudless and cold blue. The boy dropped down by her side and put one arm under her and the

other over her and began methodically kissing her face, making little noises like a fish. He did not remove his hat but it was pushed far enough back not to interfere. When her glasses got in his way, he took them off of her and slipped them into his pocket.

The girl at first did not return any of the kisses but presently she began to   *60* and after she had put several on his cheek, she reached his lips and remained there, kissing him again and again as if she were trying to draw all the breath out of him. His breath was clear and sweet like a child's and the kisses were sticky like a child's. He mumbled about loving her and about knowing when he first seen her that he loved her, but the mumbling was like the sleepy fretting of a child being put to sleep by his mother. Her mind, throughout this, never stopped or lost itself for a second to her feelings. "You ain't said you loved me none," he whispered finally, pulling back from her. "You got to say that."

She looked away from him off into the hollow sky and then down at a black   *61* ridge and then down farther into what appeared to be two green swelling lakes. She didn't realize he had taken her glasses but this landscape could not seem exceptional to her for she seldom paid any close attention to her surroundings.

"You got to say it," he repeated. "You got to say you love me."

She was always careful how she committed herself. "In a sense," she began,   *62* "if you use the word loosely, you might say that. But it's not a word I use. I don't have illusions. I'm one of those people who see *through* to nothing."

The boy was frowning. "You got to say it. I said it and you got to say it," he said.

The girl looked at him almost tenderly. "You poor baby," she murmured.   *63* "It's just as well you don't understand," and she pulled him by the neck, face-down, against her. "We are all damned," she said, "but some of us have taken off our blindfolds and see that there's nothing to see. It's a kind of salvation."

The boy's astonished eyes looked blankly through the ends of her hair. "Okay," he almost whined, "but do you love me or don'tcher?"

"Yes," she said and added, "in a sense. But I must tell you something.   *64* There mustn't be anything dishonest between us." She lifted his head and looked him in the eye. "I am thirty years old," she said. "I have a number of degrees."

The boy's look was irritated but dogged. "I don't care," he said. "I don't   *65* care a thing about what all you done. I just want to know if you love me or don'tcher?" and he caught her to him and wildly planted her face with kisses until she said, "Yes, yes."

"Okay then," he said, letting her go. "Prove it."

She smiled, looking dreamily out on the shifty landscape. She had seduced   *66* him without even making up her mind to try. "How?" she asked, feeling that he should be delayed a little.

He leaned over and put his lips to her ear. "Show me where your wooden leg joins on," he whispered.

The girl uttered a sharp little cry and her face instantly drained of color.   *67* The obscenity of the suggestion was not what shocked her. As a child she had sometimes been subject to feelings of shame but education had removed the last traces of that as a good surgeon scrapes for cancer; she would no more have felt it over what he was asking than she would have believed in his Bible. But she was as sensitive about the artificial leg as a peacock about his tail. No one ever touched it but her. She took care of it as someone else would his soul, in private and almost with her own eyes turned away. "No," she said.

68   "I known it," he muttered, sitting up. "You're just playing me for a sucker."

"Oh no no!" she cried. "It joins on at the knee. Only at the knee. Why do you want to see it?"

The boy gave her a long penetrating look. "Because," he said, "it's what makes you different. You ain't like anybody else."

69   She sat staring at him. There was nothing about her face or her round freezing-blue eyes to indicate that this had moved her; but she felt as if her heart had stopped and left her mind to pump her blood. She decided that for the first time in her life she was face to face with real innocence. This boy, with an instinct that came from beyond wisdom, had touched the truth about her. When after a minute, she said in a hoarse high voice, "All right," it was like surrendering to him completely. It was like losing her own life and finding it again, miraculously, in his.

70   Very gently he began to roll the slack leg up. The artificial limb, in a white sock and brown flat shoe, was bound in a heavy material like canvas and ended in an ugly jointure where it was attached to the stump. The boy's face and his voice were entirely reverent as he uncovered it and said, "Now show me how to take it off and on."

71   She took it off for him and put it back on again and then he took it off himself, handling it as tenderly as if it were a real one. "See!" he said with a delighted child's face. "Now I can do it myself!"

72   "Put it back on," she said. She was thinking that she would run away with him and that every night he would take the leg off and every morning put it back on again, "Put it back on," she said.

"Not yet," he murmured, setting it on its foot out of her reach. "Leave it off for a while. You got me instead."

73   She gave a little cry of alarm but he pushed her down and began to kiss her again. Without the leg she felt entirely dependent on him. Her brain seemed to have stopped thinking altogether and to be about some other function that it was not very good at. Different expressions raced back and forth over her face. Every now and then the boy, his eyes like two steel spikes, would glance behind him where the leg stood. Finally she pushed him off and said, "Put it back on me now."

74   "Wait," he said. He leaned the other way and pulled the valise toward him and opened it. It had a pale blue spotted lining and there were only two Bibles in it. He took one of these out and opened the cover of it. It was hollow and contained a pocket flask of whiskey, a pack of cards, and a small blue box with printing on it. He laid these out in front of her one at a time in an evenly-

spaced row, like one presenting offerings at the shrine of a goddess. He put the blue box in her hand. THIS PRODUCT TO BE USED ONLY FOR THE PRE-VENTION OF DISEASE, she read, and dropped it. The boy was unscrewing the top of the flask. He stopped and pointed, with a smile, to the deck of cards. It was not an ordinary deck but one with an obscene picture on the back of each card. "Take a swig," he said, offering her the bottle first. He held it in front of her, but like one mesmerized, she did not move.

Her voice when she spoke had an almost pleading sound. "Aren't you," she murmured, "aren't you just good country people?"

The boy cocked his head. He looked as if he were just beginning to under-   75 stand that she might be trying to insult him. "Yeah," he said, curling his lip slightly, "but it ain't held me back none. I'm as good as you any day in the week."

"Give me my leg," she said.

He pushed it farther away with his foot. "Come on now, let's begin to have us a good time," he said coaxingly. "We ain't got to know one another good yet."

"Give me my leg!" she screamed and tried to lunge for it but he pushed her down easily.

"What's the matter with you all of a sudden?" he asked, frowning as he   76 screwed the top on the flask and put it quickly back inside the Bible. "You just a while ago said you didn't believe in nothing. I thought you was some girl!"

Her face was almost purple. "You're a Christian!" she hissed. "You're a fine Christian! You're just like them all—say one thing and do another. You're a perfect Christian, you're . . ."

The boy's mouth was set angrily. "I hope you don't think," he said in a lofty   77 indignant tone, "that I believe in that crap! I may sell Bibles but I know which end is up and I wasn't born yesterday and I know where I'm going!"

"Give me my leg!" she screeched. He jumped up so quickly that she barely   78 saw him sweep the cards and the blue box into the Bible and throw the Bible into the valise. She saw him grab the leg and then she saw it for an instant slanted forlornly across the inside of the suitcase with a Bible at either side of its opposite ends. He slammed the lid shut and snatched up the valise and swung it down the hole and then stepped through himself.

When all of him had passed but his head, he turned and regarded her with a   79 look that no longer had any admiration in it. "I've gotten a lot of interesting things," he said. "One time I got a woman's glass eye this way. And you needn't to think you'll catch me because Pointer ain't really my name. I use a different name at every house I call at and don't stay nowhere long. And I'll tell you another thing, Hulga," he said, using the name as if he didn't think much of it, "you ain't so smart. I been believing in nothing ever since I was born!" and then the toast-colored hat disappeared down the hole and the girl was left, sitting on the straw in the dusty sunlight. When she turned her churn-ing face toward the opening, she saw his blue figure struggling successfully over the green speckled lake.

Mrs. Hopewell and Mrs. Freeman, who were in the back pasture, digging up onions, saw him emerge a little later from the woods and head across the meadow toward the highway. "Why, that looks like that nice dull young man that tried to sell me a Bible yesterday," Mrs. Hopewell said, squinting. "He must have been selling them to the Negroes back in there. He was so simple," she said, "but I guess the world would be better off if we were all that simple."

81   Mrs. Freeman's gaze drove forward and just touched him before he disappeared under the hill. Then she returned her attention to the evil-smelling onion shoot she was lifting from the ground. "Some can't be that simple," she said. "I know I never could."

WRITING AND DISCUSSION QUESTIONS

Informative

1. O'Connor is a master of capturing the "everydayness" of life, its "ordinary" moments, which when put under a microscope make individual lives look foolish or wasted. What facts does she reveal about Mrs. Freeman and her daughters early in the story? How do these facts affect your view of them?
2. Consider Hulga/Joy's character. Is she sympathetic or not? What is her supreme mission in life, especially in regard to philosophy and religious faith? What does she want to do for Manley Pointer?
3. Does O'Connor intend to portray Pointer as a stereotypical Southerner—as a "Bible-belt" representative—or as an exaggeration? Do his actions at the end of the story shock you?

Persuasive

1. Argue whether O'Connor intends us to read her story as a satire of Southern faith or Southern unbelief. Are there any "good country people" in the story?
2. At one point, Hulga says, "I don't have illusions. I'm one of those people who see *through* to nothing. Argue that she is or is not perceptive of her own strengths and weaknesses. By story's end, how confident is she in her ability to read human character?
3. O'Connor once told an audience that to make Christian beliefs "visible" to her readers, she had to "draw large and startling figures" for the "almost blind" characters in her stories. Identify some of the "large and startling figures" in the story, and argue that they represent the presence or absence of a particular tenet of Christianity.

Personal

1. One of the central techniques of O'Connor's fiction is the highlighting of the cliches that substitute for real thinking and cloud her characters' perception of the

way the world actually works. Mrs. Freeman and Mrs. Hopewell exchange a number of them, for instance, "some people are more alike than others." What cliches have you observed other people, and even yourself, using that might need examination and rejection?

2. Do you have any traits like those that Hulga/Joy possesses as a result of education? Do you consider yourself a person who can see through things as Hulga fancies herself? What are the dangers of Hulga's seemingly self-assured self-important attitudes toward life?

3. Mrs. Hopewell seems disappointed with Hulga/Joy's career decisions: "You could not say, 'My daughter is a philosopher.'" In what way do our parents and peers affect our perceptions of ourselves and drive us toward beliefs and attitudes that we may not consciously choose? Can this affect our very attitudes toward religious faith as well?

CHAPTER WRITING ASSIGNMENTS

1. Write a persuasive essay that explores the impact of the Law of Moses or the Sermon on the Mount on North American culture. Include such considerations: the extent to which our legal and judicial systems are based on these teachings, beneficial and detrimental influences, the extent to which influence is being eroded or altered. In view of the way our culture is headed are you optimistic or pessimistic about the twenty-first century?

2. Write a tongue-in-cheek essay that "discovers" laws or principles inadvertently left out of the Ten Commandments or Sermon on the Mount. Title your essay "The Lost Book of Moses" or "The Missing Notes from the Sermon on the Mount," and consider those twentieth-century circumstances that elicit new or different versions of the guidelines Moses or Jesus presented.

3. If you consider yourself a believer in God, craft an essay that explains your reasons for your faith to a sympathetic, but skeptical, nonbeliever. You may cite personal experience, but base your essay on historical and Biblical evidence as much as possible. If you consider yourself a nonbeliever in God, craft an essay that explains your reasons for your lack of faith to a sympathetic, but skeptical, believer. You may cite personal experience, but, again, base your essay on historical and Biblical evidence as much as possible.

4. Science and religious faith are often assumed to be in conflict. Each "side" tends to identify the other with being either "unscientific" or "superstitious." Considering the views that C. S. Lewis offers in his "Meditation in a Toolshed," develop an essay that answers these questions: do science and religion necessarily contradict? can they be reconciled? should one have more authority than the

other? Craft an essay that might be titled, "Toward a Harmony of Science and Religion" or "Refuting the Claims of Religion from a Scientific Point of View." Argue in your essay that (1) the claims of science take precedence over the claims of religion, (2) the claims of religion take precedence over those of science, or (3) some synthesis of these two positions can be achieved that parcels out different realms of authority depending on the particular issues. Whichever view you take, assume that your reader will not necessarily be sympathetic to your point of view, and thus present evidence accordingly.

5. Write an essay that examines carefully the religious faith—in its absence or presence—of the characters Hulga/Joy ("Good Country People") and Joe and Danny ("The Law"). What do they share? How do they differ? How does their religious heritage shape their view of the world?

Chapter Four

HUMANISM

The humanistic tradition began with the Greeks, and many of the ideals contained in their civilization have since contributed to Western culture's sense of human potential and achievement. Indeed, the Greeks have profoundly affected our understanding of such areas of learning and practice as politics, law, philosophy, art, architecture, logic, poetry, drama, history, biography, language, oratory, mathematics, science, and athletic competition. It is humanism that has led us to see these areas not as god-given institutions fixed for all time, but as human creations that can be continuously modified. In addition, humanism has given us such ideals as the value of the individual human being and of his or her total development—a healthy mind in a healthy body—ideals out of which modern democracy and mass education naturally grew. Although not a sudden development (for most of these contributions appeared between 800 B.C. and A.D. 200, and the most important occurred in the fifth and fourth centuries B.C.), the flowering of Greek humanism is nevertheless unprecedented in its cultural breadth and is rivaled only by Judeo–Christian thought in its influence on modern culture. So powerful and pervasive a body of thought clearly demands our attention in terms of both its historical roots and present manifestations.

THE GREEKS: CULTURAL BACKGROUNDS TO THE RISE OF HUMANISM

Although a highly religious people, the Greeks did not have the Jews' sense of being divinely chosen for some special long-term destiny. The lack of such a view

187

Bronze Zeus from Artemisium, 460–450 B.C., believed to have held a thunderbolt. Athens, National Museum. From John Boardman et al., *The Oxford History of the Classical World*, Oxford University Press, 1988, p. 284.

of themselves might have contributed to the emergence of personal freedom and freedom of thought as important values which most Greeks believed only themselves capable of pursuing and appreciating. In fact, the Greeks coined the word "barbarian" *(barbaros)*, with all its connotations of being less than fully civilized, to refer to anyone not Greek (actually, not a native speaker of Greek; the modern concept of nationhood did not exist in the ancient world).

The Greek kind of polytheism, belief in many gods, might also have encouraged their pursuit of the fullness of life. Unlike the Judiac tradition, their gods were anthropomorphic, being regularly depicted with human bodies. Their personalities were also modeled on the human, for they were capable of lofty justice and munificence and also of the pettiest human behavior. They included twelve major Olympian deities, listed here with their more familiar Roman counterparts in parentheses—Zeus (Jupiter), Hera (Juno), Athena (Minerva), Apollo, Artemis (Diana), Poseidon (Neptune), Aphrodite (Venus), Hermes (Mercury), Hephaestus (Vulcan), Ares (Mars), Demeter (Ceres), and Dionysius (Bacchus)—and two major gods of the underworld, Hades (Pluto) and Persephone (Proserpine). Each was linked with special symbols, or attributes, and areas of life. Those areas may seem sometimes contradictory: Artemis was associated both with chastity and childbirth, Athena with wisdom and warfare—and sometimes redundant: Ares was also associated with war. But taken together they seem to cover all imaginable areas of life. Each Greek community tended to give special honor to a limited number of the gods and to adopt patrons. The people of Athens, for example, believed themselves to be in the special care of Athena. On the whole though, the Greeks believed that the wise person pays homage to all the major goddesses and gods, a belief that suggested the value of all areas of human experience. Thus, honoring the gods included participating in all areas of life: engaging in physical love, for example, was as much an act of homage to Aphrodite, goddess of love, as performing what we would see as more specifically religious rites.

Greek religion focused on the fullness of life in other ways as well. Although the Greeks conceived of an afterlife, their values were centered on this life and on developing their capacities to enjoy it. The point is made explicit in Book XI of Homer's *Odyssey* when Odysseus, having performed a sacrifice to call up the dead for consultation on how he can return home, speaks with the ghost of Achilles, the greatest warrior in the Trojan War. Odysseus, believing that the position of so great a man among the dead must be royal, wonders why Achilles seems so unhappy. Achilles answers, "Better, I say, to break sod as a farm hand / for some poor country man, on iron rations, / than lord it over all the exhausted dead." In other words, he would rather be the poorest of day laborers and alive than be king of all the dead. The Greeks came, in fact, to cultivate the joy of living in all its possible dimensions: not only the natural joy that begins with merely drawing breath, but also the pleasures that come from wealth and power and the deeper delight and fullness that come from pursuits like love, art, literature, and philosophy.

This sense of fullness was exhibited also in Greek social and political life. Although speaking a common language, Greeks developed numerous independent city–states with considerable differences in social and political systems. They were no doubt influenced in this regard by their mountainous land with its many relatively isolated valleys, their irregular coast with countless harbors, and the opportunities for exchange and colonization offered by the many islands in the highly navigable and relatively placid Aegean Sea. Whether or not the cause was primarily geographical, they managed to avoid the gigantic autocracies that developed in Egypt and Mesopotamia and were able to develop the first models for the democratic state.

Democracy, however, was only one of many political systems the Greek city–states established, and the early models were too far from perfect to inspire anything like a democratic revolution. In fact, Athens, whose empire lasted only a half century, served more as an example of the failure than of the success of democracy. Yet that system had elements of what many today see as ideal: theirs was a participatory rather than a representative democracy, one in which every citizen could sit in the Assembly, the primary governing body, and many important positions were determined periodically by lot, practices that suggested the value of distributing rather than concentrating political power. These practices, as developed and adapted by the Romans, would form the basis of the U.S. Constitution.

Also from a modern point of view, however, Athenian democracy exhibited deeper flaws. In practice, far less than a majority participated because women, slaves, and the people of the subject states of Athens' empire were denied any part at all. Participatory democracy worked as well as it did in Athens because it paid citizens to attend the Assembly out of funds exacted from its subject states. In fact, Athens was more ruthless even than Sparta in establishing and maintaining its domination.

Both slavery and the exclusion of women from public life were widespread throughout the ancient world, but there were wide variations in the degree to which each was applied, even within the Greek world, and Athens was one of the worst in this regard. One scholar, Oswyn Murray, tells us that in Athens

> the family clearly served as the means of protecting and enclosing women. Women were citizens, with certain cults reserved to them and not allowed to foreign women, and they were citizens for the purposes of marriage and procreation; but otherwise they lacked all independence status. They . . . could not own any property, with the conventional exception of their clothes, their personal jewelry and personal slaves. . . . At all times the woman belonged to a family and was under the legal protection of its head.[1]

Women were, in effect, a kind of property: those deemed respectable were kept in Oriental seclusion; the others were used primarily as prostitutes. A further indication of the status of women is provided in Eva C. Keuls' description of a "peculiar quirk of Attic law":

> Under a statute attributed to Solon [early sixth century] and perhaps really initiated by him, virtually any legal action undertaken by a man was invalid if it could be shown to have been conceived "under the influence of a woman" or "through the persuasion of a woman." . . . That the charge was taken seriously in legal proceedings . . . is indicated by the fact that in 404 B.C. . . . the statute was abolished for the purpose of donations of property.[2]

Even the intellectuals held similar views, believing that women had less capacity for reason. The philosopher Aristotle, for example, held that "the deliberative faculty" in the female was "inoperative."

The existence of these contradictions presents a special challenge to our sense of historical perspective. It is not enough to notice such faults briefly, set them aside as peculiarities of a culture not our own, and then (as Western culture has traditionally done) emphasize the positive features of Greek culture and enshrine its great figures as our intellectual fathers. Perhaps this is part of the reason that our own country was born in a spirit that raised the rhetoric of personal freedom

---

[1]Murray, O. *The Oxford History of the Classical World.* New York: Oxford University Press, 1988, p. 206.
[2]Keuls, E. V. *The Reign of the Phallus: Sexual Politics in Ancient Athens,* New York: Harper & Row, 1985, p. 322.

 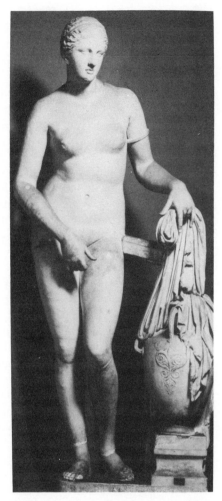

The Doryphorus (spear carrier) by Polyclitus *(left)*, Roman marble copy of a Greek bronze original from 440 B.C.; used by the artist to display his views of the ideal proportions for the human figure. The Aphrodite by Praxiteles *(right)*, Roman copy of a Greek marble original from 340 B.C.; widely held to be the greatest statue of antiquity. From John Boardman et al., *The Oxford History of the Classical World*, Oxford University Press, 1988, pp. 271, 288.

to new heights while it institutionalized slavery and continued to subjugate women.

Despite its unattractive elements, Greek culture did foster an unprecedented spirit of debate and free inquiry among its male citizens. It was this spirit that is the most important Greek contribution to humanism, for it is reflected in the disciplines of rational inquiry and critical analysis, of history, logic, metaphysics, and ethics. The growth of these intellectual disciplines helps account for the difference between the Hebrew concept of justice, and the Greek practice of asking and pursuing analytically the question of what is the best possible such system and how may it be created. Whereas the Hebrews saw all law and virtually all knowledge as coming from God and saw humanity's duty as being faithful and obedient, the Greeks raised all questions anew and sought answers based on reasoned argument and logical demonstration, principles that Western culture has come to value highly.

Another major Greek contribution to humanism that was as important to the Greeks as was rational inquiry was the expansion of aesthetic sensibilities, sensibilities we continue to value. The Greeks poured forth a flood of creative energy in the arts, most notably in architecture, sculpture, poetry, and drama. Although most of Greek art was religious—its major architecture was temples, its major sculpture represented figures of the gods, and its major poetry and drama were written for production at religious festivals—here, too, religion seemed to encourage humanistic endeavor. Because the gods were anthropomorphic, their depiction in sculpture ultimately glorified the human form. Not bound by the concept of sacred texts, Greek dramatists could engage in a kind of reverent play with the culture's ancient myths. They could speculate about events in order to comment on current issues, to probe human character, or to seek out what seemed the universal truths of human experience. Perhaps the highest expressions of human worth in Greek culture are found in the tragic dramas, in which the Greeks explored the paradoxical mixture of fallibility and dignity in the human struggle to endure the tragic conditions of life.

These and more contributions of the humanistic tradition to culture will be revealed in the readings that follow, not the least of which is the variety of ways of defining human value itself and the variety of ways that human value can be seen in relation to other values, including religious ones. Contrary to the Judeo–Christian tradition, however, humanism begins not with a god's love for humanity but with one human being's love for another.

SAPPHO, SELECTIONS

By the time of Sappho (c. 610–575 B.C.), many of the cultural patterns familiar to Classical Greece had already formed. Greek religion and mythology had been well developed six centuries earlier. The first Olympic games had been held about 776 B.C. Many of the major city–states had not only been founded but had established a Greek colonial presence throughout the Aegean Sea, including the western end of Asia Minor, and westward across the Adriatic Sea to Italy and Sicily. During the latter half of the eighth century B.C., the Greek alphabet was developed, which was a major advance over previous writing systems and one that made possible one of the greatest literary cultures the world would ever see. Also, toward the end of that century, Homer most likely wrote the great epics, the *Iliad* and *Odyssey* (loosely based on events of more than five centuries earlier), and Hesiod wrote the first systematic mythology, the *Theogony*. The first great lyric poetry, written to be sung to the accompaniment of the small harplike lyre, appeared near the end of the seventh century B.C., most notably from the pen of Sappho.

The little we know of Sappho includes her home, the city of Mytilene on Lesbos, one of the largest of the Aegean islands, part of the area close to and including western Asia Minor that the Greeks referred to as Ionia. Of noble birth, she was among several families exiled to Sicily about 600 B.C. because of political enmity, but she was allowed to return to Lesbos some years later. She was married and had at least one child, a daughter. The lovers to whom she most frequently addresses poems are women named Anaktoria and Atthis.

It is difficult for us to imagine the kind of attitudes that made possible a woman like Sappho, married, perhaps even respectable in her own society, and yet celebrating openly her passion for other women. Although sexual freedom, including a casual acceptance of homosexual love, was not unusual among Greek men, there is no indication outside of Sappho's works of its having been accepted among women. It is, therefore, difficult to imagine a Sappho flourishing in many other Greek societies, certainly not in Athens. Her culture might, in fact, have been a remnant of matriarchal cultures that prevailed throughout the Mediterranean and Near East in the ancient past until they were gradually replaced by patriarchal cultures over a period of nearly 2500 years, from approximately 3100 to 600 B.C. This transformation might have taken place by way of developments within cultures and by way of conquests by more powerful immigrating patriarchies. Indeed, some modern anthropologists see the many Greek myths of gods raping goddesses and mortal women as the vestiges of these conquests: one people conquering another was expressed as the winner's gods subjugating the loser's.

Vestigial survivals of matriarchy may also explain the degree of Sappho's emphasis on the worship of Aphrodite. Matriarchies place their greatest emphasis on the worship of goddesses, as did the people of some Aegean and western Mediterranean islands. Notable among them was Cyprus, famous for its worship of Aphrodite, which is why Sappho sometimes refers to the goddess of love as "the Kyprian." Emphasis on the worship of love, however, was unusual throughout most of Greek civilization at that time, which was largely made up of warrior societies. Although they would acknowledge the power of love, they typically considered it a cause of strife, an idea enshrined in the story of Helen, wife of the Greek Menelaos, who ran off with or was abducted by Paris, prince of Troy, and thus precipitated the Trojan War.

Whatever else we know of Sappho comes from her poetry, of which only a small fraction survives, and that in broken fragments. Because of these fragments, one might be deceived into thinking Sappho unusually modern in her apparent practice of writing very short poems embodying a single vivid image, but all of the short poems and most of the longer pieces are parts of larger poems now lost, and all the titles, which seem to set off each piece as a separate poem, have been supplied by modern editors. Despite these fragments, her work has been lavishly praised by both the ancient poets who would have had more complete versions of her work and by many of the greatest poets since. Indeed, these fragments work and have universal appeal as poems because they reveal so uncommon a combination of simplicity, honesty, and vividness.

▼

Selections
SAPPHO

120 THE LYRIC POEM

Come, holy tortoise shell,
my lyre, and become a poem.

121 NOW I BEGIN

I begin with words of air
yet they are good to hear.

122 HEADDRESS

My mother always said
that in her youth she was
exceedingly in fashion

wearing a purple ribbon
looped in her hair. But
the girl whose hair is yellower

than torchlight need wear no
colorful ribbons from Sardis—
but a garland of fresh flowers.

123 HER INNOCENCE

I do not have a rancorous spirit
but the simple heart of a child.

124 TO ANAKTORIA

Some say cavalry and others claim
infantry or a fleet of long oars
is the supreme sight on the black earth.
I say it is

the one you love. And easily proved.
Did not Helen—who far surpassed all
mortals in beauty—desert the best
of men, her king,

and sail off to Troy and forget
her daughter and dear kinsmen? Merely
the *Kyprian*'s gaze made her bend and led
her from her path;

these things remind me now
of Anaktoria who is far,
and I
for one

would rather see her warm supple step
and the sparkle of her face—than watch
all the dazzling chariots and armored
                    hoplites of Lydia.[1]

125   ALONE[2]

The moon and Pleiades
are set. Midnight,
and time spins away.
I lie in bed, alone.

126   TO EROS[3]

You burn me.

127   THE BLAST OF LOVE

Like a mountain whirlwind
punishing the oak trees,
love shattered my heart.

128   SEIZURE

To me he seems like a god
as he sits facing you and
hears you near as you speak
softly and laugh

in a sweet echo that jolts
the heart in my ribs. For now
as I look at you my voice
is empty and

can say nothing as my tongue
cracks and slender fire is quick
under my skin. My eyes are dead
to light, my ears

[1]Hoplites are elite, heavily armed infantry; Lydia is a kingdom in west central Asia Minor; Sappho uses this phrase perhaps because Lydian hoplites were of legendary beauty or perhaps, as we learn later (Fragment 141), because Anaktoria now lives in Sardis, capital of Lydia. This may also explain the reference to Sardis in Fragment 122.
[2]Authorship uncertain.
[3]Eros, the god of love.

pound, and sweat pours over me.
I convulse, paler than grass,
and feel my mind slip as I
go close to death.

129   WORLD

I could not hope
to touch the sky
with my two arms.

130   BEACH COLOR

The furzy flower of the golden broom
grew along the shore.

131   LET SLEEPING DOGS LIE

Don't stir up the small
heaps of beach jetsam.

132   TO HER GIRLFRIENDS

On this day I will sing beautifully
and make you happy, dear comrades.

133   FULL MOON

The glow and beauty of the stars
are nothing near the splendid moon
when in her roundness she burns silver
about the world.

134   THEN

In gold sandals
dawn like a thief
fell upon me.

135 THE CRICKET

When sun dazzles the earth
with straight-falling flames,
a cricket rubs its wings
scraping up a shrill song.

136 PIGEONS AT REST

The hearts in the pigeons grew cold
and their wings dropped to their sides.

137 THE HERALD

Nightingale, with your
lovely voice, you are
the herald of spring.

138 EVENING STAR

Of all stars Hesperos,[4]
is the most beautiful.

139 CEREMONY

Now the earth with many flowers
puts on her spring embroidery.

140 DEAR ATTHIS, DID YOU KNOW?

In dream Love came out of heaven
and put on his purple cloak.

141 TO ATTHIS

My Atthis, although our dear Anaktoria
lives in distant Sardis,
she thinks of us constantly, and

[4]Hesperos, the planet Venus when it was the evening star; during the part of the year when it was the morning star, Venus had another name, Phosphoros.

of the life we shared in days when for her
you were a splendid goddess,
and your singing gave her deep joy.

Now she shines among Lydian women as
when the red-fingered moon
rises after sunset, erasing

stars around her, and pouring light equally
across the salt sea
and over densely flowered fields;

and lucent dew spreads on the earth to quicken
roses and fragile thyme
and the sweet-blooming honey-lotus.

Now while our darling wanders she remembers lovely Atthis' love,
and longing sinks deep in her breast.

She cries loudly for us to come! We hear,
for the night's many tongues
carry her cry across the sea.

142   A LETTER[5]

"Sappho, if you do not come out,
I swear, I will love you no more.

O rise and free your lovely strength
from the bed and shine upon us.
Lift off your Chian nightgown, and

like a pure lily by a spring,
bathe in the water. Our Kleïs
will bring a saffron blouse and violet

tunic from your chest. We will place
a clean mantle on you, and crown
your hair with flowers. So come, darling,

with your beauty that maddens us,
and you, Praxinoa, roast the nuts
for our breakfast. One of the gods

is good to us, for on this day
Sappho, most beautiful of women,
will come with us to the white city

---

[5]The speaker may be Atthis, whose words Sappho is quoting.

of Mytilene, like a mother
among her daughters," Dearest Atthis,
can you now forget all those days?

143   TO HER FRIEND

Honestly I wish I were dead!
Although she too cried bitterly

when she left, and said to me,
"Ah, what a nightmare it is now.
Sappho, I swear I go unwillingly."

And I answered, "Go, and be happy.
But remember me, for surely you
know how we worshiped you. If not,

then I want to remind you of all
the exquisite days
we two shared; how

you took garlands of violets
and roses, and when by my side
you tied them round you in soft bands,

and you took many flowers
and flung them in loops
about your sapling throat,

how the air was rich in a scent
of queenly spices made of myrrh
you rubbed smoothly on your limbs,

and on soft beds, gently, your desire
for delicate girls
was satisfied,

and how there was no dance and no
holy shrine
we two did not share,

no sound,
no
grove."

144   TO ATTHIS

Love—bittersweet, irrepressible—
loosens my limbs and I tremble.

Yet, Atthis, you despise my being.
To chase Andromeda, you leave me.

145   TO ATTHIS

I loved you, Atthis, long ago,
when my girlhood was in full flower
and you were like a graceless child.

146   LONG DEPARTURE

Then I said to the elegant ladies:
"How you will remember when you are old
the glorious things we did in our youth!

We did many pure and beautiful things.
Now that you are leaving the city,
love's sharp pain encircles my heart."

147   A PRAYER TO APHRODITE

On your dazzling throne, Aphrodite,
sly eternal daughter of Zeus,
I beg you: do not crush me with grief,

but come to me now—as once
you heard my far cry, and yielded,
slipping from your father's house

to yoke the birds to your gold
chariot, and came. Handsome sparrows
brought you swiftly to the dark earth,

their wings whipping the middle sky.
Happy, with deathless lips, you smiled:
"What is wrong, why have you called me?

What does your mad heart desire?
Whom shall I make love you, Sappho,
who is turning her back on you?

Let her run away, soon she'll chase you;
refuse your gifts, soon she'll give them.
She will love you, though unwillingly."

Then come to me now and free me
from fearful agony. Labor
for my mad heart, and be my ally.

148   TO APHRODITE OF THE FLOWERS, AT KNOSSOS[6]

Leave Krete and come to this holy temple
where the graceful grove of apple trees
circles an altar smoking with frankincense.

Here roses leave shadow on the ground
and cold springs babble through apple branches
where shuddering leaves pour down profound sleep.

In our meadow where horses graze
and wild flowers of spring blossom,
anise shoots fill the air with aroma.

And here, Queen Aphrodite, pour
heavenly nectar into gold cups
and fill them gracefully with sudden joy.

WRITING AND DISCUSSION QUESTIONS

Informative

1. List some of the subjects that Sappho writes about. What does she have to say about them? Do any themes emerge as recurring?
2. Why would Sappho describe the dawn in lyric 134 as a thief?

Persuasive

1. It has been said that Sappho sings less of the joys of love than of the pain of loss. Argue for or against this contention.
2. There has been much speculation about Sappho's day-to-day life and of the society of women she moved in. Some scholars, for example, have speculated that she might have run a women's finishing school. Under what conditions can you imagine such a society existing? How do you suppose men entered into the picture?

---

[6]Knossos was the capital of ancient Crete.

Personal

1. How are Sappho's poems humanistic?
2. Write a few short lyrics in imitation of Sappho's poetry.

▼

THUCYDIDES, SELECTIONS FROM *THE PELOPONNESIAN WAR*

Often seen as the first true historian, Thucydides (c. 460–c. 404 B.C.) was an Athenian naval general who in 424 B.C. was exiled from Athens after he failed to save the city Amphipolis from surprise attack by the Spartan league. During his exile, which lasted for 20 years, he traveled throughout Greece collecting materials for his *History of the Peloponnesian War*. Although the Peloponnesian War lasted from 431 to 404 B.C. and is the subject of his history, Thucydides sets its stage with an introductory section, the major portion of which is reprinted here, that presents the history of Greece from its origins up until the time of the war.

The word "history" used to describe a particular literary form did not originate with Thucydides. His predecessor Herodotus (c. 484–c. 428 B.C.) completed in 425 B.C. his *Historia*, "Investigations," a chronicle of the Persian Wars (490–460 B.C.). Herodotus seems to have adopted a historian's purpose because he undertook this work, in his own words, "so that the achievements of men should not be obliterated by time." He also seems to have adopted a historian's method because his work is based on personally collected oral history. However, he often seemed interested more in a good story; he attributed events to the operations of divine will rather than analyzing their human and natural causes, and his overall view was biased by his pro-Greek vision of the war as a struggle between Persian slavery and Greek freedom.

Thucydides, on the other hand, approached his subject with a truly critical attitude. He sought in the humanistic spirit to describe the objective truth of human action. Among the indications of this are his initial reference to himself in the third person, his rejection of the tale teller's practice (especially to be found in Homer) of attributing a grandeur to the past that the present could never rival, his efforts to distinguish between fact and opinion, and his willingness to acknowledge what he does not know. An example of his critical technique is his analysis of the causes of the Trojan War: not the romantic ideas of oaths and love, but the "real" politics of power and fear.

The second selection from Thucydides is from a much later section of his history, an oration by Pericles, the dominant political figure in Athens during the 30-year period from the end of the Persian Wars to the beginning of the Peloponnesian War. This period is usually seen as the high point of Greek civilization and is called the Periclean Age. The occasion for Pericles' oration is a funeral for the Greek warriors who fell, not only in battle but from a plague that Athens suffered in the first year of the latter war; Pericles himself would die of the plague two years later. It is an opportunity for Pericles—and through him, Thucydides—to present the ideals of Athenian democracy and a central value of the humanist tradition, the importance of the individual as a citizen.

▼

The Background of Greece
THUCYDIDES

THE STATE OF GREECE FROM THE EARLIEST TIMES TO THE COMMENCEMENT OF THE PELOPONNESIAN WAR

Thucydides, an Athenian, wrote the history of the war between the Peloponnesians[1] and the Athenians, beginning at the moment that it broke out, and believing that it would be a great war, and more worthy of relation than any that had preceded it. This belief was not without its grounds. The preparations of both the combatants were in every department in the last state of perfection; and he could see the rest of the Hellenic race taking sides in the quarrel; those who delayed doing so at once having it in contemplation. Indeed this was the greatest movement yet known in history, not only of the Hellenes, but of a large part of the barbarian world—I had almost said of mankind. For though the events of remote antiquity, and even those that more immediately precede the war, could not from lapse of time be clearly ascertained, yet the evidences which an inquiry carried as far back as was practicable leads me to trust, all point to the conclusion that there was nothing on a great scale, either in war or in other matters. 1

For instance, it is evident that the country now called Hellas[2] had in ancient times no settled population; on the contrary, migrations were of frequent occurrence, the several tribes readily abandoning their homes under the pressure of superior numbers. Without commerce, without freedom of communication either by land or sea, cultivating no more of their territory than the exigencies of life required, destitute of capital, never planting their land (for they could not tell when an invader might not come and take it all away, and when he did come they had no walls to stop him), thinking that the necessities of daily sustenance could be supplied at one place as well as another, they cared little for shifting their habitation, and consequently neither built large cities nor attained to any other form of greatness. The richest soils were always most subject to this change of masters; such as the district now called Thessaly, Bœtia, most of the Peloponnese, Arcadia excepted, and the most fertile parts of the rest of 2

---

[1]Peloponnese, the lower section of the Greek peninsula south of the Gulf of Corinth; it was dominated during the fifth century B.C. by the city of Sparta, which ruled its major state, Lacedemonia.

[2]Hellas, Hellenes, the Greek terms for the whole of the Greek world and Greek peoples.

Hellas. The goodness of the land favoured the aggrandisement of particular individuals, and thus created faction which proved a fertile source of ruin. It also invited invasion. Accordingly Attica, from the poverty of its soil enjoying from a very remote period freedom from faction, never changed its inhabitants. And here is no inconsiderable exemplification of my assertion, that the migrations were the cause of there being no correspondent growth in other parts. The most powerful victims of war or faction from the rest of Hellas took refuge with the Athenians as a safe retreat; and at an early period, becoming naturalised, swelled the already large population of the city to such a height that Attica became at last too small to hold them, and they had to send out colonies to Ionia.

3   There is also another circumstance that contributes not a little to my conviction of the weakness of ancient times. Before the Trojan war there is no indication of any common action in Hellas, nor indeed of the universal prevalence of the name; on the contrary, before the time of Hellen, son of Deucalion, no such appellation existed, but the country went by the names of the different tribes, in particular of the Pelasgian. It was not till Hellen and his sons grew strong in Phthiotis, and were invited as allies into the other cities, that one by one they gradually acquired from the connection the name of Hellenes; though a long time elapsed before that name could fasten itself upon all. The best proof of this is furnished by Homer. Born long after the Trojan war, he nowhere calls all of them by that name, nor indeed any of them except the followers of Achilles from Phthiotis, who were the original Hellenes: in his poems they are called Danaans, Argives, and Achæns. He does not even use the term barbarian, probably because the Hellenes had not yet been marked off from the rest of the world by one distinctive appellation. It appears therefore that the several Hellenic communities, comprising not only those who first acquired the name, city by city, as they came to understand each other, but also those who assumed it afterwards as the name of the whole people, were before the Trojan war prevented by their want of strength and the absence of mutual intercourse from displaying any collective action.

4   Indeed, they could not unite for this expedition till they had gained increased familiarity with the sea. And the first person known to us by tradition as having established a navy is Minos.[3] He made himself master of what is now called the Hellenic sea, and ruled over the Cyclades, into most of which he sent the first colonies, expelling the Carians and appointing his own sons governors; and thus did his best to put down piracy in those waters, a necessary step to secure the revenues for his own use.

5   For in early times the Hellenes and the barbarians of the coast and islands, as communication by sea became more common, were tempted to turn pirates, under the conduct of their most powerful men; the motives being to serve their

---

[3]Minos, legendary King of Crete, one of the most powerful and sophisticated civilizations of the eastern Mediterranean until its fall about 1400 B.C., nearly a thousand years before the period of Classical Greek civilization.

own cupidity and to support the needy. They would fall upon a town unprotected by walls, and consisting of a mere collection of villages, and would plunder it; indeed, this came to be the main source of their livelihood, no disgrace
being yet attached to such an achievement, but even some glory. An illustration
of this is furnished by the honour with which some of the inhabitants of the
continent still regard a successful marauder, and by the question we find the
old poets everywhere representing the people as asking of voyagers—'Are they
pirates?'—as if those who are asked the question would have no idea of dis-
claiming the imputation, or their interrogators of reproaching them for it. The
same rapine prevailed also by land.

And even at the present day many parts of Hellas still follow the old fashion, 6
the Ozolian Locrians, for instance, the Ætolians, the Acarnanians, and that
region of the continent; and the custom of carrying arms is still kept up among
these continentals, from the old piratical habits. The whole of Hellas used once
to carry arms, their habitations being unprotected, and their communication
with each other unsafe; indeed, to wear arms was as much a part of everyday
life with them as with the barbarians. And the fact that the people in these
parts of Hellas are still living in the old way points to a time when the same
mode of life was once equally common to all. The Athenians were the first to
lay aside their weapons, and to adopt an easier and more luxurious mode of
life; indeed, it is only lately that their rich old men left off the luxury of wearing
undergarments of linen, and fastening a knot of their hair with a tie of golden
grasshoppers, a fashion which spread to their Ionian kindred, and long prevailed among the old men there. On the contrary a modest style of dressing,
more in conformity with modern ideas, was first adopted by the Lacedæonians,
the rich doing their best to assimilate their way of life to that of the common
people. They also set the example of contending naked, publicly stripping and
anointing themselves with oil in their gymnastic exercises. Formerly, even in
the Olympic contests, the athletes who contended wore belts across their mid-
dles; and it is but a few years since that the practice ceased. To this day among
some of the barbarians, especially in Asia, when prizes for boxing and wrestling
are offered, belts are worn by the combatants. And there are many other points
in which a likeness might be shown between the life of the Hellenic world of
old and the barbarian of to-day.

With respect to their towns, later on, at an era of increased facilities of navi- 7
gation and a greater supply of capital, we find the shores becoming the site of
walled towns, and the isthmuses being occupied for the purposes of commerce,
and defence against a neighbour. But the old towns, on account of the great
prevalence of piracy, were built away from the sea, whether on the islands or
the continent, and still remain in their old sites. For the pirates used to plunder
one another, and indeed all coast populations, whether seafaring or not.

The islanders, too, were great pirates. These islanders were Carians and 8
Phœnicians, by whom most of the islands were colonised, as was proved by the
following fact. During the purification of Delos by Athens in this war all the
graves in the island were taken up, and it was found that above half their

inmates were Carians: they were identified by the fashion of the arms buried with them, and by the method of interment, which was the same as the Carians still follow. But as soon as Minos had formed his navy, communication by sea became easier, as he colonised most of the islands, and thus expelled the malefactors. The coast populations now began to apply themselves more closely to the acquisition of wealth, and their life became more settled; some even began to build themselves walls on the strength of their newly-acquired riches. For the love of gain would reconcile the weaker to the dominion of the stronger, and the possession of capital enabled the more powerful to reduce the smaller towns to subjection. And it was at a somewhat later stage of this development that they went on the expedition against Troy.[4]

9   What enabled Agamemnon[5] to raise the armament was more, in my opinion, his superiority in strength, than the oaths of Tyndareus, which bound the Suitors to follow him. Indeed, the account given by those Peloponnesians who have been the recipients of the most credible tradition is this. First of all Pelops, arriving among a needy population from Asia with vast wealth, acquired such power that, stranger though he was, the country was called after him; and this power fortune saw fit materially to increase in the hands of his descendants. Eurystheus had been killed in Attica by the Heraclids. Atreus was his mother's brother; and to the hands of his relation, who had left his father on account of the death of Chrysippus, Eurystheus, when he set out on his expedition, had committed Mycenæ and the government. As time went on and Eurystheus did not return, Atreus complied with the wishes of the Mycenæans, who were influenced by fear of the Heraclids,—besides, his power seemed considerable, and he had not neglected to court the favour of the populace,—and assumed the sceptre of Mycenæ and the rest of the dominions of Eurystheus, And so the power of the descendants of Pelops came to be greater than that of the descendants of Perseus. To all this Agamemnon succeeded. He had also a navy far stronger than his contemporaries, so that, in my opinion, fear was quite as strong an element as love in the formation of the confederate expedition. The strength of his navy is shown by the fact that his own was the largest contingent, and that of the Arcadians was furnished by him; this at least is what Homer says, if his testimony is deemed sufficient. Besides, in his account of the transmission of the sceptre, he calls him

'Of many an isle, and of all Argos king.'

Now Agamemnon's was a continental power; and he could not have been master of any except the adjacent islands (and these would not be many), but through the possession of a fleet.

---

[4]Troy, or Ilium, major city in northwest Asia Minor, site of Homer's *Iliad;* the actual war that the epic is based on probably took place 1250–1200 B.C.

[5]Agamemnon, the Greek leader during the Trojan War; he was the king of Mycenae, a powerful city–state in the northeast corner of Peloponnese; "oaths" refer to Homer's story that all the suitors of the beautiful Helen had vowed to support the man she married, who turned out to be Agamemnon's brother, Menelaos; the abduction of Helen by Paris, prince of Troy, precipitated the war.

And from this expedition we may infer the character of earlier enterprises. *10*
Now Mycenæ may have been a small place, and many of the towns of that age
may appear comparatively insignificant, but no exact observer would therefore
feel justified in rejecting the estimate given by the poets and by tradition of the
magnitude of the argument. For I suppose if Lacedæmon were to become desolate, and the temples and the foundations of the public buildings were left,
that as time went on there would be a strong disposition with posterity to refuse
to accept her fame as a true exponent of her power. And yet they occupy two-
fifths of Peloponnese and lead the whole, not to speak of their numerous allies
without. Still, as the city is neither built in a compact form nor adorned with
magnificent temples and public edifices, but composed of villages after the old
fashion of Hellas, there would be an impression of inadequacy. Whereas, if
Athens were to suffer the same misfortune, I suppose that any inference from
the appearance presented to the eye would make her power to have been twice
as great as it is. We have therefore no right to be sceptical, nor to content ourselves with an inspection of a town to the exclusion of a consideration of its
power; but we may safely conclude that the armament in question surpassed all
before it, as it fell short of modern efforts; if we can here also accept the testimony of Homer's poems, in which, without allowing for the exaggeration which
a poet would feel himself licensed to employ, we can see that it was far from
equalling ours. He has represented it as consisting of twelve hundred vessels;
the Bœotian complement of each ship being a hundred and twenty men, that of
the ships of Philoctetes fifty. By this, I conceive, he meant to convey the maximum and the minimum complement: at any rate he does not specify the
amount of any others in his catalogue of the ships. That they were all rowers as
well as warriors we see from his account of the ships of Philoctetes, in which
all the men at the oar are bowmen. Now it is improbable that many supernu-
meraries sailed if we except the kings and high officers; especially as they had
to cross the open sea with munitions of war, in ships, moreover, that had no
decks, but were equipped in the old piratical fashion. So that if we strike the
average of the largest and smallest ships, the number of those who sailed will
appear inconsiderable, representing, as they did, the whole force of Hellas.
And this was due not so much to scarcity of men as of money. Difficulty of
subsistence made the invaders reduce the numbers of the army to a point at
which it might live on the country during the prosecution of the war. Even after
the victory they obtained on their arrival—and a victory there must have been,
or the fortifications of the naval camp could never have been built—there is no
indication of their whole force having been employed; on the contrary, they
seem to have turned to cultivation of the Chersonese and to piracy from want
of supplies. This was what really enabled the Trojans to keep the field for ten
years against them; the dispersion of the enemy making them always a match
for the detachment left behind. If they had brought plenty of supplies with
them, and had persevered in the war without scattering for piracy and agriculture, they would have easily defeated the Trojans in the field; since they could
hold their own against them with the division on service. In short, if they had
stuck to the siege, the capture of Troy would have cost them less time and less

trouble. But as want of money proved the weakness of earier expeditions, so from the same cause even the one in question, more famous than its predecessors, may be pronounced on the evidence of what it effected to have been inferior to its renown and to the current opinion about it formed under the tuition of the poets.

11   Even after the Trojan war Hellas was still engaged in removing and settling, and thus could not attain to the quiet which must precede growth. The late return of the Hellenes from Ilium caused many revolutions, and factions ensued almost everywhere; and it was the citizens thus driven into exile who founded the cities. Sixty years after the capture of Ilium the modern Bœotians were driven out of Arne by the Thessalians, and settled in the present Bœotia, the former Cadmeis; though there was a division of them there before, some of whom joined the expedition to Ilium. Twenty years later the Dorians and the Heraclids became masters of Peloponnese; so that much had to be done and many years had to elapse before Hellas could attain to a durable tranquillity undisturbed by removals, and could begin to send out colonies, as Athens did to Ionia and most of the islands, and the Peloponnesians to most of Italy and Sicily and some places in the rest of Hellas. All these places were founded subsequently to the war with Troy.

12   But as the power of Hellas grew, and the acquisition of wealth became more an object, the revenues of the states increasing, tyrannies were by their means established almost everywhere,—the old form of government being hereditary monarchy with definite prerogatives,—and Hellas began to fit out fleets and apply herself more closely to the sea. It is said that the Corinthians were the first to approach the modern style of naval architecture, and that Corinth was the first place in Hellas where galleys were built; and we have Ameinocles, a Corinthian shipwright, making four ships for the Samians. Dating from the end of this war, it is nearly three hundred years ago that Ameinocles went to Samos. Again, the earliest sea-fight in history was between the Corinthians and Corcyræans; this was about two hundred and sixty years ago, dating from the same time. Planted on an isthmus, Corinth had from time out of mind been a commercial emporium; as formerly almost all communication between the Hellenes within and without Peloponnese was carried on overland, and the Corinthian territory was the highway through which it travelled. She had consequently great money resources, as is shown by the epithet 'wealthy' bestowed by the old poets on the place, and this enabled her, when traffic by sea became more common, to procure her navy and put down piracy; and as she could offer a mart for both branches of the trade, she acquired for herself all the power which a large revenue affords. Subsequently the Ionians attained to great naval strength in the reign of Cyrus, the first king of the Persians, and of his son Cambyses, and while they were at war with the former commanded for a while the Ionian sea. Polycrates also, the tyrant of Samos, had a powerful navy in the reign of Cambyses with which he reduced many of the islands, and among them Rhenea, which he consecrated to the Delian Apollo. About this time also the Phocæans, while they were founding Marseilles, defeated the Car-

thaginians in a sea-fight. These were the most powerful navies. And even these, although so many generations had elapsed since the Trojan war, seem to have been principally composed of the old fifty-oars and long-boats, and to have counted few galleys among their ranks. Indeed it was only shortly before the Persian war and the death of Darius the successor of Cambyses, that the Sicilian tyrants and the Corcyræans acquired any large number of galleys. For after these there were no navies of any account in Hellas till the expedition of Xerxes; Ægina, Athens, and others may have possessed a few vessels, but they were principally fifty-oars. It was quite at the end of this period that the war with Ægina and the prospect of the barbarian invasion enabled Themistocles to persuade the Athenians to build the fleet with which they fought at Salamis; and even these vessels had not complete decks.

The navies, then, of the Hellenes during the period we have traversed were *13* what I have described. All their insignificance did not prevent their being an element of the greatest power to those who cultivated them, alike in revenue and in dominion. They were the means by which the islands were reached and reduced, those of the smallest area falling the easiest prey. Wars by land there were none, none at least by which power was acquired; we have the usual border contests, but of distant expeditions with conquest for object we hear nothing among the Hellenes. There was no union of subject cities round a great state, no spontaneous combination of equals for confederate expeditions; what fighting there was consisted merely of local warfare between rival neighbours. The nearest approach to a coalition took place in the old war between Chalcis and Eretria; this was a quarrel in which the rest of the Hellenic name did to some extent take sides.

Various, too, were the obstacles which the national growth encountered in *14* various localities. The power of the Ionians was advancing with rapid strides, when it came into collision with Persia, under King Cyrus, who, after having dethroned Crœsus and overrun everything between the Halys and the sea, stopped not till he had reduced the cities of the coast; the islands being only left to be subdued by Darius and the Phœnician navy. Again, wherever there were tyrants,[6] their habit of providing simply for themselves, of looking solely to their personal comfort and family aggrandisement, made safety the great aim of their policy, and prevented anything great proceeding from them; though they would each have their affairs with their immediate neighbours. All this is only true of the mother country, for in Sicily they attained to very great power. Thus for a long time everywhere in Hellas do we find causes which make the states alike incapable of combination for great and national needs, or of any vigorous action of their own.

But at last a time came when the tyrants of Athens and the far older tyran- *15*

---

[6]Tyrant, not a word with negative connotations in Greek history; emerging in many city–states from the seventh to the fifth centuries B.C., tyrannies represent a stage in Greece's political evolution by which single leaders, often with popular support, overthrew the ruling aristocracies. To Thucydides, their reign seems to represent a time of instability and insularity: the tyrant was typically too concerned with maintaining his own rule, often precarious, to be concerned with larger Greek issues.

nies of the rest of Hellas were, with the exception of those in Sicily, once and for all put down by Lacedæmon; for this city, though after the settlement of the Dorians, its present inhabitants, it suffered from factions for an unparalleled length of time, still at a very early period obtained good laws, and enjoyed a freedom from tyrants which was unbroken; it has possessed the same form of government for more than four hundred years, reckoning to the end of the late war, and has thus been in a position to arrange the affairs of the other states. Not many years after the deposition of the tyrants, the battle of Marathon was fought between the Medes[7] and the Athenians. Ten years afterwards the barbarian returned with the armada for the subjugation of Hellas. In the face of this great danger the command of the confederate Hellenes was assumed by the Lacedæmonians in virtue of their superior power; and the Athenians having made up their minds to abandon their city, broke up their homes, threw themselves into their ships, and became a naval people. This coalition, after repulsing the barbarian, soon afterwards split into two sections, which included the Hellenes who had revolted from the king, as well as those who had aided him in the war. At the head of the one stood Athens, at the head of the other Lacedæmon, one the first naval, the other the first military power in Hellas. For a short time the league held together, till the Lacedæmonians and Athenians quarrelled, and made war upon each other with their allies, a duel into which all the Hellenes sooner or later were drawn, though some might at first remain neutral. So that the whole period from the Median war to this, with some peaceful intervals, was spent by each power in war, either with its rival, or with its own revolted allies, and consequently afforded them constant practice in military matters, and that experience which is learnt in the school of danger.

16   The policy of Lacedæmon was not to exact tribute from her allies, but merely to secure their subservience to her interests by establishing oligarchies among them; Athens, on the contrary, had by degrees deprived hers of their ships, and imposed instead contributions in money on all except Chios and Lesbos. Both found their resources for this war separately to exceed the sum of their strength when the alliance flourished intact.

17   Having now given the result of my inquiries into early times, I grant that there will be a difficulty in believing every particular detail. The way that most men deal with traditions, even traditions of their own country, is to receive them all alike as they are delivered, without applying any critical test whatever. The general Athenian public fancy that Hipparchus was tyrant when he fell by

[7]Medes, the Persians, builders of the greatest empire in the ancient world before the Roman empire, centered in what is now Iran and extending westward to include Asia Minor and Egypt and eastward to the Indus River. The Persian King Darius, seeking revenge against Athens for supporting rebel Ionian cities, mounted an expedition that landed in Greece and was defeated by primarily Athenian forces at Marathon in 490 B.C. Ten years later, Darius' successor, Xerxes, mounted a greater expedition, which was also repulsed, this time by combined Greek forces: mainly Spartans at Thermopylae (480 B.C.), mainly Athenians in the sea battle of Salamis (480 B.C.), Spartans and Athenians at Plataea (479 B.C.). Their success created a new sense of Greek nationalism and an alliance between Athens and Sparta that was unevenly maintained for the 30 years between the Persian and Peloponnesian wars.

the hands of Harmodius and Aristogiton; not knowing that Hippias, the eldest of the sons of Pisistratus, was really supreme, and that Hipparchus and Thessalus were his brothers; and that Harmodius and Aristogiton suspecting, on the very day, nay at the very moment fixed on for the deed, that information had been conveyed to Hippias by their accomplices, concluded that he had been warned, and did not attack him, yet, not liking to be apprehended and risk their lives for nothing, fell upon Hipparchus near the temple of the daughters of Leos, and slew him as he was arranging the Panathenaic procession.

There are many other unfounded ideas current among the rest of the Hellenes, even on matters of contemporary history which have not been obscured by time. For instance, there is the notion that the Lacedæmonian kings have two votes each, the fact being that they have only one; and that there is a company of Pitane, there being simply no such thing. So little pains do the vulgar take in the investigation of truth, accepting readily the first story that comes to hand. On the whole, however, the conclusions I have drawn from the proofs quoted may, I believe, safely be relied on. Assuredly they will not be disturbed either by the lays of a poet displaying the exaggeration of his craft, or by the compositions of the chroniclers that are attractive at truth's expense; the subjects they treat of being out of the reach of evidence, and time having robbed most of them of historical value by enthroning them in the region of legend. Turning from these, we can rest satisfied with having proceeded upon the clearest data, and having arrived at conclusions as exact as can be expected in matters of such antiquity. To come to this war; despite the known disposition of the actors in a struggle to overrate its importance, and when it is over to return to their admiration of earlier events, yet an examination of the facts will show that it was much greater than the wars which preceded it. *18*

With reference to the speeches in this history, some were delivered before the war began, others while it was going on; some I heard myself, others I got from various quarters; it was in all cases difficult to carry them word for word in one's memory, so my habit has been to make the speakers say what was in my opinion demanded of them by the various occasions, of course adhering as closely as possible to the general sense of what they really said. And with reference to the narrative of events, far from permitting myself to derive it from the first source that came to hand, I did not even trust my own impressions, but it rests partly on what I saw myself, partly on what others saw for me, the accuracy of the report being always tried by the most severe and detailed tests possible. My conclusions have cost me some labour from the want of coincidence between accounts of the same occurrences by different eye-witnesses, arising sometimes from imperfect memory, sometimes from undue partiality for one side or the other. The absence of romance in my history will, I fear, detract somewhat from its interest; but if it be judged useful by those inquirers who desire an exact knowledge of the past as an aid to the interpretation of the future, which in the course of human things must resemble if it does not reflect it, I shall be content. In fine, I have written my work, not as an essay which is to win the applause of the moment, but as a possession for all time. *19*

20   The Median war, the greatest achievement of past times, yet found a speedy decision in two actions by sea and two by land. The Peloponnesian war was prolonged to an immense length, and long as it was it was short without parallel for the misfortunes that it brought upon Hellas. Never had so many cities been taken and laid desolate, here by the barbarians, here by the parties contending (the old inhabitants being sometimes removed to make room for others); never was there so much banishing and blood-shedding, now on the field of battle, now in the strife of action. Old stories of occurrences handed down by tradition, but scantily confirmed by experience, suddenly ceased to be incredible; there were earthquakes of unparalleled extent and violence; eclipses of the sun occurred with a frequency unrecorded in previous history; there were great droughts in sundry places and consequent famines, and that most calamitous and awfully fatal visitation, the plague. All this came upon them with the late war, which was begun by the Athenians and Peloponnesians by the dissolution of the thirty years' truce made after the conquest of Eubæa. To the question why they broke the treaty, I answer by placing first an account of their grounds of complaint and points of difference, that no one may ever have to ask the immediate cause which plunged the Hellenes into a war of such magnitude. The real cause I consider to be the one which was formally most kept out of sight. The growth of the power of Athens, and the alarm which this inspired in Lacedæmon made war inevitable. Still it is well to give the grounds alleged by either side, which led to the dissolution of the treaty and the breaking out of the war. . . .

▼

The Funeral Oration of Pericles

1   In the same winter the Athenians gave a funeral at the public cost to those who had first fallen in this war. It was a custom of their ancestors, and the manner of it is as follows. Three days before the ceremony, the bones of the dead are laid out in a tent which has been erected; and their friends bring to their relatives such offerings as they please. In the funeral procession cypress coffins are borne in cars, one for each tribe; the bones of the deceased being placed in the coffin of their tribe. Among these is carried one empty bier decked for the missing, that is, for those whose bodies could not be recovered. Any citizen or stranger who pleases, joins in the procession: and the female relatives are there to wail at the burial. The dead are laid in the public sepulchre in the most beautiful suburb of the city, in which those who fall in war are always buried; with the exception of those slain at Marathon, who for their singular and extraordinary valour were interred on the spot where they fell. After

the bodies have been laid in the earth, a man chosen by the state, of approved wisdom and eminent reputation, pronounces over them an appropriate panegyric; after which all retire. Such is the manner of the burying; and throughout the whole of the war, whenever the occasion arose, the established custom was observed. Meanwhile these were the first that had fallen, and Pericles, son of Xanthippus, was chosen to pronounce their eulogium. When the proper time arrived, he advanced from the sepulchre to an elevated platform in order to be heard by as many of the crowd as possible, and spoke as follows:

'Most of my predecessors in this place have commended him who made this　*2* speech part of the law, telling us that is well that it should be delivered at the burial of those who fall in battle. For myself, I should have thought that the worth which had displayed itself in deeds, would be sufficiently rewarded by honours also shown by deeds; such as you now see in this funeral prepared at the people's cost. And I could have wished that the reputations of many brave men were not to be imperilled in the mouth of a single individual, to stand or fall according as he spoke well or ill. For it is hard to speak properly upon a subject where it is even difficult to convince your hearers that you are speaking the truth. On the one hand, the friend who is familiar with every fact of the story, may think that some point has not been set forth with that fulness which he wishes and knows it to deserve; on the other, he who is a stranger to the matter may be led by envy to suspect exaggeration if he hears anything above his own nature. For men can endure to hear others praised only so long as they can severally persuade themselves of their own ability to equal the actions recounted: when this point is passed, envy comes in and with it incredulity. However, since our ancestors have stamped this custom with their approval, it becomes my duty to obey the law and to try to satisfy your several wishes and opinions as best I may.

'I shall begin with our ancestors: it is both just and proper that they should　*3* have the honour of the first mention on an occasion like the present. They dwelt in the country without break in the succession from generation to genenration, and handed it down free to the present time by their valour. And if our more remote ancestors deserve praise, much more do our own fathers, who added to their inheritance the empire which we now possess, and spared no pains to be able to leave their acquisitions to us of the present generation. Lastly, there are few parts of our dominions that have not been augmented by those of us here, who are still more or less in the vigour of life; while the mother country has been furnished by us with everything that can enable her to depend on her own resources whether for war or for peace. That part of our history which tells of the military achievements which gave us our several possessions, or of the ready valour with which either we or our fathers stemmed the tide of Hellenic or foreign aggression, is a theme too familiar to my hearers for me to dilate on, and I shall therefore pass it by. But what was the road by which we reached our position, what the form of government under which our greatness grew, what the national habits out of which it sprang; these are questions which I may try to solve before I proceed to my panegyric upon these men; since I think this to be a subject upon which on the present occasion a speaker may properly dwell, and to which the whole assemblage, whether citizens or foreigners, may listen with advantage.

4   'Our constitution does not copy the laws of neighbouring states; we are rather a pattern to others than imitators ourselves. Its administration favours the many instead of the few; this is why it is called a democracy. If we look to the laws, they afford equal justice to all in their private differences; if to social standing, advancement in public life falls to reputation for capacity, class considerations not being allowed to interfere with merit; nor again does poverty bar the way, if a man is able to serve the state, he is not hindered by the obscurity of his condition. The freedom which we enjoy in our government extends also to our ordinary life. There, far from exercising a jealous surveillance over each other, we do not feel called upon to be angry with our neighbour for doing what he likes, or even to indulge in those injurious looks which cannot fail to be offensive, although they inflict no positive penalty. But all this ease in our private relations does not make us lawless as citizens. Against this fear is our chief safeguard, teaching us to obey the magistrates and the laws, particularly such as regard the protection of the injured, whether they are actually on the statute book, or belong to that code which, although unwritten, yet cannot be broken without acknowledged disgrace.

5   'Further, we provide plenty of means for the mind to refresh itself from business. We celebrate games and sacrifices all the year round, and the elegance of our private establishments forms a daily source of pleasure and helps to banish the spleen; while the magnitude of our city draws the produce of the world into our harbour, so that to the Athenian the fruits of other countries are as familiar a luxury as those of his own.

6   'If we turn to our military policy, there also we differ from our antagonists. We throw open our city to the world, and never by alien acts exclude foreigners from any opportunity of learning or observing, although the eyes of an enemy may occasionally profit by our liberality; trusting less in system and policy than to the native spirit of our citizens; while in education, where our rivals from their very cradles by a painful discipline seek after manliness, at Athens we live exactly as we please, and yet are just as ready to encounter every legitimate danger. In proof of this it may be noticed that the Lacedæmonians do not invade our country alone, but bring with them all their confederates; while we Athenians advance unsupported into the territory of a neighbour, and fighting upon a foreign soil usually vanquish with ease men who are defending their homes. Our united force was never yet encountered by any enemy, because we have at once to attend to our marine and to despatch our citizens by land upon a hundred different services; so that, wherever they engage with some such fraction of our strength, a success against a detachment is magnified into a victory over the nation, and a defeat into a reverse suffered at the hands of our entire people. And yet if with habits not of labour but of ease, and courage not of art but of nature, we are still willing to encounter danger, we have the double advantage of escaping the experience of hardships in anticipation and of

facing them in the hour of need as fearlessly as those who are never free from them.

'Nor are these the only points in which our city is worthy of admiration. We   7
cultivate refinement without extravagance and knowledge without effeminacy; wealth we employ more for use than for show, and place the real disgrace of poverty not in owning to the fact but in declining the struggle against it. Our public men have, besides politics, their private affairs to attend to, and our ordinary citizens, though occupied with the pursuits of industry, are still fair judges of public matters; for, unlike any other nation, regarding him who takes no part in these duties not as unambitious but as useless, we Athenians are able to judge at all events if we cannot originate, and instead of looking on discussion as a stumbling-block on the way of action, we think it an indispensable preliminary to any wise action at all. Again, in our enterprises we present the singular spectacle of daring and deliberation, each carried to its highest point, and both united in the same persons; although usually decision is the fruit of ignorance, hesitation of reflection. But the palm of courage will surely be adjudged most justly to those, who best know the difference between hardship and pleasure and yet are never tempted to shrink from danger. In generosity we are equally singular, acquiring our friends by conferring not by receiving favours. Yet, of course, the doer of the favour is the firmer friend of the two, in order by continued kindness to keep the recipient in his debt; while the debtor feels less keenly from the very consciousness that the return he makes will be a payment, not a free gift. And it is only the Athenians who, fearless of consequences, confer their benefits not from calculations of expediency, but in the confidence of liberality.

'In short, I say that as a city we are the school of Hellas; while I doubt if the   8
world can produce a man, who where he has only himself to depend upon, is equal to so many emergencies, and graced by so happy a versatility as the Athenian. And that this is no mere boast thrown out for the occasion, but plain matter of fact, the power of the state acquired by these habits proves. For Athens alone of her contemporaries is found when tested to be greater than her reputation, and alone gives no occasion to her assailants to blush at the antagonist by whom they have been worsted, or to her subjects to question her title by merit to rule. Rather, the admiration of the present and succeeding ages will be ours, since we have not left our power without witness, but have shown it by mighty proofs; and far from needing a Homer for our panegyrist, or other of his craft whose verses might charm for the moment only for the impression which they gave to melt at the touch of fact, we have forced every sea and land to be the highway of our daring, and everywhere, whether for evil or for good, have left imperishable monuments behind us. Such is the Athens for which these men, in the assertion of their resolve not to lose her, nobly fought and died; and well may every one of their survivors be ready to suffer in her cause.

'Indeed if I have dwelt at some length upon the character of our country, it   9
has been to show that our stake in the struggle is not the same as theirs who have no such blessings to lose, and also that the panegyric of the men over

whom I am now speaking might be by definite proofs established. That pane-gyric is now in a great measure complete; for the Athens that I have celebrated is only what the heroism of these and their like have made her, men whose fame, unlike that of most Hellenes, will be found to be only commensurate with their deserts. And if a test of worth be wanted, it is to be found in their closing scene, and this not only in the cases in which it set the final seal upon their merit, but also in those in which it gave the first intimation of their having any. For there is justice in the claim that steadfastness in his country's battles should be as a cloak to cover a man's other imperfections; since the good action has blotted out the bad, and his merit as a citizen more than outweighed his demerits as an individual. But none of these allowed either wealth with its prospect of future enjoyment to unnerve his spirit, or poverty with its hope of a day of freedom and riches to tempt him to shrink from danger. No, holding that vengeance upon their enemies was more to be desired than any personal bless-ings, and reckoning this to be the most glorious of hazards, they joyfully deter-mined to accept the risk, to make sure of their vengeance and to let their wishes wait; and while committing to hope the uncertainty of final success, in the business before them they thought fit to act boldly and trust in themselves. Thus choosing to die resisting, rather than to live submitting, they fled only from dishonour, but met danger face to face, and after one brief moment, while at the summit of their fortune, escaped, not from their fear, but from their glory.

10   'So died these men as became Athenians. You, their survivors, must deter-mine to have as unaltering a resolution in the field, though you may pray that it may have a happier issue. And not contented with ideas derived only from words of the advantages which are bound up with the defence of your country, though these would furnish a valuable text to a speaker even before an audi-ence so alive to them as the present, you must yourselves realise the power of Athens, and feed your eyes upon her from day to day, till love of her fills your hearts; and then when all her greatness shall break upon you, you must reflect that it was by courage, sense of duty, and a keen feeling of honour in action that men were enabled to win all this, and that no personal failure in an enter-prise could make them consent to deprive their country of their valour, but they laid it at her feet as the most glorious contribution that they could offer. For this offering of their lives made in common by them all they each of them indi-vidually received that renown which never grows old, and for a sepulchre, not so much that in which their bones have been deposited, but that noblest of shrines wherein their glory is laid up to be eternally remembered upon every occasion on which deed or story shall fall for its commemoration. For heroes have the whole earth for their tomb; and in lands far from their own, where the column with its epitaph declares it, there is enshrined in every breast a record unwritten with no tablet to preserve it, except that of the heart. These take as your model, and judging happiness to be the fruit of freedom and freedom of valour, never decline the dangers of war. For it is not the miserable that would

most justly be unsparing of their lives; these have nothing to hope for: it is rather they to whom continued life may bring reverses as yet unknown, and to whom a fall, if it came, would be most tremendous in its consequences. And surely, to a man of spirit, the degradation of cowardice must be immeasurably more grievous than the unfelt death which strikes him in the midst of his strength and patriotism!

'Comfort, therefore, not condolence, is what I have to offer to the parents of *11* the dead who may be here. Numberless are the chances to which, as they know, the life of man is subject; but fortunate indeed are they who draw for their lot a death so glorious as that which has caused your mourning, and to whom life has been so exactly measured as to terminate in the happiness in which it has been passed. Still I know that this is a hard saying, especially when those are in question of whom you will constantly be reminded by seeing in the homes of others blessings of which once you also boasted: for grief is felt not so much for the want of what we have never known, as for the loss of that to which we have been long accustomed. Yet you who are still of an age to beget children must bear up in the hope of having others in their stead; not only will they help you to forget those whom you have lost, but will be to the state at once a reinforcement and a security; for never can a fair or just policy be expected of the citizen who does not, like his fellows, bring to the decision the interests and apprehensions of a father. While those of you who have passed your prime must congratulate yourselves with the thought that the best part of your life was fortunate, and that the brief span that remains will be cheered by the fame of the departed. For it is only the love of honour that never grows old; and honour it is, not gain, as some would have it, that rejoices the heart of age and helplessness.

'Turning to the sons or brothers of the dead, I see an arduous struggle *12* before you. When a man is gone, all are wont to praise him, and should your merit be ever so transcendent, you will still find it difficult not merely to over-take, but even to approach their renown. The living have envy to contend with, while those who are no longer in our path are honoured with a goodwill into which rivalry does not enter. On the other hand, if I must say anything on the subject of female excellence to those of you who will now be in widowhood, it will be all comprised in this brief exhortation. Great will be your glory in not falling short of your natural character; and greatest will be hers who is least talked of among the men whether for good or for bad.

'My task is now finished. I have performed it to the best of my ability, and *13* in words, at least, the requirements of the law are now satisfied. If deeds be in question, those who are here interred have received part of their honours already, and for the rest, their children will be brought up till manhood at the public expense: the state thus offers a valuable prize, as the garland of victory in this race of valour, for the reward both of those who have fallen and their survivors. And where the rewards for merit are greatest, there are found the best citizens.

14 'And now that you have brought to a close your lamentations for your relatives, you may depart.'

WRITING AND DISCUSSION QUESTIONS

Informative

1. Identify specific instances of Thucydides' critical attitude at work, where he weighs conflicting reports, and evaluates legends and traditional beliefs.
2. As a general and a responsible member of a democracy, Thucydides understood the workings of governments and the management of armies. Cite specific instances in which his practical experience enters into his interpretation of politics and war of the ancient past.
3. What does Thucydides see as the primary cause of the Peloponnesian War?

Persuasive

1. Thucydides is sometimes said to have been especially objective in his handling of Sparta. He was an Athenian, of course, and Sparta was his people's deadly enemy. Argue that Thucydides was objective or biased in his discussion of Sparta.
2. Compare the sense of the past found in *The Peloponnesian War* with that found in the Bible. Argue that the treatment and interpretation of the past is ''truer'' in one than in the other.
3. Summarize Pericles' ideas of the good citizen and argue whether his ideas are acceptable today. Also consider to what extent Pericles' position is affected by his speaking in a time of war. Is there a difference between what constitutes a good citizen during peace and war?

Personal

1. Thucydides' objective brand of analysis of historical events and peoples sometimes seems dull because it lacks the romance of story. What interests and delights you in Thucydides' history? What kind of history do you prefer and why?
2. Although history as a discipline strives for objective truth, most histories make some sort of case, have a governing view of the meaning and direction of events, and, thus, present an intepretation of reality based on fundamental assumptions and on ''facts'' stragetically selected from surviving records of the past. The result can never in any absolute sense be ''the truth.'' Can you identify ''interpretative'' processes at work in Thucydides? What are his assumptions about human nature? What facts does he select and why?
3. What dangers can you see in historical comment, or any kind of social comment, that applies a method of careful objectivity to some aspects of the past yet remains seriously biased with regard to others? What examples of this danger can you discuss?

4. To what extent and in what ways are Thucydides' themes and methods "humanistic"?

▼

PLATO, "THE ALLEGORY OF THE CAVE" FROM *THE REPUBLIC*

When Socrates (470–399 B.C.), Plato's (c. 427–347 B.C.) mentor and the first of the great Classical Greek philosphers, began to teach late in the fifth century B.C., he already had two centuries of Greek philosophical tradition behind him. That tradition had degenerated, however, into a combination of gamesmanship and commercialism—or so Socrates believed. These characteristics were centered in a group of thinkers called Sophists, the intellectual Pharisees of the time. Today, they would be equivalent to lawyers or law professors because they worked for pay and because they taught their students how to win an argument, no matter which side they argued, two practices that Socrates abhorred. Socrates believed that one should teach out of a pure love of knowledge and that the purpose of argument and inquiry was not to persuade but to arrive at the truth. He remains a symbol of several principles central to Greek humanism: a belief in the primary importance of the human intellect and in its capacity to perfect itself and to attain truth and a commitment to the life of the mind and to the highest standards of intellectual honesty.

Socrates is a difficult figure to describe accurately, however, because he never wrote anything himself, and what we know of him comes only from the reports of others, especially Plato, who was his greatest student. This problem is magnified by Plato's practice of using Socrates as the voice for his own ideas, which may or may not accurately reflect the teachings of Socrates. A few facts, however, are generally agreed on. Socrates was uncompromisingly committed to philosophy as a way of life. He made philosophy highly personal, emphasizing that its basis was self-knowledge and that the beginning of self-knowledge was an awareness of one's own ignorance. Only from this basis could objective analysis begin. His self-proclaimed purpose was to be a kind of gadfly, who stung people into an awareness of their own blindness. He questioned most matters of conventional wisdom: virtue, ethics, justice, piety, and so forth and did so in a time of social disorder when such questions were greatly feared. Although he developed a small, but dedicated, group of followers, he was far from popular; indeed, he was sentenced to death by Athens' democratic court on charges of not believing in the traditional gods, of introducing gods of his own, and of corrupting the youth. Thus, he was the victim of popular anti-intellectualism and was the first great martyr of humanism.

Plato's most widely read work over the centuries, the *Republic*, is concerned with articulating the nature of justice and with describing what a truly just society would be. This is the world's first major work of political philosophy; many have called it the greatest ever, and it describes the world's first fully developed utopia. Although the word *utopia* has Greek roots, it was coined as a pun in the sixteenth century A.D. by the English humanist Thomas More. *Ou topos* means "no place," and *eu topos* means "good place"; thus, *utopia* means both an imaginary and an ideal society. It represents a peculiarly humanistic concept because it is not an ideal place established by a divinity, like Eden or some Paradise yet to come, and it is not a mere dream of a state of pleasure and ease. Rather, it is a rational model of a society that human beings might construct.

Plato conceived of the state as a commonwealth, something owned not by kings and rulers, but by the people as a whole (in Latin, this concept of the state would be described as "a public thing," *res publica*, which is the source of the English word *republic*). The central problem in such a state is ensuring that the best and wisest rule. Plato believed in neither the effectiveness of traditional aristocracy where family connections determined one's right to power nor in the effectiveness of democracy where lottery and popular election determined one's right to rule. Rather, he believed that some people understand what a just state is better than others and that some people are better qualified to rule than others. He also believed that the public masses are not the best judges of who their governors ought to be. In an attempt to describe those individuals who are wisest and best qualified to rule and to explain their relation to the rest of humanity, Plato wrote what has come to be called "The Allegory of the Cave," the best known passage in the *Republic* (Book 7) and the best known of all his passages. Socrates converses here with Glaucon, Plato's brother.

▼

The Allegory of the Cave
PLATO

1   Next said I, here is a parable to illustrate the degrees in which our nature may be enlightened or unenlightened. Imagine the condition of men living in a sort of cavernous chamber underground, with an entrance open to the light and a long passage all down the cave. Here they have been from childhood, chained by the leg and also by the neck, so that they cannot move and can see only what is in front of them, because the chains will not let them turn their heads. At some distance higher up is the light of a fire burning behind them; and between the prisoners and the fire is a track with a parapet built along it, like the screen at a puppetshow, which hides the performers while they show their puppets over the top.

2   I see, said he.

Now behind this parapet imagine persons carrying along various artificial objects, including figures of men and animals in wood or stone or other materials, which project above the parapet. Naturally, some of these persons will be talking, others silent.

3   It is a strange picture, he said, and a strange sort of prisoners.

4   Like ourselves, I replied; for in the first place prisoners so confined would have seen nothing of themselves or of one another, except the shadows thrown by the fire-light on the wall of the Cave facing them, would they?

5   Not if all their lives they had been prevented from moving their heads.

6   And they would have seen as little of the objects carried past.

7   Of course.

8   Now, if they could talk to one another, would they not suppose that their words referred only to those passing shadows which they saw?

9   Necessarily.

And suppose their prison had an echo from the wall facing them? When one   *10*
of the people crossing behind them spoke, they could only suppose that the
sound came from the shadow passing before their eyes.

No doubt.   *11*

In every way, then, such prisoners would recognize as reality nothing but the   *12*
shadows of those artificial objects.

Inevitably.   *13*

Now consider what would happen if their release from the chains and the   *14*
healing of their unwisdom should come about in this way. Suppose one of them
set free and forced suddenly to stand up, turn his head, and walk with eyes
lifted to the light; all these movements would be painful, and he would be too
dazzled to make out the objects whose shadows he had been used to see. What
do you think he would say, if someone told him that what he had formerly seen
was meaningless illusion, but now, being somewhat nearer to reality and turned
towards more real objects, he was getting a truer view? Suppose further that he
were shown the various objects being carried by and were made to say, in reply
to questions, what each of them was. Would he not be perplexed and believe
the objects now shown him to be not so real as what he formerly saw?

Yes, not nearly so real.   *15*

And if he were forced to look at the fire-light itself, would not his eyes ache,   *16*
so that he would try to escape and turn back to the things which he could see
distinctly, convinced that they really were clearer than these other objects now
being shown to him?

Yes.   *17*

And suppose someone were to drag him away forcibly up the steep and rug-   *18*
ged ascent and not let him go until he had hauled him out into the sunlight,
would he not suffer pain and vexation at such treatment, and, when he had
come out into the light, find his eyes so full of its radiance that he could not
see a single one of the things that he was now told were real?

Certainly he would not see them all at once.   *19*

He would need, then, to grow accustomed before he could see things in that   *20*
upper world. At first it would be easiest to make out shadows, and then the
images of men and things reflected in water, and later on the things themselves. After that, it would be easier to watch the heavenly bodies and the sky
itself by night, looking at the light of the moon and stars rather than the Sun
and the Sun's light in the day-time.

Yes, surely.   *21*

Last of all, he would be able to look at the Sun and contemplate its nature,   *22*
not as it appears when reflected in water or any alien medium, but as it is in
itself in its own domain.

No doubt.   *23*

And now he would begin to draw the conclusion that it is the Sun that pro-   *24*
duces the seasons and the course of the year and controls everything in the visible world, and moreover is in a way the cause of all that he and his companions used to see.

25   Clearly he would come at last to that conclusion.

26   Then if he called to mind his fellow prisoners and what passed for wisdom in his former dwelling-place, he would surely think himself happy in the change and be sorry for them. They may have had a practice of honouring and commending one another, with prizes for the man who had the keenest eye for the passing shadows and the best memory for the order in which they followed or accompanied one another, so that he could make a good guess as to which was going to come next. Would our released prisonor be likely to covet those prizes or to envy the men exalted to honour and power in the Cave? Would he not feel like Homer's Achilles, that he would far sooner "be on earth as a hired servant in the house of a landless man" or endure anything rather than go back to his old beliefs and live in the old way?

27   Yes, he would prefer any fate to such a life.

28   Now imagine what would happen if he went down again to take his former seat in the Cave. Coming suddenly out of the sunlight, his eyes would be filled with darkness. He might be required once more to deliver his opinion on those shadows, in competition with the prisoners who had never been released, while his eyesight was still dim and unsteady; and it might take some time to become used to the darkness. They would laugh at him and say that he had gone up only to come back with his sight ruined; it was worth no one's while even to attempt the ascent. If they could lay hands on the man who was trying to set them free and lead them up, they would kill him.

29   Yes, they would.

30   Every feature of this parable, my dear Glaucon, is meant to fit our earlier analysis. The prison dwelling corresponds to the region revealed to us through the sense of sight, and the fire-light within it to the power of the Sun. The ascent to see the things in the upper world you may take as standing for the upward journey of the soul into the region of the intelligible; then you will be in possession of what I surmise, since that is what you wish to be told. Heaven knows whether it is true; but this, at any rate, is how it appears to me. In the world of knowledge, the last thing to be perceived and only with great difficulty is the essential Form of Goodness. Once it is perceived, the conclusion must follow that, for all things, this is the cause of whatever is right and good; in the visible world it gives birth to light and to the lord of light, while it is itself sovereign in the intelligible world and the parent of intelligence and truth. Without having had a vision of this Form no one can act with wisdom, either in his own life or in matters of state.

31   So far as I can understand, I share your belief. . . .

32   You will see, then, Glaucon, that there will be no real injustice in compelling our philosophers to watch over and care for the other citizens. We can fairly tell them that their compeers in other states may quite reasonably refuse to collaborate: there they have sprung up, like a self-sown plant, in despite of their country's institutions; no one has fostered their growth, and they cannot be expected to show gratitude for a care they have never received. "But," we shall say, "it is not so with you. We have brought you into existence for your country's sake as well as for your own, to be like ļeaders and kingbees in a hive;

you have been better and more thoroughly educated than those others and hence you are more capable of playing your part both as men of thought and as men of action. You must go down, then, each in his turn, to live with the rest and let your eyes grow accustomed to the darkness. You will then see a thousand times better than those who live there always; you will recognize every image for what it is and know what it represents, because you have seen justice, beauty, and goodness in their reality; and so you and we shall find life in our commonwealth no mere dream, as it is in most existing states, where men live fighting one another about shadows and quarrelling for power, as if that were a great prize; whereas in truth government can be at its best and free from dissension only where the destined rulers are least desirous of holding office."

WRITING AND DISCUSSION QUESTIONS

Informative

1. An allegory is a narrative in the form of an extended metaphor where everything about the imagined situation corresponds to something in life as seen by the writer. Plato's cave, for example, represents the general condition of our lives, the individuals in it represent ourselves, the shadows projected on the wall represent other things and so on. Briefly identify what each element of the allegory corresponds to in real life according to Socrates.

2. Notice that the ascent out of the cave is not easy. Not only is there the climb out into the sunlight, but another kind of "ascent," a further struggle *in* the light, follows. What is its nature, and what does it reveal about Plato's concept of learning?

Persuasive

1. Putting aside the content or supposed veracity of their teaching, argue that Christ as depicted in the Sermon on the Mount or Socrates as depicted in the *Republic* is the better teacher.

2. Plato's Socrates says that only those who have had "a vision" of "the essential Form of Goodness" can act with wisdom. This sounds like a religious-mystical vision and is one of many similarities between Socrates and religious figures like Moses and Christ. For example, all three committed their lives to the pursuit of a vision of goodness, all believed in a higher reality, and both Socrates and Christ were martyred for their beliefs. Despite these similarities, argue that there are essential differences between the humanistic teachings of Socrates and the religious teachings of Moses and Christ.

Personal

1. Plato describes the individual who has been freed from his chains in the cave and is allowed (forced) to pursue a higher vision: "suppose someone were to drag

him away forcibly up the steep and rugged ascent . . . until he had hauled him out into the sunlight." Would most people have to be dragged this way, or would most be eager to "see the light"? Which group do you most likely belong to?

2. Although democracy is generally considered a development of humanism, humanism's emphasis on excellence carries with it a tendency toward elitism that to some seems at odds with democracy. That tendency is especially apparent in the *Republic,* where the superiority, indeed, the right to rule, of an intellectual elite is emphasized. How do you see this emphasis on intellectual excellence in relation to democracy? What possible conflicts between the two have you experienced? You might consider the problems of politicians like Woodrow Wilson, Adlai Stevenson, or Eugene McCarthy, or the difference in general attitudes toward different kinds of excellence, like attitudes toward "jocks" and "brains."

▼

GIORGIO VASARI, "LEONARDO DA VINCI" FROM *LIVES OF THE PAINTERS*

In the time between Plato and the beginning of the Renaissance in Italy in the fourteenth century A.D., the humanist tradition underwent many changes, not the least of which was its acquiring a name. In the second century B.C., the Latin word *humanitas* was used by a group of cultivated individuals, mostly Romans, interested in Greek philosophy as well as Latin literature. To them, this word referred to "the dignity and grandeur of man's personality, that which distinguishes him from all the other beings on earth."[1] This sense of humanity's special value carried with it the obligation to cultivate one's personality, to educate oneself, and to respect the personality of others.

With the rise of Christianity, the Latin word remained, but its meaning shifted from the Classical sense of positive human value to a meaning restricted simply to human nature. Thus, *humanitas* suggested those qualities that distinguish humanity from greater beings—angels and God—and, therefore, emphasized humanity's limitations and frailties. Then, early in the Renaissance, certain Italian scholars renewed the interest in the study of human culture, especially as exhibited in Greek and Roman literature and philosophy, much of which, especially the Greek, was being rediscovered in the form of long-forgotten manuscripts. These scholars called themselves *umanisti,* an Italian derivation from the Latin *humanitas,* which carried both meanings from the past, a double sense of humanity's grandeur and weakness, along with close associations with Classical learning.

Indeed, it was on learning in the applied sense, education, that humanists had their first major effects. Formal education in the medieval Christian world had been designed primarily to instruct clergymen. The other major occupation for the powerful, warfare, had been thought to require physical training, not education. Renaissance humanism, however, inspired a new ideal, the scholar on horseback. This was a man (Renaissance humanism was as sexist as was Classical humanism) educated to be a ruler and a gentleman, trained in aspects of warfare ranging from swordsmanship to military tactics, but who was also able to write Ciceronian Latin (not that

[1]Schulz, F. *The Principles of Roman Law.* New York: Oxford University Press, 1936, pp. 189–90.

barbarous church Latin) and at least to read Greek, to engage scholars in philosophical debate, to entertain ladies with elegant conversation, to play some musical instrument at least tolerably well, and even to write a little poetry.

Measured against the strictest traditions of Judeo–Christian thought, Renaissance humanism seemed to shift the center of interest away from God by expanding the sense of human potential. As a result, humanism came to be associated in some minds with an areligious or even an antireligious position. Certainly, some humanists exhibited a passion for humanity and pagan culture apart from consideration of any relationship with any divine spirit. At least as commonly, however, especially in Europe north of the Alps, humanists preserved a healthy sense of human limitation while expanding human knowledge within the Christian tradition, not in opposition to it. From this point of view, human nature continued to be seen as existing for a divine purpose and as necessarily including a religious spirit. But despite exemplary Christians among their number, for instance, Saint Thomas More, humanists, on the whole, placed no special emphasis on piety. The key to what made the accomplished humanist was a variety of excellences. Few attained to such an ideal, but the man who most epitomized what has come to be called the "Renaissance man" was Leonardo da Vinci, the most important contemporary description of whom was provided by Giorgio Vasari (1511–1574).

Vasari wrote his *Lives of Excellent Italian Architects, Painters, and Sculptors* (1550, revised and expanded 1568), best known as *Lives of the Painters*, within the tradition of Renaissance humanism. The time in which it was written was characterized by a revival of ancient learning and, like the Classical Greek period, by an unusual burst of creative energy, especially of the arts in Italy. In fact, Vasari described the art of his time as a *rinascita*, a significant "rebirth" of Classical form, and was among the first to suggest the existence of what came to be called the Renaissance. Like all Renaissance humanists, he wrote in imitation of his Greek and Roman forebears, relying especially on the *Parallel Lives* by Plutarch (c. A.D. 46–c. 120), a Greek biographer and essayist. Like Plutarch, he wrote of outstanding individuals, describing them not just as a historian would but as a student of human character would, depicting their weaknesses as well as strengths, their pettiness as well as grandeur. Unlike Plutarch, who wrote about great political and military leaders, Vasari concentrated on artists. Plutarch was also a moralist who used the lives he depicted as examples of good and bad in an effort to develop an ideal of right human action. Vasari was more interested in the accomplishment of his subjects as artists and only in those moral qualities that affected their artistic success and fame.

Leonardo da Vinci (1452–1519), the subject of this selection from Vasari, is widely recognized as the most versatile genius of the Renaissance. He initiated the style of High Renaissance art, profoundly influencing the work of other greats like Michelangelo and Raphael. He is noted for scientific researches and inventions far in advance of his time—the military tank, flying machines of various types including the helicopter, and many others. He also combined his abilities in art and science in his systematic studies of anatomy (he may be called the first great medical illustrator), and his prose style went far toward creating the modern genre of scientific writing. His interest in human perception also expressed itself both in his painting and his contributions to the study of optics. Leonardo represents the Renaissance ideal of the man of genius complete on all sides.

Vasari describes Leonardo in heroic proportions as a unique combination of beauty, grace, and talent, capable of excellence in nearly all areas of human endeavor considered important at the time. The projects da Vinci conceives of are seen as heroic, and even the major defect noted in him, his tendency to leave many projects incomplete, is the result of a virtue, the grandeur of his imagination. Indeed, Vasari's description is a celebration of the highest capacities of the creative human imagination. And unlike the Greek tradition, there is no apparent concern for hubris; there is glory in outdoing all expectation, in overreaching even if it means failure, and most especially in achieving the immortality of lasting fame for such achievements.

▼

Leonardo da Vinci
GIORGIO VASARI

1   The richest gifts are occasionally seen to be showered, as by celestial influence, on certain human beings; nay, they sometimes supernaturally and marvellously congregate in one sole person; beauty, grace, and talent being united in such a manner that, to whatever the man thus favoured may turn himself, his every action is so divine as to leave all other men far behind him, and manifestly to prove that he has been specially endowed by the hand of God himself, and has not obtained his pre-eminence by human teaching, or the power of man.

2   This was seen and acknowledged by all men in the case of Leonardo da Vinci, in whom, to say nothing of his beauty of person, which yet was such that it has never been sufficiently extolled, there was a grace beyond expression, which was rendered manifest without thought or effort in every act and deed; and who had besides so rare a gift of talent and ability that, to whatever subject he turned his attention, however difficult, he presently made himself absolute master of it. Extraordinary power was in his case conjoined with remarkable facility, a mind of regal boldness and magnanimous daring; his gifts were such that the celebrity of his name extended most widely, and he was held in the highest estimation, not in his own time only, but also, and even to a greater extent, after his death; nay, this has continued, and will continue to be by all succeeding ages.

3   Truly admirable, indeed, and divinely endowed was Leonardo da Vinci; this artist was the son of Ser Piero da Vinci. He would without doubt have made great progress in learning and knowledge of the sciences, had he not been so versatile and changeful, but the instability of his character caused him to undertake many things which having commenced he afterwards abandoned. In arithmetic, for example, he made such rapid progress in the short time during which he gave his attention to it that he often confounded the master who was teaching him, by the perpetual doubts he started, and by the difficulty of the questions he proposed. He also commenced the study of music, and resolved to acquire the art of playing the lute, when, being by nature of an exalted imagination and full of the most graceful vivacity, he sang to that instrument most divinely, improvising at once the verses and the music.

4   But, though dividing his attention among pursuits so varied, he never abandoned his drawing, and employed himself much in works of relief, that being the occupation which attracted him more than any other. His father, Ser Piero,

observing this, and considering the extraordinary character of his son's genius, one day took some of his drawings and showed them to Andrea del Verrocchio, who was a very intimate friend of his, begging him earnestly to tell him whether he thought that Leonardo would be likely to secure success if he devoted himself to the arts of design. Andrea Verrocchio was amazed as he beheld the remarkable commencement made by Leonardo, and advised Ser Piero to see that he attached himself to that calling, whereupon the latter took his measures accordingly, and sent Leonardo to study in the bottega, or workshop, of Andrea.

Thither the boy resorted therefore, with the utmost readiness, and not only   5
gave his attention to one branch of art, but to all the others, of which design made a portion. Endowed with such admirable intelligence, and being also an excellent geometrician, Leonardo not only worked in sculpture (having executed certain heads in terra-cotta, of women smiling, even in his first youth, which are now reproduced in gypsum, and also others of children which might be supposed to have proceeded from the hand of a master); but in architecture likewise he prepared various designs for ground plans and the construction of entire buildings. He too it was who, though still but a youth, first suggested the formation of a canal from Pisa to Florence, by means of certain changes to be effected on the river Arno.

Leonardo likewise made designs for mills, fulling machines, and other   6
engines, which were to be acted on by means of water; but as he had resolved to make painting his profession, he gave the larger portion of time to drawing from nature. He sometimes formed models of different figures in clay, on which he would arrange fragments of soft drapery dipped in plaster; from these he would then set himself patiently to draw on very fine cambric or linen that had already been used and rendered smooth. These he executed in black and white with the point of the pencil in a most admirable manner, as may be seen by certain specimens from his own hand which I have in my book of drawings. He drew on paper also with so much care and so perfectly that no one has ever equalled him in this respect. I have a head by him in chiaroscuro, which is incomparably beautiful. Leonardo was indeed so imbued with power and grace by the hand of God, and was endowed with so marvelous a facility in reproducing his conceptions, and his memory also was always so ready and so efficient in the service of his intellect, that in discourse he won all men by his reasonings, and confounded every antagonist, however powerful, by the force of his arguments.

This master was also frequently occupied with the construction of models   7
and the preparation of designs for the removal or the perforation of mountains, to the end that they might thus be easily passed from one plain to another. By means of levers, cranes, and screws, he likewise showed how great weights might be raised or drawn, in what manner ports and havens might be cleansed and kept in order, and how water might be obtained from the lowest deeps. From speculations of this kind he never gave himself rest, and of the results of these labours and meditations there are numberless examples in drawings, &c.,

dispersed among those who practise our arts. I have myself seen very many of them.

8   Besides all this he wasted not a little time to the degree of even designing a series of cords, curiously intertwined, but of which any separate strand may be distinguished from one end to the other, the whole forming a complete circle. A very curiously complicated and exceedingly difficult specimen of these coils may be seen engraved; in the midst of it are the following words: *Leonardus Vinci Academia.* Among these models and drawings there is one, by means of which Leonardo often sought to prove to the different citizens—many of them men of great discernment—who then governed Florence, that the church of San Giovanni in that city could be raised, and steps placed beneath it, without injury to the edifice. He supported his assertions with reasons so persuasive that while he spoke the undertaking seemed feasible, although every one of his hearers, when he had departed, could see for himself that such a thing was impossible.

9   In conversation Leonardo was indeed so pleasing that he won the hearts of all hearers, and though possessing so small a patrimony that it might almost be called nothing, while he yet worked very little, he still constantly kept many servants and horses, taking extraordinary delight in the latter. He was indeed fond of all animals, ever treating them with infinite kindness and consideration; as a proof of this it is related that, when he passed places where birds were sold, he would frequently take them from their cages, and having paid the price demanded for them by the sellers, would then let them fly into the air, thus restoring to them the liberty they had lost. Leonardo was in all things so highly favoured by nature that, to whatever he turned his thoughts, mind, and spirit, he gave proof in all of such admirable power and perfection, that whatever he did bore an impress of harmony, truthfulness, goodness, sweetness and grace, wherein no other man could ever equal him.

10   Leonardo, with his profound intelligence of art, commenced various under-takings, many of which he never completed, because it appeared to him that the hand could never give its due perfection to the object or purpose which he had in his thoughts, or beheld in his imagination; seeing that in his mind he frequently formed the idea of some difficult enterprise, so subtle and so won-derful that, by means of hands, however excellent or able, the full reality could never be worthily executed and entirely realized. His conceptions were varied to infinity; philosophizing over natural objects, among others, he set himself to investigate the properties of plants, to make observations on the heavenly bod-ies, to follow the movements of the planets, the variations of the moon, and the course of the sun.

11   Having been placed, then, by Ser Piero in his childhood with Andrea Ver-rocchio, as we have said, to learn the art of the painter, that master was engaged on a picture the subject of which was San Giovanni baptizing Jesus Christ. In this, Leonardo painted an angel holding some vestments; and although he was but a youth, he completed that figure in such a manner that the angel of Leonardo was much better than the portion executed by his mas-

ter, which caused the latter never to touch colours more, so much was he displeased to find that a mere child could do more than himself.

Leonardo received a commission to prepare the cartoon for the hangings of   *12*
a door, which was to be woven in silk and gold in Flanders, thence to be despatched to the King of Portugal; the subject was the sin of our first parents in Paradise. Here the artist depicted a meadow in chiaroscuro, the high lights being in white lead, displaying an immense variety of vegetation and numerous animals, respecting which it may be truly said that, for careful execution and fidelity to nature, they are such that there is no genius in the world, however god-like, which could produce similar objects with equal truth. In the fig tree, for example, the foreshortening of the leaves and the disposition of the branches are executed with so much care that one finds it difficult to conceive how any man could have so much patience. There is besides a palm tree, in which the roundness of the fan-like leaves is exhibited to such admirable perfection and with so much art that nothing short of the genius and patience of Leonardo could have effected it. But the work for which the cartoon was prepared was never carried into execution, the drawing therefore remained in Florence, and is now in the fortunate house of the illustrious Ottaviano de' Medici, to whom it was presented, no long time since, by the uncle of Leonardo.

It is related that Ser Piero da Vinci, being at his country house, was there   *13*
visited by one of the peasants on his estate, who, having cut down a fig tree on his farm, had made a shield from part of it with his own hands, and then brought it to Ser Piero, begging that he would be pleased to cause the same to be painted for him in Florence. This the latter very willingly promised to do, the countryman having great skill in taking birds and in fishing, and being often very serviceable to Ser Piero in such matters. Having taken the shield with him to Florence therefore, without saying any thing to Leonardo as to whom it was for, he desired the latter to paint something upon it. Accordingly, he one day took it in hand, but finding it crooked, coarse, and badly made, he straightened it at the fire, and giving it to a turner, it was brought back to him smooth and delicately rounded, instead of the rude and shapeless form in which he had received it. He then covered it with gypsum, and having prepared it to his liking, he began to consider what he could paint upon it that might best and most effectually terrify whomsoever might approach it, producing the same effect with that formerly attributed to the head of Medusa.

For this purpose therefore, Leonardo carried to one of his rooms, into which *14*
no one but himself ever entered, a number of lizards, hedgehogs, newts, serpents, dragon-flies, locusts, bats, glow-worms, and every other sort of strange animal of similar kind on which he could lay his hands; from his assemblage, variously adapted and joined together, he formed a hideous and appalling monster, breathing poison and flames, and surrounded by an atmosphere of fire. This he caused to issue from a dark and rifted rock, with poison reeking from the cavernous throat, flames darting from the eyes, and vapours rising from the nostrils in such sort that the result was indeed a most fearful and monstrous

creature: at this he laboured until the odours arising from all those dead animals filled the room with a mortal fetor, to which the zeal of Leonardo and the love which he bore to art rendered him insensible or indifferent.

15   When this work, which neither the countryman nor Ser Piero any longer inquired for, was completed, Leonardo went to his father and told him that he might send for the shield at his earliest convenience, since so far as he was concerned, the work was finished. Ser Piero went accordingly one morning to the room for the shield, and having knocked at the door, Leonardo opened it to him, telling him nevertheless to wait a little without, and having returned into the room he placed the shield on the easel, and shading the window so that the light falling on the painting was somewhat dimmed, he made Ser Piero step within to look at it. But the latter, not expecting any such thing, drew back, startled at the first glance, not supposing that to be the shield, or believing the monster he beheld to be a painting, he therefore turned to rush out, but Leonardo withheld him, saying: "The shield will serve the purpose for which it has been executed; take it therefore and carry it away, for this is the effect it was designed to produce."

16   The work seemed something more than wonderful to Ser Piero, and he highly commended the fanciful idea of Leonardo; but he afterwards silently bought from a merchant another shield, whereon there was painted a heart transfixed with an arrow, and this he gave to the countryman, who considered himself obliged to him for it to the end of his life. Some time after Ser Piero secretly sold the shield painted by Leonardo to certain merchants for one hundred ducats, and it subsequently fell into the hands of the Duke of Milan, sold to him by the same merchants for three hundred ducats. . . .

17   On the death of Giovanni Galeazzo, Duke of Milan, in the year 1493, Ludovico Sforza was chosen in the same year to be his successor, when Leonardo was invited with great honour to Milan by the Duke, who delighted greatly in the music of the lute, to the end that the master might play before him. Leonardo therefore took with him a certain instrument which he had himself constructed almost wholly of silver, and in the shape of a horse's head, a new and fanciful form calculated to give more force and sweetness to the sound. Here Leonardo surpassed all the musicians who had assembled to perform before the Duke. He was besides one of the best *improvisatori* in verse existing at that time, and the Duke, enchanted with the admirable conversation of Leonardo, was so charmed by his varied gifts that he delighted beyond measure in his society, and prevailed on him to paint an altar-piece, the subject of which was the Nativity of Christ, which was sent by the Duke as a present to the Emperor.

18   For the Dominican monks of Santa Maria delle Grazie at Milan, he also painted a Last Supper, which is a most beautiful and admirable work; to the heads of the Apostles in this picture the master gave so much beauty and majesty that he was constrained to leave that of Christ unfinished, being convinced that he could not impart to it the divinity which should appertain to and distin-

guish an image of the Redeemer. But this work, remaining thus in its unfinished state, has been ever held in the highest estimation by the Milanese, and not by them only, but by foreigners also. Leonardo succeeded to perfection in expressing the doubts and anxiety experienced by the Apostles, and the desire felt by them to know by whom their Master is to be betrayed; in the faces of all appear love, terror, anger, or grief and bewilderment, unable as they are to fathom the meaning of their Lord. Nor is the spectator less struck with admiration by the force and truth with which, on the other hand, the master has exhibited the impious determination, hatred, and treachery of Judas. The whole work indeed is executed with inexpressible diligence even in its most minute part. Among other things may be mentioned the tablecloth, the texture of which is copied with such exactitude that the linen cloth itself could scarcely look more real.

It is related that the prior of the monastery was excessively importunate in pressing Leonardo to complete the picture. He could in no way comprehend wherefore the artist should sometimes remain half a day together absorbed in thought before his work, without making any progress that he could see; this seemed to him a strange waste of time, and he would fain have had him work away as he could make the men do who were digging in his garden, never laying the pencil out of his hand. Not content with seeking to hasten Leonardo, the prior even complained to the Duke, and tormented him to such a degree that the latter was at length compelled to send for Leonardo, whom he courteously entreated to let the work be finished, assuring him nevertheless that he did so because impelled by the importunities of the prior. *19*

Leonardo, knowing the Prince to be intelligent and judicious, determined to explain himself fully on the subject with him, although he had never chosen to do so with the prior. He therefore discoursed with him at some length respecting art, and made it perfectly manifest to his comprehension that men of genius are sometimes producing most when they seem to be labouring least, their minds being occupied in the elucidation of their ideas, and in the completion of those conceptions to which they afterwards give form and expression with the hand. He further informed the Duke that there were still wanting to him two heads, one of which, that of the Saviour, he could not hope to find on earth, and had not yet attained the power of presenting it to himself in imagination, with all that perfection of beauty and celestial grace which appeared to him to be demanded for the due representation of the Divinity incarnate. *20*

The second head still wanting was that of Judas, which also caused him some anxiety, since he did not think it possible to imagine a form of feature that should properly render the countenance of a man who, after so many benefits received from his Master, had possessed a heart so depraved as to be capable of betraying his Lord and the Creator of the world. With regard to that second, however, he would make search, and after all, if he could find no better, he need never be at any great loss, for there would always be the head of that troublesome and impertinent prior. This made the Duke laugh with all his heart; he declared Leonardo to be completely in the right, and the poor prior, *21* utterly confounded, went away to drive on the digging in his garden, and left Leonardo in peace. The head of Judas was then finished so successfully that it is indeed the true image of treachery and wickedness; but that of the Redeemer remained, as we have said, incomplete.

22   The admirable excellence of this picture, the beauty of its composition, and the care with which it was executed, awakened in the King of France a desire to have it removed into his own kingdom, insomuch that he made many attempts to discover architects, who might be able to secure it by defences of wood and iron, that it might be transported without injury. He was not to be deterred by any consideration of the cost that might be incurred, but the painting, being on the wall, his Majesty was compelled to forego his desire, and the Milanese retained their picture.

23   In the same refectory, and while occupied with the Last Supper, Leonardo painted the portrait of the above-named Duke Ludovico, with that of his first-born son, Maximilian: these are on the wall opposite to that of the Last Supper, and where there is a Crucifixion painted after the old manner. On the other side of the Duke is the portrait of the Duchess Beatrice, with that of Francesco, their second son: both of these princes were afterwards Dukes of Milan: the portraits are most admirably done.

24   While still engaged with the paintings of the refectory, Leonardo proposed to the Duke to cast a horse in bronze of colossal size, and to place on it a figure of the Duke, by way of monument to his memory: this he commenced, but finished the model on so large a scale that it never could be completed, and there were many ready to declare (for the judgments of men are various, and are sometimes rendered malignant by envy) that Leonardo had begun it, as he did others of his labours, without intending ever to finish it. The size of the work being such, insuperable difficulties presented themselves, as I have said, when it came to be cast; nay, the casting could not be effected in one piece, and it is very probable that, when this result was known, many were led to form the opinion alluded to above from the fact that so many of Leonardo's works had failed to receive completion. But of a truth, there is good reason to believe that the very greatness of his most exalted mind, aiming at more than could be effected, was itself an impediment, perpetually seeking to add excellence to excellence, and perfection to perfection; this was, without doubt, the true hindrance, so that, as our Petrarch has it, the work was retarded by desire.

25   All who saw the large model in clay, which Leonardo made for this work, declared that they had never seen anything more beautiful or more majestic; this model remained as he had left it until the French, with their King Louis, came to Milan, when they destroyed it totally. A small model of the same work, executed in wax, and which was considered perfect, was also lost, with a book containing studies of the anatomy of the horse, which Leonardo had prepared for his own use. He afterwards gave his attention, and with increased earnestness, to the anatomy of the human frame, a study wherein Messer Marcantonio della Torre, an eminent philosopher, and himself did mutually assist and encourage each other.

26   Messer Marcantonio was at that time holding lectures in Pavia, and wrote on

the same subject; he was one of the first, as I have heard say, who began to apply the doctrines of Galen to the elucidation of medical science, and to diffuse light over the science of anatomy, which, up to that time, had been involved in the almost total darkness of ignorance. In this attempt, Marcantonio was wonderfully aided by the genius and labour of Leonardo, who filled a book with drawings in red crayons, outlined with the pen, all copies made with the utmost care from bodies dissected by his own hand. In this book he set forth the entire structure, arrangement, and disposition of the bones, to which he afterwards added all the nerves, in their due order, and next supplied the muscles, of which the first are affixed to the bones; the second give the power of cohesion or holding firmly; and the third impart that of motion. Of each separate part he wrote an explanation in rude characters, written backwards and with the left hand, so that whoever is not practised in reading cannot understand them, since they are only to be read with a mirror.

Of these anatomical drawings of the human form, a great part is now in the   27
possession of Messer Francesco da Melzi, a Milanese gentleman, who, in the time of Leonardo, was a child of remarkable beauty, much beloved by him, and is now a handsome and amiable old man, who sets great store by these drawings, and treasures them as relics, together with the portrait of Leonardo of blessed memory. To all who read these writings it must appear almost incredible that this sublime genius could, at the same time, discourse, as he has done, of art, and of the muscles, nerves, veins, and every other part of the frame, all treated with equal diligence and success. . . .

For Francesco del Giocondo, Leonardo undertook to paint the portrait of   28
Mona Lisa, his wife, but, after loitering over it for four years, he finally left it unfinished. This work is now in the possession of King Francis of France, and is at Fontainebleau. Whoever shall desire to see how far art can imitate nature may do so to perfection in this head, wherein every peculiarity that could be depicted by the utmost subtlety of the pencil has been faithfully reproduced.

The eyes have the lustrous brightness and moisture which is seen in life, and 29
around them are those pale, red, and slightly livid circles, also proper to nature, with the lashes, which can only be copied, as these are, with the greatest difficulty. The eyebrows also are represented with the closest exactitude, where fuller and where more thinly set, with the separate hairs delineated as they issue from the skin, every turn being followed, and all the pores exhibited in a manner that could not be more natural than it is. The nose, with its beautiful and delicately roseate nostrils, might be easily believed to be alive. The mouth, admirable in its outline, has the lips uniting the rose tints of their colour with that of the face, in the utmost perfection, and the carnation of the cheek does not appear to be painted, but truly of flesh and blood. He who looks earnestly at the pit of the throat cannot but believe that he sees the beating of the pulses, and it may be truly said that this work is painted in a manner well calculated to make the boldest master tremble, and astonishes all who behold it, however well accustomed to the marvels of art.

Mona Lisa was exceedingly beautiful, and while Leonardo was painting her   30 portrait, he took the precaution of keeping some one constantly near her, to sing or play on instruments, or to jest and otherwise amuse her, to the end that she might continue cheerful, and so that her face might not exhibit the melancholy expression often imparted by painters to the likenesses they take. In this portrait of Leonardo's on the contrary, there is so pleasing an expression, and a smile so sweet, that while looking at it one thinks it rather divine than human, and it has ever been esteemed a wonderful work, since life itself could exhibit no other appearance. . . .

31 Leonardo da Vinci was a man of very high spirit, and was very generous in all his actions: it is related of him that, having once gone to the bank to receive the salary which Piero Soderini caused to be paid to him every month, the cashier was about to give him certain paper packets of pence, but Leonardo refused to receive them, remarking, at the same time, "I am no penny-painter." Not completing the picture, he was charged with having deceived Piero Soderini, and was reproached accordingly; when Leonardo so wrought with his friends, that they collected the sums which he had received and took the money to Piero Soderini with offers of restoration, but Piero would not accept them.

32 On the exaltation of Pope Leo X to the chair of St. Peter, Leonardo accompanied the Duke Giuliano de'Medici to Rome. The Pontiff was much inclined to philosophical inquiry, and was more especially addicted to the study of alchemy; Leonardo, therefore, having composed a kind of paste from wax, made of this, while it was still in its half-liquid state, certain figures of animals, entirely hollow and exceedingly slight in texture, which he then filled with air. When he blew into these figures, he could make them fly through the air, but when the air within had escaped from them they fell to the earth.

33 One day the vine-dresser of the Belvedere found a very curious lizard, and for this creature Leonardo constructed wings, made from the skins of other lizards, flayed for the purpose; into these wings he put quicksilver, so that when the animal walked, the wings moved also, with a tremulous motion. He then made eyes, horns, and a beard for the creature, which he tamed and kept in a case; he would then show it to the friends who came to visit him, and all who saw it ran away terrified.

34 He more than once, likewise, caused the intestines of a sheep to be cleansed and scraped until they were brought into such a state of tenuity that they could be held within the hollow of the hand; having then placed in a neighbouring chamber a pair of blacksmith's bellows, to which he had made fast one end of the intestines, he would blow into them until he caused them to fill the whole room, which was a very large one, insomuch that whoever might be therein was compelled to take refuge in a corner. He thus showed them transparent and full of wind, remarking that, whereas they had previously been contained within a small compass, they were now filling all space, and this, he would say, was a fit emblem of talent or genius. He made numbers of these follies in various kinds, occupied himself much with mirrors and optical instruments, and made

the most singular experiments in seeking oils for painting, and varnishes to preserve the work when executed.

About this time, he painted a small picture for Messer Baldassare Turini, of Pescia, who was Datary to Pope Leo: the subject of this work was Our Lady, with the Child in her arms, and it was executed by Leonardo with infinite care and art; but whether from the carelessness of those who prepared the ground, or because of his peculiar and fanciful mixtures for colours, varnishes, &c., it is now much deteriorated. In another small picture, he painted a little Child, which is graceful and beautiful to a miracle. These paintings are both in Pescia, in the possession of Messer Giulio Turini. It is related that Leonardo, having received a commission for a certain picture from Pope Leo, immediately began to distil oils and herbs for the varnish, whereupon the Pontiff remarked, "Alas! the while, this man will assuredly do nothing at all, since he is thinking of the end before he has made a beginning to his work." $\quad$ 35

There was perpetual discord between Michelagnolo Buonarroti and Leonardo, and the competition between them caused Michelangelo to leave Florence, the Duke Giuliano framing an excuse for him, the pretext for his departure being that he was summoned to Rome by the Pope for the façade of San Lorenzo. When Leonardo heard of this, he also departed and went to France, where the King, already possessing several of his works, was most kindly disposed towards him, and wished him to paint the cartoon of Sant'Anna; but Leonardo, according to his custom, kept the King a long time waiting with nothing better than words. $\quad$ 36

Finally, having become old, he lay sick for many months, and, finding himself near death, wrought diligently to make himself acquainted with the Catholic ritual, and with the good and holy path of the Christian religion: he then confessed with great penitence and many tears, and although he could not support himself on his feet, yet, being sustained in the arms of his servants and friends, he devoutly received the Holy Sacrament, while thus out of his bed. The King, who was accustomed frequently and affectionately to visit him, came immediately afterwards to his room, and he, causing himself out of reverence to be raised up, sat in his bed describing his malady and the different circumstances connected with it, lamenting, besides, that he had offended God and man, inasmuch as that he had not laboured in art as he ought to have done. He was then seized with a violent paroxysm, the forerunner of death, when the King, rising and supporting his head to give him such assistance and do him such favour as he could, in the hope of alleviating his sufferings, the spirit of Leonardo, which was most divine, conscious that he could attain to no greater honour, departed in the arms of the monarch, being at that time in the seventy-fifth year of his age. $\quad$ 37

The death of Leonardo caused great sorrow to all who had known him, nor was there ever an artist who did more honour to the art of painting. The radiance of his countenance, which was splendidly beautiful, brought cheerfulness to the heart of the most melancholy, and the power of his word could move the most obstinate to say, "No," or "Yes," as he desired. He possessed so great a $\quad$ 38 degree of physical strength that he was capable of restraining the most impetuous violence, and was able to bend one of the iron rings used for the knockers of doors, or a horse-shoe, as if it were lead. With the generous liberality of his nature, he extended shelter and hospitality to every friend, rich or poor, provided only that he were distinguished by talent or excellence. The poorest and most insignificant abode was rendered beautiful and honourable by his works; and as the city of Florence received a great gift in the birth of Leonardo, so did it suffer a more than grievous loss at his death.

39   To the art of painting in oil, this master contributed the discovery of a certain mode of deepening the shadows, whereby the later artists have been enabled to give great force and relief to their figures. His abilities in statuary were proved by three figures in bronze, which are over the north door of San Giovanni; they were cast by Gio. Francesco Rustici, but conducted under the advice of Leonardo, and are, without doubt, the most beautiful castings that have been seen in these later days, whether for design or finish.

40   We are indebted to Leonardo for a work on the anatomy of the horse, and for another, much more valuable, on that of man; wherefore, for the many admirable qualities with which he was so richly endowed, although he laboured much more by his word than in fact and by deed, his name and fame can never be extinguished.

WRITING AND DISCUSSION QUESTIONS

Informative

1. List the areas of learning of which Leonardo is a master, according to Vasari.
2. What are some of the major engineering projects Leonardo designed? What can be said about their scale?

Persuasive

1. Summarize Vasari's account of the "old shield" episode. What conclusions can you draw from this about Leonardo's character?
2. Describe Leonardo's response to the prior's complaints about his slowness in finishing *The Last Supper*. How convincing is his argument that artistic creation is an intellectual, as well as an imaginative, process?
3. Vasari illustrates Leonardo's generosity by citing his offering of "shelter and hospitality to every friend, rich or poor, provided only that he were distinguished by talent or excellence." How does this compare with your notion of Christian charity? What does Leonardo's kind of charity tell us about his character?

Personal

1. *Mona Lisa* may be the most famous painting in the Western world, one about which there has developed a special mystique. Compare the painting as

described by Vasari with your own impression, based both on your examination of a reproduction and on what you know or can learn about the painting's reputation.

2. Consider Vasari's portrait of Leonardo as a heroic expression of an ideal human being and compare it to your own general conception of such a being today. What significant qualities are absent from Vasari's portrait? How important are heroes like Leonardo to our conception of humanity?

▼

RALPH WALDO EMERSON, "PROSPECTS" FROM *NATURE*

Whatever works of Classical or Renaissance humanism may "really" mean, the values those readings were thought to affirm have had a profound impact on Western culture. By the eighteenth century, those values had coalesced into a body of humanistic beliefs that, for many, were something close to undeniable doctrines. To understand the radical changes in humanism that have occurred since, we should be familiar with these beliefs.

As was understood by most thinkers from the Renaissance through the eighteenth century, traditional humanism emphasized that human nature is characterized by certain universal elements and that human culture throughout time has manifested these elements. Despite such universality, however, that indicated a common humanity, traditional humanism was not marked by democratic ideals. Its tenets included, for example, the belief that human nature was permanent and uniform, unchanged by time or place; that social progress was not possible, and that the social and political experiments that failed in the past, like democracy, were not likely to succeed in the present. There could be no progress because humanity was essentially flawed, a belief humanism shared with the Judeo–Christian tradition. To suppose that any of the fundamental problems of human nature could be solved was sinful pride. In part, that is why traditional humanism admired tragedy as a literary form and emphasized the Greek concept of hubris.

This view sounds terribly pessimistic, but the optimistic side of traditional humanism, the glory of humanity, was in the capacity of individuals of genius to rise above some of those human limitations despite the dangers of hubris. This emphasis on individual genius led to traditional humanism's concern, some would say obsession, with excellence and quality. As a result, it looked at society more in hierarchical than in egalitarian terms: some groups of people—some individuals, some classes, some races, or one sex—were better than others, whether intellectually or politically, and the gradations of excellence and power in these groups constituted their proper order in society. Thus, traditional humanism was content with monarchy and admired heroes, like Plato's philosopher in the *Republic* or Vasari's Leonardo, whom only very few could hope to imitate.

Indeed, the traditional humanist looked at everything in hierarchical terms. The mind, for example, was seen as under the royal command of the will, with reason or judgment next in authority, and the passions and senses a kind of servant class at the bottom. To violate this order in the mind was analogous to violating the order in the body politic; hence, insanity and civil war were similar. Similarly, hierarchy governed the value of literary genres, with tragedy and epic the noblest forms, pastoral the least noblest, and all other genres arranged between. Literature itself, indeed artistic creation of all types, was of major importance for three reasons: it was the greatest expression of the human imagination, it was the greatest earthly achievement possible to flawed humanity, and it preserved the past and was, therefore, the major source of the accumulated knowledge of human experience. Thus, the humanist was a traditionalist, a historian, a literary scholar, and a lover of learning and of places like libraries and universities where learning was preserved, explored, and generated.

There are many individuals today who hold to most of these tenets; the writings of some can be found among the selections in Chapter 2. Humanism, however, was not frozen in the Classical mold; rather, it has developed and altered as Western culture has developed and altered, especially under the influence of the other great ideas examined in this book. The result has been the emergence of a wide variety of "humanisms."

The selection by Ralph Waldo Emerson (1803–1882) that follows exhibits several alterations of the traditional humanistic ideal, one of which, the attitude toward science, had developed within the mainstream of humanism well before Emerson. During the early Renaissance, when Vasari wrote, science retained much of its Classical respect as a proper expression of one of the admirable capabilities of the human intellect. But later, because it challenged so much of traditional knowledge, science began to be looked on with increasing suspicion by traditional humanists as well as by conservative theologians. By the early eighteenth century, the modern sense of opposition between science and the humanities was beginning to solidify. Science, they believed, is overly concerned with classification and with exactitude, with the quantifiable and the material; thus, it distracts us from the central moral concerns of life, questions about what constitutes right behavior. Emerson shares this view with traditional humanism, but rather than emphasize the need for practical morals, he calls for a greater emphasis on spiritual development.

Greater departures from the older humanistic tradition, however, are apparent in Emerson's new brand of liberal humanism, inspired by the spirit of democracy in America. Although Emerson believed that humanity was flawed, he also believed that human nature could improve and, along with it, so could humanity's social and political structures. In fact, for Emerson, the defects in humanity do not represent our real nature: to say as he does that "Man is a god in ruins" and "the dwarf of himself" is to say that our real nature—the real nature of all of us, not just the few great among us—is that of a god, a giant.

This view is linked as well with his rejection of important tenets of traditional Christianity. He did not believe, for example, in the special divinity of Christ; he saw Christ as God only in the sense that all human beings, by being, are capable of partaking in divinity. In an address he delivered to the graduating class of Harvard Divinity School in 1838, he pointed out what he considered two errors in the administration of Christianity: its emphasis on the difference between Christ and us, which calls on us to subordinate our nature to his, and its emphasis on law as imposed from above rather than as emerging naturally from our moral nature.

In rejecting these ideas, however, he was rejecting also central tenets of traditional humanism: its hierarchical way of looking at the world as well as its dependence on tradition. In his view, humanity's problems were the result of having lost touch with the real self, which must be recovered. And nature and vision are the keys to that recovery, that is, nature looked at rightly.

Emerson calls this transformation "redemption of soul," using the language of religious conversion, which is not surprising given Emerson's background. He was the descendant of a long line of distinguished New England clergymen, the son of a Unitarian minister, and himself a minister for a time. He left the ministry, however, and went on to proclaim his liberal humanistic views in books and in numerous lectures delivered across America.

In the selection, "Prospects," that follows, which is the last chapter of his long
essay *Nature* (1836), he declares his faith in humanity and gives us some sense of
what he believes we may eventually achieve.

▼

Prospects
RALPH WALDO EMERSON

In inquiries repecting the laws of the world and the frame of things,   *1*
the highest reason is always the truest. That which seems faintly possible, it is
so refined, is often faint and dim because it is deepest seated in the mind
among the eternal verities. Empirical science is apt to cloud the sight, and by
the very knowledge of functions and processes to bereave the student of the
manly contemplation of the whole. The savant becomes unpoetic. But the best
read naturalist who lends an entire and devout attention to truth, will see that
there remains much to learn of his relation to the world, and that it is not to be
learned by any addition or subtraction or other comparison of known quantities, but is arrived at by untaught sallies of the spirit, by a continual self-recov-
ery, and by entire humility. He will perceive that there are far more excellent
qualities in the student than preciseness and infallibility; that a guess is often
more fruitful than an indisputable affirmation, and that a dream may let us
deeper into the secret of nature than a hundred concerted experiments.

For the problems to be solved are precisely those which the physiologist and   *2*
the naturalist omit to state. It is not so pertinent to man to know all the individuals of the animal kingdom, as it is to know whence and whereto is this tyrannizing unity in his constitution, which evermore separates and classifies things,
endeavoring to reduce the most diverse to one form. When I behold a rich
landscape, it is less to my purpose to recite correctly the order and superposi-
tion of the strata, than to know why all thought of multitude is lost in a tranquil
sense of unity. I cannot greatly honor minuteness in details, so long as there is
no hint to explain the relation between things and thoughts; no ray upon the
metaphysics of conchology, of botany, of the arts, to show the relation of the
forms of flowers, shells, animals, architecture, to the mind and build science
upon ideas. In a cabinet of natural history, we become sensible of a certain
occult recognition and sympathy in regard to the most unwieldly and eccentric
forms of beast, fish, and insect. The American who has been confined, in his
own country, to the sight of buildings designed after foreign models, is surprised on entering York Minister or St. Peter's at Rome, by the feeling that
these structures are imitations also,—faint copies of an invisible archetype. Nor
has science sufficient humanity, so long as the naturalist overlooks that wonderful congruity which subsists between man and the world; of which he is lord,
not because he is the most subtile inhabitant, but because he is its head and

heart, and finds something of himself in every great and small thing, in every
mountain stratum, in every new law or color, fact of astronomy, or atmospheric
influence which observation or analysis lays open. A perception of this mystery
inspires the muse of George Herbert, the beautiful psalmist of the seventeenth
century. The following lines are part of his little poem on Man.

> Man is all symmetry,
> Full of proportions, one limb to another,
>   And all to all the world besides.
>   Each part may call the farthest, brother;
> For head with foot hath private amity,
>   And both with moons and tides.
>
> Nothing hath got so far
> But man hath caught and kept it as his prey;
>   His eyes dismount the highest star:
>   He is in little all the sphere.
> Herbs gladly cure our flesh, because that they
>   Find their acquaintance there.
>
> For us, the winds, do blow,
> The earth doth rest, heaven move, and fountains flow;
>   Nothing we see, but means our good,
>   As our delight, or as our treasure;
> The whole is either our cupboard of food,
>   Or cabinet of pleasure.
>
> The stars have us to bed:
> Night draws the curtain; which the sun withdraws.
>   Music and light attend our head.
>   All things unto our flesh are kind,
> In their descent and being; to our mind,
>   In their ascent and cause.
>
> More servants wait on man
> Than he'll take notice of. In every path,
>   He treads down that which doth befriend him
>   When sickness makes him pale and wan.
> Oh mighty love! Man is one world, and hath
>   Another to attend him.

3   The perception of this class of truths makes the attraction which draws men
to science, but the end is lost sight of in attention to the means. In view of this
half-sight of science, we accept the sentence of Plato, that "poetry comes
nearer to vital truth than history." Every surmise and vaticination of the mind
is entitled to a certain respect, and we learn to prefer imperfect theories, and
sentences which contain glimpses of truth, to digested systems which have no
one valuable suggestion. A wise writer will feel that the ends of study and com-

position are best answered by announcing undiscovered regions of thought, and so communicating, through hope, new activity to the torpid spirit.

I shall therefore conclude this essay with some traditions of man and nature, 4 which a certain poet sang to me; and which, as they have always been in the world, and perhaps reappear to every bard, may be both history and prophecy.

"The foundations of man are not in matter, but in spirit. But the element of 5 spirit is eternity. To it, therefore, the longest series of events, the oldest chronologies are young and recent. In the cycle of the universal man, from whom the known individuals proceed, centuries are points, and all history is but the epoch of one degradation.

"We distrust and deny inwardly our sympathy with nature. We own and dis- 6 own our relation to it, by turns. We are like Nebuchadnezzar, dethroned, bereft of reason, and eating grass like an ox. But who can set limits to the remedial force of spirit?

"A man is a god in ruins. When men are innocent, life shall be longer, and 7 shall pass into the immortal as gently as we awake from dreams. Now, the world would be insane and rabid, if these disorganizations should last for hundreds of years. It is kept in check by death and infancy. Infancy is the perpetual Messiah, which comes into the arms of fallen men, and pleads with them to return to paradise.

"Man is the dwarf of himself. Once he was permeated and dissolved by 8 spirit. He filled nature with his overflowing currents. Out from him sprang the sun and moon; from man the sun, from woman the moon. The laws of his mind, the periods of his actions externized themselves into day and night, into the year and the seasons. But, having made for himself this huge shell, his waters retired; he no longer fills the veins and veinlets; he is shrunk to a drop. He sees that the structure still fits him, but fits him colossally. Say, rather, once it fitted him, now it corresponds to him from far and on high. He adores timidly his own work. Now is man the follower of the sun, and woman the follower of the moon. Yet sometimes he starts in his slumber, and wonders at himself and his house, and muses strangely at the resemblance betwixt him and it. He perceives that if his law is still paramount, if still he have elemental power, if his word is sterling yet in nature, it is not conscious power, it is not inferior but superior to his will. It is instinct." Thus my Orphic poet sang.

At present, man applies to nature but half his force. He works on the world 9 with his understanding alone. He lives in it and masters it by a penny-wisdom; and he that works most in it is but a half-man, and whilst his arms are strong and his digestion good, his mind is embruted, and he is a selfish savage. His relation to nature, his power over it, is through the understanding, as by manure; the economic use of fire, wind, water, and the mariner's needle; steam, coal, chemical agriculture; the repairs of the human body by the dentist and the surgeon. This is such a resumption of power as if a banished king should buy his territories inch by inch, instead of vaulting at once into his throne. Meantime, in the thick darkness, there are not wanting gleams of a better light,—occasional examples of the action of man upon nature with his entire force,—with reason as well as understanding. Such examples are, the traditions of miracles in the earliest antiquity of all nations; the history of Jesus Christ; the achievements of a principle, as in religious and political revolutions, and in the abolition of the slave-trade; the miracles of enthusiasm, as those reported of Swedenborg, Hohenlohe, and the Shakers; many obscure and yet contested facts, now arranged under the name of Animal Magnetism; prayer; eloquence; self-healing; and the wisdom of children. These are examples of Reason's momentary grasp of the sceptre; the exertions of a power which exists not in time or space, but an instantaneous in-streaming causing power. The difference between the actual and the ideal force of man is happily figured by the schoolmen, in saying, that the knowledge of man is an evening knowledge, *vespertina cognitio*, but that of God is a morning knowledge, *matutina cognitio*.

10   The problem of restoring to the world original and eternal beauty is solved by the redemption of the soul. The ruin or the blank that we see when we look at nature, is in our own eye. The axis of vision is not coincident with the axis of things, and so they appear not transparent but opaque. The reason why the world lacks unity, and lies broken and in heaps, is because man is disunited with himself. He cannot be a naturalist until he satisfies all the demands of the spirit. Love is as much its demand as perception. Indeed, neither can be perfect without the other. In the uttermost meaning of the words, thought is devout, and devotion is thought. Deep calls unto deep. But in actual life, the marriage is not celebrated. There are innocent men who worship God after the tradition of their fathers, but their sense of duty has not yet extended to the use of all their faculties. And there are patient naturalists, but they freeze their subject under the wintry light of the understanding. Is not prayer also a study of truth,—a sally of the soul into the unfound infinite? No man ever prayed heartily without learning something. But when a faithful thinker, resolute to detach every object from personal relations and see it in the light of thought, shall, at the same time, kindle science with the fire of the holiest affections, then will God go forth anew into the creation.

11   It will not need, when the mind is prepared for study, to search for objects. The invariable mark of wisdom is to see the miraculous in the common. What is a day? What is a year? What is summer? What is woman? What is a child? What is sleep? To our blindness, these things seem unaffecting. We make fables to hide the baldness of the fact and conform it, as we say, to the higher law of the mind. But when the fact is seen under the light of an idea, the gaudy fable fades and shrivels. We behold the real higher law. To the wise, therefore, a fact is true poetry, and the most beautiful of gables. These wonders are brought to our own door. You also are a man. Man and woman and their social life, poverty, labor, sleep, fear, fortune, are known to you. Learn that none of these things is superficial, but that each phenomenon has its roots in the faculties and affections of the mind. Whilst the abstract question occupies your intellect, nature brings it in the concrete to be solved by your hands. It were a wise inquiry for the closet, to compare, point by point, especially at remarkable crises in life, our daily history with the rise and progress of ideas in the mind.

12   So shall we come to look at the world with new eyes. It shall answer the endless inquiry of the intellect,—What is truth? and of the affections,—What is

good? by yielding itself passive to the educated Will. Then shall come to pass what my poet said: "Nature is not fixed but fluid. Spirit alters, moulds, makes it. The immobility or bruteness of nature is the absence of spirit; to pure spirit it is fluid, it is volatile, it is obedient. Every spirit builds itself a house, and beyond its house a world, and beyond its world a heaven. Know then that the world exists for you. For you is the phenomenon perfect. What we are, that only can we see. All that Adam had, all that Cæsar could, you have and can do. Adam called his house, heaven and earth; Cæsar called his house, Rome; you perhaps call yours, a cobbler's trade; a hundred acres of ploughed land; or a scholar's garret. Yet line for line and point for point your dominion is as great as theirs, though without fine names. Build therefore your own world. As fast as you conform your life to the pure idea in your mind, that will unfold its great proportions. A correspondent revolution in things will attend the influx of the spirit. So fast will disagreeable appearances, swine, spiders, snakes, pests, madhouses, prisons, enemies, vanish; they are temporary and shall be no more seen. The sordor and filths of nature, the sun shall dry up and the wind exhale. As when the summer comes from the south the snow-banks melt and the face of the earth becomes green before it, so shall the advancing spirit create its ornaments along its path, and carry with it the beauty it visits and the song which enchants it; it shall draw beautiful faces, warm hearts, wise discourse, and heroic acts, around its way, until evil is no more seen. The kingdom of man over nature, which cometh not with observation,—a dominion such as now is beyond his dream of God,—he shall enter without more wonder than the blind man feels who is gradually restored to perfect sight."

WRITING AND DISCUSSION QUESTIONS

Informative

1. Examine Emerson's complaint about science. What are some of the words he uses to state his objections and to describe what he thinks of as better ways to examine the world?
2. Explain the distinction Emerson makes between "understanding" and "reason."
3. To help express his own view of humanity, Emerson quotes part of a poem by George Herbert. Obtain the full text of that poem, and summarize the ideas expressed in the parts Emerson did not quote.
4. Emerson says that humanity's "elemental power . . . is not conscious power, it is not inferior but superior to the will. It is instinct." Compare this statement to the traditional humanistic hierarchy of the mind.

Persuasive

1. Although "redemption of soul" sounds like another term for religious conversion, some of the ways Emerson describes this change, for instance, "to look at the world with new eyes," sound much like the experience of the philosopher who

emerges from Plato's cave. Argue which is closer to Emerson's views, the Christian concept or that of Greek humanism.

2. We have described the traditional humanistic way of looking at the world as "vertical," that is, hierarchical. Argue that what Emerson calls the "wonderful congruity which subsists between man and the world" is or is not a "horizontal" way of looking at life.

3. Emerson puts in the mouth of "a certain poet," most likely himself in a prophetic mood, a story of creation. How is that story used to define human nature, its potentialities, and the barriers to its further development? Compare this story and its implications with another version of creation you know—the Biblical version, for example.

Personal

1. Emerson says, "It were a wise inquiry for the closet [the old sense of a private room], to compare, point by point, especially at remarkable crises in life, our daily history with the rise and progress of ideas in the mind." The point of this inquiry is to discover whether the crises create our state of mind or our state of mind creates the crises. Try it for yourself.

2. Do you think Emerson's expectations about humanity are exciting and prophetic or out of all proportion to reality? Do you believe humanity is perfectible or that each individual is capable of perfecting his self?

3. To those who define humanism as a rejection of traditional religious beliefs, Emerson is clearly a humanist—on the edge, some might say, of being "a Godless humanist." Others define humanism as a body of values rooted in the past, associated with and derived from the ancient Greeks and Romans; they would see Emerson as having rejected too much of that past to be considered a humanist at all—some might call him simply "a radical." In this text, we have tried to stake out a middle ground by discussing "humanisms" and by referring to Emerson as "a liberal humanist." There are many other possible classifications and definitions. Choose or create one that satisfies you, explain why you think it is the best definition, and show how Emerson does or does not fit your definition.

▼

E. E. CUMMINGS, "I SING OF OLAF GLAD AND BIG"

The concern in traditional humanism for hierarchy involves an emphasis on rational order in all things, including the social order. Although it recognizes the importance of individual liberty, it tends to place greater emphasis on the fact that liberty is sustained and protected by the state. Even Socrates, whom we have considered a martyr to humanism, argued on the day of his execution that, having been tried and convicted according to law, however erroneously, he owed obedience to the state. This attitude, perhaps the oldest version of "My country, right or wrong," explains why most of the great literary examples from the past of admirable individuals in conflict with the state—Antigone and Hamlet, for example—are the subjects of tragedies. Indeed, only in the most extreme situations is rebelliousness treated with any sympathy. This respect for authority, order, and stability has been maintained even in democratic nations like the United States: although born in revolution and proud of its libertarian principles, it has remained singularly unsympathetic toward—indeed afraid of—revolutionaries of any kind, whether they were labor unionists or free thinkers, Marxian intellectuals or conscientious objectors, males who let their hair grow long or females who cut their hair short when opposite styles were in fashion.

Nevertheless, the liberal humanism of thinkers like Emerson has also been preserved, indeed has grown, during the twentieth century, placing greater emphasis on individual freedom and calling increased attention to how the social order can fail to secure, may actively suppress, individual freedom. These developments have occurred in response to world wars, the rise of totalitarian states, and a growing fear of the dangers of statism. In such a context, the great human being becomes the protester, one who, sometimes at great personal risk, refuses to be a part of a system she considers unjust. Such a hero is Olaf, depicted in "i sing of Olaf glad and big" (1931) by e. e. cummings (1894–1963).

Cummings was one of the most rebellious of modern poets in his ideas, his language, his experimental approach to poetic form and to punctuation, and even in the way he wrote his name—he considered capital letters pretentious. His background and early life, however, showed few signs of the rebel to come. He was the son of a Harvard sociology professor who became pastor of the famous Old South Church (Congregationalist) before cummings entered his teens. He received a B.A. degree in 1915 and an M.A. in 1916 from Harvard. Early during World War I he enlisted in a French ambulance corps and served until a French censor accused him of treasonable correspondence (the war effort was not going well and authorities were frightened and ready to take the least expression of discontent as a sign of disloyalty). As a result, cummings was interred in a French concentration camp for three months, an experience he later described in his novel *The Enormous Room* (1922). Not sufficiently disillusioned, he volunteered upon his release for the U.S. Army, which had entered the fight by then, and he served out the war.

Afterward, he went to Paris to study painting, which he pursued professionally, along with poetry, while living a bohemian life there and later in New York. In his art and life, personal liberty became a central theme.

▼

i sing of Olaf glad and big

e. e. cummings

i sing of Olaf glad and big
whose warmest heart recoiled at war:
a conscientious object-or

his wellbelovéd colonel(trig
westpointer most succinctly bred)
took erring Olaf soon in hand;
but—though an host of overjoyed

5

noncoms(first knocking on the head
him)do through icy waters roll
10 that helplessness which others stroke
with brushes recently employed
anent this muddy toiletbowl,
while kindred intellects evoke
allegiance per blunt instruments—
15 Olaf(being to all intents
a corpse and wanting any rag
upon what God unto him gave)
responds, without getting annoyed
"I will not kiss your f.ing flag"

20 straightway the silver bird looked grave
(departing hurriedly to shave)

but—though all kinds of officers
(a yearning nation's blueeyed pride)
their passive prey did kick and curse
25 until for wear their clarion
voices and boots were much the worse,
and egged the firstclassprivates on
his rectum wickedly to tease
by means of skilfully applied
30 bayonets roasted hot with heat—
Olaf(upon what were once knees)
does almost ceaselessly repeat
"there is some s. I will not eat"

our president,being of which
35 assertions duly notified
threw the yellowsonofabitch
into a dungeon,where he died

Christ(of His mercy infinite)
i pray to see;and Olaf, too

40 preponderatingly because
unless statistics lie he was
more brave than me:more blond than you.

WRITING AND DISCUSSION QUESTIONS

Informative

1. Given what happens to Olaf, is there more than one meaning to cummings'
phrase, "conscientious object-or"?

2. List the tortures to which officers and noncommissioned officers (noncoms) subject Olaf to convince him to join the war effort.
3. List some of the words and phrases cummings uses that are usually associated with patriotic documents and sayings. What is their effect in the context of this poem?
4. In the historical context in which cummings is writing (1931), is there any special significance to his implication that the military officers are "blueeyed"? Who is the "you" that Olaf is "more blond than," and what does this assertion mean?

Persuasive

1. Argue that cummings is or is not exaggerating. Argue whether or not anything approaching this kind of persecution for one's ideas could have happened in America.
2. Vasari is proud to tell us that cardinals and princes, popes and kings admire Leonardo's art, approve his arguments, and wait upon his deathbed. How impressed would cummings be with this information? Examine the differences between how each writer measures human greatness.

Personal

1. Given Olaf's physical and verbal responses, what can be said about the principles on which his responses are based?
2. No one is likely to object to describing what Olaf is subjected to as "dehumanizing." What humanistic or religious concepts of human dignity are implicit in applying that term to Olaf's treatment?

▼

AUDRE LORDE, "THE WOMEN OF DAN DANCE WITH SWORDS IN THEIR HANDS TO MARK THE TIME WHEN THEY WERE WARRIORS"

From the point of view of civil rights activists and feminists today, one of the major problems with liberal humanism is that too often it remains trapped in traditionalist assumptions no matter how liberal it is professed to be. One of the most dangerous of these assumptions, according to this viewpoint, is the belief in the universality of human nature. Accordingly, the Western white male begins with basic assumptions about what Man—correction, humanity—is and then decides (magnanimously) to include women or people of color. It is like the all-male club that decides to admit women but expects to continue operating under the same constitution and bylaws (except, of course, for the gender clause) that the original all-male group created.

The humanist of whatever kind, it would seem, must assume that there are some essentially human qualities and values that bind us *all* together. But perhaps some people are not really "just like us," in all the ways that the mainstream culture defines humanity. Perhaps some people really are different, and perhaps this difference is positive in ways that can profit the dominant culture, not simply by tolerating but by discovering, acknowledging, and even celebrating these differences. Such an attitude may provide an expanded view and appreciation of humanity.

To many women and people of color, however, the attempt to define what is unique about themselves is motivated less by a desire to enrich the whole of human culture, which will no doubt follow, than by something more basic: the need of every individual and every group to define themselves in their own terms, to be themselves, to create out of their own experience their own sense of what it means to be human. To a poet, especially a black woman poet like Audre Lorde (1934–), that means discovering long-suppressed and forgotten traditions and creating new images of the self as depicted in her poem "The Women of Dan Dance with Swords in Their Hands to Mark the Time When They Were Warriors" (1978).

Lorde was born in New York City and grew up in Manhattan, attending a Catholic school there and receiving her B.A. from Hunter College of the City University of New York and her M.L.S. from Columbia University. She held a number of positions in libraries until 1968, when her poetry earned her a National Endowment for the Arts grant and the first of a succession of academic appointments culminating in her present position as Professor of English at Hunter College. She has lectured widely throughout the United States and has published seven books of poetry, a nonfiction journal of her personal bout with cancer, a novel, and a collection of her nonfiction writings. Despite her urban background, Lorde's work is rich with a sense of joy in the life of nature and in her African roots.

"The Women of Dan" places us in Africa (Dan is an ancient name for the West African kingdom of Dahomey). It begins with the poet's declaration of what she is *not* in terms of images linked with mostly Western patriarchal gods: the sun god of which the Greek and Roman Apollo is a type, the Judeo–Christian god who sent a plague of locusts upon Egypt, and the masculine rain god of many cultures. She goes on to declare something of what she *is*.

▼

The Women of Dan Dance with Swords in Their Hands to Mark the Time When They Were Warriors

AUDRE LORDE

I did not fall from the sky
I
nor descend like a plague of locusts
to drink color and strength from the earth
and I do not come like rain
as a tribute or symbol for earth's becoming

I come as a woman
dark and open
some times I fall like night
10 softly
and terrible
only when I must die
in order to rise again.

I do not come like a secret warrior
15 with an unsheathed sword in my mouth
hidden behind my tongue
slicing my throat to ribbons
of service with a smile
while the blood runs
20 down and out
through holes in the two sacred mounds
on my chest.

I come like a woman
who I am
25 spreading out through nights
laughter and promise
and dark heat
warming whatever I touch
that is living
30 consuming
only
what is already dead.

WRITING AND DISCUSSION QUESTIONS

Informative

1. From what images other than patriarchal gods does the speaker dissociate herself?
2. In terms of what positive images does the speaker describe herself?
3. What are the connotations of the phrase, "service with a smile" (line 18)?

Persuasive

1. The title would suggest that the women of Dan are the speakers of this poem, but there is also the strong implication that the voice is the poet's, making a personal declaration. What is the purpose of this double voice?
2. There are a number of words and images associated with terror in the poem, some linked to what the speaker rejects, some to what she adopts. What is the

difference? For example, what is the difference between the sword in the mouth of the "secret warriors" and the swords in the hands of the women of Dan?

Personal

1. Describe the effect of the poet's dissociating herself from traditional patriarchal gods. Is she rejecting not only patriarchalism but the Christian tradition as well? Something to consider: in biographical notes, Lorde describes her religious persuasion as Quaker. Do you see a difference between rejecting God (the biographical note suggests that Lorde has not done this) and rejecting the image of a jealous, avenging God (the poem suggests that Lorde has done this)?

2. Is it possible to make a similar distinction with regard to humanism? List as many of the characteristics of humanism that you can, and then try to remove all traces that can be identified with racism, sexism, and ethnocentrism. What do you have left? Be sure to save your answer, and reexamine it after studying the chapters on feminism and civil rights.

3. Describe your own response to this poem. Do you find the picture of armed women joyfully dancing exhilarating or threatenting, a beautiful affirmation or an inappropriate display, or a bit of both?

4. In your own view, argue whether the features we value in human character, that is, strength, compassion, endurance, love, and so on, ought to wear a different dress for men and women.

CHAPTER WRITING ASSIGNMENTS

1. Art historian Erwin Panofsky defines humanism as "the conviction of the dignity of man, based on both the insistence on human values (rationality and freedom) and the acceptance of human limitations (fallibility and frailty); from this, two postulates result—responsibility and tolerance" (*Meaning in the Visual Arts*. Garden City, N.Y.: Doubleday, 1955, p. 2). Review the documents on humanism you have read, and measure each against Panofsky's definition. Argue whether each document fits this definition. If some do not, explain whether you would exclude them or change the definition.

2. Another implication of humanism is that its values are opposed to the values of religion, stating that the former centers its values in this life, the latter in some other or afterlife. Examine whether you find this to be a quality consistent throughout the humanistic documents you have read, and argue whether the distinction is valid.

3. Is the humanistic viewpoint necessarily more tolerant than a religious one? Explain why or why not, and distinguish in both cases between ideals and practice.

4. Explore the problem of the different definitions of humanism by writing a dialogue in which definitions are debated between two authors or two characters or an

author and a character from the readings in this chapter, for example, Vasari and Emerson, Leonardo and Olaf, and Pericles and cummings.

5. Write a similar dialogue, but with the focus on shared concepts of humanism and the problems of maintaining these concepts in the speakers' different times, for example, Sappho and Lorde, or cummings and Emerson.

6. Explain whether humanism and religion ought to be seen as contradictory and mutually exclusive or as complementary and mutually compatible.

7. Approach the same question as above in the form of a dialogue between a representative figure from your readings in this chapter and one from your readings in the previous chapter.

Chapter Five

THE SCIENTIFIC REVOLUTION

"Not to know the relative disposition of things is the state of slaves or children: to have mapped out the Universe is the boast, or at least the ambition of Philosophy."

JOHN HENRY NEWMAN (1852)

If time travelers from at least a century ago were to visit our world today, the most immediately apparent changes would be those brought about by science. They would see it in our skylines, our roads and automobiles, the microwave ovens and electric can openers in our homes, the incredible bulk of information available in the print and electronic media; a closer look would reveal a marked change in such areas as the speed of worldwide travel, our average life expectancy, our ability to exterminate a large selected group of people, and our potential for annihilating our entire species. But not all the changes brought about by science are physical; some are abstract. Many of Western humanity's basic assumptions and beliefs, indeed the notions of what differentiates belief from fact, have been shaped by the scientific revolution. Yet there are no subjects in which American students seem less interested than the sciences, except perhaps mathematics, which is one of the fundamental tools of science. Although the usefulness of science is widely recognized, relatively few of us have had our curiosity really piqued by any scientific idea, and still fewer of us understand the vital connections that have developed over the centuries between the seemingly dry facts of science and our notions of beauty, goodness, and spirit. Therefore, perhaps a broader understanding of science, that is, its background and development as a branch of study, is necessary for a fuller appreciation of its contribution to culture.

The word "science" comes from the Latin word *scientia,* meaning simply "knowledge," but the word has developed numerous additional meanings, of which two are particularly important. First, with ancient Greek and Roman philosophical movements, "science" came to mean a systematic approach to knowledge in general; second, some four hundred years ago, the most common modern meaning emerged from the scientific revolution, and "science" came to mean a systematic approach to the knowledge of the natural world based on reason and experiment.

SCIENCE BEFORE THE SCIENTIFIC REVOLUTION

Human culture, from its darkest beginnings, is full of technological discoveries, a part of science in the very broadest sense: the domestication of animals and of plants, the molding and firing of clay, the use of the wheel, the craft of shipbuilding, the invention of writing, the smelting of bronze and then of iron, and many more; each step profoundly affected developments in civilization and culture. But these discoveries, as far as known, were largely fortuitous, certainly not through any systematic study of nature. Systematic observation of nature seems to have begun when priestly groups in cultures from China to Egypt, from Mesopotamia to Pre-Columbian America, began to catalog the motions of the heavenly bodies to establish the times for planting and harvesting. Technological developments and systematic observation, by themselves, however, do not make science in the modern sense, although any increase in the body of knowledge, any addition of system to its method of accumulation, helps lay the foundation from which science can develop.

Judaism made significant, though somewhat indirect, contributions to that foundation. If the Bible is, as some have said, less a book than a collection of books, it can be described as the world's first great library. Its focus, however, was on systematic approaches to theology and moral philosophy and to some extent history but not to science. In addition, Judaism, like many cultures, had its own lore about the practical concerns of life, and much of that lore would later be seen to be scientifically justified—the dietary laws, for example, no doubt protected Jews from many diseases. Even so, the Biblical authors' justification for those laws was always theological—they were God's commands—not scientific in the modern sense. Nevertheless, the Judaic tradition fostered a profound respect for learning, which was preserved and expanded in its applications as Western culture developed. For this reason, many of the world's greatest scholars have been Jews, and in our own century, they are perhaps the most fully represented ethnic group among Nobel Prize laureates in the sciences.

The rise of humanism, associated primarily with the height of Greek civilization in the fifth century B.C., marked a major increase in the systematic study of nature. Ionian Greek scholars in the sixth century B.C. were among the first to look for naturalistic rather than theological explanations for objects and events in nature. For example, lightning to Homer in the eighth century B.C. was the action of an angry Zeus, but to the sixth century B.C. philosopher Anaximander, it was the result of pent up wind escaping suddenly from clouds. The Greeks also developed a rhetorical tradition, inspired perhaps by their democratic institutions, that demanded not only reason but demonstration, a principle that when applied to nature meant physical demonstration. But anything like real experimentation was rare, and observations often continued to be explained in terms of theological or highly questionable rationalistic assumptions. For example, Pythagoras, in the sixth century B.C., produced his famous theorem that the square of the hypotenuse of a right triangle is equal to the sum of the squares of the two sides, and he saw this and other relations as indications that mathematics revealed the basic principles of all things, an idea dear to the hearts of many modern scientists. But he saw those relations as mystic, and his "school" was as much a cult as an institution of learning. In the fourth century B.C., Aristotle saw motion as a natural attribute of all physical objects, which were believed to be composed of four fundamental substances: earth and water, whose natural motions were downward, and air and fire, whose natural motions were upward. To account for the heavenly bodies, Aristotle posited the existence of a perfect fifth element whose natural motion was circular and eternal. As obviously wrong as these ideas may appear to us now, they came to be generally accepted and remained so for the next two thousand years. Nevertheless, Aristotle's observations were often highly accurate, especially in the biological sciences in which he created the basis for modern classification systems (he recognized, for example, that whales and porpoises were mammals), contributions for which Charles Darwin, some 2200 years later, would acknowledge his indebtedness.

The contributions of humanism to science culminated in the establishment of the library of Alexandria in Egypt about 300 B.C., which stood for seven centuries and which Carl Sagan describes as "the brain and glory of the greatest city on the planet, the first true research institute in the history of the world." In addition to the seventy Hebrew scholars who produced the Septuagint, the Greek translation of the Torah, Alexandria's large community of scholars included Archimedes (third century B.C.), engineer and physicist who discovered how to mathematically describe and experimentally determine the density of an object; Euclid (third century B.C.), mathematician and physicist whose geometry is still taught today almost intact; Eratosthenes (third century B.C.), mathematician and astronomer who deduced that the earth is round and computed its diameter to within only a small percent error; Galen (second century B.C.), anatomist and physician who became the Western world's major medical authority for nearly two millennia; Ptolemy (second century A.D.), astronomer and geographer who created a model for describing the motions of heavenly bodies that prevailed in the Western world for the next millennium and a half; Hypatia, perhaps the last great mind of the Greek tradition, a woman who was slain by a fanatical Christian mob shortly before the Alexandrian library itself was destroyed early in the fifth century A.D.

As significant as the contributions of Greek humanism to science were, they fell short of initiating any scientific revolution because they caused no fundamental change in how humanity looked at or acted in the world. New theoretical knowledge remained largely within a small elite group of scholars, and any new technology was likewise too little known or too rare to inspire any faith in the fruits of scientific progress. As a result, science languished in the Roman Empire, where interest flourished in certain practical areas of learning—politics, the law, rhetoric, architecture—but where little of the Greek interest in learning for its own sake prevailed.

Although Christianity contributed little directly to the growth of science, it would be a mistake to define the relation of Christianity with science in terms of the extreme opposition suggested by the murder of Hypatia. In fact, the concept of the Incarnation, the belief that God became flesh in Christ, uniting the human and the divine, provided the basis for the argument that God thereby acknowledged the value and dignity of the flesh and of the material world; the view of the world as a stable cosmos regulated by a benevolent deity encouraged Christians to look for system and regularity in the visible world. The study of nature could not, therefore, be evil. Even so, the material world was still seen as lower than that of the spiritual, and although the Church did not oppose natural science, it did nothing to encourage it. Until the sixteenth century, there was not much in the way of any other significant forces encouraging science.

In fact, in the late Classical period, as Rome began its protracted fall and as barbarian invaders threatened its borders, interest in science declined further. Christian monastics did preserve some ancient learning, but the proportion saved was small. The library at Alexandria, for example, is reported to have contained 123 plays by Sophocles alone. Seven survive today. For the survival of Greek science, we are more indebted to Arabic culture than to Christian. In fact, Aristotle's ideas did not return to the Western world until the twelfth century when many of his works were translated into Latin from Arabic manuscripts found in libraries in Islamic Spain.

Because of interest stimulated by these translations in the High Middle Ages, the twelfth and thirteenth centuries, science in the tradition of systematic philosophy and theology began to be studied in universities modeled to some degree on the academies established by Plato and Aristotle. The medieval universities were created primarily to train clergymen and, as a result, there was much less of the spirit of free inquiry that had characterized the Classical academies and much more emphasis on mastering an established body of learning and dogma. Nevertheless, these academies provided the basis for an international community of scholars through whom new knowledge could spread. Science, in the modern sense, began to emerge when a few scholars began independently to observe nature closely and, perhaps most importantly, to conduct controlled observations and to design experiments that tested the "truths" they had been taught. Such investigations did not trigger a revolution in ideas, however; the process was much more gradual. Indeed, it was some five hundred years later when the findings of the Polish astronomer Copernicus began to undermine many of the basic assumptions that were used to explain the operations of the universe.

AUTHORITY AND THE SCIENTIFIC REVOLUTION

One of the most basic of medieval assumptions on the operation of the universe relates to a problem mentioned in the introduction to this text, the one that Owen Barfield describes as the twentieth century's "chronological snobbery," that is, our tendency to devalue the past, to see the present, the modern world, as the most civilized, informed, advanced, and important of all time. This is unquestionably a fault, but it is a relatively new fault. For most of human existence, at least for as long as language has permitted the preservation and transmission of the past, chronological snobbery has worked in the opposite direction. The greatest value has been attached to the old, to what was thought to have been established from the beginning of time, to what has withstood the test of time. In fact, one of the ways in which science has been most revolutionary is precisely in reversing this attitude. That is why a central issue surrounding the scientific revolution was the question of which authority establishes "truth."

Up to the beginning of the scientific revolution in the sixteenth and seventeenth centuries, the prime authority for truth, scientific or otherwise, was traditional in that the presumed validity of any idea was dependent on texts handed down from the ancients. Although the two major acknowledged sources of knowledge, revelation and reason, might seem to be ongoing processes, their major manifestations were in fact seen to have already taken place: revelation was embodied in the Bible; reason was embodied in the texts of the great philosophers, especially Aristotle. In effect, the Judeo–Christian concept of honoring sacred texts had been applied as well to the surviving texts of ancient philosophers—a little less rigorously, however, for in any dispute between the sacred and the worldly realms, revelation, the authority for which was divine, took precedence over reason, the authority for which was human. After the work of the great medieval philosophers, especially Thomas Aquinas, revelation and reason were seen as largely compatible, as parts of a grand system, and any gaps within it were considered as indications of the weakness of human reason, not as flaws in the system itself. No fundamentally new knowledge was expected, or desired, to emerge. Those who wanted to know the truth were to consult the ancient texts and those texts commenting on them, and any new contribution would only be in the form of further commentary.

This medieval synthesis was a tenuous one and was held together primarily by the embodiment of these traditional sources of authority in institutions. That is, knowledge was officially approved by both church and state; arguments might arise over whether church or state should exert authority in a particular case (indeed, much of medieval history concerns the working out, sometimes violently, of their rival claims), but both institutions would agree on the principle of the authority of the ancient traditions. Both saw knowledge as part of a grand and essentially coherent system because they saw authority as part of that grand system, both of which were ordained by God. Especially to those in powerful positions, whether in church or state, all authority, that of clergy over laity, of king over noble and subject, of master over servant, and of man over woman, was grounded in the past and the more ancient, the better. Any notion of change, certainly any fundamental change, was subversive, for to question any one authority was to threaten all.

During the early stages of the rise of modern science, those in authority had cause to feel threatened. When Galileo's *The Starry Messenger* was published in 1610, the Protestant Reformation was already a century old, the age of exploration (da Gama, Columbus, and Magellan) was a century and a half old, both of which introduced profound changes in a culture reluctant to change. In addition, for some time before the fall of Constantinople a century and a half earlier, a small flood of Greek scholars had been migrating to Western Europe; with the aid of ancient manuscripts unknown in the West, they initiated a revival of Plato that gradually began to challenge the dominance of Aristotle and to open a new era of philosophical speculation. In addition, Europe was far from politically stable. In fact, the religious, social, and political order all seemed threatened, and those in power struggled to maintain the old order not merely to hold on to their privileged positions but, as many sincerely believed, to keep the fabric of society from unraveling altogether.

The resulting instability and insecurity surrounding the concept of authority explains the basis for the resistance to the scientific revolution and why, in fact, it was a revolution. That resistance must be understood and kept in historical perspective in order to avoid the bewilderment often suffered by modern readers confronting relatively ancient scientific texts: why do writers like Galileo have so much trouble presenting ideas and observations that are taken for granted today? First, these authors were usually writing not to a general audience interested in scientific information but to a body of scholars wedded to a different way of looking at the phenomena in question. Second, because of the habit of bowing to tradition, the authority of the past, the audience was usually reluctant to even consider a new approach, and the writer had to take special care to be convincing without being insulting or seeming to be presumptuous. Third, there was often no common body of belief, not even a faulty theory, to explain the phenomena in question, and the writer was forced to build his field from its very foundations. Galileo is one of the more lucid of the early science writers in part because he did not have to deal with this third problem: he had a coherent theory, the Ptolemaic system, and Copernicus had already laid the new foundations for change. But in order to understand the scientific revolution in general and the Copernican revolution in particular, we need to understand a little more about the systems of cosmological thought contending against each other.

THE OLD VERSUS THE NEW MODEL
FOR THE UNIVERSE

The scientific revolution is commonly said to have begun in the middle of the sixteenth century with the publication of Copernicus' *De Revolutionibus Orbium Coelestium (Concerning the Revolutions of Celestial Bodies)* (1543). Copernicus was the first to argue on a sound mathematical basis for the universe being heliocentric, centered around the Sun, as opposed to the Ptolemaic system, which for more than fourteen centuries had embodied the dominant view, that the Earth was the center of the universe. This initial struggle in the scientific revolution, between Ptolemaic and Copernican views of the universe, illustrates the degree to which fundamental spiritual values become linked, rightly or wrongly, to the way the physical universe is conceived.

The Ptolemaic system of the universe provided a picture of order, a series of concentric circles (actually they were conceived of as spheres) with Earth at the center, surrounded in turn by the spheres of the Moon, Mercury, Venus, the Sun, Mars, Jupiter, Saturn, and finally the outermost sphere of the fixed stars (see Figure 1). Beyond that was the empyreum, the realm of God and the angels. As odd as it may appear today, the Ptolemaic system was for a millennium and a half a practical and satisfying view of the universe.

First, on the practical level, the Ptolemaic system satisfied common sense because everything in the heavens does seem to revolve around the Earth. Also, it helped explain other obvious phenomena, like the difference between the "fixed" stars, that is, those that maintain so constant a relation to each other that they are identified by their groupings or constellations, and the "planets," literally (in Greek) "wanderers," which move independently across the backdrop of the fixed stars. The Ptolemaic view was also useful because it provided a model on the basis of which the motions of the heavenly bodies could be predicted fairly accurately. Thus, it served the needs of navigation by providing reliable signposts, of agriculture by helping to mark the seasons, and of daily life by providing the basis for a calendar.

More than a practical way of viewing the universe, however, the Ptolemaic system developed into the symbol of an elaborate body of values by satisfying other needs:

1. It satisfied reason, that is, that notion of the higher kind of common sense handed down primarily from the Greeks that drew logical deductions from supposedly self-evident truths. Ptolemy accepted Aristotle's Earth-centered view, including his rationalistic notion that the heavens constituted a realm of perfection, that the sphere of the Moon marked the division between the higher and perfect celestial realm and the dull, "sublunary," imperfect world of the Earth. The "self-evident" basis for this logic was the association of matter with heaviness, lowness, and imperfection on the one hand and of spirit with lightness, height, and perfection on the other. Thus, in this scheme, there is movement from

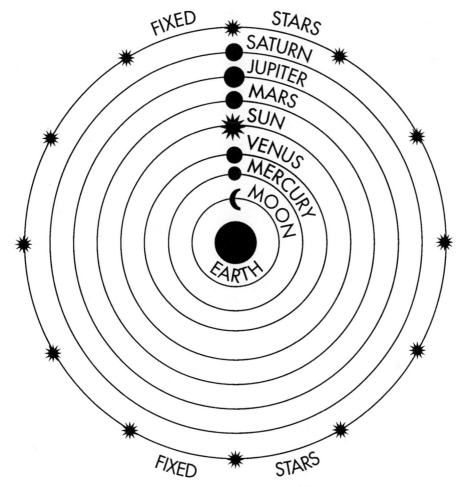

Fig. 1. The system of the world in broad outline according to the Medieval astronomers, from Armitage, A. *Sun, Stand Thou Still: The Life and Work of Copernicus.* New York: Henry Schuman, 1947, p. 140.

base matter on Earth to purified matter in the heavenly bodies to pure spirit in the empyreum. Bodies in the realm of perfected matter, according to Aristotle, were perfect spheres with smooth shining surfaces, unlike the irregular and imperfect surface of the Earth, and they moved eternally in that most perfect of two-dimensional forms, the circle.

2. It satisfied the need for a spiritual order. Although Ptolemy was not Christian, his system lent itself very well to, and by the Middle Ages had been incorporated fully into, Christian cosmology. It was easy to equate the philosophical concept of earthly imperfection with the religious concept of sin; indeed, many writers described the Earth's surface not just in terms of the idea that irregularity meant imperfection, but in terms of the metaphor of a diseased body; its irregularities were the outward signs of

spiritual corruption. Moreover, Earth was at the literal bottom of the universe, an appropriate place for fallen humanity. In fact, hell was imagined to be either on a physical level with us, on the opposite side of the globe, or in the only lower place one could get, beneath the surface.

3. It answered the need for traditional authority. Ptolemy himself was, of course, an ancient whose model was based largely on that even more ancient (by about 500 years) and most respected of philosophers, Aristotle. Moreover, the Bible in no way contradicted Ptolemy's model and in an occasional passage seemed to support the idea of the sun moving around the Earth: most notably Joshua's prayer, which God answered, that the sun stand still so his army could have more time to slaughter the Amorites (Joshua 10:12–14).

4. It answered the need for beauty. Renaissance theories of beauty placed great emphasis on geometric form and mathematical proportion. Certain geometric figures, especially the circle, and certain ratios were thought to be inherently pleasing to the eye, and some artists, Leonardo da Vinci, for example, had worked out elaborate systems for describing the proper proportions of the ideal human figure (see Figure 2). Many of the same rationalistic and aesthetic assumptions lie behind both da Vinci's famous diagram illustrating anatomical proportions and the diagram of the Ptolemaic universe. It may seem surprising, but science has always had an aesthetic side. The greatest scientific theories are distinguished by what scientists like to call their "elegance," a quality of simplicity and coherence in complexity that is really impossible to distinguish from what artists call the beautiful (Einstein once said that his theory of relativity simply had to be true; it was too beautiful not to be). Indeed, the Ptolemaic cosmology, in its wonderfully symmetrical system of concentric circles, seemed to possess this kind of elegance. And this was an elegance, like all beautiful things, that seemed to extend beyond itself to embrace within its material order the rational and spiritual order described above. It must have, indeed, seemed in the sixteenth century too beautiful not to be true.

With all of these needs that the Ptolemaic system fulfilled, that there could be any reason to challenge its authority seems surprising, but there were in fact many. Although it was quite literally the picture of simplicity in broad outline, in practice it was curiously complex. Because the planets do in fact circle the sun, accounting for their motions in an Earth-centered system required complicated adjustments (eccentrics and epicycles, they were called) that were only approximately accurate and that became increasingly complicated as inaccuracies multiplied over time. To those in the late sixteenth century who looked at it closely, the Ptolemaic system seemed to be losing its elegance, like a symphony played by an orchestra going increasingly out of tune.

The system created by the Polish astronomer Copernicus, though clearly superior to Ptolemy's from a modern scientific perspective, did not have an immediate

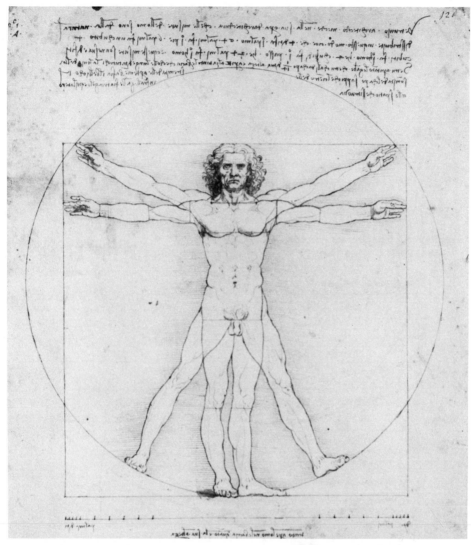

Fig. 2. From Richter, J. P., ed. *The Notebooks of Leonardo da Vinci.* New York: Dover Press, 1970, plate XVIII.

impact on the world. The reasons for this are many. As can be seen by comparing Copernicus' system (Figure 3) with Ptolemy's system (Figure 1), the two did not really appear much different at first glance; indeed, Copernicus continued to adhere to some of the old rationalistic assumptions in his preference for perfect circles. Published in Latin, *De Revolutionibus* had as its audience a small scholarly and clerical community, which limited both its spread and its threat to authority. Copernicus, moreover, did not agree to the publication of his work until he was dying so that when it appeared he would be unavailable for attack. In

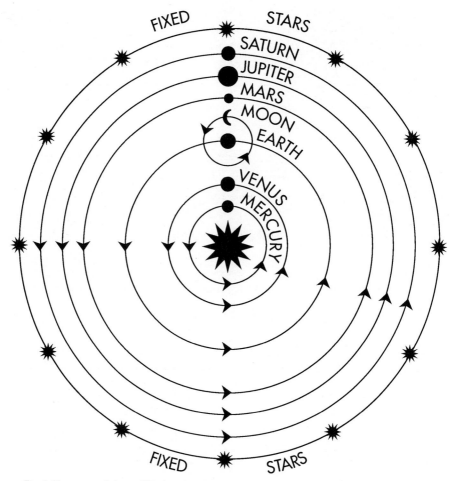

Fig. 3 The system of the world in broad outline according to Copernicus, from Armitage, A. *Sun, Stand Thou Still: The Life and Work of Copernicus.* New York: Henry Schuman, 1947, p. 141.

addition, he confined himself almost entirely to purely astronomical issues, avoiding the theological and philosophical ramifications of his system. He did provide a valuable new mathematical model for computing the positions of planets, but that model only further limited his audience to a relatively few scholars. Last, there was still not a body of sufficiently accurate and generally accepted observations against which the Copernican model could be readily tested; thus, it could be seen as merely speculative.

Nevertheless, Copernicus's work had attracted the attention of a small scientific community, and by the first decade of the seventeenth century, that work began to bear fruit. Three names stand out in this regard. First was Tycho Brahe, a Danish exile in Prague who accumulated the most accurate set of data on planetary positions available before the invention of the telescope. Next was Johannes

Kepler, the German astronomer who, with the aid of Tycho's data, determined that the planetary orbits were not circular but elliptical (Kepler's First Law of Planetary Motion) and that, in its orbit, a planet sweeps out equal areas in equal times (Kepler's Second Law). The third name is Galileo.

▼

GALILEO GALILEI, FROM *THE STARRY MESSENGER*

Galileo Galilei (1564–1642), raised the scientific revolution to a new level primarily by reaching a larger audience. He did so first by abandoning the authoritative tradition of the scholarly language of Latin and by writing *The Starry Messenger* in Italian. Therefore, any literate Italian, not just scholars, could read his book. Second, although he understood and extended Copernicus' mathematical analyses of planetary positions, he rested the bulk of his arguments on direct observation through his own specially designed telescope. Moreover, because the telescope was so obviously valuable in navigation and warfare, its use rapidly spread, and any Italian who could read his book could also confirm his observations. The radical process we associate with modern science of challenging authority through an appeal to direct observation of nature was suddenly raised to a level where institutional authority could no longer ignore it.

Born in Pisa in 1564, Galileo received the standard Classical and religious education of the well-to-do of his time. He studied medicine at the University of Pisa, where he upset his professors by challenging the major Classical authorities in that field, Aristotle and Galen. He then studied mathematics at Florence, where he took his degree. By the age of 24, he was a lecturer in mathematics at Pisa, and three years later, in 1592, he accepted the chair of mathematics at the University of Padua, where he remained for the next 18 years. He made major contributions to science in his experiments with falling bodies, the pendulum, and hydrostatics, but it was his work in astronomy that attracted the greatest immediate attention, leading to the Roman Catholic Church's condemnation of the Copernican system in 1616 and its forcing of Galileo in 1633 to recant his position in favor of the heliocentric universe.

▼

from *The Starry Messenger*
GALILEO GALILEI

Great indeed are the things which in this brief treatise I propose for   *1*
observation and consideration by all students of nature. I say great, because of
the excellence of the subject itself, the entirely unexpected and novel character

of these things, and finally because of the instrument by means of which they have been revealed to our senses.

2   Surely it is a great thing to increase the numerous host of fixed stars previously visible to the unaided vision, adding countless more which have never before been seen, exposing these plainly to the eye in numbers ten times exceeding the old and familiar stars.

3   It is a very beautiful thing, and most gratifying to the sight, to behold the body of the moon, distant from us almost sixty earthly radii,[1] as if it were no farther away than two such measures—so that its diameter appears almost thirty times larger, its surface nearly nine hundred times, and its volume twenty-seven thousand times as large as when viewed with the naked eye. In this way one may learn with all the certainty of sense evidence that the moon is not robed in a smooth and polished surface but is in fact rough and uneven, covered everywhere, just like the earth's surface, with huge prominences, deep valleys, and chasms.

4   Again, it seems to me a matter of no small importance to have ended the dispute about the Milky Way by making its nature manifest to the very senses as well as to the intellect. Similarly it will be a pleasant and elegant thing to demonstrate that the nature of those stars which astronomers have previously called "nebulous" is far different from what has been believed hitherto. But what surpasses all wonders by far, and what particularly moves us to seek the attention of all astronomers and philosophers, is the discovery of four wandering stars not known or observed by any man before us. Like Venus and Mercury, which have their own periods about the sun, these have theirs about a certain star that is conspicuous among those already known, which they sometimes precede and sometimes follow, without ever departing from it beyond certain limits. All these facts were discovered and observed by me not many days ago with the aid of a spyglass which I devised, after first being illuminated by divine grace. Perhaps other things, still more remarkable, will in time be discovered by me or by other observers with the aid of such an instrument, the form and construction of which I shall first briefly explain, as well as the occasion of its having been devised. Afterwards I shall relate the story of the observations I have made.

5   About ten months ago a report reached my ears that a certain Fleming[2] had constructed a spyglass by means of which visible objects, though very distant from the eye of the observer, were distinctly seen as if nearby. Of this truly

---

[1]The original text reads "diameters" here and in another place. That this error was Galileo's and not the printer's has been convincingly shown by Edward Rosen. The slip was a curious one, as astronomers of all schools had long agreed that the maximum distance of the moon was approximately sixty terrestrial radii. Still more curious is the fact that neither Kepler nor any other correspondent appears to have called Galileo's attention to this error; not even a friend who ventured to criticize the calculations in this very passage.

[2]Credit for the original invention is generally assigned to Hans Lipperhey, a lens grinder in Holland who chanced upon this property of combined lenses and applied for a patent on it in 1608. Lipperhey had discovered how lenses commonly available for spectacles could be used to produce a magnification of about three times. Galileo developed the idea and technology to produce much higher magnification in the first astronomical quality telescopes.

remarkable effect several experiences were related, to which some persons gave credence while others denied them. A few days later the report was confirmed to me in a letter from a noble Frenchman at Paris, Jacques Badovere,[3] which caused me to apply myself wholeheartedly to inquire into the means by which I might arrive at the invention of a similar instrument. This I did shortly afterwards, my basis being the theory of refraction. First I prepared a tube of lead, at the ends of which I fitted two glass lenses, both plane on one side while on the other side one was spherically convex and the other concave. Then placing my eye near the concave lens I perceived objects satisfactorily large and near, for they appeared three times closer and nine times larger than when seen with the naked eye alone. Next I constructed another one, more accurate, which represented objects as enlarged more than sixty times. Finally, sparing neither labor nor expense, I succeeded in constructing for myself so excellent an instrument that objects seen by means of it appeared nearly one thousand times larger and over thirty times closer than when regarded with our natural vision.

It would be superfluous to enumerate the number and importance of the advantages of such an instrument at sea as well as on land. But forsaking terrestrial observations, I turned to celestial ones, and first I saw the moon from as near at hand as if it were scarcely two terrestrial radii away. After that I observed often with wondering delight both the planets and the fixed stars, and since I saw these latter to be very crowded, I began to seek (and eventually found) a method by which I might measure their distances apart.   6

Here it is appropriate to convey certain cautions to all who intend to undertake observations of this sort, for in the first place it is necessary to prepare quite a perfect telescope, which will show all objects bright, distinct, and free from any haziness, while magnifying them at least four hundred times and thus showing them twenty times closer. Unless the instrument is of this kind it will be vain to attempt to observe all the things which I have seen in the heavens, and which will presently be set forth. Now in order to determine without much trouble the magnifying power of an instrument, trace on paper the contour of two circles or two squares of which one is four hundred times as large as the other, as it will be when the diameter of one is twenty times that of the other. Then, with both these figures attached to the same wall, observe them simultaneously from a distance, looking at the smaller one through the telescope and at the larger one with the other eye unaided. This may be done without inconvenience while holding both eyes open at the same time; the two figures will appear to be of the same size if the instrument magnifies objects in the desired proportion.   7

Such an instrument having been prepared, we seek a method of measuring distances apart. This we shall accomplish by the following contrivance.   8

---

[3]Badovere studied in Italy toward the close of the sixteenth century and is said to have been a pupil of Galileo's about 1598. When he wrote concerning the new instrument in 1609 he was in the French diplomatic service at Paris, where he died in 1620.

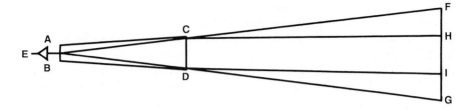

9   Let ABCD be the tube and E be the eye of the observer. Then if there were
no lenses in the tube, the rays would reach the object FG along the straight
lines ECF and EDG. But when the lenses have been inserted, the rays go along
the refracted lines ECH and EDI; thus they are brought closer together, and
those which were previously directed freely to the object FG now include only
the portion of it HI. The ratio of the distance EH to the line HI then being
found, one may by means of a table of sines determine the size of the angle
formed at the eye by the object HI, which we shall find to be but a few minutes
of arc. Now, if to the lens CD we fit thin plates, some pierced with larger and
some with smaller apertures, putting now one plate and now another over the
lens as required, we may form at pleasure different angles subtending more or
fewer minutes of arc, and by this means we may easily measure the intervals
between stars which are but a few minutes apart, with no greater error than
one or two minutes. And for the present let it suffice that we have touched
lightly on these matters and scarcely more than mentioned them, as on some
other occasion we shall explain the entire theory of this instrument.

10   Now let us review the observations made during the past two months, once
more inviting the attention of all who are eager for true philosophy to the first
steps of such important contemplations. Let us speak first of that surface of the
moon which faces us. For greater clarity I distinguish two parts of this surface,
a lighter and a darker; the lighter part seems to surround and to pervade the
whole hemisphere, while the darker part discolors the moon's surface like a
kind of cloud, and makes it appear covered with spots. Now those spots which
are fairly dark and rather large are plain to everyone and have been seen
throughout the ages; these I shall call the "large" or "ancient" spots, distinguishing them from others that are smaller in size but so numerous as to occur
all over the lunar surface, and especially the lighter part. The latter spots had
never been seen by anyone before me. From observations of these spots
repeated many times I have been led to the opinion and conviction that the surface of the moon is not smooth, uniform, and precisely spherical as a great
number of philosophers believe it (and the other heavenly bodies) to be, but is
uneven, rough, and full of cavities and prominences, being not unlike the face
of the earth, relieved by chains of mountains and deep valleys. The things I
have seen by which I was enabled to draw this conclusion are as follows.

11   On the fourth or fifth day after new moon, when the moon is seen with brilliant horns, the boundary which divides the dark part from the light does not
extend uniformly in an oval line as would happen on a perfectly spherical solid,

but traces out an uneven, rough, and very wavy line as shown in the figure below. Indeed, many luminous excrescences extend beyond the boundary into the darker portion, while on the other hand some dark patches invade the illuminated part. Moreover a great quantity of small blackish spots, entirely separated from the dark region, are scattered almost all over the area illuminated by the sun with the exception only of that part which is occupied by the large and ancient spots. Let us note, however, that the said small spots always agree in having their blackened parts directed toward the sun, while on the side opposite the sun they are crowned with bright contours, like shining summits. There is a similar sight on earth about sunrise, when we behold the valleys not yet flooded with light though the mountains surrounding them are already ablaze with glowing splendor on the side opposite the sun. And just as the shadows in the hollows on earth diminish in size as the sun rises higher, so these spots on the moon lose their blackness as the illuminated region grows larger and larger.

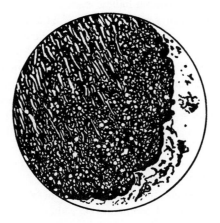

Again, not only are the boundaries of shadow and light in the moon seen to   *12* be uneven and wavy, but still more astonishingly many bright points appear within the darkened portion of the moon, completely divided and separated from the illuminated part and at a considerable distance from it. After a time these gradually increase in size and brightness, and an hour or two later they become joined with the rest of the lighted part which has now increased in size. Meanwhile more and more peaks shoot up as if sprouting now here, now there, lighting up within the shadowed portion; these become larger, and finally they too are united with that same luminous surface which extends ever further. An illustration of this is to be seen in the figure above. And on the earth, before the rising of the sun, are not the highest peaks of the mountains illuminated by the sun's rays while the plains remain in shadow? Does not the light go on spreading while the larger central parts of those mountains are becoming illuminated? And when the sun has finally risen, does not the illumination of plains and hills finally become one? But on the moon the variety of elevations and depressions appears to surpass in every way the roughness of the terrestrial surface, as we shall demonstrate further on.

13   At present I cannot pass over in silence something worthy of consideration which I observed when the moon was approaching first quarter, as shown in the previous figure. Into the luminous part there extended a great dark gulf in the neighborhood of the lower cusp. When I had observed it for a long time and had seen it completely dark, a bright peak began to emerge, a little below its center, after about two hours. Gradually growing, this presented itself in a triangular shape, remaining completely detached and separated from the lighted surface. Around it three other small points soon began to shine, and finally, when the moon was about to set, this triangular shape (which had meanwhile become more widely extended) joined with the rest of the illuminated region and suddenly burst into the gulf of shadow like a vast promontory of light, surrounded still by the three bright peaks already mentioned. Beyond the ends of the cusps, both above and below, certain bright points emerged which were quiet detached from the remaining lighted part, as may be seen depicted in the same figure. There were also a great number of dark spots in both the horns, especially in the lower one; those nearest the boundary of light and shadow appeared larger and darker, while those more distant from the boundary were not so dark and distinct. But in all cases, as we have mentioned earlier, the blackish portion of each spot is turned toward the source of the sun's radiance, while a bright rim surrounds the spot on the side away from the sun in the direction of the shadowy region of the moon. This part of the moon's surface, where it is spotted as the tail of a peacock is sprinkled with azure eyes, resembles those glass vases which have been plunged while still hot into cold water and have thus acquired a crackled and wavy surface, from which they receive their common name of "ice-cups."

14   As to the large lunar spots, these are not seen to be broken in the above manner and full of cavities and prominences; rather, they are even and uniform, and brighter patches crop up only here and there. Hence if anyone wished to revive the old Pythagorean[4] opinion that the moon is like another earth, its brighter part might very fitly represent the surface of the land and its darker region that of the water. I have never doubted that if our globe were seen from afar when flooded with sunlight, the land regions would appear brighter and the watery regions darker.[5] The large spots in the moon are also seen to be less elevated than the brighter tracts, for whether the moon is waxing or waning there are always seen, here and there along its boundary of light and shadow, certain ridges of brighter hue around the large spots (and we have

[4]Pythagoras was a mathematician and philosopher of the sixth century B.C., a semilengendary figure whose followers were credited at Galileo's time with having anticipated the Copernican system. This tradition was based upon a misunderstanding. The Pythagoreans made the earth revolve about a "central fire" whose light and heat were reflected to the earth by the sun.

[5]Leonardo da Vinci had previously suggested that the dark and light regions of the moon were bodies of land and water, though Galileo probably did not know this. Da Vinci, however, had mistakenly supposed that the water would appear brighter than the land.

attended to this in preparing the diagrams); the edges of these spots are not only lower, but also more uniform, being uninterrupted by peaks or ruggedness.

 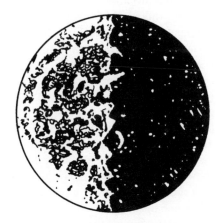

Near the large spots the brighter part stands out particularly in such a way that before first quarter and toward last quarter, in the vicinity of a certain spot in the upper (or northern) region of the moon, some vast prominences arise both above and below . . . Before last quarter this same spot is seen to be walled about with certain blacker contours which, like the loftiest mountaintops, appear darker on the side away from the sun and brighter on that which faces the sun. (This is the opposite of what happens in the cavities, for there the part away from the sun appears brilliant, while that which is turned toward the sun is dark and in shadow.) After a time, when the lighted portion of the moon's surface has diminished in size and when all (or nearly all) the said spot is covered with shadow, the brighter ridges of the mountains gradually emerge from the shade. . . .   15

There is another thing which I must not omit, for I beheld it not without a certain wonder; this is that almost in the center of the moon there is a cavity larger than all the rest, and perfectly round in shape. I have observed it near both first and last quarters, and have tried to represent it as correctly as possible. As to light and shade, it offers the same appearance as would a region like Bohemia[6] if that were enclosed on all sides by very lofty mountains arranged exactly in a circle. Indeed, this area on the moon is surrounded by such enormous peaks that the bounding edge adjacent to the dark portion of the moon is seen to be bathed in sunlight before the boundary of light and shadow reaches halfway across the same space. As in other spots, its shaded portion faces the   16

---

[6]This casual comparison between a part of the moon and a specific region on earth was later the basis of much trouble for Galileo. Even in antiquity the idea that the moon (or any other heavenly body) was of the same nature as the earth had been dangerous to hold. The Athenians banished the philosopher Anaxagoras for teaching such notions, and charged Socrates with blasphemy for repeating them.

sun while its lighted part is toward the dark side of the moon; and for a third time I draw attention to this as a very cogent proof of the ruggedness and unevenness that pervades all the bright region of the moon. Of these spots, moreover, those are always darkest which touch the boundary line between light and shadow, while those farther off appear both smaller and less dark, so that when the moon ultimately becomes full (at opposition[7] to the sun), the shade of the cavities is distinguished from the light of the places in relief by a subdued and very tenuous separation.

17   The things we have reviewed are to be seen in the brighter region of the moon. In the large spots, no such contrast of depressions and prominences is perceived as that which we are compelled to recognize in the brighter parts by the changes of aspect that occur under varying illumination by the sun's rays throughout the multiplicity of positions from which the latter reach the moon. In the large spots there exist some holes rather darker than the rest, as we have shown in the illustrations. Yet these present always the same appearance, and their darkness is neither intensified nor diminished, although with some minute difference they appear sometimes a little more shaded and sometimes a little lighter according as the rays of the sun fall on them more or less obliquely. Moreover, they join with the neighboring regions of the spots in a gentle linkage, the boundaries mixing and mingling. It is quite different with the spots which occupy the brighter surface of the moon; these, like precipitous crags having rough and jagged peaks, stand out starkly in sharp contrasts of light and shade. And inside the large spots there are observed certain other zones that are brighter, some of them very bright indeed. Still, both these and the darker parts present always the same appearance; there is no change either of shape or of light and shadow; hence one may affirm beyond any doubt that they owe their appearance to some real dissimilarity of parts. They cannot be attributed merely to irregularity of shape, wherein shadows move in consequence of varied illuminations from the sun, as indeed is the case with the other, smaller, spots which occupy the brighter part of the moon and which change, grow, shrink, or disappear from one day to the next, as owing their origin only to shadows of prominences.

18   But here I foresee that many persons will be assailed by uncertainty and drawn into a grave difficulty, feeling constrained to doubt a conclusion already explained and confirmed by many phenomena. If that part of the lunar surface which reflects sunlight more brightly is full of chasms (that is, of countless prominences and hollows), why is it that the western edge of the waxing moon, the eastern edge of the waning moon, and the entire periphery of the full moon are not seen to be uneven, rough, and wavy? On the contrary they look as precisely round as if they were drawn with a compass; and yet the whole periphery consists of that brighter lunar substance which we have declared to be filled

[7]Opposition of the sun and moon occurs when they are in line with the earth between them (full moon, or lunar eclipse); conjunction, when they are in line on the same side of the earth (new moon, or eclipse of the sun).

with heights and chasms. In fact not a single one of the great spots extends to the extreme periphery of the moon, but all are grouped together at a distance from the edge.

Now let me explain the twofold reason for this troublesome fact, and in turn *19* give a double solution to the difficulty. In the first place, if the protuberances and cavities in the lunar body existed only along the extreme edge of the circular periphery bounding the visible hemisphere, the moon might (indeed, would necessarily) look to us almost like a toothed wheel, terminated by a warty or wavy edge. Imagine, however, that there is not a single series of prominences arranged only along the very circumference, but a great many ranges of mountains together with their valleys and canyons disposed in ranks near the edge of the moon, and not only in the hemisphere visible to us but everywhere near the boundary line of the two hemispheres. Then an eye viewing them from afar will not be able to detect the separation of prominences by cavities, because the intervals between the mountains located in a given circle or a given chain will be hidden by the interposition of other heights situated in yet other ranges. This will be especially true if the eye of the observer is placed in the same straight line with the summits of these elevations. Thus on earth the summits of several mountains close together appear to be situated in one plane if the spectator is a long way off and is placed at an equal elevation. Similarly in a rough sea the tops of the waves seem to lie in one plane, though between one high crest and another there are many gulfs and chasms of such depth as not only to hide the hulls but even the bulwarks, masts, and rigging of stately ships. Now since there are many chains of mountains and chasms on the moon in addition to those around its periphery, and since the eye, regarding these from a great distance, lies nearly in the plane of their summits, no one need wonder that they appear as arranged in a regular and unbroken line.

To the above explanation another may be added; namely, that there exists *20* around the body of the moon, just as around the earth, a globe of some substance denser than the rest of the aether.[8] This may serve to receive and reflect the sun's radiations without being sufficiently opaque to prevent our seeing through it, especially when it is not illuminated. Such a globe, lighted by the sun's rays, makes the body of the moon appear larger than it really is, and if it were thicker it would be able to prevent our seeing the actual body of the moon. And it actually is thicker near the circumference of the moon; I do not mean in an absolute sense, but relatively to the rays of our vision, which cut it obliquely there. Thus it may obstruct our vision, especially when it is lighted, and cloak the lunar periphery that is exposed to the sun. . . .

That the lighter surface of the moon is everywhere dotted with protuber- *21* ances and gaps has, I think, been made sufficiently clear from the appearances already explained. It remains for me to speak of their dimensions, and to show

---

[8]The aether, or "ever-moving," was the special substance of which the sky and all the heavenly bodies were supposed to be made, a substance essentially different from all the earthly "elements." In later years Galileo abandoned his suggestion here that the moon has a vaporous atmosphere.

that the earth's irregularities are far less than those of the moon. I mean that they are absolutely less, and not merely in relation to the sizes of the respective globes. This is plainly demonstrated as follows.

22   I had often observed, in various situations of the moon with respect to the sun, that some summits within the shadowy portion appeared lighted, though lying some distance from the boundary of the light. By comparing this separation to the whole diameter of the moon, I found that it sometimes exceeded one-twentieth of the diameter. Accordingly, let CAF be a great circle of the lunar body, E its center, and CF a diameter, which is to the diameter of the earth as two is to seven.

23   Since according to very precise observations the diameter of the earth is seven thousand miles, CF will be two thousand, CE one thousand, and one-twentieth of CF will be one hundred miles. Now let CF be the diameter of the great circle which divides the light part of the moon from the dark part (for because of the very great distance of the sun from the moon, this does not differ appreciably from a great circle), and let A be distant from C by one-twentieth of this. Draw the radius EA, which, when produced, cuts the tangent line GCD (representing the illuminating ray) in the point D. Then the arc CA, or rather the straight line CD, will consist of one hundred units whereof CE contains one thousand, and the sum of the squares of DC and CE will be 1,010,000. This is equal to the square of DE; hence ED will exceed 1,004, and AD will be more than four of those units of which CE contains one thousand. Therefore the altitude AD on the moon, which represents a summit reaching up to the solar ray GCD and standing at the distance CD from C, exceeds four miles. But on the earth we have no mountains which reach to a perpendicular height of even one mile.[9] Hence it is quite clear that the prominences on the moon are loftier than those on the earth.

24   Here I wish to assign the cause of another lunar phenomenon well worthy of notice. I observed this not just recently, but many years ago, and pointed it out to some of my friends and pupils, explaining it to them and giving its true cause. Yet since it is rendered more evident and easier to observe with the aid of the telescope, I think it not unsuitable for introduction in this place, especially as it shows more cleary the connection between the moon and the earth.

25   When the moon is not far from the sun, just before or after new moon, its globe offers itself to view not only on the side where it is adorned with shining horns, but a certain faint light is also seen to mark out the periphery of the dark part which faces away from the sun, separating this from the darker background of the aether. Now if we examine the matter more closely, we shall see that not only does the extreme limb of the shaded side glow with this uncertain light, but the entire face of the moon (including the side which does not receive the glare of the sun) is whitened by a not inconsiderable gleam. At first glance

---

[9]Galileo's estimate of four miles for the height of some lunar mountains was a very good one. His remark about the maximum height of mountains on the earth was, however, quite mistaken. An English propagandist for his views, John Wilkins, took pains to correct this error in his anonymous *Discovery of a New World . . . in the Moon* (London, 1638), Prop. ix.

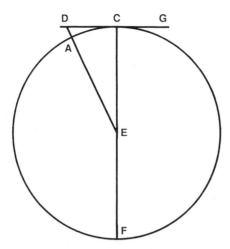

only a thin luminous circumference appears, contrasting with the darker sky coterminous with it; the rest of the surface appears darker from its contact with the shining horns which distract our vision. But if we place ourselves so as to interpose a roof or chimney or some other object at a considerable distance from the eye, the shining horns may be hidden while the rest of the lunar globe remains exposed to view. It is then found that this region of the moon, though deprived of sunlight, also shines not a little. The effect is heightened if the gloom of night has already deepened through departure of the sun, for in a darker field a given light appears brighter.

Moreover, it is found that this secondary light of the moon (so to speak) is greater according as the moon is closer to the sun. It diminishes more and more as the moon recedes from that body until, after the first quarter and before the last, it is seen very weakly and uncertainly even when observed in the darkest sky. But when the moon is within sixty degrees of the sun it shines remarkably, even in twilight; so brightly indeed that with the aid of a good telescope one may distinguish the large spots. This remarkable gleam has afforded no small perplexity to philosophers, and in order to assign a cause for it some have offered one idea and some another. Some would say it is an inherent and natural light of the moon's own; others, that it is imparted by Venus; others yet, by all the stars together; and still others derive it from the sun, whose rays they would have permeate the thick solidity of the moon. But statements of this sort are refuted and their falsity evinced with little difficulty. For if this kind of light were the moon's own, or were contributed by the stars, the moon would retain it and would display it particularly during eclipses, when it is left in an unusually dark sky. This is contradicted by experience, for the brightness which is seen on the moon during eclipses is much fainter and is ruddy, almost copper-colored, while this is brighter and whitish. Moreover the other light is variable and movable, for it covers the face of the moon in such a way that the place near the edge of the earth's shadow is always seen to be brighter than the rest of the moon; this undoubtedly results from contact of the tangent solar rays

26

with some denser zone which girds the moon about.[10] By this contact a sort of twilight is diffused over the neighboring regions of the moon, just as on earth a sort of crepuscular light is spread both morning and evening; but with this I shall deal more fully in my book on the system of the world.[11]

27   To assert that the moon's secondary light is imparted by Venus is so childish as to deserve no reply. Who is so ignorant as not to understand that from new moon to a separation of sixty degrees between moon and sun, no part of the moon which is averted from the sun can possibly be seen from Venus? And it is likewise unthinkable that this light should depend upon the sun's rays penetrating the thick solid mass of the moon, for then this light would never dwindle, inasmuch as one hemisphere of the moon is always illuminated except during lunar eclipses. And the light does diminish as the moon approaches first quarter, becoming completely obscured after that is passed.

28   Now since the secondary light does not inherently belong to the moon, and is not received from any star or from the sun, and since in the whole universe there is no other body left but the earth, what must we conclude? What is to be proposed? Surely we must assert that the lunar body (or any other dark and sunless orb) is illuminated by the earth. Yet what is there so remarkable about this? The earth, in fair and grateful exchange, pays back to the moon an illumination similar to that which it receives from her throughout nearly all the darkest gloom of night.

29   Let us explain this matter more fully. At conjunction the moon occupies a position between the sun and the earth; it is then illuminated by the sun's rays on the side which is turned away from the earth. The other hemisphere, which faces the earth, is covered with darkness; hence the moon does not illuminate the surface of the earth at all. Next, departing gradually from the sun, the moon comes to be lighted partly upon the side it turns toward us, and its whitish horns, still very thin, illuminate the earth with a faint light. The sun's illumination of the moon increasing now as the moon approaches first quarter, a reflection of that light to the earth also increases. Soon the splendor on the moon extends into a semicircle, and our nights grow brighter; at length the entire visible face of the moon is irradiated by the sun's resplendent rays, and at full moon the whole surface of the earth shines in a flood of moonlight. Now the moon, waning, sends us her beams more weakly, and the earth is less strongly lighted; at length the moon returns to conjunction with the sun, and black night covers the earth.

30   In this monthly period, then, the moonlight gives us alternations of brighter and fainter illumination; and the benefit is repaid by the earth in equal measure. For while the moon is between us and the sun (at new moon), there lies

[10]Kepler had correctly accounted for the existence of this light and its ruddy color. It is caused by refraction of sunlight in the earth's atmosphere, and does not require a lunar atmosphere as supposed by Galileo.

[11]The book thus promised was destined not to appear for more than two decades. Events which will presently be recounted prevented its publication for many years, and then it had to be modified to present the arguments for both the Ptolemaic and Copernican systems instead of just the latter as Galileo here planned. Even then it was suppressed, and the author was condemned to life imprisonment.

before it the entire surface of that hemisphere of the earth which is exposed to the sun and illuminated by vivid rays. The moon receives the light which this reflects, and thus the nearer hemisphere of the moon—that is, the one deprived of sunlight—appears by virtue of this illumination to be not a little luminous. When the moon is ninety degrees away from the sun it sees but half the earth illuminated (the western half), for the other (the eastern half) is enveloped in night. Hence the moon itself is illuminated less brightly from the earth, and as a result its secondary light appears fainter to us. When the moon is in opposition to the sun, it faces a hemisphere of the earth that is steeped in the gloom of night, and if this position occurs in the plane of the ecliptic the moon will receive no light at all, being deprived of both the solar and the terrestrial rays. In its various other positions with respect to the earth and sun, the moon receives more or less light according as it faces a greater or smaller portion of the illuminated hemisphere of the earth. And between these two globes a relation is maintained such that whenever the earth is most brightly lighted by the moon, the moon is least lighted by the earth, and vice versa.

Let these few remarks suffice us here concerning this matter, which will be more fully treated in our *System of the world*. In that book, by a multitude of arguments and experiences, the solar reflection from the earth will be shown to be quite real—against those who argue that the earth must be excluded from the dancing whirl of stars for the specific reason that it is devoid of motion and of light. We shall prove the earth to be a wandering body surpassing the moon in splendor, and not the sink of all dull refuse of the universe; this we shall support by an infinitude of arguments drawn from nature. *31*

Thus far we have spoken of our observations concerning the body of the moon. Let us now set forth briefly what has thus far been observed regarding the fixed stars. And first of all, the following fact deserves consideration: The stars, whether fixed or wandering,[12] appear not to be enlarged by the telescope in the same proportion as that in which it magnifies other objects, and even the moon itself. In the stars this enlargement seems to be so much less that a telescope which is sufficiently powerful to magnify other objects a hundredfold is scarcely able to enlarge the stars four or five times. The reason for this is as follows. *32*

When stars are viewed by means of unaided natural vision, they present themselves to us not as of their simple (and, so to speak, their physical) size, but as irradiated by a certain fulgor and as fringed with sparkling rays, especially when the night is far advanced. From this they appear larger than they would if stripped of those adventitious hairs of light, for the angle at the eye is determined not by the primary body of the star but by the brightness which extends so widely about it. This appears quite clearly from the fact that when stars first emerge from twilight at sunset they look very small, even if they are of the first magnitude; Venus itself, when visible in broad daylight, is so small *33*

---

[12]That is, planets. Among these bodies Galileo counted his newly discovered satellites of Jupiter. The term "satellites" was introduced somewhat later by Kepler.

as scarcely to appear equal to a star of the sixth magnitude. Things fall out differently with other objects, and even with the moon itself; these, whether seen in daylight or the deepest night, appear always of the same bulk. Therefore the stars are seen crowned among shadows, while daylight is able to remove their headgear; and not daylight alone, but any thin cloud that interposes itself between a star and the eye of the observer. The same effect is produced by black veils or colored glasses, through the interposition of which obstacles the stars are abandoned by their surrounding brilliance. A telescope similarly accomplishes the same result. It removes from the stars their adventitious and accidental rays, and then it enlarges their simple globes (if indeed the stars are naturally globular) so that they seem to be magnified in a lesser ratio than other objects. In fact a star of the fifth or sixth magnitude when seen through a telescope presents itself as one of the first magnitude.

34   Deserving of notice also is the difference between the appearances of the planets and of the fixed stars.[13] The planets show their globes perfectly round and definitely bounded, looking like little moons, spherical and flooded all over with light; the fixed stars are never seen to be bounded by a circular periphery, but have rather the aspect of blazes whose rays vibrate about them and scintillate a great deal. Viewed with a telescope they appear of a shape similar to that which they present to the naked eye, but sufficiently enlarged so that a star of the fifth or sixth magnitude seems to equal the Dog Star, largest of all the fixed stars. Now, in addition to stars of the sixth magnitude, a host of other stars are perceived through the telescope which escape the naked eye; these are so numerous as almost to surpass belief. One may, in fact, see more of them than all the stars included among the first six magnitudes. The largest of these, which we may call stars of the seventh magnitude, or the first magnitude of invisible stars, appear through the telescope as larger and brighter than stars of the second magnitude when the latter are viewed with the naked eye. In order to give one or two proofs of their almost inconceivable number, I have adjoined pictures of two constellations. With these as samples, you may judge of all the others.

35   In the first I had intended to depict the entire constellation of Orion, but I was overwhelmed by the vast quantity of stars and by limitations of time, so I have deferred this to another occasion. There are more than five hundred new stars distributed among the old ones within limits of one or two degrees of arc. Hence to the three stars in the Belt of Orion and the six in the Sword which were previously known, I have added eighty adjacent stars discovered recently, preserving the intervals between them as exactly as I could. To distinguish the known or ancient stars, I have depicted them larger and have outlined them doubly; the other (invisible) stars I have drawn smaller and without the extra line. I have also preserved differences of magnitude as well as possible.

---

[13]Fixed stars are so distant that their light reaches the earth as from dimensionless points. Hence their images are not enlarged by even the best telescopes, which serve only to gather more of their light and in that way increase their visibility. Galileo was never entirely clear about this distinction. Nevertheless, by applying his knowledge of the effects described here, he greatly reduced the prevailing overestimation of visual dimensions of stars and planets.

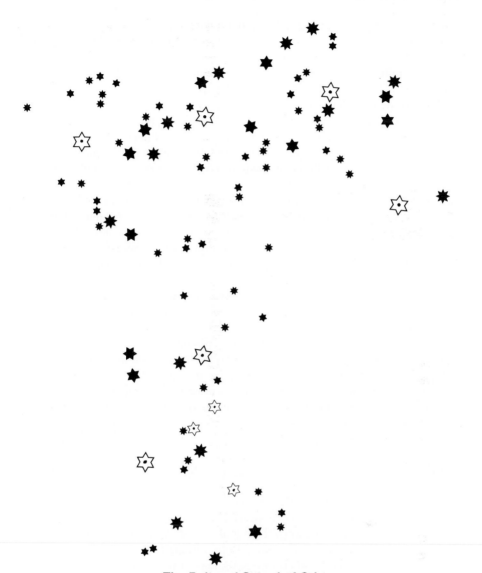

The Belt and Sword of Orion

In the second example I have depicted the six stars of Taurus known as the   *36*
Pleiades (I say six, inasmuch as the seventh is hardly ever visible) which lie
within very narrow limits in the sky. Near them are more than forty others
invisible, no one of which is much more than half a degree away from the original six. . . .

Third, I have observed the nature and the material of the Milky Way. With   *37*
the aid of the telescope this has been scrutinized so directly and with such ocu-
lar certainty that all the disputes which have vexed philosophers through so
many ages have been resolved, and we are at last freed from wordy debates

about it. The galaxy is, in fact, nothing but a congeries of innumerable stars grouped together in clusters. Upon whatever part of it the telescope is directed, a vast crowd of stars is immediately presented to view. Many of them are rather large and quite bright, while the number of smaller ones is quite beyond calculation. . . .

38   We have now briefly recounted the observations made thus far with regard to the moon, the fixed stars, and the Milky Way. There remains the matter which in my opinion deserves to be considered the most important of all—the disclosure of four PLANETS never seen from the creation of the world up to our own time, together with the occasion of my having discovered and studied them, their arrangements, and the observations made of their movements and alterations during the past two months. I invite all astronomers to apply themselves to examine them and determine their periodic times, something which has so far been quite impossible to complete, owing to the shortness of the time. Once more, however, warning is given that it will be necessary to have a very accurate telescope such as we have described at the beginning of this discourse.

39   On the seventh day of January in this present year 1610, at the first hour of night, when I was viewing the heavenly bodies with a telescope, Jupiter presented itself to me; and because I had prepared a very excellent instrument for myself, I perceived (as I had not before, on account of the weakness of my previous instrument) that beside the planet there were three starlets, small indeed, but very bright. Though I believed them to be among the host of fixed stars, they aroused my curiosity somewhat by appearing to lie in an exact straight line parallel to the ecliptic, and by their being more splendid than others of their size. Their arrangement with respect to Jupiter and each other was the following:

East   *   *   ◯   *   **West**

that is, there were two stars on the eastern side and one to the west. The most easterly star and the western one appeared larger than the other. I paid no attention to the distances between them and Jupiter, for at the outset I thought them to be fixed stars, as I have said.[14] But returning to the same investigation on January eighth—led by what, I do not know—I found a very different arrangement. The three starlets were now all to the west of Jupiter, closer together, and at equal intervals from one another as shown in the following sketch:

East   ◯   *   *   *   **West**

---

[14]The reader should remember that the telescope was nightly revealing to Galileo hundreds of fixed stars never previously observed. His unusual gifts for astronomical observation are illustrated by his having noticed and remembered these three merely by reason of their alignment, and recalling them so well that when by chance he happened to see them the following night he was certain that they had changed their positions. No such plausible and candid account of the discovery was given by the rival astronomer Simon Mayr, who four years later claimed priority.

At this time, though I did not yet turn my attention to the way the stars had 40 come together, I began to concern myself with the question how Jupiter could be east of all these stars when on the previous day it had been west of two of them. I commenced to wonder whether Jupiter was not moving eastward at that time, contrary to the computations of the astronomers, and had got in front of them by that motion.[15] Hence it was with great interest that I awaited the next night. But I was disappointed in my hopes, for the sky was then covered with clouds everywhere.

On the tenth of January, however, the stars appeared in this position with 41 respect to Jupiter:

East   ✳ ✳ ⬤   **West**

that is, there were but two of them, both easterly, the third (as I supposed) being hidden behind Jupiter. As at first, they were in the same straight line with Jupiter and were arranged precisely in the line of the zodiac. Noticing this, and knowing that there was no way in which such alterations could be attributed to Jupiter's motion, yet being certain that these were still the same stars I had observed (in fact no other was to be found along the line of the zodiac for a long way on either side of Jupiter), my perplexity was now transformed into amazement. I was sure that the apparent changes belonged not to Jupiter but to the observed stars, and I resolved to pursue this investigation with greater care and attention.

And thus, on the eleventh of January, I saw the following disposition: 42

East   ✳ ✳   ⬤   **West**

There were two stars, both to the east, the central one being three times as far from Jupiter as from the one farther east. The latter star was nearly double the size of the former, whereas on the night before they had appeared approximately equal.

I had now decided beyond all question that there existed in the heavens 43 three stars wandering about Jupiter as do Venus and Mercury about the sun, and this became plainer than daylight from observations on similar occasions which followed. Nor were there just three such stars; four wanderers complete their revolutions about Jupiter, and of their alterations as observed more precisely later on we shall give a description here. Also I measured the distances between them by means of the telescope, using the method explained before. Moreover I recorded the times of the observations, especially when more than one was made during the same night—for the revolutions of these planets are so speedily completed that it is usually possible to take even their hourly variations.

[15]Jupiter was at this time in "retrograde" motion; that is, the earth's motion made the planet appear to be moving westward among the fixed stars.

44   Thus on the twelfth of January at the first hour of night I saw the stars arranged in this way:

East   ✳ ＊⬭ ✳   **West**

The most easterly star was larger than the western one, though both were easily visible and quite bright. Each was about two minutes of arc distant from Jupiter. The third star was invisible at first, but commenced to appear after two hours; it almost touched Jupiter on the east, and was quite small. All were on the same straight line directed along the ecliptic.

45   On the thirteenth of January four stars were seen by me for the first time, in this situation relative to Jupiter:

East   ＊ ⬭ ＊✳＊   **West**

Three were westerly and one was to the east; they formed a straight line except that the middle western star departed slightly toward the north. The eastern star was two minutes of arc away from Jupiter, and the intervals of the rest from one another and from Jupiter were about one minute. All the stars appeared to be of the same magnitude, and though small were very bright, much brighter than fixed stars of the same size. . . .[16]

46   Such are the observations concerning the four Medicean planets recently first discovered by me, and although from these data their periods have not yet been reconstructed in numerical form, it is legitimate at least to put in evidence some facts worthy of note. Above all, since they sometimes follow and sometimes precede Jupiter by the same intervals, and they remain within very limited distances either to east or west of Jupiter, accompanying that planet in both its retrograde and direct movements in a constant manner, no one can doubt that they complete their revolutions about Jupiter and at the same time effect all together a twelve-year period about the center of the universe. That they also revolve in unequal circles is manifestly deduced from the fact that at the greatest elongation[17] from Jupiter it is never possible to see two of these planets in conjunction, whereas in the vicinity of Jupiter they are found united two, three, and sometimes all four together. It is also observed that the revolutions are swifter in those planets which describe smaller circles about Jupiter, since the stars closest to Jupiter are usually seen to the east when on the previous day they appeared to the west, and vice versa, while the planet which traces the largest orbit appears upon accurate observation of its returns to have a semimonthly period.

47   Here we have a fine and elegant argument for quieting the doubts of those

---

[16]Galileo's day-by-day journal of observations continued in unbroken sequence until ten days before publication of the book, which he remained in Venice to supervise. The observations omitted here contained nothing of a novel character.

[17]By this is meant the greatest angular separation from Jupiter attained by any of the satellites.

who, while accepting with tranquil mind the revolutions of the planets about the sun in the Copernican system, are mightily disturbed to have the moon alone revolve about the earth and accompany it in an annual rotation about the sun. Some have believed that this structure of the universe should be rejected as impossible. But now we have not just one planet rotating about another while both run through a great orbit around the sun; our own eyes show us four stars which wander around Jupiter as does the moon around the earth, while all together trace out a grand revolution about the sun in the space of twelve years.

And finally we should not omit the reason for which the Medicean stars *48* appear sometimes to be twice as large as at other times, though their orbits about Jupiter are very restricted. We certainly cannot seek the cause in terrestrial vapors, as Jupiter and its neighboring fixed stars are not seen to change size in the least while this increase and diminution are taking place. It is quite unthinkable that the cause of variation should be their change of distance from the earth at perigee and apogee, since a small circular rotation could by no means produce this effect, and an oval motion (which in this case would have to be nearly straight) seems unthinkable and quite inconsistent with the appearances. But I shall gladly explain what occurs to me on this matter, offering it freely to the judgment and criticism of thoughtful men. It is known that the interposition of terrestrial vapors makes the sun and moon appear large, while the fixed stars and planets are made to appear smaller. Thus the two great luminaries are seen larger when close to the horizon, while the stars appear smaller and for the most part hardly visible. Hence the stars appear very feeble by day and in twilight, though the moon does not, as we have said. Now from what has been said above, and even more from what we shall say at greater length in our *System*, it follows that not only the earth but also the moon is surrounded by an envelope of vapors, and we may apply precisely the same judgment to the rest of the planets. Hence it does not appear entirely impossible to assume that around Jupiter also there exists an envelope denser than the rest of the aether, about which the Medicean planets revolve as does the moon about the elemental sphere. Through the interposition of this envelope they appear larger when they are in perigee by the removal, or at least the attenuation, of this envelope.

Time prevents my proceeding further, but the gentle reader may expect *49* more soon.

WRITING AND DISCUSSION QUESTIONS

Informative

1. Describe the major contributions to knowledge that Galileo claims to make in *The Starry Messenger* (summarized in his first paragraphs), and explain how each contribution opposes the accepted opinion at the time.

2. Choose any of Galileo's major points (for example, that the surface of the moon is rough and uneven), and summarize how his observations support his conclusions.

Persuasive

1. Argue whether Galileo is an effective communicator according to the features of his presentation. Consider his tone, use of evidence, clarity of argument, handling of opposing views, and sense of audience.
2. Given that Galileo's new information would be seen by many to undermine the basis for faith in God, argue whether he should have withheld this information, presented it in a different manner, or done just what he did.

Personal

1. Is your own scientific knowledge based on direct experience or on something else? Choose some particular scientific issue or principle of interest to you and consider how much of your knowledge is based on faith in the processes of investigation and peer review (the validation by other scientists of the reliability of experimental methods, the logic of argument, and the honesty of the investigators involved in advancing any scientific conclusions).
2. How effective is your own judgment in distinguishing between solid conclusions based on sound observations, reasonable speculations based on limited knowledge, and nonsense? In what areas do you think it important for you or people in general to make such distinctions better?
3. Galileo still held with Copernicus that the Sun was the center not only of the solar system but of the universe. How do you suppose he would feel if he knew that the Sun is in fact only a medium-sized star two thirds of the way out on one spiral arm of a galaxy of a hundred billion stars, itself only a medium-sized galaxy in a universe of another hundred billion galaxies? How does this knowledge of your physical place in the universe affect your philosophical or theological view of your own significance or purpose?

▼

JOHN DONNE, *AN ANATOMY OF THE WORLD, THE FIRST ANNIVERSARIE*

John Donne (1572–1631) was an early seventeenth century poet roughly contemporaneous with Galileo and Shakespeare (both born in 1564). Donne's life and work are fascinating studies in themselves, spanning the period when he was mad Jack of London, a scandalous rake whose love poetry undermined the expectations of his time by its unusual combination of cynicism, bawdiness, and learning, to the later period when he was Dr. John Donne, an Anglican priest and Dean of St. Paul's Cathedral, one of the world's greatest writers of religious verse and devotional prose.

Somewhere in the transition between these two lives, Donne wrote two long poems, collected under the title *The Anniversaries* in 1611 and 1612, the occasion for which was the death of his patron's and friend's daughter. In the first of these, *An Anatomy of the World*, excerpted here, Donne relates his patron's personal grief to what he sees as a universal grief, the sense in this time of intellectual, political, and religious turmoil that the whole world was in an advanced stage of decay—in fact, the metaphor he uses is that the world is dead, and the "anatomy" he performs on its corrupted "body" is a postmortem dissection, an autopsy. In doing so, Donne sees science, the "new philosophy," as a major contributor to the world's decay. He is also obviously aware of the connections many people perceived and still perceive between scientific thought and the larger issues of moral, spiritual, and aesthetic values.

Donne may or may not have been familiar with Copernicus' work at the time he wrote *The Anatomy*. It is not likely that he had read Galileo's *Starry Messenger*, published in Italy only the year before, although he might have heard something about its contents. He is only a little more likely to have been aware of Johannes Kepler's *Astronomia Nova*, published in 1609, which supported Copernicus' heliocentric premise but argued convincingly that the planetary orbits were elliptical, not circular. Remember, though, that Copernicus was still not generally accepted at the beginning of the seventeenth century, and this was not a time when information could be spread rapidly. The latest research results were not being presented in international conferences or published in professional journals, nor were they being summarized for a less-specialized audience as they are today and disseminated almost immediately by television, radio, and popular news vehicles such as *Time* and *Newsweek*. Nevertheless, Donne was sensitive to the changes brought about by science.

▼

from *An Anatomy of the World, The First Anniversarie*
JOHN DONNE

THE NEW PHILOSOPHY

And now the springs and summers which we see,
Like sons of women after fifty be.
And new philosophy calls all in doubt;
The element of fire is quite put out;
The sun is lost, and th' earth, and no man's wit
Can well direct him where to look for it.
And freely men confess that this world's spent,
When in the planets, and the firmament
They seek so many new; they see that this

210

Is crumbled out again to his atomies,
'Tis all in pieces, all coherence gone,
All just supply, and all relation. . . .

For the world's subtlest immaterial parts
Feel this consuming wound and age's darts;
For the world's beauty is decay'd, or gone
250   —Beauty; that's colour and proportion.
We think the heavens enjoy their spherical,
Their round proportion, embracing all;
But yet their various and perplexed course,
Observed in divers ages, doth enforce
Men to find out so many eccentric parts,
Such diverse downright lines, such overthwarts,
As disproportion that pure form; it tears
The firmament in eight-and-forty shares,
And in these constellations then arise
260   New stars, and old do vanish from our eyes;
As though heaven suffered earthquakes, peace or war,
When new towers rise, and old demolish'd are.
They have impaled within a zodiac
The free-born sun, and keep twelve signs awake
To watch his steps; the Goat and Crab control,
And fright him back, who else to either pole,
Did not these tropics fetter him, might run.
For his course is not round, nor can the sun
Perfect a circle, or maintain his way
270   One inch direct; but where he rose to-day
He comes no more, but with a cozening line,
Steals by that point, and so is serpentine;
And seeming weary with his reeling thus,
He means to sleep, being now fallen nearer us.
So of the stars which boast that they do run
In circle still, none ends where he begun.
All their proportion's lame, it sinks, it swells;
For of meridians and parallels
Man hath weaved out a net, and this net thrown
280   Upon the heavens, and now they are his own.
Loth to go up the hill, or labour thus
To go to heaven, we make heaven come to us.
We spur, we rein the stars, and in their race
They're diversely content to obey our pace.
But keeps the earth her round proportion still?
Doth not a Teneriffe or higher hill
Rise so high like a rock, that one might think

The floating moon would shipwreck there and sink?
Seas are so deep that whales, being struck to-day,
Perchance to-morrow scarce at middle way   *290*
Of their wish'd journey's end, the bottom, die.
And men, to sound depths, so much line untie
As one might justly think that there would rise
At end thereof one of th' antipodes.
If under all a vault infernal be
—Which sure is spacious, except that we
Invent another torment, that there must
Millions into a straight hot room be thrust—
Then solidness and roundness have no place.
Are these but warts and pockholes in the face   *300*
Of th' earth? Think so; but yet confess, in this
The world's proportion disfigured is;
That those two legs whereon it doth rely,
Reward and punishment, are bent awry.

WRITING AND DISCUSSION QUESTIONS

Informative

1. Find as many references to astronomy as you can in Donne's poem, and briefly discuss what connections are made by these references to either the Ptolemaic or the Copernican system.

Persuasive

1. When he complains about the "eccentric parts" of the motions of heavenly bodies, Donne may be referring to the Ptolemaic system; an eccentric, mentioned in the introduction to this section, was one kind of adjustment made to make some observations fit the Ptolemaic system. Which bothers Donne the most, the fact that a new model for the universe might have replaced the old or the fact that the old model had become untenable?
2. Notice Donne's brief definition of beauty, "colour and proportion." Relate this definition to the discussion in the introduction to this section on the aesthetic appeal of the Ptolemaic system. Argue that Donne's position about the connection between the beautiful and rational order is or is not based on Ptolemaic values.

Personal

1. What connections do you see between modern science's description of order in the universe and your sense of beauty? Is the scientific incompatible with the beautiful, or is it somehow connected?

2. Donne's metaphor describing the world as a diseased human body recalls the older Christian–Ptolemaic view that corruption is tied to both the world's physical position and moral condition, in the latter as far back as the Biblical Fall. If so, Donne could be arguing not so much that the new philosophy has caused the world's sickness but that it does nothing to heal that sickness or perhaps that it deepens the sickness by diverting us from the more important concerns regarding our spiritual state. How do you see the moral effects of science? Does science increase moral awareness or decrease it? Or does science have nothing whatever to do with morality?

▼

BLAISE PASCAL, PREFACE TO THE *TREATISE ON THE VACUUM*

As the scientific revolution developed during the seventeenth century, the political conflict between tradition and science softened. The struggle for a hearing of the new approach to natural philosophy became less a political issue, except perhaps in Italy, and more a scholarly issue (in other words, an issue of academic politics rather than national politics). During this time, the conflict was variously billed as the ancients versus the moderns and the battle of the books. The battle raged on this level until well into the eighteenth century and was punctuated by several major discoveries. Englishman William Harvey convincingly demonstrated the circulation of the blood (*On the Motion of the Heart and Blood in Animals*, 1628) and proved that ancient authorities Aristotle and Galen were clearly wrong. Frenchman René Descartes invented analytical geometry (Cartesian coordinates—the familiar x and y axes used to graph equations—bear the Latin form of his name), and he developed what he considered a critical philosophical method for obtaining the truth, a method that began with radical doubt of all intellectual authority except that of the mind applying a rigorous logical method. Also, his *Discourse on Method* (1637) became what many scholars have called the philosophical basis for modern science. Dutchman Antonie van Leeuwenhoek used single-lens microscopes, through which he discovered and cataloged a vast "invisible" world utterly unknown to the ancients (some 375 reports to the British Royal Society, 1660s–1690s). Englishman Isaac Newton discovered the necessary mathematics (the calculus, independently worked out by German Gottfried Wilhelm Leibniz) and, through its application, a set of laws of motion that finally united the heavens and the earth, demonstrating with mathematical certainty that the planets and their moons all obey the same laws governing the motions of apples and cannonballs on earth (*Principia Mathematica*, 1687). Frenchman Blaise Pascal's contributions were less grand, but nevertheless significant, and his preface to the *Treatise on the Vacuum* (1648) is an illuminating example of how the battle of the books was fought in the middle of the seventeenth century.

In his thirty-nine short years, Pascal (1623–1662) distinguished himself as a mathematician, a physicist, an inventor, a theologian, and a philosopher. He began as a mathematical prodigy and by the age of 20 invented what is sometimes described as the first computer, sometimes as the first calculator, his *machine arithmétique*, a mechanical device for performing computations. He was also a profoundly religious person, undergoing two major conversions in 1646 and 1654, and produced a series of philosophical and religious writings that have earned him a reputation as one of the first truly modern theologians.

To understand his objective in the preface to the *Treatise on the Vacuum*, we need to know something about the treatise itself. Pascal had been working on experiments confirming the work of the Italian physicist Evangelista Torricelli, who found that if a glass tube more than 30 inches long filled with mercury was inverted in a bowl of mercury, the mercury in the tube would drop down to a level about 30 inches above the level in the bowl, leaving the inside of the glass tube above the 30-inch mark empty. Aristotle had said that "Nature abhors a vacuum," suggesting that it was impossible to create a vacuum, but Pascal and Torricelli had created one. Pascal goes on in the *Treatise* to argue that the mercury does not drop further because it is held up by outside air pressure, thus identifying the principle behind the barometer, which was developed some years later (in tribute to which, the fundamental unit of pressure in the metric system is today called the *pascal*). However, his major concern in the preface is to prepare a learned audience to consider an idea that goes against one of the major assumptions of his time, the belief in the authority of the ancients.

It should be noted, however, that even though Pascal rejects any absolute authority in the ancients with regard to the physical sciences, in explaining what will be later described as the idea of progress, he acknowledges the continuing indebtedness of new ideas to the past. New knowledge builds on old knowledge. That is why an aphorism commonly attributed to Newton continues to be quoted today by both scientists and historians of science: "If I have seen farther, it is by standing on the shoulders of giants."

▼

Preface to the *Treatise on the Vacuum*
BLAISE PASCAL

We have carried our respect for antiquity so far today, in matters in *1*
which it should have less influence, that we treat all its ideas as revelations and even its obscurities as mysteries; we can no longer advance new opinions without danger, and an author's text is enough to destroy the strongest arguments. . . .

Not that my intention is to correct one vice by another, and to have no *2*
esteem for the ancients because they are too much esteemed. I do not want to banish their authority to set up reason alone, although there is an attempt to establish their authority alone to the prejudice of reason. . . .

To make this important distinction with care we must consider that one *3*
group depend exclusively on memory and are purely historical, having as their only object to know what the authors have written; the other group depend exclusively on reason and are wholly dogmatic, having as their object to seek and discover hidden truths. Those of the first kind have the same limits as the books containing them. . . .

4   It is in accordance with this distinction that we should regulate differently the extent of our respect. . . .

5   In matters in which we seek to know only what authors have written, as in history, geography, jurisprudence, languages, and above all in theology, and in short wherever either the simple fact or an institution, human or divine, is the starting point, we must necessarily have recourse to books, since all that can be known about such matters is contained there. Whence it is evident that we can have the whole of that knowledge and that it is not possible to add anything to it.

6   If it is a question of knowing who was the first king of France, where the geographers put the first meridian, what words are used in a dead language, and everything of this sort, how could we find it out except from books? And who can add anything new to what they tell us about it, since we desire to know only what they contain? Authority alone can give us light on such matters. But it is in theology that authority has its chief weight because there it is insepara-ble from truth, which we know only through it; so that to give absolute certainty to things which reason can least grasp, it is sufficient to point them out in Holy Scripture (as, to show the uncertainty of the most probable things, we need only point out that they are not included there); because the principles of theol-ogy are above nature and reason, and the mind of man, too feeble to reach them by its own efforts, can arrive at this highest knowledge only if carried there by an all-powerful and supernatural force.

7   It is quite otherwise with subjects accessible to sense or reasoning: here authority is useless, only reason can know them. Authority and reason have their separate rights: a moment ago one had all the advantage; here the other is queen in her turn. But since subjects of this kind are suited to the mind's reach, it has perfect freedom to concern itself with them; its inexhaustible fertil-ity produces continually, and its discoveries can be at once without end and without interruption. . . .

8   Thus it is that geometry, arithmetic, music, physics, medicine, architecture, and all the sciences subject to experiment and reason must be added to if they are to become perfect. The ancients found them merely sketched by their prede-cessors, and we shall leave them to our successors in a more perfected state than we received them. Since their perfection depends upon time and effort, it is evident that even if our effort and time had gained us less than the labors of the ancients, separated from ours, the two together nevertheless must have more effect than either alone.

9   The clearing up of this difference should make us pity the blindness of those who advance authority alone as proof in physics instead of reason or experi-ment, and should fill us with horror at the wickedness of others who use reason alone in theology instead of the authority of Scripture and the Fathers. We must strengthen the courage of those timid souls who dare discover nothing in physics, and confound the insolence of that temerity which introduces novelty into theology. Meanwhile the misfortune of the age is such that we see many new opinions in theology altogether unknown to antiquity maintained with obsti-

nacy and received with applause; whereas those put forward in physics, though few in number, must be convicted of error, it seems, as soon as they shock, however little, received opinions. As if respect for the philosophers of antiquity were a duty but for the most ancient of the Fathers only decorum! I leave it to the judicious to observe the importance of this abuse which perverts the order of the sciences so unjustly, and I think there will be few who do not wish this . . . to be applied to other subjects, since new discoveries are inevitably errors in those matters we profane with impunity, whereas they are absolutely necessary for the perfection of so many other subjects incomparably lower, which however we would be afraid to touch.

Let us make a more just distribution of our credulity and our doubt, and set   *10* limits to our respect for the ancients. Since reason is its source, reason should also be its measure. Let us consider that if the ancients had kept to this deference of daring to add nothing to the knowledge transmitted to them and if their contemporaries had been as much opposed to accepting anything new, they would have deprived both themselves and their posterity of the fruit of their discoveries. Just as they used the discoveries handed down to them only as the means of making new ones, and that happy daring had opened the road for them to great achievements, so we should take the discoveries won for us by them in the same spirit, and following their example make these discoveries the means and not the end of our study, and thus by imitating the ancients try to surpass them. For what is more unfair than to treat our predecessors with more respect than they treated those who preceded them, and to have for them that inviolable respect they have deserved from us only because they did not themselves have it for those who had the same advantage over them? . . .

The secrets of nature are hidden. Although she is always at work, her effects   *11* are not always discovered; time reveals them from generation to generation, and although always the same in herself, she is not always equally known. The experiments which give us our knowledge of nature multiply continually; and since they are the only principles of physics, the consequences multiply in proportion. It is in this way that we can today have other ideas and new opinions without scorn and without ingratitude, since the first knowledge given us by the ancients has served as steps to our own, and since we are indebted to them for the advantage of a position higher than theirs; because placed by them part way up the ladder, we are carried higher by our slightest effort, and with less labor and less glory we find ourselves above them. It is from that height we can discover things it was impossible for them to see. Our view has a wider range, and although they knew as well as we do everything they could observe of nature, they nevertheless did not know so much and we see more than they did.

However it is a strange thing how we reverence their opinions. To contradict   *12* them counts as a crime and to add to them is an outrage, as if they had left no more truths to know. Is not this to treat man's reason with indignity and to put it on a level with animal instinct, since we thereby take away the main difference, which consists in this that the effects of reason increase continually whereas instinct always remains in the same state? Beehives were as well laid out a thousand years ago as today, and each bee forms that hexagon as exactly the first time as the last. It is the same with everything animals make by that hidden motion. Nature teaches them in response to the pressure of necessity; but this frail knowledge dies with its need: as they receive it without study, they do not have the happiness of preserving it; and every time they are given it, they find it new, because nature, whose object is merely to maintain animals in an order of limited perfection, infuses in them this necessary knowledge, always the same, lest they perish, and does not allow them to add to it lest they go beyond the boundaries prescribed to them. It is different with man, made only for infinity. He is ignorant in his life's first age, but he never ceases to learn as he goes forward, for he has the advantage not only of his own experience but also of his predecessors', because he always keeps in his memory the knowledge he has once acquired, and that of the ancients is always at hand in the books they have left. And since he keeps his knowledge, he can also easily increase it, so that men today are in a certain sense in the same condition in which those ancient philosophers would be if they could have prolonged their old age until now, adding to the knowledge they had what their studies might have won for them by the grace of so many centuries. Hence it is that by a special prerogative not only does each man advance from day to day in the sciences, but all men together make a continual progress as the universe grows old, because the same thing happens in the succession of men as in the different ages of an individual man. So that the whole series of men during the course of so many centuries should be considered as one self-same man, always in existence and continually learning. Whence it is seen with what injustice we respect antiquity in the persons of its philosophers; for since old age is the age furthest removed from childhood, who does not see that the old age of this universal man should be sought not in the times near his birth but in those which are most distant from it? Those whom we call ancients were in truth new in every respect, and actually formed the childhood of man; and since we have added to their knowledge the experience of the succeeding centuries, it is in ourselves that that antiquity can be found which we revere in others.

13   The ancients should be admired for the consequences they drew correctly from the little stock of principles they had, and they should be excused for those in which they lacked the advantage of experiment rather than force of reason.

14   For were they not excusable for their opinion about the Milky Way when, the weakness of their eyes as yet unaided by artifice, they attributed its color to a greater density in that part of the sky, which would more powerfully reflect the light? But would we not be inexcusable for holding to the same opinion now that with the help of the telescope we have discovered an infinity of little stars there, whose more abundant light has made us recognize the true cause of that whiteness?

15   Did they not also have cause to say that all corruptible bodies were contained within the sphere of the moon's heaven, when during the course of so many centuries they had never yet observed corruption or generation beyond

this space? But should we not give contrary assurance when the whole earth has seen with its eyes comets burst into flame and vanish far beyond that sphere?

Thus it is that concerning the vacuum the ancients were right to say that nature did not permit it, because all their experiments had always led to the observation that she abhorred it and could not endure it. But if the new experiments had been known to them, perhaps they would have found reason to affirm what they had reason to deny because the vacuum had not yet appeared. Therefore in making the judgment that nature did not permit a vacuum, they meant to speak of nature only as they knew her; since to make the judgment in general it would not be enough to have seen it true in a hundred instances or in a thousand or in any other number however great, for if there remained a single case to examine, it alone would suffice to prevent the general definition, and if a single case were opposed, it alone. . . . For in all matters whose proof is by experiment and not by demonstration no universal assertion can be made except by the general enumeration of all the parts and all the different cases. Thus when we say the diamond is the hardest of all bodies, we mean of all bodies we know, and we neither can nor should include those we do not know. And when we say that gold is the heaviest of all bodies, it would be rash of us to include in this general proposition bodies not yet in our knowledge, although it is not impossible they are in nature. Similarly when the ancients asserted that nature did not permit a vacuum, they meant she did not permit a vacuum in all the experiments they had seen, and they could not without rashness include experiments they did not know. But if they had known them, undoubtedly they would have drawn the same consequences as we do and would by their avowal have given them the authority of that antiquity which men today want to make the sole principle of the sciences. 16

Thus without contradicting the ancients we can assert the opposite of what they said; and finally whatever the weight of antiquity, truth should always have the advantage, even when newly discovered, since it is always older than every opinion men have held about it, and only ignorance of its nature could imagine it began to be at the time it began to be known. 17

WRITING AND DISCUSSION QUESTIONS

Informative

1. Pascal does not entirely reject the authority of the past. In fact, he insists that in some areas ancient authority should be unquestioned. Explain how Pascal distinguishes between areas of learning and knowledge that are subject to ancient authority and those that are not.

2. Describe the discoveries of Galileo that Pascal makes specific reference to in arguing that there is a body of new knowledge about which the ancients were not aware.

3. Pascal's argument for the possibility of progress in the "sciences subject to experiment and reason," paradoxically, is based on the weakness of human reason. Explain.

Persuasive

1. Pascal carefully prepares his readers for receiving information that will contradict many of their assumptions. Galileo did not; he assumed instead that his audience would simply be as convinced by the facts as he was. What does this difference tell you about the two writers' personalities? Argue that one attitude is more appropriate than the other in a scientist. Ought a scientist to concern himself with his readers' feelings and prejudices, or is his business only the facts?
2. In arguing that the ancients "used the discoveries handed down to them only as the means of making new ones" and that the best way to imitate them is to try to surpass them, Pascal could be seen as reviving an important and long disused principle of humanism. Argue whether or not Pascal qualifies as a humanist.

Personal

1. Descartes and Pascal both began as extraordinarily able and innovative mathematicians. Descartes believed that a single rational method could ultimately reveal all truth with the clarity and certainty of the geometric theorem. Pascal, although respecting and using the rational method as it applied to nature, saw all knowledge, even the newest, as falling short of universality and as always subject to revision on the basis of new evidence or some as yet unexamined case. Which position do you believe is the most truly scientific?
2. Whether or not his influence was direct, several of Pascal's ideas would later emerge in interesting new combinations. His distinction between areas of knowledge, those based on reason and experiment as opposed to those based on memory, would become a major distinction between the sciences and the humanities. Do you think this is a valid or useful distinction? Pascal's idea of how scientific knowledge builds on the past had already been articulated by Francis Bacon as the idea of progress (*The Advancement of Learning,* 1605). This idea would combine with the distinction between the sciences and the humanities, especially in Thomas Macaulay ("Lord Bacon" 1837), to become the basis for the argument that the sciences are superior to the humanities and deserve more study. How do you see the relative importance of the sciences and the humanities?

CHARLES DARWIN, FROM *THE ORIGIN OF SPECIES*

Although Charles Darwin (1809–1882) was the grandson of Erasmus Darwin (1731–1802), one of the earlier thinkers to speculate about an evolutionary universe, as a young man he had little interest in science and not much commitment to anything else. He pursued medical training for a while but found its study boring and its practice (surgery) gruesome. He turned to the ministry by default rather than by any great desire, taking his B.A. from Cambridge in 1831, when he was offered the opportunity to sail with H.M.S. *Beagle* on a five-year, round-the-world voyage of discovery. This was the experience that made him a scientist.

During his voyage, Darwin was especially impressed with the unusual varieties of life that were found in isolated places like Australia, the Galapagos Islands, and New Zealand, and he began to think seriously about their origins. Fairly soon after his return, by 1837 or 1838, he had worked out his major ideas, but these were not printed until 1859. Part of the reason for this delay was Darwin's reclusive spirit, but part also was the intellectual climate of the time, which did not make easy the argument for a natural process of biological development.

The reasons for this intellectual climate had their origins in the previous century. During the eighteenth century, many thinkers had developed a sense of reconciliation between science and religion based largely on the discoveries of Newton at the end of the seventeenth century and a set of assumptions involving what is called "the argument from design." Newton's major contribution in this regard was his study of motion, which suggested that all actions were controlled by universal laws. The argument from design, one of several traditional "proofs" of the existence of God, states that the existence of order in the universe necessarily implies a divine source of that order; more specifically, after Newton, mathematically precise and experimentally demonstrable natural law was seen as proof of the existence of a divine lawgiver. These beliefs were linked with a mechanical model of the universe. That is, the universe was a grand mechanism created by God, who also created the natural laws governing its operations. As a mechanism, the universe was a static structure, most commonly described in terms of a clock, designed so that every part had a predetermined function, and "change" referred only to the revolutions of parts within that structure.

This view not only seemed to satisfy reason, but seemed compatible with the Biblical version of Creation as well. Because the world was an essentially fixed structure, it was not critical to determine when it was created; therefore, Biblical chronology was as good as any (the standard date for creation was 4004 B.C., computed early in the eighteenth century from Biblical genealogies by the Anglican Bishop Usher). Indeed, for some, the growth of science seemed to contribute to a kind of "natural theology," a process defined in the title of the major work summing up these ideas for the eighteenth century, William Paley's *Natural Theology, or Evidences of the Existence and Attributes of the Deity Collected from the Appearances of Nature* (1802). For thinkers like Paley, who used the image of a watch to represent organisms, the more one looked at the incredible intricacies of the machinery of natural design, the perfect adaptations of organisms to survive in their environment, the more one must be convinced by these "evidences" of the wisdom and benevolence of the divine watchmaker, their creator.

What has been described above can be referred to as the static or clock model of the universe, which as a scientific model is analogous to the Ptolemaic universe. Just as the Copernican revolution brought about the displacement of the Ptolemaic system in the sixteenth and seventeenth centuries, in the nineteenth century, the Darwinian revolution, the emergence of an evolutionary or developmental model, brought about the displacement of the static model. The similarities between these two revolutions are that they struck a major blow to humanity's anthropocentric assumptions about the universe and they extended concepts of natural physical laws in important new dimensions. The crucial difference between the two is that the Copernican revolution extended this sense of law spatially, to the planets and stars, applying to the entire physical universe, whereas the Darwinian revolution extended this sense of law temporally, describing the processes by which the universe came to be as we know it, processes operating since the unimaginably distant past by the same laws that govern the present.

What drove science to exploring a new model in this case was similar to what caused the Copernican revolution, the gradual accumulation of new information that seemed increasingly incompatible with the old model. The sources of that information were the newly developing sciences of geology and paleontology.

The crucial geological discovery was what has been called "deep time." Geologists realized, first of all, that "sedimentary" rock had been created by the accumulation of sediments in the bottom of seas and other low-lying areas over so long a period of time that the weight of accumulations above had compressed the sediments into rock. Indeed, there were whole series of layers (or strata) of such sedimentary rock hundreds of feet thick that would have required even longer periods of time to create. Moreover, some of those whole series of strata, originally laid down horizontally, had been somehow turned vertical, been worn down, and had hundreds of feet of new horizontal strata laid on top of them, creating a kind of giant multilayered underground "T" that geologists call an "unconformity" and that would have required even vaster expanses of time to create. These are the kinds of observations that led to the conception of deep time, the recognition that the world might be a thousand, maybe ten thousand *times* as old as Bishop Usher's Biblically based estimate. (Today's estimates would be more than 70,000 times as old—the earth is now believed to have formed 4.3 to 4.6 billion years ago, the universe from 15 to 20 billion years ago.)

Paleontology, the study of fossils, the petrified remains of organic life embedded in rocks, also uncovered a number of incompatibilities with the static model. Just as geology reveals a kind of dynamic history of earth in deep time, the fossils embedded in rocks reveal a similar kind of history of organic life. In broad outline, this history suggests a long period in which there was no life at all followed by periods during which increasingly complex life forms appeared. The movement toward more complex forms, however, which some might find a reassuring sign of rational order, is not one-directional or consistent. Regression seems to take place as well as progress, and whole orders of living creatures sometimes disappear. Indeed, the oft-cited extinction of the dinosaurs is only the best known of several mass extinctions found in the fossil record.

During the early 1800s, still long before Darwin's *Origin of Species*, geology (which then included paleontology) split into two camps, although this division was not clear at the time. The first group, which today we would call creationists, clung to the static model, associating themselves with a few central concepts: special creation, the belief that God miraculously created the material world, including every living thing in it, at a specific point in time or at a series of specific points corresponding to the Biblical days of Creation; fixity of species, the belief that each living species as created by God is capable of wide variation within itself but is incapable of divergence into any other species; catastrophism, the belief that marked changes in the geological record were signs of specific catastrophes, like Noah's Flood, instituted by God. Some of those who supported this model were willing to expand their notion of the scale of time somewhat beyond the Biblical estimate of a 6000-year-old earth, but few accepted the idea of an earth existing on the scale of deep time.

The second group, which today we would call evolutionists, though taking no consistent position on the ultimate origin of the universe or of life, insisted on the scientific principle of explaining natural phenomena, including the origins of species in the world, in terms of natural causes. They too associated themselves with a few central concepts: uniformitarianism, the belief that nature operates according to the same laws today as it did any time in the past (this concept is defined in the subtitle of the major work by Charles Lyell, a major influence on Darwin, *Principles of Geology, Being an Attempt to Explain the Former Changes of the Earth's Surface, by Reference to Causes Now in Operation*, 1830); gradualism, the belief that changes, even those that appear "sudden" relative to deep time, took place slowly by the gradual accumulation of small changes over long periods of time, not by sudden catastrophes; mutability of species, the belief that the great variety of organic life on earth came to be, as in the concept of gradualism, by the slow accumulation of small changes in species and their transformation into others.

The crucial problem with the early evolutionary model was the lack of any reasonable scientific mechanism for the transformation of species. Many speculations were offered: that an organism's "need" somehow generated new organs or that the use or disuse of an organ generated its development or disappearance, but these mechanisms lacked clear evidence to support them. Darwin's chief contribution was describing a convincing mechanism and effectively illustrating it through his own extensive observations.

The great variety of life forms Darwin observed seemed directly analogous to the wide variations within species that were produced in domestic breeding programs for animals like pigeons and dogs, a process involving *artificial* selection of desired traits. For Darwin to propose that such a process could account naturally for the development of the wide variety of species on earth, he needed only the concept of deep time, already provided by geology, and the postulation of a mechanism for the *natural* selection of favorable variations.

A central element in defining the mechanism of natural selection came to Darwin by way of an economist, Thomas Malthus, whose *Essay on the Principle of Population* (1798) argued that in human society, population tended to increase more rapidly than the means of subsistence. In Malthus' mathematical terms, "Population, when unchecked, increases in a geometrical ratio [2, 4, 8, 16, 32, . . .]. . . . The means of subsistence could not possibly be made to increase faster than in an arithmetical ratio [2, 4, 6, 8, 10, . . .]." Malthus was making a point about the limits to human progress, but Darwin saw this kind of population pressure in a broader biological perspective. It established the basic condition of a "struggle for existence" in which varieties of a species with traits favorable to their survival have a greater chance of passing on those traits to their progeny.

Darwin's central purpose was to extend Lyell's efforts in geology to biology, to explain earlier changes in plant and animal life "by reference to causes now in operation," and his argument was inescapably logical. Given the problem of geometrical population increase—indeed, in nature many species have a reproductive potential not on the 2×2 scale illustrated above, but on a 1000×1000 scale—there must be a great struggle for survival. Given the wide variability of features within a species, some of those features must be more conducive to survival than others. Assuming that beneficial features can be inherited, some traits would tend, therefore, to be "naturally selected" and passed to descendants. Given the wide dispersion of species over a variety of changing environments and given the hundreds of millions of years provided by deep time, members of a species must have diverged into new species, eventually producing the almost infinite variety of life alive today and observable in the fossil record.

Darwin's major scientific impact has been the establishment of evolution as the chief unifying principle in biology, a principle that has stood up well in absorbing major new developments, in areas ranging from geology and paleontology, which originally inspired the new model, to genetics and molecular biology. His influence, however, has extended far beyond biology, for better and for worse. Among the worst extensions of Darwinism was the misapplication of the concept of the survival of the fittest to economics, thereby justifying in the name of science the most rapacious forms of capitalism, something Darwin never suggested (discussed later in the chapter on Marx). Others misapplied evolutionary theory in arguing that certain races were more "highly evolved" than others or even that men were more highly evolved than women, issues that are examined in the readings after the Darwin selection. More fruitful extensions by astrophysicists and nuclear physicists have applied the evolutionary model to trace the development of the universe back to its origin in the Big Bang, which is believed to mark the very beginning of time.

Perhaps the greatest impact of evolutionary theory on culture as a whole, however, has been its philosophical and theological implications, including those stemming from its extension to human origins. Darwin himself did not extend the theory to humanity until the *Descent of Man, and Selection in Relation to Sex* (1871), but his critics anticipated and opposed it almost immediately after the publication of the *Origin of Species*. To Darwin's critics, the inevitable implication of that extension would be to debase and despiritualize humanity, to see us as just another animal species, however highly evolved, the accidental result of the operations of natural law, not the crowning glory of creation for which everything else was made. To many who championed Darwin, these implications were seen as liberating humanity from its ancient prejudices and its false sense of superiority: just as the Copernican revolution destroyed our geocentrism, the Darwinian revolution destroyed our anthropocentrism. Still, others managed to reconcile their religious beliefs to an evolutionary model by conceiving of creation as ultimately directed by God but operating through natural law in a process continuing throughout all time; thus, change is the law of life and of the whole universe, including human nature. Before leaping too far into the broader implications of these ideas, however, we would do well to look carefully at their humbler origins in the observations of a scientist who did his best to leave the philosophical and theological debates to others.

▼

from *The Origin of Species*[1]

CHARLES DARWIN

CHAPTER IV

Natural Selection; or the Survival of the Fittest

Summary of Chapter

1   If under changing conditions of life organic beings present individual differences in almost every part of their structure, and this cannot be disputed; if there be, owing to their geometrical rate of increase, a severe struggle for life at some age, season, or year, and this certainly cannot be disputed;

---

[1]The present text is excerpted from the sixth edition of the *Origin* (1872), the last edition during Darwin's lifetime.

then, considering the infinite complexity of the relations of all organic beings to each other and to their conditions of life, causing an infinite diversity in structure, constitution, and habits, to be advantageous to them, it would be a most extraordinary fact if no variations had ever occurred useful to each being's own welfare, in the same manner as so many variations have occurred useful to man. But if variations useful to any organic being ever do occur, assuredly individuals thus characterised will have the best chance of being preserved in the struggle for life; and from the strong principle of inheritance, these will tend to produce offspring similarly characterised. This principle of preservation, or the survival of the fittest, I have called Natural Selection. It leads to the improvement of each creature in relation to its organic and inorganic conditions of life; and consequently, in most cases, to what must be regarded as an advance in organisation. Nevertheless, low and simple forms will long endure if well fitted for their simple conditions of life.

Natural selection, on the principle of qualities being inherited at correspond- 2 ing ages, can modify the egg, seed, or young, as easily as the adult. Amongst many animals, sexual selection[2] will have given its aid to ordinary selection, by assuring to the most vigorous and best adapted males the greatest number of offspring. Sexual selection will also give characters useful to the males alone, in their struggles or rivalry with other males; and these characters will be transmitted to one sex or to both sexes, according to the form of inheritance which prevails.

Whether natural selection has really thus acted in adapting the various forms 3 of life to their several conditions and stations, must be judged by the general tenor and balance of evidence given in the following chapters. But we have already seen how it entails extinction; and how largely extinction has acted in the world's history, geology plainly declares. Natural selection, also leads to divergence of character; for the more organic beings diverge in structure, habits, and constitution, by so much the more can a large number be supported on the area,—of which we see proof by looking to the inhabitants of any small spot, and to the productions naturalised in foreign lands. Therefore, during the modification of the descendants of any one species, and during the incessant struggle of all species to increase in numbers, the more diversified the descendants become, the better will be their chance of success in the battle for life. Thus the small differences distinguishing varieties of the same species, steadily tend to increase, till they equal the greater differences between species of the same genus, or even of distinct genera. . . .

Natural selection, as has just been remarked, leads to divergence of charac- 4 ter and to much extinction of the less improved and intermediate forms of life. On these principles, the nature of the affinities, and the generally well-defined

---

[2]Sexual selection, a special form of natural selection, refers to the patterns of mating choices within a species. The female peacock, for example, seems to prefer males with the largest and brightest expanse of tail feathers, a preference that selects and develops that feature within the males of that species.

distinctions between the innumerable organic beings in each class throughout the world, may be explained. It is a truly wonderful fact—the wonder of which we are apt to overlook from familiarity—that all animals and all plants throughout all time and space should be related to each other in groups, subordinate to groups, in the manner which we everywhere behold—namely, varieties of the same species most closely related, species of the same genus less closely and unequally related, forming sections and sub-genera, species of distinct genera much less closely related, and genera related in different degrees, forming sub-families, families, orders, sub-classes and classes. The several subordinate groups in any class cannot be ranked in a single file, but seem clustered round points, and these round other points, and so on in almost endless cycles. If species had been independently created, no explanation would have been possible of this kind of classification; but it is explained through inheritance and the complex action of natural selection, entailing extinction and divergence of character. . . .

5   The affinities of all the beings of the same class have sometimes been represented by a great tree. I believe this simile largely speaks the truth. The green and budding twigs may represent existing species; and those produced during former years may represent the long succession of extinct species. At each period of growth all the growing twigs have tried to branch out on all sides, and to overtop and kill the surrounding twigs and branches, in the same manner as species and groups of species have at all times overmastered other species in the great battle for life. The limbs divided into great branches, and these into lesser and lesser branches, were themselves once, when the tree was young, budding twigs, and this connection of the former and present buds by ramifying branches may well represent the classification of all extinct and living species in groups subordinate to groups. Of the many twigs which flourished when the tree was a mere bush, only two or three, now grown into great branches, yet survive and bear the other branches; so with the species which lived during long-past geological periods, very few have left living and modified descendants. From the first growth of the tree, many a limb and branch has decayed and dropped off; and these fallen branches of various sizes may represent those whole orders, families, and genera which have now no living representatives, and which are known to us only in a fossil state. As we here and there see a thin straggling branch springing from a fork low down in a tree, and which by some chance has been favoured and is still alive on its summit, so we occasionally see an animal like the Ornithorhynchus or Lepidosiren,[3] which in some small degree connects by its affinities two large branches of life, and which has apparently been saved from fatal competition by having inhabited a protected station. As buds give rise by growth to fresh buds, and these, if vigorous, branch out and overtop on all sides many a feebler branch, so by generation I believe it has been with the great Tree of Life, which fills with its dead and broken branches the crust of the earth, and covers the surface with its ever-branching and beautiful ramifications. . . .

[3]Ornithorhynchus, the duck-billed platypus; Lepidosiren, a South American lungfish.

CHAPTER X

On the Imperfection of the Geological Record

In the sixth chapter I enumerated the chief objections which might be justly 6 urged against the views maintained in this volume. Most of them have now been discussed. One, namely the distinctness of specific forms, and their not being blended together by innumerable transitional links, is a very obvious difficulty. I assigned reasons why such links do not commonly occur at the present day under the circumstances apparently most favourable for their presence, namely, on an extensive and continuous area with graduated physical conditions. I endeavoured to show, that the life of each species depends in a more important manner on the presence of other already defined organic forms, than on climate, and, therefore, that the really governing conditions of life do not graduate away quite insensibly like heat or moisture. I endeavoured, also, to show that intermediate varieties, from existing in lesser numbers than the forms which they connect, will generally be beaten out and exterminated during the course of further modification and improvement. The main cause, however, of innumerable intermediate links not now occurring everywhere throughout nature, depends on the very process of natural selection, through which new varieties continually take the places of and supplant their parent-forms. But just in proportion as this process of extermination has acted on an enormous scale, so must the number of intermediate varieties, which have formerly existed, be truly enormous. Why then is not every geological formation and every stratum full of such intermediate links? Geology assuredly does not reveal any such finely-graduated organic chain; and this, perhaps, is the most obvious and serious objection which can be urged against the theory. The explanation lies, as I believe, in the extreme imperfection of the geological record.

In the first place, it should always be borne in mind what sort of intermediate 7 ate forms must, on the theory, have formerly existed. I have found it difficult, when looking at any two species, to avoid picturing to myself forms *directly* intermediate between them. But this is a wholly false view; we should always look for forms intermediate between each species and a common but unknown progenitor; and the progenitor will generally have differed in some respects from all its modified descendants. To give a simple illustration: the fantail and pouter pigeons are both descended from the rock-pigeon; if we possessed all the intermediate varieties which have ever existed, we should have an extremely close series between both and the rock-pigeon; but we should have no varieties directly intermediate between the fantail and pouter; none, for instance, combining a tail somewhat expanded with a crop somewhat enlarged, the characteristic features of these two breeds. These two breeds, moreover, have become so much modified, that, if we had no historical or indirect evidence regarding their origin, it would not have been possible to have determined, from a mere comparison of their structure with that of the rock-pigeon, C. livia, whether they had descended from this species or from some allied form, such as C. oenas.

8   So, with natural species, if we look to forms very distinct, for instance to the horse and tapir, we have no reason to suppose that links directly intermediate between them ever existed, but between each and an unknown common parent. The common parent will have had in its whole organisation much general resemblance to the tapir and to the horse; but in some points of structure may have differed considerably from both, even perhaps more than they differ from each other. Hence, in all such cases, we should be unable to recognise the parent-form of any two or more species, even if we closely compared the structure of the parent with that of its modified descendants, unless at the same time we had a nearly perfect chain of the intermediate links.

9   It is just possible by the theory, that one of two living forms might have descended from the other; for instance, a horse from a tapir; and in this case *direct* intermediate links will have existed between them. But such a case would imply that one form had remained for a very long period unaltered, whilst its descendants had undergone a vast amount of change; and the principle of competition between organism and organism, between child and parent, will render this a very rare event; for in all cases the new and improved forms of life tend to supplant the old and unimproved forms.

10   By the theory of natural selection all living species have been connected with the parent-species of each genus, by differences not greater than we see between the natural and domestic varieties of the same species at the present day; and these parent-species, now generally extinct, have in their turn been similarly connected with more ancient forms; and so on backwards, always converging to the common ancestor of each great class. So that the number of intermediate and transitional links, between all living and extinct species, must have been inconceivably great. But assuredly, if this theory be true, such have lived upon the earth.

On the Lapse of Time, as Inferred from the Rate of Deposition and Extent of Denudation

11   Independently of our not finding fossil remains of such infinitely numerous connecting links, it may be objected that time cannot have sufficed for so great an amount of organic change, all changes having been effected slowly. It is hardly possible for me to recall to the reader who is not a practical geologist, the facts leading the mind feebly to comprehend the lapse of time. He who can read Sir Charles Lyell's grand work on the Principles of Geology, which the future historian will recognise as having produced a revolution in natural science, and yet does not admit how vast have been the past periods of time, may at once close this volume. Not that it suffices to study the Principles of Geology, or to read special treatises by different observers on separate formations, and to mark how each author attempts to give an inadequate idea of the duration of each formation, or even of each stratum. We can best gain some idea of past time by knowing the agencies at work, and learning how deeply the surface of the land has been denuded, and how much sediment has been depos-

ited. As Lyell has well remarked, the extent and thickness of our sedimentary formations are the result and the measure of the denudation which the earth's crust has elsewhere undergone. Therefore a man should examine for himself the great piles of superimposed strata, and watch the rivulets bringing down mud, and the waves wearing away the sea-cliffs, in order to comprehend something about the duration of past time, the monuments of which we see all around us. . . .

On the Poorness of Palaeontological Collections

Now let us turn to our richest geological museums, and what a paltry display   *12* we behold! That our collections are imperfect is admitted by every one. The remark of that admirable palaeontologist, Edward Forbes, should never be forgotten, namely, that very many fossil species are known and named from single and often broken specimens, or from a few specimens collected on some one spot. Only a small portion of the surface of the earth has been geologically explored, and no part with sufficient care, as the important discoveries made every year in Europe prove. No organism wholly soft can be preserved. Shells and bones decay and disappear when left on the bottom of the sea, where sediment is not accumulating.

. . . Those who believe that the geological record is in any degree perfect,   *13* will undoubtedly at once reject the theory. For my part, following out Lyell's metaphor, I look at the geological record as a history of the world imperfectly kept, and written in a changing dialect; of this history we possess the last volume alone, relating only to two or three countries. Of this volume, only here and there a short chapter has been preserved; and of each page, only here and there a few lines. Each word of the slowly-changing language, more or less different in the successive chapters, may represent the forms of life, which are entombed in our consecutive formations, and which falsely appear to have been abruptly introduced. On this view, the difficulties above discussed are greatly diminished, or even disappear. . . .

CHAPTER XV

Recapitulation and Conclusion

As this whole volume is one long argument, it may be convenient to the   *14* reader to have the leading facts and inferences briefly recapitulated.

That many and serious objections may be advanced against the theory of   *15* descent with modification through variation and natural selection, I do not deny. I have endeavored to give to them their full force. Nothing at first can appear more difficult to believe than that the more complex organs and instincts have been perfected, not by means superior to, though analogous with, human reason, but by the accumulation of innumerable slight variations, each good for the individual possessor. Nevertheless, this difficulty, though appearing to our imagination insuperably great, cannot be considered real if we admit the following propositions, namely, that all parts of the organisation and instincts offer, at least, individual differences—that there is a struggle for existence leading to the preservation of profitable deviations of structure or instinct—and, lastly, that gradations in the state of perfection of each organ may have existed, each good of its kind. The truth of these propositions cannot, I think, be disputed.

16   It is, no doubt, extremely difficult even to conjecture by what gradations many structures have been perfected, more especially amongst broken and failing groups of organic beings, which have suffered much extinction, but we see so many strange gradations in nature, that we ought to be extremely cautious in saying that any organ or instinct, or any whole structure, could not have arrived at its present state by many graduated steps. There are, it must be admitted, cases of special difficulty opposed to the theory of natural selection; and one of the most curious of these is the existence in the same community of two or three defined castes of workers or sterile female ants; but I have attempted to show how these difficulties can be mastered. . . .

17   On this doctrine of the extermination of an infinitude of connecting links, between the living and extinct inhabitants of the world, and at each successive period between the extinct and still older species, why is not every geological formation charged with such links? Why does not every collection of fossil remains afford plain evidence of the gradation and mutation of the forms of life? Although geological research has undoubtedly revealed the former existence of many links, bringing numerous forms of life much closer together, it does not yield the infinitely many fine gradations between past and present species required on the theory; and this is the most obvious of the many objections which may be urged against it. Why, again, do whole groups of allied species appear, though this appearance is often false, to have come in suddenly on the successive geological stages? Although we now know that organic beings appeared on this globe, at a period incalculably remote, long before the lowest bed of the Cambrian system was deposited, why do we not find beneath this system great piles of strata stored with the remains of the progenitors of the Cambrian fossils? For on the theory, such strata must somewhere have been deposited at these ancient and utterly unknown epochs of the world's history.

18   I can answer these questions and objections only on the supposition that the geological record is far more imperfect than most geologists believe. The number of specimens in all our museums is absolutely as nothing compared with the countless generations of countless species which have certainly existed. The parent-form of any two or more species would not be in all its characters directly intermediate between its modified offspring, any more than the rock-pigeon is directly intermediate in crop and tail between its descendants, the

pouter and fantail pigeons. We should not be able to recognise a species as the parent of another and modified species, if we were to examine the two ever so closely, unless we possessed most of the intermediate links; and owing to the imperfection of the geological record, we have no just right to expect to find so many links. If two or three, or even more linking forms were discovered, they would simply be ranked by many naturalists as so many new species, more especially if found in different geological sub-stages, let their differences be ever so slight. . . .

Such is the sum of the several chief objections and difficulties which may be   *19* justly urged against the theory; and I have now briefly recapitulated the answers and explanations which, as far as I can see, may be given. I have felt these difficulties far too heavily during many years to doubt their weight. But it deserves especial notice that the more important objections relate to questions on which we are confessedly ignorant; nor do we know how ignorant we are. We do not know all the possible transitional gradations between the simplest and the most perfect organs; it cannot be pretended that we know all the varied means of distribution during the long lapse of years, or that we know how imperfect is the Geological Record. Serious as these several objections are, in my judgment they are by no means sufficient to overthrow the theory of descent with subsequent modification.

Now let us turn to the other side of the argument. Under domestication we   *20* see much variability, caused, or at least excited, by changed conditions of life; but often in so obscure a manner, that we are tempted to consider the variations as spontaneous. Variability is governed by many complex laws,—by correlated growth, compensation, the increased use and disuse of parts, and the definite action of the surrounding conditions. There is much difficulty in ascertaining how largely our domestic productions have been modified; but we may safely infer that the amount has been large, and that modifications can be inherited for long periods. As long as the conditions of life remain the same, we have reason to believe that a modification, which has already been inherited for many generations, may continue to be inherited for an almost infinite number of generations. On the other hand, we have evidence that variability when it has once come into play, does not cease under domestication for a very long period; nor do we know that it ever ceases, for new varieties are still occasionally produced by our oldest domesticated productions.

Variability is not actually caused by man; he only unintentionally exposes   *21* organic beings to new conditions of life, and then nature acts on the organisation and causes it to vary. But man can and does select the variations given to him by nature, and thus accumulates them in any desired manner. He thus adapts animals and plants for his own benefit or pleasure. He may do this methodically, or he may do it unconsciously by preserving the individuals most useful or pleasing to him without any intention of altering the breed. It is certain that he can largely influence the character of a breed by selecting, in each successive generation, individual differences so slight as to be inappreciable except by an educated eye. This unconscious process of selection has been the great agency in the formation of the most distinct and useful domestic breeds. That many breeds produced by man have to a large extent the character of natural species, is shown by the inextricable doubts whether many of them are varieties or aboriginally distinct species.

22   There is no reason why the principles which have acted so efficiently under domestication should not have acted under nature. In the survival of favoured individuals and races, during the constantly-recurrent Struggle for Existence, we see a powerful and ever-acting form of Selection. The struggle for existence inevitably follows from the high geometrical ratio of increase which is common to all organic beings. This high rate of increase is proved by calculation,—by the rapid increase of many animals and plants during a succession of peculiar seasons, and when naturalised in new countries. More individuals are born than can possibly survive. A grain in the balance may determine which individuals shall live and which shall die,—which variety or species shall increase in number, and which shall decrease, or finally become extinct. As the individuals of the same species come in all respects into the closest competition with each other, the struggle will generally be most severe between them; it will be almost equally severe between the varieties of the same species, and next in severity between the species of the same genus. On the other hand the struggle will often be severe between beings remote in the scale of nature. The slightest advantage in certain individuals, at any age or during any season, over those with which they come into competition, or better adaptation in however slight a degree to the surrounding physical conditions, will, in the long run, turn the balance.

23   With animals having separated sexes, there will be in most cases a struggle between the males for the possession of the females. The most vigorous males, or those which have most successfully struggled with their conditions of life, will generally leave most progeny. But success will often depend on the males having special weapons, or means of defense, or charms; and a slight advantage will lead to victory. . . .

24   If then, animals and plants do vary, let it be ever so slightly or slowly, why should not variations or individual differences, which are in any way beneficial, be preserved and accumulated through natural selection, or the survival of the fittest? If man can by patience select variations useful to him, why, under changing and complex conditions of life, should not variations useful to nature's living products often arise, and be preserved or selected? What limit can be put to this power, acting during long ages and rigidly scrutinising the whole constitution, structure, and habits of each creature,—favouring the good and rejecting the bad? I can see no limit to this power, in slowly and beautifully adapting each form to the most complex relations of life. The theory of natural selection, even if we look no farther than this, seems to be in the highest

degree probable. I have already recapitulated, as fairly as I could, the opposed difficulties and objections: now let us turn to the special facts and arguments in favour of the theory. . . .

It can hardly be supposed that a false theory would explain, in so satisfac-   *25*
tory a manner as does the theory of natural selection, the several large classes of facts above specified. It has recently been objected that this is an unsafe method of arguing; but it is a method used in judging of the common events of life, and has often been used by the greatest natural philosophers. The undulatory theory of light has thus been arrived at; and the belief in the revolution of the earth on its own axis was until lately supported by hardly any direct evidence. It is no valid objection that science as yet throws no light on the far higher problem of the essence or origin of life. Who can explain what is the essence of the attraction of gravity? No one now objects to following out the results consequent on this unknown element of attraction; notwithstanding that Leibnitz formerly accused Newton of introducing "occult qualities and miracles into philosophy."

I see no good reason why the views given in this volume should shock the   *26*
religious feelings of any one. It is satisfactory, as showing how transient such impressions are, to remember that the greatest discovery ever made by man, namely, the law of the attraction of gravity, was also attacked by Leibnitz, "as subversive of natural, and inferentially of revealed, religion." A celebrated author and divine has written to me that "he has gradually learnt to see that it is just as noble a conception of the Deity to believe that He created a few original forms capable of self-development into other and needful forms, as to believe that He required a fresh act of creation to supply the voids caused by the action of His laws." . . .

But the chief cause of our natural unwillingness to admit that one species   *27*
has given birth to clear and distinct species, is that we are always slow in admitting great changes of which we do not see the steps. The difficulty is the same as that felt by so many geologists, when Lyell first insisted that long lines of inland cliffs had been formed, the great valleys excavated, by the agencies which we see still at work. The mind cannot possibly grasp the full meaning of the term of even a million years; it cannot add up and perceive the full effects of many slight variations, accumulated during an almost infinite number of generations.

Although I am fully convinced of the truth of the views given in this volume   *28*
under the form of an abstract, I by no means expect to convince experienced naturalists whose minds are stocked with a multitude of facts all viewed, during a long course of years, from a point of view directly opposite to mine. It is so easy to hide our ignorance under such expressions as the "plan of creation," "unity of design," &c., and to think that we give an explanation when we only re-state a fact. Any one whose disposition leads him to attach more weight to

unexplained difficulties than to the explanation of a certain number of facts will certainly reject the theory. A few naturalists, endowed with much flexibility of mind, and who have already begun to doubt the immutability of species, may be influenced by this volume; but I look with confidence to the future,—to young and rising naturalists, who will be able to view both sides of the question with impartiality. Whoever is led to believe that species are mutable will do good service by conscientiously expressing his conviction; for thus only can the load of prejudice by which this subject is overwhelmed be removed. . . .

29   Authors of the highest eminence seem to be fully satisfied with the view that each species has been independently created. To my mind it accords better with what we know of the laws impressed on matter by the Creator, that the production and extinction of the past and present inhabitants of the world should have been due to secondary causes, like those determining the birth and death of the individual. When I view all beings not as special creations, but as the lineal descendants of some few beings which lived long before the first bed of the Cambrian system was deposited, they seem to me to become ennobled. Judging from the past, we may safely infer that not one living species will transmit its unaltered likeness to a distant futurity. And of the species now living very few will transmit progeny of any kind to a far distant futurity; for the manner in which all organic beings are grouped, shows that the greater number of species in each genus, and all the species in many genera, have left no descendants, but have become utterly extinct. We can so far take a prophetic glance into futurity as to foretell that it will be the common and widely-spread species, belonging to the larger and dominant groups within each class, which will ultimately prevail and procreate new and dominant species. As all the living forms of life are the lineal descendants of those which lived long before the Cambrian epoch, we may feel certain that the ordinary succession by generation has never once been broken, and that no cataclysm has desolated the whole world. Hence we may look with some confidence to a secure future of great length. And as natural selection works solely by and for the good of each being, all corporeal and mental endowments will tend to progress towards perfection.[4]

30   It is interesting to contemplate a tangled bank, clothed with many plants of many kinds, with birds singing on the bushes, with various insects flitting about, and with worms crawling through the damp earth, and to reflect that these elaborately constructed forms, so different from each other, and dependent upon each other in so complex a manner, have all been produced by laws acting around us. These laws, taken in the largest sense, being Growth with Reproduction; Inheritance which is almost implied by reproduction; Variability from the indirect and direct action of the conditions of life, and from use and

[4]We are not sure what exactly Darwin meant by "progress towards perfection," but modern understanding sees it as a tendency toward better adaptation of organisms toward their environment, not a claim that evolution leads to perfection. In fact, natural selection often produces highly imperfect "solutions."

disuse[5]: a Ratio of Increase so high as to lead to a Struggle for Life, and as a consequence to Natural Selection, entailing Divergence of Character and the Extinction of less-improved forms. Thus, from the war of nature, from famine and death, the most exalted object which we are capable of conceiving, namely, the production of the higher animals, directly follows. There is grandeur in this view of life, with its several powers, having been originally breathed by the Creator into a few forms or into one; and that, whilst this planet has gone cycling on according to the fixed law of gravity, from so simple a beginning endless forms most beautiful and most wonderful have been, and are being evolved.

WRITING AND DISCUSSION QUESTIONS

Informative

1. Point out as many specific references as you can find to comparisons Darwin makes between artificial and natural selection.
2. Explain the meaning of the following words and their importance to Darwin's argument: variation, improvement, diversification, the tree of life.

Persuasive

1. Define "intermediate forms," and argue, as would Darwin, that their apparent absence would not undermine his theory. How does this concept relate to the imperfection of the fossil record?
2. On the basis that the fossil record does not now and is not likely ever to "yield the infinitely many fine gradations between past and present species required on the theory," argue that Darwin's theory can or cannot be maintained. What is the usefulness of a theory like evolution that cannot ever be fully proven?

Personal

1. In a passage added by Darwin since the original 1859 edition of his work, he compares certain theological attacks on his theory to Leibniz's reaction to Newton's concept of gravity. He might as well have compared himself to Galileo—certainly it will be easier for us to consider that comparison. Is it valid to do so? What is the difference, if any, between a religiously based attack on Galileo and one on Darwin?
2. Darwin refers to Lyell's metaphor describing the geological record as a history of

---

[5]Darwin's reference to variability arising "from use and disuse" is odd because it is a theory fundamentally different from his own and one associated with the eighteenth-century French zoologist Lamarck, whose ideas Darwin rejected. Modern scientists likewise have found nothing to support the use or disuse theory. For example, if you decide to become a weight lifter and develop very large muscles, you will not as a result develop any kind of genetic tendency toward such muscles, and your larger muscles will not be inheritable.

the world imperfectly kept. Pursue this metaphor by writing your own "Meditation upon a Rock." Pick up any rock, contemplate it for a day or two, then write down everything you know or can imagine about the rock as a "word" or a record on the history of the earth. Last, how would your meditation or discourse differ from that of a scientist?

▼

STEPHEN JAY GOULD, "WOMEN'S BRAINS" AND "SEX, DRUGS, DISASTERS, AND THE EXTINCTION OF DINOSAURS"

A Professor of Geology at Harvard University and Curator of Invertebrate Paleontology and Alexandar Agassiz Professor of Zoology in Harvard's Museum of Comparative Zoology, Stephen Jay Gould (1941–) is one of the most lucid of modern writers on the sciences. His books include *Ever Since Darwin* (1977), *Ontogeny and Phylogeny* (1977), *The Panda's Thumb* (1980), *The Mismeasure of Man* (1981), *Hen's Teeth and Horse's Toes* (1983), *The Flamingo's Smile* (1985), and *Time's Arrow, Time's Cycle* (1987). "This View of Life," his column appearing for over a decade in the journal *Natural History*, won the 1980 National Magazine Award for Essays and Criticism and is the source for many of the essays later collected in several of the books listed above. His two essays that follow exhibit an approach peculiar to the last half of the twentieth century in the way they consider the viability of a scientific theory. These essays could not have been written without the change that occurred in the first half of this century in the way science itself is viewed, a change that constitutes, in fact, another kind of scientific revolution.

Despite Pascal's warning that scientific knowledge is always provisional, that its certainty is dependent on the unlikely possibility that we have examined all relevant cases, science grew in the eighteenth and nineteenth centuries under the assumption that it was delivering the eternal truths of nature. The history of science was, therefore, seen as the progressive displacement of the darkness of ignorance and superstition by the light of scientific truth. Ironically, although science began by questioning all claims to authority, it established itself as the new authority; although it was originally an outgrowth of humanism, it forgot the humanist doctrine of human fallibility. It was inevitable, however, that eventually the new scientific knowledge would radically displace, not old superstition, but not-so-old science.

Both the overconfidence of science and the radical change in what was believed to be scientific truth are especially apparent in physics. Robert P. Crease and Charles C. Mann reveal something of that overconfidence:

> At Harvard University, for instance, [during the 1880s] the then-head of the physics department, John Trowbridge, felt compelled to warn bright graduate students away from physics. The essential business of science is finished, he told them. All that remains is to dot a few *i*'s and cross a few *t*'s, a task best left to the second-rate. In 1894, Albert Michelson of the University of Chicago, one of the most prominent experimenters of the day and the future recipient of a Nobel

Prize, told an audience that "it seems probable that most of the grand underlying principles have been firmly established and that further advances are to be sought chiefly in the rigorous application of these principles to all phenomena which come under our notice. . . . [T]he future truths of physics are to be looked for in the sixth place of decimals."[1]

It is amazing that such statements could have been made immediately before the explosion of new knowledge that occurred during the next three decades, knowledge involving the structure of the atom, relativity, the interchangeability of matter and energy, and much more. Each of these reorientations was not based simply on an acquisition of new data, but each was a revolution in its own right.

For example, by the first decade of the twentieth century, scientists realized that the atom had an internal structure much like a solar system, with the major part of its mass concentrated in a very small central nucleus and with the major part of its volume made up of electrons in orbit around the nucleus. However, theories that attempted to account for the motion of these electrons using mechanical laws failed utterly. As has been discussed, the discovery late in the seventeenth century, based primarily on Newton, that nature operated according to precise, mathematically definable laws had an enormous impact on science and culture. Equally momentous was the discovery early in the twentieth century, as Nobel laureate Richard P. Feynman puts it, "that Newton's laws of motion were quite wrong in atoms."[2]

Gould's first essay in these readings, "Women's Brains," illustrates some of the changes that resulted from these revelations, changes in how science itself is perceived. Science is not a process of pure induction, a body of conclusions that emerge inevitably and necessarily from the data. Its hypotheses emerge instead from a variety of sources, including cultural presuppositions and pure guesswork. Scientific theories of a particular time, therefore, can be as near *or* far from universal truth and as much a unique expression of a culture as its art, literature, music, religion, or philosophy.

What then is science, and how does it differ from these other cultural expressions? Answers to these questions are central to Gould's approach in his second essay in these readings, "Sex, Drugs, Disasters, and the Extinction of Dinosaurs," an approach based on the work of two modern historians of science, Karl R. Popper and Thomas S. Kuhn. In such works as *The Logic of Scientific Discovery* (1934) and *Conjectures and Refutations: The Growth of Scientific Knowledge* (1962), Popper argues that scientific knowledge is never complete and, most important, can never be proven. Scientific theories are essentially conjectures that can be tested; consistently negative results can prove a theory false (in Popper's terms, an experiment can "falsify" the theory), but positive results can only provisionally "confirm" or corroborate the theory, which may mean it is true only in this case, or that class of cases, but never absolutely or certainly. Popper continues:

Those among our theories which turn out to be highly resistant to criticism, which appear to us at a certain moment of time to be better approximations to truth than other known theories, may be described, together with the reports of their tests, as "the science" of that time. Since none of them can be positively justified [i.e., proven], it is essentially their critical and progressive character—the fact

[1]Crease, R. P., and C. C. Mann. *The Second Creation: Makers of the Revolution in 20th Century Physics.* New York: Macmillan, 1986, p. 10.
[2]Feynman, R. P., *QED: The Strange Theory of Light and Matter*, Princeton: Princeton U.P., 1985, p. 5.

that we can *argue* about their claim to solve our problems better than their com-petitors—which constitutes the rationality of science.[3]

Thus, science differs from other areas of knowledge in that it deals with problems that can be solved; it proposes hypotheses that can be tested and confirmed or, as Gould does with Broca's theory in "Women's Brains," that can be falsified.

Kuhn, in *The Structure of Scientific Revolutions* (1962), offers a similar concep-tion of scientific knowledge in slightly different terms. He defines "normal science" in any particular area for any particular time as a coherent body of knowledge pos-sessing two characteristics: it is generally accepted by the scientific community, and it is "sufficiently open-ended to leave all sorts of problems for the redefined group of practitioners to resolve"[4]; that is, it generates more science. Gould uses a com-bination of Popper's and Kuhn's criteria to decide among competing theories that may account for the extinction of the dinosaurs.

Kuhn offers another interesting insight: he uses the word "paradigm" to refer to any particular way of conceiving of, organizing, and working within a specific body of knowledge. The Ptolemaic system of conceiving of the cosmos would be such a paradigm. The Copernican revolution, indeed any of the radical reassessments of scientific knowledge already discussed, would be what Kuhn calls "a paradigm shift," signaling a scientific revolution, which is the subject of his book. Kuhn also analyzes how paradigms emerge, weaken, and are replaced by new ones. This chapter on science as a great idea has been shaped to a large degree by Kuhn's ideas, which put science into historical and cultural perspective. As Kuhn points out, the learning of any science involves an initiation into the current scientific paradigm; in this case, the "science" is the history of science, and in the history of science, the central principle of the current paradigm is revolution. This is an important concept because it clarifies that science, or more specifically what is taught as science, is not the "truth" about nature, but is the best approximation to the truth at a particular point in time. Science provides a great many facts, but they are facts organized according to the current paradigm, the overarching model, or even set of models that the sci-entific community agrees on as making the best sense out of the known facts, as solving the most problems, and as best generating new questions that are solvable and testable.

▼

Women's Brains
STEPHEN JAY GOULD

1   In the prelude to *Middlemarch*, George Eliot lamented the unful-filled lives of talented women:

> Some have felt that these blundering lives are due to the inconvenient indefiniteness with
> which the Supreme Power has fashioned the natures of women: if there were one level of

---

[3]Popper, K. R., *Conjectures and Refutations: The Growth of Scientific Knowledge.* New York: Basic Books, 1962, p. vii.
  [4]Kuhn, T. S., *The Structure of Scientific Revolutions* 2nd ed. Chicago: U. of Chicago Press, 1970, p. 10.

feminine incompetence as strict as the ability to count three and no more, the social lot of women might be treated with scientific certitude.

Eliot goes on to discount the idea of innate limitation, but while she wrote in 2 1872, the leaders of European anthropometry were trying to measure "with scientific certitude" the inferiority of women. Anthropometry, or measurement of the human body, is not so fashionable a field these days, but it dominated the human sciences for much of the nineteenth century and remained popular until intelligence testing replaced skull measurement as a favored device for making invidious comparisons among races, classes, and sexes. Craniometry, or measurement of the skull, commanded the most attention and respect. Its unquestioned leader, Paul Broca (1824–80), professor of clinical surgery at the Faculty of Medicine in Paris, gathered a school of disciples and imitators around himself. Their work, so meticulous and apparently irrefutable, exerted great influence and won high esteem as a jewel of nineteenth-century science.

Broca's work seemed particularly invulnerable to refutation. Had he not   3 measured with the most scrupulous care and accuracy? (Indeed, he had. I have the greatest respect for Broca's meticulous procedure. His numbers are sound. But science is an inferential exercise, not a catalog of facts. Numbers, by themselves, specify nothing. All depends upon what you do with them.) Broca depicted himself as an apostle of objectivity, a man who bowed before facts and cast aside superstition and sentimentality. He declared that "there is no faith, however respectable, no interest, however legitimate, which must not accommodate itself to the progress of human knowledge and bend before truth." Women, like it or not, had smaller brains than men and, therefore, could not equal them in intelligence. This fact, Broca argued, may reinforce a common prejudice in male society, but it is also a scientific truth. L. Manouvrier, a black sheep in Broca's fold, rejected the inferiority of women and wrote with feeling about the burden imposed upon them by Broca's numbers:

> Women displayed their talents and their diplomas. They also invoked philosophical authorities. But they were opposed by *numbers* unknown to Condorcet or to John Stuart Mill. These numbers fell upon poor women like a sledge hammer, and they were accompanied by commentaries and sarcasms more ferocious than the most misogynist imprecations of certain church fathers. The theologians had asked if women had a soul. Several centuries later, some scientists were ready to refuse them a human intelligence.

Broca's argument rested upon two sets of data: the larger brains of men in   4 modern societies, and a supposed increase in male superiority through time. His most extensive data came from autopsies performed personally in four Parisian hospitals. For 292 male brains, he calculated an average weight of 1,325 grams; 140 female brains averaged 1,144 grams for a difference of 181 grams, or 14 percent of the male weight. Broca understood, of course, that part of this difference could be attributed to the greater height of males. Yet he made no attempt to measure the effect of size alone and actually stated that it cannot account for the entire difference because we know, a priori, that women are not as intelligent as men (a premise that the data were supposed to test, not rest upon):

> We might ask if the small size of the female brain depends exclusively upon the small size of her body. Tiedemann has proposed this explanation. But we must not forget that women are, on the average, a little less intelligent than men, a difference which we should not exaggerate but which is, nonetheless, real. We are therefore permitted to suppose that the relatively small size of the female brain depends in part upon her physical inferiority and in part upon her intellectual inferiority.

5   In 1873, the year after Eliot published *Middlemarch*, Broca measured the cranial capacities of prehistoric skulls from L'Homme Mort cave. Here he found a difference of only 99.5 cubic centimeters between males and females, while modern populations range from 129.5 to 220.7. Topinard, Broca's chief disciple, explained the increasing discrepancy through time as a result of differing evolutionary pressures upon dominant men and passive women:

> The man who fights for two or more in the struggle for existence, who has all the responsibility and the cares of tomorrow, who is constantly active in combating the environment and human rivals, needs more brain than the woman whom he must protect and nourish, the sedentary woman, lacking any interior occupations, whose role is to raise children, love, and be passive.

6   In 1879, Gustave Le Bon, chief misogynist of Broca's school, used these data to publish what must be the most vicious attack upon women in modern scientific literature (no one can top Aristotle). I do not claim his views were representative of Broca's school, but they were published in France's most respected anthropological journal. Le Bon concluded:

> In the most intelligent races, as among the Parisians, there are a large number of women whose brains are closer in size to those of gorillas than to the most developed male brains. This inferiority is so obvious that no one can contest it for a moment; only its degree is worth discussion. All psychologists who have studied the intelligence of women, as well as poets and novelists, recognize today that they represent the most inferior forms of human evolution and that they are closer to children and savages than to an adult, civilized man. They excel in fickleness, inconstancy, absence of thought and logic, and incapacity to reason. Without doubt there exist some distinguished women, very superior to the average man, but they are as exceptional as the birth of any monstrosity, as, for example, of a gorilla with two heads; consequently, we may neglect them entirely.

7   Nor did Le Bon shrink from the social implications of his views. He was horrified by the proposal of some American reformers to grant women higher education on the same basis as men:

> A desire to give them the same education, and, as a consequence, to propose the same goals for them, is a dangerous chimera. . . . The day when, misunderstanding the inferior occupa-

tions which nature has given her, women leave the home and take part in our battles; on this day a social revolution will begin, and everything that maintains the sacred ties of the family will disappear.

Sound familiar?[1]

I have reexamined Broca's data, the basis for all this derivative pronounce- 8 ment, and I find his numbers sound but his interpretation ill-founded, to say the least. The data supporting his claim for increased difference through time can be easily dismissed. Broca based his contention on the samples from L'Homme Mort alone—only seven male and six female skulls in all. Never have so little data yielded such far ranging conclusions.

In 1888, Topinard published Broca's more extensive data on the Parisian 9 hospitals. Since Broca recorded height and age as well as brain size, we may use modern statistics to remove their effect. Brain weight decreases with age, and Broca's women were, on average, considerably older than his men. Brain weight increases with height, and his average man was almost half a foot taller than his average woman. I used multiple regression, a technique that allowed me to assess simultaneously the influence of height and age upon brain size. In an analysis of the data for women, I found that, at average male height and age, a woman's brain would weigh 1,212 grams. Correction for height and age reduces Broca's measured difference of 181 grams by more than a third, to 113 grams.

I don't know what to make of this remaining difference because I cannot 10 assess other factors known to influence brain size in a major way. Cause of death has an important effect: degenerative disease often entails a substantial diminution of brain size. (This effect is separate from the decrease attributed to age alone.) Eugene Schreider, also working with Broca's data, found that men killed in accidents had brains weighing, on average, 60 grams more than men dying of infectious diseases. The best modern data I can find (from American hospitals) records a full 100-gram difference between death by degenerative arteriosclerosis and by violence or accident. Since so many of Broca's subjects were very elderly women, we may assume that lengthy degenerative disease was more common among them than among the men.

More importantly, modern students of brain size still have not agreed on a 11 proper measure for eliminating the powerful effect of body size. Height is partly adequate, but men and women of the same height do not share the same body build. Weight is even worse than height, because most of its variation reflects nutrition rather than intrinsic size—fat versus skinny exerts little influence upon the brain. Manouvrier took up this subject in the 1880s and argued that muscular mass and force should be used. He tried to measure this elusive property in various ways and found a marked difference in favor of men, even

---

[1]When I wrote this essay, I assumed that Le Bon was a marginal, if colorful, figure. I have since learned that he was a leading scientist, one of the founders of social psychology, and best known for a seminal study on crowd behavior, still cited today (*La psychologie des foules*, 1895), and for his work on unconscious motivation.

in men and women of the same height. When he corrected for what he called "sexual mass," women actually came out slightly ahead in brain size.

12   Thus, the corrected 113-gram difference is surely too large; the true figure is probably close to zero and may as well favor women as men. And 113 grams, by the way, is exactly the average difference between a 5 foot 4 inch and a 6 foot 4 inch male in Broca's data. We would not (especially us short folks) want to ascribe greater intelligence to tall men. In short, who knows what to do with Broca's data? They certainly don't permit any confident claim that men have bigger brains than women.

13   To appreciate the social role of Broca and his school, we must recognize that his statements about the brains of women do not reflect an isolated prejudice toward a single disadvantaged group. They must be weighed in the context of a general theory that supported contemporary social distinctions as biologically ordained. Women, blacks, and poor people suffered the same disparagement, but women bore the brunt of Broca's argument because he had easier access to data on women's brains. Women were singularly denigrated but they also stood as surrogates for other disenfranchised groups. As one of Broca's disciples wrote in 1881: "Men of the black races have a brain scarcely heavier than that of white women." This juxtaposition extended into many other realms of anthropological argument, particularly to claims that, anatomically and emotionally, both women and blacks were like white children—and that white children, by the theory of recapitulation, represented an ancestral (primitive) adult stage of human evolution. I do not regard as empty rhetoric the claim that women's battles are for all of us.

14   Maria Montessori did not confine her activities to educational reform for young children. She lectured on anthropology for several years at the University of Rome, and wrote an influential book entitled *Pedagogical Anthropology* (English edition, 1913). Montessori was no egalitarian. She supported most of Broca's work and the theory of innate criminality proposed by her compatriot Cesare Lombroso. She measured the circumference of children's heads in her schools and inferred that the best prospects had bigger brains. But she had no use for Broca's conclusions about women. She discussed Manouvrier's work at length and made much of his tentative claim that women, after proper correction of the data, had slightly larger brains than men. Women, she concluded, were intellectually superior, but men had prevailed heretofore by dint of physical force. Since technology has abolished force as an instrument of power, the era of women may soon be upon us: "In such an epoch there will really be superior human beings, there will really be men strong in morality and in sentiment. Perhaps in this way the reign of women is approaching, when the enigma of her anthropological superiority will be deciphered. Woman was always the custodian of human sentiment, morality and honor."

15   This represents one possible antidote to "scientific" claims for the constitutional inferiority of certain groups. One may affirm the validity of biological distinctions but argue that the data have been misinterpreted by prejudiced men with a stake in the outcome, and that disadvantaged groups are truly superior.

In recent years, Elaine Morgan has followed this strategy in her *Descent of Women*, a speculative reconstruction of human prehistory from the woman's point of view—and as farcical as more famous tall tales by and for men.

I prefer another strategy. Montessori and Morgan followed Broca's philosophy to reach a more congenial conclusion. I would rather label the whole enterprise of setting a biological value upon groups for what it is: irrelevant and highly injurious. George Eliot well appreciated the special tragedy that biological labeling imposed upon members of disadvantaged groups. She expressed it for people like herself—women of extraordinary talent. I would apply it more widely—not only to those whose dreams are flouted but also to those who never realize that they may dream—but I cannot match her prose. In conclusion, then, the rest of Eliot's prelude to *Middlemarch:* 16

> The limits of variation are really much wider than anyone would imagine from the sameness of women's coiffure and the favorite love stories in prose and verse. Here and there a cygnet is reared uneasily among the ducklings in the brown pond, and never finds the living stream in fellowship with its own oary-footed kind. Here and there is born a Saint Theresa, foundress of nothing, whose loving heartbeats and sobs after an unattained goodness tremble off and are dispersed among hindrances instead of centering in some long-recognizable deed.

WRITING AND DISCUSSION QUESTIONS

Informative

1. In discussing Paul Broca's work, Gould makes a crucial distinction: "science is an inferential exercise, not a catalog of facts." Illustrate this point by briefly describing the accuracy of Broca's method of data collection and the accuracy of his conclusions drawn from the data.
2. Maria Montessori accepted some of Broca's conclusions but not others. On what basis does she seem to have made this distinction?

Persuasive

1. Gould's discussion reveals how social presuppositions can dictate supposedly scientific results and lead to contradictions. Why, for example, is Gustave Le Bon concerned about the social consequences of giving women the same education as men if women are intellectually inferior to men? Can you think of any other such contradictions in similar arguments? For example, Nazis argued that Jews were racially inferior to "Aryans" and at the same time claimed that Jews were taking over the world, an indication, one would suppose in applying evolutionary principles in this way to "races," of their superior fitness.
2. Summarize the arguments you have heard for the inferiority of any racial, ethnic, sexual, or economic group, and argue that the scientific basis for those claims is based on presuppositions.

Personal

1. Suppose Broca had discovered that the women's brains he weighed were heavier than the men's. How do you think he would have responded? Would he have remained the objective scientist and bent before the truth, or would he have found a way to interpret the data consistent with his belief that "women are, on average, a little less intelligent than men"? To what extent can you be found guilty of interpreting data to support your own presuppositions?

2. Gould points out that "individious comparisons among races, classes, and sexes," even after skull measurement had been discredited, continued to be made on the "scientific" basis of intelligence testing. What do you know about the controversies surrounding the validity of intelligence tests? Has the practice of intelligence testing touched you in any way? Has your reading of Gould's essay changed the way you look at this practice?

3. Gould warns against the dangers of attaching value to biological groups, of implying that some are inherently better than others. List the biologically based groups to which you belong. Imagine a "scientific" argument to support the inferiority or superiority of one, and describe your life in a society in which belief in that argument is widespread.

▼

Sex, Drugs, Disasters, and the Extinction of Dinosaurs

1   Science, in its most fundamental definition, is a fruitful mode of inquiry, not a list of enticing conclusions. The conclusions are the consequence, not the essence.

2   My greatest unhappiness with most popular presentations of science concerns their failure to separate fascinating claims from the methods that scientists use to establish the facts of nature. Journalists, and the public, thrive on controversial and stunning statements. But science is, basically, a way of knowing—in P. B. Medawar's apt words, "the art of the soluble." If the growing corps of popular science writers would focus on *how* scientists develop and defend those fascinating claims, they would make their greatest possible contribution to public understanding.

3   Consider three ideas, proposed in perfect seriousness to explain that greatest of all titillating puzzles—the extinction of dinosaurs. Since these three notions invoke the primally fascinating themes of our culture—sex, drugs, and violence—they surely reside in the category of fascinating claims. I want to show

why two of them rank as silly speculation, while the other represents science at its grandest and most useful.

Science works with testable proposals. If, after much compilation and scru- 4
tiny of data, new information continues to affirm a hypothesis, we may accept it provisionally and gain confidence as further evidence mounts. We can never be completely sure that a hypothesis is right, though we may be able to show with confidence that it is wrong. The best scientific hypotheses are also generous and expansive: they suggest extensions and implications that enlighten related, and even far distant, subjects. Simply consider how the idea of evolution has influenced virtually every intellectual field.

Useless speculation, on the other hand, is restrictive. It generates no testable 5
hypothesis, and offers no way to obtain potentially refuting evidence. Please note that I am not speaking of truth or falsity. The speculation may well be true; still, if it provides, in principle, no material for affirmation or rejection, we can make nothing of it. It must simply stand forever as an intriguing idea. Useless speculation turns in on itself and leads nowhere; good science, containing both seeds for its potential refutation and implications for more and different testable knowledge, reaches out. But, enough preaching. Let's move on to dinosaurs, and the three proposals for their extinction.

1. Sex: Testes function only in a narrow range of temperature (those of mammals hang externally in a scrotal sac because internal body temperatures are too high for their proper function). A worldwide rise in temperature at the close of the Cretaceous period caused the testes of dinosaurs to stop functioning and led to their extinction by sterilization of males.
2. Drugs: Angiosperms (flowering plants) first evolved toward the end of the dinosaurs' reign. Many of these plants contain psychoactive agents, avoided by mammals today as a result of their bitter taste. Dinosaurs had neither means to taste the bitterness nor livers effective enough to detoxify the substances. They died of massive overdoses.
3. Disasters: A large comet or asteroid struck the earth some 65 million years ago, lofting a cloud of dust into the sky and blocking sunlight, thereby suppressing photosynthesis and so drastically lowering world temperatures that dinosaurs and hosts of other creatures became extinct.

Before analyzing these three tantalizing statements, we must establish a basic ground rule often violated in proposals for the dinosaurs' demise. *There is no separate problem of the extinction of dinosaurs.* Too often we divorce specific events from their wider contexts and systems of cause and effect. The fundamental fact of dinosaur extinction is its synchrony with the demise of so many other groups across a wide range of habitats, from terrestrial to marine.

The history of life has been punctuated by brief episodes of mass extinction. 6
A recent analysis by University of Chicago paleontologists Jack Sepkoski and

Dave Raup, based on the best and most exhaustive tabulation of data ever assembled, shows clearly that five episodes of mass dying stand well above the "background" extinctions of normal times (when we consider all mass extinctions, large and small, they seem to fall in a regular 26-million-year cycle . . .). The Cretaceous debacle, occurring 65 million years ago and separating the Mesozoic and Cenozoic eras of our geological time scale, ranks prominently among the five. Nearly all the marine plankton (single-celled floating creatures) died with geological suddenness; among marine invertebrates, nearly 15 percent of all families perished, including many previously dominant groups, especially the ammonites (relatives of squids in coiled shells). On land, the dinosaurs disappeared after more than 100 million years of unchallenged domination.

7   In this context, speculations limited to dinosaurs alone ignore the larger phenomenon. We need a coordinated explanation for a system of events that includes the extinction of dinosaurs as one component. Thus it makes little sense, though it may fuel our desire to view mammals as inevitable inheritors of the earth, to guess that dinosaurs died because small mammals ate their eggs (a perennial favorite among untestable speculations). It seems most unlikely that some disaster peculiar to dinosaurs befell these massive beasts— and that the debacle happened to strike just when one of history's five great dyings had enveloped the earth for completely different reasons.

8   The testicular theory, an old favorite from the 1940s, had its root in an interesting and thoroughly respectable study of temperature tolerances in the American alligator, published in the staid *Bulletin of the American Museum of Natural History* in 1946 by three experts on living and fossil reptiles—E. H. Colbert, my own first teacher in paleontology; R. B. Cowles; and C. M. Bogert.

9   The first sentence of their summary reveals a purpose beyond alligators: "This report describes an attempt to infer the reactions of extinct reptiles, especially the dinosaurs, to high temperatures as based upon reactions observed in the modern alligator." They studied, by rectal thermometry, the body temperatures of alligators under changing conditions of heating and cooling. (Well, let's face it, you wouldn't want to try sticking a thermometer under a 'gator's tongue.) The predictions under test go way back to an old theory first stated by Galileo in the 1630s—the unequal scaling of surfaces and volumes. As an animal, or any object, grows (provided its shape doesn't change), surface areas must increase more slowly than volumes—since surfaces get larger as length squared, while volumes increase much more rapidly, as length cubed. Therefore, small animals have high ratios of surface to volume, while large animals cover themselves with relatively little surface.

10   Among cold-blooded animals lacking any physiological mechanism for keeping their temperatures constant, small creatures have a hell of a time keeping warm—because they lose so much heat through their relatively large surfaces. On the other hand, large animals, with their relatively small surfaces, may lose heat so slowly that, once warm, they may maintain effectively constant tempera-

tures against ordinary fluctuations of climate. (In fact, the resolution of the "hot-blooded dinosaur" controversy that burned so brightly a few years back may simply be that, while large dinosaurs possessed no physiological mechanism for constant temperature, and were not therefore warm-blooded in the technical sense, their large size and relatively small surface area kept them warm.)

Colbert, Cowles, and Bogert compared the warming rates of small and large   *11* alligators. As predicted, the small fellows heated up (and cooled down) more quickly. When exposed to a warm sun, a tiny 50-gram (1.76-ounce) alligator heated up one degree Celsius every minute and a half, while a large alligator, 260 times bigger at 13,000 grams (28.7 pounds), took seven and a half minutes to gain a degree. Extrapolating up to an adult 10-ton dinosaur, they concluded that a one-degree rise in body temperature would take eighty-six hours. If large animals absorb heat so slowly (through their relatively small surfaces), they will also be unable to shed any excess heat gained when temperatures rise above a favorable level.

The authors then guessed that large dinosaurs lived at or near their optimum   *12* temperatures; Cowles suggested that a rise in global temperatures just before the Cretaceous extinction caused the dinosaurs to heat up beyond their optimal tolerance—and, being so large, they couldn't shed the unwanted heat. (In a most unusual statement within a scientific paper, Colbert and Bogert then explicitly disavowed this speculative extension of their empirical work on alligators.) Cowles conceded that this excess heat probably wasn't enough to kill or even to enervate the great beasts, but since testes often function only within a narrow range of temperature, he proposed that this global rise might have sterilized all the males, causing extinction by natural contraception.

The overdose theory has recently been supported by UCLA psychiatrist   *13* Ronald K. Siegel. Siegel has gathered, he claims, more than 2,000 records of animals who, when given access, administer various drugs to themselves—from a mere swig of alcohol to massive doses of the big H. Elephants will swill the equivalent of twenty beers at a time, but do not like alcohol in concentrations greater than 7 percent. In a silly bit of anthropocentric speculation, Siegel states that "elephants drink, perhaps, to forget . . . the anxiety produced by shrinking rangeland and the competition for food."

Since fertile imaginations can apply almost any hot idea to the extinction of   *14* dinosaurs, Siegel found a way. Flowering plants did not evolve until late in the dinosaurs' reign. These plants also produced an array of aromatic, amino-acid-based alkaloids—the major group of psychoactive agents. Most mammals are "smart" enough to avoid these potential poisons. The alkaloids simply don't taste good (they are bitter); in any case, we mammals have livers happily supplied with the capacity to detoxify them. But, Siegel speculates, perhaps dinosaurs could neither taste the bitterness nor detoxify the substances once ingested. He recently told members of the American Psychological Association: "I'm not suggesting that all dinosaurs OD'd on plant drugs, but it certainly was a factor." He also argued that death by overdose may help explain why so many dinosaur fossils are found in contorted positions. (Do not go gentle into that good night.)

15   Extraterrestrial catastrophes have long pedigrees in the popular literature of extinction, but the subject exploded again in 1979, after a long lull, when the father-son, physicist-geologist team of Luis and Walter Alvarez proposed that an asteroid, some 10 km in diameter, struck the earth 65 million years ago (comets, rather than asteroids, have since gained favor. . . . Good science is self-corrective).

16   The force of such a collision would be immense, greater by far than the megatonnage of all the world's nuclear weapons. . . . In trying to reconstruct a scenario that would explain the simultaneous dying of dinosaurs on land and so many creatures in the sea, the Alvarezes proposed that a gigantic dust cloud, generated by particles blown aloft in the impact, would so darken the earth that photosynthesis would cease and temperatures drop precipitously. (Rage, rage against the dying of the light.) The single-celled photosynthetic oceanic plankton, with life cycles measured in weeks, would perish outright, but land plants might survive through the dormancy of their seeds (land plants were not much affected by the Cretaceous extinction, and any adequate theory must account for the curious pattern of differential survival). Dinosaurs would die by starvation and freezing; small, warm-blooded mammals, with more modest requirements for food and better regulation of body temperature, would squeak through. "Let the bastards freeze in the dark," as bumper stickers of our chauvinistic neighbors in sunbelt states proclaimed several years ago during the Northeast's winter oil crisis.

17   All three theories, testicular malfunction, psychoactive overdosing, and asteroidal zapping, grab our attention mightily. As pure phenomenology, they rank about equally high on any hit parade of primal fascination. Yet one represents expansive science, the others restrictive and untestable speculation. The proper criterion lies in evidence and methodology; we must probe behind the superficial fascination of particular claims.

18   How could we possibly decide whether the hypothesis of testicular frying is right or wrong? We would have to know things that the fossil record cannot provide. What temperatures were optimal for dinosaurs? Could they avoid the absorption of excess heat by staying in the shade, or in caves? At what temperatures did their testicles cease to function? Were late Cretaceous climates ever warm enough to drive the internal temperatures of dinosaurs close to this ceiling? Testicles simply don't fossilize, and how could we infer their temperature tolerances even if they did? In short, Cowles's hypothesis is only an intriguing speculation leading nowhere. The most damning statement against it appeared right in the conclusion of Colbert, Cowles, and Bogert's paper, when they admitted: "It is difficult to advance any definite arguments against this hypothesis." My statement may seem paradoxical—isn't a hypothesis really good if you can't devise any arguments against it? Quite the contrary. It is simply untestable and unusable.

Siegel's overdosing has even less going for it. At least Cowles extrapolated   *19*
his conclusion from some good data on alligators. And he didn't completely
violate the primary guideline of siting dinosaur extinction in the context of a
general mass dying—for rise in temperature could be the root cause of a general catastrophe, zapping dinosaurs by testicular malfunction and different
groups for other reasons. But Siegel's speculation cannot touch the extinction
of ammonites or oceanic plankton (diatoms make their own food with good
sweet sunlight; they don't OD on the chemicals of terrestrial plants). It is simply a gratuitous, attention-grabbing guess. It cannot be tested, for how can we
know what dinosaurs tasted and what their livers could do? Livers don't fossilize any better than testicles.

The hypothesis doesn't even make any sense in its own context. Angio-   *20*
sperms were in full flower ten million years before dinosaurs went the way of
all flesh. Why did it take so long? As for the pains of a chemical death
recorded in contortions of fossils, I regret to say (or rather I'm pleased to note
for the dinosaurs' sake) that Siegel's knowledge of geology must be a bit deficient: muscles contract after death and geological strata rise and fall with
motions of the earth's crust after burial—more than enough reason to distort a
fossil's pristine appearance.

The impact story, on the other hand, has a sound basis in evidence. It can   *21*
be tested, extended, refined and, if wrong, disproved. The Alvarezes did not
just construct an arresting guess for public consumption. They proposed their
hypothesis after laborious geochemical studies with Frank Asaro and Helen
Michael had revealed a massive increase of iridium in rocks deposited right at
the time of extinction. Iridium, a rare metal of the platinum group, is virtually
absent from indigenous rocks of the earth's crust; most of our iridium arrives
on extraterrestrial objects that strike the earth.

The Alvarez hypothesis bore immediate fruit. Based originally on evidence   *22*
from two European localities, it led geochemists throughout the world to examine other sediments of the same age. They found abnormally high amounts of
iridium everywhere—from continental rocks of the western United States to
deep sea cores from the South Atlantic.

Cowles proposed his testicular hypothesis in the mid-1940s. Where has it   *23*
gone since then? Absolutely nowhere, because scientists can do nothing with it.
The hypothesis must stand as a curious appendage to a solid study of alligators.
Siegel's overdose scenario will also win a few press notices and fade into obliv-
ion. The Alvarezes' asteroid falls into a different category altogether, and much
of the popular commentary has missed this essential distinction by focusing on
the impact and its attendant results, and forgetting what really matters to a scientist—the iridium. If you talk just about asteroids, dust, and darkness, you
tell stories no better and no more entertaining than fried testicles or terminal
trips. It is the iridium—the source of testable evidence—that counts and forges
the crucial distinction between speculation and science.

The proof, to twist a phrase, lies in the doing. Cowles's hypothesis has gen-   *24*
erated nothing in thirty-five years. Since its proposal in 1979, the Alvarez

hypothesis has spawned hundreds of studies, a major conference, and attendant publications. Geologists are fired up. They are looking for iridium at all other extinction boundaries. Every week exposes a new wrinkle in the scientific press. Further evidence that the Cretaceous iridium represents extraterrestrial impact and not indigenous volcanism continues to accumulate. As I revise this essay in November 1984 (this paragraph will be out of date when the book is published), new data include chemical "signatures" of other isotopes indicating unearthly provenance, glass spherules of a size and sort produced by impact and not by volcanic eruptions, and high-pressure varieties of silica formed (so far as we know) only under the tremendous shock of impact.

25   My point is simply this: Whatever the eventual outcome (I suspect it will be positive), the Alvarez hypothesis is exciting, fruitful science because it generates tests, provides us with things to do, and expands outward. We are having fun, battling back and forth, moving toward a resolution, and extending the hypothesis beyond its original scope. . . .

26   As just one example of the unexpected, distant cross-fertilization that good science engenders, the Alvarez hypothesis made a major contribution to a theme that has riveted public attention in the past few months—so-called nuclear winter. . . . In a speech delivered in April 1982, Luis Alvarez calculated the energy that a ten-kilometer asteroid would release on impact. He compared such an explosion with a full nuclear exchange and implied that all-out atomic war might unleash similar consequences.

27   This theme of impact leading to massive dust clouds and falling temperatures formed an important input to the decision of Carl Sagan and a group of colleagues to model the climatic consequences of nuclear holocaust. Full nuclear exchange would probably generate the same kind of dust cloud and darkening that may have wiped out the dinosaurs. Temperatures would drop precipitously and agriculture might become impossible. Avoidance of nuclear war is fundamentally an ethical and political imperative, but we must know the factual consequences to make firm judgments. I am heartened by a final link across disciplines and deep concerns—another criterion, by the way, of science at its best. A recognition of the very phenomenon that made our evolution possible by exterminating the previously dominant dinosaurs and clearing a way for the evolution of large mammals, including us, might actually help to save us from joining those magnificent beasts in contorted poses among the strata of the earth.

WRITING AND DISCUSSION QUESTIONS

Informative

1. Identify as many statements by Gould as you can find that echo Popper's or Kuhn's criteria (see Gould introduction, pp. 309–310) for what constitutes good

science. Note that although Gould cites neither source, to accuse him of plagiarism would be unfair. Popper's and Kuhn's criteria have become such well-accepted approaches to the current scientific paradigm that such references are no longer necessary—anymore than a scientist would think it necessary today to cite Darwin when using the model of biological evolution.

2. Briefly summarize the major reasons why the sex and drugs theories for dinosaur extinction are not good science, and why the disaster hypothesis is.

Persuasive

1. In addition to sex, drugs, and disasters, Gould briefly mentions another and older theory to explain dinosaur extinction, competition with mammals. What kind of presuppositions and ideologies prevalent during the first half of this century made this explanation seem plausible, even preferable despite the fact that it offered no help in explaining the well-known and simultaneous mass extinction of so much of marine life? Notice that the mammalian competition hypothesis required the view that dinosaurs were inferior in important ways to mammals.

2. Argue that the dismissal of the mammalian competition theory is part of the reason many generally assumed features of dinosaurs, including their cold bloodedness and lack of intelligence, are currently being radically revised. Does this suggest further ideological connections?

3. What reasons, other than purely scientific ones, can explain why some scientists may prefer any of the three major theories discussed by Gould? Argue that prejudices in themselves will or will not render these theories invalid.

4. Among the questions asked at the end of the Darwin selection was this: "What is the usefulness of a theory like evolution that cannot ever be fully proven?" Having read the Gould selections and the introduction to them, explain whether you find yourself better equipped to answer this question.

Personal

1. How satisfied are you with Gould's explanation of the best choice? Are you disturbed by his acknowledgment that an untestable hypothesis, *even if true,* is still bad science?

2. Choose any body of knowledge that is generally considered marginally scientific or pseudoscientific—telekinesis, telepathy, UFOs, creationism, astrology, palmistry, and so on. Assess the "scientific" basis and the approach in these bodies of knowledge according to Popper's and Kuhn's criteria and according to your own criteria.

3. As stated in the introduction to this selection, learning a science is an initiation into the current scientific paradigm, which is often ignored in our science classes. How important is it that your teachers introduce a concept with something like, "This is the current model"?

▼

ROBERT JAY LIFTON, "THIS WORLD IS NOT THIS WORLD" FROM *THE NAZI DOCTORS: MEDICAL KILLING AND THE PSYCHOLOGY OF GENOCIDE*

Perhaps more than any other person working in the medical or psychological sciences, Robert Jay Lifton (1926–) has chronicled the experiences of extreme violence and suffering caused by "educated" men and women who are distinctly products of an "advanced" technological age. Whether it be those who survived the atomic bombing of Hiroshima, the pilots who dropped bombs on Vietnam, the medical personnel who became indispensible to Hitler's "final solution," or the planners who have amassed more than 40,000 nuclear warheads, Lifton has used his psychiatric training to become an intimate witness to man's inhumanity to man.

A doctor of medicine himself, Lifton is Distinguished Professor of Psychiatry and Psychology at John Jay College and the Graduate Center of the City University of New York. The twelve books he has written collectively reveal how human the commission of even the most unspeakable atrocities can be. He undertook the study for one of his most important books, *The Nazi Doctors: Medical Killing and the Psychology of Genocide* (1986), the first chapter of which appears below, as a logical consequence of his work on survivors and perpetrators of monstrous evil and because he is a Jew. His friends, however, advised him to stay away from the topic, fearing that in conducting the study, which would require many years and immersion in gruesome atrocities, condemnation might be replaced by kinds of insight that would somehow lessen the horror. Lifton responded by saying that "to avoid probing the sources of evil seemed to me, in the end, a refusal to call forth our capacity to engage and combat it. Such avoidance contains not only fear of contagion but an assumption that Nazis or any other evil has no relationship whatsoever to the rest of us—to more general human capacities." In other words, the scientist can help us make sense of acts by "ordinary" people (for example, the killing of more than one million children) that seem incomprehensible.

Scientists, being after all ordinary people, have often served as instruments of evil policies, and it is especially ironic that during the twentieth century practitioners of the medical sciences, the healing arts, have appeared prominently in such roles. One can note Soviet psychiatrists who lock up dissidents, Chilean doctors serving as torturers, South African doctors who cover up reports of blacks killed in prison, or doctors of many nationalities including our own who have worked to develop the most insidious instruments of mind control and chemical and biological warfare. But Lifton realized there was a significant new element to be examined in Nazi doctors, their "biological visions that justified genocide as a means of national and racial healing." Only a person schooled in the science of psychology could begin to make sense of the foundations of a virulently anti-Semitic racial ideology.

Just as pseudoscience was used in the nineteenth century to reinforce sexism (summarized in Gould's "Women's Brains"), a racial ideology built on what seemed a solid science to millions was used to exterminate an entire culture of Jews in Europe. The fact that hundreds of thousands of educated persons—lawyers, doctors, civil servants, and professors—participated, not to mention the millions who watched and did nothing, begs for an explanation. Part of that explanation is that the ideology of hate was convincing because it was dressed in a metaphor of "scientific" healing.

▼

This World Is Not This World

ROBERT JAY LIFTON

APPROACHING AUSCHWITZ

I gained an important perspective on Auschwitz from an Israeli den- *1* tist who had spent three years in that camp. We were completing a long interview, during which he had told me about many things, including details of SS dentists' supervision of prisoners' removal of gold fillings from the teeth of fellow Jews killed in the gas chambers. He looked about the comfortable room in his house with its beautiful view of Haifa, sighed deeply, and said, "This world is not this world." What I think he meant was that, after Auschwitz, the ordinary rhythms and appearances of life, however innocuous or pleasant, were far from the truth of human existence. Underneath those rhythms and appearances lay darkness and menace.

The comment also raises the question of our capacity to approach Ausch- *2* witz. From the beginning there has been enormous resistance on the part of virtually everyone to knowledge of what the Nazis were doing and have done there. That resistance has hardly abated, whatever the current interest in what we call "the Holocaust." Nor have more recent episodes of mass slaughter done much to overcome it. For to permit one's imagination to enter into the Nazi killing machine—to begin to experience that killing machine—is to alter one's relationship to the entire human project. One does not want to learn about such things.

Psychologically speaking, nothing is darker or more menacing, or harder to *3* accept, than the participation of physicians in mass murder. However technicized or commercial the modern physician may have become, he or she is still supposed to be a healer—and one responsible to a tradition of healing, which all cultures revere and depend upon. Knowledge that the doctor has joined the killers adds a grotesque dimension to the perception that "this world is not this world." During my work I gained the impression that, among Germans and many others, this involvement of physicians was viewed as the most shameful of all Nazi behavior.

When we think of the crimes of Nazi doctors, what come to mind are their *4* cruel and sometimes fatal human experiments. Those experiments, in their precise and absolute violation of the Hippocratic oath, mock and subvert the very idea of the ethical physician, of the physician dedicated to the well-being of patients. I shall examine those human experiments from the standpoint of the regime's medical and political ideology.

5   Yet when we turn to the Nazi doctor's role in Auschwitz, it was not the experiments that were most significant. Rather it was his participation in the killing process—indeed his supervision of Auschwitz mass murder from beginning to end. This aspect of Nazi medical behavior has escaped full recognition—even though we are familiar with photographs of Nazi doctors standing at the ramp and performing their notorious "selections" of arriving Jews, determining which were to go directly to the gas chamber and which were to live, at least temporarily, and work in the camp. Yet this medicalized killing had a logic that was not only deeply significant for Nazi theory and behavior but holds for other expressions of genocide as well.

6   In this book I will examine both the broad Nazi "biomedical vision" as a central psychohistorical principle of the regime, and the psychological behavior of individual Nazi doctors. We need to look at both dimensions if we are to understand more about how Nazi doctors—and Nazis in general—came to do what they did.

7   The very extremity of Auschwitz and related Nazi murder renders it close to unreality. A distinguished European physician, who had struggled with Nazi brutality for forty years—first as an inmate of Auschwitz and other camps and then as an authority on medical consequences of that incarceration—said to me very quietly at the end of a long interview, "You know, I still can't really believe that it happened—that a group of people would round up all of the Jews in Europe and send them to a special place to kill them." He was saying that the Auschwitz "other world" is beyond belief. The wonder is that there is not an even greater tendency than actually exists to accept the directly false contention that Nazi mass murder did not take place.

8   Also at issue for us here is the relationship of Nazi doctors to the human species. Another Auschwitz survivor who knew something about them asked me, "Were they *beasts* when they did what they did? Or were they *human beings?*" He was not surprised by my answer: they were and are men, which is my justification for studying them; and their behavior—Auschwitz itself—was a product of specifically *human* ingenuity and cruelty.

9   I went on to tell this survivor of the ordinariness of most Nazi doctors I had interviewed. Neither brilliant nor stupid, neither inherently evil nor particularly ethically sensitive, they were by no means the demonic figures—sadistic, fanatic, lusting to kill—people have often thought them to be. My friend replied, "But it is *demonic* that they were *not* demonic." He could then raise his second question, really the one he had in mind in the first place: "How did they become killers?" That question can be addressed, and this book is in the way of an answer.

10   What my survivor friend was struggling with—what I have struggled with throughout this study—is the disturbing psychological truth that participation in mass murder need not require emotions as extreme or demonic as would seem appropriate for such a malignant project. Or to put the matter another way, ordinary people can commit demonic acts.

11   But that did not mean that Nazi doctors were faceless bureaucratic cogs or

automatons. As human beings, they were actors and participants who manifested certain kinds of behavior for which they were responsible, and which we
can begin to identify.

There are several dimensions, then, to the work. At its heart is the transfor-   *12*
mation of the physician—of the medical enterprise itself—from healer to
killer. That transformation requires us to examine the interaction of Nazi political ideology and biomedical ideology in their effects on individual and collective
behavior. That in turn takes us to the significance of medicalized killing for
Nazi mass murder in general—and for large-scale killing and genocide on the
part of others. Finally, the work has relevance for broad questions of human
control over life and death—for physicians everywhere, for science and scientists and other professionals in general, for institutions of various kinds—and
also for concepts of human nature and ultimate human values. I can no more
than touch on most of these general issues, having made a decision to focus on
Nazi doctors and medicalized killing, and then on issues of mass murder. But
my hope is that others will find here experience that might help them explore
any of the searing moral issues implicit in this study.

That hope raises the important question of specificity and generality. I   *13*
believe that one must stress the specificity of the Nazi killing project, especially
concerning Jews: its unique characteristics, and the particular forces that
shaped it. But having done that, one must also search for larger *principles* suggested by that unique project. No other event or institution can or should be
equated with Auschwitz; but nor should we deny ourselves the opportunity to
explore its general relevance for genocide and for situations of a very different
order in which psychological and moral questions may be considerably more
ambiguous. . . .

THE INTERVIEWS[1]

My assumption from the beginning, in keeping with my twenty-five years of   *14*
research, was that the best way to learn about Nazi doctors was to talk to them;
interviews became the pragmatic core of the study. But I knew that, even more
than in earlier work, I would have to supplement the interviews with extensive
reading in and probing of all related issues—having to do not only with observations by others on Nazi medical behavior but with the Nazi era in general, as
well as with German culture and history and with overall patterns of victimiza-
tion in general and anti-Jewishness in particular.

From the beginning I sought counsel from authorities on every aspect of the   *15*
era—historians, social scientists, novelists and playwrights (some themselves
survivors of camps)—about ways of understanding the regime and its behavior;
about readings, libraries, trial documents, and other sources; and about other

---

[1] I have used pseudonyms consisting of a first name and last initial for the people I interviewed for this book
and a few others. In addition, I have altered certain identifying details that do not affect the substance of the
interviews, and in a few cases refrained from specific citations.

people to talk to. With the help of foundation grants I began to travel: preliminary trips to Germany in January 1978 and to Israel and Poland in May and June of that year. I lived in Munich from September 1978 through April 1979, during which time I did the greater part of the interviews, mostly in Germany and Austria, but also again in Poland and Israel, as well as in France, England, Norway, and Denmark. In January 1980, I did more work in Israel and Germany; and in March of that year, I interviewed three Auschwitz survivors in Australia. I have never been so intense a traveler nor so engrossed or pained a psychological investigator.

16   I interviewed three groups of people. The central group consisted of twenty-nine men who had been significantly involved at high levels with Nazi medicine, twenty-eight of them physicians and one a pharmacist. Of that group of twenty-eight doctors, five had worked in concentration camps (three in Auschwitz) either as SS physicians assigned there or in connection with medical experiments; six had some association with the "euthanasia" (direct medical killing) program; eight were engaged in medical policy making and in developing and implementing Nazi medical-ideological theory; six held other important medical positions which involved them in tainted behavior and ideological conflict; and three were engaged mainly in military medicine which brought them in contact with (or led them to seek distance from) massive Nazi killing of Jews behind the lines in Eastern Europe.

17   I interviewed a second group of twelve former Nazi nonmedical professionals of some prominence: as lawyers, judges, economists, teachers, architects, administrators, and Party officials. My purpose here was to probe the experiences of professionals in general under the Nazis and their relationship to ideology as well as to obtain background information about medical and related policies.

18   Very different was the third group I interviewed: eighty former Auschwitz prisoners who had worked on medical blocks, more than half of them doctors. The majority were Jewish (interviewed in the United States, Israel, Western Europe, and Australia); but they included two non-Jewish groups, Poles (interviewed in Krakow, Warsaw, and London) and former political prisoners (interviewed mostly in various parts of Western Europe, notably Vienna). I focused on their encounters with and observations of Nazi doctors and Auschwitz medical policies in general.

19   Concerning the two groups of former Nazis, especially the doctors, arrangements were never simple. It seemed clear from the beginning that I could best approach them through introductions from Germans of some standing in their society who were sympathetic to my research. The process was enhanced by a formal appointment I was given as a fellow at the Max Planck Institute for Research in Psychopathology and Psychotherapy, directed by Dr. Paul Matussek. My first task was to locate former Nazi doctors of standing in the regime—which I did with the help of assistants, through books, knowledgeable scholars, hearsay, and intensive address searches. When a name and address had been uncovered, Professor Matussek would send a form letter, which he

and I had carefully constructed, to that person. The letter described me as a prominent American psychiatric researcher who was conducting a study of the "stresses and conflicts" of German physicians under National Socialism; mentioned my earlier work on Hiroshima and Vietnam; emphasized my commitment to confidentiality; and urged the person in question to cooperate fully with me. In the case of positive replies, I wrote a brief letter mentioning my desire to understand events of that time as accurately as possible.

The recipients of those letters undoubtedly understood that "stresses and [20] conflicts" were euphemisms for more sinister matters. But for varying psychological reasons of their own, about 70 percent of those approached agreed to see me. Some felt they should show this courtesy to a "colleague" from abroad introduced to them by a person of great medical standing in their country. The amount of time that had passed since the Nazi period permitted some of them to look upon it as something they could now begin to talk about. Indeed to do so could afford them an opportunity to affirm a post-Nazi identity. I had the impression that many of these former Nazi doctors retained pockets of guilt and shame, to which they did not have access—that is, unconscious or numbed forms of quiet self-condemnation. Those unacknowledged feelings were consistent with a need to talk.

But their way of dealing with those feelings was frequently the opposite of [21] self-confrontation: rather, the dominant tendency among these Nazi doctors was to present themselves to me as decent people who tried to make the best of a bad situation. And they wanted a confirmation from me of this view of themselves. Moreover, as elderly men—the youngest were in their late fifties, most were in their late sixties or older, and one was ninety-one—they were at the stage of life when one likes to "review" one's past in order to assert its meaning and affirm its legacy beyond impending death.

Some part of these men wished to be heard: they had things to say that most [22] of them had never said before, least of all to people around them. Yet none of them—not a single former Nazi doctor I spoke to—arrived at a clear ethical evaluation of what he had done, and what he had been part of. They could examine events in considerable detail, even look at feelings and speak generally with surprising candor—but almost in the manner of a third person. The narrator, morally speaking, was not quite present.

I had to consider many levels of truth and untruth. I tried to learn all I [23] could about each Nazi doctor before seeing him, and afterward to compare and cross-check details and interpretations with those available from other sources: from interviews with other former Nazi doctors and with nonmedical professionals; from interviews with former inmates and victims, especially those who had been physicians at Auschwitz; from written accounts of all forms of Nazi medical behavior, especially those writings that appeared relatively soon after the war; and from a great variety of books and documents, including trial records as well as diaries and letters when available. All this additional information was necessary for evaluation not only of willful falsehood or (more often) distortion but of questions of memory as well. We were discussing events that had occurred thirty or forty or more years before; persistent forgetting and manifestations of psychic numbing could blend with self-serving distortion. Yet I also encountered vivid and accurate recall, along with surprising candor and self-revelation. I had to combine all of this information in making interpretive judgments; but in the end, I felt I had learned much about the Nazi doctors I interviewed, and about Nazi doctors in general.

24   I spent four or more hours with the majority of Nazi doctors, usually during two or more interviews. But arrangements varied greatly according to their availability and their importance to the work. I saw some only once, and one terminated the interview after just half an hour. But I saw others for much longer periods, several for a total of twenty to thirty hours in a series of day-long meetings. The great majority of interviews had to be interpreted. As in past work, I was able to train a few regular assistants to interpret in a fashion that permitted quick and relatively direct exchange. Whatever its limitations, the presence of an interpreter in several cases provided a certain advantage: a buffer that enabled Nazi doctors, when uncomfortable and conflicted, to deal more freely with highly charged matters than they might have been able to do in direct, and therefore more threatening, exchange. The intensity that developed in these interviews was no less than that in those relatively few interviews I was able to conduct in English (because of the fluency of the interviewee). In both of those situations, with no exception, these German doctors agreed to my tape-recording the interviews, so that I had a precise record of what was said and was able to work later from the original German.

25   An ironic element in the approach was the requirement (made by the Yale University Committee on Research with Human Subjects, and generally followed in American research) that I obtain "informed consent" from the Nazi doctors. The requirement itself stemmed from the Nuremberg Medical Trial, and was therefore a consequence of the misbehavior of the very doctors I was interviewing or their associates. That touch of humanity seemed exactly right. Therefore, in correspondence with these doctors before our meeting, I reaffirmed the principles of confidentiality and of their right to raise any issues or questions they wished as well as to cease to participate in a particular interview or the research in general at any time. These principles were stated in written forms I asked each doctor to sign, sometimes at the beginning or the end of the first interview and at other times during the second meeting or through the mail (depending upon my estimate of whether introducing the form at a particular time would intensify an already stressful situation and thereby interfere with the work).

26   Among the doctors I interviewed, two were in the midst of trials stemming from their Nazi activities. Another had served a long jail sentence. And many of them had been held for periods of up to several years after the war without formal trial. On the whole, however, they were not the most identifiable criminal group of the doctors: members of that group had either been put to death at Nuremberg and subsequent trials or else died of natural causes years before,

having been for the most part relatively senior at the time of their crimes. But the ones I did see, as I shall describe, were hardly free of evil, sometimes murderous, behavior.

I decided not to mention my Jewishness in preliminary correspondence with   *27* these doctors. Some undoubtedly suspected I was Jewish, though none asked me directly. On the one occasion when the matter came up specifically, the doctor concerned (during an interview near the end of the work) referred to an article in *Time* magazine describing the research and mentioning the fact that I was Jewish. His unctuous reference to the "tragic history" of our two peoples tended to confirm my impression that, had I emphasized my Jewishness from the beginning, this information would have colored and limited responses during the interviews and caused a much higher percentage of former Nazi doctors to refuse to see me. Whether talked about or not, however, my Jewishness was in some way significantly present in every interview, surely in my approach and probably in perceptions at some level of consciousness on the part of the German doctors.

Concerning the interview sequence, I first described briefly the purpose,   *28* method, and ground rules of the research, including a casual reference to my policy of recording interviews. Upon obtaining a doctor's agreement to proceed, I asked a few factual questions about his immediate situation, but essentially began by asking him to trace his educational, especially medical, background. Because those experiences were relatively less emotionally loaded than subsequent ones, he could establish a pattern of fairly free discourse along with a kind of medical dialogue with me. It would also usually require him to describe the impact of the early Nazi period on his medical study and work and on his life in general. I would then usually ask more about the man's family and cultural background, before examining in detail what he did and experienced during the Nazi years. The doctors knew that this was what I had come for, and many plunged energetically into those experiences. They tended to be less ready for detailed questions about feelings and conflicts—and about images and dreams, aspirations and self-judgments. But over the course of the interviews, the doctors came to reveal a great deal in these areas as well. With a little encouragement, these doctors—like other people I have interviewed in different research—entered readily into the interview's combined pattern of focused explorations on the one hand, and spontaneous associations on the other.

The atmosphere tended to vary from uneasy to cordial. There could be periods of genuine rapport, usually alternating with tensions, various forms of distancing, and reassertion on the part of both the Nazi doctor and myself of our essentially antithetical existences. I shall have more to say later about the worldviews these doctors expressed; but generally most adopted a rather characteristic post-Second World War, conservative political and social stance which included criticism of Nazi excesses but support for relatively authoritarian elements in German society and a certain uneasiness about what the young might be up to. Every once in a while there would be a flash of nostalgia for the Nazi times, for an era when life had intensity and meaning, whatever the conflicts engendered.

30   I never quite got over the sense of strangeness I experienced at sitting face to face with men I considered to be on the opposite side of the victimizing barricade, so to speak. Nor did I cease to feel a certain embarrassment and shame over my efforts to enter their psychological world. These feelings could be compounded when, as in a few cases, I found things to like about a man, and felt myself engaging his humanity. My central conflict, then, had to do with my usual sense of the psychological interview as an essentially friendly procedure, and my considerably less than friendly feelings toward these interviewees. I worked always within that conflict. I frequently had the impulse to divest myself of the conflict by means of aggressive moral confrontation. For the most part, I resisted that impulse—though my psychological probing could resemble such confrontation and certainly left little doubt concerning my perspective. But it was necessary to maintain that distinction; and the psychological probing, rather than moral confrontation, was required for eliciting the kind of behavioral and motivational information I sought. That distinction was also necessary, I later realized, for maintaining something important to me, my own professional identity in doing the work. So much so that it would probably be accurate to say that for me psychological probing *was* a form of moral confrontation. Yet I must add that there were moments when I wanted not only to confront but to accuse—indeed in some way attack—the man sitting opposite me. With it all, I experienced, and still experience, an obligation to be *fair* to these former Nazi doctors—that is, to make as accurate and profound an overall assessment as I am able.

31   With Auschwitz survivors the atmosphere of the interviews was entirely different. Just about all of them (with the exception of one who felt too upset by these matters to talk to me) involved themselves immediately in a common effort toward understanding Nazi doctors and what they did in the camp and elsewhere. The former inmates proved to be invaluable observers on both counts. Not surprisingly, my closest personal identification was with Jewish survivor physicians. In many cases they had come from families and social and ethnic backgrounds not too different from my own, and from areas close to my grandparents' original homes. I could not help contrasting their ordeal with my own privileged existence, and would come from these interviews literally reeling, sometimes close to tears. But I also had moving interviews with non-Jewish doctors from Poland and various other parts of Europe, many of whom had been sent to Auschwitz because of having tried to help Jews. An exception to this fundamental sympathy was one painful but revealing interview with an anti-Semitic Polish doctor who had worked closely with the Nazis and whom I shall discuss later in the book.

32   The interviews I conducted were unlike any I had previously attempted. Over their course I experienced every kind of emotion—from rage to anxiety to revulsion, and (with survivors) to admiration, shared pain, guilt, and help-

lessness—and now and then the wish that I had never begun the whole enterprise. I had nightmares about Auschwitz, sometimes involving my wife and children. When I mentioned these to my survivor friend just after I had begun the research, when they were most frequent, he looked at me without particular sympathy but perhaps with a glimmer of approval, and said softly, "Good. Now you can do the work." That helped me.

Yet, whatever the pain involved, I was not for the most part depressed or   33
extremely distraught, and in fact experienced considerable energy in carrying out the study. I was immersed in its active requirements—the elaborate arrangements in organizing and carrying out the interviews and the general sense of a task that had to be completed. The pain hit me a bit harder when I returned to the United States in the spring of 1979 and sat down alone in my study to contemplate and begin to order what I had learned. Now I was no longer in motion, my only task was to imagine myself into Auschwitz and other killing centers, as I have been attempting to do ever since. Of course, one moves imaginatively in and out of such places—one cannot stay in them too long. Contributing to my well-being in the recent part of the work was the very struggle to bring form to the material. Over the course of such an enterprise, self-discipline is made possible by the anticipation of combating an evil and those responsible for it, of having one's say.

THE LIMITS OF PSYCHOLOGICAL EXPLANATION

Psychological research is always a moral enterprise, just as moral judgments   34
inevitably include psychological assumptions. Consider, for instance, Hannah Arendt's celebrated judgment on Adolf Eichmann and the "banality of evil."[2] That phrase has emerged as a general characterization of the entire Nazi project. What I have noted about the ordinariness of Nazi doctors as men would seem to be further evidence of her thesis. But not quite. Nazi doctors were banal, but what they did was not. Repeatedly in this study, I describe banal men performing demonic acts. In doing so—or in *order* to do so—the men themselves changed; and in carrying out their actions, they themselves were no longer banal. By combining psychological and moral considerations, one can better understand the nature of the evil and the motivations of the men.

My goal in this study is to uncover psychological conditions conducive to   35
evil. To make use of psychology in that way, one must try to avoid specific pitfalls. Every discipline courts illusions of understanding that which is not understood; depth psychology, with its tenuous and often defensive relationship to science, may be especially vulnerable to that illusion. Here I recall the cautionary words of a French-speaking, Eastern European survivor physician: "The professor would like to understand what is not understandable. We ourselves who were there, and who have always asked ourselves the question and will ask

[2]Hannah Arendt, *Eichmann in Jerusalem: A Report on the Banality of Evil* (New York: Viking, 1963).

it until the end of our lives, we will never understand it, because it cannot be understood."

36   More than being merely humbling, this passage suggests an important principle: that certain events elude our full understanding, and we do best to acknowledge that a partial grasp, a direction of understanding, is the best to be expected of any approach. It is an eloquent rejection of psychological reductionism: the collapsing of complex events into single, all-embracing explanations, in ways that sweep away rather than illuminate the interlocking structures and motivations behind those events. In that kind of reductionism, one can sacrifice psychological accuracy no less than moral sensitivity.

37   Another pitfall, even in the absence of reductionism, has to do with "understanding" as a replacement for moral judgment: with the principle contained in the frequently invoked French aphorism *Tout comprendre c'est tout pardonner.* But here I would say that if such full understanding were to include a grasp of moral as well as psychological issues, the second part of the aphorism—"forgiving all"—would not follow. The danger has to be recognized, and it can be overcome only by one's remaining aware of the moral context of psychological work.

38   Partly to address some of these moral questions in connection with social and historical experience, the early psychoanalyst Otto Rank called his last major work *Beyond Psychology* (1941).[3] Rank had long been preoccupied with ethical principles he believed Freud and others had excluded from psychological work, largely because psychology itself was entrapped in its own scientific ideology. By implication, that kind of scientific-psychological ideology could reduce Auschwitz, or its SS medical practitioners, to a particular mechanism or set of mechanisms. The question of evil would then not be raised. In that sense we may say that, to address moral issues one need not remain entirely *beyond* psychology, but must constantly look at matters that most psychology has ignored. Even then we do well to acknowledge, as Rank did, that psychology can explain just so much. Concerning Auschwitz and Nazi genocide, there is a great deal about which we will remain in ignorance, but we must learn what we can.

39   Of considerable importance here is one's psychological model or paradigm. My own departs from the classic Freudian model of instinct and defense and stresses life continuity, or the symbolization of life and death.[4] The paradigm includes both an immediate and an ultimate dimension. The immediate dimension—our direct psychological involvement—includes struggles with connection and separation, integrity and disintegration, movement and stasis. Separation, disintegration, and stasis are death equivalents, images that relate to concerns about death; while the experiences of connection, integrity, and movement are associated with a sense of vitality and with symbolizations of life. The

[3]Otto Rank, *Beyond Psychology* (New York: Dover, 1958 [1941]).

[4]Robert Jay Lifton, *The Life of the Self: Toward a New Psychology* (New York: Basic Books, 1983 [1976]; *The Broken Connection: On Death and the Continuity of Life* (New York: Basic Books, 1983 [1979]).

ultimate dimension addresses larger human involvements, the sense of being connected to those who have gone before and to those who will follow our own limited life span. We thus seek a *sense* of immortality, of living on in our children, works, human influences, religious principles, or in what we look upon as eternal nature. This sense can also be achieved by the experience of transcendence: of a special psychic state so intense that within it time and death disappear—the classic experience of mystics.

One must address this ultimate dimension—what Otto Rank called "immor- *40* tality systems"[5]—if one is to begin to grasp the force of the Nazi projection of the "Thousand Year Reich." The same is true of the Nazi concept of the *Volk*—a term not only denoting "people" but conveying for many German thinkers "the union of a group of people with a transcendental 'essence' . . . [which] might be called 'nature' or 'cosmos' or 'mythos,' but in each instance . . . was fused to man's innermost nature, and represented the source of his creativity, his depth of feeling, his individuality, and his unity with other members of the *Volk*."[6] Here we may say that *Volk* came to embody an immortalizing connection with eternal racial and cultural substance. And that connection begins to put us in touch with the Nazi version of "revolutionary immortality."[7]

The paradigm also delimits the researcher's combined attitude of advocacy *41* and detachment: articulating one's inevitable moral advocacies, rather than bootlegging them in via a claim to absolute moral neutrality; and, at the same time, maintaining sufficient detachment to apply the technical and scientific principles of one's discipline. My own advocacies include those related to my being an American, a physician, a psychiatrist, a Jew, and a human being concerned with forces of destruction in our world—and to my generally critical stance on ethical, social, and political questions.

The balance sought in dealing with these staggering experiences, however *42* difficult to maintain, is what Martin Buber described as one of "distance and relation."

MEDICALIZED KILLING

In Nazi mass murder, we can say that a barrier was removed, a boundary *43* crossed: that boundary between violent imagery and periodic killing of victims (as of Jews in pogroms) on the one hand, and systematic genocide in Auschwitz and elsewhere on the other. My argument in this study is that the medicalization of killing—the imagery of killing in the name of healing—was crucial to that terrible step. At the heart of the Nazi enterprise, then, is the destruction of the boundary between healing and killing.

[5]See Lifton, *Broken Connection* [3], chap. 1.
[6]George L. Mosse, *The Crisis of German Ideology: Intellectual Origins of the Third Reich* (New York: Grosset & Dunlap, 1964), p. 4.
[7]Robert Jay Lifton, *Revolutionary Immortality: Mao Tse-tung and the Chinese Cultural Revolution* (New York: W. W. Norton, 1971 [1968]).

44   Early descriptions of Auschwitz and other death camps focused on the sadism and viciousness of Nazi guards, officers, and physicians. But subsequent students of the process realized that sadism and viciousness alone could not account for the killing of millions of people. The emphasis then shifted to the bureaucracy of killing: the faceless, detached bureaucratic function originally described by Max Weber, now applied to mass murder.[8] This focus on numbed violence is enormously important, and is consistent with what we shall observe to be the routinization of all Auschwitz function.

45   Yet these emphases are not sufficient in themselves. They must be seen in relation to the visionary motivations associated with ideology, along with the specific individual-psychological mechanisms enabling people to kill. What I call "medicalized killing" addresses these motivational principles and psychological mechanisms, and permits us to understand the Auschwitz victimizers— notably Nazi doctors—both as part of a bureaucracy of killing and as individual participants whose attitudes and behavior can be examined.

46   Medicalized killing can be understood in two wider perspectives. The first is the "surgical" method of killing large numbers of people by means of a controlled technology making use of highly poisonous gas; the method employed became a means of maintaining distance between killers and victims. This distancing had considerable importance for the Nazis in alleviating the psychological problems experienced (as attested over and over by Nazi documents) by the *Einsatzgruppen* troops who carried out face-to-face shooting of Jews in Eastern Europe—problems that did not prevent those troops from murdering 1,400,000 Jews.[9]

47   I was able to obtain direct evidence on this matter during an interview with a former *Wehrmacht* neuropsychiatrist who had treated large numbers of *Einsatzgruppen* personnel for psychological disorders. He told me that these disorders resembled combat reactions of ordinary troops: severe anxiety, nightmares, tremors, and numerous bodily complaints. But in these "killer troops," as he called them, the symptoms tended to last longer and to be more severe. He estimated that 20 percent of those doing the actual killing experienced these symptoms of psychological decompensation. About half of that 20 percent associated their symptoms mainly with the "unpleasantness" of what they had to do, while the other half seemed to have moral questions about shooting people in that way. The men had greatest psychological difficulty concerning shooting women and children, especially children. Many experienced a sense of guilt in their dreams, which could include various forms of punishment or retribution. Such psychological difficulty led the Nazis to seek a more "surgical" method of killing.

[8]See Raul Hilberg, *The Destruction of the European Jews* (Chicago: Quadrangle, 1967 [1961]); Richard L. Rubenstein, *The Cunning of History: Mass Death and the American Future* (New York: Harper & Row, 1975); Arendt, *Eichmann* [1]. Hilberg's expanded edition of his classic work was too recent to consult fully for this book; see *The Destruction of the European Jews*, 3 vols., rev. and definitive ed. (New York: Holmes & Meier, 1985).

[9]Hilberg, *Destruction* [7], p. 256.

But there is another perspective on medicalized killing that I believe to be   *48*
insufficiently recognized: *killing as a therapeutic imperative.* That kind of motivation was revealed in the words of a Nazi doctor quoted by the distinguished
survivor physician Dr. Ella Lingens-Reiner. Pointing to the chimneys in the distance, she asked a Nazi doctor, Fritz Klein, "How can you reconcile that with
your [Hippocratic] oath as a doctor?" His answer was, "Of course I am a doctor and I want to preserve life. And out of respect for human life, I would
remove a gangrenous appendix from a diseased body. The Jew is the gangrenous appendix in the body of mankind."[10]

The medical imagery was still broader. Just as Turkey during the nineteenth   *49*
century (because of the extreme decline of the Ottoman empire) was known as
the "sick man of Europe," so did pre-Hitler ideologues and Hitler himself
interpret Germany's post-First World War chaos and demoralization as an "illness," especially of the Aryan race. Hitler wrote in *Mein Kampf,* in the mid-
1920s, that *"anyone who wants to cure this era, which is inwardly sick and rotten, must first of all summon up the courage to make clear the causes of this
disease."*[11] The diagnosis was racial. The only genuine "culture-creating" race,
the Aryans, had permitted themselves to be weakened to the point of endangered survival by the "destroyers of culture," characterized as "the Jew." The
Jews were agents of "racial pollution" and "racial tuberculosis," as well as
parasites and bacteria causing sickness, deterioration, and death in the host
peoples they infested. They were the "eternal bloodsucker," "vampire," "germ
carrier," "peoples' parasite," and "maggot in a rotting corpse."[12] The cure
had to be radical: that is (as one scholar put it), by "cutting out the 'canker of
decay,' propagating the worthwhile elements and letting the less valuable wither
away, . . . [and] 'the extirpation of all those categories of people considered to
be worthless or dangerous.'"[13]

Medical metaphor blended with concrete biomedical ideology in the Nazi   *50*
sequence from coercive sterilization to direct medical killing to the death
camps. The unifying principle of the biomedical ideology was that of a deadly
racial disease, the sickness of the Aryan race; the cure, the killing of all Jews.

Thus, for Hans Frank, jurist and General Governor of Poland during the   *51*
Nazi occupation, "the Jews were a lower species of life, a kind of vermin,
which upon contact infected the German people with deadly diseases." When
the Jews in the area he ruled had been killed, he declared that "now a sick

---

[10]A slightly different, published version is found in Ella Lingens-Reiner, *Prisoners of Fear* (London: Gol-
lancz, 1948), pp. 1–2.

[11]Adolf Hitler, *Mein Kampf* (Boston: Houghton Mifflin, 1943 [1925–26]), p. 435.

[12]Ibid., pp. 150, 300–308, 312–13. For scholarly treatments of Hitler's (and earlier) metaphors for the
Jews, see Eberhard Jäckel, *Hitler's Weltanschauung: A Blueprint for Power* (Middletown, Conn.: Wesleyan
University Press, 1972 [1969]); Rudolph Binion, *Hitler Among the Germans* (New York: Elsevier, 1976); Lucy
S. Dawidowicz, *The War Against the Jews, 1933–1945* (New York: Holt, Rinehart & Winston, 1975), pp. 19–
21, 55–56; Uriel Tal, *Christians and Jews in Germany: Religion, Politics and Ideology in the Second Reich,
1870–1914* (Ithaca: Cornell University Press, 1975), pp. 259–89.

[13]Hans Buchheim, quoted in Helmut Krausnick, "The Persecution of the Jews," in Krausnick et al., *Anatomy of the SS State* (New York: Walker, 1968 [1965]), p. 15.

Europe would become healthy again."[14] It was a religion of the will—the will as "an all-encompassing metaphysical principle";[15] and what the Nazis "willed" was nothing less than total control over life and death. While this view is often referred to as "social Darwinism," the term applies only loosely, mostly to the Nazi stress on natural "struggle" and on "survival of the fittest." The regime actually rejected much of Darwinism; since evolutionary theory is more or less democratic in its assumption of a common beginning for all races, it is therefore at odds with the Nazi principle of inherent Aryan racial virtue.[16]

52   Even more specific to the biomedical vision was the crude genetic imagery, combined with still cruder eugenic visions. Here Heinrich Himmler, as high priest, spoke of the leadership's task as being "like the plant-breeding specialist who, when he wants to breed a pure new strain from a well-tried species that has been exhausted by too much cross-breeding, first goes over the field to cull the unwanted plants."[17]

53   The Nazi project, then, was not so much Darwinian or social Darwinist as a vision of absolute control over the evolutionary process, over the biological human future. Making widespread use of the Darwinian term "selection," the Nazis sought to take over the functions of nature (natural selection) and God (the Lord giveth and the Lord taketh away) in orchestrating their own "selections," their own version of human evolution.

54   In these visions the Nazis embraced not only versions of medieval mystical anti-Semitism but also a newer (nineteenth- and twentieth-century) claim to "scientific racism." Dangerous Jewish characteristics could be linked with alleged data of scientific disciplines, so that a "mainstream of racism" formed from "the fusion of anthropology, eugenics, and social thought."[18] The resulting "racial and social biology" could make vicious forms of anti-Semitism seem intellectually respectable to learned men and women.

55   One can speak of the Nazi state as a "biocracy." The model here is a theocracy, a system of rule by priests of a sacred order under the claim of divine prerogative. In the case of the Nazi biocracy, the divine prerogative was that of cure through purification and revitalization of the Aryan race: "From a dead mechanism which only lays claim to existence for its own sake, there must be formed a living organism with the exclusive aim of serving a higher idea." Just as in a theocracy, the state itself is no more than a vehicle for the divine purpose, so in the Nazi biocracy was the state no more than a means to achieve *"a mission of the German people on earth"*: that of *"assembling and preserving the*

[14]Hilberg, *Destruction* [7], p. 12.

[15]J. P. Stern, *Hitler: The Führer and the People* (Glasgow: Fontana/Collins, 1971), p. 70. The celebration of that religious impulse was epitomized by the gigantic Nuremberg rally of 1934, whose theme, "The Triumph of the Will," became the title of Leni Riefenstahl's noted film. Riefenstahl, in an interview with an assistant of mine, made clear that Hitler himself provided that slogan.

[16]Mosse, *German Ideology* [5], p. 103.

[17]Himmler, quoted in Krausnick, "Persecution" [12], p. 14.

[18]George L. Mosse, *Toward the Final Solution: A History of European Racism* (New York: Fertig, 1978), p. 77.

most valuable stocks of basic racial elements in this [Aryan] *people . . .* [and] *. . . raising them to a dominant position.*"[19] The Nazi biocracy differed from a classical theocracy in that the biological priests did not actually rule. The clear rulers were Adolf Hitler and his circle, not biological theorists and certainly not the doctors. (The difference, however, is far from absolute: even in a theocracy, highly politicized rulers may make varying claims to priestly authority.) In any case, Nazi ruling authority was maintained in the name of the higher biological principle.

Among the biological authorities called forth to articulate and implement   56
"scientific racism"—including physical anthropologists, geneticists, and racial theorists of every variety—doctors inevitably found a unique place. It is they who work at the border of life and death, who are most associated with the awesome, death-defying, and sometimes death-dealing aura of the primitive shaman and medicine man. As bearers of this shamanistic legacy and contemporary practitioners of mysterious healing arts, it is they who are likely to be called upon to become biological activists.

I have mentioned my primary interest in Nazi doctors' participation in medi-   57
calized or biologized killing. We shall view their human experiments as related to the killing process and to the overall Nazi biomedical vision. At Nuremberg, doctors were tried only limitedly for their involvement in killing, partly because its full significance was not yet understood.[20]

In Auschwitz, Nazi doctors presided over the murder of most of the one mil-   58
lion victims of that camp. Doctors performed selections—both on the ramp among arriving transports of prisoners and later in the camps and on the medical blocks. Doctors supervised the killing in the gas chambers and decided when the victims were dead. Doctors conducted a murderous epidemiology, sending to the gas chamber groups of people with contagious diseases and sometimes including everyone else who might be on the medical block. Doctors ordered and supervised, and at times carried out, direct killing of debilitated patients on the medical blocks by means of phenol injections into the bloodstream or the heart. In connection with all of these killings, doctors kept up a pretense of medical legitimacy: for deaths of Auschwitz prisoners and of outsiders brought there to be killed, they signed false death certificates listing spurious illnesses. Doctors consulted actively on how best to keep selections running smoothly; on how many people to permit to remain alive to fill the slave labor requirements of the I. G. Farben enterprise at Auschwitz; and on how to burn the enormous numbers of bodies that strained the facilities of the crematoria.

In sum, we may say that doctors were given much of the responsibility for   59
the murderous ecology of Auschwitz—the choosing of victims, the carrying through of the physical and psychological mechanics of killing, and the balanc-

---

[19]Hitler, *Mein Kampf* [10], pp. 397–98.
[20]*Nuremberg Medical Case*, especially vol. I, pp. 8–17 (the indictment) and 27–74 (opening statement by Chief Prosecutor Telford Taylor, 9 December 1946); personal interview with James M. McHaney, prosecutor of the Medical Case.

ing of killing and work functions in the camp. While doctors by no means ran Auschwitz, they did lend it a perverse medical aura. As one survivor who closely observed the process put the matter, "Auschwitz was like a medical operation," and "the killing program was led by doctors from beginning to end."

60   We may say that the doctor standing at the ramp represented a kind of omega point, a mythical gatekeeper between the worlds of the dead and the living, a final common pathway of the Nazi vision of therapy via mass murder.

WRITING AND DISCUSSION QUESTIONS

Informative

1. What does Lifton mean when he says, "The reversal of healing and killing became an organizing principle of the work"? What, in other words, was the logic behind Nazi killing? Why does Lifton see sadism as an incomplete explanation?

2. How does Lifton interpret the Israeli dentist's words, "This world is not this world"? How does his interpretation explain our resistance to or hesitation in studying evil?

3. Lifton is asked whether the Nazi doctors were humans or beasts. What is his answer and what is the significance of the question? What interpretation of Arendt's phrase, "the banality of evil," does Lifton offer?

4. How did Lifton approach his subjects? Why was the "informed consent" requirement ironic?

5. What is the relation between Nazi "scientific racism" and Darwinism?

Persuasive

1. Describe some of the reactions of the doctors to Lifton's questions. Why did many try to characterize themselves as decent folks?

2. What role did "distancing" have in "medicalized killing"? In what sense is the same distancing characteristic of life in our industrialized culture?

3. What value do you see in studying genocides like those that occurred in Cambodia in the late 1970s or Armenia in the early part of this century?

4. Lifton reveals his own responses—"from rage to anxiety to revulsion, and (with survivors) to admiration, shared pain, guilt, and hopelessness"—including his struggles to maintain his "professional identity." Argue that these revelations of personal response are or are not relevant or appropriate. Consider the difference between professional identity and scientific objectivity, and the extent to which moral and ethical issues should enter into such a study.

Personal

1. Could anything like what Lifton describes happen again? What tendencies to totalitarianism do you see today in the United States? How does science or pseudoscience enter into these tendencies?

2. Albert Camus, speaking from his own experiences during World War II as a member of the French anti-Nazi underground, has stated that we must strive to be neither victims nor executioners, that we must avoid institutions and actions that create these categories. Is this possible? Before answering, carefully consider the ways you can be victimized and can victimize others, however distanced you may be.

3. Do you think the Holocaust was a Jewish or a human tragedy?

CHAPTER WRITING ASSIGNMENTS

1. Choose some important area of scientific development—such as the discovery of the atom; relativity; quantum theory; the full extent of the electromagnetic spectrum; red shift and the expanding universe; or DNA—and examine whether and why it may be considered a scientific revolution. Explore not only the technological implications, but also the impact on culture. What fundamental assumptions or values has the new idea forced us to rethink?

2. In his famous essay, *The Two Cultures,* written more than three decades ago, British author C. P. Snow argues that the worlds of the scientist and the humanist are so different that they represent not just divergent views, but divided cultures. He also argues, however, that, as a whole, scientists are far more knowledgeable in and appreciative of the humanities than humanists are of the sciences and that in fact the responsibility for this division rests primarily in the humanistic bias of the larger culture and its educational systems. The results are widespread ignorance of science and the perpetuation of the division between the two cultures. Argue whether this is an accurate assessment of the situation today.

3. What problems or dangers do you see in maintaining a democratic society based on complex technology when the majority of educated people in that society are ignorant of the science on which the technology is based?

4. Science excites antipathy among many people partly because some thinkers have seen it as displacing older value systems. In 1827, for example, Thomas Babington Macaulay praised scientific learning and its contributions to progress by deprecating the "ancient philosophy," by which he meant the humanistic tradition: "The ancient philosophy was a treadmill, not a path. It was made up of revolving questions, of controversies which were always beginning again. It might indeed sharpen and invigorate the minds of those who devoted themselves to it. . . . But such disputes could add nothing to the stock of knowledge." In 1866, Thomas Henry Huxley similarly praised science at the expense of religion, arguing that "the man of science has learned to believe in justification, not by faith, but by verification" and that "as our race approaches its maturity," it will discover "that there is but one kind of knowledge and but one method of acquiring it." What is your response to such claims?

5. According to your readings in this chapter, argue whether science ought to be seen as in conflict with, complementary to, or irrelevant to humanism.

6. Pursue the same argument in terms of the relation between science and religion.

7. Write a dialogue that explores the argument in question 5 or 6 by using any two writers.

8. Choose some source of science news intended for a general audience—the science section of *Newsweek* or *Time,* for example, or, if you are more ambitious, *Science News* or the "Science and the Citizen" section of *Scientific American*—and read their recent offerings over a period of a few weeks or months. Note the items you find especially interesting, and those you think are important or significant, and with that information, report why the general public should make an effort to stay informed on scientific matters.

9. Consider the difference between scientific advancements, like the development of atomic theory or the discovery of DNA, and technology, like computers or birth control pills. Explain which has the greater impact on our values, scientific theory or its applications.

Chapter Six

THE DEMOCRATIC REVOLUTION

Imagine being stranded on a desert island with a group of your peers. There is ample food and shelter, and the climate is hospitable. You feel assured of rescue but believe that it will come only after a prolonged stay. The central problem and challenge of your group, then, is to organize yourselves so that certain necessities of living can be obtained and evenly distributed. You are aware that without this organization, harm may come to those who are weaker and less able to fend for themselves. In fact, any individual or group, whether weak or strong, becomes vulnerable if unfair organization results in a faction that gains a disproportionate share of power. Clearly, the island scenario above reflects the story in William Golding's novel *Lord of the Flies*, and is one view of the continuing story of individual human beings thrown into groups and left to prosper or die.

The central problem of any group, then, that assembles to live together, whether on a mainland or a deserted island, whether as a family or a society, is balancing the conflicting claims of freedom and authority, of individual liberty and communal need. All government starts by recognizing the validity of these claims and then by attempting to resolve the conflicts rising among them. One example of this conflicting claim is the wartime military draft, which requires individuals to relinquish their rights to personal liberty by submitting to the defense needs of their country (as was so controversial during the Vietnam war). Other familiar claims raise similar controversial issues: prayer in public schools (how can the interests of those who do not want to pray and those who do want to pray be simultaneously respected?), and capital punishment (is the community

343

protected and is it justified in denying the "right to life" of the few who may have committed a capital offense?). A society earns its right to call itself successful and civilized when it works out an optimal balance between these conflicting claims. At the same time that it protects or maximizes individual needs and liberties, it also provides for a reasonable degree of security and protection of the public good. The history of democracy in the last 2500 years reveals increasingly effective ways of working out this balance.

Societies have not only sought a balance of individual freedoms and collective goods, but they have also appealed to different kinds of authority to work out that balance. While the early Jews and Christians appealed to revelation and the word of God as their authority, the ancient Greeks appealed to reason, dialogue, and debate. Rather than kings and rulers dictating what was acceptable, the freemen of Athens, through a representative council of free male citizens, governed the city. They gained the right to do this through heredity (by virture of being free Athenian males), and chaotic as the system was, taxes, laws, wars, and the rights and obligations of citizenship were debated regularly by hundreds of men in the assembly or town square. Thus, the institution of the city–state that was governed by principle and reason was born. The Greek "democracy," sadly though, only lasted several hundred years.

From our standpoint today, it may seem oppressive and intolerable that the great majority of ancient Greeks, that is, slaves, women, and subject peoples were effectively excluded from the decision-making processes. Even so, the dominant governance systems throughout the West up until the seventeenth century, until the beginning of the Enlightenment, limited participation even further. For women, the oppression lasted longer: suffrage in this country did not come for them until 1920. And for American blacks, it was delayed even longer: the civil rights movement of the 1960s was the real beginning of liberation and participation. There are a number of reasons that explain why the people continued to practice obedience to some higher authority for so many hundreds of years. First, obedience to the authority of priest or king, or some combination of these two, was easy for the masses of peasants, serfs, and slaves, for such obedience was a habit. It required little thought or risk and depended on the identification and patronage of a few strong male leaders who invested themselves with special powers. In fact, kings and nobles successfully claimed they were closer to God than were the common classes and, therefore, represented God on earth; thus, they ruled with "divine right." Second, the political benefits, rights, and privileges accruing to the masses were few by our standards, but there was still a modicum of order and the opportunity of some meagre gains, such as protection from starvation.

Two things had to happen before obedience to higher authority was no longer practiced by the common classes, which would lead to their full participation in government. First, the authority of the old institutions of church and state had to come into question. The power of religious and secular rulers was grounded in revelation and based on heredity, and before that power could be shared with greater numbers of people, a fundamental shift in thinking had to occur. People's concerns regarding life were typically focused on preparation for heaven, not earth; therefore, before any change in political order could occur, it would have to be preceded by a change in this perspective, a change that would emphasize life on earth. Second, a new form of authority would have to recognize the rights and powers of the people, replacing the powers vested in priests and kings. As the growing middle classes began to place more faith in their own rights, as well as in reason and change, they demanded more liberties and political freedoms and eventually the right of rebellion.

The first great rebellion of the common classes against a tyrannical central power was the French Revolution of 1789. Although surely an act of brutish violence and force, the French Revolution was ultimately about ideas, ideas that changed the prevailing thought about the individual's relationship to society. (A number of smaller peasant revolts and what is referred to as the Glorious Revolution preceded the French Revolution, but these did not have the long-standing impact of the more important French Revolution.) According to Vartan Gregoran, president of Brown University,

> The French Revolution espoused for the first time in the history of the West a truly universal civilization, transcending cultural, national, ethnic, social and racial boundaries by proclaiming the fundamental and inviolable rights of all the peoples of the world to freedom and equality. Insofar as it translated those ideals into a living reality, the French Revolution can be said to have founded the modern era and to have given shape for the first time to the principles and institutions by which we now define our purposes and measure our achievements in public life.[1]

The combined efforts of three political philosophers would lay the foundation for the ideas just described and, ultimately, for the French and American Revolutions. In the seventeenth and eighteenth centuries, Thomas Hobbes, John Locke, and Jean-Jacques Rousseau established the basic vocabulary and principles that changed the thinking about government. Hobbes introduced the idea of people living in a state of nature, and though all were equal, all were selfish and innately brutish and needed controls imposed upon them, if for nothing else, at least for self-preservation. Thus, Hobbes justified the absolute rule of the monarch, which though it protected people, it deprived them of many rights. Locke and Rousseau also believed in the equality of man, but were not as cynical. They also believed that people lived in a state of nature but that this nature was not a jungle that illicited only savage instincts. Rather, it was a political society based on natural laws and rights stemming from God. In such a society agreements could be arrived at through forms of state governance established to protect its citizens. Thus, a social contract, much like God's covenant with the early Jews

---

[1] *New York Times*, March 12, 1989, p. 26.

as expressed in Genesis and Exodus, would guide relations in a society (except the covenant is among people, not between people and God). It should become clear that democracies, especially those in the last 200 years, have worked out the institutions and practices to balance individual rights with the public good much more effectively than the Greeks had. The success of the democratic government, in fact, accounts in large part for the changes we have recently seen in the Soviet Union and Eastern Europe.

Thomas Jefferson and other "founding fathers" of the United States codified these principles in three documents that would not only stand the severe test of more than 200 years, but also serve as the governance model for numerous other countries, many in the Third World. Our Declaration of Independence laid out the basis by which a government or state is entitled to govern. Importantly, the Declaration established that the consent and the human rights of the governed take precedence over the will and whims of the state. The Constitution, which is not included as a reading in this text, defines the structure and operation of that government, establishing a division of power into three branches and a system of checks and balances that has somewhat effectively ensured a fair distribution of wealth and power. Last, the Bill of Rights, the first ten amendments of the Constitution, defines and protects individual rights.

▼

JOHN LOCKE, FROM "AN ESSAY CONCERNING THE TRUE ORIGINAL, EXTENT, AND END OF CIVIL GOVERNMENT"

Along with other political thinkers like Thomas Hobbes and Jean-Jacques Rousseau, John Locke (1632–1704) contributed greatly to our understanding of what is generally called "social contract theory"; one aspect of the theory is concerned with what happens when individuals live in groups. Other than his reputation as a political philosopher, he is also known as the founder of the British school of empiricism. Educated at Oxford University, Locke received his bachelor's degree in 1656, became a lecturer in 1660, and taught Greek, rhetoric, and philosophy. While preparing for a master's degree in philosophy and while studying medicine, he met the influential Earl of Shaftesbury who was on a chance visit to Oxford. Providing medical attention to the politician, Locke found that he and Shaftesbury thought along the same lines, in as much as both men were strongly committed to freedom for the common person. As a result, Locke spent the better part of the next two decades working for Shaftesbury, who propelled Locke into numerous political battles.

In the 1680s, before Locke wrote the selection that follows, rumors of a plot to murder King Charles II (ruled England 1660–1685), a Protestant, and to replace him with his brother, James II, a Roman Catholic, circulated widely. Locke's employer, Shaftesbury, was at the time the First Minister of King Charles II, and he was becoming increasingly influential. To secure his furture as Minister and his relationship to the king, Shaftesbury tried to pass a law excluding Roman Catholics from the succession. The supporters of James II countered with an argument for the divine right of kings, which would allow James II, in the event of his succession, to choose whatever religion pleased him. To support his own case, James II reissued a book written by Robert Filmer championing the divine right of kings. Shaftesbury asked his friend Locke to respond to this book.

In 1690, Locke published *Two Treatises of Government*. The first treatise was primarily a refutation of the principles of absolute monarchy and the divine right of kings, which were used throughout the centuries by strong and often tyrannical individuals as the basis for their authority. The second treatise, excerpted here, is Locke's argument of the true origin of government. This treatise uses the results of the previous argument against the divine right of kings as points of departure for developing the idea of a governmnet based on human liberty and human rights.

During the previous thousand years or so, a number of arguments based on both reason and scripture had been developed to justify the political status quo, which in Europe, for the most part, was monarchy founded on divine right. In fact, loyalty to the established monarch had come to be seen in most states as a religious obligation, not merely a civil one. Rebellion was not simply a crime, but a sin. This was an issue, however, that a number of circumstances forced England to radically rethink. In that predominantly Protestant country, the attempt of Catholic King James II (who ruled England from 1685–1688) to reinstitute Roman Catholicism as the established church of England would have serious implications. Therefore, Locke grounded his arguments in both scripture and reason, and he examined scripture to refute previous arguments and to cite Biblical precedent for his claims. He examined the state of nature to redefine some of the fundamental, rational assumptions about the nature of humanity.

Just two years before the publication of Locke's *Two Treatises*, King James II had been deposed by the English Parliament, and a new monarchy had then been set up in the clearly Protestant persons of William and Mary. Locke's publication was only one of many attempts, though the farthest reaching, to come to terms with this political conflict and to justify what the English called this Glorious Revolution of 1688, glorious because there had been no civil war, James II had left for France, and no blood had been shed. This conflict demonstrated that some control could be exerted over the monarchy and that political compromises could be made.

Locke is the creator of a philosophical concept called the "social contract," which is an agreement between persons and the community or state they inhabit. For any persons trying to live together, each must exert some control over his impulses if the group is to survive as a cooperative entity. This is as true of a family as it is of a school group or a townspeople. Such control can work only if a bargain is struck: the individual agrees to do certain things for the "state," and the "state" agrees to provide something in return. To illustrate, a college student in a dormitory will agree to make certain accommodations for this neighbors, such as not playing the tuba at 3:00 AM; in return, he will be promised a degree of civility and courtesy from all of the other students in the dormitory. Completing the analogy, for instance, if I expect the community to provide me with education, health, and security, I must be willing, in return, to keep my side of the bargain and provide my community with productive services that contribute to the welfare of others, to obey reasonable laws, and to defend my community when it is threatened.

On a broader scale, Locke referred to the individual living without restraint as someone existing within a "state of nature." To function in a community, though, people must strive to live in a "state of equality," that is, "no one ought to harm another in his life, health, liberty or possessions."

▼

from *An Essay Concerning the True Original, Extent, and End of Civil Government*
JOHN LOCKE

I

1 1. It having been shewn in the foregoing discourse,

1. That Adam had not, either by natural right of fatherhood, nor by positive donation from God, any such authority over his children, or dominion over the world, as is pretended.
2. That if he had, his heirs yet had no right to it.
3. That if his heirs had, there being no law of nature nor positive law of God that determines which is the right heir in all cases that may arise, the right of succession, and consequently of bearing rule, could not have been certainly determined.
4. That if even that had been determined, yet the knowledge of which is the eldest line of Adam's posterity being so long since utterly lost, that in the races of mankind and families of the world, there remains not to one above another, the least pretence to be the eldest house, and to have the right of inheritance.

2 All these premises having, as I think, been clearly made out, it is impossible that the rulers now on earth should make any benefit, or derive any the least shadow of authority from that, which is held to be the fountain of all power, *Adam's private dominion and paternal jurisdiction;* so that he that will not give just occasion to think that all government in the world is the product only of force and violence, and that men live together by no other rules but that of beasts, where the strongest carries it, and so lay a foundation for perpetual disorder and mischief, tumult, sedition, and rebellion (things that the followers of that hypothesis so loudly cry out against), must of necessity find out another rise of government, another original of political power, and another way of designing and knowing the persons that have it, than what Sir Robert Filmer hath taught us.

3 2. To this purpose, I think it may not be amiss, to set down what I take to be political power; that the power of a magistrate over a subject may be distinguished from that of a father over his children, a master over his servant, a husband over his wife, and a lord over his slave. All which distinct powers happening sometimes together in the same man, if he be considered under these different relations, it may help us to distinguish these powers one from another, and shew the difference betwixt a ruler of a commonwealth, a father of a family, and a captain of a galley.

3. Political power, then, I take to be a right of making laws with penalties of 4
death, and consequently all less penalties, for the regulating and preserving of property, and of employing the force of the community, in the execution of such laws, and in the defence of the commonwealth from foreign injury; and all this only for the public good.

II

Of the State of Nature

4. To understand political power aright, and derive it from its original, we 5
must consider, what state all men are naturally in, and that is, a state of perfect freedom to order their actions, and dispose of their possessions and persons, as they think fit, within the bounds of the law of nature, without asking leave, or depending upon the will of any other man.

A state also of equality, wherein all the power and jurisdiction is reciprocal, 6
no one having more than another; there being nothing more evident, than that creatures of the same species and rank, promiscuously born to all the same advantages of nature, and the use of the same faculties, should also be equal one amongst another without subordination or subjection, unless the lord and master of them all should, by any manifest declaration of his will, set one above another, and confer on him, by an evident and clear appointment, an undoubted right to dominion and sovereignty.

5. This equality of men by nature, the judicious Hooker looks upon as so 7
evident in itself, and beyond all question, that he makes it the foundation of that obligation to mutual love amongst men, on which he builds the duties they owe one another, and from whence he derives the great maxims of justice and charity. His words are:

'The like natural inducement hath brought men to know that it is no less 8
their duty, to love others than themselves; for seeing those things which are equal, must needs all have one measure; if I cannot but wish to receive good, even as much at every man's hands, as any man can wish unto his own soul, how should I look to have any part of my desire herein satisfied, unless myself be careful to satisfy the like desire, which is undoubtedly in other men. We all being of one and the same nature; to have any thing offered them repugnant to this desire, must needs in all respects grieve them as much as me; so that if I do harm, I must look to suffer, there being no reason that others should shew greater measure of love to me, than they have by me shewed unto them; my

desire therefore to be loved of my equals in nature, as much as possible may be, imposeth upon me a natural duty of bearing to themward fully the like affection; from which relation of equality between ourselves and them that are as ourselves, what several rules and canons natural reason hath drawn, for direction of life, no man is ignorant.' *Eccl, Pol.*, lib. i.

9 6. But though this be a state of liberty, yet it is not a state of licence: though man in that state have an uncontrollable liberty to dispose of his person or possessions, yet he has not liberty to destroy himself, or so much as any creature in his possession, but where some nobler use than its bare preservation calls for it. The state of nature has a law of nature to govern it, which obligates every one, and reason, which is that law, teaches all mankind, who will but consult it, that being all equal and independent, no one ought to harm another in his life, health, liberty, or possessions: for men being all the workmanship of one omnipotent, and infintely wise maker; all the servants of one sovereign master, sent into the world by his order, and about his business; they are his property, whose workmanship they are, made to last during his, not one another's pleasure: and being furnished with like faculties, sharing all in one community of nature, there cannot be supposed any such subordination among us, that may authorize us to destroy one another, as if we were made for one another's uses, as the inferior ranks of creatures are for ours. Every one, as he is bound to preserve himself, and not to quit his station wilfully, so by the like reason, when his own preservation comes not in competition, ought he as much as he can to preserve the rest of mankind, and not unless it be to do justice on an offender, take away, or impair the life, or what tends to the preservation of the life, the liberty, health, limb or goods of another.

10 7. And that all men may be restrained from invading others rights, and from doing hurt to one another, and the law of nature be observed, which willeth the peace and preservation of all mankind, the execution of the law of nature is, in that state, put into every man's hands, whereby every one has a right to punish the transgressors of that law to such a degree, as may hinder its violation. For the law of nature would, as all other laws that concern men in this world, be in vain, if there were nobody that in the state of nature had a power to execute that law, and thereby preserve the innocent and restrain offenders. And if any one in the state of nature may punish another for any evil he has done, every one may do so: for in that state of perfect equality where naturally there is no superiority or jurisdiction of one over another, what any may do in prosecution of that law, every one must needs have a right to do.

11 8. And thus, in the state of nature, one man comes by a power over another; but yet no absolute or arbitrary power, to use a criminal, when he has got him in his hands, according to the passionate heats, or boundless extravagancy of his own will; but only to retribute to him, so far as calm reason and conscience dictates, what is proportionate to his transgression, which is so much as may serve for reparation and restraint: for these two are the only reasons why one man may lawfully do harm to another, which is that we call punishment. In transgressing the law of nature, the offender declares himself to live by another rule than that of reason and common equity, which is that measure God has set

to the actions of men for their mutual secruity, and so he becomes dangerous to mankind, the tie, which is to secure them from injury and violence, being slighted and broken by him, which being a trespass against the whole species, and the peace and safety of it, provided for by the law of nature, every man upon this score, by the right he hath to preserve mankind in general, may restrain, or where it is necessary, destroy things noxious to them, and so may bring such evil on any one, who hath transgressed that law, as may make him repent the doing of it, and thereby deter him, and, by his example others, from doing the like mischief. And in this case, and upon this ground, every man hath a right to punish the offender, and be executioner of the law of nature.

9. I doubt not but this will seem a very strange doctrine to some men; but *12* before they condemn it, I desire them to resolve me, by what right any prince or state can put to death, or punish an alien, for any crime he commits in their country. 'Tis certain their laws, by virture of any sanction they receive from the promulgated will of the legislative, reach not a stranger: they speak not to him, or, if they did, is bound to hearken to them. The legislative authority, by which they are in force over the subjects of that commonwealth, hath no power over him. Those who have the supreme power of making laws in England, France or Holland, are to an Indian, but like the rest of the world, men without authority: and therefore, if by the law of nature every man hath not a power to punish offences against it, as he soberly judges the case to require, I see not how the magistrate of any community can punish an alien of another country; since, in reference to him, they can have no more power than what every man naturally may have over another.

10. Besides the crime which consists in violating the law, and varying from *13* the right rule of reason, whereby a man so far becomes degenerate, and declares himself to quit the principles of human nature and to be a noxious creature, there is commonly injury done, and some person or other, some other man receives damage by his transgression; in which case he who hath received any damage, has, besides the right of punishment common to him with other men, a particular right to seek reparation from him that has done it: and any other person, who finds it just, may also join with him that is injured, and assist him in recovering from the offender so much as may make satisfaction for the harm he has suffered.

11. From these two distinct rights, the one of punishing the crime for *14* restraint, and preventing the like offence, which right of punishing is in every-body; the other of taking reparation, which belongs only to the injured party, comes it to pass that the magistrate, who by being magistrate hath the common right of punishing put into his hands, can often, where the public good demands not the execution of the law, remit the punishment of criminal offences by his own authority, but yet cannot remit the satisfaction due to any private man for the damage he has received. That, he who has suffered the damage has a right to demand in his own name, and he alone can remit: the damnified person has this power of appropriating to himself the goods or ser-vice of the offender, by right of self-preservation, as every man has a power to punish the crime, to prevent its being committed again, by the right he has of

preserving all mankind, and doing all reasonable things he can in order to that end: and thus it is, that every man, in the state of nature, has a power to kill a murderer, both to deter others from doing the like injury, which no reparation can compensate, by the example of the punishment that attends it from every body, and also to secure men from the attempts of a criminal, who having renounced reason, the common rule and measure God hath given to mankind, hath, by the unjust violence and slaughter he hath committed upon one, declared war against all mankind, and therefore may be destroyed as a lion or a tiger, one of those wild savage beasts, with whom men can have no society nor security: and upon this is grounded that great law of nature, *Whoso sheddeth man's blood, by man shall his blood be shed*. And Cain was so fully convinced, that every one had a right to destroy such a criminal, that after the murder of his brother, he cries out, *Every one that findeth me shall slay me;* so plain was it writ in the hearts of all mankind.

15   12. By the same reason may a man in the state of nature punish the lesser breaches of that law. It will perhaps be demanded, with death? I answer, each transgression may be punished to that degree, and with so much severity, as will suffice to make it an ill bargain to the offender, give him cause to repent, and terrify others from doing the like. Every offence, that can be committed in the state of nature, may in the state of nature be also punished equally, and as far forth as it may, in a commonwealth: for though it would be besides my present purpose, to enter here into the particulars of the law of nature, or its measures of punishment; yet, it is certain there is such a law, and that too as intelligible and plain to a rational creature, and a studier of that law, as the positive laws of commonwealths: nay, possibly plainer; as much as reason is easier to be understood, than the fancies and intricate contrivances of men, following contrary and hidden interests put into words; for so truly are a great part of the municipal laws of countries, which are only so far right, as they are founded on the law of nature, by which they are to be regulated and interpreted.

16   13. To this strange doctrine, *viz.* That in the state of nature every one has the executive power of the law of nature, I doubt not but it will be objected, that it is unreasonable for men to be judges in their own cases, that self-love will make men partial to themselves and their friends: and on the other side, ill-nature, passion and revenge will carry them too far in punishing others; and hence nothing but confusion and disorder will follow; and that therefore God hath certainly appointed government to restrain the partiality and violence of men. I easily grant that civil government is the proper remedy for the inconveniences of the state of nature, which must certainly be great where men may be judges in their own case, since 'tis easy to be imagined, that he who was so unjust as to do his brother an injury, will scarce be so just as to condemn himself for it; but I shall desire those who make this objection, to remember, that absolute monarchs are but men; and if government is to be the remedy of those evils, which necessarily follow from men's being judges in their own cases, and the state of nature is therefore not to be endured, I desire to know what kind of government that is, and how much better it is than the state of nature, where

one man commanding a multitude, has the liberty to be judge in his own case, and may do to all his subjects whatever he pleases, without the least question or control of those who execute his pleasure? and in whatsoever he doth, whether led by reason, mistake or passion, must be submitted to? which men in the state of nature are not bound to do one to another. And if he that judges, judges amiss in his own, or any other case, he is answerable for it to the rest of mankind.

14. 'Tis often asked as a mighty objection, where are, or ever were there any men in such a state of nature? To which it may suffice as an answer at present, that since all princes and rulers of *independent* governments all through the world, are in a state of nature, 'tis plain the world never was, nor never will be, without numbers of men in that state. I have named all governors of *independent* communities, whether they are, or are not, in league with others: for 'tis not every compact that puts an end to the state of nature between men, but only this one of agreeing together mutually to enter into one community, and make one body politic; other promises, and compacts, men may make one with another, and yet still be in the state of nature. The promises and bargains for truck, etc. between the two men in the desert island, mentioned by Garcilasso de la Vega, in his history of Peru; or between a Swiss and an Indian, in the woods of America, are binding to them, though they are perfectly in a state of nature, in reference to one another: for truth and keeping of faith belongs to men as men, and not as members of society. 17

15. To those that say, there were never any men in the state of nature, I will not only oppose the authority of the judicious Hooker, *Eccl. Pol.* lib. i. *sect.* 10, where he says, 'the laws which have been hitherto mentioned, *i.e.*, the laws of nature, do bind men absolutely, even as they are men, although they have never any settled fellowship, never any solemn agreement amongst themselves what to do, or not to do: but forasmuch as we are not by ourselves sufficient to furnish ourselves with competent store of things, needful for such a life as our nature doth desire, a life fit for the dignity of man; therefore to supply those defects and imperfections which are in us, as living singly and solely by ourselves, we are naturally induced to seek communion and fellowship with others: this was the cause of men uniting themselves at first in politic societies.' But I moreover affirm, that all men are naturally in that state, and remain so, till by their own consents they make themselves members of some politic society; and I doubt not in the sequel of this discourse, to make it very clear. 18

WRITING AND DISCUSSION QUESTIONS

Informative

1. Locke opens his essay by arguing against the divine right of kings as the basis for political power. According to Locke, what ought to be the legitimate source of political power?

2. Locke describes a state of nature and a law of nature. Explain each and how a law of nature should work.
3. Paragraph 6 is essential to Locke's argument for equality. Explain Locke's view on equality.
4. Trace the use of faith and scripture through Locke's essay. What particular use of religion does he make in his argument?

Persuasive

1. Argue for or against the validity of the political analogy between family and the state.
2. Argue that God and faith play a major role in Locke's thinking, even more than do observation and reason.
3. Argue for or against the position taken by Filmer, that liberty allows one ''to do what he lists, to live as he pleases, and not to be tied by any laws.''
4. Argue that Locke's concept of the contract between the governor and the governed is analogous to the idea of a covenant between God and the Jews.

Personal

1. Describe one freedom you willingly or unwillingly give up for the benefit of the community.
2. Are people today excessively interested in self at the cost of family and community interests? Explain your position on this question.
3. Describe your relationship to the U.S., state, or local government as one of full, moderate, or minimal interest and participation. Explain why you have settled into such an arrangement.
4. Given your attitudes and lifestyle, is Locke's argument reasonable?
5. What dangers do you see in accepting the social contract? Is it possible to be too obedient to the state or too responsive only to one's own impulses?

▼

THOMAS JEFFERSON, THE DECLARATION OF INDEPENDENCE

Thomas Jefferson (1743–1826) was the third president of the United States, primary author of the Declaration of Independence, American statesman here and abroad, and lifelong advocate of agrarian democracy. A graduate of William and Mary College in 1762, he studied law and helped to form the Virginia Committee of Correspondence, for which, as a member, he prepared a paper opposing the British Parliament's authority over the colonists. Never an effective public speaker, he nevertheless won respect as a skilled rhetorician and wrote numerous addresses and resolutions.

As a delegate to the Second Continental Congress in 1775, Jefferson served on the committee drafting the Declaration of Independence, which was wholly his work except for minor alterations from Adams, Franklin, and others on the floor of Congress. In spirit and detail, it reflects the writings of John Locke, with whose work Jefferson was familiar.

The version of the Declaration reprinted here is taken from Jefferson's autobiography. You will note the indication of changes made as the document was being discussed and edited by the delegates of the Second Continental Congress. In particular, the bracketed sections in italics were the parts stricken by the delegates, and the sections in small capital letters were the parts they substituted.

Some of the changes suggest that Jefferson was rather a firebrand, perhaps overstating the case for effect. For instance, "unremitting injuries and usurpations" was changed to "repeated injuries and usurpations," and to the charge that the king had been "depriving us of the benefits of trial by jury" was added the qualifier "in many cases." One can see the concern of members of the Congress for the image this document would project. As angry and determined as many no doubt were, they did not want to exaggerate their claims and thereby leave themselves open to the charge of being a group of crazy radicals. It is the reasoned restraint that gives the final document its strength, and it is the suggestions of people like Adams and Franklin that helped to keep its tone dignified.

Of especial importance is the Congress' excision of Jefferson's declaration against slavery. It is refreshing to realize that there were individuals like Jefferson at this time who, when he declared that all men were created equal, did not exclude people of darker skin from humanity. Indeed, when he refers to slavery as a "cruel war against human nature itself," to its perpetrator as "the CHRISTIAN [his caps] king of Great Britain," and to its victims as "MEN" [also his caps] who are "bought and sold," Jefferson leaves no room for doubt that he is condemning the practice on both rational and religious grounds. Yet this entire section was removed by the Congress—no doubt for sound political reasons. Because so many of the colonies were economically dependent on slavery, a declaration of independence that condemned slavery would not have passed, and if an attempt had been made to fight out the slavery issue at this time, there might not have been a United States of America. One might well wonder whether the price was worth paying. In any case, the issue was swept under the rug, a decision for which this nation would suffer for a long time.

Generally, Jefferson worked against the aristocracy of wealth and birth. He denied the originality of his work on the Declaration when he wrote "I did not consider it any part of my charge to invent new ideas, but to place before mankind the common sense of the subject, in terms so plain and firm as to command their assent." Nevertheless, the Declaration represents a primary historical document of great power and interest.

▼

The Declaration of Independence
THOMAS JEFFERSON

[JULY 4, 1776]

When, in the course of human events, it becomes necessary for one *1* people to dissolve the political bands which have connected them with another, and to assume among the powers of the earth the separate and equal station to which the laws of nature and of nature's God entitle them, a decent respect to the opinions of mankind requires that they should declare the causes which impel them to the separation.

2   We hold these truths to be self evident: that all men are created equal; that they are endowed by their Creator with CERTAIN [*inherent and*] inalienable rights; that among these are life, liberty, and the pursuit of happiness; that to secure these rights, governments are instituted among men, deriving their just powers from the consent of the governed; that whenever any form of government becomes destructive of these ends, it is the right of the people to alter or to abolish it, and to institute new government, laying its foundation on such principles, and organizing its powers in such form, as to them shall seem most likely to effect their safety and happiness. Prudence, indeed, will dictate that governments long established should not be changed for light and transient causes; and accordingly all experience hath shown that mankind are more disposed to suffer while evils are sufferable, than to right themselves by abolishing the forms to which they are accustomed. But when a long train of abuses and usurpations, [*begun at a distinguished period and*] pursuing invariably the same object, evinces a design to reduce them under absolute despotism, it is their right, it is their duty to throw off such government, and to provide new guards for their future security. Such has been the patient sufferance of these colonies; and such is now the necessity which constrains them to ALTER [*expunge*] their former systems of government. The history of the present king of Great Britain is a history of REPEATED [*unremitting*] injuries and usurpations, ALL HAVING [*among which appears no solitary fact to contradict the uniform tenor of the rest, but all have*] in direct object the establishment of an absolute tyranny over these states. To prove this, let facts be submitted to a candid world [*for the truth of which we pledge a faith yet unsullied by falsehood*].

3   He has refused his assent to laws the most wholesome and necessary for the public good.

4   He has forbidden his governors to pass laws of immediate and pressing importance, unless suspended in their operation till his assent should be obtained; and, when so suspended, he has utterly neglected to attend to them.

5   He has refused to pass other laws for the accommodation of large districts of people, unless those people would relinquish the right of representation in the legislature, a right inestimable to them, and formidable to tyrants only.

6   He has called together legislative bodies at places unusual, uncomfortable, and distant from the depository of their public records, for the sole purpose of fatiguing them into compliance with his measures.

7   He has dissolved representative houses repeatedly [*and continually*] for opposing with manly firmness his invasions on the rights of the people.

8   He has refused for a long time after such dissolutions to cause others to be elected, whereby the legislative powers, incapable of annihilation, have returned to the people at large for their exercise, the state remaining, in the meantime, exposed to all the dangers of invasion from without and convulsions within.

He has endeavored to prevent the population of these states; for that pur- *9*
pose obstructing the laws for naturalization of foreigners, refusing to pass others to encourage their migrations hither, and raising the conditions of new
appropriations of lands.

He has OBSTRUCTED [*suffered*] the administration of justice BY [*totally to cease* *10*
in some of these states] refusing his assent to laws for establishing judiciary
powers.

He has made [*our*] judges dependent on his will alone for the tenure of their *11*
office, and the amount and payment of their salaries.

He has erected a multitude of new offices, [*by a self-assumed power*] and *12*
sent hither swarms of new officers to harass our people and eat out their
substance.

He has kept among us in times of peace standing armies [*and ships of war*] *13*
without the consent of our legislatures.

He has affected to render the military independent of, and superior to, the *14*
civil power.

He has combined with others to subject us to a jurisdiction foreign to our *15*
constitutions and unacknowledged by our laws, giving his assent to their acts of
pretended legislation for quartering large bodies of armed troops among us; for
protecting them by a mock trial from punishment for any murders which they
should commit on the inhabitants of these states; for cutting off our trade with
all parts of the world; for imposing taxes on us without our consent; for depriving us IN MANY CASES of the benefits of trial by jury; for transporting us beyond
seas to be tried for pretended offences; for abolishing the free system of
English laws in a neighboring province, establishing therein an arbitrary government, and enlarging its boundaries, so as to render it at once an example
and fit instrument for introducing the same absolute rule into these COLONIES
[*states*]; for taking away our charters, abolishing our most valuable laws, and
altering fundamentally the forms of our governments; for suspending our own
legislatures, and declaring themselves invested with power to legislate for us in
all cases whatsoever.

He has abdicated government here BY DECLARING US OUT OF HIS PROTECTION, *16*
AND WAGING WAR AGAINST US [*withdrawing his governors, and declaring us out of
his allegiance and protection*].

He has plundered our seas, ravaged our coasts, burnt our towns, and *17*
destroyed the lives of our people.

He is at this time transporting large armies of foreign mercenaries to com- *18*
plete the works of death, desolation and tyranny already begun with circumstances of cruelty and perfidy SCARCELY PARALLELED IN THE MOST BARBAROUS AGES,
AND TOTALLY unworthy the head of a civilized nation.

He has constrained our fellow citizens taken captive on the high seas, to *19*
bear arms against their country, to become the executioners of their friends
and brethren, or to fall themselves by their hands.

He has EXCITED DOMESTIC INSURRECTION AMONG US, AND HAS endeavored to *20*
bring on the inhabitants of our frontiers, the merciless Indian savages, whose

known rule of warfare is an undistinguished destruction of all ages, sexes and conditions [*of existence*].

21   [*He has incited treasonable insurrection of our fellow citizens, with the allurements of forfeiture and confiscation of our property.*

22   *He has waged cruel war against human nature itself, violating its most sacred rights of life and liberty in the persons of a distant people who never offended him, captivating and carrying them into slavery in another hemisphere, or to incur miserable death in their transportation hither. This piratical warfare, the opprobrium of INFIDEL powers, is the warfare of the CHRISTIAN king of Great Britain. Determined to keep open a market where MEN should be bought and sold, he has prostituted his negative for suppressing every legislative attempt to prohibit or to restrain this execrable commerce. And that this assemblage of horrors might want no fact of distinguished die, he is now exciting those very people to rise in arms among us, and to purchase that liberty of which he has deprived them, by murdering the people on whom he also obtruded them: thus paying off former crimes committed against the LIBERTIES of one people, with crimes which he urges them to commit against the LIVES of another.*]

23   In every stage of these oppressions we have petitioned for redress in the most humble terms: our repeated petitions have been answered only by repeated injuries.

24   A prince whose character is thus marked by every act which may define a tyrant is unfit to be the ruler of a FREE people [*who mean to be free. Future ages will scarcely believe that the hardiness of one man adventured, within the short compass of twelve years only, to lay a foundation so broad and so undisguised for tyranny over a people fostered and fixed in principles of freedom.*]

25   Nor have we been wanting in attentions to our British brethren. We have warned them from time to time of attempts by their legislature to extend AN UNWARRANTABLE [*a*] jurisdiction over US [*these our states*]. We have reminded them of the circumstances of our emigration and settlement here, [*no one of which could warrant so strange a pretension: that these were effected at the expense of our own blood and treasure, unassisted by the wealth or the strength of Great Britain: that in constituting indeed our several forms of government, we had adopted one common king, thereby laying a foundation for perpetual league and amity with them: but that submission to their parliament was no part of our constitution, nor ever in idea, if history may be credited: and,*] WE HAVE appealed to their native justice and magnanimity AND WE HAVE CONJURED THEM BY [*as well as to*] the ties of our common kindred to disavow these usurpations which WOULD INEVITABLY [*were likely to*] interrupt our connection and correspondence. They too have been deaf to the voice of justice and of consanguinity. WE MUST THEREFORE [*and when occasions have been given them, by the regular course of their laws, of removing from their councils the disturbers of our harmony, they have, by their free election, re-established them in power. At this very time too, they are permitting their chief magistrate to send over not only soldiers of our common blood, but Scotch and foreign mercenaries to invade and destroy us. These facts have given the last stab to agonizing affection, and manly spirit bids us to renounce forever these unfeeling brethren. We must endeavor to forget*

our former love for them, and hold them as we hold the rest of mankind, ene-mies in war, in peace friends. We might have a free and a great people together; but a communication of grandeur and of freedom, it seems, is below their dig-nity. Be it so, since they will have it. The road to happiness and to glory is open to us, too. We will tread it apart from them, and] acquiesce in the necessity which denounces our [*eternal*] separation AND HOLD THEM AS WE HOLD THE REST OF MANKIND, ENEMIES IN WAR, IN PEACE FRIENDS!

We, therefore, the representatives of the United States of America in Gen-eral Congress assembled, appealing to the supreme judge of the world for the rectitude of our intentions, do in the name, and by the authority of the good people of these COLONIES, SOLEMNLY PUBLISH AND DECLARE, THAT THESE UNITED COL-ONIES ARE, AND OF RIGHT OUGHT TO BE FREE AND INDEPENDENT STATES; THAT THEY ARE ABSOLVED FROM ALL ALLEGIANCE TO THE BRITISH CROWN, AND THAT ALL POLITICAL CON-NECTION BETWEEN THEM AND THE STATE OF GREAT BRITAIN IS, AND OUGHT TO BE, TOTALLY DISSOLVED; [*states reject and renounce all allegiance and subjection to the kings of Great Britain and all others who may hereafter claim by, through or under them; we utterly dissolve all political connection which may heretofore have subsisted between us and the people or parliament of Great Britain: and finally we do assert and declare these colonies to be free and independent states,*] and that as free and independent states, they have full power to levy war, con-clude peace, contract alliances, establish commerce, and to do all other acts and things which independent states may of right do. 26

And for the support of this declaration, with a firm reliance on the protection of divine providence, we mutually pledge to each other our lives, our fortunes, and our sacred honor. 27

WRITING AND DISCUSSION QUESTIONS

Informative

1. The "laws of nature and of nature's God entitle" us to "separate and equal sta-tion [with the British]." Briefly explain what Jefferson and his coauthors mean. (You may refer to Locke.)
2. On what bases do the authors of the Declaration justify rebellion?
3. According to Jefferson and his coauthors, what are the functions of government?
4. In the Declaration, what statements are made based primarily on faith? What is meant by the claim that some things are "self-evident"?
5. In the Declaration, what are the most serious complaints made against the British Crown? Which are based on observable truth?

Persuasive

1. The members of Congress were mostly landed gentry and from the upper class. Argue that despite this class distinction, the seeds of democracy planted in the Declaration made its framers significantly different from the aristrocratic British.

2. Argue that Jefferson's revolutionary vision has or has not been achieved in America.
3. The Declaration was written and published well after the Revolutionary War started. Argue that the publication of the document served purposes other than merely justifying to England the outbreak of war.

Personal

1. Explain the important differences and similarities between Jefferson's conception of independence and your own.
2. What modern circumstances would justify rebellion or civil disobedience?
3. When does the end justify the means? For example, in the case of the American colonies, a variety of circumstances justified, in their eyes, the risk of death, war, civil chaos, and social disruption. How do you determine when the end of a conflict is of sufficient benefit to justify the means of such cost and suffering?

▼

JAMES MADISON, FEDERALIST PAPER NO. 10

After declaring independence and successfully winning a war, the 13 American colonies faced the pressing task of deciding to what degree, if any, a union of the separate states should be established. Although several colonies argued for the priority of states' rights, others argued for a loose league, which won out, as defined in the Articles of Confederation. When this compact soon proved unworkable and unable to meet needs like defense and commerce, a Constitutional Convention was held in Philadelphia in 1787. The federal Constitution was the result in 1788.

The 85 Articles referred to as the Federalist Papers were written by James Madison, Alexander Hamilton, and John Jay to aid in the ratification of the Constitution. Although the writers were not publicly identified at the time the Federalist Papers were written, James Madison (1751–1836) is credited with writing the selection that follows, Federalist Paper No. 10, in 1787, more than a decade after the Declaration of Independence was adopted in 1776 and several years before the Bill of Rights was added to the Constitution in 1791. In 1809, Madison became the fourth U.S. president, succeeding Jefferson.

Madison had a real stake in ratifying the new Constitution. His argument in Federalist Paper No. 10 is designed to answer both the more liberal interests, who were afraid that the newly proposed system placed too much power in the central government, and the more conservative interests, who believed that a democracy could not survive because it would either be split by factionalism or dominated by a tyrannical majority. Madison's approach was to concede the conservative argument insofar as it applied to a fully participatory democracy like Athens—he does not mention Athens, but that is the major example of both an achieved and a failed democracy likely to be in his and his readers' minds. He goes on to argue that the kind of federal republic established by the Constitution avoids those dangers while still making possible, through the representative system, a truly popular government.

In Paper No. 10, Madison argues only the broad principle of the federal republic as an effective means to do what Locke believed government should do, protect our natural rights. Madison is not arguing in Hobbesian terms (that is, the belief that humans are base animals in need of constant vigilance and control) that an absolute authority has to be established to avoid a war of each against all, but in Lockean terms that a democratic system can be established which prevents powerful interest groups from becoming judges in their own cases. In other papers, Madison or Hamilton (Jay wrote only No. 5) argued that other possible abuses would be prevented by the system created in the Constitution of different branches of the government, the separation of powers, and the checks and balances, among others.

To understand the practical and contemporary implications of Paper No. 10, consider whether contemporary interest groups have exerted undue control on central government. For instance, does the group that has come to be called "the military industrial complex" really control the country, as Dwight Eisenhower (a five-star general and 34th president of the United States) said it could? Also, in the 1960s when U.S. Special Forces troops were sent into Guatemala to repress social and land reform movements, did the decision to use military force have anything to do with the fact that a major landholder in Guatemala was American Fruit Company and that its major stockholders included important government officials Henry Cabot Lodge and John Foster Dulles?

More contemporary examples of potential abuses of the common good come to mind. When the savings and loan industry was deregulated in the mid 1980s, was the decision to deregulate made by powerful individuals in banking or by some bankers making a great deal of money with the general public being stuck with a considerable bill for the federally insured deposits in numerous failed savings and loan institutions? Or given the current struggle in Washington between environmentalist and powerful oil and mining lobbies, how imminent is the opening of new federal parklands for industrial development? By adding the activities of the gun lobby and numerous other PACs (political action committees that lobby in Washington), the potential for abuse is very high.

▼

Federalist Paper No. 10
JAMES MADISON

Among the numerous advantages promised by a well-constructed Union, none deserves to be more accurately developed than its tendency to break and control the violence of faction. The friend of popular governments never finds himself so much alarmed for their character and fate as when he contemplates their propensity to this dangerous vice. He will not fail, therefore, to set a due value on any plan which, without violating the principles to which he is attached, provides a proper cure for it. The instability, injustice, and confusion introduced into the public councils have, in truth, been the mortal diseases under which popular governments have everywhere perished, as they continue to be the favorite and fruitful topics from which the adversaries to liberty derive their most specious declamations. The valuable improvements made by the American constitutions on the popular models, both ancient and modern, cannot certainly be too much admired; but it would be an unwarrantable partiality to contend that they have as effectually obviated the danger on this side, as was wished and expected. Complaints are everywhere heard from our most considerate and virtuous citizens, equally the friends of public and private faith and of public and personal liberty, that our governments are too unstable, that the public good is disregarded in the conflicts of rival parties, and that measures are too often decided, not according to the rules of justice and the rights of the minor party, but by the superior force of an interested and overbearing majority. However anxiously we may wish that these complaints had no foundation, the evidence of known facts will not permit us to deny that they are in some degree true. It will be found, indeed, on a candid review of our situation, that some of the distresses under which we labor have been erroneously charged on the operation of our governments; but it will be found, at the same time, that other causes will not alone account for many of our heaviest misfortunes; and, particularly, for that prevailing and increasing distrust of public engagements and alarm for private rights which are echoed from one end of the continent to the other. These must be chiefly, if not wholly, effects of the unsteadiness and injustice with which a factious spirit has tainted our public administration.

2   By a faction I understand a number of citizens, whether amounting to a majority or minority of the whole, who are united and actuated by some common impulse of passion, or of interest, adverse to the rights of other citizens, or to the permanent and aggregate interests of the community.

3   There are two methods of curing the mischiefs of faction: the one, by removing its causes; the other, by controlling its effects.

4   There are again two methods of removing the causes of faction: the one, by destroying the liberty which is essential to its existence; the other, by giving to every citizen the same opinions, the same passions, and the same interests.

5   It could never be more truly said than of the first remedy that it was worse than the disease. Liberty is to faction what air is to fire, an aliment without which it instantly expires. But it could not be a less folly to abolish liberty, which is essential to political life, because it nourishes faction than it would be to wish the annihilation of air, which is essential to animal life, because it imparts to fire its destructive agency.

6   The second expedient is as impracticable as the first would be unwise. As long as the reason of man continues fallible, and he is at liberty to exercise it, different opinions will be formed. As long as the connection subsists between his reason and his self-love, his opinions and his passions will have a reciprocal influence on each other; and the former will be objects to which the latter will attach themselves. The diversity in the faculties of men, from which the rights of property originate, is not less an insuperable obstacle to a uniformity of interests. The protection of these faculties is the first object of government. From the protection of different and unequal faculties of acquiring property, the possession of different degrees and kinds of property immediately results; and from the influence of these on the sentiments and views of the respective proprietors ensues a division of the society into different interests and parties.

7   The latent causes of faction are thus sown in the nature of man; and we see

them everywhere brought into different degrees of activity, according to the different circumstances of civil society. A zeal for different opinions concerning religion, concerning government, and many other points, as well of speculation as of practice; and attachment to different leaders ambitiously contending for pre-eminence and power; or to persons of other descriptions whose fortunes have been interesting to the human passions, have, in turn, divided mankind into parties, inflamed them with mutual animosity, and rendered them much more disposed to vex and oppress each other than to co-operate for their common good. So strong is this propensity of mankind to fall into mutual animosities that where no substantial occasion presents itself the most frivolous and fanciful distinctions have been sufficient to kindle their unfriendly passions and excite their most violent conflicts. But the most common and durable source of factions has been the various and unequal distribution of property. Those who hold and those who are without property have ever formed distinct interests in society. Those who are creditors, and those who are debtors, fall under a like discrimination. A landed interest, a manufacturing interest, a mercantile interest, a moneyed interest, with many lesser interests, grow up of necessity in civilized nations, and divide them into different classes, actuated by different sentiments and views. The regulation of these various and interfering interests forms the principal task of modern legislation and involves the spirit of party and faction in the necessary and ordinary operations of government.

No man is allowed to be a judge in his own cause, because his interest   8
would certainly bias his judgment, and, not improbably, corrupt his integrity. With equal, nay with greater reason, a body of men are unfit to be both judges and parties at the same time; yet what are many of the most important acts of legislation but so many judicial determinations, not indeed concerning the rights of single persons, but concerning the rights of large bodies of citizens? And what are the different classes of legislators but advocates and parties to the causes which they determine? Is a law proposed concerning private debts? It is a question to which the creditors are parties on one side and the debtors on the other. Justice ought to hold the balance between them. Yet the parties are, and must be, themselves the judges; and the most numerous party, or in other words, the most powerful faction must be expected to prevail. Shall domestic manufacturers be encouraged, and in what degree, by restrictions on foreign manufacturers? are questions which would be differently decided by the landed and the manufacturing classes, and probably by neither with a sole regard to justice and the public good. The apportionment of taxes on the various descriptions of property is an act which seems to require the most exact impartiality; yet there is, perhaps, no legislative act in which greater opportunity and temptation are given to a predominant party to trample on the rules of justice. Every shilling with which they overburden the inferior number is a shilling saved to their own pockets.

It is in vain to say that enlightened statesmen will be able to adjust these   9
clashing interests and render them all subservient to the public good. Enlightened statesmen will not always be at the helm. Nor, in many cases, can such

an adjustment be made at all without taking into view indirect and remote considerations, which will rarely prevail over the immediate interest which one party may find in disregarding the rights of another or the good of the whole.

10   The inference to which we are brought is that the *causes* of faction cannot be removed and that relief is only to be sought in the means of controlling its *effects.*

11   If a faction consists of less than a majority, relief is supplied by the republican principle, which enables the majority to defeat its sinister views by regular vote. It may clog the administration, it may convulse the society; but it will be unable to execute and mask its violence under the forms of the Constitution. When a majority is included in a faction, the form of popular government, on the other hand, enables it to sacrifice to its ruling passion or interest both the public good and the rights of other citizens. To secure the public good and private rights against the danger of such a faction, and at the same time to preserve the spirit and the form of popular government, is then the great object to which our inquiries are directed. Let me add that it is the great desideratum by which alone this form of government can be rescued from the opprobrium under which it has so long labored and be recommended to the esteem and adoption of mankind.

12   By what means is this object attainable? Evidently by one of two only. Either the existence of the same passion or interest in a majority at the same time must be prevented, or the majority, having such coexistent passion or interest, must be rendered, by their number and local situation, unable to concert and carry into effect schemes of oppression. If the impulse and the opportunity be suffered to coincide, we well know that neither moral nor religious motives can be relied on as an adequate control. They are not found to be such on the injustice and violence of individuals, and lose their efficacy in proportion to the number combined together, that is, in proportion as their efficacy becomes needful.

13   From this view of the subject it may be concluded that a pure democracy, by which I mean a society consisting of a small number of citizens, who assemble and administer the government in person, can admit of no cure for the mischiefs of faction. A common passion or interest will, in almost every case, be felt by a majority of the whole; a communication and concert results from the form of government itself; and there is nothing to check the inducements to sacrifice the weaker party or an obnoxious individual. Hence it is that such democracies have ever been spectacles of turbulence and contention; have ever been found incompatible with personal security or the rights of property; and have in general been as short in their lives as they have been violent in their deaths. Theoretic politicians, who have patronized this species of government, have erroneously supposed that by reducing mankind to a perfect equality in their political rights, they would at the same time be perfectly equalized and assimilated in their possessions, their opinions, and their passions.

14   A republic, by which I mean a government in which the scheme of representation takes place, opens a different prospect and promises the cure for which

we are seeking. Let us examine the points in which it varies from pure democracy, and we shall comprehend both the nature of the cure and the efficacy which it must derive from the Union.

The two great points of difference between a democracy and a republic are: 15 first, the delegation of the government, in the latter, to a small number of citizens elected by the rest; secondly, the greater number of citizens and greater sphere of country over which the latter may be extended.

The effect of the first difference is, on the one hand, to refine and enlarge 16 the public views by passing them through the medium of a chosen body of citizens, whose wisdom may best discern the true interest of their country and whose patriotism and love of justice will be least likely to sacrifice it to temporary or partial considerations. Under such a regulation it may well happen that the public voice, pronounced by the representatives of the people, will be more consonant to the public good than if pronounced by the people themselves, convened for the purpose. On the other hand, the effect may be inverted. Men of factious tempers, of local prejudices, or of sinsiter designs, may, by intrigue, by corruption, or by other means, first obtain the suffrages, and then betray the interests of the people. The question resulting is, whether small or extensive republics are most favorable to the election of proper guardians of the public weal; and it is clearly decided in favor of the latter by two obvious considerations.

In the first place it is to be remarked that however small the republic may 17 be the representatives must be raised to a certain number in order to guard against the cabals of a few; and that however large it may be they must be limited to a certain number in order to guard against the confusion of a multitude. Hence, the number of representatives in the two cases not being in proportion to that of the constituents, and being proportionally greatest in the small republic, it follows that if the proportion of fit characters be not less in the large than in the small republic, the former will present a greater option, and consequently a greater probability of a fit choice.

In the next place, as each representative will be chosen by a greater number 18 of citizens in the large than in the small republic, it will be more difficult for unworthy candidates to practise with success the vicious arts by which elections are too often carried; and the suffrages of the people being more free, will be more likely to center on men who possess the most attractive merit and the most diffusive and established characters.

It must be confessed that in this, as in most other cases, there is a mean, on 19 both sides of which inconveniencies will be found to lie. By enlarging too much the number of electors, you render the representative too little acquainted with all their local circumstances and lesser interests; as by reducing it too much, you render him unduly attached to these, and too little fit to comprehend and pursue great and natural objects. The federal Constitution forms a happy combination in this respect; the great and aggregate interests being referred to the national, the local and particular to the State legislatures.

The other point of difference is the greater number of citizens and extent of 20 territory which may be brought within the compass of republican than of democratic government; and it is this circumstance principally which renders factious combinations less to be dreaded in the former than in the latter. The smaller the society, the fewer probably will be the distinct parties and interests composing it; the fewer the distinct parties and interests, the more frequently will a majority be found of the same party; and the smaller the number of individuals composing a majority, and the smaller the compass within which they are placed, the more easily will they concert and execute their plans of oppression. Extend the sphere and you take in a greater variety of parties and interests; you make it less probable that a majority of the whole will have a common motive to invade the rights of other citizens; or if such a common motive exists, it will be more difficult for all who feel it to discover their own strength and to act in unison with each other. Besides other impediments, it may be remarked that, where there is a consciousness of unjust or dishonorable purposes, communication is always checked by distrust in proportion to the number whose concurrence is necessary.

21   Hence, it clearly appears that the same advantage which a republic has over a democracy in controlling the effects of faction is enjoyed by a large over a small republic—is enjoyed by the Union over the States composing it. Does this advantage consist in the substitution of representatives whose enlightened views and virtuous sentiments render them superior to local prejudices and to schemes of injustice? It will not be denied that the representation of the Union will be most likely to possess these requisite endowments. Does it consist in the greater security afforded by a greater variety of parties, against the event of any one party being able to outnumber and oppress the rest? In an equal degree does the increased variety of parties comprised within the Union increase this security. Does it, in fine, consist in the greater obstacles opposed to the concert and accomplishment of the secret wishes of an unjust and interested majority? Here again the extent of the Union gives it the most palpable advantage.

22   The influence of factious leaders may kindle a flame within their particular States but will be unable to spread a general conflagration through the other States. A religious sect may degenerate into a political faction in a part of the Confederacy; but the variety of sects dispersed over the entire face of it must secure the national councils against any danger from the source. A rage for paper money, for an abolition of debts, for an equal divison of property, or for any other improper or wicked project, will be less apt to pervade the whole body of the Union than a particular member of it, in the same proportion as such a malady is more likely to taint a particular county or district than an entire State.

23   In the extent and proper structure of the Union, therefore, we behold a republican remedy for the diseases most incident to republican government. And according to the degree of pleasure and pride we feel in being republicans ought to be our zeal in cherishing the spirit and supporting the character of federalists.

Publius

WRITING AND DISCUSSION QUESTIONS

Informative

1. According to Madison, what is a faction? How do factions oppose what Madison refers to as the public or common good? Why is Madison worried about factions?
2. What does Madison mean by the "superior force of an interested and overbearing majority"?
3. What are Madison's recommendations for handling the problem of factions? What two cures does he cite and which does he favor?

Persuasive

1. Argue that a "republic" is preferable to a "pure democracy." Consider the dangers inherent in a republic.
2. What argument does Madison offer to explain how a republic can be designed to handle the abuses inherent in a democracy? Argue that a republic is a form of government that does or does not handle abuses effectively.

Personal

1. What factions or interest groups do you belong to? What interests do you have and what pressures do you exert as a member of a student body, a particular nationality, religion, economic class, or other group? What abuses can you anticipate coming from such pressure on your local, state, or federal representatives?
2. What examples in American history of clearly unjust laws and practices, supported by a particular faction, can you think of that clearly threatened the common good?

▼

BILL OF RIGHTS

It may be said that there are only three great ideas behind democracy. One can be called the "majoritarian principle." According to this principle, the majority of people should have the largest representation in government and the largest control over how that government operates. Thus, by having significant access to the governing powers, the majority can exert some control over the decisions that affect their daily lives. This idea is often called "majority rule."

The second great idea behind democracy can be called the "minority principle" and is generally much less understood but certainly is just as important as the majoritarian principle. This is the principle that protects the minority against the majority's domination of central government and against unjust laws gaining too much power over individuals and small interest groups.

The third great idea behind democracy is the principle of individual and property rights. All individuals have the right to a fair slice of the national pie, a right to a livelihood, a family, and participation in the larger gains of a society.

What is unique about this country, in fact, is not the first principle, which was established in our Constitution, however important that is. Most countries today have documents very similar to our own that guarantee and define citizen representation by a majority principle and that define government operation and the balance of its various powers. Instead, what is unique about our form of democracy and what inspires countless individuals living in repressive regimes to risk their lives in coming here is the minority principle embodied in the Bill of Rights and our courts' willingness to defend it.

The Bill of Rights is the first ten amendments to the Constitution. These amendments were added in 1791, soon after ratification of the Constitution because during the debate over ratification many of the delegates expressed their dissatisfaction with the general assurances and supposed common agreement over what exactly those "natural rights of man" were that a government, in Locke's terms, was supposed to protect. They wanted those natural rights clearly defined and appended to the Consitution. In fact, many delegates were concerned that the Constitution would not have been ratified if the early addition of these amendments had not been assured.

The Bill of Rights is important because it embodies the foundation of our liberties. In the words of attorney Ira Glasser, "It's the idea that even in a democracy the majority doesn't get to rule everything; that there are certain individual rights and individual liberties that are protected from the tyranny of the majority; that just because there are more whites than blacks doesn't mean that whites can take away from blacks the right to vote or the right to live."[1]

In the Bill of Rights, most of the ten amendments are expressed in the negative ("no law," "not be infringed," and "No soldier"). Many of these are responses to grievances expressed in the Declaration of Independence and are attempts to protect the individual from an intrusive or tyrannical government or even from an overweening or tyrannical majority.

▼

Bill of Rights

ARTICLES IN ADDITION TO, AND AMENDMENT OF, THE CONSTITUTION OF THE UNITED STATES OF AMERICA, PROPOSED BY CONGRESS, AND RATIFIED BY THE LEGISLATURES OF THE SEVERAL STATES PURSUANT TO THE FIFTH ARTICLE OF THE ORIGINAL CONSTITUTION.

Amendment I [1791]

Congress shall make no law respecting an establishment of religion, or prohibiting the free exercise thereof; or abridging the freedom of speech, or of the press; or the right of the people peaceably to assemble, and to petition the Government for a redress of grievances.

---

[1]Glasser, I. *From Presidential Politics and the ACLU.* p. 2.

Amendment II [1791]

A well regulated Militia, being necessary to the security of a free state, the right of the people to keep and bear Arms, shall not be infringed.

Amendment III [1791]

No Soldier shall, in time of peace be quartered in any house, without the consent of the Owner, nor in time of war, but in a manner to be prescribed by law.

Amendment IV [1791]

The right of the people to be secure in their persons, houses, papers, and effects, against unreasonable searches and seizures, shall not be violated and no Warrants shall issue, but upon probable cause, supported by Oath or affirmation, and particularly describing the place to be searched, and the persons or things to be seized.

Amendment V [1791]

No person shall be held to answer for a capital, or otherwise infamous crime, unless on a presentment or indictment of a Grand Jury, except in cases arising in the land or naval forces, or in the Militia, when in actual service in time of War or public danger; nor shall any person be subject for the same offence to be twice put in jeopardy of life or limb; nor shall be compelled in any criminal case to be a witness against himself, nor be deprived of life, liberty, or property, without due process of law; nor shall private property be taken for public use, without just compensation.

Amendment VI [1791]

In all criminal prosecutions, the accused shall enjoy the right to a speedy and public trial, by an impartial jury of the State and district wherein the crime shall have been committed, which district shall have been previously ascertained by law, and to be informed of the nature and cause of the accusation; to be confronted with the witnesses against him; to have compulsory process for obtaining witnesses in his favor, and to have the Assistance of Counsel for his defence.

Amendment VII [1791]

In Suits at common law, where the value in controversy shall exceed twenty dollars, the right of trial by jury shall be preserved, and no fact tried by jury, shall be otherwise re-examined in any Court of the United States, than according to the rules of the common law.

Amendment VIII [1791]

Excessive bail shall not be required, nor excessive fines imposed, nor cruel and unusual punishments inflicted.

Amendment IX [1791]

The enumeration in the Constitution, of certain rights, shall not be construed to deny or disparage others retained by the people.

Amendment X [1791]

The powers not delegated to the United States by the Constitution, nor prohibited by it to the States, are reserved to the States respectively, or to the people.

WRITING AND DISCUSSION QUESTIONS

Informative

1. Identify one particular issue each amendment deals with. For this issue, describe the potential form of government intrusion into and abuse of individual rights and liberties that made the writing of each amendment necessary.
2. What does the First Amendment appear to be saying about the separation of church and state, the abridging of freedom of speech and press, the right of assembly, and the right to petition for redress of grievances?

Persuasive

1. Choose a social issue like abortion, capital punishment, gun control, the sale of pornography, requiring the Pledge of Allegiance in schools, the right of hate groups like Neo-Nazis to march, or the right to fly the Confederate flag (to many a symbol of racial segregation) from a statehouse building. Argue your position on one of these issues, basing it on your reading of the Bill of Rights.
2. Which one of the first ten amendments seems to have been most abused or most subject to abuse? Do you think the individual liberty it protects is important enough to justify the potential abuse?

Personal

1. High school principals have recently been granted broad rights to censor high school newspapers if they think reactions to their contents may undermine order or authority in the school. How do you stand on this basic First Amendment question? Should the benefit of the doubt go to the safety of the school or the importance of the freedom of speech?

ALEXIS DE TOCQUEVILLE,
FROM *DEMOCRACY IN AMERICA*

Alexis de Tocqueville (1805–1859) was a French aristocrat and statesman who traveled the 32 days required in 1831 to cross the Atlantic to observe firsthand in the United States the great and unprecedented experiment in democracy. The result was *Democracy in America* (1835), probably the most profound study of American democracy ever written. To this day, scholars look to his writing and predictions, and many of those predictions seem to have been proved true.

It will be helpful to understand the historical period and context in which Tocqueville worked. Despite the egalitarian rhetoric of the American Revolution, the first 40 years of the republic was characterized by a relatively aristocratic administration of government. There were fairly substantial property qualifications for voting in most states, and a few old families, especially in Virginia, dominated national politics. Tocqueville arrived shortly after the beginning of the Jacksonian revolution (Jackson's presidency was from 1829 to 1837), which was perhaps the first major populist movement in the nation. During this movement, egalitarianism reached a height that would have frightened Madison and might well have made even the more-liberal Jefferson uncomfortable. It would have seemed reasonable for a French aristocrat, like Tocqueville, at this time to point out that "if it is your object to refine the habits, embellish the manners, and cultivate the arts, to promote the love of poetry, beauty, and glory . . . , [then] avoid the government of a democracy."

Even though Tocqueville had aristocratic views and was slightly distrustful of democracy, he was practical and objective enough to realize that democracy offered much that would be of crucial importance to Europe. Despite the debacle of the French Revolution of 1789 and the rise and fall by 1815 of Napoleon's empire, it was clear to men like Tocqueville that Europe was nevertheless moving in the direction of democracy (there had been another and less-violent French Revolution as recently as 1830). Conditions in Europe are important for us to bear in mind when reading Tocqueville's account in America, for the primary audience is not American, but European. His purpose is to analyze America as a model of success and failure, of strength and weakness, from which he hopes Europe, especially France, will benefit. In various passages throughout his book, Tocqueville specifically refers to deteriorating conditions in Europe and addresses the urgent need to implement some form of democracy to avoid further chaos:

> I do not say it is easy to teach men how to exercise political rights, . . . but . . . I add, that, if ever there was a time at which such an attempt ought to be made, that time is now. Do you not see that religious belief is shaken and the divine notion of right is declining?—that morality is debased and the notion of moral right is fading away? . . . If, in the midst of this general disruption, you do not succeed in connecting the notion of right with that of private interest, which is the only immutable point in the human heart, what means have you of governing the world except by fear?

Tocqueville's official mission was to study prisons, but during his visit in America he became interested in how democracy was practiced. In the nine months he spent traveling across the country, he talked to farmers, merchants, Indians, and politicians. He observed that the people were so diverse that their race and ethnic origins could not be identified. He found Americans "pushy," yet he marveled at their excitement and energy. At the same time, he worried about the tumult of a common folk constructing a government and a new society. He feared freedom was mostly the opportunity to express greed and make money. Greed, given free reign, could result in the few gaining an undue advantage over the many. It also could result in the many tyrannizing the few. Voters could elect those who supported their own narrow interests, and Tocqueville wondered about the electability of a truly noble person who had as his intentions the common good. Over all, he was impressed by the tremendous productive energy of democracy and the power of self-interest to energize a whole society.

The crucial question arising from this selection is whether that union of right, private interest, and public good that Tocqueville saw as characteristic of democracy has ever effectively existed in our country and whether we are struggling successfully toward that goal today.

What is clear is that political thinkers still reckon with Tocqueville's observations today: the transformation of the tyrany of the majority into the loud cries of hundreds of interest groups, many of them appearing to "buy" votes with contributions, pressuring legislators; the continuing threats to First Amendment rights; the danger inherent in a lax or easily impressed majority that often elects the person with the popular and slick image rather than the most-qualified candidate; the danger of the state being the primary dispenser of charity for the poor and homeless; the importance to our standard of living of our productive "industry and commerce"; and the threat to ethnic minorities of "inequality of condition."

▼

from *Democracy in America*
ALEXIS DE TOCQUEVILLE

11. ADVANTAGES OF DEMOCRACY IN THE UNITED STATES

1 . . . The defects and weaknesses of a democratic government may readily be discovered; they are demonstrated by flagrant instances, whilst its salutary influence is insensible, and, so to speak, occult. A glance suffices to detect its faults, but its good qualities can be discerned only by long observation. The laws of the American democracy are frequently defective or incomplete; they sometimes attack vested rights, or sanction others which are dangerous to the community; and even if they were good, their frequency would still be a great evil. How comes it, then, that the American republics prosper and continue? . . .

2 Democratic laws generally tend to promote the welfare of the greatest possible number; for they emanate from the majority of the citizens, who are subject to error, but who cannot have an interest opposed to their own advantage. The

laws of an aristocracy tend, on the contrary, to concentrate wealth and power in the hands of the minority; because an aristocracy, by its very nature, constitutes a minority. It may therefore be asserted, as a general proposition, that the purpose of a democracy in its legislation is more useful to humanity than that of an aristocracy. This is, however, the sum total of its advantages.

Aristocracies are infinitely more expert in the science of legislation than *3* democracies ever can be. They are possessed of a self-control which protects them from the errors of temporary excitement; and they form far-reaching designs, which they know how to mature till a favorable opportunity arrives. Aristocratic government proceeds with the dexterity of art; it understands how to make the collective force of all its laws converge at the same time to a given point. Such is not the case with democracies, whose laws are almost always ineffective or inopportune. The means of democracy are therefore more imperfect than those of aristocracy, and the measures which it unwittingly adopts are frequently opposed to its own cause; but the object it has in view is more useful. . . .

An analogous observation may be made respecting public officers. It is easy *4* to perceive that the American democracy frequently errs in the choice of the individuals to whom it intrusts the power of the administration. . . . The men who are intrusted with the direction of public affairs in the United States are frequently inferior, both in capacity and morality, to those whom an aristocracy would raise to power. But their interest is identified and confounded with that of the majority of their fellow-citizens. They may frequently be faithless, and frequently mistaken; but they will never systematically adopt a line of conduct hostile to the majority; and they cannot give a dangerous or exclusive tendency to the government.

The maladministration of a democratic magistrate, moreover, is an isolated *5* fact, which has influence only during the short period for which he is elected. Corruption and incapacity do not act as common interests, which may connect men permanently with one another. A corrupt or incapable magistrate will not concert his measures with another magistrate, simply because the latter is as corrupt and incapable as himself; and these two men will never unite their endeavors to promote the corruption and inaptitude of their remote posterity. The ambition and the manœuvres of the one will serve, on the contrary, to unmask the other. The vices of a magistrate, in democratic states, are usually wholly personal. . . .

In the United States, where the public officers have no class-interests to pro- *6* mote, the general and constant influence of the government is beneficial, although the individuals who conduct it are frequently unskilled, and sometimes contemptible. There is, indeed, a secret tendency in democratic institutions, which makes the exertions of the citizens subservient to the prosperity of the community, in spite of their vices and mistakes; whilst in aristocratic institutions, there is a secret bias, which, notwithstanding the talents and virtues of those who conduct the government, leads them to contribute to the evils which oppress their fellow-creatures. In aristocratic governments, public men may frequently do harm without intending it; and in democratic states, they bring about good results which they never thought of.

Public Spirit.

7   There is one sort of patriotic attachment, which principally arises from that instinctive, disinterested, and undefinable feeling which connects the affections of man with his birthplace. This natural fondness is united with a taste for ancient customs, and a reverence for traditions of the past; those who cherish it love their country as they love the mansion of their fathers. They love the tranquillity which it affords them; they cling to the peaceful habits which they have contracted within its bosom; they are attached to the reminiscences which it awakens; and they are even pleased by living there in a state of obedience. This patriotism is sometimes stimulated by religious enthusiasm, and then it is capable of making prodigious efforts. It is in itself a kind of religion: it does not reason, but it acts from the impulse of faith and sentiment. In some nations, the monarch is regarded as a personification of the country; and, the fervor of patriotism being converted into the fervor of loyalty, they take a sympathetic pride in his conquests, and glory in his power. There was a time, under the ancient monarchy, when the French felt a sort of satisfaction in the sense of their dependence upon the arbitrary will of their king; and they were wont to say with pride, "We live under the most powerful king in the world." But, like all instinctive passions, this kind of patriotism incites great transient exertions, but no continuity of effort. It may save the state in critical circumstances, but often allows it to decline in times of peace. Whilst the manners of a people are simple, and its faith unshaken,—whilst society is steadily based upon traditional institutions, whose legitimacy has never been contested,—this instinctive patriotism is wont to endure.

8   But there is another species of attachment to country, which is more rational than the one we have been describing. It is, perhaps, less generous and less ardent, but it is more fruitful and more lasting: it springs from knowledge; it is nurtured by the laws; it grows by the exercise of civil rights; and, in the end, it is confounded with the personal interests of the citizen. A man comprehends the influence which the well-being of his country has upon his own; he is aware that the laws permit him to contribute to that prosperity, and he labors to promote it, at first because it benefits him, and secondly because it is in part his own work.

9   But epochs sometimes occur in the life of a nation, when the old customs of a people are changed, public morality is destroyed, religious belief shaken, and the spell of tradition broken, whilst the diffusion of knowledge is yet imperfect, and the civil rights of the community are ill secured, or confined within narrow limits. The country then assumes a dim and dubious shape in the eyes of the citizens; they no longer behold it in the soil which they inhabit, for that soil is to them an inanimate clod; nor in the usages of their forefathers, which they have learned to regard as a debasing yoke; nor in religion, for of that they

doubt; nor in the laws, which do not originate in their own authority; nor in the legislator, whom they fear and despise. The country is lost to their senses; they can neither discover it under its own nor under borrowed features, and they retire into a narrow and unenlightened selfishness. They are emancipated from prejudice, without having acknowledged the empire of reason; they have neither the instinctive patriotism of a monarchy, nor the reflecting patriotism of a republic; but they have stopped between the two in the midst of confusion and distress.

In this predicament, to retreat is impossible; for a people cannot recover the   10
sentiments of their youth, any more than a man can return to the innocent tastes of childhood: such things may be regretted, but they cannot be renewed. They must go forward, and accelerate the union of private with public interests, since the period of disinterested patriotism is gone by forever.

I am certainly far from affirming, that, in order to obtain this result, the   11
exercise of political rights should be immediately granted to all men. But I maintain that the most powerful, and perhaps the only, means of which we still possess of interesting men in the welfare of their country, is to make them par- takers in the government. At the present time, civic zeal seems to me to be inseparable from the exercise of political rights; and I think that the number of citizens will be found to augment or decrease in Europe in proportion as those rights are extended.

How happens it that in the United States, where the inhabitants arrived but   12
as yesterday upon the soil which they now occupy, and brought neither customs nor traditions with them there; where they met each other for the first time with no previous acquaintance; where, in short, the instinctive love of country can scarcely exist;—how happens it that every one takes as zealous an interest in the affairs of his township, his county, and the whole State, as if they were his own? It is because every one, in his sphere, takes an active part in the govern- ment of society. The lower orders in the United States understand the influence exercised by the general prosperity upon their own welfare; simple as this observation is, it is too rarely made by the people. Besides, they are wont to regard this prosperity as the fruit of their own exertions. The citizen looks upon the fortune of the public as his own, and he labors for the good of the State, not merely from a sense of pride or duty, but from what I venture to term cupidity.

It is unnecessary to study the institutions and the history of the Americans in   13
order to know the truth of this remark, for their manners render it sufficiently evident. As the American participates in all that is done in his country, he thinks himself obliged to defend whatever may be censured in it; for it is not only his country which is then attacked, it is himself. The consequence is, that his national pride resorts to a thousand artifices, and descends to all the petty tricks of personal vanity.

Nothing is more embarrassing, in the ordinary intercourse of life, than this   14
irritable patriotism of the Americans. A stranger may be well inclined to praise many of the institutions of their country, but he begs permission to blame some

things in it,—a permission which is inexorably refused. America is therefore a free country, in which, lest anybody should be hurt by your remarks, you are not allowed to speak freely of private individuals, or of the state; of the citizens, or of the authorities; of public or of private undertakings; or, in short, of anything at all, except, perhaps, the climate and the soil; and even then, Americans will be found ready to defend both, as if they had concurred in producing them.

15 In our times, we must choose between the patriotism of all and the government of a few; for the social force and activity which the first confers are irreconcilable with the pledges of tranquillity which are given by the second.

Notion of Rights.

16 After the general idea of virtue, I know no higher principle than that of right; or rather these two ideas are united in one. The idea of right is simply that of virtue introduced into the political world. It was the idea of right which enabled men to define anarchy and tyranny; and which taught them how to be independent without arrogance, and to obey without servility. The man who submits to violence is debased by his compliance; but when he submits to that right of authority which he acknowledges in a fellow-creature, he rises in some measure above the person who gives the command. There are no great men without virtue; and there are no great nations,—it may almost be added, there would be no society,—without respect for right; for what is a union of rational and intelligent beings who are held together only by the bond of force? . . .

17 The government of the democracy brings the notion of political rights to the level of the humblest citizens, just as the dissemination of wealth brings the notion of property within the reach of all men; to my mind, this is one of its greatest advantages. I do not say it is easy to teach men how to exercise political rights; but I maintain that, when it is possible, the effects which result from it are highly important; and I add, that, if there ever was a time at which such an attempt ought to be made, that time is now. Do you not see that religious belief is shaken, and the divine notion of right is declining?—that morality is debased, and the notion of moral right is therefore fading away? Argument is substituted for faith, and calculation for the impulses of sentiment. If, in the midst of this general disruption, you do not succeed in connecting the notion of right with that of private interest, which is the only immutable point in the human heart, what means will you have of governing the world except by fear? When I am told that the laws are weak and the people are turbulent, that passions are excited and the authority of virtue is paralyzed, and therefore no measures must be taken to increase the rights of democracy, I reply, that, for these very reasons, some measures of the kind ought to be taken; and I believe that governments are still more interested in taking them than society at large, for governments may perish, but society cannot die.

18 But I do not wish to exaggerate the example which America furnishes. There the people were invested with political rights at a time when they could not be

abused, for the inhabitants were few in number, and simple in their manners. As they have increased, the Americans have not augmented the power of the democracy; they have rather extended its domain.

It cannot be doubted that the moment at which political rights are granted to   *19* a people that had before been without them is a very critical one,—that the measure, though often necessary, is always dangerous. A child may kill before he is aware of the value of life; and he may deprive another person of his property, before he is aware that his own may be taken from him. The lower orders, when first they are invested with political rights, stand, in relation to those rights, in the same position as the child does to the whole of nature; and the celebrated adage may then be applied to them, *Homo puer robustus.* This truth may be perceived even in America. The States in which the citizens have enjoyed their rights longest, are those in which they make the best use of them.

It cannot be repeated too often, that nothing is more fertile in prodigies than   *20* the art of being free; but there is nothing more arduous than the apprenticeship of liberty. It is not so with despotism: despotism often promises to make amends for a thousand previous ills; it supports the right, it protects the oppressed, and it maintains public order. The nation is lulled by the temporary prosperity which it produces, until it is roused to a sense of its misery. Liberty, on the contrary, is generally established with difficulty in the midst of storms; it is perfected by civil discord; and its benefits cannot be appreciated until it is already old.

Respect for the Law.

It is not always feasible to consult the whole people, either directly or indi-   *21* rectly, in the formation of the law; but it cannot be denied that, when this is possible, the authority of the law is much augmented. This popular origin, which impairs the excellence and the wisdom of legislation, contributes much to increase its power. There is an amazing strength in the expression of the will of a whole people; and when it declares itself, even the imagination of those who would wish to contest it is overawed. The truth of this fact is well known by parties; and they consequently strive to make out a majority whenever they can. If they have not the greater number of voters on their side, they assert that the true majority abstained from voting; and if they are foiled even there, they have recourse to those who had no right to vote.

In the United States, except slaves, servants, and paupers supported by the   *22* townships, there is no class of persons who do not exercise the elective franchise, and who do not indirectly contribute to make the laws. Those who wish to attack the laws must consequently either change the opinion of the nation, or trample upon its decision.

A second reason, which is still more direct and weighty, may be adduced: in   *23* the United States, every one is personally interested in enforcing the obedience of the whole community to the law; for as the minority may shortly rally the majority to its principles, it is interested in professing that respect for the decrees of the legislator which it may soon have occasion to claim for its own. However irksome an enactment may be, the citizen of the United States complies with it, not only because it is the work of the majority, but because it is his own, and he regards it as a contract to which he is himself a party.

24   In the United States, then, that numerous and turbulent multitude does not exist, who, regarding the law as their natural enemy, look upon it with fear and distrust. It is impossible, on the contrary, not to perceive that all classes display the utmost reliance upon the legislation of their country, and are attached to it by a kind of parental affection.

25   I am wrong, however, in saying all classes; for as, in America, the European scale of authority is inverted, the wealthy are there placed in a position analogous to that of the poor in the Old World, and it is the opulent classes who frequently look upon the law with suspicion. I have already observed that the advantage of democracy is not, as has been sometimes asserted, that it protects the interests of all, but simply that it protects those of the majority. In the United States, where the poor rule, the rich have always something to fear from the abuse of their power. This natural anxiety of the rich may produce a secret dissatisfaction; but society is not disturbed by it, for the same reason which withholds the confidence of the rich from the legislative authority, makes them obey its mandates: their wealth, which prevents them from making the law, prevents them from withstanding it. Amongst civilized nations, only those who have nothing to lose ever revolt; and if the laws of a democracy are not always worthy of respect, they are always respected; for those who usually infringe the laws cannot fail to obey those which they have themselves made, and by which they are benefited, whilst the citizens who might be interested in the infraction of them are induced, by their character and station, to submit to the decisions of the legislature, whatever they may be. Besides, the people in America obey the law, not only because it is their work, but because it may be changed if it be harmful; a law is observed because, first, it is a self-imposed evil, and, secondly, it is an evil of transient duration.

Political Activity which Pervades the United States.

26   . . . It is not impossible to conceive the surprising liberty which the Americans enjoy; some idea may likewise be formed of their extreme equality; but the political activity which pervades the United States must be seen in order to be understood. No sooner do you set foot upon American ground, than you are stunned by a kind of tumult; a confused clamor is heard on every side; and a thousand simultaneous voices demand the satisfaction of their social wants. Everything is in motion around you; here, the people of one quarter of a town are met to decide upon the building of a church; there, the election of a representative is going on; a little further, the delegates of a district are posting to the town in order to consult some local improvements; in another place, the laborers of a village quit their ploughs to deliberate upon the project of a road or a public school. Meetings are called for the sole purpose of declaring their disapprobation of the conduct of the government; whilst in other assemblies,

citizens salute the authorities of the day as the fathers of their country. Societies are formed which regard drunkenness as the principal cause of the evils of the state, and solemnly bind themselves to give an example of temperance. The great political agitation of American legislative bodies, which is the only one that attracts the attention of foreigners, is a mere episode, or a sort of continuation, of that universal movement which originates in the lowest classes of the people, and extends successively to all the ranks of society. It is impossible to spend more effort in the pursuit of happiness.

The cares of politics engross a prominent place in the occupations of a citi- 27
zen in the United States; and almost the only pleasure which an American knows is to take a part in the government, and to discuss its measures. This feeling pervades the most trifling habits of life; even the women frequently attend public meetings, and listen to political harangues as a recreation from their household labors. Debating clubs are, to a certain extent, a substitute for theatrical entertainments: an American cannot converse, but he can discuss; and his talk falls into a dissertation. He speaks to you as if he was addressing a meeting; and if he should chance to become warm in the discussion, he will say "Gentlemen" to the person with whom he is conversing.

In some countries, the inhabitants seem unwilling to avail themselves of the 28
political privileges which the law gives them; it would seem that they set too high a value upon their time to spend it on the interests of the community; and they shut themselves up in a narrow selfishness, marked out by four sunk fences and a quickset hedge. But if an American were condemned to confine his activity to his own affairs, he would be robbed of one half of his existence; he would feel an immense void in the life which he is accustomed to lead, and his wretchedness would be unbearable. I am persuaded, that, if ever a despotism should be established in America, it will be more difficult to overcome the habits which freedom has formed, than to conquer the love of freedom itself.

This ceaseless agitation which democratic government has introduced into 29
the political world, influences all social intercourse. I am not sure that, upon the whole, this is not the greatest advantage of democracy; and I am less inclined to applaud it for what it does, than for what it causes to be done. It is incontestable that the people frequently conduct public business very ill; but it is impossible that the lower orders should take a part in public business without extending the circle of their ideas, and quitting the ordinary routine of their thoughts. The humblest individual who co-operates in the government of society acquires a certain degree of self-respect; and as he possesses authority, he can command the services of minds more enlightened than his own. He is canvassed by a multitude of applicants, and, in seeking to deceive him in a thousand ways, they really enlighten him. He takes a part in political undertakings which he did not originate, but which give him a taste for undertakings of the kind. New improvements are daily pointed out to him in the common property, and this gives him the desire of improving that property which is his own. He is perhaps neither happier nor better than those who came before him, but he is better informed and more active. I have no doubt that the democratic institutions of the United States, joined to the physical constitution of the country, are

the cause (not the direct, as is so often asserted, but the indirect cause) of the prodigious commercial activity of the inhabitants. It is not created by the laws, but the people learn how to promote it by the experience derived from legislation.

30   When the opponents of democracy assert that a single man performs what he undertakes better than the government of all, it appears to me that they are right. The government of an individual, supposing an equality of knowledge on either side, is more consistent, more persevering, more uniform, and more accurate in details, than that of a multitude, and it selects with more discrimination the men whom it employs. If any deny this, they have never seen a democratic government, or have judged upon partial evidence. It is true that, even when local circumstances and the dispositions of the people allow democratic institutions to exist, they do not display a regular and methodical system of government. Democratic liberty is far from accomplishing all its projects with the skill of an adroit despotism. It frequently abandons them before they have borne their fruits, or risks them when the consequences may be dangerous; but in the end, it produces more than any absolute government; if it does fewer things well, it does a greater number of things. Under its sway, the grandeur is not in what the public administration does, but in what is done without it or outside of it. Democracy does not give the people the most skillful government, but it produces what the ablest governments are frequently unable to create; namely, an all-pervading and restless activity, a superabundant force, and an energy which is inseparable from it, and which may, however unfavorable circumstances may be, produce wonders. These are the true advantages of democracy.

31   In the present age, when the destinies of Christendom seem to be in suspense, some hasten to assail democracy as a hostile power, whilst it is yet growing; and others already adore this new deity which is springing forth from chaos. But both parties are imperfectly acquainted with the object of their hatred or their worship; they strike in the dark, and distribue their blows at random.

32   We must first understand what is wanted of society and its government. Do you wish to give a certain elevation to the human mind, and teach it to regard the things of this world with generous feelings, to inspire men with a scorn of mere temproal advantages, to form and nourish strong convictions, and keep alive the spirit of honorable devotedness? Is it your object to refine the habits, embellish the manners, and cultivate the arts, to promote the love of poetry, beauty, and glory? Would you constitute a people fitted to act powerfully upon all other nations, and prepared for those high enterprises which, whatever be their results, will leave a name forever famous in history? If you believe such to be the principal object of society, avoid the government of the democracy, for it would not lead you with certainty to the goal.

33   But if you hold it expedient to divert the moral and intellectual activity of man to the production of comfort, and the promotion of general well-being; if a clear understanding be more profitable to man than genius; if your object be not to stimulate the virtues of heroism, but the habits of peace; if you had

rather witness vices than crimes, and are content to meet with fewer noble deeds, provided offences be diminished in the same proportion; if, instead of living in the midst of a brilliant society, you are contented to have prosperity around you; if, in short, you are of opinion that the principal object of a government is not to confer the greatest possible power and glory upon the body of the nation, but to insure the greatest enjoyment, and to avoid the most misery, to each of the individuals who comprise it,—if such be your desire, then equalize the conditions of men, and establish democratic institutions.

But if the time be past at which such a choice was possible, and if some   *34* power superior to that of man already hurries us, without consulting our wishes, towards one or the other of these two governments, let us endeavor to make the best of that which is allotted to us, and, by finding out both its good and its evil tendencies, be able to foster the former and repress the latter to the utmost.

12. UNLIMITED POWER OF THE MAJORITY IN THE UNITED STATES AND ITS CONSEQUENCES.

The very essence of democratic government consists in the absolute sovereignty *35* of the majority; for there is nothing in democratic states which is capable of resisting it. Most of the American constitutions have sought to increase this natural strength of the majority by artificial means.

The legislature is, of all political institutions, the one which is most easily *36* swayed by the will of the majority. The Americans determined that the members of the legislature should be elected by the people *directly*, and for a *very brief term*, in order to subject them, not only to the general convictions, but even to the daily passions, of their constitutents. The members of both houses are taken from the same classes in society, and nominated in the same manner; so that the movements of the legislative bodies are almost as rapid, and quite as irresistible, as those of a single assembly. It is to a legislature thus constituted, that almost all the authority of the government has been intrusted.

At the same time that the law increased the strength of those authorities *37* which of themselves were strong, it enfeebled more and more those which were naturally weak. It deprived the representatives of the executive power of all stability and independence; and, by subjecting them completely to the caprices of the legislature, it robbed them of the slender influence which the nature of a democratic government might have allowed them to exercise. In several States, the judicial power was also submitted to the election of the majority; and in all of them, its existence was made to depend on the pleasure of the legislative authority, since the representatives were empowered annually to regulate the stipend of the judges.

Custom has done even more than law. A proceeding is becoming more and *38* more general in the United States, which will, in the end, do away with the guaranties of representative government: it frequently happens that the voters, in electing a delegate, point out a certain line of conduct to him, and impose upon him certain positive obligations which he is pledged to fulfil. With the exeption of the tumult, this comes to the same thing as if the majority itself held its deliberations in the market-place.

39   Several other circumstances concur to render the power of the majority in America not only preponderant, but irresistible. The moral authority of the majority is partly based upon the notion, that there is more intelligence and wisdom in a number of men united than in a single individual, and that the number of the legislators is more important than their quality. The theory of equality is thus applied to the intellects of men; and human pride is thus assailed in its last retreat by a doctrine which the minority hesitate to admit, and to which they will but slowly assent. Like all other powers, and perhaps more than any other, the authority of the many requires the sanction of time in order to appear legitimate. At first, it enforces obedience by constraint; and its laws are not *respected* until they have been long maintained.

40   The right of governing society, which the majority supposes itself to derive from its superior intelligence, was introduced into the United States by the first settlers; and this idea, which of itself would be sufficient to create a free nation, has now been amalgamated with the manners of the people and the minor incidents of social life.

41   The French, under the old monarchy, held it for a maxim that the king could do no wrong; and if he did do wrong, the blame was imputed to his advisers. This notion made obedience very easy; it enabled the subject to complain of the law, without ceasing to love and honor the lawgiver. The Americans entertain the same option with respect to the majority.

42   The moral power of the majority is founded upon yet another principle, which is, that the interests of the many are to be preferred to those of the few. It will readily be perceived that the respect here professed for the rights of the greater number must naturally increase or diminish according to the state of parties. When a nation is divided into several great irreconcilable interests, the privilege of the majority is often overlooked, because it is intolerable to comply with its demands.

43   If there existed in America a class of citizens whom the legislating majority sought to deprive of exclusive privileges which they had possessed for ages, and to bring down from an elevated station to the level of the multitude, it is probable that the minority would be less ready to submit to its laws. But as the United States were colonized by men holding equal rank, there is as yet no natural or permanent disagreement between the interests of its different inhabitants.

44   There are communities in which the members of the minority can never hope to draw over the majority to their side, because they must then give up the very point which is at issue between them. Thus, an aristocracy can never become a majority whilst it retains its exclusive privileges, and it cannot cede its privileges without ceasing to be an aristocracy.

45   In the United States, political questions cannot be taken up in so general and absolute a manner; and all parties are willing to recognize the rights of the

majority, because they all hope at some time to be able to exercise them to their own advantage. The majority, therefore, in that country, exercise a prodigious actual authority, and a power of opinion which is nearly as great; no obstacles exist which can impede or even retard its progress, so as to make it heed the complaints of those whom it crushes upon its path. This state of things is harmful in itself, and dangerous for the future. . . .

Tyranny of the Majority.

I hold it to be an impious and detestable maxim, that, politically speaking,   *46*
the people have a right to do anything; and yet I have asserted that all authority originates in the will of the majority. Am I, then, in contradiction with myself?

A general law, which bears the name of justice, has been made and sanc-   *47*
tioned, not only by a majority of this or that people, but by a majority of mankind. The rights of every people are therefore confined within the limits of what is just. A nation may be considered as a jury which is empowered to represent society at large, and to apply justice, which is its law. Ought such a jury, which represents society, to have more power than the society itself, whose laws it executes?

When I refuse to obey an unjust law, I do not contest the right of the major-   *48*
ity to command, but I simply appeal from the sovereignty of the people to the sovereignty of mankind. Some have not feared to assert that a people can never outstep the boundaries of justice and reason in those affairs which are peculiarly its own; and that consequently full power may be given to the majority by which they are represented. But this is the language of a slave.

A majority taken collectively is only an individual, whose opinions, and fre-   *49*
quently whose interests, are opposed to those of another individual, who is styled a minority. If it be admitted that a man possessing absolute power may misuse that power by wronging his adversaries, why should not a majority be liable to the same reproach? Men do not change their characters by uniting with each other; nor does their patience in the presence of obstacles increase with their strength. For my own part, I cannot believe it; the power to do everything, which I should refuse to one of my equals, I will never grant to any number of them.

I do not think, for the sake of preserving liberty, it is possible to combine   *50*
several principles in the same government so as really to oppose them to one another. The form of government which is usually termed *mixed* has always appeared to me a mere chimera. Accurately speaking, there is no such thing as a *mixed government*, in the sense usually given to that word, because, in all communities, some one principle of action may be discovered which preponderates over the others. England, in the last century,—which has been especially cited as an example of this sort of government,—was essentially an aristocratic state, although it comprised some great elements of democracy; for the laws and customs of the country were such that the aristocracy could not but preponderate in the long run, and direct public affairs according to its own will.

The error arose from seeing the interests of the nobles perpetually contending with those of the people, without considering the issue of the contest, which was really the important point. When a community actually has a mixed government,—that is to say, when it is equally divided between adverse principles,—it must either experience a revolution, or fall into anarchy.

51   I am therefore of opinion, that social power superior to all others must always be placed somewhere; but I think that liberty is endangered when this power finds no obstacles which can retard its course, and give it time to moderate its own vehemence.

52   Unlimited power is in itself a bad and dangerous thing. Human beings are not competent to exercise it with discretion. God alone can be omnipotent, because his wisdom and his justice are always equal to his power. There is no power on earth so worthy of honor in itself, or clothed with rights so sacred, that I would admit its uncontrolled and all-predominant authority. When I see that the right and the means of absolute command are conferred on any power whatever, be it called a people or a king, an aristocracy or a democracy, a monarchy or a republic, I say there is the germ of tyranny, and I seek to live elsewhere, under other laws.

53   In my opinion, the main evil of the present democractic institutions of the United States does not arise, as is often asserted in Europe, from their weakness, but from their irresistible strength. I am not so much alarmed at the excessive liberty which reigns in that country, as at the inadequate securities which one finds there against tyranny.

54   When an individual or a party is wronged in the United States, to whom can he apply for redress? If to public opinion, public opinion constitutes the majority; if to the legislature, it represents the majority, and implicitly obeys it; if to the executive power, it is appointed by the majority, and serves as a passive tool in its hands. The public force consists of the majority under arms; the jury is the majority invested with the right of hearing judicial cases; and in certain States, even the judges are elected by the majority. However iniquitous or absurd the measure of which you complain, you must submit to it as well as you can.

55   If, on the other hand, a legislative power could be so constituted as to represent the majority without necessarily being the slave of its passions, an executive so as to retain a proper share of authority, and a judiciary so as to remain independent of the other two powers, a government would be formed which would still be democratic, without incurring hardly any risk of tyranny.

56   I do not say that there is a frequent use of tyranny in America, at the present day; but I maintain that there is no sure barrier against it, and that the causes which mitigate the government there are to be found in the circumstances and the manners of the country, more than in its laws.

Effects of the Omnipotence of the Majority upon the Arbitrary Authority of American Public Officers.

57   A distinction must be drawn between tyranny and arbitrary power. Tyranny may be exercised by means of the law itself, and in that case it is not arbitrary;

arbitrary power may be exercised for the public good, in which case it is not tyrannical. Tyranny usually employs arbitrary means, but, if necessary, it can do without them.

In the United States, the omnipotence of the majority, which is favorable to   58
the legal despotism of the legislature, likewise favors the arbitrary authority of the magistrate. The majority has absolute power both to make the law and to watch over its execution; and as it has equal authority over those who are in power, and the community at large, it considers public officers as its passive agents, and readily confides to them the task of carrying out its designs. The details of their office, and the privileges which they are to enjoy, are rarely defined beforehand. It treats them as a master does his servants, since they are always at work in his sight, and he can direct or reprimand them at any instant.

In general, the American functionaries are far more independent within the   59
sphere which is prescribed to them than the French civil officers. Sometimes, even, they are allowed by the popular authority to exceed those bounds; and as they are protected by the opinion, and backed by the power, of the majority, they dare do things which even a European, accustomed as he is to arbitrary power, is astonished at. By this means, habits are formed in the heart of a free country which may some day prove fatal to its liberties.

Power Exercised by the Majority in America upon Opinion.

It is in the examination of the exercise of thought in the United States, that   60
we clearly perceive how far the power of the majority surpasses all the powers with which we are acquainted in Europe. Thought is an invisible and subtile power, that mocks all the efforts of tyranny. At the present time, the most absolute monarchs in Europe cannot prevent certain opinions hostile to their authority from circulating in secret through their dominions, and even in their courts. It is not so in America; as long as the majority is still undecided, discussion is carried on; but as soon as its decision is irrevocably pronounced, every one is silent, and the friends as well as the opponents of the measure unite in assenting to its propriety. The reason of this is perfectly clear: no monarch is so absolute as to combine all the powers of society in his own hands, and to conquer all opposition, as a majority is able to do, which has the right both of making and of executing the laws.

The authority of a king is physical, and controls the actions of men without   61
subduing their will. But the majority possesses a power which is physical and moral at the same time, which acts upon the will as much as upon the actions, and represses not only all contest, but all controversy.

I know of no country in which there is so little independence of mind and   62
real freedom of discussion as in America. In any constitutional state in Europe, every sort of religious and political theory may be freely preached and disseminated; for there is no country in Europe so subdued by any single authority, as not to protect the man who raises his voice in the cause of truth from the consequences of his hardihood. If he is unfortunate enough to live under an absolute government, the people are often upon his side; if he inhabits a free country, he can, if necessary, find a shelter behind the throne. The aristocratic part

of society supports him in some countries, and the democracy in others. But in a nation where democratic institutions exist, organized like those of the United States, there is but one authority, one element of strength and success, with nothing beyond it.

63   In America, the majority raises formidable barriers around the liberty of opinion: within these barriers, an author may write what he pleases; but woe to him if he goes beyond them. Not that he is in danger of an *auto-da-fé*, but he is exposed to continued obloquy and persecution. His political career is closed forever, since he has offended the only authority which is able to open it. Every sort of compensation, even that of celebrity, is refused to him. Before publishing his opinions, he imagined that he held them in common with others; but no sooner has he declared them, than he is loudly censured by his opponents, whilst those who think like him, without having the courage to speak out, abandon him in silence. He yields at length, overcome by the daily effort which he has to make, and subsides into silence, as if he felt remorse for having spoken the truth.

64   Fetters and headsmen were the coarse instruments which tyranny formerly employed; but the civilization of our age has perfected despotism itself, though it seemed to have nothing to learn. Monarchs had, so to speak, materialized oppression: the democratic republics of the present day have rendered it as entirely an affair of the mind, as the will which it is intended to coerce. Under the absolute sway of one man, the body was attacked in order to subdue the soul; but the soul escaped the blows which were directed against it, and rose proudly superior. Such is not the course adopted by tyranny in democratic republics; there the body is left free, and the soul is enslaved. The master no longer says, "You shall think as I do, or you shall die"; but he says, "You are free to think differently from me, and to retain your life, your property, and all that you possess; but you are henceforth a stranger among your people. You may retain your civil rights, but they will be useless to you, for you will never be chosen by your fellow-citizens, if you solicit their votes; and they will affect to scorn you, if you ask for their esteem. You will remain among men, but you will be deprived of the rights of mankind. Your fellow-creatures will shun you like an impure being; and even those who believe in your innocence will abandon you, lest they should be shunned in their turn. Go in peace! I have given you your life, but it is an existence worse than death."

65   Absolute monarchies had dishonored despotism; let us beware lest democratic republics should reinstate it, and render it less odious and degrading in the eyes of the many, by making it still more onerous to the few.

66   Works have been published in the proudest nations of the Old World, expressly intended to censure the vices and the follies of the times: Labruyère inhabited the palace of Louis XIV., when he composed his chapter upon the Great, and Moliere criticised the courtiers in the pieces which were acted before the court. But the ruling power in the United States is not to be made game of. The smallest reproach irritates its sensibility, and the slightest joke which has any foundation in truth renders it indignant; from the forms of its language up to the solid virtues of its character, everything must be made the

subject of encomium. No writer, whatever be his eminence, can escape paying this tribute of adulation to his fellow-citizens. The majority lives in the perpetual utterance of self-applause; and there are certain truths which the Americans can only learn from strangers or from experience.

If America has not as yet had any great writers, the reason is given in these 67
facts; there can be no literary genius without freedom of opinion, and freedom of opinion does not exist in America. The Inquisition has never been able to prevent a vast number of anti-religious books from circulating in Spain. The empire of the majority succeeds much better in the United States, since it actually removes any wish to publish them. Unbelievers are to be met with in America, but there is no public organ of infidelity. Attempts have been made by some governments to protect morality by prohibiting licentious books. In the United States, no one is punished for this sort of book, but no one is induced to write them; not because all the citizens are immaculate in conduct, but because the majority of the community is decent and orderly.

In this case the use of the power is unquestionably good; and I am discuss- 68
ing the nature of the power itself. This irresistible authority is a constant fact, and its judicious exercise is only an accident.

Effects of the Tyranny of the Majority upon the National Character of the Americans.

The tendencies which I have just mentioned are as yet but slightly percepti- 69
ble in political society; but they already exercise an unfavorable influence upon the national character of the Americans. I attribute the small number of distinguished men in political life to the ever-increasing despotism of the majority in the United States.

When the American Revolution broke out, they arose in great numbers; for 70
public opinion then served, not to tyrannize over, but to direct the exertions of individuals. Those celebrated men, sharing the agitation of mind common at that period, had a grandeur peculiar to themselves, which was reflected back upon the nation, but was by no means borrowed from it.

In absolute governments, the great nobles who are nearest to the throne flat- 71
ter the passions of the sovereign, and voluntarily truckle to his caprices. But the mass of the nation does not degrade itself by servitude; it often submits from weakness, from habit, or from ignorance, and sometimes from loyalty. Some nations have been known to sacrifice their own desires to those of the sovereign with pleasure and pride, thus exhibiting a sort of independence of mind in the very act of submission. These nations are miserable, but they are not degraded. There is a great difference between doing what one does not approve, and feigning to approve what one does; the one is the weakness of a feeble person, the other befits the temper of a lackey.

In free countries, where every one is more or less called upon to give his 72
opinion on affairs of state,—in democratic republics, where public life is incessantly mingled with domestic affairs, where the sovereign authority is accessible on every side, and where its attention can always be attracted by vocifera-

tion,—more persons are to be met with who speculate upon its weaknesses, and live upon ministering to its passions, than in absolute monarchies. Not because men are naturally worse in these states than elsewhere, but the temptation is stronger and of easier access at the same time. The result is a more extensive debasement of character.

73   Democratic republics extend the practice of currying favor with the many, and introduce it into all classes at once: this is the most serious reproach that can be addressed to them. This is especially true in democratic states organized like the American republics, where the power of the majority is so absolute and irresistible that one must give up his rights as a citizen, and almost abjure his qualities as a man, if he intends to stray from the track which it prescribes.

74   In that immense crowd which throngs the avenues to power in the United States, I found very few men who displayed that manly candor and masculine independence of opinion which frequently distinguished the Americans in former times, and which constitutes the leading feature in distinguished characters wheresoever they may be found. It seems, at first sight, as if all the minds of the Americans were formed upon one model, so accurately do they follow the same route. A stranger does, indeed, sometimes meet with Americans who dissent from the rigor of these formularies,—with men who deplore the defects of the laws, the mutability and the ignorance of democracy,—who even go so far as to observe the evil tendencies which impair the national character, and to point out such remedies as it might be possible to apply; but no one is there to hear except yourself, and you, to whom these secret reflections are confided, are a stranger and a bird of passage. They are very ready to communicate truths which are useless to you, but they hold a different language in public. . . .

The Greatest Dangers of the American Republics Proceed from the Omnipotence of the Majority.

75   Governments usually perish from impotence or from tyranny. In the former case, their power escapes from them; it is wrested from their grasp in the latter. Many observers who have witnessed the anarchy of democratic states, have imagined that the government of those states was naturally weak and impotent. The truth is, that, when war is once begun between parties, the government loses its control over society. But I do not think that a democratic power is naturally without force or resources; say, rather, that it is almost always by the abuse of its force, and the misemployment of its resources, that it becomes a failure. Anarchy is almost always produced by its tyranny or its mistakes, but not by its want of strength.

76   It is important not to confound stability with force, or the greatness of a thing with its duration. In democratic republics, the power which directs society is not stable; for it often changes hands, and assumes a new direction. But, whichever way it turns, its force is almost irresistible. The governments of the American republics appear to me to be as much centralized as those of the

absolute monarchies of Europe, and more energetic than they are. I do not, therefore, imagine that they will perish from weakness.

If ever the free institutions of America are destroyed, that even may be   77
attributed to the omnipotence of the majority, which may at some future time urge the minorities to desperation, and oblige them to have recourse to physical force. Anarchy will then be the result, but it will have been brought about by despotism.

Mr. Madison expresses the same opinion in the Federalist, No. 51. "It is of   78
great importance in a republic, not only to guard the society against the oppression of its rulers, but to guard one part of the society against the injustice of the other part. Justice is the end of government. It is the end of civil society. It ever has been, and ever will be, pursued until it be obtained, or until liberty be lost in the pursuit. In a society, under the forms of which the stronger faction can readily unite and oppress the weaker, anarchy may as truly be said to reign as in a state of nature, where the weaker individual is not secured against the violence of the stronger; and as, in the latter state, even the stronger individuals are prompted by the uncertainty of their condition to submit to a government which may protect the weak as well as themselves, so, in the former state, will the more powerful factions be gradually induced by a like motive to wish for a government which will protect all parties, the weaker as well as the more powerful. It can be little doubted, that, if the State of Rhode Island was separated from the Confederacy and left to itself, the insecurity of right under the popular form of government within such narrow limits would be displayed by such reiterated oppressions of the factious majorities, that some power altogether independent of the people would soon be called for by the voice of the very factions whose misrule had proved the necessity of it."

Jefferson also said: "The executive power in our government is not the only,   79
perhaps not even the principal, object of my solicitude. The tyranny of the legislature is really the danger most to be feared, and will continue to be so for many years to come. The tyranny of the executive power will come in its turn, but at a more distant period."

I am glad to cite the opinion of Jefferson upon this subject rather than that   80
of any other, because I consider him the most powerful advocate democracy has ever had.

WRITING AND DISCUSSION QUESTIONS

Informative

1. What does Tocqueville see as the advantages of democracy over aristocracy? What does he say about the advantages of democracy in the sections on ''Public Spirit'' and ''Notion of Rights''?
2. How do chosen leaders in democracy compare to those in aristocracy, especially in leadership capacity and morality? In the Bush-Dukakis presidential election, most

voters were disgusted by the crass level of national discourse. How can you relate Tocqueville's comments on choice of public officials to the presidential selection process?

3. In the section "Respect for the Law," Tocqueville writes of citizen participation in lawmaking. Which excluded group does he fail to mention? Is this omission significant in any way? What does he mean by "In the United States, where the poor rule, the rich have always something to fear from the abuse of their power"?

Persuasive

1. Summarize Tocqueville's thoughts in the section on "Political Activity which Pervades the United States." Argue that the role of the active citizen in government has or has not changed.

2. What does Tocqueville consider to be the dangers of giving full political rights to young nation–states? Considering world events, argue that Tocqueville was or was not correct in his predictions here.

3. Using Tocqueville's definition of "tyranny of the majority," argue that the United States is or is not a country where there is "so little independence of mind and real freedom of discussion."

Personal

1. Does the majority in America contribute to mediocre leadership and general impairment of the national character? Can you think of several examples, such as the mindless fare that dominates much of television, that demonstrate the dangers of mass values in setting low and often vulgar standards?

2. Imagine yourself to be Alexis de Tocqueville, transported in time from the 1830s to the present. You have another nine months to tour America and to test your predictions and observations made previously. Summarize your present-day impressions and compare them with those made in the 1830s.

3. Imagine that Tocqueville is being interviewed for television by your favorite television personality—Ted Koppel, Connie Chung, Mike Douglas, Oprah, or Geraldo. Write out the interview, questions, and responses.

▼

MARTIN LUTHER KING, JR., "LETTER FROM BIRMINGHAM JAIL"

Martin Luther King, Jr. (1929–1968) has become synonymous with the struggle of black people and the poor to overcome oppression and to gain civil rights. He was born the son of a Baptist minister, was graduated from Morehouse College and Grozer Theological Seminary, and he earned his Ph.D. from Boston University. Influenced by Mahatma Gandhi's philosophy of nonviolent change, he became pastor at a church in Montgomery, Alabama, in 1955, where he used the tactics of economic boycott and civil disobedience to protest the segregation of public bus transportation.

In 1957, King moved to Atlanta, where he served with his father as pastor of the Ebenezer Baptist Church. At that time, he also organized the influential civil rights organization, the Southern Christian Leadership Conference.

In the decade that followed, King led demonstrations against segregation throughout the South. His marches were often met with violence, and sometimes he was arrested and jailed. Although he was successful in changing many of the oppressive Jim Crow laws and conditions in the country at the time (Jim Crow laws refer to the system of legal and traditional sanctions, most notably segregation against black people in the American South), King's importance extended far beyond the mere opening up of public buses and accommodations. As theologian Father James Bacik has written,

> King was an outstanding public theologian who demonstrated great insight and unusual creativity in applying the Christian faith to public policy questions. He was an activist theologian who developed his thinking through involvement in the liberation struggles of his times, rather than through abstract speculation on Christian doctrine. He was an American theologian, rooted in his black Southern Baptist religious heritage, who was also able to speak a universal message which continues to inspire people of all races and creeds.[1]

In 1963 from a Birmingham jail, King wrote the letter that follows on margins of newspapers and on toilet paper and smuggled it to an aide. It was his response to a statement signed by eight clergymen, who critized him for his "unwise and untimely" demonstrations. A year later, he was awarded the Nobel Peace Prize. He was assassinated in 1968.

▼

Letter from Birmingham Jail
MARTIN LUTHER KING, JR.

My Dear Fellow Clergymen:

While confined here in the Birmingham city jail, I came across your recent   *1*
statement calling my present activities "unwise and untimely." Seldom do I pause to answer criticism of my work and ideas. If I sought to answer all the criticisms that cross my desk, my secretaries would have little time for anything other than such correspondence in the course of the day, and I would have no time for constructive work. But since I feel that you are men of genuine good will and that your criticisms are sincerely set forth, I want to try to answer your statement in what I hope will be patient and reasonable terms.

I think I should indicate why I am here in Birmingham, since you have been   *2*
influenced by the view which argues against "outsiders coming in." I have the

[1]James J. Bacik, "Martin Luther King, Jr.," *Contemporary Theologians*, Vol. 6, No. 8, Chicago: Thomas More Association. Jan. 26, 1984.

honor of serving as president of the Southern Christian Leadership Conference, an organization operating in every southern state, with headquarters in Atlanta, Georgia. We have some eighty-five affiliated organizations across the South, and one of them is the Alabama Christian Movement for Human Rights. Frequently we share staff, educational, and financial resources with our affiliates. Several months ago the affiliate here in Birmingham asked us to be on call to engage in a nonviolent direct-action program if such were deemed necessary. We readily consented, and when the hour came we lived up to our promise. So I, along with several members of my staff, am here because I was invited here. I am here because I have organizational ties here.

3   But more basically, I am in Birmingham because injustice is here. Just as the prophets of the eighth century B.C. left their villages and carried their "thus saith the Lord" far beyond the boundaries of their home towns, and just as the Apostle Paul left his village of Tarsus and carried the gospel of Jesus Christ to the far corners of the Greco-Roman world, so am I compelled to carry the gospel of freedom beyond my own home town. Like Paul, I must constantly respond to the Macedonian call for aid.

4   Moreover, I am cognizant of the interrelatedness of all communities and states. I cannot sit idly by in Atlanta and not be concerned about what happens in Birmingham. Injustice anywhere is a threat to justice everywhere. We are caught in an inescapable network of mutuality, tied in a single garment of destiny. Whatever affects one directly, affects all indirectly. Never again can we afford to live with the narow, provincial "outside agitator" idea. Anyone who lives inside the United States can never be considered an outsider anywhere within its bounds.

5   You deplore the demonstrations taking place in Birmingham. But your statement, I am sorry to say, fails to express a similar concern for the conditions that brought about the demonstrations. I am sure that none of you would want to rest content with the superficial kind of social analysis that deals merely with effects and does not grapple with underlying causes. It is unfortunate that demonstrations are taking place in Birmingham, but it is even more unfortunate that the city's white power structure left the Negro community with no alternative.

6   In any nonviolent campaign there are four basic steps: collection of the facts to determine whether injustices exist; negotiation; self-purification; and direct action. We have gone through all these steps in Birmingham. There can be no gainsaying the fact that racial injustice engulfs this community. Birmingham is probably the most thoroughly segregated city in the United States. Its ugly record of brutality is widely known. Negroes have experienced grossly unjust treatment in the courts. There have been more unsolved bombings of Negro homes and churches in Birmingham than in any other city in the nation. These are the hard, brutal facts of the case. On the basis of these conditions, Negro leaders sought to negotiate with the city fathers. But the latter consistently refused to engage in good-faith negotiation.

7   Then, last September, came the opportunity to talk with leaders of Bir-

mingham's economic community. In the course of the negotiations, certain promises were made by the merchants—for example, to remove the stores' humiliating racial signs. On the basis of these promises, the Reverend Fred Shuttlesworth and the leaders of the Alabama Christian Movement for Human Rights agreed to a moratorium on all demonstrations. As the weeks and months went by, we realized that we were the victims of a broken promise. A few signs, briefly removed, returned; the others remained.

As in so many past experiences, our hopes had been blasted, and the   8
shadow of deep disappointment settled upon us. We had no alternative except to prepare for direct action, whereby we would present our very bodies as a means of laying our case before the conscience of the local and the national community. Mindful of the difficulties involved, we decided to undertake a process of self-purification. We began a series of workshops on nonviolence, and we repeatedly asked ourselves: "Are you able to accept blows without retaliating?" "Are you able to endure the ordeal of jail?" We decided to schedule our direct-action program for the Easter season, realizing that except for Christmas, this is the main shopping period of the year. Knowing that a strong economic-withdrawal program would be the by-product of direct action, we felt that this would be the best time to bring pressure to bear on the merchants for the needed change.

Then it occurred to us that Birmingham's mayoral election was coming up in   9
March, and we speedily decided to postpone acton until after election day. When we discovered that the Commissioner of Public Safety, Eugene "Bull" Connor, had piled up enough votes to be in the run-off, we decided again to postpone action until the day after the run-off so that the demonstrations could not be used to cloud the issues. Like many others, we wanted to see Mr. Connor defeated, and to this end we endured postponement after postponement. Having aided in this community need, we felt that our direct-action program could be delayed no longer.

You may well ask, "Why direct action? Why sit-ins, marches, and so forth?   10
Isn't negotiation a better path?" You are quite right in calling for negotiation. Indeed, this is the very purpose of direct action. Nonviolent direct action seeks to create such a crisis and foster such a tension that a community which has constantly refused to negotiate is forced to confront the issue. It seeks so to dramatize the issue that it can no longer be ignored. My citing the creation of tension as part of the work of the nonviolent-resister may sound rather shocking. But I must confess that I am not afraid of the word "tension." I have earnestly opposed violent tension, but there is a type of constructive, nonviolent tension which is necessary for growth. Just as Socrates felt that it was necessary to create a tension in the mind so that individuals could rise from the bondage of myths and half-truths to the unfettered realm of creative analysis and objective appraisal, so must we see the need for nonviolent gadflies to create the kind of tension in society that will help men rise from the dark depths of prejudice and racism to the majestic heights of understanding and brotherhood.

11   The purpose of our direct-action program is to create a situation so crisis-packed that it will inevitably open the door to negotiation. I therefore concur with you in your call for negotiation. Too long has our beloved Southland been bogged down in a tragic effort to live in monologue rather than dialogue.

12   One of the basic points in your statement is that the action that I and my associates have taken in Birmingham is untimely. Some have asked: "Why didn't you give the new city administration time to act?" The only answer that I can give to this query is that the new Birmingham administration must be prodded about as much as the outgoing one, before it will act. We are sadly mistaken if we feel that the election of Albert Boutwell as mayor will bring the millennium to Birmingham. While Mr. Boutwell is a much more gentle person than Mr. Connor, they are both segregationists, dedicated to maintenance of the status quo. I have hoped that Mr. Boutwell will be reasonable enough to see the futility of massive resistance to desegregation. But he will not see this without pressure from devotees of civil rights. My friends, I must say to you that we have not made a single gain in civil rights without determined legal and nonviolent pressure. Lamentably, it is an historical fact that privileged groups seldom give up their privileges voluntarily. Individuals may see the moral light and voluntarily give up their unjust posture; but, as Reinhold Niebuhr has reminded us, groups tend to be more immoral than individuals.

13   We know through painful experience that freedom is never voluntarily given by the oppressor; it must be demanded by the oppressed. Frankly, I have yet to engage in a direct-action campaign that was "well timed" in the view of those who have not suffered unduly from the disease of segregation. For years now I have heard the word "Wait!" It rings in the ear of every Negro with piercing familiarity. This "Wait" has almost always meant "Never." We must come to see, with one of our distinguished jurists, that "justice too long delayed is justice denied."

14   We have waited for more than 340 years for our constitutional and God-given rights. The nations of Asia and Africa are moving with jetlike speed toward gaining political independence, but we still creep at horse-and-buggy pace toward gaining a cup of coffee at a lunch counter. Perhaps it is easy for those who have never felt the stinging darts of segregation to say, "Wait." But when you have seen vicious mobs lynch your mothers and fathers at will and drown your sisters and brothers at whim; when you have seen hate-filled policemen curse, kick, and even kill your black brothers and sisters; when you see the vast majority of your twenty million Negro brothers smothering in an airtight cage of poverty in the midst of an affluent society; when you suddenly find your tongue twisted and your speech stammering as you seek to explain to your six-year-old daughter why she can't go to the public amusement park that has just been advertised on television, and see tears welling up in her eyes when she is told that Funtown is closed to colored children, and see ominous clouds of inferiority beginning to form in her little mental sky, and see her beginning to distort her personality by devleoping an unconscious bitterness toward white people; when you have to concoct an answer for a five-year-old

son who is asking, "Daddy, why do white people treat colored people so mean?"; when you take a cross-country drive and find it necessary to sleep night after night in the uncomfortable corners of your automobile because no motel will accept you; when you are humiliated day in and day out by nagging signs reading "white" and "colored"; when your first name becomes "nigger," your middle name becomes "boy" (however old you are) and your last name becomes "John," and your wife and mother are never given the respected title "Mrs."; when you are harried by day and haunted by night by the fact that you are a Negro, living constantly at tiptoe stance, never quite knowing what to expect next, and are plagued with inner fears and outer resentments; when you are forever fighting a degenerating sense of "nobodiness"—then you will understand why we find it difficult to wait. There comes a time when the cup of endurance runs over, and men are no longer willing to be plunged into the abyss of despair. I hope, sirs, you can understand our legitimate and unavoidable impatience.

You express a great deal of anxiety over our willingness to break laws. This *15* is certainly a legitimate concern. Since we so diligently urge people to obey the Supreme Court's decision of 1954 outlawing segregation in the public schools, at first glance it may seem rather paradoxical for us consciously to break laws. One may well ask: "How can you advocate breaking some laws and obeying others?" The answer lies in the fact that there are two types of laws: just and unjust. I would be the first to advocate obeying just laws. One has not only a legal but a moral responsibility to obey just laws. Conversely, one has a moral responsibility to disobey unjust laws. I would agree with St. Augustine that "an unjust law is no law at all."

Now, what is the difference between the two? How does one determine *16* whether a law is just or unjust? A just law is a man-made code that squares with the moral law or the law of God. An unjust law is a code that is out of harmony with the moral law. To put it in the terms of St. Thomas Aquinas: An unjust law is a human law that is not rooted in eternal law and natural law. Any law that uplifts human personality is just. Any law that degrades human personality is unjust. All segregation statutes are unjust because segregation distorts the soul and damages the personality. It gives the segregator a false sense of superiority and the segregated a false sense of inferiority. Segregation, to use the terminology of the Jewish philosopher Martin Buber, substitutes an "I-it" relationship for an "I-thou" relationship and ends up relegating persons to the status of things. Hence segregation is not only politically, economically, and sociologically unsound, it is morally wrong and sinful. Paul Tillich has said that sin is separation. Is not segregation an existential expression of man's tragic separation, his awful estrangement, his terrible sinfulness? Thus it is that I can urge men to obey the 1954 decision of the Supreme Court, for it is morally right; and I can urge them to disobey segregation ordinances, for they are morally wrong.

Let us consider a more concrete example of just and unjust laws. An unjust *17* law is a code that a numerical or power majority group compels a minority group to obey but does not make binding on itself. This is *difference* made legal. By the same token, a just law is a code that a majority compels a minority to follow and that it is willing to follow itself. This is *sameness* made legal.

18   Let me give another explanation. A law is unjust if it is inflicted on a minority that, as a result of being denied the right to vote, had no part in enacting or devising the law. Who can say that the legislature of Alabama which set up that state's segregation laws was democratically elected? Throughout Alabama all sorts of devious methods are used to prevent Negroes from becoming registered voters, and there are some counties in which, even though Negroes constitute a majority of the population, not a single Negro is registered. Can any law enacted under such circumstances be considered democratically structured?

19   Sometimes a law is just on its face and unjust in its application. For instance, I have been arrested on a charge of parading without a permit. Now, there is nothing wrong in having an ordinance which requires a permit for a parade. But such an ordinance becomes unjust when it is used to maintain segregation and to deny citizens the First-Amendment privilege of peaceful assembly and protest.

20   I hope you are able to see the distinction I am trying to point out. In no sense do I advocate evading or defying the law, as would the rabid segregationist. That would lead to anarchy. One who breaks an unjust law must do so openly, lovingly, and with a willingness to accept the penalty. I submit that an individual who breaks a law that conscience tells him is unjust, and who willingly accepts the penalty of imprisonment in order to arouse the conscience of the community over its injustice, is in reality expressing the highest respect for law.

21   Of course, there is nothing new about this kind of civil disobedience. It was evidenced sublimely in the refusal of Shadrach, Meshach, and Abednego to obey the laws of Nebuchadnezzar, on the ground that a higher moral law was at stake. It was practiced superbly by the early Christians, who were willing to face hungry lions and the excruciating pain of chopping blocks rather than submit to certain unjust laws of the Roman Empire. To a degree, academic freedom is a reality today because Socrates practiced civil disobedience. In our own nation, the Boston Tea Party represented a massive act of civil disobedience.

22   We should never forget that everything Adolf Hitler did in Germany was "legal" and everything the Hungarian freedom fighters did in Hungary was "illegal." It was "illegal" to aid and comfort a Jew in Hitler's Germany. Even so, I am sure that, had I lived in Germany at the time, I would have aided and comforted my Jewish brothers. If today I lived in a Communist country where certain principles dear to the Christian faith are suppressed, I would openly advocate disobeying that country's antireligious laws.

23   I must make two honest confessions to you, my Christian and Jewish brothers. First, I must confess that over the past few years I have been gravely disappointed with the white moderate. I have almost reached the regrettable conclusion that the Negro's great stumbling block in his stride toward freedom is

not the White Citizen's Counciler or the Ku Klux Klanner, but the white moderate, who is more devoted to "order" than to justice; who prefers a negative peace which is the absence of tension to a positive peace which is the presence of justice; who constantly says, "I agree with you in the goal you seek, but I cannot agree with your methods of direct action"; who paternalistically believes he can set the timetable for another man's freedom; who lives by a mythical concept of time and who constantly advises the Negro to wait for a "more convenient season." Shallow understanding from people of good will is more frustrating than absolute misunderstanding from people of ill will. Lukewarm acceptance is much more bewildering than outright rejection.

I had hoped that the white moderate would understand that law and order   24
exist for the purpose of establishing justice and that when they fail in this purpose they become the dangerously structured dams that block the flow of social progress. I had hoped that the white moderate would understand that the present tension in the South is a necessary phase of the transition from an obnoxious negative peace, in which the Negro passively accepted his unjust plight, to a substantive and positive peace, in which all men will respect the dignity and worth of human personality. Actually, we who engage in nonviolent direct action are not the creators of tension. We merely bring to the surface the hidden tension that is already alive. We bring it out in the open, where it can be seen and dealt with. Like a boil that can never be cured so long as it is covered up but must be opened with all its ugliness to the natural medicines of air and light, injustice must be exposed, with all the tenison its exposure creates, to the light of human conscience and the air of national opinion, before it can be cured.

In your statement you assert that our actions, even though peaceful, must be   25
condemned because they precipitate violence. But is this a logical assertion? Isn't this like condemning a robbed man because his possession of money precipitated the evil act of robbery? Isn't this like condemning Socrates because his unswerving commitment to truth and his philosophical inquiries precipitated the act by the misguided populace in which they made him drink hemlock? Isn't this like condemning Jesus because his unique God-consciouness and never-ceasing devotion to God's will precipitated the evil act of crucifixion? We must come to see that, as the federal courts have consistently affirmed, it is wrong to urge an individual to cease his efforts to gain his basic constitutional rights because the quest may precipitate violence. Society must protect the robbed and punish the robber.

I had also hoped that the white moderate would reject the myth concerning   26
time in relation to the struggle for freedom. I have just received a letter from a white brother in Texas. He writes: "All Christians know that the colored people will receive equal rights eventually, but it is possible that you are in too great a religious hurry. It has taken Christianity almost two thousand years to accomplish what it has. The teachings of Christ take time to come to earth." Such an attitude stems from a tragic misconception of time, from the strangely irrational notion that there is something in the very flow of time that will inevitably cure

all ills. Actually, time itself is neutral; it can be used either destructively or constructively. More and more I feel that the people of ill will have used time much more effectively than have the people of good will. We will have to repent in this generation not merely for the hateful words and actions of the bad people, but for the appalling silence of the good people. Human progress never rolls in on wheels of inevitability; it comes through the tireless efforts of men willing to be co-workers with God, and without this hard work, time itself becomes an ally of the forces of social stagnation. We must use time creatively, in the knowledge that the time is always ripe to do right. Now is the time to make real the promise of democracy and transform our pending national elegy into a creative psalm of brotherhood. Now is the time to lift our national policy from the quicksand of racial injustice to the solid rock of human dignity.

27   You speak of our activity in Birmingham as extreme. At first I was rather disappointed that fellow clergymen would see my nonviolent efforts as those of an extremist. I began thinking about the fact that I stand in the middle of two opposing forces in the Negro community. One is a force of complacency, made up in part of Negroes who, as a result of long years of oppression, are so drained of self-respect and a sense of "somebodiness" that they have adjusted to segregation; and in part of a few middle-class Negroes who, because of a degree of academic and economic security and because in some ways they profit by segregation, have become insensitive to the problems of the masses. The other force is one of bitterness and hatred, and it comes perilously close to advocating violence. It is expressed in the various black nationalist groups that are springing up across the nation, the largest and best-known being Elijah Muhammad's Muslim movement. Nourished by the Negro's frustration over the continued existence of racial discrimination, this movement is made up of people who have lost faith in America, who have absolutely repudiated Christianity, and who have concluded that the white man is an incorrigible "devil."

28   I have tried to stand between these two forces, saying that we need emulate neither the "do-nothingism" of the complacent nor the hatred and despair of the black nationalist. For there is the more excellent way of love and nonviolent protest. I am grateful to God that, through the influence of the Negro church, the way of nonviolence became an integral part of our struggle.

29   If this philosophy had not emerged, by now many streets of the South would, I am convinced, be flowing with blood. And I am further convinced that if our white brothers dismiss as "rabblerousers" and "outside agitators" those of us who employ nonviolent direct action, and if they refuse to support our nonviolent efforts, millions of Negroes will, out of frustration and despair, seek solace and security in black-nationalist ideologies—a development that would inevitably lead to a frightening racial nightmare.

30   Oppressed people cannot remain oppressed forever. The yearning for freedom eventually manifests itself, and that is what has happened to the American Negro. Something within has reminded him of his birthright of freedom, and something without has reminded him that it can be gained. Consciously or unconsciously, he has been caught up by the *Zeitgeist*, and with his black

brothers of Africa and his brown and yellow brothers of Asia, South America, and the Caribbean, the United States Negro is moving with a sense of great urgency toward the promised land of racial justice. If one recognizes this vital urge that has engulfed the Negro community, one should readily understand why public demonstrations are taking place. The Negro has many pent-up resentments and latent frustrations, and he must release them. So let him march; let him make prayer pilgrimages to the city hall; let him go on freedom rides—and try to understand why he must do so. If his repressed emotions are not released in nonviolent ways, they will seek expression through violence; this is not a threat but a fact of history. So I have not said to my people, "Get rid of your discontent." Rather, I have tried to say that this normal and healthy discontent can be channeled into the creative outlet of nonviolent direct action. And now this approach is being termed extremist.

But though I was initially disappointed at being categorized as an extremist, *31* as I continued to think about the matter I gradually gained a measure of satisfaction from the label. Was not Jesus an extremeist for love: "Love your enemies, bless them that curse you, do good to them that hate you, and pray for them which despitefully use you, and persecute you." Was not Amos an extremist for justice: "Let justice roll down like waters and righteousness like an ever-flowing stream." Was not Paul an extremist for the Christian gospel: "I bear in my body the marks of the Lord Jesus." Was not Martin Luther an extremist: "Here I stand; I cannot do otherwise, so help me God." And John Bunyan: "I will stay in jail to the end of my days before I make a butchery of my conscience." And Abraham Lincoln: "This nation cannot survive half slave and half free." And Thomas Jefferson: "We hold these truths to be self-evident, that all men are created equal. . . ." So the question is not whether we will be extremists, but what kind of extremists we will be. Will we be extremists for hate or for love? Will we be extremists for the preservation of injustice or for the extension of justice? In that dramatic scene on Calvary's hill three men were crucified. We must never forget that all three were crucified for the same crime—the crime of extremism. Two were extremists for immorality, and thus fell below their environment. The other, Jesus Christ, was an extremist for love, truth, and goodness, and thereby rose above his environment. Perhaps the South, the nation, and the world are in dire need of creative extremists.

I had hoped that the white moderate would see this need. Perhaps I was too *32* optimistic; perhaps I expected too much. I suppose I should have realized that few members of the oppressor race can understand the deep groans and passionate yearnings of the oppressed race, and still fewer have the vision to see that injustice must be rooted out by strong, persistent, and determined action. I am thankful, however, that some of our white brothers in the South have grasped the meaning of this social revolution and committed themselves to it. They are still all too few in quantity, but they are big in quality. Some—such as Ralph McGill, Lillian Smith, Harry Golden, James McBride Dabbs, Ann Braden, and Sarah Patton Boyle—have written about our struggle in eloquent and prophetic terms. Others have marched with us down nameless streets of the South. They have languished in filthy, roach-infested jails, suffering the abuse and brutality of policemen who view them as "dirty nigger-lovers." Unlike so many of their moderate brothers and sisters, they have recognized the urgency of the moment and sensed the need for powerful "action" antidotes to combat the disease of segregation.

33   Let me take note of my other major disappointment. I have been so greatly disappointed with the white church and its leadership. Of course, there are some notable exceptions. I am not unmindful of the fact that each of you has taken some significant stands on this issue. I commend you, Reverend Stallings, for your Christian stand on this past Sunday, in welcoming Negroes to your worship service on a nonsegregated basis. I commend the Catholic leaders of this state for integrating Spring Hill College several years ago.

34   But despite these notable exceptions, I must honestly reiterate that I have been disappointed with the church. I do not say this as one of those negative critics who can always find something wrong with the church. I say this as a minister of the gospel, who loves the church; who was nurtured in its bosom; who has been sustained by its spiritual blessings and who will remain true to it as long as the cord of life shall lengthen.

35   When I was suddenly catapulted into the leadership of the bus protest in Montgomery, Alabama, a few years ago, I felt we would be supported by the white church. I felt that the white ministers, priests, and rabbis of the South would be among our strongest allies. Instead, some have been outright opponents, refusing to understand the freedom movement and misrepresenting its leaders; all too many others have been more cautious than courageous and have remained silent behind the anesthetizing security of stained glass windows.

36   In spite of my shattered dreams, I came to Birmingham with the hope that the white religious leadership of this community would see the justice of our cause and, with deep moral concern, would serve as the channel through which our just grievances could reach the power structure. I had hoped that each of you would understand. But again I have been disappointed.

37   I have heard numerous southern religious leaders admonish their worshipers to comply with a desegregation decision because it is the law, but I have longed to hear white ministers declare: "Follow this decree because integration is morally right and because the Negro is your brother." In the midst of blatant injustices inflicted upon the Negro, I have watched white churchmen stand on the sideline and mouth pious irrelevancies and sanctimonious trivialities. In the midst of a mighty struggle to rid our nation of racial and economic injustice, I have heard many ministers say: "Those are social issues, with which the gospel has no real concern." And I have watched many churches commit themselves to a completely otherworldly religion which makes a strange, un-Biblical distinction between body and soul, beteween the sacred and the secular.

38   I have traveled the length and breadth of Alabama, Mississippi, and all the other southern states. On sweltering summer days and crisp autumn mornings I have looked at the South's beautiful churches with their lofty spires pointing heavenward. I have beheld the impressive outlines of her massive religious-edu-

cation buildings. Over and over I have found myself asking: "What kind of people worship here? Who is their God? Where were their voices when the lips of Governor Barnett dripped with words of interposition and nullification? Where were they when Governor Wallace gave a clarion call for defiance and hatred? Where were their voices of support when bruised and weary Negro men and women decided to rise form the dark dungeons of complacency to the bright hills of creative protest?"

Yes, these questions are still in my mind. In deep disappointment I have 39 wept over the laxity of the church. But be assured that my tears have been tears of love. There can be no deep disappointment where there is not deep love. Yes, I love the church. How could I do otherwise? I am in the rather unique position of being the son, the grandson, and the great-grandson of preachers. Yes, I see the church as the body of Christ. But, oh! How we have blemished and scarred that body through social neglect and through fear of being nonconformists.

There was a time when the church was very powerful—in the time when the 40 early Christians rejoiced at being deemed worthy to suffer for what they believed. In those days the church was not merely a thermometer that recorded the ideas and principles of popular opinion, it was a thermostat that transformed the mores of society. Whenever the early Christians entered a town, the people in power became disturbed and immediately sought to convict the Christians for being "disturbers of the peace" and "outside agitators." But the Christians pressed on, in the conviction that they were "a colony of heaven," called to obey God rather than man. Small in number they were big in commitment. They were too God-intoxicated to be "astronomically intimidated." By their effort and example they brought an end to such ancient evils as infanticide and gladiatorial contests.

Things are different now. So often the contemporary church is a weak, inef- 41 fectual voice with an uncertain sound. So often it is an archdefender of the staus quo. Far from being disturbed by the presence of the church, the power structure of the average community is consoled by the church's silent—and often even vocal—sanction of things as they are.

But the judgment of God is upon the church as never before. If today's 42 church does not recapture the sacrificial spirit of the early church, it will lose its authenticity, forfeit the loyalty of millions, and be dismissed as an irrelevant social club with no meaning for the twentieth century. Every day I meet young people whose disappointment with the church has turned into outright disgust.

Perhaps I have once again been too optimistic. Is organized religion too 43 inextricably bound to the status quo to save our nation and the world? Perhaps I must turn my faith to the inner spiritual church, the church within the church, as the true *ekklesia* and the hope of the world. But again I am thankful to God that some noble souls from the ranks of organized religion have broken loose from the paralyzing chains of conformity and joined us as active partners in the struggle for freedom. They have left their secure congregations and walked the streets of Albany, Georgia, with us. They have gone down the highways of the

South on tortuous rides for freedom. Yes, they have gone to jail with us. Some have been dismissed from their churches, have lost the support of their bishops and fellow ministers. But they have acted in the faith that right defeated is stronger than evil triumphant. Their witness has been the spiritual salt that has preserved the true meaning of the gospel in these troubled times. They have carved a tunnel of hope through the dark mountain of disappointment.

44 I hope the church as a whole will meet the challenge of this decisive hour. But even if the church does not come to the aid of justice, I have no despair about the future. I have no fear about the outcome of our struggle in Birmingham, even if our motives are at present misunderstood. We will reach the goal of freedom in Birmingham and all over the nation, because the goal of America is freedom. Abused and scorned though we may be, our destiny is tied up with America's destiny. Before the pilgrims landed at Plymouth, we were here. Before the pen of Jefferson etched the majestic words of the Declaration of Independence across the pages of history, we were here. For more than two centuries our forebears labored in this country without wages; they made cotton king; they built the homes of their masters while suffering gross injustice and shameful humiliation—and yet out of a bottomless vitality they continued to thrive and develop. If the inexpressible cruelties of slavery could not stop us, the opposition we now face will surely fail. We will win our freedom because the sacred heritage of our nation and the eternal will of God are embodied in our echoing demands.

45 Before closing I feel impelled to mention one other point in your statement that has troubled me profoundly. You warmly commended the Birmingham police force for keeping "order" and "preventing violence." I doubt that you would have so warmly commended the police force if you had seen its dogs sinking their teeth into unarmed, nonviolent Negroes. I doubt that you would so quickly commend the policemen if you were to observe their ugly and inhumane treatment of Negroes here in the city jail; if you were to watch them push and curse old Negro women and young Negro girls; if you were to see them slap and kick old Negro men and young boys; if you were to observe them, as they did on two occasions, refuse to give food because we wanted to sing our grace together. I cannot join you in your praise of the Birmingham police department.

46 It is true that the police have exercised a degree of discipline in handling the demonstrators. In this sense they have conducted themselves rather "nonviolently" in public. But for what purpose? To preserve the evil system of segregation. Over the past few years I have consistently preached that nonviolence demands that the means we use must be as pure as the ends we seek. I have tried to make clear that it is wrong to use immoral means to attain moral ends. But now I must affirm that it is just as wrong, or perhaps even more so, to use moral means to preserve immoral ends. Perhaps Mr. Connor and his policemen have been rather nonviolent in public, as was Chief Pritchett in Albany, Georgia, but they have used the moral means of nonviolence to maintain the immoral end of racial injustice. As. T. S. Eliot has said, "The last temptation is the greatest treason: To do the right deed for the wrong reason."

I wish you had commended the Negro sit-inners and demonstrators of Bir-   47
mingham for their sublime courage, their willingness to suffer, and their amazing discipline in the midst of great provocation. One day the South will recognize its real heroes. They will be the James Merediths, with the noble sense of
purpose that enables them to face jeering and hostile mobs, and with the agonizing loneliness that characterizes the life of the pioneer. They will be old,
oppressed, battered Negro women, symbolized in a seventy-two-year-old
woman in Montgomery, Alabama, who rose up with a sense of dignity and with
her people decided not to ride segregated buses, and who responded with
ungrammatical profundity to one who inquired about her weariness: "My feets
is tired, but my soul is at rest." They will be the young high school and college
students, the young ministers of the gospel and a host of their elders, coura-
geously and nonviolently sitting in at lunch counters and willingly going to jail
for conscience sake. One day the South will know that when these disinherited
children of God sat down at lunch counters, they were in reality standing up for
what is best in the American dream and for the most sacred values in our
Judeo-Christian heritage, thereby bringing our nation back to those great wells
of democracy which were dug deep by the founding fathers in their formulation
of the Constitution and the Declaration of Independence.

Never before have I written so long a letter. I'm afraid it is much too long to   48
take your precious time. I can assure you that it would have been much shorter
if I had been writing from a comfortable desk, but what else can one do when
he is alone in a narrow jail cell, other than write long letters, think long
thoughts, and pray long prayers?

If I have said anything in this letter that overstates the truth and indicates an   49
unreasonable impatience, I beg you to forgive me. If I have said anything that
understates the truth and indicates my having a patience that allows me to settle for anyting less than brotherhood, I beg God to forgive me.

I hope this letter finds you strong in the faith. I also hope that circumstances   50
will soon make it possible for me to meet each of you, not as an integrationist
or a civil-rights leader but as a fellow clergyman and a Christian brother. Let
us all hope that the dark clouds of racial prejudice will soon pass away and the
deep fog of misunderstanding will be lifted from our fear-drenched communities, and in some not too distant tomorrow the radiant stars of love and brotherhood will shine over our great nation with all their scintillating beauty.

>Yours for the cause of Peace and Brotherhood,
>MARTIN LUTHER KING, JR.

WRITING AND DISCUSSION QUESTIONS

Informative

1. One of the central issues of the letter is the tactics King was using to promote
   change in the racial laws and conditions of the South. What is nonviolent direct

action and what are its historical precedents? How does King use the Judeo–Christian heritage and American history to buttress his argument?

2. How does King define a "just law"? What is an unjust law? How does King apply these definitions to segregation?

3. What rhetorical devices and techniques does King use to express his concern for oppressed people? How do these affect you as a reader? Note such techniques as direct address of the second person "you," the use of question and answer or "call and response" (a standard form of dialogue in black churches) sections, parallel sentence structures, metaphor, and diction.

4. On what basis does King strongly criticize the white moderate?

Persuasive

1. Argue that "injustice anywhere is a threat to justice everywhere." Explain, in your argument, the basis for such an observation and to what degree you think it is valid.

2. What is King's attitude toward the institutional church? How does he see the separation of moral and social issues from the gospel? Argue that religious institutions are or are not generally culpable for their inaction in this regard.

Personal

1. In the more than 20 years since King's assassination, do you think the optimism he expressed in the letter (paragraph 44) is justified? From what you have seen, has there been progression in such areas as integration of the races and the elimination of poverty? Consider what has happened to blacks regarding unemployment, family, and education.

2. Describe the racial climate on your campus. Reflect on it, as would King, in terms of the values central to the Judeo–Christian tradition and democracy.

CHAPTER WRITING ASSIGNMENTS

1. Examine the "ways of knowing" that were used to demonstrate humanity's fundamental rights as citizens under democratic rule. In Locke, Jefferson, and others, to what degree are equal rights self-evident? To what degree are faith, reason, and observation used to demonstrate the importance of individual rights?

2. In democracy, the covenant or contract between the citizen and the state identifies rights and obligations of the citizen. What are the differences and similarities between the democratic concept of the covenant and concepts presented in previous chapters?

3. Tocqueville, Madison, Jefferson, and others identified the most dangerous form of tyranny in America as the abuse of power by the majority through legislative

pressure groups and assemblies. Provide what you believe to be contemporary examples of legislative fiat. Do special interest groups reenforce the "darker side" of the legislative process?

4. Interview an articulate person regarding his or her political life. What are the reasons for this person's political activity or inactivity? What is his notion of a democracy and of citizen freedom and responsibility in that system? What political positions does she hold? Which has she taken public?

5. What political position—liberal, conservative, libertarian, or reactionary—has this chapter turned you toward or away from? What significant conflicts or questions about democracy have been raised in your mind? How has your political consciousness changed as a result of this chapter?

6. Compare King's "Letter from Birmingham Jail" with Jefferson's "Declaration of Indepencence." Granting whatever major differences there may be in the situations (for example, King was responding to an unjust set of laws, whereas Jefferson was responding to an unjust government), are principles that each appeals to similar or different? Given the responses of each, which do you think was the more extreme?

7. What do you find to be the single greatest idea in democracy? What makes it a great idea, and what are its shortcomings?

8. Define the perfect democracy. How could one be established? Do we live in something approaching the ideal state? Has the United States succeeded in making the dream of the "founding fathers" come true? That is, has a government been established that maximizes the aspirations and liberties of individuals while preserving some reasonable order and minimizing government restraint? Is there a reasonable order and is there maximum liberty for the individual? Is there an excessive emphasis on one at the expense of the other?

The Formative Ideas

Chapter Seven

MARXISM AND ECONOMICS

Karl Marx (1818–1883) may have had more impact—directly or indirectly—on life and thought than any other thinker of the past two centuries. More than half the people of the world live in political and economic systems modeled in some sense after his ideas, and most of the rest live in systems strongly influenced and affected by Marxian thought. Yet until recently, Marx has been little studied in the United States except by historians and political scientists. The reasons for this neglect are many and complex, but all are related to the extremes of opinion about his life and works. Many of Marx's supporters have treated him as the prophet of a new order, almost a god, and approached his works as if they were sacred texts. Many of his opponents have considered him as satanic and his ideas as subversive of all that is decent and virtuous. In the United States, anticommunism has become so ingrained that many people consider the mere reading of Marx a dangerous and revolutionary act. However, anyone interested in ideas in general and modern thought in particular cannot afford to neglect him.

The study of Marx is no less important today even though it seems that Marxism as a political philosophy has demonstrated its failure. The last century and a half has seen similar exaggerated predictions of the death of democracy, of capitalism, and even of God, all since proved to be at least highly premature. Likewise, to predict that Marx will end up in the dustbin of history would be premature at this time. For the present, however, an understanding of Marx and his heritage is essential for a proper assessment of the historical events rapidly unfolding before us: the collapse of the Berlin wall, the abolition of the exclusive power of Communist parties throughout Eastern Europe and Russia, the stalled democratic movement in China, and perhaps most important, the continuing revolutionary struggles in underdeveloped countries throughout the world.

Achieving such an understanding, however, is not easy. Part of the reason is the specialized terminology Marx introduced, like "bourgeoisie," "proletariat," "class struggle," and "dialectical materialism." Even more confusing are the many differences between Marx's own ideas and "Marxism," that is, the subsequent and practical applications of Marx's thought by others such as Lenin and Mao. An additional form of his name, "Marxian," denotes approaches to any kind of intellectual or artistic endeavor influenced by Marx but not necessarily "Marxist."

HISTORICAL BACKGROUNDS TO MARXISM

A central tenet of Marx is that the course of history is determined by economics. Whether this is true for all of history is a subject for debate, but the nineteenth century was undoubtedly a time of major change, and economic factors were among the major forces driving that change. The historical developments most affecting Marx's thought center on the Industrial Revolution, the discovery and application in the late eighteenth century of new and highly efficient systems of power and production. This resulted in not only greater production, but profound social and political dislocations. We can get a quick idea of the changes occurring in the nineteenth century by contrasting England in 1800 and 1900. In 1800, the nation's major area of production was agricultural, its major population was rural, and its political system was a somewhat republican structure largely managed by a landed aristocracy. By 1900, England had become an industrial urban democracy, and its population had quadrupled. But to understand the dislocations these changes wrought, what they meant for the day-to-day lives and the toll they exacted in human misery, demands a closer look.

The vast majority of those masses that left the country were driven to the cities by joblessness and hunger, but what they found there was little better. Some of England's largest cities at mid-century had been little more than villages in 1800, having grown at a rate approaching 50% each decade. The established systems by which communities cared for their poor and sick and managed their public services were based on village economics and perspectives and were ill-adapted to handling teeming urban masses. Simple things like housing, roads, sewerage, lighting, and crime control became problems of unprecedented proportions. Effective ways of managing these problems were much slower in developing than were more efficient ways to manufacture pins or weave textiles. Indeed, any real sense of community was slow to develop in the new industrial cities, and the laboring poor, isolated in slums remote from the notice of more prosperous citizens, became an alienated and anonymous mass.

The working poor, the "lucky" ones who had jobs, were indeed the "wage slaves" of Marx's descriptions. In the 1830s and 1840s, before the first regulatory laws were passed, men, women, and children, some as young as five years, were working in mines, factories, and workshops from 12 to 16 hours a day. They labored in the most appalling conditions of heat, cold, and bodily peril, without any job security, worker's compensation, unemployment benefits, social security, or any opportunity for education. Women and children had to work because wages were barely enough to provide for one person's sustenance, much less a family. The sick, the injured, and the few who survived the workplace into anything like old age were simply cast off to die. It is a measure of how bad things were that the Ten Hours Bill of 1847, which limited only the labor of women and children and only in some industries to 10 hours each day and which included grossly inadequate enforcement provisions, was considered unusually progressive. Because the laboring classes were effectively cut off from political power, better legislation came slowly, and when it was enacted, it was largely the result of the limited sense of compassion of the prosperous. Although the franchise was gradually expanded, property qualifications for voting remained throughout the century (for example, Birmingham, one of England's growing industrial cities, in 1851 had a population of nearly a quarter million, some 8000 of whom could vote in Parliamentary elections). For most of the century, labor unions, which were considered conspiracies in restraint of trade, were outlawed. As a result, although the trade union movement began in the 1820s, unions in England were not effective until the Parliamentary acts of 1875 fully recognized the right of collective bargaining (similar legislation was not passed in the United States until 1913). As bad as all this may seem, England, in terms of its attitude toward labor, was the most progressive industrialized nation in the world.

Certainly, some parts of England became reasonably prosperous, whereas other parts remained relatively untouched by the Industrial Revolution. However, where economic growth did occur, it generally carried with it some redistribution of wealth. The middle class was growing, and the center of wealth was shifting away from the old aristocracy toward the new industrial rich, but the gap between the moneyed classes and the growing numbers of abjectly poor widened. Growth in trade resulted in the development of a truly international economy, but the fever of unregulated growth also resulted in the first series of great world depressions, referred to in the nineteenth century as financial panics. In the half century before Marx's *Communist Manifesto* (1848), there were three such disasters, in 1825–1826, 1836–1837, and 1847, in which everyone suffered, as in all depressions, but in which the working classes suffered the most.

Along with economic dislocations came political revolution, in France in 1830 and then in France, Italy, and Germany in 1848, but these were mainly manifestations of nationalism or of liberalism, and were largely middle-class revolts against the old aristocracies, *les anciens regimes,* as they were called. Help for the working poor would be a long time in coming.

Despite these problems, however, a spirit of optimism prevailed among the educated classes, sometimes wildly enthusiastic, sometimes guarded. The Victorian world looks to us in many ways as rather placid, but the sense of change that world experienced was unprecedented. As well as providing new and more products, the Industrial Revolution changed the land itself; it removed the barriers of distance and time with the invention of the railroad and telegraph. The mechanization of the textile industry not only made it possible to clothe the century's exploding population, but its waste cloth provided the raw material for paper, which helped fuel the world's first information explosion. As a result of such changes, Thomas Babington Macaulay, as early as the 1820s, spoke of his time as "an age of transition," a time on the brink of some great and far-reaching historical change. The intellectual life of the century was filled with a sense that the old world, the old order, was passing, yielding place to some new as yet unknown world. It was a time, therefore, that both fostered and resisted the spirit of revolution.

THE INDUSTRIAL REVOLUTION AND THE GREAT IDEAS

Marxism has grown into a world force partly because, as we have seen, established social systems were slow to respond to changing conditions. Also slow to respond effectively were most of Western humanity's intellectual and spiritual traditions. Whether this was because some or all of those traditions were fundamentally flawed is debatable, but a historical perspective can help to provide well-informed and cautious judgments.

Consider the issue of child labor for example. Until the nineteenth century, Western economy was based primarily on agriculture. In most lands, the fundamental unit of agricultural labor was the family, and from time immemorial, all members contributed to the needs of their family, which often required hard labor. Although undoubtedly child abuse occurred in such a system, no one objected to child labor itself, and the thought of state interference in such practices was unthinkable. Such attitudes, however, had to be radically rethought in the new industrial society. It was not that the old systems had no sense of social responsibility, but that the new systems required new definitions of that responsibility and new social and political mechanisms for safeguarding it, and that took time. The same again was true of attitudes toward the spiritual and intellectual traditions.

The Judeo–Christian Tradition

Christianity, the dominant religion in Western culture, had always concerned itself more with the soul than with the body, more with the next life than with this one. Although the pulpit inveighed against materialism, what came to be popularly known as the Protestant Work Ethic, especially by the middle classes, tended to identify wealth and prosperity with God's reward for virtue and hard work, and poverty with idleness and vice. To many Christians and their various leaders, then, social reform simply meant repentance, and caring for the poor meant only charity. The idea of instituting new social programs to take care of these problems, especially state-sponsored ones, seemed to go against all popular notions of God's plan for society. Judaism seems always to have been more socially responsive, but as a minority religion that was discriminated against, its impact on society as a whole was relatively small during the nineteenth century.

In most European states, established religions allied themselves with the political status quo and taught that the social order was ordained by God and that proper humility meant accepting one's ordained position in society. Thus, most established religions neglected the spiritual, as well as the physical, needs of the poor; the urban slums had few churches and fewer clergy willing to serve there.

Nevertheless, some seeds of social consciousness could be found among nineteenth-century religious groups, especially some of the Scriptural Protestants, which were denominations advocating that individuals establish personal relationships with God based on their readings of the Bible. These religious groups stood committed to evangelizing, in part, through teaching all believers to read, and a few of the groups made significant attempts to reach the poor. Among the best examples of the Scriptural Protestants were the Evangelicals in England who became active early in the century. They not only established Bible schools, but they publicized the lot of the working poor and promoted legislation to improve their education and working conditions. In the latter third of the century, William Booth, founder of the Salvation Army, argued forcefully for what is the basis of Christian socialism, that delivering humanity from sin was tied to delivering humanity from material degradation. He advocated a plan of social reform that included shelters for "lost women," prevention homes for girls in moral danger, employment bureaus, vocational training programs, legal assistance and bank services for the poor, missing persons bureaus, and model suburban villages. His ideas, however, met great opposition, both religious and secular, and in the popular mind, he was categorized as someone between a harmless fanatic and a subversive.

Humanism

Like the church, the mainstream of the humanistic tradition was not sensitive to the conditions of the poor, and it too lagged behind events in providing solutions or in awakening social consciousness. Poets like William Blake, John Keats, and Percy Shelley early in the century and Tennyson and Browning later brought attention to the over-simplifications of the new science and the dehumanizing effects of the new commercialism; they called for a revolution of the human heart, but few paid any heed to poets. Essayists like John Ruskin and Thomas Carlyle attacked the industrial systems that transformed workers into machines. Even so, the solutions they offered were too rooted in the past to effectively deal with the social problems caused by industrialism. For example, Ruskin advocated a return to a handcraft economy; Carlyle called for the reform of society through a "new" kind of feudal leadership to be exerted by those he called "captains of industry." The first solution was impractical, for the population had already grown to the point where reversion to less-efficient means of production would be disastrous, and the second solution was unpopular because of its promotion of elitism and militaristic control (such a plan would later be associated with Nazism). Popular novelists like Charles Dickens attacked with realistic fiction many of the same problems the poets and essayists had, inspiring sympathy and promoting reform through vivid and compassionate portraits of the poor, but the mainstream of the humanistic tradition disdained popular writers.

The Democratic Revolution

An obvious solution to the problems of industrialization would seem to have been democracy, especially as the nineteenth century progressed and the great American experiment proved its own permanence. However, Europe generally was less encouraged by the American Revolution than it was frightened by the results of the French (1789): the Reign of Terror and the guillotine, the transformation of what began as a republic into an autocratic empire, and the years of Napoleonic wars. Moreover, democratic systems were far more difficult to establish in the old world. Class structures were more firmly established, and Europe did not have America's frontier, with seemingly unlimited resources and opportunities both for escape from potential oppression and for individual advancement. Political and economic power in Europe, the wealth and the means of production, were solidly in the hands of the aristocracy and the middle class; and the moneyed classes were less willing to trust the working class with any kind of political power. Even in America, such a step was not taken until the 1820s, when the franchise was expanded, making possible the era of Jacksonian democracy in the 1830s.

Thus, the French Revolution, though based on the declared ideals of liberty, equality, and fraternity, became essentially a revolt of the middle class against the old aristocracy, and the lot of the working class showed no improvement. Indeed, to those more sympathetic to the lower classes, the ideals of the French Revolution seemed to have been betrayed, and from before 1800 through the middle of the nineteenth century, early socialist reformers, especially in France, were attacking bourgeois society. (We shift now to the terminology associated with Marx, which he adopted from the French reformers: *bourgeoisie* and *proletariat* are simply the French words for "middle class" and "working class.")

Indeed, in the early nineteenth century thinkers like Henri de Saint-Simon, Charles Fourier, and Pierre-Joseph Proudhon established a pattern of attack that Marx would adopt and expand. Bourgeois society, they believed, was rapaciously acquisitive and hypocritical, exploiting the labor of the proletariat while conspiring to keep them ignorant. Bourgeois liberalism, while advocating personal liberty, defended mainly the right to keep the profits earned by "free" exchange in the market, a position that ignored the great mass of those without property. Those with only their labor to sell in a subsistence labor market had no opportunity for profit. For them, the market was in no way free, and liberty defined in these terms was to the laboring poor a cruel joke. Bourgeois religion perpetuated social ills by attributing human misery to Adam's curse, God's just response for human sinfulness, rather than to inadequate social systems. The principles of competition and private property seemed to stand in the way of any kind of real equality, and to many reformers, a more radical kind of revolution, one that would overthrow the bourgeoisie as well as the last remnants of the old aristocracy and that would eliminate private property altogether, seemed the only way to a just and democratic society.

The Scientific Revolution

Science bred the faith in humanity's power to control nature that in many ways was the force behind the Industrial Revolution, and science through technological applications improved transportation and communication and increased production. Unfortunately, too many people did not share in these benefits. It was in the quest for solutions to this problem that the scientific spirit had its greatest impact on Marx, a quest beginning with a group of thinkers in the late eighteenth and early nineteenth centuries who tried to find laws as simple as Newton's laws of motion to describe human economic behavior. They included the creators of the new science of economics, Adam Smith, Thomas Malthus, and David Ricardo.

Smith argued in *Wealth of Nations* (1776) that economic life is shaped by a number of natural developments, the most important of which is the division of labor, which is the notion that the best goods can be created by specialists, individuals dedicating themselves to producing what they can do best and trading the fruits of their labor for their other needs. Social classes developed, and property was distributed as each kind of labor and product found its own market value. Indeed, for Smith, the perception that the best possible economic relations developed naturally was a kind of revelatory wonder. It suggested, as Newton's laws had suggested to others, the rationality and care of the divine law giver: to compete in an open market and to earn the most profit, each individual strove to make the best possible goods; thus, in naturally pursuing one's own selfish ends, one naturally served the whole community. In the past, these processes had too often been misunderstood and misapplied, especially as expressed by nationalistic and militaristic ambitions, but Smith imagined utopian consequences of the implementation of his ideas. Allowed to develop naturally, aggressiveness and competition would be turned to productive rather than destructive ends; the energy of human selfishness would, by the natural laws of economics, be harnessed to trade instead of war; and the prosperity and wealth of all nations and peoples would result. This theory came to be called *laissez faire*, a French phrase meaning "to let alone." It became the dominant economic theory of industrialized nations of the nineteenth century and is the origin of modern market economic theory. In the nineteenth century, it also became mixed up in a number of moral and social controversies.

The great beauty of laissez faire theory for many was that by pursuing one's own selfish ends the good of the larger community would follow. Nature would take care of one's responsibilities to humanity. This tendency to exalt selfishness as a virtue was given a peculiar impetus by Malthus and Ricardo. As noted in the introduction to Darwin in Chapter 5, Malthus argued in his *Essay on the Principle of Population* (1798) that while the technological means of subsistence in human society tend to increase at an arithmetic rate, the population tends to increase geometrically. This meant that the great mass of humanity is inescapably condemned to a life at the level of bare subsistence. Rather than destroy laissez faire theory, however, Malthus only undermined Smith's utopian hopes. Laissez faire was now thought able to deliver only the best possible world, but that one would be far from ideal.

Ricardo developed Smith's and Malthus' ideas further in his *Principles of Political Economy and Taxation* (1817), in which he worked out his own system of laws regulating the distribution of wealth. The most notable of his formulations was the Law of Wages: the natural price of labor is the amount necessary to enable the worker to subsist and to perpetuate his species "without increase or dimunition." To lower wages below this point was to starve the worker, but to raise wages would create only temporary prosperity; workers would simply have more children, and the new wage would again become the "natural" one of mere subsistence. Another of Ricardo's laws, derived also from Malthus, stated that as population increases and less-productive resources are forced into use, profits must necessarily decline; thus, a more compassionate employer who raises wages above the subsistence level will risk losing his business, and likewise a national policy of compassion will threaten the economic fabric of society.

Such "laws" now seem far less certain—people who are better paid and educated seem to become more concerned with the quality of their lives and tend to have fewer children, not more; despite dire predictions, and notwithstanding periods of financial panic, profits in England rose throughout the century. However, to the hard-headed economists and the clear-eyed capitalists of the nineteenth century, a more benevolent attitude toward the working class was simply foolish sentimentality. In fact, in the second half of the century, Darwin's theories would be expropriated to further support these ideas: according to what came to be called "social Darwinism," the wealthy were so because of their natural superiority and energy, and the poor were so because of their natural inferiority and laziness. Economic classes demonstrated that in the struggle for economic survival the fittest had survived; the upper classes were, therefore, justified in their lack of concern for the lower classes. To work for the betterment of the poor would be to violate the laws of nature and imperil not only one's own survival and that of the nation, but perhaps that of the human race as well.

Other explorations of the science of the first half of the nineteenth century, however, seemed to hold the potential for more hopeful results. At least one thinker began to wonder if something like the materialistic, developmental models sought by geologists and biologists to account for the natural world might account for history. That thinker was, of course, Karl Marx.

KARL MARX, FROM *THE COMMUNIST MANIFESTO*

Karl Marx (1818–1883) was born in Trier in Rhineland Prussia, now part of West Germany, of middle-class Jewish parents. His father had converted to Christianity the year before Karl's birth, and the young Marx exhibited a strong sense of Christian devotion and self-sacrifice in his adolescent years. After one academic year (1835–1836) at the University of Bonn, he went on to the University of Berlin to study philosophy and law. While there, he lost his Christian faith, though not his sense of devotion and self-sacrifice, and discovered the work of the German philosopher G.F.W. Hegel (1770–1831). He decided to abandon his father's ambitions for his own law career, dedicated himself to philosophy, earned a Ph.D. at the Univeristy of Jena, and developed into a political radical. In 1842, he accepted the editorship of a newspaper and discovered his own power as a political journalist. He was so effective, in fact, that the authorities shut him down. He emigrated to Paris in 1843, where he pursued his career as a radical journalist and came in contact with some of the major radical thinkers of his time. Also, in Paris in 1844, he met the young Friedrich Engels (1820–1895), the son of a rich Prussian manufacturer, who became his life-long friend, collaborator, and a major source of financial support, which Marx sorely needed. From 1845 to 1849, he suffered a series of expulsions because of his ideas, which took him to Brussels, then to Germany, and finally to London, where he lived in exile for the rest of his life. In the meantime, he had become associated in 1847 with a London-based radical group known as the Communist League, which commissioned Marx to draft, in German, a manifesto declaring its doctrines. The result was the now-famous *Communist Manifesto* (1848).

Marx's theories represent a continuation and expansion of the scientific revolution. His approach is based on the belief that history can be understood scientifically as a rational and coherent process. Marx recognized, however, that historical change was far more complicated than anything that could be described in terms of Newtonian mathematics or the laws of the "classical economists," a term coined by Marx to describe the founders of that science. To analyze history scientifically, Marx like Darwin needed a developmental model. To find one, he turned to a method developed by Hegel called "dialectic."

Dialectic is a method of inquiry derived from Plato. The Platonic dialectic arrives at truth by critically exposing the contradictions in opposing arguments. Hegel expanded the term to apply to the contradictions, the contending forces, inherent in reality and the processes by which those forces develop in relation to each other. His most famous formulation is the description of change in a pattern of thesis, antithesis, and synthesis. In simple terms, this means that every idea (thesis) generates its opposite (antithesis); the clash of these ideas results not in the victory of one, but in a new idea or set of ideas (synthesis), which in turn becomes a new thesis, generating an antithesis, and so on in a continuous process of development. Thus, dialectic in this modern sense is a way of looking at reality as process.

Hegel saw this process as the progressive manifestation of Spirit in matter, a development driven by God or the Absolute. Marx saw the process in empirical terms, as the natural way in which complex systems of any kind develop—not as a simple, unidirectional chain of causes and effects, but as a multidirectional network of causation. Indeed, this concept of dialectical empiricism is among the most seminal of Marx's ideas. When we look at any portion of reality as a complex system of interacting parts, where changes in one part affect all the other parts and where the system itself evolves, we are thinking dialectically. Many scientists and thinkers who may be far from Marx philosophically or politically may still have been profoundly influenced by this aspect of Marxian thought. This view is inherent, for example, in such divergent areas as modern applications of evolutionary theory, the latest approaches to literary criticism and linguistics, systems approaches to a wide variety of phenomena from ecology to industrial management, and even to quantum theory and the new mathematical study of chaos.

Marx is distinguished from other dialectical thinkers in two general ways. First, his major historical concern was political economy. Second, he is philosophically a materialist. That is, in the tradition going back to the ancient Greek philosophers Democritus and Epicurus, he believed that the material world was the ultimate reality. That is why his philosophy has been called "dialectical materialism," although Marx never used this phrase himself.

Studying history in dialectic terms, however, led Marx to many profoundly disturbing conclusions. First, history is a series of revolutions or changes driven by economic forces. Alterations in the means of production or in the mediums of exchange inspire class struggles, which in turn lead to political revolutions. That is why the first major division of the *Manifesto* opens with the declaration, "The history of all hitherto existing society is the history of class struggle." That is, classes have always existed in society, divisions between those who possess economic power and those who do not, between oppressors and oppressed, exploiters and exploited, often including several levels of relative power and powerlessness.

Second, to Marx, class struggle in itself is not wrong. In fact, he considered class structures of various sorts a historical necessity, natural ways that social organisms have adapted to the economic conditions of their life just as biological organisms adapt to their environment. This is the key to why Marx rejected the classical economists. For them, the basic factors that determine economic life are simple and eternal and the laws derived from them are universal; such a view provided no accounting for change, for history. On the other hand, Marx's sense of change leads to the disturbing conclusion that not only economic conditions, but right and wrong are products of historical necessity. Thus, moral law is no more an absolute than is political law for both are defined by the classes in power to maintain social and political stability in ways that also maintain their own power.

Marx does not suggest that the powerful cynically create moral law to serve their own interests; they may sincerely believe in the absolute truth of their sense of law, and a given view of "truth" or "good" may be entirely appropriate for its time. For instance, as mentioned in the introduction to this chapter, child labor in an agricultural economy is a viable, in fact a necessary, practice; however, the definition of what constitutes appropriate child labor was modified throughout the eighteenth and nineteenth centuries as people became more socially conscious. In a dialectic view of history, change is inevitable, new economic conditions develop, and those changes cause social change, which in turn force political change. Political change, however, can only take place in the form of revolution, because a privileged class never surrenders its power voluntarily. Thus "wrong" becomes redefined by revolutionary factions to mean resistance to the forces of historical change.

In his own time, Marx saw signs of the processes of historical change accelerating and of the class struggle coming to an end. With the final defeat of the old aristocracy by the bourgeoisie, class struggle was reduced to a final conflict between the two remaining classes, the bourgeoisie and the proletariat. At the same time, the bourgeoisie, in its victory over the aristocracy, was forging the conditions of its own ultimate defeat. Industrialization was itself creating a massive proletariat and concentrating them in cities where they could organize and become a political force. The financial crises of the time were clear indications that bourgeois dominance was weakening, and in establishing a world market, the bourgeoisie was breaking down national boundaries and loyalties, creating a new sense of world culture, and setting the stage for a worldwide communist revolution.

from *The Communist Manifesto*

KARL MARX

A spectre is haunting Europe—the spectre of Communism. All the   *1*
Powers of old Europe have entered into a holy alliance to exorcise this spectre:
Pope and Czar, Metternich and Guizot, French Radicals and German police-
spies.

Where is the party in opposition that has not been decried as Communistic   *2*
by its opponents in power? Where the Opposition that has not hurled back the
branding reproach of Communism, against the more advanced opposition parties, as well as against its reactionary adversaries?

Two things result from this fact.   *3*

I. Communism is already acknowledged by all European Powers to be itself
a Power.

II. It is high time that Communists should openly, in the face of the whole
world, publish their views, their aims, their tendencies, and meet this nursery
tale of the Spectre of Communism with a Manifesto of the party itself.

To this end, Communists of various nationalities have assembled in London,   *4*
and sketched the following Manifesto, to be published in the English, French,
German, Italian, Flemish and Danish languages.

I

Bourgeois and Proletarians

The history of all hitherto existing society is the history of class struggles.   *5*

Freeman and slave, patrician and plebeian, lord and serf, guild-master and   *6*
journeyman, in a word, oppressor and oppressed, stood in constant opposition
to one another, carried on an uninterrupted, now hidden, now open fight, a
fight that each time ended, either in a revolutionary re-constitution of society at
large, or in the common ruin of the contending classes.

In the earlier epochs of history, we find almost everywhere a complicated   *7*
arrangement of society into various orders, a manifold gradation of social rank.
In ancient Rome we have patricians, knights, plebeians, slaves; in the Middle
Ages, feudal lords, vassals, guild-masters, journeymen, apprentices, serfs: in
almost all of these classes, again, subordinate gradations.

The modern bourgeois society that has sprouted from the ruins of feudal   *8* society has not done away with class antagonisms. It has but established new classes, new conditions of oppression, new forms of struggle in place of the old ones.

9   Our epoch, the epoch of the bourgeoisie, possesses, however, this distinctive feature: it has simplified the class antagonisms. Society as a whole is more and more splitting up into two great hostile camps, into two great classes directly facing each other: Bourgeoisie and Proletariat.

10   From the serfs of the Middle Ages sprang the chartered burghers of the earliest towns. From these burgesses the first elements of the bourgeoisie were developed.

11   The discovery of America, the rounding of the Cape, opened up fresh ground for the rising bourgeoisie. The East-Indian and Chinese markets, the colonisation of America, trade with the colonies, the increase in the means of exchange and in commodities generally, gave to commerce, to navigation, to industry, an impulse never before known, and thereby, to the revolutionary element in the tottering feudal society, a rapid development.

12   The feudal system of industry, under which industrial production was monopolised by closed guilds, now no longer sufficed for the growing wants of the new markets. The manufacturing system took its place. The guild-masters were pushed on one side by the manufacturing middle class; division of labour between the different corporate guilds vanished in the face of division of labour in each single workshop.

13   Meantime the markets kept ever growing, the demand ever rising. Even manufacture no longer sufficed. Thereupon, steam and machinery revolutionised industrial production. The place of manufacture was taken by the giant, Modern Industry, the place of the industrial middle class, by industrial millionaires, the leaders of whole industrial armies, the modern bourgeois.

14   Modern industry has established the world-market, for which the discovery of America paved the way. This market has given an immense development to commerce, to navigation, to communication by land. This development has, in its turn, reacted on the extension of industry; and in proportion as industry, commerce, navigation, railways extended, in the same proportion the bourgeoisie developed, increased its capital, and pushed into the background every class handed down from the Middle Ages.

15   We see, therefore, how the modern bourgeoisie is itself the product of a long course of development, of a series of revolutions in the modes of production and of exchange.

16   Each step in the development of the bourgeoisie was accompanied by a corresponding political advance of that class. An oppressed class under the sway of the feudal nobility, an armed and self-governing association in the mediaeval commune; here independent urban republic (as in Italy and Germany), there taxable "third estate" of the monarchy (as in France), afterwards, in the period of manufacture proper, serving either the semi-feudal or the absolute monarchy as a counterpoise against the nobility, and, in fact, corner-stone of the great monarchies in general, the bourgeoisie has at last, since the establishment of

Modern Industry and of the world-market, conquered for itself, in the modern representative State, exclusive political sway. The executive of the modern State is but a committee for managing the common affairs of the whole bourgeoisie.

The bourgeoisie, historically, has played a most revolutionary part. *17*

The bourgeoisie, wherever it has got the upper hand, has put an end to all *18* feudal, patriarchal, idyllic relations. It has pitilessly torn asunder the motley feudal ties that bound man to his "natural superiors," and has left remaining no other nexus between man and man than naked self-interest, than callous "cash payment." It has drowned the most heavenly ecstacies of religious fervour, of chivalrous enthusiasm, of philistine sentimentalism, in the icy water of egotistical calculation. It has resolved personal worth into exchange value, and in place of the numberless indefeasible chartered freedoms, has set up that single, unconscionable freedom—Free Trade. In one word, for exploitation, veiled by religious and political illusions, it has substituted naked, shameless, direct, brutal exploitation.

The bourgeoisie has stripped of its halo every occupation hitherto honoured *19* and looked up to with reverent awe. It has converted the physician, the lawyer, the priest, the poet, the man of science, into its paid wage-labourers.

The bourgeoisie has torn away from the family its sentimental veil, and has *20* reduced the family relation to a mere money relation.

The bourgeoisie has disclosed how it came to pass that the brutal display of *21* vigour in the Middle Ages, which Reactionists so much admire, found its fitting complement in the most slothful indolence. It has been the first to show what man's activity can bring about. It has accomplished wonders far surpassing Egyptian pyramids, Roman aqueducts, and Gothic cathedrals; it has conducted expeditions that put in the shade all former Exoduses of nations and crusades.

The bourgeoisie cannot exist without constantly revolutionising the instru- *22* ments of production, and thereby the relations of production, and with them the whole relations of society. Conservation of the old modes of production in unaltered form, was, on the contrary, the first condition of existence for all earlier industrial classes. Constant revolutionising of production, uninterrupted disturbance of all social conditions, everlasting uncertainty and agitation distinguish the bourgeois epoch from all earlier ones. All fixed, fast-frozen relations, with their train of ancient and venerable prejudices and opinions, are swept away, all new-formed ones become antiquated before they can ossify. All that is solid melts into air, all that is holy is profaned, and man is at last compelled to face with sober senses, his real conditions of life, and his relations with his kind.

The need of a constantly expanding market for its products chases the bour- *23* geoisie over the whole surface of the globe. It must nestle everywhere, settle everywhere, establish connexions everywhere.

The bourgeoisie has through its exploitation of the world-market given a cos- *24* mopolitan character to production and consumption in every country. To the great chagrin of Reactionists, it has drawn from under the feet of industry the national ground on which it stood. All old-established national industries have

been destroyed or are daily being destroyed. They are dislodged by new industries, whose introduction becomes a life and death question for all civilised
nations, by industries that no longer work up indigenous raw material, but raw
material drawn from the remotest zones; industries whose products are consumed, not only at home, but in every quarter of the globe. In place of the old
wants, satisfied by the productions of the country, we find new wants, requiring
for their satisfaction the products of distant lands and climes. In place of the
old local and national seclusion and self-sufficiency, we have intercourse in
every direction, universal inter-dependence of nations. And as in material, so
also in intellectual production. The intellectual creations of individual nations
become common property. National one-sidedness and narrow-mindedness
become more and more impossible, and from the numerous national and local
literatures, there arises a world literature.

25   The bourgeoisie, by the rapid improvement of all instruments of production,
by the immensely facilitated means of communication, draws all, even the most
barbarian, nations into civilisation. The cheap prices of its commodities are the
heavy artillery with which it batters down all Chinese walls, with which it forces
the barbarians' intensely obstinate hatred of foreigners to capitulate. It compels
all nations, on pain of extinction, to adopt the bourgeois mode of production; it
compels them to introduce what it calls civilisation into their midst, *i.e.*, to
become bourgeois themselves. In one word, it creates a world after its own
image.

26   The bourgeoisie has subjected the country to the rule of the towns. It has
created enormous cities, has greatly increased the urban population as compared with the rural, and has thus rescued a considerable part of the population from the idiocy of rural life. Just as it has made the country dependent on
the towns, so it has made barbarian and semi-barbarian countries dependent on
the civilised ones, nations of peasants on nations of bourgeois, the East on the
West.

27   The bourgeoisie keeps more and more doing away with the scattered state of
the population, of the means of production, and of property. It has agglomer-
ated population, centralised means of production, and has concentrated property in a few hands. The necessary consequence of this was political centralisation. Independent, or but loosely connected provinces, with separate interests,
laws, governments and systems of taxation, became lumped together into one
nation, with one government, one code of laws, one national class-interest, one
frontier and one customs-tariff.

28   The bourgeoisie, during its rule of scarce one hundred years, has created
more massive and more colossal productive forces than have all preceding generations together. Subjection of Nature's forces to man, machinery, application
of chemistry to industry and agriculture, steam-navigation, railways, electric tel-
egraphs, clearing of whole continents for cultivation, canalisation of rivers,
whole populations conjured out of the ground—what earlier century had even a
presentiment that such productive forces slumbered in the lap of social labour?

29   We see then: the means of production and of exchange, on whose founda-

tion the bourgeoisie built itself up, were generated in feudal society. At a certain stage in the development of these means of production and of exchange, the conditions under which feudal society produced and exchanged, the feudal organisation of agriculture and manufacturing industry, in one word, the feudal relations of property became no longer compatible with the already developed productive forces; they became so many fetters. They had to be burst asunder; they were burst asunder.

Into their place stepped free competition, accompanied by a social and political constitution adapted to it, and by the economical and political sway of the bourgeois class. 30

A similar movement is going on before our own eyes. Modern bourgeois society with its relations of production, of exchange and of property, a society that has conjured up such gigantic means of production and of exchange, is like the sorcerer, who is no longer able to control the powers of the nether world whom he has called up by his spells. For many a decade past the history of industry and commerce is but the history of the revolt of modern productive forces against modern conditions of production, against the property relations that are the conditions for the existence of the bourgeoisie and of its rule. It is enough to mention the commercial crises that by their periodical return put on its trial, each time more threateningly, the existence of the entire bourgeois society. In these crises a great part not only of the existing products, but also of the previously created productive forces, are periodically destroyed. In these crises there breaks out an epidemic that, in all earlier epochs, would have seemed an absurdity—the epidemic of over-production. Society suddenly finds itself put back into a state of momentary barbarism; it appears as if a famine, a universal war of devastation had cut off the supply of every means of subsistence; industry and commerce seem to be destroyed; and why? Because there is too much civilisation, too much means of subsistence, too much industry, too much commerce. The productive forces at the disposal of society no longer tend to further the development of the conditions of bourgeois property; on the contrary, they have become too powerful for these conditions, by which they are fettered, and so soon as they overcome these fetters, they bring disorder into the whole of bourgeois society, endanger the existence of bourgeois property. The conditions of bourgeois society are too narrow to comprise the wealth created by them. And how does the bourgeoisie get over these crises? On the one hand by enforced destruction of a mass of productive forces; on the other, by the conquest of new markets, and by the more thorough exploitation of the old ones. That is to say, by paving the way for more extensive and more destructive crises, and by diminishing the means whereby crises are prevented. 31

The weapons with which the bourgeoisie felled feudalism to the ground are now turned against the bourgeoisie itself. 32

But not only has the bourgeoisie forged the weapons that bring death to itself; it has also called into existence the men who are to wield those weapons—the modern working class—the proletarians. 33

In proportion as the bourgeoisie, *i.e.*, capital, is developed, in the same pro- 34 portion is the proletariat, the modern working class, developed—a class of labourers, who live only so long as they find work, and who find work only so long as their labour increases capital. These labourers, who must sell themselves piecemeal, are a commodity, like every other article of commerce, and are consequently exposed to all the vicissitudes of competition, to all the fluctuations of the market.

35   Owing to the extensive use of machinery and to division of labour, the work of the proletarians has lost all individual character, and, consequently, all charm for the workman. He becomes an appendage of the machine, and it is only the most simple, most monotonous, and most easily acquired knack, that is required of him. Hence, the cost of production of a workman is restricted, almost entirely, to the means of subsistence that he requires for his maintenance, and for the propagation of his race. But the price of a commodity, and therefore also of labour, is equal to its cost of production. In proportion, therefore, as the repulsiveness of the work increases, the wage decreases. Nay more, in proportion as the use of machinery and division of labour increases, in the same proportion the burden of toil also increases, whether by prolongation of the working hours, by increase of the work exacted in a given time or by increased speed of the machinery, etc.

36   Modern industry has converted the little workshop of the patriarchal master into the great factory of the industrial capitalist. Masses of labourers, crowded into the factory, are organised like soldiers. As privates of the industrial army they are placed under the command of a perfect hierarchy of officers and sergeants. Not only are they slaves of the bourgeois class, and of the bourgeois State; they are daily and hourly enslaved by the machine, by the overlooker, and, above all, by the individual bourgeois manufacturer himself. The more openly this despotism proclaims gain to be its end and aim, the more petty, the more hateful and the more embittering it is.

37   The less the skill and exertion of strength implied in manual labour, in other words, the more modern industry becomes developed, the more is the labour of men superseded by that of women. Differences of age and sex have no longer any distinctive social validity for the working class. All are instruments of labour, more or less expensive to use, according to their age and sex.

38   No sooner is the exploitation of the labourer by the manufacturer, so far, at an end, and he receives his wages in cash, than he is set upon by the other portions of the bourgeoisie, the landlord, the shopkeeper, the pawnbroker, etc.

39   The lower strata of the middle class—the small tradespeople, shopkeepers, and retired tradesmen generally, the handicraftsmen and peasants—all these sink gradually into the proletariat, partly because their diminutive capital does not suffice for the scale on which Modern Industry is carried on, and is swamped in the competition with the large capitalists, partly because their specialised skill is rendered worthless by new methods of production. Thus the proletariat is recruited from all classes of the population.

40   The proletariat goes through various stages of development. With its birth begins its struggle with the bourgeoisie. At first the contest is carried on by

individual labourers, then by the workpeople of a factory, then by the operatives of one trade, in one locality, against the individual bourgeois who directly exploits them. They direct their attacks not against the bourgeois conditions of production, but against the instruments of production themselves; they destroy imported wares that compete with their labour, they smash to pieces machinery, they set factories ablaze, they seek to restore by force the vanished status of the workman of the Middle Ages.

At this stage the labourers still form an incoherent mass scattered over the *41* whole country, and broken up by their mutual competition. If anywhere they unite to form more compact bodies, this is not yet the consequence of their own active union, but of the union of the bourgeoisie, which class, in order to attain its own political ends, is compelled to set the whole proletariat in motion, and is moreover yet, for a time, able to do so. At this stage, therefore, the proletarians do not fight their enemies, but the enemies of their enemies, the remnants of absolute monarchy, the landowners, the non-industrial bourgeois, the petty bourgeoisie. Thus the whole historical movement is concentrated in the hands of the bourgeoisie; every victory so obtained is a victory for the bourgeoisie.

But with the development of industry the proletariat not only increases in *42* number; it becomes concentrated in greater masses, its strength grows, and it feels that strength more. The various interests and conditions of life within the ranks of the proletariat are more and more equalised, in proportion as machinery obliterates all distinctions of labour, and nearly everywhere reduces wages to the same low level. The growing competition among the bourgeois, and the resulting commercial crises, make the wages of the workers ever more fluctuating. The unceasing improvement of machinery, ever more rapidly developing, makes their livelihood more and more precarious; the collisions between individual workmen and individual bourgeois take more and more the character of collisions between two classes. Thereupon the workers begin to form combinations (Trades' Unions) against the bourgeois; they club together in order to keep up the rate of wages; they found permanent associations in order to make provision beforehand for these occasional revolts. Here and there the contest breaks out into riots.

Now and then the workers are victorious, but only for a time. The real fruit *43* of their battles lies, not in the immediate result, but in the ever-expanding union of the workers. This union is helped on by the improved means of communication that are created by modern industry and that place the workers of different localities in contact with one another. It was just this contact that was needed to centralise the numerous local struggles, all of the same character, into one national struggle between classes. But every class struggle is a political struggle. And that union, to attain which the burghers of the Middle Ages, with their miserable highways, required centuries, the modern proletarians, thanks to railways, achieve in a few years.

This organisation of the proletarians into a class, and consequently into a *44* political party, is continually being upset again by the competition between the workers themselves. But it ever rises up again, stronger, firmer, mightier. It compels legislative recognition of particular interests of the workers, by taking advantage of the divisions among the bourgeoisie itself. Thus the ten-hours' bill in England was carried.

45 Altogether collisions between the classes of the old society further, in many ways, the course of development of the proletariat. The bourgeoisie finds itself involved in a constant battle. At first with the aristocracy; later on, with those portions of the bourgeoisie itself, whose interests have become antagonistic to the progress of industry; at all times, with the bourgeoisie of foreign countries. In all these battles it sees itself compelled to appeal to the proletariat, to ask for its help, and thus, to drag it into the political arena. The bourgeoisie itself, therefore, supplies the proletariat with its own elements of political and general education, in other words, it furnishes the proletariat with weapons for fighting the bourgeoisie.

46 Further, as we have already seen, entire sections of the ruling classes are, by the advance of industry, precipitated into the proletariat, or are at least threatened in their conditions of existence. These also supply the proletariat with fresh elements of enlightenment and progress.

47 Finally, in times when the class struggle nears the decisive hour, the process of dissolution going on within the ruling class, in fact within the whole range of old society, assumes such a violent, glaring character, that a small section of the ruling class cuts itself adrift, and joins the revolutionary class, the class that holds the future in its hands. Just as, therefore, at an earlier period, a section of the nobility went over to the bourgeoisie, so now a portion of the bourgeoisie goes over to the proletariat, and in particular, a portion of the bourgeois ideologists, who have raised themselves to the level of comprehending theoretically the historical movement as a whole.

48 Of all the classes that stand face to face with the bourgeoisie today, the proletariat alone is a really revolutionary class. The other classes decay and finally disappear in the face of Modern Industry; the proletariat is its special and essential product.

49 The lower middle class, the small manufacturer, the shopkeeper, the artisan, the peasant, all these fight against the bourgeoisie, to save from extinction their existence as fractions of the middle class. They are therefore not revolutionary, but conservative. Nay more, they are reactionary, for they try to roll back the wheel of history. If by chance they are revolutionary, they are so only in view of their impending transfer into the proletariat, they thus defend not their present, but their future interests, they desert their own standpoint to place themselves at that of the proletariat.

50 The "dangerous class," the social scum, that passively rotting mass thrown off by the lowest layers of old society, may, here and there, be swept into the movement by a proletarian revolution, its conditions of life, however, prepare it far more for the part of a bribed tool of reactionary intrigue.

51 In the conditions of the proletariat, those of old society at large are already virtually swamped. The proletarian is without property; his relation to his wife

and children has no longer anything in common with the bourgeois family-relations; modern industrial labour, modern subjection to capital, the same in England as in France, in America as in Germany, has stripped him of every trace of national character. Law, morality, religion, are to him so many bourgeois prejudices, behind which lurk in ambush just as many bourgois interests.

All the preceding classes that got the upper hand, sought to fortify their   52
already acquired status by subjecting society at large to their conditions of appropriation. The proletarians cannot become masters of the productive forces of society, except by abolishing their own previous mode of appropriation, and thereby also every other previous mode of appropriation. They have nothing of their own to secure and to fortify, their mission is to destroy all previous securities for, and insurances of, individual property.

All previous historical movements were movements of minorities, or in the   53
interests of minorities. The proletarian movement is the self-conscious, independent movement of the immense majority, in the interests of the immense majority. The proletariat, the lowest stratum of our present society, cannot stir, cannot raise itself up, without the whole superincumbent strata of official society being sprung into the air.

Though not in substance, yet in form, the struggle of the proletariat with the   54
bourgeoisie is at first a national struggle. The proletariat of each country must, of course, first of all settle matters with its own bourgeoisie.

In depicting the most general phases of the development of the proletariat,   55
we traced the more or less veiled civil war, raging within existing society, up to the point where that war breaks out into open revolution, and where the violent overthrow of the bourgeosie lays the foundation for the sway of the proletariat.

Hitherto, every form of society has been based, as we have already seen, on   56
the antagonism of oppressing and oppressed classes. But in order to oppress a class, certain conditions must be assured to it under which it can, at least, continue its slavish existence. The serf, in the period of serfdom, raised himself to membership in the commune, just as the petty bourgeois, under the yoke of feudal absolutism, managed to develop into a bourgeois. The modern labourer, on the contrary, instead of rising with the progress of industry, sinks deeper and deeper below the conditions of existence of his own class. He becomes a pauper, and pauperism develops more rapidly than population and wealth. And here it becomes evident, that the bourgeoisie is unfit any longer to be the ruling class in society, and to impose its conditions of existence upon society as an over-riding law. It is unfit to rule because it is incompetent to assure an existence to its slave within his slavery, because it cannot help letting him sink into such a state, that it has to feed him, instead of being fed by him. Society can no longer live under this bourgeoisie, in other words, its existence is no longer compatible with society.

The essential condition for the existence, and for the sway of the bourgeois   57
class, is the formation and augmentation of capital; the condition for capital is wage-labour. Wage-labour rests exclusively on competition between the labourers. The advance of industry, whose involuntary promoter is the bourgeoisie,

replaces the isolation of the labourers, due to competition, by their revolutionary combination, due to association. The development of Modern Industry, therefore, cuts from under its feet the very foundation on which the bourgeoisie produces and appropriates products. What the bourgeoisie, therefore, produces, above all, is its own grave-diggers. Its fall and the victory of the proletariat are equally inevitable.

II

Proletarians and Communists

58 In what relation do the Communists stand to the proletarians as a whole?

59 The Communists do not form a separate party opposed to other working-class parties.

60 They have no interests separate and apart from those of the proletariat as a whole.

61 They do not set up any sectarian principles of their own, by which to shape and mould the proletarian movement.

62 The Communists are distinguished from the other working-class parties by this only: 1. In the national struggles of the proletarians of the different countries, they point out and bring to the front the common interests of the entire proletariat, independently of all nationality. 2. In the various stages of development which the struggle of the working class against the bourgeoisie has to pass through, they always and everywhere represent the interests of the movement as a whole.

63 The Communists, therefore, are on the one hand, practically, the most advanced and resolute section of the working-class parties of every country, that section which pushes forward all others; on the other hand, theoretically, they have over the great mass of the proletariat the advantage of clearly understanding the line of march, the conditions, and the ultimate general results of the proletarian movement.

64 The immediate aim of the Communists is the same as that of all the other proletarian parties: formation of the proletariat into a class, overthrow of the bourgeois supremacy, conquest of political power by the proletariat.

65 The theoretical conclusions of the Communists are in no way based on ideas or principles that have been invented, or discovered, by this or that would-be universal reformer.

66 They merely express, in general terms, actual relations springing from an existing class struggle, from a historical movement going on under our very eyes. The abolition of existing property relations is not at all a distinctive feature of Communism.

67 All property relations in the past have continually been subject to historical change consequent upon the change in historical conditions.

68 The French Revolution, for example, abolished feudal property in favour of bourgeois property.

The distinguishing feature of Communism is not the abolition of property   *69*
generally, but the abolition of bourgeois property. But modern bourgeois private property is the final and most complete expression of the system of producing and appropriating products, that is based on class antagonisms, on the
exploitation of the many by the few.

In this sense, the theory of the Communists may be summed up in the single   *70*
sentence: Abolition of private property.

We Communists have been reproached with the desire of abolishing the right   *71*
of personally acquiring property as the fruit of a man's own labour, which
property is alleged to be the groundwork of all personal freedom, activity and
independence.

Hard-won, self-acquired, self-earned property! Do you mean the property of   *72*
the petty artisan and of the small peasant, a form of property that preceded the
bourgeois form? There is no need to abolish that; they development of industry
has to a great extent already destroyed it, and is still destroying it daily.

Or do you mean modern bourgeois private property?   *73*

But does wage-labour create any property for the labourer? Not a bit. It cre-   *74*
ates capital, *i.e.*, that kind of property which exploits wage-labour, and which
cannot increase except upon condition of begetting a new supply of wage-
labour for fresh exploitation. Property, in its present form, is based on the
antagonism of capital and wage-labour. Let us examine both sides of this
antagonism.

To be a capitalist, is to have not only a purely personal, but a social *status*   *75*
in production. Capital is a collective product, and only by the united action of
many members, nay, in the last resort, only by the united action of all members of society, can it be set in motion.

Capital is, therefore, not a personal, it is a social power.   *76*

When, therefore, capital is converted into common property, into the prop-   *77*
erty of all members of society, personal property is not thereby transformed
into social property. It is only the social character of the property that is
changed. It loses its class-character.

Let us now take wage-labour.   *78*

The average price of wage-labour is the minimum wage, *i.e.*, that quantum   *79*
of the means of subsistence, which is absolutely requisite to keep the labourer
in bare existence as a labourer. What, therefore, the wage-labourer appropriates by means of his labour, merely suffices to prolong and reproduce a bare
existence. We by no means intend to abolish this personal appropriation of the
products of labour, an appropriation that is made for the maintenance and
reproduction of human life, and that leaves no surplus wherewith to command
the labour of others. All that we want to do away with, is the miserable character of this appropriation, under which the labourer lives merely to increase capital, and is allowed to live only in so far as the interest of the ruling class
requires it.

In bourgeois society, living labour is but a means to increase accumulated   *80*
labour. In Communist society, accumulated labour is but a means to widen, to
enrich, to promote the existence of the labourer.

81   In bourgeois society, therefore, the past dominates the present; in Communist society, the present dominates the past. In bourgeois society capital is independent and has individuality, while the living person is dependent and has no individuality.

82   And the abolition of this state of things is called by the bourgeois, abolition of individuality and freedom! And rightly so. The abolition of bourgeois individuality, bourgeois independence, and bourgeois freedom is undoubtedly aimed at.

83   By freedom is meant, under the present bourgeois conditions of production, free trade, free selling and buying.

84   But if selling and buying disappears, free selling and buying disappears also. This talk about free selling and buying, and all the other "brave words" of our bourgeoisie about freedom in general, have a meaning, if any, only in contrast with restricted selling and buying, with the fettered traders of the Middle Ages, but have no meaning when opposed to the Communistic abolition of buying and selling, of the bourgeois conditions of production, and of the bourgeoisie itself.

85   You are horrified at our intending to do away with private property. But in your existing society, private property is already done away with for nine-tenths of the population; its existence for the few is solely due to its non-existence in the hands of those nine-tenths. You reproach us, therefore, with intending to do away with a form of property, the necessary condition for whose existence is the non-existence of any property for the immense majority of society.

86   In one word, you reproach us with intending to do away with your property. Precisely so; that is just what we intend.

87   From the moment when labour can no longer be converted into capital, money, or rent, into a social power capable of being monopolised, *i.e.*, from the moment when individual property can no longer be transformed into bourgeois property, into capital, from that moment, you say, individuality vanishes.

88   You must, therefore, confess that by "individual" you mean no other person than the bourgeois, than the middle-class owner of property. This person must, indeed, be swept out of the way, and made impossible.

89   Communism deprives no man of the power to appropriate the products of society; all that it does is to deprive him of the power to subjugate the labour of others by means of such appropriation.

90   It has been objected that upon the abolition of private property all work will cease, and universal laziness will overtake us.

91   According to this, bourgeois society ought long ago to have gone to the dogs through sheer idleness; for those of its members who work, acquire nothing, and those who acquire anything, do not work. The whole of this objection is but another expression of the tautology: that there can no longer be any wage-labour when there is no longer any capital.

92   All objections urged against the Communistic mode of producing and appropriating material products, have, in the same way, been urged against the Communistic modes of producing and appropriating intellectual products. Just as, to the bourgeois, the disappearance of class property is the disappearance of pro-

duction itself, so the disappearance of class culture is to him identical with the disappearance of all culture.

That culture, the loss of which he laments, is, for the enormous majority, a 93 mere training to act as a machine.

But don't wrangle with us so long as you apply, to our intended abolition of 94 bourgeois property, the standard of your bourgeois notions of freedom, culture, law, &c. Your very ideas are but the outgrowth of the conditions of your bourgeois production and bourgeois property, just as your jurisprudence is but the will of your class made into a law for all, a will, whose essential character and direction are determined by the economical conditions of existence of your class.

The selfish misconception that induces you to transform into eternal laws of 95 nature and of reason, the social forms springing from your present mode of production and form of property—historical relations that rise and disappear in the progress of production—this misconception you share with every ruling class that has preceded you. What you see clearly in the case of ancient property, what you admit in the case of feudal property you are of course forbidden to admit in the case of your own bourgeois form of property.

Abolition of the family! Even the most radical flare up at this infamous pro- 96 posal of the Communists.

On what foundation is the present family, the bourgeois family, based? On 97 capital, on private gain. In its completely developed form this family exists only among the bourgeoisie. But this state of things finds its complement in the practical absence of the family among the proletarians, and in public prostitution.

The bourgeois family will vanish as a matter of course when its complement 98 vanishes, and both will vanish with the vanishing of capital.

Do you charge us with wanting to stop the exploitation of children by their 99 parents? To this crime we plead guilty.

But, you will say, we destroy the most hallowed of relations, when we 100 replace home education by social.

And your education! Is not that also social, and determined by the social 101 conditions under which you educate, by the intervention, direct or indirect, of society, by means of schools, &c.? The Communists have not invented the intervention of society in education; they do but seek to alter the character of that intervention, and to rescue education from the influence of the ruling class.

The bourgeois clap-trap about the family and education, about the hallowed 102 co-relation of parent and child, becomes all the more disgusting, the more, by the action of Modern Industry, all family ties among the proletarians are torn asunder, and their children transformed into simple articles of commerce and instruments of labour.

But you Communists would introduce community of women, screams the 103 whole bourgeoisie in chorus.

The bourgeois sees in his wife a mere instrument of production. He hears 104 that the instruments of production are to be exploited in common, and, naturally, can come to no other conclusion than that the lot of being common to all will likewise fall to the women.

105   He has not even a suspicion that the real point aimed at is to do away with the status of women as mere instruments of production.

106   For the rest, nothing is more ridiculous than the virtuous indignation of our bourgeois at the community of women which, they pretend, is to be openly and officially established by the Communists. The Communists have no need to introduce community of women; it has existed almost from time immemorial.

107   Our bourgeois, not content with having the wives and daughters of their proletarians at their disposal, not to speak of common prostitutes, take the greatest pleasure in seducing each other's wives.

108   Bourgeois marriage is in reality a system of wives in common and thus, at the most, what the Communists might possibly be reproached with, is that they desire to introduce, in substitution for a hypocritically concealed, an openly legalised community of women. For the rest, it is self-evident that the abolition of the present system of production must bring with it the abolition of the community of women springing from that system, *i.e.*, of prostitution both public and private.

109   The Communists are further reproached with desiring to abolish countries and nationality.

110   The working men have no country. We cannot take from them what they have not got. Since the proletariat must first of all acquire political supremacy, must rise to be the leading class of the nation, must constitute itself *the* nation, it is, so far, itself national, though not in the bourgeois sense of the word.

111   National differences and antagonisms between peoples are daily more and more vanishing, owing to the development of the bourgeoisie, to freedom of commerce, to the world-market, to uniformity in the mode of production and in the conditions of life corresponding thereto.

112   The supremacy of the proletariat will cause them to vanish still faster. United action, of the leading civilised countries at least, is one of the first conditions for the emancipation of the proletariat.

113   In proportion as the exploitation of one individual by another is put an end to, the exploitation of one nation by another will also be put an end to. In proportion as the antagonism between classes within the nation vanishes, the hostility of one nation to another will come to an end.

114   The charges against Communism made from a religious, a philosophical, and, generally, from an ideological standpoint, are not deserving of serious examination.

115   Does it require deep intuition to comprehend that man's ideas, views and conceptions, in one word, man's consciousness, changes with every change in the conditions of his material existence, in his social relations and in his social life?

116   What else does the history of ideas prove, than that intellectual production

changes its character in proportion as material production is changed? The ruling ideas of each age have ever been the ideas of its ruling class.

When people speak of ideas that revolutionise society, they do but express *117* the fact, that within the old society, the elements of a new one have been created, and that the dissolution of the old ideas keeps even pace with the dissolution of the old conditions of existence.

When the ancient world was in its last throes, the ancient religions were *118* overcome by Christianity. When Christian ideas succumbed in the 18th century to rationalist ideas, feudal society fought its death battle with the then revolutionary bourgeoisie. The ideas of religious liberty and freedom of conscience merely gave expression to the sway of free competition within the domain of knowledge.

"Undoubtedly," it will be said, "religious, moral, philosophical and juridical *119* ideas have been modified in the course of historical development. But religion, morality, philosophy, political science, and law, constantly survived this change."

"There are, besides, eternal truths, such as Freedom, Justice, etc., that are *120* common to all states of society. But Communism abolishes eternal truths, it abolishes all religion, and all morality, instead of constituting them on a new basis: it therefore acts in contradiction to all past historical experience."

What does this accusation reduce itself to? The history of all past society has *121* consisted in the development of class antagonisms, antagonisms that assumed different forms at different epochs.

But whatever form they may have taken, one fact is common to all past *122* ages, viz., the exploitation of one part of society by the other. No wonder, then, that the social consciousness of past ages, despite all the multiplicity and variety it displays, moves within certain common forms, or general ideas, which cannot completely vanish except with the total disappearance of class antagonisms.

The Communist revolution is the most radical rupture with traditional property *123* relations; no wonder that its development involves the most radical rupture with traditional ideas.

But let us have done with the bourgeois objections to Communism. *124*

We have seen above, that the first step in the revolution by the working *125* class, is to raise the proletariat to the position of ruling class, to win the battle of democracy.

The proletariat will use its political supremacy to wrest, by degrees, all capi- *126* tal from the bourgeoisie, to centralise all instruments of production in the hands of the State, *i.e.*, of the proletariat organised as the ruling class; and to increase the total of productive forces as rapidly as possible.

Of course, in the beginning, this cannot be effected except by means of des- *127* potic inroads on the rights of property, and on the conditions of bourgeois production; by means of measures, therefore, which appear economically insufficient and untenable, but which, in the course of the movement, outstrip themselves, necessitate further inroads upon the old social order, and are unavoidable as a means of entirely revolutionising the mode of production.

128　　These measures will of course be different in different countries.

129　　Nevertheless in the most advanced countries, the following will be pretty generally applicable.

1. Abolition of property in land and application of all rents of land to public purposes.

2. A heavy progressive or graduated income tax.

3. Abolition of all right of inheritance.

4. Confiscation of the property of all emigrants and rebels.

5. Centralisation of credit in the hands of the State, by means of a national bank with State capital and an exclusive monopoly.

6. Centralisation of the means of communication and transport in the hands of the State.

7. Extension of factories and instruments of production owned by the State, the bringing into cultivation of waste-lands, and the improvement of the soil generally in accordance with a common plan.

8. Equal liability of all to labour. Establishment of industrial armies, especially for agriculture.

9. Combination of agriculture with manufacturing industries; gradual abolition of the distinction between town and country, by a more equable distribution of the population over the country.

10. Free education for all children in public schools. Abolition of children's factory labour in its present form. Combination of education with industrial production, &c., &c.

130　　When, in the course of development, class distinctions have disappeared, and all production has been concentrated in the hands of a vast association of the whole nation, the public power will lose its political character. Political power, properly so called, is merely the organised power of one class for oppressing another. If the proletariat during its contest with the bourgeoisie is compelled, by the force of circumstances, to organise itself as a class, if, by means of a revolution, it makes itself the ruling class, and, as such, sweeps away by force the old conditions of production, then it will, along with these conditions, have swept away the conditions for the existence of class antagonisms and of classes generally, and will thereby have abolished its own supremacy as a class.

131　　In place of the old bourgeois society, with its classes and class antagonisms, we shall have an association, in which the free development of each is the condition for the free development of all. . . .

IV

Position of the Communists in Relation to the Various Existing Opposition Parties

Section II has made clear the relations of the Communists to the existing working-class parties, such as the Chartists in England and Agrarian Reformers in America.   *132*

The Communists fight for the attainment of the immediate aims, for the enforcement of the momentary interests of the working class; but in the movement of the present, they also represent and take care of the future of that movement. In France the Communists ally themselves with the Social-Democrats, against the conservative and radical bourgeoisie, reserving, however, the right to take up a critical position in regard to phrases and illusions traditionally handed down from the great Revolution.   *133*

In Switzerland they support the Radicals, without losing sight of the fact that this party consists of antagonistic elements, partly of Democratic Socialists, in the French sense, partly of radical bourgeois.   *134*

In Poland they support the party that insists on an agrarian revolution as the prime condition for national emancipation, that party which fomented the insurrection of Cracow in 1846.   *135*

In Germany they fight with the bourgeoisie whenever it acts in a revolutionary way, against the absolute monarchy, the feudal squirearchy, and the petty bourgeoisie.   *136*

But they never cease, for a single instant, to instil into the working class the clearest possible recognition of the hostile antagonism between bourgeoisie and proletariat, in order that the German workers may straightway use, as so many weapons against the bourgeoisie, the social and political conditions that the bourgeoisie must necessarily introduce along with its supremacy, and in order that, after the fall of the reactionary classes in Germany, the fight against the bourgeoisie itself may immediately begin.   *137*

The Communists turn their attention chiefly to Germany, because that country is on the eve of a bourgeois revolution that is bound to be carried out under more advanced conditions of European civilisation, and with a much more developed proletariat, than that of England was in the seventeenth, and of France in the eighteenth century, and because the bourgeois revolution in Germany will be but the prelude to an immediately following proletarian revolution.   *138*

In short, the Communists everywhere support every revolutionary movement against the existing social and political order of things.   *139*

In all these movements they bring to the front, as the leading question in each, the property question, no matter what its degree of development at the time.   *140*

Finally, they labour everywhere for the union and agreement of the democratic parties of all countries.   *141*

142   The Communists disdain to conceal their views and aims. They openly declare that their ends can be attained only by the forcible overthrow of all existing social conditions. Let the ruling classes tremble at a Communistic revolution. The proletarians have nothing to lose but their chains. They have a world to win.

WORKING MEN OF ALL COUNTRIES, UNITE!

WRITING AND DISCUSSION QUESTIONS

Informative

1. Marx explains how "the modern bourgeoisie is itself the product of a long course of development." Briefly summarize that development, and explain the role of feudalism, medieval guilds, and the Age of Exploration in that development.
2. "The bourgeoisie cannot exist without constantly revolutionising the instruments of production, and thereby the relations of production, and with them the whole relations of society." Explain this chain of causes. How in Marx's view does changing the instruments of production lead to changes in the relations of society?
3. Why do labor unions arise and what is their place in Marx's view of the development of the proletariat? Does Marx consider whether they may become a sufficient force to balance the power of the bourgeoisie?
4. What reasons does Marx give for his declaration "that the bourgeoisie is unfit any longer to be the ruling class in society"?
5. In his discussion of the family, Marx raises the question of education. What is the connection?
6. What are some of the specific assumptions that form the basis of Marx's dream of a society in which "the free development of each is the condition for the free development of all"?

Persuasive

1. Marx claimed that "national one-sidedness and narrow-mindedness" would break down as a result of the developing world market, paving the way for a world state. Argue the accuracy of this claim in the light of recent resurgences of nationalism in the Middle East and Eastern Europe. Consider also that in 1992, nearly a century and a half after the *Manifesto,* Europe will begin to function, in terms of trade, like a single nation, ostensibly to be more competitive in the world market. Was Marx simply wrong or did he underestimate the time required for the predicted changes? Consider this question in larger terms by selecting several of Marx's predictions about economic changes: are there more that either have already or seem about to come true than have not?
2. Marx was not alone in noting that one result of industrialization during the nineteenth century was the dehumanization of labor itself: no joy remained in the work, as the worker "becomes an appendage of the machine, and it is only the most

simple, most monotonous, and most easily acquired knack that is required of him."
Argue that this is or is not still a problem in modern industry.
3. The forces of labor, as Marx predicted, have coalesced politically into a labor party in nearly all the industrialized nations of Europe but not in the United States. Why not?
4. Marx thought that the laboring class, once it gained political power, would "destroy all previous securities for, and insurances of, individual property." Why did he think this must happen? Why has it not happened in most industrialized nations?
5. Examine the list of 10 "measures" Marx considered "unavoidable as a means of entirely revolutionising the mode of production," which he lists near the end of Part II. Which of them have been incorporated into capitalistic societies? Which do you think are incompatible with a free society?
6. How different is Marx's concern for the material bases of society, value, and institutions from Smith's and Ricardo's insistence on the role of greed in creating an ideal—or at least the best possible—system? Who is more materialistic?
7. Compare and contrast the *Manifesto* with the Declaration of Independence in terms of the ideologies that lie behind each. Which do you think offers a more adequate view of human nature and human relationships?

Personal

1. Marx claims that the triumph of bourgeois values "has put an end to all feudal, patriarchal, idyllic relations . . . and has left remaining no other nexus between man and man than naked self-interest, than callous 'cash payment.'" Many people today who are not Marxists may agree with this statement and argue that the phrase "business ethics" is a contradiction in terms. How much room do you think capitalism has left for the operation of values and ideals other than making money?
2. Marx believed that individuality and freedom, the great ideals of the bourgeoisie, are limited by the economic conditions of capitalism to the freedom and individuality of only a privileged class. Explain why this might have seemed true in mid-nineteenth-century Europe, and argue what degree of truth you can see in this belief now in the last decade of the twentieth century.
3. Consider Marx's argument that a "selfish misconception" we share "with every ruling class" induces us "to transform into eternal laws of nature and reason, the social forms springing from [our] present mode of production and form of property." From your own understanding of history, how true has this been? Do you think Marx himself fell into his own version of this "selfish misconception"? Do you think any truths or values remain apart from any historical context?
4. Marx advocated public education for all children, which many opposed because they believed it would undermine the family. Today, though public education is generally advocated for all, many Americans are still concerned that it may be undermining the values on which the institution of the family is based. What are the

central issues in those arguments? Has our society dealt adequately with the issue of what values should be taught in our schools? How do today's arguments in favor of public education differ from or resemble Marx's?

5. Attacks on communists in Marx's time included the charge that they advocated the abolition of the family, which certainly was not one of Marx's claims. Marx argued instead that the family would simply disappear, that in fact it was already being abolished by the bourgeoisie, especially in the way women were treated. How true do you think his arguments were about the exploitation of women? How true do you think they are today?

▼

CHARLES BEARD, FROM *ECONOMIC ORIGINS OF JEFFERSONIAN DEMOCRACY*

By 1900, the original versions of both capitalism and communism had begun to change. Capitalist economies in industrialized nations were beginning to solve some of their worst abuses, recognizing in deed, if not in theory, that even a "free" market required some government control. Contrary to both Ricardo's and Marx's predictions, profits for capitalists and real wages for the working class had increased, at least enough to keep unrest at the level of the strike or riot but short of outright revolution. Marx had been established as the major voice of socialist theory, but numerous controversies had risen over how he was to be interpreted and applied. Among the most notable critics near the turn of the century was a young Russian revolutionary calling himself Lenin, who argued that Marx was "wrong" mainly because he failed to anticipate how colonial imperialism would both mask and delay the developments he predicted: working men in industrialized nations were not miserable enough to rise because they were not in fact the lowest class; they and their bourgeois Western economies were being supported by the exploited colonial masses of Africa, China, Latin America, and elsewhere. But while these battles concerning interpretation were being fought both theoretically and in the streets, Marx's ideas were influencing, in subtle ways, Western thought, including the academic disciplines and especially history.

History is not the past, but an interpretation of the past. Therefore, every work of history has behind it a historian's assumptions about what drives events: divine will; some racial, ethnic, or national destiny; powerful personalities; the force of great ideas; or the pressures of economics. The last of these is among the least-popular approaches to history because it may depress a reader to conceive of great human events being caused primarily by crass materialistic forces like money, property, the means of production, and class conflict, and because to look at history this way may seem too much like Marxism. Yet one measure of Marx's significance is the extent to which both Marxist and non-Marxist students of society began to stress the importance of economic conditions and to use much of his basic terminology for their studies.

Charles Beard (1874–1948) was not a Marxist. He was, however, an eminent American historian and political scientist who pursued a system of interpreting history inspired to a significant degree by Marx. In his *Economic Interpretation of the Constitution* (1913), he upset cherished, popular notions about the origins of the Federal government by calling attention to the role of property and class conflict in the ratification of the U.S. Constitution. In Beard's hands, the story of the Constitution's origins was not so much one of the emergence of great political ideals as it was a conflict over concrete economic interests. "The financiers, public creditors, traders, commercial men, manufacturers, and allied groups, centering mainly in the larger seaboard towns," supported ratification while "the farmers, particularly in the inland regions, and the debtors" mainly opposed it. It was in short a conflict "between the capitalistic and agrarian classes."

To Beard, the result of his discovery was neither dismaying nor evidence of the need for a proletarian dictatorship. If the origins of the American government were less than idyllic and if America in his lifetime was still less than perfect, Beard nevertheless believed that American history demonstrated the feasibility of the gradual emergence of a true social democracy. In *The Rise of American Civilization* (1927), written with his wife Mary Beard, he positioned the Golden Age of American Democracy in the future, not the past. In his attempt to promote that future, however, he did more than write; he functioned as a reformer and gadfly. A professor of history at Columbia University from 1904 to 1917, he resigned in protest over the dismissal of two colleagues for their opposition to the United States' entry into World War I. In 1918, he helped organize the New School for Social Research in New York City. Although strongly supporting the New Deal in the 1930s and 1940s, he attacked Franklin Delano Roosevelt's foreign policy, arguing in his last book that Roosevelt had forced Japan to war. He was one of the earliest and most eminent of American historians to argue the point, now considered a commonplace and implied earlier in this introduction, that a historian's view of history is "not a purely objective discovery."

Following is an excerpt from the opening chapter of Beard's *Economic Origins of Jeffersonian Democracy* (1915), in which he briefly summarizes the bases for his conclusions in the *Economic Interpretation of the Constitution*, before carrying on the argument to show how the same class conflict continued in the early decades under the new Constitution.

▼

from *Economic Origins of Jeffersonian Democracy*
CHARLES A. BEARD

CHAPTER I

The Federalist-Republican Antagonism and the Conflict Over the Constitution

 An examination into the origins of Jeffersonian Democracy naturally *1* opens with an inquiry whether there was any connection between that party and the large body of citizens who opposed the establishment of the Constitution of the United States. In the struggle over the adoption of that instrument, there appeared, it is well known, a sharp antagonism throughout almost the entire country. The views of competent contemporary observers and of modern students of the period are in accord on that point. Of this there can be no doubt. Chief Justice Marshall, a member of the Virginia ratifying convention and a Federalist of high standing, who combined with his unusual opportunities for personal observation his mastery of President Washington's private correspondence, informs us that the parties to the conflict over the Constitution were in some states evenly balanced, that in many instances the majority in favor of the new system was so small that its intrinsic merits alone would not have carried the day, that in some of the adopting states a majority of the people were in the opposition, and that in all of them the new government was accepted with reluctance only because a dread of dismemberment of the union overcame hostility to the proposed fundamental law.[1]

2   A half a century after Marshall thus described the contest over the ratification of the Constitution, Hildreth, a patient and discriminating student of the Federalist period, on turning over the sources in a fresh light, came to the same conclusion.[2] He frankly declared that it was exceedingly doubtful whether, upon a fair canvass, a majority of the people, in several of the states which ratified the Constitution, actually favored its adoption; that in the powerful states of Massachusetts, New York, Pennsylvania, and Virginia, the majority in favor of the new frame of government was very uncertain, so uncertain, in fact, as to raise the question whether there had been any majority at all; and that everywhere the voters of the states were sharply divided into two well-marked political parties. Bancroft, whose devotion to the traditions of the Constitution is never to be questioned, was no less emphatic than Hildreth in his characterization of the contest for the new political order as a hard-fought battle ending in victory snatched from the very jaws of defeat.[3] From the day of Hildreth and Bancroft to this, no serious student of the eighteenth century has doubted at least the severity and even balance of the conflict over the Constitution. Only those publicists concerned with the instant need of political controversies have been bold enough to deny that the fundamental law of the land was itself the product of one of the sharpest partisan contests in the history of the country.

3   This stubbornly fought battle over the Constitution was in the main economic in character, because the scheme of government contemplated was designed to effect, along with a more adequate national defence, several commercial and financial reforms of high significance, and at the same time to afford an efficient check upon state legislatures that had shown themselves prone to assault acquired property rights, particularly of personality, by means of paper money and other agrarian measures. To speak more precisely, the contest over the Constitution was not primarily a war over abstract political ideals, such as state's rights and centralization, but over concrete economic issues, and the political division which accompanied it was substantially along the lines of the

---

[1] *Life of Washington* (2d ed.), Vol. II, p. 127.
[2] Hildreth, *History of the United States* (1856), Vol. IV, pp. 25 ff.
[3] *History of the Constitution of the United States* (1882), Vol. II, pp. *passim*.

interests affected—the financiers, public creditors, traders, commercial men, manufacturers, and allied groups, centering mainly in the larger seaboard towns, being chief among the advocates of the Constitution, and the farmers, particularly in the inland regions, and the debtors being chief among its opponents. That other considerations, such as the necessity for stronger national defence, entered into the campaign is, of course, admitted, but with all due allowances, it may be truly said that the Constitution was a product of a struggle between capitalistic and agrarian interests.

This removal of the Constitution from the realm of pure political ethics and   4
its establishment in the dusty way of earthly strife and common economic endeavor is not, as some would have us believe, the work of profane hands. It has come about through the gathering of the testimony of contemporary witnesses of undoubted competency and through the researches of many scholars. Although in the minds of some, the extent of the economic forces may be exaggerated and the motives of many leaders in the formation and adoption of the Constitution may be incorrectly interpreted, the significant fact stands out with increasing boldness that the conflict over the new system of government was chiefly between the capitalistic and agrarian classes.

Occupying an influential position in the former of these classes were the   5
holders of the state and continental debt amounting to more than all the rest of the fluid capital in the United States. No less an important person than Washington assigned the satisfaction of the claims of the public creditors as the chief reason for the adoption of the Constitution, for he held that unless provisions were made for the payment of the debt, the country might as well continue under the old order of the Articles of Confederation. "I had endulged the expectation," he wrote to Jefferson, "that the New Government would enable those entrusted with its administration to do justice to the public creditors and retrieve the National character. But if no means are to be employed but requisitions, that expectation will be in vain and we may well recur to the old Confederation."[4]

Without doubting the fact that the standard of honor which Washington here   6
set up was a consideration in the minds of many, it is no less a fact that the numerous holders of the public debt themselves formed a considerable centre corps in the political army waging the campaign for the adoption of the Constitution. For instance, a prominent Federalist of Connecticut, Chauncey Goodrich, a man placed by his connections and experience in a position to observe closely the politics of that and surrounding states, wrote, in 1790, that "perhaps without the active influence of the creditors, the government could not have been formed, and any well-grounded dissatisfaction on their part will make its movements dull and languid, if not worse."[5] The willingness of a number of Northern men to break up the Union before the new government was fairly launched because they could not secure a satisfactory settlement of

[4]*Documentary History of the Constitution*, Vol. IV, p. 40.
[5]Gibbs, *Administrations of Washington and Adams*, Vol. I, p. 37.

the debt is proof that Goodrich had correctly gauged the weight of the public creditors in the battle for the Constitution.

7   To the testimony of Virginia and Connecticut in this matter of the influence of public creditors and allied interests in the formation and ratification of the Constitution we may add that of New York, then as now one of the first financial centres, speaking through a witness of such high authority that the most incredulous would hardly question it,—Alexander Hamilton, the first Secretary of the Treasury under the new system. He had been a member of the Convention which drafted the Constitution. He was intimately associated with the leaders in the movement for ratification. He shared in the preparation of that magnificent polemic, *The Federalist.* But above all, he was, as Secretary of the Treasury, in full possession of the names of those who funded continental and state securities after the Constitution was adopted. No one in all the United States, therefore, had such excellent opportunities to know the real forces which determined the constitutional conflict. What Goodrich could surmise, Hamilton could test by reference to the Treasury ledgers at his elbow. That the public creditors were "very influential" and the allied property interests, that is, in the main, capitalistic interests, were "very weighty" in securing the adoption of the Constitution, he distinctly avowed, although he wisely refrained from estimating exactly their respective values in the contest. In an unfinished manuscript on the funding system, he considered this matter at length, saying: "The public creditors, who consisted of various descriptions of men, a large proportion of them very meritorious and very influential, had had a considerable agency in promoting the adoption of the new Constitution, for this peculiar reason, among the many weighty reasons which were common to them as citizens and proprietors, that it exhibited the prospect of a government able to do justice to their claims. Their disappointment and disgust quickened by the sensibility of private interest, could not but have been extreme [if the debt had not been properly funded]. There was also another class of men, and a very weighty one, who had had great share in the establishment of the Constitution, who, though not personally interested in the debt, considered maxims of public credit as of the essence of good government, *as intimately connected by the analogy and sympathy of principles with the security of property in general,* and as forming an inseparable portion of the great system of political order. These men, from sentiment, would have regarded their labors in supporting the Constitution as in a great measure lost; they would have seen the disappointment of their hopes in the unwillingness of the government to do what they esteemed justice, and to pursue what they called an honorable policy; and they would have regarded this failure as an augury of the continuance of the fatal system which had for some time prostrated the national honor, interest, and happiness. The disaffection of a part of these classes of men might have carried a considerable reinforcement to the enemies of the government."[6]

[6]Hamilton, *Works* (Lodge ed.), Vol. VII, p. 418. The smaller edition, not the Federal edition, is cited throughout this volume.

Other contemporaries stressed other features in the conflict, but nevertheless 8 agreed that it had been primarily economic in character. For instance, Fisher Ames, of Massachusetts, who had been a member of the state ratifying convention, laid emphasis upon the commercial rather than the financial aspects of the constitutional battle. Speaking in the House of Representatives, on March 28, 1789, he said: "I conceive, sir, that the present Constitution was dictated by commercial necessity more than any other cause. The want of an efficient government to secure the manufacturing interests and to advance our commerce, was long seen by men of judgment and pointed out by patriots solicitous to promote our general welfare."[7] The inevitable inference from this remark is that, in Ames's opinion, men of commercial and manufacturing interests must have seen the possibilities of economic advantage in the adoption of the Constitution, and naturally arrayed themselves on its side.

More than a decade after the conflict over the Constitution, when many of 9 the great actors in that drama had passed away, and there had been ample time and opportunity to reflect deeply upon the nature and causes of that struggle, Chief Justice Marshall described it, in effect, though not in exact terms, as a war between mercantile, financial, and capitalistic interests generally, on the one hand, and the agrarian and debtor interests, on the other.[8] Half a century later, Hildreth, whose work has been cited above, came to substantially identical conclusions. He declared that "in most of the towns and cities, and seats of trade and mechanical industry, the friends of the Constitution formed a very decided majority. Much was hoped from the organization of a vigorous national government and the exercise of extensive powers vested in it for the regulation of commerce." In North Carolina and Rhode Island, the states which first rejected the Constitution, Hildreth continued, the trouble was the state paper money which destroyed the rights of creditors. In Massachusetts he found the "weight of talent, wealth, and influence" on the Federal side. In Virginia, the opponents of the Constitution included many of the great planters and "the backwoods population almost universally," and the opposition of the planters was to be, in part, ascribed to the fear of having to pay their debts due to British merchants in case the Constitution went into effect. In New York it was the City and the southern counties, not the interior agricultural regions, that supported the new scheme of national government.[9]

By a strange coincidence, Charles Francis Adams gave to the world the 10 same economic interpretation of the Constitution in the very year that Hildreth published his history. In his life of his grandfather, the President, Mr. Adams, who enjoyed the unrivalled advantage of having access to documents closed to all his contemporaries, represented the adoption of the fundamental law of the United States as a triumph of property over the propertyless. The social disorder which preceded the federal Convention of 1787, Mr. Adams attributed to

---

[7] P. W. Ames, *Speeches of Fisher Ames*, p. 12.
[8] Beard, *Economic Interpretation of the Constitution*, p. 296.
[9] *Op. cit.*, Vol. IV, pp. 25 ff.

"the upheaving of the poorest classes to throw off all law of debtor and creditor," and the Convention itself, he declared, "was the work of commercial people in the seaport towns, of the planters of the slave-holding states, of the officers of the revolutionary army, and the property holders everywhere. . . . That among the opponents of the Constitution are to be ranked a great majority of those who had most strenuously fought the battle of independence of Great Britain is certain. . . . Among the federalists, it is true, were to be found a large body of the patriots of the Revolution, almost all the general officers who survived the war, and a great number of the substantial citizens along the line of the seaboard towns and populous regions, all of whom had heartily sympathized in the policy of resistance. But these could never have succeeded in effecting the establishment of the Constitution, had they not received the active and steady cooperation of all that was left in America of attachment to the mother country, as well as of the moneyed interest, which ever points to strong government as surely as the needle to the pole."[10]

11   That which representative men of the eighteenth century definitely understood, and Hildreth implied in a somewhat rambling fashion was completely demonstrated by Professor O. G. Libby in his study of the *Geographical Distribution of the Vote on the Constitution in the Thirteen States:* the support for the Constitution came from the centres of capitalistic interest and the opposition came from the agrarians and those burdened with debts. To adduce further evidence in support of Professor Libby's thesis is merely to add documentation to that which has been satisfactorily established.[11]

WRITING AND DISCUSSION QUESTIONS

Informative

1. What authorities does Beard cite in making his case for the economic forces behind the Constitutional debate? Are they reliable sources that effectively support his argument?

2. In waging the Revolutionary War, the new nation had incurred a considerable public debt, and the Articles of Confederation, the document that empowered the government before the Constitution was ratified, provided no means by which the central government could raise the money to pay that debt. How do Washington and Hamilton characterize the state of the government operating under the Articles?

3. The Preamble to the Constitution declares that "We the People of the United States" ordained and established that document. According to Beard, to what extent is this true?

---

[10]C. F. Adams, *The Works of John Adams*, Vol. I, p. 441.

[11]Beard, *Economic Interpretation of the Constitution*. It is curious that this volume raised such a storm of criticism in certain quarters when the leading ideas set forth in it had long been accepted by students of the economic aspects of American history.

Persuasive

1. Consider the full text of the Preamble, where the reasons for establishing the Constitution are listed: "We the People of the United States, in order to form a more perfect union, establish Justice, insure domestic tranquility, provide for the common defence, promote the general Welfare, and secure the Blessings of Liberty to ourselves and our Posterity, do ordain and establish this Constitution of the United States of America." It does not mention anything much like the words quoted by Beard of Washington, "to do justice to the public creditors," or of Hamilton, to maintain "the security of property." Why not? Argue that the Preamble is or is not biased.
2. Review the selections from Alexis de Tocqueville's *Democracy in America,* which appear in Chapter 6. What indications did he see of class conflict as described by Beard in America, and how did they enter into his assessment of the internal dangers facing the young nation?

Personal

1. The Bill of Rights, as you know, was not part of the original Constitution. Was this an indication, do you think, that the original framers of the Constitution thought of "liberty" in terms more of the security of property than of free speech, a free press, or even freedom of religion?
2. It has long been popular for the people of the United States to conceive of the national character in terms of images drawn from both agrarian and frontier experience, where the central struggle was with the land or its aboriginal inhabitants. Yet, if Beard is correct, farmers, planters, and backwoodsmen, who according to President John Quincey Adams' grandson (and President John Adams' great-grandson) C. F. Adams, were "a great majority of those who had most strenuously fought the battle of independence of Great Britain" and were the interests most opposed to acceptance of the Constitution. How does this knowledge affect your conception of the national character?
3. Are there other popular ways of conceiving of the national character that reveal a knowledge of class consciousness? Choose a popular film— *Who Framed Roger Rabbit?* or *Platoon,* for example—and examine it as a Marxian drama.
4. Do you see any economic, geographic, and class divisions as significant in today's Democratic and Republican parties as those Beard found among the Federalists and anti-Federalists?

CLIFFORD ODETS, *WAITING FOR LEFTY*

The 1930s was a difficult time for Americans. The Great Depression began with the stock market crash in 1929 and produced widespread misery throughout the next decade. Desperately hungry people languished in the cities, and farmers and ranchers were hardly able to afford the cost of raising produce and livestock, much less the cost of shipping to urban markets. Large numbers of the unemployed migrated across the nation in search of work where there was none. It was a time when many people's faith in the capitalistic, democratic republic was severely shaken and when the specter of communism was feared. This fear, however, was not new; it had been rising during hard times and waning during good times since at least the 1870s. Also, this fear was directed at domestic discontent agitated not so much by newly formed communist regimes (fear of Russian-inspired communism would not set in until the late 1940s) as by the foreign ideas that had been widely circulated since the 1840s. This agitation was intensified by the increasing number of intellectuals supporting left-wing movements and by a right-wing response, which although following an argument more than a half century old, was acquiring a more-violent expression. The old argument was the branding of all attempts by workers to help themselves collectively, or by others to encourage them to do so, as communist inspired and, therefore, as against all decent human values. This response is a major theme of Clifford Odets' *Waiting for Lefty*, a play inspired in part by a New York City taxi drivers' strike in 1934.

Waiting for Lefty is one of two long one-act plays by Odets that opened together on Broadway in March 1935. This was a difficult year with the ongoing Depression entering its sixth season and with only the first faint glimmers of improvement beginning to show from Franklin Roosevelt's New Deal. It was also an ominous year: the first Nazi Bundist groups began sprouting in America, but their significance was unknown to most Americans because the spirit of isolationism was at its height in this country. Only a few people—mainly intellectuals—were paying attention to the rise of national socialist dictatorships in Italy and Germany. Odets was one of those few, and his other one-act play in March of 1935, *Till the Day I Die*, was an anti-Nazi piece that critics thought was good drama but unnecessarily alarmist. Critics, however, were more impressed with his blend of drama and politics in *Awake and Sing*, which had opened earlier that year, and in *Paradise Lost* that opened later that year. All four plays were successful Broadway productions, and by the end of that productive year, the critics were calling Odets a "revolutionary oracle," the "darling of the proletariat," and a "prophet of the Left." Early in 1938, after a profitable time writing for Hollywood and after another Broadway hit *(Golden Boy)*, *The New Yorker* profiled him as "Revolution's Number One Boy." These epithets, however, were compliments more than they were condemnations. It should be borne in mind that few Americans, because of the United States' isolationism and because of Russia's closed society, were aware of the worst results of communism, that is, Stalin's brand of Marxism–Leninism. In Russia, the forced collectivization of farms began in 1929, and in only half a decade as a result of this policy, 16 million persons died by execution and starvation in the Ukraine alone. Also, the notorious purges that began in 1934 sent millions more to execution or imprisonment in labor camps before the decade ended.

Odets seemed an unlikely Marxist, even for the 1930s. After his success, old friends commented that he looked more like "a well groomed capitalist playboy," and while in Hollywood, he is said to have been making about $2500 a week, which during the Depression was an astronomical sum. Although he was a member of the Communist party for a brief period in the early 1930s, his Marxism, like that of many American intellectuals, was his own and was exercised independently of any political affiliation.

Odets (1906–1963) was born in Philadelphia of Jewish Lithuanian immigrants. The family soon moved to the Bronx, where, despite their own middle-class prosperity, Odets grew up close enough to poverty to develop a social conscience. His revolutionary spirit, however, may have had more to do with his theater experience. He left high school before graduation to work in radio and theater, and he managed to become part of the famous Theatre Guild, playing minor roles in the late 1920s.

Later, he joined the Group Theatre, which was a group that split from the Guild in 1931 and which became famous for its emphasis on Stanislavsky's "method" approach to acting and for its interest in Marxism. American theater in the 1920s had already established itself as a major voice of social protest and included attacks on bourgeois materialism by dramatists like Eugene O'Neill, Elmer Rice, and Maxwell Anderson. Thus, when Odets began play writing, he was entering an established tradition, although his approach, at least in some plays, was more propagandistic than most. It was this propagandistic bent in a world troubled by social and economic strife that made Odets' voice particularly relevant to his time. As a result, by 1938 *Waiting for Lefty* was being produced all over the world, serving, in Odet's words, as "a kind of light-machine-gun that you wheeled in to use whenever there was any kind of strike trouble."

▼

Waiting for Lefty
CLIFFORD ODETS

As the curtain goes up we see a bare stage. On it are sitting six or seven men in a semi-circle. Lolling against the proscenium down left is a young man chewing a toothpick: a gunman. A fat man of porcine appearance is talking directly to the audience. In other words he is the head of a union and the men ranged behind him are a committee of workers. They are now seated in interesting different attitudes and present a wide diversity of type, as we shall soon see. The fat man is hot and heavy under the collar, near the end of a long talk, but not too hot: he is well fed and confident. His name is HARRY FATT.

FATT: You're so wrong I ain't laughing. Any guy with eyes to read knows it. Look at the textile strike—out like lions and in like lambs. Take the San Francisco tie-up—starvation and broken heads. The steel boys wanted to walk out too, but they changed their minds. It's the trend of the times, that's what it is. All we workers got a good man behind us now. He's top man of the country—looking out for our interests—the man in the White House is the one I'm referrin' to. That's why the times ain't ripe for a strike. He's working day and night—

VOICE *(from the audience):* For who? *(The* GUNMAN *stirs himself.)*

FATT: For you! The records prove it. If this was the Hoover régime, would I say don't go out, boys? Not on your tintype! But things is different now. You read the papers as well as me. You know it. And that's why I'm against the strike. Because we gotta stand behind the man who's standin' behind us! The whole country—

ANOTHER VOICE: Is on the blink! *(The* GUNMAN *looks grave.)*

FATT: Stand up and show yourself, you damn red! Be a man, let's see what you look like! *(Waits in vain.)* Yellow from the word go! Red and yellow makes a dirty color, boys. I got my eyes on four or five of them in the union here.

What the hell'll they do for you? Pull you out and run away when trouble starts. Give those birds a chance and they'll have your sisters and wives in the whore houses, like they done in Russia. They'll tear Christ off his bleeding cross. They'll wreck your homes and throw your babies in the river. You think that's bunk? Read the papers! Now listen, we can't stay here all night. I gave you the facts in the case. You boys got hot suppers to go to and—

ANOTHER VOICE: Says you!

GUNMAN: Sit down, Punk!

ANOTHER VOICE: Where's Lefty? *(Now this question is taken up by the others in unison.* FATT *pounds with gavel.)*

FATT: That's what I wanna know. Where's your pal, Lefty? You elected him chairman—where the hell did he disappear?

VOICES: We want Lefty! Lefty! Lefty!

FATT *(pounding):* What the hell is this—a circus? You got the committee here. This bunch of cowboys you elected. *(Pointing to man on extreme right end.)*

MAN: Benjamin.

FATT: Yeah, Doc Benjamin. *(Pointing to other men in circle in seated order):* Benjamin, Miller, Stein, Mitchell, Phillips, Keller. It ain't my fault Lefty took a run-out powder. If you guys—

A GOOD VOICE: What's the committee say?

OTHERS: The committee! Let's hear from the committee! (Fatt *tries to quiet the crowd, but one of the seated men suddenly comes to the front. The* GUNMAN *moves over to center stage, but* FATT *says:)*

FATT: Sure, let him talk. Let's hear what the red boys gotta say! *(Various shouts are coming from the audience.* FATT *insolently goes back to his seat in the middle of the circle. He sits on his raised platform and relights his cigar. The* GUNMAN *goes back to his post.* JOE, *the new speaker, raises his hand for quiet. Gets it quickly. He is sore.)*

JOE: You boys know me. I ain't a red boy one bit! Here I'm carryin' a shrapnel that big I picked up in the war. And maybe I don't know it when it rains! Don't tell me red! You know what we are? The black and blue boys! We been kicked around so long we're black and blue from head to toes. But I guess anyone who says straight out he don't like it, he's a red boy to the leaders of the union. What's this crap about goin' home to hot suppers? I'm asking to your faces how many's got hot suppers to go home to? Anyone who's sure of his next meal, raise your hand! A certain gent sitting behind me can raise them both. But not in front here! And that's why we're talking strike—to get a living wage!

VOICE: Where's Lefty?

JOE: I honest to God don't know, but he didn't take no run-out powder. That Wop's got more guts than a slaughter house. Maybe a traffic jam got him, but he'll be here. But don't let this red stuff scare you. Unless fighting for a living scares you. We gotta make up our minds. My wife made up my mind last week, if you want the truth. It's plain as the nose on Sol Feinberg's face we need a strike. There's us comin' home every night—eight, ten hours on the cab. "God," the wife says, "eighty cents ain't money—don't buy beans almost. You're workin' for the company," she says to me, "Joe! you ain't workin' for me or the family no more!" She says to me, "If you don't start . . ."

I. JOE AND EDNA

The lights fade out and a white spot picks out the playing space within the space of seated men. The seated men are very dimly visible in the outer dark, but more prominent is FATT *smoking his cigar and often blowing the smoke in the lighted circle.*

A tired but attractive woman of thirty comes into the room, drying her hands on an apron. She stands there sullenly as JOE *comes in from the other side, home from work. For a moment they stand and look at each other in silence.*

JOE: Where's all the furniture, honey?

EDNA: They took it away. No installments paid.

JOE: When?

EDNA: Three o'clock.

JOE: They can't do that.

EDNA: Can't? They did it.

JOE: Why, the palookas, we paid three-quarters.

EDNA: The man said read the contract.

JOE: We must have signed a phony. . . .

EDNA: It's a regular contract and you signed it.

JOE: Don't be so sour, Edna. . . . *(Tries to embrace her.)*

EDNA: Do it in the movies, Joe—they pay Clark Gable big money for it.

JOE: This is a helluva house to come home to. Take my word!

EDNA: Take MY word! Whose fault is it?

JOE: Must you start that stuff again?

EDNA: Maybe you'd like to talk about books?

JOE: I'd like to slap you in the mouth!

EDNA: No you won't.

JOE *(sheepishly)*: Jeez, Edna, you get me sore some time. . . .

EDNA: But just look at me—I'm laughing all over!

JOE: Don't insult me. Can I help it if times are bad? What the hell do you want me to do, jump off a bridge or something?

EDNA: Don't yell. I just put the kids to bed so they won't know they missed a meal. If I don't have Emmy's shoes soled tomorrow, she can't go to school. In the meantime let her sleep.

JOE: Honey, I rode the wheels off the chariot today. I cruised around five hours without a call. It's conditions.

EDNA: Tell it to the A & P!

JOE: I booked two-twenty on the clock. A lady with a dog was lit . . . she gave me a quarter tip by mistake. If you'd only listen to me—we're rolling in wealth.

EDNA: Yeah? How much?

JOE: I had "coffee and—" in a beanery. *(Hands her silver coins.)* A buck four.

EDNA: The second month's rent is due tomorrow.

JOE: Don't look at me that way, Edna.

EDNA: I'm looking through you, not at you. . . . Everything was gonna be so ducky! A cottage by the waterfall, roses in Picardy. You're a four-star-bust! If you think I'm standing for it much longer, you're crazy as a bedbug.

JOE: I'd get another job if I could. There's no work—you know it.

EDNA: I only know we're at the bottom of the ocean.

JOE: What can I do?

EDNA: Who's the man in the family, you or me?

JOE: That's no answer. Get down to brass tacks. Christ, gimme a break, too! A coffee and java all day. I'm hungry, too, Babe. I'd work my fingers to the bone if—

EDNA: I'll open a can of salmon.

JOE: Not now. Tell me what to do!

EDNA: I'm not God!

JOE: Jeez, I wish I was a kid again and didn't have to think about the next minute.

EDNA: But you're not a kid and you do have to think about the next minute. You got two blondie kids sleeping in the next room. They need food and clothes. I'm not mentioning anything else—But we're stalled like a flivver in the snow. For five years I laid awake at night listening to my heart pound. For God's sake, do something, Joe, get wise. Maybe get your buddies together, maybe go on strike for better money. Poppa did it during the war and they won out. I'm turning into a sour old nag.

JOE *(defending himself):* Strikes don't work!

EDNA: Who told you?

JOE: Besides that means not a nickel a week while we're out. Then when it's over they don't take you back.

EDNA: Suppose they don't! What's to lose?

JOE: Well, we're averaging six-seven dollars a week now.

EDNA: That just pays for the rent.

JOE: That is something, Edna.

EDNA: It isn't. They'll push you down to three and four a week before you know it. Then you'll say, "That's somethin'," too!

JOE: There's too many cabs on the street, that's the whole damn trouble.

EDNA: Let the company worry about that, you big fool! If their cabs didn't make a profit, they'd take them off the streets. Or maybe you think they're in business just to pay Joe Mitchell's rent!

JOE: You don't know a-b-c, Edna.

EDNA: I know this—your boss is making suckers outa you boys every minute. Yes, and suckers out of all the wives and the poor innocent kids who'll grow up with crooked spines and sick bones. Sure, I see it in the papers, how good orange juice is for kids. But dammit our kids get colds one on top of the other. They look like little ghosts. Betty never saw a grapefruit. I took her to the store last week and she pointed to a stack of grapefruits. "What's that!" she said. My God, Joe—the world is supposed to be for all of us.

JOE: You'll wake them up.

EDNA: I don't care, as long as I can maybe wake you up.

JOE: Don't insult me. One man can't make a strike.

EDNA: Who says one? You got hundreds in your rotten union!

JOE: The union ain't rotten.

EDNA: No? Then what are they doing? Collecting dues and patting your back?

JOE: They're making plans.

EDNA: What kind?

JOE: They don't tell us.

EDNA: It's too damn bad about you. They don't tell little Joey what's happening in his bitsie witsie union. What do you think it is—a ping pong game?

JOE: You know they're racketeers. The guys at the top would shoot you for a nickel.

EDNA: Why do you stand for that stuff?

JOE: Don't you wanna see me alive?

EDNA (*after a deep pause*): No . . . I don't think I do, Joe. Not if you can lift a finger to do something about it, and don't. No, I don't care.

JOE: Honey, you don't understand what—

EDNA: And any other hackie that won't fight . . . let them all be ground to hamburger!

JOE: It's one thing to—

EDNA: Take your hand away! Only they don't grind me to little pieces! I got different plans. (*Starts to take off her apron.*)

JOE: Where are you going?

EDNA: None of your business.

JOE: What's up your sleeve?

EDNA: My arm'd be up my sleeve, darling, if I had a sleeve to wear. (*Puts neatly folded apron on back of chair.*)

JOE: Tell me!

EDNA: Tell you what?

JOE: Where are you going?

EDNA: Don't you remember my old boy friend?

JOE: Who?

EDNA: Bud Haas. He still has my picture in his watch. He earns a living.

JOE: What the hell are you talking about?

EDNA: I heard worse than I'm talking about.

JOE: Have you seen Bud since we got married?

EDNA: Maybe.

JOE: If I thought . . . (*He stands looking at her.*)

EDNA: See much? Listen, boy friend, if you think I won't do this it just means you can't see straight.

JOE: Stop talking bull!

EDNA: This isn't five years ago, Joe.

JOE: You mean you'd leave me and the kids?

EDNA: I'd leave *you* like a shot!

JOE: No. . . .

EDNA: Yes! (Joe *turns away, sitting in a chair with his back to her. Outside the lighted circle of the playing stage we hear the other seated members of the strike committee. "She will . . . she will . . . it happens that way," etc. This group should be used throughout for various comments, political, emotional and as general chorus. Whispering. . . . The fat boss now blows a heavy cloud of smoke into the scene.*)

JOE (*finally*): Well, I guess I ain't got a leg to stand on.

EDNA: No?

JOE (*suddenly mad*): No, you lousy tart, no! Get the hell out of here. Go pick up that bull-thrower on the corner and stop at some cushy hotel downtown. He's probably been coming here every morning and laying you while I hacked my guts out!

EDNA: You're crawling like a worm!

JOE: You'll be crawling in a minute.

EDNA: You don't scare me that much! (*Indicates a half inch on her finger.*)

JOE: This is what I slaved for!

EDNA: Tell it to your boss!

JOE: He don't give a damn for you or me!

EDNA: That's what I say.

JOE: Don't change the subject!

EDNA: This is the subject, the *exact subject!* Your boss makes this subject. I never saw him in my life, but he's putting ideas in my head a mile a minute. He's giving your kids that fancy disease called the rickets. He's making a jelly-fish outa you and putting wrinkles in my face. This is the subject every inch of the way! He's throwing me into Bud Haas' lap. When in hell will you get wise—

JOE: I'm not so dumb as you think! But you are talking like a red.

EDNA: I don't know what that means. But when a man knocks you down you get up and kiss his fist! You gutless piece of boloney.

JOE: One man can't—

EDNA (*with great joy*): I don't say one man! I say a hundred, a thousand, a whole million, I say. But start in your own union. Get those hack boys together! Sweep out those racketeers like a pile of dirt! Stand up like men and fight for the crying kids and wives. Goddamnit! I'm tired of slavery and sleepless nights.

JOE (*with her*): Sure, sure! . . .

EDNA: Yes. Get brass toes on your shoes and know where to kick!

JOE (*suddenly jumping up and kissing his wife full on the mouth*): Listen, Edna, I'm goin' down to 174th Street to look up Lefty Costello. Lefty was saying the other day . . . (*He suddenly stops.*) How about this Haas guy?

EDNA: Get out of here!

JOE: I'll be back! (*Runs out. For a moment* EDNA *stands triumphant. There is a blackout and when the regular lights come up,* JOE MITCHELL *is concluding what he has been saying):*

JOE: You guys know this stuff better than me. We gotta walk out!

(Abruptly he turns and goes back to his seat.)

Blackout

II. LAB ASSISTANT EPISODE

Discovered: MILLER, *a lab assistant, looking around; and* FAYETTE, *an industrialist.*

FAY: Like it?

MILLER: Very much. I've never seen an office like this outside the movies.

FAY: Yes, I often wonder if interior decorators and bathroom fixture people don't get all their ideas from Hollywood. Our country's extraordinary that way. Soap, cosmetics, electric refrigerators—just let Mrs. Consumer know they're used by the Crawfords and Garbos—more volume of sale than one plant can handle!

MILL: I'm afraid it isn't that easy, Mr. Fayette.

FAY: No, you're right—gross exaggeration on my part. Competition is cut-throat today. Market's up flush against a stone wall. The astronomers had better hurry—open Mars to trade expansion.

MILL: Or it will be just too bad!

FAY: Cigar?

MILL: Thank you, don't smoke.

FAY: Drink?

MILL: Ditto, Mr. Fayette

FAY: I like sobriety in my workers . . . the trained ones, I mean. The pollacks and niggers, they're better drunk—keeps them out of mischief. Wondering why I had you come over?

MILL: If you don't mind my saying—very much.

FAY *(patting him on the knee):* I like your work.

MILL: Thanks.

FAY: No reason why a talented young man like yourself shouldn't string along with us— a growing concern. Loyalty is well repaid in our organization. Did you see Siegfried this morning?

MILL: He hasn't been in the laboratory all day.

FAY: I told him yesterday to raise you twenty dollars a month. Starts this week.

MILL: You don't know how happy my wife'll be.

FAY: Oh, I can appreciate it. *(He laughs.)*

MILL: Was that all, Mr. Fayette?

FAY: Yes, except that we're switching you to laboratory A tomorrow. Siegfried knows about it. That's why I had you in. The new work is very important.

Siegfried recommended you very highly as a man to trust. You'll work directly under Dr. Brenner. Make you happy?

MILL: Very. He's an important chemist!

FAY *(leaning over seriously):* We think so, Miller. We think so to the extent of asking you to stay within the building throughout the time you work with him.

MILL: You mean sleep and eat in?

FAY: Yes. . . .

MILL: It can be arranged.

FAY: Fine. You'll go far, Miller.

MILL: May I ask the nature of the new work?

FAY *(looking around first):* Poison gas. . . .

MILL: Poison!

FAY: Orders from above. I don't have to tell you from where. New type poison gas for modern warfare.

MILL: I see.

FAY: You didn't know a new war was that close, did you?

MILL: I guess I didn't.

FAY: I don't have to stress the importance of absolute secrecy.

MILL: I understand!

FAY: The world is an armed camp today. One match sets the whole world blazing in forty-eight hours. Uncle Sam won't be caught napping!

MILL *(addressing his pencil):* They say 12 million men were killed in that last one and 20 million more wounded or missing.

FAY: That's not our worry. If big business went sentimental over human life there wouldn't be big business of any sort!

MILL: My brother and two cousins went in the last one.

FAY: They died in a good cause.

MILL: My mother says "no!"

FAY: She won't worry about you this time. You're too valuable behind the front.

MILL: That's right.

FAY: All right, Miller. See Siegfried for further orders.

MILL: You should have seen my brother—he could ride a bike without hands. . . .

FAY: You'd better move some clothes and shaving tools in tomorrow. Remember what I said—you're with a growing organization.

MILL: He could run the hundred yards in 9:8 flat. . . .

FAY: Who?

MILL: My brother. He's in the Meuse-Argonne Cemetery. Mama went there in 1926. . . .

FAY: Yes, those things stick. How's your handwriting Miller, fairly legible?

MILL: Fairly so.

FAY: Once a week I'd like a little report from you.

MILL: What sort of report?

FAY: Just a few hundred words once a week on Dr. Brenner's progress.

MILL: Don't you think it might be better coming from the Doctor?

FAY: I didn't ask you that.

MILL: Sorry.

FAY: I want to know what progress he's making, the reports to be purely confidential—between you and me.

MILL: You mean I'm to watch him?

FAY: Yes!

MILL: I guess I can't do that. . . .

FAY: Thirty a month raise . . .

MILL: You said twenty. . . .

FAY: Thirty!

MILL: Guess I'm not built that way.

FAY: Forty. . . .

MILL: Spying's not in my line, Mr. Fayette!

FAY: You use ugly words, Mr. Miller!

MILL: For ugly activity? Yes!

FAY: Think about it, Miller. Your chances are excellent. . . .

MILL: No.

FAY: You're doing something for your country. Assuring the United States that when those goddamn Japs start a ruckus we'll have offensive weapons to back us up! Don't you read your newspapers, Miller?

MILL: Nothing but Andy Gump.

FAY: If you were on the inside you'd know I'm talking cold sober truth! Now, I'm not asking you to make up your mind on the spot. Think about it over your lunch period.

MILL: No.

FAY: Made up your mind already?

MILL: Afraid so.

FAY: You understand the consequences?

MILL: I lose my raise—

MILL: And my job!

Simultaneously: FAY: And your job!

MILL: You misunderstand—

MILL: Rather dig ditches first!

FAY: That's a big job for foreigners.

MILL: But sneaking—and making poison gas—that's for Americans?

FAY: It's up to you.

MILL: My mind's made up.

FAY: No hard feelings?

MILL: Sure hard feelings! I'm not the civilized type, Mr. Fayette. Nothing suave or sophisticated about me. Plenty of hard feelings! Enough to want to bust you and all your kind square in the mouth! *(Does exactly that.)*

Blackout

III. THE YOUNG HACK AND HIS GIRL

Opens with girl and brother. FLORENCE *waiting for* SID *to take her to a dance.*

FLOR: I gotta right to have something out of life. I don't smoke, I don't drink. So if Sid wants to take me to a dance, I'll go. Maybe if you was in love you wouldn't talk so hard.

IRV: I'm saying it for your good.

FLOR: Don't be so good to me.

IRV: Mom's sick in bed and you'll be worryin' her to the grave. She don't want that boy hanging around the house and she don't want you meeting him in Crotona Park.

FLOR: I'll meet him anytime I like!

IRV: If you do, yours truly'll take care of it in his own way. With just one hand, too!

FLOR: Why are you all so set against him?

IRV: Mom told you ten times—it ain't him. It's that he ain't got nothing. Sure, we know he's serious, that he's stuck on you. But that don't cut no ice.

FLOR: Taxi drivers used to make good money.

IRV: Today they're makin' five and six dollars a week. Maybe you wanta raise a family on that. Then you'll be back here living with us again and I'll be supporting two families in one. Well . . . over my dead body.

FLOR: Irv, I don't care—I love him!

IRV: You're a little kid with half-baked ideas!

FLOR: I stand there behind the counter the whole day. I think about him—

IRV: If you thought more about Mom it would be better.

FLOR: Don't I take care of her every night when I come home? Don't I cook supper and iron your shirts and . . . you give me a pain in the neck, too. Don't try to shut me up! I bring a few dollars in the house, too. Don't you see I want something else out of life. Sure, I want romance, love, babies. I want everything in life I can get.

IRV: You take care of Mom and watch your step!

FLOR: And if I don't?

IRV: Yours truly'll watch it for you!

FLOR: You can talk that way to a girl. . . .

IRV: I'll talk that way to your boy friend, too, and it won't be with words! Florrie, if you had a pair of eyes you'd see it's for your own good we're talking. This ain't no time to get married. Maybe later—

FLOR: "Maybe Later" never comes for me, though. Why don't we send Mom to a hospital? She can die in peace there instead of looking at the clock on the mantelpiece all day.

IRV: That needs money. Which we don't have!

FLOR: Money, Money, Money!

IRV: Don't change the subject.

FLOR: This is the subject!

IRV: You gonna stop seeing him? *(She turns away.)* Jesus, kiddie, I remember when you were a baby with curls down your back. Now I gotta stand here yellin' at you like this.

FLOR: I'll talk to him, Irv.

IRV: When?

FLOR: I asked him to come here tonight. We'll talk it over.

IRV: Don't get soft with him. Nowadays is no time to be soft. You gotta be hard as a rock or go under.

FLOR: I found that out. There's the bell. Take the egg off the stove I boiled for Mom. Leave us alone Irv. *(SID comes in—the two men look at each other for a second. IRV exits.)*

SID *(enters):* Hello, Florrie.

FLOR: Hello, Honey. You're looking tired.

SID: Naw, I just need a shave.

FLOR: Well, draw your chair up to the fire and I'll ring for brandy and soda . . . like in the movies.

SID: If this was the movies I'd bring a big bunch of roses.

FLOR: How big?

SID: Fifty or sixty dozen—the kind with long, long stems—big as that. . . .

FLOR: You dope. . . .

SID: Your Paris gown is beautiful.

FLOR *(acting grandly):* Yes, Percy, velvet panels are coming back again. Madame La Farge told me today that Queen Marie herself designed it.

SID: Gee . . . !

FLOR: Every princess in the Balkans is wearing one like this. *(Poses grandly.)*

SID: Hold it. *(Does a nose camera—thumbing nose and imitating grinding of camera with other hand. Suddenly she falls out of the posture and swiftly goes to him, to embrace him, to kiss him with love. Finally):*

SID: You look tired, Florrie.

FLOR: Naw, I just need a shave. *(She laughs tremulously.)*

SID: You worried about your mother?

FLOR: No.

SID: What's on your mind?

FLOR: The French and Indian War.

SID: What's on your mind?

FLOR: I got us on my mind, Sid. Night and day, Sid!

SID: I smacked a beer truck today. Did I get hell! I was driving along thinking of US, too. You don't have to say it—I know what's on your mind. I'm rat poison around here.

FLOR: Not to me. . . .

SID: I know to who . . . and I know why. I don't blame them. We're engaged now for three years. . . .

FLOR: That's a long time. . . .

SID: My brother Sam joined the navy this morning—get a break that way. They'll send him down to Cuba with the hootchy-kootchy girls. He don't know from nothing, that dumb basket ball player!

FLOR: Don't you do that.

SID: Don't you worry, I'm not the kind who runs away. But I'm so tired of being a dog, Baby, I could choke. I don't even have to ask what's going on in your mind. I know from the word go, 'cause I'm thinking the same things, too.

FLOR: It's yes or no—nothing in between.

SID: The answer is no—a big electric sign looking down on Broadway!

FLOR: We wanted to have kids. . . .

SID: But that sort of life ain't for dogs which is us. Christ, Baby! I get like thunder in my chest when we're together. If we went off together I could maybe look the world straight in the face, spit in its eye like a man should do. God-damnit, it's trying to be a man on the earth. Two in life together.

FLOR: But something wants us to be lonely like that—crawling alone in the dark. Or they want us trapped.

SID: Sure, the big shot money men want us like that.

FLOR: Highly insulting us—

SID: Keeping us in the dark about what is wrong with us in the money sense. They got the power and mean to be damn sure they keep it. They know if they give in just an inch, all the dogs like us will be down on them together—an ocean knocking them to hell and back and each singing cuckoo with stars coming from their nose and ears. I'm not raving, Florrie—

FLOR: I know you're not, I know.

SID: I don't have the words to tell you what I feel. I never finished school. . . .

FLOR: I know. . . .

SID: But it's relative, like the professors say. We worked like hell to send him to college—my kid brother Sam, I mean—and look what he done—joined the navy! The damn fool don't see the cards is stacked for all of us. The money man dealing himself a hot royal flush. Then giving you and me a phony hand like a pair of tens or something. Then keep on losing the pots 'cause the cards is stacked against you. Then he says, what's the matter you can't win—no stuff on the ball, he says to you. And kids like my brother believe it 'cause they don't know better. For all their education, they don't know from nothing. But wait a minute! Don't he come around and say to you—this millionaire with a jazz band—listen Sam or Sid or what's-your-name, you're no good, but here's a chance. The whole world'll know who you are. Yes sir, he says, get up on that ship and fight those bastards who's making the world a lousy place to live in. The Japs, the Turks, the Greeks. Take this gun—kill the slobs like a real hero, he says, a real American. Be a hero! And the guy you're poking at? A real louse, just like you, 'cause they don't let him catch more than a pair of tens, too. On that foreign soil he's a guy like me and Sam, a guy who wants his baby like you and hot sun on his face! They'll teach Sam to point the guns the wrong way, that dumb basket ball player!

FLOR: I got a lump in my throat, Honey.

SID: You and me—we never even had a room to sit in somewhere.

FLOR: The park was nice . . .

SID: In winter? The hallways . . . I'm glad we never got together. This way we don't know what we missed.

FLOR *(in a burst):* Sid, I'll go with you—we'll get a room somewhere.

SID: Naw . . . they're right. If we can't climb higher than this together—we better stay apart.

FLOR: I swear to God I wouldn't care.

SID: You would, you would—in a year, two years, you'd curse the day. I seen it happen.

FLOR: Oh, Sid. . . .

SID: Sure, I know. We got the blues, Babe—the 1935 blues. I'm talkin' this way 'cause I love you. If I didn't, I wouldn't care. . . .

FLOR: We'll work together, we'll—

SID: How about the backwash? Your family needs your nine bucks. My family—

FLOR: I don't care for them!

SID: You're making it up, Florrie. Little Florrie Canary in a cage.

FLOR: Don't make fun of me.

SID: I'm not, Baby.

FLOR: Yes, you're laughing at me.

SID: I'm not. *(They stand looking at each other, unable to speak. Finally, he turns to a small portable phonograph and plays a cheap, sad, dance tune. He makes a motion with his hand; she comes to him. They begin to dance slowly. They hold each other tightly, almost as though they would merge into each other. The music stops, but the scratching record continues to the end of the scene. They stop dancing. He finally looses her clutch and seats her on the couch, where she sits, tense and expectant.)*

SID: Hello, Babe.

FLOR: Hello. *(For a brief time they stand as though in a dream.)*

SID *(finally):* Good-bye, Babe. *(He waits for an answer, but she is silent. They look at each other.)*

SID: Did you ever see my Pat Rooney imitation? *(He whistles Rosy O'Grady and soft-shoes to it. Stops. He asks:)*

SID: Don't you like it?

FLOR *(finally):* No. *(Buries her face in her hands. Suddenly he falls on his knees and buries his face in her lap.)*

Blackout

IV. LABOR SPY EPISODE

FATT: You don't know how we work for you. Shooting off your mouth won't help. Hell, don't you guys ever look at the records like me? Look in your own industry. See what happened when the hacks walked out in Philly three months ago! Where's Philly? A thousand miles away? An hour's ride on the train.

VOICE: Two hours!!

FATT: Two hours . . . what the hell's the difference. Let's hear from someone who's got the practical experience to back him up. Fellers, there's a man here who's seen the whole parade in Philly, walked out with his pals, got knocked down like the rest—and blacklisted after they went back. That's why he's here. He's got a mighty interestin' word to say. *(Announces): Tom Clayton! (As* CLAYTON *starts up from the audience,* FATT *gives him a hand which is sparsely followed in the audience.* CLAYTON *comes forward.)*

Fellers, this is a man with practical strike experience—Tom Clayton from little ole Philly.

CLAYTON *a thin, modest individual:* Fellers, I don't mind your booing. If I thought it would help us hacks get better living conditions, I'd let you walk all over me, cut me up to little pieces. I'm one of you myself. But what I wanna say is that Harry Fatt's right. I only been working here in the big town five weeks, but I know conditions just like the rest of you. You know how it is— don't take long to feel the sore spots, no matter where you park.

CLEAR VOICE *(from audience):* Sit down!

CLAYTON: But Fatt's right. Our officers is right. The time ain't ripe. Like a fruit don't fall off the tree until it's ripe.

CLEAR VOICE: Sit down, you fruit!

FATT *(on his feet):* Take care of him, boys.

VOICE *(in audience, struggling):* No one takes care of me. *(Struggle in house and finally the owner of the voice runs up on stage, says to speaker):*

SAME VOICE: Where the hell did you pick up that name! Clayton! This rat's name is Clancy, from the old Clancys, way back! Fruit! I almost wet myself listening to that one!

FATT *(gunman with him):* This ain't a barn! What the hell do you think you're doing here!

SAME VOICE: Exposing a rat!

FATT: You can't get away with this. Throw him the hell outa here.

VOICE *(preparing to stand his ground):* Try it yourself. . . . When this bozo throws that slop around. You know who he is? That's a company spy.

FATT: Who the hell are you to make—

VOICE: I paid dues in this union for four years, that's who's me! I gotta right and this pussy-footed rat ain't coming in here with ideas like that. You know his record. Lemme say it out—

FATT: You'll prove all this or I'll bust you in every hack outfit in town!

VOICE: I gotta right. I gotta right. Looka *him,* he don't say boo!

CLAYTON: You're a liar and I never seen you before in my life!

VOICE: Boys, he spent two years in the coal fields breaking up any organization he touched. Fifty guys he put in jail. He's ranged up and down the east coast—shipping, textiles, steel—he's been in everything you can name. Right now—

CLAYTON: That's a lie!

VOICE: Right now he's working for that Bergman outfit on Columbus Circle who furnishes rats for any outfit in the country, before, during, and after strikes. *(The man who is the hero of the next episode goes down to his side with other committee men.)*

CLAYTON: He's trying to break up the meeting, fellers!

VOICE: We won't search you for credentials. . . .

CLAYTON: I got nothing to hide. Your own secretary knows I'm straight.

VOICE: Sure. Boys, you know who this sonovabitch is?

CLAYTON: I never seen you before in my life!

VOICE: Boys, I slept with him in the same bed sixteen years. HE'S MY OWN LOUSY BROTHER!!

FATT *(after pause):* Is this true? *(No answer from* CLAYTON.*)*

VOICE *(to* CLAYTON*):* Scram, before I break your neck! *(*CLAYTON *scrams down center aisle.* VOICE *says, watching him:* Remember his map—he can't change that—Clancy! *(Standing in his place says):* Too bad you didn't know about this, Fatt! *(After a pause.)* The Clancy family tree is bearing nuts! *(Standing isolated clear on the stage is the hero of the next episode.)*

Blackout

V. INTERNE EPISODE

Dr. Barnes, an elderly distinguished man, is speaking on the telephone. He wears a white coat.

DR. BARNES: No, I gave you my opinion twice. You outvoted me. You did this to Dr. Benjamin yourself. That is why you can tell him yourself. *(Hangs up phone, angrily. As he is about to pour himself a drink from a bottle on the table, a knock is heard.)*

BARNES: Who is it?

BENJAMIN *(without):* Can I see you a minute, please?

BARNES *(hiding the bottle):* Come in, Dr. Benjamin, come in.

BENJ: It's important—excuse me—they've got Leeds up there in my place— He's operating on Mrs. Lewis—the historectomy—it's my job. I washed up, prepared . . . they told me at the last minute. I don't mind being replaced, Doctor, but Leeds is a damn fool! He shouldn't be permitted—

BARNES *(dryly):* Leeds is the nephew of Senator Leeds.

BENJ: He's incompetent as hell.

BARNES *(obviously changing subject, picks up lab. jar):* They're doing splendid work in brain surgery these days. This is a very fine specimen. . . .

BENJ: I'm sorry, I thought you might be interested.

BARNES *(still examining jar):* Well, I am, young man, I am! Only remember it's a charity case!

BENJ: Of course. They wouldn't allow it for a second, otherwise.

BARNES: Her life in in danger?

BENJ: Of course! You know how serious the case is!

BARNES: Turn your gimlet eyes elsewhere, Doctor. Jigging around like a cricket on a hot grill won't help. Doctors don't run these hospitals. He's the Senator's nephew and there he stays.

BENJ: It's too bad.

BARNES: I'm not calling you down either. *(Plopping down jar suddenly.)* God-damnit, do you think it's my fault?

BENJ *(about to leave):* I know . . . I'm sorry.

BARNES: Just a minute. Sit down.

BENJ: Sorry, I can't sit.

BARNES: Stand then!

BENJ *(sits):* Understand, Dr. Barnes, I don't mind being replaced at the last minute this way, but . . . well, this flagrant bit of class distinction—because she's poor—

BARNES: Be careful of words like that—"class distinction." Don't belong here. Lots of energy, you brilliant young men, but idiots. Discretion! Ever hear that word?

BENJ: Too radical?

BARNES: Precisely. And some day like in Germany, it might cost you your head.

BENJ: Not to mention my job.

BARNES: So they told you?

BENJ: Told me what?

BARNES: They're closing Ward C next month. I don't have to tell you the hospital isn't self-supporting. Until last year that board of trustees met deficits. . . . You can guess the rest. At a board meeting Tuesday, our fine feathered friends discovered they couldn't meet the last quarter's deficit—a neat little sum well over $100,000. If the hospital is to continue at all, its damn—

BENJ: Necessary to close another charity ward!

BARNES: So they say. . . . *(A wait.)*

BENJ: But that's not all?

BARNES *(ashamed):* Have to cut down on staff too . . .

BENJ: That's too bad. Does it touch me?

BARNES: Afraid it does.

BENJ: But after all I'm top man here. I don't mean I'm better than others, but I've worked harder.

BARNES: And shown more promise. . . .

BENJ: I always supposed they'd cut from the bottom first.

BARNES: Usually.

BENJ: But in this case?

BARNES: Complications.

BENJ: For instance? *(BARNES hesitant.)*

BARNES: I like you, Benjamin. It's one ripping shame.

BENJ: I'm no sensitive plant—what's the answer?

BARNES: An old disease, malignant, tumescent. We need an anti toxin for it.

BENJ: I see.

BARNES: What?

BENJ: I met that disease before—at Harvard first.

BARNES: You have seniority here, Benjamin.

BENJ: But I'm a Jew! (BARNES *nods his head in agreement.* BENJ *stands there a moment and blows his nose.*)

BARNES *(blows his nose):* Microbes!

BENJ: Pressure from above?

BARNES: Don't think Kennedy and I didn't fight for you!

BENJ: Such discrimination, with all those wealthy brother Jews on the board?

BARNES: I've remarked before—doesn't seem to be much difference between wealthy Jews and rich Gentiles. Cut from the same piece!

BENJ: For myself I don't feel sorry. My parents gave up an awful lot to get me this far. They ran a little dry goods shop in the Bronx until their pitiful savings went in the crash last year. Poppa's peddling neckties. . . . Saul Ezra Benjamin—a man who's read Spinoza all his life.

BARNES: Doctors don't run medicine in this country. The men who know their jobs don't run anything here, except the motormen on trolley cars. I've seen medicine change—plenty—anesthesia, sterilization—but not because of rich men—in *spite* of them! In a rich man's country your true self's buried deep. Microbes! Less. . . . Vermin! See this ankle, this delicate sensitive hand? Four hundred years to breed that. Out of a revolutionary background! Spirit of '76! Ancestors froze at Valley Forge! What's it all mean! Slops! The honest workers were sold out then, in '76. The Constitution's for rich men then and now. Slops! *(The phone rings.)*

BARNES *(angrily):* Dr. Barnes. *(Listens a moment, looks at* BENJAMIN.*)* I see. *(Hangs up, turns slowly to the younger Doctor.)* They lost your patient. *(*BENJ *stands solid with the shock of this news but finally hurls his operation gloves to the floor.)*

BARNES: That's right . . . that's right. Young, hot, go and do it! I'm very ancient, fossil, but life's ahead of you, Dr. Benjamin, and when you fire the first shot say, "This one's for old Doc Barnes!" Too much dignity—bullets. Don't shoot vermin! Step on them! If I didn't have an invalid daughter—

*(*BARNES *goes back to his seat, blows his nose in silence):* I have said my piece, Benjamin.

BENJ: Lots of things I wasn't certain of. Many things these radicals say . . . you don't believe theories until they happen to you.

BARNES: You lost a lot today, but you won a great point.

BENJ: Yes, to know I'm right? To really begin believing in something? Not to say, "What a world!", but to say, "Change the world!" I wanted to go to Russia. Last week I was thinking about it—the wonderful opportunity to do good work in their socialized medicine—

BARNES: Beautiful, beautiful!

BENJ: To be able to work—

BARNES: Why don't you go? I might be able—

BENJ: Nothing's nearer what I'd like to do!

BARNES: Do it!

BENJ: No! Our work's here—America! I'm scared. . . . What future's ahead, I don't know. Get some job to keep alive—maybe drive a cab—and study and work and learn my place—

BARNES: And step down hard!

BENJ: Fight! Maybe get killed, but goddamn! We'll go ahead! *(*BENJAMIN *stands with clenched fist raised high.)*

Blackout

AGATE: *Ladies and Gentlemen,* and don't let anyone tell you we ain't got some ladies in this sea of upturned faces! Only they're wearin' pants. Well, maybe I don't know a thing; maybe I fell outa the cradle when I was a kid and ain't been right since—you can't tell!

VOICE: Sit down, cockeye!

AGATE: Who's paying you for those remarks, Buddy?—Moscow Gold? Maybe I got a *glass eye,* but it come from working in a factory at the age of eleven. They hooked it out because they didn't have a shield on the works. But I wear it like a medal 'cause it tells the world where I belong—deep down in the working class! We had delegates in the union there—all kinds of secretaries and treasurers . . . walkin' delegates, but not with blisters on their feet! Oh no! On their fat little ass from sitting on cushions and raking in mazuma. *(*SECRETARY *and* GUNMAN *remonstrate in words and actions here.)* Sit down, boys. I'm just sayin' that about unions in general. I know it ain't true here! Why no, our officers is all aces. Why, I seen our own secretary Fatt walk outa his way not to step on a cockroach. No boys, don't think—

FATT *(breaking in):* You're out of order!

AGATE *(to audience):* Am I outa order?

ALL: No, no. Speak. Go on, etc.

AGATE: Yes, our officers is all aces. But I'm a member here—and no experience in Philly either! Today I couln't wear my union button. The damnest thing happened. When I take the old coat off the wall, I see she's smoking. I'm a sonovagun if the old union button isn't on fire! Yep, the old celluloid was makin' the most god-awful stink: the landlady come up and give me hell! You know what happened? That old union button just blushed itself to death! Ashamed! Can you beat it?

FATT: Sit down, Keller! Nobody's interested!

AGATE: Yes they are!

GUNMAN: Sit down like he tells you!

AGATE *(continuing to audience):* And when I finish—*(His speech is broken by* FATT *and* GUNMAN *who physically handle him. He breaks away and gets to other side of stage. The two are about to make for him when some of the committee*

*men come forward and get in between the struggling parties. Agate's shirt has
been torn.)*

AGATE *(to audience):* What's the answer, boys? The answer is, if we're reds
because we wanna strike, then we take over their salute too! Know how they do
it? *(Makes Communist salute.)* What is it! An uppercut! The good old uppercut
to the chin! Hell, some of us boys ain't even got a shirt to our backs. What's
the boss class tryin' to do—make a nudist colony outa us? *(The audience
laughs and suddenly* AGATE *comes to the middle of the stage so that the other
cabmen back him up in a strong clump.)*

AGATE: Don't laugh! Nothing's funny! This is your life and mine! It's skull
and bones every incha the road! Christ, we're dyin' by inches! For what? For
the debutant-ees to have their sweet comin' out parties in the Ritz! Poppa's got
a daughter she's gotta get her picture in the papers. Christ, they make 'em with
our blood. Joe said it. Slow death or fight. It's war! *(Throughout this whole
speech* AGATE *is backed up by the other six workers, so that from their activity it
is plain that the whole group of them are saying these things. Several of them
may take alternate lines out of this long last speech.)*

You Edna, God love your mouth! Sid and Florrie, the other boys, old Doc
Barnes—fight with us for right! It's war! Working class, unite and fight! Tear
down the slaughter house of our old lives! Let freedom really ring.

These slick slobs stand here telling us about bogeymen. That's a new one
for the kids—the reds is bogeymen! But the man who got me food in 1932, he
called me Comrade! The one who picked me up where I bled—he called me
Comrade too! What are we waiting for. . . . Don't wait for Lefty! He might
never come. Every minute—*(This is broken into by a man who has dashed up
the center aisle from the back of the house. He runs up on stage, says):*

MAN: Boys, they just found Lefty!

OTHERS: What? What? What?

SOME: Shhh. . . . Shhh. . . .

MAN: They found Lefty. . . .

AGATE: Where?

MAN: Behind the car barns with a bullet in his head!

AGATE *(crying):* Hear it, boys, hear it? Hell, listen to me! Coast to coast!
HELLO AMERICA! HELLO. WE'RE STORMBIRDS OF THE WORKING-
CLASS. WORKERS OF THE WORLD. . . . OUR BONES AND BLOOD! And
when we die they'll know what we did to make a new world! Chirst, cut us up
to little pieces. We'll die for what is right! put fruit trees where our ashes are!

(To audience): Well, what's the answer?

ALL: STRIKE!

AGATE: LOUDER!

ALL: STRIKE!

AGATE AND OTHERS ON STAGE: AGAIN!

ALL: STRIKE, STRIKE, STRIKE!!!

Curtain

WRITING AND DISCUSSION QUESTIONS

Informative

1. Describe Harry Fatt's way of dealing with dissent in his union. What ideas associated with Marxism or Marxism–Leninism does he attribute to dissenters?

2. In Scene V, the Interne Episode, why does Dr. Barnes think Dr. Benjamin's use of the words "class distinction" is lacking in "discretion"?

3. In the last scene identify all the verbal echoes you can find of Marx's language in Agate's speeches. Identify also any non-Marxist references, like the religious oaths.

4. What is the point of the title? How does that point relate to Marx's insistence that the emancipation of the working class be accomplished by the working class?

Persuasive

1. Argue that Odets uses the scenes between Joe and Edna, Irving and Florence, and Florence and Sid to show how poverty undermines family relationships, actual and potential.

2. Describe Odets' attitude toward war and its causes as revealed in this play. Argue that such an attitude is centrally related to Marxist thought.

3. This play centers on the taxi drivers' strike, but scenes II and V, the Lab Assistant and Interne Episodes, have little to do with taxis. What are the connections? What are the larger problems that taxi company bosses and corrupt union officials are only a part of? Do you see any relation between those larger problems and what came in the 1960s and 1970s to be called the "military industrial complex"?

4. Argue whether Odets shows a lack of faith in democracy or in the existing political and economic system as a means of fostering a democratic society. What seems to be the basis for his argument that a different system would result in a more democratic society?

5. Odets is certainly concerned with the material well being of humanity, but so was William Booth, founder of the Salvation Army. Argue that Odets does or does not share Marx's philosophical materialism. If you think there is not enough information in the play to argue a position, pursue the same issue by exploring these questions: What are the major values Odets argues for? How compatible are they with your notion of Marxism and with traditional religious faith?

6. In Scene V, the Interne Episode, Odets attacks "the rich" as the sources of a number of problems, including contempt for charity cases and anti-Semitism. The first could easily be related to class divisions, but how does the second relate to class? Defend or attack Odets' pattern of blaming all social ills on the class system and of assuming that all such ills would disappear if that system were abolished.

7. Read one of Odet's later plays, *The Country Girl* (1950) or *Flowering Peach* (1954), or view one of his films, *None But the Lonely Heart,* which the National Board of Review named the best film of 1944, or *Sweet Smell of Success* (1957), and explore what traces of Marxist themes and issues were still to be found in his work at that time.

Personal

1. Do you think that Odets agrees with Marx that the family is being destroyed by capitalism, that the family must ultimately disappear?
2. Some critics have dismissed *Lefty* as a piece of "agitprop," agitation and propaganda. Do you agree? Is this only a historical curiosity, or does it possess any lasting literary or dramatic value?
3. Assuming that Odets exposes real problems, do you think the extent of revolution he advocates was necessary? Why does the strike turn into a rally to change the world?

▼

TONI CADE BAMBARA, "THE LESSON" FROM *GORILLA MY LOVE*

Whether Marx was right that the history of all society is the history of class struggle, it is impossible to doubt that class struggle is an important aspect of history. Charles Beard has shown that this is so even in America, where class divisions are usually assumed to be less important and less well defined than in the so-called old world. It is also clear that Marxist thought has had its greatest appeal where class divisions have been most pronounced, and Clifford Odets has shown how frustrating it can be for one who believes himself oppressed in what is supposed to be a freely competitive society: the cards are stacked against him, and when he loses, "the money man . . . says, what's the matter you can't win—no stuff on the ball." This frustration is even worse when the class divisions are defined in terms of visibly ethnic differences like skin color. Injustice seems inescapable and becomes so much a part of life that for many it is not even seen as injustice. But once perceived, there is released the kind of anger that breeds revolutionary thought. This is the kind of situation Toni Cade Bambara deals with in her short story "The Lesson."

Bambara was born Toni Cade in New York City in 1939; in 1970, she added Bambara, a name she learned was associated with her grandmother's family. She grew up in the New York City boroughs of Harlem, Bedford-Stuyvesant, Queens, and Jersey City, New Jersey. Her education was an unusually rich combination of the informal and the formal. Of her informal education she has said, "As a kid with an enormous appetite for knowledge and a gift for imagining myself anywhere in the universe, I always seemed to be drawn to the library or to some music spot or to 125th Street and Seventh Avenue, Speaker's Corner, to listen to Garveyites, Father Diviners, Rastafarians, Muslims, trade unionists, communists, Pan-Africanists." Her formal education included a B.A. in theater arts and English from Queens College, City University of New York (1959), and an M.A. in modern American fiction from City College of New York (1964). In between, she managed to study most of one year in Europe at the University of Florence and the Ecole de Mime Etienne Decroux in Paris, to work in New York as a social worker and as a recreational and occupational therapist for a hospital psychiatric division, to volunteer her time directing or coordinating numerous local neighborhood programs, and to write.

She has gone on to teach at several colleges and universities, including positions as associate professor at Livingston College in New Jersey and writer in residence at Spellman College in Atlanta. During this time, she continued her involvement in civil rights and community issues, especially those related to blacks and women. She has also edited two first-of-their-kind anthologies, *The Black Woman* (1970) and *Tales and Stories for Black Folks* (1971); has published two short story collections, from the first of which, *Gorilla My Love* (1972), the story below is taken; and has written a novel, *The Salt Eaters* (1980).

"The Lesson" takes place in the late 1940s or early 1950s, certainly before the mid-century civil rights movement began in America. The story illustrates how oppression breeds its greatest ally, ignorance, which deprives its victims not only of the means of improving themselves, but even of the knowledge of that oppression. Mrs. Moore, one of the two central characters, is one of those heroic black women who struggled against that ignorance to pass on her own sense of dignity and purpose and create the basis in awareness for change.

▼

The Lesson
TONI CADE BAMBARA

Back in the days when everyone was old and stupid or young and foolish and me and Sugar were the only ones just right, this lady moved on our block with nappy hair and proper speech and no makeup. And quite naturally we laughed at her, laughed the way we did at the junk man who went about his business like he was some big-time president and his sorry-ass horse his secretary. And we kinda hated her too, hated the way we did the winos who cluttered up our parks and pissed on our handball walls and stank up our hallways and stairs so you couldn't halfway play hide-and-seek without a goddamn gas mask. Miss Moore was her name. The only woman on the block with no first name. And she was black as hell, cept for her feet, which were fish-white and spooky. And she was always planning these boring-ass things for us to do, us being my cousin, mostly, who lived on the block cause we all moved North the same time and to the same apartment then spread out gradual to breathe. And our parents would yank our heads into some kinda shape and crisp up our clothes so we'd be presentable for travel with Miss Moore, who always looked like she was going to church, though she never did. Which is just one of the things the grownups talked about when they talked behind her back like a dog. But when she came calling with some sachet she'd sewed up or some gingerbread she'd made or some book, why then they'd all be too embarrassed to turn her down and we'd get handed over all spruced up. She'd been to college and said it was only right that she should take responsibility for the young ones' education, and she not even related by marriage or blood. So they'd go for it. Specially Aunt Gretchen. She was the main gofer in the family. You got some ole dumb shit foolishness you want somebody to go for, you send for Aunt Gretchen. She been screwed into the go-along for so long, it's a blood-deep natural thing with her. Which is how she got saddled with me and Sugar and Junior in the first place while our mothers were in a la-de-da apartment up the block having a good ole time.

So this one day Miss Moore rounds us all up at the mailbox and it's puredee hot and she's knockin herself out about arithmetic. And school suppose to let up in summer I heard, but she don't never let up. And the starch in my pinafore scratching the shit outta me and I'm really hating this nappy-head bitch and her goddamn college degree. I'd much rather go to the pool or to the show where it's cool. So me and Sugar leaning on the mailbox being surly, which is a Miss Moore word. And Flyboy checking out what everybody brought for lunch. And Fat Butt already wasting his peanut-butter-and-jelly sandwich like the pig he is. And Junebug punchin on Q.T.'s arm for potato chips. And Rosie Giraffe shifting from one hip to the other waiting for somebody to step on her foot or ask her if she from Georgia so she can kick ass, preferably Mercedes'. And Miss Moore asking us do we know what money is, like we a bunch of retards. I mean real money, she say, like it's only poker chips or monopoly papers we lay on the grocer. So right away I'm tired of this and say so. And would much rather snatch Sugar and go to the Sunset and terrorize the West Indian kids and take their hair ribbons and their money too. And Miss Moore files that remark away for next week's lesson on brotherhood, I can tell. And finally I say we oughta get to the subway cause it's cooler and besides we might meet some cute boys. Sugar done swiped her mama's lipstick, so we ready.

So we heading down the street and she's boring us silly about what things cost and what our parents make and how much goes for rent and how money ain't divided up right in this country. And then she gets to the part about we all poor and live in the slums, which I don't feature. And I'm ready to speak on that, but she steps out in the street and hails two cabs just like that. Then she hustles half the crew in with her and hands me a five-dollar bill and tells me to calculate 10 percent tip for the driver. And we're off. Me and Sugar and Junebug and Flyboy hangin out the window and hollering to everybody, putting lipstick on each other cause Flyboy a faggot anyway, and making farts with our sweaty armpits. But I'm mostly trying to figure how to spend this money. But they all fascinated with the meter ticking and Junebug starts laying bets as to how much it'll read when Flyboy can't hold his breath no more. Then Sugar lays bets as to how much it'll be when we get there. So I'm stuck. Don't nobody want to go for my plan, which is to jump out at the next light and run off to the first bar-b-que we can find. Then the driver tells us to get the hell out cause we there already. And the meter reads eighty-five cents. And I'm stalling to figure out the tip and Sugar say give him a dime. And I decide he don't need it bad as I do, so later for him. But then he tries to take off with Junebug foot still in the door so we talk about his mama something ferocious. Then we check out that we on Fifth Avenue and everybody dressed up in stockings. One lady in a fur coat, hot as it is. White folks crazy.

"This is the place," Miss Moore say, presenting it to us in the voice she uses at the museum. "Let's look in the windows before we go in."

"Can we steal?" Sugar asks very serious like she's getting the ground rules squared away before she plays. "I beg your pardon," say Miss Moore, and we fall out. So she leads us around the windows of the toy store and me and Sugar screamin, "This is mine, that's mine, I gotta have that, that was made for me, I was born for that," till Big Butt drowns us out.

"Hey, I'm goin to buy that there."

"That there? You don't even know what it is stupid."

"I do so," he say punchin on Rosie Giraffe. "It's a microscope."

"Whatcha gonna do with a microscope, fool?"

"Look at things."

"Like what, Ronald?" ask Miss Moore. And Big Butt ain't got the first notion. So here go Miss Moore gabbing about the thousands of bacteria in a drop of water and the somethinorother in a speck of blood and the million and one living things in the air around us is invisible to the naked eye. And what she say that for? Junebug go to town on that "naked" and we rolling. Then Miss Moore ask what it cost. So we all jam into the window smudgin it up and the price tag say $300. So then she ask how long'd take for Big Butt and Junebug to save up their allowances. "Too long," I say, "Yeh," adds Sugar, "outgrown it by that time." And Miss Moore say no, you never outgrow learning instruments. "Why, even medical students and interns and," blah, blah, blah. And we ready to choke Big Butt for bringing it up in the first damn place.

"This here costs four hundred eighty dollars," says Rosie Giraffe. So we pile up all over her to see what she pointin out. My eyes tell me it's a chunk of glass cracked with something heavy, and different-color inks dripped into the splits, then the whole thing put into a oven or something. But for $480 it don't make sense.

"That's a paperweight made of semi-precious stones fused together under tremendous pressure," she explains slowly, with her hands doing the mining and all the factory work.

"So what's a paperweight?" asks Rosie Giraffe.

"To weigh paper with, dumbbell," say Flyboy, the wise man from the East.

"Not exactly," say Miss Moore, which is what she say when you warm or way off too. "It's to weigh paper down so it won't scatter and make your desk untidy." So right away me and Sugar curtsy to each other and then to Mercedes who is more the tidy type.

"We don't keep paper on top of the desk in my class," say Junebug, figuring Miss Moore crazy or lyin one.

"At home, then," she say. "Don't you have a calendar and pencil case and a blotter and a letter-opener on your desk at home where you do your homework?" And she know damn well what our homes look like cause she nosys around in them every chance she gets.

"I don't even have a desk," say Junebug. "Do we?"

"No. And I don't get no homework neither," says Big Butt.

"And I don't even have a home," say Flyboy like he do at school to keep the white folks off his back and sorry for him. Send this poor kid to camp posters, is his specialty.

"I do," says Mercedes. "I have a box of stationery on my desk and a picture of my cat. My godmother bought the stationery and the desk. There's a big rose on each sheet and the envelopes smell like roses."

"Who wants to know about your smelly-ass stationery," say Rosie Giraffe fore I can get my two cents in.

"It's important to have a work area all your own so that . . ."

"Will you look at this sailboat, please," say Flyboy, cuttin her off and pointin to the thing like it was his. So once again we tumble all over each other to gaze at this magnificent thing in the toy store which is just big enough to maybe sail two kittens across the pond if you strap them to the posts tight. We all start reciting the price tag like we in assembly. "Handcrafted sailboat of fiberglass at one thousand one hundred ninety-five dollars."

"Unbelievable," I hear myself say and am really stunned. I read it again for myself just in case the group recitation put me in a trance. Same thing. For some reason this pisses me off. We look at Miss Moore and she lookin at us, waiting for I dunno what.

"Who'd pay all that when you can buy a sailboat set for a quarter at Pop's, a tube of glue for a dime, and a ball of string for eight cents? It must have a motor and a whole lot else besides," I say. "My sailboat cost me about fifty cents."

"But will it take water?" say Mercedes with her smart ass.

"Took mine to Alley Pond Park once," say Flyboy. "String broke. Lost it. Pity."

"Sailed mine in Central Park and it keeled over and sank. Had to ask my father for another dollar."

"And you got the strap," laugh Big Butt. "The jerk didn't even have a string on it. My old man wailed on his behind."

Little Q.T. was staring hard at the sailboat and you could see he wanted it bad. But he too little and somebody'd just take it from him. So what the hell. "This boat for kids, Miss Moore?"

"Parents silly to buy something like that just to get all broke up," say Rosie Giraffe.

"That much money it should last forever," I figure.

"My father'd buy it for me if I wanted it."

"Your father, my ass," say Rosie Giraffe getting a chance to finally push Mercedes.

"Must be rich people shop here," say Q.T.

"You are a very bright boy," say Flyboy. "What was your first clue?" And he rap him on the head with the back of his knuckles, since Q.T. the only one he could get away with. Though Q.T. liable to come up behind you years later and get his licks in when you half expect it.

"What I want to know is," I says to Miss Moore though I never talk to her, I wouldn't give the bitch that satisfaction, "is how much a real boat costs? I figure a thousand'd get you a yacht any day."

"Why don't you check that out," she says, "and report back to the group?" Which really pains my ass. If you gonna mess up a perfectly good swim day least you could do is have some answers. "Let's go in," she say like she got something up her sleeve. Only she don't lead the way. So me and Sugar turn the corner to where the entrance is, but when we get there I kinda hang back.

Not that I'm scared, what's there to be afraid of, just a toy store. But I feel funny, shame. But what I got to be shamed about? Got as much right to go in as anybody. But somehow I can't seem to get hold of the door, so I step away from Sugar to lead. But she hangs back too. And I look at her and she looks at me and this is ridiculous. I mean, damn, I have never ever been shy about doing nothing or going nowhere. But then Mercedes steps up and then Rosie Giraffe and Big Butt crowd in behind and shove, and next thing we all stuffed into the doorway with only Mercedes squeezing past us, smoothing out her jumper and walking right down the aisle. Then the rest of us tumble in like a glued-together jigsaw done all wrong. And people looking at us. And it's like the time me and Sugar crashed into the Catholic church on a dare. But once we got in there and everything so hushed and holy and the candles and the bowin and the handkerchiefs on all the drooping heads, I just couldn't go through with the plan. Which was for me to run up to the altar and do a tap dance while Sugar played the nose flute and messed around in the holy water. And Sugar kept givin me the elbow. Then later teased me so bad I tied her up in the shower and turned it on and locked her in. And she'd be there till this day if Aunt Gretchen hadn't finally figured I was lying about the boarder takin a shower.

Same thing in the store. We all walkin on tiptoe and hardly touchin the games and puzzles and things. And I watched Miss Moore who is steady watchin us like she waitin for a sign. Like Mama Drewery watches the sky and sniffs the air and takes note of just how much slant is in the bird formation. Then me and Sugar bump smack into each other, so busy gazing at the toys, specially the sailboat. But we don't laugh and go into our fat-lady bump-stomach routine. We just stare at that price tag. Then Sugar run a finger over the whole boat. And I'm jealous and want to hit her. Maybe not her, but I sure want to punch somebody in the mouth.

"Watcha bring us here for, Miss Moore?"

"You sound angry, Sylvia. Are you mad about something?" Givin me one of them grins like she tellin a grown-up joke that never turns out to be funny. And she's lookin very closely at me like maybe she planning to do my portrait from memory. I'm mad, but I won't give her that satisfaction. So I slouch around the store bein very bored and say, "Let's go."

Me and Sugar at the back of the train watchin the tracks whizzin by large then small then getting gobbled up in the dark. I'm thinkin about this tricky toy I saw in the store. A clown that somersaults on a bar then does chin-ups just cause you yank lightly at his leg. Cost $35. I could see me askin my mother for a $35 birthday clown. "You wanna who that costs what?" she'd say, cocking her head to the side to get a better view of the hole in my head. Thirty-five dollars could buy new bunk beds for Junior and Gretchen's boy. Thirty-five dollars and the whole household could go visit Granddaddy Nelson in the country. Thirty-five dollars would pay for the rent and the piano bill too. Who are these people that spend that much for performing clowns and $1000 for toy sailboats? What kinda work they do and how they live and how come we ain't in on it? Where we are is who we are, Miss Moore always pointin out. But it don't necessarily have to be that way, she always adds then waits for somebody to say that poor people have to wake up and demand their share of the pie and don't none of us know what kind of pie she talking about in the first damn place. But she ain't so smart cause I still got her four dollars from the taxi and she sure ain't gettin it. Messin up my day with this shit. Sugar nudges me in my pocket and winks.

Miss Moore lines us up in front of the mailbox where we started from, seem like years ago, and I got a headache for thinkin so hard. And we lean all over each other so we can hold up under the draggy-ass lecture she always finishes us off with at the end before we thank her for borin us to tears. But she just looks at us like she readin tea leaves. Finally she say, "Well, what did you think of F. A. O. Schwarz?"

Rosie Giraffe mumbles, "White folks crazy."

"I'd like to go there again when I get my birthday money," says Mercedes, and we shove her out the pack so she has to lean on the mailbox by herself.

"I'd like a shower. Tiring day," say Flyboy.

Then Sugar surprises me by sayin, "You know, Miss Moore, I don't think all of us here put together eat in a year what that sailboat costs." And Miss Moore lights up like somebody goosed her. "And?" she say, urging Sugar on. Only I'm standin on her foot so she don't continue.

"Imagine for a minute what kind of society it is in which some people can spend on a toy what it would cost to feed a family of six or seven. What do you think?"

"I think," say Sugar pushing me off her feet like she never done before, cause I whip her ass in a minute, "that this is not much of a democracy if you ask me. Equal chance to pursue happiness means an equal crack at the dough, don't it?" Miss Moore is besides herself and I am disgusted with Sugar's treachery. So I stand on her foot one more time to see if she'll shove me. She shuts up, and Miss Moore looks at me, sorrowfully I'm thinkin. And somethin weird is goin on, I can feel it in my chest.

"Anybody else learn anything today?" lookin dead at me. I walk away and Sugar has to run to catch up and don't even seem to notice when I shrug her arm off my shoulder.

"Well, we got four dollars anyway," she says.

"Uh hunh."

"We could go to Hascombs and get half a chocolate layer and then go to the Sunset and still have plenty money for potato chips and ice cream sodas."

"Uh hunh."

"Race you to Hascombs," she say.

We start down the block and she gets ahead which is O.K. by me cause I'm going to the West End and then over to the Drive to think this day through. She can run if she want to and even run faster. But ain't nobody gonna beat me at nuthin.

WRITING AND DISCUSSION QUESTIONS

Informative

1. Notice the physical features of Mrs. Moore that Sylvia, the narrator, dislikes: "nappy hair and proper speech and no makeup . . . [and] black as hell." Why are these features significant to Sylvia? What do they reveal about Mrs. Moore?
2. Describe Sylvia's attitude toward education. What specific elements of her environment account for that attitude?
3. The $35.00 toy clown becomes an economic yardstick for Sylvia. Compare the toy clown with all the other things the $35.00 could pay for, and consider what that clown would cost in today's dollars.

Persuasive

1. What is the significance of the lady dressed in a fur coat in the summer and of Sylvia's response, "White folks crazy"? Argue that the story is or is not critical of "white" behaviors and attitudes. Why is the same response being spoken by another of the youngsters near the end of the story?
2. What is Mrs. Moore trying to teach the youngsters about "real money," and why is it important? How does it relate to what Bambara considers the root cause of injustice in her society?
3. Trace the development of Sylvia's emotional responses. Why is she surly, then bored, ashamed as she starts to enter the toy store, and then angry? Why is so much of her anger directed at her cousin Sugar? Is another kind of emotion emerging at the end of the story when she says, "But ain't nobody gonna beat me at nuthin"?
4. Compare Bambara's depiction of the family with Odets' depiction. Odets shows families suffering under the pressures of poverty, and Bambara shows a family all but disintegrated. What accounts for the difference?
5. Argue that Mrs. Moore is either an educator or agitator. Is it possible to work among a deprived group as an educator without being an agitator?

Personal

1. Argue whether America's racial problems are really problems of class. Might our society better handle racial problems if they were approached as class problems?
2. On the basis of this story (admittedly a small sample on which to base a generalization), would you describe Bambara as Marxist, Marxian, or something else? To what extent do you think Marx can help us deal with the social problems revealed in the story?
3. It is common to hear from the pulpit and to read in magazines and newspapers of the disintegration of the American family. Review some you have heard, and consider how often poverty is described as a major cause of this problem. What do you conclude about the state of social consciousness in America?
4. It is sometimes said that anticapitalist arguments are basically arguments for the

redistribution of wealth, that is, taking from the wealthy and giving to the poor. It is also sometimes said that all arguments for the redistribution of wealth are basically pro-Marxist. Is either statement fair? Would you consider government-sponsored social relief programs or the graduated income tax as means of redistributing wealth?

5. Faced with the problem of injustice as it is presented in Bambara's story, how would you define the difference between the ideal response of a Jew or Christian, a humanist, and a Marxist? Describe what you think is the best response (one or some combination of these three, or something entirely your own), making clear your criteria for what you consider "best."

▼

PAUL JOHNSON, "THE CAPITALISM & MORALITY DEBATE"

Paul Johnson (1928–) is a distinguished British historian and chronicler of the history of ideas whose works on Judaism, *A History of the Jews* (1987), and Christianity, *The History of Christianity* (1985), have received plaudits internationally for their careful historical accuracy and sensitivity. His *Modern Times* (1983) is considered by many a classic historical overview of the twentieth century, its major events and ideas, and its links to the past. A more recent and more controversial book, *Intellectuals* (1988), surveys the lives of prominent thinkers—among them Jean-Jacques Rousseau, Karl Marx, and Ernest Hemingway—in a provocative philosophical critique of what Johnson believes is their dubious intellectual contributions.

In this essay, Johnson confronts the moral dilemmas that capitalism seems to raise. If one grants that the free enterprise and market system is indeed best suited to creating wealth for the majority of a society's citizens, how then does one deal with the apparent gap between the standard of living of the rich and the poor in such a society? In accepting the premise that Marxist and socialist governments and economic systems are on the wane worldwide, Johnson asks how we may confront the issue of whether capitalism's arguably amoral stance can yield equitable and ethical relationships in society at large.

▼

The Capitalism & Morality Debate
PAUL JOHNSON

The decade of the 1980s has proved to be an ideological water- *1*
shed. It has been marked by a huge resurgence of the power and efficacy of the capitalist market system and a corresponding collapse of confidence in the

capacity of socialist "command economies." This loss of confidence in collectivism is the culmination of many decades of trial and misfortune. The truth is that, during the twentieth century, large parts of the world have given the collectivst alternative to capitalism a long, thorough, and staggeringly costly trial, and it seems to have failed absolutely everywhere. It was during the 1980s that this realization dawned even in the quarters most reluctant to admit it—among the rulers of the socialist-style states. Many of them are turning back—in despondency, almost in despair—to the despised market disciplines they had rejected.

2   Meanwhile the capitalist world is racing ahead and is creating wealth on a scale never before dreamed of. It is clear that capitalism, being a natural force rather than a contrived ideology, springing from instincts deep in our human natures, is modifying itself all the time, and we cannot foresee how it will evolve over the next century. But I am willing to predict, as a result of our experiences in this one, that never again will any considerable body of opinion seriously doubt its wealth-producing capacity or seek to replace it with something fundamentally different. We are near the end of an historical epoch in which capitalism has survived the collectivist assault and is now firmly reestablished as the world's primary way of conducting its economic business.

3   So where does this leave us? It leaves us, I suggest, with a considerable moral dilemma. I can state the dilemma in one sentence: how do we give a moral dimension to this triumphant reassertion of capitalism? For one thing we know: whereas wealth creation is essential to men's well-being, especially in a world where population is expanding so rapidly, it cannot in itself make men and women happy. We are creatures of the spirit as well as of the flesh, and we cannot be at ease with ourselves unless we feel we are fulfilling, however vaguely or imperfectly, a moral purpose. It is in this respect that capitalism, as such, is inadequate.

4 It is not that capitalism is immoral. Clergymen who insist that it is and preach against it are themselves confused, as were their predecessors a hundred years ago who insisted that any form of socialism was immoral. One can be a good Christian and a capitalist, just as one can be a good Christian and practice collectivism.

5   The trouble with capitalism is quite otherwise. It lies in its moral neutrality, its indifference to the notion of moral choices. Capitalism and the market system which gives it its efficiency and its power is single-minded in its thrust—that is why it is so productive. It is blind to all other factors: blind to class, race, and color, to religion and sex, to nationality and creed, to good and evil. It is materialist, impersonal, and non-human. It responds with great speed and accuracy to all the market factors. In a way it is like a marvelous natural computer. But it cannot make distinctions for which it is not programmed. It does not and cannot possess a soul and it therefore lacks a moral inclination one way or the other.

6   Indeed it is precisely because capitalism is morally indifferent—and so pro-

ductive of great miseries as well as great blessings—that many idealists early in the nineteenth century saw it as evil, rejected it entirely, and sought to replace it. We have come to the end of that line of argument. We have discovered there is no effective substitute for the market. We have to accept capitalism as the primary means whereby wealth is produced and begin the process of moralization within its terms of reference. I say "begin," but in a sense we have been doing it for two hundred years—by factories acts, mines acts, by monopoly and fair-trading legislation, and by all the countless laws we devise to restrict ways in which the market system can be distorted by man's cupidity.

But these are merely negative attempts to correct the excesses of capitalism.   *7* They do not in themselves give capitalism a positive moral purpose. That is a quite different and much more difficult matter. The moment you start trying to give capitalism a moral purpose, you risk interfering with the basic market mechanism which provides its wealth-creating power. If, for instance, you try to use capitalism to promote greater equality of wealth by imposing on it a steeply progressive, redistributive system of taxation, you frustrate the way in which it rewards its chief dynamic force, the acquisitive impulse, and you are liable to end by making everyone poorer. Or if, to take another example, you try to redistribute power within capitalism by balancing managerial authority by trade union privileges, you either choke the entrepreneurial spirit or you eliminate profits—the system's life-blood—or, as a rule, you do both, and so again you end by making everyone poorer.

Almost all efforts to provide capitalism itself with a positive moral purpose   *8* run into the same difficulty. Great Britain, between 1945 and the end of the 1970s, was a classic case where repeated and often ingenious attempts were made to cudgel capitalism into a system of national redistribution of wealth. It was part socialism, part corporatism, and wholly inefficient. It was baptized by the moral-sounding name of "the mixed economy." In fact, by the end of the 1970s, it had come to resemble an ancient piece of do-it-yourself machinery, constructed by amateurs, held together by adhesive tape and emitting old-fashioned steam from every joint. The British economy had become one of the least efficient and productive in the Western world. In 1979 Mrs. Thatcher and her government began the return to true capitalism, but even after a decade of common sense reforms and rapid improvements in productivity, we calculate it will still take us another ten years or so to catch up with Germany and France, while the United States and Japan are still further beyond our reach.

That is the price of trying to make capitalism do something which is not in   *9* its nature to do—promote equality. The price is paid in the shape of reduced national wealth and income—lower general living standards, inadequate health care, a run-down transport system, impoverished social services, underfunded schools. These results have been repeated, in varying degrees, everywhere else in the world where attempts to invest capitalism with positive moral functions have been made. We have to accept that the market system, while exceedingly robust when left to itself, rapidly becomes sick and comatose once you try to force it to do things contrary to its nature. The more you interfere with its mechanism by imposing moral objectives the less efficiently it works. Indeed, under a sufficient weight of moral obligation, it will seize up altogether.

10 How do we escape from this difficulty? How can we practice capitalism, with its unrivaled capacity to produce wealth, within the framework of a society that recognizes moral objectives? To put it another way: is it possible to harness the power of market capitalism to moral purposes without destroying its dynamism? That is the real, practical question that faces humanity. And I often wish our Christian theologians would address themselves to it, instead of peremptorily dismissing capitalism as intrinsically evil, as so many of them thoughtlessly do.

11   I do not pretend the problem is easily solved. On the other hand, I think it is defeatist to regard it as inherently insoluble. It is a mistake to try to turn capitalism itself into a moral animal. But I think it is possible to run it in tandem with public policies that make use of its energy while steering it in a moral direction. Let me indicate a number of ways in which I believe this can happen.

12   First, and in some ways the most important, is to provide the capitalist economy with an overall legal framework which has a moral basis. This can only be done if we accept that a fundamental object of the just society is to establish, so far as is humanly possible, absolute equality before the law. Equality of wealth is a utopian fantasy whose hopeless pursuit usually leads to tyranny. But equality before the law is a reasonable objective, whose attainment—albeit in an imperfect form—is well within the reach of civilized modern societies. Moreover, this form of equality responds to a strong human need: for whereas few of us really want equality of possessions, or believe it possible, all of us want fairness. The notion of a fair society is an attractive concept, and one toward which progress can undoubtedly be made. Moreover equality before the law is a necessary adjunct to the competitive nature of capitalism: the end result cannot be equality, but from start to finish the rules must apply equally to all.

13   What do we mean by equality before the law? We mean that the law must make no distinction of birth or caste, race or color, sex or tribe, wealth or poverty. It must hold the scales of justice blindfolded. In a curiously paradoxical way, the capitalist system similarly makes no distinction about the nature of men and women. Hence for the law so to distinguish is a gross interference with the market mechanism and makes it less efficient. Equality before the law reinforces the natural power of capitalism, so that in this case moral purpose and wealth creation go hand in hand. Inequality before the law takes many forms, some of them grotesque, as in the Republic of South Africa or the Soviet Union, some more subtle. Even in advanced Western societies like the United States, where the principle is well understood and established, the ability to buy more law than your neighbor is a ubiquitous source of inequality. In no society that I know is full equality before the law established in practice, and I do not say that it can be realized perfectly and overnight anywhere. But it is one form of equality that can be broadly attained without destructive side-effects, and systematic progress toward it is an essential object of any society that wishes to place capitalism in a context of justice.

Another way to combine capitalism with moral purpose is for society to   *14*
endorse the related but broader concept of equality of opportunity. It is one of
the miracles of the human condition that all of us, however humble, possess
talents of one kind or another, waiting to be of service. The notion that all of us
have something to contribute is God-given and stands at the heart of the Judeo-
Christian tradition. The range of talents is as infinite as human variety itself,
and the society that is swiftest to identify them in each, and put them to use,
will certainly be the most efficient (as well as just). Here again, capitalism and
justice pursue the same ends, for capitalism thrives on meritocracy—one of the
prime functions of the market is to identify and reward objective merit—and it
creates wealth most rapidly when all obstacles to equality of opportunity, social
and historic as well as purely legal, are removed. This aspect of equality is a
vital element in the moral legitimation of capitalism, for an economic structure
in which every man and woman, in theory at least, can progress from the lowest to the highest place cannot be held to be intrinsically unjust.

I say "in theory." What about in practice? It is unrealistic to talk of equality   *15*
of opportunity without taking drastic measures to make high-quality education
generally available to those who can profit from it. I know that in practice we
are not going to get a society where all will be able to benefit from the standards of the best schools and colleges. To begin with, throughout human history the most gifted teachers have always been in limited supply—there are
never enough to go around. In any case, the culture and habits of industry,
which parents transmit to their children, make absolute equality of opportunity
unattainable. But it is one thing to concede the difficulties, quite another to
accept the present system of educational inequality, which exists to some
degree in every country in the world. There is no single way, in my view, more
likely to make capitalism morally acceptable, to anchor its functions in justice,
than by giving the poor access, by merit, to high quality education of every
kind and at every stage. And it is implicit in this objective that we identify
merit, of every variety, at the earliest possible age—another respect in which
we tend to be woefully inept.

Of course, to educate the poor, according to aptitude, to the highest stan-   *16*
dards is enormously expensive. But it is the great merit of capitalism that it
does produce wealth in immense quantities for such necessary purposes; and
the more people we educate efficiently, the more wealth the system will produce. The matter is increasingly urgent for, as capitalism advances itself, it
demands ever more refined skills at each level. If training in them is not available for all who can benefit, inequalities—both within societies and between
them—will increase instead of diminish, and the moral credentials of the
system will inevitably be subjected to growing challenge. We have, in
short, to educate ourselves into justice, and to do so with all deliberate
speed.

But we must not stop at access to education. We must see to it that there is   *17*
more readiness of access to the capitalist system itself. I believe that the notion
of "democratic capitalism" is a genuine one, and that its realization, to some
degree at least, is within our grasp. There are many ways in which it can be

brought about. Some are old. Some we have only recently discovered. Some are yet to be devised.

18 In the last half-century and more, we have found that to take an industry into public ownership in no way democratizes it—quite the contrary. Nationalization, whether in the form of a monolithic public corporation, as in the old British system, or through so-called "workers' control," as in Yugoslavia, for example, merely puts the business firmly into the hands of bureaucratic or union elites, or indeed both. But it is now possible, as has been found in Britain and elsewhere, to float public corporations so that they become the property of millions of small stockholders.

19   Let us not deceive ourselves that this conveys control of them to the masses. But it does spread ownership widely, and it does introduce an element of mass financial participation in the system that is new and healthy. It gives millions of humble, ordinary people a sense that they are no longer entirely victims of the system: that they act, as well as are acted upon; that to some small degree they have a stake in society. It is a source of pride, of reassurance, even of security, and it is thus morally significant.

20   Democratic capitalism also lends itself to the old but unrealized idea of co-ownership by giving the workforce easy entry into the purchase of stock. Over 90 percent, for instance, of those who work for the recently privatized British corporation British Telecom now hold stock in the firm—thus bridging the destructive and needless chasm that separates owners and workers and that promotes class warfare. In any great capitalist enterprise, the community of interest between those who own, run, and work for it is, or ought to be, far greater than any conflict of interest. Access of workers to stock is the surest way of demonstrating this fundamental truth, which is often obscured by political sloganeering. This is particularly important in industries where the work is hard and dangerous and the profits high, such as mining and offshore oil extraction, to give two obvious examples. Democratic capitalism, and especially the worker-stock ownership aspect of it, serves to refute one of the gravest charges against capitalist practice—that it is, by its very nature, exploitative.

21   Stock ownership is not, however, the only or even the best way in which the notion of democratic capitalism can be pursued. One of the most important but least-understood disadvantages of the so-called "mixed economy" is that, in its inevitable drift to corporatism, it involves tripartite deals between government, labor unions, and large-scale capital. Such deals invariably leave out small businesses. In Britain, for instance, it is only since we have begun to dismantle mixed-economy corporatism that the needs of small businesses, and equally important, of those wishing to start them, have played any part in the formation of government policy.

22   Why have we been so remiss? Now that most of the world is necessarily turning its back on the soil, to start one's own business has replaced that fundamental human urge to farm one's own land—it is an expression of the natural creativity in man, and as such a profoundly moral impulse. Sensible, practical assistance in helping people to set up their own businesses, and to ensure a

climate of fairness in which they operate, is the best way to promote, at one and the same time, equality of opportunity, democratic capitalism, and, not least, the efficiency and acceptability of the system as a whole. There is almost invariably a strong correlation between the number of small business starts and soundly based economic expansion. So here again the interests of justice and the process of wealth creation coincide.

Popular access to capitalism at a national level has its international counter- *23* part in access to markets. The vigorous promotion of free trade is an important way in which capitalism is legitimized morally. Protectionism in any form tends to undermine capitalist efficiency by creating privileged industries, and it is unacceptable morally because it deprives the consumer of the full fruits of the market. It always appears to have advantages for new, small, and weak econo- mies—or for old established ones meeting new and ruthless competition. But in the long term, and often in the short term too, these advantages are greatly outweighed by the drawbacks. Equally objectionable are barter deals between states, or deals between states and big international corporations. All these attempts to escape the rigors of competition invariably produce corruption and fraud and bring out the worst aspects both of big government and of capitalism itself. One might put it this way: international free trade is the global version of equality of opportunity.

But just as equal opportunities within a society are unlikely to become reality *24* without general access to high-quality education, so free trade will not in prac- tice be generally accepted, especially among the poorer countries, until the huge discrepancies between nations in technical and commercial skills are diminished. I do not think that the normal workings of the international market will be recognized as just and reasonable until we narrow this gap, so much more important in the long run than any more obvious gap in living standards or financial resources. Yet here, perhaps, is the best way in which richer nations can effectively help the poorer ones.

Old-style aid is now discredited, and I think rightly so, for certainly there *25* are few more foolish things than for a rich nation to salve its conscience by transferring cash to the government of a poor one, thus as a rule keeping an inefficient and unpopular tyranny in power. But it is another matter to use our resources to train the disadvantaged masses of the Third World—and indeed the emerging ex-communist world too—in the skills of market capitalism. By widening the availability of such skills, we do many things simultaneously: we benefit the poorer countries by enabling them to compete; we benefit ourselves by making it possible for them to open their markets to us; we strengthen the system by giving it universality as well as fairness; and consumers everywhere find goods cheaper as competition increases. Here again, the process of placing capitalism in a moral context has the additional advantage of adding to its wealth-creating power. To sum up my case: doing the right thing morally usu- ally proves to be commercially the right thing to do as well.

However, I willingly concede that there is an important flaw in my argument. *26* And it applies whether one looks at individual societies or at the global community—within nations and between them. However thoroughly one applies the principle of equality before the law, however ingeniously one provides equality of opportunity and universal access to high-quality education, bitter experience seems to show that a great many people remain in deprivation, misery, and hopelessness. It is not enough to provide individuals with an exit from this underclass. Its very existence, as a class, perpetuating itself from generation to generation, is or at least seems to be a categorical indictment of the capitalist market system itself.

27   In fact it does not truly reflect upon the market. The market can be made fair—to give it moral legitimacy it *must* be made fair—but what it cannot be made to do, at least not without wrecking it, is to discriminate in favor of failure. And we have to face the fact that many human beings, in any society, will fail however fair the rules and however wide the opportunities. There is overwhelming evidence that market capitalism can conquer mass want and create a very general affluence anywhere in the world. What we now have to demonstrate is that the societies in which capitalism is the energizing force can cope with the minority problem of failure. It is, in my judgment, the biggest single task our societies face today: a problem which is at one and the same time moral, economic, and political.

28   It is *moral* because we cannot accept, on a permanent basis, the exclusion of perhaps a fifth of society from a life of modest decency. Earlier ages had to reconcile themselves to permanent mass poverty. We *know* a solution can be found, and we have an inescapable moral obligation to find it.

29   It is *economic* because it is waste on a colossal scale. Often up to 50 percent of budgets are absorbed by coping with poverty. And it is not just material waste but waste of minds and hearts.

30   It is *political* because the percentage involved is too small to effect change through the democratic process. Thus, there is an inherent tendency to resort to violence, often with racial overtones—and a violence which possesses a kind of moral authority all its own.

31   The solutions tried up to now have been collectivist ones, so they have all failed. I believe we must now turn to entrepreneurial solutions and seek to use the problem-solving mechanism of market capitalism, which has never failed us yet, to provide the answers.

32 The need is urgent, because the problem is already reproducing itself at the international level. It is right, as I have argued, to press steadily for the expansion of free trade, and for the richer nations to finance training programs and other devices to make such expansion fair and profitable to all. The majority of the global population can be progressively drawn into such a system.

33   But it would be misleading to suggest that all the nations are at present eligible. Indeed an underclass of nations, mainly but not exclusively in Africa, is developing too. What we observe in large parts of Africa is what might be called the Haiti Syndrome: entities nominally classified as states which have virtually fallen out of the international economy and which seemingly cannot provide for their citizens elementary justice or allow them to provide for them-

selves the basic necessities of life. In many cases, the miseries of these underclass nations are envenomed by civil war and frontier disputes among themselves. As they are at present organized and governed, there is nothing that capitalism can do for them—and socialism, to which most have resorted, merely compounds their problems. Indeed such underclass states seem inevitably to attract the worst exponents both of capitalism at its most unscrupulous and socialism at its most destructive. Where lies the remedy? Indeed, is there a remedy?

Certainly there is no obvious remedy within the common assumptions of the   34
late twentieth century—that all states, whatever their origins and nature, are equally sovereign. In the nineteenth century, the existence of such failed societies, with abysmally low and falling living standards exacerbated by chronic violence, would have attracted the attentions of one or other of the colonial powers. Sooner or later a colonial power would have moved in, from moral motives as well as from hope of commercial and political gain. That would be inconceivable now.

Or would it? Has not the failure of decolonization, in some areas at least,   35
been as spectacular and tragic as the general failure of collectivism? And is it unthinkable to revive the notion of national trusteeship, once so important a part of the League of Nations' work in the 1920s and 1930s? And if trusteeship is a valid concept, worth discussing in the international context, is it, or something like it, a useful idea to mull over in the context of the intractable problem of the internal underclass?

What I am suggesting is that in exploring the future potentialities of the cap-   36
italist market system and in devising ways in which society can consolidate its moral acceptability, we should keep an open mind to fresh ideas. We are at the end of one ideological era, the era in which collectivism was tried and found wanting. One thing history surely teaches is that when old ideas die, others rush in to fill the vacuum. For men and women need ideas as much as they need food and drink. If sensible and creative ideas are not forthcoming, we can be certain that dangerous and destructive ones will emerge to exert their spell. It is essential that those of us whose roots are still within the Judeo-Christian system of ethics, who value freedom, who strive for the just society, and who recognize the enormous productive potential of market capitalism should be fertile in ideas in the coming battle for minds. For if we get the ideas right, the opportunities for mankind in the next century are almost without limit.

WRITING AND DISCUSSION QUESTIONS

Informative

1. Explain Johnson's claim that capitalism is morally neutral.
2. According to Johnson, why do efforts to "provide capitalism itself with a positive moral purpose" fail?
3. The market, Johnson posits, can be made "fair," but it cannot be asked to "dis-

criminate in favor of failure.'' What does he mean by this? Must ''democratic capitalism'' always be willing to accept a certain measure of individual failure so that
the vast majority may reasonably prosper?

Persuasive

1. Capitalism cannot ''promote equality,'' says Johnson, if by that we mean some-
    thing other than equality ''before the law.'' What does *equality* entail: equal
    opportunity, equal legal status, preferred status for underrepresented groups, or
    something else? Do you agree with Johnson's basic understanding of how equality
    must work in a free market society? In what sense might his view of ''equality'' dif-
    fer from that defined in the Declaration of Independence? Argue your position.
2. According to Johnson, how can capitalism be ''combined with moral purpose''?
    Argue that these attempted adjustments would or would not avoid the same trap
    that plagues noncapitalist or anticapitalist societies, that is, the eventual state con-
    trol of individual lives.
3. How may Johnson's concessions about capitalism's ''failure'' to provide moral
    guidance within a society serve the Marxist critique of the ''bourgeoisie''? Argue
    whether such objections can be made against capitalism without subscribing to
    Marxist economics? Does opposition to capitalism's ''excesses'' commit one to a
    socialist or centrally planned economy?
4. Johnson argues on the one hand that capitalism is morally neutral, and on the
    other that ''doing the right thing morally usually proves to be commercially the right
    thing to do as well.'' Argue whether these views are contradictory or compatible.

Personal

1. At one point in his argument, Johnson links ''the notion that all of us have some-
    thing to contribute'' to society to the Judeo-Christian tradition. What is his basis for
    attributing this social platitude to the Biblical worldview? Do you find it plausible to
    credit the Bible for this notion?
2. While talking about some of capitalism's weaknesses, Johnson primarily focuses
    upon the problems of socialist economies and their typical ''nationalization,'' a
    system wherein an economy—its means of production, its jobs, prices of goods,
    the training of workers and diversity of occupations available—is controlled by
    the state. Is there any middle ground between the totalitarian state and modern
    democracies? Or does any semblance of economic control by the state lend itself
    to totalitarian control in the lives of individuals?
3. Johnson speaks of ''democratic capitalism.'' Can there not also be ''democratic
    socialism''? How would such a society be structured, and do any such societies
    exist now?
4. Although Johnson sees capitalism as a ''natural force,'' ''the primary means
    whereby wealth is produced,'' he concedes that some ''underclass nations'' are
    not at present capable of appreciating its benefits. Reminding us to ''keep an
    open mind to fresh ideas,'' he suggests a modified form of colonialism as a possi-

ble solution to this problem. Explore what you think to be the ethics of this solution from a perspective based on your notion of one of the Great Ideas you have studied so far.

5. The degree of capitalist individualism or of socialist collectivism found to be appropriate to any given country is likely to be more a matter of national or regional cultural traditions than of universal law, whether the source of that law is some notion of morality or of historical necessity. How would Marx and Johnson each respond to this statement? How do you?

6. Imagine yourself to be Toni Cade Bambara. Having read Johnson's essay, how satisfied would you be with his analysis of the relation between capitalism and morality and the solutions he offers for the problem of the underclass?

▼

MIKHAIL GORBACHEV, "ON REAL SOCIALISM" FROM *PERESTROIKA*

Mikhail Gorbachev (1931–) perhaps needs little annotation or identification, having served as the President of the Soviet Union and General Secretary of the Soviet Communist party and having been awarded the 1990 Nobel Peace Prize. Gorbachev's remarkable initiatives in restructuring Soviet society ("perestroika") and in opening the avenues of debate and dialogue among leaders, educators, and citizens of his nation ("glasnost") are widely credited with the movement toward democracy in Eastern Europe and in the Soviet Union itself. In essence, Gorbachev's remarkable shift away from hardline Marxism and his encouragement of democratic processes in Soviet domestic policy have made "legal," as it were, the discussion, debate, and even rejection of certain lines of Marxist thought. The volatile, fragile nature of the coming again of "freedom" in a nation haunted by a totalitarian past, however, requires caution and sobriety in predicting what the future may hold. In this essay, from his book, *Perestroika*, published in the West in 1987, Gorbachev carefully explains his new understanding of socialism and how it can be revised to serve a more modern, perhaps less turbulent, world.

▼

On Real Socialism
MIKHAIL GORBACHEV

The essence of our internationalist principle is: making important,   *1* meaningful decisions at home, and carefully weighing up what this will mean for socialism as a whole. It goes without saying that no socialist country can successfully move forward in a healthy rhythm without understanding, solidarity and mutually beneficial cooperation with the other fraternal nations, or at times even without their help.

ON REAL SOCIALISM

2 When we embarked on the course of perestroika, we proceeded from the premise that restructuring was working, and would continue to work. To strengthen socialism as a whole in that restructuring is the cause of the whole Soviet people, and is designed to raise our society to a qualitatively new level. This is the first point.

3 The second point is that both the course we have chosen and the need to pick up our pace have made us look at how to develop cooperation with other socialist countries in a broad historical context. The resulting conclusion—and the fraternal parties have all reached this conclusion—is that greater dynamism should be imparted to our cooperation, that this sphere too is ready for a kind of restructuring. Our thoughts, and later our initiatives, were based on the following.

4 Over the postwar decades socialism has become a strong international formation and a major factor in world politics. A socialist form of economy functions in a large group of countries. The foundations have been laid for an international socialist division of labor. Multilateral organizations of socialist states have gained a varied experience of activity. Scientific and cultural exchanges have assumed large proportions. Of course, this does not mean that the development of world socialism always proceeded successfully.

5 The initial economic level of countries that have taken the socialist path of development differed considerably. Even today it is far from identical. This is one of the difficulties in realizing socialism's overall potential and in perfecting the mechanisms of integration.

6 Socialism has gone through complicated phases of development. In the first postwar decades, only the Soviet Union had any experience in the building of a new society. It had to be responsible for everything that was happening, for good and bad. The character of economic relations with other socialist countries was also in line with this; these relations developed with emphasis on Soviet raw materials and fuel supplies and on the Soviet Union's aid in creating basic industries. In the field of state building, too, the fraternal socialist states largely relied on the Soviet example. To an extent, this was inevitable. Assertions concerning the imposition of the "Soviet model" distort this objective necessity of that time. The first socialist state's experience and help on the whole fostered the other countries' efforts to build a new society.

7 But it was not without losses, and rather serious ones at that. Drawing on the Soviet experience, some countries failed duly to consider their own specifics. Even worse, a stereotyped approach was given an ideological tint by some of our theoreticians and especially practical leaders who acted as almost the sole guardians of truth. Without taking into consideration the novelty of problems and the specific features of different socialist countries, they sometimes displayed suspicion toward those countries' approaches to certain problems.

On the other hand, there grew in a number of socialist countries tendencies   8
towards a certain introversion, which gave rise to subjective assessments and
actions. Moreover, the socialist nations have been a target of massive pressure
from imperialism—political, military, economic and ideological—ever since
their birth.

In some cases all this led to certain objective processes and to the emer-   9
gence of problems that were not noticed in time by the ruling party and the
leadership. As regards our friends in the socialist countries, they usually kept
quiet, even when they noticed something of concern. Frankness was frowned
upon, and could be "misunderstood," so to speak. Some socialist countries
went through serious crises in their development. Such was the case, for
instance, in Hungary in 1956, in Czechoslovakia in 1968, and in Poland in
1956 and then again in the early 1980s. Each of these crises had its own specific features. They were dealt with differently. But the fact is that a return to
the old order did not occur in any of the socialist nations. I want to note here
that it was not socialism that was to blame for the difficulties and complexities
of the socialist countries' development, but, chiefly, miscalculations by the ruling parties. And, of course, the West can also be "credited" with helping,
through its constant and stubborn attempts to undermine the development of
the socialist states, to trip them up.

Through hard, and at times bitter, trials the socialist countries accumulated   10
their experience in carrying out socialist transformations. The ruling communist
parties' practice, as well as theoretical work, gradually produced a fuller and
more precise idea of the methods, ways and means for a socialist transformation of society. Marx, Engels and Lenin, who theoretically substantiated the
principles on which the concept of socialism is founded, did not seek to give a
detailed picture of the future society. And this is in general impossible to do.
This picture acquired its outlines and is still in the making as a result of the
revolutionary creative work of all the socialist states.

There were also serious falterings in relations between socialist countries.   11
Particularly grave was the disruption of the USSR's friendly relations with
Yugoslavia, with the People's Republic of China and with Albania. In general
there were enough bitter lessons. But communists learned. We are still learning
today.

In general, an advantage of socialism is its ability to learn. To learn how to   12
solve the problems being raised by life. To learn how to avert crisis situations
which our opponents try to create and use against us. To learn how to resist
attempts to stratify the socialist world and pit some countries against others. To
learn how to prevent conflicts of interest between different socialist states, by
harmonizing these interests and finding mutually acceptable solutions to the
most complex problems.

What has world socialism achieved by the mid-1980s? Now we can safely   13
state that the socialist system has firmly established itself in a large group of
nations, that the socialist countries' economic potential has been steadily

increasing, and that its cultural and spiritual values are profoundly moral and that they ennoble people.

14   But in this case one may ask: if all is so well, why is perestroika exciting so much interest concerning relations between the socialist countries? Well, it's a legitimate question.

15   Generally speaking, the answer is simple enough: the initial phase of world socialism's rise and development is over, but the forms of relations which were established at that time have remained virtually unchanged. Furthermore, negative accretions in these relations were not examined with a sufficient degree of frankness, which means that not everything obstructing their development and preventing them from entering a new, contemporary stage was identified. Meanwhile, each socialist country, each socialist society, has accumulated considerable potential of its own in every field of life. Socialism's prestige and possibilities would be directly harmed if we clung to the old forms of cooperation or limited ourselves to them.

16   Indeed, beginning with the end of the 1970s, contacts between leaders of fraternal countries became more and more for show rather than for real business. There was less trust in them and their approach was more businesslike.

17   Now many things have changed. Over the past two and a half years the Soviet Union and its friends in the socialist community have jointly carried out great work. This needs to be, and is being, continued. The entire range of political, economic and humanitarian relations with the socialist countries is being cast anew. This is dictated by the objective needs of each country's development and by the international situation as a whole, rather than by emotions.

TOWARD NEW RELATIONS

18   The role of the Soviet Union in the socialist community in the conditions of perestroika is determined by the objective position of our country. Whether things are going well in our country or whether they are going poorly, this inevitably affects everyone. But the level of interaction we are now reaching is the result of more than just the work we are doing at home. It is first and foremost the result of the joint activities and concerted efforts of the fraternal countries. And we have thoroughly discussed every aspect of cooperation with our friends and allies.

19   We all proceed from the premise that at this crucial stage in world development, socialism must show in full measure the dynamism of its political and economic system, a humane way of life. Socialist community relations are already being readapted to the requirements of the time. We are far from euphoric: the work is just gaining momentum. But the major goals have been defined.

20   What do these reference points imply? First of all, the entire framework of

political relations between the socialist countries must be strictly based on absolute independence. This is the view held by the leaders of all fraternal countries. The independence of each Party, its sovereign right to decide the issues facing its country and its responsibility to its nation are the unquestionable principles.

We are also firmly convinced that the socialist community will be successful   *21* only if every party and state cares for both its own and common interests, if it respects its friends and allies, heeds their interests and pays attention to the experience of others. Awareness of this relationship between domestic issues and the interests of world socialism is typical of the countries of the socialist community. We are united, in unity resides our strength, and from unity we draw our confidence that we will cope with the issues set forth by our time.

Collaboration between the ruling communist parties is pivotal to cooperation   *22* between the socialist countries. Over the past few years we have had meetings and detailed discussions with the leadership of every fraternal country. The forms of this cooperation are also being renewed. A new, and probably key, link in this is the institution of multilateral working meetings between the leaders of fraternal countries. Such meetings enable us to confer, promptly and in a comradely manner, on the entire range of issues of socialist development and its domestic and foreign aspects.

The extension, in the complicated international situation, of the term of the   *23* Warsaw Treaty, by virtue of a unanimous decision, was a crucial event. Regular meetings of the Warsaw Treaty's Political Consultative Committee pave the way for an accumulation of the ideas and initiatives of its participants, and allow them to "synchronize their watches," so to speak.

What is intended is the harmonization of the initiatives of each fraternal   *24* country with a common line in international affairs. Experience has shown how important both components of the formula are. No fraternal country—and we attribute this to the USSR in full measure—can resolve its tasks on the international scene if it is isolated from the general course. Likewise, a coordinated foreign policy of our states can be efficient only provided the contribution of each country to the common cause is duly taken into account.

As far as economic relations are concerned, we have been developing them   *25* on the basis of consistent observance of the principles of mutual advantage and mutual assistance. We have reached an understanding that all of us are now in need of a breakthrough in science and technology and in the economic field. To this end, we have elaborated and adopted a comprehensive program for scientific and technological progress aimed at sharply increasing production efficiency, at doubling and even tripling productivity by the year 2000. Is this utopian? No. The socialist community has everything it needs to accomplish this task, including a formidable production capability, a vast number of research and engineering projects, as well as enough natural resources and manpower. Our plan-based system, too, enables us to channel considerable resources towards satisfying needs of prior importance.

26   The leaders of the member-states of the Council for Mutual Economic Assistance (CMEA), as a result of discussions, arrived at the conclusion that all structural components of the socialist system must function more efficiently. This is what all of us agree on. But it does not mean, of course, that these processes will proceed in an identical way in all socialist countries. For each nation has its own traditions, peculiarities and ways in which its political institutions function. In principle, all socialist countries are in one way or another going through the process of searching for renewal and profound transformations. But each country, that is its leadership and its people, decides independently what scope, scale, forms, rates and methods these transformations should have. There are no differences on that score; there are only specific features.

27   The French Prime Minister, Jacques Chirac, asked me: "Do you think the spirit of perestroika will bear its impact on all socialist states of Eastern Europe?" I said the influence is mutual. We borrow something from the experience of our friends and they take from us what they think suits them best. In short, it is a process of mutual exchange and enrichment.

28   Speaking honestly, it seems to me that the point was raised out of more than a desire to know how we had been doing. It was to a certain extent prompted by rumors about some of our friends being in "disagreement" with the Soviet leadership's line towards perestroika. What can I say about this? We have no serious disagreements with our friends and allies. We are used to speaking frankly and in a businesslike manner. And, to my mind, we gain more from a critical and earnest evaluation of our moves and initiatives than from loud applause for just anything we have done. That's the first point. The second, and I will repeat it in this context, is that we do not claim we are the only ones to know the truth. Truth is sought in a joint quest and effort.

29   But let me say a few more words about economic affairs. We see direct links between companies and enterprises and specialization as the chief reserve and leverage for deepening our integration. It is exactly along these lines that we are restructuring our foreign economic activities and removing barriers preventing enterprises from finding appropriate partners in fraternal countries and deciding on their own how to cooperate with them. We are launching joint socialist companies, including those expected to meet our countries' needs for the most sophisticated goods more quickly. Such companies are being set up in services, construction and transport. The Soviet Union is prepared to offer them some lucrative orders. We are also prepared to consider the possibility of involving Western businessmen in the activities of such companies.

30   We hope to accelerate the process of integration in the forthcoming few years. To this end, the CMEA should increasingly focus on two major issues.

31   First, it will coordinate economic policies, elaborate long-term programs for cooperation in some crucial fields and promote major joint research and engineering programs and projects. In doing so it is possible and expedient to cooperate with non-socialist countries and their organizations, the EEC above all.

Second, the CMEA will focus on the development and coordination of nor-   *32*
mative standards for the integration mechanism, as well as on legal and economic conditions for direct cooperation links, including, of course, the fixing of
prices.

We want the CMEA to have less administrative regimentation, fewer commit-   *33*
tees and commissions, and to pay greater attention to economic incentives, initiative, the socialist spirit of enterprise, and to an increase in the involvement of
work collectives in the process. We and our friends think that the CMEA must
get rid of a surplus of paper work and bureaucratic muddle.

In no way does the CMEA infringe on the independence of any participating   *34*
state and its sovereign right to be in charge of its own resources and capabilities and to do everything for the benefit of its people. The CMEA is not a
supranational organization. In decision-making it relies on the principle of consensus, rather than on a majority vote. The only important thing is that any
country's lack of desire or interest to participate in a project should not serve
as a restraint on others. Anyone who wants to participate is welcome to do so;
if not, one can wait and see how the others are doing. Every country is free to
decide if it is prepared for such cooperation and how far it is going to be
involved. I believe this is the only correct approach.

We also have a task of great magnitude concerning cooperation in the intel-   *35*
lectual sphere. Change is imperative here too. In fact, each of the socialist
countries is a social laboratory testing the various forms and methods of the
socialist constructive effort. This is why, in our view, exchanging experience in
socialist construction, and summing up such experience, is becoming increasingly significant.

We Soviet communists, as we consider the future of socialism, proceed from   *36*
Lenin's idea that this future will be created through a series of efforts made by
various countries. This is why we naturally believe that a good way to judge the
earnestness of a ruling party is to look at how it uses its own experience, as
well as the experience of its friends, and the world experience. As for the value
of this experience, we have one criterion here: social and political practice—
the results of social development and economic growth, and the strengthening
of socialism in practice. Our science, our press and our specialists are now
analyzing the experience of the fraternal countries on a much broader
scale and much more actively so as to apply it creatively to Soviet
conditions.

For their part, these countries show an immense interest in what is happen-   *37*
ing in the USSR. I saw this when I met with the leaders of the socialist countries and with rank-and-file citizens during my trips abroad. Here is a small
illustration. During my visit to Czechoslovakia, I had the opportunity to talk
with people on the streets and in the factories of Prague; they would tell me:
"What you're doing now is the right thing!" One young man noted: "So it boils
down to: 'Speak the truth, love the truth, and wish others the truth.'" I added:
"And act according to the truth. This is the most difficult science." I went on

to say: "Life is harder than any school; not everything comes easy. Sometimes you have to retreat, and then advance. It is agonizing to think, analyze and re-analyze, but you shouldn't be afraid of this."

38   The general conclusion of the Soviet leadership is that we can reach a new level of friendship between the socialist countries by developing ties among their work collectives and their individuals as well as through an exchange of experience. Our ties in all spheres are becoming more vigorous. We've made a good start. The solid network of contacts along Party, state and public lines plays an important and even decisive part in the cooperation among the fraternal countries. We have various types of contacts—from those between enterprises, work teams, families, children's and youth organizations, universities and schools, creative unions and cultural figures and individuals, to permanent business ties between department officials, members of governments and Central Committee secretaries.

39   A few words about our relations with the People's Republic of China, where very interesting and in many respects fruitful ideas are being realized in the process of the "four modernizations." We view China as a great socialist power, and are taking definite steps to ensure that the development of Sino-Soviet relations takes place in a spirit of good-neighborliness and cooperation. There has already been a definite improvement. We believe that the period of alienation is past. We invite our Chinese comrades to work together with us to develop good relations between our two countries and peoples.

40   The current stage of historical development puts a strict demand on the socialist states: to pick up the pace, to move to the economically, scientifically and technologically most advanced positions, and convincingly to demonstrate the attractiveness of the socialist way of life.

41   We have been frank and self-critical in our assessment of the past development and have borne our share of the blame for failures in the socialist community. Our friends were quick to respond. This has paved the way for restructuring relations, for bringing them to a new, contemporary level.

42   Together we have achieved a great deal in recent years in politics, economics and in the exchange of information. If everything is not yet successful, this does not make us nervous. We are working persistently, exploring fresh approaches. The main thing is that we are convinced of the importance of cooperation and the need to enhance it. At the current stage in history, which is in effect a turning point, the ruling parties of the socialist countries are aware of the great extent of their responsibility, nationally and internationally, and are persistently looking for further ways to accelerate social development. An orientation toward scientific and technological progress, people's creative endeavor and the development of democracy is the guarantee that in the coming period socialism will, contrary to the prophecies of all ill-wishers, reveal even more fully its real potential.

43   Revolutionary changes are becoming part and parcel of the vast socialist world. They are gaining momentum. This applies to the socialist countries, but it is also a contribution to the progress of world civilization.

WRITING AND DISCUSSION QUESTIONS

Informative

1. "Perestroika" literally means "restructuring." According to President Gorbachev, what kinds of restructuring have occurred in the Soviet Union as a result of his reforms?
2. According to Gorbachev, what are the causes of the apparent failure of socialism in some countries? In what ways does he believe socialism can be altered to provide a better standard of living for those nations where it has not produced a thriving economy?
3. One could hardly have predicted the changes toward democracy in the Soviet Union itself and its former satellite nations, even given this document from Gorbachev. Yet, what principles are enunciated here that foretell the possibility of the radical changes witnessed recently? What evidence is there in this essay that Gorbachev might acquiesce in the independence and thus secession of some states in the Soviet Union?

Persuasive

1. In defending an idea or faith before an unsympathetic audience, the claim is often made that the idea itself is sound but that the understanding and implementation of that idea have been poor. In other words, it is the perversion of the idea that needs to be criticized and rejected. One might say of theory X, for example, "Do not judge the validity of the idea by the way so-and-so has used it because he did not really understand it. Give us enough time and the right circumstances, and we will show you that X works." Argue that President Gorbachev is offering a similar defense regarding the idea of socialism.
2. In a famous phrasing, former President Reagan once referred to the Soviet Union as "an evil empire." In what way was such a characterization plausible? In what way was it not? How does this essay by President Gorbachev lend credence to Reagan's view? In what way may it refute it?
3. In what way is Gorbachev's restructuring faithful to traditional Marxism's emphasis on class struggle, the redistribution of wealth, and the state ownership of the means of production? In what ways does it depart?

Personal

1. Do you automatically distrust President Gorbachev here? Do you suspect him of some subtle manipulation or deceit in describing the new Soviet system?
2. Consider Gorbachev's statement: "In general, an advantage of socialism is its ability to learn." What has "socialism" learned, in your opinion, in the past decade that would explain these remarkable changes in Soviet policy and political relationship with the United States and the West? Does capitalism have anything to "learn"?
3. Imagine that you are a U.S. president writing an essay to be read by the Soviet

people in which you explain the American "system" and how it works. What topics and examples would you include?

▼

VÁCLAV HAVEL,
"THE GREAT MORAL STAKE OF THE MOMENT"

Recent events in Eastern Europe and the Soviet Union, especially those occurring in late 1989 and early 1990, propelled an outspoken playwright, Václav Havel (1937–), into the presidency of Czechoslovakia. The events leading up to his election are dramatic and worth noting. Not for the first time, he was arrested on October 27, 1989, for his political criticisms of the communist government of his country. One month later, activist musician Mikhail Koscak informed him that he would be proposed as candidate for president of Czechoslovakia. Miraculously, on December 29, 1989, Václav Havel was unanimously elected president.

Havel, like Poland's Solidarity leader, Lech Walesa, is a man whose stirring words are gaining the rapt attention of the world. His words have an uncanny moral and rhetorical power, and his recent speeches, in fact, have been compared to those of Abraham Lincoln. One in particular, given on February 21, 1990, shortly after his election to the presidency, stirred the U.S. Congress to no fewer than five standing ovations and frequent shouts of "Bravo!" One excerpt from that speech demonstrates that Havel is no ordinary political leader but a moral visionary:

> Without a global revolution in the sphere of human consciousness, nothing will change for the better in the sphere of our being. . . .
>
> We still don't know how to put morality ahead of politics, science and economy. We are still incapable of understanding that the only genuine backbone of all our actions, if they are to be moral, is responsibility—responsibility to something higher than my family, my country, my company, my success.
>
> If I subordinate my political behavior to this imperative, mediated to me by my conscience, I can't go far wrong. If, on the contrary, I were not guided by this voice, not even 10 presidential schools with 2000 of the best political scientists in the world could help me.
>
> This is why I ultimately decided, after resisting for a long time, to accept the burden of political responsibility. I am not the first; nor will I be the last intellectual to do this.
>
> When Thomas Jefferson wrote that governments are instituted among men deriving their just powers from the consent of the governed, it was a simple and important act of the human spirit. What gave meaning to that act, however, was the fact that the author backed it up with his life. It was not just his words; it was his deed as well.

Havel's ideas and actions have profound implications for the future of Marxism and economics in the world. He acknowledges in almost all of his writings that Marxism is swiftly declining, to be replaced, in both Eastern Europe and the Soviet Union, by an economy leaning more toward a free market system. Clearly, a free market economy reflects the kinds of values inherent in social and political democracy, where all are free to pursue their own creative and spiritual potential, which in Havel's words, lies "nowhere else than in the human heart, in the human power to reflect, in

human meekness and in human responsibility." Havel is seeking to give voice to
individual rights and individual responsibilities, which will transform the world into
what Lincoln called "the family of Man."

▼

The Great Moral Stake of the Moment
VÁCLAV HAVEL

*The following contains excerpts from Václav Havel's New Year's Day
1990 Inaugural address to Czechoslovakia:*

For the past 40 years on this day you have heard my predecessors utter   *1*
variations on the same theme, about how our country is prospering, how many
more billion tons of steel we have produced, how happy we all are, how much
we trust our government and what beautiful prospects lie ahead. I do not think
you put me into this office so that I, too, should lie to you.

Our country is not prospering. The great creative and spiritual potential of   *2*
our nation is not being used to its fullest. Whole sectors of industry are producing things in which no one is interested, while things we need are in short
supply.

The state, which calls itself a state of the working people, is humiliating and   *3*
exploiting the workers. Our outdated economy is squandering energy. . . . A
country which could once be proud of the standard of education of its people
spends so little on education that today it ranks 72nd in the world. We have
laid waste to our soil and the rivers and the forests our forefathers bequeathed
us, and we have the worst environment in all of Europe today. . . .

The worst thing is that we are living in a decayed moral environment. We   *4*
have become morally ill, because we have become accustomed to saying one
thing and thinking another. We have learned not to believe in anything, not to
care about one another and only to look after ourselves. Notions such as love,
friendship, compassion, humility and forgiveness have lost their depth and
dimension, and for many of us they represent merely some kind of psychological idiosyncrasy, or appear as some kind of stray relic from times past, something rather comical in the era of computers and space rockets. . . .

The previous regime, armed with its arrogant and intolerant ideology, deni-   *5*
grated man into a production force and nature into a production tool. In this
way it attacked their very essence and the relationship between them. It made
talented people who were capable of managing their own affairs . . . into cogs
in some kind of monstrous, ramshackle, smelly machine whose purpose no one
can understand. It can do nothing more than slowly but surely wear itself
down, along with all the cogs in it.

6   When I talk about a decayed moral environment . . . I mean all of us, because all of us have become accustomed to the totalitarian system, accepted it as an inalterable fact and thereby kept it running. In other words, all of us are responsible, each to a different degree, for keeping the totalitarian machine running. None of us is merely a victim of it, because all of us helped to create it together.

7   Why do I mention this? It would be very unwise to see the sad legacy of the past 40 years as something alien, handed down to us by some distant relatives. On the contrary, we must accept this legacy as something which we have brought upon ourselves. If we can accept this, then we will understand that it is up to all of us to do something about it. We cannot lay all the blame on those who ruled us before, not only because this would not be true but also because it could detract from the responsibility each of us now faces—the responsibility to act on our own initiative, freely, sensibly and quickly. . . .

8   Throughout the world, people are surprised that the acquiescent, humiliated, skeptical Czechoslovak people who apparently no longer believed in anything suddenly managed to find the enormous strength in the space of a few weeks to shake off the totalitarian system in a completely decent and peaceful way. We ourselves are also surprised at this, and we ask where the young people, in particular, who have never known any other system, find the source of their aspirations for truth, freedom of thought, political imagination, civic courage and civic foresight. How is it that their parents, the generation which was considered lost, also joined in with them? How is it possible that so many immediately grasped what had to be done? . . .

9   Of course, for our freedom today we also had to pay a price. Many of our people died in prison in the '50s, many were executed, thousands of human lives were destroyed, hundreds of thousands of talented people were driven abroad. . . . Those who resisted totalitarian government were persecuted, [as were] those who simply managed to remain true to their own principles and think freely. None of those who paid the price in one way or another for our freedom today should be forgotten. . . .

10   Neither should we forget that other nations paid an even higher price for their freedom today, and thus also paid indirectly for us, too. The rivers of blood which flowed in Hungary, Poland, Germany and recently in such a horrific way in Romania, as well as the sea of blood shed by the nations of the Soviet Union, should not be forgotten . . . it was these great sacrifices which wove the tragic backdrop for today's freedom or gradual liberation of the Soviet-bloc nations, and the backdrop of our newly charged freedom, too. . . .

11   This, it seems to me, is the great moral stake of the present moment. It contains the hope that in the future we will no longer have to suffer the complex of those who are permanently indebted to someone else. Now it is up to us alone whether this hope comes to fruition, and whether our civic, national and political self-confidence reawakens in a historically new way.

WRITING AND DISCUSSION QUESTIONS

Informative

1. What observations does Havel make on the state of Czechoslovakia as he enters office? What, in particular, does he say about citizen collusion with the rule of communism?
2. What does Havel mean by ''a decayed moral environment''? What relationship does he see between a political system and people's moral values?
3. What view of Marxism does Havel suggest here, especially in paragraph 5?

Persuasive

1. Argue that Havel is right or wrong for holding the people of his country, and not just the rulers, responsible for the totalitarian system. What is the intended effect of spreading the blame?

Personal

1. Speculate on the answer to the question Havel raises in paragraph 8: ''How is it possible that so many grasped what had to be done?''

▼

Words on Words

Václav Havel received the Friedenpreis des Deutschen Buchandels, the Peace Prize of the German Booksellers Association, on October 15, 1989. He wrote the following as his acceptance speech.

The prize which it is my honor to receive today is called a peace prize and has been awarded to me by booksellers, in other words, people whose business is the dissemination of words. It is therefore appropriate, perhaps, that I should reflect here today on the mysterious link between words and peace, and in general on the mysterious power of words in human history.   *1*

In the beginning was the Word; so it states on the first page of one of the most important books known to us. What is meant in that book is that the Word of God is the source of all creation. But surely the same could be said, figuratively speaking, of every human action? And indeed, words can be said to be the very source of our being, and in fact the very substance of the cosmic life-form we call Man. Spirit, the human soul, our self-awareness, our ability to generalize and think in concepts, to perceive the world as the world (and not just as our locality), and lastly, our capacity for knowing that we will die—and living in spite of that knowledge: surely all these are mediated or actually created by words?   *2*

3   If the Word of God is the source of God's entire creation then that part of God's creation which is the human race exists as such only thanks to another of God's miracles—the miracle of human speech. And if this miracle is the key to the history of mankind, then it is also the key to the history of society. Indeed it might well be the former just because it is the latter. For the fact is that if they were not a means of communication between two or more human "I"s, then words would probably not exist at all.

4   All these things have been known to us—or people have at least suspected them—since time immemorial. There has never been a time when a sense of the importance of words was not present in human consciousness.

5   But that is not all: thanks to the miracle of speech, we know probably better than the other animals that we actually know very little, in other words we are conscious of the existence of mystery. Confronted by mystery—and at the same time aware of the virtually constitutive power of words for us—we have tried incessantly to address that which is concealed by mystery, and influence it with our words. As believers, we pray to God, as magicians we summon up or ward off spirits, using words to intervene in natural or human events. As subjects of modern civilization—whether believers or not—we use words to construct scientific theories and political ideologies with which to tackle or redirect the mysterious course of history—successfully or otherwise.

6   In other words, whether we are aware of it or not, and however we explain it, one thing would seem to be obvious: we have always believed in the power of words to change history—and rightly so, in a sense.

7   Why "rightly so"?

8   Is the human word truly powerful enough to change the world and influence history? And even if there were epochs when it did exert such a power, does it still do so today?

9   You live in a country with considerable freedom of speech. All citizens without exception can avail themselves of that freedom for whatever purpose, and no one is obliged to pay the least attention, let alone worry their heads over it. You might, therefore, easily get the impression that I overrate the importance of words quite simply because I live in a country where words can still land people in prison.

10   Yes, I do live in a country where the authority and radioactive effect of words are demonstrated every day by the sanctions which free speech attracts. Just recently, the entire world commemorated the bicentenary of the great French Revolution. Inevitably we recalled the famous Declaration of the Rights of Man and of Citizens, which states that every citizen has the right to own a printing press. During the same period, i.e., exactly two hundred years after that Declaration, my friend Frantisek Stárek was sent to prison for two-and-a-half years for producing the independent cultural journal *Vokno*—not on some private printing press but with a squeaky, antediluvian duplicator. Not long before, my friend Ivan Jirous was sentenced to sixteen months' imprisonment for berating, on a typewriter, something that is common knowledge: that our country has seen many judicial murders and that even now it is possible for a

person unjustly convicted to die from ill-treatment in prison. My friend Petr Cibulka is in prison for distributing samizdat texts and recordings of nonconformist singers and bands.

Yes, all that is true. I do live in a country where a writers' congress or some   11 speech at it is capable of shaking the system. Could you conceive of something of the kind in the Federal Republic of Germany? Yes, I live in a country which, twenty-one years ago, was shaken by a text from the pen of my friend Ludvik Vaculík. And as if to confirm my conclusions about the power of words, he entitled his statement: "Two Thousand Words." Among other things, that manifesto served as one of the pretexts for the invasion of our country one night by five foreign armies. And it is by no means fortuitous that as I write these words, the present regime in my country is being shaken by a single page of text entitled—again as if to illustrate what I am saying—"A few words." Yes, I really do inhabit a system in which words are capable of shaking the entire structure of government, where words can prove mightier than ten military divisions, where Solzhenitsyn's words of truth were regarded as something so dangerous that it was necessary to bundle their author into an airplane and transport him. Yet, in the part of the world I inhabit the word Solidarity was capable of shaking an entire power bloc.

All that is true. Reams have been written about it and my distinguished   12 predecessor in this place, Lev Kopelev,[1] spoke about it also.

But it is a slightly different matter that concerns me here. It is not my inten-   13 tion solely to speak about the incredible importance that unfettered words assume in totalitarian conditions. Nor do I wish to demonstrate the mysterious power of words by pointing exclusively to those countries where a few words can count for more than a whole train of dynamite somewhere else.

I want to talk in more general terms and consider the wider and more con-   14 troversial aspects of my topic.

We live in a world in which it is possible for a citizen of Great Britain to find   15 himself the target of a lethal arrow aimed—publicly and unashamedly—by a powerful individual in another country merely because he had written a particular book. That powerful man apparently did it in the name of millions of his fellow believers. And moreover, it is possible in this world that some portion of those millions—one hopes only a small portion—will identify with the death sentence pronounced.

What's going on? What does it mean? Is it no more than an icy blast of   16 fanaticism, oddly finding a new lease on life in the era of the various Helsinki agreements, and oddly resuscitated by the rather crippling results of the rather crippling Europeanization of worlds which initially had no interest in the import of foreign civilization, and on account of that ambivalent commodity ended up saddled with astronomical debts they can never repay?

It certainly is all that.   17

But it is something else as well. It is a symbol.   18

[1]Lev Kopelev received the Peace Prize of the German Booksellers Association in 1981.

19   It is a symbol of the mysteriously ambiguous power of words.

20   In truth, the power of words is neither unambiguous nor clear-cut. It is not merely the liberating power of Walesa's words or the alarm-raising power of Sakharov's. It is not just the power of Rushdie's—clearly misconstrued—book.

21   The point is that alongside Rushdie's words we have Khomeini's. Words that electrify society with their freedom and truthfulness are matched by words that mesmerize, deceive, inflame, madden, beguile, words that are harmful—lethal, even. The word as arrow.

22   I don't think I need to go to any lengths to explain to you of all people the diabolic power of certain words: you have fairly recent first-hand experience of what indescribable historical horrors can flow, in certain political and social constellations, from the hypnotically spellbinding, though totally demented, words of a single, average, petit bourgeois. Admittedly I fail to understand what it was that transfixed a large number of your fathers and mothers, but at the same time I realize that it must have been something extremely compelling as well as extremely insidious if it was capable of beguiling, albeit only briefly, even that great genius who lent such modern and penetrating meaning to the words: *"Sein," "Da-Sein,"* and *"Existenz."*

23   The point I am trying to make is that words are a mysterious, ambiguous, ambivalent, and perfidious phenomenon. They are capable of being rays of light in a realm of darkness, as Belinsky once described Ostrovsky's *Storm.* They are equally capable of being lethal arrows. Worst of all, at times they can be the one and the other. And even both at once!

24   The words of Lenin—what were they? Liberating or, on the contrary, deceptive, dangerous, and ultimately enslaving? This is still a bone of contention among aficionados of the history of communism and the controversy is likely to go on raging for a good while yet. My own impression of these words is that they were invariably frenzied.

25   And what about Marx's words? Did they serve to illuminate an entire hidden plane of social mechanisms, or were they just the inconspicuous germ of all the subsequent appalling gulags. I don't know: most likely they are both at once.

26   And what about Freud's words? Did they disclose the secret cosmos of the human soul, or were they no more than the fountainhead of the illusion now benumbing half of America that it is possible to shed one's torments and guilt by having them interpreted away by some well-paid specialist?

27   But I'd go further and ask an even more provocative question: What was the true nature of Christ's words? Were they the beginning of an era of salvation and among the most powerful cultural impulses in the history of the world—or were they the spiritual source of the crusades, inquisitions, the cultural extermination of the Americas, and, later, the entire expansion of the white race that was fraught with so many contradictions and had so many tragic consequences, including the fact that most of the human world has been consigned to that wretched category known as the "Third World"? I still tend to think that His words belonged to the former category, but at the same time I cannot ignore the umpteen books that demonstrate that, even in its purest and earliest form,

there was something unconsciously encoded in Christianity which, when combined with a thousand and one other circumstances, including the relative permanence of human nature, could in some way pave the way spiritually, even for the sort of horrors I mentioned.

Words can have histories too. 28

There was a time, for instance, when, for whole generations of the down- 29
trodden and oppressed, the word socialism was a mesmerizing synonym for a just world, a time when, for the ideal expressed in that word, people were capable of sacrificing years and years of their lives, and their very lives even. I don't know about your country, but in mine, that particular word—"socialism"—was transformed long ago into just an ordinary truncheon used by certain cynical, parvenu bureaucrats to bludgeon their liberal-minded fellow citizens from morning until night, labeling them "enemies of socialism" and "antisocialist forces." It's a fact: in my country, for ages now, that word has been no more than an incantation that should be avoided if one does not wish to appear suspect. I was recently at an entirely spontaneous demonstration, not dissident-organized, protesting the sell-off of one of the most beautiful parts of Prague to some Australian millionaires. When one of the speakers there, loudly decrying the project, sought to bolster his appeal to the government by declaring that he was fighting for his home in the name of socialism, the crowd started to laugh. Not because they had anything against a just social order, but quite simply because they heard a word which has been incanted for years and years in every possible and impossible context by a regime that only knows how to manipulate and humiliate people.

What a weird fate can befall certain words! At one moment in history, coura- 30
geous, liberal-minded people can be thrown into prison because a particular word means something to them, and at another moment, people of the selfsame variety can be thrown into prison because that word has ceased to mean anything to them, because it has changed from a symbol of a better world into the mumbo jumbo of a doltish dictator.

No word—at least not in the rather metaphorical sense I am employing the 31
word "word" here—comprises only the meaning assigned to it by an etymological dictionary. The meaning of every word also reflects the person who utters it, the situation in which it is uttered, and the reason for its utterance. The selfsame word can, at one moment, radiate great hopes, at another, it can emit lethal rays. The selfsame word can be true at one moment and false the next, at one moment illuminating, at another, deceptive. On one occasion it can open up glorious horizons, on another, it can lay down the tracks to an entire archipelago of concentration camps. The selfsame word can at one time be the cornerstone of peace, while at another, machine-gun fire resounds in its every syllable.

Gorbachev wants to save socialism through the market economy and free 32
speech, while Li Peng protects socialism by massacring students, and Ceausescu by bulldozing his people.

What does that word actually mean on the lips of the one and the lips of the 33 other two? What is this mysterious thing that is being rescued in such disparate ways?

34   I referred to the French Revolution and that splendid declaration that accompanied it. That declaration was signed by a gentleman who was later among the first to be executed in the name of that superbly humane text. And hundreds and possibly thousands followed him. *Liberté, Egalité, Fraternité*— what superb words! And how terrifying their meaning can be. Freedom: the shirt unbuttoned before execution. Equality: the constant speed of the guillotine's fall on different necks. Fraternity: some dubious paradise ruled by a Supreme Being!

35   The world now reechoes to the wonderfully promising word "perestroika." We all believe that it harbors hopes for Europe and the whole world.

36   I am bound to admit, though, that I sometimes shudder at the thought that this word might become just one more incantation, and in the end turn into yet another truncheon for someone to beat us with. It is not my own country I am thinking of: when our rulers utter that word it means about the same as the word "our monarch" when uttered by the Good Soldier Svejk. No, what I have in mind is the fact that even the intrepid man who now sits in the Kremlin occasionally, and possibly only from despair, accuses striking workers, rebellious nations or national minorities, or holders of rather too unusual minority opinions, of "jeopardizing perestroika." I can understand his feelings. It is terribly difficult to fulfill the enormous task he has undertaken. It all hangs by the finest of threads and almost anything could break that thread. Then we would all fall into the abyss. But even so I cannot help wondering whether all this "new thinking"does not contain some disturbing relics of the old. Does it not contain some echoes of former stereotyped thinking and the *ancien régime*'s verbal rituals? Isn't the word perestroika starting to resemble the word socialism, particularly on the odd occasion when it is discreetly hurled at the very people who, for so long, were unjustly lambasted with the word socialism?

37   Your country made an enormous contribution to modern European history. I refer to the first wave of détente: the celebrated *"Ostpolitik."*

38   But even that word managed at times to be well and truly ambivalent. It signified, of course, the first glimmer of hope of a Europe without cold wars or iron curtains. At the same time—unhappily—there were also occasions when it signified the abandonment of freedom: the basic precondition for all real peace. I still vividly recall how, at the beginning of the Seventies, a number of my West German colleagues and friends avoided me for fear that contact with me—someone out of favor with the government here—might needlessly provoke that government and thereby jeopardize the fragile foundations of nascent détente. Naturally I am not mentioning it on account of myself personally, let alone out of any sort of self-pity. After all, even in those days it was rather I who pitied them, since it was not I but they who were voluntarily renouncing their freedom. I mention it only in order to demonstrate yet again from another angle how easy it is for a well-intentioned cause to be transformed into the

betrayal of its own good intentions—and yet again because of a word whose meaning does not seem to have been kept under adequate observation. Something like that can happen so easily that it almost takes you unawares: it happens inconspicuously, quietly, by stealth—and when at last you realize it, there is only one option left to you: belated astonishment.

However, that is precisely the fiendish way that words are capable of betraying us—unless we are constantly circumspect about their use. And frequently—alas—even a fairly minor and momentary lapse in this respect can have tragic and irreparable consequences, consequences far transcending the nonmaterial world of mere words and penetrating deep into a world that is all too material. *39*

I'm finally getting around to that beautiful word "peace." *40*

For forty years now I have read it on the front of every building and in every shop window in my country. For forty years, an allergy to that beautiful word has been engendered in me as in every one of my fellow citizens because I know what the word has meant here for the past forty years: ever mightier armies ostensibly to defend peace. *41*

In spite of that lengthy process of systematically divesting the word "peace" of all meaning—worse than that, investing it instead with quite the opposite meaning to that given in the dictionary—a number of Don Quixotes in Charter 77 and several of their younger colleagues in the Independent Peace Association have managed to rehabilitate the word and restore its original meaning. Naturally, though, they had to pay a price for their "semantic perestroika"— i.e., standing the word "peace" back on its feet again: almost all the youngsters who fronted the Independent Peace Association were obliged to spend a few months inside for their pains. It was worth it, though. One important word has been rescued from total debasement. And it is not just a question of saving a word, as I have been trying to explain throughout my speech. Something far more important is saved. *42*

The point is that all important events in the real word—whether admirable or monstrous—are always spearheaded in the realm of words. *43*

As I've already stated, my intention here today is not to convey to you the experience of one who has learned that words still count for something when you can still go to prison for them. My intention was to share with you another lesson that we in this corner of the world have learned about the importance of words. I am convinced it is a lesson which has universal application: namely, that it always pays to be suspicious of words and to be wary of them, and that we can never be too careful in this respect. *44*

There can be no doubt that distrust of words is less harmful than unwarranted trust in them. *45*

Besides, to distrust words, and indict them for the horrors that might slumber unobtrusively within them—isn't this, after all, the true vocation of the intellectual? I recall that André Glucksmann, the dear colleague who preceded me here today, once spoke in Prague about the need for intellectuals to emu- *46* late Cassandra: to listen carefully to the words of the powerful, to be watchful of them, to forewarn of their danger, and to proclaim their dire implications or the evil they might invoke.

47   There is something that should not escape our attention and it concerns the fact that for centuries we—the Germans and the Czechs—had all sorts of problems with living together in Central Europe. I cannot speak for you, but I think I can rightly say that as far as we Czechs are concerned, the age-old animosities, prejudices and passions, constantly fuelled and fanned in numerous ways over the centuries, have evaporated in the course of recent decades. And it is by no means coincidental that this has happened at a time when we have been saddled with a totalitarian regime. Thanks to this regime we have developed a profound distrust of all generalizations, ideological platitudes, clichés, slogans, intellectual stereotypes, and insidious appeals to various levels of our emotions, from the baser to the loftier. As a result, we are now largely immune to all hypnotic enticements, even of the traditionally persuasive national or nationalistic variety. The stifling pall of hollow words that have smothered us for so long has cultivated in us such a deep mistrust of the world of deceptive words that we are now better equipped than ever before to see the human world as it really is: a complex community of thousands of millions of unique, individual human beings in whom hundreds of beautiful characteristics are matched by hundreds of faults and negative tendencies. They must never be lumped together into homogeneous masses beneath a welter of hollow clichés and sterile words, and then en bloc—as "classes," "nations," or "political forces"—extolled or denounced, loved or hated, maligned or glorified.

48   This is just one small example of the good that can come from treating words with caution. I have chosen the example especially for the occasion, i.e., for the moment when a Czech has the honor to address an audience that is overwhelmingly German.

49   In the beginning of everything is the word.

50   It is a miracle to which we owe the fact that we are human.

51   But at the same time it is a pitfall and a test, a snare and a trial.

52   More so, perhaps, than it appears to you who have enormous freedom of speech, and might therefore assume that words are not so important.

53   They are.

54   They are important everywhere.

55   The selfsame word can be humble at one moment and arrogant the next. And a humble word can be transformed quite easily and imperceptibly into an arrogant one, whereas it is a very difficult and protracted process to transform an arrogant word into one that is humble. I tried to demonstrate this by referring to the fate of the word "peace" in my country.

56   As we approach the end of the second millennium, the world, and particularly Europe, finds itself at a peculiar crossroads. It is a long time since there were so many grounds for hoping that everything will turn out well. At the same time, there have never been so many reasons for us to fear that if everything went wrong the catastrophe would be final.

It is not hard to demonstrate that all the main threats confronting the world today, from atomic war and ecological disaster to social and civilizational catastrophe—by which I mean the widening gulf between rich and poor individuals and nations—have hidden within them just one root cause: the imperceptible transformation of what was originally a humble message into an arrogant one. *57*

Arrogantly, Man started to believe that, as the pinnacle and lord of creation, he had a total understanding of nature and could do what he liked with it. *58*

Arrogantly, he started to think that as the possessor of reason he was capable of understanding totally his own history and therefore of planning a life of happiness for all. This even gave him the right, in the name of an ostensibly better future for all—to which he had found the one and only key—to sweep from his path all those who did not fall for his plan. *59*

Arrogantly, he started to think that since he was capable of splitting the atom he was now so perfect that there was no longer any danger of nuclear arms rivalry, let alone nuclear war. *60*

In all those cases he was fatally mistaken. That is bad. But in each case he is already beginning to realize his mistake. And that is good. *61*

Having learned all those lessons, we should all fight together against arrogant words and keep a weather eye out for any insidious germs of arrogance in words that are seemingly humble. *62*

Obviously this is not just a linguistic task. Responsibility for and toward words is a task which is intrinsically ethical. *63*

As such, however, it is situated beyond the horizon of the visible world, in that realm wherein dwells the Word that was in the beginning and is not the word of Man. *64*

I won't explain why this is so. It has been explained far better than I ever could by your great forebear Immanuel Kant. *65*

WRITING AND DISCUSSION QUESTIONS

Informative

1. Summarize Havel's attitude toward the "realm of words," especially toward the dangers of "arrogant words" that are seemingly humble (4th from the last paragraph). What, in particular, does he say about the words of Walesa, Sakharov, Rushdie, and Khomeini? How do you think words can be both healing and inflaming?

2. Explain Havel's dual sense of the power of words, especially the words used by Lenin, Marx, and Freud. Why does he single out these thinkers? What does his recognition of the two-sided potential of their words suggest about the power of words to effect change in the world?

3. What is Havel's two-sided view of Christ's words? Which side does he favor? What does Havel mean when he says that Christ could pave the way to horrors as well as to an era of salvation?

4. Why does Havel have the same fears for the word ''perestroika'' (restructuring) as he does for ''socialism''?

Persuasive

1. Havel claims that arrogance is very much at the root of the worst threats confronting the world today. Argue in support of his contention by defining and then by providing examples of the results of arrogance.
2. Why are people so anxious to believe words and so hesitant to develop the kind of distrust Havel recommends? Argue that an intellectual like Havel is particularly well suited for political leadership, especially when one recognizes the importance of cultivating doubt over certainty and of preferring knowledge over ignorance?

Personal

1. What words have people in Western democracies become careless about? What ideals have turned to empty slogans?

CHAPTER WRITING ASSIGNMENTS

1. History seems to have shown that although Adam Smith and David Ricardo oversimplified the laws of economics there is a good bit of truth in what they said: free market economies have been the most successful. However, the development of the free market system, and even the definition of what constitutes a free market economy, has changed over the years. Indeed, today, most operate under controls that early in this century would have been considered Marxist. Marx, too, oversimplified the laws of economics in projecting the disappearance of capitalism and the emergence of a classless society, but much of what he said remains true, even in the face of recent changes in major socialist economies. Argue some variation on this thesis: modern economic and political history can be seen as the working out of a Marxian dialectic between a capitalist thesis and a Marxist antithesis; the result has been a synthesis that neither old style capitalists or Marxists anticipated.

2. Some economists today see even more truth in the classic economic theories, especially in Ricardo's Malthusianism. Only in the last third of this century has much of the world become aware that world population is increasing while resources are dwindling. We could well be moving toward a Malthusian world of bare subsistence for the vast majority. Do you think we will revert again to some of the abuses of nineteenth-century capitalism or of twentieth-century collectivism, or do you think we can solve such problems more equitably and humanely? Given the possibility of worldwide want, what values do you think will most sustain us, those

embodied in the Judeo–Christian, the humanistic, the Marxian, some other (for example, science), or some combination of traditions like Christian socialism?

3. Some people may argue that we are already in a Malthusian world. As citizens of one of the wealthiest nations, we are simply too far removed from world hunger to realize that we are a small minority, a privileged class. Because of our wealth, we have operated in a ''free'' world market with all sorts of advantages. Already, though, that seems to be changing. How do you think we will maintain our privileged status? Or if not, how are we likely to accommodate its loss?

4. According to *Forbes Magazine,* the number of billionaires in the United States has been nearly doubling on a yearly basis in recent years: 14 in 1985, 26 in 1986, 49 in 1987. This and the fact that during the 1980s the real median income of the top 40% of U.S. households has risen substantially while the real median income of the bottom 40% has fallen have suggested to many economists that the middle class is disappearing and we are moving toward a two-tiered society, as in many Third-World countries in which society comprises an affluent minority and a desperately poor majority. What signs, if any, do you see of this trend? Do you think it is a serious trend? If the trend should continue, do you think that some elements of Marxism will become appealing to Americans?

5. Marxism has always had the strongest appeal and has been most feared in noncommunist societies where class divisions have been the greatest— prerevolutionary Russia, China, and Cuba, for example, or many present underindustrialized countries. Do you think that the kind of revisions that socialist governments have undergone recently in Eastern Europe will substantially change that appeal? Is it possible to bring such societies to a state of more equitable distribution of wealth without some form of socialism?

6. Consider a particular terrorist movement as a test case. The traditional way of dealing with terrorism—even in Marxist societies—has been to increase security and to exterminate the terrorists. The ideal Marxian response, even though the terrorism itself may be a Marxist tactic, would be to discover the root cause of oppression that first inspired the terrorism and to eradicate that cause. In the case you have chosen, analyze which seems to be the most practical solution, both for the short and long term.

7. A major argument of the feminist movement has been the Marxian one that the traditional family is based on the exploitation of women. If true, can this situation be altered in ways other than Marx's prediction of the disappearance of the family as a social institution? Can the family be reaffirmed in ways that provide women full equality with men? How do economic factors affect these possibilities? For example, if economic changes are making it increasingly necessary for most families to have two primary wage earners to achieve or maintain their desired

standard of living, is it not true that an adjustment becomes necessary in the direction of equality in household and parental duties?

8. How do you think Marx's thought can be used today, if at all? Now that we seem to have less to fear from Marxism than we have at any time in the last century, can Marx's work be more intelligently explored and more fruitfully applied, or is it more likely to fade into obscurity?

Chapter Eight

FREUD AND STUDY OF THE MIND

Imagine trying to explain someone's behavior, perhaps even your own, without being able to use terms like inferiority complex, neurotic, overactive imagination, Freudian slip, psychosomatic, unconscious, psychoanalyze, defense mechanism, fixation, libidinous, and conditioned. These concepts, so much a part of our daily conversation and thinking, come from the field of psychology and from the scientific inquiry into the nature of the mind. Each in some way names and interprets an aspect of personality or behavior; that is, each explains the outward behavior of an individual by attempting to penetrate the "inner self." Our familiarity with and casual use of technical nomenclature like this demonstrates the impact psychology as a discipline has had on our culture.

Yet, as one psychologist has observed, psychology has a long past but a short history. That is to say, although humankind has always had an interest in exploring and altering human behavior and has discovered or invented various techniques to investigate and render explanations for the mind or "soul," it has only been in the past century or so (from about 1870) that there has existed a sustained, rigorous, scientific attempt at the study of the mind. We owe to modern psychology in large measure our understanding of—and, often, our basic belief in—the "self," the reality of the mind, the connection between thought and action and between one's self-image and one's external image. Arriving at a definition of psychology is difficult, and the definition will vary according to one's approach to the mind; a brief historical survey will illustrate the various approaches to psychology and provide a context for the readings that follow.

THE ORIGINS OF PSYCHOLOGY

Psychology as a distinct discipline separate from, say, philosophy, biology, or anthropology, is less than 100 years old. Nevertheless, most ancient cultures, including the Hebrews, Greeks, Chinese, and Native American Indians, had religious, philosophical, and mythological traditions that described and explained the human being—specificially, what constitutes the life force or "inner person" that directs the outer body. Within the Biblical tradition, for instance, the Hebrew worldview saw humankind—man or woman—as consisting of body and soul: the "outer shell," or body, was subject to decay and death, whereas the "inner self," or soul, was immutable and animated by the external. Likewise, early Christian teaching emphasized loving God with "heart, soul, and mind" (Matthew 22:37): the *heart* emphasizing our emotional nature, the *soul* our spiritual nature, and the *mind* our intellectual nature. Both the Hebrew Scriptures and the New Testament are firm in ascribing good or evil human behavior to the person's response to the law and will of God. Also, an individual's personality was interpreted in terms of the community's welfare. For instance, Godly character—rooted in eternal standards revealed by God's prophets and teachers—were believed to bring forth peace, justice, righteousness, and joy; by contrast, sinful acts, would bring ruin, inequality, strife, and hatred to a culture. As may be obvious, such judgments regarding human behavior result less from observation and hypothesis than from adherence to a code within an authoritative religious community.

The Greeks are foremost in the ancient Western world for their inquiry into the nature of behavior and for sophisticated speculation on the nature of mind and body. Plato (427–347 B.C.), in the *Republic*, gave great attention to individuality and its sources, musing about heredity and environment and their influence on human personality and destiny. In his other dialogues, particularly, the *Phaedrus* and the *Phaedo*, Plato took up the topics of the immortality of the soul, or *psyche*, and the problem of its unity, especially in relation to moral choice. Plato attempted to define the qualities in a man or woman that permitted or obstructed the pursuit of truth and beauty. Plato believed that the soul is immortal, that it gives the body purpose and direction, and that it is divided into three parts: reason, emotion, and appetite. In one of his examples to explain how these components function, a thirsty traveler happens upon an unsanitary well; his physical body urges a drink, his inner emotion stirs a strong desire to do so, but his overarching reason compels him to forego the drink to survive. For Plato, as with most ancient Greek philosophers, reason was considered superior to appetite or emotion. Also, Plato believed that only the indivisible could be eternal, and thus, he long wrestled with the philosophical problem of how the soul, being divisible, could also be immortal, a paradox he never quite resolved.

Plato's pupil, Aristotle (384–322 B.C.), was much more interested in what one would call the more practical issues of psychology: memory, intelligence, motivation, sleep and dreaming, and human development. His interests were many, and he wrote separate treatises on politics, rhetoric, poetics, logic, and mathematics. His chief contributions to ancient psychology may be located in his *De*

Anima ("On the Soul"), wherein he investigates the nature of the mind as a branch of biology; elsewhere, Aristotle similarly investigates the nature of perception. According to these studies, perception causes a physical change in the perceiver; to "see" a white flower means that the eye or some part of it becomes white itself; to taste a grape means that the tongue in some sense becomes grape-like. Like Plato, Aristotle believed in a soul-like entity that directs the body, but unlike Plato, he believed that the soul is a unified "I" in its perceptions. Aristotle's various works have had considerable influence through the ages in many disciplines. His contribution to psychology is the legacy of founding conclusions based on physical observation and inductive reasoning.

THE BIRTH OF MODERN PSYCHOLOGY

Throughout the Middle Ages, the religious viewpoints of the Judeo–Christian heritage and the philosophical traditions of Greek humanism informed scholarly opinion about human behavior and, thus, the study of the mind. By the sixteenth century, however, as suggested in Chapter 6, the authority of science as stemming from empirical observation began to affect every discipline, including the fledgling field of psychology, which would be housed for two centuries in the discipline of philosophy. Perhaps it is Francis Bacon (1561–1626) whom we should credit for laying the foundation of psychology in the post-Renaissance for his insistence on empirical inquiry into the influence of habit, education, correction, and other conditions on human behavior. A more obvious influence is certainly René Descartes (1596–1650), whose delineation of the mind–body problem has remained an active philosophical and psychological puzzle for subsequent scholars and researchers. Descartes' famous declaration, "I think, therefore I am," arose from his program to doubt everything except the inescapable fact of his own existence. His refusal to trust the information gathered by his imperfect senses and his rigorous evaluation of that sensory experience to corroborate "facts" or "feelings" were deliberate features of his method of inquiry. This skepticism ultimately led him to argue for a dualism of mind and body; the mind is filled with innate ideas, which are put there by God, and it has no physical component. It, therefore, has no direct contact with the external world but, nevertheless, appears to direct the physical body. Questions concerning the form or character of the "mind's" existence and the manner of its contact with the tangible world, and related questions, haunted the disciplines of philosophy, psychology, and theology throughout the seventeenth and eighteenth centuries.

Immanuel Kant (1724–1804) sought to clarify the issues in the Cartesian mind–body problem from the philosopher's perspective. He argued that the mind itself contains structures that help it assimilate and then to evaluate sensory experience, and that neither reason nor empirical inquiry alone can yield unassailable knowledge. Philosophers and scientists before Kant, including Aristotle and John Locke, had debated whether the mind is a passive receiver or creative projector of meaning and knowledge. Kant argued that the mind is both: in his "transcendental idealism," he argued that the mind while collecting sensory information acts in a passive role and while synthesizing this information acts in a creative role. He also declared that no object of inquiry, whether it is the "thing-in-itself" or the human mind, can ever be truthfully known by merely applying the scientific method, which, of course, must incorporate sensory data. Kant himself doubted that psychology would ever become a "science" because he believed that experimental evaluation of mental phenomena was not possible. Nevertheless, Kant's "philosophy of mind" indirectly helped to defuse some of the extremes of materialism that had dominated empirical science and to legitimize the view that the mind and its "mental states" are real entities that have an existence independent from the body and its organs.

From the standpoint of empirical science, the work of experimental physiologists in the nineteenth century made important discoveries about the brain and nervous system that yielded insights into the mind–body problem. Hermann von Helmholtz (1821–1894), a German physicist, measured the speed of the nerve impulse, offered a theory of color perception, and explained auditory discrimination between musical tones; whereas in France, Paul Broca (1824–1880) identified the portion of the brain that controls speech. Similarly, the German psychophysicist Gustav Fechner (1801–1887) quantified the intensity of stimulus and sensitivity, thereby establishing a physiological connection between mind and body. These advances established the climate for a more rigorous and focused inquiry into the relationships between behavior, mind, brain, and body and helped establish the field now known as psychology.

Historians of psychology generally credit Wilhelm Wundt (1832–1920) with establishing the discipline of modern psychology. Wundt opened the first laboratory dedicated to psychological inquiry, and his view that psychology was the study of immediate experience attracted widespread attention. Such study necessarily required the observation of experience, but because the only real witness to "psychological events" is the person herself, Wundt believed that the way to "get at" the mind is through introspection, or self-observation, using specially designed criteria to record, evaluate, and correlate these observations. Wundt believed that "thinking about one's own thoughts" would yield data as compelling as those derived from the experimental observation of nature. Wundt is responsible in large measure for the field of structuralist psychology, which reduces the discipline to three main tasks: the analysis of thought processes according to component parts, the analysis of the interconnection among these processes, and the analysis of the laws that govern these interconnections.

Although Wundt's structuralism dominated the early years of psychology, it was quickly surpassed in popularity by other "schools of psychology" that attempted to account for other, more problematic aspects of behavior. Associationist psychology, begun by the late-eighteenth-century psychologist David Hartley (1705–1757), attempted to account for the existence of "complex" ideas, for example, "loyalty," that cannot be reduced to mere appetite, innate ideas, or experience. Such a concept must come from the association of smaller, less complex ideas; thus, loyalty is seen as a combination or association of such ideas as the love for self, a trust in friendship, the hope for survival in remaining united, and so on. Ivan Pavlov (1849–1936), a Russian physiologist, extended this associative notion from ideas to stimulus–response. From his experiments on animals, he argued that human behavior can be influenced by certain stimuli, particularly reward and punishment. For instance, one behavior can be encouraged by the stimuli of reward, whereas another behavior can be discouraged by the stimuli of punishment. The contemporary school of behaviorist psychology, discussed below, has clear roots in the work of Pavlov.

Functionalist psychology is a distinctively American school of psychology, associated with the work of William James (1842–1910), who defined psychology in terms of an organism adapting to its environment. Influenced by the evolutionary biology of Charles Darwin, James and his followers emphasized the prospect of changing human behavior through adjustment and education, thus expanding psychology's research interests beyond the description of mental states to the determination of appropriate strategies for altering behavior. James' *Varieties of Religious Experience* examines the reports of individuals who claimed a belief in an "unseen order" and declares that beliefs that emanate from "the will to believe" are good if they fulfill the individual who possesses them and if he or she did not proselytize on their behalf. James, along with American educator John Dewey (1859–1942), thus helped create the philosophical basis for pragmatism, which posits that any sincerely held belief that somehow benefits the holder may be said to be "true." This truth is relative and not absolute and is part of the fabric of a pluralism that James deeply adhered to. "An unfinished universe" leaves open choices and advances for individuals that no rigid body of facts or codes of ethics could permit. His major work, *Principles of Psychology*, is still regarded by professional psychologists as a remarkable compendium of insights into psychological inquiry and the themes of individuality, choice, and purpose.

The name most often associated with the study of psychology, however, is that of the Viennese physician and psychologist, Sigmund Freud (1856–1939). In the minds of some, Freud *is* psychology, even though, historically speaking, he is simply the founder of psychoanalysis, which is one more school or method of psychological inquiry. Psychoanalysis is so entrenched in the popular mind as the central mode of psychological therapy and procedure that it is difficult to distinguish psychology as a discipline from Freud's single contribution. More will be said about Freud and his work in the introduction to his reading selection.

THE CONTEMPORARY STUDY OF THE MIND

Psychology is today a rich and diverse field of study that encompasses many kinds of cross-disciplinary inquiry, including such hybrid fields as psychobiology, psychogenetics, psychosociology, psycholinguistics, and psychohistory. The prefix *psycho*, used in each of these terms, indicates an emphasis on determining the "mental" sources of human behavior, often in a strictly neurological-oriented inquiry. That is to say, many contemporary theorists in psychology tend to explain how the mind works in terms of physiological mechanisms and how dysfunctions in behavior are caused by the organic breakdown of these mechanisms. In the midst of this flourishing of psychological inquiry, two schools of contemporary inquiry into the mind deserve special comment.

First, behaviorism as a school of psychology, which has its roots in the turn-of-the-century work of structuralists like Ivan Pavlov, has continued to hold a prominent place in modern psychology because of the prestige of its chief spokesman, B. F. Skinner (1904–1990). Skinner, like most behaviorists, does not find the hypothesis of "the mind" persuasive. He argues against the idea that there are mental states that can be accurately measured or profitably ascribed to "humanness"; rather, he prefers to locate psychology within the realm of describing overt behavior. To the behavioral psychologist, each individual's actions can be explained or described in terms of a complex set of stimuli and responses; there are no "thought processes" to account for the reasons a person behaves in a certain way. Instead, there can be only an account of those conditioning factors that have, in their reinforcement over time, brought the individual to the bundle of reactions that he comprises. Behaviorism is among the most-criticized forms of psychological study because it rejects most of the categories and moral frameworks traditionally used to define "human."

A second and most intriguing aspect of contemporary inquiry into the study of mind is the work in artificial intelligence (AI). This branch of study seeks to determine in what sense the mind is a "computer," whether computers "think," and the direction that analogies flow in designing computers to simulate human thinking, that is, whether the computer behaves like the mind or whether the mind behaves like the computer. Strictly speaking, AI is the science of creating machines to perform the functions of the human mind. Holding a conversation, answering questions, and discovering or reclassifying knowledge are some of the activities that AI scientists have pursued in their imaginative pursuit of "cloning" the human mind. However, AI is not the study of computers or robots, but of human intelligence—its components, strategies for learning, and modes of contemplation and discovery. AI is concerned, then, with human thinking in general, with perception, and with information gathering. Is there something called "creativity" that can be located in the brain—something that can be stimulated or simulated in others or in machines? What is the nature of "tacit" knowledge, that is, knowledge that human beings can use but not articulate? How does the mind as an entity "speak to" the body? These are all questions traditional to the field of psychology that have been in large part subsumed by AI research in the past 30 years.

The distinctive contribution of AI inquiry into these kinds of questions is its emphasis on the use of models and analogies to illuminate the way the mind works. Some of the practical byproducts of such research have been the "word processor" that allows the composition of texts, speech synthesis and recognition that allows machines to "talk," and medical diagnostic equipment that uses spectroscopy to identify dysfunctions in the body. The social and religious implications of AI are as wide ranging as they are for psychology. Inevitably, what is regarded as uniquely human or prohibitively "male" or "female" traits are challenged by data and applications of AI.

In the readings that follow, arranged chronologically, the impact of psychology and its methods is traced from the time of Freud to the present. Each selection, as have the selections in previous chapters, indicates the shifting and often surprising conceptions of humankind within a particular sphere of inquiry. Psychologists no more have the final truth on what it means to be human than do the philosophers, theologians, physical and political scientists, and others. They do have, in good measure, the aura of a "special insight" that accompanies any field with a vocabulary and methodolgy not easily explained or paraphrasable.

▼

SIGMUND FREUD, FROM *THE INTERPRETATION OF DREAMS*

No brief summary can do justice to the broad scope of practice and theory that Sigmund Freud's (1856–1939) psychoanalysis represents to the study of the mind and the field of psychology. Simply put, psychoanalysis postulates the existence of an unconscious mind that influences the way an individual behaves. By using various techniques, the psychoanalyst attempts to identify the past events, usually from childhood, that may unlock the key to the patient's present behavior. The psychiatrist's "couch," the techniques of hypnosis and free association, the trek into a patient's past to uncover the hidden traumas of childhood are the staples of psychoanalysis and, because so well known, are now stereotypical of therapists generically labeled "Freudian." These stereotypes belie, however, the extraordinary impact Freud's work has had not only on the medical and academic study of the mind, but also on philosophy, politics, linguistics, anthropology, and literature. Freud has played a very prominent role in shaping Western culture in this century, even if his specific therapy strategies and general notions of the way the mind works have been more or less eclipsed by later associates and modern researchers and theorists in this field.

From Freud, we have the vocabulary of "id," "ego," and "superego," "the unconscious," and many other standard psychological terms that are now used daily to account for behavior. In many ways, Freud's work represents less a theory of the mind than a theory of personality: how individuals are shaped by the events of their lives, especially during childhood; by relations with father, mother, siblings, friends, and acquaintances; by what others have done "to" and "about" them; and by how "repression" of these experiences has led to problems and weaknesses in the personality. Some critics argue that there is a tendency toward determinism in Freudian psychology, that is, toward the belief that an individual's choices and self-image are "fixed" so thoroughly by past events that the prospect of change is accompanied by a long, arduous path of deeper and deeper probes into childhood and adolescent behavior. Freud, early in his career, used hypnosis as a means to uncover these past events, but he soon abandoned it in favor of free association, in which a patient responds spontaneously to words or ideas provided by the therapist. In an early work, *Studies on Hysteria* (1895), Freud posited that many of his patients' maladjustments were based on their suppression of hatred for one or more parents. Also, in some cases, Freud opined that the Oedipus or Electra complex was at work, that is, the sexual desire by the son or daughter for the parent of the opposite sex and the bitter rivalry toward the parent of the same sex.

In his later work, often considered his most important contribution and the chief document in the history of psychoanalysis, *The Interpretation of Dreams* (1899), Freud argued that dreams represent a kind of fulfillment of unconscious desires, or wish fulfillment, and that other neuroses or mental problems could be attributed to the repression of such desires, especially sexual ones. It should be noted that, by his own admission, Freud was hostile to religion, specifically the Judeo–Christian heritage and its notion of "Father–God"; Freud argued that one's belief in an all-powerful deity derives solely from one's childhood impression of a father who was an all-powerful family head. In *The Future of an Illusion* (1927), Freud argued that no adult should "remain a child forever" in pursuing a faith that requires absolute obedience to a deity, especially one, he argued, that is absent. Freud categorized religious belief and behavior predicated on that belief as simply a regression to childish desires for security and the sublimation of sexual or aggressive drives. Presently, Freud's work has been refined and restated in ways that he perhaps would not recognize; yet Freud has not lost his relevance, for other branches of psychology, both practice and theory, continue to be built upon his original inquiry into the nature of mind and behavior.

In *The Interpretation of Dreams*, Freud, using his own dream and its interpretation, offers an early statement of the nature of dreams and their connection to the conscious mind and its apparent desire for what Freud labeled "wish fulfillment."

▼

from *The Interpretation of Dreams*
SIGMUND FREUD

PREAMBLE

1   During the summer of 1895 I had been giving psycho-analytic treatment to a young lady who was on very friendly terms with me and my family. It will be readily understood that a mixed relationship such as this may be a source of many disturbed feelings in a physician and particularly in a psychotherapist. While the physician's personal interest is greater, his authority is less; any failure would bring a threat to the old-established friendship with the patient's family. This treatment had ended in a partial success; the patient was relieved of her hysterical anxiety but did not lose all her somatic symptoms. At that time I was not yet quite clear in my mind as to the criteria indicating that a hysterical case history was finally closed, and I proposed a solution to the patient which she seemed unwilling to accept. While we were thus at variance, we had broken off the treatment for the summer vacation.—One day I had a visit from a junior colleague, one of my oldest friends, who had been staying

with my patient, Irma, and her family at their country resort. I asked him how he had found her and he answered: 'She's better, but not quite well.' I was conscious that my friend Otto's words, or the tone in which he spoke them, annoyed me. I fancied I detected a reproof in them, such as to the effect that I had promised the patient too much; and, whether rightly or wrongly, I attributed the supposed fact of Otto's siding against me to the influence of my patient's relatives, who, as it seemed to me, had never looked with favour on the treatment. However, my disagreeable impression was not clear to me and I gave no outward sign of it. The same evening I wrote out Irma's case history, with the idea of giving it to Dr. M. (a common friend who was at that time the leading figure in our circle) in order to justify myself. That night (or more probably the next morning) I had the following dream, which I noted down immediately after waking.[1]

DREAM OF JULY 23RD–24TH, 1895

A large hall—numerous guests, whom we were receiving.—Among them was Irma. I at once took her on one side, as though to answer her letter and to reproach her for not having accepted my 'solution' yet. I said to her: 'If you still get pains, it's really only your fault.' She replied: 'If you only knew what pains I've got now in my throat and stomach and abdomen—it's choking me'—I was alarmed and looked at her. She looked pale and puffy. I thought to myself that after all I must be missing some organic trouble. I took her to the window and looked down her throat, and she showed signs of recalcitrance, like women with artificial dentures. I thought to myself that there was really no need for her to do that.—She then opened her mouth properly and on the right I found a big white patch; at another place I saw extensive whitish grey scabs upon some remarkable curly structures which were evidently modelled on the turbinal bones of the nose.—I at once called in Dr. M., and he repeated the examination and confirmed it. . . . Dr. M. looked quite different from usual; he was very pale, he walked with a limp and his chin was clean-shaven. . . . My friend Otto was now standing beside her as well, and my friend Leopold was percussing her through her bodice and saying: 'She has a dull area low down on the left.' He also indicated that a portion of the skin on the left shoulder was infiltrated. (I noticed this, just as he did, in spite of her dress.) . . . M. said: 'There's no doubt it's an infection, but no matter; dysentery will supervene and the toxin will be eliminated.' . . . We were directly aware, too, of the origin of the infection. Not long before, when she was feeling unwell, my friend Otto had given her an injection of a preparation of propyl, propyls . . . propionic acid . . . trimethylamin (and I saw before me the formula for this printed in heavy type). . . . Injections of that sort ought not to be made so thoughtlessly. . . . And probably the syringe had not been clean.

2

---

[1][*Footnote added* 1914:] This is the first dream which I submitted to a detailed interpretation.

3   This dream has one advantage over many others. It was immediately clear what events of the previous day provided its starting-point. My preamble makes that plain. The news which Otto had given me of Irma's condition and the case history which I had been engaged in writing till far into the night continued to occupy my mental activity even after I was asleep. Nevertheless, no one who had only read the preamble and the content of the dream itself could have the slightest notion of what the dream meant. I myself had no notion. I was astonished at the symptoms of which Irma complained to me in the dream, since they were not the same as those for which I had treated her. I smiled at the senseless idea of an injection of propionic acid and at Dr. M.'s consoling reflections. Towards its end the dream seemed to me to be more obscure and compressed than it was at the beginning. In order to discover the meaning of all this it was necessary to undertake a detailed analysis.

ANALYSIS

4   *The hall—numerous guests, whom we were receiving.* We were spending that summer at Bellevue, a house standing by itself on one of the hills adjoining the Kahlenberg.[2] The house had formerly been designed as a place of entertainment and its reception-rooms were in consequence unusually lofty and hall-like. It was at Bellevue that I had the dream, a few days before my wife's birthday. On the previous day my wife had told me that she expected that a number of friends, including Irma, would be coming out to visit us on her birthday. My dream was thus anticipating this occasion: it was my wife's birthday and a number of guests, including Irma, were being received by us in the large hall at Bellevue.

5   *I reproached Irma for not having accepted my solution; I said: 'If you still get pains, it's your own fault.'* I might have said this to her in waking life, and I may actually have done so. It was my view at that time (though I have since recognized it as a wrong one) that my task was fulfilled when I had informed a patient of the hidden meaning of his symptoms: I considered that I was not responsible for whether he accepted the solution or not—though this was what success depended on. I owe it to this mistake, which I have now fortunately corrected, that my life was made easier at a time when, in spite of all my inevitable ignorance, I was expected to produce therapeutic successes.—I noticed, however, that the words which I spoke to Irma in the dream showed that I was specially anxious not to be responsible for the pains which she still had. If they were her fault they could not be mine. Could it be that the purpose of the dream lay in this direction?

6   *Irma's complaint: pains in her throat and abdomen and stomach; it was choking her.* Pains in the stomach were among my patient's symptoms but were not very prominent; she complained more of feelings of nausea and disgust.

[2][A hill which is a favourite resort in the immediate neighborhood of Vienna.]

Pains in the throat and abdomen and constriction of the throat played scarcely any part in her illness. I wondered why I decided upon this choice of symptoms in the dream but could not think of an explanation at the moment.

She looked pale and puffy. My patient always had a rosy complexion. I   7
began to suspect that someone else was being substituted for her.

I was alarmed at the idea that I had missed an organic illness. This, as may   8
well be believed, is a perpetual source of anxiety to a specialist whose practice is almost limited to neurotic patients and who is in the habit of attributing to hysteria a great number of symptoms which other physicians treat as organic. On the other hand, a faint doubt crept into my mind—from where, I could not tell—that my alarm was not entirely genuine. If Irma's pains had an organic basis, once again I could not be held responsible for curing them; my treatment only set out to get rid of *hysterical* pains. It occurred to me, in fact, that I was actually *wishing* that there had been a wrong diagnosis; for, if so, the blame for my lack of success would also have been got rid of.

I took her to the window to look down her throat. She showed some recalci-   9
trance, like women with false teeth. I thought to myself that really there was no need for her to do that. I had never had any occasion to examine Irma's oral cavity. What happened in the dream reminded me of an examination I had carried out some time before of a governess: at a first glance she had seemed a picture of youthful beauty, but when it came to opening her mouth she had taken measures to conceal her plates. This led to recollections of other medical examinations and of little secrets revealed in the course of them—to the satisfaction of neither party. *'There was really no need for her to do that'* was no doubt intended in the first place as a compliment to Irma; but I suspected that it had another meaning besides. (If one carries out an analysis attentively, one gets a feeling of whether or not one has exhausted all the background thoughts that are to be expected.) The way in which Irma stood by the window suddenly reminded me of another experience. Irma had an intimate woman friend of whom I had a very high opinion. When I visited this lady one evening I had found her by a window in the situation reproduced in the dream, and her physician, the same Dr. M., had pronounced that she had a diphtheritic membrane. The figure of Dr. M. and the membrane reappear later in the dream. It now occurred to me that for the last few months I had had every reason to suppose that this other lady was also a hysteric. Indeed, Irma herself had betrayed the fact to me. What did I know of her condition? One thing precisely: that, like my Irma of the dream, she suffered from hysterical choking. So in the dream I had replaced my patient by her friend. I now recollected that I had often played with the idea that she too might ask me to relieve her of her symptoms. I myself, however, had thought this unlikely, since she was of a very reserved nature. She was *recalcitrant,* as was shown in the dream. Another reason was that *there was no need for her to do it:* she had so far shown herself strong enough to master her condition without outside help. There still remained a few features that I could not attach either to Irma or to her friend: *pale; puffy; false teeth.* The false teeth took me to the governess whom I have already men-

tioned; I now felt inclined to be satisfied with *bad* teeth. I then thought of someone else to whom these features might be alluding. She again was not one of my patients, nor should I have liked to have her as a patient, since I had noticed that she was bashful in my presence and I could not think she would make an amenable patient. She was usually pale, and once, while she had been in specially good health, she had looked puffy.[3] Thus I had been comparing my patient Irma with two other people who would also have been recalcitrant to treatment. What could the reason have been for my having exchanged her in the dream for her friend? Perhaps it was that I should have *liked* to exchange her: either I felt more sympathetic towards her friend or had a higher opinion of her intelligence. For Irma seemed to me foolish because she had not accepted my solution. Her friend would have been wiser, that is to say she would have yielded sooner. She would then have *opened her mouth properly,* and have told me more than Irma.[4]

10   *What I saw in her throat: a white patch and turbinal bones with scabs on them.* The white patch reminded me of diphtheritis and so of Irma's friend, but also of a serious illness of my eldest daughter's almost two years earlier and of the fright I had had in those anxious days. The scabs on the turbinal bones recalled a worry about my own state of health. I was making frequent use of cocaine at that time to reduce some troublesome nasal swellings, and I had heard a few days earlier that one of my women patients who had followed my example had developed an extensive necrosis of the nasal mucous membrane. I had been the first to recommend the use of cocaine, in 1885,[5] and this recommendation had brought serious reproaches down on me. The misuse of that drug had hastened the death of a dear friend of mine. This had been before 1895 [the date of the dream].

11   *I at once called in Dr. M., and he repeated the examination.* This simply corresponded to the position occupied by M. in our cicle. But the '*at once*' was sufficiently striking to require a special explanation. It reminded me of a tragic event in my practice. I had on one occasion produced a severe toxic state in a woman patient by repeatedly prescribing what was at that time regarded as a harmless remedy (sulphonal), and had hurriedly turned for assistance and support to my experienced senior colleague. There was a subsidiary detail which confirmed the idea that I had this incident in mind. My patient—who succumbed to the poison—had the same name as my eldest daughter. It had never occurred to me before, but it struck me now almost like an act of retri-

---

[3] The still-unexplained complaints about *pains in the abdomen* could also be traced back to this third figure. The person in question was, of course, my own wife; the pains in the abdomen reminded me of one of the occasions on which I had noticed her bashfulness. I was forced to admit to myself that I was not treating either Irma or my wife very kindly in this dream; but it should be observed by way of excuse that I was measuring them both by the standard of the good and amenable patient.

[4] I had a feeling that the interpretation of this part of the dream was not carried far enough to make it possible to follow the whole of its concealed meaning. If I had pursued my comparison between the three women, it would have taken me far afield.—There is at least one spot in every dream at which it is unplumbable—a navel, as it were, that is its point of contact with the unknown.

[5] [This is a misprint . . . for '1884', the date of Freud's first paper on cocaine.]

bution on the part of destiny. It was as though the replacement of one person by another was to be continued in another sense: this Mathilde for that Mathilde, an eye for an eye and a tooth for a tooth. It seemed as if I had been collecting all the occasions which I could bring up against myself as evidence of lack of medical conscientiousness.

Dr. M. was pale, had a clean-shaven chin and walked with a limp. This was   12
true to the extent that his unhealthy appearance often caused his friends anxiety. The two other features could only apply to someone else. I thought of my elder brother, who lives abroad, who is clean-shaven and whom, if I remembered right, the M. of the dream closely resembled. We had had news a few days earlier that he was walking with a limp owing to an arthritic affection of his hip. There must, I reflected, have been some reason for my fusing into one the two figures in the dream. I then remembered that I had a similar reason for being in an ill-humour with each of them: they had both rejected a certain suggestion I had recently laid before them.

My friend Otto was now standing beside the patient and my friend Leopold   13
was examining her and indicated that there was a dull area low down on the
left. My friend Leopold was also a physician and a relative of Otto's. Since they both specialized in the same branch of medicine, it was their fate to be in competition with each other, and comparisons were constantly being drawn between them. Both of them acted as my assistants for years while I was still in charge of the neurological outpatients' department of a children's hospital. Scenes such as the one represented in the dream used often to occur there. While I was discussing the diagnosis of a case with Otto, Leopold would be examining the child once more and would make an unexpected contribution to our decision. The difference between their characters was like that between the bailiff Bräsig and his friend Karl:[6] one was distinguished for his quickness, while the other was slow but sure. If in the dream I was contrasting Otto with the prudent Leopold, I was evidently doing so to the advantage of the latter. The comparison was similar to the one between my disobedient patient Irma and the friend whom I regarded as wiser than she was. I now perceived another of the lines along which the chain of thought in the dream branched off: from the sick child to the children's hospital.—*The dull area low down on the left* seemed to me to agree in every detail with one particular case in which Leopold had struck me by his thoroughness. I also had a vague notion of something in the nature of a metastatic affection; but this may also have been a reference to the patient whom I should have liked to have in the place of Irma. So far as I had been able to judge, she had produced an imitation of a tuberculosis.

A portion of the skin on the left shoulder was infiltrated. I saw at once that   14
this was the rheumatism in my own shoulder, which I invariably notice if I sit up late into the night. Moreover the wording in the dream was most ambiguous: *'I noticed this, just as he did. . . .'* I noticed it in my own body, that is. I was

---

[6][The two chief figures in the once popular novel, *Ut mine Stromtid*, written in Mecklenburg dialect, by Fritz Reuter (1862–64.) There is an English translation, *An Old Story of my Farming Days* (London, 1878).]

struck, too, by the unusual phrasing: 'a portion of the skin was infiltrated'. We are in the habit of speaking of 'a left upper posterior infiltration', and this would refer to the lung and so once more to tuberculosis.

15   *In spite of her dress.* This was in any case only an interpolation. We naturally used to examine the children in the hospital undressed: and this would be a contrast to the manner in which adult female patients have to be examined. I remember that it was said of a celebrated clinician that he never made a physical examination of his patients except through their clothes. Further than this I could not see. Frankly, I had no desire to penetrate more deeply at this point.

16   *Dr. M. said: 'It's an infection, but no matter. Dysentery will supervene and the toxin will be eliminated.'* At first this struck me as ridiculous. But nevertheless, like all the rest, it had to be carefully analysed. When I came to look at it more closely it seemed to have some sort of meaning all the same. What I discovered in the patient was a local diphtheritis. I remembered from the time of my daughter's illness a discussion on diphtheritis and diphtheria, the latter being the general infection that arises from the local diphtheritis. Leopold indicated the presence of a general infection of this kind from the existence of a dull area, which might thus be regarded as a metastatic focus. I seemed to think, it is true, that metastases like this do not in fact occur with diphtheria: it made me think rather of pyaemia.

17   *No matter.* This was intended as a consolation. It seemed to fit into the context as follows. The content of the preceding part of the dream had been that my patient's pains were due to a severe organic affection. I had a feeling that I was only trying in that way to shift the blame from myself. Psychological treatment could not be held responsible for the persistence of diphtheritic pains. Nevertheless I had a sense of awkwardness at having invented such a severe illness for Irma simply in order to clear myself. It looked so cruel. Thus I was in need of an assurance that all would be well in the end, and it seemed to me that to have put the consolation into the mouth precisely of Dr. M. had not been a bad choice. But here I was taking up a superior attitude towards the dream, and this itself required explanation.

18   And why was the consolation so nonsensical?

19   *Dysentery.* There seemed to be some remote theoretical notion that morbid matter can be eliminated through the bowels. Could it be that I was trying to make fun of Dr. M.'s fertility in producing far-fetched explanations and making unexpected pathological connections? Something else now occurred to me in relation to dysentery. A few months earlier I had taken on the case of a young man with remarkable difficulties associated with defaecating, who had been treated by other physicians as a case of 'anaemia accompanied by malnutrition'. I had recognized it as a hysteria, but had been unwilling to try him with my psychotherapeutic treatment and had sent him on a sea voyage. Some days before, I had had a despairing letter from him from Egypt, saying that he had had a fresh attack there which a doctor had declared was dysentery. I suspected that the diagnosis was an error on the part of an ignorant practitioner who had allowed himself to be taken in by the hysteria. But I could not help

reproaching myself for having put my patient in a situation in which he might have contracted some organic trouble on top of his hysterical intestinal disorder. Moreover, 'dysentery' sounds not unlike 'diphtheria'—a word of ill omen which did not occur in the dream.[7]

Yes, I thought to myself, I must have been making fun of Dr. M. with the *20*
consoling prognosis 'Dysentery will supervene, etc.': for it came back to me that, years before, he himself had told an amusing story of a similar kind about another doctor. Dr. M. had been called in by him for consultation over a patient who was seriously ill, and had felt obliged to point out, in view of the very optimistic view taken by his colleague, that he had found albumen in the patient's urine. The other, however, was not in the least put out: 'No matter', he had said, 'the albumen will soon be eliminated!'—I could no longer feel any doubt, therefore, that this part of the dream was expressing derision at physicians who are ignorant of hysteria. And, as though to confirm this, a further idea crossed my mind: 'Does Dr. M. realize that the symptoms in his patient (Irma's friend) which give grounds for fearing tuberculosis also have a hysterical basis? Has he spotted this hysteria? or has he been taken in by it?'

But what could be my motive for treating this friend of mine so badly? That *21*
was a very simple matter. Dr. M. was just as little in agreement with my 'solution' as Irma herself. So I had already revenged myself in this dream on two people: on Irma with the words 'If you still get pains, it's your own fault', and on Dr. M. by the wording of the nonsensical consolation that I put into his mouth.

We were directly aware of the origin of the infection. This direct knowledge *22*
in the dream was remarkable. Only just before we had had no knowledge of it, for the infection was only revealed by Leopold.

When she was feeling unwell, my friend Otto had given her an injection. Otto *23*
had in fact told me that during his short stay with Irma's family he had been called in to a neighbouring hotel to give an injection to someone who had suddenly felt unwell. These injections reminded me once more of my unfortunate friend who had poisoned himself with cocaine. I had advised him to use the drug internally [i.e., orally] only, while morphia was being withdrawn; but he had at once given himself cocaine *injections*.

A preparation of propyl . . . propyls . . . propionic acid. How could I have *24*
come to think of this? During the previous evening, before I wrote out the case history and had the dream, my wife had opened a bottle of liqueur, on which the word 'Ananas'[8] appeared and which was a gift from our friend Otto: for he had a habit of making presents on every possible occasion. It was to be hoped, I thought to myself, that some day he would find a wife to cure him of the habit. This liqueur gave off such a strong smell of fusel oil that I refused to touch it. My wife suggested our giving the bottle to the servants, but I—with

---

[7][The German words *'Dysenterie'* and *'Dyphtherie'* are more alike than the English ones.]

[8]I must add that the sound of the word 'Ananas' bears a remarkable resemblance to that of my patient Irma's family name.

even greater prudence—vetoed the suggestion, adding in a philanthropic spirit that there was no need for *them* to be poisoned either. The smell of fusel oil (amyl . . .) evidently stirred up in my mind a recollection of the whole series— propyl, methyl, and so on—and this accounted for the propyl preparation in the dream. It is true that I carried out a substitution in the process: I dreamt of propyl after having smelt amyl. But substitutions of this kind are perhaps legitimate in organic chemistry.

25   *Trimethylamin.* I saw the chemical formula of this substance in my dream, which bears witness to a great effort on the part of my memory. Moreover, the formula was printed in heavy type, as though there had been a desire to lay emphasis on some part of the context as being of quite special importance. What was it, then, to which my attention was to be directed in this way by trimethylamin? It was to a conversation with another friend who had for many years been familiar with all my writings during the period of their gestation, just as I had been with his.[9] He had at that time confided some ideas to me on the subject of the chemistry of the sexual processes, and had mentioned among other things that he believed that one of the products of sexual metabolism was trimethylamin. Thus this substance led me to sexuality, the factor to which I attributed the greatest importance in the origin of the nervous disorders which it was my aim to cure. My patient Irma was a young widow; if I wanted to find an excuse for the failure of my treatment in her case, what I could best appeal to would no doubt be this fact of her widowhood, which her friends would be glad to see changed. And how strangely, I thought to myself, a dream like this is put together! The other woman, whom I had as a patient in the dream instead of Irma, was also a young widow.

26   I began to guess why the formula for trimethylamin had been so prominent in the dream. So many important subjects converged upon that one word. Trimethylamin was an allusion not only to the immensely powerful factor of sexuality, but also to a person whose agreement I recalled with satisfaction whenever I felt isolated in my opinions. Surely this friend who played so large a part in my life must appear again elsewhere in these trains of thought. Yes. For he had a special knowledge of the consequences of affections of the nose and its accessory cavities; and he had drawn scientific attention to some very remarkable connections between the turbinal bones and the female organs of sex (Cf. the three curly structures in Irma's throat.) I had had Irma examined by him to see whether her gastric pains might be of nasal origin. But he suffered himself from suppurative rhinitis, which caused me anxiety; and no doubt there was an allusion to this in the pyaemia which vaguely came into my mind in connection with the metastases in the dream.

[9](This, as the editors correctly point out, was Wilhelm Fliess. In fact, Fliess played a far larger part in the making of this dream than either Freud, or his editors, acknowledge. Shortly before Freud dreamt this dream, Fliess had been involved in an appalling piece of malpractice: operating on the nose of one of Freud's patients, he had left a piece of gauze in her nose and nearly killed her. One motive for this famous dream was the exculpation not just of himself, but of Fliess. (For details, see Peter Gay, *Freud*, pp. 83–87.)}.

Injections of that sort ought not to be made so thoughtlessly. Here an accusa-　*27*
tion of thoughtlessness was being made directly against my friend Otto. I
seemed to remember thinking something of the same kind that afternoon when
his words and looks had appeared to show that he was siding against me. It had
been some such notion as: 'How easily his thoughts are influenced! How
thoughtlessly he jumps to conclusions!'—Apart from this, this sentence in the
dream reminded me once more of my dead friend who had so hastily resorted
to cocaine injections. As I have said, I had never contemplated the drug being
given by injection. I noticed too that in accusing Otto of thoughtlessness in handling chemical substances I was once more touching upon the story of the
unfortunate Mathilde, which gave grounds for the same accusation against
myself. Here I was evidently collecting instances of my conscientiousness, but
also of the reverse.

And probably the syringe had not been clean. This was yet another accusa-　*28*
tion against Otto, but derived from a different source. I had happened the day
before to meet the son of an old lady of eighty-two, to whom I had to give an
injection of morphia twice a day. At the moment she was in the country and he
told me that she was suffering from phlebitis. I had at once thought it must be
an infiltration caused by a dirty syringe. I was proud of the fact that in two
years I had not caused a single infiltration; I took constant pains to be sure that
the syringe was clean. In short, I was conscientious. The phlebitis brought me
back once more to my wife, who had suffered from thrombosis during one of
her pregnancies; and now three similar situations came to my recollection
involving my wife, Irma and the dead Mathilde. The identity of these situations
had evidently enabled me to substitute the three figures for one another in the
dream.

I have now completed the interpretation of the dream.[10] While I was carry-　*29*
ing it out I had some difficulty in keeping at bay all the ideas which were
bound to be provoked by a comparison between the content of the dream and
the concealed thoughts lying behind it. And in the meantime the 'meaning' of
the dream was borne in upon me. I became aware of an intention which was
carried into effect by the dream and which must have been my motive for
dreaming it. The dream fulfilled certain wishes which were started in me by the
events of the previous evening (the news given me by Otto and my writing out
of the case history). The conclusion of the dream, that is to say, was that I was
not responsible for the persistence of Irma's pains, but that Otto was. Otto had
in fact annoyed me by his remarks about Irma's incomplete cure, and the
dream gave me my revenge by throwing the reproach back on to him. The
dream acquitted me of the responsibility for Irma's condition by showing that it
was due to other factors—it produced a whole series of reasons. The dream

[10][*Footnote added* 1909:] Though it will be understood that I have not reported everything that occurred
to me during the process of interpretation. {As some of Freud's most alert early readers, like Karl Abraham
and Carl G. Jung, noted, he had silently passed over all the sexual elements in this dream interpretation.}

represented a particular state of affairs as I should have wished it to be. *Thus its content was the fulfilment of a wish and its motive was a wish.*

30   Thus much leapt to the eyes. But many of the details of the dream also became intelligible to me from the point of view of wish-fulfilment. Not only did I revenge myself on Otto for being too hasty in taking sides against me by representing him as being too hasty in his medical treatment (in giving the injection); but I also revenged myself on him for giving me the bad liqueur which had an aroma of fusel oil. And in the dream I found an expression which united the two reproaches: the injection was of a preparation of propyl. This did not satisfy me and I pursued my revenge further by contrasting him with his more trustworthy competitor. I seemed to be saying: 'I like *him* better than *you*.' But Otto was not the only person to suffer from the vials of my wrath. I took revenge as well on my disobedient patient by exchanging her for one who was wiser and less recalcitrant. Nor did I allow Dr. M. to escape the consequences of his contradiction but showed him by means of a clear allusion that he was an ignoramus on the subject. ('*Dysentery will supervene*, etc.') Indeed I seemed to be appealing from him to someone else with greater knowledge (to my friend who had told me of trimethylamin) just as I had turned from Irma to her friend and from Otto to Leopold. 'Take these people away! Give me three others of my choice instead! Then I shall be free of these undeserved reproaches!' The groundlessness of the reproaches was proved for me in the dream in the most elaborate fashion. *I* was not to blame for Irma's pains, since she herself was to blame for them by refusing to accept my solution. *I* was not concerned with Irma's pains, since they were of an organic nature and quite incurable by psychological treatment. Irma's pains could be satisfactorily explained by her widowhood (cf. the trimethylamin) which *I* had no means of altering. Irma's pains had been caused by Otto giving her an incautious injection of an unsuitable drug—a thing *I* should never have done. Irma's pains were the result of an injection with a dirty needle, like my old lady's phlebitis—whereas *I* never did any harm with my injections. I noticed, it is true, that these explanations of Irma's pains (which agreed in exculpating me) were not entirely consistent with one another, and indeed that they were mutually exclusive. The whole plea—for the dream was nothing else—reminded one vividly of the defence put forward by the man who was charged by one of his neighbours with having given him back a borrowed kettle in a damaged condition. The defendant asserted first, that he had given it back undamaged; secondly, that the kettle had a hole in it when he borrowed it; and thirdly, that he had never borrowed a kettle from his neighbour at all. So much the better: if only a single one of these three lines of defence were to be accepted as valid, the man would have to be acquitted.

31   Certain other themes played a part in the dream, which were not so obviously connected with my exculpation from Irma's illness: my daughter's illness and that of my patient who bore the same name, the injurious effect of cocaine, the disorder of my patient who was travelling in Egypt, my concern about my wife's health and about that of my brother and of Dr. M., my own physical ail-

ments, my anxiety about my absent friend who suffered from suppurative rhinitis. But when I came to consider all of these, they could all be collected into a single group of ideas and labelled, as it were, 'concern about my own and other people's health—professional conscientiousness'. I called to mind the obscure disagreeable impression I had had when Otto brought me the news of Irma's condition. This group of thoughts that played a part in the dream enabled me retrospectively to put this transient impression into words. It was as though he had said to me: 'You don't take your medical duties seriously enough. You're not conscientious; you don't carry out what you've undertaken.' Thereupon, this group of thoughts seemed to have put itself at my disposal, so that I could produce evidence of how highly conscientious I was, of how deeply I was concerned about the health of my relations, my friends and my patients. It was a noteworthy fact that this material also included some disagreeable memories, which supported my friend Otto's accusation rather than my own vindication. The material was, as one might say, impartial; but nevertheless there was an unmistakable connection between this more extensive group of thoughts which underlay the dream and the narrower subject of the dream which gave rise to the wish to be innocent of Irma's illness.

I will not pretend that I have completely uncovered the meaning of this   *32*
dream or that its interpretation is without a gap. I could spend much more time over it, derive further information from it and discuss fresh problems raised by it. I myself know the points from which further trains of thought could be followed. But considerations which arise in the case of every dream of my own restrain me from pursuing my interpretative work. If anyone should feel tempted to express a hasty condemnation of my reticence, I would advise him to make the experiment of being franker than I am. For the moment I am satisfied with the achievement of this one piece of fresh knowledge. If we adopt the method of interpreting dreams which I have indicated here, we shall find that dreams really have a meaning and are far from being the expression of a fragmentary activity of the brain, as the authorities have claimed. *When the work of interpretation has been completed, we perceive that a dream is the fulfilment of a wish.*

WRITING AND DISCUSSION QUESTIONS

Informative

1. Summarize Freud's dream. Compare the dream itself with Freud's preamble that explains the identity of Irma. What features do the dream and the day's prior events share?
2. What are the chief components Freud uses as the foundation for his interpretation? What links does he make between a preexisting circumstance in the waking world and that of his dream?
3. On what basis does Freud conclude that his dream's content was the fulfillment of

a wish? What is the "method of interpretation" to which Freud refers and urges the psychoanalytic community to adopt at the end of the account?

Persuasive

1. Argue that Freud's interpretation is or is not plausible. Are there alternative explanations for various elements? To what extent do you believe his "method" is valid?
2. To what extent does Freud's work actually shed light on the source and power of dreams? What does it tell us about the "unconscious" and its ability to influence behavior? Is this information useful or trivial?

Personal

1. Dream interpretation has been a part of human society since recorded history. The Biblical story of Joseph, for instance, attests to the importance of dreams and their interpretations to all segments of society. What part do you think dreams actually play in an individual's life? Are dreams significant only as wish fulfillment, or do they have other purposes?
2. Do you have a recurring dream? Speculate on its source and meaning. Which of its elements may be linked to daily events, persons, or situations? Is the dream pleasing or displeasing? Do you welcome it or fear it?

▼

WILLIAM JAMES, FROM *THE WILL TO BELIEVE*

William James (1842–1910) came from an illustrious New York family that included his brother Henry James and sister Alice James, both accomplished writers. After attempting a career as an artist, James turned to the natural sciences and earned a medical degree. While fighting fits of depression and hallucinations, James claimed to have, in effect, "cured himself" by an act of the will: "My first act of free will shall be to believe in free will." His personal exploration of the mind's powers to will itself into different states of consciousness—to believe something more healthy or profitable to the body, for instance—led him into his unique contribution to the study of psychology. After taking a position in physiology at Harvard University, James soon decided that he did not possess the strength to perform laboratory work acceptably and, therefore, turned to the new field of psychology. James' brand of psychological inquiry was heavily influenced by the work of Charles Darwin, from whom he drafted the notion of an organism's ability to adapt to changing environment. Believing that the human mind itself represents an organism capable of responding creatively to its environment, James argued that the mind can exert extraordinary control over the destiny of an individual. And his arguments went far in establishing the idea of pragmatism; that is, if one believes something to be true, and thereby acts on that truth, the actual or objective truth of that proposition is inconsequential. In this selection, the first half of his famous treatise, *The Will to Believe* (1897), James argues that the rationality or irrationality of religious faith is not important; what is important is that religious faith is beneficial as long as the individual "accepts" it as true.

from *The Will to Believe*
WILLIAM JAMES

. . . What then do we now mean by the religious hypothesis? Sci-   *1*
ence says things are; morality says some things are better than other things;
and religion says essentially two things.

First, she says that the best things are the more eternal things, the overlap-   *2*
ping things, the things in the universe that throw the last stone, so to speak,
and say the final word. "Perfection is eternal"—this phrase of Charles Secré-
tan—seems a good way of putting this first affirmation of religion, an affirmation which obviously cannot yet be verified scientifically at all.

The second affirmation of religion is that we are better off even now if we   *3*
believe her first affirmation to be true.

Now, let us consider what the logical elements of this situation are *in case*   *4*
the religious hypothesis in both its branches be really true. (Of course, we must
admit that possibility at the outset. If we are to discuss the question at all, it
must involve a living option. If for any of you religion be a hypothesis that cannot, by any living possibility, be true, then you need go no farther. I speak to
the "saving remnant" alone.) So proceeding, we see, first, that religion offers
itself as a *momentous* option. We are supposed to gain, even now, by our
belief, and to lose by our non-belief, a certain vital good. Secondly, religion is
a *forced* option, so far as that good goes. We cannot escape the issue by
remaining sceptical and waiting for more light, because, although we do avoid
error in that way *if religion be untrue*, we lose the good, *if it be true*, just as
certainly as if we positively chose to disbelieve. It is as if a man should hesitate
indefinitely to ask a certain woman to marry him because he was not perfectly
sure that she would prove an angel after he brought her home. Would he not
cut himself off from that particular angel-possibility as decisively as if he went
and married someone else? Scepticism, then, is not avoidance of option; it is
option of a certain particular kind of risk. *Better risk loss of truth than chance
of error*—that is your faith-vetoer's exact position. He is actively playing his
stake as much as the believer is; he is backing the field against the religious
hypothesis, just as the believer is backing the religious hypothesis against the
field. To preach scepticism to us as a duty until "sufficient evidence" for religion be found, is tantamount therefore to telling us, when in presence of religious hypothesis, that to yield to our fear of its being error is wiser and better
than to yield to our hope that it may be true. It is not intellect against all passions, then; it is only intellect with one passion laying down its law. And by
what, forsooth, is the supreme wisdom of this passion warranted? Dupery for
dupery, what proof is there that dupery through hope is so much worse than
dupery through fear? I, for one, can see no proof; and I simply refuse obedi-

ence to the scientist's command to imitate his kind of option, in a case where my own stake is important enough to give me the right to choose my own form of risk. If religion be true and the evidence for it be still insufficient, I do not wish, by putting your extinguisher upon my nature (which feels to me as if it had after all some business in this matter), to forfeit my sole chance in life of getting upon the winning side—that chance depending, of course, on my willingness to run the risk of acting as if my passional need of taking the world religiously might be prophetic and right.

5   All this is on the supposition that it really may be prophetic and right, and that, even to us who are discussing the matter, religion is a live hypothesis which may be true. Now, to most of us religion comes in a still further way that makes a veto on our active faith even more illogical. The more perfect and more eternal aspect of the universe is represented in our religions as having personal form. The universe is no longer a mere *It* to us, but a *Thou*, if we are religious; and any relation that may be possible from person to person might be possible here. For instance, although in one sense we are passive portions of the universe, in another we show a curious autonomy, as if we were small active centres on our own account. We feel, too, as if the appeal of religion to us were made to our own active good-will, as if evidence might be forever withheld from us unless we met the hypothesis half-way. To take a trivial illustration: just as a man who in a company of gentlemen made no advances, asked a warrant for every concession, and believed no one's word without proof, would cut himself off by such churlishness from all the social rewards that a more trusting spirit would earn—so here, one who should shut himself up in snarling logicality and try to make the gods extort his recognition willy-nilly, or not get it at all, might cut himself off forever from his only opportunity of making the gods' acquaintance. This feeling, forced on us we know not whence, that by obstinately believing that there are gods (although not to do so would be so easy both for our logic and our life) we are doing the universe the deepest service we can, seems part of the living essence of the religious hypothesis. If the hypothesis *were* true in all its parts, including this one, then pure intellectualism, with its veto on our making willing advances, would be an absurdity; and some participation of our sympathetic nature would be logically required. I, therefore, for one, cannot see my way to accepting the agnostic rules for truth-seeking, or wilfully agree to keep my willing nature out of the game. I cannot do so for this plain reason, that *a rule of thinking which would absolutely prevent me from acknowledging certain kinds of truth if those kinds of truth were really there, would be an irrational rule.* That for me is the long and short of the formal logic of the situation, no matter what the kinds of truth might materially be.

6   I confess I do not see how this logic can be escaped. But sad experience makes me fear that some of you may still shrink from radically saying with me, *in abstracto*, that we have the right to believe at our own risk any hypothesis that is live enough to tempt our will. I suspect, however, that if this is so, it is because you have got away from the abstract logical point of view altogether,

and are thinking (perhaps without realizing it) of some particular religious hypothesis which for you is dead. The freedom to "believe what we will" you apply to the case of some patent superstition; and the faith you think of is the faith defined by the schoolboy when he said, "Faith is when you believe something that you know ain't true." I can only repeat that this is misapprehension. *In concreto*, the freedom to believe can only cover living options which the intellect of the individual cannot by itself resolve; and living options never seem absurdities to him who has them to consider. When I look at the religious question as it really puts itself to concrete men, and when I think of all the possibilities which both practically and theoretically it involves, then this command that we shall put a stopper on our heart, instincts, and courage, and *wait*—acting of course meanwhile more or less as if religion were *not* true[1]—till doomsday, or till such time as our intellect and senses working together may have raked in evidence enough—this command, I say, seems to me the queerest idol ever manufactured in the philosophic cave. Were we scholastic absolutists, there might be more excuse. If we had an infallible intellect with its objective certitudes, we might feel ourselves disloyal to such a perfect organ of knowledge in not trusting to it exclusively, in not waiting for its releasing word. But if we are empiricists, if we believe that no bell in us tolls to let us know for certain when truth is in our grasp, then it seems a piece of idle fantasticality to preach so solemnly our duty of waiting for the bell. Indeed we *may* wait if we will—I hope you do not think that I am denying that—but if we do so, we do so at our peril as much as if we believed. In either case we *act*, taking our life in our hands. No one of us ought to issue vetoes to the other, nor should we bandy words of abuse. We ought, on the contrary, delicately and profoundly to respect one another's mental freedom: then only shall we bring about the intellectual republic; then only shall we have that spirit of inner tolerance without which all our outer tolerance is soulless, and which is empiricism's glory; then only shall we live and let live, in speculative as well as in practical things. . . .

WRITING AND DISCUSSION QUESTIONS

Informative

1. According to James, what claims does religion make? How do the claims of religion differ from those of science?
2. Why does James believe that religious faith must be a "living option," or plausi-

---

[1]"Since belief is measured by action, he who forbids us to believe religion to be true, necessarily also forbids us to act as we should if we did believe it to be true. The whole defence of religous faith hinges upon action. If the action required or inspired by the religious hypothesis is in no way different from that dictated by the naturalistic hypothesis, then religious faith is a pure superfluity, better pruned away, and controversy about its legitimacy is a piece of idle trifling, unworthy of serious minds. I myself believe, of course, that the religious hypothesis gives to the world an expression which specifically determines our reactions, and makes them in a large part unlike what they might be on a purely naturalistic scheme of belief." (James's note)

ble, before it can be analyzed and discussed? How does this view of skepticism affect his understanding of religion?

3. What does James propose to do with those who differ on the matter of the validity of religious faith?

Persuasive

1. Argue for or against James' contention that religious faith in some sense "personalizes" the universe ("The universe is no longer a mere *It* to us, but a *Thou*."). What are the implications in conceiving of the universe as being made up of impersonal forces or as being "alive" in itself?

2. James defends religion against certain criticisms drawn from science and the scientific method. Argue that he is or is not successful.

3. James disagrees with what he calls "agnostic rules of truth-seeking" because they "would absolutely prevent me from acknowledging certain kinds of truth if those kinds of truth were really there," and thus would be "irrational." Do you accept his objection? What alternatives are there for *truth seeking*?

Personal

1. To what extent is religious faith—Christianity, Judaism, Islamism, and Buddhism, for example—a "living option" to you? How does one begin to wrestle with or distinguish between the claims of competing religious faiths?

2. Explain whether or not James' point boils down to, "if it feels good and if it does not hurt anyone else, do it."

3. James is often credited with founding the philosophy or social practice of "pragmatism," the belief that the validity of an idea is measured by how well it "works" in the limited context in which it is applied, as opposed to its values as a transcendent or eternal truth. Do you see evidence of pragmatism at work in your culture and in your own life? Is it impossible to live one's life in the light or pursuit of truths that transcend the immediate situation and that apply in all contexts?

▼

B. F. SKINNER, "WHAT IS MAN?"

Until he retired, Burrhus Frederic Skinner (1904–1990) taught experimental psychology at Harvard University. One of the more controversial psychologists of the twentieth century, Skinner is associated with the behaviorist school of psychology, which places supreme importance on studying the observable responses of living creatures to external stimuli. One of the premises of behaviorism as defined by Skinner is that people are not "free" or "autonomous" creatures, but are products of the network of stimuli that exist in their environments. That is to say, Skinner argues that we do not exercise free choice as much as respond to conditioning—the stimuli of family, friends, culture, the unconscious—and to the countless other influences that reinforce certain kinds of behavior while discouraging others.

In his books *Walden Two* (1948), *Beyond Freedom and Dignity* (1971), and *About Behaviorism* (1974), Skinner articulates his position that most of the aspects of individuality that humankind cherishes are, in fact, illusions—illusions that must be dispelled in order for society to survive and to operate more productively. In "What Is Man?" (1971), Skinner describes the method of scientific inquiry used in his behaviorism and then illustrates his method in defining "man." As he reaches his conclusion, he offers a proposal for a radically different human community—made possible by stripping away our "romantic" ideals that he believes have enslaved rather than conferred true freedom and dignity upon us.

▼

What Is Man?
B. F. SKINNER

As a science of behavior follows the strategy of physics and biology, *1* the autonomous agent to which we have traditionally attributed behavior is replaced by the environment—the environment in which the species evolved and in which the behavior of the individual is shaped and maintained.

Take, for example, a "cognitive" activity, *attention*. A person responds to *2* only a small part of the stimuli impinging upon him. The traditional view is that he himself determines which stimuli are to be effective—by paying attention to them. Some kind of inner gatekeeper allows some stimuli to enter and keeps all others out. A sudden or strong stimulus may break through and "attract" attention, but the person himself is otherwise in control. An analysis of the environmental circumstances reverses the relation. The kinds of stimuli that break through by "attracting attention" do so because they have been associated in the evolutionary history of the species or the personal history of the individual with important—e.g., dangerous—things. Less forceful stimuli attract attention only to the extent that they have figured in contingencies of reinforcement.

We can arrange contingencies that insure that an organism—even such a *3* simple organism as a pigeon—will attend to one object and not to another, or to one property of an object, such as its color, and not to another, such as its shape. The inner gatekeeper is replaced by the contingencies that the person has been exposed to and that select the stimuli he reacts to.

FACE

In the traditional view a person perceives the world around him and acts upon *4* it to make it known to him. It has even been argued that the world would not exist if no one perceived it. The action is exactly reversed in an environmental analysis. There would, of course, be no perception if there were no world to perceive, but we would not perceive an existing world if there were no appropriate contingencies.

5   We say that a baby perceives his mother's face and knows it. Our evidence is that the baby responds in one way to his mother's face and in other ways to other faces or other things. He makes this distinction not through some mental act of perception but because of prior contingencies. Some of these may be contingencies of survival. The face and facial expressions of the human mother have been associated with security, warmth, food and other important things during both the evolution of the species and the life of the child.

6   The role of the environment is particularly subtle when what is known is the knower himself. If there is no external world to initiate knowing, must we not then say that the knower himself acts first? This is, of course, the field of consciousness or awareness which a scientific analysis of behavior is often accused of ignoring. The charge is a serious one and should be taken seriously.

7   Man is said to differ from the other animals mainly because he is "aware of his own existence." He knows what he is doing; he knows that he has had a past and will have a future; he alone follows the classical injunction, "Know thyself." Any analysis of human behavior that neglected these facts would be defective indeed. And some analyses do. "Methodological behaviorism" limits itself to what can be observed publicly; mental processes may exist, but their nature rules them out of scientific consideration. The "behaviorists" in political science and many logical positivists in philosophy have followed a similar line. But we can study self-observation, and we must include it in any reasonably complete account of human behavior. Rather than ignore consciousness, an experimental analysis of behavior has put much emphasis on certain crucial issues. The question is not whether a man can know himself but what he knows when he does so.

SKIN

8   The problem arises in part from the indisputable fact of privacy: a small part of the universe is enclosed within a human skin. It would be foolish to deny the existence of that private world, but it is also foolish to assert that because it is private its nature is different from the world outside. The difference is not in the stuff that composes the private world but in its accessibility. There is an exclusive intimacy about a headache or heartache that has seemed to support the doctrine that knowing is a kind of possession.

9   The difficulty is that although privacy may bring the knower closer to what he knows, it interferes with the process through which he comes to know anything. As we have seen, contingencies under which a child learns to describe his feelings are necessarily defective; the verbal community cannot use the same procedures for this that it uses to teach a child to describe objects. There are, of course, natural contingencies under which we learn to respond to private stimuli, and they generate behavior of great precision; we could not walk if

we were not stimulated by parts of our own body. But very little awareness is associated with this kind of behavior and, in fact, we behave in these ways most of the time without being aware of the stimuli to which we are responding. We do not attribute awareness to other species that obviously use similar private stimuli. To "know" private stimuli is more than to respond to them.

HELP

The verbal community specializes in self-descriptive contingencies. It asks: What did you do yesterday? Why did you do that? How do you feel about that? The answers help persons adjust to each other effectively. And it is because such questions are asked that a person responds to himself and his behavior in the special way called knowing or being aware. Without the help of a verbal community all behavior would be unconscious. Consciousness is a social product. It is not only *not* the special field of autonomous man, it is not within the range of a solitary man. 10

And it is not within the range of accuracy of anyone. The privacy that seems to confer intimacy upon self-knowledge makes it impossible for the verbal community to maintain precise contingencies. Introspective vocabularies are by nature inaccurate, and that is one reason why they have varied so widely among schools of philosophy and psychology. Even a carefully trained observer runs into trouble when he studies new private stimuli. 11

AWARE

Theories of psychotherapy that emphasize awareness assign a role to autonomous man that is the function of contingencies of reinforcement. Awareness may help if the problem is in part a lack of awareness, and "insight" into one's condition may help if one then takes remedial action. But awareness or insight alone is not always enough, and may be too much. One need not be aware of one's behavior or the conditions controlling it in order to behave effectively— or ineffectively. 12

The extent to which a man *should* be aware of himself depends upon the importance of self-observation for effective behavior. Self-knowledge is valuable only to the extent that it helps to meet the contingencies under which it has arisen. 13

THINK

Perhaps the last stronghold of autonomous man is the complex "cognitive" activity called thinking. Because it is complex, it has yielded only slowly to explanation in terms of contingencies of reinforcement. We say that a person *forms a concept or an abstraction,* but all we see is that certain kinds of contin- 14 gencies of reinforcement have brought a response under the control of a single property of a stimulus. We say that a person *recalls* or *remembers* what he has seen or heard, but all we see is that the present occasion evokes a response, possibly in weakened or altered form, acquired on another occasion. We say that a person *associates* one word with another, but all we observe is that one verbal stimulus evokes the response previously made to another. Rather than suppose that it is therefore autonomous man who forms concepts or abstractions, recalls or remembers, and associates, we can put matters in good order simply by noting that these terms do not refer to forms of behavior.

15   A person may take explicit action, however, when he solves a problem. The creative artist may manipulate a medium until something of interest turns up. Much of this can be done covertly, and we are then likely to assign it to a different dimensional system; but it can always be done overtly, perhaps more slowly but also often more effectively, and with rare exceptions it must have been learned in overt form. The culture constructs special contingencies to promote thinking. It teaches a person to make fine discriminations by making differential reinforcement more precise. It teaches techniques to use in solving problems. It provides rules that make it unnecessary to expose a person to the contingencies from which the rules derive, and it provides rules for finding rules.

16   Self-control or self-management is a special kind of problem-solving that, like self-knowledge, raises all the issues associated with privacy. It is always the environment that builds the behavior with which we solve problems, even when the problems are found in the private world inside the skin. We have not investigated the matter of self-control in a very productive way, but the inadequacy of our analysis is no reason to fall back on a miracle-working mind. If our understanding of contingencies of reinforcement is not yet sufficient to explain all kinds of thinking, we must remember that the appeal to mind explains nothing at all.

INSIDE

17 In shifting control from autonomous man to the observable environment we do not leave an empty organism. A great deal goes on inside the skin, and physiology will eventually be able to tell us more about it. It will explain why behavior indeed relates to the antecedent events of which we can show it to be a function.

18   People do not always correctly understand the assignment. Many physiologists regard themselves as looking for the "physiological correlates" of mental events. They regard physiological research as simply a more scientific version of introspection. But physiological techniques are not, of course, designed to detect or measure personalities, feelings, or thoughts. At the moment neither introspection nor physiology supplies very adequate information about what is

going on inside a man as he behaves, and since they are both directed inward they have the same effect of diverting attention from the external environment.

Much of the misunderstanding about an inner man comes from the meta- *19* phor of storage. Evolutionary and environmental histories change an organism, but they are not stored within it. Thus we observe that babies suck their mothers' breasts and can easily imagine that a strong tendency to do so has survival value, but much more is implied by a "sucking instinct" regarded as something a baby possesses that enables it to suck. The concept of "human nature" or "genetic endowment" is dangerous when we take it in that sense. We are closer to human nature in a baby than in an adult, or in a primitive culture than in an advanced one, in the sense that environmental contingencies are less likely to have obscured the genetic endowment, and it is tempting to dramatize that endowment by implying that earlier stages have survived in concealed form: man is a naked ape. But anatomists and physiologists will not find an ape, or for that matter, instincts. They will find anatomical and physiological features that are the product of an evolutionary history.

SIN

It is often said too that the personal history of the individual is stored within *20* him as a "habit." The cigarette habit is talked of as being something more than the behavior said to show that a person possesses it. But the only other information we have is about the reinforcers and the schedules of reinforcement that make a person smoke a great deal. The contingencies are not stored; they simply leave a person changed.

The issue has had a curious place in theology. Does man sin because he is *21* sinful or is he sinful because he sins? Neither question points to anything very useful. To say that a man is sinful because he sins is to give an operational definition of sin. To say that he sins because he is sinful is to trace his behavior to a supposed inner trait. But whether a person engages in the kind of behavior called sinful depends upon circumstances not mentioned in either question. The sin assigned as an inner possession (the sin a person "knows") is to be found in a history of reinforcement.

SELF

It is the nature of an experimental analysis of human behavior to strip away the *22* functions previously assigned to autonomous man and transfer them one by one to the controlling environment. The analysis leaves less and less for autonomous man to do. But what about man himself? Is there not something about a person—a self—that is more than a living body?

A self is a repertoire of behavior appropriate to a given set of contingencies, *23* and a substantial part of the conditions to which a person is exposed may play a dominant role. Under other conditions a person may sometimes report, "I'm not myself today" or "I couldn't have done what you said I did, because that's not like me." The identity conferred upon a self arises from the contingencies responsible for the behavior.

SPLIT

24 Two or more repertoires generated by different sets of contingencies compose two or more selves. A person possesses one repertoire appropriate to his life with his friends and another appropriate to his life with his family. A problem of identity arises when a person finds himself with family and friends at the same time.

25   Self-knowledge and self-control imply two selves in this sense. The self-knower is almost always a product of social contingencies, but the self that is known may come from other sources. The controlling self (the conscience or superego) is of social origin, but the controlled self is more likely to be the product of genetic susceptibilities to reinforcement (the id or the Old Adam). The controlling self generally represents the interests of others; the controlled self the interests of the individual.

STRANGER

26 The picture that emerges from a scientific analysis is not of a body with a person inside but of a body that *is* a person in the sense that it displays a complex repertoire of behavior. The picture is, of course, unfamiliar. The man we thus portray is a stranger, and from the traditional point of view he may not seem to be a man at all.

27   C. S. Lewis put it bluntly: "Man is being abolished."

28   There is clearly some difficulty in identifying the man to whom Lewis referred. He cannot have meant the human species; far from being abolished, it is filling the earth. Nor are individual men growing less effective or productive. What is being abolished is autonomous man—the inner man, the homunculus, the possessing demon, the man defended by the literatures of freedom and dignity.

29   His abolition is long overdue. Autonomous man is a device we use to explain what we cannot explain in any other way. We constructed him from our ignorance, and as our understanding increases, the very stuff of which he is composed vanishes. Science does not dehumanize man, it de-homunculizes him, and it must do so if it is to prevent the abolition of the human species.

30   To man *qua* man we readily say good riddance. Only by dispossessing autonomous man can we turn to the real causes of human behavior—from the inferred to the observed, from the miraculous to the natural, from the inaccessible to the manipulable.

PURPOSE

It is often said that in doing so we must treat the man who survives as a mere   *31*
animal. "Animal" is a pejorative term—but only because "man" has been
made spuriously honorific. Joseph Wood Krutch argued that the traditional
view supports Hamlet's exclamation "How like a god!" while Pavlov emphasized "How like a dog!" But that was a step forward. A god is the archetypal
pattern of an explanatory fiction, of a miracle-working mind, of the metaphysical. Man is much more than a dog, but like a dog he is within range of a scientific analysis.

An important role of autonomous man has been to give direction to human   *32*
behavior, and it is often said that in dispossessing an inner agent we leave man
without a purpose: "Since a scientific psychology must regard human behavior
objectively, as determined by necessary laws, it must represent human behavior
as unintentional." But "necessary laws" would have this effect only if they
referred exclusively to antecedent conditions. Intention and purpose refer to
selective consequences, the effects of which we can formulate in "necessary
laws." Has life, in all the forms in which it exists on the surface of the earth, a
purpose? And is this evidence of intentional design? The primate hand evolved
in order that the primate could more successfully manipulate things, but its
purpose was to be found not in a prior design but rather in the process of
selection. Similarly, in operant conditioning—when a pianist acquires the
behavior of playing a smooth scale for example—we find the purpose of the
skilled movement of the hand in the consequences that follow it. In neither the
evolution of the human hand nor in the acquired use of the hand is any prior
intention or purpose at issue.

There is a difference between biological and individual purpose in that the   *33*
latter can be felt. No one could have felt the purpose in the development of the
human hand, but a person can in a sense feel the purpose with which he plays
a smooth scale. But he does not play a smooth scale *because* he feels the purpose of doing so; what he feels is a by-product of his behavior and of its consequences. The relation of the human hand to the contingencies of survival under
which it evolved is, of course, out of reach of personal observation; the relation
of the behavior to contingencies of reinforcement that have generated it is not.

CONTROL

As a scientific analysis of behavior dispossesses autonomous man and turns the   *34*
control he had been said to exert over to the environment, the individual may
seem particularly vulnerable. He is henceforth to be controlled by the world
around him, and in large part by other men. Is he not then simply a victim?
Certainly, men have been victims, as they have been victimizers, but the word
is too strong. It implies despoliation, which is by no means an essential consequence of interpersonal control. But even under benevolent control is the indi-

vidual not helpless—"at a dead end in his long struggle to control his own destiny"?

35   It is only autonomous man who has reached a dead end. Man himself may be controlled by his environment, but it is an environment almost wholly of his own making. The physical environment of most persons is largely man-made— the walls that shelter them, the tools they use, the surfaces they walk on—and the social environment is obviously man-made. It generates the language a person speaks, the customs he follows, and the behavior he exhibits with respect to the ethical, religious, governmental, economic, educational and psychotherapeutic institutions that control him.

36   The evolution of a culture is in fact a kind of gigantic exercise in self-control. As the individual controls himself by manipulating the world he lives in, so the human species has constructed an environment in which its members behave in a highly effective way. Mistakes have been made, and we have no assurance that the environment man has constructed will continue to provide gains that outstrip the losses. But man as we know him, for better or for worse, is what man has made of man.

ROLES

37 This will not satisfy those who cry "Victim!" C. S. Lewis protested: ". . . the power of man to make himself what he pleases . . . means . . . the power of some men to make other men what they please." This is inevitable in the nature of cultural evolution. We must distinguish the controlling self from the controlled self even when they are both inside the same skin, and when control is exercised through the design of an external environment, the selves are, with minor exceptions, distinct.

38   The person who, purposely or not, introduces a new cultural practice is only one among possibly billions it will affect. If this does not seem like an act of self-control, it is only because we have misunderstood the nature of self-control in the individual.

39   When a person changes his physical or social environment "intentionally"— that is, in order to change human behavior, possibly including his own—he plays two roles: one as a controller, as the designer of a controlling culture, and another as the controlled, as the product of a culture. There is nothing inconsistent about this; it follows from the nature of the evolution of a culture, with or without intentional design.

40   The human species probably has undergone little genetic change in recorded time. We have only to go back a thousand generations to reach the artists of the caves of Lascaux.[1] Features bearing directly on survival (such as resistance to disease) change substantially in a thousand generations, but the child of one

---

[1]The reference is to the prehistoric paintings of animals on the walls of caves at Lascaux, in southern France.

of the Lascaux artists transplanted to the world of today might be almost indistinguishable from a modern child.

Man has improved himself enormously in the same period of time by chang- 41
ing the world he lives in. Modern religious practices developed over a hundred
generations and modern government and law developed in fewer than a hundred. Perhaps no more than 20 generations have been needed to produce
modern economic practices, and possibly no more than four or five to produce
modern education, psychotherapy, and the physical and biological technologies
that have increased man's sensitivity to the world around him and his power to
change that world.

CHANGE

Man has "controlled his own destiny," if that expression means anything at all. 42
The man that man has made is the product of the culture man has devised. He
has emerged from two quite different processes of evolution: biological and cultural. Both may now accelerate because both are subject to intentional design.
Men have already changed their genetic endowment by breeding selectively and
by changing contingencies of survival, and for a long time they have introduced
cultural practices as cultural mutations. They may now begin to do both with a
clearer eye to the consequences.

STAGE

The individual is the carrier of both his species and his culture. Cultural prac- 43
tices like genetic traits are transmitted from individual to individual. Even
within the most regimented culture every personal history is unique. But the
individual remains merely a stage in a process that began long before he came
into existence and will long outlast him. He has no ultimate responsibility for a
species trait or a cultural practice, even though it was he who underwent the
mutation or introduced the practice that became part of the species or culture.

Even if Lamarck had been right in supposing that the individual could 44
change his genetic structure through personal effort, we should have to point to
the environmental circumstances responsible for the effort, as we shall have to
do when geneticists begin to change the human endowment. And when an individual engages in the intentional design of a cultural practice, we must turn to
the culture that induces him to do so and supplies the art or science he uses.

END

One of the great problems of individualism, seldom recognized as such, is 45
death—the inescapable fate of the individual, the final assault on freedom and
dignity. Death is one of those remote events that are brought to bear on behav-

ior only with the aid of cultural practices. What we see is the death of others, as in Pascal's famous metaphor: "Imagine a number of men in chains, all under sentence of death, some of whom are each day butchered in the sight of others; those remaining see their own condition in that of their fellows, and looking at each other with grief and despair await their turn. This is an image of the human condition."

46   Some religions have made death more important by picturing a future existence in heaven or hell, but the individualist has a special reason to fear death: it is the prospect of personal annihilation. The individualist can find no solace in reflecting upon any contribution that will survive him. He has refused to be concerned for the survival of his culture and is not reinforced by the fact that the culture will long survive him. In the defense of his own freedom and dignity he had denied the contributions of the past and must therefore relinquish all claim upon the future.

PICTURES

47 Science probably has never demanded a more sweeping change in a traditional way of thinking about a subject, nor has there ever been a more important subject. In the traditional picture a person perceives the world around him, selects features to be perceived, discriminates among them, judges them good or bad, changes them to make them better (or worse), and may be held responsible for his action and justly rewarded or punished for its consequences. In the scientific picture a person is a member of a species shaped by evolutionary contingencies of survival, displaying behavioral processes that bring him under the control of the environment in which he lives, and largely under the control of a social environment that he and millions of others like him have constructed and maintained during the evolution of a culture. The direction of the controlling relation is reserved: a person does not act upon the world; the world acts upon him.

48   It is difficult to accept such a change simply on intellectual grounds and nearly impossible to accept its implications. The reaction of the traditionalist is usually described in terms of feelings. One of these, to which the Freudians have appealed in explaining the resistance to psychoanalysis, is wounded vanity. Freud himself expounded, as Ernest Jones said, "the three heavy blows which narcissism or self-love of mankind has suffered at the hands of science. The first was cosmological and was dealt by Copernicus; the second was biological and was dealt by Darwin; the third was psychological and was dealt by Freud."

49   But what are the signs or symptoms of wounded vanity, and how shall we explain them? What people do about a scientific picture of man is to call it wrong, demeaning and dangerous, to argue against it, and to attack those who propose or defend it. These are signs of wounded vanity only to the extent that the scientific formulation destroys accustomed reinforcers. If a person can no

longer take credit or be admired for what he does, then he seems to suffer a loss of dignity or worth, and behavior previously reinforced by credit or admiration will undergo extinction. Extinction often leads to aggressive attack.

FUTILITY

Another effect of the scientific picture has been described as a loss of faith or 50 "nerve," as a sense of doubt or powerlessness, or as discouragement, depression, or despondency. A person is said to feel that he can do nothing about his own destiny, but what he feels is a weakening of old responses that are no longer reinforced.

Another effect is a kind of nostalgia. Old repertoires break through as tradi- 51 tionalists seize upon and exaggerate similarities between present and past. They call the old days the good old days, when people recognized the inherent dignity of man and the importance of spiritual values. These fragments of outmoded behavior tend to be wistful—that is, they have the character of increasingly unsuccessful behavior.

RAINBOW

These reactions to a scientific conception of man are, of course, unfortunate. 52 They immobilize men of good will, and anyone concerned with the future of his culture will do what he can to correct them. No theory changes what it is a theory about. We change nothing because we look at it, talk about it, or analyze it in a new way. Keats drank confusion to Newton for analyzing the rainbow, but the rainbow remained as beautiful as ever and became for many even more beautiful.

Man has not changed because we look at him, talk about him, and analyze 53 him scientifically. His achievements in science, government, religion, art and literature remain as they have always been, to be admired as one admires a storm at sea or autumn foliage or a mountain peak, quite apart from their origins and untouched by a scientific analysis. What does change is our chance of doing something about the subject of a theory. Newton's analysis of the light in a rainbow was a step in the direction of the laser.

PERILS

The traditional conception of man is flattering; it confers reinforcing privileges. 54 It is therefore easy to defend and difficult to change. It was designed to build up the individual as an instrument of countercontrol, and it did so effectively, but in such a way as to limit future progress.

We have seen how the literatures of freedom and dignity, with their concern 55 for autonomous man, have perpetuated the use of punishment and condoned the use of only weak nonpunitive techniques. It is not difficult to demonstrate a connection between the unlimited right of the individual to pursue happiness and the catastrophes threatened by unchecked breeding, the unrestrained affluence that exhausts resources and pollutes the environment, and the imminence of nuclear war.

56   Physical and biological technologies have alleviated pestilence and famine and the painful, dangerous and exhuasting features of daily life, and a behavioral technology can begin to alleviate other kinds of ills. In the analysis of human behavior it is just possible that we are slightly beyond Newton's position in the analysis of light, for we are beginning to make technological applications, and there are wonderful possibilities—all the more wonderful because traditional approaches have been so ineffective.

57   It is hard to imagine a world in which people live together without quarreling, maintain themselves by producing the food, shelter and clothing they need, enjoy themselves and contribute to the enjoyment of others in art, music, literature and games, consume only a reasonable part of the resources of the world and add as little as possible to its pollution, bear no more children than they can raise decently, continue to explore the world around them and discover better ways of dealing with it, and come to know themselves and the world around them accurately and comprehensively. Yet all this is possible. We have not yet seen what man can make of man.

WRITING AND DISCUSSION QUESTIONS

Informative

1. Explain the "science of behavior" as Skinner illustrates it. What are its premises, and how does it explain phenomena? How is it different from other methods of observation and interpretation of data?
2. How does Skinner define "thinking"? How does his definition fit into his criticism of "autonomous man"?
3. "To man *qua* man we readily say good riddance." Which "man" is Skinner happy to dispense with? What is gained or lost in leaving this particular conception of "man" behind?

Persuasive

1. Argue that it is or is not important to "define" man, or humanity. Describe your approach in answering the question, "What is humanity?" For instance, would your approach have a scientific basis, or do you believe another basis would be better?
2. Argue for or against Skinner's behaviorism. Is it merely inconsistent in places or completely implausible? Skinner writes as if he expects opposition. Where in his essay does he pause as if to anticipate and then to respond to objections? What is objectionable about behaviorism?

3. One could easily compare and contrast C. S. Lewis' "Meditation in a Toolshed" (Chapter 3) with B. F. Skinner's "What Is Man?" to reveal the underpinnings of both men's viewpoints. Skinner, in fact, occasionally cites Lewis while articulating his own point of view. What quarrel does Skinner have with Lewis' conception of humanity?

Personal

1. Skinner uses section headers like "Self," "Stranger," "Purpose," to organize his presentation. Under each rubric, he offers his observations on how his behaviorism explains the phenomenon or concept. Respond to two or three of these concepts.
2. Skinner concludes with "We have not yet seen what man can make of man." Is this statement ominous or optimistic? How do you respond to it?
3. In what sense can it be important to prevent the "abolition of the human species," as Skinner puts it, at the expense of "autonomous" man? Is "man" more like a "god" (Hamlet) or a "dog" (Pavlov)? Is our belief in the uniqueness of individual humanity merely a superstition? What is there to preserve if "personhood" is dismissed?

WALKER PERCY, "THE MYSTERY OF LANGUAGE" FROM *THE MESSAGE IN THE BOTTLE*

Walker Percy (1916–1990), a celebrated American novelist, was born in Birmingham, Alabama, to a traditional, aristocratic Southern family. After his father's suicide, he was raised by his uncle Will Percy, himself a well-known writer. Percy eventually earned a B.A. from the University of North Carolina, and then received a medical degree in psychiatry from Columbia University in 1941. Percy never embarked on a medical practice, however, having contracted tuberculosis during his medical internship. During his convalescence from the disease, Percy read the works of Kierkegaard (1813–1855) and other religious philosophers and underwent a dramatic conversion to Christianity.

Percy's six novels typically explore the latent search for God in the hearts of disillusioned protagonists—loners, dreamers, and iconoclasts who reject the world in anticipation of something better. One of the signs of God that Percy's characters uncover in their search is the profound fact and mystery of human language—the creation of and communication with symbol and metaphor. This very fact of human language makes it more than an elevated form of animal communication; it is also a manifestation of divine order and of a person's well being. In his most recent novel, *The Thanatos Syndrome*, the protagonist, Dr. Tom More, is a clinical psychologist who begins to diagnose the maladies of his patients by observing the problems in their own speech and their out-of-character use of language.

Percy has also written two volumes of nonfiction, *Lost in the Cosmos* (1980), a satire of pop psychology and self-help books, and *The Message in the Bottle* (1975), a collection of essays about the nature of human language and what it reveals about our place in the universe. The essay presented here, "The Mystery of Language," is drawn from that collection and provides some of Percy's main themes in his inquiry

into language. Because we take language for granted, Percy argues, we forget what
a remarkable phenomenon it is and what it reveals about our true nature and, even,
our origins.

▼

The Mystery of Language
WALKER PERCY

1   Language is an extremely mysterious phenomenon. By mysterious I
do not mean that the events which take place in the brain during an exchange
of language are complex and little understood—although this is true too. I
mean, rather, that language, which at first sight appears to be the most familiar
sort of occurrence, an occurrence which takes its place along with other occurrences in the world—billiard balls hitting other billiard balls, barkings of dogs,
cryings of babies, sunrises, and rainfalls—is in reality utterly different from
these events. The importance of a study of language, as opposed to a scientific
study of a space-time event like a solar eclipse or rat behavior, is that as soon
as one scratches the surface of the familiar and comes face to face with the
nature of language, one also finds himself face to face with the nature of man.

2   If you were to ask the average educated American or Englishman or Pole, or
anyone else acquainted with the scientific temper of the last two hundred years,
what he conceived the nature of language to be, he would probably reply in
more or less the following way:

3   When I speak a word or sentence and you understand me, I utter a series of
peculiar little sounds by which I hope to convey to you the meaning I have in
mind. The sounds leave my mouth and travel through the air as waves. The
waves strike the tympanic membrane of your outer ear and the motion of the
membrane is carried to the inner ear, where it is transformed into electrical
impulses in the auditory nerve. This nerve impulse is transmitted to your brain,
where a very complex series of events takes place, the upshot of which is that
you "understand" the words; that is, you either respond to the words in the
way I had hoped you would or the words arouse in you the same idea or expectation or fear I had in mind. Your understanding of my sounds depends upon
your having heard them before, upon a common language. As a result of your
having heard the word *ball* in association with the thing ball, there has occurred
a change in your brain of such a character that when I say *ball* you understand
me to mean ball.

4   This explanation of language is not, of course, entirely acceptable to a lin-
guist or a psychologist. But it is the *sort* of explanation one would give to a
question of this kind. It is the sort of explanation to be found in the *Book of
Knowledge* and in a college psychology textbook. It may be less technical or a
great deal more technical—no doubt modern philosophers of meaning would

prefer the term *response* to *idea* in speaking of your understanding of my words—but, technical or not, we agree in general that something of the kind takes place. The essence of the process is a series of events in space-time: muscular events in the mouth, wave events in the air, electrocolloidal events in the nerve and brain.

The trouble is that this explanation misses the essential character of lan-   5
guage. It is not merely an oversimplified explanation; it is not merely an incomplete or one-sided explanation. It has nothing at all to do with language considered as language.

What I wish to call attention to is not a new discovery, a new piece of   6
research in psycholinguistics which revolutionizes our concept of language as the Michelson-Morley experiment revolutionized modern physics. It is rather the extraordinary sort of thing language is, which our theoretical view of the world completely obscures. This extraordinary character of language does not depend for its unveiling upon a piece of research but is there under our noses for all to see. The difficulty is that it *is* under our noses; it is too close and too familiar. Language, symbolization, is the stuff of which our knowledge and awareness of the world are made, the medium through which we see the world. Trying to see it is like trying to see the mirror by which we see everything else.

There is another difficulty. It is the fact that language cannot be explained in   7
the ordinary terminology of explanations. The terminology of explanations is the native attitude of the modern mind toward that which it does not understand—and is its most admirable trait. That attitude is briefly this: Here is a phenomenon . . . how does it work? The answer is given as a series of space-time events. This is how C works; you see, this state of affairs A leads to this state of affairs B, and B leads to C. This attitude goes a long way toward an understanding of billiards, of cellular growth, of anthills and sunrises. But it cannot get hold of language.

All of the space-time events mentioned in connection with the production of   8
speech do occur, and without them there would be no language. But language is something else besides these events. This does not mean that language cannot be understood but that we must use another frame of reference and another terminology. If one studies man at a so-to-speak sublanguage level, one studies him as one studies anything else, as a phenomenon which is susceptible of explanatory hypothesis. A psychologist timing human responses moves about in the same familiar world of observer and data-to-be-explained as the physiologist and the physicist. But as soon as one deals with language not as a sequence of stimuli and responses, not as a science of phonetics or comparative linguistics, but as the sort of thing language is, one finds himself immediately in uncharted territory.

The usual version of the nature of language, then, turns upon the assump-   9
tion that human language is a marvelous development of a type of behavior found in lower animals. As Darwin expressed it, man is not the only animal that can use language to express what is passing in his mind: "The *Cebus azarae* monkey in Paraguay utters at least six distinct sounds which excite in

other monkeys similar emotions." More recent investigations have shown that bees are capable of an extraordinary dance language by which they can communicate not only direction but distance.

10   This assumption is of course entirely reasonable. When we study the human ear or eye or brain we study it as a development in continuity with subhuman ears and eyes and brains. What other method is available to us? But it is here that the radical difference between the sort of thing that language is and the sort of thing that the transactions upon the billiard table are manifests itself to throw us into confusion. This method of finding our way to the nature of language, this assumption, does not work. It not only does not work; it ignores the central feature of human language.

11   The oversight and the inability to correct it have plagued philosophers of language for the past fifty years. To get to the heart of the difficulty we must first understand the difference between a sign and a symbol.

12   A sign is something that directs our attention to something else. If you or I or a dog or a cicada hears a clap of thunder, we will expect rain and seek cover. It will be seen at once that this sort of sign behavior fits in very well with the explanatory attitude mentioned above. The behavior of a man or animal responding to a natural sign (thunder) or an artificial sign (Pavlov's buzzer) can be explained readily as a series of space-time events which takes place because of changes in the brain brought about by past association.

13   But what is a symbol? A symbol does not direct our attention to something else, as a sign does. It does not direct at all. It "means" something else. It somehow comes to contain within itself the thing it means. The word *ball* is a sign to my dog and a symbol to you. If I say *ball* to my dog, he will respond like a good Pavlovian organism and look under the sofa and fetch it. But if I say *ball* to you, you will simply look at me and, if you are patient, finally say "What about it?" The dog responds to the word by looking for the thing; you conceive the ball through the word *ball*.

14   Now we can, if we like, say that the symbol is a kind of sign, and that when I say the word *ball*, the sound strikes your ear drum, arrives in your brain, and there calls out the idea of a ball. Modern semioticists do, in fact, try to explain a symbol as a kind of sign. But this doesn't work. As Susanne Langer has observed, this leaves out something, and this something is the most important thing of all.

15   The thing that is left out is the relation of denotation. The word *names* something. The symbol symbolizes something. Symbolization is qualitatively different from sign behavior; the thing that distinguishes man is his ability to symbolize his experience rather than simply respond to it. The word *ball* does all the things the psychologist says it does, makes its well-known journey from tongue to brain. But it does something else too: it names the thing.

16   So far we have covered ground which has been covered much more adequately by Susanne Langer and the great German philosopher of the symbol, Ernst Cassirer. The question I wish to raise here is this: What are we to make of this peculiar act of naming? If we can't construe it in terms of space-time

events, as we construe other phenomena—solar eclipses, gland secretion, growth—then how can we construe it?

The longer we think about it, the more mysterious the simplest act of nam-   *17* ing becomes. It is, we begin to realize, quite without precedent in all of natural history as we know it. But so, you might reply, is the emergence of the eye without precedent, so is sexual reproduction without precedent. These are nevertheless the same *kinds* of events, which have gone before. We can to a degree understand biological phenomena in the same terms in which we understand physical phenomena, as a series of events and energy exchanges, with each event arising from and being conditioned by a previous event. This is not to say that biology can be reduced to physical terms but only that we can make a good deal of sense of it as a series of events and energy exchanges.

But naming is *generically* different. It stands apart from everything else that   *18* we know about the universe. The collision of two galaxies and the salivation of Pavlov's dog, different as they are, are far more alike than either is like the simplest act of naming. Naming stands at a far greater distance from Pavlov's dog than the latter does from a galactic collision.

Just what is the act of denotation? What took place when the first man   *19* uttered a mouthy little sound and the second man understood it, not as a sign to be responded to, but as "meaning" something they beheld in common? The first creature who did this is almost by minimal empirical definition the first man. What happened is of all things on earth the one thing we should know best. It is the one thing we do most; it is the warp and woof of the fabric of our consciousness. And yet it is extremely difficult to look *at* instead of through and even more difficult to express once it is grasped.

Naming is unique in natural history because for the first time a being in the   *20* universe stands apart from the universe and affirms some other being to be what it is. In this act, for the first time in the history of the universe, "is" is spoken. What does this mean? If something important has happened, why can't we talk about it as we talk about everything else, in the familiar language of space-time events?

The trouble is that we are face to face with a phenomenon which we can't   *21* express by our ordinary phenomenal language. Yet we are obliged to deal with it; it happens, and we cannot dismiss it as a "semantical relation." We sense, moreover, that this phenomenon has the most radical consequences for our thinking about man. To refuse to deal with it because it is troublesome would be fatal. It is as if an astronomer developed a theory of planetary motion and said that his theory holds true of planets A, B, C, and D but that planet E is an exception. It makes zigzags instead of ellipses. Planet E is a scandal to good astronomy; therefore we disqualify planet E as failing to live up to the best standards of bodies in motion.

This is roughly the attitude of some modern semanticists and semioticists   *22* toward the act of naming. If the relation of symbol to thing symbolized be considered as anything other than a sign calling forth a response, then this relation is "wrong." Say whatever you like about a pencil, Korzybski used to say, but never say it is a pencil. The word is not the thing, said Chase; you can't eat the word *oyster*. According to some semanticists, the advent of symbolization is a major calamity in the history of the human race. Their predicament is not without its comic aspects. Here are scientists occupied with a subject matter of which they, the scientists, disapprove. For the sad fact is that we shall continue to say "This is a pencil" rather than "This object I shall refer to in the future by the sound *pencil*."

23 By the semanticists' own testimony we are face to face with an extraordinary phenomenon—even though it be "wrong." But if, instead of deploring this act of naming as a calamity, we try to see it for what it is, what can we discover?

24 When I name an unknown thing or hear the name from you, a remarkable thing happens. In some sense or other, the thing is said to "be" its name or symbol. The semanticists are right: this round thing is certainly not the word *ball*. Yet unless it becomes, in some sense or other, the word *ball* in our consciousness, we will never know the ball! Cassirer's thesis was that everything we know we know through symbolic media, whether words, pictures, formulae, or theories. As Mrs. Langer put it, symbols are the vehicles of meaning.

25 The transformation of word into thing in our consciousness can be seen in the phenomenon of false onomatopoeia. The words *limber, flat, furry, fuzzy, round, yellow, sharp* sound like the things they signify, not because the actual sounds resemble the thing or quality, but because the sound has been transformed in our consciousness to "become" the thing signified. If you don't believe this, try repeating one of these words several dozen times: All at once it will lose its magic guise as symbol and become the poor drab vocable it really is.

26 This modern notion of the symbolic character of our awareness turns out to have a very old history, however. The Scholastics, who incidentally had a far more adequate theory of symbolic meaning in some respects than modern semioticists, used to say that man does not have a direct knowledge of essences as do the angels but only an indirect knowledge, a knowledge mediated by symbols. John of St. Thomas observed that symbols come to contain within themselves the thing symbolized *in alio esse*, in another mode of existence.

27 But what has this symbolic process got to do with the "is" I mentioned earlier, with the unprecedented affirmation of existence? We know that the little copula "is" is a very late comer in the evolution of languages. Many languages contain no form of the verb "to be." Certainly the most primitive sentence, a pointing at a particular thing and a naming, does not contain the copula. Nevertheless it is a *pairing*, an apposing of word and thing, an act the very essence of which is an "is-saying," an affirming of the thing to be what it is for both of us.

28 Once we have grasped the nature of symbolization, we may begin to see its significance for our view of man's place in the world. I am assuming that we share, to begin with, an empirical-realistic view of the world, that we believe that there are such things as rocks, planets, trees, dogs, which can be at least partially known and partially explained by science, and that man takes his

place somewhere in the scheme. The faculty of language, however, confers upon man a very peculiar position in this scheme—and not at all the position we establish in viewing him as a "higher organism."

The significance of language may be approached in the following way. In our ordinary theoretical view of the world, we see it as a process, a dynamic succession of energy states. There are subatomic particles and atoms and molecules in motion; there are gaseous bodies expanding or contracting; there are inorganic elements in chemical interaction; there are organisms in contact with an environment, responding and adapting accordingly, there are animals responding to each other by means of sign behavior.   *29*

This state of affairs we may think of as a number of terms in interaction, each with all the others. Each being is in the world, acting upon the world and itself being acted upon by the world.   *30*

But when a man appears and names a thing, when he says this is water and water is cool, something unprecedented takes place. What the third term, man, does is not merely enter into interaction with the others—though he does this too—but stand apart from two of the terms and say that one "is" the other. The two things which he pairs or identifies are the *word* he speaks or hears and the *thing* he sees before him.   *31*

This is not only an unprecedented happening; it is also, as the semanticists have noted, scandalous. A is clearly not B. But were it not for this cosmic blunder, man would not be man; he would never be capable of folly and he would never be capable of truth. Unless he says that A is B, he will never know A or B; he will only respond to them. A bee is not as foolish as man, but it also cannot tell the truth. All it can do is respond to its environment.   *32*

What are the consequences for our thinking about man? There are a great many consequences, epistemological, existential, religious, psychiatric. There is space here to mention only one, the effect it has on our *minimal* concept of man. I do not mean our concept of his origin and his destiny, which is, of course, the province of religion. I mean, rather, our working concept, as our minimal working concept of water is a compound of hydrogen and oxygen.   *33*

An awareness of the nature of language must have the greatest possible consequences for our minimal concept of man. For one thing it must reveal the ordinary secular concept of man held in the West as not merely inadequate but quite simply mistaken. I do not refer to the Christian idea of man as a composite of body and soul, a belief which is professed by some and given lip service by many but which can hardly be said to be a working assumption of secular learning. We see man—when I say we, I mean 95 per cent of those who attend American high schools and universities—as the highest of the organisms: He stands erect, he apposes thumb and forefinger, his language is far more complex than that of the most advanced *Cebus azarae*. But the difference is quantitative, not qualitative. Man is a higher organism, standing in direct continuity with rocks, soil, fungi, protozoa, and mammals.   *34*

This happens not to be true, however, and in a way it is unfortunate. I say unfortunate because it means the shattering of the old dream of the Enlighten-   *35* ment—that an objective-explanatory-causal science can discover and set forth all the knowledge of which man is capable. The dream is drawing to a close. The existentialists have taught us that what man is cannot be grasped by the sciences of man. The case is rather that man's science is one of the things that man does, a mode of existence. Another mode is speech. Man is not merely a higher organism responding to and controlling his envirnoment. He is, in Heidegger's words, that being in the world whose calling it is to find a name for Being, to give testimony to it, and to provide for it a clearing.

WRITING AND DISCUSSION QUESTIONS

Informative

1. What does Percy find remarkable or unusual about language? What unique qualities, according to Percy, does language possess compared with other seemingly natural and unremarkable phenomena? Why does he say language "cannot be explained in the ordinary terminology of explanation"?

2. Explain Percy's definition of "sign" and "symbol." How does his distinction between the two serve his exposition of the "mystery" of language?

3. Naming, says Percy, is generically different from denoting or defining a term or even describing it. How is it different? Why does Percy press this point so firmly?

Persuasive

1. Percy argues against the notion that human speech and writing is merely a response to a stimulus, a simple process of "muscular events in the mouth, wave events in the air. . . . etc." His claim is that "man is not merely a higher organism," but in fact he is "that being in the world whose calling it is to find a name for Being." Argue that this is or is not a religious claim. Is language an instance of uniqueness that sets humans apart?

2. Compare and contrast Percy's view of humanness with those of John Searle and B. F. Skinner as presented in this chapter. Which of their views of humanness appeals to you? Why?

Personal

1. Percy uses the word "mystery" to describe language. Do you consider it a mystery? Has scientific methodology and explanation stripped away the mystery of most human phenomena? Percy draws our attention to "the old dream of the Enlightenment—that an objective-explanatory-causal science can discover and set forth all the knowledge of which man is capable." Do you find all phenonema explainable in terms of "natural" causes? What do you find mysterious about yourself or the world?

2. In Genesis, one of the tasks given to Adam is the "naming" of the other creatures. How does Percy's explanation of the power of naming shed light on the

relationships between man and woman and between humankind and nature implied in the Genesis narrative?

▼

JOHN SEARLE "CAN COMPUTERS THINK?" FROM *MINDS, BRAINS, AND SCIENCE*

John Searle is a professor of philosophy at the University of California, Berkeley, among whose interests are exploring and clarifying the relationships among the mind, language, and artificial intelligence. What sets Searle apart from other philosophers is his lucid prose style, crafted for divergent audiences; he speaks to his fellow philosophers and to nonphilosophers with equal ease. Searle's book *Minds, Brains, and Science* (1987) offers a skeptical look at the claims made by the researchers of artificial intelligence about the thinking capabilities of computers. His special task is to offer a solution to the "mind–body problem," which he defines this way:

> How can we account for the relationships between two apparently completely different things? On the one hand, there are mental things, such as our thoughts and feelings; we think of them as subjective, conscious, and immaterial. On the other hand, there are physical things; we think of them as having mass, as extended into space, and as causally interacting with other physical things.

> Because many solutions to the mind–body problem end up denying the existence of or downgrading the status of one or other of these phenomena, Searle has sought a different tack. He argues against the naive materialist conception of the mind; that is the mind is not a real entity but only the construction of a biological process over which the human being has no control. Against some utopian claims, then, Searle denies that the human mind is merely a biological computer. His larger concern is, thus, defending the common sense view that human beings are, in fact, conscious, free, rational agents. In this selection from *Minds, Brains and Science*, he questions whether "computers can think"; in his opposition to this notion, Searle articulates important and useful criteria for determining what is a uniquely human quality.

▼

Can Computers Think?
JOHN SEARLE

Though we do not know in detail how the brain functions, we do   *1* know enough to have an idea of the general relationships between brain processes and mental processes. Mental processes are caused by the behaviour of elements of the brain. At the same time, they are realised in the structure that is made up of those elements. I think this answer is consistent with the standard biological approaches to biological phenomena. Indeed, it is a kind of commonsense answer to the question, given what we know about how the world works. However, it is very much a minority point of view. The prevailing view in philosophy, psychology, and artificial intelligence is one which emphasises the analogies between the functioning of the human brain and the functioning of digital computers. According to the most extreme version of this view, the brain is just a digital computer and the mind is just a computer program. One could summarise this view—I call it 'strong artificial intelligence', or 'strong AI'—by saying that the mind is to the brain, as the program is to the computer hardware.

2   This view has the consequence that there is nothing essentially biological about the human mind. The brain just happens to be one of an indefinitely large number of different kinds of hardware computers that could sustain the programs which make up human intelligence. On this view, any physical system whatever that had the right program with the right inputs and outputs would have a mind in exactly the same sense that you and I have minds. So, for example, if you made a computer out of old beer cans powered by windmills; if it had the right program, it would have to have a mind. And the point is not that for all we know it might have thoughts and feelings, but rather that it must have thoughts and feelings, because that is all there is to having thoughts and feelings: implementing the right program.

3   Most people who hold this view think we have not yet designed programs which are minds. But there is pretty much general agreement among them that it's only a matter of time until computer scientists and workers in artificial intelligence design the appropriate hardware and programs which will be the equivalent of human brains and minds. These will be artificial brains and minds which are in every way the equivalent of human brains and minds.

4   Many people outside of the field of artificial intelligence are quite amazed to discover that anybody could believe such a view as this. So, before criticising it, let me give you a few examples of the things that people in this field have actually said. Herbert Simon of Carnegie-Mellon University says that we already have machines that can literally think. There is no question of waiting for some future machine, because existing digital computers already have thoughts in exactly the same sense that you and I do. Well, fancy that! Philosophers have been worried for centuries about whether or not a machine could think, and now we discover that they already have such machines at Carnegie-Mellon. Simon's colleague Alan Newell claims that we have now discovered (and notice that Newell says 'discovered' and not 'hypothesised' or 'considered the possibility', but we have *discovered*) that intelligence is just a matter of physical symbol manipulation; it has no essential connection with any specific kind of biological or physical wetware or hardware. Rather, any system whatever that is capable of manipulating physical symbols in the right way is capable of intelligence in the same literal sense as human intelligence of human beings. Both Simon and Newell, to their credit, emphasise that there is nothing metaphorical about these claims; they mean them quite literally. Freeman Dyson is quoted as having said that computers have an advantage over the rest of us when it comes to

evolution. Since consciousness is just a matter of formal processes, in computers these formal processes can go on in substances that are much better able to survive in a universe that is cooling off than beings like ourselves made of our wet and messy materials. Marvin Minsky of MIT say that the next generation of computers will be so intelligent that we will 'be lucky if they are willing to keep us around the house as household pets'. My all-time favourite in the literature of exaggerated claims on behalf of the digital computer is from John McCarthy, the inventor of the term 'artificial intelligence'. McCarthy says even 'machines as simple as thermostats can be said to have beliefs'. And indeed, according to him, almost any machine capable of problem-solving can be said to have beliefs. I admire McCarthy's courage. I once asked him: 'What beliefs does your thermostat have?' And he said: 'My thermostat has three beliefs—it's too hot in here, it's too cold in here, and it's just right in here.' As a philosopher, I like all these claims for a simple reason. Unlike most philosophical theses, they are reasonably clear, and they admit of a simple and decisive refutation. It is this refutation that I am going to undertake in this chapter.

The nature of the refutation has nothing whatever to do with any particular   5
stage of computer technology. It is important to emphasise this point because the temptation is always to think that the solution to our problems must wait on some as yet uncreated technological wonder. But in fact, the nature of the refutation is completely independent of any state of technology. It has to do with the very definition of a digital computer, with what a digital computer is.

It is essential to our conception of a digital computer that its operations can   6
be specified purely formally; that is, we specify the steps in the operation of the computer in terms of abstract symbols—sequences of zeroes and ones printed on a tape, for example. A typical computer 'rule' will determine that when a machine is in a certain state and it has a certain symbol on its tape, then it will perform a certain operation such as erasing the symbol or printing another symbol and then enter another state such as moving the tape one square to the left. But the symbols have no meaning; they have no semantic content; they are not about anything. They have to be specified purely in terms of their formal or syntactical structure. The zeroes and ones, for example, are just numerals; they don't even stand for numbers. Indeed, it is this feature of digital computers that makes them so powerful. One and the same type of hardware, if it is appropriately designed, can be used to run an indefinite range of different programs. And one and the same program can be run on an indefinite range of different types of hardwares.

But this feature of programs, that they are defined purely formally or syntac-   7
tically, is fatal to the view that mental processes and program processes are identical. And the reason can be stated quite simply. There is more to having a mind than having formal or syntactical processes. Our internal mental states, by definition, have certain sorts of contents. If I am thinking about Kansas City or wishing that I had a cold beer to drink or wondering if there will be a fall in interest rates, in each case my mental state has a certain mental content in addition to whatever formal features it might have. That is, even if my thoughts

occur to me in strings of symbols, there must be more to the thought than the abstract strings, because strings by themselves can't have any meaning. If my thoughts are to be *about* anything, then the strings must have a *meaning* which makes the thoughts about those things. In a word, the mind has more than a syntax, it has a semantics. The reason that no computer program can ever be a mind is simply that a computer program is only syntactical, and minds are more than syntactical. Minds are semantical, in the sense that they have more than a formal structure, they have a content.

8   To illustrate this point I have designed a certain thought-experiment. Imagine that a bunch of computer programmers have written a program that will enable a computer to simulate the understanding of Chinese. So, for example, if the computer is given a question in Chinese, it will match the question against its memory, or data base, and produce appropriate answers to the questions in Chinese. Suppose for the sake of argument that the computer's answers are as good as those of a native Chinese speaker. Now then, does the computer, on the basis of this, understand Chinese, does it literally understand Chinese, in the way that Chinese speakers understand Chinese? Well, imagine that you are locked in a room, and in this room are several baskets full of Chinese symbols. Imagine that you (like me) do not understand a word of Chinese, but that you are given a rule book in English for manipulating these Chinese symbols. The rules specify the manipulations of the symbols purely formally, in terms of their syntax, not their semantics. So the rule might say: 'Take a squiggle-squiggle sign out of basket number one and put it next to a squoggle-squoggle sign from basket number two.' Now suppose that some other Chinese symbols are passed into the room, and that you are given further rules for passing back Chinese symbols out of the room. Suppose that unknown to you the symbols passed into the room are called 'questions' by the people outside the room, and the symbols you pass back out of the room are called 'answers to the questions'. Suppose, furthermore, that the programmers are so good at designing the programs and that you are so good at manipulating the symbols, that very soon your answers are indistinguishable from those of a native Chinese speaker. There you are locked in your room shuffling your Chinese symbols and passing out Chinese symbols in response to incoming Chinese symbols. On the basis of the situation as I have described it, there is no way you could learn any Chinese simply by manipulating these formal symbols.

9   Now the point of the story is simply this: by virtue of implementing a formal computer program from the point of view of an outside observer, you behave exactly as if you understood Chinese, but all the same you don't understand a word of Chinese. But if going through the appropriate computer program for understanding Chinese is not enough to give *you* an understanding of Chinese, then it is not enough to give *any other digital computer* an understanding of Chinese. And again, the reason for this can be stated quite simply. If you don't understand Chinese, then no other computer could understand Chinese because no digital computer, just by virtue of running a program, has anything that you don't have. All that the computer has, as you have, is a formal program for

manipulating uninterpreted Chinese symbols. To repeat, a computer has a syntax, but no semantics. The whole point of the parable of the Chinese room is to remind us of a fact that we knew all along. Understanding a language, or indeed, having mental states at all, involves more than just having a bunch of formal symbols. It involves having an interpretation, or a meaning attached to those symbols. And a digital computer, as defined, cannot have more than just formal symbols because the operation of the computer, as I said earlier, is defined in terms of its ability to implement programs. And these programs are purely formally specifiable—that is, they have no semantic content.

We can see the force of this argument if we contrast what it is like to be   *10* asked and to answer questions in English, and to be asked and to answer questions in some language where we have no knowledge of any of the meanings of the words. Imagine that in the Chinese room you are also given questions in English about such things as your age or your life history, and that you answer these questions. What is the difference between the Chinese case and the English case? Well again, if like me you understand no Chinese and you do understand English, then the difference is obvious. You understand the questions in English because they are expressed in symbols whose meanings are known to you. Similarly, when you give the answers in English you are producing symbols which are meaningful to you. But in the case of the Chinese, you have none of that. In the case of the Chinese, you simply manipulate formal symbols according to a computer program, and you attach no meaning to any of the elements.

Various replies have been suggested to this argument by workers in artificial *11* intelligence and in psychology, as well as philosophy. They all have something in common; they are all inadequate. And there is an obvious reason why they have to be inadequate, since the argument rests on a very simple logical truth, namely, syntax alone is not sufficient for semantics, and digital computers insofar as they are computers have, by definition, a syntax alone.

I want to make this clear by considering a couple of the arguments that are   *12* often presented against me.

Some people attempt to answer the Chinese room example by saying that   *13* the whole system understands Chinese. The idea here is that though I, the person in the room manipulating the symbols do not understand Chinese, I am just the central processing unit of the computer system. They argue that it is the whole system, including the room, the baskets full of symbols and the ledgers containing the programs and perhaps other items as well, taken as a totality, that understands Chinese. But this is subject to exactly the same objection I made before. There is no way that the system can get from the syntax to the semantics. I, as the central processing unit have no way of figuring out what any of these symbols means; but then neither does the whole system.

Another common response is to imagine that we put the Chinese under-   *14* standing program inside a robot. If the robot moved around and interacted causally with the world, wouldn't that be enough to guarantee that it understood Chinese? Once again the inexorability of the semantics-syntax distinction overcomes this manoeuvre. As long as we suppose that the robot has only a computer for a brain then, even though it might behave exactly as if it understood Chinese, it would still have no way of getting from the syntax to the semantics of Chinese. You can see this if you imagine that I am the computer. Inside a room in the robot's skull I shuffle symbols without knowing that some of them come in to me from television cameras attached to the robot's head and others go out to move the robot's arms and legs. As long as all I have is a formal computer program, I have no way of attaching any meaning to any of the symbols. And the fact that the robot is engaged in causal interactions with the outside world won't help me to attach any meaning to the symbols unless I have some way of finding out about that fact. Suppose the robot picks up a hamburger and this triggers the symbol for hamburger to come into the room. As long as all I have is the symbol with no knowledge of its causes or how it got there, I have no way of knowing what it means. The causal interactions between the robot and the rest of the world are irrelevant unless those causal interactions are represented in some mind or other. But there is no way they can be if all that the so-called mind consists of is a set of purely formal, syntactical operations.

15   It is important to see exactly what is claimed and what is not claimed by my argument. Suppose we ask the question that I mentioned at the beginning: 'Could a machine think?' Well, in one sense, of course, we are all machines. We can construe the stuff inside our heads as a meat machine. And of course, we can all think. So, in one sense of 'machine', namely that sense in which a machine is just a physical system which is capable of performing certain kinds of operations, in that sense, we are all machines, and we can think. So, trivially, there are machines that can think. But that wasn't the question that bothered us. So let's try a different formulation of it. Could an artefact think? Could a man-made machine think? Well, once again, it depends on the kind of artefact. Suppose we designed a machine that was molecule-for-molecule indistinguishable from a human being. Well then, if you can duplicate the causes, you can presumably duplicate the effects. So once again, the answer to that question is, in principle at least, trivially yes. If you could build a machine that had the same structure as a human being, then presumably that machine would be able to think. Indeed, it would be a surrogate human being. Well, let's try again.

16   The question isn't: 'Can a machine think?' or: 'Can an artefact think?' The question is: 'Can a digital computer think?' But once again we have to be very careful in how we interpret the question. From a mathematical point of view, anything whatever can be described *as if* it were a digital computer. And that's because it can be described as instantiating or implementing a computer program. In an utterly trivial sense, the pen that is on the desk in front of me can be described as a digital computer. It just happens to have a very boring computer program. The program says: 'Stay there.' Now since in this sense, anything whatever is a digital computer, because anything whatever can be described as implementing a computer program, then once again, our question

gets a trivial answer. Of course our brains are digital computers, since they implement any number of computer programs. And of course our brains can think. So once again, there is a trivial answer to the question. But that wasn't really the question we were trying to ask. The question we wanted to ask is this: 'Can a digital computer, as defined, think?' That is to say: 'Is instantiating or implementing the right computer program with the right inputs and outputs, sufficient for, or constitutive of, thinking?' And to this question, unlike its predecessors, the answer is clearly 'no'. And it is 'no' for the reason that we have spelled out, namely, the computer program is defined purely syntactically. But thinking is more than just a matter of manipulating meaningless symbols, it involves meaningful semantic contents. These semantic contents are what we mean by 'meaning'.

It is important to emphasise again that we are not talking about a particular   *17* stage of computer technology. The argument has nothing to do with the forthcoming, amazing advances in computer science. It has nothing to do with the distinction between serial and parallel processes, or with the size of programs, or the speed of computer operations, or with computers that can interact causally with their environment, or even with the invention of robots. Technological progress is always grossly exaggerated, but even subtracting the exaggeration, the development of computers has been quite remarkable, and we can reasonably expect that even more remarkable progress will be made in the future. No doubt we will be much better able to simulate human behaviour on computers than we can at present, and certainly much better than we have been able to in the past. The point I am making is that if we are talking about having mental states, having a mind, all of these simulations are simply irrelevant. It doesn't matter how good the technology is, or how rapid the calculations made by the computer are. If it really is a computer, its operations have to be defined syntactically, whereas consciousness, thoughts, feelings, emotions, and all the rest of it involve more than a syntax. Those features, by definition, the computer is unable to *duplicate* however powerful may be its ability to *simulate*. The key distinction here is between duplication and simulation. And no simulation by itself ever constitutes duplication.

What I have done so far is give a basis to the sense that those citations I   *18* began this talk with are really as preposterous as they seem. There is a puzzling question in this discussion though, and that is: 'Why would anybody ever have thought that computers could think or have feelings and emotions and all the rest of it?' After all, we can do computer simulations of any process whatever that can be given a formal description. So, we can do a computer simulation of the flow of money in the British economy, or the pattern of power distribution in the Labour party. We can do computer simulation of rain storms in the home counties, or warehouse fires in East London. Now, in each of these cases, nobody supposes that the computer simulation is actually the real thing; no one supposes that a computer simulation of a storm will leave us all wet, or a computer simulation of a fire is likely to burn the house down. Why on earth would anyone in his right mind suppose a computer simulation of mental processes actually had mental processes? I don't really know the answer to that, since the idea seems to me, to put it frankly, quite crazy from the start. But I can make a couple of speculations.

19   First of all, where the mind is concerned, a lot of people are still tempted to some sort of behaviourism. They think if a system behaves as if it understood Chinese, then it really must understand Chinese. But we have already refuted this form of behaviourism with the Chinese room argument. Another assumption made by many people is that the mind is not a part of the biological world, it is not a part of the world of nature. The strong artificial intelligence view relies on that in its conception that the mind is purely formal; that somehow or other, it cannot be treated as a concrete product of biological processes like any other biological product. There is in these discussions, in short, a kind of residual dualism. AI partisans believe that the mind is more than a part of the natural biological world; they believe that the mind is purely formally specifiable. The paradox of this is that the AI literature is filled with fulminations against some view called 'dualism', but in fact, the whole thesis of strong AI rests on a kind of dualism. It rests on a rejection of the idea that the mind is just a natural biological phenomenon in the world like any other.

20   I want to conclude this chapter by putting together the thesis of the last chapter and the thesis of this one. Both of these theses can be stated very simply. And indeed, I am going to state them with perhaps excessive crudeness. But if we put them together I think we get a quite powerful conception of the relations of minds, brains and computers. And the argument has a very simple logical structure, so you can see whether it is valid or invalid. The first premise is:

1. *Brains cause minds.*

Now, of course, that is really too crude. What we mean by that is that mental processes that we consider to constitute a mind are caused, entirely caused, by processes going on inside the brain. But let's be crude, let's just abbreviate that as three words—brains cause minds. And that is just a fact about how the world works. Now let's write proposition number two:

2. *Syntax is not sufficient for semantics.*

That proposition is a conceptual truth. It just articulates our distinction between the notion of what is purely formal and what has content. Now, to these two propositions—that brains cause minds and that syntax is not sufficient for semantics—let's add a third and a fourth:

3. *Computer programs are entirely defined by their formal, or syntactical, structure.*

That proposition, I take it, is true by definition; it is part of what we mean by the notion of a computer program.

4. *Minds have mental contents; specifically, they have semantic contents.*

And that, I take it, is just an obvious fact about how our minds work. My thoughts, and beliefs, and desires are about something, or they refer to something, or they concern states of affairs in the world; and they do that because their content directs them at these states of affairs in the world. Now, from these four premises, we can draw our first conclusion; and it follows obviously from premises 2, 3, and 4:

CONCLUSION 1. *No computer program by itself is sufficient to give a system a mind. Programs, in short, are not minds, and they are not by themselves sufficient for having minds.*

Now, that is a very powerful conclusion, because it means that the project of trying to create minds solely by designing programs is doomed from the start. And it is important to re-emphasise that this has nothing to do with any particular state of technology or any particular state of the complexity of the program. This is a purely formal, or logical, result from a set of axioms which are agreed to by all (or nearly all) of the disputants concerned. That is, even most of the hardcore enthusiasts for artificial intelligence agree that in fact, as a matter of biology, brain processes cause mental states, and they agree that programs are defined purely formally. But if you put these conclusions together with certain other things that we know, then it follows immediately that the project of strong AI is incapable of fulfilment.

However, once we have got these axioms, let's see what else we can derive. Here is a second conclusion:

CONCLUSION 2. *The way that brain functions cause minds cannot be solely in virtue of running a computer program.*

And this second conclusion follows from conjoining the first premise together with our first conclusion. That is, from the fact that brains cause minds and that programs are not enough to do the job, it follows that the way that brains cause minds can't be solely by running a computer program. Now that also I think is an important result, because it has the consequence that the brain is not, or at least is not just, a digital computer. We saw earlier that anything can trivially be described as if it were a digital computer, and brains are no exception. But the importance of this conclusion is that the computational properties of the brain are simply not enough to explain its functioning to produce mental states. And indeed, that ought to seem a commonsense scientific conclusion to us anyway because all it does is remind us of the fact that brains are biological engines; their biology matters. It is not, as several people in artificial intelligence have claimed, just an irrelevant fact about the mind that it happens to be realised in human brains.

Now, from our first premise, we can also derive a third conclusion:

CONCLUSION 3. *Anything else that caused minds would have to have causal powers at least equivalent to those of the brain.*

And this third conclusion is a trivial consequence of our first premise. It is a bit like saying that if my petrol engine drives my car at seventy-five miles an hour, then any diesel engine that was capable of doing that would have to have a power output at least equivalent to that of my petrol engine. Of course, some other system might cause mental processes using entirely different chemical or biochemical features from those the brain in fact uses. It might turn out that there are beings on other planets, or in other solar systems, that have mental states and use an entirely different biochemistry from ours. Suppose that Martians arrived on earth and we concluded that they had mental states. But suppose that when their heads were opened up, it was discovered that all they had inside was green slime. Well still, the green slime, if it functioned to produce consciousness and all the rest of their mental life, would have to have causal powers equal to those of the human brain. But now, from our first conclusion, that programs are not enough, and our third conclusion, that any other system would have to have causal powers equal to the brain, conclusion four follows immediately:

Conclusion 4. *For any artefact that we might build which had mental states equivalent to human mental states, the implementation of a computer program would not by itself be sufficient. Rather the artefact would have to have powers equivalent to the powers of the human brain.*

The upshot of this discussion I believe is to remind us of something that we have known all along: namely, mental states are biological phenomena. Consciousness, intentionality, subjectivity and mental causation are all a part of our biological life history, along with growth, reproduction, the secretion of bile, and digestion.

WRITING AND DISCUSSION QUESTIONS

Informative

1. What does Searle say is the "prevailing view" in philosophy, psychology, and artificial intelligence regarding the "mind–body problem"? What does he mean by "strong AI"?
2. If one defines intelligence as "physical symbol manipulation," do computers "think"? What problems does Searle have with this definition? Explain his objections. How does he define "digital computer," and of what consequence is it to his refutation of the notion that computers think?
3. Explain his "Chinese room" analogy and the objections other philosophers have voiced against it. What is Searle's defense against these objections?

Persuasive

1. Searle essentially argues that intelligence or thinking cannot be reduced to mere "syntax," or the arrangement of symbols, because "semantics," or meaning making, is at the heart of human thinking. How would Walker Percy and B. F. Skinner respond to his contention? Argue that Searle's stance addresses the issues raised by behaviorism.
2. Consider Searle's conclusion: "mental states are biological phenomena." Argue for or against this conclusion. What claim is being made? How does it differ from those he refutes?

Personal

1. Is there anything intrinsically insulting or wrong-headed to you in calling the brain a "computer" and the mind a "program"? What other metaphors have been used to describe the brain?
2. If you are a computer user, explain those elements of the computer that strike you as "human like." In what ways does it function differently or better than the human mind? Can the mind perform tasks that the computer cannot and vice versa?

CHAPTER WRITING ASSIGNMENTS

1. In what sense does psychology deserve to be thought of as a science? Consider the views in this chapter from thinkers as diverse as Freud, James, Skinner, Percy, and Searle. If psychological inquiry and research can accommodate such diversity, in what sense is it a coherent discipline? Can its "knowledge" be taken seriously given the various tenets that appear to be mutually exclusive? Write an essay that explores the practice and defines the nature of psychology.

2. How would a devout Jew or Christian, a committed feminist, or a Marxist respond to B. F. Skinner's conception of "man?" Respond to Skinner by adopting the viewpoint of one such person.

3. Until recently, homosexuality had been labeled by psychologists and by society as a whole as an "aberration." How have views toward homosexuality changed in the past two decades? What accounts for the change? Presently, how do standard psychological texts and "treatments" define and refer to homosexuality? Write an essay that offers a historical perspective on the source and meaning of homosexual orientation and behavior.

4. Current debate between abortion rights activists and right-to-life activists focuses on what constitutes "personhood." In what ways can the work of psychologists, philosophers, and researchers of artificial intelligence shed light on this debate? How is personhood legally and medically defined by both sides of the abortion debate? Craft an essay that explores the issue of personhood and how it may be resolved in the abortion debate.

Chapter Nine

EXISTENTIALISM

Existentialism is a philosophy that represents an important turning point in the history of ideas. In the nineteenth century, existential thinkers began questioning the precepts originating with the Greeks and generally adhered to up through the nineteenth century that the world was divinely ordered and that faith and reason could be used to understand that order, to give meaning to individuality, and to solve problems concerning the just society. The old notions of an ordered and stable world gave way to a world of rapid change, of increasing uncertainty, and of growing anxiety. The forces that caused such changes are many and include the advances in science, the Industrial Revolution, the promotion of democracy and the ideal of the individual, rapid population growth, and unstable class structures to name a few. Despite these many changes, though, the ancient and modern world continued to share one principle in common and that was the emphasis on reason.

Although it is hard to define the term "existentialism," it can be understood as representing a number of ideas, for instance, the importance of individual freedom and of the acceptance of responsibility; a skepticism toward established ideologies such as religions and various forms of government, which are considered as closed frameworks that have abused the process of reason in providing solutions and accurate views of the world; a belief that the vast majority of humanity is trapped in a dulled routine and alienated from a dynamic existence; and the moral obligation to accept one's myriad choices and to act authentically. In short, most existentialists believe: (1) humans are individually free to make choices; (2) even so, most persons do not exercise that freedom; rather, they allow their genetic inheritance and their environment to choose for them; (3) humans are only what they make of themselves; and (4) those who do not make their own choices lead "inauthentic" lives.

According to existentialism, life comes to have meaning for the individual, only when that individual has risen above the external forces that control his life. An analogy may help to make this idea clear. Imagine a leaf falling from a tree, buffeted here and there by occasional gusts of wind. The leaf is at the mercy of nature's apparently random forces. Typically, an individual, while moving through life, has as little control over her own path as does the leaf falling to the ground. Existentialists tend to believe that the loss of this full control derives from one's imprisonment in routine and conventional behavior—in other words, from an ignorance and even a fear of the mutliple options for and consequences of acting. For many people in the West, an awakening to the stultifying effects of routine and convention, to life's complexities and paradoxes, and to the aloneness of every individual occurs sometime in the high school or college years. Some existentialists like Albert Camus (1913–1960) would say that the alternative to such awakening is a form of intellectual suicide, where one denies the choices and responsibilities present in every situation, by submitting instead to a readily available and previously shaped idea system as offered, for instance, by a religion or political organization.

The breaking with routine is important to existentialism, but it would be misleading to imply that the philosophy is by definition nonconformist. The goal of existentialism is to reflect critically on one's choices, to become self-conscious and fully responsible for the choices and commitments one makes. Thus, it is entirely possible that an existentialist will choose to believe in God, to be an atheist, and to be pro-choice or pro-life. An important trait of existentialists is that they deliberately and carefully reflect on the "authentic," that is, self-conscious compared with self-deceptive, choices they are capable of making.

Existentialists, because they are antideterministic, see routine and convention as anathema. Existentialism asserts that we are our choices; that is, we are who we are not through an unfolding of our genetic inheritance or the external forces of our environment including the routines and conventions of society, all of which tend to shape our attitudes and behaviors, but through our capacity to choose and to act. The excuse that "I am the product of my society and upbringing" is unacceptable to the existentialist. At all stages of one's life, one is responsible for choosing what to make of, and acting upon, the manifestation of one's heritage and present environment.

The primary focus of existentialism is on persons as individuals and on the concrete particulars of existence. From this focus, there follows a skepticism of abstract idea systems and a fear of individual existence becoming buried by abstract theorizing. The basis for such fear is that any individual who is involved in theorizing risks adopting the posture of a spectator who ultimately falls away from a life of action and commitment. Because of their emphasis on the individual and exercise of freedom, existentialists are generally opposed to religious orthodoxies, political systems, and conventional moralities, especially if these conventions do not allow the individual to exercise choice and action.

The collapse of routine in an individual life is reflected in certain important events in the development of Western civilization. Sometime in the early nineteenth century, the confidence in the human experience that many thinkers had expressed on and off for over two thousand years collapsed for many intellectuals. The ancient Greeks, in magnificent sculptural tributes to the human form and in Homeric epics depicting the hero's dignity in overcoming tragic circumstances, offered typical expressions of this confidence. For Plato, the essence of our world consisted of things and Ideas, and the actual things of this world (chairs, tables, persons, emotions, and actual governments) were merely reflections of transcendent phemonena of the world of Ideas. Because a particular thing, emotion, or government does not last forever, though the Idea behind that thing, emotion, or government (Tableness, Love, or Democracy) never perishes, the Ideas are more real in that they are eternal. The task of the individual, for Plato then, is to strive to know the Ideas and to move toward their actualization—to come closer to the Ideals of Love, Goodness, Beauty, and Democracy. There was a sustaining hope that human reason could, through study and work, result in the highest of human aspirations. (It would be wrong, though, to leave the impression that optimism about human reason and development was the only characteristic of the Greek mind. One must acknowledge the darker vision of Greek tragedy and the skepticism of Socrates.)

With the burning of the library at Alexandria in A.D. 391 and the growth of the Roman Empire, the influence of ancient Greece declined. During an interval of over a thousand years, that is, the Middle Ages, the Christian cosmos was so thoroughly charted that there seemed to be little room for uncertainty about the role and proper conduct of the individual in society. In the fourteenth century, at the beginning of the Renaissance, the optimism of the Greeks toward perfection of the individual was renewed and continued through the seventeenth century, the Enlightenment, and into the eighteenth century with its emphasis on human reason, particularly the scientific method. In that period of several hundred years, confidence in the supposedly unlimited human capacities to solve problems and the inevitability of progress grew steadily, especially with the writings of Copernicus, Galileo, Newton, and Locke. The scientific method was being used to uncover the universal laws of nature and offered the expectation that almost anything could be measured and quantified. The American and French Revolutions further championed the rights of the individual, and their success further reinforced the optimism about progress.

In the nineteenth century came the discovery of many biological principles, suggesting that nature could be controlled. For instance, from genetics came the improvement of plant and animal species and from microbiology came the elimination of age-old diseases. The Industrial Revolutions in England and America increased hope for the millions who were overworked and lived in squalor. The invention of labor-saving devices like the railroad and the cotton gin and the vast array of consumer products continued this optimism into the twentieth century.

ORIGINS OF EXISTENTIALISM IN THE NINETEENTH CENTURY

Despite the scientific achievements and the continual advance toward individual liberty, all was not rosy in the nineteenth and beginning of the twentieth centuries, for the situation of the common person continued to be characterized by poverty, misery, and powerlessness. Some governments attempted to improve the lot of the common person by protective legislation, but by and large, business interests and the propertied classes exploited the laborers. The established Church too often neglected the poor in order to aggrandize itself. (Yet, in many previous centuries, the Church almost single-handedly sustained the poor in some nations by providing education, housing, and care.) In the cities, inhuman living and working conditions prevailed. Marxism appeared in response to these conditions and inspired "successful" revolutions in Russia and China, after which communist governments were instituted. The governments, though, soon devolved into totalitarian states, whose programmatic terrorism took the lives of over 50 million persons and sapped the strength and will of countless others. Such "utopian" ideologies based on what appeared to be high ideals resulted in extreme human suffering, which may have been more severe than the original conditions that inspired the revolution.

Two nineteenth-century thinkers articulated the deep-seated doubts buried in the directions Western civilization was heading. These two thinkers, Kierkegaard and Nietzsche, laid the foundation for the wave of existentialism that washed over France and the United States during World War II.

The Danish theologian Søren Kierkegaard (1813–1855) believed that the only truth one could accept was supremely subjective, by which he meant neither a radical relativism nor an antirationalism. Rather, he emphasized the importance of subjective moments of reflection, separating oneself from all systems and institutions to examine the range of choices and consequences. Kierkegaard preached that man's most important act was to choose: not just that one *can* choose, but that one *must* choose.

To trace the development of this conclusion, it must be understood that in Kierkegaard's most important works published in the 1840s (*Either/Or, Repetition, Fear and Trembling, Philosophical Fragments, The Concept of Dread, Stages on Life's Way, Attack on Christendom,* and *The Present Age*), he proposed that there are three stages of growth for each individual. Initially, in what he called the "aesthetic" stage, one lives, absorbed and affected by what occurs around him, passionately pursuing the pleasurable and interesting and avoiding the boring. Kierkegaard's treatment of Don Juan is important because it shows that pursuit of the interesting can be a part of a life of integrity, though it cannot be the highest governing principle, for it lacks the capacity to find the ever new and the ever interesting. One who lives from moment to moment seeking physical pleasure fails to make judgments and decisions about which experience has greater long-term importance. One who lives according to philosophical abstraction, because he is no more than a spectator of the human drama, fails also to make critically relevant decisions. Like the leaf described above, the life of one who lives in the aesthetic stage is ultimately controlled by outside phenomena.

Being unable to make lasting and satisfying choices in life, the "aesthete" soon despairs of a life of immediacy and moves toward the second stage of existence, the "ethical." Eventually he rejects altogether the life based merely on the pleasurable and interesting. Although it does not seem to matter to Kierkegaard which ethical standard the individual chooses, what is important is the intensity and sincerity with which choices are made. The first stage, characterized by an aimless pursuit of momentary pleasures followed by boredom, gives way to a purposive life that is more secure. It is a life governed by universal principles, which give shape to authenticity and a well-developed sense of self. The individual is capable of making important decisions and commitments and of honest and fair social interactions. However, the second stage fails to bring permanent peace of mind, for in arriving at a strong and inward knowledge of the self, one discovers human fallibility, self-deception, and the weakness of will. One committed only to the ethical life does not possess the strength of character necessary to fully commit to a broad and strong moral path and, thus, is alienated from God. He experiences deep doubts, which brings remorse and guilt, over his choice of ethical standards and his various commitments.

The "religious" phase is the last for Kierkegaard, and in it, the individual seeks to know and serve God; to arrive at this stage, the individual must rise beyond the ethical sphere and its concern for self-knowledge and duty and make a "leap of faith." Such a leap seemingly defies reason and fully embraces human finiteness. It listens to a voice that rises beyond reason. The Biblical story of Abraham's near sacrifice of his son Isaac typifies the movement from the ethical to the religious sphere, where the good father, who would do anything to preserve and nurture the life of his son, submits through faith to what he realizes is a higher moral demand, God's call to sacrifice.

As critic Nathan Scott explains, Kierkegaard's analysis of human stages of development soon led him to a radical indictment of the Lutheran Church of his day. Everywhere in the Europe of his time, Kierkegaard observed social structures that worked to prevent persons from reckoning with their own individual and subjective beings, making growth through these stages impossible; instead, the group was the controlling force of the time. In denouncing the pervasiveness of group and "herd" behavior, Kierkegaard attacked the Lutheran State Church of Denmark, observing that the clergy were not witnessing on behalf of Christ; rather, they were preoccupied with the business of perpetuating their lavish buildings, delivering successful sermons, and being "simply another bulwark of bourgeois respectability."[1] Baptism, confirmation, and church attendance were supposed to constitute a true Christianity, but were fairly infrequent; also, the difficulty and strain of maintaining faith in the absence of good reasons, the hardships of remaining steadfast, and the challenge to an ethical integrity were too rarely acknowledged.

---

[1]Scott, Nathan, *Mirrors of Man in Existentialism*. New York, Collins, 1969, pp. 31–57.

In effect, Kierkegaard disturbed the certainties around him by claiming that any idea system (religious or philosophical) that has the effect of imposing a purpose or essence on persons (or including the view that essences are determined) has utterly failed. The French philospher Jean-Paul Sartre (1905–1980) was to claim more than a century later that "existence precedes essence"; that is, one begins life by merely existing, with no given purpose or essence. The ultimate freedom to choose who and what we are, in the midst of a world in which purpose and meaning are not givens (or ready-made parts of the human character) obligates us to make our own decisions. Ultimately, we are each alone to contemplate the universe and, through the exercise of our freedom, to realize our purpose. The result, both Kierkegaard and Sartre realized, is the dread and despair of being alone, without family, friends, church, or other idea system to serve as support. However, despair and anarchy were not the end points of either philosopher's thought. Both pursued lives of constructive action, Kierkegaard through his writings and Sartre through his writings and his political activities, and both urged others on to such lives.

In his analysis of social and religious conditions of his time, Kierkegaard affirmed God's ultimate love and care for his creatures. His own purpose was to disclose the sham in the institutionalized church and to revive the power and authority of sacred scripture.

German philosopher Friedrich Nietzsche (1844–1900), who is the second nineteenth-century philospher to lay the foundation for existentialism, took a more radical step by denying the fundamental vitality of the Christian scripture as practiced by those around him and by claiming that God was, indeed, dead. Although Nietzsche never read Kierkegaard's writings, the two men shared similar ideas. Both loathed the controlling power of the Church and the middle-class masses, what Nietzsche referred to as the "power of the flock and no shepherd." Also, both seemed to share similar personalities in that they were combative and given to introspection.

Nietzsche's father was a Lutheran pastor who died by the time Friedrich was five. Raised by his mother and grandmother, surrounded also by his sister and two maiden aunts, Nietzsche studied philosophy at the University of Bonn, where he was a brilliant student. Somewhat like Kierkegaard, who had a slight humpback, Nietzsche was physically frail and at times psychologically unstable, qualities which some think made the men outsiders and, therefore, capable of penetratingly unconventional insights. That should not, however, be taken as a sign that Nietzsche's mind was impaired, which it was not until his last years, when he had a nervous breakdown and is said to have gone mad.

In 1868, Nietzsche developed a close relationship with the famous composer Richard Wagner; to understand Nietzsche's important concept of "the will to power," it is important to understand this relationship. Both men shared an enthusiasm for the writings of the German philosopher Arthur Schopenhauer (1788–1860) who also was associated with the idea of will, and a repulsion for the mediocrity and stagnation they sensed in bourgeois German society. Wagner's operas and symphonies dramatized the greatness and magnitude he hoped the German culture would attain; Nietzsche was drawn to Wagner's ideas and to his German paganism, which Wagner hoped would lead to a new Germany.

However, problems soon developed in the relationship. The roots of Nietzsche's parting with Wagner lay in Wagner's aversion to Christianity's Jewish roots and the centrality of humility, meekness, and love in the Judeo–Christian tradition, undercutting what Wagner believed was the importance of power. In 1882, when Wagner's opera *Parsifal*, based on the essentially Christian quest for the Holy Grail, was staged, it was the racial doctrine inherent in that work that caused Nietzsche to break relations. Nietzsche's discomfort with the ideas that later evolved into the monstrous evil of Hitler's race ideology did not become clear to the world until long after his death, for his sister Elizabeth selectively edited her brother's works in ways that made them appear to support the idea of an exclusive super race. In fact, Nietzsche had always rejected anti-Semitism and nationalism, advocating cultural diversity and race mixture.

Modern scholars have convincingly shown that the center of Nietzsche's thought is not to champion the power of a superior "man" over others deemed racially inferior; rather, it is his realization that the loss of a faith that had been nurtured for centuries signaled nothing less than the death of God and a major turning point for the world. Nietsche's will to power referred to his ideals or personal integrity and commitment to excellence through subjective moments of the will. His clearest statement of that position occurs in *The Gay Science* (1882):

> Do we not hear anything yet of the noise of the gravediggers who are burying God? Do we not smell anything yet of God's decomposition? Gods too decompose. God is dead. . . . And we have killed him. . . . What was holiest and most powerful of all that the world has yet owned has bled to death under our knives. Who will wipe this blood off us? . . . Is not the greatness of this deed too great for us? Must not we ourselves become gods simply to seem worthy of it?

Like Kierkegaard, Nietzsche observed that faith was not subjectively signifi-cant in the lives of his contemporaries. Nietzsche's importance is that he offered the news to the world that the Church had lost its prophetic power, that God had been killed by humans, that those humans were, therefore, on trial, and that we must search out a way of living without faith in God and with doubt and uncer-tainty. Nietzsche did not analytically speculate about the existence of God as many philosophers had; rather, his conclusion was based on a kind of empirical observation—God simply did not exist for most Europeans and was, in effect, dead. Nietzsche realized that what was new about humanity's plight was that the great foundation of faith, the great rock of the Judeo–Christian tradition that had served humanity for more than three thousand years, was for him and so many others gone, and nothing was left in its place. Nietzsche was, therefore, not claim-ing that there was no God; he was saying that God was no longer a culturally significant and determining influence. Finding God "dead" in the souls of his contemporaries, Nietzsche observed the fundamentally secular nature of society and speculated about the implications.

Nietzsche asked what it meant to live in a world in which religion could no longer deliver the all-encompassing guidelines for action and reason for living, a world in which people looked elsewhere (to material success, to teachers, and to newspapers) for direction, in which all were alone in a world without any meaning apart from that which people created for themselves. Nietzsche realized that being alone without God meant living in a great void, but it also had another side. If God could not look out for humanity, then humanity was responsible for all creatures and all events on earth. Nietzsche realized that there was an exhiliration in that burden that humanity must establish values and laws and must chart the waters and lands. He called the responsibility we must face "a reevaluation," by which he meant a reinvention of purpose and meaning, a redefinition of value itself. Thus, in his masterpiece, *Thus Spake Zarathustra* (1892), and in his collection of notes *The Will to Power*, Nietzsche urged a new type of human to emerge whom he called *Übermensch* (variously translated as "overman" or "superman"). For such a person, the "will to power" meant the striving for greater achievement, creativity, and vitality, for a transcendence all persons were capable of.[2] Here again there is movement away from the ancient world with its frequent assumptions of a fixed reality and of a definite place and purpose for each person; for Nietzsche, dynamic growth or becoming, not being, was the fundamental reality.

These early existentialists reminded the European middle class that it was fast becoming too comfortable with its successes and reminded the Church that it had forgotten the central message of Christ. As Jacob Bronowski reminded us, we are not creatures of the landscape; we are shapers of the landscape and even, more important, shapers of ourselves. For both these early existentialists, Christianity was becoming a rigid and dangerous bulwark of conservatism, encouraging conformity and complacency, and thus insensitivity. For Kierkegaard, the Christian, and for Nietzsche, the atheist, the goal of their philosophies was a revitalization of faith.

THE DEVELOPMENT OF EXISTENTIALISM IN THE TWENTIETH CENTURY

The development of existentialism in the twentieth century occurred most dramatically after World War II, when the philosophy crossed the frontier of academic life into the world of practical affairs. Through the first half of this century, despite its nineteenth-century origins, existentialism was ignored in academic circles and was not generally accepted as a "philosophy." It took a second great world war to change that, especially from a European perspective. With the rise of the Third Reich, the crisis of meaning and purpose that existentialists talked about resounded at the feet of a whole civilization.

It is one thing to argue the meaninglessness of existence, to throw terms like "meaning," "the death of God," and "choice" around; it is quite another to

[2]Scott, p. 81.

experience it. The world of 1933–1945 seemed utterly in the hands of madmen, who were able to assume and maintain power because of the profound silence, or really acquiescence, on the part of millions of people and on the part of the establsihed institutions of church, state, and culture that shirked their primary responsibility, the protection of civilization. No abstraction, this was the inescapably blatant and disastrous failure of traditional institutions. The average citizen had but two choices: to acquiesce (that is, to cooperate, to submit, to be silent) or to resist. This was a context in which being authentic (that is, making responsible and thoughtful choices and reevaluating one's values) itself seemed absurd, for the likelihood of failure, torture, and death far outweighed that for success. Given the circumstances, it is remarkable indeed that a resistance effort even existed, for from 1940 to 1943 it must have seemed to resisters like Albert Camus or theologian Dietrich Bonhoeffer that Hitler's claim was true, that the Reich would last a thousand years.

For people in the Nazi concentration camps, of course, conditions were much worse, as the story by the Polish writer and Auschwitz prisoner, Tadeusz Borowski, which follows, shows. To maintain one's humanity while living in the most brutal of conditions was almost the only form of resistance available. How radically one must reevaluate, in Nietzsche's terms, when one is in a world devoid of value—no justice, no mercy, no sense of God or humanity, no law—except punishment and death. There seemed to be no ethically responsible choices, only existence or nothingness. For most, there was no choice whatever, only death.

World War II, then, invited the world to witness the systematic atrocities of the "advanced," "industrialized," and "cultured" regime of the Nazis. Although "civilization" was shocked, it did little. Clearly, there was reason for despair. If God was dead, or as Holocaust survivor Elie Wiesel said, only absent and on leave, then anything was possible, even genocide. In response to such events, twentieth-century existentialists interpreted life as an absurdity, in a world where each new technological marvel was matched by a new wave of destruction, resulting in an unsettling realization that we do not really have a firm grasp on our lives.

The high priest of the second, modern wave of existentialism was Frenchman Jean-Paul Sartre (1905–1980). We should also mention the French novelist Albert Camus (1913–1960), German philosopher Martin Heidegger (1889–1976), feminist Simone de Beauvoir (1908–1986), the French Roman Catholic Gabriel Marcel (1889–1973), and the Jewish philosopher Martin Buber (1878–1965). The variety of these voices should make it clear that existentialism is not a system only for atheists. What is common among all these writers is their belief in the centrality of the experience of the individual who hangs onto life without the support of limiting ideologies or systems, who grapples with complex modern phenomena, the decline of religion, the sense of rootlessness, and the feeling that, in the words of William Barrett, each man is "solitary and unsheltered before his own death," and who maintains that there is an obligation for affirming moral integrity and authentic behavior.

The readings that follow include more literary than philosophical works.

Indeed, existentialism lends itself to expression in literature more completely than any other philosophy because of its emphasis on individuality, on the skepticism of abstract theorizing, on the dramas of individual choice within social and institutional settings, and on living in extreme (or absurd) situations.

▼

MATTHEW ARNOLD, "DOVER BEACH"

Educated at Rugby, Winchester, where his clergyman father was headmaster, and at Balliol College, Oxford University, where he earned the reputation as a dandy and a wit, Matthew Arnold (1822–1888) became a fellow at Oried College soon after he was graduated. For 35 years, he served as inspector of schools, which gave him the chance to travel widely throughout England and observe the conditions of a country quickly changing from an agrarian to an industrial society. In 1851, he married Fanny Wightman, who bore him six children. Part of "Dover Beach" (1867) dates from his honeymoon experience.

Most of Arnold's reputation stems from his extensive prose writings on education, literature, politics, and society. Repeatedly in his works, he asked how one should live the good life in an emerging industrial culture. Although Arnold is not considered an existential thinker, the poem that follows clearly demonstrates the cultural shift toward existentialism and away from traditional religion in the nineteenth century. He spoke with an urbane and informed voice that inspired trust, and he gained a wide following throughout much of his career.

On his own poetry, Arnold once wrote in a letter to his mother, "My poems represent, on the whole, the main movement of the mind of the last quarter of a century, and thus they will probably have their day as people become conscious to themselves of what that movement of mind is, and interested in the literary productions which reflect it." One critic wrote that "as a poet he usually records his own experiences, his own feelings of loneliness and isolation as a lover, his longing for a serenity that he cannot find, his melancholy sense of the passing of youth. . . ."

▼

Dover Beach
MATTHEW ARNOLD

The sea is calm to-night.
The tide is full, the moon lies fair
Upon the straits;—on the French coast, the light
Gleams and is gone; the cliffs of England stand,
Glimmering and vast, out in the tranquil bay.   5
Come to the window, sweet is the night air!
Only, from the long line of spray
Where the sea meets the moon-blanch'd land,

Listen, you hear the grating roar
10   Of pebbles which the waves draw back, and fling,
At their return, up the high strand,
Begin, and cease, and then again begin,
With tremulous cadence slow, and bring
The eternal note of sadness in.

15   Sophocles[1] long ago
Heard it on the Ægæan, and it brought
Into his mind the turbid ebb and flow
Of human misery; we
Find also in the sound a thought,
20   Hearing it by this distant northern sea.

The Sea of Faith
Was once, too, at the full, and round earth's shore
Lay like the folds of a bright girdle furl'd.
But now I only hear
25   Its melancholy, long, withdrawing roar,
Retreating, to the breath
Of the night-wind, down the vast edges drear
And naked shingles[2] of the world.

Ah, love, let us be true
30   To one another! for the world, which seems
To lie before us like a land of dreams,
So various, so beautiful, so new,
Hath really neither joy, nor love, nor light,
Nor certitude, nor peace, nor help for pain;
35   And we are here as on a darkling plain
Swept with confused alarms of struggle and flight,
Where ignorant armies clash by night.

WRITING AND DISCUSSION QUESTIONS

Informative

1. How would you summarize the development of the poem? What prompts the narrator to begin his meditation? What relationship do you see between the sea at Dover Beach in stanza 1, the Aegean Sea in stanza 2, and the "Sea of Faith" in stanza 3? How is the sea an effective image here?

[1]Sophocles: the reference is probably to his play *Antigone*, in which Antigone compares her own curse to the flow of the Aegean Sea adjacent to Greece.
[2]naked shingles: pebble beaches.

2. What does "Sea of Faith" suggest? Is it a positive image? Does it suggest strong or precarious support? What does it mean that the sea is withdrawing?
3. Note Arnold's use of metaphors, especially the "eternal note of sadness," "the turbid ebb and flow / Of human misery," "The Sea of Faith," and "a land of dreams." How do these metaphors reflect his attitude toward change in the world?
4. What existential themes does the poem contain? Consider the centrality and freedom of the individual, the skepticism toward any idea system or ideology, and the emphasis on choice.

Persuasive

1. Which development do you think most dramatically accounts for the loss of faith in the nineteenth century: science, democracy, the industrial revolution, Marxism, or Darwinian science? What epistemology replaces faith as the dominant way of knowing?
2. Is the tone of the poem hopeful, pessimistic, or cynical?
3. What single value does the narrator of the poem cling to? Does it seem reasonable that this value could stand up to the cataclysmic changes occurring in the mid-nineteenth century?

Personal

1. How would you describe the contemporary state of faith? Is it still in retreat? If it is not like a "sea" anymore, what is it like?

▼

FRANZ KAFKA, "THE PROBLEM OF OUR LAWS" and "AN OLD MANUSCRIPT" FROM *THE COMPLETE STORIES*

It is a distinctive mark of the twentieth century to hear the adjective "Kafkan" or "Kafkaesque" used to describe today's living conditions. Although Franz Kafka (1883–1924) is not conventionally classified as an existential writer, his life, parables, stories, and novels suggest much of the alienation, uncertainty, and gloom of part of the philosophy. In fact, his name is commonly used to refer to the state of undeserved terror and the presence of the surreal and grotesque.

Kafka was born in Prague, Czechoslovakia, where he earned a doctorate in law from the German university there. Although he was a brilliant law student, he never practiced; instead, he went to work for a government insurance agency. Twice engaged to the same woman, Kafka experienced a stormy five-year relationship with her, during which time he completed many of his most famous stories, including "The Metamorphosis," and most of his novel *The Trial*.

A corrosive and all-consuming alienation pervaded his life, which probably accounted for the brooding sense of isolation and nightmare in the lives of his fictional characters. He was a Jew and was, thus, separated from the predominantly Christian society, and as a religious skeptic, he failed to identify with his family's Judaism. He lacked a sense of his national identity because he was a German-speaking minority in the Slavic Austro-Hungarian monarchy; and as the often sickly son (he had a tubercular condition) of an oppressive father, he grew away from close attachments to his family. Increasingly, he believed himself to be a victim, but he could not comprehend who was punishing him and what wrongs he had committed to deserve the suffering.

▼

The Problem of Our Laws
FRANZ KAFKA

1   Our laws are not generally known; they are kept secret by the small group of nobles who rule us. We are convinced that these ancient laws are scrupulously administered; nevertheless it is an extremely painful thing to be ruled by laws that one does not know. I am not thinking of possible discrepancies that may arise in the interpretation of the laws, or of the disadvantages involved when only a few and not the whole people are allowed to have a say in their interpretation. These disadvantages are perhaps of no great importance. For the laws are very ancient; their interpretation has been the work of centuries, and has itself doubtless acquired the status of law; and though there is still a possible freedom of interpretation left, it has now become very restricted. Moreover the nobles have obviously no cause to be influenced in their interpretation by personal interests inimical to us, for the laws were made to the advantage of the nobles from the very beginning, they themselves stand above the laws, and that seems to be why the laws were entrusted exclusively into their hands. Of course, there is wisdom in that—who doubts the wisdom of the ancient laws?—but also hardship for us; probably that is unavoidable.

2   The very existence of these laws, however, is at most a matter of presumption. There is a tradition that they exist and that they are a mystery confided to the nobility, but it is not and cannot be more than a mere tradition sanctioned by age, for the essence of a secret code is that it should remain a mystery. Some of us among the people have attentively scrutinized the doings of the nobility since the earliest times and possess records made by our forefathers—records which we have conscientiously continued—and claim to recognize amid the countless number of facts certain main tendencies which permit of this or that historical formulation; but when in accordance with these scrupulously tested and logically ordered conclusions we seek to adjust ourselves somewhat for the present or the future, everything becomes uncertain, and our work seems only an intellectual game, for perhaps these laws that we are trying to

unravel do not exist at all. There is a small party who are actually of this opinion and who try to show that, if any law exists, it can only be this: The Law is whatever the nobles do. This party see everywhere only the arbitrary acts of the nobility, and reject the popular tradition, which according to them possesses only certain trifling and incidental advantages that do not offset its heavy drawbacks, for it gives the people a false, deceptive, and overconfident security in confronting coming events. This cannot be gainsaid, but the overwhelming majority of our people account for it by the fact that the tradition is far from complete and must be more fully inquired into, that the material available, prodigious as it looks, is still too meager, and that several centuries will have to pass before it becomes really adequate. This view, so comfortless as far as the present is concerned, is lightened only by the belief that a time will eventually come when the tradition and our research into it will jointly reach their conclusion, and as it were gain a breathing space, when everything will have become clear, the law will belong to the people, and the nobility will vanish. This is not maintained in any spirit of hatred against the nobility; not at all, and by no one. We are more inclined to hate ourselves, because we have not yet shown ourselves worthy of being entrusted with the laws. And that is the real reason why the party who believe that there is no law have remained so few—although their doctrine is in certain ways so attractive, for it unequivocally recognizes the nobility and its right to go on existing.

Actually one can express the problem only in a sort of paradox: Any party   3
that would repudiate not only all belief in the laws, but the nobility as well, would have the whole people behind it; yet no such party can come into existence, for nobody would dare to repudiate the nobility. We live on this razor's edge. A writer once summed the matter up in this way: The sole visible and indubitable law that is imposed upon us is the nobility, and must we ourselves deprive ourselves of that one law?

Translated by Willa and Edwin Muir

WRITING AND DISCUSSION QUESTIONS

Informative

1. What is the narrator's attitude toward the laws and toward the nobles who administer them? Is there any ambivalence in either of these attitudes?
2. What is the "small party" of which the narrator speaks in the second paragraph? Why do they take exception to the nobility, and why do the majority of the people reject the nobility's position? What do the majority do and why?
3. For many, the "tradition sanctioned by age" tends to give credibility to the laws, however painful they may be. What comfort is given to people by this attitude, especially when the people generally do not believe themselves to be "worthy of being entrusted with the laws"?

Persuasive

1. What does Kafka mean by "our laws"? Is there a religious and moral, as well as legal and political, sense to the term? Argue that the ambiguity is functional in that the law can mean many things.
2. Critics have commented that when Kafka read his parables and stories aloud, his audience almost always laughed. What irony and humor, often of an unreal, surrealist variety, permeate this parable? What is the source of the irony and humor?

Personal

1. What makes the parable almost immediately comprehensible to a modern audience?

▼

An Old Manuscript

1   It looks as if much had been neglected in our country's system of defense. We have not concerned ourselves with it until now and have gone about our daily work; but things that have been happening recently begin to trouble us.

2   I have a cobbler's workshop in the square that lies before the Emperor's palace. Scarcely have I taken my shutters down, at the first glimmer of dawn, when I see armed soldiers already posted in the mouth of every street opening on the square. But these soldiers are not ours, they are obviously nomads from the North. In some way that is incomprehensible to me they have pushed right into the capital, although it is a long way from the frontier. At any rate, here they are; it seems that every morning there are more of them.

3   As is their nature, they camp under the open sky, for they abominate dwelling houses. They busy themselves sharpening swords, whittling arrows, and practicing horsemanship. This peaceful square, which was always kept so scrupulously clean, they have made literally into a stable. We do try every now and then to run out of our shops and clear away at least the worst of the filth, but this happens less and less often, for the labor is in vain and brings us besides into danger of falling under the hoofs of the wild horses or of being crippled with lashes from the whips.

4   Speech with the nomads is impossible. They do not know our language, indeed they hardly have a language of their own. They communicate with each other much as jackdaws do. A screeching as of jackdaws is always in our ears. Our way of living and our institutions they neither understand nor care to understand. And so they are unwilling to make sense even out of our sign language. You can gesture at them till you dislocate your jaws and your wrists and still they will not have understood you and will never understand. They often

make grimaces; then the whites of their eyes turn up and foam gathers on their lips, but they do not mean anything by that, not even a threat; they do it because it is their nature to do it. Whatever they need, they take. You cannot call it taking by force. They grab at something and you simply stand aside and leave them to it.

From my stock, too, they have taken many good articles. But I cannot com- 5
plain when I see how the butcher, for instance, suffers across the street. As soon as he brings in any meat the nomads snatch it all from him and gobble it up. Even their horses devour flesh; often enough a horseman and his horse are lying side by side, both of them gnawing at the same joint, one at either end. The butcher is nervous and does not dare to stop his deliveries of meat. We understand that, however, and subscribe money to keep him going. If the nomads got no meat, who knows what they might think of doing; who knows anyhow what they may think of, even though they get meat every day.

Not long ago the butcher thought he might at least spare himself the trouble 6
of slaughtering, and so one morning he brought along a live ox. But he will never dare to do that again. I lay for a whole hour flat on the floor at the back of my workshop with my head muffled in all the clothes and rugs and pillows I had simply to keep from hearing the bellowing of that ox, which the nomads were leaping on from all sides, tearing morsels out of its living flesh with their teeth. It had been quiet for a long time before I risked coming out; they were lying overcome around the remains of the carcass like drunkards around a wine cask.

This was the occasion when I fancied I actually saw the Emperor himself at 7
a window of the palace; usually he never enters these outer rooms but spends all his time in the innermost garden; yet on this occasion he was standing, or so at least it seemed to me, at one of the windows, watching with bent head the goings-on before his residence.

"What is going to happen?" we all ask ourselves. "How long can we endure 8
this burden and torment? The Emperor's palace has drawn the nomads here but does not know how to drive them away again. The gate stays shut; the guards, who used to be always marching out and in with ceremony, keep close behind barred windows. It is left to us artisans and tradesmen to save our country; but we are not equal to such a task; nor have we even claimed to be capable of it. This is a misunderstanding of some kind; and it will be the ruin of us."

Translated by Willa and Edwin Muir

WRITING AND DISCUSSION QUESTIONS

Informative

1. Who is the narrator? Is it significant that he is a cobbler? What is his attitude toward the event occurring around him? Is his attitude typical of most ordinary citizens?

2. What tone is suggested by the opening line? How would an existentialist view both the narrator's place in that society and his attitude toward that place? What examples of understatement are in the parable? What does the understatement say about the narrator's plight?
3. What drew the nomads to the narrator's city? What is suggested about the Emperor's role in the apparent "invasion"?

Persuasive

1. Most of Kafka's parables, including this one, do not seem to be placed in any historical location or time. What is the effect of this "floating" quality?
2. Some critics contend that Kafka carried a sense of undetermined guilt around with him. What evidence from this narrative supports that observation?

Personal

1. In what sense does this parable have a universal quality? In what sense can it be said that the parable speaks for all our lives? (Kafka once commented that the parables and stories were really incomprehensible but that "the cares we have to struggle with every day: that is a different matter.")

▼

JEAN-PAUL SARTRE, "EXISTENTIALISM"

If Camus' brand of existentialism developed amidst the poverty-stricken peasantry of Algiers, Jean-Paul Sartre's (1905–1980) emerged as he once said, in reaction to his maternal grandfather, the bourgeois, quasi-scholarly Professor Charles Schweitzer, with whom he spent his formative years. In Sartre's own words, "Docile by virtue of circumstance, by taste and by custom, I came to rebellion later only because I carried submission to an extreme."

As Sartre said in his autobiography, "I began my life as I shall no doubt end it: amidst books." Sartre was schooled at École Normale Supérieure in Paris, where he concentrated in psychology and philosophy. He taught at a variety of universities in France until World War II broke out, when he was briefly taken as a prisoner. By feigning a case of vertigo, he convinced the Nazis to release him. Like Albert Camus (1913–1960), who was a close friend until a break over Sartre's later sympathy with Marxism, Sartre was a leader in the French Resistance to the Nazi occupation. Although he wrote his first two pieces of fiction, "The Wall" (1948) and *Nausea* before the war, his most productive period came during and shortly after the war when he wrote his most famous plays, *The Flies* (1943) and *No Exit* (1947), and his major philosophical treatise, *Being and Nothingness* (1943). His autobiography, *Words*, was published in 1964, when he was offered the Nobel Prize for literature, which he refused in order to avoid the institutional fame it accorded. His long-time companion was feminist Simone de Beauvoir (1908–1986); they never married, in part to avoid the snares of "bourgeois" marriage.

Deriving from his concepts of "being" and "nothingness" and implied in his principle that "existence precedes essence," Sartre belongs to the atheistic school of existentialism, whereas others like Martin Buber (1878–1965), Gabriel Marcel (1889–1973), and Paul Tillich (1886–1965) clearly see no conflict between a belief in God and the existential concept of complete personal responsibility. It would, however, be misleading to imply that there is no room for positive action in Sartre's view of a world absent of God. Indeed, Sartre has been one of the leading thinkers, a man of great conscience, in this century, in part because he has so passionately championed human freedom and, in turn, the lot of the worker. As a result, Sartre has been very sympathetic to Marxism, even if that at times meant buying into an idea system at the cost of some personal freedom.

Critic Nathan Scott summed up Sartre's influences:

> Admittedly, Sartre—standing as he does so immediately in the line of Nietzsche—is . . . in his atheism and his consistently tragic perspective on the human situation, a very "absolute" kind of existentialist. But his great purpose over more than forty years has been that of helping us to discover how to live where Orestes in *The Flies* finally discovers himself to be—"on the far side of despair." And thus his *example* is felt to be among the most inspiring on the intellectual landscape of our time.[1]

What follows is Sartre's famous lecture delivered in 1946. It was published in England under the title "Esixtentialism and Humanism." While it cannot be taken as the definitive statement of existentialism, it is widely read and respected.

▼

Existentialism
JEAN-PAUL SARTRE

Man is nothing else but what he makes of himself. Such is the first   1
principle of existentialism. It is also what is called subjectivity, the name we are labeled with when charges are brought against us. But what do we mean by this, if not that man has a greater dignity than a stone or table? For we mean that man first exists, that is, that man first of all is the being who hurls himself toward a future and who is conscious of imagining himself as being in the future. Man is at the start a plan which is aware of itself, rather than a patch of moss, a piece of garbage, or a cauliflower; nothing exists prior to this plan; there is nothing in heaven; man will be what he will have planned to be. Not what he will want to be. Because by the word "will" we generally mean a conscious decision, which is subsequent to what we have already made of ourselves. I may want to belong to a political party, write a book, get married; but all that is only a manifestation of an earlier, more spontaneous choice that is called "will." But if existence really does precede essence, man is responsible

[1]Scott, p. 183.

for what he is. Thus, existentialism's first move is to make every man aware of what he is and to make the full responsibility of his existence rest on him. And when we say that a man is responsible for himself, we do not only mean that he is responsible for his own individuality, but that he is responsible for all men.

2   The word "subjectivism" has two meanings, and our opponents play on the two. Subjectivism means, on the one hand, that an individual chooses and makes himself; and, on the other, that it is impossible for man to transcend human subjectivity. The second of these is the essential meaning of existentialism. When we say that man chooses his own self, we mean that every one of us does likewise; but we also mean by that that in making this choice he also chooses all men. In fact, in creating the man that we want to be, there is not a single one of our acts which does not at the same time create an image of man as we think he ought to be. To choose to be this or that is to affirm at the same time the value of what we choose, because we can never choose evil. We always choose the good, and nothing can be good for us without being good for all.

3   If, on the other hand, existence precedes essence, and if we grant that we exist and fashion our image at one and the same time, the image is valid for everybody and for our whole age. Thus, our responsibility is much greater than we might have supposed, because it involves all mankind. If I am a working-man and choose to join a Christian trade union rather than be a Communist, and if by being a member, I want to show that the best thing for man is resignation, that the kingdom of man is not of this world, I am not only involving my own case—I want to be resigned for everyone. As a result, my action has involved all humanity. To take a more individual matter, if I want to marry, to have children, even if this marriage depends solely on my own circumstances or passion or wish, I am involving all humanity in monogamy and not merely myself. Therefore, I am responsible for myself and for everyone else. I am creating a certain image of man of my own choosing. In choosing myself, I choose man.

4   This helps us understand what the actual content is of such rather grandiloquent words as anguish, forlornness, despair. As you will see, it's all quite simple.

5   First, what is meant by anguish? The existentialists say at once that man is anguish. What that means is this: the man who involves himself and who realizes that he is not only the person he chooses to be, but also a lawmaker who is, at the same time, choosing all mankind as well as himself, cannot help escape the feeling of his total and deep responsibility. Of course, there are many people who are not anxious; but we claim that they are hiding their anxiety, that they are fleeing from it. Certainly, many people believe that when they do something, they themselves are the only ones involved, and when someone says to them, "What if everyone acted that way?" they shrug their shoulders and answer, "Everyone doesn't act that way." But really, one should always ask himself, "What would happen if everybody looked at things that way?" There is no escaping this disturbing thought except by a kind of double-deal-

ing. A man who lies and makes excuses for himself by saying "not everybody does that," is someone with an uneasy conscience, because the act of lying implies that a universal value is conferred upon the lie.

Anguish is evident even when it conceals itself. This is the anguish that Kier-   6
kegaard called the anguish of Abraham. You know the story: an angel has ordered Abraham to sacrifice his son; if it really were an angel who has come and said, "You are Abraham, you shall sacrifice your son," everything would be all right. But everyone might first wonder, "Is it really an angel, and am I really Abraham? What proof do I have?"

There was a madwoman who had hallucinations; someone used to speak to   7
her on the telephone and give her orders. Her doctor asked her, "Who is it who talks to you?" She answered, "He says it's God." What proof did she really have that it was God? If an angel comes to me, what proof is there that it's an angel? And if I hear voices, what proof is there that they come from heaven and not from hell, or from the subconscious, or a pathological condition? What proves that they are addressed to me? What proof is there that I have been appointed to impose my choice and my conception of man on humanity? I'll never find any proof or sign to convince me of that. If a voice addresses me, it is always for me to decide that this is the angel's voice; if I consider that such an act is a good one, it is I who will choose to say that it is good rather than bad.

Now, I'm not being singled out as an Abraham, and yet at every moment   8
I'm obliged to perform exemplary acts. For every man, everything happens as if all mankind had its eyes fixed on him and were guiding itself by what he does. And every man ought to say to himself, "Am I really the kind of man who has the right to act in such a way that humanity might guide itself by my actions?" And if he does not say that to himself, he is masking his anguish.

There is no question here of the kind of anguish which would lead to quiet-   9
ism, to inaction. It is a matter of a simple sort of anguish that anybody who has had responsibilities is familiar with. For example, when a military officer takes the responsibility for an attack and sends a certain number of men to death, he chooses to do so, and in the main he alone makes the choice. Doubtless, orders come from above, but they are too broad; he interprets them, and on this inter- pretation depend the lives of ten or fourteen or twenty men. In making a deci- sion he cannot help having a certain anguish. All leaders know this anguish. That doesn't keep them from acting; on the contrary, it is the very condition of their action. For it implies that they envisage a number of possibilities, and when they choose one, they realize that it has value only because it is chosen. We shall see that this kind of anguish, which is the kind that existentialism describes, is explained, in addition, by a direct responsbility to the other men whom it involves, It is not a curtain separating us from action, but is part of action itself.

When we speak of forlornness, a term Heidegger was fond of, we mean only   10
that God does not exist and that we have to face all the consequences of this. This existentialist is strongly opposed to a certain kind of secular ethics which

would like to abolish God with the least possible expense. About 1880, some French teachers tried to set up a secular ethics which went something like this: God is a useless and costly hypothesis; we are discarding it; but, meanwhile, in order for there to be an ethics, a society, a civilization, it is essential that certain values be taken seriously and that they be considered as having an *a priori* existence. It must be obligatory, *a priori*, to be honest, not to lie, not to beat your wife, to have children, etc., etc. So we're going to try a little device which will make it possible to show that values exist all the same, inscribed in a heaven of ideas, though otherwise God does not exist. In other words—and this, I believe, is the tendency of everything called reformism in France—nothing will be changed if God does not exist. We shall find ourselves with the same norms of honesty, progress, and humanism, and we shall have made of God an outdated hypothesis which will peacefully die off by itself.

11   The existentialist, on the contrary, thinks it very distressing that God does not exist, because all possibility of finding values in a heaven of ideas disappears along with Him; there can no longer be an *a priori* Good, since there is no infinite and perfect consciousness to think it. Nowhere is it written that the Good exists, that we must be honest, that we must not lie; because the fact is we are on a plane where there are only men. Dostoievsky said, "If God didn't exist, everything would be possible." That is the very starting point of existentialism. Indeed, everything is permissible if God does not exist, and as a result man is forlorn, because neither within him nor without does he find anything to cling to. He can't start making excuses for himself.

12   If existence really does precede essence, there is no explaining things away by reference to a fixed and given human nature. In other words, there is no determinism, man is free, man is freedom. On the other hand, if God does not exist, we find no values or commands to turn to which legitimize our conduct. So, in the bright realm of values, we have no excuse behind us, nor justification before us. We are alone, with no excuses.

13   That is the idea I shall try to convey when I say that man is condemned to be free. Condemned, because he did not create himself, yet, in other respects is free; because, once thrown into the world, he is responsible for everything he does. The existentialist does not believe in the power of passion. He will never agree that a sweeping passion is a ravaging torrent which fatally leads a man to certain acts and is therefore an excuse. He thinks that man is responsible for his passion.

14   The existentialist does not think that man is going to help himself by finding in the world some omen by which to orient himself. Because he thinks that man will interpret the omen to suit himself. Therefore, he thinks that man, with no support and no aid, is condemned every moment to invent man. Ponge, in a very fine article, has said, "Man is the future of man." That's exactly it. But if it is taken to mean that this future is recorded in heaven, that God sees it, then it is false, because it would really no longer be a future. If it is taken to mean that, whatever a man may be, there is a future to be forged, a virgin future before him, then this remark is sound. But then we are forlorn.

To give you an example which will enable you to understand forlornness   *15*
better, I shall cite the case of one of my students who came to see me under
the following circumstances: his father was on bad terms with his mother, and,
moreover, was inclined to be a collaborationist,[1] his older brother had been
killed in the German offensive of 1940, and the young man, with somewhat
immature but generous feelings, wanted to avenge him. His mother lived alone
with him, very much upset by the half-treason of her husband and the death of
her older son; the boy was her only consolation.

The boy was faced with the choice of leaving for England and joining the   *16*
Free French forces—that is, leaving his mother behind—or remaining with his
mother and helping her to carry on. He was fully aware that the woman lived
only for him and that his going off—and perhaps his death—would plunge her
into despair. He was also aware that every act that he did for his mother's sake
was a sure thing, in the sense that it was helping her to carry on, whereas every
effort he made toward going off and fighting was an uncertain move which
might run aground and prove completely useless; for example, on his way to
England he might, while passing through Spain, be detained indefinitely in a
Spanish camp; he might reach England or Algiers and be stuck in an office at a
desk job. As a result, he was faced with two very different kinds of action: one,
concrete, immediate, but concerning only one individual; the other concerned
an incomparably vaster group, a national collectivity, but for that very reason
was dubious, and might be interrupted en route. And, at the same time, he was
wavering between two kinds of ethics. On the one hand, an ethics of sympathy,
of personal devotion; on the other, a broader ethics, but one whose efficacy was
more dubious. He had to choose between the two.

Who could help him choose? Christian doctrine? No. Christian doctrine says,   *17*
"Be charitable, love your neighbor, take the more rugged path, etc., etc." But
which is the more rugged path? Whom should he love as a brother? The fighting man or his mother? Which does the greater good, the vague act of fighting
in a group, or the concrete one of helping a particular human being to go on
living? Who can decide *a priori?* Nobody. No book of ethics can tell him. The
Kantian ethics says, "Never treat any person as a means, but as an end." Very
well, if I stay with my mother, I'll treat her as an end and not as a means; but
by virtue of this very fact, I'm running the risk of treating the people around
me who are fighting, as means; and, conversely, if I go to join those who are
fighting. I'll be treating them as an end, and, by doing that, I run the risk of
treating my mother as a means.

If values are vague, and if they are always too broad for the concrete and   *18*
specific case that we are considering, the only thing left for us is to trust our
instincts. That's what this young man tried to do; and when I saw him, he said,
"In the end, feeling is what counts. I ought to choose whichever pushes me in
one direction. If I feel that I love my mother enough to sacrifice everything else
for her—my desire for vengeance, for action, for adventure—then I'll stay

---

[1]With the occupying German army, or its puppet government in Vichy.

with her. If, on the contrary, I feel that my love for my mother isn't enough, I'll leave."

19   But how is the value of a feeling determined? What gives his feeling for his mother value? Precisely the fact that he remained with her. I may say that I like so-and-so well enough to sacrifice a certain amount of money for him, but I may say so only if I've done it. I may say "I love my mother well enough to remain with her" if I have remained with her. The only way to determine the value of this affection is, precisely, to perform an act which confirms and defines it. But, since I require this affection to justify my act, I find myself caught in a vicious circle.

20   On the other hand, Gide has well said that a mock feeling and a true feeling are almost indistinguishable; to decide that I love my mother and will remain with her, or to remain with her by putting on an act, amount somewhat to the same thing. In other words, the feeling is formed by the acts one performs; so, I cannot refer to it in order to act upon it. Which means that I can neither seek within myself the true condition which will impel me to act, nor apply to a system of ethics for concepts which will permit me to act. You will say, "At least, he did go to a teacher for advice." But if you seek advice from a priest, for example, you have chosen this priest; you already knew, more or less, just about what advice he was going to give you. In other words, choosing your adviser is involving yourself. The proof of this is that if you are a Christian, you will say, "Consult a priest." But some priests are collaborating, some are just marking time, some are resisting. Which to choose? If the young man chooses a priest who is resisting or collaborating, he has already decided on the kind of advice he's going to get. Therefore, in coming to see me he knew the answer I was going to give him, and I had only one answer to give: "You're free, choose, that is, invent." No general ethics can show you what is to be done; there are no omens in the world. The Catholics will reply, "But there are." Granted—but, in any case, I myself choose the meaning they have.

21   When I was a prisoner, I knew a rather remarkable young man who was a Jesuit. He had entered the Jesuit order in the following way: he had had a number of very bad breaks; in childhood, his father died, leaving him in poverty, and he was a scholarship student at a religious institution where he was constantly made to feel that he was being kept out of charity; then, he failed to get any of the honors and distinctions that children like; later on, at about eighteen, he bungled a love affair; finally, at twenty-two, he failed in military training, a childish enough matter, but it was the last straw.

22   This young fellow might well have felt that he had botched everything. It was a sign of something, but of what? He might have taken refuge in bitterness or despair. But he very wisely looked upon all this as a sign that he was not made for secular triumphs, and that only the triumphs of religion, holiness, and faith were open to him. He saw the hand of God in all this, and so he entered the order. Who can help seeing that he alone decided what the sign meant?

23   Some other interpretation might have been drawn from this series of setbacks; for example, that he might have done better to turn carpenter or revolu-

tionist. Therefore, he is fully responsible for the interpretation. Forlornness implies that we ourselves choose our being. Forlornness and anguish go together.

As for despair, the term has a very simple meaning. It means that we shall 24 confine ourselves to reckoning only with what depends upon our will, or on the ensemble of probabilities which make our action possible. When we want something, we always have to reckon with probabilities. I may be counting on the arrival of a friend. The friend is coming by rail or streetcar; this supposes that the train will arrive on schedule, or that the streetcar will not jump the track. I am left in the realm of possibility; but possibilities are to be reckoned with only to the point where my action comports with the ensemble of these possibilities, and no further. The moment the possibilities I am considering are not rigorously involved by my action, I ought to disengage myself from them, because no God, no scheme, can adapt the world and its possibilities to my will. When Descartes said, "Conquer yourself rather than the world," he meant essentially the same thing.

The Marxists to whom I have spoken reply, "You can rely on the support of 25 others in your action, which obviously has certain limits because you're not going to live forever. That means: rely on both what others are doing elsewhere to help you, in China, in Russia, and what they will do later on, after your death, to carry on the action and lead it to its fulfillment, which will be the revolution. You even *have* to rely upon that, otherwise you're immoral." I reply at once that I will always rely on fellow-fighters insofar as these comrades are involved with me in a common struggle, in the unity of a party or a group in which I can more or less make my weight felt; that is, one whose ranks I am in as a fighter and whose movements I am aware of at every moment. In such a situation, relying on the unity and will of the party is exactly like counting on the fact that the train will arrive on time or that the car won't jump the track. But, given that man is free and that there is no human nature for me to depend on, I cannot count on men whom I do not know by relying on human goodness or man's concern for the good of society. I don't know what will become of the Russian revolution; I may make an example of it to the extent that at the present time it is apparent that the proletariat plays a part in Russia that it plays in no other nation. But I can't swear that this will inevitably lead to a triumph of the proletariat. I've got to limit myself to what I see.

Given that men are free and that tomorrow they will freely decide what man 26 will be, I cannot be sure that, after my death, fellow-fighters will carry on my work to bring it to its maximum perfection. Tomorrow, after my death, some men may decide to set up Fascism, and the others may be cowardly and muddled enough to let them do it. Fascism will then be the human reality, so much the worse for us.

Actually, things will be as man will have decided they are to be. Does that 27 mean that I should abandon myself to quietism? No. First, I should involve myself; then, act on the old saw, "Nothing ventured, nothing gained." Nor does it mean that I shouldn't belong to a party, but rather that I shall have no illusions and shall do what I can. For example, suppose I ask myself, "Will socialization, as such, ever come about?" I know nothing about it. All I know is that I'm going to do everything in my power to bring it about. Beyond that, I can't count on anything. Quietism is the attitude of people who say, "Let others do what I can't do." The doctrine I am presenting is the very opposite of quietism, since it declares, "There is no reality except in action." Moreover, it goes further, since it adds, "Man is nothing else than his plan; he exists only to the extent that he fulfills himself; he is therefore nothing else than the ensemble of his acts, nothing else than his life."

28   According to this, we can understand why our doctrine horrifies certain people. Because often the only way they can bear their wretchedness is to think, "Circumstances have been against me. What I've been and done doesn't show my true worth. To be sure, I've had no great love, no great friendship, but that's because I haven't met a man or woman who was worthy. The books I've written haven't been very good because I haven't had the proper leisure. I haven't had children to devote myself to because I didn't find a man with whom I could have spent my life. So there remains within me, unused and quite viable, a host of propensities, inclinations, possibilities, that one wouldn't guess from the mere series of things I've done."

29   Now, for the existentialist there is really no love other than one which manifests itself in a person's being in love. There is no genius other than one which is expressed in works of art; the genius of Proust is the sum of Proust's works; the genius of Racine is his series of tragedies. Outside of that, there is nothing. Why say that Racine could have written another tragedy, when he didn't write it? A man is involved in life, leaves his impress on it, and outside of that there is nothing. To be sure, this may seem a harsh thought to someone whose life hasn't been a success. But, on the other hand, it prompts people to understand that reality alone is what counts, that dreams, expectations, and hopes warrant no more than to define a man as a disappointed dream, as miscarried hopes, as vain expectations. In other words, to define him negatively and not positively. However, when we say, "You are nothing else than your life," that does not imply that the artist will be judged solely on the basis of his works of art; a thousand other things will contribute toward summing him up. What we mean is that a man is nothing else than a series of undertakings, that he is the sum, the organization, the ensemble of the relationships which make up these undertakings.

30   When all is said and done, what we are accused of, at bottom, is not our pessimism, but an optimistic toughness. If people throw up to us our works of fiction in which we write about people who are soft, weak, cowardly, and sometimes even downright bad, it's not because these people are soft, weak, cowardly, or bad; because if we were to say, as Zola did, that they are that way because of heredity, the workings of environment, society, because of biological or psychological determinism, people would be reassured. They would say, "Well, that's what we're like, no one can do anything about it." But when the existentialist writes about a coward, he says that this coward is responsible for his cowardice. He's not like that because he has a cowardly heart or lung or

brain; he's not like that on account of his physiological make-up; but he's like that because he has made himself a coward by his acts. There's no such thing as a cowardly constitution; there are nervous constitutions; there is poor blood, as the common people say, or strong constitutions. But the man whose blood is poor is not a coward on that account, for what makes cowardice is the act of renouncing or yielding. A constitution is not an act; the coward is defined on the basis of the acts he performs. People feel, in a vague sort of way, that this coward we're talking about is guilty of being a coward, and the thought frightens them. What people would like is that a coward or a hero be born that way. . . .

From these few reflections it is evident that nothing is more unjust than the 31 objections that have been raised against us. Existentialism is nothing else than an attempt to draw all the consequences of a coherent atheistic position. It isn't trying to plunge man into despair at all. But if one calls every attitude of unbelief despair, like the Christians, then the word is not being used in its original sense. Existentialism isn't so atheistic that it wears itself out showing that God doesn't exist. Rather, it declares that even if God did exist, that would change nothing. There you've got our point of view. Not that we believe that God exists, but we think that the problem of His existence is not the issue. In this sense existentialism is optimistic, a doctrine of action, and it is plain dishonesty for Christians to make no distinction between their own despair and ours and then to call us despairing.

WRITING AND DISCUSSION QUESTIONS

Informative

1. "Man is nothing else but what he makes of himself." What does that mean, especially in terms of religion, politics, family, and self? What would a diametrically opposite position be?

2. We are "responsible for all men. . . . In fact, in creating the man that we want to be, there is not a single one of our acts which does not at the same time create an image of man as we think he ought to be." Explain these statements. What kind of relationship to the world does this position imply?

3. How do the so-called existential emotions (anguish, forlornness, and despair) figure into Sartre's philosophy as presented in this essay?

4. Characterize Sartre's atheism as stated in this essay. How does he arrive at atheism, and what are the implications? Is Sartre's position as stated in the essay's first two paragraphs necessarily opposed to religion? Where does he most directly reject God?

Persuasive

1. Much of Sartre's essay is a defense against claims of subjectivism. Other thinkers attack Sartre for his nihilism, utter gloominess, and anarchy. How would you evalu-

ate his position against one or several of these attacks? Take the position that Sartre, in this essay, is not a pessimist.

2. How would Sartre address a Marxist or Christian critic of his position? Defend Sartre against such critics.

Personal

1. The opening paragraph argues that most of us are not responsible for our own attitudes, that we have not made ourselves, that we are what others (family, peers, country, and God) have made of us. By allowing other persons or forces to create us, we would, according to Sartre, have committed a form of intellectual suicide. How would you acknowledge those sides of yourself that you were not fully responsible for forming? For example, to what degree is your religious affiliation or your attitudes on capital punishment, abortion, or flag burning convenient rather than carefully thought out?

▼

ALBERT CAMUS, FROM *THE MYTH OF SISYPHUS*

Albert Camus (1913–1960) once observed that we had only three choices in life: physical suicide, a total escape from the challenge presented by existence; intellectual suicide, a refusal to confront one's freedom and choices; or revolt, a creative attack on the absurdity, injustice, and suffering around one. Some insight into how Camus discovered these choices is gained when one understands the milieu in which Camus grew up. Born at Mandovi, Algeria, Camus grew up in poverty. His father died during World War I soon after his son's birth, and afterward, Camus' mother moved the family to Algiers. There, she worked as a domestic servant, and Camus came to know the extremes of poverty and suffering. Still, he grew up on the shores of the magnificent Mediterranean Sea, which he called "the happy sea" and which instilled in him the stance of the solitary thinker and the sensual delight of light and color. Camus never regarded the poverty of his childhood as a calamity because, as he said, "it was always balanced by the richness of light." He later said in an interview, "Misery kept me from believing that all was not well under the sun."

With a scholarship to the University of Algiers, Camus studied philosophy and worked as an actor and director of his own theater company. In 1942, he left Algiers for Nazi-occupied Paris to obtain a newspaper job. He had already completed his first novel, *The Stranger* (1942), an essay, *The Myth of Sisyphus* (1942), and his play *Caligula* (1944). He soon became editor of a major underground Resistance paper, *Combat*. In 1944 when France was liberated, Camus became a national hero as a writer and activist. In 1957, he was awarded the Nobel Prize for Literature. In 1960, he died young in a freak car accident at the age of 47.

Camus, with his friend Sartre, became a central figure for the generation that grew up during and after World War II because he saw so clearly the consequences of indifference, which he dramatized in his greatest novel, *The Plague* (1947), the story of a small African town visited unexpectedly by the bubonic plague. As a symbol of the Nazi and fascist scourge sweeping through Europe, the plague challenges the people of the town to act. Few meet the challenge, mostly because they are indifferent, self-occupied, or anxious to exploit the terror for their private gain. Only a few mount the kind of revolt that Camus believed could save Europe and the rest of the world. Thus, Camus' life and writings worked to inspire a younger generation, which desperately sought a foundation of meaning.

▼

from *The Myth of Sisyphus*
ALBERT CAMUS

The gods had condemned Sisyphus to ceaselessly rolling a rock to   *1*
the top of a mountain, whence the stone would fall back of its own weight. They had thought with some reason that there is no more dreadful punishment than futile and hopeless labor.

If one believed Homer, Sisyphus was the wisest and most prudent of mor-   *2*
tals. According to another tradition, however, he was disposed to practice the profession of highwayman. I see no contradiction in this. Opinions differ as to the reasons why he became the futile laborer of the underworld. To begin with, he is accused of a certain levity in regard to the gods. He stole their secrets. Ægina, the daughter of Æsopus, was carried off by Jupiter. The father was shocked by that disappearance and complained to Sisyphus. He, who knew of the abduction, offered to tell about it on condition that Æsopus would give water to the citadel of Corinth. To the celestial thunderbolts he preferred the benediction of water. He was punished for this in the underworld. Homer tells us also that Sisyphus had put Death in chains. Pluto could not endure the sight of his deserted, silent empire. He dispatched the god of war, who liberated Death from the hands of her conqueror.

It is said also that Sisyphus, being near to death, rashly wanted to test his   *3*
wife's love. He ordered her to cast his unburied body into the middle of the public square. Sisyphus woke up in the underworld. And there, annoyed by an obedience so contrary to human love, he obtained from Pluto permission to return to earth in order to chastise his wife. But when he had seen again the face of this world, enjoyed water and sun, warm stones and the sea, he no longer wanted to go back to the infernal darkness. Recalls, signs of anger, warnings were of no avail. Many years more he lived facing the curve of the gulf, the sparkling sea, and the smiles of earth. A decree of the gods was necessary. Mercury came and seized the impudent man by the collar and, snatching him from his joys, led him forcibly back to the underworld, where his rock was ready for him.

You have already grasped that Sisyphus is the absurd hero. He *is*, as much   *4*
through his passions as through his torture. His scorn of the gods, his hatred of death, and his passion for life won him that unspeakable penalty in which the

whole being is exerted toward accomplishing nothing. This is the price that must be paid for the passions of this earth. Nothing is told us about Sisyphus in the underworld. Myths are made for the imagination to breathe life into them. As for this myth, one sees merely the whole effort of a body straining to raise the huge stone, to roll it and push it up a slope a hundred times over; one sees the face screwed up, the cheek tight against the stone, the shoulder bracing the clay-covered mass, the foot wedging it, the fresh start with arms outstretched, the wholly human security of two earth-clotted hands. At the very end of his long effort measured by skyless space and time without depth, the purpose is achieved. Then Sisyphus watches the stone rush down in a few moments toward that lower world whence he will have to push it up again toward the summit. He goes back down to the plain.

5   It is during that return, that pause, that Sisyphus interests me. A face that toils so close to stones is already stone itself! I see that man going back down with a heavy yet measured step toward the torment of which he will never know the end. That hour like a breathing-space which returns as surely as his suffering, that is the hour of consciousness. At each of those moments when he leaves the heights and gradually sinks toward the lairs of the gods, he is superior to his fate. He is stronger than his rock.

6   If this myth is tragic, that is because its hero is conscious. Where would his torture be, indeed, if at every step the hope of succeeding upheld him? The workman of today works every day in his life at the same tasks, and this fate is no less absurd. But it is tragic only at the rare moments when it becomes conscious. Sisyphus, proletarian of the gods, powerless and rebellious, knows the whole extent of his wretched condition: it is what he thinks of during his descent. The lucidity that was to constitute his torture at the same time crowns his victory. There is no fate that cannot be surmounted by scorn.

7   If the descent is thus sometimes performed in sorrow, it can also take place in joy. This word is not too much. Again I fancy Sisyphus returning toward his rock, and the sorrow was in the beginning. When the images of earth cling too tightly to memory, when the call of happiness becomes too insistent, it happens that melancholy rises in man's heart: this is the rock's victory, this is the rock itself. The boundless grief is too heavy to bear. These are our nights of Gethsemane. But crushing truths perish from being acknowledged. Thus, Œdipus at the outset obeys fate without knowing it. But from the moment he knows, his tragedy begins. Yet at the same moment, blind and desperate, he realizes that the only bond linking him to the world is the cool hand of a girl. Then a tremendous remark rings out: "Despite so many ordeals, my advanced age and the nobility of my soul make me conclude that all is well." Sophocles' Œdipus, like Dostoevsky's Kirilov, thus gives the recipe for the absurd victory. Ancient wisdom confirms modern heroism.

8   One does not discover the absurd without being tempted to write a manual of happiness. "What! by such narrow ways—?" There is but one world, however. Happiness and the absurd are two sons of the same earth. They are

inseparable. It would be a mistake to say that happiness necessarily springs from the absurd discovery. It happens as well that the feeling of the absurd springs from happiness. "I conclude that all is well," says Œdipus, and that remark is sacred. It echoes in the wild and limited universe of man. It teaches that all is not, has not been, exhausted. It drives out of this world a god who had come into it with dissatisfaction and a preference for futile sufferings. It makes of fate a human matter, which must be settled among men.

All Sisyphus' silent joy is contained therein. His fate belongs to him. His rock is his thing. Likewise, the absurd man, when he contemplates his torment, silences all the idols. In the universe suddenly restored to its silence, the myriad wondering little voices of the earth rise up. Unconscious, secret calls, invitations from all the faces, they are the necessary reverse and price of victory. There is no sun without shadow, and it is essential to know the night. The absurd man says yes and his effort will henceforth be unceasing. If there is a personal fate, there is no higher destiny, or at least there is but one which he concludes is inevitable and despicable. For the rest, he knows himself to be the master of his days. At that subtle moment when man glances backward over his life, Sisyphus returning toward his rock, in that slight pivoting he contemplates that series of unrelated actions which becomes his fate, created by him, combined under his memory's eye and soon sealed by his death. Thus, convinced of the wholly human origin of all that is human, a blind man eager to see who knows that the night has no end, he is still on the go. The rock is still rolling. *9*

I leave Sisyphus at the foot of the mountain! One always finds one's burden again. But Sisyphus teaches the higher fidelity that negates the gods and raises rocks. He too concludes that all is well. This universe henceforth without a master seems to him neither sterile nor futile. Each atom of that stone, each mineral flake of that night-filled mountain, in itself forms a world. The struggle itself toward the heights is enough to fill a man's heart. One must imagine Sisyphus happy. *10*

WRITING AND DISCUSSION QUESTIONS

Informative

1. Sisyphus, from Greek mythology, was a legendary king of Corinth who accused Zeus of abducting the daughter of an acquaintance. Zeus was so angered that he condemned Sisyphus in Hades to roll a large stone up a hill only to have it roll down again. In what sense is that story appropriate for Camus' purposes? Why does Camus cite Sisyphus as his absurd hero?

2. In the fifth paragraph, Camus says that it is "during [Sisyphus'] return" that Sisyphus interests him. Why?

3. In what particular sense is Sisyphus a hero? What do you think Camus means by "his scorn of the gods, his hatred of death, and his passion for life," winning the

title "hero" for confronting the ultimate penalty of pushing a rock up and down a hill, a seemingly futile behavior? How is Sisyphus superior to his fate? How does he surmount his fate "by scorn"? And where does Camus find Sisyphus' joy?

Persuasive

1. Argue that Sisyphus' plight does or does not fairly represent the human situation. If you do not think Sisyphus is a good symbol for humankind, identify another figure from mythology, or one from religion, that is a better representation.
2. What attitude toward one's circumstances in life is stated or implied in this essay? Argue that the attitude is either optimistic or pessimistic.

Personal

1. Camus compared Sisyphus to the working persons of the twentieth century whose lives, he says, are equally absurd, but not tragic. What do you think Camus means by this distinction?
2. What does the rock symbolize for you? What apparently monotonous, routine, and repetitive activities that may be inherently meaningless can take on greater meaning and significance when they become conscious, that is, when one sees them as a premeditated response to the absurd conditions of life?

▼

SAMUEL BECKETT, *Act Without Words*

Samuel Beckett (1906–1990) is best known as a playwright of what is called "the theater of the absurd," which is based on many of the philosophical premises of existentialism, but especially on the idea that God does not exist and that the individual is alone and, therefore, faces an overwhelming immensity of choices with a sense of dread. Life, this thinking goes, does not exist apart from individually derived thought and action; that is, because there is no God, there are no moral or spiritual absolutes that establish value and codes of conduct. We find ourselves alone in an alien and indifferent world. Playwrights who are identified with the theater of the absurd believe that the dramatic stage should reflect these existential ideas thematically and structurally. It is not uncommon, then, to see characters living in garbage cans or waiting for messages from mysterious figures who never appear.

Beckett's most well-known work is probably *Waiting for Godot* (1955), the story of two tramps, Estragon and Vladimir, who wait eternally for the mysterious Godot to come. As critic Martin Esslin comments, the play suggests that we have been "projected into a world (without being asked whether we wanted to come into it), [and] the fact that we are now here seems to imply that we have a purpose to fulfill, an appointment to keep—and yet we are never quite sure what the appointment is, what its purpose might be."[1] The implication of this apparently ambiguous view of the human situation is that life is full of paralysis, ignorance, word games, and momentary flashes of human feeling.

[1]Martin Esslin, *The Theatre of the Absurd.* N.Y.: Penguin Books, 1980, p. 59.

Beckett was born at Foxrock, near Dublin, Ireland, and was raised as a Protestant by his religious mother. Educated at Trinity College, Dublin, he went on to teach in Belfast and then traveled to Paris to lecture, where he met and became good friends with the novelist James Joyce. In 1938, Beckett took up permanent residency in Paris and has been a prolific writer of criticism, novels, and plays, and has had a major impact on several contemporary playwrights like Pinter, Fugard, and Stoppard. He was awarded the Nobel Prize for Literature in 1969.

▼

Act Without Words I

A Mime for One Player

SAMUEL BECKETT

Desert. Dazzling light.

The man is flung backwards on stage from right wing. He falls, gets up immediately, dusts himself, turns aside, reflects.

Whistle from right wing.

He reflects, goes out right.

Immediately flung back on stage he falls, gets up immediately, dusts himself, turns aside, reflects.

Whistle from left wing.

He reflects, goes out left.

Immediately flung back on stage he falls, gets up immediately, dusts himself, turns aside, reflects.   *10*

Whistle from left wing.

He reflects, goes towards left wing, hesitates, thinks better of it, halts, turns aside, reflects.

A little tree descends from flies, lands. It has a single bough some three yards from ground and at its summit a meager tuft of palms casting at its foot a circle of shadow.

He continues to reflect.

Whistle from above.

He turns, sees tree, reflects, goes to it, sits down in its shadow, looks at his hands.

A pair of tailor's scissors descends from flies, comes to rest before tree, a   *20*
yard from ground.

He continues to look at his hands.

Whistle from above.

He looks up, sees scissors, takes them and starts to trim his nails.

The palms close like a parasol, the shadow disappears.

He drops scissors, reflects.

A tiny carafe, to which is attached a huge label inscribed WATER, descends from flies, comes to rest some three yards from ground.

He continues to reflect.

30 Whistle from above.

He looks up, sees carafe, reflects, gets up, goes and stands under it, tries in vain to reach it, renounces, turns aside, reflects.

A big cube descends from flies, lands.

He continues to reflect.

Whistle from above.

He turns, sees cube, looks at it, at carafe, reflects, goes to cube, takes it up, carries it over and sets it down under carafe, tests its stability, gets up on it, tries in vain to reach carafe, renounces, gets down, carries cube back to its place, turns aside, reflects.

40 A second smaller cube descends from flies, lands.

He continues to reflect.

Whistle from above.

He turns, sees second cube, looks at it, at carafe, goes to second cube, takes it up, carries it over and sets it down under carafe, tests its stability, gets up on it, tries in vain to reach carafe, renounces, gets down, takes up second cube to carry it back to its place, hesitates, thinks better of it, sets it down, goes to big cube, takes it up, carries it over and puts it on small one, tests their stability, gets up on them, the cubes collapse, he falls, gets up immediately, brushes himself, reflects.

50 He takes up small cube, puts it on big one, tests their stability, gets up on them and is about to reach carafe when it is pulled up a little way and comes to rest beyond his reach.

He gets down, reflects, carries cubes back to their place, one by one, turns aside, reflects.

A third still smaller cube descends from flies, lands.

He continues to reflect.

Whistle from above.

He turns, sees third cube, looks at it, reflects, turns aside, reflects.

The third cube is pulled up and disappears in flies.

60 Beside carafe a rope descends from flies, with knots to facilitate ascent.

He continues to reflect.

Whistle from above.

He turns, sees rope, reflects, goes to it, climbs up it and is about to reach carafe when rope is let out and deposits him back on ground.

He reflects, looks around for scissors, sees them, goes and picks them up, returns to rope and starts to cut it with scissors.

The rope is pulled up, lifts him off ground, he hangs on, succeeds in cutting rope, falls back on ground, drops scissors, falls, gets up again immediately, brushes himself, reflects.

70 The rope is pulled up quickly and disappears in flies.

With length of rope in his possession he makes a lasso with which he tries to lasso carafe.

The carafe is pulled up quickly and disappears in flies.

He turns aside, reflects.

He goes with lasso in his hand to tree, looks at bough, turns and looks at cubes, looks again at bough, drops lasso, goes to cubes, takes up small one, carries it over and sets it down under bough, goes back for big one, takes it up and carries it over under bough, makes to put it on small one, hesitates, thinks better of it, sets it down, takes up small one and puts it on big one, tests their stability, turns aside and stoops to pick up lasso.   *80*

The bough folds down against trunk.

He straightens up with lasso in his hand, turns and sees what has happened.

He drops lasso, turns aside, reflects.

He carries back cubes to their place, one by one, goes back for lasso, carries it over to cubes and lays it in a neat coil on small one.

He turns aside, reflects.

Whistle from right wing.

He reflects, goes out right.

Immediately flung back on stage he falls, gets up immediately, brushes himself, turns aside, reflects.   *90*

Whistle from left wing.

He does not move.

He looks at his hands, looks around for scissors, sees them, goes and picks them up, starts to trim his nails, stops, reflects, runs his finger along blade of scissors, goes and lays them on small cube, turns aside, opens his collar, frees his neck and fingers it.

The small cube is pulled up and disappears in flies, carrying away rope and scissors.

He turns to take scissors, sees what has happened.

He turns aside, reflects.   *100*

He goes and sits down on big cube.

The big cube is pulled from under him. He falls. The big cube is pulled up and disappears in flies.

He remains lying on his side, his face towards auditorium, staring before him.

The carafe descends from flies and comes to rest a few feet from his body.

He does not move.

Whistle from above.

He does not move.

The carafe descends further, dangles and plays about his face.   *110*

He does not move.

The carafe is pulled up and disappears in flies.

The bough returns to horizontal, the palms open, the shadow returns.

Whistle from above.

He does not move.

The tree is pulled up and disappears in flies.

He looks at his hands.

CURTAIN

WRITING AND DISCUSSION QUESTIONS

Informative

1. This play is often interpreted as a reenactment of the Tantalus story from Greek mythology. Tantalus was a legendary king of Lydia who for his crimes was condemned in Hades both to stand in water up to his chin that receded when he tried to take a drink and to stand below fruit hanging above his head that moved away when he reached for it. Therefore, Tantalus becomes a symbol of someone who must learn to bear the constant suffering of being taunted and teased, thus the word "tantalized." How well does the myth fit Beckett's play?

2. How would you summarize the plot? What kinds of behavior does "the man" repeatedly engage in, and how, if at all, does he change at the end? What is he able to control, and what is beyond his control?

Persuasive

1. Some observers of the theater of the absurd argue that it does not present a view of unrelieved gloom, but rather comic relief. Argue that the predominant mood in this play is either tragic or comic.

2. Characterize the force that moves the carafe out of the man's hands. Argue that it is or is not God. Is it too capricious and mean spirited to be considered God?

3. The man is initially flung around the stage in what may be seen as a violent introduction to the world. Argue that the play can be seen as a symbolic reenactment of a life cycle.

Personal

1. If humans derive dignity from anything, it is that they do not refuse to move and reflect on their predicament. In what sense is this a fair or unfair representation of your sense of the human condition?

TADEUSZ BOROWSKI, "THE PEOPLE WHO WALKED ON" FROM *THIS WAY FOR THE GAS, LADIES AND GENTLEMEN*

As suggested in the introduction to this chapter, the Nazi terror and occupation of so much of Europe during World War II created an existential crisis for all who were touched as bystanders, victims, resisters, or perpetrators. The growing body of Holocaust and World War II literature written by the likes of Elie Wiesel, Primo Levi, Charlotte Delbo, Jersy Kosinski, and Albert Camus constitutes a chilling testimony to the existential dilemmas of that period, especially the problem of how the individual is to act responsibly when the costs are normally death. One of the greatest writers in this genre is the Pole Tadeusz Borowski (1922–1951), who was considered the greatest hope of Polish literature until he, ironically, turned a gas valve on himself on July 1, 1951. Borowski's collection of twelve short narratives, *This Way for the Gas, Ladies and Gentlemen* (1967), mostly blend fact and fiction, recounting aspects of a year he spent at the Auschwitz death camp in Poland.

Borowski became a political prisoner in Auschwitz in 1944 after the Nazis arrested him for underground resistance activities. The stories that have come out of his ordeal are important because they attempt to work out the guilt and responsibility of an articulate bystander who participated directly in the infamous selections for the ovens, who bought women, and who generally contributed to the "hierarchy of fear." One of the most striking stories in the collection is reprinted below; it is about a political prisoner who works at odd jobs such as roofing in Birkenau and the receiving transports at the station at Auschwitz, the most notorious and deadly of Hitler's death camps. In the story, the narrator–bystander describes his daily leisure and work routines, and with cool detachment, he comments that "Between two throw-ins in a soccer game, right behind my back, three thousand people had been put to death." It becomes clear to the reader that the narrator, in fighting for his own survival, is doing so at the cost of his humanity. Having had to deal with such survival in his life might help explain why the author, Borowski, committed suicide six years after his liberation.

It will be helpful to understand something about life in the death camps, how difficult or nearly impossible any form of resistance was. The terror and degradation were so extreme that many scholars believe that the only form of resistance was a minimal maintenance of human emotion and dignity, which was physically difficult when one had to live in temperature extremes on only 200–300 calories each day and sleep in excrement at night. Critic Terrance Des Pres, in writing about life in the Soviet Gulag prison system and the Nazi camps, commented that

> All [survivors suggest] images of existence at its limit, a case of the worst world possible. From it comes the definition of extremity as a situation in which men and women must live without accommodation; . . . all were places in which the human self was stripped of spiritual as well as physical mediations, until literally nothing was left to persist through pain and time but the body itself.[1]

▼

The People Who Walked On
TADEUSZ BOROWSKI

It was early spring when we began building a soccer field on the broad clearing behind the hospital barracks. The location was excellent: the gypsies to the left, with their roaming children, their lovely, trim nurses, and their women sitting by the hour in the latrines; to the rear—a barbed-wire fence, and behind it the loading ramp with the wide railway tracks and the end-

---

[1]Des Pres, Terrance. *The Survivor: An Anatomy of Life in the Death Camps*, N.Y.: Oxford University Press, 1976, p. 214.

less coming and going of trains; and beyond the ramp, the women's camp—
Frauen Konzentration Lager. No one, of course, ever called it by its full name.
We simply said F.K.L.[1]—that was enough. To the right of the field were the
crematoria, some of them at the back of the ramp, next to the F.K.L., others
even closer, right by the fence. Sturdy buildings that sat solidly on the ground.
And in front of the crematoria, a small wood which had to be crossed on the
way to the gas.

2   We worked on the soccer field throughout the spring, and before it was finished we starting planting flowers under the barracks window and decorating
the blocks with intricate zigzag designs made of crushed red brick. We planted
spinach and lettuce, sunflowers and garlic. We laid little green lawns with grass
transplanted from the edges of the soccer field, and sprinkled them daily with
water brought in barrels from the lavatories.

3   Just when the flowers were about to bloom, we finished the soccer field.

4   From then on, the flowers were abandoned, the sick lay by themselves in the
hospital beds, and we played soccer. Every day, as soon as the evening meal
was over, anybody who felt like it came to the field and kicked the ball around.
Others stood in clusters by the fence and talked across the entire length of the
camp with the girls from the F.K.L.

5   One day I was goalkeeper. As always on Sundays, a sizeable crowd of hospital orderlies and convalescent patients had gathered to watch the game. Keeping goal, I had my back to the ramp. The ball went out and rolled all the way
to the fence. I ran after it, and as I reached to pick it up, I happened to glance
at the ramp.

6   A train had just arrived. People were emerging from the cattle cars and
walking in the direction of the little wood. All I could see from where I stood
were bright splashes of colour. The women, it seemed, were already wearing
summer dresses; it was the first time that season. The men had taken off their
coats, and their white shirts stood out sharply against the green of the trees.
The procession moved along slowly, growing in size as more and more people
poured from the freight cars. And then it stopped. The people sat down on the
grass and gazed in our direction. I returned with the ball and kicked it back
inside the field. It travelled from one foot to another and, in a wide arc,
returned to the goal. I kicked it towards a corner. Again it rolled out into the
grass. Once more I ran to retrieve it. But as I reached down, I stopped in
amazement—the ramp was empty. Out of the whole colourful summer procession, not one person remained. The train too was gone. Again the F.K.L.
blocks were in unobstructed view, and again the orderlies and the patients
stood along the barbed-wire fence calling to the girls, and the girls answered
them across the ramp.

7   Between two throw-ins in a soccer game, right behind my back, three thousand people had been put to death.

8   In the following months, the processions to the little wood moved along two

---

[1]*Frauen Konzentration Lager* was the women's concentration ward.

roads: one leading straight from the ramp, the other past the hospital wall. Both led to the crematoria, but some of the people had the good fortune to walk beyond them, all the way to the Zauna, and this meant more than just a bath and a delousing, a barber's shop and a new prison suit. It meant staying alive. In a concentration camp, true, but—alive.

Each day, as I got up in the morning to scrub the hospital floors, the people 9 were walking—along both roads. Women, men, children. They carried their bundles.

When I sat down to dinner—and not a bad one, either—the people were 10 walking. Our block was bathed in sunlight; we threw the doors and the windows wide open and sprinkled the floors with water to keep the dust down. In the afternoons I delivered packages which had been brought that morning from the Auschwitz post office. The clerk distributed mail. The doctors dressed wounds and gave injections. There was, as a matter of fact, only one hypodermic needle for the entire block. On warm evenings I sat at the barracks door reading *Mon frère Yves* by Pierre Loti—while the procession continued on and on, along both roads.

Often, in the middle of the night, I walked outside; the lamps glowed in the 11 darkness above the barbed-wire fences. The roads were completely black, but I could distinctly hear the far-away hum of a thousand voices—the procession moved on and on. And then the entire sky would light up; there would be a burst of flame above the wood . . . and terrible human screams.

I stared into the night, numb, speechless, frozen with horror. My entire body 12 trembled and rebelled, somehow even without my participation. I no longer controlled my body, although I could feel its every tremor. My mind was completely calm, only the body seemed to revolt.

Soon afterwards, I left the hospital. The days were filled with important 13 events. The Allied Armies had landed on the shores of France. The Russian front, we heard, had started to move west towards Warsaw.

But in Birkenau, day and night long lines of trains loaded with people waited 14 at the station. The doors were unsealed, the people started walking—along both roads.

Located next to the camp's labour sector was the deserted, unfinished Sector 15 C. Here only, the barracks and the high voltage fence around them had been completed. The roofs, however, were not yet covered with tar sheets, and some of the blocks still had no bunks. An average Birkenau block, furnished with three tiers of bunks, could hold up to five hundred people. But every block in Sector C was now being packed with a thousand or more young women picked from among the people on the ramp . . . Twenty-eight blocks—over thirty thousand women. Their heads were shaved and they were issued little sleeveless summer dresses. But they were not given underwear. Nor spoons, nor bowls, nor even a rag to clean themselves with. Birkenau was situated on marshes, at the foot of a mountain range. During the day, the air was warm and so transparent that the mountains were in clear view, but in the morning they lay shrouded in a thick, icy mist. The mornings were cold and penetrating.

For us, this meant merely a refreshing pause before a hot summer day, but the women, who only twenty yards to our right had been standing at roll-call since five in the morning, turned blue from the cold and huddled together like a flock of partridges.

16   We named the camp—Persian Market. On sunny, warm days the women would emerge from the barracks and mill around in the wide aisles between the blocks. Their bright summer dresses and the gay kerchiefs on their shaved heads created the atmosphere of a busy, colourful market—a Persian Market because of its exotic character.

17   From afar, the women were faceless and ageless. Nothing more than white blotches and pastel figures.

18   The Persian Market was not yet completed. The Wagner Kommando began building a road through the sector, packing it down with a heavy roller. Others fiddled around with the plumbing and worked on the washrooms that were to be installed throughout all the sectors of Birkenau.[2] Still others were busy stocking up the Persian Market with the camp's basic equipment—supplies of blankets, metal cups and spoons—which they arranged carefully in the warehouses under the direction of the chief supervisor, the assigned S.S.[3] officer. Naturally, much of the stuff evaporated immediately, expertly 'organized' by the men working on the job.

19   My comrades and I laid a roof over the shack of every Block Elder[4] in the Persian Market. It was not done on official order, nor did we work out of charity. Neither did we do it out of a feeling of solidarity with the old serial numbers, the F.K.L. women who had been placed there in all the responsible posts. In fact, we used 'organized' tar-boards and melted 'organized' tar, and for every roll of tar-board, every bucket of tar, an Elder had to pay. She had to pay the Kapo, the Kommandoführer, the Kommando 'bigwigs'. She could pay in various ways: with gold, food, the women of her block, or with her own body. It depended.

20   On a similar basis, the electricians installed electricity, the carpenters built and furnished the shacks, using 'organized' lumber, the masons provided metal stoves and cemented them in place.

21   It was at that time that I came to know the anatomy of this strange camp. We would arrive there in the morning, pushing a cart loaded with tar-sheets and tar. At the gate stood the S.S. women-guards, hippy blondes in black leather boots. They searched us and let us in. Then they themselves went to inspect the blocks. Not infrequently they had lovers among the masons and the carpenters. They slept with them in the unfinished washrooms or the Block Elders' shacks.

22   We would push our cart into the camp, between the barracks, and there, on some little square, would light a fire and melt the tar. A crowd of women would

---

[2]The receiving station for Auschwitz and the killing center.
[3]*Schutzstaffel*, or Hitler's elite party military organization.
[4]Senior inmate supervisor.

immediately surround us. They begged us to give them anything, a penknife, a handkerchief, a spoon, a pencil, a piece of paper, a shoe string, or bread.

'Listen, you can always manage somehow,' they would say. 'You've been in   23
the camp a long time and you've survived. Surely you have all you need. Why won't you share it with us?'

At first we gave them everything we happened to have with us, and then   24
turned our pockets inside out to show we had nothing more. We took off our shirts and handed them over. But gradually we began coming with empty pockets and gave them nothing.

These women were not so much alike as it had seemed when we looked at   25
them from another sector, from a distance of twenty metres.

Among them were small girls, whose hair had not been shaved, stray little   26
cherubs from a painting of the Last Judgment. There were young girls who gazed with surprise at the women crowding around us, and who looked at us, coarse, brutal men, with contempt. Then there were married women, who desperately begged for news of their lost husbands, and mothers trying to find a trace of their children.

'We are so miserable, so cold, so hungry,' they cried. 'Tell us, are they at   27
least a little bit better off?'

'They are, if God is just,' we would answer solemnly, without the usual   28
mocking and teasing.

'Surely they're not dead?' the women asked, looking searchingly into our   29
faces.

We would walk away without a word, eager to get back to work.   30

The majority of the Block Elders at the Persian Market were Slovak girls   31
who managed to communicate in the the language of the new inmates. Every one of these girls had behind her several years of concentration camp. Every one of them remembered the early days of the F.K.L., when female corpses piled up along the barracks walls and rotted, unremoved, in hospital beds— and when human excrement grew into monstrous heaps inside the blocks.

Despite their rough manner, they had retained their femininity and human   32
kindness. Probably they too had their lovers, and probably they too stole margarine and tins of food in order to pay for blankets and dresses, but . . .

. . . but I remember Mirka, a short, stocky 'pink' girl. Her shack was all   33
done up in pink too, with pink ruffled curtains across the window that faced the block. The pink light inside the shack set a pink glow over the girl's face, making her look as if she were wrapped in a delicate misty veil. There was a Jew in our Kommando with very bad teeth who was in love with Mirka. He was always running around the camp trying to buy fresh eggs for her, and then throwing them, protected in soft wrapping, over the barbed-wire fence. He would spend many long hours with her, paying little attention to the S.S. women inspecting the barracks or to our chief who made his rounds with a tremendous revolver hanging from his white summer uniform.

One day Mirka came running over to where several of us were laying a roof.   34
She signalled frantically to the Jew and called, turning to me:

35   'Please come down! Maybe you can help too!'

36   We slid off the roof and down the barracks door. Mirka grabbed us by the hands and pulled us in the direction of her shack. There she led us between the cots and pointing to a mass of colourful quilts and blankets on top of which lay a child, she said breathlessy:

37   'Look, it's dying! Tell me, what can I do? What could have made it so sick so suddenly?'

38   The child was asleep, but very restless. It looked like a rose in a golden frame—its burning cheeks were surrounded by a halo of blond hair.

39   'What a pretty child,' I whispered.

40   'Pretty!' cried Mirka. 'All you know is that it's pretty! But it can die any moment! I've had to hide it so they wouldn't take it to the gas! What if an S.S. woman finds it? Help me!'

41   The Jew put his arm around her shoulders. She pushed him away and suddenly burst into sobs. I shrugged, turned around, and left the barracks.

42   In the distance, I could see trains moving along the ramp. They were bringing new people who would walk in the direction of the little wood. One Canada group[5] was just returning from the ramp, and along the wide camp road passed another Canada group going to take its place. Smoke was rising above the treetops. I seated myself next to the boiling bucket of tar and, stirring it slowly, sat thinking for a long time. At one point a wild thought suddenly shot across my mind: I too would like to have a child with rose-coloured cheeks and light blond hair. I laughed aloud at such a ridiculous notion and climbed up on the roof to lay the hot tar.

43   And I remember another Block Elder, a big redhead with broad feet and chapped hands. She did not have a separate shack, only a few blankets spread over the bed and instead of walls a few other blankets thrown across a piece of rope.

44   'I mustn't make them feel,' she would say, pointing to the women packed tightly in the bunks, 'that I want to cut myself off from them. Maybe I can't given them anything, but I won't take anything away from them either.'

45   'Do you believe in life after death?' she asked me once in the middle of some lighthearted conversation.

46   'Sometimes,' I answered cautiously. 'Once I believed in it when I was in jail, and again once when I came close to dying here in the camp.'

47   'But if a man does evil, he'll be punished, won't he?'

48   'I suppose so, unless there are some criteria of justice other than the man-made criteria. You know . . . the kind that explain causes and motivations, and erase guilt by making it appear insignificant in the light of the overall harmony of the universe. Can a crime committed on one level be punishable on a different one?'

49   'But I mean in a normal, human sense!' she exclaimed.

50   'It ought to be punished. No question about it.'

---

[5]Kapos or prisoners who helped unload the trains in the death camps.

'And you, would you do good if you were able to?'   *51*

'I seek no rewards. I build roofs and want to survive the concentration   *52*
camp.'

'But do you think that they', she pointed with her chin in an indefinite direc-   *53*
tion, 'can go unpunished?'

'I think that for those who have suffered unjustly, justice alone is not   *54*
enough. They want the guilty to suffer unjustly too. Only this will they understand as justice.'

'You're a pretty smart fellow! But you wouldn't have the slightest idea how   *55*
to divide bread justly, without giving more to your own mistress!' she said bitterly and walked into the block. The women were lying in the rows of bunks,
head to head. Their faces were still, only the eyes seemed alive, large and shining. Hunger had already started in this part of the camp. The redheaded Elder
moved from bunk to bunk, talking to the women to distract them from their
thoughts. She pulled out the singers and told them to sing, the dancers—and
told them to dance, the poets—and made them recite poetry.

'All the time, endlessly, they ask me about their mothers, their fathers. They   *56*
beg me to write to them.'

'They've asked me too. It's just too bad.'   *57*

'Ah, you! You come and then you go, but me? I plead with them, I beg   *58*
them—if anyone is pregnant, don't report to the doctor, if anyone is sick, stay
in the barracks! But do you think they believe me? It's no good, no matter how
hard you try to protect them. What can you do if they fall all over themselves
to get to the gas?'

One of the girls was standing on top of a table singing a popular tune. When   *59*
she finished, the women in the bunks began to applaud. The girl bowed, smiling. The redheaded Elder covered her face with her rough hands.

'I can't stand it any longer! It's too disgusting!' she whispered. And suddenly   *60*
she jumped up and rushed over to the table. 'Get down!' she screamed at the
singer.

The women fell silent. She raised her arm.   *61*

'Quiet!' she shouted, though nobody spoke a word. 'You've been asking me   *62*
about your parents and your children. I haven't told you. I felt sorry for you.
But now I'll tell you, so that you know, because they'll do the same with you if
you get sick! Your children, your husbands and your parents are not in another
camp at all. They've been stuffed into a room and gassed! Gassed, do you
understand? Like millions of others, like my own mother and father. They're
burning in deep pits and in ovens . . . The smoke which you see above the
rooftops doesn't come from the brick plant at all, as you're being told. It's
smoke from your children! Now go on and sing.' She finished calmly, pointing
her finger at the terrified singer. Then she turned around and walked out of the
barracks.

It was undeniable that the conditions in both Auschwitz and Birkenau were   *63*
steadily improving. At the beginning, beating and killing were the rule, but later
this became only sporadic. At first, you had to sleep on the floor lying on your

side because of the lack of space, and could turn over only on command; later you slept in bunks, or wherever you wished, sometimes even in bed. Originally, you had to stand at roll-call for as long as two days at a time, later—only until the second gong, until nine o'clock. In the early years, packages were forbidden, later you could receive 500 grams, and finally as much as you wanted. Pockets of any kind were at first strictly taboo, but eventually even civilian clothes could sometimes be seen around Birkenau. Life in the camp became 'better and better' all the time—after the first three or four years. We felt certain that the horrors could never again be repeated, and we were proud that we had survived. The worse the Germans fared at the battle front, the better off we were. And since they fared worse and worse . . .

64   At the Persian Market, time seemed to move in reverse. Again we saw the Auschwitz of 1940. The women greedily gulped down the soup which nobody in our blocks would even think of touching. They stank of sweat and female blood. They stood at roll-call from five in the morning. When they were at last counted, it was almost nine. Then they were given cold coffee. At three in the afternoon the evening roll-call began and they were given dinner: bread with some spread. Since they did not work, they did not rate the *Zulage*, the extra work ration.

65   Sometimes they were driven out of the barracks in the middle of the day for an additional roll-call. They would line up in tight rows and march along the road, one behind the other. The big, blonde S.S. women in leather boots plucked from among them all the skinny ones, the ugly ones, the big-bellied ones—and threw them inside the Eye. The so-called Eye was a closed circle formed by the joined hands of the barracks guards. Filled out with women, the circle moved like a macabre dance to the camp gate, there to become absorbed by the great, camp-wide Eye. Five hundred, six hundred, a thousand selected women. Then all of them started on their walk—along the two roads.

66   Sometimes an S.S. woman dropped in at one of the barracks. She cased the bunks, a woman looking at other women. She asked if anyone cared to see a doctor, if anyone was pregnant. At the hospital, she said, they would get milk and white bread.

67   They scrambled out of the bunks and, swept up into the Eye, walked to the gate—towards the little wood.

68   Just to pass the time of day—for there was little for us to do at the camp— we used to spend long hours at the Persian Market, either with the Block Elders, or sitting under the barracks walls, or in the latrines. At the Elders' shacks you drank tea or dozed off for an hour or two in their beds. Sitting under the barracks wall you chatted with the carpenters and the bricklayers. A few women were usually hanging around, dressed in pretty little pullovers and wearing sheer stockings. Any one of them could be had for a piece of bright silk or a shiny trinket. Since time began, never has there been such an easy market for female flesh!

69   The latrines were built for the men and the women jointly, and were separated only by wooden boards. On the women's side, it was crowded and noisy,

on ours, quiet and pleasantly cool inside the concrete enclosure. You sat there by the hour conducting love dialogues with Katia, the pretty little latrine girl. No one felt any embarrassment or thought the set-up uncomfortable. After all, one had already seen so much . . .

That was June. Day and night the people walked—along the two roads.   *70* From dawn until late at night the entire Persian Market stood at roll-call. The days were warm and sunny and the tar melted on the roofs. Then came the rains, and with them icy winds. The mornings would dawn cold and penetrating. Then the fair weather returned once again. Without interruption, the trains pulled up to the ramp and the people walked on . . . Often we had to stand and wait, unable to leave for work, because they were blocking the roads. They walked slowly, in loose groups, sometimes hand in hand. Women, old men, children. As they passed just outside the barbed-wire fence they would turn their silent faces in our direction. Their eyes would fill with tears of pity and they threw bread over the fence for us to eat.

The women took the watches off their wrists and flung them at our feet, ges-   *71* turing to us to take them.

At the gate, a band was playing foxtrots and tangos. The camp gazed at the   *72* passing procession. A man has only a limited number of ways in which he can express strong emotions or violent passions. He uses the same gestures as when what he feels is only petty and unimportant. He utters the same ordinary words.

'How many have gone by so far? It's been almost two months since mid-   *73* May. Counting twenty thousand per day . . . around one million!'

'Eh, they couldn't have gassed that many every day. Though . . . who the   *74* hell knows, with four ovens and scores of deep pits . . .'

'Then count it this way: from Koszyce and Munkacz, almost 600,000. They   *75* got 'em all, no doubt about it. And from Budapest? 300,000, easily.'

'What's the difference?'   *76*

'*Ja,* but anyway, it's got to be over soon. They'll have slaughtered every sin-   *77* gle one of them.'

'There's more, don't worry.'   *78*

You shrug your shoulders and look at the road. Slowly, behind the crowd of   *79* people, walk the S.S. men, urging them with kindly smiles to move along. They explain that it is not much farther and they pat on the back a little old man who runs over to a ditch, rapidly pulls down his trousers, and wobbling in a funny way squats down. An S.S. man calls to him and points to the people disappearing round the bend. The little old man nods quickly, pulls up his trousers and, wobbling in a funny way, runs at a trot to catch up.

You snicker, amused at the sight of a man in such a big hurry to get to the   *80* gas chamber.

Later, we started working at the warehouses, spreading tar over their drip-   *81* ping roofs. The warehouses contained mountains of clothing, junk, and not-yet-disembowelled bundles. The treasures taken from the gassed people were piled up at random, exposed to the sun and the rain.

82   Every day, after lighting a fire under the bucket of tar, we went to 'organize' a snack. One of us would bring a pail of water, another a sack of dry cherries or prunes, a third some sugar. We stewed the fruit and then carried it up on the roof for those who took care of the work itself. Others fried bacon and onions and ate it with corn bread. We stole anything we could get our hands on and took it to the camp.

83   From the warehouse roofs you could see very clearly the flaming pits and the crematoria operating at full speed. You could see the people walk inside, undress. Then the S.S. men would quickly shut the windows and firmly tighten the screws. After a few minutes, in which we did not even have time to tar a piece of roofing board properly, they opened the windows and the side doors and aired the place out. Then came the *Sonderkommando*[6] to drag the corpses to the burning pits. And so it went on, from morning until night—every single day.

84   Sometimes, after a transport had already been gassed, some late-arriving cars drove around filled with the sick. It was wasteful to gas them. They were undressed and Oberscharführer Moll either shot them with his rifle or pushed them live into a flaming trench.

85   Once, a car brought a young woman who had refused to part from her mother. Both were forced to undress, the mother led the way. The man who was to guide the daughter stopped, struck by the perfect beauty of her body, and in his awe and admiration he scratched his head. The woman, noticing this coarse, human gesture, relaxed. Blushing, she clutched the man's arm.

86   'Tell me, what will they do to me?'

87   'Be brave,' said the man, not withdrawing his arm.

88   'I am brave! Can't you see, I'm not even ashamed of you! Tell me!'

89   'Remember, be brave, come. I shall lead you. Just don't look.'

90   He took her by the hand and led her on, his other hand covering her eyes. The sizzling and the stench of the burning fat and the heat gushing out of the pit terrified her. She jerked back. But he gently bent her head forward, uncovering her back. At that moment Oberscharführer fired, almost without aiming. The man pushed the woman into the flaming pit, and as she fell he heard her terrible, broken scream.

91   When the Persian Market, the gypsy camp and the F.K.L. became completely filled with the women selected from among the people from the ramp, a new camp was opened up across from the Persian Market. We called it Mexico. It, too, was not yet completed, and there also they began to install shacks for the Block Elders, electricity, and windows.

92   Each day was just like another. People emerged from the freight cars and walked on—along both roads.

93   The camp inmates had problems of their own: they waited for packages and letters from home, they 'organized' for their friends and mistresses, they speculated, they schemed. Nights followed days, rains came after the dry spells.

---

[6]Jewish prisoners who unloaded bodies from the gas chambers.

Towards the end of the summer, the trains stopped coming. Fewer and   94
fewer people went to the crematoria. At first, the camp seemed somehow empty
and incomplete. Then everybody got used to it. Anyway, other important events
were taking place: the Russian offensive, the uprising and burning of Warsaw,
the transports leaving the camp every day, going West towards the unknown,
towards new sickness and death; the revolt at the crematoria and the escape of
a *Sonderkommando* that ended with the execution of all the escapees.

And afterwards, you were shoved from camp to camp, without a spoon, or a   95
plate, or a piece of rag to clean yourself with.

Your memory retains only images. Today, as I think back on that last sum-   96
mer in Auschwitz, I can still see the endless, colourful procession of people solemnly walking–along both roads; the woman, her head bent forward, standing
over the flaming pit; the big redheaded girl in the dark interior of the barracks,
shouting impatiently:

'Will evil be punished? I mean in human, normal terms!'   97

And I can still see the Jew with bad teeth, standing beneath my high bunk   98
every evening, lifting his face to me, asking insistently:

'Any packages today? Couldn't you sell me some eggs for Mirka? I'll pay in   99
marks. She is so fond of eggs . . .'

WRITING AND DISCUSSION QUESTIONS

Informative

1. Describe the routine at Birkenau as witnessed by the narrator. What is his attitude toward the killings?
2. What dehumanizing techniques does the narrator witness? How does he react to the atrocities he witnesses?
3. How does the narrator use specific persons (Mirka, the dying child, the big red-head, or the young woman with her mother) to communicate a sense of his life at the death camp? To what degree are the prisoners real to him? How does their realness affect his reaction?
4. What is the effect of Borowski's narrating the story in the first person? Does it suggest an acceptance of responsibility for what happens?

Persuasive

1. One observer of people in extreme situations, Robert Jay Lifton, speculated that survival was possible only through what he called ''psychic numbing,'' a process of denying one's true feelings. Argue that the narrator does or does not numb himself.
2. Argue for or against the narrator's complicity in the events of the death camp. In what sense does he find himself in an existential situation? What choices does he face and how does he treat each of them?
3. What view of God and divine justice is suggested by the story?

4. What is the predominant tone of the narrative: one of unremitting bitterness, despair, resignation, empathy, or cold indifference? Choose one and support your position.

Personal

1. How credible is the narrator's story for you? To what degree do you identify with his experience?

▼

THOM GUNN, "ON THE MOVE"

Thom Gunn (1929–) was born in Gravesend, England, where his father was a journalist. His family moved a number of times early in Thom's life because his father worked for several newspapers. After serving two years in the British Army, Thom moved to Paris, where he worked in the subway and tried to write fiction on the side. He later attended college and was graduated from Trinity College, Cambridge University in 1953; while there, he published his first poems. After a short stay in Rome, Gunn entered Stanford University in California as a graduate student. He has lived and taught in San Francisco ever since, except for a year in Texas and occasional trips home to England.

Gunn is a member of a school of poetry called "The Movement," which seeks what a critic called "greater concreteness and a less high-flown diction" than the modernist masters Pound and Eliot. Gunn rejected them because he believed they had jettisoned traditional poetic resonances by deciding, in Gunn's words, "to strengthen the images while either banishing concepts or, where they couldn't avoid them, treating them to the same free association as images." Gunn has praised poets like Gary Snyder and Ted Hughes, whose works rely as much as Gunn's on a respect for the natural, concrete world. Gunn is also concerned with the sense of movement as it reflects the existential concept of choice and exercise of will, of which the poem that follows is one of his best-known illustrations.

▼

On the Move

'Man, you gotta Go.'

THOM GUNN

The blue jay scuffling in the bushes follows
Some hidden purpose, and the gust of birds
That spurts across the field, the wheeling swallows,
Have nested in the trees and undergrowth.
Seeking their instinct, or their poise, or both,

One moves with an uncertain violence
Under the dust thrown by a baffled sense
Or the dull thunder of approximate words.

On motorcycles, up the road, they come:
Small, black, as flies hanging in the heat, the Boys,
Until the distance throws them forth, their hum
Bulges to thunder held by calf and thigh.
In goggles, donned impersonality,
In gleaming jackets trophied with the dust,
They strap in doubt—by hiding it, robust—
And almost hear a meaning in their noise.

Exact conclusion of their hardiness
Has no shape yet, but from known whereabouts
They ride, direction where the tires press.
They scare a flight of birds across the field:
Much that is natural, to the will must yield.
Men manufacture both machine and soul,
And use what they imperfectly control
To dare a future from the taken routes.

It is a part solution, after all.
One is not necessarily discord
On earth; or damned because, half animal,
One lacks direct instinct, because one wakes
Afloat on movement that divides and breaks.
One joins the movement in a valueless world,
Choosing it, till, both hurler and the hurled,
One moves as well, always toward, toward.

A minute holds them, who have come to go:
The self-defined, astride the created will
They burst away; the towns they travel through
Are home for neither bird nor holiness,
For birds and saints complete their purposes.
At worst, one is in motion; and at best,
Reaching no absolute, in which to rest,
One is always nearer by not keeping still.

WRITING AND DISCUSSION QUESTIONS

Informative

1. Describe the bluejay, the ''gust of birds,'' and ''the wheeling swallows'' as the
   poem's narrator sees them. What controls their behavior? What qualities does the
   speaker attribute to them?

2. What is the narrator's view of "the Boys" who ride motorcycles? Who or what controls their movements? What is their purpose? What is the role of nature or instinct in their lives? What attitude toward them is suggested in stanza 3?
3. What is the relationship between the Boys and the birds? What important similarities and differences suggest an existential problem, a solution to which is suggested in stanza 4? Why are "the Boys" an effective symbol of "movement in a valueless world"? What is meant by "a valueless world"?

Persuasive

1. Explain what the narrator means when he says "men manufacture both machine and soul." What existential idea is suggested by this? Argue that the poem is essentially existential in character.
2. The narrator implies in the last stanza that the Boys fall short of being saints. What conclusion about them does he come to, suggested by the last three lines?
3. What do we come "nearer" to "by not keeping still"? Argue that the narrator's attitude toward human movement is essentially a constructive and creative act or that it is a source of "discord" and disarray.

Personal

1. Do you think the poem is antireligious? Is it impossible for a belief in God to coexist with the belief that we "dare a future from the taken routes"?
2. How does the speaker's attitude toward motorcycle groups compare to yours?

CHAPTER WRITING ASSIGNMENTS

1. Some critics have argued that existentialism is a "philosophy of despair." Based on your readings, how accurate is that description, especially when you consider Sartre's description of humanity as alone, "abandoned on earth in the midst of [our] infinite responsibilities, without help, with no other aim than the one [we] set for [ourselves]"? To what degree does the sense of our aloneness and complete responsibility lead to a sense not of despair, but of power and meaningfulness? Can existentialism be considered a great idea if it is permeated by despair?

2. To what degree does existentialism speak to the modern experience today? To what degree are we all outsiders, estranged from others, our institutions, and even our fullest selves? Does living in an industrial society alienate us from fuller and more meaningful lives? What are some of the manifestations of this alienation in the work place, in our youth, and in our art and music? Is existentialism a functional philosophy for the modern world?

3. From one of the following works of literature, analyze an alienated hero, that is, one who has abandoned or been abandoned by the institutions and conventions of society: Holden Caufield from J. D. Salinger's *The Catcher in the Rye*, Rabbit

from John Updike's *Rabbit Run,* Yossarian from Joseph Heller's *Catch 22,* the young man in Edward Albee's *The American Dream,* Celie in Alice Walker's *The Color Purple,* or Milkman in Toni Morrison's *Song of Solomon.* How closely does the character fit the main features of existentialism? How and why has the alienation occurred?

4. Read an essay from one of the chief existential thinkers, Kierkegaard, Nietzsche, Heidegger, Buber, or Marcel, who made their reputations as philosophers and not as writers of literature. Examine one of the key themes of the philosophy to see how different writers treat it.

5. Contrast existentialism from the atheist's and the theist's point of view, for example Sartre or Nietzsche contrasted with Kierkegaard, Buber, or Marcel. How central to the philosophy of each thinker is the belief or disbelief in God?

6. Of the great ideas you have studied so far, which seems closest to existentialism? Which seems most different? Can existentialism be said to derive from any of the ideas, especially its dominant way of knowing and its implications for action?

Chapter Ten

ETHNICITY AND CIVIL RIGHTS

It is a scene etched in the memory of most people who lived through the late 1950s during the rise of the civil rights movement in America. A fifty-three-year-old black woman enters the city bus in Montgomery, Alabama, in 1955, and is told abruptly by the bus driver that she must give up her seat to a white woman. She refuses, and there ensues one of the climactic moral and legal battles for the conscience of a nation in the twentieth century. America was to be changed forever—bitterly torn by the issue of ethnic bigotry but invigorated by justice finally measured out. Her name was Rosa Parks, and her defiance of this deeply embedded prejudice against her people led directly to the boycotts and sit-ins that introduced Americans to the dynamic, young, and articulate Southern minister from Atlanta, Georgia, Dr. Martin Luther King, Jr.

As discovered in Chapter 6, with the rise of post-Enlightenment democratic governments, men and, eventually, women were permitted virtually for the first time in human history to seek self-government. With this came the enunciation of "rights," both those regarded as broadly "inalienable," or basic *human* rights, and others conceived as *civil* rights bestowed on individuals by virtue of their being citizens of a particular locality, region, or nation. If I am a person, then I deserve the basic rights—so says the Declaration of Independence—of life, liberty, and the pursuit of happiness. The concept of civil rights, however, extends beyond such basic human rights to include other personal freedoms, such as the right to seek one's own identity, purpose, and meaning in life without institutional or governmental interference; and practical freedoms, such as the choice to live in a particular neighborhood; the equal opportunity to compete for jobs and pro-

614

fessions; the liberty to form associations to work toward changes in a political system; the complementary rights to adequate education, housing, and health care; and, above all, the assurance of fair legal representation.

The "idea" of civil rights is, in essence, that of a further, more explicit elaboration of what is in implied in "liberty" and "the pursuit of happiness." Thus, from one point of view, it is inconceivable that a government founded on principles so profoundly dedicated to individual freedoms could deliberately deny such rights to any person or groups of persons. But in examining the idea of civil rights in the history of western democracies, one discovers the disappointing truth that in the past four centuries, the civil rights of individuals have often been withheld, predicated on the basis of ethnicity. Such rights—prescribed and regulated by those in power and, thus, in a position to deny many privileges—have been frequently captive to an unarticulated ethnocentrism, or the belief that one majoritarian ethnic heritage is superior to another.

To be secure in, content with, and proud of one's ethnic heritage are natural and positive attitudes and should be celebrated and perpetuated. However, there remains in the United States, and perhaps Western culture in general, a tendency to do the opposite, to feel called on to abandon or hide one's heritage in order to become a generic, "assimilated citizen." Many believe there is a tendency of those in positions of power and authority to use ethnic heritage as an *exclusionary* or as a *meritorious* principle to make unfair distinctions on many levels. This quite clearly is an affront to nearly every moral creed revealed to or devised by humankind. School segregation, literacy tests for voting, and the use of quotas for enrollments in college and some professions are widespread examples of unfair treatment.

Historically, democracies have been built on two competing notions of civil rights. One line of thinking perceives civil rights as the prerogative of the government, that is, that citizens have those rights and only those rights that the government—through the executive, judicial, and legislative branches—specifically grants to the people. The second view is that civil rights include any and all rights that the government does not specifically deny its citizens. These two views of civil rights are obviously in tension, and there are often competing claims in civil rights disputes. An issue like abortion, for instance, illustrates how difficult it is to disentangle such claims: one side argues that "the right of privacy" establishes a principle by which a woman, alone, should be able to make a decision about her pregnancy, and another side posits that the right to privacy cannot extend to the killing of an independent, unborn human being. Is it the government's prerogative to bestow or withhold the "civil right" to abortion; or is it simply the government's responsibility to recognize abortion as an inalienable civil right?

The importance of civil rights comes into sharpest focus, however, when one observes the effects of discrimination, or the denial of civil rights, to individuals based on their ethnic identity, skin color, or religious heritage. The same post-Enlightenment impulse to create democratic change also bears the tragic record, and the twentieth century is by no means excluded, of systematic and premeditated oppression of individuals, families, tribes, and ethnic and racial groups by governments and powerful lobbies. The result of such institutionalized oppression has meant not only programmatic poverty, fractured families, disenfranchisement from the processes of social change, and general demoralization and dehumanization, but too often death by outright murder or by neglect, disease, or abandonment. When civil rights are denied or suppressed by groups in power, whether that power is a formal, governmental authority or the tacit authority in a school, workplace, or neighborhood, the result is inevitably social disintegration.

Although recently, feminists, homosexuals, and fundamentalist Christians, to name only a few groups, have all sought legal remedies to situations they regard as violations of their civil rights, those most often the victims of discrimination are people of color, people who are visibly ethnic. Although one can disguise one's political commitments by remaining silent or being dishonest to avoid discrimination, one cannot change skin color. In the twentieth century, particularly in the United States, Native Americans, African-Americans, Hispanics, and Asian-Americans have all been targets of civil rights discrimination, sometimes blatant, often subtle, but nearly always pervasive.

Truly, the discussion of civil rights is often bound up in a search for appropriate terminology that describes the situation and plight of victims of discrimination. The term "minority," for instance, once used to describe groups who were numerically underrepresented in a population, is no longer regarded as an appropriate designation, chiefly because it defines groups in terms of who they *are not* instead of who they *are* and it connotes inferiority for those not deemed in the "majority." Likewise, the terms "prejudice" and "bigotry" have now given way to more global terms like "racism" and "ethnocentricity." This semantic problem, in fact, illustrates the difficulty of confronting the issue of civil rights objectively and sensitively; the very words one uses to describe the disadvantaged predicament of groups within a society may alienate or malign the groups even when the intention is to seek their welfare. The majority in a society naturally struggles with the rights of its "minority" members, if only to articulate the threat they feel to their standing or power: "What do 'they,' 'those people' want? Can't 'they' get a job or go to school or quit having children?" It is the experience of the "other" group, the underprivileged, that many of us lack and need to be informed of.

The social scientist Joe R. Feagin helpfully places the terms "race" and "ethnic group" in perspective. He points out that while phrases like "Jewish race" or "Black race" are popularly used, they are inaccurate and potentially dangerous concepts when interpreted as distinct categories of human beings based on physical or psychological characteristics transmitted by descent. As Feagin points out:

> A racial group is not something which is naturally generated as part of the self-evident order of the universe, but is a social group which persons inside or outside the group have decided is important to single out as inferior or superior, typically on the basis of real or alleged physical characteristics subjectively selected.[1]

[1] Feagin, J. R. *Racial and Ethnic Relations.* Princeton, N.J.: Prentice-Hall, 1976, p. 7.

Consequently, he defines "racism" as "an ideology which considers a group's unchangeable physical characteristics to be linked in a direct, causal way to psychological or intellectual characteristics, and which on this basis distinguishes between superior and inferior groups."[2] When transplanted Europeans, who had rarely thought of black men and women as other than primitives and slaves, encountered them—as well as Native Americans in the New World—they could rarely overcome this association to treat them with dignity and mutual respect. Immigrants from Ireland and Italy were once widely defined by white, Anglo-Saxons as an inferior "racial" group. In Nazi Germany, the hatred directed at Jews was in part based on the identification of Jews as a "race" with supposedly inferior genetic characteristics—an example of a loathsome and dogmatic social theory denying not only the *civil* but the *human* right to live. Judaism, of course, defines not a "race," or biological entity, but a culture, a faith, and one of the oldest on earth.

Increasingly social scientists, and sensitive and sympathetic citizens in general, are moving away from *race*-oriented terms and concepts that are clearly based on culturally biased or biologically unsound notions that extend, instead of end, discriminatory thinking. Potentially more useful as a descriptive term is *ethnicity*, or ethnic group. All human beings, regardless of skin color, physical structure, or religious heritage, belong to an ethnic group. The term "ethnic" comes from the Greek word *ethnos*, which means simply "nation." There presently are broad and narrow uses of the term and, frankly, "ethnic" can also be misused for the sake of making distinctions or exclusions that deprive persons of their civil rights.

Feagin's definition, however, is a helpful one to use in furthering our understanding of the dynamics of civil rights and the idea of ethnic heritage: "an ethnic group [is] a group which is socially distinguished or set apart, by others and/or by itself, primarily on the basis of cultural or nationality characteristics."[3] Ethnicity means a "shared sense of peoplehood" that transcends mere biology or geography and that includes one's native language, literature, and the cultural experiences of a shared past. Such an identity has meaning, however, only when it is *self-defined*, that is, defined from within the context of the group. To impose an external identity or set of cultural values on a group is potentially an excuse to further deprive the group of its sense of social importance and relevance and to alienate that group. For instance, to categorize an ethnic group as intellectually inferior to another, or to regard one ethnic group's language, literature, or music as "more primitive" or "less prestigious" than another only perpetuates a social and ethnocentric discrimination. The meaning, relevance, and pride in an ethnic identity must arise authentically from the people who comprise that ethnic group.

In the United States, it is the *visibly ethnic*, or people of color, who have most often been the victims of civil rights discrimination, and it is their story that is prominently explored in the readings in this chapter. Murray Friedman, vice chair of the U.S. Civil Rights Commission, has observed that since the turn of the century, the civil rights movement has been beset by two fundamental and, seem-

[2]Feagin, J. R. p. 6.
[3]Feagin, J. R. p. 3.

ingly, mutually exclusive motives: to seek full social and political equality, that is, integration, and to emphasize some degree of separate-but-equal status with economic and community strength.[4] Another version of this dilemma is the "melting pot" metaphor. Is a Western democracy like the United States a "melting pot" that subsumes and assimilates the various ethnic backgrounds that form one distinctive "American culture"? Or is such a metaphor simply another label for an ethnocentrism that disenfranchises and discriminates against individuals and groups on the basis of their "marginality" and "minority" status? Should immigrants to the United States seek to preserve their cultural backgrounds while merging into the "mainstream" of American society or form separatist communities that attempt to "coexist" with rather than merge with the dominant culture?

Whatever the answers are to these dilemmas, it is clear that throughout the nineteenth and twentieth centuries, the concept of the melting pot exerted considerable pressure on immigrants to minimize their ethnic identity and to merge with mainstream American culture. Of the light-skinned groups, those who maintained their ethnoreligious identity suffered the most, especially the Jews, whereas those who assimilated within the dominant culture merged relatively easily in a generation or two. But the visibly ethnic always look different; they have remained an easy target for bigotry.

Although Lincoln's *Emancipation Proclamation* freed slaves from the oppression of slavery, oppression continued in far more subtle forms for almost 100 years. This plight of black men and women has been the primary focus in the civil rights struggle, though recent associations such as Rev. Jesse Jackson's Rainbow Coalition have successfully incorporated a number of different ethnic groups, including Hispanics and Native American Indians in the fight for civil rights.

The selections in this chapter contain voices from different points of view that confront the issues raised by ethnicity and civil rights. Rather than provide a general introduction to the civil rights movement, which traces the early battles of ex-slaves like Frederick Douglass up through to the volatile civil rights movements of the 1960s led by Dr. Martin Luther King, Jr., we have provided each selection with a capsule introduction to the writer's time and place, which should establish the context of each writer's thoughts.

▼

FREDERICK DOUGLASS, "ORATION, DELIVERED IN CORINTHIAN HALL, ROCHESTER, JULY 5, 1852"

It is difficult to underestimate the impact of slavery on the moral conscience of the United States in the nineteenth century. This issue, as it epitomizes the struggle for equality and civil rights better than any other, can be seen as the predominant issue of the young nation as it sought to establish its democracy based on "inalienable rights" bestowed on it by a benevolent creator. One American who became the cen-

[4]"What To Read on Civil Rights," *Policy Review* (Summer, 1988) p. 79.

tral figure in the debate over the issue and the destiny of its ten million black men, women, and children was himself a fugitive slave: Frederick Douglass. As Richard Barksdale and Keneth Kinnamon express it, Douglass possessed "the splendid mixture of verbal eloquence, wisdom, passion, and anger" that made him the most effective spokesman for the emancipation of his people.[1] In 1838, at the age of 21, Douglass fled his slave quarters in Maryland to the freedom awaiting him in Massachusetts. From that base, he inaugurated his leadership role among blacks in the fight against slavery.

Douglass' tactics differed from those of William Lloyd Garrison, the white abolitionist whose emphasis on moral persuasion and secession from the proslavery South made little headway in the battle against slavery. Douglass sought solutions that made the black citizen an equal partner with other citizens in the shaping of America's destiny, rejecting calls for black colonization and other segregationist proposals. Fired with the degrading personal experience of slavery, Douglass' conversations with the volatile, crusading John Brown of Springfield, Massachusetts, led him to the conclusion that only a strong, invading military force could end the slave plantation stranglehold on the South—a bold and ambitious proposal that, when it gained consensus, ultimately led to the Civil War. In his autobiographical writings and speeches, Douglass evinces great oratorical skill, a command of rhetorical flourish, grand metaphor, and precision in diction that elevate him above his peers in the antislavery movement. In his speech, "Oration, Delivered in Corinthian Hall, Rochester, July 5, 1852," 9 years before the beginning of the Civil War, Douglass urges his audience to recognize the consequences of slavery for the nation's conscience, to take responsibility for its evident continuance, and to join him in rescuing America's glorious destiny from the hands of evil slaveowners. It reflects Douglass' passion and eloquence, and as well, remains a textbook example of effective nineteenth-century speechmaking. After a relatively flowery introduction, the speech becomes an impassioned plea for direct action to end slavery. Our excerpt begins with Douglass' main argument.

▼

Oration, Delivered in Corinthian Hall, Rochester, July 5, 1852

FREDERICK DOUGLASS

THE PRESENT

My business, if I have any here to-day, is with the present. The accepted time with God and his cause is the ever-living now.

1

> Trust no future, however pleasant,
>   Let the dead past bury its dead;
> Act, act in the living present,
>   Heart within, and God overhead.

1.*Black Writers of America* (New York: Macmillan, 1972), p. 85.

We have to do with the past only as we can make it useful to the present and to the future. To all inspiring motives, to noble deeds which can be gained from the past, we are welcome. But now is the time, the important time. Your fathers have lived, died, and have done their work, and have done much of it well. You live and must die, and you must do your work. You have no right to enjoy a child's share in the labor of your fathers, unless your children are to be blest by your labors. You have no right to wear out and waste the hard-earned fame of your fathers to cover your indolence. Sydney Smith tells us that men seldom eulogize the wisdom and virtues of their fathers, but to excuse some folly or wickedness of their own. This truth is not a doubtful one. There are illustrations of it near and remote, ancient and modern. It was fashionable, hundreds of years ago, for the children of Jacob to boast, we have "Abraham to our father," when they had long lost Abraham's faith and spirit. That people contented themselves under the shadow of Abraham's great name, while they repudiated the deeds which made his name great. Need I remind you that a similar thing is being done all over this country to-day? Need I tell you that the Jews are not the only people who built the tombs of the prophets, and garnished the sepulchres of the righteous? Washington could not die till he had broken the chains of his slaves. Yet his monument is built up by the price of human blood, and the traders in the bodies and souls of men, shout—"We have Washington to *'our father.'* "—Alas! that it should be so; yet so it is.

> The evil that men do, lives after them,
> The good is oft' interred with their bones.

2   Fellow-citizens, pardon me, allow me to ask, why am I called upon to speak here to-day? What have I, or those I represent, to do with your national independence? Are the great principles of political freedom and of natural justice, embodied in that Declaration of Independence, extended to us? and am I, therefore, called upon to bring our humble offering to the national altar, and to confess the benefits and express devout gratitude for the blessings resulting from your independence to us?

3   Would to God, both for your sakes and ours, that an affirmative answer could be truthfully returned to these questions! Then would my task be light, and my burden easy and delightful. For *who* is there so cold, that a nation's sympathy could not warm him? Who so obdurate and dead to the claims of gratitude, that would not thankfully acknowledge such priceless benefits? Who so stolid and selfish, that would not give his voice to swell the hallelujahs of a nation's jubilee, when the chains of servitude had been torn from his limbs? I am not that man. In a case like that, the dumb might eloquently speak, and the "lame man leap as an hart."

4   But, such is not the state of the case. I say it with a sad sense of the disparity between us. I am not included within the pale of this glorious anniversary! Your high independence only reveals the immeasurable distance between us. The blessings in which you, this day, rejoice, are not enjoyed in common.—

The rich inheritance of justice, liberty, prosperity and independence, bequeathed by your fathers, is shared by you, not by me. The sunlight that brought life and healing to you, has brought stripes and death to me. This Fourth of July is *yours*, not *mine*. *You* may rejoice, *I* must mourn. To drag a man in fetters into the grand illuminated temple of liberty, and call upon him to join you in joyous anthems, were inhuman mockery and sacrilegious irony. Do you mean, citizens, to mock me, by asking me to speak to-day? If so, there is a parallel to your conduct. And let me warn you that it is dangerous to copy the example of a nation whose crimes, towering up to heaven, were thrown down by the breath of the Almighty, burying that nation in irrecoverable ruin! I can to-day take up the plaintive lament of a peeled and woe-smitten people!

"By the rivers of Babylon, there we sat down. Yea! we wept when we remembered Zion. We hanged our harps upon the willows in the midst thereof. For there, they that carried us away captive, required of us a song; and they who wasted us required of us mirth, saying, Sing us one of the songs of Zion. How can we sing the Lord's song in a strange land? If I forget thee, O Jerusalem, let my right hand forget her cunning. If I do not remember thee, let my tongue cleave to the roof of my mouth."   5

Fellow-citizens; above your national, tumultuous joy. I hear the mournful wail of millions! whose chains, heavy and grievous yesterday, are, to-day, rendered more intolerable by the jubilee shouts that reach them. If I do forget, if I do not faithfully remember those bleeding children of sorrow this day, "may my right hand forget her cunning, and may my tongue cleave to the roof of my mouth!" To forget them, to pass lightly over their wrongs, and to chime in with the popular theme, would be treason most scandalous and shocking, and would make me a reproach before God and the world. My subject, then, fellow-citizens, is AMERICAN SLAVERY. I shall see, this day, and its popular characteristics, from the slave's point of view. Standing, there, identified with the American bondman, making his wrongs mine, I do not hesitate to declare, with all my soul, that the character and conduct of this nation never looked blacker to me than on this 4th of July! Whether we turn to the declarations of the past, or to the professions of the present, the conduct of the nation seems equally hideous and revolting. America is false to the past, false to the present, and solemnly binds herself to be false to the future. Standing with God and the crushed and bleeding slave on this occasion, I will, in the name of humanity which is outraged, in the name of liberty which is fettered, in the name of the constitution and the Bible, which are disregarded and trampled upon, dare to call in question and to denounce, with all the emphasis I can command, everything that serves to perpetuate slavery—the great sin and shame of America! "I will not equivocate; I will not excuse;" I will use the severest language I can command; and yet not one word shall escape me that any man, whose judgment is not blinded by prejudice, or who is not at heart a slaveholder, shall not confess to be right and just.   6

But I fancy I hear some one of my audience say, it is just in this circumstance that you and your brother abolitionists fail to make a favorable impres-   7 sion on the public mind. Would you argue more, and denounce less, would you persuade more, and rebuke less, your cause would be much more likely to succeed. But, I submit, where all is plain there is nothing to be argued. What point in the anti-slavery creed would you have me argue? On what branch of the subject do the people of this country need light? Must I undertake to prove that the slave is a man? That point is conceded already. Nobody doubts it. The slaveholders themselves acknowledge it in the enactment of laws for their government. They acknowledge it when they punish disobedience on the part of the slave. There are seventy-two crimes in the State of Virginia, which, if committed by a black man, (no matter how ignorant he be,) subject him to the punishment of death; while only two of the same crimes will subject a white man to the like punishment.—What is this but the acknowledgement that the slave is a moral, intellectual and responsible being. The manhood of the slave is conceded. It is admitted in the fact that Southern statute books are covered with enactments forbidding, under severe fines and penalties, the teaching of the slave to read or to write.—When you can point to any such laws, in reference to the beasts of the field, then I may consent to argue the manhood of the slave. When the dogs in your streets, when the fowls of the air, when the cattle on your hills, when the fish of the sea, and the reptiles that crawl, shall be unable to distinguish the slave from a brute, *then* will I argue with you that the slave is a man!

8   For the present, it is enough to affirm the equal manhood of the negro race. Is it not astonishing that, while we are ploughing, planting and reaping, using all kinds of mechanical tools, erecting houses, constructing bridges, building ships, working in metals of brass, iron, copper, silver and gold; that, while we are reading, writing and cyphering, acting as clerks, merchants and secretaries, having among us lawyers, doctors, ministers, poets, authors, editors, orators and teachers; that, while we are engaged in all manner of enterprises common to other men, digging gold in California, capturing the whale in the Pacific, feeding sheep and cattle on the hill-side, living, moving, acting, thinking, planning, living in families as husbands, wives and children, and, above all, confessing and worshipping the Christian's God, and looking hopefully for life and immortality beyond the grave, we are called upon to prove that we are men!

9   Would you have me argue that man is entitled to liberty? that he is the rightful owner of his own body? You have already declared it. Must I argue the wrongfulness of slavery? Is that a question for Republicans? Is it to be settled by the rules of logic and argumentation, as a matter beset with great difficulty, involving a doubtful application of the principle of justice, hard to be understood? How should I look to-day, in the presence of Americans, dividing, and subdividing a discourse, to show that men have a natural right to freedom? speaking of it relatively, and positively, negatively, and affirmatively. To do so, would be to make myself ridiculous, and to offer an insult to your understanding.—There is not a man beneath the canopy of heaven, that does not know that slavery is wrong *for him.*

10   What, am I to argue that it is wrong to make men brutes, to rob them of

their liberty, to work them without wages, to keep them ignorant of their relations to their fellow men, to beat them with sticks, to flay their flesh with the lash, to load their limbs with irons, to hunt them with dogs, to sell them at auction, to sunder their families, to knock out their teeth, to burn their flesh, to starve them into obedience and submission to their masters? Must I argue that a system thus marked with blood, and stained with pollution, *is wrong?* No! I will not. I have better employment for my time and strength, than such arguments would imply.

What, then, remains to be argued? Is it that slavery is not divine; that God   *11*
did not establish it; that our doctors of divinity are mistaken? There is blasphemy in the thought. That which is inhuman, cannot be divine! *Who* can reason on such a proposition? They that can, may; I cannot. The time for such argument is past.

At a time like this, scorching irony, not convincing argument, is needed. O!   *12*
had I the ability, and could I reach the nation's ear, I would, to-day, pour out a fiery stream of biting ridicule, blasting reproach, withering sarcasm, and stern rebuke. For it is not light that is needed, but fire; it is not the gentle shower, but thunder. We need the storm, the whirlwind, and the earthquake. The feeling of the nation must be quickened; the conscience of the nation must be roused; the propriety of the nation must be startled; the hypocrisy of the nation must be exposed; and its crimes against God and man must be proclaimed and denounced.

What, to the American slave, is your 4th of July? I answer; a day that   *13*
reveals to him, more than all other days in the year, the gross injustice and cruelty to which he is the constant victim. To him, your celebration is a sham; your boasted liberty, an unholy license; your national greatness, swelling vanity; your sounds of rejoicing are empty and heartless; your denunciations of tyrants, brass fronted impudence; your shouts of liberty and equality, hollow mockery; your prayers and hymns, your sermons and thanksgivings, with all your religious parade, and solemnity, are, to him, mere bombast, fraud, deception, impiety, and hypocrisy—a thin veil to cover up crimes which would disgrace a nation of savages. There is not a nation on the earth guilty of practices, more shocking and bloody, than are the people of these United States, at this very hour.

Go where you may, search where you will, roam through all the monarchies   *14*
and despotisms of the old world, travel through South America, search out every abuse, and when you have found the last, lay your facts by the side of the every day practices of this nation, and you will say with me, that, for revolting barbarity and shameless hypocrisy, America reigns without a rival.

THE INTERNAL SLAVE TRADE

Take the American slave-trade, which we are told by the papers, is especially   *15*
prosperous just now. Ex-Senator Benton tells us that the price of men was

never higher than now. He mentions the fact to show that slavery is in no danger. This trade is one of the peculiarities of American institutions. It is carried on in all the large towns and cities in one half of this confederacy; and millions are pocketed every year, by dealers in this horrid traffic. In several states, this trade is a chief source of wealth. It is called (in contradistinction to the foreign slave-trade) *"the internal slave-trade."* It is, probably, called so, too, in order to divert from it the horror with which the foreign slave-trade is contemplated. That trade has long since been denounced by this government, as piracy. It has been denounced with burning words, from the high places of the nation, as an execrable traffic. To arrest it, to put an end to it, this nation keeps a squadron, at immense cost, on the coast of Africa. Everywhere, in this country, it is safe to speak of this foreign slave-trade, as a most inhuman traffic, opposed alike to the laws of God and of man. The duty to extirpate and destroy it is admitted even by our DOCTORS OF DIVINITY. In order to put an end to it, some of these last have consented that their colored brethren (nominally free) should leave this country, and establish themselves on the western coast of Africa! It is, however, a notable fact, that, while so much execration is poured out by Americans, upon those engaged in the foreign slave-trade, the men engaged in the slave-trade between the states pass without condemnation, and their business is deemed honorable.

16   Behold the practical operation of this internal slave-trade, the American slave-trade, sustained by American politics and American religion. Here you will see men and women, reared like swine, for the market. You know what is a swine-drover? I will show you a man-drover. They inhabit all our Southern States. They perambulate the country, and crowd the highways of the nation, with droves of human stock. You will see one of these human flesh jobbers, armed with pistol, whip, and bowie-knife, driving a company of a hundred men, women, and children, from the Potomac to the slave market at New Orleans. These wretched people are to be sold singly, or in lots, to suit purchasers. They are food for the cotton-field, and the deadly sugar-mill. Mark the sad procession, as it moves wearily along, and the inhuman wretch who drives them. Hear his savage yells and his blood-chilling oaths, as he hurries on his affrighted captives! There, see the old man, with locks thinned and gray. Cast one glance, if you please, upon that young mother, whose shoulders are bare to the scorching sun, her briny tears falling on the brow of the babe in her arms. See, too, that girl of thirteen, weeping, *yes!* weeping, as she thinks of the mother from whom she has been torn! The drove moves tardily. Heat and sorrow have nearly consumed their strength; suddenly you hear a quick snap, like the discharge of a rifle; the fetters clank, and the chain rattles simultaneously; your ears are saluted with a scream, that seems to have torn its way to the centre of your soul! The crack you heard, was the sound of the slave-whip; the scream you heard, was from the woman you saw with the babe. Her speed had faltered under the weight of her child and her chains! that gash on her shoulder tells her to move on. Follow this drove to New Orleans. Attend the auction; see men examined like horses; see the forms of women rudely and brutally exposed to the shocking gaze of American slave-buyers. See this drove sold

and separated for ever; and never forget the deep, sad sobs that arose from that scattered multitude. Tell me citizens, WHERE, under the sun, you can witness a spectacle more fiendish and shocking. Yet this is but a glance at the American slave-trade, as it exists, at this moment, in the ruling part of the United States.

I was born amid such sights and scenes. To me the American slave-trade is   *17* a terrible reality. When a child, my soul was often pierced with a sense of its horrors. I lived on Philpot Street, Fell's Point, Baltimore, and have watched from the wharves, the slave ships in the Basin, anchored from the shore, with their cargoes of human flesh, waiting for favorable winds to waft them down the Chesapeake. There was, at that time, a grand slave mart kept at the head of Pratt Street, by Austin Woldfolk. His agents were sent into every town and county in Maryland, announcing their arrival, through the papers, and on flaming *"hand-bills,"* headed CASH FOR NEGROES. These men were generally well dressed men, and very captivating in their manners. Ever ready to drink, to treat, and to gamble. The fate of many a slave has depended upon the turn of a single card; and many a child has been snatched from the arms of its mother, by bargains arranged in a state of brutal drunkenness.

The flesh-mongers gather up their victims by dozens, and drive them,   *18* chained, to the general depot at Baltimore. When a sufficient number have been collected here, a ship is chartered, for the purpose of conveying the forlorn crew to Mobile, or to New Orleans. From the slave prison to the ship, they are usually driven in the darkness of night; for since the anti-slavery agitation, a certain caution is observed.

In the deep still darkness of midnight, I have been often aroused by the   *19* dead heavy footsteps, and the pitious cries of the chained gangs that passed our door. The anguish of my boyish heart was intense; and I was often consoled, when speaking to my mistress in the morning, to hear her say that the custom was very wicked; that she hated to hear the rattle of the chains, and the heart-rending cries. I was glad to find one who sympathized with me in my horror.

Fellow-citizens, this murderous traffic is, to-day, in active operation in this boasted republic. In the solitude of my spirit, I see clouds of dust raised on the   *20* highways of the South; I see the bleeding footsteps; I hear the doleful wail of fettered humanity, on the way to the slave-markets, where the victims are to be sold like *horses, sheep,* and *swine,* knocked off to the highest bidder. There I see the tenderest ties ruthlessly broken, to gratify the lust, caprice and rapacity of the buyers and sellers of men. My soul sickens at the sight.

> Is this the land your Fathers loved,
>   The freedom which they toiled to win?
> Is this the earth whereon they moved?
>   Are these the graves they slumber in?

But a still more inhuman, disgraceful, and scandalous state of things   *21* remains to be presented.

By an act of the American Congress, not yet two years old, slavery has been   *22* nationalized in its most horrible and revolting form. By that act, Mason & Dixon's line has been obliterated; New York has become as Virginia; and the power to hold, hunt, and sell men, women and children, as slaves, remains no longer a mere state institution, but is now an institution of the whole United States. The power is co-extensive with the star-spangled banner, and American Christianity. Where these go, may also go the merciless slave-hunter. Where these are, man is not sacred. He is a bird for the sportsman's gun. By that most foul and fiendish of all human decrees, the liberty and person of every man are put in peril. Your broad republican domain is hunting ground for *men.* *Not* for thieves and robbers, enemies of society, merely, but for men guilty of no crime. Your law-makers have commanded all good citizens to engage in this hellish sport. Your President, your Secretary of State, your *lords, nobles,* and ecclesiastics, enforce, as a duty you owe to your free and glorious country, and to your God, that you do this accursed thing. Not fewer than forty Americans, have, within the past two years, been hunted down, and, without a moment's warning, hurried away in chains, and consigned to slavery, and excruciating torture. Some of these have had wives and children, dependent on them for bread; but of this, no account was made. The right of the hunter to his prey, stands superior to the right of marriage, and to *all* rights in this republic, the rights of God included! For black men there are neither law, justice, humanity, nor religion. The Fugitive Slave *Law* makes MERCY TO THEM, A CRIME: and bribes the judge who tries them. An American JUDGE GETS TEN DOLLARS FOR EVERY VICTIM HE CONSIGNS to slavery, and five, when he fails to do so. The oath of any two villains is sufficient, under this hell-black enactment, to send the most pious and exemplary black man into the remorseless jaws of slavery! His own testimony is nothing. He can bring no witnesses for himself. The minister of American justice is bound, by the law to hear but *one* side; and *that* side, is the side of the oppressor. Let this damning fact be perpetually told. Let it be thundered around the world, that, in tyrant-killing, king-hating, people-loving, democratic, Christian America, the seats of justice are filled with judges, who hold their offices under an open and palpable *bribe*, and are bound, in deciding in the case of a man's liberty, *to hear only his accusers!*

23   In glaring violation of justice, in shameless disregard of the forms of administering law, in cunning arrangement to entrap the defenceless, and in diabolical intent, this Fugitive Slave Law stands alone in the annals of tyrannical legislation. I doubt if there be another nation on the globe, having the brass and the baseness to put such a law on the statute-book. If any man in this assembly thinks differently from me in this matter, and feels able to disprove my statements, I will gladly confront him at any suitable time and place he may select.

RELIGIOUS LIBERTY

24 I take this law to be one of the grossest infringements of Christian Liberty, and, if the churches and ministers of our country were not stupidly blind, or most wickedly indifferent, they, too, would so regard it.

At the very moment that they are thanking God for the enjoyment of civil   25
and religious liberty, and for the right to worship God according to the dictates
of their own consciences, they are utterly silent in respect to a law which robs
religion of its chief significance, and makes it utterly worthless to a world lying
in wickedness. Did this law concern the *"mint, anise* and *cummin"*—abridge
the right to sing psalms, to partake of the sacrament, or to engage in any of the
ceremonies of religion, it would be smitten by the thunder of a thousand pulpits. A general shout would go up from the church, demanding *repeal, repeal,
instant repeal!*—And it would go hard with that politician who presumed to
solicit the votes of the people without inscribing this motto on his banner. Further, if this demand were not complied with, another Scotland would be added
to the history of religious liberty, and the stern old covenanters would be
thrown into the shade. A John Knox would be seen at every church door, and
heard from every pulpit, and Fillmore would have no more quarter than was
shown by Knox, to the beautiful, but treacherous Queen Mary of Scotland.—
The fact that the church of our country, (with fractional exceptions,) does not
esteem "the Fugitive Slave Law" as a declaration of war against religious liberty, implies that that church regards religion simply as a form of worship, an
empty ceremony, and *not* a vital principle, requiring active benevolence, justice, love and good will towards man. It esteems sacrifice above mercy; psalm-
singing above right doing; solemn meetings above practical righteousness. A
worship that can be conducted by persons who refuse to give shelter to the
houseless, to give bread to the hungry, clothing to the naked, and who enjoin
obedience to a law forbidding these acts of mercy, is a curse, not a blessing to
mankind. The Bible addresses all such persons as "scribes, pharisees, hypocrites, who pay tithe of *mint, anise,* and *cummin,* and have omitted the weight-
ier matters of the law, judgment, mercy and faith."

THE CHURCH RESPONSIBLE

But the church of this country is not only indifferent to the wrongs of the slave,   26
it actually takes sides with the oppressors. It has made itself the bulwark of
American slavery, and the shield of American slave-hunters. Many of its most
eloquent Divines, who stand as the very lights of the church, have shamelessly
given the sanction of religion, and the bible, to the whole slave system.—They
have taught that man may, properly, be a slave; that the relation of master and
slave is ordained of God; that to send back an escaped bondman to his master
is clearly the duty of all the followers of the Lord Jesus Christ; and this horrible
blasphemy is palmed off upon the world for christianity.

For my part, I would say, welcome infidelity! welcome atheism! welcome   27
anything! in preference to the gospel, *as preached by those Divines!* They convert the very name of religion into an engine of tyranny, and barbarous cruelty,
and serve to confirm more infidels, in this age, than all the infidel writings of
Thomas Paine, Voltaire, and Bolingbroke, put together, have done. These ministers make religion a cold and flinty-hearted thing, having neither principles of

right action, nor bowels of compassion. They strip the love of God of its beauty, and leave the throne of religion a huge, horrible, repulsive form. It is a religion for oppressors, tyrants, man-stealers, and *thugs*. It is not that *"pure and undefiled religion"* which is from above, and which is *"first pure, then peaceable, easy to be entreated,* full of mercy and good fruits, *without partiality, and without hypocrisy."* But a religion which favors the rich against the poor; which exalts the proud above the humble; which divides mankind into two classes, tyrants and slaves; which says to the man in chains, *stay there;* and to the oppressor, *oppress on;* it is a religion which may be professed and enjoyed by all the robbers and enslavers of mankind; it makes God a respecter of persons, denies his fatherhood of the race, and tramples in the dust the great truth of the brotherhood of man. All this we affirm to be true of the popular church, and the popular worship of our land and nation—a religion, a church and a worship which, on the authority of inspired wisdom, we pronounce to be an abomination in the sight of God. In the language of Isaiah, the American church might be well addressed, "Bring no more vain oblations; incense is an abomination unto me: the new moons and Sabbaths, the calling of assemblies, I cannot away with; it is iniquity, even the solemn meeting. Your new moons, and your appointed feasts my soul hateth. They are a trouble to me; I am weary to bear them; and when ye spread forth your hands I will hide mine eyes from you. Yea! when ye make many prayers, I will not hear. YOUR HANDS ARE FULL OF BLOOD; cease to do evil, learn to do well, seek judgment; relieve the oppressed; judge for the fatherless; plead for the widow."

28   The American church is guilty, when viewed in connection with what it is doing to uphold slavery; but it is superlatively guilty when viewed in connection with its ability to abolish slavery.

29   The sin of which it is guilty is one of omission as well as of commission. Albert Barnes but uttered what the common sense of every man at all observant of the actual state of the case will receive as truth, when he declared that "There is no power out of the church that could sustain slavery an hour, if it were not sustained in it."

30   Let the religious press, the pulpit, the sunday school, the conference meeting, the great ecclesiastical, missionary, bible and tract associations of the land array their immense powers against slavery, and slave-holding; and the whole system of crime and blood would be scattered to the winds, and that they do not do this involves them in the most awful responsibility of which the mind can conceive.

31   In prosecuting the anti-slavery enterprise, we have been asked to spare the church, to spare the ministry; but *how*, we ask, could such a thing be done? We are met on the threshold of our efforts for the redemption of the slave, by the church and ministry of the country, in battle arrayed against us; and we are compelled to fight or flee. From *what* quarter, I beg to know, has proceeded a fire so deadly upon our ranks, during the last two years, as from the Northern pulpit? As the champions of oppressors, the chosen men of American theology have appeared—men, honored for their so called piety, and their real learning.

The LORDS of Buffalo, the SPRINGS of New York, the LATHROPS of Auburn, the COXES and SPENCERS of Brooklyn, the GANNETS and SHARPS of Boston, the DEW-EYS of Washington, and other great religious lights of the land, have, in utter denial of the authority of *Him,* by whom they professed to be called to the ministry, deliberately taught us, against the example of the Hebrews, and against the remonstrance of the Apostles, they teach *that we ought to obey man's law before the law of God.*

My spirit wearies of such blasphemy; and how such men can be supported, 32 as the "standing types and representative of Jesus Christ," is a mystery which I leave others to penetrate. In speaking of the American church, however, let it be distinctly understood that I mean the *great mass* of the religious organizations of our land. There are exceptions, and I thank God that there are. Noble men may be found, scattered all over these Northern States, of whom Henry Ward Beecher, of Brooklyn, Samuel J. May, of Syracuse, and my esteemed friend[1] on the platform, are shining examples; and let me say further, that, upon these men lies the duty to inspire our ranks with high religious faith and zeal, and to cheer us on in the great mission of the slave's redemption from his chains.

RELIGION IN ENGLAND AND RELIGION IN AMERICA

One is struck with the difference between the attitude of the American church 33 towards the anti-slavery movement, and that occupied by the churches in England towards a similar movement in that country. There, the church, true to its mission of ameliorating, elevating, and improving the condition of mankind, came forward promptly, bound up the wounds of the West Indian slave, and restored him to his liberty. There, the question of emancipation was a high religious question. It was demanded, in the name of humanity, and according to the law of the living God. The Sharps, the Clarksons, the Wilber-forces, the Buxtons, the Burchells, and the Knibbs, were alike famous for their piety, and for their philanthropy. The anti-slavery movement *there,* was not an anti-church movement, for the reason that the church took its full share in prosecuting that movement: and the anti-slavery movement in this country will cease to be an anti-church movement, when the church of this country shall assume a favorable, instead of a hostile position towards that movement.

Americans! your republican politics, not less than your republican religion, 34 are flagrantly inconsistent. You boast of your love of liberty, your superior civilization, and your pure christianity, while the whole political power of the nation, (as embodied in the two great political parties,) is solemnly pledged to support and perpetuate the enslavement of three millions of your countrymen. You hurl your anathemas at the crowned headed tyrants of Russia and Austria, and pride yourselves on your Democratic institutions, while you yourselves con-

[1]Rev. R. R. Raymond.

sent to be the mere *tools* and *body-guards* of the tyrants of Virginia and Carolina. You invite to your shores fugitives of oppression from abroad, honor them with banquets, greet them with ovations, cheer them, toast them, salute them, protect them, and pour out your money to them like water; but the fugitives from your own land, you advertise, hunt, arrest, shoot and kill. You glory in your refinement, and your universal education; yet you maintain a system as barbarous and dreadful, as ever stained the character of a nation—a system begun in avarice, supported in pride, and perpetuated in cruelty. You shed tears over fallen Hungary, and make the sad story of her wrongs the theme of your poets, statesmen and orators, till your gallant sons are ready to fly to arms to vindicate her cause against her oppressors; but, in regard to the ten thousand wrongs of the American slave, you would enforce the strictest silence, and would hail him as an enemy of the nation who dares to make those wrongs the subject of public discourse! You are all on fire at the mention of liberty for France or for Ireland; but are as cold as an iceberg at the thought of liberty for the enslaved of America.—You discourse eloquently on the dignity of labor; yet, you sustain a system which, in its very essence, casts a stigma upon labor. You can bare your bosom to the storm of British artillery, to throw off a three-penny tax on tea; and yet wring the last hard earned farthing from the grasp of the black laborers of your country. You profess to believe "that, of one blood, God made all nations of men to dwell on the face of all the earth," and hath commanded all men, everywhere to love one another; yet you notoriously hate, (and glory in your hatred,) all men whose skins are not colored like your own. You declare, before the world, and are understood by the world to declare, that you *"hold these truths to be self evident, that all men are created equal; and are endowed by their Creator with certain inalienable rights; and that, among these are, life, liberty, and the pursuit of happiness;"* and yet, you hold securely, in a bondage, which according to your own Thomas Jefferson, *"is worse than ages of that which your fathers rose in rebellion to oppose,"* a seventh part of the inhabitants of your country.

35   Fellow-citizens! I will not enlarge further on your national inconsistencies. The existence of slavery in this country brands your republicanism as a sham, your humanity as a base pretence, and your christianity as a lie. It destroys your moral power abroad; it corrupts your politicians at home. It saps the foundation of religion; it makes your name a hissing, and a bye-word to a mocking earth. It is the antagonistic force in your government, the only thing that seriously disturbs and endangers your *Union*. It fetters your progress; it is the enemy of improvement, the deadly foe of education; it fosters pride; it breeds insolence; it promotes vice; it shelters crime; it is a curse to the earth that supports it; and yet, you cling to it, as if it were the sheet anchor of all your hopes. Oh! be warned! be warned! a horrible reptile is coiled up in your nation's bosom; the venomous creature is nursing at the tender breast of your youthful republic; *for the love of God, tear away,* and fling from you the hideous monster, and *let the weight of twenty millions, crush and destroy it forever!*

THE CONSTITUTION

But it is answered in reply to all this, that precisely what I have now denounced   *36*
is, in fact, guaranteed and sanctioned by the Constitution of the United States;
that, the right to hold, and to hunt slaves is a part of that Constitution framed
by the illustrious Fathers of this Republic.

Then, I dare to affirm, notwithstanding all I have said before, your fathers   *37*
stooped, basely stooped.

> To palter with us in a double sense:
> And keep the word of promise to the ear,
> But break it to the heart.

And instead of being the honest men I have before declared them to be,   *38*
they were the veriest imposters that ever practised on mankind. *This* is the
inevitable conclusion, and from it there is no escape; but I differ from those
who charge this baseness on the framers of the Constitution of the United
States. *It is a slander upon their memory,* at least, so I believe. There is not
time now to argue the constitutional question at length; nor have I the ability to
discuss it as it ought to be discussed. The subject has been handled with mas-
terly power by Lysander Spooner, Esq., and last, though not least, by Gerritt
Smith, Esq. These gentlemen have, as I think, fully and clearly vindicated the
Constitution from any design to support slavery for an hour.

Fellow-citizens! there is no matter in respect to which, the people of the   *39*
North have allowed themselves to be so ruinously imposed upon, as that of the
pro-slavery character of the Constitution. In *that* instrument I hold there is neither warrant, license, nor sanction of the hateful thing; but interpreted, as it
ought to be interpreted, the Constitution is a GLORIOUS LIBERTY DOCUMENT.
Read its preamble, consider its purposes. Is slavery among them? Is it at the
gateway? or is it in the temple? it is neither. While I do not intend to argue this
question on the present occasion, let me ask, if it be not somewhat singular
that, if the Constitution were intended to be, by its framers and adopters, a
slaveholding instrument, why neither *slavery, slaveholding,* nor *slave* can anywhere be found in it. What would be thought of an instrument, drawn up,
legally drawn up, for the purpose of entitling the city of Rochester to a track of
land, in which no mention of land was made? Now, there are certain rules of
interpretation, for the proper understanding of all legal instruments. These
rules are well established. They are plain, common-sense rules, such as you
and I, and all of us, can understand and apply, without having passed years in
the study of law. I scout the idea that the question of the constitutionality, or
unconstitutionality of slavery, is not a question for the people. I hold that every
American citizen has a right to form an opinion of the constitution, and to propagate that opinion, and to use all honorable means to make his opinion the pre-

vailing one. Without this right, the liberty of an American citizen would be as insecure as that of a Frenchman. Ex-Vice-President Dallas tells us that the constitution is an object to which no American mind can be too attentive, and no American heart too devoted. He further says, the constitution, in its words, is plain and intelligible, and is meant for the homebred, unsophisticated understandings of our fellow-citizens. Senator Berrien tells us that the Constitution is the fundamental law, that which controls all others. The charter of our liberties, which every citizen has a personal interest in understanding thoroughly. The testimony of Senator Breese, Lewis Cass, and many others that might be named, who are everywhere esteemed as sound lawyers, so regard the constitution. I take it, therefore, that it is not presumption in a private citizen to form an opinion of that instrument.

40   Now, take the constitution according to its plain reading, and I defy the presentation of a single pro-slavery clause in it. On the other hand it will be found to contain principles and purposes, entirely hostile to the existence of slavery.

41   I have detained my audience entirely too long already. At some future period I will gladly avail myself of an opportunity to give this subject a full and fair discussion.

42   Allow me to say, in conclusion, notwithstanding the dark picture I have this day presented, of the state of the nation, I do not despair of this country. There are forces in operation, which must inevitably, work the downfall of slavery. *"The arm of the Lord is not shortened,"* and the doom of slavery is certain. I, therefore, leave off where I began, with *hope*. While drawing encouragement from "the Declaration of Independence," the great principles it contains, and the genius of American Institutions, my spirit is also cheered by the obvious tendencies of the age. Nations do not now stand in the same relation to each other that they did ages ago. No nation can now shut itself up, from the surrounding world, and trot round in the same old path of its fathers without interference. The time *was* when such could be done. Long established customs of hurtful character could formerly fence themselves in, and do their evil work with social impunity. Knowledge was then confined and enjoyed by the privileged few, and the multitude walked on in mental darkness. But a change has now come over the affairs of mankind. Walled cities and empires have become unfashionable. The arm of commerce has borne away the gates of the strong city. Intelligence is penetrating the darkest corners of the globe. It makes its pathway over and under the sea, as well as on the earth. Wind, steam, and lightning are its chartered agents. Oceans no longer divide, but link nations together. From Boston to London is now a holiday excursion. Space is comparatively annihilated.—Thoughts expressed on one side of the Atlantic, are distinctly heard on the other.

43   The far off and almost fabulous Pacific rolls in grandeur at our feet. The Celestial Empire, the mystery of ages, is being solved. The fiat of the Almighty, *"Let there be Light,"* has not yet spent its force. No abuse, no outrage whether in taste, sport or avarice, can now hide itself from the all-pervading light. The iron shoe, and crippled foot of China must be seen, in contrast with nature.

Africa must rise and put on her yet unwoven garment. "Ethiopia shall stretch out her hand unto God."

WRITING AND DISCUSSION QUESTIONS

Informative

1. Explain the setting for Douglass' speech; what makes the date, subject matter, and audience particularly charged with significance?
2. There are numerous Biblical allusions in Douglass' speech; account for his decision to link his speech with Biblical themes. How does it enhance his speech for his presumed audience? To what extent is the antislavery cause dependent on the work of church folk and other religious believers?
3. Examine Douglass' references to the Constitution and the Declaration of Independence. How do they, and the 4th of July, serve to heighten the impact of his argument?

Persuasive

1. In his original delivery Douglass ends his speech with a poem written by fellow, white abolitionist, William Lloyd Garrison, who was opposed to the use of force in ending slavery. Why does Douglass elect to end his oration with reference to an opponent's views? Argue that this is or is not an effective way to conclude.
2. Compare Douglass' speech in scope, intent and impact with that of Dr. King's "Letter from Birmingham Jail." What do they have in common? In what way do they differ? Argue that one or the other is more effective for its time and place.

Personal

1. What risks does Douglass take in his indictment of churches and ministers for their responsibility for the continuation of slavery? Did it take special courage for him to so address his audience?
2. If you had not heard of Frederick Douglass before reading this text, speculate on the reasons why. Is it a matter of his absence from important history texts? Your own limited reading? The obscurity of the roots of slavery and the abolitionist movement? Critics of public school history texts have come under criticism for neglecting the contributions of blacks and other ethnic groups. Do you think this is a valid charge?

▼

ZORA NEALE HURSTON, "THE GILDED SIX-BITS"

Zora Neale Hurston (1903–1960), was born and grew up in the all-black town of Eatonville, Florida, and made it the literal and psychological setting of most of her fiction. After a childhood of family turmoil in which her mother died and her apparently irresponsible father remarried, Hurston attended Howard University in Washington, D.C., later winning a scholarship to Barnard College in 1924 in New York. While there, she became part of what literary historians refer to as the "Harlem Renaissance," a group of black writers who emerged as important spokespersons for new literary styles and themes. Spared some of the more traumatic contacts with racism in her youth, Hurston's work generally does not deal directly with racial or civil rights themes. Nevertheless, she makes a major contribution to our understanding of the context of civil rights in her faithful, anthropological accounts of life in the black communities of the South in the early part of this century. Her reliable record of black folklore, the vocabulary and syncopation of black language, and the tensions among segregated blacks caught between the values and dreams of the larger white culture and their own authentic experience as former slaves is invaluable in documenting the poor status of blacks in their quest for identity. *Their Eyes Were Watching God* (1937), a biographical novel, remains the most admired of her fictional works, and her nonfiction essays on black community life found many outlets in mainstream publications during the 1930s and 1940s. Despite her early successes, Hurston died in poverty at age 57 in Fort Pierce, Florida. Her reputation as a chronicler of black experience in America has been triumphantly revived recently with the attention paid to her by such renowned black women writers as Alice Walker and Toni Morrison. The short story presented here, "The Gilded Six-Bits," partakes of the same strengths of narration and use of authentic dialogue characteristic of *Their Eyes Were Watching God*. First published in 1933, this well-crafted tale provides the reader with a glimpse of the social milieu of poor blacks and the dim prospects for movement into the larger culture.

▼

The Gilded Six-Bits
ZORA NEALE HURSTON

It was a Negro yard around a Negro house in a Negro settlement that looked to the payroll of the G and G Fertilizer works for its support.

But there was something happy about the place. The front yard was parted in the middle by a sidewalk from gate to door-step, a sidewalk edged on either side by quart bottles driven neck down into the ground on a slant. A mess of homey flowers planted without a plan but blooming cheerily from their helter-skelter places. The fence and house were whitewashed. The porch and steps scrubbed white.

The front door stood open to the sunshine so that the floor of the front room could finish drying after its weekly scouring. It was Saturday. Everything clean from the front gate to the privy house. Yard raked so that the strokes of the rake would make a pattern. Fresh newspaper cut in fancy edge on the kitchen shelves.

Missie May was bathing herself in the galvanized washtub in the bedroom.

Her darkbrown skin glistened under the soapsuds that skittered down from her wash rag. Her stiff young breasts thrust forward aggressively like broadbased cones with the tips lacquered in black.

She heard men's voices in the distance and glanced at the dollar clock on the dresser.

"Humph! Ah'm way behind time t'day! Joe gointer be heah 'fore Ah git mah clothes on if Ah don't make haste."

She grabbed the clean meal sack at hand and dried herself hurriedly and began to dress. But before she could tie her slippers, there came the ring of singing metal on wood. Nine times.

Missie May grinned with delight. She had not seen the big tall man come stealing in the gate and creep up the walk grinning happily at the joyful mischief he was about to commit. But she knew that it was her husband throwing silver dollars in the door for her to pick up and pile beside her plate at dinner. It was this way every Saturday afternoon. The nine dollars hurled into the open door, he scurried to a hiding place behind the cape jasmine bush and waited.

Missie May promptly appeared at the door in mock alarm.

"Who dat chunkin' money in mah do'way?" she demanded. No answer from the yard. She leaped off the porch and began to search the shrubbery. She peeped under the porch and hung over the gate to look up and down the road. While she did this, the man behind the jasmine darted to the china berry tree. She spied him and gave chase.

"Nobody ain't gointer be chunkin' money at me and Ah not do 'em nothin'," she shouted in mock anger. He ran around the house with Missie May at his heels. She overtook him at the kitchen door. He ran inside but could not close it after him before she crowded in and locked with him in a rough and tumble. For several minutes the two were a furious mass of male and female energy. Shouting, laughing, twisting, turning, tussling, tickling each other in the ribs; Missie May clutching onto Joe and Joe trying, but not too hard, to get away.

"Missie May, take yo' hand out mah pocket!" Joe shouted out between laughs.

"Ah ain't, Joe, no lessen you gwine gimme whateve' it is good you got in yo' pocket. Turn it go, Joe, do Ah'll tear yo' clothes."

"Go on tear 'em. You de one dat pushes de needles round heah. Move yo' hand Missie May."

"Lemme git dat paper sack out yo' pocket. Ah bet its candy kisses."

"Tain't. Move yo' hand. Woman ain't got no business in a man's clothes nohow. Go away."

Missie May gouged way down and gave an upward jerk and triumphed.

"Unhhunhh! Ah got it. It 'tis so candy kisses. Ah knowed you had somethin' for me in yo' clothes. Now Ah got to see whut's in every pocket you got."

Joe smiled indulgently and let his wife go through all of his pockets and take out the things that he had hidden there for her to find. She bore off the chewing gum, the cake of sweet soap, the pocket handkerchief as if she had wrested them from him, as if they had not been bought for the sake of this friendly battle.

"Whew! dat play-fight done got me all warmed up." Joe exclaimed. "Got me some water in de kittle?"

"Yo' water is on de fire and yo' clean things is cross de bed. Hurry up and wash yo'self and git changed so we kin eat. Ah'm hongry." As Missie said this, she bore the steaming kettle into the bedroom.

"You ain't hongry, sugar." Joe contradicted her. "Youse jes' a little empty. Ah'm de one whut's hongry. Ah could eat up camp meetin', back off 'ssocia-tion, and drink Jurdan dry. Have it on de table when Ah git out de tub."

"Don't you mess wid mah business, man. You git in yo' clothes. Ah'm a real wife, not no dress and breath. Ah might not look lak one, but if you burn me, you won't git a thing but wife ashes."

Joe splashed in the bedroom and Missie May fanned around in the kitchen. A fresh red and white checked cloth on the table. Big pitcher of buttermilk beaded with pale drops of butter from the churn. Hot fried mullet, crackling bread, ham hock atop a mound of string beans and new potatoes, and perched on the window-sill a pone of spicy potato pudding.

Very little talk during the meal but that little consisted of banter that pre-tended to deny affection but in reality flaunted it. Like when Missie May reached for a second helping of the tater pone. Joe snatched it out of her reach.

After Missie May had made two or three unsuccessful grabs at the pan, she begged, "Aw, Joe gimme some mo' dat tater pone."

"Nope, sweetenin' is for us men-folks. Y'all pritty lil frail eels don't need nothin' lak dis. You too sweet already."

"Please, Joe."

"Naw, naw. Ah don't want you to git no sweeter than whut you is already. We goin' down de road a lil piece t'night so you go put on yo' Sunday-go-to-meetin' things."

Missie May looked at her husband to see if he was playing some prank. "Sho nuff, Joe?"

"Yeah. We goin' to de ice cream parlor."

"Where de ice cream parlor at, Joe?"

"A new man done come heah from Chicago and he done got a place and took and opened it up for a ice cream parlor, and bein' as it's real swell, Ah wants you to be one de first ladies to walk in dere and have some set down."

"Do Jesus, Ah ain't knowed nothin' 'bout it. Who de man done it?"

"Mister Otis D. Slemmons, of spots and places—Memphis, Chicago, Jack-sonville, Philadelphia and so on."

"Dat heavy-set man wid his mouth full of gold teethes?"

"Yeah. Where did you see 'im at?"

"Ah went down to de sto' tuh git a box of lye and Ah seen 'im standing' on de corner talkin' to some of de mens, and Ah come on back and went to scrubbin de floor, and he passed and tipped his hat whilst Ah was scourin' de steps. Ah thought Ah never seen *him* befo'.''

Joe smiled pleasantly. "Yeah, he's up to date. He got de finest clothes Ah ever seen on a colored man's back.''

"Aw, he don't look no better in his clothes than you do in yourn. He got a puzzlegut on 'im and he so chuckle-headed, he got a pone behind his neck.''

Joe looked down at his own abdomen and said wistfully, "Wisht Ah had a build on me lak he got. He ain't puzzle-gutted, honey. He jes' got a corperation. Dat make 'm look lak a rich white man. All rich mens is got some belly on 'em.''

"Ah seen de pitchers of Henry Ford and he's a spare-built man and Rockefeller look lak he ain't got but one gut. But Ford and Rockefeller and dis Slemmons and all de rest kin be as many-gutted as dey please, Ah'm satisfied wid you jes' lak you is, baby. God took pattern after a pine tree and built you noble. Youse a pritty man, and if Ah knowed any way to make you mo' pritty still Ah'd take and do it.''

Joe reached over gently and toyed with Missie May's ear. "You jes' say dat cause you love me, but Ah know Ah can't hold no light to Otis D. Slemmons. Ah ain't never been nowhere and Ah ain't got nothin' but you.''

Missie May got on his lap and kissed him and he kissed back in kind. Then he went on. "All de womens is crazy 'bout 'im everywhere he go.''

"How you know dat, Joe?''

"He tole us so hisself.''

"Dat don't make it so. His mouf is cut crossways ain't it? Well, he kin lie jes' lak anybody else.''

"Good Lawd, Missie! You womens sho is hard to sense into things. He's got a five-dollar gold piece for a stick-pin and he got a ten-dollar gold piece on his watch chain and his mouf is jes' crammed full of gold teethes. Sho wisht it wuz mine. And whut make it so cool, he got money 'cumulated. And womens give it all to 'im.''

"Ah don't see whut de womens see on 'im. Ah wouldn't give 'im a wink if de sheriff wuz after 'im.''

"Well, he tole us how de white womens in Chicago give 'im all dat gold money. So he don't 'low nobody to touch it at all. Not even put dey finger on it. Dey tole 'im not to. You kin make 'miration at it, but don't tetch it.''

"Whyn't he stay up dere where dey so crazy 'bout im?''

"Ah reckon dey done made 'im vast-rich and he wants to travel some. He say dey wouldn't leave 'im hit a lick of work. He got mo' lady people crazy 'bout him than he kin shake a stick at.''

"Joe, Ah hates to see you so dumb. Dat stray nigger jes' tell y'all anything and y'all b'lieve it.''

"Go 'head on now, honey and put on yo' clothes. He talkin' 'bout his pritty womens--Ah want 'im to see *mine*.''

Missie May went off to dress and Joe spent the time trying to make his stomach punch out like Slemmons' middle. He tried the rolling swagger of the stranger, but found that his tall bone-and-muscle stride fitted ill with it. He just had time to drop back into his seat before Missie May came in dressed to go.

On the way home that night Joe was exultant. "Didn't Ah say old Otis was swell? Can't he talk Chicago talk? Wuzn't dat funny whut he said when great big fat old Ida Armstrong come in? He asted me, 'Who is dat broad wid de forte shake?' Dat's a new word. Us always thought forty was a set of figgers but he showed us where it means a whole heap of things. Sometimes he don't say forty, he jes' say thirty-eight and two and dat mean de same thing. Know whut he tole me when Ah wuz payin for our ice cream? He say, 'Ah have to hand it to you, Joe. Dat wife of yours is jes' thirty-eight and two. Yessuh, she's forte!' Ain't he killin'?"

"He'll do in case of a rush. But he sho is got uh heap uh gold on 'im. Dat's de first time Ah ever seed gold money. It lookted good on him sho nuff, but it'd look a whole heap better on you."

"Who, me? Missie May youse crazy! Where would a po' man lak me git gold money from?"

Missie May was silent for a minute, then she said, "Us might find some goin' long de road some time. Us could."

"Who would be losin' gold money round heah? We ain't even seen none dese white folks wearin' no gold money on dey watch chain. You must be figgerin' Mister Packard or Mister Cadillac goin' pass through heah."

"You don't know whut been lost 'round heah. Maybe somebody way back in memorial times lost they gold money and went on off and it ain't never been found. And then if we wuz to find it, you could wear some "thout havin' no gang of womens lak dat Slemmons say he got."

Joe laughed and hugged her. "Don't be so wishful 'bout me. Ah'm satisfied de way Ah is. So long as Ah be yo' husband, Ah don't keer 'bout nothin' else. Ah'd ruther all de other womens in de world to be dead than for you to have de toothache. Less we go to bed and git our night rest."

It was Saturday night once more before Joe could parade his wife in Slemmons' ice cream parlor again. He worked the night shift and Saturday was his only night off. Every other evening around six o'clock he left home, and dying dawn saw him hustling home around the lake where the challenging sun flung a flaming sword from east to west across the trembling water.

That was the best part of life--going home to Missie May. Their whitewashed house, the mock battle on Saturday, the dinner and ice cream parlor afterwards, church on Sunday nights when Missie out-dressed any woman in town--all, everything was right.

One night around eleven the acid ran out at the G. and G. The foreman knocked off the crew and let the steam die down. As Joe rounded the lake on his way home, a lean moon rode the lake in a silver boat. If anybody had asked Joe about the moon on the lake, he would have said he hadn't paid it any attention. But he saw it with his feelings. It made him yearn painfully for Missie. Creation obsessed him. He thought about children. They had been married more than a year now. They had money put away. They ought to be making little feet for shoes. A little boy child would be about right.

He saw a dim light in the bedroom and decided to come in through the kitchen door. He could wash the fertilizer dust off himself before presenting himself to Missie May. It would be nice for her not to know that he was there until he slipped into his place in bed and hugged her back. She always liked that.

He eased the kitchen door open slowly and silently, but when he went to set his dinner bucket on the table he bumped it into a pile of dishes, and something crashed to the floor. He heard his wife gasp in fright and hurried to reassure her.

"Iss me, honey. Don't git skeered."

There was a quick, large movement in the bedroom. A hustle, a thud, and a stealthy silence. The light went out.

What? Robbers? Murderers? Some varmint attacking his helpless wife, perhaps. He struck a match, threw himself on guard and stepped over the door-sill into the bedroom.

The great belt on the wheel of Time slipped and eternity stood still. By the match light he could see the man's legs fighting with his breeches in his frantic desire to get them on. He had both chance and time to kill the intruder in his helpless condition--half in and half out of his pants--but he was too weak to take action. The shapeless enemies of humanity that live in the hours of Time had waylaid Joe. He was assaulted in his weakness. Like Samson awakening after his haircut. So he just opened his mouth and laughed.

The match went out and he struck another and lit the lamp. A howling wind raced across his heart, but underneath its fury he heard his wife sobbing and Slemmons pleading for his life. Offering to buy it with all that he had. "Please, suh, don't kill me. Sixty-two dollars at de sto'. Gold money."

Joe just stood. Slemmons looked at the window, but it was screened. Joe stood out like a roughbacked mountain between him and the door. Barring him from escape, from sunrise, from life.

He considered a surprise attack upon the big clown that stood there laughing like a chessy cat. But before his fist could travel an inch, Joe's own rushed out to crush him like a battering ram. Then Joe stood over him.

"Git into yo' damn rags, Slemmons, and dat quick."

Slemmons scrambled to his feet and into his vest and coat. As he grabbed his hat, Joe's fury overrode his intentions and he grabbed at Slemmons with his left hand and struck at him with his right. The right landed. The left grazed the front of his vest. Slemmons was knocked a somersault into the kitchen and fled through the open door. Joe found himself alone with Missie May, with the golden watch charm clutched in his left fist. A short bit of broken chain dangled between his fingers.

Missie May was sobbing. Wails of weeping without words, Joe stood, and after awhile he found out that he had something in his hand. And then he stood and felt without thinking and without seeing with his natural eyes. Missie May kept on crying and Joe kept on feeling so much and not knowing what to do with all his feelings, he put Slemmons' watch charm in his pants pocket and took a good laugh and went to bed.

"Missie May, whut you cryin' for?"

"Cause Ah love you so hard and Ah know you don't love *me* no mo'."

Joe sank his face into the pillow for a spell then he said huskily, "You don't know de feelings of dat yet, Missie May."

"Oh Joe, honey, he said he wuz gointer give me dat gold money and he jes' kept on after me—"

Joe was very still and silent for a long time. Then he said. "Well, don't cry no mo', Missie May. Ah got yo' gold piece for you."

The hours went past on their rusty ankles. Joe still and quiet on one bed-rail and Missie May wrung dry of sobs on the other. Finally the sun's tide crept upon the shore of night and drowned all its hours. Missie May with her face stiff and streaked towards the window saw the dawn come into her yard. It was day. Nothing more. Joe wouldn't be coming home as usual. No need to fling open the front door and sweep off the porch, making it nice for Joe. Never no more breakfast to cook; no more washing and starching of Joe's jumper-jackets and pants. No more nothing. So why get up?

With this strange man in her bed, she felt embarrassed to get up and dress. She decided to wait till he had dressed and gone. Then she would get up, dress quickly and be gone forever beyond reach of Joe's looks and laughs. But he never moved. Red light turned to yellow, then white.

From beyond the no-man's land between them came a voice. A strange voice that yesterday had been Joe's.

"Missie May, ain't you gonna fix me no breakfus'?"

She sprang out of bed. "Yeah, Joe. Ah didn't reckon you wuz hongry."

No need to die today. Joe needed her for a few more minutes anyhow.

Soon there was a roaring fire in the cook stove. Water bucket full and two chickens killed. Joe loved fried chicken and rice. She didn't deserve a thing and good Joe was letting her cook him some breakfast. She rushed hot biscuits to the table as Joe took his seat.

He ate with his eyes in his plate. No laughter, no banter.

"Missie May, you ain't eatin' yo' breakfus'."

"Ah don't choose none, Ah thank yuh."

His coffee cup was empty. She sprang to refill it. When she turned from the stove and bent to set the cup beside Joe's plate, she saw the yellow coin on the table tween them.

She slumped into her seat and wept into her arms.

Presently Joe said calmly, "Missie May, you cry too much. Don't look back lak Lot's wife and turn to salt."

The sun, the hero of every day, the impersonal old man that beams as brightly on death as on birth, came up every morning and raced across the blue dome and dipped into the sea of fire every evening. Water ran down hill and birds nested.

Missie knew why she didn't leave Joe. She couldn't. She loved him too much, but she could not understand why Joe didn't leave her. He was polite, even kind at times, but aloof.

There were no more Saturday romps. No ringing silver dollars to stack beside her plate. No pockets to rifle. In fact the yellow coin in his trousers was like a monster hiding in the cave of his pockets to destroy her.

She often wondered if he still had it, but nothing could have induced her to ask nor yet to explore his pockets to see for herself. Its shadow was in the house whether or no.

One night Joe came home around midnight and complained of pains in the back. He asked Missie to rub him down with liniment. It had been three months since Missie had touched his body and it all seemed strange. But she rubbed him. Grateful for the chance. Before morning, youth triumphed and Missie exulted. But the next day, as she joyfully made up their bed, beneath her pillow she found the piece of money with the bit of chain attached.

Alone to herself, she looked at the thing with loathing, but look she must. She took it into her hands with trembling and saw first thing that it was no gold piece. It was a gilded half dollar. Then she knew why Slemmons had forbidden anyone to touch his gold. He trusted village eyes at a distance not to recognize his stick-pin as a gilded quarter, and his watch charm as a four-bit piece.

She was glad at first that Joe had left it there. Perhaps he was through with her punishment. They were man and wife again. Then another thought came clawing at her. He had come home to buy from her as if she were any woman in the long house. Fifty cents for her love. As if to say that he could pay as well as Slemmons. She slid the coin into his Sunday pants pocket and dressed herself and left his house.

Half way between her house and the quarters she met her husband's mother, and after a short talk she turned and went back home. Never would she admit defeat to that woman who prayed for it nightly. If she had not the substance of marriage she had the outside show. Joe must leave *her*. She let him see she didn't want his old gold four-bits too.

She saw no more of the coin for some time though she knew that Joe could not help finding it in his pocket. But his health kept poor, and he came home at least every ten days to be rubbed.

The sun swept around the horizon, trailing its robes of weeks and days. One morning as Joe came in from work, he found Missie May chopping wood. Without a word he took the ax and chopped a huge pile before he stopped.

"You ain't got no business choppin' wood, and you know it."

"How come? Ah been choppin' it for de last longest."

"Ah ain't blind. You makin' feet for shoes."

"Won't you be glad to have a lil baby chile, Joe?"

"You know dat 'thout astin' me."

"Iss gointer be a boy chile and de very spit of you."

"You reckon, Missie May?"

"Who else could it look lak?"

Joe said nothing, but he thrust his hand deep into his pocket and fingered something there.

It was almost six months later Missie May took to bed and Joe went and got his mother to come wait on the house.

Missie May was delivered of a fine boy. Her travail was over when Joe came in from work one morning. His mother and the old women were drinking great bowls of coffee around the fire in the kitchen.

The minute Joe came into the room his mother called him aside.

"How did Missie May make out?" he asked quickly.

"Who, dat gal? She strong as a ox. She gointer have plenty mo'. We done fixed her wid de sugar and lard to sweeten her for de nex' one."

Joe stood silent awhile.

"You ain't ast 'bout de baby, Joe. You oughter be mighty proud cause he sho is de spittin' image of yuh, son. Dat's yourn all right, if you never git another one, dat un is yourn. And you know Ah'm mighty proud too, son, cause Ah never thought well of you marryin' Missie May cause her ma used tuh fan her foot around right smart and Ah been mighty skeered dat Missie May wuz gointer git misput on her road."

Joe said nothing. He fooled around the house till late in the day then just before he went to work, he went and stood at the foot of the bed and asked his wife how she felt. He did this every day during the week.

On Saturday, he went to Orlando to make his market. It had been a long time since he had done that.

Meat and lard, meal and flour, soap and starch. Cans of corn and tomatoes. All the staples. He fooled around town for awhile and bought bananas and apples. Way after while he went around to the candy store.

"Hello, Joe," the clerk greeted him. "Ain't seen you in a long time."

"Nope, Ah ain't been heah. Been round in spots and places."

"Want some of them molasses kisses you always buy?"

"Yessuh." He threw the gilded half dollar on the counter. "Will dat spend?"

"Whut is it, Joe? Well, I'll be doggone! A gold-plated four-bit piece. Where'd you git it, Joe?"

"Offen a stray nigger dat come through Eatonville. He had it on his watch chain for a charm--goin' round making out iss gold money. Ha ha! He had a quarter on his tie pin and it wuz all golded up too. Tryin' to fool people. Makin' out he so rich and everything. Ha! Ha! Tryin' to tole off folkses wives from home."

"How did you git it, Joe? Did he fool you, too?"

"Who, me? Naw suh! He ain't fooled me none. Know whut Ah done? He come round me wid his smart talk. Ah hauled off and knocked 'im down and took his old four-bits way from 'im. Gointer buy my wife some good ole lasses kisses wid it. Gimme fifty cents worth of dem candy kisses."

"Fifty cents buys a mighty lot of candy kisses, Joe. Why don't you split it up and take some chocolate bars, too. They eat good, too."

"Yessuh, dey do, but Ah wants all dat in kisses. Ah got a lil boy chile home now. Tain't a week old yet, but he kin suck a sugar tit and maybe eat one them kisses hisself."

Joe got his candy and left the store. The clerk turned to the next customer. "Wisht I could be like these darkies. Laughin' all the time. Nothin' worries 'em."

Back in Eatonville, Joe reached his own front door. There was the ring of singing metal on wood. Fifteen times. Missie May couldn't run to the door, but she crept there as quickly as she could.

"Joe Banks, Ah hear you chunkin' money in mah do'way. You wait till Ah got mah strength back and Ah'm gointer fix you for dat."

WRITING AND DISCUSSION QUESTIONS

Informative
1. What is the social status of Missie May and Joe in Eatonville? Is there any class structure in the town, or is it a town of equals?
2. Why is the image of Otis D. Slemmons so sterling in Eatonville, and particularly among the town's women? What is the symbol of his wealth and charm? Why does Joe think he "can't hold no light" to him? What does Joe do for a living?
3. Explain Joe's behavior after discovering Slemmons in bed with his wife. Why does he decide to let him escape? Why does he choose to reconcile with his wife and resume his life as if nothing had happened?

Persuasive
1. Argue that the story's title helps underscore the theme of the emptiness of black aspirations and the accommodation to the values of the dominant culture outside of Eatonville.
2. Hurston effectively captures the cadence and pronunciation of the Southern Black dialect; how does it serve her narrative? To what extent does it make the story difficult to read? Why or why not?
3. Interpret the ending of the story. Are Joe and Missie May destined to "live happily ever after"? Defend your interpretation.

Personal
1. Imagine a story with similar husband and wife characters in an all-white town nearby Eatonville. How differently would the story be told? What choices would white characters have that Hurston's black characters do not?
2. Otis Slemmons is mentioned by Missie May in the same breath as Henry Ford and John D. Rockefeller. Who are these men, and why would she associate them with

Slemmons? To what extent is Joe revealing his own system of values in admitting "Wisht Ah had a build on me lak he [Slemmons] got"? Do you find yourself comparing your appearance and goals with those of famous or wealthy celebrities?

▼

RICHARD RODRIGUEZ, "BILINGUALISM AND CHILDHOOD'S END" FROM *HUNGER OF MEMORY*

Richard Rodriguez (1944–) is a freelance writer who came to public attention in 1982 with the publication of his poignant memoir, *Hunger of Memory: The Education of Richard Rodriguez*. In this book, Rodriguez traces his slow intellectual development as a young Mexican–American who could not speak English to his eventual scholarship at the prestigious University of California, Berkeley, where he earned a Ph.D. in comparative literature. In this excerpt, Rodriguez articulates the painful changes that took place in his own consciousness and in his family life after he acquired and then adopted English—his "public" language—in preference to the "private" language of his home. Since its publication, Rodriguez's view on bilingual education and the problems of assimilation have been both critically acclaimed and attacked by intellectuals and educators who debate whether his personal experience is either instructive or normative in resolving the civil rights issues that nonnative speakers of English face in a democratic nation.

▼

Bilingualism and Childhood's End
RICHARD RODRIGUEZ

1   Supporters of bilingual education today imply that students like me miss a great deal by not being taught in their family's language. What they seem not to recognize is that, as a socially disadvantaged child, I considered Spanish to be a private language. What I needed to learn in school was that I had the right—and the obligation—to speak the public language of *los gringos*. The odd truth is that my first-grade classmates could have become bilingual, in the conventional sense of that word, more easily than I. Had they been taught (as upper-middle-class children are often taught early) a second language like Spanish or French, they could have regarded it simply as that: another public language. In my case such bilingualism could not have been so quickly achieved. What I did not believe was that I could speak a single public language.

2   Without question, it would have pleased me to hear my teachers address me

in Spanish when I entered the classroom. I would have felt much less afraid. I would have trusted them and responded with ease. But I would have delayed— for how long postponed?—having to learn the language of public society. I would have evaded—and for how long could I have afforded to delay?—learning the great lesson of school, that I had a public identity.

Fortunately, my teachers were unsentimental about their responsibility. What they understood was that I needed to speak a public language. So their voices would search me out, asking me questions. Each time I'd hear them I'd look up in surprise to see a nun's face frowning at me. I'd mumble, not really meaning to answer. The nun would persist, "Richard, stand up. Don't look at the floor. Speak up. Speak to the entire class, not just to me!" But I couldn't believe that the English language was mine to use. (In part, I did not want to believe it.) I continued to mumble. I resisted the teacher's demands. (Did I somehow suspect that once I learned public langauge my pleasing family life would be changed?) Silent, waiting for the bell to sound, I remained dazed, diffident, afraid. 3

Because I wrongly imagined that English was intrinsically a public language and Spanish an intrinsically private one, I easily noted the difference between classroom language and the language of home. At school, words were directed to a general audience of listeners. ("Boys and girls.") Words were meaningfully ordered. And the point was not self-expression alone but to make oneself understood by many others. The teacher quizzed: "Boys and girls, why do we use that word in this sentence? Could we think of a better word to use there? Would the sentence change its meaning if the words were differently arranged? And wasn't there a better way of saying much the same thing?" (I couldn't say. I wouldn't try to say.) 4

Three months. Five. Half a year passed. Unsmiling, ever watchful, my teachers noted my silence. They began to connect my behavior with the difficult progress my older sister and brother were making. Until one Saturday morning three nuns arrived at the house to talk to our parents. Stiffly, they sat on the blue living room sofa. From the doorway of another room, spying the visitors, I noted the incongruity—the clash of two worlds, the faces and voices of school intruding upon the familiar setting of home. I overheard one voice gently wondering, "Do your children speak only Spanish at home, Mrs. Rodriguez?" While another voice added, "That Richard especially seems so timid and shy." 5

That Rich-heard! 6

With great tact the visitors continued, "It is possible for you and your husband to encourage your children to practice their English when they are home?" Of course, my parents complied. What would they not do for their children's well-being? And how could they have questioned the Church's authority which those women represented? In an instant, they agreed to give up the language (the sounds) that had revealed and accentuated our family's closeness. The moment after the visitors left, the change was observed. "*Ahora,* speak to us *en inglés,*" my father and mother united to tell us. 7

At first, it seemed a kind of game. After dinner each night, the family gath- 8 ered to practice "our" English. (It was still then *inglés,* a language foreign to us, so we felt drawn as strangers to it.) Laughing, we would try to define words we could not pronounce. We played with strange English sounds, often overanglicizing our pronunciations. And we filled the smiling gaps of our sentences with familiar Spanish sounds. But that was cheating, somebody shouted. Everyone laughed. In school, meanwhile, like my brother and sister, I was required to attend a daily tutoring session. I needed a full year of special attention. I also needed my teachers to keep my attention from straying in class by calling out, *Rich-heard*—their English voices slowly prying loose my ties to my other name, its three notes, *Ri-car-do.* Most of all I needed to hear my mother and father speak to me in a moment of seriousness in broken—suddenly heartbreaking—English. The scene was inevitable: One Saturday morning I entered the kitchen where my parents were talking in Spanish. I did not realize that they were talking in Spanish however until, at the moment they saw me, I heard their voices change to speak English. Those *gringo* sounds they uttered startled me. Pushed me away. In that moment of trivial misunderstanding and profound insight, I felt my throat twisted by unsounded grief. I turned quickly and left the room. But I had no place to escape to with Spanish. (The spell was broken.) My brother and sisters were speaking English in another part of the house.

9   Again and again in the days following, increasingly angry, I was obliged to hear my mother and father: "Speak to us *en inglés.*" *(Speak.)* Only then did I determine to learn classroom English. Weeks after, it happened: One day in school I raised my hand to volunteer an answer. I spoke out in a loud voice. And I did not think it remarkable when the entire class understood. That day, I moved very far from the disadvantaged child I had been only days earlier. The belief, the calming assurance that I belonged in public, had at last taken hold.

10   Shortly after, I stopped hearing the high and loud sounds of *los gringos.* A more and more confident speaker of English, I didn't trouble to listen to *how* strangers sounded, speaking to me. And there simply were too many English-speaking people in my day for me to hear American accents anymore. Conversations quickened. Listening to persons who sounded eccentrically pitched voices, I usually noted their sounds for an initial few seconds before I concentrated on *what* they were saying. Conversations became content-full. Transparent. Hearing someone's *tone* of voice—angry or questioning or sarcastic or happy or sad—I didn't distinguish it from the words it expressed. Sound and word were thus tightly wedded. At the end of a day, I was often bemused, always relieved, to realize how "silent," though crowded with words, my day in public had been. (This public silence measured and quickened the change in my life.)

11   At last, seven years old, I came to believe what had been technically true since my birth: I was an American citizen.

12   But the special feeling of closeness at home was diminished by then. Gone was the desperate, urgent, intense feeling of being at home; rare was the experience of feeling myself individualized by family intimates. We remained a lov-

ing family, but one greatly changed. No longer so close; no longer bound tight by the pleasing and troubling knowledge of our public separateness. Neither my older brother nor sister rushed home after school anymore. Nor did I. When I arrived home there would often be neighborhood kids in the house. Or the house would be empty of sounds.

Following the dramatic Americanization of their children, even my parents   *13* grew more publicly confident. Especially my mother. She learned the names of all the people on our block. And she decided we needed to have a telephone installed in the house. My father continued to use the word *gringo*. But it was no longer charged with the old bitterness or distrust. (Stripped of any emotional content, the word simply became a name for those Americans not of Hispanic descent.) Hearing him, sometimes, I wasn't sure if he was pronouncing the Spanish word *gringo* or saying gringo in English.

Matching the silence I started hearing in public was a new quiet at home.   *14* The family's quiet was partly due to the fact that, as we children learned more and more English, we shared fewer and fewer words with our parents. Sentences needed to be spoken slowly when a children addressed his mother or father. (Often the parent wouldn't understand.) The child would need to repeat himself. (Still the parent misunderstood.) The young voice, frustrated, would end up saying, "Never mind"—the subject was closed. Dinners would be noisy with the clinking of knives and forks against dishes. My mother would smile softly between her remarks; my father at the other end of the table would chew and chew at his food, while he stared over the heads of his children.

My *mother!* My *father!* After English became my primary language, I no   *15* longer knew what words to use in addressing my parents. The old Spanish words (those tender accents of sound) I had used earlier—*mamá* and *papá*—I couldn't use anymore. They would have been too painful reminders of how much had changed in my life. On the other hand, the words I heard neighborhood kids call *their* parents seemed equally unsatisfactory. *Mother* and *Father*; *Ma, Papa, Pa, Dad, Pop* (how I hated the all-American sound of that last word especially)—all these terms I felt were unsuitable, not really terms of address for *my* parents. As a result, I never used them at home. Whenever I'd speak to my parents, I would try to get their attention with eye contact alone. In public conversations, I'd refer to "my parents" or "my mother and father."

My mother and father, for their part, responded differently, as their children   *16* spoke to them less. She grew restless, seemed troubled and anxious at the scarcity of words exchanged in the house. It was she who would question me about my day when I came home from school. She smiled at small talk. She pried at the edges of my sentences to get me to say something more. (What?) She'd join conversations she overheard, but her intrusions often stopped her children's talking. By contrast, my father seemed reconciled to the new quiet. Though his English improved somewhat, he retired into silence. At dinner he spoke very little. One night his children and even his wife helplessly giggled at his garbled English pronunciation of the Catholic Grace before Meals. Thereafter he made his wife recite the prayer at the start of each meal, even on formal occasions, when there were guests in the house. Hers became the public voice of the family. On official business, it was she, not my father, one would usually hear on the phone or in stores, talking to strangers. His children grew so accustomed to his silence that, years later, they would speak routinely of his shyness. (My mother would often try to explain: Both his parents died when he was eight. He was raised by an uncle who treated him like little more than a menial servant. He was never encouraged to speak. He grew up alone. A man of few words.) But my father was not shy, I realized, when I'd watch him speaking Spanish with relatives. Using Spanish, he was quickly effusive. Especially when talking with other men, his voice would speak, flicker, flare alive with sounds. In Spanish, he expressed ideas and feelings he rarely revealed in English. With firm Spanish sounds, he conveyed confidence and authority English would never allow him.

17 The silence at home, however, was finally more than a literal silence. Fewer words passed between parents and child, but more profound was the silence that resulted from my inattention to sounds. At about the time I no longer bothered to listen with care to the sounds of English in public, I grew careless about listening to the sounds family members made when they spoke. Most of the time I heard someone speaking at home and didn't distinguish his sounds from the words people uttered in public. I didn't even pay much attention to my parents' accented and ungrammatical speech. At least not at home. Only when I was with them in public would I grow alert to their accents. Though, even then, their sounds caused me less and less concern. For I was increasingly confident of my own public identity.

18 I would have been happier about my public success had I not sometimes recalled what it had been like earlier, when my family had conveyed its intimacy through a set of conveniently private sounds. Sometimes in public, hearing a stranger, I'd hark back to my past. A Mexican farmworker approached me downtown to ask directions to somewhere. "¿Hijito . . . ?" he said. And his voice summoned deep longing. Another time, standing beside my mother in the visiting room of a Carmelite convent, before the dense screen which rendered the nuns shadowy figures, I heard several Spanish-speaking nuns—their busy, singsong overlapping voices—assure us that yes, yes, we were remembered, all our family was remembered in their prayers. (Their voices echoed faraway family sounds.) Another day, a dark-faced old woman—her hand light on my shoulder—steadied herself against me as she boarded a bus. She murmured something I couldn't quite comprehend. Her Spanish voice came near, like the face of a never-before-seen relative in the instant before I was kissed. Her voice, like so many of the Spanish voices I'd hear in public, recalled the golden age of my youth. Hearing Spanish then, I continued to be a careful, if sad, listener to sounds. Hearing a Spanish-speaking family walking behind me, I turned to look. I smiled for an instant, before my glance found the Hispanic-looking faces of strangers in the crowd going by.

19 Today I hear bilingual educators say that children lose a degree of "individuality" by becoming assimilated into public society. (Bilingual schooling was popularized in the seventies, that decade when middle-class ethnics began to

resist the process of assimilation—the American melting pot.) But the bilingualists simplistically scorn the value and necessity of assimilation. They do not seem to realize that there are *two* ways a person is individualized. So they do not realize that while one suffers a diminished sense of *private* individuality by becoming assimilated into public society, such assimilation makes possible the achievement of *public* individuality.

The bilingualists insist that a student should be reminded of his difference   20 from others in mass society, his heritage. But they equate mere separateness with individuality. The fact is that only in private—with intimates—is separateness from the crowd a prerequisite for individuality. (An intimate draws me apart, tells me that I am unique, unlike all others.) In public, by contrast, full individuality is achieved, paradoxically, by those who are able to consider themselves members of the crowd. Thus it happened for me: Only when I was able to think of myself as an American, no longer an alien in *gringo* society, could I seek the rights and opportunities necessary for full public individuality. The social and political advantages I enjoy as a man result from the day that I came to believe that my name, indeed, is *Rich-heard Road-ree-guess.* It is true that my public society today is often impersonal. (My public society is usually mass society.) Yet despite the anonymity of the crowd and despite the fact that the individuality I achieve in public is often tenuous—because it depends on my being one in a crowd—I celebrate the day I acquired my new name. Those middle-class ethnics who scorn assimilation seem to me filled with decadent self-pity, obsessed by the burden of public life. Dangerously, they romanticize public separateness and they trivialize the dilemma of the socially disadvantaged.

My awkward childhood does not prove the necessity of bilingual education.   21 My story discloses instead an essential myth of childhood—inevitable pain. If I rehearse here the changes in my private life after my Americanization, it is finally to emphasize the public gain. The loss implies the gain: The house I returned to each afternoon was quiet. Intimate sounds no longer rushed to the door to greet me. There were other noises inside. The telephone rang. Neighborhood kids ran past the door of the bedroom where I was reading my schoolbooks—covered with shopping-bag paper. Once I learned public langauge, it would never again be easy for me to hear intimate family voices. More and more of my day was spent hearing words. But that may only be a way of saying that the day I raised my hand in class and spoke loudly to an entire roomful of faces, my childhood started to end.

WRITING AND DISCUSSION QUESTIONS

Informative

1. What is Rodriguez' quarrel with the suporters of bilingual education? Is it the intention of his essay to attack bilingualism?

2. Rodriguez attempts to contrast the "public language" of the school with the "pri-

vate'' language of the home and family. What does each represent to him? What does he believe is gained or lost in acquiring the ''public'' language?
3. How do Rodriguez' anecdotes about schooling heighten the reader's identification with him? What is the rhetorical effect of spelling out the Anglo pronunciation of his name as *Rich-heard Road-ree-guess?*

Persuasive

1. Argue that the ultimate cost of mastering English to Rodriguez was the loss of his cultural identity. Would Rodriguez agree or disagree with you?
2. How would a proponent of bilingual education, or the education of non-English speaking children in their own native tongue, argue against Rodriguez? Is there a way to do both: preserve one's cultural heritage and literature as available in one's native tongue and embrace the more dominant tongue for public commerce?
3. How much of one's personal ethnic heritage is bound up in the language of the home and the collected literature of one's background? Argue that the ''you'' that you have become is primarily a product of either your education or your family influences. Has your education deprived you of elements important to ethnic pride?

Personal

1. Is it of any value anymore to seek an ''unhyphenated'' America, that is, to be an American who chooses not to draw attention to his or her ethnic heritage (e.g., African–American, Jewish–American, Mexican–American, Anglo–American)? To what extent do you wish to be identified by and with your skin color or historical lineage? Is the most important feature of your citizenship your background or your present status in the existing culture?
2. In his last paragraph, Rodriguez identifies a particular linguistic episode as signaling the end of his childhood. What was this incident? Is there such an incident in your own experience that corresponds with his?
3. What civil rights issues are raised by Rodriguez' strong advocacy of assmiliation into the larger culture? Is it possible to use Rodriguez' arguments as a brief to deny civil rights or subtly minimize them for nonnative speakers of English?

▼

JAMES BALDWIN, ''IF BLACK ENGLISH ISN'T A LANGUAGE, THEN TELL ME, WHAT IS?''

When James Baldwin (1924–1979) died in France, he left behind a canon of fictional and nonfictional works that is a virtual compendium of the black experience in

America. For many years between 1950 and 1979, Baldwin was not only an exemplar of superior insight into the trials and travails of the black American, but in his own right one of America's major writers. As one critic observed of Baldwin, "more than any other writer, [Baldwin] can make one feel what it is really like to be a black man in a white man's world; and he is especially expert at evoking, not merely the brutally overt physical confrontations between black and white, but the subtle unease that lurks beneath all traffic between the colors." Born in Harlem, Baldwin knew firsthand ghetto life and its toil taken on the lives of young black men and women caught in a web of despair: drug trafficking, poor housing and educational opportunities, and general destitution were the heritage of his neighborhoods. Baldwin's survival skills and well-tuned literacy forged a way out of this predicament; after his formal education, a series of prestigious fellowships funded a career as a writer. Among his works were novels and plays, and many essays that chronicled his view of the place and destiny of blacks in an America where the expatriate Baldwin found little to praise. His *The Fire Next Time* (1963) represents a document that helped fuel the passions of disenfranchised blacks to achieve civil rights. The essay presented here, written for the *New York Times* in 1979, provides a kind of counterstatement to Richard Rodriguez' argument against bilingualism. In it, Baldwin documents the relationship between language and experience, posing crucial questions about the politics of language education and use in a democracy.

▼

If Black English Isn't a Language, Then Tell Me, What Is?
JAMES BALDWIN

The argument concerning the use, or the status, or the reality, of 1
black English is rooted in American history and has absolutely nothing to do with the question the argument supposes itself to be posing. The argument has nothing to do with language itself but with the *role* of language. Language, incontestably, reveals the speaker. Language, also, far more dubiously, is meant to define the other—and, in this case, the other is refusing to be defined by a language that has never been able to recognize him.

People evolve a language in order to describe and thus control their circum- 2
stances, or in order not to be submerged by a reality that they cannot articulate. (And, if they cannot articulate it, they *are* submerged.) A Frenchman living in Paris speaks a subtly and crucially different language from that of the man living in Marseilles; neither sounds very much like a man living in Quebec; and they would all have great difficulty in apprehending what the man from Guadeloupe, or Martinique, is saying, to say nothing of the man from Senegal—although the "common" language of all these areas is French. But

each has paid, and is paying, a different price for this "common" language, in which, as it turns out, they are not saying, and cannot be saying, the same things: They each have very different realities to articulate, or control.

3   What joins all languages, and all men, is the necessity to confront life, in order, not inconceivably, to outwit death: The price for this is the acceptance, and achievement, of one's temporal identity. So that, for example, though it is not taught in the schools (and this has the potential of becoming a political issue) the south of France still clings to its ancient and musical Provençal, which resists being described as a "dialect." And much of the tension in the Basque countries, and in Wales, is due to the Basque and Welsh determination not to allow their languages to be destroyed. This determination also feeds the flames in Ireland for among the many indignities the Irish have been forced to undergo at English hands is the English contempt for their language.

4   It goes without saying, then, that language is also a political instrument, means, and proof of power. It is the most vivid and crucial key to identity: it reveals the private identity, and connects one with, or divorces one from, the larger, public, or communal identity. There have been, and are, times, and places, when to speak a certain language could be dangerous, even fatal. Or, one may speak the same language, but in such a way that one's antecedents are revealed, or (one hopes) hidden. This is true in France, and is absolutely true in England: The range (and reign) of accents on that damp little island make England coherent for the English and totally incomprehensible for everyone else. To open your mouth in England is (if I may use black English) to "put your business in the street": You have confessed your parents, your youth, your school, your salary, your self-esteem, and alas, your future.

5   Now, I do not know what white Americans would sound like if there had never been any black people in the United States, but they would not sound the way they sound. *Jazz*, for example, is a very specific sexual term, as in *jazz me, baby*, but white people purified it into the Jazz Age. *Sock it to me*, which means, roughly, the same thing, has been adopted by Nathaniel Hawthorne's descendants with no qualms or hesitations at all, along with *let it all hang out* and *right on! Beat to his socks*, which was once the black's most total and despairing image of poverty, was transformed into a thing called the Beat Generation, which phenomenon was, largely, composed of *uptight*, middle-class white people, imitating poverty, trying to *get down*, to get *with it*, doing their *thing*, doing their despairing best to be *funky*, which we, the blacks, never dreamed of doing—we *were* funky, baby, like *funk* was going out of style.

6   Now, no one can eat his cake, and have it, too, and it is late in the day to attempt to penalize black people for having created a language that permits the nation its only glimpse of reality, a language without which the nation would be even more *whipped* than it is.

7   I say that this present skirmish is rooted in American history, and it is. Black English is the creation of the black diaspora. Blacks came to the United States chained to each other, but from different tribes: Neither could speak the other's language. If two black people, at that bitter hour of the world's history,

had been able to speak to each other, the institution of chattel slavery could never have lasted as long as it did. Subsequently, the slave was given, under the eye, and the gun, of his master, Congo Square, and the Bible—or, in other words, and under these conditions, the slave began the formation of the black church, and it is within this unprecedented tabernacle that black English began to be formed. This was not, merely, as in the European example, the adoption of a foreign tongue, but an alchemy that transformed ancient elements into a new language: *A language comes into existence by means of brutal necessity, and the rules of the language are dictated by what the language must convey.*

There was a moment, in time, and in this place, when my brother, or my   8 mother, or my father, or my sister, had to convey to me, for example, the danger in which I was standing from the white man standing just behind me, and to convey this with a speed, and in a language, that the white man could not possibly understand, and that, indeed, he cannot understand, until today. He cannot afford to understand it. This understanding would reveal to him too much about himself, and smash that mirror before which he has been frozen for so long.

Now, if this passion, this skill, this (to quote Toni Morrison) "sheer intelli-   9 gence," this incredible music, the mighty achievement of having brought a people utterly unknown to, or despied by "history"—to have brought this people to their present, troubled, troubling, and unassailable and unanswerable place—if this absolutely unprecedented journey does not indicate that black English is a language, I am curious to know what definition of language is to be trusted.

A people at the center of the Western world, and in the midst of so hostile a   10 population, has not endured the transcended by means of what is patronizingly called a "dialect." We, the blacks, are in trouble, certainly, but we are not doomed, and we are not inarticulate because we are not compelled to defend a morality that we know to be a lie.

The brutal truth is that the bulk of the white people in America never had   11 any interest in educating black people, except as this could serve white purposes. It is not the black child's language that is in question, it is not his language that is despised: It is his experience. A child cannot be taught by anyone who despises him, and a child cannot afford to be fooled. A child cannot be taught by anyone whose demand, essentially, is that the child repudiate his experience, and all that gives him sustenance, and enter a limbo in which he will no longer be black, and in which he knows that he can never become white. Black people have lost too many black children that way.

And, after all, finally, in a country with standards so untrustworthy, a coun-   12 try that makes heroes of so many criminal mediocrities, a country unable to face why so many of the nonwhite are in prison, or on the needle, or standing, futureless, in the streets—it may very well be that both the child, and his elder, have concluded that they have nothing whatever to learn from the people of a country that has managed to learn so little.

WRITING AND DISCUSSION QUESTIONS

Informative

1. How does Baldwin define "language"? Why is his way of defining language crucial to the development of his argument?
2. Are you acutely aware of the distinctive elements Baldwin points out in his discussion of black English and their effect on the way English is spoken and written in America? What other vocabulary items, phrases, ways of expressions can you trace to black culture? Do you regard these as good or bad influences?
3. Baldwin argues that one's language alters the way one views the world, and, likewise, how the world views oneself. What does he mean that language is a "political instrument"? What evidence does Baldwin offer for this assertion?

Persuasive

1. To what extent must someone who is submerged in an oppressive situation adopt the language, modes of reasoning, and general manner of behavior of the oppressor to win freedom? Baldwin's own eloquence seems to be to his advantage in arguing for the legitimacy of his cause; could he have argued his case just as well in a less-prestigious black dialect?
2. What is the place in education for recognizing and celebrating difference in cultural heritage and background? To what degree should educators seek diversity instead of commonality and uniformity? Argue the case for or against cultural diversity and language education in higher education.

Personal

1. In what way does one's language, not only vocabulary and syntax, but also accent and intonation, affect the way one is perceived and treated? Have you ever felt victimized, or seen someone else victimized, by the attitude of someone in authority who regards your language use as somehow inferior or substandard?
2. In the end, do you agree with Baldwin that the complaint sometimes voiced against black English is essentially an indictment of black experience and behavior, that when educators and politicians raise questions about the propriety of black English, they are actually making political commentary? Apply Richard Rodriguez' argument to Baldwin. Is it possible to argue that black English is at once something to be celebrated as well as something to be exchanged eventually for a more "public" language? How would Baldwin reply to Rodriguez?

▼

ANNE WORTHAM (WITH BILL MOYERS), "AN INTERVIEW ON RACISM IN AMERICAN CULTURE"

Anne Wortham (1941–), a black sociologist, is a controversial educator because of her dissenting views on the civil rights movement, its premises, and some of its heroes. Interviewed for Bill Moyers' PBS program, "A World of Ideas," Wortham speaks frankly about her own struggle for individuality while growing up in the foment of civil rights activism in the 1950s and 1960s. Here she explains its effects on her own thinking regarding equality and civil rights. Her book, *The Other Side of Racism*, attempts to reassess the effects of racism on American culture and offers an alternative set of defintions and solutions to the problems of prejudice and bigotry in our society. Bill Moyers is a well-known television personality and media journalist who once served as President John F. Kennedy's press secretary. His book, *A World of Ideas* (1989), is the source of this interview.

▼

An Interview on Racism in American Culture
ANNE WORTHAM (with BILL MOYERS)

MOYERS: Your writings have made you a controversial figure, one who criticizes the Civil Rights movement and its leaders for promoting reverse racism and the welfare state. How would you describe yourself to a stranger who genuinely wanted to know what you stand for?

WORTHAM: I like to say that I'm an individualist. I believe that life is a very important adventure that has to be carried out by individuals—in cooperation with other individuals, yes, but always lived by individuals. I take full responsibility for myself and for the kind of life I create and the relationships I have with other people. I believe very strongly in individual freedom, both internal freedom and external freedom.

MOYERS: Internal freedom being the power to make choices and external freedom being freedom from the restraint of society, of others.

WORTHAM: Freedom from the restraint of society and within that context, therfore, freedom to realize my highest potential but to take responsibility for any failures or lack of knowledge that I have.

MOYERS: Well, that doesn't sound very controversial.

WORTHAM: I think most people would say that they do.

MOYERS: Why, then, are you so controversial?

WORTHAM: The controversy emerges when we begin to ask the question, "But what do you mean by being an individualist? What do you mean by freedom? What do you mean by liberty?"

I read a series of articles recently on the effect of television on the American family and the American character. Throughout these articles there is a bashing of individualism on the grounds that individualism is irresponsible, narcissistic, self-centered. It is, in fact, self-centeredness that is being criticized as "individualism." But this is an incorrect understanding of individualism. The kind of individualism that I espouse is self-responsible. Self-responsibility can never be transformed into self-centeredness.

MOYERS: You said one of the reasons you looked forward to teaching at Washington and Lee is that they still practice good manners there—good manners is not a self-centered characteristic, it is an expression of living in society.

WORTHAM: Yes, and it is a statement of self-respect and respect for other human beings. It is a device for maintaining civility in human relations. The reason one would have allegiance to good manners and etiquette is because one values being human. And because one values being human, one values oneself and others. You would not want to give to another person more or less respect than you would yourself as a human being.

MOYERS: So individualism does not mean, "I have the right to do whatever I want to do, whenever I want to do it"?

WORTHAM: One has only the right to be oneself—within the boundaries of respect for others. There is a boundary between you and others. That's why we have etiquette. Behind the walls of etiquette and decorum is the autonomy of the individual. The reason etiquette was developed in the first place was to maintain individual freedom.

MOYERS: Here we sit under a sign that says "No Smoking"—and you don't because—

WORTHAM:—because there is a sign which is a statement addressed to me and to everyone else which says that we, the administrators of the institution, prefer not to have smoking in this setting.

MOYERS: And you go along with that even though, individually, you believe you have the right to smoke.

WORTHAM: Yes, but I don't have the right to abuse an institutional rule, and by doing so, to contradict my unsigned, tacit agreement with the institution that by being a part of it, by accepting its invitation to work here, I shall honor certain rules. One doesn't sign anything—it is just understood in a civilized society.

MOYERS: "Civilized society"—what do you mean by that?

WORTHAM: A civilized society is one whose members expect that each will address at all times, as far as possible, the rational in man; that even when I may want to bash you over the head, I will be checked by my awareness of you as a rational entity, and I will not resort to force as an expression of my disagreement with you or even my feeling that you have been unjust to me; that in my disagreements with you, I will rely on the power of persuasion.

MOYERS: So that even if I act irrationally toward you, you're going to treat me as a rational person.

WORTHAM: I remind myself that this is an irrational person who is betraying rationality and therefore himself.

MOYERS: So what happens inside when we all betray rationality?

WORTHAM: Well, we are very clever beings, you see. Rationality has the capacity for betraying itself. Rational men have the capacity to be irrational and to institutionalize irrationality. We've seen that in Nazi Germany.

MOYERS: It's what Joseph Heller wrote about in *Catch-22*. Irrationality becomes a bureaucratic process.

WORTHAM: Yes, and the unfortunate thing is that it becomes so absurd that it's funny. Literary critics and analysts have always commented on absurdity being comical, but in real life, it's another cup of tea altogether! There you get bureaucracy gone mad. Max Weber was very much aware of this. He worried that the very thing that made freedom, enlightenment, and civilization possible also had the capacity to turn on itself.

MOYERS: You once said, "By most standards, I'm not supposed to exist." What did you mean?

WORTHAM: There are theories of social determinism which view people as being not a product of their thinking, or of their interpretations of the world around them, but as being solely a product of their environment—as being social products.

In the sixties, in undergraduate school, I would meet people who were surprised by me. At first I was baffled by their surprise. Then I understood the reason for their surprise, and I was not only baffled but angry and hurt that Northerners I met had a vision of life among blacks in the South which did not match my own experience. Both black and white Northerners approached me as a caricature, as their version of what a black growing up in the South in the fifties should be. They thought I should be someone who was scarred by racism, who had certain pathologies, who was very race-conscious, who was suspicious of whites. They had a script. They were prepared to love me unconditionally just because I was a socially defined historical victim. So you see, when I say I'm not supposed to exist, I'm saying that the history written recently of blacks and women in America does not count on people like me.

MOYERS: How did the reality of Anne Wortham challenge their image of you?

WORTHAM: Well, for one thing, I was innocent. At first, I didn't even understand their script. They thought that as a victim I should have understood what my saviors were after—and I didn't. Then when I did understand, I just reacted naturally, which was to refuse their offer of liberation, and their interpretation of me as someone who hated all whites. Their mission was to convince me that they were among the good whites.

Behind those walls of segregation, my father was a Christian. To the extent that he ever talked about whites—and we rarely talked about whites in our house—but whenever he did, he said to forget about the Constitution and our neighbors and everybody else, because God said you should love everybody. Growing up, I had this drummed into my head, so it was very difficult when the late sixties came along for me to reconcile the idea that I should love everyone until they show you that they shouldn't be loved with the idea that I should hate all whites because they are whites. I just didn't have it in me, and that upset some people. They wanted me to be their Martin Luther King, and I didn't even like Martin Luther King. I was scared of him. I was utterly afraid of that man.

MOYERS: Of Martin Luther King? Why?

WORTHAM: Because something told me he was saying things that were not right for me. His vision made me as a black person morally superior to whites.

Whites would be redeemed by their acknowledging me as an equal. The kid in me said, "I don't want to do all of this. I don't like this."

MOYERS: But hadn't you been discriminated against when you were growing up in the fifties?

WORTHAM: But you see, these are two different things. I'm telling you now—having understood in retrospect—why I was so miserable in the early sixties. I was going through absolute hell because I had peer pressure from everywhere. If you were a student, you had to go and march and do this and that. Certainly, I wanted civil rights. But I thought that something else was being asked of me in addition—and of everybody else, for that matter. We were demanding civil rights, but I felt that we were also asking our country to give us some kind of special recognition that required a diminution of other Americans.

MOYERS: But all that was being asked was that everybody stop discriminating against you.

WORTHAM: That's not what I heard when I was twenty years old. I heard something else from the Civil Rights movement. Now, here I was, a twenty-year-old black kid who had grown up in a relatively sheltered environment in Jackson, Tennessee, whose sense of morality had been very straightforward. When I was in high school, I worked as a maid for whites, so that I knew whites intimately—though most Southern blacks do. The relationship of whites and blacks in the South is a very complex one. Now, in 1962, all of the students were participating in the movement. To be a good citizen as a student, you had to be an activist student.

MOYERS: And you refused.

WORTHAM: I refused. My problem was, "How do I refuse without incurring the wrath of my peers?" I just sort of snuck into the background. I didn't like myself for doing that.

I'll tell you a story. One day in 1961 or '62, we were out on the campus green at Tuskegee. A student was urging us to go down to the town of Tuskegee and show our solidarity with all the student marchers. The tension in the air was thick, electrifying. You felt as though everything you stood for was on the line, that you now had to do something. I was standing there, and one of the students came over to me and asked "What are you going to do? Are you going downtown?" Now, here's one of these moments of your life, and a choice has to be made. She said, "I don't know what to do."

I said, "Look, I think we should both go up to our dorm rooms and let down the shades and keep the lights off, and we should think and be quiet and we should decide up there. I don't think we should decide out here."

Now, at that time, I had no grand theory about the mechanics of being an individual, and of maintaining the truth of one's identity within a larger society. I didn't have any theory or even any great understanding. I was just going on gut reactions about what you do. And the thing you do is that you don't give up your own story. You don't give up the authenticity of yourself.

MOYERS: What's sacred to you?

WORTHAM: It's the authenticity that is sacred. It is the one thing that is yours.

MOYERS: Your story.

WORTHAM: Your story, your life. It is the thing that you die for, ultimately, if you have to. It is the only thing that you die for.

MOYERS: If you had gone out and marched on the streets and protested, would you have been giving up your story? Would you have been giving up what's sacred to you?

WORTHAM: Yes, I would have. Now, perhaps someone else wouldn't have. What I wanted was an understanding from those other persons, who might have thought their story was to be a civil rights activist. I wanted them to understand that I had for myself a different life vocation, that my story was to be written differently. That doesn't deny the validity of some of the things that were being done in the Civil Rights movement. But one doesn't always have to be an activist to contribute to society or to have a good life.

MOYERS: Did you want the freedom to vote?

WORTHAM: I wanted the freedom to vote, but you see, I wanted to vote to encourage the development of institutions that will see to it that my neighbor will not impinge on the free and frutiful writing of my own story, and of his. I want that vote to make sure that he and I can disagree in peace, that we can go our separate ways without interfering with each other in harmful and malicious ways.

MOYERS: What was it that caused you not to join the Civil Rights movement? What did you think they were asking of you that you didn't want to give?

WORTHAM: They were asking me to condemn all white Americans. That's what I felt at the time. And I couldn't do it.

MOYERS: But what about those who had kept your father from being a first-class citizen and would have kept you from being a first-class citizen if they could have—those who discriminated, who persecuted, who broke the law to keep you an outsider?

WORTHAM: They were wrong, absolutely wrong. You see, it depends on your definition of your situation. Actually, everything I say begins with this. When I left home to go to Tuskegee, I met black students form the deep South, whose relationships with whites were totally different from ours. A lot of Northern whites don't know this, but we down South know this—the intensity of anger and outrage is colored by these personal experiences.

In our household, whites were simply people, some of whom were very bad and did horrible things. My father didn't hate all whites, he hated "the government," which was known as "Uncle Sam" in our house. The government was the one who gave whites the power to do all these horrible things. And the government was not only doing those sorts of things, but the government was a chronic thief, who took your money. My father would say, "Watch out for Uncle Sam. He'll get in your back pocket any minute." If there was any sort of downhome animus, it was toward the government. The strategy was to rely on yourself, to be as creative as possible to get around segregation and discrimination. The attitude was "Discrimination is terrible, but you've got to live, you've got to put your kids through school. You can't waste psychological energy on feeling downtrodden. Man, you've got to get up in the morning." And he would always tell us, "You know, you've got to get up and get out there."

MOYERS: That was pure Booker T. Washington, you know.

WORTHAM: Of course it was.

MOYERS: He said, "If you learn to do something better than someone else, you'll make your way in the world."

WORTHAM: I was taught this. In fact, my father used to say to us, not knowing that it was Booker T. Washington who spoke these words, "Cast your bucket down." He also used to say, "Knowledge is power," not knowing from where that expression came.

So my view of whites was not that they were so all-powerful as individual people. They never become a stereotype in my mind. I never gave them the power that it seemed the civil rights message had to impute to them in order to make its redress. And I felt that I was being asked somehow to diminish myself by attributing to just another human being who was doing horrible things, that he was somehow much more powerful and a different kind of human being. I was not going to make whites that important. They aren't that important. They never were that important.

MOYERS: They were important enough to exercise state power over you.

WORTHAM: They were that important—but they were not important enough to define who I am.

MOYERS: How did you react when Rosa Parks sat on the bus, and the movement began to swell in the streets, and Martin Luther King emerged, and suddenly there was finally a movement of black Americans to protest this power of coercion?

WORTHAM: Well, I must tell you, I was like a lot of black kids. History doesn't say this, especially history as told on TV, but I had lessons to get. Mrs. Johnson in my English class said, "You must have those papers in by Friday, and if you don't get an A, that's it!" The ethos in our segregated black school was: "Without your high school diploma—forget everyting."

When the Civil Rights movement came along, we felt it was wonderful that this thing was happening. It seemed there was this event that was going on that was related to our everyday life but was not central to the business of everyday life.

Now there are a lot of people who would be very upset by my disclosing this very mundane aspect of getting on in the world—but this is what was going on. We were not all running out into the street joining movements. I knew very little about the details of the early Civil Rights movement. Most of it I learned after I had got to college. Some of it was imparted to us in classes—not very much, mind you. In fact, the most I learned was when I actually began the formal study of race and ethnic relations.

MOYERS: But you were bent on getting up and out.

WORTHAM: I had lessons to get. My mother died when I was nine. I had a house to clean. My father had to get up in the morning and go to work. He was breaking into the business of being an independent salesman. He had to deal with the segregation and prejudice of the day. So the Civil Rights movement was a current event, and not just for my family. It was that way for a lot of families.

MOYERS: If everybody had been like you and your father, do you think the change would have come that finally liberated blacks?

WORTHAM: Oh no, no, you must have activists. No, I'm not setting up a kind of model. This is why part of the history that I am now imparting isn't told. There is a mistaken belief that you must make a choice between public activism and private striving, that you must put a very sterile, very politicized face on black history.

There were activists in our community who were marching. There were some, like my father, who didn't and who didn't like the marchers, either. He didn't like the NAACP in our town. The NAACP people were all those doctors and teachers that he wanted us to grow up to be like. He was striving by proxy to outdo them. He didn't like them. He also thought that they were very unrealistic. In fact, at one point, he actually wrote a letter to them and said, "Look, you people want us to boycott the supermarkets. We should be trying to figure out how we can have our own market."

MOYERS: When you finally enountered these Northern Yankees, what actually happened? What convinced you that they saw you as a stereotype?

WORTHAM: They wanted me to give them a story, and the story they wanted was that I wasn't getting my essays written for Mrs. Johnson, and that my segregated high school was terrible, and that I was getting an inferior education. Actually, we now know that my education behind those walls of segregation was far better than the integrated education of the kids in the urban swamps today. This is not a justification of segregation—I'm applauding Mrs. Johnson here. But they wanted the story, and I didn't have it to give them.

They also wanted me to be angry. Later, as I moved into the professional world, the Black Power movement was at its height. I worked at NBC and ABC and the people I met wanted a Black Power pose, and I didn't have it. Not only did I disagree with the Black Power ideology, but I just don't have it in my personality. So, in the most subtle relations, where certain tacit understandings are at work, the typical Northern Yankee wanted to be seen as being more understanding toward me than I required of him. All I required of him was his respect. I didn't require his compassion. The Republicans haven't understood that, you see—

MOYERS: What do you mean?

WORTHAM: Conservative Republicans have thought that they had to show that they were as compassionate as liberals, Democrats, and other people on the left when they should have challenged the nature of the compassion. I've often found, having worked among Northern liberals a great deal, that their compassion lacks respect. An analogy is that abolitionist who really, deep down in his heart, thought that blacks were inferior, though he wanted them freed. He really thought that they were inferior to him.

MOYERS: And respect means?

WORTHAM: Respect means that you leave me alone, that you don't build up in your own mind scenarios for my salvation and that you respect me enough to trust me, even when I'm an idiot, even when I'm wrong.

MOYERS: And to say so if you are an idiot.

WORTHAM: Absolutely. If I am an idiot, tell me, disagree with me. Harold Cruse has written a book in which he touches on this very thing. The history of the Civil Rights movement began with this misunderstanding among its white participants: that they would not demand of blacks what they demanded in their own self-help organizations.

MOYERS: Did you find these Northerners who wanted to love you were asking more than you could give them?

WORTHAM: Yes. They were asking for my sanction. I was the altar before which they stood, and they were asking me to redeem them, which is what Martin Luther King promised them that I would give them.

MOYERS: And you didn't want to give it to them.

WORTHAM: I can't. Nobody can. We cannot give this to each other. I cannot give you a sense of the importance of your life. I can confirm it. I can nod my head and say yes, but I cannot make it so for you. That you must do for yourself. I can't do it for you.

MOYERS: You're saying, "I can't do it at the expense of not being what I am—"

WORTHAM: —Yes—

MOYERS: "—and if I played it your way, if I'd been the beaten-down, put-upon little person that you thought I should be, I would have been betraying myself because I wasn't that person."

WORTHAM: I would have been betraying myself. They would have had a fine old time of loving me and being compassionate and so forth, but they would have nullified that by disrespecting me. If we have to ask of any other human being that for us to love him, he must be something that is closer to our view of him or of our grand scheme of how human beings ought to be, then our own obligation to him is simply not to love him. That is the way to respect him. If he doesn't earn our love, then just don't love him. Don't harm him, don't force him to do anything—just walk away.

But there are some people who can't keep their hands off other people. They just won't. It takes a lot of courage to leave other people alone, you see.

MOYERS: Was slavery an evil?

WORTHAM: Oh, absolutely. It always is.

MOYERS: Is racism an evil?

WORTHAM: Absolutely. Racism is evil in whatever form it takes. However, it is not something that whites have a monopoly on. Blacks are also racist. My grandmother was on certain days.

MOYERS: In what way?

WORTHAM: I remember sitting on her front porch. She would sometimes go on about those "crackers."

MOYERS: A cracker, we should say, for people who don't know—

WORTHAM: A cracker in the South is a lower-class white—sometimes called "white trash," sometimes called "redneck." It's really sort of funny, because you could have the white gentry demeaning white crackers just as spiritedly as you could have any black demeaning them. Blacks look down on white crackers, too.

MOYERS: You have yourself acknowledged that with the exception of the American Indian, no ethnic group has suffered more injustices at the hands of government or its fellow citizens than black Americans.

WORTHAM: Yes.

MOYERS: But you also say the debt's been paid, the protection and preservation of the human rights and liberty of Negroes, as you wrote, is no longer a dream deferred. Do you really believe that's so?

WORTHAM: Yes, insofar as the relationship of blacks to the state is concerned.

MOYERS: You mean the state no longer says, "You cannot vote, you cannot eat here, you cannot go to school."

WORTHAM: In fact, the state has gone beyond that to oppressing us in different ways. It has given us all that any just and moral government or liberal state can give to its citizens, and that is equal rights before the law. One of the paradoxes of democracy and one of the gambles that we make is that citizens have the freedom to redefine their situation. The situation has been defined so that blacks are historical victims and that the state owes them more than just simply what it gives—not gives, actually, but acknowledges. I don't hold to the view that the state gives rights. It simply acknowledges rights that already exist, and institutionalizes those. If rights are thought of as being given, then rights become privileges, things that the state doles out to people. Then blacks can claim, "Look, we are in need of these most, we are behind the most," et cetera. And to make that claim against fellow citizens who have their own list of claims, the life of the black community has to become almost totally politicized, and the individual life of a black has to become politicized.

MOYERS: So you are opposed to affirmative action?

WORTHAM: Yes.

MOYERS: Busing?

WORTHAM: Yes.

MOYERS: Employment quotas?

WORTHAM: Yes.

MOYERS: On the principle that—

WORTHAM: —on the principle that first of all, to institute such policies requires that the state violate the rights of all of its citizens, including those who advocate those policies. And secondly, that even if one disagreed on philosophical grounds, such things don't work. They obscure or ignore the fact that blacks and other minorities make choices that are not always consistent with the statistics. In certain situations, there are not always enough blacks in the population to meet a quota, say, in a given police department or a given sociology department or a given university.

MOYERS: But that hasn't been the problem, of course. The problem has been that the police departments and universities wouldn't open the doors.

WORTHAM: My opposition to affirmative action quotas is the imposition of them on the private sector. So far as the public sector is concerned, the government should make sure that it has equal opportunity operating. If the only way to have opportunities available for blacks in all levels of government is to make sure that you recruit people in black communities who are interested in such occupations, then in fact you give some preferential attention to blacks in the recruitment realm, but only at this level.

MOYERS: Why do you rule out affirmative action in the private sector?

WORTHAM: When I talk about affirmative action for government, I'm talking about recruiting job applicants within particular fields within the government. I don't say that the government should make sure that it hires these people, or that it is unjust if government doesn't. It is unjust only if it refuses to let these people in, or doesn't make an extra effort to make sure that those who want to be policemen or firemen can be.

The private sector can't afford to do this. It is a misuse of its funds to do so. The private sector ends up looking for people who don't want to be in these positions or who sometimes are not qualified to be in these positions. We're finding this in academia with people who want to take positions for the income, but who have no sense of commitment to these jobs, and who would rather be doing something else.

MOYERS: That's a harsh judgment.

WORTHAM: It is a very harsh judgment. But there are backstair horror stories, especially in academia, of some of the effects of affirmative action, and there's a lot of mismatching going on because of the pressure to find a career, and the pressure of the university to have an affirmative action program. Why? Because it needs to show the government it is not discriminating, and because if it does not have such a program, it is thereby considerd to be discriminating. Many times, this is not necessarily the case.

This relationship of university to government I would see abolished totally, and the relationship also with business and government I would see abolished. I can't be for affirmative action. It simply cements that relationship, and it makes minorities pawns in this game.

MOYERS: If we say to a young black in the ghetto, "You're free to get a job," and there are no jobs, or if we say to a single-parent family in the ghetto, "You're free to get a house," but there's no affordable housing, are we not perpetrating a cruel hoax on them?

WORTHAM: No, we are being realistic. If we want to be a goal-directed government rather than a government that is based on the rule of law, then fine. But the ideal is that we are a government that wants to respect the rule of law, and if that is the case, then we cannot—at any point ever—justify violating the rights of members of the majority for the sake of the well-being of members of minority groups.

MOYERS: So what if the majority wants to say that because Anne Wortham is black, she won't be allowed to vote?

WORTHAM: Yes, but that's on a different level, you see. Once, I, a black, have the right to vote, I have the freedom to try to persuade my government that my fellow citizens who are white should not have the freedom to deny me entry into their restaurant.

MOYERS: Do you have the freedom to try to persuade your government to set up an economic program that will give advantages to young black kids in the ghetto who need help?

WORTHAM: I have the freedom to do it, which is not to say I approve of the freedom to do it. I do not approve of that particular strategy.

MOYERS: Why?

WORTHAM: I think that one of the unfortunate consequences of the Civil Rights movement was that the economic advancement of the black community and other minorities was defined as being outside the national economy. It pained me so much one day to hear President Reagan trying so hard to make this point. He never did. I read not long ago that Reagan had a message that he could have taken to the minorities and to blacks, which would have been a direct extention of his own basic philosophy—which he's betrayed all over the board, but that's another story. But he never was able to make the point. The point is this: You cannot save the minority community by destroying America. You cannot do it. You cannot save those young black kids in the ghetto who don't have jobs by destroying the American economy.

MOYERS: Job programs for ghetto kids are destroying America?

WORTHAM: That's not the connection I'm making. I'm not saying that by doing so, you destroy America. I am saying that you should not see their fate as being outside the larger problem of what we do about our budget deficits, our overspending, and so forth. We won't look at how we can help them in the correct light. A lot of the programs of the sixties not only did no good, but also they cost us a lot of money.

MOYERS: You've said that minorities could change the direction of American politics for the better by breaking their alliance with the government.

WORTHAM: Yes. You would think, with a history such as ours, that we would have understood two things: first, that the government, while we need it, ultimately cannot be our friend, and also that we don't need it to be our friend, really. It is just an instrument. If minorities broke their alliance with the government, they would depend more on themselves. We would acknowledge the legacy of Booker T. Washington, which is slowly coming back to legitimacy now. We should have kept that side of our story, which some today will call the conservative side of black history and black culture. You see, we would not be here were it not for our own efforts. Most of our history has been in relationship to a government that has not been very kind. Government is not a savior—the American federal government has not acted as a liberator. Civil rights for minorities was no great favor, for Christ's sake! This is what they should have done two hundred years ago. We should have retained a kind of skepticism of the state that my father had, and that in fact, a lot of Southern blacks always had. Our view of the state was always skeptical as opposed to Northern blacks, who tended to be more trusting. Ironically, although the Civil Rights movement came out of the South, it began to take on the Northern view of the state as being a benevolent institution. It isn't. It can't be, ultimately.

MOYERS: But it's all right in your scheme of things for blacks to organize to achieve social equality.

WORTHAM: No, that's not what I said. I don't believe in social equality. I believe in equality under the law.

MOYERS: Is it acceptable to organize politically to gain social advantage?

WORTHAM: It's acceptable—but I would not think that political organization would be the way to go at this point. What we need is economic advancement, and economic advancement can't be very substantial if it is done through politics.

MOYERS: You say in your book that blacks and whites should "simply exist as traders, exchanging material and intellectual values for their mutual benefit."

WORTHAM: Yes.

MOYERS: Does that mean the only bond between us is cash and materials—is economic?

WORTHAM: The trading metaphor is meant to convey more than economics. The economic trading relationship is one which Booker T. Washington understood—that if I have something to offer, and if it is good enough, you will buy it. And if you don't buy it, it's because it wasn't as good as this guy's over here. It shouldn't be because this fellow over here was able to use politics to prevent me from even competing with him, or, if once I'm at the door, make it so that in order to compete with him I must have special government contracts and engage in what we now call sleaze politics in order to have an advantage. The advantage should always be merely on the basis of what you offer in the particular situation.

MOYERS: You're obviously aware that you're criticized by many blacks for making what they call the worn-out arguments on behalf of racism that whites used to make.

WORTHAM: Yes. Because of my views, I have difficulties finding a job. Fortunately, I will go to Washington and Lee in January, and I hope that phase of my career is now over. But prior to now, it's been rather difficult. In one of my job interviews two years ago, it was asked of me, very seriously, by the faculty of a Northern urban university, whether I would encourage my students to employ the bootstrap method of mobility. They were concerned that I would, not that I wouldn't.

MOYERS: And your answer?

WORTHAM: Of course I would. I said that I don't teach any particular ideology, that I would come there to teach my subject, but that in talking with students about their careers, I will always tell them, "Look at your assets, look at what you have, and try to do with what you have. Don't first begin thinking of what you can take from the other fellow. That's not a way to go, because in the end, you will lose, especially if what the other fellow has got is a great deal of power." These faculty members were Northern white liberals who would say that I'm advocating benign neglect. But they would want me to neglect black students by encouraging them *not* to pull themselves up by their bootstraps—which is the very thing that white Americans have done.

You know, I don't understand this. What kind of friend is this? I'm merely advocating for blacks what the whites do for themselves. But if I say it, I am encouraging something that is against my race, and so forth and so on. I don't need friends like these. The black community doesn't need friends like these, who tell us to deny the self-help element of our heritage. My father feels that he has been totally ignored in all of this. He's very angry because no one gives him credit for having raised his five children on his own and put all of them through college without any help from Uncle Sam. It's not in the history books. He's very bitter.

MOYERS: Are you bitter?

WORTHAM: No, I'm not bitter. I understand it. But my father is bitter that people say we don't do anything on our own. They say that we always need the government to come in and help us do things. He wants to be known as the man who raised five kids and sent them through college.

MOYERS: You wrote an essay once called "Silence," in which you said, "But all these people have identity. They have a place. They know of fear, anger, anxiety, sadness, graft, hate, inferiority, superiority. I know only of contempt for them, and loneliness for myself, because I could not belong. I could never belong."

WORTHAM: Where did you find that? That essay was written the summer of 1963, when I was twenty. There is something wrong with that statement. I felt that I didn't belong. I was in Washington preparing for my Peace Corps orientation training, and everyone was gearing up for the March on Washington. Everyone knew what they were supposed to be doing that summer. And there I was, feeling that I couldn't do what they were doing and that I was very much alone. I don't feel that now. I didn't know at that time that the ideas I had, which were snatches of thought and floating abstractions, had been thought by people long ago, that I could find them in the Founding Fathers, and in the Greeks, and in literature.

I didn't know where to go. I now know, and I don't feel alone at all. I also don't have contempt. I was then someone who knew that she disagreed but who didn't want to pay the price of disagreement. It wasn't until I was much older that I understood that if I was going to disagree, there was a price to pay. I don't like it, but I'll pay it.

MOYERS: Why do you quote Shakespeare in your book? "Things without remedy should be without regard. What is done is done."

WORTHAM: What I mean by that is that one reaches a point at which you understand that history was here before you, and will go on after you, and that if you tie your own personal destiny, the vocation of your life, to public events, then you ultimately end up burning yourself out in activism—or you get out of the picture altogether, you commit suicide, or you go and sit in a corner somewhere and suck your thumb. So you have to reach a point at which you can say, "I am rational enough, I understand enough of life, and of myself as an individual human being, to know that I am limited in what I can do, and I am limited in what I know. My number one obligation is to fulfill my life's purpose. I cannot save the world. Even if I wanted to, I can't." This is a very realistic statement, not a statement of defeat, or retreat. It is a reorientation.

MOYERS: Do you get tired of being asked questions about race?

WORTHAM: Yes, I do, sometimes. It gets weary. But I have the most interesting conversations and all sorts of opportunities to discuss issues. Sometimes I realize that I allow people to say things they would never say to someone else who is black and female. And so I do.

MOYERS: If legal racism is not a problem any more, why are blacks poorer than whites on the whole? Why do they have less political power? Why do they have fewer job opportunities?

WORTHAM: There are no easy answers. Any way I respond will be inadequate. The coming of political rights and economic opportunities that flow from political rights occurred at a point when the American economy was changing.

MOYERS: Blacks are getting free just as the economy is fundamentally changing?

WORTHAM: Yes. So we have a huge labor force of unskilled and skilled laborers for whom there are just no jobs. That's one layer of analysis at which you can stop, but that does not make the story human, that is not the same as talking about a particular man who's willing to work, but who cannot work, not simply because of prejudice, although that's a factor, but far more importantly because the job does not exist. You see, my father had a high school education and built every house we lived in because the national economy, even under segregation, was different. In a way, my father was economically freer. Although he couldn't vote, he sent me to college. I can vote, but I can't send any kid to college, and I certainly can't buy a house, as my father did. I make enough to just keep going. And I have all the things that he thought he was giving me to prevent just the sort of bind that I'm in. It says nothing about prejudice and racism; it is a reflection of how much the national economy has declined. I don't mean to say that those things don't exist, but that it's just more complicated. I think if we allow that, then we truly appreciate and understand the plight of the black poor—and all poor. But if we keep simply labeling the problem as racism, all we do is put up a screen between ourselves and those we say we care about. We don't really understand their lives at all.

WRITING AND DISCUSSION QUESTIONS

Informative

1. How does Wortham's experience as a young black woman during the early civil rights movement differ from that of others she mentions? What specifics does she cite as formative influences on her view of the movement? What were her experiences with white students?

2. What appears to be the main theme of Wortham's interview? What does she mean when she says that "Northerners" were asking for her "sanction" and to redeem them? What examples does Wortham offer for her view that blacks can have racist attitudes? Do you find her examples credible?

3. Wortham opposes what she calls the "welfare state." In one place she suggests that the government should not and cannot "be our friend." What does she imply about the role of the state in creating and maintaining freedom and civil rights?

Persuasive

1. Wortham uses the term "bootstrap method of mobility" to describe certain of her approaches to advising students. What do you think her attitude is toward Booker T. Washington? Why might this be an offensive concept to other black activists? Argue the case.

2. What is Wortham's basic argument: that inequality of the "rules" in a culture, however racist, cannot account for the relative status of one ethnic group in a society *or* that such rules are not the *sole* determining factor? Examine her reasoning and respond to her argument. How does it affect one's stance toward disadvantaged groups in a society if one believes basic civil rights have already been achieved by a formerly disenfranchised ethnic group? Defend your point of view.

Personal

1. What is your view of *affirmative action*—those policies designed to guarantee equal or, in some cases, preferential access to educational and job opportunities? Does Wortham's interview show significant opposition to the premises of an affirmative action program? How do you think the problems of bigotry and racism have affected opportunities among blacks, Hispanics, and other nonwhites? Is affirmative action a reasonable remedy for such preexisting problems?

2. Is there such a thing as "reverse racism"? How does one balance concerns for equal opportunity in employment and education when it appears that the dominant culture and its ethnic representatives are already advantaged by the status quo? Have you ever felt either victimized or advantaged by affirmative action rules?

▼

ALICE WALKER, "EVERYDAY USE"

There is no more celebrated author among black women writers in contemporary letters than Alice Walker (1944–). Author of the best-selling and Pulitzer Prize-winning work, *The Color Purple* (1982), and the recent ground-breaking, mythically ambitious novel, *Temple of My Familiar* (1989), Walker has assumed a place in American fiction and nonfiction of supreme importance. Born in Georgia, the youngest of eight children, Walker graduated from Sarah Lawrence College in New York and returned to the South to work in the civil rights movement. During her involvement in that movement, Walker began to write fiction and nonfiction in support of the movement's ideals, eventually moving toward more overtly feminist themes in her discussion of ethnic heritage. In the short story, "Everyday Use" (1973), Walker traces the influence of mothers on black consciousness and their sense of identity in a hostile world. In addition to her collected essays and novels, Walker has also published a biography of Langston Hughes, an important black poet of the twentieth century, three books of poems, and two collections of short stories.

▼

"Everyday Use"

FOR YOUR GRANDMAMMA

ALICE WALKER

1   I will wait for her in the yard that Maggie and I made so clean and wavy yesterday afternoon. A yard like this is more comfortable than most people know. It is not just a yard. It is like an extended living room. When the hard clay is swept clean as a floor and the fine sand around the edges lined with tiny, irregular grooves, anyone can come and sit and look up into the elm tree and wait for the breezes that never come inside the house.

2   Maggie will be nervous until after her sister goes: she will stand hopelessly in corners, homely and ashamed of the burn scars down her arms and legs, eying her sister with a mixture of envy and awe. She thinks her sister has held life always in the palm of one hand, that "no" is a word the world never learned to say to her.

3   You've no doubt seen those TV shows where the child who has "made it" is confronted, as a surprise, by her own mother and father, tottering in weakly from backstage. (A pleasant surprise, of course: What would they do if parent and child came on the show only to curse out and insult each other?) On TV mother and child embrace and smile into each other's faces. Sometimes the mother and father weep, the child wraps them in her arms and leans across the table to tell how she would not have made it without their help. I have seen these programs.

4   Sometimes I dream a dream in which Dee and I are suddenly brought together on a TV program of this sort. Out of a dark and soft-seated limousine I am ushered into a bright room filled with many people. There I meet a smiling, gray, sporty man like Johnny Carson who shakes my hand and tells me what a fine girl I have. Then we are on the stage and Dee is embracing me with tears in her eyes. She pins on my dress a large orchid, even though she has told me once that she thinks orchids are tacky flowers.

5   In real life I am a large, big-boned woman with rough, manworking hands. In the winter I wear flannel nightgowns to bed and overalls during the day. I

can kill and clean a hog as mercilessly as a man. My fat keeps me hot in zero weather. I can work outside all day, breaking ice to get water for washing; I can eat pork liver cooked over the open fire minutes after it comes steaming from the hog. One winter I knocked a bull calf straight in the brain between the eyes with a sledge hammer and had the meat hung up to chill before nightfall. But of course all this does not show on television. I am the way my daughter would want me to be: a hundred pounds lighter, my skin like an uncooked barley pancake. My hair glistens in the hot bright lights. Johnny Carson has much to do to keep up with my quick and witty tongue.

But that is a mistake. I know even before I wake up. Who ever knew a   6
Johnson with a quick tongue? Who can even imagine me looking a strange white man in the eye? It seems to me I have talked to them always with one foot raised in flight, with my head turned in whichever way is farthest from them. Dee, though. She would always look anyone in the eye. Hesitation was not part of her nature.

"How do I look, Mama?" Maggie says, showing just enough of her thin body   7
enveloped in pink skirt and red blouse for me to know she's there, almost hidden by the door.

"Come out into the yard," I say.   8

Have you ever seen a lame animal, perhaps a dog run over by some care-   9
less person rich enough to own a car, sidle up to someone who is ignorant enough to be kind to him? That is the way my Maggie walks. She has been like this, chin on chest, eyes on ground, feet in shuffle, ever since the fire that burned the other house to the ground.

Dee is lighter than Maggie, with nicer hair and a fuller figure. She's a   10
woman now, though sometimes I forget. How long ago was it that the other house burned? Ten, twelve years? Sometimes I can still hear the flames and feel Maggie's arms sticking to me, her hair smoking and her dress falling off her in little black papery flakes. Her eyes seemed stretched open, blazed open by the flames reflected in them. And Dee. I see her standing off under the sweet gum tree she used to dig gum out of; a look of concentration on her face as she watched the last dingy gray board of the house fall in toward the red-hot brick chimney. Why don't you do a dance around the ashes? I'd wanted to ask her. She had hated the house that much.

I used to think she hated Maggie, too. But that was before we raised the   11
money, the church and me, to send her to Augusta to school. She used to read to us without pity; forcing words, lies, other folks' habits, whole lives upon us two, sitting trapped and ignorant underneath her voice. She washed us in a river of make-believe, burned us with a lot of knowledge we didn't necessarily need to know. Pressed us to her with the serious way she read, to shove us away at just the moment, like dimwits, we seemed about to understand.

Dee wanted nice things. A yellow organdy dress to wear to her graduation   12
from high school; black pumps to match a green suit she'd made from an old suit somebody gave me. She was determined to stare down any disaster in her efforts. Her eyelids would not flicker for minutes at a time. Often I fought off

the temptation to shake her. At sixteen she had a style of her own: and knew what style was.

13   I never had an education myself. After second grade the school was closed down. Don't ask me why: in 1927 colored asked fewer questions than they do now. Sometimes Maggie reads to me. She stumbles along good-naturedly but can't see well. She knows she is not bright. Like good looks and money, quickness passed her by. She will marry John Thomas (who has mossy teeth in an earnest face) and then I'll be free to sit here and I guess just sing church songs to myself. Although I never was a good singer. Never could carry a tune. I was always better at a man's job. I used to love to milk till I was hooked in the side in '49. Cows are soothing and slow and don't bother you, unless you try to milk them the wrong way.

14   I have deliberately turned my back on the house. It is three rooms, just like the one that burned, except the roof is tin; they don't make shingle roofs any more. There are no real windows, just some holes cut in the sides, like the portholes in a ship, but not round and not square, with rawhide holding the shutters up on the outside. This house is in a pasture, too, like the other one. No doubt when Dee sees it she will want to tear it down. She wrote me once that no matter where we "choose" to live, she will manage to come see us. But she will never bring her friends. Maggie and I thought about this and Maggie asked me, "Mama, when did Dee ever *have* any friends?"

15   She had a few. Furtive boys in pink shirts hanging about on washday after school. Nervous girls who never laughed. Impressed with her they worshiped the well-turned phrase, the cute shape, the scalding humor that erupted like bubbles in lye. She read to them.

16   When she was courting Jimmy T she didn't have much time to pay to us, but turned all her faultfinding power on him. He *flew* to marry a cheap city girl from a family of ignorant flashy people. She hardly had time to recompose herself.

17   When she comes I will meet—but there they are!

18   Maggie attempts to make a dash for the house, in her shuffling way, but I stay her with my hand. "Come back here," I say. And she stops and tries to dig a well in the sand with her toe.

19   It is hard to see them clearly through the strong sun. But even the first glimpse of leg out of the car tells me it is Dee. Her feet were always neat-looking, as if God himself had shaped them with a certain style. From the other side of the car comes a short, stocky man. Hair is all over his head a foot long and hanging from his chin like a kinky mule tail. I hear Maggie suck in her breath. "Uhnnnh," is what it sounds like. Like when you see the wriggling end of a snake just in front of your foot on the road. "Uhnnnh."

20   Dee next. A dress down to the ground, in this hot weather. A dress so loud it hurts my eyes. There are yellows and oranges enough to throw back the light of the sun. I feel my whole face warming from the heat waves it throws out. Earrings gold, too, and hanging down to her shoulders. Bracelets dangling and making noises when she moves her arm up to shake the folds of the dress out

of her armpits. The dress is loose and flows, and as she walks closer, I like it. I hear Maggie go "Uhnnnh" again. It is her sister's hair. It stands straight up like the wool on a sheep. It is black as night and around the edges are two long pigtails that rope about like small lizards disappearing behind her ears.

"Wa-su-zo-Tean-o!" she says, coming on in that gliding way the dress   *21* makes her move. The short stocky fellow with the hair to his navel is all grinning and he follows up with "Asalamalakim, my mother and sister!" He moves to hug Maggie but she falls back, right up against the back of my chair. I feel her trembling there and when I look up I see the perspiration falling off her chin.

"Don't get up," says Dee. Since I am stout it takes something of a push.   *22* You can see me trying to move a second or two before I make it. She turns, showing white heels through her sandals, and goes back to the car. Out she peeks next with a Polaroid. She stoops down quickly and lines up picture after picture of me sitting there in front of the house with Maggie cowering behind me. She never takes a shot without making sure the house is included. When a cow comes nibbling around the edge of the yard she snaps it and me and Maggie *and* the house. Then she puts the Polaroid in the back seat of the car, and comes up and kisses me on the forehead.

Meanwhile Asalamalakim is going through motions with Maggie's hand.   *23* Maggie's hand is as limp as a fish, and probably as cold, despite the sweat, and she keeps trying to pull it back. It looks like Asalamalakim wants to shake hands but wants to do it fancy. Or maybe he don't know how people shake hands. Anyhow, he soon gives up on Maggie.

"Well," I say. "Dee."

"No, Mama," she says. "Not 'Dee,' Wangero Leewanika Kemanjo!"

"What happened to 'Dee'?" I wanted to know.

"She's dead," Wangero said. "I couldn't bear it any longer, being named after the people who oppress me."

"You know as well as me you was named after your aunt Dicie," I said.   *24* Dicie is my sister. She named Dee. We called her "Big Dee" after Dee was born.

"But who was *she* named after?" asked Wangero.

"I guess after Grandma Dee," I said.

"And who was she named after?" asked Wangero.

"Her mother," I said, and saw Wangero was getting tired. "That's about as far back as I can trace it," I said. Though, in fact, I probably could have carried it back beyond the Civil War through the branches.

"Well," said Asalamalakim, "there you are."   *25*

"Uhnnnh," I heard Maggie say.

"There I was not," I said, "before 'Dicie' cropped up in our family, so why should I try to trace it that far back?"

He just stood there grinning, looking down on me like somebody inspecting a Model A car. Every once in a while he and Wangero sent eye signals over my head.

"How do you pronounce this name?" I asked.

26   "You don't have to call me by it if you don't want to," said Wangero.

"Why shouldn't I?" I asked. "If that's what you want us to call you, we'll call you."

"I know it might sound awkward at first," said Wangero.

"I'll get used to it," I said. "Ream it out again."

Well, soon we got the name out of the way. Asalamalakim had a name twice as long and three times as hard. After I tripped over it two or three times he told me to just call him Hakim-a-barber. I wanted to ask him was he a barber, but I didn't really think he was, so I didn't ask.

27   "You must belong to those beef-cattle peoples down the road," I said. They said "Asalamalakim" when they met you, too, but they didn't shake hands. Always too busy: feeding the cattle, fixing the fences, putting up salt-lick shelters, throwing down hay. When the white folks poisoned some of the herd the men stayed up all night with rifles in their hands. I walked a mile and a half just to see the sight.

Hakim-a-barber said, "I accept some of their doctrines, but farming and raising cattle is not my style." (They didn't tell me, and I didn't ask, whether Wangero (Dee) had really gone and married him.)

We sat down to eat and right away he said he didn't eat collards and pork was unclean. Wangero, though, went on through the chitlins and corn bread, the greens and everything else. She talked a blue streak over the sweet potatoes. Everything delighted her. Even the fact that we still used the benches her daddy made for the table when we couldn't afford to buy chairs.

"Oh, Mama!" she cried. Then turned to Hakim-a-barber. "I never knew how lovely these benches are. You can feel the rump prints," she said, running her hands underneath her and along the bench. Then she gave a sigh and her hand closed over Grandma Dee's butter dish. "That't it!" she said. "I knew there was something I wanted to ask you if I could have." She jumped up from the table and went over in the corner where the churn stood, the milk in it clabber by now. She looked at the churn and looked at it.

"This churn top is what I need," she said. "Didn't Uncle Buddy whittle it out of a tree you all used to have?"

28   "Yes," I said.

"Uh huh," she said happily. "And I want the dasher, too."

"Uncle Buddy whittle that, too?" asked the barber.

Dee (Wangero) looked up at me.

"Aunt Dee's first husband whittled the dash," said Maggie so low you almost couldn't hear her. "His name was Henry, but they called him Stash."

29   "Maggie's brain is like an elephant's," Wangero said, laughing. "I can use the churn top as a centerpiece for the alcove table," she said, sliding a plate over the churn, "and I'll think of something artistic to do with the dasher."

30   When she finished wrapping the dasher the handle stuck out. I took it for a moment in my hands. You didn't even have to look close to see where hands

pushing the dasher up and down to make butter had left a kind of sink in the wood. In fact, there were a lot of small sinks; you could see where thumbs and fingers had sunk into the wood. It was beautiful light yellow wood, from a tree that grew in the yard where Big Dee and Stash had lived.

After dinner Dee (Wangero) went to the trunk at the foot of my bed and started rifling through it. Maggie hung back in the kitchen over the dishpan. Out came Wangero with two quilts. They had been pieced by Grandma Dee and then Big Dee and me had hung them on the quilt frames on the front porch and quilted them. One was in the Lone Star pattern. The other was Walk Around the Mountain. In both of them were scraps of dresses Grandma Dee had worn fifty and more years ago. Bits and pieces of Grandpa Jarrell's Paisley shirts. And one teeny faded blue piece, about the size of a penny matchbox, that was from Great Grandpa Ezra's uniform that he wore in the Civil War.

"Mama," Wangero said sweet as a bird. "Can I have these old quilts?"

I heard something fall in the kitchen, and a minute later the kitchen door slammed.

"Why don't you take one or two of the others?" I asked. "These old things was just done by me and Big Dee from some tops your grandma pieced before she died."

"No," said Wangero. "I don't want those. They are stitched around the borders by machine."

"That'll make them last better," I said.

"That's not the point," said Wangero. "These are all pieces of dresses Grandma used to wear. She did all this stiching by hand. Imagine!" She held the quilts securely in her arms, stroking them.

"Some of the pieces, like those lavender ones, come from old clothes her mother handed down to her," I said, moving up to touch the quilts. Dee (Wangero) moved back just enough so that I couldn't reach the quilts. They already belonged to her.

"Imagine!" she breathed again, clutching them closely to her bosom.

"The truth is," I said, "I promised to give them quilts to Maggie, for when she marries John Thomas."

She gasped like a bee had stung her.

"Maggie can't appreciate these quilts!" she said. "She'd probably be backward enough to put them to everyday use."

"I reckon she would," I said. "God knows I been saving 'em for long enough with nobody using 'em. I hope she will!" I didn't want to bring up how I had offered Dee (Wangero) a quilt when she went away to college. Then she had told me they were old-fashioned, out of style.

"But they're *priceless!*" she was saying now, furiously; for she has a temper. "Maggie would put them on the bed and in five yeears they'd be in rags. Less than that!" "She can always make some more," I said. "Maggie knows how to quilt."

31

32

33

Dee (Wangero) looked at me with hatred. "You just will not understand. The point is these quilts, *these* quilts!"

34   "Well," I said, stumped. "What would *you* do with them?"

"Hang them," she said. As if that was the only thing you *could* do with quilts.

Maggie by now was standing in the door. I could almost hear the sound her feet made as they scraped over each other.

"She can have them, Mama," she said, like somebody used to never winning anything, or having anything reserved for her. "I can 'member Grandma Dee without the quilts."

35   I looked at her hard. She had filled her bottom lip with checkerberry snuff and it gave her face a kind of dopey, hangdog look. It was Grandma Dee and Big Dee who taught her how to quilt herself. She stood there with her scarred hands hidden in the folds of her skirt. She looked at her sister with something like fear but she wasn't mad at her. This was Maggie's portion. This was the way she knew God to work.

36   When I looked at her like that something hit me in the top of my head and ran down to the soles of my feet. Just like when I'm in church and the spirit of God touches me and I get happy and shout. I did something I never had done before: hugged Maggie to me, then dragged her on into the room, snatched the quilts out of Miss Wangero's hands and dumped them into Maggie's lap. Maggie just sat there on my bed with her mouth open.

"Take one or two of the others," I said to Dee.

But she turned without a word and went out to Hakim-a-barber.

"You just don't understand," she said, as Maggie and I came out to the car.

"What don't I understand?" I wanted to know.

37   "Your heritage," she said. And then she turned to Maggie, kissed her, and said, "You ought to try to make something of yourself, too, Maggie. It's really a new day for us. But from the way you and Mama still live you'd never know it."

38   She put on some sunglasses that hid everything above the tip of her nose and her chin.

39   Maggie smiled; maybe at the sunglasses. But a real smile, not scared. After we watched the car dust settle I asked Maggie to bring me a dip of snuff. And then the two of us sat there just enjoying, until it was time to go in the house and go to bed.

WRITING AND DISCUSSION QUESTIONS

Informative

1. How do the churn and the quilts in "Everyday Use" exemplify the different values of Dee and Maggie's mother toward the modern world? Explain the different

reactions Maggie and Dee have toward these items and what they mean to each of them.
2. Is Dee's homecoming successful? Is her mother simply misunderstanding her or is there a real break in their respective set of values?
3. Consider the unusual chronology of the narrative. How does Walker frame the story, that is, does she begin the story in the past or the present? What effect does the sudden shift to the arrival of Dee and her friend have on your perception of the setting?

Persuasive

1. It might be said that the two daughters represent two views of the world that lay beyond their mother's home. Argue that one or the other is more realistic and, therefore, more suited to living and thriving in the society that helped create their poverty in the first place.
2. The statement is made that Dee rarely had friends. Why might this be the case?
3. Whom do you think Walker wants the reader to identify with in the story?

Personal

1. What values has Dee brought home from college with her? How do they differ from her mother's? Has your educational experience created conflicts with your parents and siblings? If so, in what form?
2. Are there artifacts in your family that bear a meaning beyond their "everyday usefulness." Who has assigned them this value? Are there conflicts over who they belong to? What should be done with them?

CHAPTER WRITING ASSIGNMENTS

1. One of the common themes running through all of the selections in this chapter is the power of literacy, of the command of language to facilitate change among the oppressed. Trace this recognition of the power of language in the careers and published works of two or three of the leaders of the civil rights movement in American culture. Write an essay that affirms the power of their ideas, which enables them to be effective speakers and writers.

2. Consider the proposition: the nonwhite individual in the 1990s is in a much better position than he or she was at the end of the civil rights movement in the 1960s and is approaching full equality and enfranchisement in the political system. Argue for or against it, offering solid evidence from current events and recent history to support your argument.

3. Write an essay that explores the nature of abortion rights. Is this a "civil rights"

issue? Whose rights are primary in resolving the matter: the mother, the father, the unborn child, or the state itself? To what extent is abortion a privacy issue, a moral issue, or a medical issue?

4. To what extent do you believe the Holocaust of Nazi Germany, resulting in the death of six million Jews, an aberration? To what extent did it represent the inevitable result of racist policies and state-sponsored discrimination? Argue this proposition: A holocaust such as happened in Nazi Germany could never happen again in a healthy, functioning democracy.

Chapter Eleven

FEMINISM

Risk

JOANNA RUSS

He didn't like this future world, oh no he didn't, our old friend John Hemingway London Rockne Knievel Dickey Wayne. It wasn't risky enough. He had been a racing-car driver way back then (before he was frozen) and he couldn't stand cars that protected you in head-on collisions and roads that wouldn't let you collide with anything in the first place. Nor did he like the medical advances which had made it impossible to die of anything (except extreme old age) or the sports they practiced for health and fun (but never for danger). Nor was it possible to be better at something than anybody else. That is, you could be, but who cared? He wanted to go deep-sea diving, glider crashing, mountain-climbing, alligator-wrestling, lion-shooting, novel-writing, and even worse things. So he went before a parliament of these sensitive-but-bland men and women who had resurrected him from the cryogenics chambers of an earlier day and said loudly, legs planted far apart (he favored the one with the silver pins in it a little, though):

"MAN IS NOT MAN WITHOUT RISK!"

Then he said, even louder:

"MANHOOD—IDENTITY—EVEN LIFE ITSELF—DEMAND THE CONSTANT TEST OF DANGER!"

They said, "Oh dear." Their eyes got very round. They murmured worriedly amongst themselves. He thought he might have to throw a temper tantrum (the

679

kind he used to put on so well in front of the news cameras) but that proved
unnecessary. They debated politely. They put their hands over their faces. They
said most of the unfrozen people seemed to like this new world. They said there
really was no accounting for tastes, was there, after all.

  But finally they said, Very well; you shall have your Risk.
  And they inoculated him with Bubonic Plague.

As science fiction writer Joanna Russ suggests in her playful fable "Risk" printed
above, the times they are a changin'. Men like Ernest Hemingway and John
Wayne who have cultivated their machismo qualities, those exaggerated "male"
behaviors that stress toughness and hardness, are not very happy in the fable
with the emerging gender roles, where women can be assertive and men do not
have to be. This reversal of roles has happened because we are in the midst of
a great revolution in thinking, feminism. Whatever one's position on feminism is,
whether people call themselves feminists, are neutral, or are violently opposed to
the philosophy behind the idea, they cannot call themselves educated persons if
their understanding of this important idea does not cause more than the typical
knee-jerk response. Feminism as an organized system of thought is barely 200
years old, but it is a far-reaching and revolutionary idea that touches every significant part of modern life, many believe as far reaching in its implications for
society as religion, humanism, and science have been. Because feminism forces
us to reexamine the role gender plays in our personal, political, and even spiritual
lives and because so many people feel so strongly about it, studying feminism
can be especially difficult.

  Whether we want to admit it, we are in the midst of a feminist revolution.
Unlike most of the other ideas in this text, whose initial impact occurred in the
relatively distant past, feminism is very much happening now. Once we accept
this as a given, it becomes apparent that the newer a revolutionary idea is, the
more controversial the idea may seem. Somehow, the passing of time helps us to
adjust to new ideas. Even though new ideas about gender may make us very
uncomfortable, they may also challenge and improve our lives; thus, it becomes
incumbent on us to examine the new ways of thinking about being male or female
and test them against traditional ways. Doing this, we may find ourselves admitting that there is, has been, and may always be a conflict between most men and
women. Often the conflict appears in playful ways and is, therefore, harmless;
but too frequently, it ends in abuse and pain, as in rape, divorce, and wife battering. Sometimes the conflict has political, ideological, and religious dimensions,
as with abortion, child custody laws, and state-supported child care.

  The difficulty in studying feminism does not derive just from the fact that the
revolution is still occurring. It also stems from the fact that feminism is a complex
idea that seeks to combine the personal, the religious, and the political. Because
that combination can invoke our defenses and personal prejudices, the best
stance to take in studying feminism may be to step outside the present, at least
outside our strongest opinions on the subject, and examine feminism as a histor-

ical phenomenon, much as this textbook has approached each of the previous eight ideas.

At its simplest, feminism is both an organized system of thought and the struggle for social, economic, and educational equality for women. Feminism views most societies as "patriarchal," an organizational scheme that grants greater power to men than to women by denying women equal status, power, and access to those resources needed to develop full lives. Feminists generally believe that the power of patriarchy derives from its gender system, which assigns particular traits to men and women on the basis of their sex. Once this assignment is made, a number of conclusions follow. First, the seeming "fact" that it is "natural" for women to be sensitive, emotional, cooperative, submissive, and nurturing. Second, that men "should be" aggressive, logical, and unemotional. If one accepts these premises, it follows that men are more suitable for doing the business of the world, whereas women are more suitable for work in the home. The world outside the home is where so much of the power resides, so women find themselves at a disadvantage. Most feminists believe that biological differences do not explain these roles or the inequality of the genders. Rather, it is the traditional social and political make-up of society that gives importance and autonomy to men. Thus, the power of patriarchy stems from its pervasiveness: it is so hard to change because many people assume it is anchored in our biology as well as all previous ideas, religion, humanism, science, and so on, that have shaped who we are. Because it is central to what we do and how we think, it begins to seem unalterable.

Clearly, feminism is not just the attempt to understand and eliminate exploitation or subordination of females by males; feminism is also a new perspective on knowledge, a way of knowing (like revelation, reason, and science) that uses gender as a category of analysis. Such a new way of knowing would point out that most history is written by men, that history has been shaped by the male viewpoint and male values, that the "great books of the western world" are written mostly by white men of European descent not because women are incapable of such feats, that male dominance has affected the way we view history and shape reality, and that so much writing by women has been systematically suppressed. Such a way of knowing would describe a feminist epistemology (an approach to knowledge shaped by a consciousness of gender) dramatically different from one shaped by men. It would explain why so many women, especially in the last century, who tried to compete with men outside the home, thereby violating the conventions of "female decorum," found themselves driven to depression and suicide.

Although the feminist struggle for equality has occurred mainly in the last 200 years in the United States and Great Britain, its roots are ancient. There are profemale texts from ancient Greece (Sappho's poetry and some of Aristophanes' plays) and from the Middle Ages (Lilith is often considered the first feminist). Women's resistance was strengthened in the Enlightenment and through the humanism of the eighteenth century, both of which asserted the dignity and equality of all persons. More recently, feminism has become more of a worldwide movement. Wherever and whenever feminist struggles are occurring, it is clear that massive historical forces have helped to determine the relative success or failure of the idea. Specifically, as social conditions changed from feudal monarchy to industrial democracy, women began in the late eighteenth and nineteenth centuries to demand full equality and opportunity in all walks of life.

The power and importance of struggle for women's equality stems from the fact that with all the rhetoric of equality apparent in such works as Plato's *Republic*, Locke's *Treatise on Government*, and Jefferson's declaration that "all men are created equal," women were still, over the last 4000 or more years, regarded as physically, emotionally, and intellectually inferior to men. Traditionally tied to the home as child bearers and by the division of labor that sent men into the external world while women stayed in the home, women were further subjugated to men by law and theology. Legally, women could not own property, participate in business, or gain control over the lives of their children. Theologically, men have often used the Fall, as well as other portions of scripture, to justify women's subordination; as early as in Geneisis 3:16, God says to Eve, "I will greatly multiply thy sorrow and thy conception; in sorrow thou shalt bring forth children; and thy desire *shall be* to thy husband and he shall rule over thee."

A dramatic example of how strong antifemale attitudes were in the very recent past is contained in a best-selling book at the turn of the last century in England. Viennese theorist Otto Weininger's *Sex and Character* (1903) had, in the words of literary critic Ford Maddox Ford (1873–1939), "spread through the serious male society of England as if it had been an epidemic," and it was just as popular in Europe. Weininger's theory was that in a distant animal, brutish past, we had all been bisexual. Progress had come to civilization when we began to differentiate ourselves sexually. Art critic Bran Dijkstra summarized the theory when he wrote:

> In the mathematical equation which created the sexual, i.e. reproductive entity in nature, the masculine represented the positive pole, the feminine the negative. Woman might be the locus of the physical—one might say, the mechanical—reproduction of humanity, but the male was the locus of the brain, of humanity's capacity for spiritual understanding. Therefore, the more truly male men became, the more spiritual he would be, whereas the more completely feminine women became, the more materalistic and brainless she would be.[1]

To this day most feminists believe that such attitudes persist, that males do control a grossly disproportionate amount of economic and political power in the world, and we are facing in the feminist movement a monumental power struggle. What Martin Luther King, Jr. (1929–1968) said in regard to race surely applies as well to sex: "Lamentably, it is an historical fact that privileged groups seldom give up their privileges voluntarily."

---

[1] B. Dijkstra, *Idols of Perversity: Fantasies of Feminine Evil in Fin de Siecle Culture* (New York: Oxford University Press, 1986), 218–219.

The most important nineteenth-century declaration of women's equality was issued at Seneca Falls, New York, at a convention organized by women in 1848. This conference is important because it was the first time women gathered to speak of their living conditions and it was the first time that the rights of women were documented. The two most important participants were Elizabeth Cady Stanton (1815–1902) and Lucretia Mott (1793–1880), who drafted the declaration and used the Declaration of Independence as a model. Earlier, an antislavery conference in London had barred women from attending. This exclusion galvanized the women to meet at Seneca Falls. Often referred to as the "first wave" of the feminist movement, Seneca Falls demanded everything from the vote to full opportunity in education and business.

Although many of these rights have been secured in the advanced countries of the Western world, most feminists believe that the feminist revolution is by no means complete. While suffrage was won in the United States in 1920 through ratification of the 19th Amendment, the first wave of feminism did not have the impact the suffragettes had hoped for. Even with the vote for women, little seemed to change. Still treated as the weaker sex, for women little changed in the way of politics, economics, or their role in society. The 1960s, 1970s, and 1980s have witnessed a rebirth of feminism, often referred to as the "second wave" or the "Women's Liberation Movement." Two important works that paved the way for the second wave are Simone de Beauvoir's (1908–1986) *The Second Sex* (1952) and Betty Friedan's *The Feminine Mystique* (1963). French writer, existentialist, and companion of philospher Jean-Paul Sartre (1908–1980) and filmmaker Claude Lanzmann, de Beauvoir spent her life in revolt against bourgeois values she had been raised to respect. Her fight for women's rights was a natural outgrowth of that conflict. Critic Liliane Lazar summarizes the essential message of *The Second Sex*, which "postulates that man conceived of himself as the essential being and has made the woman the unessential being, the other, the second." Beauvoir's other main postulate is that there is no biological law that determines feminine nature, and all notions of feminine nature are, therefore, cultural or artificial. "One is not born, but rather one becomes a woman."

Friedan's groundbreaking early work was a similar attack on the expectations that women could succeed only through childbearing and domestic life. Three years after she wrote *The Feminine Mystique*, Friedan founded the National Organization for Women (NOW) and served as its president unitl 1970. By the 1970s NOW had over 400 local chapters, pressing for reform legislation in such areas as abortion rights, child care centers, equal pay for equal work, the elimination of gender bias in educational testing, and for elimination of cultural stereotyping of women and men in the media and in education. By the 1980s, NOW had grown dramatically, and the National Women's Political Caucus, organized in 1971 to strengthen the position of women in politics, had 73,000 members. Other women's groups, such as the Black Feminist Organization (1973) and the Coalition of Labor Union Women (1974), abound. As feminist Ellen Berry writes, "Today, it is possible to describe a world in which the idea of a woman working seriously at a career is no longer laughable, in which the choice to remain single no longer makes a woman an old maid, and in which contraception and a degree of sexual freedom are taken for granted." Nevertheless, feminists believe those gains are no reason for complacency, because deeply engrained attitudes of male superiority, which privilege men, still exist.

Again, there are reasons feminists believe that the battle is not yet over. Although Congress passed the Eqaul Rights Amendment in 1972, the amendment has not been able to get the support of the 38 states required to bar sex discrimination nationally (Opponents argue that laws already protect women in the United States and that the Equal Rights Amendment is too open ended and places power in the hands of the courts, not the people). In addition, the poverty rate of women has risen rapidly (a phenomenon referred to as the "feminization of poverty") and the fundamentalist Right has been mounting serious threats to what many feminists see as women's reproductive freedom.

The second wave of feminism is a single, unified movement only in its goal of equality for women. Clearly, feminists differ in how they think equality should be achieved. One basic division has to do with whether they believe that change can occur within our system, or whether the system itself needs changing. "Liberal" feminists think that liberal democracy and its principles of individual rights guaranteeing freedom to all do not need changing. They just want these principles appled fairly and equally to women. They argue for better enforcement of current employment laws regarding equal opportunity, sexual harrassment on the job, equal pay for equal work, and sexually balanced application of the laws concerning divorce and child support.

This group may also be divided into two subgroups, as defined by writer Judi Loesch: first, there are the "assimilationist" or "equality" feminists, who insist that men and women be treated equally in law and social relations. They are against special benefits for women in situations like pregnancy and child custody; then, there are the "social" feminists, who believe that it is the "dual burden women carry to maintain a home and family *and* function in the workforce that disadvantages them and demands extra compensation if they are to gain equality outside the home."[2]

On the other hand, "socialist" feminists believe that the liberal framework is in error in assuming that change can occur given just the liberal traditions of democracy. They focus on institutions and material conditions, and want structural changes in ownership, law, and economic systems. For example, Friedrich Engels (1820–1895) believed women were oppressed because of the economic structure of a capitalistic, industrial system that vests power in the owners of land and capital. The poverty, slums, and subhuman working conditions he witnessed in England led him to speak sharply against a system that exploited women (and men in the proletariat class).

A third group is often referred to as "radical" feminists. They see gender differences as the basis of all difference in power and status and urge the revolt of the "colonized" (women) against the "colonizer" (men). One extreme outcome

---

[2]J. Loesch, "Social Feminism: Reweavng Society." *Social Justice Review* (July/August, 1987): 22.

of the radical position is that women refuse to participate in the male order and, instead, form their own separate societies to discover a "woman's culture." Generally, these feminists urge radical transformation, from the social to the personal and the political.

Another important group among feminists is people of color. This is a growing and important movement, especially in the United States, where black, Hispanic, Native American, and Asian women have too often been excluded from the mainstream of feminist thought. The fact that the "patriarchy" assailed by feminists is in large measure white and Western makes the inclusion of these women critical. (This bias of patriarchy is often referred to as its Eurocentric quality because the men who shaped the ideas of Western society were mostly white Europeans.)

Clearly, such classification systems are never universally agreed on. Some feminists may consider reproductive rights, including legalized abortion, as an essential part of liberal feminism. Those who believe in the "right to life," on the other hand, may fully agree with the economic issues like equal pay but oppose abortion and consider those who support it as "radical" feminists.

Feminism stirs deep feelings, and it remains the subject of one of the great debates of contemporary life. Often one's view of the feminist revolution depends on one's vantage point, and it is important to keep this in mind while developing a thoughtful position on the subject. Nevertheless, the revolution of feminism contains much vitality and diversity, as the readings that follow show.

▼

ELIZABETH CADY STANTON AND LUCRETIA MOTT, "DECLARATION OF SENTIMENTS AND RESOLUTIONS, SENECA FALLS"

The Seneca Falls Declaration represents the most important event in the nineteenth-century women's movement, really the beginning of the modern struggle for women's equality. The motivating event for the gathering in Seneca Falls, New York, in 1848 was the attendance eight years earlier of Elizabeth Cady Stanton and Lucretia Mott at the World's Anti-Slavery Convention in London, where they were witness to the exclusion of women as delegates, solely on the basis of their gender. The two women agreed there and then to do something about the discrimination.

Stanton was the central force behind the meeting convened at Seneca Falls. She later wrote:

My experiences at the World's Anti-Slavery Convention, all I had read of the legal status of women, and the oppression I saw everywhere, together swept across my soul, intensified now by many personal experiences . . . In this tempest-tossed condition of mind I received an invitation to spend the day with Lucretia Mott. . . . I poured out the torrent of my long-accumulating discontent with such vehemence and indignation that I stirred myself, as well as the rest of the party.

Stanton, with the assistance of Mott and others, drafted the Declaration, using the Declaration of Independence with a deliberate irony. This imitation was fitting, especially because political reforms in working conditions were very much in the air at the time as people demanded that the democratic principles of the American and French Revolutions be upheld; it is also more than coincidental that Marx and Engels wrote and presented the *Communist Manifesto* to the world that very same year, in 1848.

▼

Declaration of Sentiments and Resolutions, Seneca Falls

ELIZABETH CADY STANTON AND LUCRETIA MOTT

. . . In this tempest-tossed condition of mind I received an invitation to spend the day with Lucretia Mott. . . . I poured out the torrent of my long-accumulating discontent with such vehemence and indignation that I stirred myself, as well as the rest of the party."

Then and there the decision was made to call a woman's rights meeting. Only a few days before the convention was scheduled to begin, Stanton, with Lucretia Mott and others, drew up the Seneca Falls Declaration of Sentiments and Resolutions, using the Declaration of Independence as a model.

This use of the Declaration of Independence was particularly appropriate to the time. For in 1848, in England, France, Germany, Austria and elsewhere, people were taking to the streets, seeking the fulfillment of liberal democratic rights proclaimed in the great documents of the French and American Revolutions and, in many instances, demanding new economic rights for workers. Presaging the political and social storms of the future, that very same year Marx and Engels penned and issued the *Communist Manifesto.*

About three hundred persons appeared at the chapel in Seneca Falls on the appointed day. James Mott, husband of Lucretia, chaired the convention. The Declaration of Sentiments was read to the assembly and adopted. Eleven resolutions were adopted unanimously; a twelfth—that pertaining to granting women elective franchise—passed by a narrow margin only after Frederick Douglass stoutly defended it from the floor.

1   When, in the course of human events, it becomes necessary for one portion of the family of man to assume among the people of the earth a position different from that which they have hitherto occupied, but one to which the laws of nature and of nature's God entitle them, a decent respect to the opinions of mankind requires that they should declare the causes that impel them to such a course.

2   We hold these truths to be self-evident: that all men and women are created equal; that they are endowed by their Creator with certain inalienable rights;

that among these are life, liberty, and the pursuit of happiness; that to secure these rights governments are instituted, deriving their just power from the consent of the governed. Whenever any form of government becomes destructive of these ends, it is the right of those who suffer from it to refuse allegiance to it, and to insist upon the institution of a new government, laying its foundation on such principles, and organizing its powers in such form, as to them shall seem most likely to effect their safety and happiness. Prudence, indeed, will dictate that governments long established should not be changed for light and transient causes; and accordingly all experience hath shown that mankind are more disposed to suffer, while evils are sufferable, than to right themselves by abolishing the forms to which they were accustomed. But when a long train of abuses and usurpations, pursuing invariably the same object evinces a design to reduce them under absolute despotism, it is their duty to throw off such government, and to provide new guards for their future security. Such has been the patient sufferance of the women under this government, and such is now the necessity which constrains them to demand the equal station to which they are entitled.

The history of mankind is a history of repeated injuries and usurpations on 3 the part of man toward woman, having in direct object the establishment of an absolute tyranny over her. To prove this, let facts be submitted to a candid world.

He has never permitted her to exercise her inalienable right to the elective 4 franchise.

He has compelled her to submit to laws, in the formation of which she had 5 no voice.

He has withheld from her rights which are given to the most ignorant and 6 degraded men—both natives and foreigners.

Having deprived her of this first right of a citizen, the elective franchise, 7 thereby leaving her without representation in the halls of legislation, he has oppressed her on all sides.

He has made her, if married, in the eye of the law, civilly dead. 8

He has taken from her all right in property, even to the wages she earns. 9

He has made her, morally, an irresponsible being, as she can commit many 10 crimes with impunity, provided they be done in the presence of her husband. In the covenant of marriage, she is compelled to promise obedience to her husband, he becoming, to all intents and purposes, her master—the law giving him power to deprive her of her liberty, and to administer chastisement.

He has so framed the laws of divorce, as to what shall be the proper causes, 11 and in case of separation, to whom the guardianship of the children shall be given, as to be wholly regardless of the happiness of women—the law, in all cases, going upon a false supposition of the supremacy of man, and giving all power into his hands.

After depriving her of all rights as a married woman, if single, and the 12 owner of property, he has taxed her to support a government which recognizes her only when her property can be made profitable to it.

13   He has monopolized nearly all the profitable employments, and from those she is permitted to follow, she receives but a scanty remuneration. He closes against her all the avenues to wealth and distinction which he considers most honorable to himself. As a teacher of theology, medicine, or law, she is not known.

14   He has denied her the facilities for obtaining a thorough education, all colleges being closed against her.

15   He allows her in Church, as well as State, but a subordinate position, claiming Apostolic authority for her exclusion from the ministry, and, with some exceptions, from any public participation in the affairs of the Church.

16   He has created a false public sentiment by giving to the world a different code of morals for men and women, by which moral delinquencies which exclude women from society, are not only tolerated, but deemed of little account in man.

17   He has usurped the prerogative of Jehovah himself, claiming it as his right to assign for her a sphere of action, when that belongs to her conscience and to her God.

18   He has endeavored, in every way that he could, to destroy her confidence in her own powers, to lessen her self-respect, and to make her willing to lead a dependent and abject life.

19   Now, in view of this entire disfranchisement of one-half the people of this country, their social and religious degradation—in view of the unjust laws above mentioned, and because women do feel themselves aggrieved, oppressed, and fraudulently deprived of their most sacred rights, we insist that they have immediate admission to all the rights and privileges which belong to them as citizens of the United States.

20   In entering upon the great work before us, we anticipate no small amount of misconception, misrepresentation, and ridicule; but we shall use every instrumentality within our power to effect our object. We shall employ agents, circulate tracts, petition the State and National legislatures, and endeavor to enlist the pulpit and the press in our behalf. We hope this Convention will be followed by a series of Conventions embracing every part of the country.

RESOLUTIONS

21 Whereas, The great precept of nature is conceded to be, that "man shall pursue his own true and substantial happiness." Blackstone in his Commentaries remarks, that this law of Nature being coeval with mankind, and dictated by God himself, is of course superior in obligation to any other. It is binding over all the globe, in all countries and at all times; no human laws are of any validity if contrary to this, and such of them as are valid, derive all their force, and all their validity, and all their authority, mediately and immediately, from this original; therefore,

22   *Resolved*, That such laws as conflict, in any way, with the true and substan-

tial happiness of woman, are contrary to the great precept of nature and of no validity, for this is "superior in obligation to any other."

Resolved, That all laws which prevent woman from occupying such a station 23 in society as her conscience shall dictate, or which place her in a position inferior to that of man, are contrary to the great precept of nature, and therefore of no force or authority.

Resolved, That woman is man's equal—was intended to be so by the Crea- 24 tor, and the highest good of the race demands that she should be recognized as such.

Resolved, That the women of this country ought to be enlightened in regard 25 to the laws under which they live, that they may no longer publish their degradation by declaring themselves satisfied with their present position, nor their ignorance, by asserting that they have all the rights they want.

Resolved, That inasmuch as man, while claiming for himself intellectual 26 superiority, does accord to woman moral superiority, it is pre-eminently his duty to encourage her to speak and teach, as she has an opportunity, in all religious assemblies.

Resolved, That the same amount of virtue, delicacy, and refinement of 27 behavior that is required of woman in the social state, should also be required of man, and the same transgressions should be visited with equal severity on both man and woman.

Resolved, That the objection of indelicacy and impropriety, which is so often 28 brought against woman when she addresses a public audience, comes with a very ill-grace from those who encourage, by their attendance, her appearance on stage, in the concert, or in feats of the circus.

Resolved, That woman has too long rested satisfied in the circumscribed lim- 29 its which corrupt customs and a perverted application of the Scriptures have marked out for her, and that it is time she should move in the enlarged sphere which her great Creator has assigned her.

Resolved, That it is the duty of the women of this country to secure to them- 30 selves their sacred right to the elective franchise.

Resolved, That the equality of human rights results necessarily from the fact 31 of the identity of the race in capabilities and responsibilities.

Resolved, therefore, That, being invested by the Creator with the same capa- 32 bilities, and the same consciousness of responsibility for their exercise, it is demonstrably the right and duty of woman, equally with man, to promote every righteous cause by every righteous means; and especially in regard to the great subjects of morals and religion, it is self-evidently her right to participate with her brother in teaching them, both in private and in public, by writing and by speaking, by any instrumentalities proper to be used, and in any assemblies proper to be held; and this being a self-evident truth growing out of the divinely implanted principles of human nature, any custom or authority adverse to it, whether modern or wearing the hoary sanction of antiquity, is to be regarded as a self-evident falsehood, and at war with mankind.

[At the last session Lucretia Mott offered and spoke to the following 33 resolution:]

34   *Resolved,* That the speedy success of our cause depends upon the zealous and untiring efforts of both men and women, for the overthrow of the monopoly of the pulpit, and for the securing to woman an equal participation with men in the various trades, professions, and commerce.

WRITING AND DISCUSSION QUESTIONS

Informative

1. Based on what specific democratic principles does the Declaration justify taking steps to institute a "new government" or severe social reforms? From whom does Stanton take "the great precept of nature"?
2. Which of the "facts" submitted to support the claim of male oppression seem most important? Which of these grievances seem to have been the most resistant to change in the last century and a half?
3. Why do you think Stanton used the Declaration of Independence as a model? How closely does she imitate the earlier document? What kind of authority, if any, is gained by the imitation?
4. Are there any assumptions about gender behavior here? Traditionally, of course, women have been considered to be more emotional, more sensitive, more artistic, and more compassionate than men, even though these traits are not likely theirs by nature. To what degree do these assumptions hold up here? Is Stanton using these behaviors in particular rhetorical ways to make a point?

Persuasive

1. How are men pictured here? Assuming Stanton's claims are accurate, what kind of morality have men followed? How is Stanton using "male" behavior as a persuasive device? Argue your position.
2. There are a number of different references to church and God in the Declaration. Argue that this is merely a rhetorical ploy or that Stanton, in fact, bases her call for equality on traditional Judeo–Christian principles.
3. For thousands of years the word "man" was assumed to mean "thinking person" and was used interchangeably for male or female. The generic nouns and pronouns used in the Seneca Falls Declaration are "man" and "he/him," something that would upset many modern feminists. Why do you think these early feminists did not focus on such language issues? What advantages or disadvantages do you see in using language that is gender neutral, such as "person" or "his/her"? Argue that gender-neutral language is or is not important.

Personal

1. Where do you personally draw the lines when fighting for women's rights? Of these issues, which do you support and why: affirmative action, equal pay for equal work, equal service in the armed services, reproductive rights, child care facilities at work, and maternity leave and benefits.

2. To what degree do you think that the resolutions stated in the Declaration have been successfully achieved today? Is the feminist struggle largely won?

▼

SOJOURNER TRUTH, "AIN'T I A WOMAN?"

As most of us know, black Americans' emancipation from slavery meant neither freedom from racism, for the black people of the United States, nor freedom from sexism, for black American women. In fact, many social scientists believe that racism against blacks, especially those who are poor, continues to be one of the most costly problems we face in terms of the lives of the victims as well as to the health of the country. Others think that the greatest problem is now poverty and that racism does not account for a significant degree of oppression.

The writings of Sojourner Truth demonstrate how deep the problems of racism go. Born a slave in New York, she was a forceful speaker at antislavery meetings from the time she gained her freedom in 1827. Although she was given the name Isabella while a slave, she replaced it with the symbolic "Sojourner Truth," speaking any place she could against the evils of both racism and sexism. At the First National Women's Rights Convention in Worcester, Massachusetts, in 1850, she persuaded the white participants (she was the only black person present) to pass a resolution declaring black female slaves, particularly the million and a half slave women of the South, as the "most grossly wronged and foully outraged of all women."

Part of Truth's importance in the women's movement stems from the frequent accusation that the white middle class dominates it, with the exclusion of the poor and ethnic minorities. Of course, if that were the case, it could not succeed in its primary goal of equality for all women. The potential for real racism in the women's movement was evident even in mid-nineteenth century America, for Truth made the remarks that follow at a women's convention in Akron, Ohio, only by overcoming the resistance of many women who feared that publicity of her presence would confuse the women's cause with abolition. But Frances Gage, who transcribed Truth's remarks for posterity and presided over the meeting, insisted on letting her speak.

Truth's opening was a direct response to several male clergy in attendance who opposed equality for women. Their arguments were varied: one was based on the manhood of Christ; another on man's "greater intellect"; and another on the temptation and sin of Eve. When the atmosphere was at its most turbulent, Sojourner Truth rose, in Gage's words, "slowly from her seat . . ., and she moved slowly and solemnly to the front, laid her old bonnet at her feet, and turned her great speaking eyes to me. There was a hissing sound of disapprobation above and below."

▼

Ain't I a Woman?
SOJOURNER TRUTH

Well, children, where there is so much racket there must be some-   1
thing out of kilter. I think that 'twixt the negroes of the South and the women at

the North, all talking about rights, the white men will be in a fix pretty soon. But what's all this here talking about?

2   That man over there says that women need to be helped into carriages, and lifted over ditches, and to have the best place everywhere. Nobody ever helps me into carriages, or over mud-puddles, or gives me any best place! And ain't I a woman? Look at me! Look at my arm! I have ploughed and planted, and gathered into barns, and no man could head me! And ain't I a woman? I could work as much and eat as much as a man—when I could get it—and bear the lash as well! And ain't I a woman? I have borne thirteen children, and seen them most all sold off to slavery, and when I cried out with my mother's grief, none but Jesus heard me! And ain't I a woman?

3   Then they talk about this thing in the head; what's this they call it? [Intellect, someone whispers.] That's it, honey. What's that got to do with women's rights or negro's rights? If my cup won't hold but a pint, and yours holds a quart, wouldn't you be mean not to let me have my little half-measure full?

4   Then that little man in black there, he says women can't have as much rights as men 'cause Christ wasn't a woman! Where did your Christ come from? Where did your Christ come from? From God and a woman! Man had nothing to do with Him.

5   If the first woman God ever made was strong enough to turn the world upside down all alone, these women together ought to be able to turn it back, and get it right side up again! And now they is asking to do it, the men better let them.

6   Obliged to you for hearing me, and now old Sojourner ain't got nothing more to say.

WRITING AND DISCUSSION QUESTIONS

Informative

1. According to Truth, what images of women appear to have kept them in their place?
2. What is Truth's argument in favor of women's rights? Apart from the logic of the argument, what is its tone? How may its effectiveness rely on more than its logic? How, for example, does Truth counter the argument that Eve was a sinner and a temptress?
3. The third paragraph has spurred some debate. What is Truth saying here about women's intellect? What argument is she making in favor of women's and blacks' rights?

Persuasive

1. How do you think institutional religion uses Christ's discipleship to argue against women's rights? Truth counters that argument by saying that Christ came from a

woman. Take a side in this debate, which still goes on today over such issues as the right of women to become priests, ministers, and rabbis.

2. In responding to her adversaries at the meeting, Truth rejects the authority of the past, as it is expressed in Christ's maleness and Eve's sin, while arguing for equal rights for women. What kind of authority does she put in its place? Argue that she is or is not effective.

Personal

1. Which black females speak effectively today for the rights of black women? Consider looking into the lives of persons like Toni Morrison, Alice Walker, Barbara Jordan, Shirley Chisholm, or Ruby Dee. How successful has their struggle for equality been, especially as poverty, racism and sexism all conspire to keep them down?

▼

JOHN STUART MILL, FROM *THE SUBJECTION OF WOMEN*

John Stuart Mill (1806–1873) is perhaps the greatest nineteenth-century defender of individual liberties. His writing is characterized by the brilliance of his logic and the thoroughness of his arguments and cases. He tackled the political and religious problems of his age with a vengeance that has come to have a profound effect on twentieth-century thinking. His essay *On Liberty* (1859) is one of the greatest treatises on free speech ever written.

Under the influence of his father, James Mill, John was home-schooled in London. Mill's father had serious doubts about institutional schooling's ability to develop the intellect, and he apparently succeeded in educating his son at home. At age three, Mill read Greek; he read Latin and was proficient at arithmetic at age eight; and he had mastered logic at age 12. As he writes in his *Autobiography* (1873), by the time he was 14 years old, he had more than a two-decade advantage over his peers.

Mill's sensitivities for others developed partly as the result of a nervous breakdown he experienced in his early twenties. Further, in 1851, he married Harriet Taylor, who convinced him that women deserved more recognition and influence in society. Mill wrote later that she was "the inspirer" of his best writing. Eighteen years after his marriage, 1869, he wrote *The Subjection of Women*, which has become a classic on women's liberation and surely demonstrates that one does not have to be a woman to write an authoritative and convincing defense of feminism. A decade earlier, in *On Liberty*, we see Mill's stunning defense of the minority against the power and tyranny of the majority, which helps explain why he was so ready to come to the defense of women.

▼

from *The Subjection of Women*
JOHN STUART MILL

1   The object of this Essay is to explain as clearly as I am able, the grounds of an opinion which I have held from the very earliest period when I had formed an opinion at all on social or political matters, and which, instead of being weakened or modified, has been constantly growing stronger by the progress of reflection and the experience of life: That the principle which regulates the existing social relations between the two sexes—the legal subordination of one sex to the other—is wrong in itself, and now one of the chief hindrances to human improvement; and that it ought to be replaced by a principle of perfect equality, admitting no power or privilege on the one side, nor disability on the other.

2   Some will object, that a comparison cannot fairly be made between the government of the male sex and the forms of unjust power which I have adduced in illustration of it, since these are arbitrary, and the effect of mere usurpation, while it on the contrary is natural. But was there ever any domination which did not appear natural to those who possessed it? There was a time when the division of mankind into two classes, a small one of masters and numerous one of slaves, appeared, even to the most cultivated minds, to be a natural, and the only natural, condition of the human race. No less an intellect, and one which contributed no less to the progress of human thought, than Aristotle, held this opinion without doubt or misgiving; and rested it on the same premises on which the same assertion in regard to the dominion of men over women is usually based, namely that there are different natures among mankind, free natures, and slave natures; that the Greeks were of a free nature, the barbarian races of Thracians and Asiatics of a slave nature. But why need I go back to Aristotle? Did not the slaveowners of the Southern United States maintain the same doctrine, with all the fanaticism with which men cling to the theories that justify their passions and legitimate their personal interests? Did they not call heaven and earth to witness that the dominion of the white man over the black is natural, that the black race is by nature incapable of freedom, and marked out for slavery? some even going as far as to say that the freedom of manual laborers is an unnatural order of things anywhere. Again, the theorists of absolute monarchy have always affirmed it to be the only natural form of government; issuing from the patriarchal, which was the primitive and spontaneous form of society, framed on the model of the paternal, which is anterior to society itself, and, as they contend, the most natural authority of all. . . . So true is it that unnatural generally means only uncustomary, and that everything which

is usual appears natural. The subjection of women to men being a universal custom, any departure from it quite naturally appears unnatural. But how entirely, even in this case, the feeling is dependent on custom, appears by ample experience. Nothing so much astonishes the people of distant parts of the world, when they first learn anything about England, as to be told that it is under a queen: the thing seems to them so unnatural as to be almost incredible. To Englishmen this does not seem in the least degree unnatural, because they are used to it; but they do feel it unnatural that women should be soldiers or members of parliament. In the feudal ages, on the contrary, war and politics were not thought unnatural to women, because not unusual; it seemed natural that women of the privileged classes should be of manly character, inferior in nothing but bodily strength to their husbands and fathers. The independence of women seemed rather less unnatural to the Greeks than to other ancients, on account of the fabulous Amazons (whom they believed to be historical), and the partial example afforded by the Spartan women; who, though no less subordinate by law than in other Greek states, were more free in fact, and being trained to bodily exercises in the same manner with men, gave ample proof that they were not naturally disqualified for them. There can be little doubt that Spartan experience suggested to Plato, among many other of his doctrines, that of the social and political equality of two sexes.

But, it will be said, the rule of men over women differs from all these others 3 in not being a rule of force: it is accepted voluntarily, women make no complaint, and are consenting parties to it. In the first place, a great number of women do not accept it. Ever since there have been women able to make their sentiments known by their writings (the only mode of publicity which society permits to them), an increasing number of them have recorded protests against their present social condition: and recently many thousands of them, headed by the most eminent women known to the public, have petitioned Parliament for their admission to the Parliamentary Suffrage. The claim of women to be educated as solidly, and in the same branches of knowledge, as men, is urged with growing intensity, and with a great prospect of success; while the demand for their admission into professions and occupations hitherto closed against them, becomes every year more urgent. Though there are not in this country, as there are in the United States, periodical Conventions and an organized party to agitate for the Rights of Women, there is a numerous and active Society organized and managed by women, for the more limited object of obtaining the political franchise. Nor is it only in our own country and in America that women are beginning to protest, more or less collectively, against the disabilities under which they labor. France, and Italy, and Switzerland, and Russia now afford examples of the same thing. How many more women there are who silently cherish similar aspirations, no one can possibly know; but there are abundant tokens how many *would* cherish them, were they not so strenuously taught to repress them as contrary to the proprities of their sex. . . .

All causes, social and natural, combine to make it unlikely that women 4 should be collectively rebellious to the power of men. They are so far in a position different from all other subject classes, that their masters require something more from them than actual service. Men do not want solely the obedience of women, they want their sentiments. All men, except the most brutish, desire to have, in the woman most nearly connected with them, not a forced slave but a willing one, not a slave merely, but a favorite. They have therefore put everything in practice to enslave their minds. The masters of all other slaves rely, for maintaining obedience, on fear; either fear of themselves, or religious fears. The masters of women wanted more than simple obedience, and they turned the whole force of education to effect their purpose. All women are brought up from the very earliest years in the belief that their ideal of character is the very opposite to that of men; not self-will, and government by self-control, but submission, and yielding to the control of others. All the moralities tell them that it is the duty of women, and all the current sentimentalities that it is their nature, to live for others; to make complete abnegation of themselves, and to have no life but in their affections. And by their affections are meant the only ones they are allowed to have—those to the men with whom they are connected, or to the children who constitute an additional and indefeasible tie between them and a man. When we put together three things—first, the natural attraction between opposite sexes; secondly, the wife's entire dependence on the husband, every privilege or pleasure she has being either his gift, depending entirely on his will; and lastly, that the principal object of human pursuit, consideration, and all objects of social ambition, can in general be sought or obtained by her only through him, it should be a miracle if the object of being attractive to men had not become the polar star of feminine education and formation of character. And, this great means of influence over the minds of women having been acquired, an instinct of selfishness made men avail themselves of it to the utmost as a means of holding women in subjection, by representing to them meekness, submissiveness, and resignation of all individual will into the hands of a man, as an essential part of sexual attractiveness. Can it be doubted that any of the other yokes which mankind have succeeded in breaking, would have subsisted till now if the same means had existed, and had been as sedulously used, to bow down their minds to it? If it had been made the object of the life of every young plebeian to find personal favor in the eyes of some patrician, of every young serf with some seigneur; if domestication with him, and a share of his personal affections, had been held out as the prize which they all should look out for, the most gifted and aspiring being able to reckon on the most desirable prizes; and if, when this prize had been obtained, they had been shut out by a wall of brass from all interest not centering in him, all feelings and desires but those which he shared or inculcated; would not serfs and seigneurs, plebeians and patricians, have been as broadly distinguished at this day as men and women are? and would not all but a thinker here and there, have believed the distinction to be a fundamental and unalterable fact in human nature?

5   The preceding considerations are amply sufficient to show that custom, however universal it may be, affords in this case no presumption, and ought not to

create any prejudice, in favor of the arrangements which place women in social and political subjection to men. But I may go farther, and maintain that the course of history, and the tendencies of progressive human society, afford not only no presumption in favor of this system of inequality of rights, but a strong one against it; and that, so far as the whole course of human improvement up to this time, the whole stream of modern tendencies, warrants any inference on the subject, it is, that this relic of the past is discordant with the future, and must necessarily disappear.

For, what is the peculiar character of the modern world—the difference   6
which chiefly distinguishes modern institutions, modern social ideas, modern life itself, from those of times long past? It is, that human beings are no longer born to their place in life, and chained down by an inexorable bond to the place they are born to, but are free to employ their faculties, and such favorable chances as offer, to achieve the lot which may appear to them most desirable.

On the other point which is involved in the just equality of women, their   7
admissibility to all the functions and occupations hitherto retained as the monopoly of the stronger sex, I should anticipate no difficulty in convincing anyone who has gone with me on the subject of the equality of women in the family. I believe that their disabilities elsewhere are only clung to in order to maintain their subordination in domestic life; because the generality of the male sex cannot yet tolerate the idea of living with an equal. Were it not for that, I think that almost everyone, in the existing state of opinion in politics and political economy, would admit the injustice of excluding half the human race from the greater number of lucrative occupations, and from almost all high social functions; ordaining from their birth either that they are not, and cannot by any possibility become, fit for employments which are legally open to the stupidest and basest of the other sex, or else that however fit they may be, those employments shall be interdicted to them, in order to be preserved for the exclusive benefit of males. In the last two centuries, when (which was seldom the case) any reason beyond the mere existence of the fact was thought to be required to justify the disabilities of women, people seldom assigned as a reason their inferior mental capacity; which, in times when there was a real trial of personal faculties (from which all women were not excluded) in the struggles of public life, no one really believed in. The reason given in those days was not women's unfitness, but the interest of society, by which was meant the interest of men: just as the *raison d'état*, meaning the convenience of the government, and the support of existing authority, was deemed a sufficient explanation and excuse for the most flagitious crimes. In the present day, power holds a smoother language, and whomsoever it oppresses, always pretends to do so for their own good: accordingly, when anything is forbidden to women, it is thought necessary to say, and desirable to believe, that they are incapable of doing it, and that they depart from their real path of success and happiness when they aspire to it. But to make this reason plausible (I do not say valid), those by whom it is urged must be prepared to carry it to a much greater length than anyone ven-

tures to do in the face of present experience. It is not sufficient to maintain that women on the average are less gifted than men on the average, with certain of the higher mental faculties, or that a smaller number of women than of men are fit for occupations and functions of the highest intellectual character. It is necessary to maintain that no women at all are fit for them, and that the most eminent women are inferior in mental faculties to the most mediocre of the men on whom those functions at present devolve. For if the performance of the function is decided either by competition, or by any mode of choice which secures regard to the public interest, there needs to be no apprehension that any important employments will fall into the hands of women inferior to average men, or to the average of their male competitors. The only result would be that there would be fewer women than men in such employments; a result certain to happen in any case, if only from the preference always likely to be felt by the majority of women for the one vocation in which there is nobody to compete with them. Now, the most determined depreciator of women will not venture to deny, that when we add the experience of recent times to that of ages past, women, and not a few merely, but many women, have proved themselves capable of everything, perhaps without a single exception, which is done by men, and of doing it successfully and creditably. The utmost that can be said is, that there are many things which none of them have succeeded in doing as well as they have been done by some men—many in which they have not reached the very highest rank. But there are extremely few, dependent only on mental faculties, in which they have not attained the rank next to the highest. Is not this enough, and much more than enough, to make it a tyranny to them, and a detriment to society, that they should not be allowed to compete with men for the exercise of these functions? Is it not a mere truism to say, that such functions are often filled by men far less fit for them than numbers of women, and who would be beaten by women in any fair field of competition? What difference does it make that there may be men somewhere, fully employed about other things, who may be still better qualified for the things in question than these women? Does not this take place in all competitions? Is there so great a superfluity of men fit for high duties, that society can afford to reject the service of any competent person? Are we so certain of always finding a man made to our hands for any duty or function of social importance which falls vacant, that we lose nothing by putting a ban upon one-half of mankind, and refusing beforehand to make their faculties available, however distinguished they may be? And even if we could do without them, would it be consistent with justice to refuse to them their fair share of honor and distinction, or to deny to them the equal moral right of all human beings to choose their occupation (short of injury to others) according to their own preferences, at their own risk? Nor is the injustice confined to them: it is shared by those who are in a position to benefit by their services. To ordain that any kind of persons shall not be physicians, or shall not be advocates, or shall not be members of parliament, is to injure not them only, but all who employ physicians or advocates, or elect members of parliament, and who are deprived of the stimulating effect of greater competition on the exertions of the competitors, as well as restricted to a narrower range of individual choice. . . .

There remains a question, not of less importance than those already dis- 8
cussed, and which will be asked the most importunately by those opponents whose conviction is somewhat shaken on the main point. What good are we to expect from the changes proposed in our customs and institutions? Would mankind be at all better off if women were free? If not, why disturb their minds, and attempt to make a social revolution in the name of an abstract right? . . .

To which let me first answer, the advantage of having the most universal and 9
pervading of all human relations regulated by justice instead of injustice. The vast amount of this gain to human nature, it is hardly possible, by any explanation or illustration, to place in a stronger light than it is placed by the bare statement, to anyone who attaches a normal meaning to words. All the selfish propensities, the self-worship, the unjust self-preference, which exist among mankind, have their source and root in, and derive their principal nourishment from, the present constitution of the relation between men and women. Think what it is to a boy, to grow up to manhood in the belief that without any merit or any exertion of his own, though he may be the most frivolous and empty or the most ignorant and stolid of mankind, by the mere fact of being born a male he is by right the superior of all and every one of an entire half of the human race: including probably some whose real superiority to himself he has daily or hourly occasion to feel; but even if in his whole conduct he habitually follows a woman's guidance, still, if he is a fool, she thinks that of course she is not, and cannot be, equal in ability and judgment to himself; and if he is not a fool, he does worse—he sees that she is superior to him, and believes that, notwithstanding her superiority, he is entitled to command and she is bound to obey. What must be the effect on his character, of this lesson? And men of the cultivated classes are often not aware how deeply it sinks into the immense majority of male minds. For, among right-feeling and well-bred people, the inequality is kept as much as possible out of sight; above all, out of sight of the children. As much obedience is required from boys to their mother as to their father: they are not permitted to domineer over their sisters, nor are they accustomed to see these postponed to them, but the contrary; the compensations of the chivalrous feeling being made prominent, while the servitude which requires them is kept in the background. Well brought-up youths in the higher classes thus often escape the bad influences of the situation in their early years, and only experience them when, arrived at manhood, they fall under the dominion of facts as they really exist. Such people are little aware, when a boy is differently brought up, how early the notion of his inherent superiority to a girl arises in his mind; how it grows with his growth and strengthens with his strength; how it is inoculated by one schoolboy upon another; how early the youth thinks himself superior to his mother, owing her perhaps forbearance, but no real respect; and how sublime and sultan-like a sense of superiority he feels, above all, over the

woman whom he honors by admitting her to a partnership of his life. Is it imagined that all this does not pervert the whole manner of existence of the man, both as an individual and as a social being? It is an exact parallel to the feeling of a hereditary king that he is excellent above others by being born a king, or a noble by being born a noble. The relation between husband and wife is very like that between lord and vassal, except that the wife is held to more unlimited obedience than the vassal was. However the vassal's character may have been affected, for better and for worse, by his subordination, who can help seeing that the lord's was affected greatly for the worse? whether he was led to believe that his vassals were really superior to himself, or to feel that he was placed in command over people as good as himself, for no merits of labors of his own, but merely for having, as Figaro says, taken the trouble to be born. The self-worship of the monarch, or of the feudal superior, is matched by the self-worship of the male. Human beings do not grow up from childhood in the possession of unearned distinctions, without pluming themselves upon them. Those whom privileges not acquired by their merit, and which they feel to be disproportioned to it, inspire with additional humility, are always the few, and the best few. The rest are only inspired with pride, and the worst sort of pride, that which values itself upon accidental advantages, not of its own achieving. Above all, when the feeling of being raised above the whole of the other sex is combined with personal authority over one individual among them; the situation, if a school of conscientious and affectionate forbearance to those whose strongest points of character are conscience and affection, is to men of another quality a regularly constituted Academy or Gynmasium for training them in arrogance and overbearingness; which vices, if curbed by the certainty of resistance in their intercourse with other men, their equals, break out towards all who are in a position to be obliged to tolerate them, and often revenge themselves upon the unfortunate wife for the involuntary restraint which they are obliged to submit to elsewhere.

10   The example afforded, and the educaton given to the sentiments, by laying the foundation of domestic existence upon a relation contradictory to the first principles of social justice, must, from the very nature of man, have a perverting influence of such magnitude, that it is hardly possible with our present experience to raise our imaginations to the conception of so great a change for the better as would be made by its removal. All that education and civilization are doing to efface the influences on character of the law of force, and replace them by those of justice, remains merely on the surface, as long as the citadel of the enemy is not attacked. The principle of the modern movement in morals and politics, is that conduct, and conduct alone, entitles to respect: that not what men are, but what they do, constitutes their claim to deference; that, above all, merit, and not birth, is the only rightful claim to power and authority. If no authority, not in its nature temporary, were allowed to one human being over another, society would not be employed in building up propensities with one hand which it has to curb with the other. The child would really, for the

first time in man's existence on earth, be trained in the way he should go, and when he was old there would be a chance that he would not depart from it. But so long as the right of the strong to power over the weak rules in the very heart of society, the attempt to make the equal right of the weak the principle of its outward actions will always be an uphill struggle; for the law of justice, which is also that of Christianity, will never get possession of men's inmost sentiments; they will be working against it, even when bending to it.

The second benefit to be expected from giving to women the free use of   *11* their faculties, by leaving them the free choice of their employments, and opening to them the same field of occupation and the same prizes and encouragements as to other human beings, would be that of doubling the mass of mental faculties available for the higher service of humanity. Where there is now one person qualified to benefit mankind and promote the general improvement, as a public teacher, or an administrator of some branch of public or social affairs, there would then be a chance of two. Mental superiority of any kind is at present everywhere so much below the demand; there is such a deficiency of persons competent to do excellently anything which it requires any considerable amount of ability to do; that the loss to the world, by refusing to make use of one-half of the whole quantity of talent it possesses, is extremely serious. It is true that this amount of mental power is not totally lost. Much of it is employed, and would in any case be employed, in domestic management, and in the few other occupations open to women and from the remainder indirect benefit is in many individual cases obtained, through the personal influence of individual women over individual men. But these benefits are partial; their range is extremely circumscribed; and if they must be admitted, on the one hand, as a deduction from the amount of fresh social power that would be acquired by giving freedom to one-half of the whole sum of human intellect, there must be added, on the other, the benefit of the stimulus that would be given to the intellect of men by the competition; or (to use a more true expression) by the necessity that would be imposed on them of deserving precedency before they could expect to obtain it. . . .

WRITING AND DISCUSSION QUESTIONS

Informative

1. Mill uses an elaborate scaffolding of logic to argue for women's rights, but he returns again and again to the benefits such changes would bring. What are these benefits, and how do they fit into his argument?
2. How and why does Mill reject the argument that the subjection of women is natural? Identify several ways in which ''custom'' is often used to demonstrate that it is unnatural to change the relative status of the sexes.
3. How does Mill treat the apparent silence and voluntary acceptance by women of

"the rule of men over women"? Why, according to Mill, are women not "collectively rebellious"? How does Mill account for the meekness and submissiveness of the women he observed?

Persuasive

1. How does Mill's view of "modern social ideas, modern life itself" become the basis of his argument against inequality? Do you agree with his view of modern life? How does his view of modern culture differ from yours? How else can one define modern culture, and will a different definition result in a different conclusion with regard to women's role?
2. Mill claims that "the male sex cannot yet tolerate the idea of living with an equal" in the family. Can you think of other reasons that conspire to keep women in the home? Do childrearing and the "division of labor" justify women spending more time in the home?

Personal

1. Mill makes a dramatic statement when he says in paragaph 9 that "All the selfish propensities, the self-worship, the unjust self-precedence, which exist among mankind, have their source and root in, and derive their principal nourishment from, the present constitution of the relation between men and women." Then, he describes the growth of a boy from childhood to manhood. Do you think he has overstated his case? To what degree does Mill's description of growing up fit your own experience?
2. In paragraph 10 Mill refers to the Christian "law of justice" and its belief in "equal rights of the weak." According to your own experience, how has religion treated women? Do you think Mill has insulted women by including them under the category of "weak"?

▼

VIRGINIA WOOLF, "THE PATRIARCHY" FROM *A ROOM OF ONE'S OWN*

Virginia Woolf's (1882–1941) *A Room of One's Own* (1929) is perhaps the most convincing and imaginative treatise on the psychological and material bases for women's silence and exclusion ever written, considered by many to be *the* classic of the twentieth-century women's movement. A stunning analysis of the effects of male dominance on women's artistic productivity and a call for the end of gender bias, the narrative was originally delivered as a series of lectures to an art society in England in 1928. Part fantasy, part literary criticism, part history, and part study of the creative process, the lectures ask why women have been left out for so long—out of money, the status, and the power, the and relegated to the bedroom and kitchen. For answers, we are taken to the great universities and museums of England, where the British empire was shaped and where the roots of modern Western civilization were planted. Critics have almost universally heralded Woolf's book, placing it beside the great works on the great ideas. What is especially striking about Woolf's writing, said a reviewer for *Yale Review*, is "Its quiet, demure laughter . . . *A Room of One's Own* offers us, among other good things, a meditation, delicately whimsical and deeply true. . . ."

Virginia Woolf was an innovater in many areas. She was a successful diarist, literary critic, and novelist, and was one of the pioneers of the style of stream of consciousness, or interior monologue, so important to Modernist literature of the twentieth century. Woolf is also known for her pacifism, early making the connection between patriarchy and fascism. In 1895, shortly after her mother's death, and in 1915 she suffered nervous breakdowns; in 1941, Woolf committed suicide by drowning.

Reading *A Room of One's Own* may initially pose problems for the reader because Woolf presents her analysis of patriarchy through a fantasy of several episodes in different places in London. In the first chapter, she asks her audience, which has asked her to speak on "women and fiction," to imagine a woman, whose name is Mary Seton, stepping onto the lawn at "Oxbridge," her symbol for Oxford and Cambridge Universities. The second chapter, which is reprinted below, takes place at the British Museum. She speculates on what would happen to her character Mary Seton there, as she thinks about the lot of women over the last several centuries.

▼

The Patriarchy
VIRGINIA WOOLF

The scene, if I may ask you to follow me, was now changed. The   *1*
leaves were still falling, but in London now, not Oxbridge,[1] and I must ask you
to imagine a room, like many thousands, with a window looking across people's
hats and vans and motor-cars to other windows, and on the table inside the
room a blank sheet of paper on which was written in large letters WOMEN AND
FICTION, but no more. The inevitable sequel to lunching and dining at Oxbridge
seemed, unfortunately, to be a visit to the British Museum. One must strain off
what was personal and accidental in all these impressions and so reach the
pure fluid, the essential oil of truth. For that visit to Oxbridge and the luncheon
and the dinner had started a swarm of questions. Why did men drink wine and
women water? Why was one sex so prosperous and the other so poor? What
effect has poverty on fiction? What conditions are necessary for the creation of
works of art?—a thousand questions at once suggested themselves. But one
needed answers, not questions; and an answer was only to be had by consulting
the learned and the unprejudiced, who have removed themselves above the
strife of tongue and the confusion of body and issued the result of their reasoning and research in books which are to be found in the British Museum. If

---

[1]Oxbridge is an imaginary university; Woolf derived its name by combining Oxford and Cambridge Universities.

truth is not to be found on the shelves of the British Museum, where I asked myself, picking up a notebook and a pencil, is truth?

2   Thus provided, thus confident and enquiring, I set out in the pursuit of truth. The day, though not actually wet, was dismal, and the streets in the neighborhood of the Museum were full of open coal-holes, down which sacks were showering; four-wheeled cabs were drawing up and depositing on the pavement corded boxes containing, presumably, the entire wardrobe of some Swiss or Italian family seeking fortune or refuge or some other desirable commodity which is to be found in the boarding-houses of Bloomsbury in the winter. The usual hoarse-voiced men paraded the streets with plants on barrows. Some shouted; others sang. London was like a workshop. London was like a machine. We were all being shot backwards and forwards on this plain foundation to make some pattern. The British Museum was another department of the factory. The swing-doors swung open; and there one stood under the vast dome, as if one were a thought in the huge bald forehead which is so spendidly encircled by a band of famous names. One went to the counter; one took a slip of paper; one opened a volume of the catalogue, and. . . . . the five dots here indicate five separate minutes of stupefaction, wonder, and bewilderment. Have you any notion how many books are written about women in the course of one year? Have you any notion how many are written by men? Are you aware that you are, perhaps, the most discussed animal in the universe? Here had I come with a notebook and a pencil proposing to spend a morning reading, supposing that at the end of the morning I should have transferred the truth to my notebook. But I should need to be a herd of elephants, I thought, and a wilderness of spiders, desperately referring to the animals that are reputed longest lived and most multitudinously eyed, to cope with all this. I should need claws of steel and beak of brass even to penetrate the husk. How shall I ever find the grains of truth embedded in all this mass of paper, I asked myself, and in despair began running my eye up and down the long list of titles. Even the names of the books gave me food for thought. Sex and its nature might well attract doctors and biologists; but what was surprising and difficult of explanation was the fact that sex—woman, that is to say—also attracts agreeable essayists, light-fingered novelists, young men who have taken the M.A. degree; men who have taken no degree; men who have no apparent qualification save that they are not women. Some of these books were, on the face of it, frivolous and facetious; but many, on the other hand, were serious and prophetic, moral and hortatory. Merely to read the titles suggested innumerable schoolmasters, innumerable clergymen mounting their platforms and pulpits and holding forth with a loquacity which far exceeded the hour usually allotted to such discourse on this one subject. It was a most strange phenomenon; and apparently—here I consulted the letter M—one confined to male sex. Women do not write books about men—a fact that I could not help welcoming with relief, for if I had first to read all that men have written about women, then all that women have written about men, the aloe that flowers once in a hundred years would flower twice before I could set pen to paper. So, making a perfectly arbitrary choice

of a dozen volumes or so, I sent my slips of paper to lie in the wire tray, and waited in my stall, among the other seekers for the essential oil of truth.

What could be the reason, then, of this curious disparity, I wondered, draw- 3 ing cartwheels on the slips of paper provided by the British taxpayer for other purposes. Why are women, judging from this catalogue, so much more interesting to men than men to women? A very curious fact it seemed, and my mind wandered to picture the lives of men who spend their time writing books about women; whether they were old or young, married or unmarried, red-nosed or hump-backed—anyhow, it was flattering, vaguely, to feel oneself the object of such attention, provided that it was not entirely bestowed by the crippled and the infirm—so I pondered until all such frivolous thoughts were ended by an avalanche of books sliding down on the desk in front of me. Now the trouble began. The student who has been trained in research at Oxbridge has no doubt some method of shepherding his question past all distractions till it runs into its answer as a sheep runs into its pen. The student by my side, for instance, who was copying assiduously from a scientific manual was, I felt sure, extracting pure nuggets of the essential ore every ten minutes or so. His little grunts of satisfaction indicated so much. But if, unfortunately, one has had no training in a university, the question far from being shepherded to its pen flies like a frightened flock hither and thither, helter-skelter, pursued by a whole pack of hounds. Professors, schoolmasters, sociologists, clergymen, novelists, essayists, journalists, men who had no qualification save that they were not women, chased my simple and single question—Why are women poor?—until it became fifty questions; until the fifty questions leapt frantically into mid-stream and were carried away. Every page in my notebook was scribbled over with notes. To show the state of mind I was in, I will read you a few of them, explaining that the page was headed quite simply, WOMEN AND POVERTY, in block letters; but what followed was something like this:

> *Condition in Middle Ages of,*
> *Habits in the Fiji islands of,*
> *Worshipped as goddesses by,*
> *Weaker in moral sense than,*
> *Idealism of,*
> *Greater conscientiousness of,*
> *South Sea Islanders, age of puberty among,*
> *Attractiveness of,*
> *Offered as sacrifice to,*
> *Small size of brain of,*
> *Profounder sub-consciousness of,*
> *Less hair on the body of,*
> *Mental, moral and physical inferiority of,*
> *Love of children of,*
> *Greater length of life of,*
> *Weaker muscles of,*

> *Strength of affections of,*
> *Vanity of,*
> *Higher education of,*
> *Shakespeare's opinion of,*
> *Lord Birkenhead's opinion of,*
> *Dean Inge's opinion of,*
> *La Bruyère's opinion of,*
> *Dr. Johnson's opinion of,*
> *Mr. Oscar Browning's opinion of, . . .*

Here I drew breath and added, indeed, in the margin, Why does Samuel Butler[2] say, "Wise men never say what they think of women"? Wise men never say anything else apparently. But, I continued, leaning back in my chair and looking at the vast dome in which I was a single but by now somewhat harassed thought, what is so unfortunate is that wise men never think the same thing about women. Here is Pope.[2]

> *Most women have no character at all.*

And here is La Bruyère.

> *Les femmes sont extrêmes; elles sont meilleures ou pires que les*
> *hommes—*[3]

a direct contradiction by keen observers who were contemporary. Are they capable of education or incapable? Napoleon thought them incapable. Dr. Johnson[4] thought the opposite. Have they souls or have they not souls? Some savages say they have none. Others, on the contrary, maintain that women are half divine and worship them on that account. Some sages hold that they are shallower in the brain; others that they are deeper in the consciousness. Goethe honoured them; Mussolini despises them. Wherever one looked men thought about women and thought differently. It was impossible to make head or tail of it all, I decided, glancing with envy at the reader next door who was making the neatest abstracts, headed often with an A or a B or a C, while my own notebook rioted with the wildest scribble of contradictory jottings. It was distressing, it was bewildering, it was humiliating. Truth had run through my fingers. Every drop had escaped.

4   I could not possibly go home, I reflected, and add as a serious contribution to the study of women and fiction that women have less hair on their bodies than men, or that the age of puberty among the South Sea Islanders is nine— or is it ninety?—even the handwriting had become in its distraction indecipher-

---

[2]Alexander Pope (1688–1744), British Neoclassical poet.
[3]"The women are extreme; they are better or worse than men."
[4]Dr. Samuel Johnson (1709–1784), British essayist.

able. It was disgraceful to have nothing more weighty or respectable to show after a whole morning's work. And if I could not grasp the truth about W. (as for brevity's sake I had come to call her) in the past, why bother about W. in the future? It seemed pure waste of time to consult all those gentlemen who specialise in women and her effect on whatever it may be—politics, children, wages, morality—numerous and learned as they are. One might as well leave their books unopened.

But while I pondered I had unconsciously, in my listlessness, in my despera- 5 tion, been drawing a picture where I should, like my neighbour, have been writing a conclusion. I had been drawing a face, a figure. It was the face and figure of Professor von X. engaged in writing his monumental work entitled *The Mental, Moral, and Physical Inferiority of the Female Sex.* He was not in my picture a man attractive to women. He was heavily built; he had a great jowl; to balance that he had very small eyes; he was very red in the face. His expression suggested that he was labouring under some emotion that made him jab his pen on the paper as if he were killing some noxious insect as he wrote, but even when he had killed it that did not satisfy him; he must go on killing it; and even so, some cause for anger and irritation remained. Could it be his wife, I asked, looking at my picture. Was she in love with a cavalry officer? Was the cavalry officer slim and elegant and dressed in astrachan? Had he been laughed at, to adopt the Freudian theory, in his cradle by a pretty girl? For even in his cradle the professor, I thought, could not have been an attractive child. Whatever the reason, the professor was made to look very angry and very ugly in my sketch, as he wrote his great book upon the mental, moral, and physical inferiority of women. Drawing pictures was an idle way of finishing an unprofitable morning's work. Yet it is in our idleness, in our dreams, that the submerged truth sometimes comes to the top. A very elementary exercise in psychology, not to be dignified by the name of psycho-analysis, showed me, on looking at my notebook, that the sketch of the angry professor had been made in anger. Anger had snatched my pencil while I dreamt. But what was anger doing there? Interest, confusion, amusement, boredom—all these emotions I could trace and name as they succeeded each other throughout the morning. Had anger, the black snake, been lurking among them? Yes, said the sketch, anger had. It referred me unmistakably to the one book, to the one phrase, which had roused the demon; it was the professor's statement about the mental, moral, and physical inferiority of women. My heart had leapt. My cheeks had burnt. I had flushed with anger. There was nothing specially remarkable, however foolish, in that. One does not like to be told that one is naturally the inferior of a little man—I looked at the student next me—who breathes hard, wears a ready-made tie, and has not shaved this fortnight. One has certain foolish vanities. It is only human nature, I reflected, and began drawing cartwheels and circles over the angry professor's face till he looked like a burning bush or a flaming comet—anyhow, an apparition without human semblance or significance. The professor was nothing now but a faggot burning on the top of Hampstead Heath. Soon my own anger was explained and done with; but curiosity remained. How explain the anger of the professors? Why were they angry? For when it came to analysing the impression left by these books there was always an element of heat. This heat took many forms; it showed itself in satire, in sentiment, in curiosity, in reprobation. But there was another element which was often present and could not immediately be identified. Anger, I called it. But it was anger that had gone underground and mixed itself with all kinds of other emotions. To judge from its odd effects, it was anger disguised and complex, not anger simple and open.

6   Whatever the reason, all these books, I thought, surveying the pile on the desk, are worthless for my purposes. They were worthless scientifically, that is to say, though humanly they were full of instruction, interest, boredom, and very queer facts about the habits of the Fiji islanders. They had been written in the red light of emotion and not in the white light of truth. Therefore they must be returned to the central desk and restored each to his own cell in the enormous honeycomb. All that I had retrieved from that morning's work had been the one fact of anger. The professors—I lumped them together thus—were angry. But why, I asked myself, having returned the books, why, I repeated, standing under the colonnade among the pigeons and the prehistoric canoes, why are they angry? And, asking myself this question, I strolled off to find a place for luncheon. What is the real nature of what I call for the moment their anger? I asked. Here was a puzzle that would last all the time that it takes to be served with food in a small restaurant somewhere near the British Museum. Some previous luncher had left the lunch edition of the evening paper on a chair, and, waiting to be served, I began idly reading the headlines. A ribbon of very large letters ran across the page. Somebody had made a big score in South Africa. Lesser ribbons announced that Sir Austen Chamberlain was at Geneva. A meat axe with human hair on it had been found in a cellar, Mr. Justice—commented in the Divorce Courts upon the Shamelessness of Women. Sprinkled about the paper were other pieces of news. A film actress had been lowered from a peak in California and hung suspended in mid-air. The weather was going to be foggy. The most transient visitor to this planet, I thought, who picked up this paper could not fail to be aware, even from this scattered testimony, that England is under the rule of a partriarchy. Nobody in their senses could fail to detect the dominance of the professor. His was the power and the money and the influence. He was the proprietor of the paper and its editor and sub-editor. He was the Foreign Secretary and the Judge. He was the cricketer; he owned the racehorses and the yachts. He was the director of the company that pays two hundred per cent to its shareholders. He left millions to charities and colleges that were ruled by himself. He suspended the film actress in mid-air. He will decide if the hair on the meat axe is human; he it is who will acquit or convict the murderer, and hang him, or let him go free. With the exception of the fog he seemed to control everything. Yet he was angry. I knew that he was angry by this token. When I read what he wrote about women I thought, not of what he was saying, but of himself. When an arguer argues dispassionately he thinks only of the argument; and the reader cannot help thinking of the

argument too. If he had written dispassionately about women, had used indisputable proofs to establish his argument and had shown no trace of wishing that the result should be one thing rather than another, one would not have been angry either. One would have accepted the fact, as one accepts the fact that a pea is green or a canary yellow. So be it, I should have said. But I had been angry because he was angry. Yet it seemed absurd, I thought, turning over the evening paper, that a man with all this power should be angry. Or is anger, I wondered, somehow, the familiar, the attendant sprite on power? Rich people, for example, are often angry because they suspect that the poor want to seize their wealth. The professors, or patriarchs, as it might be more accurate to call them, might be angry for that reason partly, but partly for one that lies a little less obviously on the surface. Possibly they were not "angry" at all; often, indeed, they were admiring, devoted, exemplary in the relations of private life. Possibly when the professor insisted a little too emphatically upon the inferiority of women, he was concerned not with their inferiority, but with his own superiority. That was what he was protecting rather hot-headedly and with too much emphasis, because it was a jewel to him of the rarest price. Life for both sexes—and I looked at them, shouldering their way along the pavement—is arduous, difficult, a perpetual struggle. It calls for gigantic courage and strength. More than anything, perhaps, creatures of illusion as we are, it calls for confidence in oneself. Without self-confidence we are as babes in the cradle. And how can we generate this imponderable quality, which is yet so invaluable, most quickly? By thinking that other people are inferior to oneself. By feeling that one has some innate superiority—it may be wealth, or rank, a straight nose, or the portrait of a grandfather by Romney—for there is no end to the pathetic devices of the human imagination—over other people. Hence the enormous importance to a patriarch who has to conquer, who has to rule, of feeling that great numbers of people, half the human race indeed, are by nature inferior to himself. It must indeed be one of the chief sources of his power. But let me turn the light of this observation on to real life, I thought. Does it help to explain some of those psychological puzzles that one notes in the margin of daily life? Does it explain my astonishment the other day when Z, most humane, most modest of men, taking up some book by Rebecca West and reading a passage in it, exclaimed, "The arrant feminist! She says that men are snobs!" The exclamation, to me so surprising—for why was Miss West an arrant feminist for making a possibly true if uncomplimentary statement about the other sex?—was not merely the cry of wounded vanity; it was a protest against some infringement of his power to believe in himself. Women have served all these centuries as looking-glasses possessing the magic and delicious power of reflecting the figure of man at twice its natural size. Without that power probably the earth would still be swamp and jungle. The glories of all our wars would be unknown. We should still be scratching the outlines of deer on the remains of mutton bones and bartering flints for sheepskins or whatever simple ornament took our unsophisticated taste. Supermen and Fingers of Destiny would never have existed. The Czar and the Kaiser would never have worn their crowns or lost them. Whatever may be their use in civilised societies, mirrors are essential to all violent and heroic action. That is why Napoleon and Mussolini both insist so emphatically upon the inferiority of women, for if they were not inferior, they would cease to enlarge. That serves to explain in part the necessity that women so often are to men. And it serves to explain how restless they are under her criticism; how impossible it is for her to say to them this book is bad, this picture is feeble, or whatever it may be, without giving far more pain and rousing far more anger than a man would do who gave the same criticism. For if she begins to tell the truth, the figure in the looking-glass shrinks; his fitness for life is diminished. How is he to go on giving judgement, civilising natives, making laws, writing books, dressing up, and speechifying at banquets, unless he can see himself at breakfast and at dinner at least twice the size he really is? So I reflected, crumbling my bread and stirring my coffee and now and again looking at the people in the street. The looking-glass vision is of supreme importance because it charges the vitality; it stimulates the nervous system. Take it away and man may die, like the drug fiend deprived of his cocaine. Under the spell of that illusion, I thought, looking out of the window, half the people on the pavement are striding to work. They put on their hats and coats in the morning under its agreeable rays. They start the day confident, braced, believing themselves desired at Miss Smith's tea party; they say to themselves as they go into the room, I am the superior of half the people here, and it is thus that they speak with that self-confidence, that self-assurance, which have had such profound consequences in public life and lead to such curious notes in the margin of the private mind.

7   But these contributions to the dangerous and fascinating subject of the psychology of the other sex—it is one, I hope, that you will investigate when you have five hundred a year of your own—were interrupted by the necessity of paying the bill. It came to five shillings and ninepence. I gave the waiter a ten-shilling note and he went to bring me change. There was another ten-shilling note in my purse; I noticed it, because it is a fact that still takes my breath away—the power of my purse to breed ten-shilling notes automatically. I open it and there they are. Society gives me chicken and coffee, bed and lodging, in return for a certain number of pieces of paper which were left me by an aunt, for no other reason than that I share her name.

8   My aunt, Mary Beton, I must tell you, died by a fall from her horse when she was riding out to take the air in Bombay. The news of my legacy reached me one night about the same time that the act was passed that gave votes to women. A solicitor's letter fell into the post-box and when I opened it I found that she had left me five hundred pounds a year for ever. Of the two—the vote and the money—the money, I own, seemed infinitely the more important. Before that I had made my living by cadging odd jobs from newpapers, by reporting a donkey show here or a wedding there; I had earned a few pounds by addressing envelopes, reading to old ladies, making artificial flowers, teaching the alphabet to small children in a kindergarten. Such were the chief occupations that were open to women before 1918. I need not, I am afraid, describe in any detail the hardness of the work, for you know perhaps women

who have done it; nor the difficulty of living on the money when it was earned, for you may have tried. But what still remains with me as a worse infliction than either was the poison of fear and bitterness which those days bred in me. To begin with, always to be doing work that one did not wish to do, and to do it like a slave, flattering and fawning, not always necessarily perhaps, but it seemed necessary and the stakes were too great to run risks; and then the thought of that one gift which it was death to hide—a small one but dear to the possessor—perishing and with it myself, my soul—all this became like a rust eating away the bloom of the spring, destroying the tree at its heart. However, as I say, my aunt died; and whenever I change a ten-shilling note a little of that rust and corrosion is rubbed off; fear and bitterness go. Indeed I thought, slipping the silver into my purse, it is remarkable, remembering the bitterness of those days, what a change of temper a fixed income will bring about. No force in the world can take from me my five hundred pounds. Food, house, and clothing are mine for ever. Therefore not merely do effort and labour cease, but also hatred and bitterness. I need not hate any man; he cannot hurt me. I need not flatter any man; he has nothing to give me. So imperceptibly I found myself adopting a new attitude towards the other half of the human race. It was absurd to blame any class or any sex, as a whole. Great bodies of people are never responsible for what they do. They are driven by instincts which are not within their control. They too, the patriarchs, the professors, had endless difficulties, terrible drawbacks to contend with. Their education had been in some ways as faulty as my own. It had bred in them defects as great. True, they had money and power, but only at the cost of harbouring in their breasts an eagle, a vulture, for ever tearing the liver out and plucking at the lungs—the instinct for possession, the rage for acquisition which drives them to desire other people's fields and goods perpetually; to make frontiers and flags; battleships and poison gas; to offer up their own lives and their children's lives. Walk through the Admiralty Arch (I had reached that monument), or any other avenue given up to trophies and cannon, and reflect upon the kind of glory celebrated there. Or watch in the spring sunshine the stockbroker and the great barrister going indoors to make money and more money and more money when it is a fact that five hundred pounds a year will keep one alive in the sunshine. These are unpleasant instincts to harbour, I reflected. They are bred of the conditions of life; of the lack of civilisation, I thought, looking at the statue of the Duke of Cambridge, and in particular at the feathers in his cocked hat, with a fixity that they have scarcely ever received before. And, as I realised these drawbacks, by degrees fear and bitterness modified themselves into pity and toleration; and then in a year or two, pity and toleration went, and the greatest release of all came, which is freedom to think of things in themselves. That building, for example, do I like it or not? Is that picture beautiful or not? Is that in my opinion a good book or a bad? Indeed my aunt's legacy unveiled the sky to me, and substituted for the large and imposing figure of a gentleman, which Milton recommended for my perpetual adoration, a view of the open sky.

So thinking, so speculating, I found my way back to my house by the river. 9
Lamps were being lit and an indescribable change had come over London since

the morning hour. It was as if the great machine after labouring all day had made with our help a few yards of something very exciting and beautiful—fiery fabric flashing with red eyes, a tawny monster roaring with hot breath. Even the wind seemed flung like a flag as it lashed the houses and rattled the hoardings.

10   In my little street, however, domesticity prevailed. The house painter was descending his ladder; the nursemaid was wheeling the perambulator carefully in and out back to nursery tea; the coalheaver was folding his empty sacks on top of each other; the woman who keeps the green-grocer's shop was adding up the day's takings with her hands in red mittens. But so engrossed was I with the problem you have laid upon my shoulders that I could not see even these usual sights without referring them to one centre. I thought how much harder it is now than it must have been even a century ago to say which of these employments is the higher, the more necessary. Is it better to be a coal-heaver or a nursemaid; is the charwoman who has brought up eight children of less value to the world than the barrister who has made a hundred thousand pounds? It is useless to ask such questions; for nobody can answer them. Not only do the comparative values of the charwomen and lawyers rise and fall from decade to decade, but we have no rods with which to measure them even as they are at the moment. I had been foolish to ask my professor to furnish me with "indisputable proofs" or this or that in his argument about women. Even if one could state the value of any one gift at the moment, those values will change; in a century's time very possibly they will have changed completely. Moreover, in a hundred years, I thought, reaching my own doorstep, women will have ceased to be the protected sex. Logically they will take part in all the activities and exertions that were once denied them. The nursemaid will heave coal. The shop-woman will drive an engine. All assumptions founded on the facts observed when women were the protected sex will have disappeared—as, for example (here a squad of soldiers marched down the street), that women and clergymen and gardeners live longer than other people. Remove that protection, expose them to the same exertions and activities, make them soldiers and sailors and engine-drivers and dock labourers, and will not women die off so much younger, so much quicker, than men that one will say, "I saw a woman today," as one used to say, "I saw an aeroplane." Anything may happen when womanhood has ceased to be a protected occupation, I thought, opening the door. But what bearing has all this upon the subject of my paper, Women and Fiction? I asked, going indoors.

WRITING AND DISCUSSION QUESTIONS

Informative

1. Chapter two, reprinted here, asks what the effect of poverty is on fiction and on women. How does the narrator's shift to the British Museum from Oxbridge move the reader to the question of poverty? When she looks for books on women and poverty, what does she find?

2. Who is Professor Von X, and why does he make the narrator so angry? What is the basis for his apparent anger? How would the world be different without the power of patriarchy?
3. The narrator has come into a modest inheritance. How has that changed her life? What are the costs of money and power, that is, what disadvantages of these sources of dominance does the narrator identify?

Persuasive

1. Summarize Woolf's argument for feminism, basing it on the need for a bank account and a room of one's own. Develop the symbol of the money and room so that you see the implications of these two phenomena. Argue that money and personal work space are or are not what women need in order to develop their fullest potentialities.
2. How are males depicted, especially males like Von X? Argue that the descriptions are or are not fair. Can you imagine other reasons why women may not have written, especially in preindustrial societies where women were more bound to the home?
3. Examine Woolf's style, that is, her use of anecdote, literary analysis, fantasy, symbol, history, case study, and reason. Argue that her approach projects a more or less effective argument than would a straightforward expository approach.

Personal

1. Speculate on the women you know who do or do not have rooms of their own, figuratively speaking. What are the difficulties, for women, of having both marriage and career? What inequalities tend to persist in homes where men and women try to share household "duties" and careers?
2. How current do you think Woolf's picture of Professor Von X is, that is, is the kind of man represented by Von X a thriving species, an extinct species, or something in between?
3. Oxbridge University, Woolf's symbol of education, access, and upward mobility, is the great barrier to the achievement of women's aspirations, because it is strictly a male domain. Do you think that gender barriers have been removed from our educational institutions? Consider possible gender bias in testing, federal or local support for athletic teams, and sexist behavior by male faculty.

▼

ALICE MUNRO, "THE OFFICE" FROM *DANCE OF THE HAPPY SHADES*

The story that follows makes a wonderful companion to Woolf's *A Room of One's Own*. "The Office" is about one modern woman's struggle to find a place of her own and about a man who seems troubled by her insistence on independence. Thus, it suggests that the program women have called for is not so easily achieved. Alice

Munro (1931–), its author, is best known for her short stories that explore the psychological dimensions of the lives of ordinary people caught in very ordinary situations. She writes about Canadians living mostly in small towns, attempting to sort out the confusing roles imposed on them in an advanced industrial society.

Munro was raised in Wingham, Ontario, where she first came to know the lives of the rural people who would fill her stories. She attended the University of Western Ontario, where she published her first stories.

▼

The Office
ALICE MUNRO

1   The solution to my life occurred to me one evening while I was ironing a shirt. It was simple but audacious. I went into the living room where my husband was watching television and I said, "I think I ought to have an office."

2   It sounded fantastic, even to me. What do I want an office for? I have a house; it is pleasant and roomy and has a view of the sea; it provides appropriate places for eating and sleeping, and having baths and conversations with one's friends. Also I have a garden; there is no lack of space.

3   No. But here comes the disclosure which is not easy for me: I am a writer. That does not sound right. Too presumptuous; phony, or at least unconvincing. Try again. I write. Is that better? I *try* to write. That makes it worse. Hypocritical humility. Well then?

4   It doesn't matter. However I put it, the words create their space of silence, the delicate moment of exposure. But people are kind, the silence is quickly absorbed by the solicitude of friendly voices, crying variously, how wonderful, and good for *you*, and well, that *is* intriguing. And what do you write, they inquire with spirit. Fiction, I reply, bearing my humiliation by this time with ease, even a suggestion of flippancy, which was not always mine, and again, again, the perceptible circles of dismay are smoothed out by such ready and tactful voices—which have however exhausted their stock of consolatory phrases, and can say only, "*Ah!*"

5   So this is what I want an office for (I said to my husband): to write in. I was at once aware that it sounded like a finicky requirement, a piece of rare self-indulgence. To write, as everyone knows, you need a typewriter, or at least a pencil, some paper, a table and chair; I have all these things in a corner of my bedroom. But now I want an office as well.

6   And I was not even sure that I was going to write in it, if we come down to that. Maybe I would sit and stare at the wall; even that prospect was not unpleasant to me. It was really the sound of the word "office" that I liked, its sound of dignity and peace. And purposefulness and importance. But I did not

care to mention this to my husband, so I launched instead into a high-flown explanation which went, as I remember, like this:

A house is all right for a man to work in. He brings his work into the house,   7
a place is cleared for it; the house rearranges itself as best it can around him. Everybody recognizes that his work *exists*. He is not expected to answer the telephone, to find things that are lost, to see why the children are crying, or feed the cat. He can shut his door. Imagine (I said) a mother shutting her door, and the children knowing she is behind it; why, the very thought of it is outrageous to them. A woman who sits staring into space, into a country that is not her husband's or her children's is likewise known to be an offence against nature. So a house is not the same for a woman. She is not someone who walks into the house, to make use of it, and will walk out again. She *is* the house; there is no separation possible.

(And this is true, though as usual when arguing for something I am afraid I   8
do not deserve, I put it in too emphatic and emotional terms. At certain times, perhaps on long spring evenings, still rainy and sad, with the cold bulbs in bloom and a light too mild for promise drifting over the sea, I have opened the windows and felt the house shrink back into wood and plaster and those humble elements of which it is made, and the life in it subside, leaving me exposed, empty-handed, but feeling a fierce and lawless quiver of freedom, of loneliness too harsh and perfect for me now to bear. Then I know how the rest of the time I am sheltered and encumbered, how insistently I am warmed and bound.)

"Go ahead, if you can find one cheap enough," is all my husband had to   9
say to this. He is not like me, he does not really want explanations. That the heart of another person is a closed book, is something you will hear him say frequently, and without regret.

Even then I did not think it was something that could be accomplished. Per-   10
haps at bottom it seemed to me too improper a wish to be granted. I could almost more easily have wished for a mink coat, for a diamond necklace; these are things women do obtain. The children, learning of my plans, greeted them with the most dashing skepticism and unconcern. Nevertheless I went down to the shopping centre which is two blocks from where I live; there I had noticed for several months, and without thinking how they could pertain to me, a couple of For Rent signs in the upstairs windows of a building that housed a drugstore and a beauty parlour. As I went up the stairs I had a feeling of complete unreality; surely renting was a complicated business, in the case of offices; you did not simply knock on the door of the vacant premises and wait to be admitted; it would have to be done through channels. Also, they would want too much money.

As it turned out, I did not even have to knock. A woman came out of one of   11
the empty offices, dragging a vacuum cleaner, and pushing it with her foot, towards the open door across the hall, which evidently led to an apartment in the rear of the building. She and her husband lived in this apartment; their name was Malley; and it was indeed they who owned the building and rented out the offices. The rooms she had just been vacuuming were, she told me, fit-

ted out for a dentist's office, and so would not interest me, but she would show me the other place. She invited me into her aprtment while she put away the vacuum and got her key. Her husband, she said with a sigh I could not interpret, was not at home.

12   Mrs. Malley was a black-haired, delicate-looking woman, perhaps in her early forties, slatternly but still faintly appealing, with such arbitrary touches of femininity as the thin line of bright lipstick, the pink feather slippers on obviously tender and swollen feet. She had the swaying passivity, the air of exhaustion and muted apprehension, that speaks of a life spent in close attention on a man who is by turns vigorous, crotchety and dependent. How much of this I saw at first, how much decided on later is of course impossible to tell. But I did think that she would have no children, the stress of her life, whatever it was, did not allow it, and in this I was not mistaken.

13   The room where I waited was evidently a combination living room and office. The first things I noticed were models of ships—galleons, clippers, Queen Marys—sitting on the tables, the window sills, the television. Where there were no ships there were potted plants and a clutter of what are sometimes called "masculine" ornaments—china deer heads, bronze horses, huge ashtrays of heavy, veined, shiny material. On the walls were framed photographs and what might have been diplomas. One photo showed a poodle and a bulldog, dressed in masculine and feminine clothing, and assuming with dismal embarrassment a pose of affection. Written across it was "Old Friends." But the room was really dominated by a portrait, with its own light and a gilded frame; it was of a good-looking, fair-haired man in middle age, sitting behind a desk, wearing a business suit and looking pre-eminently prosperous, rosy and agreeable. Here again, it is probably hindsight on my part that points out that in the portrait there is evident also some uneasiness, some lack of faith the man has in this role, a tendency he has to spread himself too bountifully and insistently, which for all anyone knows may lead to disaster.

14   Never mind the Malleys. As soon as I saw that office, I wanted it. It was larger than I needed, being divided in such a way that it would be suitable for a doctor's office. (We had a chiropractor in here but he left, says Mrs. Malley in her regretful but uninformative way.) The walls were cold and bare, white with a little grey, to cut the glare for the eyes. Since there were no doctors in evidence, nor had been, as Mrs. Malley freely told me, for some time, I offered twenty-five dollars a month. She said she would have to speak to her husband.

15   The next time I came my offer was agreed upon, and I met Mr. Malley in the flesh. I explained, as I had already done to his wife, that I did not want to make use of my office during regular business hours, but during the weekends and sometimes in the evening. He asked me what I would use it for, and I told him, not without wondering first whether I ought to say I did stenography.

He absorbed the information with good humour. "Ah, you're a writer."

"Well yes. I write."

"Then we'll do our best to see you're comfortable here," he said expansively. "I'm a great man for hobbies myself. All these ship-models, I do them in my spare time, they're a blessing for the nerves. People need an occupation for their nerves. I daresay you're the same."

"Something the same," I said, resolutely agreeable, even relieved that he saw my behaviour in this hazy and tolerant light. At least he did not ask me, as I half-expected, who was looking after the children, and did my husband approve? Ten years, maybe fifteen, had greatly softened, spread and defeated the man in the picture. His hips and thighs had now a startling accumulation of fat, causing him to move with a sigh, a cushiony settling of flesh, a ponderous matriarchal discomfort. His hair and eyes had faded, his features blurred, and the affable, predatory expression had collapsed into one of troubling humility and chronic mistrust. I did not look at him. I had not planned, in taking an office, to take on the responsibility of knowing any more human beings.

On the weekend I moved in, without the help of my family, who would have *16* been kind. I brought my typewriter and a card table and chair, also a little wooden table on which I set a hot plate, a kettle, a jar of instant coffee, a spoon and a yellow mug. That was all. I brooded with satisfaction on the bareness of my walls, the cheap dignity of my essential furnishings, the remarkable lack of things to dust, wash or polish.

The sight was not so pleasing to Mr. Malley. He knocked on my door soon *17* after I was settled and said that he wanted to explain a few things to me— about unscrewing the light in the outer room, which I would not need, about the radiator and how to work the awning outside the window. He looked around at everything with gloom and mystification and said it was an awfully uncomfortable place for a lady.

"It's perfectly all right for me," I said, not as discouragingly as I would have liked to, because I always have a tendency to placate people whom I dislike for no good reason, or simply do not want to know. I make elaborate offerings of courtesy sometimes, in the foolish hope that they will go away and leave me alone.

"What you want is a nice easy chair to sit in, while you're waiting for inspiration to hit. I've got a chair down in the basement, all kinds of stuff down there since my mother passed on last year. There's a bit of carpet rolled up in a corner down there, it isn't doing anybody any good. We could get this place fixed up so's it'd be a lot more homelike for you."

But really, I said, but really I like it as it is.

"If you want to run up some curtains, I'd pay you for the material. Place needs a touch of colour, I'm afraid you'll get morbid sitting in here."

Oh, no, I said, and laughed, I'm sure I won't. *18*

"It'd be a different story if you was a man. A woman wants things a bit cosier."

So I got up and went to the window and looked down into the empty Sunday *19* street through the slats of the Venetian blind, to avoid the accusing vulnerability of his fat face and I tried out a cold voice that is to be heard frequently in my thoughts but has great difficulty getting out of my cowardly mouth. "Mr. Malley, please don't bother me about this any more. I said it suits me. I have everything I want. Thanks for showing me about the light."

20   The effect was devastating enough to shame me. "I certainly wouldn't dream of bothering you," he said, with precision of speech and aloof sadness. "I merely made these suggestions for your comfort. Had I realized I was in your way, I would of left some time ago." When he had gone I felt better, even a little exhilarated at my victory though still ashamed of how easy it had been. I told myself that he would have had to be discouraged sooner or later, it was better to have it over with at the beginning.

21   The following weekend he knocked on my door. His expression of humility was exaggerated, almost enough so to seem mocking, yet in another sense it was real and I felt unsure of myself.

"I won't take up a minute of your time," he said. "I never meant to be a nuisance. I just wanted to tell you I'm sorry I offended you last time and I apologize. Here's a little present if you will accept it."

He was carrying a plant whose name I did not know; it had thick, glossy leaves and grew out of a pot wrapped lavishly in pink and silver foil.

"There," he said, arranging this plant in a corner of my room. "I don't want any bad feelings with you and me. I'll take the blame. And I thought, maybe she won't accept furnishings, but what's the matter with a nice little plant, that'll brighten things up for you."

22   It was not possible for me, at this moment, to tell him that I did not want a plant. I hate house plants. He told me how to take care of it, how often to water it and so on; I thanked him. There was nothing else I could do, and I had the unpleasant feeling that beneath his offering of apologies and gifts he was well aware of this and in some way gratified by it. He kept on talking, using the words *bad feelings, offended, apologize.* I tried once to interrupt, with the idea of explaining that I had made provision for an area in my life where good feelings, or bad, did not enter in, that between him and me, in fact, it was not necessary that there be any feelings at all; but this struck me as a hopeless task. How could I confront, in the open, this craving for intimacy? Besides, the plant in its shiny paper had confused me.

"How's the writing progressing?" he said, with an air of putting all our unfortunate differences behind him.

"Oh, about as usual."

"Well if you ever run out of things to write about, I got a barrelful." Pause. "But I guess I'm just eatin' into your time here," he said with a kind of painful buoyancy. This was a test, and I did not pass it. I smiled, my eyes held by that magnificent plant; I said it was all right.

"I was just thinking about the fellow was in here before you. Chiropractor. You could of wrote a book about him."

23   I assumed a listening position, my hands no longer hovering over the keys. If cowardice and insincerity are big vices of mine, curiosity is certainly another.

"He had a good practice built up here. The only trouble was, he gave more adjustments than was listed in the book of chiropractory. Oh, he was adjusting right and left. I came in here after he moved out, and what do you think I found? Soundproofing! This whole room was soundproofed, to enable him to make his adjustments without disturbing anybody. This very room you're sitting writing your stories in.

"First we knew of it was a lady knocked on my door one day wanted me to provide her with a passkey to his office. He'd locked his door against her.

"I guess he just got tired of treating her particular case. I guess he figured he'd been knocking away at it long enough. Lady well on in years, you know, and him just a young man. He had a nice young wife too and a couple of the prettiest children you ever would want to see. Filthy some of the things that go on in this world."

It took me some time to realize that he told this story not simply as a piece   *24* of gossip, but as something a writer would be particularly interested to hear. Writing and lewdness had a vague delicious connection in his mind. Even this notion, however, seemed so wishful, so infantile, that it struck me as a waste of energy to attack it. I knew now I must avoid hurting him for my own sake, not for his. It had been a great mistake to think that a little roughness would settle things.

The next present was a teapot. I insisted that I drank only coffee and told   *25* him to give it to his wife. He said that tea was better for the nerves and that he had known right away I was a nervous person, like himself. The teapot was covered with gilt and roses and I knew that it was not cheap, in spite of its extreme hideousness. I kept it on my table. I also continued to care for the plant, which thrived obscenely in the corner of my room. I could not decide what else to do. He bought me a wastebasket, a fancy one with Chinese mandarins on all eight sides; he got a foam rubber cushion for my chair. I despised myself for submitting to this blackmail. I did not even really pity him; it was just that I could not turn away, I could not turn away from that obsequious hunger. And he knew himself my tolerance was bought; in a way he must have hated me for it.

When he lingered in my office now he told me stories of himself. It occurred *26* to me that he was revealing his life to me in the hope that I would write it down. Of course he had probably revealed it to plenty of people for no particular reason, but in my case there seemed to be a special, even desperate necessity. His life was a series of calamities, as people's lives often are; he had been let down by people he had trusted, refused help by those he had depended on, betrayed by the very friends to whom he had given kindness and material help. Other people, mere strangers and passersby, had taken time to torment him gratuitously, in novel and inventive ways. On occasion, his very life had been threatened. Moreover his wife was a difficulty, her health being poor and her temperament unstable; what was he to do? You see how it is, he said, lifting his hands, but I live. He looked to me to say yes.

I took to coming up the stairs on tiptoe, trying to turn my key without mak- *27* ing a noise; this was foolish of course because I could not muffle my typewriter. I actually considered writing in longhand, and wished repeatedly for the evil chiropractor's soundproofing. I told my husband my problem and he said it was not a problem at all. Tell him you're busy, he said. As a matter of fact I did tell him; every time he came to my door, always armed with a little gift or an errand, he asked me how I was and I said that today I was busy. Ah, then, he said, as he eased himself through the door, he would not keep me a minute. And all the time, as I have said, he knew what was going on in my mind, how I weakly longed to be rid of him. He knew but could not afford to care.

28   One evening after I had gone home I discovered that I had left at the office a letter I had intended to post, and so I went back to get it. I saw from the street that the light was on in the room where I worked. Then I saw him bending over the card table. Of course, he came in at night and read what I had written! He heard me at the door, and when I came in he was picking up my wastebasket, saying he thought he would just tidy things up for me. He went out at once. I did not say anthing, but found myself trembling with anger and gratification. To have found a just cause was a wonder, an unbearable relief.

29   Next time he came to my door I had locked it on the inside. I knew his step, his chummy cajoling knock. I continued typing loudly, but not uninterruptedly, so he would know I heard. He called my name, as if I was playing a trick; I bit my lips together not to answer. Unreasonably as ever, guilt assailed me but I typed on. That day I saw the earth was dry around the roots of the plant; I let it alone.

30   I was not prepared for what happened next. I found a note taped to my door, which said that Mr. Malley would be obliged if I would step into his office. I went at once to get it over with. He sat at his desk surrounded by obscure evidences of his authority; he looked at me from a distance, as one who was now compelled to see me in a new and sadly unfavourable light; the embarrassment which he showed seemed not for himself, but me. He started off by saying, with a rather stagey reluctance, that he had known of course when he took me in that I was a writer.

"I didn't let that worry me, though I have heard things about writers and artists and that type of person that didn't strike me as very encouraging. You know the sort of thing I mean."

This was something new; I could not think what it might lead to.

"Now you came to me and said, Mr. Malley, I want a place to write in. I believed you. I gave it to you. I didn't ask any questions. That's the kind of person I am. But you know the more I think about it, well, the more I am inclined to wonder."

"Wonder what?" I said.

31   "And your own attitude, that hasn't helped to put my mind at ease. Locking yourself in and refusing to answer your door. That's not a normal way for a person to behave. Not if they got nothing to hide. No more than it's normal for a young woman, says she has a husband and kids, to spend her time rattling away on a typewriter."

"But I didn't think that—"

He lifted his hand, a forgiving gesture. "Now all I ask is, that you be open and aboveboard with me, I think I deserve that much, and if you are using that office for any other purposes, or at any other times than you let on, and having your friends or whoever they are up to see you—"

"I don't know what you mean."

"And another thing, you claim to be a writer. Well I read quite a bit of material, and I never have seen your name in print. Now maybe you write under some other name?"

"No," I said.   32

"Well I don't doubt there are writers whose names I haven't heard," he said genially. "We'll let that pass. Just you give me your word of honour there won't be any more deceptions, or carryings-on, et cetera, in that office you occupy—"

My anger was delayed somehow, blocked off by a stupid incredulity. I only   33
knew enough to get up and walk down the hall, his voice trailing after me, and lock the door. I thought—I must go. But after I had sat down in my own room, my work in front of me, I thought again how much I liked this room, how well I worked in it, and I decided not to be forced out. After all, I felt, the struggle between us had reached a deadlock. I could refuse to open the door, refuse to look at his notes, refuse to speak to him when we met. My rent was paid in advance and if I left now it was unlikely that I would get any refund. I resolved not to care. I had been taking my manuscript home every night, to prevent his reading it, and now it seemed that even this precaution was beneath me. What did it matter if he read it, any more than if the mice scampered over it in the dark? Several times after this I found notes on my door. I intended not to read them, but I always did. His accusations grew more specific. He had heard voices in my room. My behaviour was disturbing his wife when she tried to take her afternoon nap. (I never came in the afternoons, except on weekends.) He had found a whisky bottle in the garbage.

I wondered a good deal about that chiropractor. It was not comfortable to   34
see how the legends of Mr. Malley's life were built up.

As the notes grew more virulent our personal encounters ceased. Once or   35
twice I saw his stooped, sweatered back disappearing as I came into the hall. Gradually our relationship passed into something that was entirely fantasy. He accused me now, by note, of being intimate with people from *Numero Cinq*. This was a coffee-house in the neighborhood, which I imagine he invoked for symbolic purposes. I felt that nothing much more would happen now, the notes would go on, their contents becoming possibly more grotesque and so less likely to affect me.

He knocked on my door on a Sunday morning, about eleven o'clock. I had   36
just come in and taken my coat off and put my kettle on the hot plate.

This time it was another face, remote and transfigured, that shone with the   37
cold light of intense joy at discovering the proofs of sin.

"I wonder," he said with emotion, "if you would mind following me down the hall?"

I followed him. The light was on in the washroom. This washroom was mine and no one else used it, but he had not given me a key for it and it was always open. He stopped in front of it, pushed back the door and stood with his eyes cast down, expelling his breath discreetly.

"Now who done that?" he said, in a voice of pure sorrow.

38   The walls above the toilet and above the washbasin were covered with drawings and comments of the sort you see sometimes in public washrooms on the beach, and in town hall lavatories in the little decaying towns where I grew up. They were done with a lipstick, as they usually are. Someone must have got up here the night before, I thought, possibly some of the gang who always loafed and cruised around the shopping centre on Saturday nights.

"It should have been locked," I said, coolly and firmly as if thus to remove myself from the scene. "It's quite a mess."

"It sure is. It's pretty filthy language, in my book. Maybe it's just a joke to your friends, but it isn't to me. Not to mention the art work. That's a nice thing to see when you open a door on your own premises in the morning."

I said, "I believe lipstick will wash off."

"I'm just glad I didn't have my wife see a thing like this. Upsets a woman that's had a nice bringing up. Now why don't you ask your friends up here to have a party with their pails and brushes? I'd like to have a look at the people with that kind of a sense of humour."

39   I turned to walk away and he moved heavily in front of me.

"I don't think there's any question how these decorations found their way onto my walls."

"If you're trying to say I had anything to do with it," I said, quite flatly and wearily, "you must be crazy."

"How did they get there then? Whose lavatory is this? Eh, whose?"

"There isn't any key to it. Anybody can come up here and walk in. Maybe some kids off the street came up here and did it last night after I went home, how do I know?"

40   "It's a shame the way the kids gets blamed for everything, when it's the elders that corrupts them. That's a thing you might do some thinking about, you know. There's laws. Obscenity laws. Applies to this sort of thing and literature too as I believe."

41   This is the first time I ever remember taking deep breaths, consciously, for purposes of self-control. I really wanted to murder him. I remember how soft and loathsome his face looked, with the eyes almost closed, nostrils extended to the soothing odour of righteousness, the odour of triumph. If this stupid thing had not happened, he would never have won. But he had. Perhaps he saw something in my face that unnerved him, even in this victorious moment, for he drew back to the wall, and began to say that actually, as a matter of fact, he had not really felt it was the sort of thing I personally would do, more the sort of thing that perhaps certain friends of mine—I got into my own room, shut the door.

42   The kettle was making a fearful noise, having almost boiled dry. I snatched it off the hot plate, pulled out the plug and stood for a moment choking on rage. This spasm passed and I did what I had to do. I put my typewriter and paper on the chair and folded the card table. I screwed the top tightly on the

instant coffee and put it and the yellow mug and the teaspoon into the bag in which I had brought them; it was still lying folded on the shelf. I wished childishly to take some vengeance on the potted plant, which sat in the corner with the flowery teapot, the wastebasket, the cushion, and—I forgot—the little plastic pencil sharpener behind it.

When I was taking things down to the car Mrs. Malley came. I had seen little of her since that first day. She did not seem upset, but practical and resigned. 43

"He is lying down," she said. "He is not himself."

She carried the bag with the coffee and the mug in it. She was so still I felt my anger leave me, to be replaced by an absorbing depression. 44

I have not yet found another office. I think that I will try again some day, but not yet. I have to wait at least until that picture fades that I see so clearly in my mind, though I never saw it in reality—Mr. Malley with his rags and brushes and a pail of soapy water, scrubbing in his clumsy way, his deliberately clumsy way, at the toilet walls, stooping with difficulty, breathing sorrowfully, arranging in his mind the bizarre but somehow never quite satisfactory narrative of yet another betrayal of trust. While I arrange words, and think it is my right to be rid of him. 45

WRITING AND DISCUSSION QUESTIONS

Informative

1. The narrator begins by saying "The solution to my life occurred to me one evening while I was ironing a shirt." This sentence seems to compact into one woman's life the problems addressed by the women's movement. In light of the whole story, to what problem do you think the narrator is referring when she talks about a solution? In what sense would an office be a solution to her life? If there is room at home, is not an office an unnecessary indulgence?
2. How does the narrator characterize herself in the story? What adjectives and adverbs lend insight into her reasons for moving out of the house?
3. What do you learn about Mr. Malley from his own room and office, as well as from the narrator's view of him, his wife, and the way he responds to the narrator? What is his view of women? How do you explain his gifts and the accusations he directs at the narrator?
4. Why does Malley break down in the story? How do you explain his increasingly violent behavior?

Persuasive

1. Argue for or against the position that the narrator, with "space" at home, needs an office outside the home.
2. Argue that Mr. Malley's gifts are or are not sincere tokens of his concern for the conditions under which the narrator works.
3. Argue that Mr. Malley is or is not just as much a victim as the narrator is.

Personal

1. One of the special burdens of women's liberation is that the liberated woman often chooses both to raise a family and to develop a career. What particular problems are attached to that dual lifestyle, as you have observed them in the story or in your own experience? Do you think sharing house work and child rearing with the husband is an effective way out of that dilemma?

2. Some readers see the story as an exploration of male jealousy of female creativity and of the male abhorrence of a woman not making a man the center of her world. Is this view consistent with your view of the story? Do you see a general relationship between psychological violence and physical violence?

▼

SUSAN GLASPELL, *TRIFLES*

Susan Glaspell (1882–1948), a modern-day Judith Shakespeare (the imaginary sister of Shakespeare Virginia Woolf invents in *A Room of One's Own*), wrote numerous plays, novels, and stories about the plight of women of her time. She was born in Davenport, Iowa, and was graduated from Drake University. Early in her career, in 1915, she organized the Provincetown Players, a theatrical troupe, with her husband George Cram Cook. *Trifles* was originally written for the group that performed in Provincetown. Other plays she wrote were *The Verge* (1921), a study of a disturbed woman driven insane, and *Alison's House*, which suggested the life of Emily Dickinson and won the Pulitzer Prize in 1930.

Trifles is a disturbing play about the murder of a withdrawn, but "decent," man and is disturbing not only because of the dark picture it draws of the men in the play, but also because of the actions of the women in taking the law into their own hands. Some critics have said that this is a play about women bonding in part because they "read" the world differently, and more accurately, than men. Others see in it the effects of isolation, a lack of community and love, and psychological violence. Glaspell's short story "A Jury of Her Peers" is a later prose version of the play reprinted here.

▼

Trifles
SUSAN GLASPELL

Scene

The kitchen in the now abandoned farm-house of John Wright, a gloomy kitchen, and left without having been put in order—unwashed pans under the sink, a loaf of bread outside the bread-box, a dish-towel on the table—other signs of incompleted work. At the rear the outer door opens and the

SHERIFF *comes in followed by the* COUNTY ATTORNEY *and* HALE. *The* SHERIFF *and* HALE *are men in middle life, the* COUNTY ATTORNEY *is a young man; all are much bundled up and go at once to the stove. They are followed by the two women— the Sheriff's wife first; she is a slight wiry woman, with a thin nervous face.* MRS. HALE *is larger and would ordinarily be called more comfortable looking, but she is disturbed now and looks fearfully about as she enters. The women have come in slowly, and stand close together near the door.*

COUNTY ATTORNEY *(rubbing his hands)* This feels good. Come up to the fire, ladies.

MRS. PETERS *(after taking a step forward)* I'm not—cold.

SHERIFF *(unbuttoning his overcoat and stepping away from the stove as if to mark the beginning of official business)* Now, Mr. Hale, before we move things about, you explain to Mr. Henderson just what you saw when you came here yesterday morning.

COUNTY ATTORNEY By the way, has anything been moved? Are things just as you left them yesterday?

SHERIFF *(looking about)* It's just the same. When it dropped below zero last night I thought I'd better send Frank out this morning to make a fire for us— no use getting pneumonia with a big case on, but I told him not to touch anything except the stove—and you know Frank.

COUNTY ATTORNEY Somebody should have been left here yesterday.

SHERIFF Oh—yesterday. When I had to send Frank to Morris Center for that man who went crazy—I want you to know I had my hands full yesterday. I knew you could get back from Omaha by to-day and as long as I went over everything here myself—

COUNTY ATTORNEY Well, Mr. Hale, tell just what happened when you came here yesterday morning.

HALE Harry and I had started to town with a load of potatoes. We came along the road from my place and as I got here I said, "I'm going to see if I can't get John Wright to go in with me on a party telephone." I spoke to Wright about it once before and he put me off, saying folks talked too much anyway, and all he asked was peace and quiet—I guess you know about how much he talked himself; but I thought maybe if I went to the house and talked about it before his wife, though I said to Harry that I didn't know as what his wife wanted made much difference to John—

COUNTY ATTORNEY Let's talk about that later, Mr. Hale. I do want to talk about that, but tell now just what happened when you got to the house.

HALE I didn't hear or see anything; I knocked at the door, and still it was all quiet inside. I knew they must be up, it was past eight o'clock. So I knocked again, and I thought I heard somebody say "Come in." I wasn't sure, I'm not sure yet, but I opened the door—this door *(indicating the door by which the two women are still standing)* and there in that rocker—*(pointing to it)* sat Mrs. Wright.

(They all look at the rocker.)

COUNTY ATTORNEY What—was she doing?

HALE She was rockin' back and forth. She had her apron in her hand and was kind of—pleating it.

COUNTY ATTORNEY And how did she—look?

HALE Well, she looked queer.

COUNTY ATTORNEY How do you mean—queer?

HALE Well, as if she didn't know what she was going to do next. And kind of done up.

COUNTY ATTORNEY How did she seem to feel about your coming?

HALE Why, I don't think she minded—one way or other. She didn't pay much attention. I said, "How do, Mrs. Wright, it's cold, aint it?" And she said "Is it?"—and went on kind of pleating at her apron. Well, I was surprised; she didn't ask me to come up to the stove, or to set down, but just sat there, not even looking at me, so I said, "I want to see John." And then she—laughed. I guess you would call it a laugh. I thought of Harry and the team outside, so I said a little sharp: "Can't I see John?" "No," she says, kind o'dull like. "Ain't he home?" says I. "Yes," says she, "he's home." "Then why can't I see him?" I asked her out of patience. "'Cause he's dead," says she. "Dead?" says I. She just nodded her head, not getting a bit excited, but rockin' back and forth. "Why—where is he?" says I, not knowing what to say. She just pointed upstairs—like that *(himself pointing to the room above)*. I got up, with the idea of going up there. I walked from there to here—then I says, "Why, what did he die of?" "He died of a rope around his neck," says she, and just went on pleatin' at her apron. Well, I went out and called Harry. I thought I might—need help. We went upstairs and there he was lyin'—

COUNTY ATTORNEY I think I'd rather have you go into that upstairs, where you can point it all out. Just go on now with the rest of the story.

HALE Well, my first thought was to get that rope off. It looked . . . *(Stops, his face twitches.)* . . . but Harry, he went up to him, and he said, "No, he's dead all right, and we'd better not touch anything." So we went back down stairs. She was still sitting that same way. "Has anybody been notified?" I asked. "No," says she, unconcerned. "Who did this, Mrs. Wright?" said Harry. He said it business-like—and she stopped pleatin' of her apron. "I don't know," she says. "You don't *know*?" says Harry. "No," says she. "Weren't you sleepin' in the bed with him?" says Harry. "Yes, says she, "but I was on the inside." "Somebody slipped a rope around his neck and strangled him and you didn't wake up?" says Harry. "I didn't wake up," she said after him. We must 'a looked as if we didn't see how that could be, for after a minute she said, "I sleep sound." Harry was going to ask her more questions, but I said maybe we ought to let her tell her story first to the coroner, or the sheriff, so Harry went fast as he could to Rivers' place, where there's a telephone.

COUNTY ATTORNEY And what did Mrs. Wright do when she knew that you had gone for the coroner?

HALE She moved from that chair to this over here . . . *(Pointing to a small chair in the corner.)* . . . and just sat there with her hands held together and looking down. I got a feeling that I ought to make some conversation, so I said

I had come in to see if John wanted to put in a telephone, and at that she started to laugh, and then she stopped and looked at me—scared. *(The* COUNTY ATTORNEY, *who has had his notebook out, makes a note.)* I dunno, maybe it wasn't scared. I wouldn't like to say it was. Soon Harry got back, and then Dr. Lloyd came, and you, Mr. Peters, and so I guess that's all I know that you don't.

COUNTY ATTORNEY *(looking around)* I guess we'll go upstairs first—and then out to the barn and around there. *(To the* SHERIFF.*)* You're convinced that there was nothing important here—nothing that would point to any motive?

SHERIFF Nothing here but kitchen things.

(The COUNTY ATTORNEY, *after again looking around the kitchen, opens the door of a cupboard closet. He gets up on a chair and looks on a shelf. Pulls his hand away, sticky.)*

COUNTY ATTORNEY Here's a nice mess.

(The women draw nearer.)

MRS. PETERS *(to the other woman)* Oh, her fruit; it did freeze. *(To the Lawyer.)* She worried about that when it turned so cold. She said the fire'd go out and her jars would break.

SHERIFF Well, can you beat the woman! Held for murder and worryin' about her preserves.

COUNTY ATTORNEY I guess before we're through she may have something more serious than preserves to worry about.

HALE Well, women are used to worrying over trifles.

(The two women move a little closer together.)

COUNTY ATTORNEY *(with the gallantry of a young politician)* And yet, for all their worries, what would we do without the ladies? *(The women do not unbend. He goes to the sink, takes a dipperful of water from the pail and, pouring it into a basin, washes his hands. Starts to wipe them on the roller-towel, turns it for a cleaner place.)* Dirty towels! *(Kicks his foot against the pans under the sink.)* Not much of a housekeeper, would you say, ladies?

MRS. HALE *(stiffly)* There's a great deal of work to be done on a farm.

COUNTY ATTORNEY To be sure. And yet . . . *(With a little bow to her.)* . . . I know there are some Dickson county farmhouses which do not have such roller towels.

(He gives it a pull to expose its full length again.)

MRS. HALE Those towels get dirty awful quick. Men's hands aren't always as clean as they might be.

COUNTY ATTORNEY Ah, loyal to your sex, I see. But you and Mrs. Wright were neighbors. I suppose you were friends, too.

MRS. HALE *(shaking her head)* I've not seen much of her of late years. I've not been in this house—it's more than a year.

COUNTY ATTORNEY And why was that? You didn't like her?

MRS. HALE I like her all well enough. Farmers' wives have their hands full, Mr. Henderson. And then—

COUNTY ATTORNEY Yes—?

MRS. HALE *(looking about)* It never seemed a very cheerful place.

COUNTY ATTORNEY No—it's not cheerful. I shouldn't say she had the home-making instinct.

MRS. HALE Well, I don't know as Wright had, either.

COUNTY ATTORNEY You mean that they didn't get on very well?

MRS. HALE No, I don't mean anything. But I don't think a place'd be any cheerful for John Wright's being in it.

COUNTY ATTORNEY I'd like to talk more of that a little later. I want to get the lay of things upstairs now.

(He goes to the left, where three steps lead to a stair door.)

SHERIFF I suppose anything Mrs. Peters does'll be all right. She was to take in some clothes for her, you know, and a few little things. We left in such a hurry yesterday.

COUNTY ATTORNEY Yes, but I would like to see what you take, Mrs. Peters, and keep an eye out for anything that might be of use to us.

MRS. PETERS Yes, Mr. Henderson.

(The women listen to the men's steps on the stairs, then look about the kitchen.)

MRS. HALE I'd hate to have men coming into my kitchen, snooping around and criticizing.

(She arranges the pans under sink which the Lawyer had shoved out of place.)

MRS. PETERS Of course it's no more than their duty.

MRS. HALE Duty's all right, but I guess that deputy sheriff that came out to make the fire might have got a little of this on. *(Gives the roller towel a pull.)* Wish I'd thought of that sooner. Seems mean to talk about her for not having things slicked up when she had to come away in such a hurry.

MRS. PETERS *(who has gone to a small table in the left rear corner of the room, and lifted one end of a towel that covers a pan)* She had bread set. *(Stands still.)*

MRS. HALE *(eyes fixed on a loaf of bread beside the bread-box, which is on a low shelf at the other side of the room. Moves slowly toward it.)* She was going to put this in there. *(Picks up loaf, then abruptly drops it. In a manner of returning to familiar things.)* It's a shame about her fruit. I wonder if it's all gone. *(Gets up on the chair and looks.)* I think there's some here that's all right, Mrs. Peters. Yes—here; *(Holding it toward the window.)* this is cherries, too. *(Looking again.)* I declare I believe that's the only one. *(Gets down, bottle in her hand. Goes to the sink and wipes it off on the outside.)* She'll feel awful bad after all her hard work in the hot weather. I remember the afternoon I put up my cherries last summer. *(She puts the bottle on the big kitchen table, center of the room, front table. With a sigh, is about to sit down in the rocking-chair. Before she is seated realizes what chair it is: with a slow look at it, steps back. The chair which she has touched rocks back and forth.)*

MRS. PETERS Well, I must get those things from the front room closet. *(She goes to the door at the right, but after looking into the other room, steps back.)* You coming with me, Mrs. Hale? You could help me carry them.

(They go in the other room: reappear, MRS. PETERS *carrying a dress and skirt,* MRS. HALE *following with a pair of shoes.)*

MRS. PETERS My, it's cold in there.

(She puts the clothes on the big table, and hurries to the stove.)

MRS. HALE *(examining the skirt)* Wright was close. I think maybe that's why she kept so much to herself. She didn't even belong to the Ladies' Aid. I suppose she felt she couldn't do her part, and then you don't enjoy things when you feel shabby. She used to wear pretty clothes and be lively, when she was Minnie Foster, one of the town girls singing in the choir. But that—oh, that was thirty years ago. This all you was to take in?

MRS. PETERS She said she wanted an apron. Funny thing to want, for there isn't much to get you dirty in jail, goodness knows. But I suppose just to make her feel more natural. She said they was in the top drawer in this cupboard. Yes, here. And then her little shawl that always hung behind the door. *(Opens stair door and looks.)* Yes, here it is.

(Quickly shuts door leading upstairs.)

MRS. HALE *(abruptly moving toward her)* Mrs. Peters?

MRS. PETERS Yes, Mrs Hale?

MRS. HALE Do you think she did it?

MRS. PETERS *(in a frightened voice)* Oh, I don't know.

MRS. HALE Well, I don't think she did. Asking for an apron and her little shawl. Worrying about her fruit.

MRS. PETERS *(starts to speak, glances up, where footsteps are heard in the room above. In a low voice)* Mr. Peters says it looks bad for her. Mr. Henderson is awful sarcastic in a speech and he'll make fun of her sayin' she didn't wake up.

MRS. HALE Well, I guess John Wright didn't wake when they was slipping that rope under his neck.

MRS. PETERS No, it's strange. It must have been done awfully crafty and still. They say it was such a—funny way to kill a man, rigging it all up like that.

MRS. HALE That's just what Mr. Hale said. There was a gun in the house. He says that's what he can't understand.

MRS. PETERS Mr. Henderson said coming out that what was needed for the case was a motive; something to show anger, or—sudden feeling.

MRS. HALE *(who is standing by the table)* Well, I don't see any signs of anger around here. *(She puts her hand on the dish towel which lies on the table, stands looking down at table, one half of which is clean, the other half messy.)* It's wiped here. *(Makes a move as if to finish work, then turns and looks at loaf of bread outside the bread-box. Drops towel. In that voice of coming back to familiar things.)* Wonder how they are finding things upstairs? I hope she had it a little more red-up up there. You know, it seems kind of *sneaking.* Locking her up in town and then coming out here and trying to get her own house to turn against her!

MRS. PETERS But, Mrs. Hale, the law is the law.

MRS. HALE I s'pose 'tis. *(Unbuttoning her coat.)* Better loosen up your things, Mrs. Peters. You won't feel them when you go out.

(MRS. PETERS *takes off her fur tippet, goes to hang it on hook at back of room, stands looking at the under part of the small corner table.*)

MRS. PETERS She was piecing a quilt. (*She brings the large sewing basket and they look at the bright pieces.*)

MRS. HALE It's log cabin pattern. Pretty, isn't it? I wonder if she was goin' to quilt it or just knot it?

(*Footsteps have been heard coming down the stairs. The* SHERIFF *enters, followed by* HALE *and the* COUNTY ATTORNEY.)

SHERIFF They wonder if she was gong to quilt it or just knot it. (*The men laugh, the women looked abashed.*)

COUNTY ATTORNEY (*rubbing his hands over the stove*) Frank's fire didn't do much up there, did it? Well, let's go out to the barn and get that cleared up.

(*The men go outside.*)

MRS. HALE (*resentfully*) I don't know as there's anything so strange, our takin' up our time with little things while we're waiting for them to get the evidence. (*She sits down at the big table smoothing out a block with decision.*) I don't see as it's anything to laugh about.

MRS. PETERS (*apologetically*) Of course they've got awful important things on their minds.

(*Pulls up a chair and joins* MRS. HALE *at the table.*)

MRS. HALE (*examining another block*) Mrs. Peters, look at this one. Here, this is the one she was working on, and look at the sewing! All the rest of it has been so nice and even. And look at this! It's all over the place! Why, it looks as if she didn't know what she was about!

(*After she has said this they look at each other, then start to glance back at the door. After an instant* MRS. HALE *has pulled at a knot and ripped the sewing.*)

MRS. PETERS Oh, what are you doing, Mrs. Hale?

MRS. HALE (*mildly*) Just pulling out a stitch or two that's not sewed very good. (Threading a needle.) Bad sewing always made me fidgety.

MRS. PETERS (*nervously*) I don't think we ought to touch things.

MRS. HALE I'll just finish up this end. (*Suddenly stopping and leaning forward.*) Mrs. Peters?

MRS. PETERS Yes, Mrs. Hale?

MRS. HALE What do you suppose she was so nervous about?

MRS. PETERS Oh—I don't know. I don't know as she was nervous. I sometimes sew awful queer when I'm just tired. (MRS. HALE *starts to say something, looks at* MRS. PETERS, *then goes on sewing.*) Well, I must get these things wrapped up. They may be through sooner than we think. (*Putting apron and other things together.*) I wonder where I can find a piece of paper, and string.

MRS. HALE In that cupboard, maybe.

MRS. PETERS (*looking in cupboard*) Why, here's a bird-cage (*Holds it up.*) Did she have a bird, Mrs. Hale?

MRS. HALE Why, I don't know whether she did or not—I've not been here for so long. There was a man around last year selling canaries cheap, but I don't know as she took one; maybe she did. She used to sing real pretty herself.

MRS. PETERS *(glancing around)* Seems funny to think of a bird here. But she must have had one, or why should she have a cage? I wonder what happened to it?

MRS. HALE. I s'pose maybe the cat got it.

MRS. PETERS No, she didn't have a cat. She's got that feeling some people have about cats—being afraid of them. My cat got in her room and she was real upset and asked me to take it out.

MRS. HALE My sister Bessie was like that. Queer, ain't it?

MRS. PETERS *(examining the cage)* Why, look at this door. It's broke. One hinge is pulled apart.

MRS. HALE *(looking too)* Looks as if some one must have been rough with it.

MRS. PETERS Why, yes.

(She brings the cage forward and puts it on the table.)

MRS. HALE I wish if they're going to find any evidence they'd be about it. I don't like this place.

MRS. PETERS But I'm awful glad you came with me, Mrs. Hale. It would be lonesome for me sitting here alone.

MRS. HALE It would, wouldn't it? *(Dropping her sewing.)* But I tell you what I do wish, Mrs. Peters. I wish I had come over some times when *she* was here. I—*(Looking around the room.)*—wish I had.

MRS. PETERS But of course you were awful busy, Mrs. Hale—your house and your children.

MRS. HALE I could've come. I stayed away because it weren't cheerful—and that's why I ought to have come. I—I've never liked this place. Maybe because it's down in a hollow and you don't see the road. I dunno what it is, but it's a lonesome place and always was. I wish I had come over to see Minnie Foster sometimes. I can see now—

(Shakes her head.)

MRS. PETERS Well, you mustn't reproach yourself, Mrs. Hale. Somehow we just don't see how it is with other folks until—something comes up.

MRS. HALE Not having children makes less work—but it makes a quiet house, and Wright out to work all day, and no company when he did come in. Did you know John Wright, Mrs. Peters?

MRS. PETERS Not to know him; I've seen him in town. They say he was a good man.

MRS. HALE Yes—good; he didn't drink, and kept his word as well as most, I guess, and paid his debts. But he was a hard man, Mrs. Peters. Just to pass the time of day with him. *(Shivers.)* Like a raw wind that gets to the bone. *(Pauses, her eye falling on the cage.)* I should think she would 'a wanted a bird. But what do you suppose went with it?

MRS. PETERS I don't know, unless it got sick and died.

(She reaches over and swings the broken door, swings it again, both women watch it.)

MRS. HALE You weren't raised round here, were you? (MRS. PETERS *shakes her head.*) You didn't know—her?

MRS. PETERS Not till they brought her yesterday.

MRS. HALE She—come to think of it, she was kind of like a bird herself—real sweet and pretty, but kind of timid and—fluttery. How—she—did—change. (*Silence; then as if struck by a happy thought and relieved to get back to every day things.*) Tell you what, Mrs. Peters, why don't you take the quilt in with you? It might take up her mind.

MRS. PETERS Why, I think that's a real nice idea, Mrs. Hale. There couldn't possibly be any objection to it, could there? Now, just what would I take? I wonder if her patches are in here—and her things.

(*They look in the sewing basket.*)

MRS. HALE Here's some red. I expect this has got sewing things in it. (*Brings out a fancy box.*) What a pretty box. Looks like something somebody would give you. Maybe her scissors are in here. (*Opens box. Suddenly puts her hand to her nose.*) Why—(MRS. PETERS *bends nearer, then turns her face away.*) There's something wrapped up in this piece of silk.

MRS. PETERS Why, this isn't her scissors.

MRS. HALE (*lifting the silk*) Oh, Mrs. Peters—it's—

(*Mrs. Peters bends closer.*)

MRS. PETERS It's the bird.

MRS. HALE (*jumping up*) But, Mrs. Peters—look at it. Its neck! Look at its neck! It's all—other side *to.*

MRS. PETERS Somebody—wrung—its neck.

(*Their eyes meet. A look of growing comprehension, of horror. Steps are heard outside. Mrs. Hale slips box under quilt pieces, and sinks into her chair. Enter* SHERIFF *and* COUNTY ATTORNEY. MRS. PETERS *rises.*)

COUNTY ATTORNEY (*as one turning from serious things to little pleasantries*) Well, ladies, have you decided whether she was going to quilt it or knot it?

MRS. PETERS We think she was going to—knot it.

COUNTY ATTORNEY Well, that's interesting. I'm sure. (*Seeing the bird-cage.*) Has the bird flown?

MRS. HALE (*putting more quilt pieces over the box*) We think the—cat got it.

COUNTY ATTORNEY (*preoccupied*) Is there a cat?

(*Mrs. Hale glances in a quick covert way at* MRS. PETERS.)

MRS. PETERS Well, not now. They're superstitious, you know. They leave.

COUNTY ATTORNEY (*to* SHERIFF PETERS, *continuing an interrupted conversation*) No sign at all of any one having come from the outside. Their own rope. Now let's go up again and go over it piece by piece. (*They start upstairs.*) It would have to have been some one who knew just the— (MRS. PETERS *sits down. The two women sit there not looking at one another, but as if peering into something and at the same time holding back. When they talk now it is in the manner of feeling their way over strange ground as if afraid of what they are saying, but as if they can not help saying it.*)

MRS. HALE She liked the bird. She was going to bury it in that pretty box.

MRS. PETERS (*in a whisper*) When I was a girl—my kitten—there was a boy took a hatchet, and before my eyes—and before I could get there—*(Covers her face an instant.)* If they hadn't held me back I would have—*(Catches herself, looks upstairs where steps are heard, falters weakly)*—hurt him.

MRS. HALE *(with a slow look around her)* I wonder how it would seem never to have had any children around. *(Pause.)* No, Wright wouldn't like the bird—a thing that sang. She used to sing. He killed that, too.

MRS. PETERS *(moving uneasily)* We don't know who killed the bird.

MRS. HALE I knew John Wright.

MRS. PETERS It was an awful thing was done in this house that night, Mrs. Hale. Killing a man while he slept, slipping a rope around his neck that choked the life out of him.

MRS. HALE His neck. Choked the life out of him.

(Her hand goes out and rests on the bird-cage.)

MRS. PETERS *(with rising voice)* We don't know who killed him. We don't *know.*

MRS. HALE *(her own feeling not interrupted)* If there'd been years and years of nothing, then a bird to sing to you, it would be awful—still, after the bird was still.

MRS. PETERS *(something within her speaking)* I know what stillness is. When we homesteaded in Dakota, and my first baby died—after he was two years old, and me with no other then—

MRS. HALE *(moving)* How soon do you suppose they'll be through, looking for the evidence?

MRS. PETERS I know what stillness is. *(Pulling herself back.)* The law has got to punish crime, Mrs. Hale.

MRS. HALE *(not as if answering that)* I wish you'd seen Minnie Foster when she wore a white dress with blue ribbons and stood up there in the choir and sang. *(A look around the room.)* Oh, I *wish* I'd come over here once in a while. That was a crime! That was a crime! Who's going to punish that?

MRS. PETERS *(looking upstairs)* We mustn't—take on.

MRS. HALE I might have known she needed help! I know how things can be— for women. I tell you, it's queer, Mrs. Peters. We live close together and we live far apart. We all go through the same things—it's all just a different kind of the same thing. *(Brushes her eyes, noticing the bottle of fruit, reaches out for it.)* If I was you I wouldn't tell her her fruit was gone. Tell her it *ain't.* Tell her it's all right. Take this in to prove it to her. She—she may never know whether it was broke or not.

MRS. PETERS *(takes the bottle, looks about for something to wrap it in; takes petticoat from the clothes brought from the other room, very nervously begins winding this around the bottle. In a false voice)* My, it's a good thing the men couldn't hear us. Wouldn't they just laugh. Getting all stirred up over a little thing like a—dead canary. As if that could have anything to do with—with— wouldn't they *laugh!*

(The men are heard coming down stairs.)

MRS. HALE *(under her breath)* Maybe they would—maybe they wouldn't.

COUNTY ATTORNEY No, Peters, it's all perfectly clear except a reason for doing it. But you know juries when it comes to women. If there was some definite thing. Something to show—something to make a story about—a thing that would connect up with this strange way of doing it.

(The women's eyes meet for an instant. Enter HALE *from outer door.)*

HALE Well, I've got the team around. Pretty cold out there.

COUNTY ATTORNEY I'm going to stay here a while by myself. *(To the* SHERIFF.*)* You can send Frank out for me, can't you? I want to go over everything. I'm not satisfied that we can't do better.

SHERIFF Do you want to see what Mrs. Peters is going to take in?

(The Lawyer goes to the table, picks up the apron, laughs.)

COUNTY ATTORNEY Oh, I guess they're not very dangerous things the ladies have picked out. *(Moves a few things about, disturbing the quilt pieces which cover the box. Steps back.)* No, Mrs. Peters doesn't need supervising. For that matter, a sheriff's wife is married to the law. Ever think of it that way, Mrs. Peters?

MRS. PETERS Not—just that way.

SHERIFF *(chuckling)* Married to the law. *(Moves toward the other room.)* I just want you to come in here a minute, George. We ought to take a look at these windows.

COUNTY ATTORNEY *(scoffingly)* Oh, windows!

SHERIFF We'll be right out, Mr. Hale.

(HALE goes outside. The SHERIFF *follows the* COUNTY ATTORNEY *into the other room. Then* MRS. HALE *rises, hands tight together, looking intensely at* MRS. PETERS, *whose eyes make a slow turn, finally meeting* MRS. HALES. *A moment* MRS. HALE *holds her, then her own eyes point the way to where the box is concealed. Suddenly Mrs. Peters throws back quilt pieces and tries to put the box in the bag she is wearing. It is too big. She opens box, starts to take bird out, cannot touch it, goes to pieces, stands there helpless. Sound of a knob turning in the other room. Mrs. Hale snatches the box and puts it in the pocket of her big coat. Enter County Attorney and Sheriff.)*

COUNTY ATTORNEY *(facetiously)* Well, Henry, at least we found out that she was not going to quilt it. She was going to—what is it you call it, ladies?

MRS. HALE *(her hand against her pocket)* We call it—knot it, Mr. Henderson.

(Curtain)

WRITING AND DISCUSSION QUESTIONS

Informative

1. Although Mrs. Wright never admits to killing her husband, there are a number of clues that suggest she might have. What are these? What do her past and Mr. Wright's personality tell us about a possible motive for a murder?

2. The picture we get of the men in the play suggests that what is important to them is very different from what is of value to the three women in the play. From the way

they speak and behave, what is learned about the men? How do their values affect the outcome of the investigation?

3. What important differences do you see between Mrs. Hale and Mrs. Peters? Do you see any changes in their values and attitudes as the play progresses?
4. The men jokingly ask several times about the quilt Mrs. Wright was making. Do quilting and knotting have any significance beyond the stitch Mrs. Wright was using and beyond the clue of the botched stitch?

Persuasive

1. Many readers are sympathetic to the women in the play, even as Mrs. Peters and Mrs. Hale become judge and jury by not disclosing evidence that might well convict Mrs. Wright. What picture do we get of the law in the play? Argue that the two women are or are not sympathetic characters.
2. Readers are generally split over whether to condemn or sympathize with Mrs. Wright's apparent murder of her husband. What position do you take? Remember that the play occurs at a time when women's rights were severely curtailed, especially in comparison to today.

Personal

1. Battering of women has become a significantly visible problem today, inspiring considerable media attention. What do you know about the causes of these abusive incidents?
2. The two women in the play make a tacit compact not to reveal what they know to the "authorities." They most likely do this because they have little or no faith in the male-controlled legal system. Would you agree or disagree that the legal system today, as apparently run by men, is flawed, flawed significantly enough to justify breaking it?

▼

MARY DALY, "AFTER THE DEATH OF GOD THE FATHER"

Mary Daly (1928–), a professor of theology at Boston College and author of a number of studies of the influence of religion on our lives, sent shock waves through the academic community when she published *Beyond God the Father* in 1973. Her roots lie in the humanistic tradition of the 1950s and 1960s, but nobody expected such a conclusive indictment of the Judeo–Christian tradition. Daly followed her first book with *Gyn/Ecology: The Meta-Ethics of Radical Feminism* (1978) and *Pure Lust* (1984). As feminist Karen Gould describes her, Daly merges theological and spiritual realms and is viewed as the most important female theologian and philosopher of feminism in 30 years.

Daly is chiefly concerned with the polarizations that a dualistic way of thinking has forced us into, polarizations that go to the roots of our thinking about who we are, oppositions like male/female, master/slave, Jesus/Mary, female culpability and guilt (through Eve and the Fall)/male salvation (through male symbols like Christ and a male God). These arise, Daly believes, as the result of deep-seated attitudes with which the Judeo–Christian tradition views males and females. More specifically, dualism is the primary epistemology (way of knowing) of a patriarchal system.

The result of the dominance of patriarchal thinking is that women have had to live "on the boundary" of patriarchy, so that they will not, as a result of living inside it, be negated by it. Instead, Daly believes, they must reject virtues like meekness, obedience, and sacrifice, represented by Mary and the female image in patriarchy, in favor of a more generative God, one of becoming rather than of being.

▼

After the Death of God the Father

WOMEN'S LIBERATION AND THE TRANSFORMATION OF CHRISTIAN CONSCIOUSNESS

MARY DALY

1   The women's liberation movement has produced a deluge of books and articles. Their major task has been exposition and criticism of our male-centered heritage. In order to reveal and drive home to readers the oppressive character of our cultural institutions, it was necessary to do careful research, to trot out passages from leading philosophers, psychologists, statesmen, poets, historians, saints and theologians which make the reader's hair stand on end by the blatancy of their misogynism. Part of the task also has been the tracing of the subtle psychological mechanisms by which society has held men up and women down. This method of exposition and analysis reached its crescendo within this past year when Kate Millet's *Sexual Politics* rocketed her into the role of American counterpart to Simone de Beauvoir.

2   As far as the level of creative research is concerned, that phase of the work is finished. The skeletons in our cultural closet have been hauled out for inspection. I do not mean to imply that there are not countless more of the same to be uncovered (just the other day I noticed for the first time that Berdyaev blandly affirms there is "something base and sinister in the female element." Etcetera). Nor do I mean that the task of communicating the message is over. Millions have yet to hear the news, let alone to grasp its import. Certainly it would be a mistake and a betrayal to trivialize the fact that our culture is so diseased. That has always been a major tactic in the fine art of suppressing the rage of women. No, what I am saying is that Phase One of critical research and writing in the movement has opened the way for the logical next step in creative thinking. We now have to ask how the women's revolution can and should change our whole vision of reality. What I intend to do here is to sketch some of the ways in which it can influence Western religious thought.

The Judaic-Christian tradition has served to legitimate sexually imbalanced 3
patriarchial society. Thus, for example, the image of the Father God, spawned in the human imagination and sustained as plausible by patriarchy, has in turn rendered service to this type of society by making its mechanisms for the oppression of women appear right and fitting. If God in "his" heaven is a father ruling "his" people then it is in the "nature" of things and according to divine plan and the order of the universe that society be male-dominated. Theologian Karl Barth found it appropriate to write that woman is "ontologically" subordinate to man. Within this context a mystification of roles takes place: the husband dominating his wife represents God himself. What is happening, of course, is the familiar mechanism by which the images and values of a given society are projected into a realm of beliefs, which in turn justify the social infrastructure. The belief system becomes hardened and objectified, seeming to have an unchangeable independent existence and validity of its own. It resists social change which would rob it of its plausibility. Nevertheless, despite the vicious circle, change does occur in society, and ideologies die, though they die hard.

As the women's revolution begins to have its effect upon the fabric of soci- 4
ety, transforming it from patriarchy into something that never existed before—into a diarchal situation that is radically new—it will, I believe, become the greatest single potential challenge to Christianity to rid itself of its oppressive tendencies or go out of business. Beliefs and values that have held sway for thousands of years will be questioned as never before: It is also very possibly the greatest single hope for survival of religious consciousness in the West.

At this point it is important to consider the objection that the liberation of 5
women will only mean that new characters will assume the same old roles, but that nothing will change essentially in regard to structure, ideology, or values. This objection is often based upon the observation that the very few women in "masculine" occupations seem to behave very much as men do. This is really not to the point for it fails to recognize that the effect of tokenism is not to change stereotypes or social systems but to preserve these. What I am discussing here is an emergence of women such as has never taken place before. It is naive to assume that the coming of women into equal power in society generally and in the church in particular will simply mean uncritical acceptance of values formerly given priority by men. Rather, I suggest that it will be a catalyst for transformation of our culture.

The roles and structures of patriarchy have been developed and sustained in 6
accordance with an artifical polarization of human qualities into the traditional sexual stereotypes. The image of the person in authority and the accepted understanding of "his" role have corresponded to the eternal masculine stereotype, which implies hyperrationality, "objectivity," aggressivity, the possession of dominating and manipulative attitudes toward persons and environment and the tendency to construct boundaries between the self (and those identified with the self) and "the other." The caricature of a human being which is repre-

sented by this stereotype depends for its existence upon the opposite caricature—the eternal feminine (hyper-emotional, passive, self-abasing, etc.). By
becoming whole persons women can generate a counterforce to the stereotype
of the leader as they challenge the artificial polarization of human characteristics. There is no reason to assume that women who have the support of their
sisters to criticize the masculine stereotype will simply adopt it as a model for
themselves. More likely they will develop a wider range of qualities and skills
in themselves and thereby encourage men to engage in a comparably liberating
procedure (a phenomenon we are beginning to witness already in men's liberation groups). This becoming of *whole* human beings will affect the values of our
society, for it will involve a change in the fabric of human consciousness.

7   Accordingly, it is reasonable to anticipate that this change will affect the
symbols which reflect the values of our society, including religious symbols.
Since some of these have functioned to justify oppression, women and men
would do well to welcome this change. Religious symbols die when the cultural
situation that supported them ceases to give them plausibility. This should pose
no problem to authentic faith, which accepts the relativity of all symbols and
recognizes that fixation upon any of them as absolute in itself is idolatrous.

8   The becoming of new symbols is not a matter that can arbitrarily be decided
around a conference table. Rather they grow out of a changing communal situation and experience. This does not mean that theologically we are consigned
to the role of passive spectators. We are called upon to be attentive to what the
new experience of the becoming of women is revealing to us, and to foster the
evolution of consciousness beyond the oppressiveness and imbalance reflected
and justified by symbols and doctrines throughout the millennia of patriarchy.

9   This imbalance is apparent first of all in the biblical and popular image of
the great patriarch in heaven who rewards and punishes according to his mysterious and arbitrary will. The fact that the effects of this image have not always
been humanizing is evident to any perceptive reader of history. The often cruel
behavior of Christians toward unbelievers and even toward dissenters among
themselves is shocking evidence of the function of that image in relation to values and behavior.

10   Sophisticated thinkers, of course, have never intellectually identified God
with an elderly parent in heaven. Nevertheless it is important to recognize that
even when very abstract conceptualizations of God are formulated in the mind,
images have a way of surviving in the imagination in such a way that a person
can function on two different and even apparently contradictory levels at the
same time. Thus one can speak of God as spirit and at the same time imagine
"him" as belonging to the male sex. Such primitive images can profoundly
affect conceptualizations which appear to be very refined and abstract. Even the
Yaweh of the future, so cherished by the theology of hope, comes through on
an imaginative level as exclusively a He-God, and it is perhaps consistent with
this that theologians of hope have attempted to develop a political theology
which takes no explicit cognizance of the devastation wrought by sexual politics.

11   The widespread conception of the "Supreme Being" as an entity distinct

from this world but controlling it according to plan and keeping human beings in a state of infantile subjection has been a not too subtle mask of the divine patriarch. The Supreme Being's plausibility, and that of the static worldview which accompanies this projection has, of course, declined. This was a projection founded in specifically patriarchal infrastructures and sustained as subjectively real by the usual processes of generating plausibility. The sustaining power of the social infrastructures has been eroded by a number of developments in recent history, including the general trend toward democratization of society and the emergence of technology with the accompanying sense of mastery over the world and man's destiny. However, it is the women's movement which appears destined to play the key-role in the overthrow of such oppressive elements in traditional theism, precisely because it strikes at the source of the imbalance reflected in traditional beliefs.

The women's movement will present a growing threat to patriarchal religion *12* less by attacking it than by simply leaving it behind. Few of the leaders in the movement evince an interest in institutional religion, having recognized it as an instrument of their betrayal. Those who see their commitment to the movement as consonant with concern for the religious heritage are aware that the Christian tradition is by no means bereft of elements which foster genuine experiences and intimations of transcendence. The problem is that their liberating potential is choked off in the surrounding atmosphere of the images, ideas, values, and structures of patriarchy. What will, I think, become possible through the social change coming from radical feminism is a more acute and widespread perception of qualitative differences between those conceptualizations of God and of the human relationship to God which are oppressive in their implications, and those which encourage self-actualization and social commitment.

The various theologies that hypostatize transcendence invariably use this *13* "God" to legitimate oppression, particularly that of women. These are irredeemably anti-feminine and therefore anti-human. In contrast to this, a more authentic language of transcendence does not hypostatize or objectify God and consequently does not lend itself to such use. So for example, Tillich's way of speaking about God as ground and power of being would be very difficult to use for the legitimation of any sort of oppression. It grows out of awareness of that reality which is both transcendent and immanent, not reducible to or adequately represented by such expressions as person, father, supreme being. Awareness of this reality is not achieved by playing theological games but by existential courage. I am not saying that a liberated consciousness necessarily will use Tillich's language of transcendence. That of Whitehead, James, Jaspers, to mention a few—or an entirely new language—may do as well or better. But it remains true that the driving revelatory force which will make possible an authenticity of religious consciousness is courage in the face of anxiety.

Since the projections of patriarchal religion have been blocking the dynamics *14* of existential courage by offering the false security of alienation—that is, of self-reduction to stereotyped roles—there is reason to see hope for the emergence of genuine religious consciousness in the massive challenge to patriarchy which is now in its initial stages. The becoming of women may be not only the doorway to deliverance from the omnipotent Father in all of his disguises—a deliverance which secular humanism has passionately fought for—but also a doorway to something, that is, the beginning for many of a more authentic search for transcendence, that is, for God.

15   The imbalance in Christian ideology resulting from sexual hierarchy is manifested not only in the doctrine of God but also in the notion of Jesus as the unique God-man. A great deal of Christian doctrine concerning Jesus has been docetic, that is, it has not really seriously accepted the fact that Jesus was a human being. An effect of the liberation of women will very likely be the loss of plausibility of Christological formulas which come close to reflecting a kind of idolatry in regard to the person of Jesus. As it becomes better understood that God is transcendent and unobjectifiable—or else not at all—it will become less plausible to speak of Jesus as the Second Person of the Trinity who "assumed" a human nature. Indeed, the prevalent emphasis upon the total uniqueness and supereminence of Jesus will, I think, become less meaningful. To say this is not at all to deny his extraordinary character and mission. The point is to attempt a realistic assessment of certain ways of using his image (which in all likelihood he himself would repudiate). It is still not uncommon for priests and ministers, when confronted with the issue of women's liberation, to assert that God become incarnate uniquely as a male, and then to draw arguments for male supremacy from this. Indeed, the tradition itself tends to justify such assertions. The underlying—and often explicit—assumption in the minds of theologians down through the centuries has been that the divinity could not have deigned to become incarnate in the "inferior" sex, and the "fact" that "he" did not do so reinforces the belief in masculine superiority. The transformation of society by the erosion of male dominance will generate serious challenges to such assumptions of the Christological tradition.

16   It will, I think, become increasingly evident that exclusively masculine symbols for the ideal of "incarnation" will not do. As a uniquely masculine divinity loses credibility, so also the idea of a unique divine incarnation in a human being of the male sex may give way in the religious consciousness to an increased awareness of the divine presence in all human beings, understood as expressing and in a real sense incarnating—although always inadequately—the power of being. The seeds of this awareness are already present, of course, in the traditional doctrine that all human beings are made to the image of God and in a less than adequate way in the doctrine of grace. Now it should become possible to work out with increasing realism the implication in both of these doctrines that human beings are called to self-actualization and to the creation of a community that fosters the becoming of women and men. This means that no completely adequate models can be taken from the past. It may be that we will witness a remythologizing of Western religion. Certainly, if the need for parental symbols for God persists, something like the Father-Mother God proposed by Mary Baker Eddy will be more acceptable to the new woman and the new man than the Father God of the past. A symbolism for incarnation of the

divine in human beings may continue to be needed in the future, but it is highly unlikely that women or men will continue to find plausible that symbolism which is epitomized in the image of the Virgin kneeling in adoration before her own son. Perhaps this will be replaced by the emergence of bisexual imagery which is not hierarchical. The experience of the past brought forth a new Adam and a new Eve. Perhaps the future will bring a new Christ and a new Mary. For the present, it would appear that we are being called upon to recognize the poverty of all symbols and the fact of our past idolatry regarding them, and to turn to our own resources for bringing about the radically new in our own lives.

The manifestation of God in Jesus was an eschatological event whose fulfilled reality lies in the future. The Jesus of the Gospels was a free person who challenged ossified beliefs and laws. Since he was remarkably free of prejudice against women and treated them as equals insofar as the limitations of his culture would allow, it is certain that he would be working with them for their liberation today. This awakening of women to their human potentiality by creative action as they assume equal partnership with men in society can bring about a manifestation of God in themselves which will be the Second Coming of God incarnate, fulfilling the latent promise in the original revelation that men and women are made to the image of God.   17

Behind the Mask

It should be evident, then, that women's liberation is an event that can challenge authoritarian, exclusive and non-existential notions of faith and revelation. Since women have been extra-environmentals, to use a McLuhanish term, that is, since they have not been part of the authority structure which uses "faith" and "revelation" to reinforce the mechanisms of alienation, their emergence can effect a more widespread criticalness of idolatry which is often masked by these ideas. There could result from this a more general understanding of faith as a state of ultimate concern and commitment and a heightened sense of relativity concerning the symbols it uses to express this commitment. An awareness might also emerge—not merely in the minds of a theological elite, but in the general consciousness—that revelation is an ongoing experience.   18

The becoming of women implies also a transvaluation of values in Christian morality. As the old order is challenged and as men and women become freed to experience a wholeness of personality which the old polarizations impeded, the potentiality will be awakened for a change in moral consciousness which will go far beyond Nietzsche's merely reactionary rejection of Christian values.   19

Much of the traditional theory of Christian virtue appears to be the product of reactions on the part of men—perhaps guilty reactions—to the behavioral excesses of the stereotypic male. There has been theoretical emphasis upon charity, meekness, obedience, humility, self-abnegation, sacrifice, service. Part of the problem with this moral ideology is that it became generally accepted not   20 by men but by women, who have hardly been helped by an ethic which reinforced their abject situation. This emphasis upon the passive virtues, of course, has not challenged exploitativeness but supported it. Part of the syndrome is the prevailing notion of sin as an offense against those in power, or against "God" (the two are often equated). Within the perspective of such a privatized morality the structures themselves of oppression are not seen as sinful.

21   Consistent with all of this is the fact that the traditional Christian moral consciousness has been fixated upon the problems of reproductive activity in a manner totally disproportionate to its feeble political concern. This was summed up several years ago in Archbishop Roberts' remark that "if contraceptives had been dropped over Japan instead of bombs which merely killed, maimed and shriveled up thousands alive there would have been a squeal of outraged protest from the Vatican to the remotest Mass center in Asia." Pertinent also is Simone de Beauvoir's remark that the church has reserved its uncompromising humanitarianism for man in the fetal condition. Although theologians today acknowledge that this privatized morality has failed to cope with the structures of oppression, few seriously face the possibility that the roots of this distortion are deeply buried in the fundamental and all-pervasive sexual alienation which the women's movement is seeking to overcome.

22   It is well-known that Christians under the spell of the jealous God who represents the collective power of his chosen people can use religion to justify that "us and them" attitude which is disastrous in its consequences for the powerless. It is less widely understood that the projection of "the other"—easily adaptable to national, racial and class differences—has basically and primordially been directed against women. Even the rhetoric of racism finds its model in sexism.

23   The consciousness-raising which is beginning among women is evoking a qualitatively new understanding of the subtle mechanisms which produce and destroy "the other," and a consequent empathy with all of the oppressed. This gives grounds for the hope that their emergence can generate a counterforce to the exploitative mentality which is destroying persons and the environment. Since the way men and women are seen in society is a prime determinant in the whole social system and ideology, radical women refuse to see their movement as simply one among others. What I am suggesting is that it might be the only chance for the turning of human beings from a course leading to the deterioration and perhaps the end of life on this planet.

24   Those who see their concern for women's liberation as consonant with an envolving Christianity would be unrealistic to expect much comprehension from the majority of male ecclesiastics. Such writers as Gordon Rattrey Taylor *(The Biological Time Bomb)*, Robert Francoeur *(Utopian Motherhood)*, and others keep beeping out the message that we are moving into a world in which human sexuality is no longer merely oriented to reproduction of the species—which means that the masculine and feminine mystiques are doomed to evaporate. Within the theological community, however, the predictable and almost universal response has been what one might call the ostrich syndrome. Whereas the

old theology justified sexual oppression, the new theology for the most part simply ignores it and goes on in comfortable compatibility with it, failing to recognize its deep connection with such other major problems as war, racism and environmental pollution. The work of fostering religious consciousness which is explicitly incompatible with sexism will require an extraordinary degree of creative rage, love and hope.

WRITING AND DISCUSSION QUESTIONS

Informative

1. Daly believes the second phase of the feminist movement will challenge our view of reality, in particular our entire conception of the Judeo–Christian tradition. What elements of that tradition, specifically, does she think will be or are being challenged? In what sense is that tradition represented by patriarchy? According to Daly, how does that patriarchy translate into religious practice in Judaism and Christianity?
2. Daly writes of a polarization of human qualities that results from the dualities inherent in the Judeo–Christian tradition. What do you think she means by this, especially by concepts like "divine patriarch" and "sexual hierarchy"? What alternate view of religion does she advocate?
3. Daly is particulary concerned with much of Christianity's views of the incarnation of Jesus "uniquely as a male," leading to "arguments for male superiority. . . ." How would women's role in society and in the Church, as well as their view of themselves, be affected by the view that because Christ was a male, only males should fill the most important roles in the Church?

Persuasive

1. Daly reserves some of her bitterest attacks for Christianity and its apparent subordination of women. Argue that her opinions do or do not measure up to the evidence of Christian practice.
2. Daly believes that women's liberation will dramatically change our view of religion. Argue for or against that view.

Personal

1. Daly urges us to adopt a religion "which encourage(s) self-actualization and social commitment." Given your own experience of institutional religion, how close has your church, synagogue, or mosque come to that goal? If you are not a part of an organized religion now, did the failure of religion to work toward such a goal account for your choice not to join a church or synagogue?
2. If virtues like meekness, obedience, and sacrifice are so disadvantageous to women, as Daly claims, does that mean that such virtues have no function or use by anyone in society? If that is the case, what kind of society will we have, one dominated by pride, disobedience, and self-indulgence?

▼

JUDY CHICAGO, FROM *THROUGH THE FLOWER: MY STRUGGLE AS A WOMAN ARTIST*

The international art world does not know what to make of artist–writer and Jewish–feminist Judy Chicago (1939–). Her monumental multimedia work "The Dinner Party," completed in 1979, portrays, in an open-centered triangular table, 46.5 feet on each side, the lives of 39 women who have made major contributions to history [the inverted triangle is an ancient symbol of women's power]. Each woman, from the Primordial Goddess, an Amazon woman, Sappho, Sojourner Truth, and Susan B. Anthony to Georgia O'Keeffe, has her story told with a porcelain plate, goblet, and needlework runners, which together form a banquet dinnertable setting. "The Dinner Party" opened at the San Francisco Museum of Modern Art to vitriolic reviews from many male critics and deep affections from most of the thousands who stood in long lines to see it. Chicago's idea was daunting: to assemble all the great women of Western history at one table and to do it in female-oriented media of china painting and needlework. After five years, $200,000, and additional hundreds of thousands of dollars in donated time from over 400 artists, both female and male, the project opened, a feminist counterpart to the Sistine Chapel and a female variation on "The Last Supper."

Part of Chicago's purpose, and a major source of the hostility the project received, was to make an artistic statement in female imagery, especially after centuries of male, phallic imagery. Each of the 39 plates imaginatively departs from a vaginally suggestive butterfly image, the symbol of rebirth for centuries and the trademark of much of Chicago's art since 1972. In Chicago's words, written in 1974:

> . . . there is a big gap between my feelings as a woman and the visual language of the male culture. Whenever I want to deal with the issue of vulnerability, emotional exposure, or primitive feelings, the only image I can think of is a vagina, probably because those aspects of the human experience have been relegated to the sphere of the "feminine" and then deprecated. My struggle has been and is to find a way to let the female experience be represented in such a way that it can stand for those areas of human experience that male society denies, thus challenging the prevailing values. I don't know how to do that yet. Neither does anyone else. It is the the major problem those of us face who are trying to forge a new language, one that is relevant to women's experience.[1]

It is apparent that Chicago has begun to find the images and the language to express the female experience.

Still, the reviews of "The Dinner Party" were mixed, as one would expect from such controversial material. Many female critics praised it. Typical of these was art critic Lucy Lippard:

> The Dinner Party . . . is good art, though a leading art magazine refused to cover the show because it was "merely sociology." The more time I spent with The Dinner Party, with prolonged views across the table when the brilliant color of the needlework is best seen and with detailed scrutiny of the extraordinary ornament of each plate and runner, the more immersed I became in the beauty of pattern, texture, form and the more I was moved by the networks being revealed.[2]

"The Dinner Party" nevertheless experienced a rather tortured life. After it opened in San Francisco, the rest of its planned museum tour was cancelled in large part because of its subject matter, and it went into crates in a warehouse. A grassroots campaign to resurrect the work, with hundreds of donations by individuals who demanded that it be seen again, brought it to Houston in 1980. It moved from city to city by this pattern, as Chicago's fans raised dollar after dollar. Major museums in New York, Chicago, and Los Angeles still refused to show "The Dinner Party."

As the excerpt below, from Chicago's autobiography *Through the Flower*, shows, Chicago is more than an isolated feminist artist working to open the art world to women. Because women are so often excluded from establishment art circles controlled by men, Chicago created her own women's art networks. In 1970, she founded the first feminist art program in Fresno; soon after, she founded the first women's art space, the first women's art school and then the Los Angeles Women's Building, each a place where women can go and be accepted and taken seriously as professionals.

Chicago generally works from day to day, often not knowing where her next dollar will come from. The reason for her near-fanatical devotion to her art is suggested in her own words: "Art has an incredible capacity to change people's lives. Art, the way it is now, is as imprisoned as women—and as powerless. We need art that affirms

---

[1] Unpublished statement distributed at lectures, 1974.

[2] L. Lippard, "Setting a New Place: Judy Chicago's Dinner Party," in *Get the Message: A Decade of Art for Social Change.* (New York: Dutton, 1984), 110.

our experience, that transforms us, and empowers us." Chicago's mission as an artist, in her words, has been "to express aspects of the human experience that have been forgotten in, omitted from or distorted by history and to represent those who have not been able to speak for themselves."[3] After "The Dinner Party," she "broke the silence about birth" in "The Birth Project," a needlework collection that grew out of her interest in creation myths and that sees the birth process as a metaphor for creation. After successive trips to libraries and art archives turned up almost no images of birth, she went directly to women, gathering their testimony about birth. Her next project was "Powerplay," in which she examined the consequences of power on men and the world.

In what is perhaps her most ambitious project, she has since 1985 worked on "The Holocaust Project," "again speaking for the voiceless, examining the ways in which the Holocaust grew out of the development of Western civilization and the price we have paid for that development." With her husband, Donald Woodman, Chicago traveled for two months through the devastated Jewish centers of Europe and through Hitler's death camps. The result, which will open in Chicago 1992, is again a monumental multimedia statement about the dispossessed and the marginalized, about the fabric of Western civilization that devalues life and those who do not fit the particular mold defined by the totalitarian state.

To prepare for The Holocaust Project, Chicago read widely on the Holocaust, spoke to Holocaust scholars, viewed and studied survivor testimony, and studied the art created by the victims and the survivors. In this project, Chicago has dared to approach a forbidding topic so much in the media today because she believes that "it has been presented in a narrow and biased way—either omitting the Jewish experience or emphasizing it while excluding the experiences of other victims."[4] The result of this attempt at integration is a work that looks at the perpetrators and victims within a very wide boundary, and includes images of the Church, the Roosevelt administration, the Native American, the homosexual, the buffalo, and the female victim of Hitler. In "The Holocaust Project," Chicago confronts our tendency to avoid, deny, and distort the monstrous evil that is part of our heritage. "Art can contribute to our evolution by enlarging our consciousness,"[5] she says.

[3]Unpublished statement distributed at lectures, 1988.
[4]Unpublished statement distributed at lectures, 1988.
[5]Unpublished statement distributed at lectures, 1988.

An effective publicist of her own work, Chicago has written four books: *Through the Flower: My Struggle as a Woman Artist,* excerpts of which follow; *The Dinner Party: A Symbol of Our Heritage; Embroidering Our Heritage: The Dinner Party Needlework;* and *The Birth Project.*

▼

from *Through the Flower: My Struggle as a Woman Artist*
JUDY CHICAGO

Making a Professional Life

After I returned from New York, Lloyd and I became increasingly   *1* more involved with each other. After Jerry's death,[6] I had several affairs, all of which depressed me enormously and made me think that I would have to spend the rest of my life alone. The men with whom I became involved either used me sexually, expected me to "take care" of them, were threatened by my work, or, if they could relate to my work, were unable to relate to me personally. Lloyd seemed to be the only man I knew who cared about *me,* who could relate to my work, and who wanted to be involved with me in other ways as well. At the beginning of 1965, we moved into a loft in Pasadena. At that time, we began a slow struggle to build a loving and equalized relationship, in which we could both be ourselves. For the next few years, my energies were divided between my work in the studio and developing a mature relationship with Lloyd.

It was after I left school that my professional life really began. With it came   *2* another dose of discrimination, this time worse than before. It seemed that as my work got better, the resistance to acknowledging that a woman could be an artist grew stronger. After we moved to Pasadena, male artists came to visit and made it clear that they were interested in Lloyd, not me. Gallery and museum people refused to see my work, or if they did, ignored it, or at most, gave me an inappropriate or patronizing response. One museum curator dropped by our studio almost every month. One time, Lloyd asked him if he had seen my new work, and when he said "No," suggested that he go into the studio we shared. My piece, which was quite large, was against one wall. As we

---

[6]Jerry is Chicago's deceased husband.

walked into the room, the curator went over to a sculpture of Lloyd's that he had seen many times and became completely absorbed in looking at it, asking Lloyd if he had changed the color. Embarrassed, Lloyd said "No" and asked him why he wasn't looking at my piece. When the man still refused to turn around, Lloyd covered his sculpture and demanded that the man look at my work. Finally, he looked at it and mumbled something about it being very beautiful. But by this time I was too hurt to respond, and just fled from the studio crying. Later, when the piece was in a show in New York and much acclaimed, this same man went around bragging about how he visited me all the time. Earlier, he had told me that neither he nor his wife wanted much to do with me because I was too "direct."

3   During the next five years, I was continually made to feel by men in the art world that there was something "wrong" with me. They'd say things like "Gee, Judy, I like your work, but I just can't cut it that you're a woman." Or male artists who lived in the neighborhood would come over and be astonished that I wouldn't cook for them or cater to their needs. I heard stories from people about how someone said that I was a "bitch" or a "castrater," which hurt me deeply. If I showed work and Lloyd didn't, then I was held responsible for his not being shown, and I was accused of having "cut his balls off." the same thing applied if I did a good work and he did a work that wasn't as good as his last piece. It seemed like I couldn't win. But I wouldn't give up. I knew that what I was confronting came out of the fact that I was a woman, but whenever I tried to talk about that openly, I would be put down with statements like, "Come on, Judy, the suffrage movement is over," and treated as if I were a leper.

4   All through this period, I worked and I showed my work in galleries and museums. The two people who helped me most were my dealer and Lloyd; they supported me and stood up for me. My earlier naïveté about my situation as a woman artist was giving way to a clear understanding that my career was going to be a long, hard struggle. Fortunately, I knew that I was okay—that the problem was in the culture and not in me, but it still hurt. And I still felt that I had to hide my womanliness and be tough in both my personality and my work. My imagery was becoming increasingly more "neutralized." I began to work with formal rather than symbolic issues. But I was never interested in "formal issues" as such. Rather, they were something that my content had to be hidden behind in order for my work to be taken seriously. Because of this duplicity, there always appeared to be something "not quite right" about my pieces according to the prevailing aesthetic. It was not that my work was false. It was rather that I was caught in a bind. In order to be myself, I had to express those things that were most real to me, and those included the struggles I was having as a woman, both personally and professionally. At the same time, if I wanted to be taken seriously as an artist, I had to suppress anything in my work that would mark it as having been made by a woman. I was trying to find a way to be myself, still function within the framework of the art community, and be recognized as an artist. This required focusing upon issues that

were essentially derived from what men had designated as being important, while still trying to make my own way. However, I certainly do not wish to repudiate the work that I made in this period, because much of it was good work within the confines of what was permissible.

In 1967, I was working on a piece for a big sculpture show. The piece was called "Ten Part Cylinder" and was made from the forms in which freeway pillars are cast. I needed a large amount of money to finish the piece, and a collector friend of mine introduced me to a man who, he said, was interested in helping me. This man owned a large company that dealt in plastics, and I thought his involvement in plastics was the reason for his interest in my sculpture, which was to be finished with Fiberglas. We went to lunch, and at lunch I discovered the real reason for his offered help. He felt that women "needed help" from men because they were inferior, and he "liked to help women." He went on to say that if a male artist were to ask him for help, it would be very degrading to the artist, and he would refuse, because "men should take care of themselves."

I can remember my throat constricting and my stomach becoming tight. On the one hand, this man was willing to give me all the money I needed to finish my piece, but it meant that I would have to live with the fact that I accepted help from a person who considered me inferior and was only helping me as a way of proving that inferiority since, by accepting the money, I would be reinforcing his belief. I felt a painful and familiar conflict.

Perhaps today I would tell him off and walk out. Then, because I had accepted the idea that I had to be "tough enough" to do whatever I had to do in order to get my work done, I accepted his offer, feeling terrible about it. Was it any wonder that in my work I was trying to move as far away as possible from revealing that I was a woman? Being a woman and being an artist spelled only one thing: pain.

Although I was struggling to deny anything in my work that could mark me as a woman, some aspects of my femaleness were intrinsically involved with both my day-to-day activity as an artist and in my developing aesthetic. In fighting for my rights in the art world I was acting out of a feminist consciousness before I knew what to call my point of view. When I worked in my studio I came into contact with those areas of my personality structure that had been crippled by female role conditioning. This was particularly true in relation to my expectations of the male art authorities, who I tended to see as a child sees a parent. I kept expecting to gain approval from them, particularly since I had grown up expecting to be loved for whatever I did. It was a continual shock to me to discover that instead of love and approval, I encountered hostility and rejection. Now it is clear to me that to expect men to validate one for challenging male dominance (which is what a woman artist implicitly does, simply by being a woman and an artist) is entirely fantastic. But, at the time, I kept going out into the world with my vulnerability and my need for love and acceptance, only to slowly and painfully realize that I had to change my expectations.

Instead of looking to the male world to approve of me and my work, I had to learn to approve of myself and to see myself, not as a child to be approved of by someone "out there," but rather as a creator with something to give to the world. In some strange way, the rejection I faced strengthened me, but only because it forced me to learn to live on my own hook, to use *my* values, instincts, and judgments as my guides. . . .

9   If I as a woman was seen stereotypically during this period, my relationship with Lloyd was utterly incomprehensible to the people around us, and to some extent this is still true. From the time I first met him, when I was eighteen and he was twenty, he loved me and I cared for him, but I hadn't been able to accept him for a long time because he didn't fit male stereotypes any more than I fit female ones. To the degree that I acted in typically unfemale ways, he acted in ways that were similarly nonmale. As I was able to be assertive and ambitious, he was able to be supportive and noncompetitive, which was harder for me to accept because aspiring toward "masculine" standards when you are a woman has more status than demanding that you have the right to be "feminine" if you are a man. Though neither of us could fit into the narrow confines of role expectation, both of us had absorbed some of the cultural attitudes that there was something "wrong with us" because of that. We both knew that the standard male-female relationship as it existed in the society could not contain our personalities. Even my relationship with Jerry (as it had been) was not developed enough to accommodate me at that point in my growth, so it could not serve as a model for us. Lloyd and I had to struggle together to make a relationship that could allow us *both* to realize our personal ambitions. I think we had shied away from that difficult task for a long time and had avoided becoming involved with one another until we both had developed to the point that we could take on a struggle to make an equalized relationship at a time in history when there was no support for such an effort.

10   Then, the first material from the slowly developing women's movement reached the West Coast. When I read it, I couldn't believe it. Here were women saying the things I had been feeling, saying them out loud. I trembled when I read them, remembering the put-downs I encountered whenever I had tried to express the facts of my life as a woman artist. I had so internalized the taboo about mentioning it that I shuddered with terror reading Valerie Solanas' book, *The Scum Manifesto,* and some of the early journals of the women's movement. Even though I thought Solanas extreme, I recognized the truth of many of her observations, and I identified with all the material in those early tracts as I had never identified with anything in my whole life.

11   As I read, I slowly allowed the information to seep into my pores, realizing that at last there was an alternative to the isolation, the silence, the repressed anger, the rejection, the depreciation, and the denial I had been facing. If these women could say how they felt, so could I. Coincidentally, I had been invited by several colleges in the area to speak about my work. I decided to use the

opportunities to express my real feelings, to reveal what I had been going through as a woman and an artist. I was so scared. My voice shook, I could hardly talk. I spoke about the isolation and the rejection, the put-downs and the distortions. I spoke about my anger toward men because they had used me sexually. Everyone was shocked; there were angry reactions from the men. I drove home and trembled in terror at the fantasies that told me that something terrible was going to happen because I was saying the unsayable. I was telling the truth about my experiences as a woman, and I felt sure that I would be punished for it, that someone would break into my studio and destroy all my paintings or would shoot me or beat me up.

For one entire year, I lived in terror. I recognized that my fear reflected how   *12* deeply I had internalized society's taboos about revealing my real feelings. I had been told that if I told men the truth, I would "castrate" them, and I was afraid that they would retaliate. But I felt that I *had* to reach out and take this opportunity to be myself, offered implicitly by the women's movement. I accepted the fear as part of my day-to-day experience and just felt it every day, every time I attempted to reveal my own point of view. Even now, five years later, each time I make another step in exposing my real feelings, the fears engulf me again. The difference is that I have tangible support from women now; then I was alone and had only a few books to tell me that there were other women who were also speaking out. . . .

FRESNO AND THE WOMEN'S PROGRAM

Before I was hired at Fresno State, I discussed my ideas for a female art class   *13* with the Art Department chairman, a man who considered himself a "liberal." He was very sympathetic toward my plan to offer a class for women only, and we discussed the fact that a great many young women entered the beginning art classes and few emerged from the schools into professional life. He agreed with me that something should be done about that, and he seemed to understand my desire to give back some of my own acquired knowledge to younger women. I did not discuss my experiences in the male art community, nor did I mention my plan to develop an alternative context for women. I stressed my interest in helping young women become artists and, because Fresno was outside of the sophisticated art world, there was little real comprehension of the implications of my plan.

I posted signs in the halls of the Art Department inviting young women who   *14* wanted to be artists to come to a meeting where I discussed my ideas about a class. On the posters and in my remarks, I stressed that the women should want to be artists because I felt that my struggle, if it was relevant to other women, was so primarily to those who had already developed to the point that they had a desire to "do" something with their lives. However, one of the first things that I discovered in working with the class was that asking the women if they wanted to be artists was not a reliable question because many of them did not have the assurance that they could actually become what they said they wanted to become. Once I knew that I *wanted* to be an artist, I had made myself into one. I did not understand that wanting doesn't always lead to action. Many of the women had been raised without the sense that they could mold and shape their own lives, and so, wanting to be an artist but without the ability to realize their wants was, for some of them, only an idle fantasy, like wanting to go to the moon.

15   I had made a tentative plan for the class. I suspected, from my own struggle, that the reason women had trouble realizing themselves as artists was related to their conditioning as women. I had found that society's definition of me as a woman was in conflict with my own sense of personhood (and, after all, it was a *person* who was making art). Due to my own determination, I had been able to stand up to this conflict and to function in the face of it. If my situation was similar to other women's, then my struggle was a metaphor for the struggle out of role conditioning that a woman would have to make if she were to realize herself. I was sure that this process would take some time, and so I set up the class with the idea that I would work intensely with the fifteen women I had chosen for a year. When I began to realize how primitive their self-images were, I began to doubt whether a year would be long enough, as it seemed that before I could even help them make art, I would have to help them feel that they were "all right" as people.

16   I had decided that the class should meet away from the campus because I had had ample demonstrations of how intimidated many young women are in the presence of men. When I had lectured in the Los Angeles area, speaking about my ideas for a female art community and expressing the facts of my personal struggle, I had held question-and-answer periods afterward. Frequently, only men would raise their hands. Feeling that it was ludicrous to discuss these issues only with men, I had asked the men to leave. Only after they had gone did the women begin to assert themselves, soon becoming lively and uninhibited. The change that so often takes place in women when men are present was further illustrated to me after my all-female class started in Fresno. During the first semester, I also taught a mixed class, and several of the women from the all-female class were in that. On Monday, in the segregated class, the women were assertive, eager, and outspoken. On Tuesday, in the mixed class, the same women became passive and withdrawn. It is not that the men did anything overt to cause the women to retreat; rather, their presence reminded the women of society's tacit and all-pervasive instruction that they should not be too aggressive, so that the men's egos would not be threatened. This ever-present command seemed to be lifted only when men were not around, for me then as well as them.

17   In order to have a space in which we could explore ourselves without the intimidating presence of men, I felt that we should have a studio away from the school. Besides, being an artist meant having a studio, and if I wanted the women to experience themselves as artists, I thought the first step would be for them to do what artists do—find a studio, fix it up, then begin to work in it.

The fixing-up process seemed a natural way for the women to learn to use tools, develop building skills, and gain confidence in themselves physically. I remembered my own phony bravado in the industrial arts shop and felt committed to providing a way for the women to learn craft without either having to "come on tough" or feel embarrassed about their awkwardness. I also thought that, once the studio was complete, we would get an old car and fix it up, thus further extending mechanical skills and also helping the women build a sense of independence. I wanted them to feel that they could "take care of themselves"—something, it turned out, few of them felt.

Only after these processes had taken place did I plan to move into artmaking, but my plans changed and adapted themselves to the natural flow of the group. The first meeting of the class freaked me out. The fifteen students and I were sitting around at the home of one of the women. The women were chit-chatting, talking about clothes and boyfriends in a very superficial manner. I sat quietly for a while, waiting for them to start talking about their feelings about the class, their excitement or fear, their ideas about art, a book one of them had read, anything that would indicate some intellectual interest. But the conversation never altered from its course—clothes, boyfriends, casual experiences, food. I couldn't believe it. I had been with art students before. There was generally *some* discussion about something having to do with art or the arts in general. I suddenly felt panicked. What had I gotten myself into? This was just like high school. I had run away from this . . . I didn't wnat to be identified with women like these . . . "chicks," who concerned themselves with trivial issues. I didn't know what to do . . . I wanted to escape. I forced myself to stay, to take responsibility for my feelings. Right then, I made the most important step in my commitment to women: to always reveal exactly how I felt. I said: "You know you are boring the hell out of me. You're supposed to be art students. Art students talk about art and books and movies and ideas. You're not talking about anything."

Dead silence. I thought: "Already the first day and I, with my big mouth, have blown it." Then I heard a soft voice saying: "Well, maybe the reason we don't talk about anything is that nobody ever asked us what we thought." I was very moved. I realized that no one had ever demanded of these women that they reach their potential. They began to tell me about their lives and relationships, about how, when they went to parties, the men did most of the "serious talking." True, many of them had been pressured by their parents into getting good grades, but getting good grades was one thing, and establishing personal goals and identities was another. They were always introduced as Sue or Carol or Nancy, just "girls" who were expected to go along with the men. (Later, we developed a practice of always introducing ourselves and each other by our full names and shaking hands, looking full into the face of the person to whom we were being introduced.) We discussed the idea of making demands upon each other, about learning to exchange ideas, feelings, and thoughts. Soon the room was filled with discussion and excitement. It would not be until the following year that I would begin to understand the full implications of making demands

18

19

upon personalities who were accustomed to being protected, not pushed. But I had to be involved with female education for several years before its dynamic became clear. . . .

AFTERWORD

20 It is 1982—twenty-five years since I left the city of my birth to go to school in California; over twenty years since I first exhibited my work; almost that long since my first husband died; a decade since I took the name of my hometown as my own; seven years since *Through the Flower* was published; almost four years since I became divorced and three years since "The Dinner Party" was premiered—a good time to look back and talk about where I've been. It never occurred to me I'd be a writer as well as an artist even though by now I have published three books. I think of writing as a sideline; my studio work always comes first. Over the years I've created a lot of art; I work constantly. My life has had a sameness for over two decades—a result of working in the studio every day.

21   Recently, I saw Emanuel Jacobson, my teacher at the Art Institute when I was in my teens. He heard me give a lecture about my work and afterward he told me I was exactly the same as when I was fourteen years old. I don't know why I liked that remark so much—perhaps because it made me feel connected to my youth. All I know is that my whole life has been a struggle and that I've finally become used to the fact that that is what it will be until the end. Material possessions have never meant very much to me; I still live from month to month. All that matters to me is to keep on working and to keep on fighting through my work for women to be free. The story that I told in *Through the Flower* conveyed a great deal about what I'd done during the first half of my professional life. I'll pick up the thread of that tale beginning in 1972.

22   By then, my imagery was becoming clearer, and I felt the desire to use a brush again, instead of a spray gun, as I wanted a kind of detail that only brush painting allows. While on a trip along the Northwest coast of America, I stopped at an antique shop where I was enchanted by a beautifully painted porcelain plate. It was there that I first discovered the visual potential of china painting. (China painting is the process of applying successive layers of paint to an already glazed ceramic surface. Repeated firings melt the paint into the glaze.) When I returned home, I looked for a china painting teacher, having decided that this technique would lend itself to my new imagery.

23   My interest in china painting took me into a female subculture, for in the last fifty years china painting has been entirely in the hands of women. My experiences with china painters were in sharp contrast with my earlier apprenticeships which, of course, had all been with men. This was the first time it was a distinct advantage to be a woman artist. I enjoyed the warm, homey atmosphere of china painting classes, though I shuddered at the unprofessional presentation of work at china-painting exhibitions. Still, these exhibitions were

always crowded, which interested me, as the audiences for most modern art exhibitions are usually very small. By then, I was trying to make my work accessible beyond the confines of the art world. And it was clear from the china painting shows that there were many people interested in art, though they were alienated from the contemporary art world.

In addition to learning the techniques of china painting during my two-year   24 apprenticeship, I was deeply affected by being around "the world of the china painter." I had never known women such as these—women who lived tradi- tional female lives and fit their creative work into the structure of those lives. Many even painted on their kitchen tables when they weren't in use for meals. And yet, there were also a number of very serious professionals, who supported themselves through their work. One such woman was Rosemarie Radmaker, who helped build a bridge between me and the traditional china painters, some of whom could not believe that I intended to honor their work.

I met Rosemarie when she came to an exhibit of my first china-painted   25 pieces, two series of works entitled "Butterfly Goddesses and Other Speci- mens" and "Six Views from the Womantree." In the first series, a group of thirty porcelain miniatures, I had begun to develop an imagery which universal- ized the female form that I had finally revealed in "The Rejection Quintet." In the "Butterfly Goddesses and Other Specimens," I took that vaginal shape and transformed it, creating a variety of natural forms, butterflies and even female deities. Some of the pieces incorporated historical images like the Venus of Willendorf, an ancient female fetish. Many prefigured "The Dinner Party" images and some were, in fact, actual studies for the plates. The "Woman- trees" evolved from an experience I had at a park in London. I saw a great tree there with a large central cavity into which I immediately climbed. Once inside, I felt myself to be simultaneously identified with the tree and apart from it. This resulted in a series of images that were, like many of my works, about being inside and outside at the same time.

When Rosemarie introduced herself to me, I shook her hand nervously since 26 I had no idea how a china painter would respond to my show. She was, how- ever, very supportive, and later she became my china painting consultant on "The Dinner Party." There was a direct link between my experiences with the china painters and the development of "The Dinner Party."

Like most classically trained artists, I had grown up with a certain prejudice   27 against crafts, and my notion of china painting was that it was a hobby of "little old ladies." Meeting the china painters changed my attitudes, and my relation- ship with Rosemarie showed me that the capacity for female identification existed in many women, even those who would never call themselves feminists. Additionally, the fact that some of the china painters were really artists, though they were not recognized as such, led me to reexamine my ideas about being an artist and about the nature of art. Seeing the cups and saucers and plates which many of the china painters worked on suggested to me the idea of a table setting as an appropriate form for what I wanted to express. By the time I had finished studying china painting, I had begun my new, major work.

28   This work, which occupied me for five years, grew out of my conviction that as long as women's achievements were excluded from human history, all women would face the same conflicts I had faced and would meet the same resistance I had encountered as I tried to express my ideas and fulfill my talents. This enraged me because it meant that women's energies, instead of being directed in positive ways, would be continually squandered in the struggle to merely participate in human culture rather than to actually shape it. I decided to try and create a work of art that could convey the sense of women's real contributions and symbolize the tragedy of women's containment.

29   In order to do this, I developed the idea of a "dinner party," which was to be a sort of reinterpretation of the Last Supper from the point of view of those who'd done the cooking throughout history. The guests at this dinner party were to be presented as images on plates, a reference to the way in which history had consumed rather than revered women of achievement. By early 1975, my concept for "The Dinner Party" had expanded to become a symbolic history of women in Western civilization. Moreover, I had decided that this subject could be expressed in more than one form. Although I intended to create a traveling exhibition, I knew that many would be unable to see the show. Therefore, I planned to express the same content through a book (which eventually became two volumes) and a film. Because my belief in the power of art to change consciousness was steadily growing, I wanted my work to reach a broad audience so that the information contained in it could have as profound an impact as possible. I wanted to structure the work so it would attract those who attended china painting exhibitions as well as the art world elite.

30   Fortunately, Johanna Demetrakas, who had chronicled "Womanhouse," became interested in "The Dinner Party" project and spent three and a half years documenting the intense studio process that was involved in finishing the work. Her film, *Right Out of History: The Making of Judy Chicago's Dinner Party*, brought the experience of "The Dinner Party" to many people who might otherwise never have been exposed to it.

31   My two-volume book, *The Complete Dinner Party*, which was published by Anchor Press/Doubleday, offered another form of dealing with the subject of women's history. The first volume, *The Dinner Party: A Symbol of Our Heritage*, described the creation of the thirty-nine plates representing the various mythological figures and historical personages at the banquet table and summarized the historical information symbolized by the porcelain floor on which the table rests. I also tried to give a sense of my personal struggle and of the studio process. In the second volume, *Embroidering Our Heritage: The Dinner Party Needlework*, I discussed the sacramental nature of the "The Dinner Party" as it is expressed in the needlework, which, along with china painting, is used extensively in the exhibition. (My experience studying china painting had led to a general interest in women's traditional art forms and, even before I incorporated needlework into "The Dinner Party," I had become interested in embroidery.)

32   Between 1974 and 1976, I worked on some pieces not intended for "The

Dinner Party." Among these was the triptych "Did You Know Your Mother
Had a Sacred Heart?", my first work that included needlework. The three sections rest on an embroidered cloth which repeats the images on the side panels.
The work is based on traditional medieval altars that present the Virgin Mary
as the source of all life. It is an extension of the goddess imagery in the porcelain miniatures. Both dealt with the idea of the feminine as universal and holy,
a theme that pervades much of my recent work.

By 1976, I had completed nineteen of the thirty-nine plates to be included   *33*
in "The Dinner Party" as well as most of the conceptual work. I planned to
structure the piece as an equilateral triangle, open in the center, with thirteen
place settings on each wing. (The triangle is an ancient symbol of the Goddess,
and I chose an equilateral shape to stand for the goal of feminism—an equalized world.) In addition to the plates, I would include a napkin, flatware, and a
goblet or chalice, all of which would be set on tables covered with white linen
cloths. These cloths would be embroidered with the names and brief descriptions of the women represented on the plates.

Originally, I intended to embroider these phrases in circles slightly larger   *34*
than the fourteen-inch painted plates, much like I had written around the small
discs in the center of my porcelain miniatures, but I had to abandon this idea
because of technical difficulties. Instead, I decided to use needlework in a more
expressive way, especially after discovering that I had a natural ability to design
for embroidery. At first, I just extended the imagery of the plates onto individual "runners" that covered the tablecloths; then I began to treat the runners as
metaphors for the historic context or milieu in which each woman lived. (The
development of the needlework in "The Dinner Party" is thoroughly discussed
in *Embroidering Our Heritage: The Dinner Party Needlework.*

Until 1976, I continued to work as I always had—alone in my studio. But it   *35*
became clear to me that I needed help with the research for "The Dinner
Party," with the embroidery and, most of all, with the ceramics (having decided
that I wanted the images on the plates to slowly become dimensional as a metaphor for women's increasing freedom). It was then that I began to work with
Diane Gelon, who began by doing research and eventually became "The Dinner Party" Project Coordinator; Susan Hill, who supervised the fabrication of
the runners and assisted me on the needlework book; and Leonard Skuro, who
developed the basic ceramic technology for the sculptural plates. But I had no
idea that opening my studio to first three and eventually four hundred people
would so transform both my artmaking process and my personal life. The effect
of "The Dinner Party" is discussed in my two other books; here I am going to
concentrate on how working with so many people affected my development as
an artist.

During the remaining three years it took to complete "The Dinner Party,"   *36*
my solitary artmaking activity became public. For the first time since I was a
student, other people watched me work. Even though my second husband,
Lloyd, and I shared a studio, we had entirely separate spaces. Moreover, part
of what had made our marriage work was our sense of connection as isolated

artists. Suddenly, I was involved with many different people whose very presence attested to the importance of my work. It must have been very difficult for him, but, to tell the truth, I barely noticed, for I was swept up by the momentum of what I had put in motion.

37   I had decided to place the table on a porcelain floor that would be inscribed with the names of hundreds of other women of achievement. These names would be grouped around each of the place settings and would suggest that the women represented at the table had emerged from a long tradition of female accomplishment. This, I hoped, would challenge the myth that successful women had "pulled themselves up by their bootstraps," an idea which makes women who find it impossible to succeed without support feel that there is something wrong with them. I had learned from my study of history that most women of achievement had enjoyed a liberal historic period, a positive environment, or a supportive family or personal relationship. (The Heritage Floor, which provides both a literal and symbolic foundation for the banquet table, is described in *The Dinner Party: A Symbol of Our Heritage*, which also contains short biographies of the 999 women included.)

38   I can't remember very much of those three years—mostly I just worked. Regardless of whether I was tired or sick or depressed, I forced myself into the studio every day. As more and more people joined the project, their energy helped sustain mine. But ultimately, I knew the piece was my responsibility, and I had to grow to carry the load. For the first time in my life, I was working to my capacity. But in order to accomplish this, I had to break my last link with female role conditioning and, in so doing, shatter my personal life.

39   Although I had always had equalized relationships with men, there was one place where I had consistently held back. I was totally committed to my life as an artist, but there was a part of me that had never completely "let go." I now understand that this was because I always felt that I couldn't allow myself to forget about life's duties or to be emotionally irresponsible, though I'd seen men do both many times. Anaïs Nin once remarked that she didn't think women could ever completely disconnect from the needs of others, but she was wrong. I discovered that I could block out everything and everyone when I had work to do. And I also discovered that, when I did that on a consistent basis, I needed to be taken care of at the end of every day.

40   By becoming fully myself creatively, without realizing it I put myself outside the structure of most female/male relationships. I became the one who needed to be nurtured rather than the nurturer. But women are the ones who are brought up to be nurturing, while men, even when they'd like to be, rarely have the skills. Moreover, my experience has repeatedly demonstrated that many men are frightened by the unfamiliarity of being asked for something they're not used to doing. As difficult as this situation was for me, and still is, the opportunity to work to my full potential has been worth the emotional deprivation and pain. . . .

41   In March 1979, the exhibition had its first showing at the San Francisco Museum of Modern Art. I had no idea how my work would be received but all

my fears dissolved by opening night. Five thousand people arrived, and it seemed as if everyone was crowded around me offering congratulations and covering me with flowers, jewelry, and other gifts. Women threw their arms around my neck and thanked me with tears in their eyes and everyone stood patiently in line to see the work, something that never happens at openings. Then, article after article appeared, locally and nationally. Most of them were positive, but soon "The Dinner Party" was being dismissed as "controversial," even though attendance at the exhibition reached 100,000 by closing day, when people waited six or seven hours to get in to the show. . . .

By the time it left Chicago, nearly half a million people had seen the show. *42* This outpouring of support and response attests to the power of art and the hunger among women for symbols that affirm us. But the refusal of our institutions to be responsive to the clear public desire to see "The Dinner Party" raises the question of whether our society is prepared to honor and preserve women's symbols the way it has cared for those created by men.

We as women have a right to ask, "What is art? What do *we* want it to be?" *43* and to see our answers validated. "The Dinner Party" challenges assumptions about what constitutes art and that is what it is intended to do. It offers a vision of art that is high in quality, yet relevant in content to a wide audience. But it focuses on women's experiences rather than men's. The institutional resistance to the exhibition suggests that those who control the definition of art are still not ready—despite some signs of change—to accept that female-oriented content can be the basis for important and potentially universal art. This has led to a problem for me as an artist that is still unresolved.

WRITING AND DISCUSSION QUESTIONS

Informative

1. Chicago describes the obstacles she faced in the mid-1960s as a woman artist. What kinds of barriers does she describe? Are all of them external? Why do men seem to resent and oppose her? What connections to Virginia Woolf's and Alice Munro's narratives do you see here?

2. Chicago describes the developing relationship with her friend Lloyd, whom she married some years after her first husband Jerry had died in an automobile accident. How would you characterize her relationship with Lloyd? To what degree is such a relationship more "normal" today than it was then?

3. How would you describe the growing process Chicago went through before she could fully accept her real feelings and wishes concerning art? How is that process reflected in what happened at the Fresno State female art class?

Persuasive

1. Chicago writes that "The Dinner Party" "grew out of my conviction that as long as women's achievements were excluded from human history, all women would

face the same conflicts I had faced and would meet the same resistance I had encountered. . . ." What assumptions does she make in this statement? Argue that these assumptions are or are not valid.

2. Chicago is often accused of doing "crafts," not "art." What are some important differences between arts and crafts? Which art form has more status? Why? Argue that china painting and needlework do or do not deserve less status than the more traditional arts. How should we judge nontraditional media, used primarily by women to express ideas that are not only nontraditional but that flout established traditions about the role of women in history? Are they art? If not, what are they? Politics? Sociology? Do we need new criteria to judge a project like "The Dinner Party"?

Personal

1. How "universal" is Chicago's story? Do you think it applies to most other women artists? How would Woolf explain the apparent absence of women artists, composers, sculptors, and playwrights? Does Chicago's story apply to women in non-art careers? How much do you think the world has changed concerning women's opportunities in the last 25 years? What evidence do you have for saying this?
2. What is your personal reaction to "The Dinner Party"? Would you pay to see it? Do you think it is important art? Are you bothered by the specifically "female" imagery in it?

CHAPTER WRITING ASSIGNMENTS

1. Many people believe that feminism is a single belief system, but this is not so. Investigate two different modern feminist thinkers, focusing on one aspect of their thinking, such as the role of men in the movement, tactics for engendering change, the importance of pornography to the movement, or the awareness of female poverty. Thinkers you might examine are Betty Friedan, Mary Daly, Kate Millett, Susan Griffin, Gloria Steinem, Germaine Greer, Phillis Schafly, Adrienne Rich, Audre Lourde, or Paula Gunn Allen. Or study the National Organization for Women, which will also reflect the conflicts and differences within the women's movement. Research NOW to determine its diverse goals and multiple tactics.

2. Interview three different women or men to see what the effects of the feminist movement have been on their lives and whether it has stymied. Start by exploring their knowledge of and attitudes toward feminism.

3. Look at the role of women in societies other than the United States. Has the gender system in countries in Africa, Asia, or South America, for example, granted women lower value and power, limited access to resources, and less opportunity to control their own lives?

4. Study a common situation or problem from the perspective of gender: early childhood schooling, fashion, math education, career choice, choice of college major, advertising, or leisure activities. Become knowledgeable about the trends and thinking in these areas to determine whether there are gender implications.

AUTHOR-TITLE INDEX

CREDITS